[redacted]

[redacted]

[redacted]

[redacted]

THEOLOGICAL DICTIONARY
OF THE
OLD TESTAMENT

THEOLOGICAL DICTIONARY
OF THE
OLD TESTAMENT

EDITED BY

G. JOHANNES BOTTERWECK
AND
HELMER RINGGREN

Translated by

DAVID E. GREEN

Volume V
יהוה ־ חמר
ḥmr–YHWH

WILLIAM B. EERDMANS PUBLISHING COMPANY
GRAND RAPIDS, MICHIGAN

Translated from
THEOLOGISCHES WÖRTERBUCH ZUM ALTEN TESTAMENT
Band III, Lieferungen 1-4
Published 1977-1980 by
VERLAG W. KOHLHAMMER GMBH STUTTGART, W. GERMANY

Library of Congress Cataloging in Publication Data
Botterweck, G. Johannes
Theological dictionary of the Old Testament
Translation of Theologisches Wörterbuch zum Alten Testament.
Includes rev. ed. of v. 1-2.
Includes bibliographical references.
1. Bible. O.T.—Dictionaries—Hebrew. 2. Hebrew language—Dictionaries—English.
I. Ringgren, Helmer, 1917— joint author. II. Title.
BS440.B5713 221.4'4'0321 73-76170

ISBN 0-8028-2338-6 (set)
Volume V 0-8028-2329-7

Printed in the United States of America

CONSULTING EDITORS

George W. Anderson
Henri Cazelles
David Noel Freedman
Shemaryahu Talmon
Gerhard Wallis

CONTRIBUTORS

P. R. Ackroyd, London
G. André, Uppsala
C. Barth, Basel
A. Baumann, Wolfsburg
J. Bergman, Uppsala
†G. J. Botterweck, Bonn (Editor)
R. E. Clements, Cambridge
W. Dommershausen, Trier
†H. Eising, Münster
H.-J. Fabry, Bonn
D. N. Freedman, Ann Arbor
J. Gamberoni, Paderborn
L. T. Geraty, South Lancaster
G. Giesen, Düren
V. Hamp, Munich
G. F. Hasel, Berrien Springs
F. J. Helfmeyer, Cologne
I. Höver-Johag, Bonn
H. A. Hoffner, Chicago
O. Kaiser, Cappel
A. S. Kapelrud, Oslo
D. Kellermann, Tübingen
E. Kutsch, Erlangen
C. Locher, Zürich
N. Lohfink, Frankfurt am Main
J. R. Lundbom, New Haven
H. Lutzmann, Münster
F. Maass, Denzlingen
G. Mayer, Mainz
L. A. Mitchel, Angwin
H.-P. Müller, Halstenbek
M. P. O'Connor, Ann Arbor
B. Otzen, Aarhus
H. D. Preuss, Neuendettelsau
H. Ringgren, Uppsala (Editor)
J. Schüpphaus, Bonn
K.-D. Schunck, Rostock
K. Seybold, Basel
W. von Soden, Münster
M. Tsevat, Cincinnati
S. Wagner, Leipzig
G. Wallis, Halle
H.-J. Zobel, Greifswald

CONTENTS

ABBREVIATIONS

AANLR	*Atti dell' Academia Nazionale dei Lincei, Rendiconti*, Rome
AASOR	*Annual of the American Schools of Oriental Research,* New Haven, Ann Arbor, Durham
AB	*The Anchor Bible*, ed. W. F. Albright and D. N. Freedman, Garden City
ABL	R. F. Harper, *Assyrian and Babylonian Letters*, Chicago, 1892-1914, 14 vols.
ABoT	*Ankara Arkeoloji Müzesinde bulunan Boğazköy Tableteri* (Istanbul, 1948)
ABR	*Australian Biblical Review,* Melbourne
acc.	accusative
AcOr	*Acta orientalia*, Copenhagen
AcOrASH	*Acta orientalia, Academiae Scientiarum Hungaricae*, Budapest
act.	active
ADAI.Ä	*Abhandlungen des Deutschen Archäologischen Instituts*, Cairo, *Ägyptolische Reihe*, Glückstadt
adj.	adjective
ADPV	*Abhandlungen des deutschen Palästinavereins*, Wiesbaden
AfO	*Archiv für Orientforschung*, Graz
AG	*Analecta gregoriana*, Rome
ÄgAbh	*Ägyptologische Abhandlungen*, Wiesbaden
AHAW	*Abhandlungen der Heidelberger Akademie der Wissenschaften*
AHDO	*Archives d'histoire du droit oriental*, Brussels
AHw	W. von Soden, *Akkadisches Handwörterbuch,* Wiesbaden, 1959—
AION	*Annali dell'Istituto Universitario Orientali di Napoli*
AJSL	*The American Journal of Semitic Languages and Literatures*, Chicago
AKGW	*Abhandlungen der Königlichen Gesellschaft der Wissenschaften zu Göttingen*
Akk.	Akkadian
ALBO	*Analecta lovaniensia biblica et orientalia,* Louvain
ALUOS	*Annual of the Leeds University Oriental Society*
Amhar.	Amharic
AnAcScFen	*Annales Academiae Scientarum Fennicae*, Helsinki
AnBibl	*Analecta biblica*, Rome
AncIsr	R. de Vaux, *Ancient Israel: Its Life and Institutions*, Eng. trans., New York, 1961
ANEP	*The Ancient Near East in Pictures*, ed. J. B. Pritchard, Princeton, ^{2}1955, ^{3}1969
ANET	*Ancient Near Eastern Texts Relating to the OT,* ed. J. B. Pritchard, Princeton, ^{2}1955, ^{3}1969
AnOr	*Analecta orientalia*, Rome
AnSt	*Anatolian Studies*, London
AO	*Der Alte Orient,* Leipzig
AOAT	*Alter Orient und AT,* Neukirchen-Vluyn
AOB	*Altorientalische Bilder zum AT,* ed. H. Gressmann, Berlin, Leipzig, ^{2}1927
AOBib	*Altorientalische Bibliothek*, Leipzig
AOS	*American Oriental Series*, New Haven
AP	A. E. Cowley, *Aramaic Papyri of the Fifth Century B.C.*, Oxford, 1923

APN	K. Tallqvist, *Assyrian Personal Names. ASSF,* 43/1, 1914; repr. 1966
APNM	H. B. Huffmon, *Amorite Personal Names in the Mari Texts*, Baltimore, 1965
Arab.	Arabic
Aram.	Aramaic
ArbT	*Arbeiten zur Theologie*, Stuttgart
ARM	*Archives royales de Mari*, Paris
ArOr	*Archiv orientâlní*, Prague
ARW	*Archiv für Religionswissenschaft,* Leipzig, Berlin
AS	*Assyriological Studies*, Chicago
ASOR	American Schools of Oriental Research
ASSF	*Acta Societatis Scientarum Fennicae*, Helsinki
Assyr.	Assyrian
ASTI	*Annual of the Swedish Theological Institute in Jerusalem*, Leiden
AT	Altes Testament, Ancien Testament, etc.
ATA	*Alttestamentliche Abhandlungen*, Münster
ATD	*Das AT Deutsch,* ed. V. Herntrich and A. Weiser, Göttingen
AThANT	*Abhandlungen zur Theologie des Alten und Neuen Testaments*, Zurich
AUM	*Andrews University Monographs*, Berrien Springs
AuS	G. Dalman, *Arbeit und Sitte in Palästina,* Gütersloh, 1928-1942, repr. 1964, 7 vols.
AUSS	*Andrews University Seminary Studies*, Berrien Springs
BA	*The Biblical Archaeologist,* New Haven, Ann Arbor, Durham
Bab.	Babylonian, Babylonian Talmud
BAfO	*Beihefte zur Archiv für Orientforschung*, Graz
BASOR	*Bulletin of the American Schools for Oriental Research,* New Haven, Ann Arbor, Durham
BAss	*Beiträge zu Assyriologie und semitischen Sprachwissenschaft,* Leipzig
BAT	*Die Botschaft des ATs*, Stuttgart
BBB	*Bonner biblische Beiträge*
BBLAK	*Beiträge zur biblischen Landes- und Altertumskunde*, Stuttgart
BDB	Brown-Driver-Briggs, *A Hebrew and English Lexicon of the OT,* Oxford, 1907
BDBAT	*Beiheft zur Dielheimer Blätter zum AT*
BE	Babylonian Expedition of the University of Pennsylvania, Philadelphia, *Series A, Cuneiform Texts*, ed. H. V. Hilprecht, 1893-1914
BeO	*Bibbia e oriente*, Milan
BETL	*Bibliotheca ephemeridum theologicarum lovaniensium*, Paris, Gembloux
BEvTh	*Beiträge zur evangelische Theologie*, Munich
BFChTh	*Beiträge zur Förderung christlicher Theologie*, Gütersloh
BHHW	*Biblisch-Historisches Handwörterbuch,* ed. L. Rost and B. Reicke, Göttingen, 1962-1966, 3 vols.
BHK	*Biblia hebraica*, ed. R. Kittel, Stuttgart, ^{3}1929
BHS	*Biblia hebraica stuttgartensia*, ed. K. Elliger and W. Rudolph, Stuttgart, 1966-1977
BHTh	*Beiträge zur historischen Theologie*, Tübingen
Bibl	*Biblica*, Rome
Bibl. d'étude	*Bibliothèque d'étude*, Institut français d'archéologie orientale, Cairo
bibliog.	bibliography
BietOr	*Biblica et orientalia*, Rome
BIFAO	*Bulletin de l'institut français d'archéologie orientale*, Cairo
BiLe	*Bibel und Leben*, Düsseldorf

BiOr	*Bibliotheca orientalis*, Leiden
BK	*Biblischer Kommentar AT*, ed. M. Noth and H. W. Wolff, Neukirchen-Vluyn
BL	*Bibel-Lexikon*, ed. H. Haag, Einsiedeln, 1951, ^{2}1968
BLe	H. Bauer-P. Leander, *Historische Grammatik der hebräischen Sprache des ATs*, 1918-1922, repr. Hildesheim, 1962
BMAP	E. G. Kraeling, *The Brooklyn Museum Aramaic Papyri*, New Haven, 1953
BOT	*De Boeken van het OT*, Roermond en Maaseik
BRL	K. Galling, *Biblisches Reallexikon*, Tübingen, 1937, ^{2}1977
BSAW	*Berichte über die Verhandlungen der Sächsischen Akademie der Wissenschaften zu Leipzig*
BSt	*Biblische Studien*, Neukirchen-Vluyn
BT	*The Bible Translator*, London
BTS	*Bible et terre sainte*
BuA	B. Meissner, *Babylonien und Assyrien*, Heidelberg, 1920-25, 2 vols.
BVC	*Bible et vie chrétienne*, Paris
BWANT	*Beiträge zur Wissenschaft vom Alten und Neuen Testament*, Stuttgart
BWL	W. G. Lambert, *Babylonian Wisdom Literature*, Oxford, 1960
BZ	*Biblische Zeitschrift*, Paderborn
BZAW	*Beihefte zur ZAW*, Berlin
ca.	*circa*
CAD	*The Assyrian Dictionary of the Oriental Institute of the University of Chicago*, 1956—
CahRB	*Cahiers de la RB*, Paris
CAT	*Commentaire de l'AT*, Neuchâtel
CBQ	*Catholic Biblical Quarterly*, Washington
CBSC	*The Cambridge Bible for Schools and Colleges*, Cambridge
CD A,B	Damascus Document, manuscript A, B
CH	Code of Hammurabi
ChrÉg	*Chronique d'Égypte*, Brussels
CIHeb	*Corpus inscriptionum hebraicum*, ^{2}1974
CIH	*Corpus Inscriptionum Himyariticarum* (= *CIS*, IV)
CIJ	*Corpus inscriptionum judaicarum*, Rome, 1936—
CIS	*Corpus inscriptionum semiticarum*, Paris, 1881—
CML	G. R. Driver, *Canaanite Myths and Legends*, Edinburgh, 1956
comm.	commentary
conj.	conjecture
const.	construct
ContiRossini	K. Conti Rossini, *Chrestomathia arabica meridionalis ephigraphica*, Rome, 1931
COT	*Commentaar op het OT*, ed. G. C. Aalders, Kampen, 1955-57, 2 vols.
CT	*Cuneiform Texts from Babylonian Tablets . . . in the British Museum*, London, 1896—
CT	*The Egyptian Coffin Texts*, ed. A. de Buck and A. H. Gardiner, Chicago, 1935-1947
cyl.	cylinder
DBS	*Dictionnaire de la Bible, Supplement*, ed. L. Pirot, A. Robert, H. Cazelles, and A. Feuillet, Paris, 1926—
Dem.	Demotic
DISO	C. F. Jean-J. Hoftijzer, *Dictionnaire des inscriptions sémitiques de l'ouest*, Leiden, 1965

diss.	dissertation
DJD	*Discoveries in the Judean Desert,* Oxford, 1955—
DKAW	*Denkschriften der Kaiserlichen Akademie der Wissenschaften*
DMOA	*Documenta et monumenta orientis antiqui,* Leiden
EA	Tell el-Amarna tablets
EB	*Die Heilige Schrift in deutscher Übersetzung. Echter-Bibel,* Würzburg
Egyp.	Egyptian
EH	*Europäische Hochschulschriften,* Bern
EHAT	*Exegetisches Handbuch zum AT,* Münster
Einl.	Einleitung
EMiqr	*Enṣiqlōpedyā miqrā'it,* Jerusalem, 1950—
EncBTh	*Encyclopedia of Biblical Theology,* ed. J. B. Bauer, Eng. trans., London, 1970, 3 vols.
EncJud	*Encyclopedia judaica,* Jerusalem, 1971-72, 16 vols.
EnEl	Enuma Elish
Eng.	English
ERE	*Encyclopedia of Religion and Ethics,* ed. J. Hastings, New York, 1913-1927, 13 vols.
esp.	especially
EstBíb	*Estudios bíblicos,* Madrid
Ethiop.	Ethiopic
ETL	*Ephemerides theologicae lovanienses,* Louvain
EvTh	*Evangelische Theologie,* Munich
ExpT	*Expository Times,* London
fem.	feminine
FRLANT	*Forschungen zur Religion und Literatur des Alten und Neuen Testaments,* Göttingen
FuF	*Forschungen und Fortschritte,* Berlin
FzB	*Forschung zur Bibel,* Stuttgart
GaG	W. von Soden, *Grundriss der akkadischen Grammatik. AnOr,* 33 (1952)
GesB	W. Gesenius-F. Buhl, *Hebräisches und aramäisches Handwörterbuch,* Berlin, ^{17}1921
GGA	*Göttingische Gelehrte Anzeigen*
GHK	*Göttinger Hand-Kommentar zum AT,* ed. W. Nowack
Gilg.	Gilgamesh epic
GK	W. Gesenius-E. Kautsch, *Hebräische Grammatik,* Halle, ^{28}1909 (= Kautsch-Cowley, *Gesenius' Hebrew Grammar,* Oxford, ^{2}1910)
Gk.	Greek
Greg	*Gregorianum,* Rome
GSAT	*Gesammelte Studien zum AT,* Munich
GThT	*Gereformeerd theologisch Tijdschrift,* Baarn, Aalten, Kampen
HAT	*Handbuch zum AT,* ed. O. Eissfeldt, ser. 1, Tübingen
HDB	*Dictionary of the Bible,* ed. J. Hastings, 4 vols., 1898-1902; rev. ed., 1 vol., New York, 1963
Heb.	Hebrew
Herm	*Hermeneia,* Philadelphia
HG	J. Friedrich, *Die hethitischen Gesetze. DMOA,* 7 (1959)
Hitt.	Hittite
HKAT	*Handkommentar zum AT,* Göttingen
HSAT	*Die heilige Schrift des ATs,* ed. E. Kautsch and A. Bertholet, Tübingen, ^{4}1922-23

HSM	*Harvard Semitic Monographs*, Cambridge, Mass.
HThR	*Harvard Theological Review*, Cambridge, Mass.
HUCA	*Hebrew Union College Annual*, Cincinnati
Hurr.	Hurrian
HwbIsl	*Handwörterbuch des Islam*, A. J. Wensinck and J. H. Kramers, Leiden, 1941
IB	*The Interpreter's Bible*, ed. G. A. Buttrick, Nashville, 1962, 4 vols.; *Supplement*, ed. K. Crim, 1976
ICC	*The International Critical Commentary*, Edinburgh
IEJ	*Israel Exploration Journal*, Jerusalem
IG	*Inscriptiones graecae*, Berlin, 1873—
impf.	imperfect
impv.	imperative
inf.	infinitive
in loc.	on this passage
Int	*Interpretation*, Richmond
Introd.	Introduction
IPN	M. Noth, *Die israelitischen Personennamen. BWANT*, 46[3/10], 1928, repr. 1966
Iran.	Iranian
Ja	Enumeration according to A. Jamme (Old South Arabic)
JAC	*Jahrbuch für Antike und Christentum*, Münster
JANES	*Journal of the Ancient Near Eastern Society of Columbia University*, New York
JAOS	*Journal of the American Oriental Society*, Boston, New Haven
JBL	*Journal of Biblical Literature*, New York, New Haven, Philadelphia, Missoula, Chico
JBR	*Journal of Bible and Religion*, Boston
JCS	*Journal of Cuneiform Studies*, New Haven, Cambridge, Mass.
JEA	*Journal of Egyptian Archaeology*, London
JEOL	*Jahrbericht van het Vooraziatisch-Egyptisch Gezelschap "Ex Oriente Lux,"* Leiden
JJS	*Journal of Jewish Studies*, London
JNES	*Journal of Near Eastern Studies*, Chicago
JPOS	*Journal of the Palestine Oriental Society*, Jerusalem
Joüon	P. Joüon, *Grammaire de l'hébreu biblique*, ²1947, repr. Rome, 1965
JPTh	*Jahrbücher für protestantische Theologie*, Leipzig
JQR	*Jewish Quarterly Review*, Philadelphia
JSJ	*Journal for the Study of Judaism in the Persian, Hellenistic and Roman Period*, Leiden
JSS	*Journal of Semitic Studies*, Manchester
JTS	*Journal of Theological Studies*, Oxford
Jud	*Judaica*, Zurich
K	*Kethibh*
KAH	*Keilschrifttexte aus Assur historischen Inhalts;* I, ed. L. Messerschmidt, *WVDOG*, 16, 1911; II, ed. O. Schroeder, *WVDOG*, 37, 1922
KAI	H. Donner-W. Röllig, *Kanaanäische und aramäische Inschriften*, Wiesbaden, ²1966-69, 3 vols.
KAR	*Keilschrifttexte aus Assur religiösen Inhalts*, ed. E. Ebeling, *WVDOG*, 28, 1919; 34, 1923
KAT	*Kommentar zum AT*, ed. E. Sellin and J. Herrmann, Leipzig, Gütersloh
KAV	*Keilschrifttexte aus Assur verschiedenen Inhalts*, ed. O. Schroeder, *WVDOG*, 35, 1920

KB	*Keilschriftliche Bibliothek*, ed. E. Schrader, Berlin, 1889-1900
KBL	L. Koehler-W. Baumgartner, *Hebräisches und aramäisches Lexikon zum AT*, Leiden, ^{1}1955, ^{2}1958, ^{3}1967—
KBo	*Keilschrifttexte aus Boghazköi*, *WVDOG*, 30, 36, 68-70, 72-, Leipzig, 1915-1923; Berlin, 1954—
KEHAT	*Kurzgefasstes exegetisches Handbuch zum AT*, ed. O. F. Fridelin, Leipzig, 1812-1896
KHC	*Kurzer Handcommentar zum AT*, ed. K. Marti, Tübingen
KlPauly	*Der kleine Pauly*, ed. K. Ziegler and W. Sontheimer, Stuttgart, 1964—
KlSchr	*Kleine Schriften* (A. Alt, 1953-59, ^{3}1964; O. Eissfeldt, 1963-68)
KTU	*Die keilalphabetischen Texte aus Ugarit*, I, ed. M. Dietrich, O. Loretz, and J. Sanmartín, *AOAT*, 24, 1976
KUB	Staatliche Museen zu Berlin, Vorderasiatische Abteilung (later Deutsche Orient-Gesellschaft), *Keilschrifturkunden aus Boghazköi*, 1921—
KuD	*Kerygma und Dogma*, Göttingen
Lane	E. W. Lane, *An Arabic-English Lexicon*, London, 1863-1893, repr. 1968, 8 vols.
LAPO	*Littératures anciennes du Proche-Orient*, Paris
Lat.	Latin
Leslau, *Contributions*	W. Leslau, *Ethiopic and South Arabic Contributions to the Hebrew Lexicon*, Los Angeles, 1958
LexÄg	W. Helck-E. Otto, *Lexikon der Ägyptologie*, Wiesbaden, 1972—
LexHebAram	F. Zorrell, *Lexicon hebraicum et aramaicum Veteris Testamenti*, Rome, 1966
LexLingAeth	A. Dillmann, *Lexicon linguae aethiopicae*, Leipzig, 1865
LexLingAram	E. Vogt, *Lexicon linguae aramaicae Veteris Testamenti documentis antiquis illustratum*, Rome, 1971
LexSyr	C. Brockelmann, *Lexicon syriacum*, Halle, 1928, ^{2}1968
LidzEph	M. Lidzbarski, *Ephemeris für semitische Epigraphik*, Giessen, 1900-1915
LidzNE	M. Lidzbarski, *Handbuch der nordsemitischen Epigraphik*, Weimar, 1898
lit.	literally
LThK	*Lexikon für Theologie und Kirche*, 1930-38, ^{2}1957—
LUÅ	*Lunds Universitets Årsskrift*
LXX	Septuagint (LXX^A, Codex Alexandrinus; LXX^B, Codex Vaticanus; LXX$^{S[1,2]}$, Codex Sinaiticus, correctors 1, 2, etc.)
Mand.	Mandaic
masc.	masculine
MDAI	*Mitteilungen des deutschen Archäologischen Instituts in Kairo*, Wiesbaden
MDAW	*Mitteilungen der Deutschen Akademie der Wissenschaft zu Berlin*, Institut für Orientforschung
MdD	E. S. Drower-R. Macuch, *Mandaic Dictionary*, Oxford, 1963
MDP	*Mémoires de la Délégation française en Perse*, Paris, 1900
MEOL	*Mededeelingen en Verhandelingen van het Vooraziatisch-Egyptisch Gezelschap "Ex Oriente Lux,"* Leiden
Min.	Minoan
MPL	J. P. Migne, *Patrologia latina*, Paris, 1844-1864, 221 vols.
ms(s).	manuscript(s)
MT	Masoretic Text
MThS	*Münchener theologische Studien*
MThZ	*Münchener theologische Zeitschrift*
MUSJ	*Mélanges de l'Université St. Joseph*, Beirut

n(n).	note(s)
Nab.	Nabatean
NAWG	*Nachrichten der Akademie der Wissenschaften in Göttingen*
NCB	*New Century Bible*, London
NCBC	*The New Century Bible Commentary,* Grand Rapids
NEB	*New English Bible*, Oxford, 1961-1970
NIDNTT	*The New International Dictionary of NT Theology,* ed. L. Coenen, E. Beyreuther, and H. Bietenhard, Eng. trans., Grand Rapids, 1976
NovT	*Novum Testamentum*, Leiden
N.S.	New Series
NT	New Testament, Neues Testament, etc.
NTL	*The New Testament Library,* Philadelphia
NTT	*Norsk teologisk Tidsskrift,* Oslo
obj.	object
OBO	*Orbis biblicus et orientalis*, Fribourg, Göttingen
obv.	obverse of a papyrus or tablet
OECT	*Oxford Editions of Cuneiform Texts*, ed. S. Langdon, Oxford, 1923—
OIP	*Oriental Institute Publications*, Chicago, 1924—
OLZ	*Orientalistische Literaturzeitung*, Leipzig, Berlin
Or	*Orientalia*, Rome
OrAnt	*Oriens antiquus*, Rome
OrBibLov	*Orientalia et biblica lovaniensia*
OrNeer	*Orientalia neerlandica*, Leiden
OrSuec	*Orientalia suecana*, Uppsala
OSA	Old South Arabic
OT	Old Testament, Oude Testament, etc.
OTL	*The Old Testament Library,* Philadelphia
OTS	*Oudtestamentische Studiën*, Leiden
OuTWP	*De Ou Testamentiese Werkgemeenskap in Suid-Afrika*, Pretoria
p(p).	page(s)
PAAJR	*Proceedings of the American Academy for Jewish Research,* Philadelphia
Palmyr.	Palmyrene
par.	parallel/and parallel passages
pass.	passive
PBS	University Museum, University of Pennsylvania, *Publications of the Babylonian Section*, Philadelphia
PEQ	*Palestine Exploration Quarterly,* London
perf.	perfect
Phil.-hist. Kl.	Philosophische-historische Klasse
Phoen.	Phoenician
PJ	*Palästinajahrbuch,* Berlin
pl(s).	plate(s)
pl.	plural
PLO	*Porta linguarum orientalium*, Wiesbaden
PNU	F. Grondähl, *Personennamen der Texte aus Ugarit,* Rome, 1967
POS	*Pretoria Oriental Series*, Leiden
PredOT	*De Prediking van het OT,* Nijkerk
prep.	preposition
PRU	*Le Palais royal d'Ugarit,* ed. C. F.-A. Schaeffer and J. Nougayrol, Paris

ptcp.	participle
Pun.	Punic
PW	A. Pauly-G. Wissowa, *Real-Encyclopädie der classischen Altertumswissenschaft,* Stuttgart, 1839; supplements, 1903-1956, 11 vols.; ser. 2, 1914-1948
Pyr.	K. Sethe, *Die altägyptischen Pyramidentexte,* Leipzig, 1908-1922, 4 vols.
Q	*Qere*
R	H. C. Rawlinson, *The Cuneiform Inscriptions of Western Asia,* London, 1861-1909, 4 vols.
RA	*Revue d'assyriologie et d'archéologie orientale,* Paris
RAC	*Reallexikon für Antike und Christentum,* ed. T. Klauser, Stuttgart, 1950—
RÄR	H. Bonnet, *Reallexikon der ägyptischen Religionsgeschichte,* Berlin, 1952
RB	*Revue biblique,* Paris
RdM	*Die Religionen der Menschheit,* ed. C. M. Schröder, Stuttgart
RÉg	*Revue d'égyptologie,* Paris
repr.	reprint, reprinted
RÉS	*Revue des études sémitique,* Paris
RÉS (with number of text)	*Répertoire d'épigraphie sémitique,* Paris
RevBíbl	*Revista bíblica,* Buenos Aires
RevExp	*Review and Expositor,* Louisville
RevQ	*Revue de Qumrân,* Paris
RGG	*Die Religion in Geschichte und Gegenwart,* Tübingen, ed. H. Gunkel-L. Zscharnack, ²1927-1931, 5 vols.; ed. K. Galling, ³1957-1965, 6 vols.
RHA	*Revue hittite et asiatique,* Paris
RHPR	*Revue d'histoire et de philosophie religieuses,* Strasbourg, Paris
RHR	*Revue de l'histoire des religions,* Paris
RivBibl	*Rivista biblica,* Rome
RLA	*Reallexikon der Assyriologie,* ed. G. Ebeling-B. Meissner, Berlin, 1932—
RS	Ras Shamra text
RScR	*Recherches de science religieuse,* Paris
RSF	*Rivista di studi fenici,* Rome
RSP	*Ras Shamra Parallels,* ed. L. R. Fisher, *et al.*, I, *AnOr,* 49, 1972; II, *AnOr,* 50, 1975
RSV	*Revised Standard Version,* New York, 1946, 1952
RT	*Recueil de travaux relatifs à la philologie et à l'archéologie égyptiennes et assyriennes,* Paris
RThL	*Revue théologique de Louvain*
RyNP	G. Ryckmans, *Les noms propres sud-sémitiques. Bibliothèque de muséon,* 2, 1934-35, 3 vols.
Sam.	Samaritan
SAW	*Sitzungsberichte der Österreichischen Akademie der Wissenschaften in Wien*
SBAW	*Sitzungsberichte der Bayerischen Akademie der Wissenschaften,* Munich
SDAW	*Sitzungsberichte der Deutschen Akademie der Wissenschaften zu Berlin*
SBS	*Stuttgarter Bibel-Studien*
SBT	*Studies in Biblical Theology,* London, Chicago
Schaff-Herzog	*The New Schaff-Herzog Encyclopedia of Religious Knowledge,* New York, 1912, ²1949-1952
SchThU	*Schweizerische theologische Umschau,* Bern

ScrHier	*Scripta hierosolymitana*, Jerusalem
Sef	*Sefarad. Revista de la Escuela de Estudios hebraicos del Instituto Arias Montano*, Madrid
Sem	*Semitica*, Paris
ser.	series
sg.	singular
SNumen	*Supplements to Numen*, Leiden
SNVAO	*Skrifter utgitt av det Norske Videnskaps-Akadem i Oslo*
Soq.	Soqoṭri
SOTS Mon	*Society for Old Testament Study Monograph*, Cambridge
SPIB	*Scripta Pontificii Instituti Biblici*, Rome
SSAW	*Sitzungsberichte der Sächsischen Akademie der Wissenschaften zu Leipzig*
SSN	*Studia semitica neerlandica*, Assen
StAns	*Studia anselmiana*, Rome
StANT	*Studien zum Alten und Neuen Testament*, Munich
St.-B.	H. L. Strack-P. Billerbeck, *Kommentar zum NT aus Talmud und Midrasch*, Munich, 1922-1961, 6 vols.
StDI	*Studia et documenta ad iura orientis antiqui pertinentia*, Leiden
StFrib	*Studia friburgensia*, Freiburg
StFS	*Studia Francisci Scholten*, Leiden
StJLA	*Studies in Judaism in Late Antiquity*, Leiden
StOr	*Studia orientalia*, Helsinki
StPb	*Studia postbiblica*, Leiden
StTh	*Studia theologica*, Lund, Aarhus
StudGen	*Studium generale*, Heidelberg
StUNT	*Studien zur Umwelt des NTs*, Göttingen
subj.	subject
subst.	substantive
Sum.	Sumerian
Sup.	Supplement(s)
Šurpu	E. Reiner, *Šurpu. A Collection of Sumerian and Akkadian Incantations. BAfO*, 11, 1958
Synt.	C. Brockelmann, *Hebräische Syntax*, Neukirchen-Vluyn, 1956
Syr.	Syriac
Syr.	*Syria. Revue d'art oriental et d'archéologie*, Paris
SVT	*Supplements to VT*, Leiden
TAPhS	*Transactions of the American Philosophical Society*, Philadelphia
Targ.	Targum
TCL	*Textes cunéiformes du Musée du Louvre*, Paris, 1910—
TCS	*Texts from Cuneiform Sources*, Locust Valley, N. Y.
TDNT	*Theological Dictionary of the NT*, ed. G. Kittel-G. Friedrich, Eng. trans., Grand Rapids, 1964-1976, 10 vols.
TDOT	*Theological Dictionary of the OT*, ed. G. J. Botterweck-H. Ringgren, Eng. trans., Grand Rapids, 1974—
THAT	*Theologisches Handwörterbuch zum AT*, ed. E. Jenni-C. Westermann, Munich, 1971-76, 2 vols.
ThB	*Theologische Bücherei*, Munich
Theol.	Theology (of)
ThLB	*Theologisches Literaturblatt*, Leipzig

ThLZ — *Theologische Literaturzeitung*, Leipzig, Berlin
ThSt — *Theologische Studien*, Zurich
ThT — *Theologisch Tijdschrift*, Wageningen
ThZ — *Theologische Zeitschrift*, Basel
Tigr. — Tigriña
TigrWB — E. Littmann-M. Höfner, *Wörterbuch der Tigre-Sprache*, Wiesbaden, 1962
TIM — *Texts in the Iraq Museum*, I-VII, Wiesbaden, 1965-1971; VIII, Baghdad, 1975; IX-, Leiden, 1976—
trans. — translation, translated by
TrThZ — *Trierer theologische Zeitschrift*
TU — *Texte und Untersuchungen der altchristlichen Literatur*, Leipzig, Berlin
TynB — *Tyndale Bulletin*, London
UF — *Ugarit-Forschungen*, Neukirchen-Vluyn
Ugar. — Ugaritic
UEOL — *Uitgaven van het Vooraziatisch-Egyptisch Gezelschap "Ex Oriente Lux,"* Leiden
Urk. — *Urkunden des ägyptischen Altertums*, Leipzig, 1903—
UT — C. H. Gordon, *Ugaritic Textbook, AnOr*, 38, 1965
UUA — *Uppsala universitetsårsskrift*
VAB — *Vorderasiatische Bibliothek*, Leipzig, 1907-1916
VAS — *Vorderasiatische Schriftdenkmäler der königlichen Museen zu Berlin*
VD — *Verbum domini*, Rome
VG — C. Brockelmann, *Grundriss der vergleichenden Grammatik der semitischen Sprachen*, Berlin, 1908-1913, repr. 1961, 2 vols.
vo. — verso, on the reverse of a papyrus or tablet
VT — *Vetus Testamentum*, Leiden
Vulg. — Vulgate
WbÄS — A. Erman-H. Grapow, *Wörterbuch der ägyptischen Sprache*, Leipzig, 1926-1931, repr. 1963, 6 vols.
WbMyth — *Wörterbuch der Mythologie*, ed. H. W. Haussig, Stuttgart, 1961
WdF — *Wege der Forschung*, Darmstadt
Wehr — H. Wehr, *A Dictionary of Modern Written Arabic*, ed. J. M. Cowan, Ithaca, 1961, ^{4}1968
Whitaker — R. E. Whitaker, *A Concordance of the Ugaritic Language*, Cambridge, Mass., 1972
WMANT — *Wissenschaftliche Monographien zum Alten und Neuen Testament*, Neukirchen-Vluyn
WO — *Die Welt des Orients*, Göttingen
WTM — J. Levy, *Wörterbuch über die Talmudim und Midraschim*, Leipzig, ^{2}1924, repr. 1963, 4 vols.
WUS — J. Aistleitner, *Wörterbuch der ugaritischen Sprache. BSAW*, Phil.-hist. Kl., 106/3, 1963, ^{4}1974
WVDOG — *Wissenschaftliche Veröffentlichungen der Deutschen Orient-Gesellschaft* (Berlin), Leipzig
WZ — *Wissenschaftliche Zeitschrift*
WZKM — *Wiener Zeitschrift für die Kunde des Morgenlandes*
Ya'ud. — Ya'udic
YOSBT — *Yale Oriental Series, Babylonian Texts*, New Haven
ZA — *Zeitschrift für Assyriologie*, Leipzig, Berlin
ZÄS — *Zeitschrift für ägyptische Sprache und Altertumskunde*, Leipzig, Berlin
ZAW — *Zeitschrift für die alttestamentliche Wissenschaft*, Giessen, Berlin

ZDMG	*Zeitschrift der Deutschen Morgenländischen Gesellschaft,* Leipzig, Wiesbaden
ZDPV	*Zeitschrift des Deutschen Palästina-Vereins,* Leipzig, Stuttgart, Wiesbaden
ZMR	*Zeitschrift für Missionskunde und Religionswissenschaft,* Berlin
ZNW	*Zeitschrift für die neutestamentliche Wissenschaft,* Giessen, Berlin
ZThK	*Zeitschrift für Theologie und Kirche,* Tübingen
ZVR Sond	*Sonderabdruck aus der Zeitschrift für vergleichende Rechtswissenschaft,* Stuttgart
→	cross-reference within this Dictionary
<	derived from
>	whence derived, to

TRANSLITERATION

VOWELS

◌ַ	a
◌ֲ	^{a}
◌ָ	ā
◌ֶ	e
◌ֱ	^{e}
◌ֶי	ey
◌ֵ	ē
◌ֵי	ê
◌ְ	^{e}
◌ִ	i
◌ִי	î
◌ָ	o
◌ֳ	^{o}
◌ֹ	ō
וֹ	ô
◌ֻ	u
וּ	û
◌ָה	â
◌ָיו	āw
◌ַי	ay
◌ָי	āy

CONSONANTS

א	’
בּ	b
ב	ḇ
גּ	g
ג	ḡ
דּ	d
ד	ḏ
ה, הּ	h
ו	w
ז	z
ח	ḥ
ט	ṭ
י	y
כּ	k
כ	ḵ
ל	l
מ	m
נ	n
ס	s
ע	‘
פּ	p
פ	p̄
צ	ṣ
ק	q
ר	r
שׂ	ś
שׁ	š
תּ	t
ת	ṯ

חמר *ḥmr;* חֹמֶר *ḥōmer;* חֵמָר *ḥēmār*

Contents: I. Roots, Etymology. II. 1. "Foam"; 2. "Glow, Burn"; 3. *ḥōmer,* "Clay"; 4. *ḥēmār,* "Bitumen."

I. Roots, Etymology. *KBL*³ distinguishes five roots *ḥmr;* assignment to the various roots, especially of the few instances of the verb, remains uncertain.

From the root *ḥmr* I, which appears in Jewish Aram. *ḥᵃmar,* "burden, heap up, aggravate" (Middle Heb. *ḥāmar,* "drive asses," is probably a denominative from → חֲמוֹר *ḥᵃmôr* [*chᵃmôr*], "ass"), is derived *ḥōmer* III, the "homer" as a measure of volume. In Akkadian, too, *imēru* means both "ass" and a measure of volume. Here, too, should probably be assigned the expression *ḥºmārim ḥºmārim,* "in heaps," of Ex. 8:10 (Eng. v. 14), referring to the plague of frogs in Egypt, and the phrase *ḥᵃmôr ḥᵃmōrāṯāyim* in Jgs. 15:16 (Samson's poem), if the traditional interpretation, "heaps upon heaps," is actually correct; it is often read *ḥāmôr ḥᵃmartîm,* "I have truly flayed them" (from *ḥmr* IV, see below). Nyberg[1] considers the phrase to be paronomasia used for emphasis, and translates, "of an ass indeed"; cf. Jgs. 5:30 for the syntax.

The root *ḥmr* II appears in Arab. *ḫamara,* "cover," "leaven," Aram. (Jewish Aram., Christian Palestinian Aram., Syr., Mand.) *ḥᵃmîrā'* (Sam. *'myr*), Arab. *ḫamīr,* "leaven," "that which is leavened," Egyp. Aram. *ḥᵃmîr,* "leavened,"[2] Tigré *ḥamra,* "ferment." In Biblical Hebrew, the verb *ḥāmar,* "foam,"[3] *ḥemer,* "wine," and *ḥōmer,* "surging" (Hab. 3:15), are attested.

The root *ḥmr* III appears in Middle Heb. *ḥāmar* and Arab. *ḥamara* II, "roast," "burn," Jewish Aram. *ḥᵃmar,* "glow," Arab. *ḥmr* IX and XI, "be red," *'aḥmar,* "red," Akk. *emēru,* "be reddened,"[4] and Tigré *ḥamar,* "reddish brown."[5] In Biblical Hebrew, the form *ḥºmarmar* (Lam. 1:20; 2:11, with *mē'îm* as subject; Job 16:16, with *pānîm* as subject), usually translated "burn, glow,"[6] is assigned here, together with the hiphil

ḥmr. R. J. Forbes, *Bitumen and Petroleum in Antiquity* (Leiden, 1936); *idem, Studies in Ancient Technology,* I (Leiden, ²1964), 1-125; G. Pettinato, *Das altorientalische Menschenbild und die sumerischen und akkadischen Schöpfungsmythen. AHAW,* 1971/1; A. Schwarzenbach, *Die geographische Terminologie im Hebräischen des ATs* (Leiden, 1954).

1 H. S. Nyberg, *Hebreisk Grammatik* (Uppsala, 1952), §92b.
2 *DISO,* 90.
3 See II.1 below.
4 *AHw,* I, 214.
5 Leslau, *Contributions,* 21.
6 See II.2 below.

form *taḥmîr,* "cause to burn" (Sir. 4:2f.), as well as → חמור *ḥ^a^mōr* [*ch^a^môr*], "ass," *ḥōmer,* "clay," and *ḥēmār,* "bitumen" (?).

The root *ḥmr* IV is associated with Arab. *ḥamara,* "scrape," "flay"; it is found only as a conjectural reading *ḥāmôr ḥ^a^martîm*[7] in Jgs. 15:16.

The root *ḥmr* V is attested only once, in Ex. 2:3, where it occurs as a verb derived from *ḥēmār,* "bitumen," with the meaning "daub with bitumen." Clearly the noun *ḥēmār* belongs here as a primary noun.

II. 1. *"Foam."* The verb *ḥāmar,* "foam," appears only in Ps. 46:4(3), where it is applied to the foaming and roaring (*hāmâ*) waters of chaos as they advance: even if the world is returned to chaos, Yahweh who is present in Zion will provide security. The verb may also occur in Ps. 75:9(8) (*w^e^yayin ḥāmar*), which speaks of the cup of wrath in Yahweh's hand. But the perfect tense of the verb is not really appropriate to the context, and the reading *yên ḥemer* seems preferable. In any case, the meaning is "foaming wine."

From the same root is derived also the noun *ḥemer,* "wine" (Dt. 32:14; Sir. 31:30 [Gk. 34:30]; probably also Isa. 27:2); cf. Arab. *ḫamr,* "wine," Ugar. *ḫmr,* usually translated "wine, intoxicating beverage," but rendered as "wine-bowl, vat" by Dahood[8] (→ יין *yayin*). The Deuteronomy passage speaks of wine as a symbol of the fertility of the land; Sir. 31:30 stands within a lengthy warning against excess in drinking; Isa. 27:2 contains an allusion to Isa. 5:1ff., the Song of the Vineyard, so that the reading of 1QIs^a^ (*ḥwmr* instead of *ḥmr*) can hardly be correct. Many manuscripts read *ḥemeḏ,* i.e., a "pleasant" vineyard, which is quite possible; it is hardly necessary to explicate *kerem* with a word for "wine."

2. *"Glow, Burn."* The reduplicating form *ḥ^o^marmar* occurs 3 times. In Job 16:16, the subject is *pānîm:* "My face glows (burns) with weeping." The translation "grows red" may also be considered on the basis of Arab. *'aḥmar,* "red." In Lam. 1:20; 2:11, the subject is *mēʿay,* "my interior"; the translation could be either "be in tumult" (*ḥmr* II, "ferment") or "glow, burn" (*ḥmr* III). The translation "redden" proposed by Gradwohl[9] is unlikely. Driver[10] cites Akk. *emēru*[11] and translates "is contorted." Wilson[12] cites Akk. *ḫurḫummatu*[13] and takes the "foaming up" of fermenting wine, etc., as a metaphor for a glowing face.

Here also belongs the hiphil form *taḥmîr* in Sir. 4:3, with *mēʿîm* as its object, meaning either "stir up" or "cause to burn."

---

[7] See above.

[8] M. Dahood, "Hebrew-Ugaritic Lexicography II," *Bibl,* 45 (1964), 408f.

[9] R. Gradwohl, *Die Farben im AT: Eine terminologische Studie. BZAW,* 83 (1963), 17.

[10] G. R. Driver, review of *CAD,* III [1959], *JSS,* 5 (1960), 157.

[11] *AHw,* I, 214: "distend" from breast, intestines; not like *KBL*[3]*: emermēru!*

[12] J. V. K. Wilson, "Hebrew and Akkadian Philological Notes," *JSS,* 7 (1962), 173.

[13] Cf. *AHw,* I, 359; but von Soden, *GaG,* §57d.

3. *ḥōmer, "Clay."* The word *ḥōmer* meaning "clay" occurs 15 times.[14] It stands as a kind of earth or soil in combination or parallelism with → טיט *ṭîṭ* (Isa. 41:25; Nah. 4:14) or → עפר *'āphār* [*'āpār*] (Job 4:19; 27:16; 30:19; cf. 10:9), and also with *'ēper* (Job 13:12; 30:19). It appears alone in Isa. 10:6. It is mentioned as a building material: in Ex. 1:14 together with *l^eḇēnîm,* "bricks"; in Gen. 11:3, which lists *ḥēmār,* "bitumen," as being used for mortar; and in Nah. 3:14, where *ṭîṭ, ḥōmer,* and brick-molds are used in preparation for a siege. In metaphorical usage, *ḥōmer* stands for weakness and rejection: Assyria tramples its enemies like *ḥōmer* in the street (Isa. 10:6), Cyrus will trample his enemies like *ḥōmer* and *ṭîṭ* (Isa. 41:25), human wisdom and human accomplishments are like ashes and *ḥōmer* (Job 13:12; cf. 30:19). But it can also symbolize a large quantity: silver is piled up like *'āpār* and clothing like *ḥōmer* (Job 27:16).

Above all, *ḥōmer* appears as the potter's raw material (Isa. 41:25); it thus serves frequently to symbolize mankind in relationship to the omnipotence of God. Jeremiah sees a potter working with *ḥōmer* (Jer. 18:4) and realizes that the house of Israel is like clay in God's hand (v. 6): God can do with his people as he wills. At the same time, however, one senses behind this image the conviction that God has a purpose in what he does: he intends to make a good vessel. Isa. 29:16 and 45:9 express the idea that mankind must not question what God does—to do so would be like a pot rebelling against the potter. Isa. 64:7(8) calls God the father of Israel; he has shaped the nation as a potter shapes his clay. Both God's power and his care and pity are emphasized.

The same image probably stands behind several statements in the book of Job that describe mankind as being made out of clay: "Remember that thou hast made me like clay, and thou wilt turn me to dust (*'āpār*) again" (10:9). Here *ḥōmer* appears more or less synonymous with *'āpār,* and the notion of mankind's origin out of the dust is clearly the same as in Gen. 2:7 (cf. 3:19). On the other hand, Job 33:6 appears to preserve a recollection of the Akkadian idea. Elihu says, "I, too, was formed (*qrṣ,* "pinched off") from a piece of clay." Various Akkadian texts relate how mankind was formed from clay (*ṭiṭṭu*) when a god pinched off (*karāṣu*) a lump of clay.[15] The same idea reappears several times in the Dead Sea scrolls, in 1QS 11:22 even with *qrṣ*. In the Hodayoth, mankind is very often referred to as *yeṣer ḥōmer* (1QH 1:21; 3:24; 4:29; 11:3; 12:26 [associated with their return to *'āpār*[16]]; 12:32; 18:12). The emphasis is always on mankind's weakness and sinfulness; these statements are based on the Qumran doxologies that celebrate mankind's lowliness.[17]

4. *ḥēmār, "Bitumen."* The noun *ḥēmār* is the most common word for "bitumen" or "asphalt," a mineral known to have been found in antiquity near the Dead Sea (Gen.

---

[14] Schwarzenbach, 132f.

[15] See Pettinato, 41ff.

[16] See H. J. Fabry, *Die Wurzel Šûb in der Qumran-Literatur. BBB,* 46 (1975), 110-120.

[17] See H.-W. Kuhn, *Enderwartung und gegenwärtiges Heil. StUNT,* 4 (1966), 27f.

14:10)[18] and in Mesopotamia[19] (Akk. *iṭṭû*,[20] *napṭu*[21]). The use of asphalt is attested as early as the third millennium. In the OT it is mentioned as mortar for bricks (Gen. 11:3) and as a caulking compound for Noah's ark (Gen. 6:14, where, however, the word used is *kōper*, borrowed from Akk. *kupru*[22]) and the basket in which Moses was placed on the Nile (Ex. 2:3).

Ringgren

---

18 See P. C. Hammond, "The Nabataean Bitumen Industry at the Dead Sea," *BA*, 22 (1959), 40-48.

19 See G. Ebeling, "Erdöl, Erdpech," *RLA*, II (1938), 462f.

20 *AHw*, I, 408.

21 *Ibid.*, II, 742.

22 *Ibid.*, I, 509.

חָנָה *ḥānâ*; מַחֲנֶה *maḥ*[a]*neh*

Contents: I. Ancient Near East: 1. Egyptian; 2. Akkadian; 3. Phoenician and Aramaic Inscriptions; 4. Qumran; 5. LXX and Deuterocanonical Writings. II. Israel: 1. Seminomadic Camps; 2. Military Camps; 3. The Desert Camp: a. Outward Form (Organization); b. The Desert Camp in the Earlier Source Strata; c. The Priestly Notion of the Camp: Model and Purpose; d. Tent and Camp; e. Conclusions; 4. The Camp of God; 5. Miscellanea; 6. Conclusions.

ḥānâ. A. Alt, "Zelte und Hütten," *Alttestamentliche Studien F. Nötscher . . . gewidmet. BBB*, 1 (1950), 16-25 = *KlSchr*, III (1959), 233-242, cited hereafter; A. Besters, "Le sanctuaire central dans Jud XIX–XXI," *ETL*, 41 (1965), 20-41; W. Beyerlin, *Origins and History of the Oldest Sinaitic Traditions* (Eng. trans., Oxford, 1966); M. Buber, *Kingship of God* (Eng. trans., New York, 1967); G. Dalman, *AuS*, VI (1939); G. Fohrer, "AT—'Amphiktyonie' und 'Bund?' " *ThLZ*, 91 (1966), 801-816, 839-904; T. E. Fretheim, "The Priestly Document: Anti-Temple?" *VT*, 18 (1968), 313-329; M. Görg, *Das Zelt der Begegnung. BBB*, 27 (1967); M. Haran, "The Nature of the "'Ōhel Mô'ēdh' in Pentateuchal Sources," *JSS*, 5 (1960), 50-65; R. Hartmann, "Zelt und Lade," *ZAW*, 37 (1917/18), 209-244; J. Kaufmann, "Probleme der israelitisch-Jüdischen Religionsgeschichte," *ZAW*, 48 (1930), 23-43; R. Kilian, "Die Hoffnung auf Heimkehr in der Priesterschrift," *BiLe*, 7 (1966), 39-51; H.-J. Kraus, *Gottesdienst in Israel: Studien zur Geschichte des Laubhüttenfestes. BEvTh*, 19 (1954, ²1962); *idem*, *Worship in Israel* (Eng. trans., Richmond, 1966); A. Kuschke, "Die Lagervorstellung der priesterschriftlichen Erzählung," *ZAW*, 63 (1971), 74-105; S. Lehming, "Erwägungen zur Zelttradition," *Gottes Wort und Gottes Land. Festschrift H. W. Hertzberg* (Göttingen, 1965), 110-132; G. W. MacRae, "The Meaning and Evolution of the Feast of Tabernacles," *CBQ*, 22 (1960), 251-276; A. Malamat, "The Danite Migration and the Pan-Israelite Exodus-Conquest: A Biblical Narrative Pattern," *Bibl*, 51 (1970), 1-16; M. Noth, *Das System der Zwölf Stämme Israels. BWANT*, 52[4/1] (²1966); *idem*, "Der Wallfahrtsweg zum Sinai (Nu 33)," *PJ*, 36 (1940), 5-28 = his *Aufsätze zur biblischen Landes- und Altertumskunde* (Neukirchen-Vluyn, 1971), I, 55-74; G. von Rad, "The Form-Critical Problem of the Hexateuch," in his *The Problem of the Hexateuch and Other Essays* (Eng. trans., New York, 1966), 1-78; *idem*, "The Tent and the Ark," *Kirchliche Zeitschrift*, 42 (1931), 476-498 = *Hexateuch*, 103-124; *idem*, *Der heilige Krieg im alten Israel* (Göttingen, ⁵1969); *idem*, *Studies in Deuteronomy. SBT*, 9 (Eng. trans. 1953); *idem*, *Die Priesterschrift im Hexateuch:*

I. Ancient Near East.

1. *Egyptian.* The Egyptian equivalent to Heb. *ḥānâ, ḫny,*[1] means "alight," "settle down," "make a stop," "linger." The stop appears to be temporary in nature, as can been seen from the "alighting" of birds, as well as from the meanings "pass through a place" and "dance," together with the term *ḫny.t,* applied to wandering women, and the word *ḫn,* which means "rebel" (unstable).

2. *Akkadian.* In Assyrian, *ḫanû* means "coming from Ḫana."[2] Dossin[3] connects *ḫanû* with Heb. *ḥānâ,* although Kupper[4] cites a different verb *ḫanûm,* "intervene on someone's behalf."[5] Cf. also Finet,[6] who suggests the meaning "fat" for *ḫānû: (immeru) ḫa-nu-û,* "fat sheep." There is also a verb *ḫunnû,* "shelter (sheep)."[7]

The semantically related word *nâḫum,* "rest," "be quiet,"[8] corresponds to Heb. → נוּחַ *nûaḥ* and also to Ugar. *nḫ,* "rest," "be satisfied,"[9] which designates a social class, a type of soldier mentioned in a list from Alalakh along with the *ṣābē namē,* "people living outside of villages and towns."[10]

Soldiers of the "Ḫanaites" are found at Mari and Suprum.[11] The "Ḫanaites" have their camp beside the Euphrates (*Ḫana ša nawêm*[12]), but also live in cities (*ālānu*).[13] They are thus nomads making the transition to settled life;[14] they raise cattle and occasionally engage in raiding.[15] At their head stand the elders and the *sugagu,* "a class of nobles."[16] Their camp (*na-wu-ú-um,* "collection of nomads, troops, or sheep"[17]),

---

literarisch untersucht und theologisch logisch gewertet. BWANT, 65[4/13] (1934), 166-189 = "Die Theologie der Priesterschrift," in *GSAT,* II. *ThB,* 48 (1973), 165-188; L. Rost, *Die Vorstufen von Kirche und Synagoge im AT. BWANT,* 78[4/24] (1938, ²1967); R. Schmitt, *Zelt und Lade als Thema alttestamentlicher Wissenschaft* (Gütersloh, 1972); R. Smend, *Yahweh War and Tribal Confederation* (Eng. trans., Nashville, 1970); E. Täubler, *Biblische Studien: Die Epoche der Richter* (Göttingen, 1958); G. Wallis, "Die Stadt in den Überlieferungen der Genesis," *ZAW,* 78 (1966), 133-148; M. Weber, *Ancient Judaism* (Eng. trans., Glencoe, Ill., 1952).

[1] *WbÄS,* III, 287f.

[2] *CAD,* VI (1956), 82f.; *AHw,* I, 321.

[3] G. Dossin, *Correspondance de Iasmaḫ-Addu. ARM,* V (1952), 128.

[4] J. R. Kupper, *Les nomades en Mésopotamie au temps des rois de Mari* (Paris, 1957), 43, n. 2.

[5] *AHw,* I, 321: *ḫanû* II.

[6] A. Finet, *Répertoire analytique das tomes I à V. ARM,* XV (1954; repr. 1978), 204, citing *ARM,* V, 15, 7.

[7] *AHw,* I, 356.

[8] Cf. Finet, *ARM,* XV, 229.

[9] See *WUS,* no. 1772.

[10] *CAD,* VI, 82; cf. Kupper, *Nomades,* 45: *ṣābē namē,* "people of the countryside"; *AHw,* II, 729: *namû* = *nawû,* "steppe."

[11] Kupper, *Nomades,* 1.

[12] G. Dossin, *Correspondance de Šamši-Addu et de ses fils. ARM,* I (1949; repr. 1978), 6, 26, 41, etc.

[13] Kupper, *Nomades,* 12f.

[14] *Ibid.,* 15.

[15] *Ibid.*

[16] *Ibid.,* 16.

[17] *ARM,* XV, 294.

located in the hinterlands of the steppe (*nawûm*[18]) is under the control of Mari[19] and probably forms part of the Mari military contingent.[20]

For the meaning of *ḫanû(m)* we thus arrive at a mode of life outside of cities and towns, in camps and/or military garrisons—probably the "encampment" of semi-nomads (caravan and camel drivers?[21]) on the fringes of the settled territory, in whose presence the city dwellers had an interest for their own economic and military security.[22]

3. *Phoenician and Aramaic Inscriptions*. In Phoenician and Aramaic inscriptions, the predominant meaning of *mḥnh* is "army (encampment)";[23] cf. also the term *rb mḥnt,* used for the proconsul in Neo-Punic inscriptions.[24] One Aramaic inscription[25] states that the king "camps," i.e., rests, in the favor (= "success") of the deity; according to another,[26] the king of Assyria caused King Panammu "to rest more than the mighty kings"; this is expressed by his running "by the wheel of his lord Tiglath-pileser . . . (in the midst of the) army formations,"[27] probably "evidence of the overlord's favor toward his vassal."[28]

4. *Qumran*. With respect to the camp idea, the Qumran texts draw on the OT traditions, among other sources: the camp is military in nature (1QM 1:3; 3:4f.,14; 6:10; 14:2; 15:2; 16:3; 18:4; 19:9; etc.; 1QH 2:25). In the Damascus document, talk of the "camp" can hardly have in mind the OT camp and thus does not refer to a sojourn in the desert.[29] It does, however, have at least one element of the "desert ideology" in common with the OT notion of the desert camp:[30] a situation of separation, comparable to the purified cities of 1 Macc. 13:48 (cf. CD 12:23).[31] In these "camps" the law of God is in force (cf. CD 7:6; 10:23: the Sabbath; 19:2: marriage laws); without approval of the *m^{e}ḇaqqēr '^{a}šer lammaḥ^{a}neh,* no outsider may enter (CD 13:13). Since tents or booths are never mentioned in connection with the "camps" in the "land of Damascus," these camps should be thought of as "communities"[32] or "separate" settlements with their own specific rules (CD 7:6; 9:11; 12:23; etc.; possibly also 1QSa 2:15).[33]

---

18 *ARM,* I, 33, 95; C.-F. Jean, *Letters divers. ARM,* II (1959; repr. 1978), 103.
19 *ARM,* I, 42, 5.
20 *Ibid.*, I, 42, 5-10.
21 Kupper, *Nomades,* 15.
22 *Idem, Correspondance de Kibri-Dagan. ARM,* III (1959; repr. 1978), 10-15.
23 *KAI,* 1.2; 26 A I.7f.; 202 A.5-7, 9; 215.13, 16 (battle), 17.
24 *Ibid.*, 118.2; 120.1.
25 *Ibid.*, 214.19.
26 *Ibid.*, 215.12.
27 *Ibid.*, 215.12f.
28 *Ibid.*, II, 228.
29 J. Maier, *Die Texte vom Toten Meer* (Munich, 1960), II, 52, 57; but cf. É. Cothenet in J. Carmignac, *et al., Les textes de Qumran,* II (Paris, 1963), 188, n. 12.
30 Contra Maier, *Texte,* II, 57.
31 *Ibid.*
32 *Ibid.*
33 J. Carmignac in *Textes,* II, 25, n. 80, citing Nu. 2:3-31; 10:14-27.

5. *LXX and Deuterocanonical Writings.* The LXX usually renders *ḥānâ/maḥ*ª*neh* as *parembállein/parembolḗ,* which are technical military terms.[34] Also to the military realm belongs the scattered use of *kykloún* (Job 19:12; Isa. 29:3), *paratássein* (Ps. 26:3[Eng. 27:3]), *perikathízein* (Josh. 10:5,31,34; Jgs. 9:50), *dýnamis* (1 Ch. 12:23[22]; 2 Ch. 14:12[13]), *laós* (in the sense of "armed men," Josh. 10:5), *parátaxis* (1 S. 17:4), *pólemos* (1 S. 28:1; 2 S. 5:24; 1 K. 22:34 par. 2 Ch. 18:33). The encampments of the exodus groups, for which the verb *stratopedeúein* is used (Ex. 13:20; 14:2), are thus characterized as army encampments, in contrast to Nu. 5:2, where the desert camp is referred to as a *synagōgḗ* (place of assembly, but also a liturgical assembly) in which each has a fixed place (*táxis,* Nu. 1:52). The LXX seems to miss the theological point of 2 Ch. 31:2, rendering *maḥ*ª*nôṯ YHWH* as *oíkou kyríou.*

In the deuterocanonical books, "encamp" and "camp" refer almost exclusively to military encampment (Jth. 6:11; 7:3,12,17f.,20; 10:18; etc.; 1 Macc. 2:32; 3:3,40f.; etc.; 2 Macc. 13:15f.; 15:22), and by extension the army (Jth. 16:3; 1 Macc. 3:15,23,27; 6:40-42; etc.), siege (1 Macc. 5:5; 6:26,51; etc.), and war (1 Macc. 6:48). Jth. 7:32 also belongs in this context; the "camp" (*parembolḗ*) refers to a city in a state of military preparedness. Only Wis. 19:7 refers to the exodus camp. The divergent meanings in Sir. 11:8 (to "interrupt" a speaker) and 43:8 (the moon causing the heavenly host to encamp [?] or restraining them) are not especially significant.

II. Israel.

1. *Seminomadic Camps.* Transhumant groups are dependent on water, especially for their cattle; therefore they set up their camp in valleys during summer, like Isaac encamping in the valley of Gerar (Gen. 16:17), where he digs out the old wells (26:18). The encampment of Dan at Kiriath-jearim (Jgs. 18:11f.) appears to be of a different sort: the transmigrating Danites make a temporary stop and set up a military camp in the course of a "campaign of settlement"[35] (cf. Jgs. 18:11: six hundred men armed for war). Gen. 32:8,11(7,10) may refer to a similar camp, since the patriarch Israel is not seeking pasturage with abundant water but rather, according to Gen. 33:18-20, a place to settle. His camp, comprising women, children, male and female servants, and cattle (Gen. 32:8f.[7f.]; 33:8), is an expression of his wealth, of which he can give to appease Esau (33:8). It seems that he himself as leader of his group did not usually spend the night in the camp, i.e., in the midst of the camp, since Gen. 32:22(21) expressly emphasizes that on this night (*ballaylâ-hahû'*)—the night before his encounter with Esau—he slept in the camp (*bammaḥ*ª*neh*). His usual place was probably at the edge (entrance) of the camp (cf. also Josh. 8:13 and later military camps); probably fear of Esau's approach made him seek a secure place in the midst of the camp.

The "camp" of Joseph, or more precisely the entourage of Joseph during his mourning journey to Goren ha-Ated/Abel-mizraim (Gen. 50:9-11; a similar entourage ac-

---

[34] W. Bauer, *A Greek-English Lexicon of the NT* (Eng. trans., Chicago, ²1979), 625.

[35] Malamat, 1.

companies Naaman in 2 K. 5:15), is a traveling camp comprising chariots and horsemen (Gen. 50:9), all the servants of Pharaoh, his officials, all the elders of Egypt (50:7), Joseph, his household, his brothers, and the household of his father, "a very great camp" (50:9).

2. *Military Camps*. A military camp can come into being when gathered (*'āsap,* 1 S. 17:1; *qāḇaṣ,* 1 S. 28:1; 29:1) by the Philistine kings or by an influx of people coming to David and making his camp great *k^e maḥ^a nēh 'ᵉlōhîm* (1 Ch. 12:23[22]). Non-Israelite military camps include—besides men of military age—horses and chariots (Josh. 11:4; Jgs. 4:15f.; 1 S. 13:5; cf. 2 K. 7:7; 1 Ch. 19:7), as well as asses (2 K. 7:7); the Israelite military camp also includes cattle (2 K. 3:9). Therefore a well-watered site must be sought for the camp (Josh. 11:5; Jgs. 7:1; cf. 2 K. 3:9), usually on a plain or in a valley (Jgs. 6:33; 1 S. 29:1: the plain of Jezreel; 1 S. 4:1; 29:1: Aphek; 1 S. 4:1: Ebenezer, opposite Aphek; Jgs. 7:1: the spring of Harod, probably at the foot of Mt. Gilboa; Jgs. 7:1: in the valley by the hill of Moreh; 1 S. 17:1f.: the valley of Elah [terebinths]; 1 Ch. 11:15: the valley of Rephaim). It is surprising that the Israelites also situated their military camps on plains or in valleys, since at the outset they did not employ horses and chariots. Possibly the problem of provisioning played a role, since it is easier to guarantee provisions in the more fertile lowlands than in the hill country. The selection of the site was probably determined by the location of the object of the siege, a city located on a plain or in a valley (cf. *ḥānâ 'al* in the sense of "besiege" in Josh. 10:5,31,34; 1 S. 11:1; 2 S. 12:28).[36]

The nature of the camp varies: David's army camps in booths in the open field (2 S. 11:11); the Syrian camp consists of tents (2 K. 7:7) with booths for the king and his associates (1 K. 20:12,16). A special protected place within the camp is reserved for the king (together with his officers?) (1 S. 26:5: "the people lay in a circle about him"). This seems not to have been the regular practice, however, since Jgs. 7:13 presupposes that the commander's tent stands at the edge or entrance of the camp. This agrees with Dalman's observation[37] that among the camel-herding desert Bedouins the chief (*šēḵ*) has his tent at the camp entrance. When 1 S. 26:5 states that Saul was lying in the midst of the camp, a certain element of criticism is already implied, if the Arabic proverb cited by Dalman[38] has an "ancient history": "Only the brave man takes his place at the edge, and only the contemptible coward in the middle." The king apparently has the "first place" in the camp—an observation that will be significant for determining the site of the *'ōhel mô'ēḏ* (→ אהל *'ōhel*). The fact that the army dwells in booths will also be of importance for the question of the theological significance of *ḥānâ/maḥ^a neh.*

The size of the military camp puts the Israelites at a disadvantage. The Israelites encamp opposite the Syrians "like two little flocks of goats, but the Syrians filled the country" (1 K. 20:27). The Philistine camp numbers three thousand chariots, six thousand horses, and troops "like the sand on the seashore in multitude" (1 S. 13:5);

---

36 For pictures of what are probably Assyrian siege camps see *ANEP,* nos. 170f.

37 *AuS,* VI (1939), 28.

38 *Ibid.*

the army in the camp of the northern kings is also numerous as the sand of the sea (Josh. 11:4). The camp of the Ammonites includes thirty-two thousand chariots (1 Ch. 19:7); from the camp of the people of the East, fifteen thousand survive (Jgs. 8:10); and Saul is overcome with fear when he observes the size of the Philistine camp (1 S. 28:5). In each case (except 1 S. 28), Israel gains the victory despite the numerical superiority of the enemy and acknowledges the help of its God. The superior size of the enemy camp and the truly unexpected success of the Israelite camp provide at least one reason for Israel's faith in Yahweh.

The presence of Yahweh in the Israelite military camp. associated during the premonarchic period with the ark (1 S. 4:5f.; cf. v. 7), demands the observance of certain regulations governing purity (Dt. 23:13,15[12,14]). Here, however, the ideas associated with a nomadic camp appear to dominate (Dt. 23:15[14], *YHWH . . . mitḥallēḵ beqereḇ*), although the distinction between nomadic and military camp is fluid and can vary with the circumstances.[39]

There seems to be more noise and commotion in a military camp than in its nomadic counterpart (Ezk. 1:24; cf. 1 S. 4:6, *qôl hattᵉrûʿâ* at the arrival of the ark)—a method of "psychological warfare" in view of the short distance between the opposing camps. The daytime commotion in the camp is followed by nocturnal quiet, during which the camp is dark (Jgs. 7:22). Nighttime furnishes the Israelites—avoiding military engagements during the daylight—their best opportunity to take the enemy camp by surprise (Jgs. 7:9ff.; in the morning watch: 1 S. 11:11); but it seems that even during the daytime the camp was not always well guarded (2 S. 23:16 par. 1 Ch. 11:18).

The major component of the camp is the army; for this reason, *maḥᵃneh* is often practically synonymous with "army" (Jgs. 8:11f.; 1 S. 17:46; 2 S. 5:24; etc.); it can also mean the "camp" or army in action, i.e., "battle" (1 K. 22:34 par. 2 Ch. 18:33). There is also "entertainment" in the camp, for example, the "camp dance," which the dancing girl presumably dances naked (Cant. 7:1[6:13]).[40] The site appears to be a military camp, as appears from the admittedly puzzling mention of the (war) chariot of Amminadab (Cant. 6:12). Perhaps a reminiscence of the Egyp. *ḥny.t*[41] is also preserved in Cant. 7:1(6:13); there is the possibility of Egyptian influence in 6:12.[42] Whether the dance in 7:1(6:13) is cultic[43] or a "war dance" cannot be determined.

A camp is disbanded by the cry "Every man to his city!" (1 K. 22:36, occasioned by Ahab's death on the field).

3. *The Desert Camp.* a. *Outward Form (Organization).* The statements concerning the camp of the groups emigrating from Egypt and migrating into Canaan—especially the statements in P—exhibit a "sacral" conception of the camp alongside which "secular" details fade into the background. Among the latter we find the following: The camp consists of tents; Moses at least dwells in a tent (on Ex. 18:5, cf. v. 7), and

---

39 De Vaux, *AncIsr,* 214, citing 9.

40 H. Ringgren, *Das Hohe Lied. ATD,* XVI/2 (²1967), 286f.

41 See I.1.

42 G. Gerleman, *Ruth/Das Hohe Lied. BK,* XVIII (1965), 191f.

43 See the survey of the use of *mᵉḥôlâ* in Ringgren, *ATD,* XVI/2, 286f.

according to Lev. 14:8 and Ps. 78:28 all dwell in tents. The camp has two gates or entrances (Ex. 32:26f.); like the city gate, the camp gate appears to be a place of assembly (v. 26). Those who live in the camp obtain food from the livestock they keep (Lev. 17:3), from birds (Ex. 16:13; Nu. 11:31f.; Ps. 78:27f.), and from manna (Nu. 11:9). The presence of water plays a part in the selection of a site for the camp (Ex. 15:27; Nu. 21:12), for which reason a leader with local knowledge is needed (Nu. 10:31). The individual campsites on the route from Rameses to the plains of Moab are listed in Nu. 33:5-37,41-49. There are also other sites: Gilgal (Josh. 4:19; 5:10; 9:6; 10:6,15,43), Makkedah (10:21), and Shiloh (18:9).

The organization of the Priestly camp closely follows that of the → עדה *'ēḏâ,* which is organized hierarchically by tribe (P: *maṭṭeh*), clan (*mišpāḥâ*), and father's house (*bêṯ 'āḇ*).[44] In P, organization by tribes is less important than organization by clans;[45] indeed, even the clan organization takes a back seat to the organization by houses,[46] because "the structure of 'fathers' houses' is rooted in the postexilic community, and probably originated in the diaspora in Babylon."[47] If so, the application of this structure to the desert camp is an "obvious anachronism";[48] the same is true then also of the transfer of the clan organization to the desert period.[49] The starting point for P's description of the camp organization is probably sacral in nature, though not amphictyonic: if it is true that the *'ēḏâ* in P centers on the tent of meeting,[50] the same is probably also true of the organization of the *'ēḏâ* and the camp described in these terms. This is not the place to discuss the sacral implications of the tribe, and above all the clan and father's house. But when we examine P's sacral concept of the camp, we should also keep in mind the pre-P occurrences of *mišpāḥâ* in sacral contexts, e.g., Ex. 12:21[51] and 1 S. 20:6,29.[52]

This organization appears—at first glance—to contradict the organization of the Israelite camp "by standards" (*degel,* Nu. 1:52; 2:2f.,10,17,34; 10:14,25) and "by companies" (*ṣᵉḇā'ôṯ,* Nu. 2:32; 10:14; etc.; *pᵉquḏîm,* Nu. 2:9,16,24,31f.). Whether *degel* means "standard"[53] or a division of the army,[54] in any case this form of organization presupposes a military camp,[55] even if (especially in Nu. 2) the notion of a pilgrimage camp dominates.[56] As will be discussed later, it is possible that both notions can be traced back to a festival or festival assembly that served as a model.

Apart from Moses (and Aaron), leadership over those assembled in the (P) camp

---

44 Rost, 41-59.
45 *Ibid.,* 50.
46 *Ibid.,* 53ff.; Kuschke, 100, cf. 81.
47 *Ibid.,* 57.
48 *Ibid.*
49 *Ibid.,* 53, 55.
50 *Ibid.,* 40, cf. 59.
51 *Ibid.,* 44.
52 *Ibid.,* 47.
53 K. Galling, *BRL,* 160ff.; cf. Kuschke, 101.
54 M. Noth, *Numbers. OTL* (Eng. trans. 1968), 24; *AncIsr,* 214.
55 Kaufmann, 28.
56 Noth, *Numbers,* 24.

is exercised by the "heads" (*rā'šîm*) and "princes" (*n^e^śî'îm*).[57] The "heads" appear in P as representatives of the "fathers' houses," whose thoughts and interests they represent before the community; in this respect, according to Rost,[58] P is going by the structure of the postexilic community. The *n^e^śî'îm,* leaders of the tribes or their representatives, take part primarily in the administration of justice;[59] in the P camp they have no cultic functions.[60] If they ever did exercise such functions, they were displaced from their position by Moses and the Aaronides.[61] Their role, comparable to that of the sheikh, is appropriate to the camp situation presupposed by P in a period before or after the formation of the state. P has developed and elaborated the earlier traditions, possibly on the basis of the postexilic community organization, but more likely—on account of the sacral conception of the camp—on the basis of a sacral festival assembly. This model assembly presupposes the assembly of the tribes and is in agreement with the intentions of P: the important thing is not the permanent organization of the state, but an "interim" organization appropriate to aliens and pilgrims. Although the functions of the "heads" and "princes" transplanted by P to the desert camp are not primarily sacral in nature, their participation in sacral acts is clear ("heads": Josh. 23:2; 24:1; "princes": Nu. 7:11; cf. Ex. 34:31; "heads" and "princes": 2 Ch. 1:2; 5:2; possibly the division of the land should also be included, see Nu. 34:18; Josh. 19:51), so that it is not impossible that they performed a function in festival assemblies as well.

b. *The Desert Camp in the Earlier Source Strata.* The earlier source strata have little to say about the desert camp (using the terms *ḥānâ/maḥ^a^neh*). Apart from a few encampment and itinerary notes (Ex. 13:20; 14:2,9; 15:27; 17:1; Nu. 12:16; 21:10-13) and the reference to provision of manna (Nu. 11:9) and quails (Nu. 11:31f.) for the camp, the important texts are those that set the camp apart from the "tent" (Ex. 33:7,11; Nu. 11:30; cf. vv. 26f.) and the "mountain" (Ex. 19:17; 32:19; cf. v. 17; 19:2). It is therefore not impossible that P, which moves the "tent" into the midst of the camp, is here altering an existing tradition, yet maintaining it to the extent that the "tent" is separated from the rest of the camp by the camp of the Levites. The purity of the camp, which is emphasized by P, is already suggested by J when he recounts the exclusion of Miriam (Nu. 12:14f.). But this singular reference, which more likely involves moral rather than cultic disqualification,[62] does not alter the fact that the sacral nature of the P camp marks a notion of the camp that is *sui generis,* notwithstanding the proposed localization of the camp in the amphictyony,[63] primarily on the basis of Jgs. 21.[64]

---

57 Texts in Rost, 65, 70.
58 Pp. 68f.
59 Kuschke, 81, citing Nu. 27:2.
60 Rost, 71, 74f.; cf. *AncIsr,* 8; for a different view, see Noth, *System,* 160-62.
61 Kuschke, 80, 98.
62 *Ibid.,* 91.
63 *Ibid.,* 76.
64 *Ibid.,* 75.

c. *The Priestly Notion of the Camp: Model and Purpose*. The "amphictyony," itself now a matter of debate,[65] breaks down as a model for P's notion of the camp, as even a glance at the "showpiece" Jgs. 21f. reveals.[66] Here a clear distinction is made between the "camp" at Mizpah (Jgs. 21:8; cf. 20:1-7; 21:5; there can be no question of any amphictyonic assembly "at the sanctuary of Mizpah"[67]) and the "cultic" activities at Bethel (Jgs. 20:18,26-28; 21:2). Once again, there is no evidence for a regular cult of the amphictyony[68] or for an amphictyonic "covenant cult."[69] The lack of any sacral focus in the Mizpah camp (Jgs. 21f.) and the merely temporary stop at Bethel, which precludes the establishment of a camp (cf. Jgs. 20:23,26; 21:2, "till evening"), make recourse to an "amphictyonic assembly" unlikely as a model for P's notion of the camp.[70] The differences between the P camp and the "amphictyony" are too numerous and important: for example,[71] "the preeminent position of the priesthood" in the P camp, the "schematic, artificial-appearing arrangement of the tribes," the "essentially cultic activities" of the camp, and the characterization of the people as constituting an *'ēḏâ* rather than a *qāhāl*.[72]

Kuschke points out,[73] in the context of the question of the nature of God's presence in the camp, that the priestly notion of the tent and camp is shaped by P's account of the revelation at Sinai, a "festival legend"[74] suggesting a festival, possibly the Feast of Booths.[75] Besides the "assimilation of the community structure into the tradition of the desert period,"[76] through the P notion of the camp, the Feast of Booths or a least some pilgrimage festival may have furnished the model for this notion,[77] which would then not give the impression of being "a later sacralization."[78] On the other hand, Kraus's proposed "tent festival"[79] suffers from "the lack of clear textual evidence."[80]

At first glance, the association of the P camp with the Feast of Booths appears to be contradicted by the statement of Ex. 18:7; Lev. 14:8; Ps. 78:28 that the desert camp consisted not of booths but of tents.[81] It must be remembered, however, that in the case of the festival what was originally a dwelling of "nomads" in tents has been

---

65 Fohrer, 801-816; most recently, C. H. J. de Geus, *The Tribes of Israel. SSN*, 18 (1976), 193-209; see also O. Bächli, *Amphiktyonie im AT. ThZ Sonderband*, 6 (1977).

66 Noth, *System*, 102ff., 167.

67 Contra Noth, *ibid.*, 102, and Besters, 39f.

68 Besters, 40.

69 Noth, *System*, 113-16.

70 For an opposing view, see Beyerlin, 129.

71 Kuschke, 79-81.

72 Rost, 40, 83, 86; Kuschke, 93.

73 P. 92; cf. 81.

74 Von Rad, *Problem*, 20-26, esp. 21.

75 *Ibid.*, 34.

76 Kuschke, 100.

77 Beyerlin, 129.

78 Contra Kuschke, 81.

79 *Gottesdienst*, esp. 26f., 29, 31; *Worship*, 131-34.

80 MacRae, 260; see also H. W. Wolff, *Hosea. Herm* (Eng. trans. 1974), 215.

81 Alt, 241f.

replaced by the practice of dwelling in booths, indigenous to the settled regions.[82] It is also worth noting that Ex. 18:7 speaks solely of Moses' tent, and that even in the Davidic period the army still camped in booths (2 S. 11:11). Although we cannot be absolutely certain, there is much evidence for the Feast of Booths as a model for the P camp. In this festival, too, the notions of the military and the sacral camp probably coalesce.[83]

The phrase *yôm mô'ēḏ* in Hos. 9:5 recalls the desert period, just as Hos. 12:10(9) (*kîmê mô'ēḏ*) is linked to "Yahweh's first 'meeting' with Israel in the desert."[84] But in Hos. 9:5 this reminiscence is connected synonymously with the ḥag-YHWH, the fall harvest festival, in other words, the Feast of Booths.[85] Thus "meeting" (*mô'ēḏ*) and "Feast of Booths" are associated.

The participants in the "feast" (the fall festival or Feast of Booths)[86] at the dedication of the temple, as described in 1 K. 8 (esp. vv. 2,65), are listed as the elders of Israel, the heads of the tribes, and the leaders of the fathers' houses of the people of Israel (1 K. 8:1, *ziqnê yiśrā'ēl* . . . [*kol-rā'šê hammaṭṭôṯ neśî'ê hā'āḇôṯ liḇnê yiśrā'ēl*]; the words in brackets are omitted in the LXX). The celebration of the Feast of Booths recounted in Neh. 8:13 (and its context) also involved the heads of the fathers' houses of all the people (*rā'šê hā'āḇôṯ leḵol-hā'ām*). In both cases, therefore, we can observe a relationship between the assembly on the occasion of the Feast of Booths and the organization of the P camp, a relationship that may argue for this festival as the model for P's notion of the camp. In addition, 1 K. 8:4 speaks of the tent of meeting, "an obvious addition based on the ideology of P, intended to establish continuity with the desert sanctuary of the Mosaic period."[87]

In this case, P interprets the desert camp as a festival assembly, coming together "before Yahweh" (cf. Lev. 23:40) as for the Feast of Booths, in which "atonement" plays a role (Lev. 23:27ff.). This type of assembly is reflected in the regulations governing the purity of the camp, which aim for "the scrupulous avoidance of anything that could impugn the holiness of the God who appears above the tent in the midst of the camp."[88] We may assume that this assembly—like the Feast of Booths originally—"celebrated the festival in an enclosed area"[89] and had a fixed organization.

Temporary exclusion followed: manslaughter (Nu. 31:19) or participation in battle (Nu. 31:24), leprosy (Nu. 5:2; 12:14; Lev. 13:46; 14:8), a discharge (Nu. 5:2), contact with the "red heifer" (Nu. 19:7) and the scapegoat (Lev. 16:26,28). Those who profane the Sabbath or utter blasphemy must be stoned outside the camp (Nu. 15:35f.; Lev. 24:14). The bodies of Nadab and Abihu must be carried out of the camp (Lev. 10:4f.), as must the skin and dung of sacrificial animals (Ex. 29:14). It is not fear of contagion

---

82 Kraus, *Gottesdienst,* 26f.

83 Alt, 241f.

84 Wolff, *Hosea,* 215.

85 *Ibid.,* 156, 159; A. Weiser, *Das Buch der zwölf kleinen Propheten,* I. *ATD,* XXIV (^{6}1974), 71, 72, n. 2; T. H. Robinson, *Die zwölf kleinen Propheten. HAT,* XIV (^{3}1964), 34f.

86 M. Noth, *Könige 1-16. BK,* IX/1 (1968), 176.

87 *Ibid.,* 177; but cf. 1 K. 1:39; 2:28ff.

88 Kuschke, 91.

89 Alt, 24, n. 2.

that accounts for these regulations, but the proximity of Yahweh (Nu. 5:3). They are also dictated by the notion that the uncleanness of individuals can render the entire camp unclean (Nu. 5:2f.).

The presence of God in the camp, whether associated with the ark (Nu. 14:44) or with the tent of meeting (Nu. 2:2, etc.), demands the cultic integrity of the camp—in agreement with the Priestly interpretation of the desert camp as a festival assembly.

If the interest of P (for reasons that are in large part situational) focuses on the tent of meeting,[90] the organization of the camp around the tent becomes understandable. P is concerned primarily with an answer to the question of God's presence following national catastrophe. The answer is given in terms of a recurrent appearance of Yahweh, not associated with any fixed site.[91] This answer is supported by the account of the meeting with God at the tent of meeting, in the camp that moves from place to place at God's command (Nu. 9:17f.,20,22f.). In this case, the Priestly representation of the desert camp is an expression of a specific intention, and the detailed description of the camp's organization may have the purpose of sketching the organization of the camp of the returnees and the postexilic community.[92] P accordingly lacks an occupation tradition, since the return from exile still lies in the future.

d. *Tent and Camp.* The "tent" is assigned differing locations.[93] In E it is outside the camp (Ex. 33:7,11); in P it is in the midst of the camp (Nu. 2:2, etc.), immediately surrounded by the camp of the Levites (Nu. 1:50,53; 3:23,29,35; cf. 3:38), "that there may be no wrath upon the congregation of the people of Israel" (1:53) or in order that the Levites may be near their place of service (1:50). In both cases the camp as a whole is thought of as being at some distance from the tent of meeting, even in P (Nu. 2:2, *minneged sāḇîḇ lᵉʼōhel-mô'ēḏ*).

The origin and purpose of the distance may vary, however, and these variations are of some interest for the interpretation of the desert camp. Just as the proximity of Yahweh (esp. in P) requires that the camp be culticly pure, his proximity can become dangerous in case of cultic impurity or carelessness (cf. 2 S. 6:6f.). That camp which is under Yahweh's protection is also a camp which is threatened by his presence.[94] It is preserved from Yahweh's wrath in large measure by the "barrier" of the Levite camp (Nu. 1:53)—an important function of the priesthood. This "separating" function of the Levites appears also to be the point of 1 Ch. 9:18, where the gatekeepers (in Jerusalem) belonged to the camp of the Levites even in the desert camp.[95] Even though no gatekeepers are mentioned in the desert camp, Ex. 32:26 shows that the Levites were near the gate of the camp. Since in addition one of the functions of the Levites at that time was to keep unauthorized persons out, this also suggests the retrojection of the levitical gatekeepers into the period of the desert camp.

---

90 Von Rad, *Hexateuch,* 120; cf. 104f.; *idem, GSAT,* 179, 181f., etc.; Fretheim, 315; cf. 321.

91 Kaufmann, 33, 37; Fretheim, esp. 319.

92 Fretheim, 329.

93 For a discussion, see Schmitt, 206-209.

94 Von Rad, *OT Theol.,* I (Eng. trans., New York, 1962), 269; Kuschke, 93: the P camp is "dominated by a continual inner tension."

95 W. Rudolph, *Chronikbücher. HAT,* XXI (1955), 88.

The location of the "tent" outside the camp in E (Ex. 33:7,11)[96] is probably based on a different custom: as in the camps of camel-raising desert Bedouins, the chief has his place at the entrance to the camp.[97] The chief protects the camp, and therefore as a "man of courage" takes his position at the edge of the camp and decides on the movement of the camp. In contrast to P, E is concerned with a "tent" located at the edge of the camp, i.e., its most vulnerable spot.

Important in this connection is the description of "outside" (*ḥûṣ/miḥûṣ*) as a place of danger: there battles are fought (Jer. 21:4), there the sword rages (Ezk. 7:15; Lam. 1:20; cf. also Lam. 4:14; Ezk. 26:11; 28:23; Nah. 3:10), there robbers dwell (Hos. 7:1), and there death threatens (Jer. 9:20[21]).

Here the "tent" is set up in which the "chief" dwells to protect his camp. Although total certainty is impossible, the tent (*hā'ōhel*) that Moses pitches (*nāṭâ-lô*) outside the camp appears to be his personal tent, in other words, the leader's tent.[98]

e. *Conclusions*. The purpose of the Priestly description of the desert camp derives in large measure from the situation of the exile and the associated "openness" of the promise of the land, which suggest and justify a return to the conception of the desert camp. P was able to draw upon early camp traditions, which, however, despite the sacred tent incorporated in them, hardly prefigure the sacral aspect of P's notion of the camp. If neither an "amphictyonic assembly" nor a "tent festival" comes in question as a model, but P's camp is not based solely on a priestly fiction,[99] all that is left is recourse to a pilgrimage festival as a model, most likely the Feast of Booths. One argument in favor of this view is the fact that only P connects the Feast of Booths with the exodus (Lev. 23:42f.).[100] Earlier traditions, too, characterize this festival as a pilgrimage festival.[101] The focal point of the festival is the sanctuary,[102] and possibly the sacred tent as well (1 K. 8:4; 2 Ch. 1:3; 5:5; possibly also 1 S. 17:54[103]).

4. *The Camp of God*. In 1 Ch. 9:19, obviously recalling P's sacral notion of the camp, the desert camp is called "the camp of Yahweh." The association between that camp of Yahweh in the desert and the Jerusalem temple is established in 2 Ch. 31:2, where the temple is called the camp of Yahweh.[104] Of a different nature is the camp of Yahweh in 2 Ch. 14:12(13), where it brings confusion upon the Ethiopians taking the field against Asa at Gerar. Since this takes place without human intervention (probably through the agency of the fear of Yahweh, v. 13[14],[105] "the camp of

---

[96] Haran, 52.
[97] *AuS*, VI (1939), 28.
[98] Haran, 53; see the discussion in Görg, 151-59, esp. 155-57.
[99] Kuschke, 102.
[100] K. Elliger, *Leviticus*. *HAT*, IV (1966), 323.
[101] MacRae, 254f.; on P, 257f., 262; a possible Islamic parallel: 261f.
[102] *Ibid.*, 253, 255.
[103] H. W. Hertzberg, *I & II Samuel*. *OTL* (Eng. trans. 1964), 154.
[104] But see Rudolph, *HAT*, XXI, 304, who suggests reading *ḥaṣrôṯ*, "courts," instead of *maḥ^a nôṯ*.
[105] *Ibid.*, 244.

Yahweh" can hardly refer to the army of Judah.[106] As in Joel 2:11, the reference is to a heavenly host.

In the interpretation of Joel 2:11 (and its context) opinions differ as to whether the reference is to a swarm of locusts, or, what is more likely, an apocalyptic army or even an enemy nation, possibly from the north.[107] Wolff has correctly noticed the apocalyptic coloration of the account preserved in Joel 2:1-11, but it is questionable whether his suggested identification of this apocalyptic army with an earthly enemy is supported by the text. If, as Wolff himself notes,[108] "the manner of appearance and the character of the enemy show clear analogies to the locusts," and in addition the passage speaks of a drought or conflagration (v. 3; cf. v. 5) and the darkening of the sun, moon, and stars (v. 10), supernatural forces appear to be at work, described here as the military camp of Yahweh. In 2 Ch. 14:12(13) the camp protects Israel; in Joel 2:11 it brings disaster upon Zion (vv. 1,15), the world of nations, and the cosmos.[109]

The brief notice concerning Mahanaim in Gen. 32:2f.(1f.), at least in its present context, is probably related to this notion of a military camp. The patriarch Israel (Jacob) encounters the *mal'ᵃḵê 'ᵉlōhîm*, whom he calls *maḥᵃnēh 'ᵉlōhîm;* the toponym *maḥᵃnāyim* is traced to this encounter. This notice provides *in nuce* an account that leads up to the encounters of the patriarch with an *'îš* (Gen. 32:25ff.[24ff.]) and with Esau (33:1ff.), and possibly also with the Shechemites (33:18). Whoever the *mal'ᵃḵê 'ᵉlōhîm* and the *maḥᵃnēh 'ᵉlōhîm* may originally have been,[110] in connection with 32:25ff.(24ff.); 33:1ff.; and possibly 33:18 they appear in the context of dangerous encounters of the patriarch and their happy issue. This argues for interpreting the *maḥᵃnēh 'ᵉlōhîm* as the camp of God, although the translation "enormous camp" (cf. 1 Ch. 12:23[22])—apart from the context—cannot be ruled out.

5. *Miscellanea.* Also military in nature is the camp pitched by the angel of Yahweh around those who fear him (Ps. 34:8[7]) to deliver them (*ḥlṣ;* v. 23, *pāḏâ*). It is true that there is no immediate mention of enemies, but rather fears (v. 5[4]), troubles (vv. 7,18[6,17]), hunger (?) (v. 11[10]), and afflictions (v. 20[19]); but there is also talk of young lions (v. 11[10]),[111] evildoers (v. 17[16]), the wicked (v. 22[21]), and those who hate the righteous (v. 22[21]). These are the enemies of the righteous, about whom the angel of Yahweh encamps to protect them.[112]

Also of this type is the camp that Yahweh pitches around his house (Zec. 9:8): Yahweh encamps as a guard[113] for his house, so that no oppressor shall overrun "them." The protection of the temple[114] benefits those who dwell in Jerusalem and

---

[106] *Ibid.*

[107] H. W. Wolff, *Joel and Amos. Herm* (Eng. trans. 1977), 46; O. Kaiser, *Introd. to the OT* (Eng. trans., Minneapolis, 1975), 280ff.

[108] *Joel and Amos,* 42, etc.

[109] *Ibid.,* 48.

[110] For a basic discussion, see F. J. Helfmeyer, "Jakob in Bethel und Israel in Sichem."

[111] H.-J. Kraus, *Psalmen. BK,* XV/1 (^{4}1972), 266; cf. 267, "rich men."

[112] *Ibid.,* 269.

[113] See *BHK.*

[114] For a different interpretation, see K. Elliger, *Das Buch der zwölf kleinen Propheten,* II. *ATD,* XXV (^{7}1975), 146f.; F. Horst, *Die zwölf kleinen Propheten. HAT,* XIV, 247.

the countryside. This camp of God, described in Zec. 2:9(5) as a "wall of fire," surpasses the walls and ramparts of Tyre (Zec. 9:3f.), and thus has the function of a protecting camp.

The camp of the returning exiles is a place where they are gathered (Ezr. 8:15; *qbṣ* piel), the first camp of those returning home, which therefore serves as a kind of model. For this reason, and because of the measures ordained and carried out by Ezra in the first camp, the question of the Levites plays a role (Ezr. 8:15)—not just because of the Jerusalem temple (8:17). Through the fast proclaimed by Ezra, those assembled in the camp seek to receive a safe and successful journey from God (8:21). The concluding statement, "and (God) listened to our entreaty" (v. 23), presupposes a corresponding declaration of assurance, which by "ancient rule" could be pronounced only by a priest or prophet—another reason for Ezra's concern to have Levites in his camp, who, although entrusted with other duties, play such an important role in P's account of the desert camp.

In a list that appears among the measures taken by Nehemiah to establish new settlements, Neh. 11:25 speaks of people of Judah who had "encamped" from Beer-sheba to the valley of Hinnom (11:30). Since a fixed settlement is presupposed (11:25; *yšb*), the use of *ḥānâ* is puzzling. If this "encampment" means anything more than settlement in a specific territory,[115] the idiom may imply some political or even theological statement (no premature final distribution of cities and territories; the interim nature of Israel's permanent settlement).

The census takers of 2 S. 24:5 encamp only temporarily at Aroer, whence they depart for Gad and then to Jazer (but cf. *BHK wayyāḥēllû mē'ᵃrô'ēr,* "they began from Aroer"[116]). The instructions given the spies in Nu. 13:19 to study the cities in which the population lives and determine whether they dwell in camps or strongholds reveal two forms of settlement that differ in the way they are fortified and apparently also in origin (*maḥᵃnîm,* "open towns"; *miḇṣārîm,* "strongholds"[117]).

The predecessors of fortified towns were probably "the castles of warrior chiefs established for themselves and their personal following";[118] the predecessors of the cities described as camps were nomadic camps or "refuge places for cattle and men in dangerous regions, especially those near the desert."[119] Such cities set up as "camps" can also be distinguished from the fortified cities by their size (Nu. 13:28) and military prowess (Nu. 13:22,28,32f.).

All this suggests that in the "camp cities" we have small villages, possibly widely scattered, while the "fortified cities" may be thought of as enclosed and fortified settlements and the "seat of the army."[120]

The migration of the tribe of Dan described in Jgs. 18 presupposes that this tribe—as in the period reflected in the brief notice of Jgs. 13:25—was not yet permanently

115 See the discussion of Jgs. 13:25 below.
116 Also Hertzberg, *I & II Samuel,* 412.
117 Malamat, 6.
118 Weber, 13; cf. Wallis, 133.
119 Weber, 13f.
120 *Ibid.*

settled. This may explain why the temporary Danite territory is called the "camp of Dan" in Jgs. 13:25. An enormous camp between Zorah and Eshtaol, containing the entire tribe, can hardly be meant; instead, *maḥ^{a}nēh-ḏān* means "the entire extent of Danite territory,"[121] through which Samson moves, stirred by the spirit of Yahweh (Jgs. 13:25).

In Nah. 3:17 (cf. vv. 15f.), locusts symbolize the horde of Assyrian merchants and officials with their inconstant and therefore untrustworthy ways. Locusts come, stay for a night, and are off and away as soon as the sun comes up. To find a warm and safe place at night, they "encamp" by the walls (Nah. 3:17), their camp "in a day of cold."

The day, too, "encamps" at evening; at this time of day a guest, too, should settle down to rest and not be on his way (Jgs. 19:9). This idiom is probably borrowed from the "journey" of the sun (or the light), which rises, runs its course, and settles down to rest in the evening.

6. *Conclusions*. The use of *ḥānâ/maḥ^{a}neh* to designate the desert camp and the military camp not only predominates numerically, it is also and above all theologically significant: the "center" of the desert camp is the "tent," which according to the earlier (E) tradition (Ex. 33:7,11) was situated outside or at the edge of the camp. Since Ex. 33 is dominated by "the theme of the presence of God in the midst of his people,"[122] the situation of the "tent" was probably not dictated by the desire to set the sacred tent apart from the profane sphere of living.[123] It appears rather to be based on an ancient form of camp organization, with the tent of the leader (now the sacred tent) outside or at the edge or entrance (gate) of the camp. This form can still be observed in Ex. 32:26; Nu. 3:38; and perhaps also Gen. 32:22(21) and Jgs. 7:13. If the leader of the camp is to prevent unauthorized persons (including enemies) from entering the camp—not just the sacred tent—(Nu. 3:38), he must take up his position at the entrance to the camp, just as Ex. 32:26 strongly suggests that the Levites, whose camp is identified in Nu. 2:17 (P) with the tent of meeting, have their place near the camp gate.

The desert camp under the protection of Yahweh as its leader (Nu. 9:17f.,20,22f.; 10:34; Dt. 1:33; cf. Ex. 17:1) is a counterpart to the belief that Yahweh's angel encamps around those who fear God (Ps. 34:8[7]) and that Yahweh himself encamps at this house as a guard (Zec. 9:8), permitting no unauthorized person or enemy to enter.

The presence of God in the desert camp and the Priestly description of the desert camp as a sacral assembly explain the various regulations governing the purity of the camp. The Priestly notion of the camp implies a kind of "pansacrality" of the territory where Israel dwells that is alien to the Deuteronomistic centralization of the cult and may be conceived in opposition or as a correction.[124] Not only the tent of meeting and

---

121 Täubler, 63.
122 M. Noth, *Exodus*. *OTL* (Eng. trans. 1962), 253.
123 *Ibid.*, 255.
124 Von Rad, *OT Theol.*, I, 99; Kaufmann, 33.

its immediate levitical surroundings are "holy," but the entire camp,[125] which can therefore be called the "camp of Yahweh" (1 Ch. 9:19). The holiness of the camp derives from the presence of God, associated with his angel (Ex. 14:19f.), cloud and fire (Dt. 1:33; cf. Nu. 9:15ff.), the tent of meeting (see above), or the ark (Nu. 14:44; cf. Josh. 3:2f.). The same holds true for the military camp (Dt. 23:15[14]),[126] in which God is present (the ark: cf. 1 S. 4:5f.) and for which specific regulations are in force.[127]

It is also important not to overlook the differences between the desert camp and the military camp. If our suggestion is correct that the P camp should be interpreted as a festival assembly, there is a static element associated with the desert camp, while the military camp—in the context of the Yahweh war—bears the stamp of the "dynamic principle" and cannot be characterized as a cultic institution.[128] Of course this does not alter the holiness of the military camp, even though it is less cultic in nature than that of the desert camp in P. In both cases it is based on the presence of God, which, all in all, determines the description of the "camp."

Besides the question of how this conception and description originated, especially in P, the question of purpose is of particular theological relevance. In addition to the purposes already mentioned, P's interest in Yahweh's law and Israel's obedience is probably important in this connection, in that the encampment and departure of the desert groups take place at the command of Yahweh (Nu. 9:17-23; 10:34).

Helfmeyer

---

[125] Kraus, *Gottesdienst,* 33: "The temple zone of P is the 'camp.' "

[126] J. Wellhausen, *Israelitische und jüdische Geschichte* (^{7}1914), 24: "the military camp as the earliest sanctuary."

[127] See the survey in von Rad, *Krieg,* 7.

[128] Smend, 28, 36.

חָנַךְ *ḥānak;* חֲנֻכָּה *ḥ^a nukkâ;* *חָנִיךְ *ḥānîk*

Contents: I. Etymology. II. Occurrences and Theological Significance. III. The Hanukkah Festival.

I. Etymology. It is reasonable to assume the basic meaning "use for the first time" for the root *ḥnk*. With an impersonal object, *ḥnk* developed into the concept "initiate" (at first without religious ceremony); with a personal object, the meaning "accustom" (someone to an activity or type of conduct) stands in the foreground. Arab. *ḥanaka*

ḥānak. F.-M. Abel, "La fête de la Ḥanoucca," *RB,* 53 (1946), 538-546; H. E. del Medico, "Le cadre historique des fêtes de Hanukkah et de Purîm," *VT,* 15 (1965), 238-270; O. S. Rankin, *The Origins of the Festival of Hanukkah, the Jewish New-Age Festival* (Edinburgh, 1930); S. C. Reif, "Dedicated to חנך," *VT,* 22 (1972), 495-501; R. de Vaux, *AncIsr,* 510-14; S. Zeitlin, "Hanukkah: Its Origin and Its Significance," *JQR,* N.S. 29 (1938/39), 1-36.

(cf. *ḥanakun,* "gums") has the primary meaning of rubbing the gums of a newborn child with the juice of dates or with oil, hence "initiate" (including "initiate into something") and "make experienced" (II and IV). It is uncertain whether there is any connection with Egyp. *ḥnk.t,* "tribute, offering," or Neo-Pun. *ḥnkt* (?), "memorial tombstone."[1]

II. Occurrences and Theological Significance. The verb *ḥānaḵ* is attested only in the qal in the OT; it appears in 4 passages. According to Dt. 20:5, whoever has built a new house and has not yet "dedicated" it is exempt from military service. The same is true of the owner of a vineyard from which the first vintage has not been gathered, and of a man who is betrothed (1 Macc. 3:56; also Dt. 28:30). The Deuteronomist substitutes a humane reason ("lest another man dedicate it") for the archaic notion that was no longer known to him: anyone who puts something new to use is particularly vulnerable to demons. The legislator thus finds it unfair that an owner should not come to enjoy his newly acquired property. There is no other evidence in the OT for the "dedication" of a private house. In 1 K. 8:62-64 (par. 2 Ch. 7:4-7), the actual "dedication" of Solomon's temple is reported. Nothing is said of any special dedication or consecration ritual; instead, the temple is "put into use" and ceremonially inaugurated by the offering of mass sacrifice. The Chronicler emphasizes the solemnity of the occasion by expanding the account with the appearance of priests and Levites with musical instruments and hymns. According to 1 K. 8:64 (par. 2 Ch. 7:7), so many sacrifices were offered that additional altars had to be set up in the courtyard. In addition, the middle of the court had to be "consecrated": the author uses the piel of → קדשׁ *qdš,* which, in contrast to *ḥānaḵ,* may suggest a specific ritual.

Prov. 22:6 is an isolated aphorism concerning the value and efficacy of training children at an early age. In this context, *ḥānaḵ* means the continual "training" of the immature in the proper way of life.

The noun *ḥᵃnukkâ* occurs frequently in postexilic texts. In Nu. 7:10f.,84,88, *ḥᵃnukkaṯ hammizbēaḥ* refers to the dedication of the altar of the desert sanctuary. This takes place—after Moses has anointed and consecrated the tent, the altar, and the utensils (Nu. 7:1: → משׁח *māšaḥ,* → קדשׁ *qāḏaš*)—when the leaders of the tribes bring their rich offerings to the altar. Clearly the late author was loathe to have the comparatively modest offerings of Israel mentioned in Lev. 9 suffice for the actual "consecration of the altar."[2] There is no need to translate *ḥᵃnukkâ* in Nu. 7:10,84,88 as "dedication offering." In 2 Ch. 7:9, it is emphasized that the temple is the focal point of the cult and the place of sacrifice; *ḥᵃnukkaṯ hammizbēaḥ* is equated with the dedication of the temple (2 Ch. 7:5). In the superscription to Ps. 30, *mizmôr lᵉḏāviḏ,* the phrase *šîr-ḥᵃnukkaṯ habbayiṯ* was added at a very late date (certainly after 164 B.C.). What we have here is a liturgical direction that the psalm be sung every year at the Feast of Hanukkah.[3] What was originally an individual song of thanksgiving has thus been applied

[1] C. Schedl, "*Ḥnkt 'bnt* auf neupunischen Grabinschriften," *VT,* 12 (1962), 343-45.
[2] M. Noth, *Numbers. OTL* (Eng. trans. 1968), 63.
[3] Cf. also Talmud, *Sop.* xviii.2.

to the delivered community. According to Ezr. 6:16f., too, the dedication of the rebuilt house of God (*ḥ^a nukkaṯ bêṯ-'^e lāhā'*) involves the solemn sacrifice of burnt offerings and sin offerings. Neh. 12:27-43 recounts the dedication of the rebuilt walls of Jerusalem. The religious ceremonies designed to place the structure under Yahweh's protection are briefly described: first we are told how the festal assembly and the walls and the gates are purified; then follows a procession on the walls themselves. The purification is intended to avert any evil influences from past events; the processional circuit assures permanence for the future. The concluding sacrifices and feasting in the temple express joy and thanksgiving that the work has come to fruition. Dnl. 3:2f. describes the dedication of a divine image. The ceremonial includes the presence of numerous invited guests, the playing of various musical instruments, and prostration in worship.

The term *ḥ^a nîḵîm* ("trained men") in Gen. 14:14 for the followers of Abraham is a hapax legomenon. The root *ḥnk* appears certain. The word occurs with the same meaning in a tablet of the fifteenth century B.C. from Taanach.[4]

III. The Hanukkah Festival.

A temple dedication from the Maccabean period has gone down in history as the Feast of Hanukkah. On the 25th of Kislev in the year 167 B.C., at the command of Antiochus Epiphanes, the first pagan sacrifices were offered at Jerusalem, desecrating the temple and altar. Three years later to the very day, Judas the Maccabee, following his victories over the Seleucids, was able to rededicate the desecrated temple by means of legitimate sacrifices. It was decided to commemorate this day each year with a memorial celebration (1 Macc. 4:36-59; 2 Macc. 10:1-8). The attempt to associate the Feast of Hanukkah with the pagan observance of the winter solstice[5] is without historical foundation. The biblical term for the festival is *ho engkainismós* (1 Macc. 4:56-59; 2 Macc. 2:9-19; cf. John 10:22, *tá engkaínia*). The Hebrew name *ḥ^a nukkâ* is first attested in rabbinic literature.[6] The term used by Josephus,[7] *ta phṓta* ("Lights"), probably preserves the festival's popular name. The historical model for the purification of the temple was that of King Hezekiah (2 Ch. 29); the rededication ceremonies could be based on Solomon's dedication of the temple and the dedication of the second temple in the year 515 B.C., both of which took place in connection with the Feast of Booths. This explains the inclusion of several ceremonies associated with this festival and the eight-day celebration, beginning with 25 Kislev. Rods crowned with ivy, green branches, and palms were carried in procession, hymns were sung, especially the Hallel (Pss. 113–118), and special sacrifices were offered. In addition, Hanukkah lamps were lit in private houses during the eight days of the festival, a custom that may go back to the rekindling of the altar fire and the menorah. Even after the destruction of the temple in A.D. 70, the Feast of Hanukkah is still celebrated as the major Jewish winter festival.

Dommershausen

---

4 *KBL*³, 320.

5 For example, O. S. Rankin, "The Festival of Hanukkah," in S. H. Hooke, ed., *The Labyrinth* (London, 1935), 159-209.

6 Bab.*Šabb.* 21b.

7 *Ant.* xii.7.7.

חָנַן ḥānan; חֵן ḥēn; חַנּוּן ḥannûn; חֲנִינָה ḥ^{a}nînâ; תְּחִנָּה t^{e}ḥinnâ; תַּחֲנוּן taḥ^{a}nûn

Contents: I. 1. Etymology and Occurrences; 2. Meaning. II. Concrete Usages in the OT: 1. Grace as a Possession; 2. Grace or Favor in Human Relationships; 3. Royal Favor; 4. Favor Toward a City. III. Theological Uses: 1. Human Benevolence; 2. Brotherly Favor: Jacob and Esau; 3. Divine Favor; 4. Favor in Blessings. IV. Qumran.

I. 1. *Etymology and Occurrences.* The basic meaning of the root *ḥnn* is "grace," which is one of two primary translations for its cognate noun *ḥēn*. The noun is first a term of beauty. It denotes an aesthetically pleasing presentation or aspect of someone or something, and is properly the quality someone or something possesses. The response to this projection of beauty is also *ḥēn,* "favor." The derived sense is used in Hebrew primarily for the pleasing impression made upon one individual by another. It is possible to show *ḥēn* to the beloved ruins of Jerusalem (Ps. 102:14f.[Eng. vv. 13f.]), but this usage is rare. The verb *ḥānan* means "be gracious," being used almost exclusively in the derived sense, "show favor," but it evidently could also be used in the aesthetic sense, "possess grace" (Prov. 26:25). The same dual meaning is found in Gk. *cháris,* the word most often used to translate *ḥēn* in the LXX. Both meanings of *cháris* can be seen relatively close together in Sir. 40:17,22.

Akk. *enēnu* A is invocatory, like the Hebrew hithpael of *ḥānan,* "ask for mercy," "pray."[1] It is almost always used of someone supplicating either a god or a king. The verb *enēnu* C[2] corresponds to the Hebrew qal, "grant a privilege," "do a favor." The ruler of Elam, for example, graciously returns to his servant fields that he had earlier bought from him at full price.[3] The West Semitic loanword *enēnu* D[4] appears frequently in the Amarna letters.[5] In EA 137, Rib-addi, prince of Byblos, says to Pharaoh: "If the king, my lord, be gracious to me and return me to the city. . . ."[6] The term likewise occurs in royal correspondence. Cognate nouns *ennanātu* and *ennu*[7] are also known with the meaning "grace," "favor," or "mercy," although *eninnu* and *ennanātu*

ḥānan. D. R. Ap-Thomas, "Some Aspects of the Root HNN in the OT," *JSS,* 2 (1957), 128-148; H. Conzelmann and W. Zimmerli, "χάρις," *TDNT,* IX (1974), 372-402; M. Dahood, "Hebrew Ugaritic Lexicography II," *Bibl,* 45 (1964), 409; D. N. Freedman, "God Compassionate and Gracious," *Western Watch,* 6 (1955), 6-24; W. F. Lofthouse, "Ḥen and Ḥesed in the OT," *ZAW,* 51 (1933), 29-35; K. W. Neubauer, *Der Stamm ch n n im Sprachgebrauch des AT* (diss., Berlin, 1964); J. L. Palache, *Semantic Notes on the Hebrew Lexicon* (Eng. trans., Leiden, 1952), 32; W. L. Reed, "Some Implications of ḤĒN for OT Religion," *JBL,* 73 (1954), 36-41; H. J. Stoebe, "חנן *ḥnn* gnädig sein," *THAT,* I, 587-597; I. Willi-Plein, "חן Ein Übersetzungsproblem: Gedanken zu Sach. XII 10," *VT,* 23 (1973), 90-99.

1 *CAD,* IV (1958), 162-64; *AHw,* I, 217.
2 *CAD,* IV, 164; cf. *AHw,* I, 217, *enēnu* I.
3 *MDP,* 23, 282, 5; cf. *CAD,* IV, 164.
4 *CAD,* IV, 164f.; *AHw,* I, 217, *enēnu* I.
5 EA 137, 81; 253, 24.
6 *ANET*^{3}, 484.
7 *CAD,* IV, 168-170.

are "favors" (as in "do a favor" or "ask a favor" of someone),[8] which is not one of the meanings of *ḥēn*.

Ugar. *ḥnn* is similar to Hebrew, meaning "be gracious," "show favor."[9] Exchanges here also involve gods and kings: "Be gracious, O El,"[10] and "Secure me favor with the king."[11]

Two basic meanings are distinguished in Arab. *ḥanna:* (1) "yearn or long for," and (2) "feel tenderness or compassion," "express sympathy." The latter is more closely connected with the Hebrew root, most noticeably in the adj. *ḥannûn*. The verb *ḥanna* is used when one yearns for home, a former wife, or one's children. Common to both Arabic and Hebrew is the use of the respective verbs in situations that presuppose a prior alienation. For example, one may show favor to someone who has spurned one. In later Phoenician inscriptions from the Persian and Greek periods we find both *ḥnn* and *ḥēn*.[12] In *CIS*, I, 3, 12 a rare niphal occurs (*nḥn*); the only other known occurrence is in Jer. 22:23.[13] The use of *ḥēn* in the idiom "give favor in the eyes of" parallels common OT usage. In the Yeḥawmilk inscription,[14] the king asks his patron deity to give him "favor in the eyes of the gods and in the eyes of the people" (cf. the Pa'ala-'ashtart inscription: "and give them favor and life in the eyes of the gods and the sons of mankind"[15]). The 1st person singular suffix form *ḥny* occurs in the Larnax tes Lapethou inscription in the construct chain *mnḥt ḥny.*[16] In this phrase, "offering of my grace," "grace" has the meaning of "thanks" (as in "say grace"; Lat. *gratia*). The offering made in the sanctuary is in gratitude to Melqart for life and offspring given to the king. The verb is also found in Aramaic (Dnl. 4:24[27]; 6:12). In all cognate languages, as in Hebrew, the root was commonly employed in compounding proper names.

2. *Meaning*. a. In the OT, the verb *ḥānan* occurs primarily in the qal and hithpael. The qal has the meaning "be gracious," "show favor." The hithpael means "seek favor," mainly the favor of God, but also of mankind (Gen. 42:21). Isolated uses of the niphal, piel, and polel appear in the OT. The hiphil does not occur; the causative is expressed by *nāṯan ḥēn*, as in Gen. 39:21 (cf. also the Yeḥawmilk and Pa-'ala—'ashtart inscriptions). But only Yahweh is ever said to be able to give favor. In the absence of a hiphil, a hophal is unlikely; *yuḥan* in Isa. 26:10 and Prov. 21:10 should be read as a qal passive.

In two OT texts, *ḥnn* carries an aesthetic meaning. Prov. 26:25 contains a lone denominative piel in the phrase *kî-y^eḥannēn qôlô*, "when he speaks graciously"; Prov.

---

[8] Cf. the Old Assyrian name *Ennana-la-Aššur* in W. Mayer-G. Wilhelm, "Altassyrische Texte aus Privatsammlungen," *UF*, 7 (1975 [1976]), 319; reading of W. von Soden.

[9] *KTU*, 1.10 I, 12; 1, 65, 6; 4.75 IV, 5; 2.15, 3; 1, 17 I, 16.

[10] *KTU*, 1.65, 6.

[11] *KTU*, 2.15, 3.

[12] See Z. Harris, *A Grammar of the Phoenician Language. AOS*, 8 (1936), 102.

[13] G. A. Cooke, *A Text-Book of North-Semitic Inscriptions* (Oxford, 1903), 30f., 36.

[14] *KAI*, 10.9f.; cf. Cooke, 18f.; *ANET*³, 656.

[15] *KAI*, 48.4; Cooke, 91.

[16] *KAI*, 43.13; Cooke, 83.

22:11, another mention of gracious speech, uses an anomalous stative participle in *ḥēn śᵉpāṯāyw,* one "who is gracious of speech."[17]

In all other cases, *ḥnn* is used of favor shown in personal relationships; it can refer to ordinary acceptance or kindness, or else favor of a special nature, such as pity, mercy, or generosity. In the latter case, the usual limits established by law or custom are transcended. In Hebrew, *ḥnn* does not imply preferential treatment, a favoring of A over B (like → רצה *rāṣâ* in Dt. 33:24 and → חפץ *ḥāpēṣ* in 2 S. 20:11). Compared with *rāṣâ, ḥānan* is more active. The former refers to what satisfies the desire: delight, enjoyment, etc., and basically denotes a passive disposition. It refers more specifically to the kind of acceptance Yahweh displays when a sacrifice with its pleasing odor reaches him (Lev. 22:27; Ezk. 20:41; etc.). By contrast, *ḥānan* is active acceptance and active favor. To be gracious means to aid the poor, feed the hungry, deliver those in distress from defeat and death.[18] In all cases *ḥnn* is a positive term. It is inconceivable that one can be angry and at the same time show favor. Nor can one receive favor from someone who is at the same time angry. Favor cannot coexist with judgment. It is given or withdrawn according to whether one is positively disposed toward another. To show someone favor is perhaps a more superficial expression of oneself than to show love (→ אהב *'āhaḇ* [*'āhabh*]). Love can coexist with judgment (Prov. 3:12) and exists at a deeper level of the inner consciousness, where conflicting emotions are allowed to coexist.

b. The noun *ḥēn* occurs 67 times in the OT, only once with the article (Prov. 31:30) and once with a suffix (Gen. 39:21); it never appears in the plural. It has two basic meanings: "grace" and "favor." The latter is the more important in the OT, referring to the positive disposition one person has toward another. It can also mean "respect" (Prov. 28:23; Lam. 4:16). It appears most often in the familiar idiom *māṣā' ḥēn bᵉ'ênê,* "find favor in someone's eyes." This was a favorite expression of the Yahwist. In much later usage, *nāśā' ḥēn* replaces *māṣā' ḥēn* (Est. 2:15,17; 5:2). Only in the conditional request form *'im-māṣā'ṯî ḥēn bᵉ'êneyḵā* (Est. 7:3; cf. 5:8; 8:5) is the verb *māṣā'* retained. This idiom is more than a mere figure of speech; it describes very concretely what in fact was taken for granted in ancient Israel, as in the rest of the ancient Near East: that favor is shown on the face. Indeed, the other Hebrew word most often translated "favor" is → פנים *pānîm,* "face" (Ps. 119:58; Zec. 7:2; Mal. 1:9; Dnl. 9:13). Yahweh is frequently asked to "turn" (→ פנה *pānâ*) and show favor (Ps. 25:16; 86:16; 119:132; cf. 2 K. 13:23), i.e., turn and show his face (in mercy or kindness). To show one's face then means to be favorably disposed toward a person. In anger one's face is hidden (Ps. 13:2[1]; 27:9; 30:8[7]; etc.). Moreover, if Yahweh's face is hidden, he might not hear one's "cry for favor" (Ps. 31:23[22]; 55:2[1]). If the favor should be more than a simple expression of common courtesy, the face becomes bright. "Light of face" is a common metaphor for beneficence in the Amarna letters and the Ugaritic correspondence.[19] Ancient people tended to measure *ḥēn* more precisely by the look in

---

17 Dahood, 409.

18 Cf. d. *ḥannûn.*

19 M. Dahood, *Psalms I. AB,* XVI (1965), 26.

someone's eyes. Modern people look instead to the smile. In reality, both go together. *ḥēn* can be like *ḥāḇôḏ*. Ps. 84:12(11) says: "For Yahweh God is a sun and shield; he bestows favor (*ḥēn*) and honor (→ כבוד *kāḇôḏ*)." The brightness of a face giving *ḥēn* can also be reflected on the face that receives *ḥēn*. After Hannah finds *ḥēn* in the eyes of Eli, she departs with a *pānîm* no longer sad (1 S. 1:18; cf. Ex. 34:29-35, where Moses' face shines after his private meeting with Yahweh).

The concept of *ḥēn* is not as profound as *ḥeseḏ*. The terms rarely occur together (Gen. 19:19; Est. 2:17) and in fact are found in quite different environments, despite the fact that both can be translated "kindness" or "mercy." The word → חסד *ḥeseḏ* is a covenant term most often meaning "covenant love." It presupposes rights and obligations, and demands a favorable attitude from both parties to a relationship. A relationship built on *ḥeseḏ* is meant to be long-term. *ḥeseḏ* should be kept. In this sense it is more like *'ᵉmeṯ* (→ אמן *'āman*). But *ḥēn* is not mutually practiced by both parties. It is given by one to the other, and sustains the relationship only so long as the giver so desires. It can be given for a specific situation only. If it is given and sustained over a longer period of time, there is always the possibility that it may be withdrawn unilaterally. Unlike *ḥeseḏ*, *ḥēn* can be withdrawn without consequence, since it is given freely.

c. The word *ḥᵃnînâ* is found only once (Jer. 16:13); it is another noun meaning "favor." A similar form appears in 3Q5 2:1.

d. The adj. *ḥannûn* means "gracious," and with one possible exception (Ps. 112:4) is always used of Yahweh.

The subject for *ḥannûn wᵉraḥûm wᵉṣaddîq* in Ps. 112:4 has been problematic since ancient times. Although the triple chain is unique in the OT, *ḥannûn wᵉraḥûm* is otherwise a standard cliche applied only to Yahweh (as in Ps. 111:4). Ps. 112, however, is not a psalm about Yahweh; it is in its entirety about humankind—the righteous person (vv. 1-9) and the wicked one (v. 10). One manuscript (Alexandrinus) adds *kýrios ho Theós* (cf. RSV). But there is otherwise nothing to preclude *yᵉšārîm* from being the subject in 112:4. Note also that the cliche *(wᵉ)ṣiḏqāṯô 'ōmeḏeṯ lā'aḏ* refers to Yahweh in Ps. 111:3 and to the upright person in 112:3,9.

In most cases, *ḥannûn* occurs with *raḥûm*, "merciful"; older usage prefers *raḥûm wᵉḥannûn* (Ex. 34:6; Ps. 86:15; 103:8), while later usage prefers *ḥannûn wᵉraḥûm* (Joel 2:13; Jon. 4:2; Ps. 111:4; 112:4; 145:8; 2 Ch. 30:9; Neh. 9:17,31). The mercy a mother shows to the issue of her *reḥem* is *raḥûm*, and so also *ḥannûn* appears to carry the idea of motherly (or fatherly) compassion (cf. I.1 for the meaning of the Arabic). Yahweh is *ḥannûn* in his capacity as father (Ex. 22:26[27]). The overall goodness of Yahweh's favor can be seen from Ps. 145:8f., where *ḥannûn wᵉraḥûm* is broken up for reiteration in the following cola, with the poet substituting *ṭôḇ* for *ḥannûn* (cf. also Ps. 86:16f.: *pᵉnēh 'ēlay wᵉḥonnēnî . . . "ᵃśēh-'immî 'ôṯ lᵉṭôḇâ*).

e. The noun *tᵉḥinnâ* can mean "favor" or "mercy" (Josh. 11:20; Ezr. 9:8; the LXX translates both with *éleos;* cf. 1 Esd. 8:75), or more commonly "cry for favor," "supplication." It is often used in parallel with *tᵉpillâ*, but may also designate supplications made to other human beings (Jer. 37:20; 38:26). The chiastic ordering of terms in 1 K. 8:28, *t^e pillaṯ/t^e ḥinnāṯô—hārinnâ/hatt^e pillâ*, argues for linking *rinnâ*, "ringing cry," with *t^e ḥinnâ*, "cry of supplication."

f. The noun *taḥ^a nûn* occurs only in the pl. abstract *taḥ^a nûnîm*, "cries for favor" or "supplications."

II. Concrete Usages in the OT.

1. *Grace as a Possession*. In its aesthetic sense, *ḥēn* denotes a quality that a person, animal, or inanimate object possesses. This usage is exclusively nontheological, although the sages judge the use to which possessed grace is put as being either good or bad. The OT speaks on numerous occasions about gracious speech. It is a mark of refinement to be able to speak graciously. Such is to be desired of kings (Ps. 45:3[2]), and it is an absolute prerequisite for one who aspires to the ruling elite (Eccl. 10:12; Prov. 22:11). But gracious words can be intolerable if they mask deception. Prov. 26:25 warns of one concealing hatred: *kî-y^e ḥannēn qôlô 'al-ta'^a men-bô*, "when he speaks graciously, believe him not."

In describing women, *ḥēn* can refer to the total impression a woman makes (*'ēšeṯ-ḥēn*, Prov. 11:16), although the focus no doubt is chiefly on her carriage and speech. A youthful wife is praised by comparison to a graceful animal (Prov. 5:19). Another proverb says that a gracious woman receives honor (Prov. 11:16). But in some women *ḥēn* is also a mark of deception (Prov. 31:30), and it is commonly associated with the behavior of prostitutes (Nah. 3:4). In these latter cases, *ḥēn* certainly includes among the woman's enticing qualities her use of gracious or seductive words. Wreaths worn on the head or *garg^e rôṯ* (neck?) can be *ḥēn*, and the wisdom teachers liken their teaching to such (Prov. 1:9; 3:22; 4:9). Prov. 17:8 compares a bribe to an *'eḇen-ḥēn* (beautiful or precious stone), which again does not negate the beauty implied in *ḥēn*, but makes clear the unfortunate ends to which *ḥēn* can be used.

2. *Grace or Favor in Human Relationships*. More beautiful than gracious words or graceful forms, delicate wreaths, or precious stones are human relationships built upon *ḥēn*. In the derived sense, *ḥēn* is a human disposition. It is present in the heart of one who is positively disposed toward another.

a. *Favor as a Gift*. When used of human relationships, the verb clearly includes the idea of giving. In some passages the notion of giving is implied so strongly as to require explicit translation, e.g., Jgs. 21:22: *ḥonnûnû 'ōṯām*, "Grant them graciously to us" (cf. also III.3.b on Gen. 33:5,11). In the case of Yahweh, *ḥēn* is commonly coupled with the verb → נתן *nāṯan*, "give." It follows that *ḥēn* is in the nature of a gift. This explains in part why people must request it. It is freely given and cannot be grasped or seized by force. The giver has every right to withhold his *ḥēn*, and unless he is a person of rank, this may be done even at some risk. For the one receiving *ḥēn*, this gift is unlike most in that it never really becomes his possession. One quite literally finds favor in the eyes of another, and that is where the favor remains. It is comparable to one's reputation, which is likewise not its owner's possession. The two are nicely juxtaposed in Prov. 22:1: "A good name (→ שֵׁם *šēm*) is to be chosen rather than great riches, and favor (*ḥēn*) is better than silver or gold."

b. *Favor Sought.* Favor is sought and found, and because it can be withheld, it demands a peculiar kind of stance from the seeker, namely subordination. The ancient oriental world was a world of kings and lords, and consequently it was deemed proper to use language of deference. Typical is the expression *māṣā'ṯî ḥēn bᵉ'êneykā,* not uncommonly accompanied by bowing and prostration (Gen. 33:3ff.; 2 S. 14:22; 16:4; Ruth 2:10; Ps. 31:10[9]). Deferential language was necessary when a person of low station spoke to someone of high station. Prov. 18:23 says that while the rich may speak roughly, the poor must use entreaties (*taḥᵃnûnîm*). It is thus ironic when Job says he must ask his servant for favor (Job 19:16). But persons of means commonly employ deferential language when speaking to each other, in order not to be thought presumptuous. It is found most often in the OT when lords and kings are present, i.e., in patriarchal and royal narratives. It is even possible for a person of higher rank to speak with deference to another of lower rank. This is done when one prefers to ask for something rather than command it. Jacob, for example, speaks with deference to his son Joseph (Gen. 47:29); it cannot be assumed here that Joseph's rise to power in Egypt necessitates such language from his father. David also speaks with deference when relaying a message to Nabal (1 S. 25:8). In the case of Laban speaking to his nephew Jacob (Gen. 30:27), we have nothing more than flattery: Laban is pretending to be obligated to Jacob.

Favor can be sought at two levels. The first is the level of formality. In a specific context, *ḥēn* is sought as a preamble to a request. The expression *'im-māṣā'ṯî ḥēn bᵉ'êneykā* is an elaborate way of saying "please." The suppliant is not out to find favor per se; his main concern is having his request granted. A more profound type of favor is that which is granted for a longer period of time. On this level, *ḥēn* is a general disposition toward someone, signifying a relationship of some importance. In ordinary usage, however, requests for *ḥēn* are usually made on the first level. Laban asks Jacob's favor only that he may be allowed to speak (Gen. 30:27). Shechem requests the favor of Jacob and his sons in hope of marrying Dinah (Gen. 34:11). Jacob entreats Joseph to take an oath regarding Jacob's burial (Gen. 47:29). Joseph seeks favor from his brothers only to avert his sale (Gen. 42:21), and later he seeks the favor of Pharaoh's household when he wants to go and bury his father (Gen. 50:4). The sons of Reuben and Gad want land in Transjordan (Nu. 32:5); David wants Jonathan's permission to take leave (1 S. 20:29), provisions for his troops (1 S. 25:8), and later sanctuary from Achish (1 S. 27:5). Jeremiah presents his *tᵉḥinnâ* to Zedekiah that he may not be sent back to the house of Jonathan to die (Jer. 37:20; 38:26). Esther seeks the favor of the king that she and the Jewish people may be spared (Est. 4:8; 5:8; 7:3; 8:3,5).

c. *Favor Found.* Found favor can also be received on two levels. For specific acts of kindness, one can employ the same sort of deferential language used to seek favor. The imperfect in *'emṣā'-ḥēn bᵉ'êneykā 'ᵃḏōnî* (2 S. 16:4; Ruth 2:13) is to be translated as a present perfect: "I have surely found favor in your eyes, my lord." This is an embellished "thank you." It acknowledges favor already shown. The equally difficult form *nimṣā'-ḥēn bᵉʿênê 'ᵃḏōnî* in Gen. 47:25 appears also to be equivalent to "thank you, my lord." But favor of the more profound and lasting kind is more commonly reckoned as found. When the Yahwist says that Joseph found favor in the eyes of Potiphar (Gen. 39:4), he does not mean that Joseph did a single thing that pleased Potiphar, but rather that Joseph had overall good standing with his superior. The same is true of David with respect to Saul (1 S. 16:22) and Jonathan (1 S. 20:3). He had established a deep relationship with both men, so much so that *ḥēn* implies deep affection. The favor Ruth found in the eyes of Boaz (Ruth 2:2,10,13) as well as the favor Esther found in the eyes of King Ahasuerus (Est. 2:17; 5:2)—not to mention others who saw her (Est. 2:15)—likewise included lasting affection. Whether Joab attains lasting favor with David (2 S. 14:22) or merely exults because the king has granted his request is not clear. Neither is it clear whether Hadad had lasting favor with the pharaoh of Egypt (1 K. 11:19). For the most part, however, found favor transcends a single event and signifies a relationship of some depth. Found favor, being also a gift, can also be given in response to merit. Good sense wins *ḥēn* (Prov. 13:15), and it was apparently also given to people of skill, as we can surmise from Eccl. 9:11, although the Preacher himself is making a very different point.

d. *Loss of Favor.* Even if *ḥēn* has created a relationship of some depth, it can still be lost. Dt. 24:1 presupposes the right of a husband to give his wife a bill of divorce if she no longer finds favor in his eyes. Likewise a curse upon a guilty man consigns both him and his children to subsequent disfavor (Ps. 109:12). In this latter case, disfavor is a result of judgment, whereas in the former case judgment comes after loss of favor. The sequence is not important; what matters is that favor and judgment cannot coexist.

e. *Anticipated Favor.* Prov. 28:23, too, assumes that judgment and favor are incompatible: *môḵîaḥ 'āḏām 'aḥᵃray ḥēn yimṣā' mimmaḥᵃlîq lāšôn,* "He who rebukes a man will afterward find more favor than he who flatters with his tongue." If someone rebukes another he will no doubt lose that person's *ḥēn.* But the proverb does more than praise the rebuker over the flatterer: it says that *ḥēn* will come to the rebuker later on, but he must be willing to wait for it.

3. *Royal Favor.* In Dnl. 4:24(27), Daniel warns the king to repent of his sins and begin showing favor to the oppressed. Only so can he hope to escape a coming judgment.

4. *Favor Toward a City.* Ps. 102:15(14) records a single instance of human favor that is not directed toward another individual or group. Here the people show favor to—or more likely have pity on—the ruins of Jerusalem, which have too long lain neglected.

III. Theological Uses.

1. *Human Benevolence.* Benevolence is an act of grace shown by the rich toward the poor, or at least by an individual with means toward one who has little or no

means. It is what can be expected of a person toward his *rēaʿ*, "friend," "neighbor." Benevolence is extolled in Wisdom Literature as a prime virtue. Therefore the generous person is *ṣaddîq*, "righteous" (Ps. 37:21,26; 112:4f.). The → רשׁע *rāšāʿ*, on the contrary, is not benevolent (Prov. 21:10). Job appeals to his friends' better nature: "Be gracious to me, be gracious to me, O you my friends" (Job 19:21). If they are now exalted over Job as they maintain (v. 5), that is all the more reason to be gracious to one who stands in need. Generally speaking, someone who is gracious to the *ʿānî* will be happy (Prov. 14:21). But more important is the knowledge that showing grace to the needy honors Yahweh (Prov. 14:31). A loan to the → דל *dal* is a loan to Yahweh, and Yahweh will repay the gracious one for his deed (Prov. 19:17). According to Prov. 28:8, retribution will be meted out to the rich person who augments his wealth by extortion. In the end he gathers it only for another, namely the one who is gracious to the *dallîm*.

2. *Brotherly Favor: Jacob and Esau.* The account of Jacob and Esau in Gen. 32f. takes us to the pinnacle of the OT teaching on *ḥēn*, although the divine presence is at best peripheral. This is the dramatic episode in which the two brothers become reconciled. The Yahwist has incorporated the story into his history, but without editorializing. We might have expected him to tell us explicitly of Jacob's finding favor with Esau (cf. Gen. 6:8; 39:4), but he prefers to let the story speak for itself.

The story contains four quotations from Jacob in which he seeks *ḥēn* from Esau (Gen. 32:6[5]; 33:8,10,15). It is apparent throughout the narrative that this is not the usual request for favor.[20] Jacob does not seek Esau's *ḥēn* as preamble to something else. This *ḥēn* is the goal of his activity (32:6,8[5,7]), namely a permanent change of disposition or attitude on Esau's part.[21] Even Jacob's use of the polite *'im-nā' māṣā'tî ḥēn bᵉʿêneyḵā* shows that he has no ulterior motive. He has no request to make; instead he comes with gifts to give, and he compliments Esau with this phrase by urging him to accept them (33:10). Jacob knows that if Esau accepts the gifts it will demonstrate that Esau has accepted him as well, i.e., that Jacob has indeed found favor in his brother's eyes. The phrase is also used later when Esau's offer of men is turned down (33:15). Jacob's quest was successful, as 33:4-11 makes clear.

This event became quite important in later biblical tradition. It was remembered by Hosea (Hos. 12:5[4]): *bāḵâ wayyiṯḥannen-lô*, "he wept and sought his favor."[22] It also appears quite likely that the story served as the prototype for Jesus' parable of the lost (prodigal) son in Luke 15:11-32. In the Jacob and Esau story, favor is restored almost entirely on the human level. We get only one hint of what its significance might be in the divine economy. After Jacob and Esau have come together, Jacob says to Esau: "Truly to see your face is like seeing the face of God" (Gen. 33:10). The acceptance Jacob experiences from his brother is no less than what he might expect from a

---

[20] II.2.b.

[21] II.2.c.

[22] Lundbom; cf. W. L. Holladay, "Chiasmus, the Key to Hosea XII 3-6," *VT*, 16 (1966), 55.

gracious God. (Jacob also saw the face of God in the face of the *'îš* at the Jabbok [Gen. 32:31(30)]; Hos. 12:5[4] therefore changes *'îš* to → מלאך *mal'āk̠*.)

3. *Divine Favor.*

a. *Yahweh Himself Is Gracious.* Graciousness is a divine attribute. The adj. *ḥannûn* is used almost exclusively of Yahweh in the OT, and almost always it is joined by other adjectives in liturgical concert. Yahweh is gracious and merciful, slow to anger, and abounding in steadfast love and faithfulness (Ex. 34:6; Joel 2:13; Jon. 4:2; Ps. 86:15; 103:8; 111:4; 116:5; 145:8; Neh. 9:17,31; 2 Ch. 30:9). After the apostasy of the golden calf, and in response to Moses' specific request, Yahweh reveals his essential qualities and character: he is first of all *raḥûm wᵉḥannûn* (Ex. 34:6). The sequence is crucial. Grace comes after confession of sin even as it came before the giving of the law. Law is delicately balanced against grace, and in fact the entire conversation between Moses and Yahweh in Ex. 32–34 focuses on this subject. In the single text where *ḥannûn* is used alone (Ex. 22:26[27]), Yahweh warns that he will come as a protecting father to aid one of his children should strict justice interfere with humanitarian concerns.

The *idem per idem* constructions of Ex. 33:19 use *ḥānan* and *riḥam:* "I will be gracious to whom I will be gracious, and will show mercy on whom I will show mercy." *Idem per idem* constructions are used when one does not wish to be more specific.[23] Here in Ex. 33:19 the form has normally been taken to express Yahweh's supreme authority in dispensing grace and mercy, when, where, how, and as he pleases.[24] Its rhetorical function (likewise as in Ex. 3:14) is to terminate the debate with Moses.[25] An alternate suggestion is that the form emphasizes Yahweh's nature to be merciful and gracious (cf. Ex. 34:6f.). According to this view, Yahweh is saying to Moses, "I will surely be gracious, I will surely be merciful," or "I am the gracious one, I am the compassionate one" (cf. Ex. 3:14).[26] The form expresses the force of *ḥannûn* and *raḥûm* as attributes of God. It is assumed also that Yahweh ranks higher than humankind when he shows favor: "As the eyes of servants look to the hand of their master, as the eyes of a maid to the hand of her mistress, so our eyes look to Yahweh our God, till he have mercy upon us (*'ad̠ šeyyᵉḥonnēnû*)" (Ps. 123:2).

b. *Divine Favor to Individuals.* Whereas *ḥēn* is always a gift from one person to another, only God is ever explicitly said to "give favor" (*nāt̠an ḥēn*). He can give his own favor to someone or else negotiate favor between individuals, as in Gen. 39:21. Yahweh never seeks the favor of humans. Only in Job is there even the hint of such a thing, and then the question is raised indirectly. Speaking of the mighty Leviathan, Yahweh answers Job rhetorically: "Will he make many supplications (*taḥᵃnûnîm*) to

---

23 S. R. Driver, *The Book of Exodus. CBSC* (1911; repr. 1953), 362f.; cf. J. R. Lundbom, "God's Use of the *Idem per Idem* to Terminate Debate," *HThR*, 71 (1978), 193-201.

24 Cf. II.2.a.

25 Lundbom.

26 Cf. D. N. Freedman, "The Name of the God of Moses," *JBL*, 79 (1960), 154.

you?" (Job 40:27[41:3]). The argument here is part of a much larger *qal waḥōmer:* if Leviathan would not ask for Job's favor, how much more will Yahweh not have to ask for it (41:2b-3[10b-11])! Apparently Yahweh thought this is what Job was waiting for.

Divine favor is given to the righteous and humble (*'ānî*), i.e., the poor and oppressed. According to Ps. 84:12(11), "Yahweh bestows favor and honor (*ḥēn wᵉḵāḇôḏ yittēn*)" on "those who walk uprightly." Prov. 3:4 teaches that keeping the commandments and practicing other virtues will give one *ḥēn* in the eyes of God and human beings. The wicked person, says Isa. 26:10, should not be shown favor, for it will not help him to learn righteousness. Others who can expect Yahweh's favor are the *'ᵃniyyîm* (Ex. 22:24-26[25-27]; Prov. 3:34).

Specific individuals also seek and find divine favor. The most affirmative statements are made by the Yahwist in Genesis. Gen. 6:8, "But Noah found favor in the eyes of Yahweh," is the only statement of its kind in the entire OT. We hear of no supplications, and the assumption is that Yahweh's favor was a general disposition lasting over a long period of time. The Priestly writer gives us the further insight that Noah was a "righteous man" (*'îš ṣaddîq*), in contrast to the rest of the populace (Gen. 6:9). This shows again that the OT has no aversion to merited favor. Later the Yahwist tells us that Yahweh gave Joseph favor in the eyes of the prison warden (*wayyittēn ḥinnô bᵉ'ênê śar bêṯ-hassōhar,* Gen. 39:21). In the Jacob cycle, *ḥānan* is used twice to mean "graciously given" (Gen. 33:5,11). God has graciously given Jacob children and other possessions. Thus when ancient history is looked at from a distance, and looked at also in legends that are markedly compressed, Yahweh's favor to particular individuals is stated briefly and unequivocally. If these individuals ever sought divine favor or experienced crises where divine favor was in doubt, such was forgotten by the time these stories reached the generations of the tenth century B.C.

When we leave Genesis, a different situation obtains. Individuals seek divine favor more than they claim to have found it. Despite Yahweh's assurances that he is gracious, even the greatest figures of the OT cannot rest secure in the knowledge that they have Yahweh's continuing favor. Moses has the favor of Yahweh, but when Yahweh says he will not accompany him on the journey, Moses begins to question it (Ex. 33:12f.,16f.; 34:9). The same thing occurs later when he sees the burden he is being asked to carry as Israel's leader (Nu. 11:11). But it must also be recognized that, although Moses may have Yahweh's overall favor, this is not to say that Yahweh will grant his every request for favors. Yahweh does accede to the request that he accompany Moses on the journey, but he does not honor the oxymoronic request that Yahweh kill him (Nu. 11:15),[27] nor does he honor Moses' request to cross the Jordan: *wā'eṯḥannan 'el-YHWH bā'ēṯ hahî' lē'mōr . . .* (Dt. 3:23). David twice sought Yahweh's favor. Once, when his child was sick, he fasted and wept, saying: "Who knows whether Yahweh will be gracious to me, that the child may live" (2 S. 12:22); but the child died. And when Absalom drove him from Jerusalem, David wondered whether Yahweh in his favor would allow him to return (2 S. 15:25).[28] In this instance Yahweh was gracious. For David, then, favor is seen mainly in deliverance from trouble and death.

---

27 Zimmerli in Conzelmann and Zimmerli, 380.

28 Cf. Rib-addi, EA 137, 81.

According to the Chronicler, Manasseh also prayed for Yahweh's favor when in straits very similar to those of David. He left Jerusalem (only by hooks and chain), but like David was eventually restored to his kingdom; God heard his *tᵉḥinnâ* (2 Ch. 33:13). When Job is in distress, Bildad advises him to seek Yahweh's favor (Job 8:5). According to Bildad, Yahweh rewards the righteous and punishes sinners; therefore if Job is righteous, Yahweh will receive his cry with favor. Job, however, answers that he has sought Yahweh's favor but received no answer (Job 9:15, NEB). Daniel dutifully seeks Yahweh's favor despite the royal decree (Dnl. 6:12[11], Aramaic). This appears to refer to an act of piety performed customarily by the Jews in exile.

The Psalms are of course filled with pleas for Yahweh's favor. Although expressions of corporate worship, they nevertheless come from the heart of the individual. Very personal trials are articulated—sickness, personal enmity, loneliness, fear of death, etc. The impv. *ḥonnēnî,* "be gracious to me," is found only in the Psalms (although Job 19:21 contains the pl. *ḥonnunî*), where it occurs 17 times (Ps. 4:2[1]; 6:3[2]; 25:16; 26:11; 27:7; 30:11[10]; 31:10[9]; 41:5,11[4,10]; 51:3[1]; 56:2[1]; 57:2[1]; 86:3,16; 119:29,58,132). The hapax legomenon *ḥānᵉnēnî* (*ḥonᵉnēnî*) in 9:14(13) adds an 18th instance. The terms for "supplication(s)," *tᵉḥinnâ* (6:10[9]; 55:2[1]; 119:170) and *taḥᵃnûn* (28:2,6; 31:23[22]; 116:1; 130:2; 140:7[6]; 143:1; [86:6, *taḥᵃnûnôṯāy*]), indicate further the extent to which Yahweh's favor is sought in the Psalms. Almost all of these psalms are individual laments; the main exceptions are Pss. 4, 30, and 116, which are psalms of confidence or thanksgiving, and 119, a psalm on the Law. It may also be noteworthy that all (except for 116, 119, and 130) are ascribed by tradition to David. The psalmist usually begins his song with *ḥonnēnî*. His need may be accompanied by a consciousness of sin (25:16,18; 41:5[4]; 51:3ff.[1ff.]; 130:2ff.), or he may come as a righteous person who is being oppressed by the wicked (26; 140). In the latter situation, the psalmist is concerned to affirm his innocence, since adversity implies Yahweh's judgment to outside observers. Thus favor can be sought on either the ground of righteousness or the ground of unrighteousness coupled with repentance for sin. In Ps. 59:6(5), the poet asks Yahweh not to be gracious to the wicked. In many cases a psalm that begins with a supplication for Yahweh's favor will later incorporate the answer received, e.g., 6:3,10(2,9); 28:2,6; 31:10,23(9,22). Such psalms, whether compilations or not, tend to compress human experience. Ps. 77:10(9) (of Asaph) preserves for us the frustration of one who must wait for divine favor: "Has God forgotten to be gracious (*hᵃšāḵaḥ ḥannôṯ*), or in anger shut up his compassion?" Ps. 30 speaks of earlier favor that the psalmist sought—and evidently found—and then later adds a further plea for Yahweh's favor (vv. 9,11[8,10]).

Divine favor can also be sought indirectly through people chosen of Yahweh. In early times the divine emissary par excellence was Yahweh's *mal'aḵ;* to seek out his favor was to seek out the favor of Yahweh. Abraham wants *ḥēn* from the *mal'aḵ* in order to have him stop for a visit (Gen. 18:3), but more importantly he anticipates a possible word from Yahweh about the promised son. In the Yahwist's later reworking of this passage, it is Yahweh himself who appears to Abraham on this occasion (18:1). This messenger together with two others shows *ḥēn* to Lot by rescuing him from Sodom, and Lot's words to them, "Your servant has found favor in your sight," are words of thanks (Gen. 19:19). Lot knows that they are favorably disposed toward him, and he is naturally grateful. When the *mal'ak̲ YHWH* appears to Gideon, the latter requests a specific favor in the form of a sign to assure him that it is indeed Yahweh who is speaking with him (Jgs. 6:17). For Hannah, whose name is also derived from *ḥānan,* the divine emissary is Eli the priest. She, too, wants a child, and when Eli grants her supplication (in the name of the *'elōhê yiśrā'ēl*), she responds with a joyful "thank you": "Your maidservant has surely found favor in your eyes" (1 S. 1:18). And Hannah's own face brightens as well.[29] At a later time in Israel the *nāḇî'* became the principal messenger of God. Fifty men plead for a favorable response from the prophet Elijah that their lives may be spared (2 K. 1:13); after receiving it, they become part of the prophet's entourage.[30] The remnant left in Judah after 587 B.C. presents a *teḥinnâ* to the prophet Jeremiah, which he in turn refers to Yahweh (Jer. 42:2). Yahweh answers this supplication, but tells the people to remain in the land (42:9f.). Job looks for another kind of divine mediator, who might be gracious enough to save humankind from going down into the Pit (Job 33:24).

c. *Divine Favor to Israel.* At Sinai, Yahweh introduced himself to Israel first and foremost as a God of grace. He said it was his nature to be *raḥûm weḥannûn* (Ex. 34:6). Thus he granted Israel *ḥēn* in the eyes of the Egyptians, so that the latter would bestow gifts on them when they left Egypt (Ex. 3:21; 11:3; 12:36). But the Sinai revelation also made clear that Yahweh was a demanding God, who would not clear the guilty but would visit the iniquity of the fathers upon their children to the fourth generation (Ex. 34:7). This dual nature of Yahweh as God of grace and God of judgment finds expression throughout the OT, where grace or favor to Israel is always seen vis-à-vis judgment. During the long period of growth into nationhood, when Yahweh surely persisted in showing Israel particular favor, the OT remains strangely silent on the subject, except perhaps in some of its divine blessings.[31]

But when judgment came upon the nation, the awareness of Yahweh's favor (past and future) became acute. The prophets especially foresaw military defeats at the hand of enemies, destruction of Israelite cities and death for their inhabitants, and finally exile. All signified a loss of Yahweh's *ḥēn.* In the dedication prayer of 1 K. 8 (par. 2 Ch. 6), recorded by the Deuteronomistic historian, Solomon correctly anticipates what is to come. The prayer speaks frequently of supplication (*teḥinnâ* and hithpael of *ḥnn*) necessitated by sin and its consequences: both the present supplication Solomon is making and future supplications that the people may find it necessary to make (1 K. 8:28,30,33,38,45,47,49,52,54,59; 9:3 [cf. 2 Ch. 6:19,21,24,29,35,37,39]). These future supplications are to be made either in the temple or, if the people are outside the city, facing in the direction of the temple. With the exception of the plea for victory in battle (1 K. 8:44f. [par. 2 Ch. 6:34f.]), all are pleas for favor when the people are in some sort of distress, e.g., when they are defeated in battle (1 K. 8:33 [par. 2 Ch. 6:24]), when they are weak from lack of food, whether through famine or siege (1 K. 8:37f. [par. 2 Ch. 6:28f.]), or when they have been taken into captivity (1 K. 8:46-49

29 Cf. I.2.b.

30 J. R. Lundbom, "Elijah's Chariot Ride," *JJS*, 24 (1973), 46-49.

31 Cf. III.4.

[par. 2 Ch. 6:36-39]). In every case there is also to be a plea for forgiveness (→ סלח *sālaḥ*) of sins. Some time after Solomon concludes his prayer, Yahweh acknowledges his *t*ᵉ*ḥinnâ* (1 K. 9:3) and blesses the temple. Nothing is said about Yahweh's response to future supplications. Yahweh merely ends with a warning of judgment if apostasy ensues (9:7-9). This is the substance of Deuteronomistic theology: sin leads to loss of divine favor and issues in judgment. Implicit also in Deuteronomistic theology is the idea that Yahweh's disfavor finds expression in the hostility shown to Israel by the enemy. Favor will be shown neither to the young (Dt. 28:50) nor to the old (Lam. 4:16). The sin that precipitates Yahweh's disfavor and judgment is apostasy.

Isa. 27:11 (which presupposes the destruction of Jerusalem in 587 B.C.) states that Yahweh cannot show favor to his people because they are without discernment (→ בין *bîn*). For Jeremiah and Deuteronomy, the ultimate sin is "forsaking Yahweh and going after *'*ᵉ*lōhîm 'ᵃḥērîm*." Jeremiah says that after Yahweh withdraws his favor, the people can serve these *'*ᵉ*lōhîm 'ᵃḥērîm* "day and night" (Jer. 16:13). Jeremiah is more bitterly ironic when addressing the inhabitants of Jerusalem's royal complex: "How you will be favored (*mah-nnēḥant*) when pangs come upon you!" (Jer. 22:23). In Deuteronomistic-Jeremianic theology we also find the idea that Yahweh's favor could avert judgment. The Deuteronomistic historian says that Yahweh was gracious to Israel during the reign of Jehoahaz and had compassion on the Israelites because of his covenant with the patriarchs (2 K. 13:23). This averted destruction at the hands of Hazael, the Aramean king. Jeremiah holds out hope that Yahweh will avert judgment when he sends Baruch to the temple to read his scroll. Jeremiah says: "It may be that their supplication will come before Yahweh . . ." (Jer. 36:7). The weeping and supplication described in Jer. 3:21 may express a similar hope on the part of the people.

It is Amos who introduces the idea that Yahweh's favor would be seen in his leaving a remnant of Israel, although his tone of uncertainty gives the word an original sting: "It may be that Yahweh, the God of hosts, will be gracious to the remnant of Joseph" (Am. 5:15). Jeremiah declares that "the people who survived the sword found grace (*māṣā' ḥēn*) in the wilderness" (Jer. 31:2). Thus despite his message of judgment the prophet saw a measure of divine favor reserved for Israel that Yahweh did not originally grant to the inhabitants of Canaan (Dt. 7:2; Josh. 11:20).[32]

In the postexilic period, Ezra acknowledges Yahweh's favor in the survival of a remnant: "But now for a brief moment favor (*t*ᵉ*ḥinnâ*) has been shown by Yahweh our God, to leave us a remnant . . ." (Ezr. 9:8). In another prayer he expands the ritualized statement of Yahweh's attributes, adding that Yahweh did not forsake (→ עזב *'āzaḇ*) the people or make an end (→ כלה *kālâ*) of them, i.e., he left a remnant (Neh. 9:17,31).

Another theme reiterated by the prophets was that Yahweh would be gracious to Israel if she repented. To the people of Jerusalem, the prophet Isaiah says: "You shall weep no more. He will surely be gracious to you at the sound of your cry" (Isa. 30:19). Jeremiah anticipates the return of the northern exiles: "with weeping they shall come, and with supplications (*ûḇ*ᵉ*ṯaḥᵃnûnîm*) I will lead them back" (Jer. 31:9).

---

[32] See d. below.

Joel says to rend hearts and not garments, and return (*šûḇ*) to Yahweh, for he is *ḥannûn wᵉraḥûm* (Joel 2:13). The Chronicler records that Hezekiah addressed the remnant in the north to the effect that if they would return to Yahweh (i.e., repent: *šûḇ*) and come to Jerusalem to celebrate the Passover, then the exiles taken away by the Assyrians would be able to return (*šûḇ*) home. This would come about because Yahweh is *ḥannûn wᵉraḥûm* (2 Ch. 30:9).

As in the case of individuals, so Israel, too, must sometimes wait for Yahweh's favor. Ps. 123:3 expresses the impatience people feel after long periods of abuse: *ḥonnēnû YHWH ḥonnēnû kî-raḇ śāḇa'nû ḇûz,* "Be gracious to us, Yahweh, be gracious to us, for we have had more than enough of contempt." Ps. 102:14(13) expresses a similar sentiment with regard to the city of Zion: "It is time to favor her (*lᵉḥenᵉnâ*); the appointed time (*mô'ēḏ*) has come." The need for patience was perhaps best understood by Isaiah: "Therefore Yahweh waits to be gracious to you. . . . Blessed are all those who wait for him" (Isa. 30:18). In Isa. 33:2, the confession of the people articulates the same theme: "Yahweh, be gracious to us; we wait for thee." Later, the prayer of Daniel predicates its request for Yahweh's favor on the fact that the seventy years predicted by Jeremiah are now up and it is time for Yahweh to be gracious (Dnl. 9:2ff.). With its rhetoric of accumulation, this prayer is reminiscent of Solomon's prayer in 1 K. 8. In fact it actualizes, perhaps intentionally, what was only anticipated earlier. Now Yahweh's favor must be sought, and Daniel rather than Solomon is the intercessor for the people. He does not prostrate himself before the altar, but he does accompany his supplication with fasting, sackcloth, and ashes (Dnl. 9:3). He, too, is concerned about the temple, now lying in ruins (v. 17), and he stands before Yahweh not in righteousness (v. 18) but in repentance for the sin of himself and his people (v. 20). Daniel realizes that Yahweh's favor is his to give or withhold; it cannot be assumed as a right or compelled (v. 18; cf. Ex. 33:19). Yahweh subsequently hears Daniel's supplications and sends word to him by the angel Gabriel (Dnl. 9:20-27).

Zechariah and Malachi have different concerns that call for Yahweh's favor. In Deutero-Zechariah, the prophet speaks of "a spirit of compassion and supplication" (*rûaḥ ḥēn wᵉṯaḥᵃnûnîm*) that Yahweh will pour out upon the people of Jerusalem following the murder of their prophet (Zec. 12:10). This is in contrast to the spirit of judgment that had prevailed earlier. Malachi is concerned to upgrade the quality of sacrifice. The people are told to seek the face of God with first-rate offerings, that he may be gracious to them (Mal. 1:9).

d. *Divine Favor to Other Nations.* At the time of the conquest, Yahweh commands Moses explicitly not to be favorably disposed to the inhabitants of Canaan (Dt. 7:2; Josh. 11:20). Here *ḥānan* refers to special favor, i.e., mercy. Later, however, the book of Jonah argues that the favor available to Israel is also available to Assyria, providing of course that they repent (Jon. 4:2).

4. *Favor in Blessings.* Yahweh's favor is conveyed in the giving of blessings. On seeing his brother Benjamin after years of separation from his family, Joseph blesses him with the words: "God be gracious to you (*yoḥnᵉḵā*), my son" (Gen. 43:29). In the Aaronic benediction, the bestowal of Yahweh's favor is artfully reiterated at the

center: "Yahweh make his *face* to shine upon you, and be *gracious* to you (*wîḥunnekkā*), Yahweh lift up his *face* on you" (Nu. 6:25f.).

A similar blessing is echoed in Ps. 67:2(1): "May God be gracious to us and bless us, and make his face to shine upon us."

In an obscure passage in Zechariah, Zerubbabel, the builder of the Second Temple, is described as bringing forth the cornerstone or keystone accompanied by shouts of "Grace, grace to it!" (*ḥēn ḥēn lâ*, Zec. 4:7).[33]

Freedman, Lundbom

IV. Qumran. In the Dead Sea scrolls, *ḥnn* occurs 20 times (4 times hithpael in the formula *htnpl whtḥnn*, "prostrate oneself and supplicate," 1QH 12:4; 16:6; 17:18; 4Q184 2:4), *teḥinnâ* twice, and *ḥanînâ* once (3Q5 2:1). The verb is commonly used in the benediction formula *yḥwnkh*, "May God be gracious to you"; in most cases this "graciousness" is further specified by the mention of the attributes to be given: *bd't 'wlmym*, "with eternal knowledge" (1QS 2:3); *brwḥ rḥmym*, "with the spirit of pity" (1QH 16:9); *brwḥ d'h*, "with the spirit of knowledge" (1QM 14:25); *bkwl brkwt šmym*, "with all the blessings of heaven" (1QSb 1:5); *bkwl gmwlym*, "with all rewards" (1QSb 2:23, textually corrupt); and *brwḥ qwdš*, "with holy spirit" (2:24). This demonstration of God's favor through blessing takes on concrete form in the eternal covenant (1QSb 2:25) and in righteous judgment (2:26); it provides permanence ($11QPs^a$ 19:14,17), and permeates all human deeds (1QSb 2:27). But it is not limited to individuals; it can be called down upon the entire nation (4QDibHam 5:11). The blessing formula can also be turned into a curse (par. *'ārûr*) through negation; this curse is pronounced by the Levites over the followers of Belial (1QS 2:8).

In the Dead Sea scrolls, *teḥinnâ* means "supplication." The worshipper does not think of it as an independent prayer to God, but as a God-given gift (1QH 9:11; 11:34). The ability to "supplicate" is itself a demonstration of God's favor, along with mercy, peace, hope, and firmness of spirit.

Fabry

---

[33] Others translate *ḥēn* as "salvation," "grace," "beauty," or the like.

חָנֵף *ḥānēp*; חָנֵף *ḥānēp*; חֹנֶף *ḥōnep*; חֲנֻפָּה *ḥanuppâ*

Contents: I. 1. Occurrences; 2. Meaning; 3. Semantic Field. II. General Usage: 1. With Reference to Individuals; 2. With "Land" as Subject. III. Use in Theological Contexts: 1. In Prophetic Oracles of Judgment; 2. In the Tradition of Cultic Theology; 3. In Wisdom Thought. IV. Later Reflexes.

ḥānēp. G. R. Driver, "On Psalm 35,16," *ThZ*, 9 (1953), 468f.; *idem*, "Philological Problems," *JTS*, 47 (1946), 160-66, esp. 161f.; *idem*, "Textual and Linguistic Problems of the Book of Psalms," *HThR*, 29 (1936), 171-195, esp. 178-180; P. Joüon, "ὑποκριτής dans l'Évangile et hébreu *Hânef*," *RScR*, 20 (1930), 312-16; R. Knierim, "חנף *ḥnp* pervertiert sein," *THAT*, I, 597-99; U. Wilckens, "ὑποκρίνομαι," *TDNT*, VIII, 562-64.

I. 1. *Occurrences*. The root *ḥnp* is attested as a Canaanite loanword in Akkadian (*ḫanāpu,* "commit villainy"; cf. *taḫtinip,* "flatter [a goddess]";[1] *ḫanpu* and *ḫannipu,* "villainy, infamy"[2]); in Ugaritic (*ḫnp* verbally and nominally, the latter in the sense "impious, wicked"[3]); in OT Hebrew (verb, verbal adjective, and nouns), Middle Hebrew (piel, hiphil), and Jewish Aramaic (peal, pael, aphel) with the meaning "flatter, dissemble,"[4] as well as *ḥanᵉpā'*, *ḥᵃnuptā'* (Targ.), "impious," "impiety," Syr. *ḥanpā,* "heathen,"[5] Mand. *hanifa,* "idol," *humpana,* "dissembler, hypocrite";[6] in Arabic, *ḥanafa* (with *ḥ* rather than *ḫ* as in Ugaritic), "turn aside," whence *ḥanīf,* "orthodox," *ḥanafī,* "heathen," *ḥanafīya,* "paganism," and *aḥnaf,* "afflicted with a curvature of the foot,"[7] Libyan *3np,* "go sideways, set aside."[8] For Hebrew, two problems remain unresolved: the relationship between the verb and the noun (derivation), and the question of homonymy (*ḥnp* II, "limp," in Ps. 35:16 conj. on the basis of Libyan and Arabic[9]).

2. *Meaning*. The meaning of Heb. *ḥnp* is hard to define.[10] *GesB* gives: qal 1. "ruchlos, gottlos sein"; 2. "durch Gottlosigkeit entstellt, entweiht sein"; 3. "entweihen"; hiphil 1. "entweihen"; 2. "zu Heiden machen"; noun "Gottesverächter, Ruchloser" or "Ruchlosigkeit." *KBL*^{2,3} lists similar meanings, with the addition of "von Gott entfremdet, gottlos" for the substantive. *BDB* gives: 1. "be polluted"; 2. "profane, godless," rendering the substantives similarly as "profane, irreligious"; it derives these meanings from a basic meaning "inclining away from right," based on the Arabic. Rössler cites the meaning "abtrünnig werden,"[11] whereas Zorell gives "pollutus esse," "maculatus, nefarius." Joüon, also taking the concrete meaning in Arabic as his starting point, gives as the "sens général" for the adjective "pervers, dépravé," for the verb "corrompre, souiller (mais non 'profaner' . . .)"—except for Dnl. 11:32, where it means "séduire," approximating the postbiblical usage of Jewish Aramaic ("flatter"). Here for the first time the adjective takes on the sense of "impie, flatteur, hypocrite," the basis of the NT equivalent *hypokritḗs*.[12] According to Horst,[13] the root meaning of *ḥnp* is "act or attitude through which a state of sacral relation to the Godhead is intentionally set aside"—hence Wilckens: "wicked person, wicked-

---

1 J. van Dijk, *Cuneiform Texts. TIM,* IX (Leiden, 1976), 54, vo. 9.

2 EA 288, 7; 162, 74; cf. *AHw,* I, 320; *CAD,* VI (1956), 76, 80f.

3 *WUS,* no. 1053; *UT,* no. 981.

4 *KBL*^{2,3}.

5 *KBL*^{3}, 322: "peasant."

6 *MdD,* 125a, 136a.

7 Wehr, 210, *KBL*^{2,3}, *BDB*, *LexHebAram,* Driver.

8 O. Rössler, "Der semitische Charakter der libyschen Sprache," *ZA,* N.S. 50 (1952), 131.

9 *KBL*^{3}, Driver, I.2 below.

10 F. H. W. Gesenius, *Thesaurus philologicus criticus linguae hebraeae et chaldaeae Veteris Testamenti,* I (Leipzig, 1829), 501f.

11 P. 131.

12 Joüon, pp. 314ff.

13 F. Horst, *Hiob. BK,* XVI/1 (1968), 132.

ness."[14] Finally Knierim, like Joüon, arrives at "a concrete basic meaning 'be crooked, bent,' " which is recognizable, however, only in Ps. 35:16 (emended by Driver to *b*ᵉ*ḥanpî*) and possibly Mic. 4:11, while elsewhere the "figurative" meaning "pervert, be perverted" predominates.

Let us consider the following points. (1) All occurrences of the *ḥnp* group (with the exception of the Canaanite instances in EA and Ugaritic, as well as Ps. 35:16 [?]) involve a negative accent. (2) Both the verb and the nouns occur with only two subjects: the land or earth (*'eres,* fem. sg.) and human beings (sg. and pl.—priest, prophet, king, Job [?], psalmist [?], groups, Zion, the nation), so that a division into semantic zones is desirable. (3) In the qal, the verb is used intransitively and for the most part absolutely (sometimes with *lēḇ,* as in Job 36:13[15]), always in finite forms (twice in narrative); in the causative we find the same two secondary subjects. On the basis of these observations, we may draw the following conclusions with regard to the meaning of the root.

a. The concept lying behind the *'ereṣ* passages leads us to the concrete and figurative meaning "make dirty," "pollute," hence "desecrate," which emerges primarily from Isa. 24:5 (*taḥaṯ*); Ps. 106:38; and Nu. 35:33 ("with blood"); Jer. 3:1f.,9 (the same idea is expressed in Dt. 24:4 with *ṭm'*); and possibly Mic. 4:11 (a visible process?). This interpretation is confirmed by the LXX's preferred rendering with *miaínein* (3 times), *molýnein* (once), and *phonoktoneín* (3 times).[16] Obviously the subj. *'ereṣ,* even in metaphorical usage, evokes concrete images when used with *ḥnp.*

b. The passages with personal human subjects, which involve primarily nominal forms, signal antisocial conduct that uses hypocrisy and deception to fool oneself and others. If we note the connection with false speech (Prov. 9:11; Isa. 32:6; 9:16 [Eng. v. 17]; Jer. 23:11,15), we arrive at this paraphrase: "deceitful, distorted, hypocritical, base, sanctimonious, secretly perfidious," primarily on the basis of Prov. 11:9; Isa. 32:6; the EA passages; and Jer. 3:1 conj., all cases of deception in social relationships such as military and political loyalty, duties toward one's neighbor, and marriage.

The lexica note a Middle Hebrew and Jewish Aramaic meaning "flatter, dissemble," "hypocrite, hypocrisy,"[17] but reject this meaning for Biblical Hebrew, probably on account of the concrete sense discussed above.[18] Probably we can also see here the continued influence of the LXX, which only in two passages (Job 34:30; 36:13) uses the neutral term *hypokritḗs,* "actor," which took on a specialized meaning in the NT. It was used much more frequently in the hexaplaric translations.[19] But when we come to the meaning of Heb. *ḥnp,* this certainly does not suggest that "nowhere do words

14 P. 564.
15 Cf. Ugaritic; *KTU,* 1.18 I, 17.
16 Wilckens, 564.
17 *KBL*³, *WTM,* Jastrow.
18 Gesenius, 501; Joüon; Wilckens, esp. 565f.
19 Wilckens, 564.

of the stem חנף have the sense of dissembling or hypocrisy."[20] Instead, the aporia sensed by both Wilckens and Joüon can be resolved by the more reasonable assumption that in the OT *ḥnp* can indeed mean "hypocrisy" in the specific sense,[21] but for the LXX could be identified with the technical term belonging to the language of the Greek theatre only in clear instances (as in the passages from Sirach and Maccabees). The renderings actually used exhibit an attempt at least to preserve the negative overtones.[22]

c. If the observation is correct that *ḥnp* has a polar affinity to definitions appearing in entrance *tôrôṯ* (e.g., Job 13:16; 17:8; 27:8ff.; Isa. 33:14,15ff.),[23] we would have as the link between the two semantic fields the (hypothetical) central meaning "make oneself unrecognizable with dirt" > "make oneself unclean" and > "dissemble." The former development would be illustrated by passages such as Ps. 35:16 and Jer. 3:1ff., the latter by the line leading to Middle Hebrew, Jewish Aramaic, the Dead Sea scrolls, and the NT.

d. The basic meanings that have come down to us represent not the semantic center but rather the semantic periphery. The "Arabic" meaning "twisted" is associated with the image of "dissimulation, alienation, pretense," as also the (too) general and abstract sense "perverted." The rendering "wicked, base" or the like attempts to reproduce the root's emotional overtones (EA; Jer. 3:1; 23:11,15; Job); "godless, impious" attempts to indicate the appraisal found in Wisdom Literature and the prophets.

3. *Semantic Field.* In the semantic field there are only a few lines to trace. A relationship is established between *ḥnp* and → טמא *ṭm'* by the parallelism in Jer. 3:1 and Dt. 24:4 as well as by the context in Nu. 33:33f. and Ps. 106:38f. If the unique hothpael of *ṭm'* (pass. of the hithpael: "cause oneself to be made unclean") corresponds to the qal of *ḥnp* in Jer. 3:1, then we may assume for *ḥnp* a reflexive element not present in *ṭm':* "make oneself unclean," "deform oneself" = "dissemble." This observation is confirmed by comparison of how the stems are used. In transitive usage we find a factitive of *ṭm'* and a causative of *ḥnp,* which indicates in the case of *ḥnp* a substantial relationship with the object (secondary subj.). The verbal statements using the qal imperfect and the variations between the qal and the hiphil must be understood in the same way: the disfigurement is self-caused and the secondary subject shares responsibility.

Ps. 35:16 indicates a relationship with *qdr,* "be darkened (in dirty cloths, i.e., in mourning)," both qal and hiphil. Could the wearing of mourning disguise be the original locus of *ḥnp?*

The semantic field of the nouns is narrower, but is hard to penetrate because of problems of synonymy. In Isa. 9:16(17), the noun is linked with *mēra'*, a participle meaning "evildoer"; cf. Job 8:20. In Isa. 33:14 it appears in parallel with *ḥaṭṭā'îm,*

---

20 *Ibid.*

21 Cf. 1QS 4:10.

22 For a discussion of the problem, see G. Bornkamm, "Heuchelei," *RGG*³, III (1959), 305f.

23 See III.3 below.

"sinners"; in Job 20:5; 27:8 (cf. 15:20), it is in parallel with *r*ᵉ*šā'îm,* "the wicked." Other parallels are *šōḵ*ᵉ*ḥê 'ēl,* "forgotten by God" (Job 8:13), and *'awwāl,* "unrighteous" (Job 27:8). Antonyms include *y*ᵉ*šārîm,* "upright," and *nāqî,* "innocent" (Job 17:8; cf. 13:16); *ṣaddîqîm,* "righteous" (Prov. 11:9). The clearest passage is Isa. 32:6f., where *ḥōnep* is introduced as a term for the action of a *nāḇāl,* born of thoughts of *n*ᵉ*ḇālâ* and *'āwen;* it is ranged alongside *tô'â,* delusion uttered against Yahweh, and cruelty toward those who suffer. In such company the word exhibits the crude and blurred colors of a pejorative term: "base, filthy, perfidious." Job 15:34f. (cf. 1QS 4:9f.) establishes a relationship with the group → רמה *rāmâ* II, "deceive, betray," which does not occur in the hiphil and never refers to the land; it is more sharply defined and more concrete.

II. General Usage.

1. *With Reference to Individuals.* The use of *ḥnp* with a human subject, i.e., with denominative function, is found (besides the nominal forms) primarily in Jer. 3:1 conj.; 23:11; Mic. 4:11; Ps. 35:16 conj.; and Dnl. 11:32.

Jer. 3:1 refers to the law in Dt. 24:4, which forbids a divorced woman who has "become another man's wife" (emended on the basis of the LXX and Vulg.; the MT reads "that (!) land," possibly through the influence of 3:2,9) from returning to her first husband, for reasons having to do with purity. The passage asks whether the woman would not thus be ignoring the actions by which she had "polluted" herself according to Dt. 24:4, thus "deceiving" both herself and her first husband. Unfortunately, Jer. 3:1, which is the only place in the OT where *ḥnp* refers to a situation clearly definable in legal terms,[24] is textually uncertain. Otherwise we would have here a tangible definition of the basic semantic structure of the verb with its two dimensions.

In Jeremiah's judgment, both prophet and priest are "untrue" (Jer. 23:11), in the sense that they counterfeit the word of Yahweh and dissemble in their conduct, leading the people up the garden path with falsehood (v. 15) and deceiving themselves.[25]

Mic. 4:11 is not entirely secure textually. As the statement of the "many nations" that have assembled against Zion, an easier reading has been suggested: "Let her be stripped naked (*tēḥāśēp*), that our eye may take pleasure in Zion." But the *lectio difficilior* of the MT (*teḥ*ᵉ*nap*) can hardly be evaded: "She deceives (herself)—our eye will take pleasure in Zion."

The meaning "disguise oneself" in the sense of a ritual act would also be appropriate in the lament of Ps. 35:16 (with a syntactically necessary emendation, most likely *b*ᵉ*ḥanepî*), parallel to *b*ᵉ*ṣal'î,* "at my stumbling," in v. 15 and referring to some misfortune like a disease (v. 13): the psalmist laments that his own appropriate conduct provoked an unexpectedly hostile reaction. In this case, there would still be visible

---

[24] T. D. Martin, "The Forensic Background to Jeremiah III 1," *VT,* 19 (1969), 82-92.

[25] G. Münderlein, *Kriterien wahrer und falscher Prophetie. EH,* 23/33 (1974), 35f., 100ff.

here something of the primary meaning of the word, deriving from ritualized role-playing.[26]

Dnl. 11:32 appears likewise to assume the meaning "dissemble." Of the "contemptible person" and usurper Antiochus Epiphanes, it is prophesied that he "will cause those who violate the covenant [i.e., those with Hellenistic sympathies[27]] to dissemble (*yaḥᵃnîp̱*) through flattery." This probably does not mean renouncing their faith in Yahweh (premise), but either hiding by going underground or committing treason, being untrue to themselves.

The noun *ḥānēp̱* is especially common is the language of Wisdom (3 occurrences in Isaiah, 1 in Proverbs, 8 in Job, 3 in Sirach), where it joins "the wicked, the godless, the unrighteous," etc. as a cliche (often rendered privatively by the LXX: *ánomos, asebḗs,* etc.), so that the outlines of a differentiated usage can hardly be discerned. The use of *ḥānēp̱* to describe a person indicates a uniformly negative judgment. To this extent the word approaches a term of abuse, castigating someone for being antisocial, untrustworthy, or dishonest.

The two EA occurrences exemplify this usage: Abdiḫipa, an officer of the pharaoh and regent of Jerusalem, complains in a letter about an assault on him by Kashi, formerly Nubian mercenaries in the pharaoh's service, who are now going through Canaan in mutiny and pillaging: "the evil deed that these traitors have done against me."[28] Again, the pharaoh sends a request for extradition to the prince of Amurru, with a warrant listing by name the "opponent of the king." One is described as "an expert in wickedness [or better: deception], who has defamed the legation"—a clear reference to political offenses, dissimulation, treason.[29]

The application of the term to groups (Job 15:34) and to the words and actions of individuals (Job 34:30: a pretender to the throne; 13:16; Prov. 11:9), as well as the association with *lēḇ* (Job 36:13 and Ugaritic), reveals a semantic element of inward disposition toward deception and dissimulation. In each case, the speaker claims for himself the right to make such a judgment. Only once (Ps. 35:16) does someone predicate *ḥnp* of himself. Elsewhere the prophet castigates the nation or particular groups, confident that his judgment will be self-evident. The sage speaks in the 3rd person, achieving a paradigmatic distance without further identification (e.g., Prov. 11:9; Isa. 32:6): the subject of discussion is the *ḥānēp̱* as a type—a deceiver, a dissimulator, a hypocrite, one who puts up a front before himself and others.

The rare abstracts *ḥōnep̱* and *ḥᵃnuppâ* follow the usage of the noun and verb. It appears that *ḥōnep̱* tends more in content toward the meaning of the noun, "deception, wickedness, treachery" (Arab. "perjury," for example[30]), whereas *ḥᵃnuppâ* tends more toward the special meaning of the verb (cf. Jer. 23:15 with 23:11 and the *'ereṣ* passages).

2. *With "Land" as Subject.* Eight (or 9) of the occurrences of the verb have *'ereṣ*

---

[26] But cf. *KBL*³, 322, which associates *ḥanpî* with the root *ḥnp* II, "limp."

[27] O. Plöger, *Das Buch Daniel. KAT,* XVIII (1965), 164.

[28] EA 288, 7f.; cf. 287, 71ff.; *ANET*³, 488.

[29] EA 162, 74.

[30] J. Wellhausen, *Reste arabischen Heidentums* (Berlin, ²1897; ³1961), 187.

as the subject or (in the case of the hiphil passages) subsidiary subject (including Mic. 4:11, *ṣiyyôn*). Jer. 3:2 and 9 express a situation that appears with some frequency in this context: infidelity (*znh*) to the deity has further consequences and causes the land to be polluted; i.e., nature is involved in the result (v. 3). In Ps. 106:38, in the list of misdeeds following reference to the spilling of innocent blood through the offering of child sacrifice to the "idols of Canaan," we find the statement "the land was polluted with blood (*baddāmîm*)." The idea is continued in v. 39: "Thus they became unclean by their acts, and played the harlot in their doings." The same idea with respect to the person who commits an act is expressed in Nu. 35:33f. in terms of P's theology. Once again, the "land in which you live" (i.e., the Holy Land) has a special character: "You shall not pollute the land" (par. v. 34: "You shall not defile the land"), "for the blood (of the murder victim) pollutes the land." In addition to blood, it is infidelity and blasphemous conduct that pollute the land (Jer. 3:2,9), as well as transgression of the laws, violation of the sacral statutes, and breaking of the covenant (Isa. 24:5). In Isa. 24:5, *'ereṣ* has the sense of "earth" (*tēḇēl*). Here we find an echo of the notion that it is the earth "beneath its inhabitants" (cf. Nu. 35:33; Ps. 106:38; Jer. 3:3: "pollute") that is affected by the curse on human actions (Isa. 24:6). The conception evoked by *ḥnp* in these passages where it is associated with the land is obviously complex, first taking on clearer outlines in the priestly and cultic sphere.

III. Use in Theological Contexts.

1. *In Prophetic Oracles of Judgment.* In theological usage, *ḥnp* always has a collective subject; the noun is used in Isa. 9:16(17); 10:6, probably the earliest occurrences in the OT. The prophet applies the noun to the people and nation as a whole (9:8[9]), brought together as a unit through Yahweh's act of judgment, which constitutes them "the people of my wrath" (10:6). In Isaiah's view, their guilt is correspondingly total; it consists fundamentally in a refusal to acknowledge the situation of conflict expressed in 9:7,11,16[8,12,17]. The prophet renders his verdict accordingly: misconduct based on self-deception or even willful ignorance, "deceit and perversion, folly in every mouth" (9:16[17]). The charge is made explicit in 29:13: hypocrisy.

Jer. 3:1-5 (6-10) also focuses on *ḥnp.* The unit is organized around three meanings of the verb. First, in the metaphor of the divorced wife (v. 1a), the word is chosen to illustrate how the woman deceives herself about the possibility of a return (→ שׁוב *šûḇ*) to her former husband, which is prohibited by the law (Dt. 24:4).[31] The separation is complete; the final break with the "friend of her youth" (v. 4) cannot be canceled. Second, the deceptive intent of this conduct is clearly displayed in the application section of the oracle: the community, seemingly ready to repent, belies itself (*'iššâ zônâ,* v. 3; the simile in v. 2), hypocritically concealing its deeds. Third, the acts of "harlotry" have something contagious about them: they have polluted the land (vv. 2b,9; cf. v. 1a MT), which is devastated by lack of rain (v. 3). Thus this kind of *ḥnp* effect is itself cited as a consequence of infidelity. In developing the semantic affinities

---

[31] T. R. Hobbs, "Jeremiah 3 $_{1\text{-}5}$ and Deuteronomy 24 $_{1\text{-}4}$" *ZAW,* 86 (1974), 23-29.

of *ḥnp,* the prophetic discourse in Jer. 3:1-5 (cf. vv. 6-10) arrives at an impressive and convincing statement concerning the problem of *šûḇ.*

Seen in the light of Jer. 3:1-5 (6-10), the oracle against prophets and priests (Jer. 23:11; cf. v. 15) seems to point to a similarly structured situation: the deceptive conduct of the functionaries and the concomitant profanation of the land.

2. *In the Tradition of Cultic Theology.* The concluding parenetic remarks in Nu. 35:33f. on the theme of blood vengeance and cities of refuge, which are a late product of redaction, are based on notions of cultic theology concerning the sacred land "in which you live and in the midst of which I—Yahweh—dwell." This thematic framework provides the setting for the statement about the danger of unexpiated blood, which pollutes the whole land and can be expiated only by the blood of the one who shed it. Here *ḥnp* becomes a term for the transgression of sacral ordinances.

3. *In Wisdom Thought.* It is an important observation that in the realm of Wisdom *ḥānēp* comes to designate a particular type of conduct in which the person concerned deceives both himself and society: dissimulation and hypocrisy. In parallel with *ḥānēp* we find the man "forgotten of God" (Job 8:13), who, unlike the *ṣaddîq* (Prov. 11:9), is without *da'aṯ;* he speaks *n*ᵉ*ḇālâ* (Isa. 9:16[17]; 32:6), and his character is based on folly, madness, and iniquity (*'āwen*). He is described by the word that suggests deception and dissimulation. He who is untrue to himself and society, thus destroying himself, dangerously deceives himself and others; it is his purpose "to destroy his neighbor with his mouth" (Prov. 11:9; cf. Ps. 5:12[11]; 12:3[2]; also Isa. 32:6: "to practice ungodliness and utter error [*tô'â*] concerning Yahweh"). The choice of words shows that in this realm the phenomenon of deceptive conduct, especially on the part of individuals (cf. the Isaiah passages), is dealt with and assigned appropriate terminology; those so judged are relegated to the circle of the godless (Isa. 32:6; Job).

The term plays a particular role in the book of Job, where it is placed in the mouth of each participant in the dialogue. In all the passages, *ḥānēp* is a categorical designation alongside *rāšā'* (cf. Job 8:13b and the substantially similar Prov. 10:27) associated with conventional predications, especially in statements of Job's friends that are intended to locate Job in the vicinity of that group (8:13; 15:35 [cf. Isa. 32:6]; 20:5; 34:30 [using the king as an example]; 36:13). Examination of Job's aggressive rejection of the charge shows that in 13:16; 17:8; and 27:8 he makes use of traditional forms of expression,[32] relying in each case on notions belonging to the realm of entrance *tôrôṯ* and admittance to the sanctuary (cf. Isa. 33:14,15ff.). Indeed, in 13:16 he finds in this usage the glimmer of hope that is reinterpreted in his concluding discourse (27:8-10): it redounds to his "salvation" that he can come before God in the sanctuary, because this fact at least makes it clear that he is no *ḥānēp,* for "a *ḥānēp* shall not come before him." From this perspective, then, the *ḥānēp* stands outside the sacred precincts (cf. also 36:13). This observation casts a new light on the passages applying *ḥnp* to the land and Ps. 35:16 conj.

[32] A. Weiser, *Das Buch Hiob. ATD,* XIII (⁶1974); Horst, *in loc.*

IV. Later Reflexes. In 1QS 4:10, *ḥnp* appears as a noun in a catalog of the characteristics of the wicked spirit, following "fraud and deception" and paired with *'kzry:* "cruelty and enormous hypocrisy." The catalog continues with "terrible wrath and great folly and alien jealousy," leading up to the fruits of such a nature: "atrocities in the spirit of fornication and ways of filth in the service of uncleanness." Once again we find contextually linked the two semantic nuclei of surrender of human identity and pollution. What is attempted here is a kind of psychological categorization of hypocrisy (*ḥnp;* cf. Job 36:13).

In addition, *ḥnp* continues in Jewish Aramaic, Middle Hebrew, and Arabic as a specific term for renegades, recreants, dissidents, apostates, unbelievers, godless, and pagans. *Gen. Rab.*, p. 48 [beginning], 46ᵇ notes: "wherever in Scripture the word *ḥnp* appears, heresy [idolatry] is to be understood."[33] The development of the term within Arabic is especially interesting.[34] The Gk. *hypokrínomai* is discussed elsewhere.[35]

Seybold

---

[33] *WTM*, II, 84.
[34] Joüon, 315; Wehr, 210; *HwbIsl*, 165-67; *KBL*³, 322.
[35] Wilckens.

חֶסֶד *ḥeseḏ*

Contents: I. Semitic Dialects; Etymology; LXX. II. OT: 1. Occurrences; 2. Use. III. Secular Usage: 1. Formulaic Usage with *'āśâ* and *'im;* 2. Other Usages; 3. Summary. IV. Religious Usage: 1. Yahweh as Subject; 2. Meaning in This Context; 3. Other Syntactic Structures; 4. Liturgical Formulas; 5. The *ḥasḏê ḏāwiḏ;* 6. *ḥeseḏ* and *bᵉrîṯ;* 7. Summary. V. Qumran.

ḥeseḏ. F. Asenio, *Misericordia et veritas* (diss., Pontifical Biblical Institute, 1947). *AG*, 48 (1949); R. Bultmann, "ἔλεος," B, *TDNT*, II, 479-482; A. Caquot, "Les 'grâces de David': A propos d'Isaie 55/3 b," *Sem*, 15 (1965), 45-49; I. Elbogen, "חסד, Verpflichtung, Verheissung, Bekräftigung," *Oriental Studies. Festschrift P. Haupt* (Baltimore, 1926), 43-46; N. Glueck, *Hesed in the Bible* (Eng. trans. 1967; repr. New York, 1975); J. P. Hyatt, "The God of Love in the OT," *To Do & To Teach. Festschrift C. L. Pyatt* (Lexington, Ky., 1953), 15-26; A. Jepsen, "Gnade und Barmherzigkeit im AT," *KuD*, 7 (1961), 261-271; A. R. Johnson, "ḤESED and ḤĀSÎD," *Interpretationes ad Vetus Testamentum pertinentes. Festschrift S. Mowinckel. NTT*, 56 (1955), 100-112; W. F. Lofthouse, "Ḥen and Ḥesed in the OT," *ZAW*, 51 (1933), 29-35; U. Masing, "Der Begriff *ḥesed* im alttestamentlichen Sprachgebrauch," *Charisteria J. Kopp* (Stockholm, 1954), 27-63; J. A. Montgomery, "Hebrew *Hesed* and Greek *Charis*," *HThR*, 32 (1939), 97-102; N. H. Snaith, "The Meaning of חֶסֶד," *ExpT*, 55 (1943/44), 108-110; R. Sorg, *Ḥesed and Ḥasid in the Psalms* (St. Louis, 1953); H. J. Stoebe, *Bedeutung und Geschichte des Begriffes ḥäsäd* (diss., Münster, 1951); *idem*, "Die Bedeutung des Wortes *ḥäsäd* im AT," *VT*, 2 (1952), 244-254; *idem*, "חֶסֶד *ḥǽsǽd* Güte," *THAT*, I, 600-621; C. Wiéner, *Recherches sur l'amour pour Dieu dans l'AT* (Paris, 1957); U. G. Yarbrough, *The Significance of ḥesed in the OT* (diss., Southern Baptist Seminary, 1948/49).

I. Semitic Dialects; Etymology; LXX. The noun *ḥeseḏ* is a Hebrew word that has found its way into Middle Hebrew, Jewish Aramaic, Syriac, and Mandaic.[1] Its etymology is unknown. The root *ḥsd,* which appears just twice in Hebrew in the hithpael imperfect, is clearly denominative. Derivation from the Arabic root *ḥašada,* "band together for mutual aid,"[2] is problematical at best because of the postulated change from *š* to *s*. The LXX usually renders *ḥeseḏ* by means of *éleos* (213 times), *eleēmosýnē* (6 times), or *eleḗmos* (twice); in addition, we find *dikaiosýnē* (8 times), *cháris* (twice), and (once each) *díkaios* (Isa. 57:1), *dóxa* (Isa. 40:6), *elpís* (2 Ch. 35:26), *táxis* (Prov. 31:26[LXX v. 25]), *tá hósia* (Isa. 55:3), *oiktirmós* (Jer. 31:3[LXX 38:3]), *antilḗmptōr* (Ps. 109:12[LXX 108:12]), and *dikaiosýnē kaí éleos* (Ex. 34:7). In 6 other passages the LXX either has no corresponding equivalent or translates quite differently. It follows on the one hand that the meaning of *ḥeseḏ* must be determined from the OT texts themselves, and on the other that, in view of the LXX translation, we must reckon with some breadth of meaning.

II. OT.

1. *Occurrences*. The noun *ḥeseḏ* occurs 245 times in the OT, with the following distribution by individual books: 11 in Genesis, 4 in Exodus, 2 in Numbers, 3 in Deuteronomy, 3 in Joshua, 2 in Judges, 3 in Ruth, 16 in 1–2 Samuel, 5 in 1 Kings, 15 in 1–2 Chronicles, 3 in Ezra, 5 in Nehemiah, 2 in Esther, 3 in Job, 127 in Psalms, 10 in Proverbs, 8 in Isaiah (1 in Isaiah, 4 in Deutero-Isaiah, 3 in Trito-Isaiah), 6 in Jeremiah, 2 in Lamentations, 2 in Daniel, 6 in Hosea, 1 in Joel, 2 in Jonah, 3 in Micah, and 1 in Zechariah. It does not occur at all in Leviticus, 2 Kings, Ecclesiastes, Song of Songs, Ezekiel, Amos, Obadiah, Nahum, Habakkuk, Zephaniah, Haggai, and Malachi. Since the only passage in Proto-Isaiah (Isa. 16:5) is probably spurious, Proto-Isaiah may be included in the list of books where the word does not occur. It is evident that our term is well represented in early narrative literature, with some 49 occurrences, but becomes much less important in prophetic literature, especially that of the early period, with only 29 occurrences. It obviously occupies a special place in poetry, with 131 occurrences, but it also appears 23 times in the Chronicler's history. Although the distinction cannot be precise and the numbers must therefore be interpreted with some caution, roughly 63 of the 245 occurrences belong to the secular sphere.

2. *Use*. As a rule, *ḥeseḏ* appears in the singular. The plural is found only 18 times (Gen. 32:11[Eng. v. 10]; 2 Ch. 6:42; 32:32; 35:26; Neh. 13:14; Ps. 17:7; 25:6; 89:2,50[1,49]; 106:7,45 *Q;* 107:43; 119:41 *Q;* Isa. 55:3; 63:7 [twice]; Lam. 3:22,32 *Q*). Three of these passages belong to the secular sphere (2 Ch. 32:32; 35:26; Neh. 13:14), 13 to the religious. In addition, the *ḥasḏê ḏāwiḏ* are mentioned twice (Isa. 55:3; 2 Ch. 6:42). It should also be noted that of these occurrences probably only Gen. 32:11(10) (J) and Ps. 89 are preexilic.

---

[1] *KBL*[3].

[2] Glueck, 106f., citing F. Schulthess, *Homonyme Wurzeln in Syrischen* (Berlin, 1900), 32.

In almost half of the occurrences (124) the noun has a possessive suffix: 1st singular 10 times, 2nd masculine singular 55, 3rd masculine singular 57, 2nd and 3rd plural once each. The suffix refers to Sarah (Gen. 20), Hushai (2 S. 16), David (1 S. 20; Pss. 59,144), Ruth (Ruth 3), Nehemiah (Neh. 13), a man (Prov. 20), an idolator (Jon. 2), flesh (Isa. 40), or the Israelites (Hos. 6); in all other cases it refers to God or Yahweh.

Only rarely (16 times) is the noun found with the definite article: Gen. 21:23; 32:11(10); Dt. 7:9,12; 2 S. 2:5; 1 K. 3:6; 8:23; 2 Ch. 6:14; 24:22; Neh. 1:5 (conj.); 9:32; Ps. 130:7; Prov. 20:28; Isa. 16:5; Jer. 16:5; Dnl. 9:4. As a rule, the article refers to a specific demonstration of *ḥeseḏ* mentioned in the context.

In genitive constructions, *ḥeseḏ* appears 14 times as *nomen regens: ḥeseḏ/ḥasḏê YHWH* (1 S. 20:14; Ps. 33:5; 103:17/Ps. 89:2[1]; 107:43; Isa. 63:7; Lam. 3:22), *ḥeseḏ 'elōhîm* (2 S. 9:3; Ps. 52:10[8]), *ḥeseḏ 'ēl* (Ps. 52:3[1]), *ḥeseḏ 'elyôn* (Ps. 21:8[7]), *ḥasḏê ḏāwiḏ* (2 Ch. 6:42; Isa. 55:3), and *ḥeseḏ ne'ûrayiḵ* (Jer. 2:2). It likewise occurs 14 times as *nomen rectum: 'anšê-ḥeseḏ* (Isa. 57:1), *'îš ḥeseḏ* (Prov. 11:17; 20:6), *malḵê ḥeseḏ* (1 K. 20:31), *tôraṯ ḥeseḏ* (Prov. 31:26), *'ahaḇaṯ ḥeseḏ* (Mic. 6:8), *'elōhê ḥasdî* (Ps. 59:11[10] *Q*), *gōḏel ḥasdeḵā* (Nu. 14:19), *rōḇ ḥasd* + suffix (Neh. 13:22; Ps. 5:8[7]; 69:14[13]; 106:45 *Q*; Isa. 63:7; Lam. 3:32).

III. Secular Usage. Despite the objections raised by Jepsen,[3] it is advisable to begin with secular usage in order to determine the semantic component of *ḥeseḏ* because our term is used most concretely in relationships among humans. We can thus guard against the possibility of misinterpreting the religious use of *ḥeseḏ*.

1. *Formulaic Usage with 'āśâ and 'im.* a. The most valuable conclusions for an understanding of *ḥeseḏ* can be derived from the circumstance that almost half of the occurrences under discussion make use of a stereotyped formula: *ḥeseḏ* is constructed 25 times with *'aśâ* and *'im* (Gen. 19:19; 20:13; 21:23; 40:14; 47:29; Josh. 2:12 [twice]; etc.), once with *'āśâ* and *le* (1 K. 2:7), once in an interrogative noun clause with *'ēṯ*, "with" (2 S. 16:17), and once, having the opposite meaning, with the hiphil of *krt* and *mē'im* (1 S. 20:15). This observation alone is enough to show that in *ḥeseḏ* we are dealing with something belonging to the sphere of human interaction, where it is operative.

b. This interpersonal relationship can be defined more precisely[4] as the relationship between relatives (Sarah–Abraham, Gen. 20:13; Laban and Bethuel–Isaac, Gen. 24:49; Joseph–Israel, Gen. 47:29; Orpah/Ruth–Mahlon/Chilion/Naomi, Ruth 1:8; Kenites–Israelites, 1 S. 15:6, between host and guest (men–Lot, Gen. 19:19; Abimelech–Abraham, Gen. 21:23; Rahab–spies, Josh. 2:12,14), between friends (Jonathan–David, 1 S. 20:8,14; David–Meribbaal, 2 S. 9:1,3,7; David–Hanun, 2 S. 10:2 par. 1 Ch. 19:2; Hushai–David, 2 S. 16:17; Solomon–sons of Barzillai, 1 K. 2:7),

3 P. 265.

4 See Glueck, 35ff.

between sovereign and subjects (men of Jabesh-gilead–Saul, 2 S. 2:5; Abner–house of Saul, 2 S. 3:8; Jehoiada–Joash, 2 Ch. 24:22), and between two parties, inaugurated by an unusual act of kindness on the part of one (prisoner–Joseph, Gen. 40:14; house of Joseph–man from Bethel, Jgs. 1:24; Israelites–family of Jerubbaal [Gibeon], Jgs. 8:35).

c. The demonstration of *ḥeseḏ* consists in the sparing of Lot and the family of Rahab, or the release of the man from Bethel, who might have been killed (cf. also Sarah and Abraham in Gen. 20; in 2 Ch. 24, Joash acts in the opposite way, disregarding the *ḥeseḏ* that had been shown him). The statement that the kings of Israel are *malḵê ḥeseḏ* (1 K. 20:31) is grounded in the hope of Ben-hadad and his servants that they will not be killed. Abner likewise cites the fact that he did not hand Ish-baal over to David (2 S. 3:8), and Abimelech appeals to his reception of Abraham as a stranger (Gen. 21:23). Other acts of *ḥeseḏ* include the giving of Bethuel's own daughter to be Isaac's wife (Gen. 24:49), Joseph's agreement not to bury Israel in Egypt (Gen. 47:29), and Saul's burial by the men of Jabesh-gilead (2 S. 2:5). Finally, Gen. 40:14 involves speaking on Joseph's behalf, and 2 S. 9:1,3,7 deals with the restoration to Meribbaal of his ancestral property and in addition (as with the sons of Barzillai in 1 K. 2:7) his being given a place at the king's table. What is meant by *ḥeseḏ* can almost be paraphrased by the expression "do good" (Jgs. 8:35; 2 S. 2:6); characteristically, *haṭṭôḇâ,* like *ḥeseḏ,* is constructed with *'āśâ* and *'im* (Jgs. 8:35) or *'ēṯ* (2 S. 2:6).

d. On the basis of the passages already cited, we can make another important observation. It is often stated expressly that the one who receives an act of *ḥeseḏ* responds with a similar act of *ḥeseḏ,* or at least that the one who demonstrates *ḥeseḏ* is justified in expecting an equivalent act in return. Abimelech, for example, having taken in Abraham as a guest, asks him to show the same *ḥeseḏ* to his host and the land where he has sojourned (Gen. 21:23); Abraham so swears, and this agreement is called a covenant in v. 27. The harlot Rahab likewise asks the Israelite spies to show the same *ḥeseḏ* to the house of her father as they received from her; they, too, swear to do so (Josh. 2:12,14). Just as David asks Jonathan for an act of *ḥeseḏ,* so Jonathan also asks *ḥeseḏ* of David (1 S. 20:8,14f.); once again this is viewed against the background of the Yahweh *b^{e}rîṯ* between the two. And after the death of Jonathan, David fulfils the promise of *ḥeseḏ* in the person of Jonathan's son Meribbaal (2 S. 9). The mutuality of *ḥeseḏ* is also mentioned in 2 S. 2:5f., where David, among other things, promises to do good to the men of Jabesh-gilead because they had shown *ḥeseḏ* to Saul and buried him. Similarly, David's declaration of sympathy upon the death of Nahash, which is called *ḥeseḏ,* is occasioned by the fact that Nahash had previously shown David *ḥeseḏ* (2 S. 10:2, *ka'^{a}šer,* par. 1 Ch. 19:2, *kî*). And David's request to Solomon to show *ḥeseḏ* to the sons of Barzillai and make them his table companions is based (*kî*) on the fact that they had previously so treated David and taken him in when he was a fugitive (1 K. 2:7). There are a few other passages that, although they do not explicitly mention this mutual demonstration of *ḥeseḏ,* nevertheless imply it in their context. In Gen. 19, we must remember that Lot took in the strangers and fed them. In Gen. 40, Joseph's interpretation of his fellow prisoners' dreams justifies his request. The fact that the man from Bethel showed the spies the way into the city earned his claim to *ḥeseḏ* (Jgs. 1:24). And because the Kenites had previously shown *ḥeseḏ* to Israel, Saul's treatment of them is correspondingly friendly (1 S. 15:6). That it is among the ethical norms of human intercourse to return *ḥeseḏ* that has been received is clear from the emphatic statement that the Israelites did not show *ḥeseḏ* to the house of Jerubbaal-Gideon, even though he had done much good to Israel (Jgs. 8:35), and that Joab did not remember the *ḥeseḏ* that Jehoiada had shown him (2 Ch. 24:22).

In view of the impressive evidence for the mutuality of *ḥeseḏ*, we may venture the conjecture that even in cases where the context does not suggest such mutuality it is nevertheless implicit, because we are dealing with the closest of human bonds. In the case of Abraham and Sarah (Gen. 20:13) as well as Orpah/Ruth and Mahlon/Chilion (Ruth 1:8), it is the relationship between husband and wife; in the case of Israel and Joseph (Gen. 47:29), it is father and son; in the case of Laban/Bethuel and Isaac (Gen. 24:49), it is next of kin; and in 2 S. 16:17, it should be noted that Hushai's relationship to David is called that of a "friend" (*rēa'*).

e. Finally, it is worth noting that, of the passages just discussed, Gen. 24:49; 47:29; Josh. 2:14 use the phrase *ḥeseḏ we'ᵉmeṯ*. This expression is generally (and correctly) understood as an hendiadys, in which the second noun *'ᵉmeṯ* (→ אמן *'āman*)[5] emphasizes the permanence, certainty, and lasting validity of the demonstration or promise of *ḥeseḏ*. The same phenomenon is expressed by the phrase *'aḏ-'ôlām* in Jonathan's request that after his death David will not cut off his *ḥeseḏ* from the house of Jonathan for ever (1 S. 20:15). That demonstration of *ḥeseḏ* includes the element of *'ᵉmeṯ* is also shown by the use of *šqr*, "deal falsely," as an antonym in Gen. 21:23.

2. *Other Usages*.

a. Before we can summarize our observations, the other occurrences of *ḥeseḏ* in secular usage should be mentioned, to round out the picture that has been sketched. The active nature of *ḥeseḏ*[6] is underlined by the use of the verb *'āśâ* in Zec. 7:9 and Ps. 109:16. Similarly, the pl. *ḥᵃsāḏîm* in 2 Ch. 32:32; 35:26; Neh. 13:14 refers to the "good deeds" of Hezekiah, Josiah, and Nehemiah; in Neh. 13:14, this phrase is reinforced by the explanatory clause "that I have done for (*'āśâ* + *bᵉ*) the house of God and its furnishings." In the broader context of *ḥeseḏ* we also encounter the verbs *gāmal*, "render" (Prov. 11:17), *ḥāraš*, "devise" (Prov. 14:22), *rāḏap*, "pursue" (Prov. 21:21), and the hiphil of *yṭb*, "make good" (Ruth 3:10); in the opposite sense we find *mûš* + *min*, "refuse" (Job 6:14 conj. for *ms*[7]). The *'ahᵃḇaṯ ḥeseḏ* of Mic. 6:8 also belongs here, on account of the parallel *'ᵃśôṯ mišpāṭ*. On the basis of these observa-

[5] I, 311.

[6] See III.1.a.

[7] Most recently G. Fohrer, *Das Buch Hiob*. *KAT*, XVI (1963), 161.

tions, we can draw the general conclusion that the concept *ḥeseḏ* includes an element of action.

b. It is likewise clear that *ḥeseḏ* is a relational concept. In Ruth 3:10, the point is the relationship of Ruth to her mother-in-law and to Boaz, whom she prefers to the young men. Isa. 16:5 and Prov. 20:28 speak in general terms of the relationship between a king and his subjects. Est. 2:9,17 are concerned with the good will of Hegai and the king toward Esther, Dnl. 1:9 with that of the chief eunuch toward Daniel, and Ezr. 7:28; 9:9 with that of the Persian kings and their counselors toward Ezra. Finally, Job 6:14; Ps. 109:16; Zec. 7:9 speak of relationships among individuals. We may therefore conclude quite generally that *ḥeseḏ* is a relational concept.

c. When we turn to the concrete form taken by the demonstration of *ḥeseḏ,* we encounter at the outset ideas that are already familiar: Ezra and his colleagues are spared by the Persian king (Ezr. 9:9); Ruth prefers Boaz as a husband to the young men (Ruth 3:10); Esther receives from Hegai everything she needs to adorn her beauty, together with appropriate food and maidservants, as well as the crown and the rank of queen from the king (Est. 2:9,17); the chief eunuch does not compel Daniel to defile himself with food and drink from the king's table (Dnl. 1:9).

In addition, however, the element of doing *mišpāṭ* comes very much to the fore in this group of occurrences. In Mic. 6:8, *mišpāṭ* and *ḥeseḏ* appear in parallel in the statement of what God requires of mankind. Hos. 12:7(6) says the same: "Hold fast to *ḥeseḏ* and *mišpāṭ.*" And on a throne established upon *ḥeseḏ* shall sit a judge who seeks *mišpāṭ* and *ṣeḏeq* (Isa. 16:5). We have what amounts to an interpretative elaboration of the concept *mišpāṭ* when the absence of *ḥeseḏ* and similar concepts spoken of in Hos. 4:1 leads in v. 2 to swearing, lying, killing, stealing, adultery, and murder. In like manner, the requirement of Zec. 7:9, "Render true judgments (*mišpaṭ 'ᵉmeṯ*), show *ḥeseḏ* and *raḥᵃmîm* each to his brother," is interpreted in v. 10: "Do not oppress the widow, the fatherless, the sojourner, or the poor, and let none of you devise evil against his brother in your heart." And according to Ps. 109, forgetting to show *ḥeseḏ* leads to persecution of the poor and needy (v. 16), together with love of cursing and dislike of blessing (v. 17). Those who act according to this divine requirement can therefore be called *'anšê-ḥeseḏ* (Isa. 57:1; Prov. 11:17 [sg.]); in Isa. 57:1 we find the *ṣaddîq* in parallel, and in Prov. 11:17 the "cruel man" (*'aḵzārî*) is cited in contrast. It follows from these principles that iniquity (*'āwōn*) can be atoned for through *ḥeseḏ* and *'ᵉmeṯ.*

d. Corresponding to this shift of the concept *ḥeseḏ* into the domain of the ethical requirements imposed on mankind by God, we find also a certain change in the element of mutuality. When the *ḥeseḏ* shown Esther is ascribed to her having pleased Hegai (Est. 2:9) and to the king's loving her more than the other women (2:17), what is described is not an act but a situation that is not established by Esther's own actions. This is even clearer in Gen. 39:21; Ezr. 7:28; 9:9; Dnl. 1:9: it is ultimately God or Yahweh who brought about the demonstrations of *ḥeseḏ* on the part of the authorities to Daniel and Ezra. The other passages also display this reference to God. While Boaz responds to Ruth's demonstration of *ḥeseḏ* by saying, "May you be blessed by Yahweh" (Ruth 3:10), Nehemiah prays that God will remember favorably his good deeds (Neh. 13:14). It is as though God's blessing functions as a substitute for human acts of *ḥeseḏ* in return. In Ps. 109, conversely, a curse is invoked (v. 17) upon the one who refused to show *ḥeseḏ* to the poor and needy (vv. 12,16).

It is attractive to connect these passages with the words of the prophets in which the mutual demonstration of *ḥeseḏ* is brought into a kind of relationship to God, precisely because it is what Yahweh requires of mankind. Because people refused to hearken to Yahweh's command to practice mutual *ḥeseḏ*, the wrath of God was kindled (Zec. 7:9ff.). Yahweh has a controversy with the inhabitants of the earth because, among other things, there is no *ḥeseḏ* on earth (Hos. 4:1); the requirement of *ḥeseḏ* expresses God's will (Hos. 6:6; Mic. 6:8).

This association is likewise presupposed by the Wisdom sayings that belong in this context, to the extent that the mutual exchange of *ḥeseḏ* not only occupies an important place in their rules for the conduct of life by virtue of being made the principle by which life should be governed, but is also viewed in relationship to God, thus becoming part of the common doctrine of retribution.[8] Prov. 11:17, for example, states: "A man who is kind (*'îš ḥeseḏ*) benefits himself, but a cruel man hurts himself"; Prov. 14:22: "Those that devise evil err, but those who devise good meet *ḥeseḏ* and *'ᵉmeṯ*"; Prov. 20:28: "*ḥeseḏ* and *'ᵉmeṯ* preserve the king, and his throne is upheld by *ḥeseḏ*"; Prov. 21:21: "He who pursues *ṣᵉḏāqâ* and *ḥeseḏ* will find life and honor" (see the comms. for the text). The implicit idea, not stated here in so many words, is that acts of *ḥeseḏ* are repaid, or at least can be repaid, by God as well as by mankind. This notion is expressed unequivocally in Prov. 3:3f.: "Practice *ḥeseḏ* and you will find favor and good repute in the sight of God and man"; in Prov. 16:6: "By *ḥeseḏ* and *'ᵉmeṯ* iniquity is atoned for, and by the fear of Yahweh a man avoids evil"; and in the Wisdom saying that has found its way as an explanatory gloss into Job 6:14: "'He who withholds *ḥeseḏ* from a friend forsakes the fear of the Almighty."

e. When we finally turn to phrases using *ḥeseḏ*, we find *ḥeseḏ we'ᵉmeṯ* 4 times, all in the book of Proverbs (Prov. 3:3; 14:22; 16:6; 20:28; cf. also 20:6, with *'ᵉmûnîm*). That we are in fact dealing with an hendiadys can be seen from 16:6; only the first noun is preceded by the prep. *bᵉ*, which thus applies to the phrase as a whole, a single concept meaning "lasting, constant *ḥeseḏ*." Such *ḥeseḏ* atones for iniquity (16:6) and protects the king (20:28). Those who steadfastly practice *ḥeseḏ* find favor with God and mankind (3:3f.). Whoever does good will find lasting *ḥeseḏ* (14:22). In Isa. 16:5 (probably postexilic), too, *'ᵉmeṯ* occurs in the same context as *ḥeseḏ* (cf. also Ps. 109:12: *mōšēḵ ḥeseḏ*, "continue *ḥeseḏ*"). That true goodness is not an isolated act but rather an enduring attitude toward one's fellows is an idea already met with in Hosea, where Hos. 6:4 says of Ephraim and Judah: "Your love is like a morning cloud, like the dew that goes early away." Both images portray a fleeting *ḥeseḏ*, in the absence of

---

[8] H. Ringgren, *Sprüche, Prediger, das Hohelied, Klagelieder, das Buch Esther. ATD*, XVI (²1967), 61.

'emeṯ. It might be objected that the list in Hos. 4:1 refers to the absence of *'emeṯ*, of *ḥeseḏ*, and of *da'aṯ 'elōhîm;* the three concepts stand independent of each other and should therefore be interpreted independently. It will be noted, however, that Hos. 6:6 speaks only of *ḥeseḏ* and *da'aṯ 'elōhîm* as objects of Yahweh's desire. Neither is *'emeṯ* mentioned in Hos. 10:12 as a third term alongside *ḥeseḏ* and *da'aṯ 'elōhîm*. In Hos. 4:1, therefore, the first noun *'emeṯ* must be thought of in combination with both *ḥeseḏ* and *da'aṯ 'elōhîm*,[9] which it dominates through its initial position. The emphasis, therefore, is on the transitory nature of the *ḥeseḏ* practiced by the inhabitants of the land, which derives in turn from the absence of enduring knowledge of God.[10] There is no question of showing this *ḥeseḏ* toward God,[11] as suggested by Stoebe's "free surrender of the human heart to God."[12]

3. *Summary*. We have seen that there are three elements constitutive of the *ḥeseḏ* concept: it is active, social, and enduring. As Jepsen has rightly observed,[13] *ḥeseḏ* always designates not just a human attitude, but also the act that emerges from this attitude. It is an act that preserves or promotes life. It is intervention on behalf of someone suffering misfortune or distress. It is demonstration of friendship or piety. It pursues what is good and not what is evil. Thus the most appropriate translation of *ḥeseḏ* is "goodness," "grace," or "kindness." In the praise of the good wife, the phrase *tôraṯ-ḥeseḏ* (Prov. 31:26) can therefore be translated "kindly teaching"; standing in parallel to *ḥoḵmâ*, it refers to the woman's "gift for teaching,"[14] training others for a happy life.

The second element constitutive of our concept is its social nature. There is always someone else to whom *ḥeseḏ* is shown or from whom it is expected. The individual may be replaced by a group such as a family or clan, but we never hear of the *ḥeseḏ* of, say, the nation (not even in 1 S. 15:6); at most, the king is said to show *ḥeseḏ* toward his subjects. It is therefore clear that the concept lies in the realm of interpersonal relations. This is also clear from the fact that *ḥeseḏ* is done primarily between wife and husband, father and son, host and guest, relatives, friends, and those who have formed a relationship based on unexpected acts of kindness. We can therefore formulate our statement more precisely: *ḥeseḏ* belongs by nature to the realm of family and clan society.

The third constitutive element is also the context that most easily explains the combination of *ḥeseḏ* and *'emeṯ*, because the close and intimate society of the family requires enduring and reliable kindness as an essential element of its protective function. Kindness can most surely fulfill its function of preserving and promoting life, thus strengthening society, when it follows and is explained by certain social norms

---

[9] So also H. W. Wolff, *Hosea. Herm* (Eng. trans. 1974), 67.

[10] *Ibid.*, 67f.; *idem*, "'Wissen um Gott' bei Hosea als Urform von Theologie," *EvTh*, 12 (1952/53), 533-554 = *GSAT. ThB*, 22 ([2]1973), 182-205, esp. 197f.

[11] Jepsen, 268f.

[12] Stoebe, *VT*, 2, 250f.

[13] Jepsen, 266, and *passim*.

[14] Ringgren, *ATD*, XVI/2, 121.

such as those formulated in the *mišpāṭîm*. It follows almost automatically that the demonstration of kindness, like the *mišpāṭîm,* is heard as a divine requirement. It thus becomes extended to the sphere of humanity as a whole and becomes a mark of faith. This development can be seen in the occurrences of our concept in prophetic and Wisdom texts.

Here, too, belongs our observation that kindness frequently intends mutuality. The very fact that refusal to return an act of kindness is stigmatized as being especially reprehensible confirms the general validity of the principle that *ḥeseḏ* is mutual. This principle is also presupposed by the late passages which state that, because Yahweh requires such kindness toward one's neighbor, he will or at least can reward such an act and credit it to its doer.

It is a striking fact that the passages in which an intimate relationship is assumed, either between members of the same family or between friends, never mention this principle. This observation may serve as a hint toward answering the question of the motives behind acts of kindness. There are two fundamentally different views. Glueck, in his well-received dissertation, emphasized the close relationship of *ḥeseḏ* to → ברית *b^e^rîṯ [b^e^rîth]*, and therefore practically defined *ḥeseḏ* as the very content of *b^e^rîṯ*[15] and as "conduct in accordance with the mutual relationship of rights and duties between allies."[16] Stoebe, on the contrary, emphasized in his dissertation the points of contact between our term and → רחמים *raḥ^a^mîm,* and explained *ḥeseḏ* as "goodness or kindness . . . beyond what is expected or deserved, based solely on ready magnanimity toward others."[17] The fact that both scholars can cite appropriate texts suggests that the situation is not as clear as they assume.

If we begin with the observation that the concept of *ḥeseḏ* has its original *Sitz im Leben* in the family or clan, then the silence of these passages with respect to the principle of mutuality is explained. The fruitful and productive common life of such a close human society requires constant mutual kindness on the part of all its members. At any rate this represents the normal case. The same is true of a friendship, which is based on mutual exchange of friendly acts. In these examples it would be out of place to look for the motif of grace or mercy; it would be equally out of place to define the personal bonds in terms of legal obligations.

There is no evidence that a *b^e^rîṯ* is the prerequisite for a demonstration of *ḥeseḏ*. Abraham must swear to Abimelech (Gen. 21), and the spies to Rahab (Josh. 2), that they will return the acts of kindness that have been done them. In Gen. 21 we read also that Abraham gave various animals to Abimelech, whereupon the two men made a covenant (v. 27). In both cases, the parties belong to different and probably hostile tribes, so that the display of friendly cooperation is not an obvious expectation. Neither, of course, can mutuality be presupposed or automatically expected, since the two parties also differ greatly with respect to their strength and power. This explains why the assurances are reinforced by an oath and even a *b^e^rîṯ*. We are to understand 1 S.

[15] P. 47.
[16] P. 46.
[17] Stoebe, *VT*, 2, 248.

20:8 in a similar sense. Jonathan makes friends with David, whom his father Saul hates, making a *b^erîṯ* with David to reinforce this friendship (1 S. 18:1-3). When David finds himself in dire peril, he asks Jonathan for a demonstration of friendship on the grounds that Jonathan has made a Yahweh covenant with him, and continues: "But if there is guilt in me, slay me yourself." Thus the continuing force of the *b^erîṯ* is affirmed: the friendship has not been ended by a transgression on the part of David. It follows that here, too, *ḥesed* is not the content of the *b^erîṯ;* both *ḥesed* and *b^erîṯ* are based instead on friendship. For while *b^erîṯ* emphasizes the intensity and permanence of this friendship, *ḥesed* expresses its inherent kindness. The only connection, then, between *ḥesed* and *b^erîṯ* is the fact that the element of permanence and reliability implicit in the family or clan can be assured apart from these groups by the addition of a *b^erîṯ*. As is shown, however, by the friendships mentioned above,[18] such assurance is not absolutely necessary. This makes it clear once more that a *b^erîṯ* is not a constitutive element of *ḥesed*. Jepsen also points out a difference between Gen. 21 and 1 S. 20: Abimelech's act of kindness is the basis for his agreement with Abraham, whereas in 1 S. 20 it looks more as though Jonathan's *ḥesed* is the covenanted friendship. Jepsen rightly concludes "that there is no clear relationship between חסד and ברית."[19]

Neither is Glueck's theory that in 1 S. 20:14 *ḥesed YHWH* means the kindness growing out of the Yahweh covenant the only possible explanation. It is equally possible that *YHWH* here is a way of expressing the superlative "great kindness," in the sense of "all-inclusive"; this is certainly the case in 2 S. 9:3, which alludes to the present passage, where David shows *ḥesed 'elōhîm,* "divine kindness," i.e., "the greatest or most inclusive kindness," to a possible survivor from the family of Saul.[20]

It can be seen from this discussion that *ḥesed* refers to conduct in accord with social norms, but that the concept is not based on legal notions; it does not belong to legal terminology. This is confirmed by the observation that, at least outside the realm of family and friendship just discussed, our term involves an emotional element[21] (cf. Gen. 21:23; 40:14; Josh. 2:12,14; Jgs. 1:24; 2 S. 10:2; 1 K. 2:7; 20:31), which becomes conceptually clear and specific in relatively late texts of the OT. For example, we find the phrase *ḥesed w^eraḥ^amîm,* "merciful kindness," in Zec. 7:9 and Dnl. 1:9. That the root → חנן *ḥānan* also belongs to the semantic field of *ḥesed* is shown by Gen. 19:19 (J); 39:21 (J); Est. 2:17; Ps. 109:12. We may conclude, with Johnson, that "the term *ḥesed* connotes more than can be defined in the legal terminology of a *b^erît* . . . *ḥesed* is 'the virtue that knits together society' (W. Robertson Smith)."[22]

In Prov. 19:22, following Ringgren,[23] *ḥasdô* is to be emended to *saḥrô:* "A man's

---

[18] See III.1.b.

[19] Jepsen, 265.

[20] See D. W. Thomas, "A Consideration of Some Unusual Ways of Expressing the Superlative in Hebrew," *VT,* 3 (1953), 209-224, esp. 211-19; *idem,* "Some Further Remarks on Unusual Ways of Expressing the Superlative in Hebrew," *VT,* 18 (1968), 120-24.

[21] As Johnson (107, 110) correctly notes.

[22] P. 110.

[23] *ATD,* XVI, 78.

desire is for gain, but better a poor man than a liar." In Isa. 40:6, following Duhm,[24] *ḥemdô* should probably be read for *ḥasdô* (cf. LXX *dóxa*); Stoebe[25] supports the MT.

IV. Religious Usage.

1. *Yahweh as Subject.* Among the many passages that speak of Yahweh's kindness, we once again find a series of statements where the construction is analogous to that cited above.[26] This emphasizes the actional nature of *ḥeseḏ*. The formula *'āśâ ḥeseḏ 'im* is used 8 times with Yahweh as subject: Gen. 24:12,14; Ruth 1:8; 2 S. 2:6; 15:20 (conj. LXX); 1 K. 3:6; 2 Ch. 1:8; Job 10:12. Once we find *ḥeseḏ* constructed with *'āśâ* and *'ēṯ* (Gen. 32:11[10]) and 5 times with *'āśâ* and *lᵉ* (Ex. 20:6; Dt. 5:10; 2 S. 22:51 par. Ps. 18:51[50]; Jer. 32:18). In the opposite sense, we find *ḥeseḏ* with *'āzaḇ* and *mē'im* (Gen. 24:27) or *'ēṯ* (Ruth 2:20), or with *sûr* and *mē'im* (1 Ch. 17:13; Ps. 89:34[33]; 2 S. 7:15, read *mē'immô* for *mimmennû*; Ps. 66:20, *mē'ēṯ*). In addition, *ḥeseḏ* occurs with *'āśâ* in Jer. 9:23(24), but without a human object; and in Ps. 119:124 we find the petition: "Deal with (*'āśâ* + *'im*) thy servant according to thy kindness (*kᵉḥasdekā*)." The two latter examples will be shown below to be typical variants of what was originally the common idiom: in the first, Yahweh is spoken of in confessional (and therefore generalizing) style as the one who by nature practices (ptcp.) kindness; in the second, Yahweh's kindness can be termed the norm (*kᵉ*) by which his actions can be judged.

In addition, we find a broad range of statements with Yahweh as subject and *ḥeseḏ* as object. He "gives" (*nāṯan*, Mic. 7:20) kindness, "sends" it (*šālaḥ*, Ps. 57:4[3]), "bids" it (*mnh* piel, Ps. 61:8[7][27]), "remembers" it (*zākar*, Ps. 25:6; 98:3), "continues" it (*māšaḵ*, Jer. 31:3; Ps. 36:11[10][28]), "shows" it (*rā'â* hiphil, Ps. 85:8[7]), causes it to be heard (*šāma'* hiphil, Ps. 143:8), makes it great (*gāḇar* piel, Ps. 103:11 conj.) and wondrous (*pl'* hiphil, Ps. 17:7; 31:22[21]), or takes it away (*'āsap*, Jer. 16:5); he "commands" it (*ṣiwwâ*, Ps. 42:9[8]); he "keeps" it for individuals and groups (*nāṣar*, Ex. 34:7; *šāmar*, 1 K. 3:6; Ps. 89:29[28]); he "surrounds" (*sbb* poel, Ps. 32:10), "satisfies" (*śāḇa'* piel, Ps. 90:14), or "crowns" (*'āṭar* piel, Ps. 103:4) them with it. Yahweh's kindness is "with" the worshipper (*'im* + noun clause, Ps. 89:25[24]); he does not retain "his anger," but rather "delights" in kindness (→ חפץ *ḥāp̄ēṣ*, Mic. 7:18).

2. *Meaning in This Context.* Our observations to this point illustrate the great semantic range of the word *ḥeseḏ* in religious usage. The recipients of God's kindness include Abraham (Gen. 24), Jacob (Gen. 32:11[10]), the men of Jabesh-gilead (2 S.

---

[24] *Das Buch Jesaja* (Göttingen, ⁵1968), 292.

[25] *VT*, 2, 252.

[26] III.1.

[27] But see H.-J. Kraus, *Psalmen. BK*, XV (⁵1978) *in loc.*

[28] See III.2.e above; Ps. 85:8(7) conj.; and W. Rudolph, *Jeremia. HAT*, XII (³1968), 194. For a different interpretation, see A. Feuillet, "Note sur la traduction de Jer. XXXI 3ᶜ," *VT*, 12 (1962), 122-24.

2:5f.), the anointed of Yahweh (2 S. 22:51 par. Ps. 18:51[50]), David (2 S. 7:15; 1 K. 3:6; 1 Ch. 17:13; 2 Ch. 1:8), Job (Job 10:12), Ruth, Orpah, and Boaz (Ruth 1:8; 2:20), but also the thousand generations of the devout (Ex. 20:6; Dt. 5:10; Jer. 32:18). His kindness can mean success in finding a bride (Gen. 24:12,14,27), increase in possessions (Gen. 32:11[10]), active aid in the establishment of a dynasty (2 S. 7:15; 1 Ch. 17:13; 2 Ch. 1:8), or success and prosperity in general (2 S. 2:6; cf. 15:20). This variety shows that in demonstrations of divine *ḥeseḏ* we are dealing with the same phenomenon as in human actions. The recipients and manifestations of God's kindness largely coincide with secular usage.

There is a shift suggested, however, by the fact that besides the individual and the small, well-defined group we now find the entire people of Israel as recipients of Yahweh's kindness, which manifests itself in the acts of God that are constitutive of Israel's history and urge it forward. Yahweh in his kindness led and guided Israel (Ex. 15:13); since the deliverance from Egypt he has granted (*gāmal*) his kindness to Israel (Isa. 63:7). Since the desert period he has loved them with an everlasting love (Jer. 31:2f.). He has revealed his kindness for all nations to see in the history of Israel (Ps. 98:2f.; 117:2ff.) or in mighty natural phenomena (Job 37:13). Indeed, his kindness fills the whole earth (*mālē'*, Ps. 33:5; 119:64). Thus the community can "visualize" (*dimmâ*) the kindness of their God in the temple (Ps. 48:10[9]); they are called on to offer thanks for the kindness Yahweh has showed them (Ps. 107:8,15,21,31). But we also read that the fathers in Egypt did not remember the abundance of his kindness and rebelled at the Sea of Reeds (Ps. 106:7), whereas Yahweh relented (*niḥam*) according to (*k^e*) his kindness (v. 45). Just as Moses can pray that Yahweh will forgive the iniquity of the people "according to the greatness of thy steadfast love" (*k^{e}gōḏel ḥasdeḵā,* Nu. 14:19), so the suffering people of Israel can turn to their God in prayer for help and deliverance (Ps. 44:27[26]; 85:8[7]; Mic. 7:18,20); "for with Yahweh there is kindness, and with him is plenteous redemption" (Ps. 130:7). The knowledge that after judgment a new beginning will be given to Israel through the kindness of Yahweh is determinative for both preexilic and exilic prophecy (Isa. 54:8,10; Hos. 2:21[19], as well as exilic poetry (Lam. 3:22,32 *Q*). The active nature of Yahweh's kindness, implicit in all these passages, is further underlined by the frequent occurrence in this context of the pl. *ḥ^{a}sāḏîm,* "acts of kindness" (Ps. 17:7; 25:6; 106:7,45 *Q;* 107:43; Isa. 63:7; Lam. 3:22,32 *Q;* cf. also Ps. 89:2,50[1,49]).

How Israel understood these demonstrations of Yahweh's kindness is shown by the nouns used in parallel with *ḥeseḏ* or forming part of its semantic field. Yahweh's *ḥeseḏ* is expressed as an act of "strength" (*'ōz,* Ex. 15:13), of "victory" or "salvation" (*y^{e}šû'â,* Ps. 98:2f.; *yešaʻ*, Ps. 85:8,10[7,9]; cf. Ps. 17:7), of "justice" and "righteousness" (*mišpāṭ* and *ṣ^{e}ḏāqâ,* Jer. 9:23[24]; Ps. 33:5; cf. Ps. 85:11f.[10f.]; 89:15[14]; 98:2) or "redemption" (*p^{e}ḏûṯ,* Ps. 130:7); his deeds are "wonderful" (*niplā'ôṯ,* Ps. 106:7; 107:8,15,21,31; cf. 98:1) or "praiseworthy" (*t^{e}hillôṯ,* Isa. 63:7). God's *ḥeseḏ* is the opposite of his anger (*'ap,* Mic. 7:18; cf. Isa. 54:8); in it is expressed divine "mercy" (*raḥ^{a}mîm,* Ps. 25:6; Isa. 63:7; Jer. 16:5; Lam. 3:22; the verb *rḥm* also in Isa. 54:8,10; Lam. 3:32; *niḥam,* Ps. 106:45), as in the summary statement of Hosea: "I will betroth you to me in righteousness and in justice, in kindness and in mercy" (2:21[19]). That this gracious and merciful activity on the part of Yahweh has the quality of endurance and that Israel can rely on it is expressed by Hosea's statement immediately preceding the sentence just quoted: "I will betroth you to me for ever (*lᵉʻôlām*)," and by the statement that follows in v. 22(20): "I will betroth you to me in faithfulness (*'ᵉmûnâ*)." God's kindness is eternal because it is "from of old" (*mēʻolām*, Ps. 25:6) and endures "for ever" (*lᵉʻôlām*, Ps. 106:1; 107:1; 117:2); it is *ḥeseḏ ʻôlām* (Isa. 54:8), which is equivalent to Jeremiah's "everlasting love" (*'ahᵃḇaṯ ʻôlām*, Jer. 31:3). As we would expect from our previous observations, the noun can also be linked with *'ᵉmeṯ* (Ps. 25:10; 61:8[7]; 85:11f.[10f.]; 117:2; Mic. 7:20) or *'ᵉmûnâ* (Ps. 98:3; 100:5), and can be called an oath (*šbʻ* niphal, Mic. 7:20).

3. *Other Syntactic Structures*. These conclusions become even clearer when we turn to the next group of passages. Here we find Yahweh's kindness as the object of human action. Besides verbs that express the recalling of God's acts of kindness (*zāḵar*, Ps. 106:7; *bîn* hithpael, Ps. 107:43) or trust in them (*bāṭaḥ*, Ps. 13:6[5]; 52:10[8]; *yḥl* piel, Ps. 33:18; cf. v. 22; 147:11), we find a great number of verbs expressing proclamation: "sing of" (*rnn* piel, Ps. 59:17[16]), "sing praises" (*zmr* piel, Ps. 59:18[17]), "declare" (*ngd* hiphil, Ps. 92:3[2]), "sing of" (*šîr*, Ps. 89:2[1]; 101:1), "rejoice" (*gîl*, Ps. 31:8[7], "be glad" (*śāmaḥ*, Ps. 31:8[7]), "recount" (*zkr* hiphil, Isa. 63:7), "be declared" (*spr* pual, Ps. 88:12[11]), not "conceal" (*kḥd* piel, Ps. 40:11[10]), and possibly also "boast" (*hll* hithpael, Ps. 52:3[1][29]).

The same expressions of confidence and confession or proclamation are also associated with the other syntactic constructions of *ḥeseḏ*. God's kindness shall not "depart" (*mûš*, Isa. 54:10) from Israel; it "follows" (*rāḏap*, Ps. 23:6) the worshipper; it "preserves" (*nāṣar*, Ps. 40:12[11]; 61:8[7]), "holds up" (*sāʻaḏ*, Ps. 94:18), and "comforts" (*niḥam*, Ps. 119:76) him, or "comes" (*bô'*, Ps. 119:41) to him; it is "great" (*gāḏôl*, Ps. 86:13) towards him; it is "high" and "from everlasting to everlasting upon those who fear him" (Ps. 103:11,17; cf. 33:22). It is "good" (*ṭôḇ*, Ps. 69:17[16];[30] 109:21), indeed "better than life" (*ṭôḇ min*, Ps. 63:4[3]); it is "precious" (*yāqār*, Ps. 36:8[7]) and has no end (Ps. 77:9[8]); it extends to the heavens (Ps. 36:6[5]; 57:11[10]; 108:5[4]) or was established for ever in the heavens (Ps. 89:3[2]); it belongs to God (Ps. 62:13[12]), whose paths are kindness (Ps. 25:10), and who can be called "my gracious God" (*'ᵉlōhê ḥasdî*, Ps. 59:11 *Q*, 18[10,17]) or a God "abounding in kindness" (*raḇ-ḥeseḏ*, Ps. 86:5; 103:8).

The use of *ḥeseḏ* with particles and prepositions likewise expresses Yahweh's readiness to intervene on behalf of the worshipper and thus demonstrate his divine kindness. We find *ḥeseḏ* in combination with *bᵉ* in Ps. 31:17(16); 143:12; in Ps. 5:8(7); 69:14(13), we find *bᵉrōḇ ḥasdᵉḵā*. More common is the association with *kᵉ*: Ps. 25:7; 51:3(1); 109:26; 119:88,124,149,159 and *kᵉrōḇ*: Neh. 13:22. The noun is used with *ʻal* in Ps. 115:1; 138:2. In Ps. 6:5(4); 44:27(26) we find *lᵉmaʻan ḥasdeḵā*. Since the LXX translates this phrase in Ps. 44:27(26)(LXX 43:27) as *héneken toú onómatós sou*, thus apparently making clear that Yahweh's name and kindness are identical, our phrase may be found in Ps. 25:7: *lᵉmaʻan ṭûḇᵉḵā*, "for thy goodness' sake." Finally, in Hos. 10:12 *ḥeseḏ* is used with *lᵉpî*, "according to."

---

29 But cf. C. Schedl, "'*ḥesed 'ēl*' in Psalm 52[51], 3," *BZ*, N.S. 5 (1961), 259f.

30 But cf. Kraus, *BK*, XV, *in loc.*

As we have already seen,[31] in these contexts, too, *ḥeseḏ* can mean "life" (*ḥayyîm*, Job 10:12; also Ps. 103:4; cf. Ps. 63:4[3]; 86:13; *ḥāyâ*, Ps. 119:88,159), "care" (*pᵉqûḏâ*, Job 10:12) and a life's "harvest" (Hos. 10:12),[32] "salvation" and "deliverance" (*yᵉšû'â*, Ps. 13:6[5]; 119:41; *yeša'*, Ps. 6:5[4]; 31:17[16]; 57:4[3]; 69:14f.[13f.]; 109:21,26; *tᵉšû'â*, Ps. 40:11[10]). It is a demonstration of "justice" (*mišpāṭ*, Ps. 101:1) and of "righteousness" (*ṣᵉḏāqâ*, Hos. 10:12; Ps. 36:11[10]; cf. v. 7[6]; 40:11[10]; 88:13[12]; 103:17), of "might" (*'ōz*, Ps. 59:17f.[16f.]; 62:12[11]; cf. also *miśgāḇ*, "fortress," Ps. 59:18[17]), of miraculous power (*pele'*, Ps. 88:11,13[10,12]), and of "glory" (*kāḇôḏ*, Ps. 63:3f.[2f.]). We also find formulations in which the faith of the individual stands in the foreground. God's kindness finds expression in a word of promise (Ps. 77:9[8][33]), in his hearing and seeing the worshipper's trouble and distress (Ps. 31:8[7]; 52:9f.[8f.]; 59:11[10]; 66:20; 69:14,17[13,16]; 119:149; 138:2f.; 143:12), in forgiveness (Ps. 25:7; 51:3[1]) and admission to the sanctuary (Ps. 5:8[7]), in guidance (Ps. 143:8), instruction (Ps. 119:64,124), and just requital (Ps. 62:13[12]), in a life without torment (Ps. 32:10), and in refuge (Ps. 36:8[7]). Indeed, *ḥeseḏ* can simply be equated with goodness (*ṭôḇ*, Ps. 23:6). In all these texts, *ḥeseḏ* still refers to an act on the part of Yahweh; in Ps. 92:5f.(4f.), our term in v. 3(2) is interpreted by means of the nouns *pō'al* and *ma'ᵃśeh*. This divine activity is characterized by permanence and reliability (*'ᵉmeṯ*, Gen. 24:27; 32:11[10]; Ex. 34:6; 2 S. 2:6; 15:20; Ps. 26:3; 40:11f.[10f.]; 57:4,11[3,10]; 89:15[14]; 108:5[4]; 115:1; 138:2; *'ᵉmûnâ*, Ps. 36:6[5]; 40:11[10]; 88:12[11]; 89:2f.,25,34,50[1f.,24,33,49]; 92:3[2]), as well as by mercy (*raḥᵃmîm*, Ps. 40:12[11]; 51:3[1]; 69:17[16]; 103:4) and grace (*ḥnn*, Ps. 51:3[1]; *ḥûs*, Neh. 13:22).

4. *Liturgical Formulas*. What "God's kindness" means for Israel found concentrated and pregnant expression in two liturgical formulas. The earlier of them appears for the first time in Ex. 34, in the Yahwist's recension of the Decalog. V. 6 refers to Yahweh as "El merciful and gracious, slow to anger, and abounding in kindness and faithfulness" (*'ēl raḥûm wᵉḥannûn 'ereḵ 'appayim wᵉraḇ-ḥeseḏ w'ᵉmeṯ*). The identical formula appears in Ps. 86:15 and (with the omission of *'ēl* and *'ᵉmeṯ*) Ps. 103:8. Nu. 14:18 (J) probably represents an echo of Ex. 34:6: "Yahweh is slow to anger, and abounding in kindness." With the first two elements interchanged to *ḥannûn wᵉraḥûm*, and with *'ᵉmeṯ* omitted, the formula also appears in Joel 2:13; Jon. 4:2; Ps. 145:8 (with *gᵉḏ°l-* instead of *raḇ-ḥeseḏ*); and Neh. 9:17. In Joel and Jonah, it has been expanded by the addition of *wᵉniḥām 'al-hārā'â*, "and he repents of evil," and in Nehemiah by the prefixing of *'ᵉlôah sᵉlîḥôṯ*, "a God ready to forgive." Yahweh's readiness to forgive is also expressed in Ex. 34:7; Nu. 14:18; Jer. 32:18, formulated with *nōśē' 'āwōn* in Ex. 34 and Nu. 14, and with *mᵉšallēm 'āwōn* in Jer. 32. It may be noted that the phrase *'ōśeh ḥeseḏ la'ᵃlāpîm* in Jer. 32:18 is identical with the corresponding clause of the Elohistic Decalog in Ex. 20:6 (Dt. 5:10). This suggests the theory that the J formula clearly represents the original formulation, which was altered and transformed in the course of history. This theory lends weight to Stoebe's argument, based on

31 III.1.c, III.2.c.

32 Wolff, *Hosea*, 186.

33 S. Wagner, "אמר *'āmar*," *TDOT*, I, 342.

comparison of the J and E recensions of the Decalog, that the predication of *ḥeseḏ* of God "represents . . . an extension peculiar to the Yahwist's theology," with the words "taken from the secular domain of everyday speech."[34] In J the promise of kindness comes unconditionally at the beginning, whereas in E it follows the threat of punishment and is made conditional, "in a sense ameliorating the threat of punishment."[35]

The other liturgical formula, "Truly Yahweh is good, truly his kindness endures for ever" (*kî-ṭôḇ YHWH kî le'ôlām ḥasdô*), is found in Ps. 100:5; Jer. 33:11 (called Deuteronomistic by Rudolph[36]); similarly 1 Ch. 16:34; 2 Ch. 5:13; 7:3; Ezr. 3:11; Ps. 106:1; 107:1; 118:1,29; 136:1; shortened to *kî le'ôlām ḥasdô,* it appears also in 1 Ch. 16:41; 2 Ch. 7:6; 20:21; Ps.118:2-4; 136:1-26 (cf. Ps. 86:5, where this formula probably stands in the background). Without exception, we are dealing here with texts that are late or even very late. It follows that this formula first took on importance in the liturgy of the postexilic temple, and soon came to play a central role.

5. *The ḥasḏê ḏāwiḏ*. Although the phrase *ḥasḏê ḏāwiḏ* occurs only twice (2 Ch. 6:42; Isa. 55:3), we must devote some attention to it. We shall take it as generally accepted that *ḏāwiḏ* here is an objective genitive, so that David is the recipient of Yahweh's acts of kindness,[37] and that these acts of kindness must be interpreted as referring to the promise given to King David by the prophet Nathan, that the Davidic dynasty would endure for ever (2 S. 7, esp. v. 15). It can be asked whether the term *ḥasāḏîm* here means acts of divine favor, as it does everywhere else, or whether it means the words that promise favor, "gracious promises." But this is merely an artificial distinction. When the Chronicler has King Solomon conclude his prayer at the dedication of the temple with the earnest petition: "O Yahweh God, do not turn away the face of thy anointed one; remember thy acts of kindness to David thy servant" (2 Ch. 6:42), he is having Solomon appeal to Yahweh to remember his promise given to David and to show him, the successor to David's throne, like acts of kindness. Isa. 55:3 has the same purpose. Yahweh's promise to make a *berîṯ 'ôlām* with his people refers back to his acts of kindness toward David. The addition of *hanne'emānîm,* characterizing them as "steadfast," "enduring," "sure," underlines their unreduced validity even after the fall of the political kingship in Jerusalem. It is thus clear that for Deutero-Isaiah, too, the phrase *ḥasḏê ḏāwiḏ* refers to Yahweh's promised acts of grace, which are continually brought to pass. There can be no real distinction between God's promised acts of grace and a promise that is continually fulfilled.

Now as both texts clearly show, the phrase *ḥasḏê ḏāwiḏ* is not attested until the exilic and postexilic period. It is preceded, however, by various other formulations. When Ps. 21:8(7) states that the king who trusts in Yahweh "through the kindness of Elyon shall not be moved," it is referring to the endurance of the Jerusalem monarchy (note the predicate Elyon!), thanks to the kindness of Yahweh, in line with the prophecy

---

[34] *VT,* 2, 249f.

[35] *Ibid.,* 249.

[36] *HAT,* XII, 216.

[37] For a different view, see Caquot, 45ff.

of Nathan.[38] The same idea is expressed by 2 S. 22:51 par. Ps. 18:51(50), which states that Yahweh "gave great triumphs" (*magdîl yᵉšû'ôṯ*) to his king and "showed kindness to his anointed, to David and his descendants for ever (*'aḏ-'ôlām*)." What appears here in the form of a thanksgiving hymn is finally found in Ps. 89:50(49) as an anxious question in the context of an individual lament:[39] "Lord, where is thy kindness of old, which by thy faithfulness thou didst swear to David?" This question refers back to Yahweh's assurances as formulated in v. 25(24): "My faithfulness and my kindness shall be with him," and v. 29(28): "My kindness I will keep (*šāmar* + *lᵉ*) for him for ever (*lᵉ'ôlām*), and my covenant (*bᵉrîṯî*) will stand firm for him." Here, too, God's act of kindness refers to the preservation of the Davidic dynasty. It is safe to assume that Ps. 89 is preexilic. A major piece of evidence is 1 K. 3:6 (par. 2 Ch. 1:8), in the context of Solomon's prayer at Gibeon, where we are told that Yahweh "showed great kindness" to David and also "kept (*šāmar* + *lᵉ*) for him this great kindness" by giving him in Solomon an heir to the throne. If this text gives the impression of making a distinction between divine acts of kindness during the lifetime of David and those that concern the continuance of his dynasty, the situation is made even more complex by 1 K. 8:23f. (par. 2 Ch. 6:14f.). For Solomon's prayer at the dedication of the temple begins with these words: "O Yahweh, God of Israel, there is no God like thee, in heaven above or on earth beneath, keeping covenant and showing kindness to thy servants (*šōmēr habbᵉrîṯ wᵉhaḥeseḏ lᵉ*) who walk before thee with all their heart; who has kept (*šāmar* + *lᵉ*) with thy servant David my father what thou didst declare to him." Once more we find the construction *šāmar* + *lᵉ*; here the acts of kindness are expressly associated with the endurance of the Davidic dynasty. Even more significantly, *ḥeseḏ* is associated with *bᵉrîṯ*, and in fact the term *bᵉrîṯ* is emphasized by being placed first, so that the demonstration of kindness is interpreted as the content of the covenant. Now von Rad has pointed out[40] that the truly appropriate Hebrew expression for the content of Nathan's prophecy is the phrase *bᵉrîṯ 'ôlām* found in 2 S. 23:5. This would mean that the formulation of the prayer at the dedication of the temple should be preferred to that of the prayer at Gibeon. On the other hand, however, recent studies have pointed out that the original promise in 2 S. 7 has been developed along the lines of Deuteronomistic covenant theology, and that 2 S. 23:5 is inconceivable "before the middle of the sixth century B.C."[41] In the present context, therefore, the question is: is *ḥeseḏ* primary, or is *bᵉrîṯ*, and how should we define the relationship between the two in religious usage?

---

38 Kraus, *BK*, XV, 171; G. von Rad, *OT Theol.*, I (Eng. trans., New York, 1962), 310.

39 See Kraus, *BK*, XV, II, 616f.; for a comparison between Isa. 55 and Ps. 89, see O. Eissfeldt, "The Promises of Grace to David in Isaiah 55:1-5," *Israel's Prophetic Heritage. Festschrift J. Muilenburg* (New York, 1962), 196-207.

40 *OT Theol.*, I, 310f.

41 L. Perlitt, *Bundestheologie im AT. WMANT*, 36 (1969), 47-53; see also M. Noth, "The Laws in the Pentateuch," in his *The Laws in the Pentateuch and Other Studies* (Eng. trans., Philadelphia, 1966), 93f.; S. Herrmann, *Die prophetischen Heilserwartungen im AT. BWANT*, 85 (1965), 100-103; W. Zimmerli, *OT Theol. in Outline* (Eng. trans., Atlanta, 1978), 57.

6. *ḥeseḏ and b^erîṯ*. The answer to this question is suggested by a stereotyped formula found in 1 K. 8:23 (par. 2 Ch. 6:14) and 5 other passages, which describes God as "keeping covenant and showing kindness to" (*šōmēr habb^erîṯ w^ehaḥeseḏ l^e*) those who love him, who keep his commandments, etc. (Dt. 7:9,12; Neh. 1:5 conj.; 9:32; Dnl. 9:4). The double use of the definite article serves the purpose of making the covenant refer unambiguously to the Sinai *b^erîṯ,* with the result that *ḥeseḏ* is understood as Yahweh's faithfulness to this covenant. The same purpose is served by the combination of Yahweh's keeping covenant and Israel's keeping the commandments found in Dt. 7:9,12; Neh. 1:5; Dnl. 9:4 (cf. also Ps. 25:10). The earliest passage illustrating this usage is Dt. 7, where the style is parenetic; the other passages appear in prayers of petition. Furthermore, the fact that in 1 K. 8:23 (par. 2 Ch. 6:14) the phrase refers to the covenant with David suggests the hypothesis that it derives from Deuteronomistic or post-Deuteronomistic revision of the dedication prayer. This hypothesis is further supported by the observation that v. 24 has to make a special point of connecting the particular promise to "thy servant David" with the phrase "keeping covenant and showing kindness to thy servants who walk before thee with all their heart," borrowed from what was later to be a general formula. It follows that Deuteronomistic and especially post-Deuteronomistic theology was concerned to emphasize Yahweh's covenant, and therefore attached and subordinated the *ḥeseḏ* concept to this theologoumenon. But this means also that the *ḥeseḏ* concept in general was already available to the Deuteronomist, probably including its association with the promise to David. Finally, it may be noted that in Deuteronomy Yahweh's *ḥeseḏ*—in contrast, say, to the *b^erîṯ*—plays a very minor role: although *b^erîṯ* occurs 27 times, *ḥeseḏ* occurs only 3. With respect to our inquiry, this would mean that the formulation in the prayer at Gibeon is pre-Deuteronomistic and was borrowed from secular usage, as is attested by the phrase *ḥeseḏ ûmišpāṭ š^emōr* in Hos. 12:7(6), which is undoubtedly genuine.[42]

In addition, we also see that in Deuteronomy itself the covenant is associated with the people of Israel, but never with David or the king; instead, the portion of the law that refers to the king uses the term "choose" (*bāḥar,* Dt. 17:15), the same word used for the appointment of the Levites (Dt. 18:5; 21:5). This suggests that the interpretation of Yahweh's promise to David by means of the *b^erîṯ* concept is a pre-Deuteronomic theologoumenon.

Although a clear proof is impossible, our theory is supported by Pss. 106 and 89. Ps. 106 is influenced by Deuteronomistic theology.[43] In v. 45 we come upon the terms *b^erîṯ* and *ḥeseḏ,* standing in parallel in that order and constituting the grounds for God's relenting. Here, too, as we observed above, *ḥeseḏ* functions as the content of the *b^erîṯ.* In Ps. 89:29(28), on the contrary, God's keeping his *ḥeseḏ* precedes the parallel continuance of his *b^erîṯ.* The same statement is made in v. 50(49), where God's previous demonstrations of kindness are traced back to an oath sworn in faithfulness to David. Here, then, we come upon the opposite sequence: *ḥeseḏ* comes first, and is interpreted

---

42 Most recently Wolff, *Hosea,* 214.

43 G. Fohrer, *Introd. OT* (Eng. trans., Nashville, 1968), 291: "post-Deuteronomistic."

through the concept of the *b^{e}rîṯ* or an oath as reinforcing and strengthening the promise of *ḥeseḏ*. The same sequence of *ḥeseḏ—b^{e}rîṯ* appears in Isa. 54:10, which is likewise concerned to emphasize the eternal endurance of God's kindness (cf. v. 8).

This interpretation is reinforced by the observation that in secular usage[44] we found that mention of the *b^{e}rîṯ* fulfilled the same function in the context of promises of *ḥeseḏ*. In Gen. 21, the *b^{e}rîṯ* and oath serve to reinforce and underline the permanence of Abraham's promise to Abimelech. Since Gen. 21 is a J text, Ps. 89 may be pre-Deuteronomistic; at least there is no compelling reason to assume Deuteronomistic authorship. But this means that it is possible to hypothesize that even in the pre-Deuteronomic period the promise given to David could be expressed in terms of *ḥeseḏ* as well as *b^{e}rîṯ*.

As we saw above, following Stoebe,[45] the transference of the *ḥeseḏ* concept to Yahweh is probably due to the work of J. It seems most natural, therefore, to place the phrase *ḥasḏê ḏāwiḏ* in the context of a post-J but pre-Deuteronomic theology. This makes it unlikely that J and the circles close to him interpreted the promise to David as an eternal *b^{e}rîṯ*, not least because *b^{e}rîṯ* here means the promise itself, not the reinforcement of the promise as in Ps. 89 (cf. Gen. 21). Both *ḥeseḏ* and *b^{e}rîṯ* refer to the same circumstance and are thus mutually exclusive. This means that the phrase "everlasting *b^{e}rîṯ*" in 2 S. 23:5 comes from a pre-Deuteronomic source distinct from J.

This discussion makes it abundantly clear that in the religious language of Israel, too, it was not until the post-Deuteronomistic period—in other words, comparatively late—that the mention of *ḥeseḏ* was linked to the covenant concept in such a way as to make Yahweh's kindness the content of his covenant. It is therefore wrong to follow Glueck in calling Yahweh's *ḥeseḏ* fundamentally and comprehensively Yahweh's conduct according to the covenant.[46]

A final observation belongs in this context. In secular usage, we determined that the principle of mutuality was one of the fundamental elements of our concept.[47] It would therefore be reasonable to suppose that the demonstration of Yahweh's kindness also involves mutuality. And in fact both Glueck[48] and even more pointedly Stoebe[49] cite Jer. 2:2; 9:23(24); Hos. 4:1; 6:4,6 as referring to demonstrations of *ḥeseḏ* on the part of mankind towards God. Jepsen[50] has vigorously and rightly attacked this interpretation. With him, we interpret Hos. 4:1 against the background of Hos. 10:12; 12:7(6); Mic. 6:8; Zec. 7:9, understanding *ḥeseḏ* as conduct towards other human beings. This same is true of Jer. 9:23(24). With respect to Hos. 6:4,6, Jepsen has emphasized the close relationship between these verses and the other Hosea passages, showing that *ḥeseḏ* is properly understood as kindness that should be shown to others.

---

44 III.3.
45 IV.4.
46 See also III.3.
47 III.1.d, III.2.d.
48 Pp. 56-69.
49 *VT*, 2, 250f.
50 Pp. 268f.

In the case of Jer. 2:2 ("I remember the *ḥesed* of your youth, your love as a bride, how you followed me in the wilderness"), he points out that our noun is the object of *zākar;* as in 2 Ch. 6:42; Neh. 13:14 (cf. Ps. 98:3; 106:45), it can mean "good works." He therefore renders the verse: "I remember how you devoted yourself to good works in your youth, how you loved me when you were a bride, how at that time in the wilderness you followed me in everything."[51] Even though Jepsen is clearly aware that this interpretation of Jer. 2:2 is nothing more than a suggestion worth considering, his fundamental conclusion stands: in view of the frequency with which our term occurs in the OT, a single passage cannot bear the burden of proof. Human beings can receive the kindness of Yahweh, but they cannot do him acts of kindness. We must therefore once more note that with respect to mutuality religious usage diverges somewhat from secular usage.[52]

7. *Summary.* If we attempt to summarize our observations on the religious use of *ḥesed* in the OT, we must take into account both an agreement with secular usage and a divergence from it. This indicates once more that our concept was borrowed from the secular sphere into the religious language of Israel.

The agreement includes the active and social nature of *ḥesed* as well as the permanence of divine kindness. Everything that is said focuses on what Yahweh does for Israel and the individual worshipper. The history of Yahweh's people, past, present, and future, the life of the individual Israelite—in fact, the entire world—is the stage for the demonstration of Yahweh's kindness. Yahweh has decided in favor of Israel; he has promised life, care, alleviation of distress, and preservation—indeed, he has filled the whole earth with his kindness. He has thus granted fellowship with him to his people, to all mankind, to the whole world. And this act, like the promise and assurance of future help and fellowship, is characterized by permanence, constancy, and reliability. This is what Israel and the individual Israelite hear through Yahweh's word, including his word spoken through the mouth of his prophets. The community responds in worship, praising his kindness in hymns, confessing it, expressing their confidence and thanksgiving or pleading in laments for a new demonstration of this divine kindness. This kindness can become as it were the very essence of Yahweh, so that the worshipper in Ps. 144:2 can refer to Yahweh (among other things) as "my kindness," and Jon. 2:9(8) can call idolators those who "forsake their kindness" (*'āzaḇ ḥasdām*). In both passages, *ḥesed* stands for God himself. The same situation is evidenced by the use of the periphrastic expression "those who hope in his kindness" (*hamᵉyaḥᵃlîm lᵉḥasdô*) for the devout, found in Ps. 33:18; 147:11 (cf. 33:22). Fear of Yahweh is here equated with hope in his kindness. An essential element of Israel's faith is this constant hope in expectation of Yahweh's favor and kindness. This whole idea found its most pregnant expression in the liturgical formula "Truly Yahweh is

[51] *Ibid.*, 269.

[52] On the connection between *bᵉrîṯ* and *ḥesed,* see also M. Weinfeld, " 'Bond and Grace'—Covenantal Expressions in the Bible and in the Ancient World—A Common Heritage," *Lešonénû,* 36 (1971/72), 86-105 [Hebrew].

good, and his kindness endures for ever," which probably derives from the worship of the Second Temple.

We come now to divergences from secular usage. First we have the expansion of the realm of *ḥeseḏ* from the fellowship of family and clan to the nation of Israel and finally the whole world. This extension is intimately associated with the application of our concept to Yahweh, probably to be dated in the time of J; for J, Yahweh is both the God of Israel and the God of the entire world he created. Simultaneously with this transfer our concept acquired different nuances. Within the framework of family and clan society, despite the recognizable elements of kindness, goodness, and mercy associated with the inherent principle of mutuality, the concept had something rigid and even normative about it; when it was transferred to Yahweh, this rigidity was clearly pushed into the background. Instead, extraordinary emphasis was placed on the element of divine mercy, grace, and forbearance. Now God's kindness finds expression in his endless reconciling love, always ready to forgive. Once again, this love is expressed pregnantly in a liturgical formula: "Merciful and gracious is Yahweh, slow to anger and of great kindness." This excludes from the outset any possibility that human beings, following the secular principle of mutuality, could repay Yahweh in turn the divine kindness they have experienced or do him an act of kindness. The social nature of *ḥeseḏ* is maintained, however: God's kindness towards an individual places that individual in a new relationship with his neighbor, a relationship based on Yahweh's kindness; in his daily contacts with others he must keep the kindness he has experienced, he must practice righteousness and justice, kindness and mercy. Thus *ḥeseḏ* shapes not only the relationship of Yahweh with human beings, but also that of human beings among themselves.

These considerations suggest that it is wrong to try to define as a legal obligation this kindness of Yahweh towards Israel that is expressed by *ḥeseḏ* and the resulting mutual fellowship of the Israelites, interpreting it within the general framework of the *b^erîṯ*. When *b^erîṯ* appears in the semantic field of *ḥeseḏ,* it takes second place after *ḥeseḏ* and is used to express the permanence and constancy of Yahweh's kindness, its inviolability and trustworthiness. This holds true also for Yahweh's dynastic promise to David, which, it seems likely, originally found independent expression in terms of both *ḥeseḏ* and *b^erîṯ*. The fact that the prophecy of Nathan (2 S. 7:15) speaks of *ḥeseḏ* to formulate the contrast between David and his rejected predecessor Saul shows clearly that the kingship of David is interpreted here on the basis of the kingship of Saul, so that David, like Saul, is to be understood as a king chosen by Yahweh. The conceptual structure of election and rejection, of favor granted and withdrawn, which describes Saul's kingship, is intended to make the kingship of David, which had a fundamentally different structure from the very outset, appear to be the natural successor of Saul's kingship. If J applied the concept of *ḥeseḏ* to Yahweh, and if this took place in the era of David and Solomon, the theological interpretation of the Nathan prophecy (2 S. 7:15) as a promise of *ḥeseḏ* to David, together with the derived concept of the *ḥasḏê ḏāwiḏ,* belongs to the theological environment of J. In this case it is all the more likely that we should prefer the interpretation of the promise to David as an eternal *b^erîṯ,* an interpretation found in the last words of David (2 S. 23:5). This concept not only signals the structural difference between the kingship of David and that of Saul, but also applies the appropriate theological term *b^erîṯ* to the new and different element appearing in the dynastic promise to David.

Perhaps it was the use of both terms, *ḥeseḏ* and *b^erîṯ*, for one and the same thing, namely the dynastic promise to David, that gave rise in Israel to reflection on the relationship between Yahweh's kindness and his covenant. There may also have been other incentives, of which we are ignorant, that set such an undertaking in motion. In any event, we can observe that postexilic theology rigorously assigned the concept of *ḥeseḏ* to the category of the *b^erîṯ* idea. The kindness of Yahweh became the content of his covenant with Israel. But even in this late stage of development our concept did not become a legal term. In it we hear overtones of promise and grace, mercy and unexpected kindness, not of law and obligation.

V. Qumran.

The meaning of *ḥeseḏ* in the Dead Sea scrolls has been discussed by Zimmerli.[53] Taking as his point of departure the fact that about half the occurrences are found in the Hodayoth (28 out of 58), and that likewise more than half of the passages use the plural, "acts of kindness," Zimmerli shows that the language is biblicistic and the style deliberately plerophoric. Semantically, he notes that the word is further from *ḥēn* and closer to *b^erîṯ*. The devout person lives in *ḥeseḏ* covenant with God, and shares in the mystery that is revealed for him.

Zobel

[53] W. Zimmerli, "חסד im Schrifttum von Qumran," *Homages à A. Dupont-Sommer* (Paris, 1971), 439-449 = his *Studien zur alttestamentlichen Theologie und Prophetie* (*Gesammelte Aufsätze*, 2). *ThB*, 51 (1974), 272-283.

חָסָה *ḥāsâ*; מַחְסֶה *maḥ^aseh*; חָסוּת *ḥāsûṯ*

Contents: I. Etymology. II. OT Texts: 1. Morphology and Syntax; 2. Context; 3. "Nontheological" Usage. III. Formulas and Schemata: 1. *ḥāsâ* in the Psalms and Other Prayers; 2. *maḥ^aseh* in the Psalms; 3. *ḥāsâ*/*maḥ^aseh* in Other Books. IV. Theological Usage.

ḥāsâ. W. Beyerlin, *Die Rettung der Bedrängten in den Feindpsalmen der Einzelnen auf institutionelle Zusammenhänge untersucht. FRLANT*, 99 (1970); H. Bobzin, "Überlegungen zum althebräischen 'Tempus' system," *WO*, 7 (1973), 141-153; P. Bordreuil, "A l'ombre d'Elohim," *RHPR*, 46 (1966), 368-391; H. A. Brongers, "Merismus, Synekdoche und Hendiadys in der bibel-hebräischen Sprache," כה *1940–1965*. *OTS*, 14 (1965), 100-114; R. C. Culley, *Oral Formulaic Language in the Biblical Psalms. Near and Middle East Series*, 4 (Toronto, 1967); L. Delekat, "Zum hebräischen Wörterbuch," *VT*, 14 (1964), 7-66, esp. 28-31; *idem*, *Asylie und Schutzorakel am Zionheiligtum: Eine Untersuchung zu den privaten Feindpsalmen* (Leiden, 1967); D. Eichhorn, *Gott als Fels, Burg und Zuflucht. EH*, 23/4 (1972); P. Hugger, "Jahwe, mein Fels," *Laeta dies:*

I. Etymology.

On phonetic grounds, the origins of the word group *ḥāsâ* may be sought in Bab. and Neo-Assyr. *ḫesû(m),* "cover," "hide," with its derivative noun *meḫsû(m), maḫsû(m),* "cover" (?).[1] The meaning "hide (oneself)," attested once in a comm.,[2] does appear to come very close to the meaning of Heb. *ḥāsâ.* But the Hebrew verb is used only intransitively and its word group, as it were, only theologically. This semantic situation can hardly be explained by the etymology. More or less the same applies to a connection with Ugar. *ḥwš/ḥš.*[3] Closer to the OT is Syr. *ḥasyā,* "devout," to the extent that the variety of meanings in Syriac offers more semantic possibilities.[4] The Hebrew OT may suggest some striking points of connection with its most common (though not only) meaning, "holiness," "piety," often found in combination with *qdš'.*[5] Even this, however, can hardly be the path that leads to the predominant use of the finite verb in the OT. In Palmyrene Aramaic we find a pael of *ḥsy* with the meaning "consecrate." In Imperial Aramaic there is a masc. pl. *ḥsyn,* which many have understood as "devout."[6] Ethiop. *ḥasawa,*[7] "cover," "hide," is closer to Akkadian than to Hebrew. The meaning of *ḥāsâ* can be associated only indirectly and uncertainly with the meaning of the possible etymological equivalents in Arabic.[8]

II. OT Texts.

1. *Morphology and Syntax.* The verb occurs only in the qal. The most frequent form (attested only in the Psalms) is the 1st person singular perfect (Ps. 7:2[Eng. v. 1]; 11:1; 16:1; 25:20; 31:2[1]; 71:1; 141:8; 144:2; cf. also the equivalent 57:2[1]); other finite forms are rare. Among the other forms, the active participle predominates; the infinitive is rare. The verb *ḥāsâ* is constructed with *b^e^-*. Exceptions include: Ps. 91:4; Ruth 2:12 (*taḥaṯ-k^e^nāpāyw*); Ps. 17:7 (absolute use of the ptcp.; cf. also Prov. 14:32). The only nominal form found with any frequency, *maḥ^a^seh,* is more closely defined

---

50 Jahre Studienkolleg St. Benedikt. Münsterschwarzacher Studien, 9 (1968), 143-160; *idem, Jahwe meine Zuflucht. Münsterschwarzacher Studien,* 13 (1971); L. Kopf, "Arabische Etymologien und Parallelen zum Bibelwörterbuch," *VT,* 8 (1958), 161-215; D. Michel, *Tempora und Satzstellung in den Psalmen. Abhandlungen zur evangelischen Theologie,* 1 (Bonn, 1960); G. Pidoux, "Quelques allusions au droit d'asile dans les psaumes," *Maqqél shāqédh. Festschrift W. Vischer* (Montpellier, 1960), 191-97; J. van der Ploeg, "L'espérance dans l'AT," *RB,* 61 (1954), 481-507; L. Ruppert, *Der leidende Gerechte. FzB,* 5 (1972); H. Seebass, "בּוֹשׁ *bôš* [*bôsh*]," *TDOT,* II, 50-60; S. H. Siedl, *Gedanken zum Tempussystem im Hebräischen und Akkadischen* (Wiesbaden, 1971); W. A. van der Weiden, "Prov. XIV 32B 'Mais le juste a confiance quand il meurt,' " *VT,* 20 (1970), 339-350, esp. 340f., 344f.; A. Weiser, "πιστεύω, B. The OT Concept," *TDNT,* VI, 182-196, esp. 192f.

1 *AHw,* I, 342, 641; *CAD,* VI (1956), 176f.

2 Delekat, *VT,* 14 (1964), 28: lexical series *erimḫuš.*

3 *KTU,* 1.4 V, 51-54.

4 *LexSyr,* 245f.

5 Delekat, *VT,* 14 (1964), 29f.

6 Cf. *DISO,* 93.

7 *LexLingAeth,* 93.

8 Cf. Delekat, *loc. cit.;* Kopf, 173.

by the 1st person singular suffix (once each by the 1st person pl. [Isa. 28:15] and 3rd person sg. masc. [Ps. 14:6]); less frequently we find *l*^{e}- with suffix or noun, *b*^{e}-, or *min*. Once a genitive is used (Isa. 28:17), and once the noun is used absolutely (Job 24:8). It is not just that the occurrences are concentrated numerically in the Psalms (25 out of 37 for the verb, not counting Sir. 14:27 and 51:8; 12 out of 20 for the noun); the constructions that differ from the norm appear almost entirely outside the Psalms and prayers.

2. *Context.* As in the case of morphology and syntax, there is little variety in literary genre and context: most of the occurrences of the verb and noun are limited to prayers.

a. In the Psalms, we find *ḥāsâ*/*maḥ*^{a}*seh* primarily in individual laments, albeit not in the lament proper, but in petitions introduced as the reason or motivation for the lament, often at the beginning (Ps. 7:2[1]; 31:2[1] par. 71:1; 57:2[1]; 144:2) or in the body (Ps. 17:7; 61:4f.[3f.]; 142:6[5]; 143:9 conj.), rarely at the end (Ps. 25:20; 141:8). Less frequently forms of *ḥāsâ* occur in the hymnic section of laments (Ps. 31:20[19]; 62:8[7]; 71:7); it is more frequent again at the end (Ps. 5:12[11]; 64:11[10]; 94:22). Comparable to the hymnic or thanksgiving section of the laments are the occurrences in individual thanksgivings (Ps. 18:3,31[2,30] par. 2 S. 22:3,31; Ps. 118:8f.) and individual hymns of confidence (Ps. 11:1; 62:8f.[7f.]). These latter, like several other occurrences (Ps. 37:40; 73:28; 91:2,4,9), especially in macarisms (Ps. 2:12; 34:23[22]), belong to Wisdom Literature. Outside the Psalter we find only a few similar occurrences: Jer. 17:17b is a motivation for the petition in a lament. The only instance from a pure hymn is Sir. 51:8.

b. The word group *ḥāsâ* is used several times in Wisdom Literature outside the Psalter: Prov. 14:26,32; 30:5; Nah. 1:7; Sir. 14:27. Ps. 14:6 and Dt. 32:37 may exhibit the influence of both prophecy and Wisdom Literature.

c. In prophetic literature, the word group appears primarily in eschatological contexts (Isa. 4:6; 14:32; 25:4; 28:15,17; 57:13b; Joel 4:16[3:16]; Zeph. 3:12); in the Psalter, only Ps. 46:2[1], a Zion psalm, may belong to this group. There are two occurrences in oracles of woe: Isa. 28:15,17; 30:2f.

This survey in itself gives the impression that the word group is concentrated in a few authors, primarily of the later period.

3. *"Nontheological" Usage.* It is a well-known fact that the idioms of prayer are restricted to a small range of topics; they are highly stereotyped and fixed, and are only slightly adapted to the changing situation. As will be seen, therefore, their semantic analysis is difficult and imprecise.

A helpful starting-point is furnished by the few texts that can be called at most indirectly theological, but exhibit markedly individual features. These are Ps. 104:18, a description of nature; Jgs. 9:15, a political statement; Ruth 2:12, a religio-sociological text; and Job 24:8, a unique image. The starting-point these texts furnish is of course, in the first instance, merely logical. Nothing is being said about chronology or even a course of development. In Ps. 104:18, in the context of an "ecological" description of nature with theological overtones, *maḥ*^{a}*seh* means the "refuge" or "shelter" of the badgers (cf. the *m*^{e}*'ônôṯ* of the lions, v. 22). It spells protection, but forms part of their normal habitat, like the shelter that the poor who dwell in the desert lack in Job 24:8 (v. 10 expresses lack of clothing with the same negation, *b*^{e}*lî*). In Isa. 4:6 and 25:4, *maḥ*^{a}*seh* as a shelter against inclement weather has been incorporated into an eschatological image; in Sir. 14:27, it has been similarly incorporated into a hymnic expression.[9] Jgs. 9:15 is made unique by its context, a fable with an ironic point. The (almost nonexistent) shade cast by the bramble is the "shade of the king," the refuge and protection expected from him (cf. Lam. 4:20; 1 S. 8:5f.; 2 K. 14:8-10). In Ruth 2:12, "taking refuge under the wings of Yahweh," through what is initially adherence to the religion of Yahweh's people, means full incorporation into the social structure of this people and thus the possibility of survival.

Thus this series of unconventional passages, which are scarcely theological, documents a kind of semantic bandwidth: protection, sometimes from acute danger, but with a clear tendency in the direction of "shelter," whether in nature, an institution, or a society. There is also an element of movement or "flight" implied, in that there is constant necessary variation among the locations that constitute the habitat.

III. Formulas and Schemata.

1. *ḥāsâ in the Psalms and Other Prayers*. In the texts of prayers the word group appears in only a few schemata.

a. The schema *b*^{e}*ḵā*/*b*^{e}*YHWH ḥāsîṯi* often stands in relative independence at the beginning or towards the end of a psalm. It does not introduce the theme to be developed, but asserts the mental stance or attitude of the worshipper.

Ps. 11:1 is unique in using the full schema (without pronouns) not in direct address to Yahweh but in debate with others who are thinking pragmatically. The psalmist counters their counsel to flee with the assertion that he has decided in favor of Yahweh. This means trust in Yahweh rather than self-preservation but apparently does not imply any specific outward act, not even seeking asylum. The entire psalm may be a confession of faith: vv. 2-6 in "instruction," v. 1a in decision and attitude.

Ps. 31 opens with the same phrase, this time stylized as direct address to God: *b*^{e}*ḵā YHWH ḥāsîṯî* (v. 2[1]). Thus the psalmist finds security for his tormented and helpless life in God, whom he knows to be ready to help. To him also is addressed the petition that follows immediately: *'al-'ēḇôšâ* (v. 2b[1b]). It would mean disavowal of God himself were he to leave the devout person to his fate (cf. v. 18[17]). The account of the psalmist's troubles takes on a kind of religious rhythm through trust and confession (v. 15[14]) followed by petition (v. 18[17]). In v. 20(19), the psalmist uses a hymnic rhetorical question to extol the goodness of God *laḥōsîm bāḵ* (par. *lîrē'eyḵā*). From

[9] See below, III.3.b.

this point on, what he says of God's goodness is addressed to *kol-ham^{e}yaḥ^{a}lîm l^{e}YHWH* (v. 25b[24b]). Thus he commends his personal attitude to all, ending with an effective inclusion. The *b^{e}ḵā YHWH ḥāsîṯî* of the beginning is central, not as a particular action but as a general stance, which in the psalmist's distress (cf. v. 20b[19b]) is actualized in petition, confession of faith, confidence, and trust (vv. 2-7[1-6],15[14],18[17]; cf. Ps. 71:1-3 par. 31:2-4[1-3]). These are powerfully expressed in the characteristic verbs and nouns for deliverance, found elsewhere as well: → פלט *plṭ* (piel), → נצל *nṣl* (hiphil), → צור *ṣûr* and → סלע *sela'*, "rock," → מצודה *meṣûḏâ*, "fortress," → מאוז *mā'ôz*, → ישע *yš'* (hiphil), → נחה *nāḥâ* (hiphil), → יצא *yāṣā'* (hiphil), → פדה *pāḏâ* (qal), → פקד *pāqaḏ* (hiphil; the only verb in the 1st person sg. perf., like *ḥāsîṯî*).

In Ps. 7:2(1), also, the same exclamation precedes petitions, some expressed in the same words, for deliverance from persecutors (hiphil imperative of *yš'* and *nṣl*). We shall ignore the question of whether the "oath of purification" in vv. 4-6(3-5) (cf. Job 31; Ps. 17:3f.; 26:4-6; 137:5f.) and the petition in v. 9(8) presuppose a specific ceremony of "sacral law," with *ḥāsîṯî* having to be understood as the concrete seeking of asylum (in the sanctuary). It is impossible to draw a firm line separating outward reality from expressions indicating a subjective attitude (cf. the "rending lions" of v. 3[2] and Ps. 10:9; 17:12; 22:14,22[13,21]).

In Ps. 16:1, the uninverted verbal clause *ḥāsîṯî ḇāḵ* is preceded by a petition for preservation (*šomrēnî*). This absolute form of expression is unique in the Psalter (apart from Ps. 25:20, which is probably anthological and therefore secondary); it is not developed in the rest of the psalm. It is a deliberate stylistic device to emphasize one of the components present in *ḥāsîṯî ḇ^{e}ḵā:* the hope and expectation that Yahweh will save by way of response (*kî*!), rather than by way of reward. It is entirely up to him, who alone is the "Lord" and "good" (v. 2). The verb *'āmart* (conj. *'āmartî*) does not refer to the psalmist's own action; in this position, almost like a determinative (cf. Ps. 31:15[14]; 140:7[6]; 142:6[5]; cf. 91:2 [difficult]), it introduces a confession of faith in Yahweh (cf. Ps. 141:8; 25:15).

Ps. 25:20 is a combination of 16:1 and 31:2(1). The statement *ḥasîṯî ḇāḵ*, close to the end, summarizes the many expressions of confidence and hope. In this anthological psalm, the verb has no clear contours; it forms an inclusio in combination with *bāṭaḥ* (v. 2; but cf. 1-3). In the course of the psalm, God himself is addressed constantly as the object of hope (vv. 5-7,11,15,20f.); the psalmist, his guilt and helplessness (vv. 11b,16), retreat into the background.

In v. 8b of Ps. 141, a Wisdom meditation, our phrase precedes a petition similar to that in Ps. 31:2(1) (par. 71:1) and 25:20. But *b^{e}ḵā ḥāsîṯî* appears to have become a stylistic device.[10] The psalmist was probably trying, by combining two phrases probably somewhat worn out by extensive use, to lend more vitality to both; the result is more a psychologizing than an increase in theological potential (cf. Ps. 25:1,15; 69:3f.[2f.]; 121:1; 123:1).

At the end of certain psalms, *ḥāsâ* occurs with characteristic simplification: the subject is in the 3rd person, and the verb has Yahweh in the 3rd person as object. In

[10] Culley, 53.

Ps. 64:11(10), *wᵉḥāsâ bô,* the only verb in the perfect in this concluding verse, comes between two semantically similar statements about the rejoicing of the righteous and the singing of the "upright in heart" (cf. Ps. 5:12[11]; 31:20[19]). The two imperfects refer to temporary states; the perf. *ḥāsâ* refers to the basic, enduring decision, made once and for all—not in personal terms, but as a general didactic warning against the danger of God's tyrannical enemies (Ps. 64:6f.[5f.]; cf. Ps. 10:4,11,13; 31:23[22]; 53:2[1][11]). The reflections of Ps. 37 on the eternal problem of why the righteous suffer while the wicked enjoy good fortune lead up to a nominal clause concerning God's salvation for the righteous (v. 39). In the final verse, four imperfects of three verbs promise them help, deliverance, and salvation, concluding with the lapidary isolated statement: *kî-ḥāsû bô* (v. 40).

b. In Ps. 57:2(1), the individual hymn of lament and confidence is preceded by a solemnly repeated petition. The two motivating clauses that follow immediately are parallel, but not synonymous. The last clause of v. 2(1), formally speaking, sets a time limit. Even when interpreted as a desired goal, it is tolerable only in combination with the other clause, *ûḇᵉṣēl-kᵉnāpeyḵā 'eḥseh* (cf. Ps. 16:1). The imperfect, which is normal in this context, probably indicates an outward act to be repeated. No wonder interpreters thought of an institution to be called on in time of need: asylum.

The vocabulary of other psalms comes closer to the sphere of the sanctuary with its legal and cultic functions. In Ps. 61, an individual lament, the psalmist (a king?) addresses this wish to Yahweh: *'āgûrâ bᵉ'oholḵā 'ôlāmîm 'eḥᵉseh ḇᵉsēṯer kᵉnāpeyḵā* (v. 5[4]). In the hymnic intermezzo of another individual lament, we read that the "children of men" *bᵉṣēl kᵉnāpeyḵā yeḥᵉsāyûn:* "how precious is thy *ḥeseḏ*" (Ps. 36:8[7]). The next two verses elaborate this idea in cultic terminology that reflects both ritual and "dogma" ("fountain of life . . . thy light").

In Ps. 91, a difficult and didactic Wisdom psalm, a speaker confesses Yahweh as his *maḥsî* (v. 2); he is assured of it or summoned: *wᵉṯaḥaṯ-kᵉnapāyw teḥseh* (v. 4b): God himself will cover him with his wings. The rare word *bᵉ'eḇrāṯô* in v. 4a recalls Dt. 32:10-12. The original *Sitz im Leben* of the expression has been the source of much conjecture. The sanctuary, the cult, and the right of asylum are the focus of attention. Quantitatively, however, expressions associated with the military realm (holy war?) constitute no little portion of the environment. The question probably cannot be answered simply on the basis of the verb *ḥāsâ*. Even more difficult is the question of contemporary *Sitz im Leben,* to the extent that one may wish to go beyond the rules governing the language of prayer. The juxtaposition of perfect and imperfect in Ps. 57:2(1) may spring directly from the fixation of the formulas. That they became fixed in these particular forms may derive from their different points of reference: in the first, allusion to a fundamental decision in the past; in the second, a statement of purpose to remain actively true to this decision. A confession of faith is always present.

c. Occasionally we find *ḥāsâ* associated directly with images or allegories of God, or in close proximity to them. This has its effect on their meaning. In Ps. 144, a

---

[11] M. Dahood, *Psalms II. AB,* XVII (1968), 19.

(royal?) lament, a long series of hymnic nouns and participles (vv. 1f.) is interrupted after *māginnî* in v. 2 by the clause *ûḇô ḥāsîṯî*. The copula shows that this refers to Yahweh and not to the "shield"; but, whereas elsewhere *ḥāsîṯî* emphasizes the immediate attitude toward God, here everything focuses on the protection vouchsafed by God. The same content can be given the impersonal form of a general statement of religious dogma: Yahweh is a "shield" *le[ḵōl] haḥōsîm bô* (Ps. 18:31[30] par. 2 S. 22:31; Prov. 30:5). The word group has a stereotyped association with such images or allegories of God as protector and deliverer (e.g., Ps. 18:3[2] par. 2 S. 22:3). This is seldom so clear as in the alienated expression found in Dt. 32:37, where God asks of those who worship false gods: *'ê 'elōhêmô ṣûr ḥāsāyû ḇô*. The allegorical "rock" is in the singular, although the polemic against idols that follows uses the plural, as is appropriate (v. 38). The cultic elements are conventional (cf. Ps. 50:8-15; Jer. 7:18; Bel 1-22 [LXX Dnl. 14:1-22]). Stylistic variants include construct phrases like *ṣûr maḥsî* (Ps. 94:22) and the absolute form in Ps. 62:8(7), within a series of expressions for salvation and deliverance. It is still possible for such series to reach the level of solemn confessional assertions: *'elōhîm maḥaseh-llānû* (Ps. 62:9[8]). When third parties are involved, so that we cannot be dealing with a personal confession, the meaning probably comes very close to that of "confession" in the social or legal sense. Any cultic overtones are unintentional.

d. The idiom *ḥāsâ ḇe-* takes on a special meaning when it occurs as a relative clause or participle in macarisms or similar expressions. In Ps. 34:9(8), where the idiom is perhaps somewhat forced, the psalmist and listener are called on to "taste" and "see" that Yahweh is "good." In the parallel stich we read: *'ašrê haggeḇer yeḥeseh-bbô*— probably the one who experiences God because he strives after intimate communion and "fears" (i.e., esteems) him (cf. vv. 8,10[7,9]; 16:1f.). Ps. 34:23(22) goes beyond the end of the acrostic alphabet; it may be the concluding verse of a traditionist. Despite the difference in form, it is very close to being a macarism: "his servants" are those who *haḥōsîm bô;* Yahweh "redeems" (*pôḏeh,* ptcp.) them; they are not condemned like the wicked and those who hate the righteous.[12]

The *ḥôseh* (ptcp.) is the devout worshipper in the best sense; cf. the eschatologically tinged verse Isa. 57:13b (and 57:1f.), which sets off texts that are probably earlier: "*haḥôseh ḇî* [God] shall possess the land, and shall inherit my holy mountain." Note also Ps. 2:12: *'ašrê kol-ḥôsê ḇô* (construct!); these are clearly those who heed the admonitions of the wise (vv. 10f.) and thus escape (*pen,* v. 12a) the wrath of God.

In Sir. 51:8b we find the same construct phrase in the only universal statement within what is otherwise an individualized song of thanksgiving (vv. 1-12). In Nah. 1:7 it is dependent on *yāḏa'*, which in many passages from the Psalms refers to God's loving care (e.g., Ps. 1:6; 37:18; 44:22[21]; 94:11).[13] Ps. 5:12f.(11f.), the hymnic conclusion of a didactic individual lament, is in part equivalent to a macarism: those who *ḥôsê ḇāḵ* and *'ōhaḇê šemeḵā* (v. 12[11]) are those who have remained faithful to

12 Cf. D. Kellermann, "אשם *'āšām* [*'āshām*]," *TDOT,* I, 436.

13 Cf. W. Schottroff, "ידע *jd'* erkennen," *THAT,* I, 691-94.

God in the face of rebellion (v. 11[10]). Their reward is joy and rejoicing (cf. Ps. 63:8[7]; 64:11[10]). In the hymnic verse Ps. 31:20(19), *haḥōsîm bāḵ,* "those who fear thee," appear in apparent polemic contrast to "the sons of men" (cf. Ps. 23:5a), thus constituting a minority (cf. Ps. 31:2[1]). This religio-ethical sense is most clearly developed in Ps. 17:7, where *ḥôsîm* alone appears as the object of *môšîa'* in a unique title ascribed to Yahweh (cf. Ps. 7:11[10]). Here, too, may belong the absolute usage found in the MT of Prov. 14:32. If we reject the emendation based on the LXX, we find a good parallelism: the wicked (*rāšā'*) perishes through his evil-doing; the *ḥōseh* will be proven righteous even in death. Thus *ḥāsâ ḇ*^{e}- can stand for "religious devotion" in general, without any apparent distinctive features.

2. *maḥ*^{a}*seh in the Psalms.* The term *maḥsî* can be a simple predicate noun applied to God (Ps. 91:2,9; 142:6; cf. Ps. 14:6, *maḥsēhû*). It can be a nomen rectum after "rock" (Ps. 94:22) or a nomen regens before *'ōz* (Ps. 71:7). The relationship can also be defined by means of the 1st person suffix, either singular (Ps. 61:4[3]) or plural (Ps. 46:2[1]; 62:9[8]). In Ps. 62:9(8), the confession *'*^{e}*lōhîm maḥ*^{a}*seh-llānû* spoken on behalf of the community motivates the general exhortation "pour out your heart before him." Immediately preceding we find the personal confession *maḥsî bē'lōhîm* (Ps. 62:8[7]). Ps. 73:28b is a bit more expansive: *šattî ba'ḏōnāy YHWH maḥsî.*

Like the verb, *maḥsî* is an element of many expressions for God's protection, power, and deliverance. The syndeses vary only stylistically. The fabric of associations expresses more than the individual word. The preferential placement of *maḥ*^{a}*seh* at the beginning or the end may be significant. Ps. 73 is especially clear in its structure, which does not follow an external sequence or thematic logic but rather is guided by the aim of thanksgiving. Therefore the psalmist can conclude with the statement that his purpose is "to tell all the works of God" (Ps. 73:28b; cf. vv. 21-28a). In Ps. 73:27-28a and 14:6, *maḥ*^{a}*seh* is associated with the nearness of God, to the extent that mankind not only do not cut themselves off from this nearness or trust passively in it, but rather affirm it deliberately through their actions and attitude.

3. *ḥāsâ/maḥ*^{a}*seh in Other Books.* a. Prayers outside the Psalter furnish essentially the same picture. Whatever the dependence, if any, may be, they draw on the same customs and linguistic habits. The relevant passages therefore have already been cited in connection with the Psalms (Isa. 57:13; Nah. 1:7; Sir. 51:8; cf. Prov. 30:5).

b. The other contexts, primarily prophetic, are less stereotyped and are generally easier to date than the Psalms. The woe oracle in Isa. 30:1-3 and the judgment oracle in Isa. 28:14-22 probably come from the time of Hezekiah. The woe oracle, spoken in the 1st person by God, is directed against political and military reliance on Egypt. The words used recall the Psalms: the leaders go to Egypt "to take refuge in the protection of Pharaoh, and to seek shelter in the shadow of Egypt" (*lā'ôz b*^{e}*mā'ôz par'ōh w*^{e}*laḥsôṯ b*^{e}*ṣēl miṣrāyim,* v. 2; cf. v. 3: *heḥāsûṯ*); what they get will be *l*^{e}*ḇōšeṯ* (cf. Ps. 31:2[1]; 71:1) and *liḵlimmâ.* In Isa. 30:1f., God complains that these plans are "not mine," "not of my spirit"; the leaders have acted "without asking for my counsel." Religious language is employed deliberately for conduct contrary to God's will.

Similar usage appears in the judgment oracle: they boast that they have made a "covenant" (*b^e^rîṯ, ḥōzeh* [?]) with death and with Sheol; they have made lies their refuge and taken shelter in falsehood: *kî śamnû ḵāzāḇ maḥsēnû ûḇaššeqer nistārnû* (Isa. 28:15). God threatens that he will establish justice and righteousness, sweeping away the "refuge of lies" and the "shelter" with hail and water (v. 17).

In Joel 4:16(3:16), by contrast, we find the accustomed meaning once more in what is probably a late description of how Yahweh will judge the nations and protect his people: "Yahweh is *maḥ^a^seh* to his people, *mā'ôz* to the people of Israel." In Isa. 14:32, whose genuineness has not been disproved, representatives of those seeking foreign coalitions receive the lapidary answer: "Yahweh has founded Zion, and in her the afflicted of his people find refuge" (*ûḇâ yeḥ^e^sû '^a^niyyê 'ammô;* cf. Isa. 28:16). This is the language and ideology of the Psalms. Faced with or fearing an acute threat, they take comfort in the familiar hopes associated with the physical city of Jerusalem and its temple, unrefined hopes that were often criticized (cf. esp. Jer. 7:10 [*niṣ-ṣalnû*]-15; 26:6; Mic. 3:11).[14]

According to Zeph. 3:9-13, a roughly contemporaneous promise spoken by God, the "humble and lowly" (cf. Isa. 11:4; 14:32: 26:6) remnant of Israel "shall seek refuge in the name of Yahweh" (*w^e^ḥāsû b^e^šēm YHWH;* Zeph. 3:12; cf. Joel 3:5[2:32]). Isa. 25:4b, using the phrase *maḥseh mizzerem ṣēl mēḥōreḇ* (cf. 14:32; Zeph. 3:12) in association with the language of the Psalms (cf. v. 4a with Ps. 46:2[1]; 62:9[8]), brings new life to an original image that has lost its force (cf. Sir. 14:27). The protection expected from Yahweh constitutes the focal point. In Isa. 4:6, the same image is actually weakened by rhetorical exaggeration.

In contrast to these unframed late eschatological passages, the situation of Jer. 17:14-18 (a confession) is reasonably clear. In Jer. 17:17, "Be not a terror to me; thou art 'my refuge' in the day of evil," *maḥ^a^sî* has not only the antithetical parallel of injury but also the prepositional situation "in the day of evil." This is never the case in the Psalms (cf. Ps. 25:20; 31:2[1]; 71:1,7; 91:2,9; 94:22; 142:6[5]). Here *maḥ^a^sî* designates God as the means of escape from acute danger.

Prov. 14:26 is a crux. Despite all the syntactic problems (see the comms.), *maḥseh* stands in parallel with *miḇṭaḥ-'ōz,* the same combination found in the Psalms. Since, however, the key word connection with v. 27 has probably influenced the meaning, *maḥseh* is explained as protection against the "snares of death" (cf. Prov. 13:14; Ps. 18:6[5]). Unlike in the Psalms, *maḥseh* is not identified with God, nor is it in God; it is instead the effect or consequence of the *yir'aṯ YHWH,* in that this fear preserves life, i.e., protects against what can be imprecisely but comprehensively called "death."

IV. Theological Usage.

1. Since the use of this word group in the Psalms, which is limited to a few schemata, cannot be arranged with any assurance on the basis of date, literary genre, or *Sitz im Leben*, any attempt to derive a chronological interpretation must therefore

---

[14] Cf. O. Kaiser, *Isaiah 13–39. OTL* (Eng. trans. 1974), 47.

begin with occurrences outside the Psalter and prayers. What seems to be the earliest attested use is secular (Jgs. 9:15; possibly also Ps. 104:18 and Job 24:8 [archaizing]). The genuine Isaiah passages already presuppose a well-defined theological meaning for *ḥāsâ* and its derivatives (Isa. 28:15,17; 30:1-3). The same is true for the prophetic (Joel 4:16[3:16]) and eschatological texts, whether early (Zeph. 3:12; Isa. 14:32) or late (Isa. 4:6; 25:4f.; 57:13). Even if the earliest relevant Psalms were to be assigned a late date, the Isaiah passages just mentioned, together with Nah. 1:7 and Prov. 14:26,32; 30:5, make it likely that the theological usage, which is practically the only usage attested in the Psalter, has a very long history. Isa. 30:1-3 would lose its point if *ḥāsâ* did not have specific theological overtones.

2. Very early texts stay close to the realm of experience and observation: Jgs. 9:15; Ps. 104:18. This spontaneity is never totally lost; at least the fragmentary literary documentation gives the impression that it can later spring to life in images and metaphors: Job 24:8; Isa. 4:6; 25:4; possibly also Prov. 14:26. The problem is caused by the stereotyped and formulaic language of the Psalms. Formalized prayer is per se cultic, if the cult is not defined in very narrow terms. Recently, however, some scholars have attempted to turn *ḥāsâ* and the corresponding formulas in the Psalms into something like technical terms for specific cultic institutions, such as the right of asylum as defined in sacral law.[15] These attempts involve too much that is hypothetical and suggestive. They appear to overlook the fact that one cannot simply think of a one-way semantic street from cult to "spiritualization"; the opposite direction cannot be excluded a priori.[16] Literary and iconographic evidence shows that many stereotyped formulas can have roots far outside Israel.[17] It can hardly be shown that the word group *ḥāsâ* and its associated formulas found their way into the language of Israel's prayer only through specific institutions. Finally, it is probably true that all languages at some stage use conventional ideas from the realm of war, kingship, and cult (= ritual) for their most important concerns.

3. Finite forms of *ḥāsâ* as well as *maḥ*[a]*seh* play a role in the semantic field that is characteristic of the individual lament and the apparently related individual song of confidence (Ps. 11:1; cf. 37:40) and thanksgiving (Ps. 18:3,31[2,30]; 34:9,23[8,22]; 73:28; 94:22; 118:8f.). But they are never elements of the lament; they stand on the borderline between danger and deliverance, though still on the side of danger. Despite the tendency toward leveling and assimilation in what are often long sequences of ill-defined expressions and images, the group to which *ḥāsâ* belongs maintains a certain theologically relevant identity. The object in view is always some kind of enemy in human form, apparently never impersonal perils like disease or natural catastrophe. The only possible deliverance is God, as is stated by what are often long series of apostrophes or predicates, using metaphors drawn primarily from the realm of war, law, or cult. Usually God is mentioned directly; outside of the Psalms, we occasionally

---

15 Esp. Delekat.

16 Cf. Hugger, *Jahwe meine Zuflucht,* 69-71.

17 Cf. Bordreuil.

find instead his name (Zeph. 3:12) or Zion, the city he founded (Isa. 14:32). Thus the intellectual and affective horizon includes God, the worshipper himself and the devout on behalf of whom he speaks or intercedes, and his enemies—all persons. The central reference point is almost always the worshipper, speaking in the 1st person singular. The preferred position of *ḥāsâ/maḥ^a^seh* is at the beginning or end of the series, or serving to interrupt the monotonous sequence. A human being is always the subject; only God is the goal (this is especially clear in Ps. 143:9, if the conjecture of Delekat[18] [*'eleyḵā ḥāsîṯî*] is correct, instead of the unusual *'eleyḵā kissiṯî*). Never in any of the Psalms is any human being, place, or object viewed as the goal of refuge, not even metaphorically. Never in the Psalms is the word group defined more precisely by a specific *terminus a quo,* although neither is impossible a priori: cf. Isa. 4:6; 25:4; 28:15,17; Jer. 17:17b; Sir. 14:27; 1QH 7:17 (*wmḥsy bśr 'yn ly*). None of the comparable occurrences in the Psalms is modified by a corresponding prepositional phrase (Ps. 142:6[5]; cf. Ps. 62:8[7]; 71:7; 73:28; 91:2; 94:22). And the verb at least is never associated with appended asseverative or reinforcing questions, as is often true in the case of other verbs performing a similar function (cf., for example, Ps. 27:1; 56:5[4]; 118:6).

The *ḥāsâ/maḥ^a^seh* group is set apart from words with similar meaning through an (internal) semantic stereotyping that clearly began in the context of the Psalms. In 2 S. 22:3, for example, not far from the verb *'eḥ^e^seh* and in a series of several metaphors in which God is addressed as a protection and refuge, we find *m^e^nûsî* as an element not occurring in Ps. 18:2f.(1f.), which is otherwise identical. The physical sense of this related term is illuminated by the observation that *mānôs* can also be lost ("chance for flight"; Am. 2:14; cf. Ps. 142:5[4]; 25:35) and almost always occurs with a prepositional phrase explaining what is being fled from, even when God is the goal or place of *mānôs* (Job 11:20; Ps. 59:17[16]; Jer. 16:19).

More light is shed by several verbs and nouns that, although hardly formal parallels to our word, sometimes appear in proximity or in connection with terms that characterize its environment or are similarly constructed. These are above all *bāṭaḥ/miḇṭāḥ* (→ בטח *bāṭaḥ* [*bāṭach*]), → קוה *qāwâ* (Ps. 25:5,21; 37:34; 62:6[5]; 71:5), → יחל *yḥl* (Ps. 31:25[24]; 71:14), → חכה *ḥāḵâ* [*chākhāh*] (Ps. 33:20; Isa. 30:18; Zeph. 3:8). Especially close is the participle of *qāwâ* (cf., for example, Ps. 25:3,21).

The opposite of *ḥāsâ* is variously expressed, but always a fundamental antithesis is involved, not just an isolated failure: distance and infidelity (Ps. 73:27f.), rebellion (Ps. 5:11f.[10f.]), idolatry (Ps. 16:1,4; Isa. 57:12-13a), apostasy (Jer. 17:13).

Although it seems that originally the root was flexible and could be used in all areas, physical, psychological, and theological, and although this innate variety may never have been totally lost, as the citations from the prophets (probably secondary with respect to the Psalms) show, the laws governing the composition of prayers probably restricted its range of application, while at the same time intensifying and fixing the meaning: in the Psalms, *ḥāsâ/maḥ^a^seh* has lost the physical and psychological elements of "flight," gaining in return an exclusive reference to Yahweh in the

---

[18] *VT,* 14 (1964), 30.

sense of a fundamental decision for Yahweh over and above anything and anyone else, whether made once for all or actualized in the face of specific dangers and temptations. Although or because all the details have been eliminated, the verb above all can sum up mankind's whole relationship to God, like our "be devout," and can be used in eschatological texts. By using this word, the worshipper sets himself apart from those who seek their good fortune without or in opposition to God and try to attract others to their side; the element of personal confession is so strong that the noun appears only once with the 3rd person singular suffix, in a statement reflecting the objectivity of dogmatic theology (Ps. 14:6). In prayers, the word has become so exclusively religious and theological that it admits no synergism of intermediaries between the worshipper and God. The sense of human insufficiency presupposed and expression in the semantic field lend an element of lament to the word group. Associated with it as presupposition and consequence is an assurance of God's beneficence, his readiness and ability to help. This gives the root a place in hymns and thanksgivings, and explains why the LXX works primarily with terms meaning "confidence."[19]

Gamberoni

[19] Cf. Weiser.

חָסִיד *ḥāsîḏ*

Contents: I. Etymology, Meaning. II. Use in the OT: 1. Qualitative: Practicing *ḥeseḏ;* 2. With *'eḇeḏ;* 3. Designating the Cultic Community. III. LXX, Maccabees. IV. Discussion.

I. Etymology, Meaning. The word *ḥāsîḏ,* usually translated "godly" or "devout," is clearly derived from *ḥeseḏ*. In Hebrew the qāṭîl form sometimes produces adjectives expressing a quality, such as *ṣā'îr,* "small," or *nā'îm,* "pleasing," sometimes adjectives with passive meaning, such as *'āsîr,* "prisoner," *māšîaḥ,* "the anointed one," and sometimes action nouns, such as *qāṣîr,* "harvest."[1] The form *ḥāsîḏ* clearly belongs to

ḥāsîḏ. W. A. M. Beuken, "Ḥāsîd: Gunstgenoot," *Bijdragen,* 33 (1972), 417-435; H. A. Brongers, "De Chasidim in het Boek der Psalmen," *ThT,* 8 (1953/54), 279-297; J. Coppens, "Les Psaumes des Ḥasidim," *Festschrift A. Robert. Travaux de l'Institut Catholique de Paris,* 4 (1957), 214-224; J. H. Eaton, *Kingship and the Psalms. SBT,* N.S. 32 (1976); B. D. Eerdmans, "Essays on masoretic Psalms," *OTS,* 1 (1942), 105-296, esp. 176-257; L. Gulkowitsch, *Die Entwicklung des Begriffes Ḥāsîd im AT. Acta et commentationes Universitatis Tartuensis,* B, 32/4 (1934); L. Jacobs, "The Concept of Ḥasid in Biblical and Rabbinic Literatures," *JJS,* 8 (1957), 143-154; A. R. Johnson, "Hesed and Hāsîd," *Interpretationes ad Vetus Testamentum pertinentes. Festschrift S. Mowinckel. NTT,* 56 (1955), 100-112; J. Morgenstern, "The *ḤASÎDÎM*—Who Were They?" *HUCA,* 38 (1967), 59-73; H. J. Stoebe, "חסד *ḥǽsǽd* Güte," *THAT,* I, 600-621, esp. 618-620.

[1] P. Joüon, *Grammaire de l'Hébreu biblique* ([2]1947; repr. Rome, 1965), §88 E*b*.

the first group, thus designating a person who has or practices *ḥeseḏ*. It occurs 32 times in the OT, of which 25 are in the Psalms.

II. Use in the OT.

1. *Qualitative: Practicing ḥeseḏ*. The meaning of the word can only be approximated, since many occurrences furnish little information. Among the clearest is 2 S. 22:26 par. Ps. 18:26(Eng. v. 25): *'im-ḥāsîḏ tiṯhassāḏ*, "with the *ḥāsîḏ* thou dost show thyself *ḥāsîḏ*"; in other words, God acts towards mankind as mankind acts towards God. In parallel we find *tāmîm*, "perfect, blameless," and → נבר *nāḇār*, "pure"; in antithesis we find *'iqqēš*, "perverse," with the verb *hiṯpattēl*, "show oneself false." Thus *ḥāsîḏ* designates a desirable quality that is expressed in the mutual converse between God and mankind; starting from *ḥeseḏ*, we can derive some such meaning as "gracious." Ps. 43:1 points in the same direction, where the psalmist prays for help against *gôy lō'-ḥāsîḏ*. The context shows that we are dealing here with an *'îš-mirmâ wᵉ'awlâ*, a deceitful and unjust man. The psalmist's enemies are a "merciless and inhuman bunch."[2] Ps. 97:10 contrasts the *ḥᵃsîḏîm* with the *rᵉšā'îm;* although the text is not entirely certain, it seems to state that the *ḥᵃsîḏîm* love Yahweh and hate evil.

In Mic. 7:2, the prophet laments that the *ḥāsîḏ* and the upright (→ ישר *yāšār*) have perished from the earth, and that everyone waylays (*'āraḇ, ṣûḏ*) his neighbor. The *ḥāsîḏ* is thus ranked with the upright, in contrast to those who are treacherous and bloodthirsty. The prophet's lament recalls Ps. 12:2(1), a lament that bewails the absence of *ḥāsîḏ* and *'ᵉmûnîm* ("faithful"); this is connected with the statement that the people lie and speak with flattering lips (v. 3[2]). There is no reason to change *ḥāsîḏ* into *ḥeseḏ;* the *ḥāsîḏ* is the upright and faithful person who carries out his obligations to the community.

An equally positive meaning attaches to *ḥāsîḏ* in 1 S. 2:9, in the Song of Hannah, where we read that Yahweh will guard the feet of his *ḥᵃsîḏîm*, whereas the wicked (*rᵉšā'îm*) are cut off in darkness. The *ḥāsîḏ* is thus the opposite of the *rāšā'*, the wicked or godless; he stands under God's special protection. A similar statement in Prov. 2:8, "(God) preserves the way of his *ḥᵃsîḏîm*," is not further illuminated by an antithesis; but the context includes, in addition to the Wisdom terminology, such words as *mišpāṭ, yāšār*, and *tōm* (→ תמם *tmm*). Its purpose is to document the help, protection, and success vouchsafed those who walk according to his will.[3]

Only twice is God called *ḥāsîḏ*. The first passage, Jer. 3:12, where the statement *ḥāsîḏ 'ᵃnî* is placed in the mouth of Yahweh, shows by its context that we are dealing with a God who does not remain angry and who forgives sins. "Merciful" and "gracious" are possible translations. In the second passage, Ps. 145:17, *ḥāsîḏ* stands in parallel with *ṣaddîq;* the psalm speaks in general terms of Yahweh's graciousness and providence.

---

[2] H. Birkeland, *Die Feinde des Individuums in der israelitischen Psalmenliteratur* (Oslo, 1933), 166.

[3] H. Ringgren, *Sprüche, Prediger, das Hohelied, Klagelieder, das Buch Esther. ATD*, XVI (²1967), 18.

2. *With 'eḇeḏ.* In 3 passages from the Psalms, *ḥāsîḏ* appears to be more or less synonymous with *'eḇeḏ,* "servant" (→ עבד *'āḇaḏ*). The clearest is Ps. 86:2, where the psalmist calls himself *'eḇeḏ* and cites as justification for his prayer that his life be preserved (*šāmar, nepeš*) the fact that he is *ḥāsîḏ* (cf. Ps. 97:10, which states that God preserves the life of the godly). The psalmist also describes himself as "poor" (*'ānî*) and "needy" (*'eḇyôn*); he has enemies who are "insolent" (*zēḏ*) and "ruthless" (*'ārîṣ*) (v. 14). In Ps. 116:15, too, the context suggests identification of *ḥāsîḏ* with *'eḇeḏ:* v. 15 states that the life of the *ḥāsîḏ* is precious in the sight of Yahweh, and in v. 16 the psalmist calls himself "thy servant." The psalm appears to be a thanksgiving; the psalmist has obviously been saved from death (vv. 3, 8). Ps. 16:10 similarly gives assurance that the *ḥāsîḏ* of God will not "see the Pit," i.e., die. The speaker of this psalm cannot be defined with assurance. The psalm has features of a thanksgiving,[4] but also includes a vigorous renunciation of other gods.

Engnell[5] considers the three psalms just cited to be royal psalms, seeing in the king the servant and *ḥāsîḏ* par excellence. Eaton,[6] too, considers these to be royal psalms and describes the king as "God's pre-eminent covenant-fellow."[7] Among the royal psalms he also includes Ps. 4, where v. 4(3) contains the expression *hiplâ YHWH ḥāsîḏ lô,* "Yahweh has set apart a covenant-fellow [i.e., the king] for himself." But the text is not certain, and the reading *hiplâ ḥasdô lô* (as in Ps. 31:22[21]) seems reasonable. This category would also include Ps. 89:20(19), if we follow certain manuscripts (contra the versions) in reading the sg. *ḥ^{a}sîḏ^{e}ḵā.*[8]

3. *Designating the Cultic Community.* The qualitative sense of *ḥāsîḏ* comes less to the fore in a group of statements where the word appears as a term for the cultic community. In Ps. 50:5, the *ḥ^{a}sîḏîm* to be assembled are identical with those who "made a covenant with me by sacrifice," i.e., the covenant community, those who take part in the covenant ceremony. In Ps. 79:2, "thy *ḥ^{a}sîḏîm*" are identical with "thy servants," and in this communal lament both expressions must refer to the people of Israel. It follows, however, that these "saints" share in the sin mentioned in v. 9; it is unlikely that v. 2 refers only to an especially devout portion of the people. In Ps. 85:9(8), God speaks *šālôm* "to his people and to his *ḥ^{a}sîḏîm*"; the next verse speaks of "those who fear him." The "saints" are therefore the people, but at the same time they are obligated to fear God.

In Ps. 148:14, the three expressions "the *ḥ^{a}sîḏîm,*" "the people of Israel," and "his people" (*'ammô*) appear to be identical. We are obviously dealing with participants in the cult, who sing Yahweh's praises as representatives of the people. In Ps. 149:1, also, "the assembly (*qāhāl*) of the *ḥ^{a}sîḏîm*" that is called on to sing a new song is identical with the "sons of Zion" and "Israel" of v. 2, and probably also with "his

---

4 For a different view, see H.-J. Kraus, *Psalmen. BK,* XV/1 (^{5}1978), 120.

5 I. Engnell, "The Book of Psalms," in his *A Rigid Scrutiny* (Eng. trans., Nashville, 1969), 119f.

6 Pp. 66f., 79-81.

7 P. 151.

8 G. W. Ahlström, *Psalm 89* (Lund, 1959), 99f.; Eaton, 151; see below, II.3.

people" and "the *ᵃnāwîm*" of v. 4. The *qᵉhal ḥᵃsîḏîm* is the cultic community representing the covenant nation that shares in the *ḥeseḏ* of its God. In vv. 5 and 9 the word *ḥᵃsîḏîm* refers again to the cultic community; the "faithful" are to rejoice and glorify Yahweh, and will receive glory (*hāḏār*) through the judgment of Yahweh.

In Ps. 30:5(4), the *ḥᵃsîḏîm* are called on to praise Yahweh, i.e., to join in the thanksgiving hymn of the psalmist. Again, therefore, we must be dealing with the cultic community assembled for an act of thanksgiving. The situation is similar in Ps. 52:11(9). Here the psalmist "in the presence of the *ḥᵃsîḏîm*," i.e., the cultic community, expects his lament to be heard.

Here, too, belongs 2 Ch. 6:41, where Solomon says at the dedication of the temple: "Let thy priests, O Yahweh God, be clothed with salvation, and let thy *ḥᵃsîḏîm* rejoice in thy goodness (*ṭôḇ*)." Here *ḥᵃsîḏîm* obviously refers to the assembled multitude, the laity of the cultic community. Similarly *ḥᵃsîḏîm* appears in Ps. 132:9,16 as the complement to *kōhᵃnîm;* both terms together designate the entire temple community, here shouting with joy.

Finally, Ps. 89:20(19), mentioned above, is obscure. According to the MT, Yahweh speaks to his *ḥᵃsîḏîm* announcing the election of David. In this case the word could refer to those present at the election of the king, once more a kind of cultic community. Some manuscripts, however, read the singular, which would have to refer to the king.[9]

Of course the usage outlined here does not exclude the possibility that even in such instances *ḥāsîḏ* bears its root meaning and describes, as it were, the ideal community. If *ḥeseḏ* is connected in some cases with the notion of the covenant, there may be connotations of "faithfulness to the covenant" or "covenant fellow." On the other hand, it seems out of the question that *ḥᵃsîḏîm* might refer to a party or an especially "devout" segment of the population.

III. LXX, Maccabees. In most cases, the LXX translates *ḥāsîḏ* as *hósios*. In 2 Ch. 6:41, however, we find *huioí theoú;* in Jer. 3:12, *eleḗmōn;* in Mic. 7:2, *eulabḗs;* and in Prov. 2:8, *eulaboménoi autón.*[10]

In 1 Macc. 7:13, a group among the Israelites is designated *Asidaíoi* (i.e., *ḥᵃsîḏîm*); their aim is to reach a peaceful accommodation with the Syrians. According to Gulkowitsch,[11] this refers to "the whole nation fighting for religious freedom," not a particular party of the devout. In 2 Macc. 14:6, on the other hand, *Asidaíoi* refers to the followers of Judas Maccabeus; according to Gulkowitsch,[12] this is the term by which the nationalistic Jews prefer to call themselves. There can hardly be any doubt that the word also had religious overtones, like "faithful (to the covenant)."

Ringgren

---

9 See above, II.2.
10 Gulkowitsch, 30f.
11 *Ibid.*, 29.
12 *Ibid.*, 30.

Strangely enough, there is no firm evidence that the Qumran community used *ḥāsîḏ* to refer to itself, although the "Essene" movement (Gk. *Essēnoí,* Aram. *ḥsyn, ḥs'* [equivalent to *ḥsyd*]) is probably directly associated with the Hasidim movement of the Maccabean period.[13] It is even possible that the monastic settlement of the Essenes at Qumran was called *mṣd ḥsydyn,* "fortress of the saints," if this is the correct interpretation of the Murabba'āt letter from the period of Bar Kokhba.[14]

In a second letter (46:4), a certain Euphronius is described as living at En-gedi (belonging to Qumran?) the life of a *ḥāsîḏ* (text emended): he cares for the poor and buries the dead.

The word occurs 4 times in 11QPs[a]. The psalmists consider themselves *ḥsydym,* who in a special way document the glory of Zion and await God's reward. Probably, however, these texts come from the proto-Essene phase of separation.[15] For discussion of the term used by the Essenes for themselves, see → יחד *yāḥaḏ.*

Fabry

IV. Discussion. For earlier students of the Psalms, who considered a large number of the Psalms to be Maccabean, *ḥāsîḏ* was a term for the strict religious party that opposed the Hellenists.[16] Kittel,[17] on the contrary, sees in the *ḥ^a sîḏîm* the circle of those "living quietly in the countryside" or the especially devout, even in an earlier period. Eerdmans[18] similarily views the *ḥ^a sîḏîm* as a party or group that sought to be especially devout, upright, and honest.

Gulkowitsch takes the opposite tack. According to him, *ḥāsîḏ* was originally a term for the cultic community; only later did it take on a religio-ethical coloration. Morgenstern suggests that in several postexilic Psalms *ḥ^a sîḏîm* designates the whole company of the laity, the group called *ṣaddîqîm* in preexilic Psalms.

As was shown above, *ḥ^a sîḏîm* often (but not always) refers to the cultic community. It can hardly be assumed, however, that such a term could be used without any qualitative content; from the outset, the word must have had a positive religio-ethical meaning.

Ringgren

---

13 Cf. M. Hengel, *Judaism and Hellenism* (Eng. trans., Philadelphia, 1974), I, 251f.

14 P. Benoit, J. T. Milik, and R. de Vaux, *Les grottes de Murabb'ât. DJD,* 2 (1961), 45, 6.

15 J. A. Sanders, *The Psalms Scroll of Qumrân Cave 11 (11QPs[a]). DJD,* 2 (1965), 70.

16 A. F. Puukko, "Der Feind in den alttestamentlichen Psalmen," *OTS,* 8 (1950), 47-65.

17 R. Kittel, *Die Psalmen. KAT,* XIII ([5,6]1929).

18 Pp. 176ff., contra Brongers.

חָסֵר *ḥāsēr;* חָסֵר *ḥāsēr;* חֶסֶר *ḥeser;* חֹסֶר *ḥōser;* חֶסְרוֹן *ḥesrôn;* מַחְסוֹר *maḥsôr*

Contents: I. Etymology and Distribution: 1. Outside the Bible; 2. OT; 3. Semantic Field; 4. Idioms; 5. LXX. II. Use in the OT: 1. Concrete Usage; 2. Lack as Poverty; 3. Lack of Understanding in Wisdom Literature; 4. Lack and Abundance in Correlation with Obedience and Sin; 5. Piel as an Anthropological Term.

I. Etymology and Distribution.

1. *Outside the Bible*. The root *ḥsr* is attested in all the Semitic languages, and there is no serious debate about its meaning. The earliest occurrences are probably Ugar. *ḫsr,* "lack (verb)," and *mḫsrn,* "lack (noun)."[1] To date there are only 7 attested occurrences, mostly in economic texts.[2] There is little to support Aistleitner's attempt to intensify the meaning "lack" into "be greedy for."[3] In Old Babylonian texts we find *ḫasāru/heséru,* "break off," "defoliate,"[4] and *ḫasru(m)* and *ḫussuru,* "broken off" (*ḫeser šinnē,* "gap-toothed"[5]). The word *ḫesīru* means "something broken off" in general;[6] *ḫusirtum* refers to a "broken reed."[7] In omen texts, the stative form *ḫaser* is used of "blunted" horns (par. "broken"[8]) or breastbones[9] or parts of the liver.[10] In secular usage, the verb means something like "crumble" pieces off a clay tablet or millstone. In all these occurrences, the root designates something that is not in full possession of all its usual characteristics.

The meaning appears also in Syr. *ḥ*ᵉ*sar,* "be lacking, perish, lose," and *ḥasîrā',* "lacking."[11] In Mandaic, many occurrences of *hsr* point to the realm of sacrificial language,[12] adding to "lack" the nuance of "be deficient." In Aramaic, the verb (in combination with *l*ᵉ plus a pronominal suffix) means "lack."[13] The same is true of Middle Hebrew in the Talmud and Midrash.[14]

The root also appears in South Semitic, where it is still used in a variety of meanings: Arab. *ḫasira,* "suffer loss, be lost," and its derivatives;[15] OSA, "(remove from

---

[1] *WUS,* no. 1063; *UT,* no. 988.

[2] Whitaker, 278, 415.

[3] *KTU,* 1.6, 2, 17; cf. *CML,* 111.

[4] *AHw,* I, 329; *CAD,* VI (1956), 176.

[5] H. Zimmern, *Beiträge zur Kenntnis der babylonischen Religion. Assyriologische Bibliothek,* 12 (Leipzig, 1901), 24, 31.

[6] *AHw,* I, 342.

[7] F. Thureau-Dangin, *Textes mathématiques babyloniens. UEOL,* 1 (1938), 190, 25.

[8] E. Leichty, *The Omen Series Šumma Izbu. TCS,* 4 (1970), 172, 93.

[9] *CAD.*

[10] *AHw.*

[11] *LexSyr,* 248.

[12] *MdD,* 151, 125b.

[13] *DISO,* 94; *LexLingAram,* 66.

[14] *WTM,* II, 91f.

[15] Wehr, 238f.

the secular realm >) consecrate (a hierodule)";[16] in personal names, "turn aside";[17] Tigr. and Ge'ez *ḫasᵉra*, "be little," often with the emotional nuance "be sad, oppressed";[18] thence Amhar. *ḫaser*, "diminish, decrease,"[19] with the noun *'asar*, "penury"; and Soq. *ḫasrán*, "loss," *ḫósir*, "poor pasturage," and *di-ḫósir*, "cheap."[20]

The Hebrew nouns *ḥeser*, *ḥōser*, *maḥsôr*, "lack," as well as *ḥesrôn*, "deficit"[21] (the latter taken by Wagner[22] to be an Aramaism), also have many correlates in the other Semitic languages; for *maḥsôr*, cf. the early Canaanite *maḫzir*, "need," parallel to food and oil,[23] and Pun. *mḥsr*, "lack."[24]

2. *OT.* The root *ḥsr* appears 57 times in the OT (plus 2 conjectural occurrences). The verb *ḥāsēr* occurs 23 times (19 times in the qal, twice each in the piel and hiphil), the adjective 17 times, the substs. *ḥeser* twice, *ḥōser* 3 times (plus a conjectural occurrence in Prov. 10:21), *ḥesrôn* once, and *maḥsôr* 13 times (plus a conjectural occurrence in Jgs. 18:7, and 1QH 15:16). In addition, Sirach uses the root 18 times (6 as a verb, 12 as a subst.); in itself, this shows that we are dealing here with a term popular in Wisdom Literature. The verb in the OT is fairly evenly distributed among the various books (being found 7 times in the Pentateuch, 4 in the prophets, and 9 in the Psalms and Wisdom Literature). But the fact that 13 of the 18 occurrences of the adjective appear in Proverbs (with another in Ecclesiastes), and that 8 out of 13 occurrences of the subst. *maḥsôr* appear in Proverbs (plus 1 in the Psalms) shows the clear association with Wisdom Literature: 35 out of 59 occurrences of the root. An additional concentration appears in the Deuteronomistic literature, with 14 occurrences.

The verb *ḥāsēr* appears in various constructions in the OT. Besides an intransitive qal with the meaning "be lacking" (cf. Gen. 18:28), the verb has a personal transitive qal meaning "lack" (cf. Dt. 2:7; with *min*, Sir. 51:24). The piel has a causative sense ("deprive," Eccl. 4:8) or a comparative meaning (with *min;* "make less than," Ps. 8:6[Eng. v. 5]).[25] The hiphil appears with a transitive causative meaning "cause to lack, deprive" (Isa. 32:6) and an internally transitive meaning "have (no) lack" (Ex. 16:18). The adj. *ḥāsēr* also varies between the meanings "someone who lacks something" (e.g., 1 S. 21:16[15]), "that which is lacking" (Eccl. 6:2), and "lack" (Prov. 10:21).

3. *Semantic Field.* The semantic field "lack, be lessened" is covered by a range of more or less synonymous verbs: *ḥāḏal*, "no longer be present, cease" (Dt. 15:11; Jgs.

---

[16] W. W. Müller, "Altsüdarabische Beiträge zum hebräischen Lexikon," *ZAW*, 75 (1963), 309.

[17] *RyNP*, I, 105.

[18] *TigrWb*, 72a.

[19] W. Leslau, *Hebrew Cognates in Amharic* (Wiesbaden, 1969), 93.

[20] *Idem, Lexique soqotri* (Paris, 1938), 197, 184.

[21] *KBL*³, 325, 541.

[22] M. Wagner, *Die lexikalischen und grammatikalischen Aramaismen im alttestamentlichen Hebräisch. BZAW*, 96 (1966), 57f.

[23] EA 287, 16.

[24] *CIS*, 165, 5; *DISO*, 147.

[25] Cf. E. Jenni, *Das hebräische Pi'el* (Zurich, 1968), 73, 104.

5:6f.); *ne'dar* (niphal of *'dr* III), "be missing" (1 S. 30:19; Isa. 59:15); negated niphal of *hāyâ,* "be lacking" (Zec. 8:10); *ma'aṭ,* "be few" (Lev. 25:16), piel "become few" (Eccl. 12:3), hiphil "cause to decrease" (Ps. 107:38); sometimes also the niphal of *'āsap,* "cease, decrease" (Isa. 60:20). In the case of nouns, the semantic field is also represented by *baṣṣārâ* and *baṣṣōreṯ,* "lack, lack of rain, drought."[26] Sirach alternates *ḥāsēr* with *ṣārak̲,* "need" (8:9; 15:12; etc.; cf. 2 Ch. 2:15). Antonyms include such terms as "possess" (*bā'al* I, *yāraš, nāḥal*), "have enough" (*śāḇa'*), "be sufficient" (*śāpaq* II), and "be plentiful" (*rāḇâ, rāḇāḇ*).

4. *Idioms.* There is little range of grammatical construction in the OT. We find such construct phrases as *ḥᵃsar laḥem,* "lack of bread" (2 S. 3:29), *ḥᵃsar lēḇ* (11 times in Proverbs; 1 occurrence in 11QPsᵃ 154:7, par. *peṯî,* "simple" [cf. Prov. 9:4,16], similar to *nmhry lb,* "aghast," 1QH 2:9), and *ḥᵃsar tᵉḇûnôṯ,* "lack of understanding" (Prov. 28:16). Sirach adds some further idioms: *ḥᵃsar māzôn,* "lack of food" (Sir. 10:27); *ḥᵃsar tîrôš,* "lack of wine" (31:27); *ḥᵃsar 'ōṣmâ* (41:2), *ḥᵃsar kōaḥ,* "powerlessness" (11:12); *ḥᵃsar 'ōseq,* "lack of employment" (38:24); and *ḥᵃsar bînâ,* "lack of understanding," "foolishness" (47:23). In such phrases *ḥᵃsar* can be replaced by *'ên;* cf. Prov. 17:16; Jer. 5:21; Hos. 7:11.

5. *LXX.* The root is translated in a variety of ways by the LXX. Most common are forms of *déomai,* "lack, need" (27 times). Also common are forms of *elattoneín,* etc., "lose, get less" (19 times), and *hystereín,* "be lacking." Occasionally we find *aporeín,* "be at a loss" (Prov. 31:11), or for the piel *sterískein,* "deprive" (Eccl. 4:8). For the hiphil we find *kenón poieín* (Isa. 32:6), and for the noun *ḥōser, ékleipsis* (Dt. 28:48). The Hebrew idiom *ḥᵃsar-lēḇ* is rendered by *akárdios* (Prov. 10:13; cf. Sir. 6:20) or *áphrōn* (Prov. 10:21; 17:18).

II. Use in the OT. The roughly 77 occurrences in the OT are distributed about equally among secular, religious, and theological contexts.

1. *Concrete Usage.* In concrete contexts, the root simply indicates that something or someone is not present. This usage does not represent a fundamental condition; the verb above all can be used to designate the inchoative transition to this condition. This is the case in the P account of the Deluge (Gen. 8:3b,5), where it is not so much the case that the waters are "lacking" as that they "abate" (*ḥsr*), as is clear from the parallel expressions in J (*šûḇ, hālak̲, qll,* "recede" [vv. 3b,8,11] and the antonyms *rāḇâ, gāḇar,* "increase" [7:18]).

A similar diminution is expressed by the verb in the context of the miracle at Zarephath: the supply of meal is not "spent" (*kālâ*) and the oil does not "fail" (*ḥāsēr* with *šemen* as its semantic subject, 1 K. 17:14,16), so that the widow continues to be supplied with her necessary food.[27]

---

[26] *KBL*³, 143.

[27] For a discussion of the polemic against idolatry contained in this passage, see L. Bronner, *The Stories of Elijah and Elisha as Polemics against Baal Worship. POS,* 6 (1968), 83.

Lack implies a want of something necessary, such as bread (*leḥem*), oil (*šemen*), or wine (*yayin, tîrôš*).[28] When these basic foodstuffs are lacking (as in the case of a long siege: Ezk. 4:17; cf. Dt. 28:57), human life itself becomes marginal. Therefore even early Wisdom passages warn against the dangers of laziness and extravagance, which lead to lack of bread (Prov. 12:9; cf. also Sir. 10:27b), whereas tilling the land produces plenty of bread (*śāḇa'*, Prov. 12:11). To be without bread spells certain death; thus David can threaten the house of Joab with this as a curse (2 S. 3:29; cf. Dt. 28:48,57), and equate its effects with a discharge (*zāḇ ûmᵉṣōrā'*), fragility ("he who walks with a cane"), or death by the sword.

Amos (or one of his disciples) takes fame (called euphemistically "cleanness of teeth") as a plague sent by Yahweh intended to evoke repentance and return (→ שׁוב *šûḇ;* Am. 4:6); it has the same warning function as drought (v. 7), harvest failure (v. 9), or plague, war, and disaster (vv. 10f.). Reventlow's interpretation of this passage on the basis of a cursing ritual[29] carries slight conviction. In addition, wine and oil are luxury items, so that their lack can be understood as a diminution of the quality of life and of a high standard of living. For Ecclesiastes it is thus a sign of joy in life[30] to see no lack (*ḥāsēr*) of oil for one's hair, i.e., to use it abundantly (Eccl. 9:8). Sirach asks the hedonistic question of whether life has meaning when there is a lack of wine (Sir. 31:27). Such a lack occasions mourning, since oil and wine were created for the joy (*lᵉgîl*) of mankind.

The description of the dancing Shulammite in Cant. 7:3(2) is obscure: "Your navel is a rounded bowl that never lacks mixed wine."[31] Rudolph and Würthwein consider this statement a bawdy "euphemism for sexual intercourse," but others (e.g., Gerleman) deny that there are any erotic overtones, citing Egyptian reliefs that emphasize the navel. Perhaps the abundance of spiced wine is to be understood after the analogy of Sirach as a parabolic synecdoche for perfection of form, just as in the parallel verse the color of wheat is to be understood as a reference to the Near Eastern ideal of beauty.[32]

It is to the credit of the capable wife and a sign of her industry, vigor, and wisdom that her husband has no lack of "gain" (*šālāl*, Prov. 31:11). The interpretation offered by Thomas,[33] "and wool is not lacking [to her]," is to be rejected because it requires textual emendation.

Lack of strength (*ḥsr kwḥ/'ṣmh*) is the cause of much evil (Sir. 11:12; cf. 41:2). This lack of strength can be due to drunkenness (Sir. 31:30) or overwork (*'āmal*, 31:4). According to Sirach, this dilemma is typical of the human situation. The lazy, the hasty (Prov. 21:5), and the idle talker (Prov. 14:23) come to want, while diligent labor

---

28 Cf. *AuS*, IV, V.

29 H. Reventlow, *Das Amt des Propheten bei Amos. FRLANT,* 80 (1962), 75-90.

30 E. Würthwein, *Die fünf Megilloth. HAT,* XVIII (^{2}1969), 112ff.

31 H. Ringgren, *Sprüche, Prediger, das Hohe Lied, Klagelieder, das Buch Esther. ATD,* XVI (^{2}1967), 284ff.

32 V. Zapletal, *Der Wein in der Bibel. BSt,* 20/1 (1920).

33 D. W. Thomas, "Textual and Philological Notes on Some Passages in the Book of Proverbs," *Wisdom in Israel and in the Ancient Near East. Festschrift H. H. Rowley. SVT,* 3 (1955), 291f.

brings profit. But the one who works his fingers to the bone will perish for lack of strength. In contrast to this common experience, we find the higher wisdom that only lack of (i.e., freedom from) labor (*ḥsr ʻsq*), relief from the tasks of everyday life, constitutes the root of wisdom (*ḥoḵmâ*, Sir. 38:24). Similar statements are made in an Egyptian taunt song mocking manual laborers, the nineteenth-dynasty Instruction of Duauf.[34] In this situation, the sense of "need" conveyed by *ḥāsēr* is turned into its opposite for the sake of irony.

We occasionally find *ḥāsēr* in the context of hospitality.[35] The master of the house considers it of the utmost importance that his guests lack nothing (*'ên maḥsôr kol-dāḇār*); he provides lodging, food, drink, and escort.[36] Conversely, it is disgraceful to refuse hospitality, so that one's guest must be responsible for his own needs (bread, wine, straw, fodder); the disgrace is not lessened if an old man, even a stranger (*gēr*), takes on this obligation (Jgs. 19:9f.). Only the "atrocity of Gibeah" (Jgs. 19:22f.) could exceed such a disgrace. The faithful Israelite felt an obligation of hospitality on account of the hospitality he had received from Yahweh at the time of the exodus: "These forty years Yahweh your God has been with you; you have lacked nothing" (*lô' ḥāsartā dāḇār,* Dt. 2:7[37]). Since it is an insult to refuse hospitality, Pharaoh assures himself that Hadad is not departing because he has lacked anything (1 K. 11:22), especially since the hospitality described here had far surpassed the usual measure, involving the gift of lodging, food, and even land (*'ereṣ*) (v. 18).

For the lack (*ḥāsēr*) of persons, cf. the number of righteous persons necessary to spare a city from God's judgment (Gen. 18:28), as well as the sarcastic question asked by Achish of Gath: "Do I lack madmen, that you have brought me this fellow [David]?" (1 S. 21:16[15]).

Finally, the numerical element appears clearly in the *māšāl* of Eccl. 1:15: "What is crooked cannot be made straight, and what is lacking (*ḥesrôn*) cannot be numbered." Dahood[38] interprets the hapax legomenon *ḥesrôn* as "deficit" in mercantile bookkeeping, following Ehrlich.[39] This interpretation is most unlikely, however, since the parallel *m*e*ʻuwwāṯ,* "what is crooked," prohibits such a reading of the text. It is more likely that we are dealing with a sententious generality stating that what is disordered and lacking in the world is an unalterable element of reality.[40]

2. *Lack as Poverty.* In a large number of occurrences, *ḥāsēr* moves into the semantic field of "poverty," where it appears more or less synonymously—or at least with little apparent semantic contribution of its own—alongside → אביון *'eḇyôn* [*'ebhyôn*], →

---

[34] *ANET*³, 432-34.

[35] Cf. H. Rusche, "Gastfreundschaft im AT, im Spätjudentum und in den Evangelien unter Berücksichtigung ihres Verhältnisses zur Mission," *ZMR*, 41 (1957), 170-76.

[36] St.-B., IV, 565-571; *AuS*, VI (1939), 129-145, esp. 142.

[37] Cf. II.4.

[38] M. Dahood, "The Phoenician Background of Qohelet," *Bibl,* 47 (1966), 264-282, esp. 266.

[39] A. Ehrlich, *Randglossen zur hebräischen Bibel* (repr. Hildesheim, 1968), VI, 58.

[40] Cf. O. Loretz, *Qohelet und der alte Orient* (Freiburg, 1964), 125, and W. Zimmerli, *Prediger, ATD*, XVI, *in loc.*

דל *dal*, → עני *'ānî*, or → רוש *rāš*.[41] Wisdom Literature above all likes to make use of the root in this sense, setting it in opposition to the hiphil of *rāḇâ*, "(cause to) increase" (Prov. 22:16), *môṯār*, "profit" (Prov. 14:23; 21:5), the hiphil of *'āšar*, "be rich" (Prov. 21:17), *hôn*, "wealth" (Prov. 28:22), and *'ōšer*, "wealth," *neḵāsîm*, "possessions," and *kāḇôḏ*, "honor" (Eccl. 6:2). The teachers of wisdom inquire into the causes of "poverty" primarily in order to prevent self-inflicted poverty. This is true especially when the roots *ḥsr*, *rwš*, and *skn* are used.[42] In this case, *ḥsr* designates poverty primarily in the purely socio-economic sense of being without possessions (as the etymology suggests), without any ethical overtones (→ דל *dal*). Among the reasons cited for this kind of poverty are laziness (Prov. 6:10f.; 24:33f.), talkativeness (Prov. 14:23), extravagance and luxury (Prov. 21:17), and careless haste (Prov. 21:5).

The religious perspective can also enter this realm: the supernatural principle of justice sees to it that parsimony (understood as hardheartedness toward those in need) and jealous acquisitiveness fail of their goal (cf. Eccl. 4:8) and ultimately lead to the opposite, impoverished want (*ḥsr*, Prov. 11:24; 28:22). On the other hand, the one who fears God (→ ירא *yārē'*, Ps. 34:10[9]) and is merciful ("he who gives to the poor," *nôṯēn lārāš*, Prov. 28:27) need fear no want (*maḥsôr*). Here, however, we note that *ḥāsēr* poverty (especially outside the context of Wisdom Literature) could sometimes be thought of as undeserved. This is true for the Deuteronomist (Dt. 15:8) in the case of the *'eḇyôn* who has need (*ḥsr*) and thus comes within the protective regulations of the *šemiṭṭâ* ordinance (Dt. 15:1ff.).

Like famine (*ḥasar leḥem*),[43] lack of possessions can be traced directly to Yahweh. Together with hunger, thirst, and nakedness it can be the substance of the curse that will befall Israel in case of disobedience (Dt. 28:48). This *ḥōser-kol* will be so catastrophic that women will devour their newborn children together with the afterbirth (Dt. 28:57).

Poverty and hunger enter into people's souls, so destroying them inwardly that one can say of the *'ānî* that his soul is a *nepeš ḥasērâ*, par. *meḏuḵdāḵ* (Sir. 4:2f.). These psychical and physical (*ḥasar kōaḥ*, "powerless," Sir. 11:12) effects mean that the *'ānî* needs special care. Only a fool would disregard this need, depriving the thirsty of drink (*yaḥsîr*, par. *hārîq*, "leave unsatisfied," Isa. 32:6 [a Wisdom interpolation]; cf. *māna' mattān*, "keep back the gift," Sir. 4:3). It is precisely these effects of *ḥeser* that prevent Qoheleth (subj. uncertain[44]) from freely choosing such poverty and "depriving [himself] of pleasure" (*meḥassēr 'eṯ-napšî miṭṭôḇâ*, Eccl. 4:8; causative habitual piel[45]), above all when there is no heir to inherit the wealth that has been saved. Even someone who "has literally everything" (*'ênennû ḥāsēr lenepšô*, Eccl. 6:2)[46]

---

[41] Cf. T. Donald, "The Semantic Field of Rich and Poor in the Wisdom Literature of Hebrew and Accadian," *OrAnt*, 3 (1964), 27-41.

[42] Cf. A. Kuschke, "Arm und reich im AT mit besonderer Berücksichtigung der nachexilischen Zeit," *ZAW*, 57 (1939), 44, 47.

[43] See above, II.1.

[44] Cf. Loretz.

[45] Cf. Jenni, *Das hebräische Pi'el*, 83.

[46] For a different interpretation, see M. Dahood, "Qoheleth and Northwest Semitic Philology," *Bibl*, 43 (1962), 357f.

he could wish does not have the power to enjoy it, since God as lord of all things can dispose as he likes. Thus in the very apportionment of *ḥāsēr* and *'ōšer* God's unimpeachable righteousness is shown. It is his intent to lead his chosen people to a place where there is no *maḥsôr,* i.e., where they can dwell in security (*šqṭ*) and gain wealth (*yāraš 'eṣer*) (Jgs. 18:7 conj.; the text is a matter of much debate[47]).

Finally, poverty and hunger exhibit yet another social effect, in that they exclude the person affected from society, make him barren (*galmûḏ*), and are thus able to cut him off from his descendants (Job 30:3).

3. *Lack of Understanding in Wisdom Literature*. Lack of understanding, insight, and logic is often cited to account for inexplicable and faulty human conduct. More than 20 times (only in Wisdom Literature), *ḥāsēr* appears in combination with *lēḇ, tᵉḇûâ, bînâ* (→ בין *bîn*), or *ḥoḵmâ* (→ חכם *ḥāḵam* [*chākham*] III.1), in the semantic field of rationality, insight, and intelligence.[48] In this context it refers primarily to an intellectual defect, foolishness (like → כסיל *kᵉsîl,* "stupid," → אויל *'ᵉwîl* [*'ᵉvîl*], "fool," → סכל *sāḵāl,* "foolish," → נבל *nāḇāl,* "fool," and → פתי *peṯî,* "simple"). The fact that the phrase *ḥᵃsar da'aṯ* does not occur (cf. however *yḥsr md',* Sir. 3:13) does not mean that *ḥᵃsar lēḇ* can be defined as a purely intellectual deficiency. In Sir. 35:12 (text disputed), *ḥᵃsar lēḇ* can appear in direct antithesis to *yir'aṯ 'ēl,* "the fear of God," a human characteristic transcending the purely intellectual realm (→ ירא *yārē'*).[49]

The multiplicity of meanings conveyed by → לב *lēḇ*[50] lends complexity to the meaning of *ḥᵃsar lēḇ*. For example, it can mean the lack of a sense of responsibility (Prov. 6:32; 10:13), simple stupidity (Prov. 10:21; 11:12; 24:30, par. *'āṣēl,* "lazy"), foolishness (Prov. 7:7; 9:4,16, par. *peṯî,* "easily led astray," 12:11), and carelessness (Prov. 17:18, in giving a pledge). In such contexts the common rendering "heartless(ness)" is quite misleading, putting far too much stress on the emotional sphere; *ḥᵃsar lēḇ* never means emotional coldness but rather thoughtlessness[51] (Prov. 6:32; 11:12; 12:11; Eccl. 10:3). In Prov. 7:7, *ḥᵃsar lēḇ* means the juvenile thoughtlessness of the innocent youth, much as *ḥsr md'* (Sir. 3:13) refers to senility (cf. Sir. 3:12; Prov. 23:22).

The theological relevance of the phrase *ḥᵃsar lēḇ* appears especially in the passages in Wisdom Literature where *lēḇ*—as in Egyptian Wisdom—refers to the center of anyone who lives his life with conscious purpose, the seat of the will.[52] It is here that the divine word is heard.[53] In this sense, the lack of *lēḇ* can transcend intellectual deficiency and refer to a person's inability to perceive God's binding will. Thus in wise

---

[47] Cf. J. Gray, *Joshua, Judges, Ruth. NCBC* (1967; repr. 1986) *in loc.* and v. 10.

[48] For a discussion of the semantic field, see T. Donald, "The Semantic Field of 'Folly' in Proverbs, Job, Psalms, and Ecclesiastes," *VT,* 13 (1963), 285-292.

[49] Cf. J. Becker, *Gottesfurcht im AT. AnBibl,* 25 (1965); L. Derousseaux, *La crainte de Dieu dans l'AT* (Paris, 1970); H. P. Stähli, "ירא *yr'* fürchten," *THAT,* I, 765-778.

[50] Cf. F. Stolz, "לֵב *lēb* Herz," *THAT,* I, 861-67.

[51] H. W. Wolff, *Anthropology of the OT* (Eng. trans., Philadelphia, 1975), 48.

[52] Stolz, *THAT,* I, 863.

[53] Wolff, *Anthropology of the OT,* 53; cf. Instruction of Ptahhotep 534-563, *ANET*³, 414; Dt. 4:29, etc.; *RÄR,* 297.

men (*'anšê lēḇ*, Job 34:10), heart and tongue stand in harmony.[54] The first thing that happens to someone without *lēḇ* is that he loses control of his tongue (Eccl. 10:3). His sense of the right way vanishes, and he loses his inward orientation (Prov. 15:21). He thus lacks stability and becomes divorced from ethics and morality. In addition to "lack of knowledge" he now suffers from "lack of conscience." The fool falls victim to adultery (Prov. 6:32), self-righteous hubris (Sir. 16:23), and finally death (Prov. 10:21). It is the sense of these consequences that is lost when *lēḇ* is lacking.[55] This background gives us a deeper insight into what is meant when people say to the Pharaoh: "May your heart be with you and not leave you!"[56]

Thus the range of meanings of *ḥ^{a}sar lēḇ* extends from the innocent mental incapacity of youth or old age through intellectual stupidity and irresponsibility to unprincipled amorality. Whoever falls victim to this lack of conscience is no longer able to heed the instruction of wisdom and is irretrievably lost.

The phrase *ḥ^{a}sar t^{e}ḇûnâ* also designates a moral deficiency: the ruler so characterized (*nāgîḏ*) becomes an oppressor (Prov. 28:16). The baneful influence of Rehoboam on his people is also traced to *ḥ^{a}sar bînâ* (Sir. 47:23). Finally, lack of knowledge (*da'aṯ*) makes all wisdom (*ḥoḵmâ*) impossible (Sir. 3:25). When *nepeš* is wanting, mankind loses hope (Sir. 14:2?).

4. *Lack and Abundance in Correlation with Obedience and Sin.* Lack in its various forms is also accommodated to the schema of reward and punishment, in that a correspondence is worked out between abundance and obedience on the one hand, lack and sin on the other. Most often we find the idea that lack follows as a necessary consequence of sin or is brought about by Yahweh. In the proverbial wisdom of ancient Israel, the diligent laborer is rich, whereas the lazy person suffers want (Prov. 14:23; 21:17). Other causes of lack (hunger and poverty) can include greed (Prov. 11:24), unconsidered hastiness (Prov. 21:5; 28:22), and wickedness (*rš'*, Prov. 13:25: cf. 10:3).

Deuteronomic parenesis pictures this correspondence, brought about by Yahweh, in extreme terms: failure to obey the Torah will result in hunger, thirst, nakedness, subjugation, and want of all things (Dt. 28:48), to the point that under wartime conditions women will envy each their afterbirth (Dt. 28:57).[57] In Ezekiel's vision of the siege of Jerusalem, the people lack bread and water, and waste away under their punishment (Ezk. 4:17; vv. 12-15 [secondary] speak of unclean bread). Jeremiah ascribes *ḥ^{a}sar kōl* to disobedience toward Yahweh expressed in idolatry, but the people in the Egyptian diaspora find its cause in neglect of the cult of Anahita, the queen of heaven (Jer. 44:18).

On the other hand, there are certain expressions of faith that help protect against lack. For example, the fear of Yahweh (*yārē'*, Ps. 34:10[9]) and the act of seeking

---

[54] Ptahhotep 526-532; cf. H. H. Schmid, *Wesen und Geschichte der Weisheit. BZAW,* 101 (1966), 205.

[55] F. H. von Meyenfeldt, *Het Haart (LEB, LEBAB) in het OT* (Leiden, 1950), 164.

[56] *Urk.*, IV, 117.

[57] See above, II.2.

him (*dāraš*, v. 11[10]) count as certain means of avoiding want. This idea undoubtedly derives from Wisdom (cf. Prov. 28:27),[58] where we find the principle that social conduct such as generosity to the poor will protect the giver against want.

The keeping of the torah of Yahweh, however, is not always a guarantee in itself of escaping want. Freedom from want and deprivation is ultimately the gift of God. A sense of this dependence dominates the faith of the Israelites from the time of the exodus on. It is stated 7 times, 4 of which use *ḥāsēr.* God's help and care protect Israel from any lack during its wanderings, so that each Israelite is able to gather a sufficient quantity of manna (Ex. 16:18). For forty years, Yahweh's blessing (*brk*) showed itself in his being with (*'im*) and knowing (*yāḏa'*) his people, so that they lacked nothing (Dt. 2:7 [secondary?]);[59] cf. Neh. 9:21f., where *ḥāsēr* is understood primarily as lack of food and drink. The negation of all lack (par. *miskēnuṯ,* "scarcity," Dt. 8:9) is a characteristic of the promised land.[60] This knowledge, based on the events of the exodus and occupation, is concentrated in the confession of Ps. 23:1: "Yahweh is my shepherd, I shall not want." In this hymn of confidence—probably cultic—the psalmist takes the image of the shepherd (→ ראה *rō'eh*) from an ancient tradition that may go back to the religion of the patriarchs,[61] where it is linked with the elements of promise and assistance (being "with," *'im;* cf. Ps. 23:4 and Gen. 49:24 [J]; 48:15 [E]). Thus the epithet itself conveys the motif of trust and confidence. The rare metaphor of Yahweh as the good shepherd (cf. Ps. 28:9; 80:2[1]) is elaborated extensively in the consolation oracles of the exilic prophets (Isa. 40:10f.; Jer. 23:3; Ezk. 34:11f.; Mic. 4:6-8). The image of the shepherd's occupation (e.g., Ezk. 34:1-4) fills the phrase *lō' 'eḥsar,* "I shall not want," with a richness of meaning, the more so because the metaphor is enhanced by being applied to Yahweh. The statement *lō' 'eḥsar* means a security based on God's promise, that enjoys his guidance, protection, care, deliverance, and presence.[62]

The negation of want as a consequence of God's protective presence appears as an element in the exilic prophecy of consolation, as Isa. 51:14 shows: the prisoner is freed, he will live and have no lack of bread. The literature of the exile is nevertheless remarkably restrained in its use of the term *ḥāsēr,* a restraint that comes from the palpable misery, both material and spiritual, of this period. Is there perhaps too much of the coloring of Wisdom in our term? In 1QH 15:16, an absence of want is mentioned alongside eternal salvation and perpetual peace as characterizing the age of salvation.[63]

---

58 H.-J. Kraus, *Psalmen. BK,* XV/1 (⁵1978), 271.

59 J. G. Plöger, *Literarkritische, formgeschichtliche und stilkritische Untersuchungen zum Deuteronomium. BBB,* 26 (1967), 54.

60 G. Seitz, *Redaktionsgeschichtliche Studien zum Deuteronomium. BWANT,* 93[5/13] (1971), 304.

61 Cf. V. Maag, "Der Hirte Israels: Eine Skizze von Wesen und Bedeutung der Väterreligion," *SchThU,* 28 (1958), 2-28.

62 W. E. Gössmann, "Der Wandel des Gottesbildes in den Übersetzungen des 23. Psalms," *MThZ,* 5 (1954), 276-288.

63 Cf. H. J. Kandler, "Die Bedeutung der Armut im Schrifttum von Chirbet Qumran," *Jud,* 13 (1957), 193-209, esp. 201f.

5. *Piel as an Anthropological Term.* Ps. 8:6(5), the key passage for the doctrine of mankind as the image of God,[64] uses the piel of *ḥāsēr* as an anthropological term. Unfortunately, the other occurrences of the piel cannot be used to define the meaning more precisely, since the piel of *ḥāsēr* is itself ambiguous.[65] The definition of human nature in Ps. 8:5f.(4f.) must be seen in combination with Job 7:17; 15:14f.; and Ps. 144:3f., all of which (cf. Gen. 1:26f.) take as their point of departure the question of human nature (*mâ-'ᵉnôš*).[66]

In Ps. 8 we are probably dealing with a hymn praising God in his majesty for condescending to mankind.[67] Its cultic function is unclear.[68] The interpretations of vv. 5f.(4f.) have been a matter of debate since the LXX and Vulg., which interpret *'ᵉlōhîm* as angels and find in the hymn a mythologizing likening of the human world to the angelic world of the heavenly court.[69] But this interpretation does not yield a precise meaning for the statement *wattᵉḥassᵉrēhû mᵉ'aṭ mē'ᵉlōhîm,* since the hierarchy of the heavenly court is itself not clearly defined. If, however, we interpret *'ᵉlōhîm* as "God,"[70] we are dealing here in the *ḥsr* statement with a more explicit statement of mankind's hierarchical position relative to God; v. 5(4) is a statement about human nature.[71] In comparison with the superiority of God, *ḥsr m'ṭ* describes human nature as lower; mankind is described as "almost divine."[72] The following verses seek to describe not only the nature but also the function of mankind, using royal terminology. A primary theme of our Psalm is mankind's role as God's mandatory in the created world,[73] which they govern[74] at God's behest.[75] Their special place is defined by God's having made them only a little lower than God himself, while still prohibiting them from "being as God." Thus mankind's nearness to God both distinguishes them from the rest of creation while still preventing their identification with God. The slight distance expressed by *ḥsr m'ṭ* prohibits Israel from identifying the king with God, after the manner

---

64 K. L. Schmidt.

65 Jenni, *Das hebräische Pi'el,* 73, 104.

66 See esp. W. Zimmerli, "Was ist der Mensch?" *Göttinger Universitätsreden,* 44 (1964) = his *Studien zur Alttestamentlichen Theologie und Prophetie. Gesammelte Aufsätze,* 2. *ThB,* 51 (1974), 311-324; and M. Hengel, " 'Was ist der Mensch?' " in *Probleme biblischer Theologie. Festschrift G. von Rad* (Munich, 1971), 116-135. See also F. Maas, "אָדָם *'āḏām* ['ādhām]," *TDOT,* I, 82; T. N. D. Mettinger, "Abbild oder Urbild? 'Imago Dei' in traditionsgeschichtlicher Sicht," *ZAW,* 86 (1974), 403-424; L. Scheffczyk, ed., *Der Mensch als Bild Gottes. WdF,* 124 (1969); K. Gouders, "Gottes Schöpfung und der Auftrag des Menschen," *BiLe,* 14 (1973), 164-180.

67 K. L. Schmidt in *Der Mensch als Bild Gottes,* ed. Scheffczyk, 39.

68 Kraus, *BK,* XV/1, 66.

69 Gross, Kraus, Jenni, Zimmerli, Hengel.

70 Cf. Jerome: *paulo minus a Deo.*

71 Cf. G. von Rad, *OT Theol.,* I (Eng. trans., New York, 1962), 145: "created in the form of Elohim"; J. A. Soggin, "Zum achten Psalm," *ASTI,* 8 (1970-71), 106: "he lacks only a little of being divine"; similar interpretations in Wolff, *Anthropology of the OT,* 161, and Buber.

72 J. Ridderbos, *De Psalmen. COT* (1955), 74.

73 Caspari, von Rad, Horst.

74 Wolff.

75 Zimmerli.

of the rest of the ancient Near East. At the same time, it shows that mankind is immediately near to God. The royal tradition in the background of Ps. 8 is adopted by the NT and applied to the exalted Christ, the eschatological king (He. 2:6-9; cf. 1 Cor. 15:27).[76]

Fabry

[76] Cf. Gouders, *BiLe*, 14 (1973), 179.

חָפַז *ḥāpaz;* חִפָּזוֹן *ḥippāzôn*

Contents: 1. Root, Meaning; 2. Synonyms, LXX; 3. Use in the OT; 4. *ḥippāzôn*.

1. *Root, Meaning*. The root *ḥpz* (cf. Arab. *ḥafaza,* "spur on, agitate") serves in general as a term for panic and hasty flight. The two aspects cannot be separated, since someone in a state of panic longs to flee, and someone who is fleeing is more or less panic-stricken. All of the OT occurrences include both aspects; but the qal emphasizes panic, qal emphasizes panic, while the niphal emphasizes flight. The verb occurs 6 times in the qal, 3 times in the niphal. The noun *ḥippāzôn* occurs 3 times.

2. *Synonyms, LXX*. The meaning "be afraid" is shared by *ḥpz, rkk, yārē'*, and *'āraṣ*. Accordingly, we find all four words used more or less synonymously in Dt. 20:3 and 1QM 10:4. In 1QM 15:8 we also find *ḥtt* as a parallel. The niphal of *ḥpz* appears in Ps. 48:6(Eng. v. 5) with *tmh* and *bhl,* in Ps. 104:7 with *nûs*.

The LXX offers various translations: for the qal, we find *aisthánomai* (only in Job 40:23 for *ḥpz;*[1] Symmachus uses *kataplḗsēsthai), ékstasis, thambéomai, speúdō,* and *phobéomai;* for the niphal, *diliáō, saleúomai,* and *skepázomai*. For *ḥippāzôn* we find *spoudḗ* and *tarachḗ,* "confusion."

3. *Use in the OT.* Concretely, *ḥāpaz* is used in a comment interpolated into the story of the murder of Ishbosheth: when Mephibosheth was a child, his nurse fled with him, and because the flight was hasty (*b*[e]*ḥopzāh lānûs*) she dropped the child and he became lame (2 S. 4:4). Equally concrete is 2 K. 7:15: the Syrians fled so hastily from the siege of Samaria that they discarded their garments and weapons along the way. The *kethibh* here has *b*[e]*hēḥāp*[e]*zām,* the *qere, b*[e]*ḥopzām*—a difference in nuance but not in basic meaning. David was almost caught when he fled from Saul and Saul's men (*neḥpaz lāleḵeṯ min*), but the Philistine attack interrupted the chase (1 S. 23:26). Ps. 48:6f.(5f.) describes the panic and hasty flight of Yahweh's enemies when

[1] Cf. J. F. Schleusner, *Novus thesaurus philologico-criticus* (London, [2]1829); *LexHebAram*.

they saw Mt. Zion (cf., for example, 1 S. 14:15; Ps. 46:7ff.[6ff.]; 114:1ff.; Isa. 17:12f.; 29:5f.; 33:3).

The Israelites are called on not to fear their enemies in battle, because God fights on their side to give them victory (Dt. 20:3; the collocation of synonyms is discussed in 1 above; cf. 1QM 10:4; 15:8). Whoever thinks he has been deserted by God (Ps. 31:23[22]) or his fellows (Ps. 116:11) is overcome with consternation. The fragmentary text of 1QH 12:19 probably says much the same. In Job 40:23, *ḥpz* stands in contrast to *bāṭaḥ*. Behemoth does not need to flee in panic from the flood: he is mighty enough to stand calmly in the river.

The niphal of *ḥpz* stands in parallel with *nûs:* at Yahweh's rebuke, the personified (but not deified) waters of the abyss fled to their appointed place (Ps. 104:7).

4. *ḥippāzôn*. In all 3 of its occurrences, the noun *ḥippāzôn* alludes to the exodus from Egypt. The eating of unleavened bread in haste at the Passover is connected with the hasty flight out of Egypt (Dt. 16:3), when the people took their dough with them in their kneading bowls before it had been leavened (Ex. 12:34). Unleavened bread is baked quickly (Gen. 19:3). According to P, the Passover lamb is to be eaten in haste with unleavened bread and bitter herbs (Ex. 12:11). Those who eat are to stand ready to depart, their loins girded, their sandals on their feet, and their staff in their hands. This is the Passover of Yahweh (*pesaḥ l^eYHWH*).[2] The root *psḥ* is used for leaping movements (cf. 1 K. 18:21,26); such movements were probably engaged in during the Passover celebration to symbolize hasty flight. (Keel[3] thinks the leaping movements represent the wild jumping of demons; they would then serve an apotropaic purpose as part of the ritual.) Passover is understood as a ritual (*zikkārôn*, → זכר *zāḵar,* Ex. 12:14).

The second exodus, from Babylon, will be different. Those who return will not have to depart in haste (*b^eḥippāzôn*) or in flight (*bimnûsâ*), but can go out (*yāṣā'*, *hālaḵ*) in an orderly fashion, because God himself will go before them as leader and behind them as rear guard (Isa. 52:12), just as he did after the exodus from Egypt when the Israelites were being pursued (cf. Ex. 13:21f.; 14:19f.; Nu. 10:33f.; Isa. 58:8). In this second exodus there is no need to fear pursuit, because Babylon has ceased to be (Isa. 47).

André

---

[2] On the literary-critical problems of Ex. 12, see P. Laaf, *Die Pascha-Feier Israels. BBB*, 36 (1970), 10-18, 34, 135ff.; on the ritual, see also H. Haag, "Paque," *DBS*, VI, 1120-1149.

[3] O. Keel, "Erwägungen zum Sitz im Leben des vormosaischen Pascha und zur Etymologie von פֶּסַח," *ZAW*, 84 (1972), 414-434, esp. 433.

חָפֵץ *ḥāpēṣ;* חֵפֶץ *ḥēpeṣ*

Contents: I. 1. Etymology and Extrabiblical Occurrences; 2. Meaning; 3. Distribution; 4. LXX. II. Secular Use: 1. *ḥāpēṣ;* 2. *ḥāpēṣ* + Infinitive; 3. *ḥēpeṣ*. III. Theological Use: 1. Sacrificial Theology and Polemic; 2. Polemic against Collective Casuistry; 3. God's Pleasure and Displeasure; 4. God's Will; 5. Metaphors and Names. IV. Qumran.

I. 1. *Etymology and Extrabiblical Occurrences*. The etymology of the root *ḥpṣ* is obscure, since all its occurrences are relatively late and are limited to the realm of West Semitic (and possibly South Semitic). Our root must be distinguished from the homonymous *ḥpṣ* II, "stretch out" (Job 40:17; cf. Arab. *ḫafaḍa,* "make low,"[1] and possibly Akk. *ḫabāṣu,* "strike down [?]," "crush").[2] Outside the Hebrew OT, we find *ḥpṣ* I in Middle Hebrew and Talmudic Aramaic as the noun *ḥēpēṣ,* "object of value," *ḥ*ª*pîṣâ,* "desire," and *ḥepṣā'*, "object of value,"[3] as well as Syr. *ḥ*ᵉ*faṭ,* "be pleased, desire," ethpael "be desired,"[4] and the Phoenician-Punic name *ḥpṣb'l,* "pleasure of Ba'al,"[5] "Ba'al is pleased."[6]

The reading *mḥpṣ,* "treasures," in a Phoenician graffito from the temple of Osiris at Abydos[7] has not been confirmed. Also uncertain is the sole Punic occurrence.[8]

In the Old Aramaic Sefire stele (III.8), *ikl ḥpsy* appears in synthetic parallelism with *kl zy rḥm;* both expressions refer to the "customary exchange of gifts between potentates of antiquity"[9] and the consequent establishment of friendly relations, now to be defined in legal terms by a treaty guaranteeing loyalty and solidarity. The verbs *rḥm* and *ḥpṣ* designate the corresponding "receiving" and "giving" of good will, the latter being more precisely defined as "pleasure." The mutual good will is manifested po-

---

ḥāpēṣ. G. Gerleman, "חפץ *ḥpṣ* Gefallen haben," *THAT,* I, 623-26; H.-J. Hermisson, *Sprache und Ritus im altisraelitischen Kult. WMANT,* 19 (1965); G. Quell, "'ἀγαπάω A. Love in the OT," *TDNT,* I, 21-35; R. Rendtorff, "Priesterliche Kulttheologie und prophetische Kultpolemik," *ThLZ,* 81 (1956), 339-342; *idem, Die Gesetze in der Priesterschrift. FRLANT,* N.S. 44[62] (²1963); *idem, Studien zur Geschichte des Opfers im alten Israel. WMANT,* 24 (1967); H. Schlier, "αἱρέομαι," *TDNT,* I, 180-85; G. Schrenk, "θέλω, θέλημα," *TDNT,* III, 44-54; G. Segalla, "La volontà di Dio nei LXX in rapporto al TM: θέλημα, *rāṣôn, ḥēfeṣ,*" *RivBibl,* 13 (1965), 121-143; W. E. Staples, "The Meaning of *ḥēpeṣ* in Ecclesiastes," *JNES,* 24 (1965), 110-12; C. Wiéner, *Recherches sur l'amour pour Dieu dans l'AT* (Paris, 1957); E. Würthwein, "Amos 5, 21-27," *ThLZ,* 72 (1947), 143-152 = his *Wort und Existenz* (Göttingen, 1970), 55-67.

1 *KBL*³, 326.

2 *AHw,* I, 303.

3 *WTM,* II, 94f.

4 *LexSyr*², 249f.

5 Cooke.

6 Lane; cf. F. L. Benz, *Personal Names in the Phoenician and Punic Inscriptions. Studia Pohl,* 8 (1972), 316.

7 *LidzEph,* II, 170.

8 Poenulus 1142: *epsi,* "ma joie??"; *DISO,* 94.

9 *KAI,* II, 268.

litically in an exchange of ambassadors. Fitzmyer[10] interprets the text differently (contra Starcky, Dupont-Sommer, and *KAI*), understanding *ḥpṣ* as "business."

In Arabic especially the use of *ḥafiẓa*, "protect, observe," *ḥifẓ*, "preservation," is widespread.[11] As a substantive, it can make a thing or situation "noteworthy," and finally becomes a term meaning "thing, situation, transaction."[12] We also find *ḥpṣ*, "protect," in a Nabatean inscription[13] and in a few South Arabic contexts.[14] This etymological connection casts doubt on the distinction made by *DISO* between *ḥpṣ* I, "protect," "thing, transaction," and *ḥpṣ* II, "please."

It is likewise inappropriate to cite the OSA name *ḥfẓ*,[15] for this name (which means "hyena"[16]) clearly derives from a different root (Arab. *ḥfḍ*). It is also possible that *ḥpṣ* is connected with Akk. *ḫabāṣu* I, "be abundant," occasionally "be joyful" (par. *râšu*, "rejoice").[17]

In Hebrew, the root appears as an element in a personal name only in *ḥepṣî-ḇāh*, the mother of Hezekiah (2 K. 21:1); it means "I have pleasure in her."[18]

2. *Meaning*. The root *ḥpṣ* appears in Hebrew as a verb (only in the qal) and in nominal forms derived from the verb: the participle of verbal adj. *ḥāpēṣ*, and the verbal abstract noun *ḥēpeṣ*. The basic etymological meaning of the root cannot be defined precisely even with the help of its extrabiblical occurrences, since it exhibits—especially in South Semitic—heterogeneous semantic elements. In the south, the element of "protection" has crystallized out of the range of meanings (cf. also Ps. 37:23); in Northwest Semitic, emotional overtones predominate: "protect" develops into an intensive "care for," a joyous, affirmative "desire," and finally "have pleasure in." As a substantive, this yields "pleasure" and the "treasure" in which one has pleasure. The emotionally neutral meaning "circumstance, transaction" has also been preserved.[19]

3. *Distribution*. The verb occurs 73 times in the OT.[20] It is especially common in Isaiah (12 times), the Deuteronomistic history (10 times), and Esther (7 times), as well as the Psalms (18 times) and Wisdom Literature (10 times). It appears scarcely at all in the Pentateuch (twice) and the Chronicler's history (once). The verbal adj.

---

10 J. A. Fitzmyer, *The Aramaic Inscriptions of Sefire*. *BietOr*, 19 (1967), 97, 112.

11 Wehr, 188f.

12 Cf. L. Kopf, "Arabische Etymologien und Parallelen zum Bibelwörterbuch," *VT*, 8 (1958), 173 = his *Studies in Arabic and Hebrew Lexicography* (Jerusalem, 1976), 145; M. Wagner, *Die lexikalischen und grammatikalischen Aramaismen im alttestamentlichen Hebräisch*. *BZAW*, 96 (1966), 58; and Eccl. 3:1,17; 5:7(Eng. v. 8); 8:6; Isa. 58:13.

13 Cf. A. J. Jaussen and R. Savignac, *Mission archéologique en Arabie (Mars-Mai 1907)* (Paris, 1909-1922), no. 33,4.

14 *RÉS* 2873, 1; 3310 B, 1; ContiRossini, 150b.

15 *KBL*³, 326.

16 *RyNP*, I, 97; II, 62.

17 *AHw*, I, 303.

18 *KBL*³, 327; cf. *IPN*, 223.

19 Cf. Wagner, *Aramaismen*, 58.

20 Lisowski.

ḥāp̄ēṣ appears 12 times,[21] of which 12 occurrences are in the Psalms. The noun *ḥēp̄eṣ* occurs 38 times (8 in the Deuteronomistic history, 9 in Isaiah, only 3 in the Psalms). Sirach uses the verb and noun 7 times each.[22]

In the Dead Sea scrolls, the verb appears 7 times,[23] the noun 15 times.[24]

The verb *ḥāp̄ēṣ* designates an action that occurs frequently in a great variety of contexts. It may have as its subject Yahweh (35 times), the king (8 times), David specifically (3 times), Solomon, or Ahasuerus. Other subjects include Israel, the sons of Israel, and the nations, as well as an occasional individual, specified or not. Once by synecdoche we find *nep̄eš* for an individual (Isa. 66:3).

Both verb and noun can have a variety of objects. Personal objects of affection (a young girl, a woman, David, the saints, the *'eḇeḏ*, Israel, Cyrus, Zion, the people, priests, God, etc.) are invariably introduced by *bᵉ*. Impersonal objects are introduced by *lᵉ* or constructed absolutely. They may include possessions (gold, vineyards, bride-price, houses, offerings), abstractions (long life, help, deliverance, insight, peace, loyalty, blessing, honor, words—but also sickness, misfortune, and death), or actions (marrying, choosing, dissolving, doing what is good and pleasing before God, being just, giving alms—but also inflicting sickness and killing). Stereotyped phrases include *diḇrê-ḥēp̄eṣ* (Eccl. 12:10), *'aḇnê-ḥēp̄eṣ* (Isa. 54:12; 1QM 5:6; etc.), and *'āśâ ḥēp̄eṣ* (1 K. 5:22f.[Eng. vv. 8f.]; CD 10:20; etc.); such combinations are hard to determine.

4. *LXX*. The rendering of the LXX is as complex as the nature of the word group would lead us to expect. The verb and adjective are most frequently represented by forms of *thélein*/*ethélein* (49 times, esp. in the Psalms; elsewhere *thélein* represents *'bh*), especially when God is the subject of *ḥāp̄ēṣ*. This translation stresses above all the absolute certainty, sovereign self-assurance, and efficacy of the act; it refers to a deliberate and efficacious act of will.[25] The translation *boúlesthai* (24 times) appears primarily in negations, where it means a deliberate wish that something not take place. Five times *eudokeín* represents *ḥāp̄ēṣ;* elsewhere it usually stands for *rāṣâ*. The nuance of preference and choice is represented by the LXX through *haireín* and *hairetízein* (once each). Only twice does the LXX use *agapán* (Est. 6:9; Ps. 51:6), which elsewhere represents *'āhaḇ*, *rāḥam*, and *rāṣâ*), stressing especially the emotional element. The same verbs often paraphrase the noun *ḥēp̄eṣ*. The most frequent noun is *thélēma* (19 times); *prágma* is used 4 times, all in Ecclesiastes. The technical cultic term *rāṣôn* is also represented by *thélēma*. This translation appears "to place more stress on the element of will and less on that of love and affection."[26] An echo of erotic overtones may still be heard in the rendering of the personal name *ḥep̄ṣî-bāh* as

---

21 Mandelkern includes Nu. 14:8 and Mal. 2:17 as well.

22 D. Barthélemy and O. Rickenbacher, *Konkordanz zum hebräischen Sirach* (Göttingen, 1973), 132f.

23 K. G. Kuhn, *Konkordanz zu den Qumrantexten* (Göttingen, 1960), 75; plus two instances from Murrabba'āt letters 30:23 and 44:6; P. Benoit, J. T. Milik, and R. de Vaux, *Les grottes de Murabb'ât. DJD*, II (1961).

24 In addition to Kuhn, 3Q14 7:1; 4Q179 1 II 10.

25 Cf. Schrenk, 47.

26 *Ibid.*, 53f.

thélēma emón (Isa. 62:4). In Isa. 54:12, the LXX (*eklégesthai*) takes *ḥēpeṣ* as signifying choice or election (cf. also Ps. Sol. 9:4).

II. Secular Use.

1. *ḥāpēṣ*. The verb *ḥāpēṣ* appears some 40 times in secular contexts, although it is undeniable that many of these instances come close to being theological. It is noteworthy that *ḥāpēṣ* never refers to the desire for a secular object. Only in Isa. 13:17 do we read that during military operations the Medes ruthlessly reject all attempts to bribe them: they have no regard for (*lō' yaḥšōḇû*) silver and do not delight in gold (*zāhāḇ lō' yaḥpᵉṣû-ḇô*), i.e., they let nothing stand in the way of their military endeavors. The context here shows clearly that *ḥāpēṣ* cannot mean the mere desire for gold; the negation indicates the rejection of attempted bribery and implies superior moral and ethical qualifications.

More generally, *ḥāpēṣ* refers to actions and situations. This category includes the syntactic construction *ḥāpēṣ* + *lᵉ* + infinitive.[27] In the negotiations between Ahab and Naboth concerning the latter's vineyard, *ḥāpēṣ* designates a higher level of agreement ("you prefer") than *ṭôḇ bᵉʻêneyḵā* ("it seems good to you") with respect to the purchase or exchange (1 K. 21:2,6; cf. similarly *bāḥar,* "desire" > "prefer," Prov. 8:11).

In the realm of friendship and eroticism, *ḥāpēṣ* plays an important role. This is already suggested by the list of synonyms, which contains words like *'āhaḇ*, *ḥāšaq*, and *dāḇaq*. Such affection can spring up between males, giving rise to a variety of actions and reactions. We read in 1 S. 18:22 that Saul has delight in David (*ḥāpēṣ bᵉ*), who is also loved (*'ᵃhēḇûḵā*) at court. This affection pleases David (*yāšar bᵉʻênê*), and he agrees to become Saul's son-in-law (v. 26). Together with *'āhaḇ*, *ḥāpēṣ* stands here on the fringes of eroticism and is a term for friendly affection. Jonathan delighted much in David (*ḥāpēṣ mᵉʻōḏ*, 1 S. 19:1, par. 20:17: "he loved him as he loved his own soul," *'ahᵃḇaṯ napšô 'ᵃhēḇô*); this love finds expression in Jonathan's warning him, getting information for him, and interceding for him. The erotic connotation can be totally forgotten when *ḥāpēṣ* describes the friendship between two men as an alliance of convenience, as in 2 S. 20:17, where the same idea is expressed in the parallel half verse by the dative of possession.

In the sexual realm of love between man and woman, *ḥāpēṣ* can mean simply "delight in," but it can also designate a specific degree of affection in the hierarchy of terms defining such relationships. In Gen. 34:19, for instance, Hamor's son Shechem "had delight in" (*ḥāpēṣ bᵉ*) Jacob's daughter Dinah. This statement is clearly a summary of *dāḇaq,* "be drawn to," *'āhaḇ,* "love," and *dibber ʻal-lēḇ,* "speak tenderly to" (v. 3), and *ḥāšaq,* "long for" (v. 8). In Dt. 21:14, too, *ḥāpēṣ* is a summary term for the desire to marry a slave who has been taken as a concubine. This regulation defines the rights of such a prisoner of war who has been desired (*ḥāšaq*) and taken to wife (*laqaḥ lᵉ'iššâ*) by an Israelite (v. 11). Now when her husband no longer has

---

27 See II.2 below.

delight in her (*lō' ḥāpēṣ bāh,* v. 14), i.e., dislikes her (*śānē'*, v. 15) and dismisses her (*šillaḥ,* v. 14), she cannot lose her social status and be resold as a slave.

The development of mutual attraction as it grows between lovers can be traced in Est. 2. The woman is found pleasing (*tîṭāḇ be'ênê,* vv. 2,9) and wins favor (*tiśśā' ḥeseḏ,* v. 9), since she is attractive (*tîṭaḇ hanna'ᵃrâ*). Finally she finds personal favor (*tiśśā'-ḥēn*) and is loved (*'āhaḇ,* v. 17). According to Est. 2:14, a woman belonging to Ahasuerus' harem could not return to the king after the first night unless the king delighted in her (*kî 'im-ḥāpēṣ bāh*), delight in the sense of sexual "desire."

Still disputed is the interpretation of the adjuration in Cant. 2:7; 3:5; 8:4. The love (*hā'ahᵃḇâ*) of the lovers is not to be stirred or awakened "until it please [them] (*'ad-šetteḥpaṣ*)." Here *ḥāpēṣ* is used absolutely, probably in the sense of "have pleasure" (Rudolf:[28] "until even they have had enough"). The rendering of Würthwein,[29] "until it pleases them to leave the bridal chamber," misses the sense of *ḥāpēṣ*. Haller[30] takes the opposite approach: the lovers should not be disturbed in their pleasure until they have reached fulfillment. This interpretation also misses the mark. What is probably meant is that the lovers should be left alone with their love, and not be subjected to external influences.

We find a totally different problem when the king is the subject of *ḥāpēṣ*. In all such instances, the verb can become a term for the royal power and authority of the king, which, when exercised for the king's own pleasure or without check, can come into collision with the power of Yahweh, the universal king. David, for example, carries out his desire to have a national census in spite of all objections (2 S. 24:2f.), thus drawing the anger of Yahweh upon himself. The king should serve God with a whole heart (*lēḇ šālēm*) and a willing mind (*nepeš ḥᵃpēṣâ*) (1 Ch. 28:9); but the fundamental possibility of royal caprice impels Qoheleth later to warn against uncritical obedience to the king, for in his *dāḇār* is power, and he does whatever he pleases (*kol-'ᵃšer yaḥpōṣ ya'ᵃśeh,* Eccl. 8:3). This statement could be a deliberate reinterpretation of the almost identical ancient maxim in Prov. 21:1, according to which "the king's heart is a stream of water in the hand of Yahweh; he turns it wherever he will"—in other words, every expression of the king's power is grounded in the will of Yahweh.

The actual course of history soon demonstrated that this Wisdom maxim was an unrealistic ideal, as witness the particularly unsavory example of Jeroboam. Despite the threat uttered at Bethel by the "man of God from Judah" against the altar and sanctuary of Bethel, and despite the threat of death as punishment, Jeroboam did not turn from his evil way. Instead, he showed his capricious arrogance by filling the hand (→ מלא *mallē'*) of anyone who so desired (*heḥāpēṣ*), thus making him a priest without regard for his genealogy (1 K. 13:33). The royal power of appointment appears in the book of Esther reduced to a formula: *'îš 'ᵃšer hammeleḵ ḥāpēṣ bîqārô,* "the man whom the king delights to honor" (Est. 6:6f.,9 [twice],11). Here *ḥāpēṣ* has the meaning of an especially pressing wish or interest on behalf of Mordecai, who, having prevented an attempted assassination of the king, is now to receive honor and dignity

---

28 W. Rudolph, *Das Hohelied. KAT,* XVII/1-3 (1962), 131.

29 *Die fünf Megilloth. HAT,* XVIII (²1969), 44.

30 *Die fünf Megilloth. HAT,* XVIII (1940), 29.

(*y^eqār ûg^eḏûlâ*, 6:3), although Haman had calculated that this reward would be his (6:6).

In the Psalms especially *ḥāpēṣ* means "desire," "strive after" higher nonmaterialistic values. In Ps. 34, an individual thanksgiving with clear formal features of didactic poetry, the Wisdom teacher asks (v. 13[12]), "What man is there who desires life (*heḥāpēṣ ḥayyîm*), and covets many days (*'ōhēḇ yāmîm*), that he may enjoy good?" Faced with the complex problems of life, the psalmist finds his answer in the causal nexus of action and reward. The natural human longing for happiness is satisfied by God when people seek him (v. 11[10]) and fear him (v. 12[11]). Contrariwise, it is in the nature of enemies that they seek to snatch away life (*biqqēš nep̱eš*) and destroy it (*sāpâ*). These are the *ḥ^apēṣê rā'â*, "those who desire the hurt" of the psalmist (Ps. 40:15[14]; 70:3[2]). Similarly in a lament (Ps. 35) the sufferer prays, "Let not rejoice over me who are wrongfully my foes . . ." (v. 19), but rather all "those who desire my vindication" (*ḥ^apeṣê ṣiḏqî*, v. 27), i.e., the restoration of the proper relationship between the worshipper and Yahweh.[31] In Ps. 109:17, blessing (*b^erāḵâ*) is the object of *ḥāpēṣ*. The accused is said to have pursued the poor and needy with a curse.[32] His foes now seek to invoke the conduct/reward nexus against him by means of a curse: "He loved (*'āhaḇ*) to curse; let curses come on him! He did not like blessing (*lō'-ḥāpēṣ*); may it be far from him!" According to Sir. 15:16f., God has left the choice of fire and water, death and life, to human decision: "Reach out your hand toward what you desire (*taḥpôṣ*)" (v. 16b). Here *ḥāpēṣ* means "like, desire, seek after."

Human pleasure and desire can and should also have God's saving gifts as their object. Mankind can recognize God in his great works (*g^eḏōlîm*) in history (Ps. 111:2) and have pleasure (*ḥāpēṣ*) in them. This pleasure finds expression in wholehearted praise of Yahweh (v. 1). Experience of God and human pleasure are mutually dependent, for only "joyous inward participation can experience the mystery and wonders of Yahweh."[33] The delight of the devout is especially (*m^e'ōḏ*) in the commandments (*miṣwôṯ*) of Yahweh (Ps. 112:1; 119:35; cf. Sir. 15:15); this pleasure expresses itself in fear (→ ירא *yārē'*) of God (Ps. 112:1) and takes concrete form in generosity toward the poor (Ps. 112:5,9). In Ps. 1:2, *ḥēpeṣ b^etôraṯ YHWH* is an unmistakable sign of the upright. The wealth of parallel expressions (*hāgâ ḇ^etôrâ*, not walking in the counsel of the wicked, etc.) shows clearly that *ḥāpēṣ* means more than emotional delight: it stands rather for the joyous existential commitment of one's entire life.

In Isa. 58:2 this commitment takes the shape of active worship. Within the framework of an invective and admonition (vv. 1-12), Israel asks: "Why have we fasted, and thou seest it not . . .?" The cultic worship of the community is described in some detail: they seek God (*dāraš*, v. 2), they desire knowledge of his ways (*da'aṯ d^erāḵay yeḥpāṣûn*), they ask (*šā'al*) righteous judgments of God, and delight to draw near him (*qirḇaṯ '^elōhîm yeḥpāṣûn*). In this context, *ḥāpēṣ* clearly parallels the term used for making inquiry of God (→ שׁאל *šā'al*), originally through a prophet as intermediary.

---

[31] H.-J. Kraus, *Psalmen. BK*, XV/1 (⁵1978), 278.
[32] *Ibid.*, XV/2, 479.
[33] *Ibid.*, 467f.

Later, in communal laments or lamentation ceremonies, *ḥāpēṣ* could mean worship of Yahweh in general. Here, too, *ḥāpēṣ* proves to be a term meaning the worship of God.

Contrariwise, it is characteristic of the wicked not to desire knowledge of God's ways (*da'aṯ d^erāḵeyḵā lō' ḥāp̄āṣnû,* Job 21:14)—in other words, they do not concern themselves with his instructions and demands, which they have no intention of obeying. Thus *lo' ḥāpēṣ* comes to mean rejection. Such rejection of the word of God, which has become an object of scorn (*ḥerpâ*), is a sign of the refusal of the remnant of Israel to repent, as Jeremiah laments (Jer. 6:10). Finally, it is characteristic of the fool (*k^esîl*) to reject understanding (*t^eḇûnâ*) (Prov. 18:2; cf. Sir. 6:32; 15:15 [?]; 51:13).

Finally, the object of human desire can be God himself (Ps. 73:25) or his messenger (Mal. 3:1). It is mankind's highest happiness to find *ḥāpēṣ* only in God. His presence is felt to be precious (*ṭôb,* Ps. 73:28). The psalmist can ask in wonder: *mî-lî baššāmāyim w^e'imm^eḵā lō'-ḥāpaṣtî ḇā'āreṣ,* "Whom have I in heaven but thee? And there is nothing upon earth that I desire besides thee" (Ps. 73:25). In this delight in present communion with God we find the ultimate motif of religious assurance. This communion, this sense of unity, "is the only good that impregnates the whole of life and is not merely the supreme good among others"[34] (on the inward meaning of *ḥāpēṣ*, cf. Augustine: "restless is our heart until it rests in thee"[35]).

2. *ḥāpēṣ + Infinitive.* When *ḥāpēṣ* is constructed with the infinitive, it can suggest doing something "happily" or "joyfully," in parallel with *rāṣâ;* verbs expressing joy, however, such as *śāmaḥ, ḥāḏal, 'ālaṣ,* etc., do not appear in this context. The negation *lō' ḥāpēṣ* appears in parallel with *lō' 'āḇâ* and *mē'ēn.* Dt. 25:7f., for example, in the context of legislation concerning the levirate, deals with the case where the brother-in-law does not wish to take his brother's wife (*lō' yaḥpōṣ lāqaḥaṯ 'eṯ-y^eḇimtô*). In parallel with *ḥāpēṣ* we find *mē'ēn,* "refuse," and *lō' 'āḇâ,* "not want," so that *lō' ḥāpēṣ* emphasizes the element of will: have no pleasure, not want, refuse. Cf. also Ruth 3:13b: "if he is not willing to do the part of the next of kin for you (*lō' yaḥpōṣ l^ego'^olēḵ*). In 1 K. 9:1 we have a description of how the temple was finished and all that Solomon desired to build (*'^ašer ḥāpēṣ la'^aśôṯ;* in 2 Ch. 7:11ff. the relative clause does not appear). Here *ḥāpēṣ* is appropriately translated "desire" or simply "wish." In Jer. 42:22, *ḥāpēṣ* introduces a double infinitive: the prophet warns against wanting "to go to live" (*'^ašer ḥāpaṣtem lāḇô' lāḡûr šām*) in Egypt. Ps. 40:9(8) speaks of the "delight" of the devout in doing Yahweh's will (*la'^aśôṯ-r^eṣōn^eḵā . . . ḥāpaṣtî*); *ḥāpēṣ* emphasizes the element of will and obedience (cf. the "open ear" of v. 7[6]) as well as joy, and picks up Yahweh's rejection or refusal of sacrifice: *lō'-ḥāpaṣtā . . . lō' šā'āltā* (v. 7[6]). Egypt—the beast that dwells among the reeds—delights in war (*q^erāḇôṯ yeḥpāṣû*) and lusts after tribute (*raṣṣê-ḵāsep*) (Ps. 68:31[30]). In Job 9:3; 13:3, *ḥāpēṣ* means "wish" to contend (*lārîḇ, hôḵēaḥ*) with God; cf. also Job 33:32: "Speak, for I desire to justify you (*ḥāpaṣtî ṣadd^eqekkā*)."

---

[34] A. Weiser, *The Psalms. OTL* (Eng. trans. 1962), 515.
[35] *MPL* 32, 661.

In 1 K. 5:23(9), *ḥepṣî lāṯēṯ leḥem* refers to Hiram's desire for food in exchange for the wood he provides. In Neh. 1:11, Nehemiah prays that God will be attentive to the prayer of his servants "who delight to fear thy name" (*ʿaḇāḏeyḵā haḥapēṣîm leyirʾâ ʾeṯ-šemeḵā*), i.e., "who are deeply concerned with the worship of Yahweh."[36] In Est. 6:6, Haman asks, "Whom would the king delight to honor more than me (*lemî yaḥpōṣ hammeleḵ laʿaśôṯ yeqār yôṯēr mimmennî*)?" Here *ḥāpēṣ* has the sense of "wish."

3. *ḥēpeṣ*. In secular usage, the semantic definition of *ḥēpeṣ* depends primarily on its wide range of objects.

Yahweh caused David's *yēšaʿ* and *ḥēpeṣ* to prosper (2 S. 23:5). Various translations of *ḥēpeṣ* have been proposed: "desire," "ease," "success." According to Schulz,[37] the reference is to offspring or descendants. More likely, however, we have "salvation and desire" or "prosperity and success" as results of the *berîṯ ʿôlām*.

Sailors and travelers are glad (*yiśmeḥû*) that Yahweh has brought them to their "desired haven (*meḥôz ḥepṣām*)" (Ps. 107:30). The wicked has no "pleasure in" or "care for" his house after his death (Job 21:21). In Job 31:16, *mēḥēpeṣ dallîm* means this "desire" of the poor, which Job has never refused (*mānaʿ*), just as he has never caused the eyes of the widow to fail (*killâ*). In the commercial treaty between Hiram and Solomon, *kol-ḥepṣeḵā* or *ḥepṣî* means the "desire" for cedar, cypress, or food (1 K. 5:22-24[8-10]); according to 1 K. 9:11, Hiram provided gold "as much as he desired" (*leḵol-ḥepsô*). According to 1 S. 18:25, Saul desires no marriage present (*ʾên-ḥēpeṣ lammeleḵ bemōhar*). According to 1 K. 10:13 par. 2 Ch. 9:12, Solomon gave the queen of Sheba "all that she desired (*ʾeṯ-kol-ḥepṣāh ʾašer šāʾālâ*)."

According to Hos. 8:8, Israel is among the nations *kiḵelî ʾên-ḥēpeṣ*, like a vessel "without pleasure," "without value" (cf. Prov. 3:15; 8:11). When Israel lost its independence, it lost simultaneously respect and importance among the nations, becoming like a useless vessel. In similar fashion, Jehoiachin (Coniah) is described in Jer. 22:28 as a "despised, broken pot (*ʿeṣeḇ niḇzeh nāpûs*)," a vessel without "pleasure" or "value." According to Jer. 48:38, Yahweh has broken Moab "like a vessel for which no one cares"; Moab has become a derision and horror (*liśḥōq welimḥittâ*) to all its neighbors (v. 39).

According to the promise in Isa. 54:12, Jerusalem will be more glorious than ever, built in part of agates (*kaḏkōḏ*), carbuncles or crystal (*ʾaḇnê ʾeqdāḥ*), and precious stones (*ʾaḇnê-ḥēpeṣ*). Wisdom is better than coral (*penînîm*); jewels (*ḥapāṣîm*) cannot compare with it (Prov. 3:15; 8:11). Here *ḥapāṣîm* may be an abbreviation for *ʾaḇnê-ḥēpeṣ*. The breastplate of Aaron is "graven with precious stones (*ʾaḇnê-ḥēpeṣ*) like a seal" (Sir. 45:11b); Simon the high priest is like a vessel overlaid with gold, set with precious stones (*ʾaḇnê-ḥēpeṣ*) of all kinds (Sir. 50:9c).

On the Sabbath it is forbidden to pursue business (*ʿāśâ* or *māṣāʾ ḥēpeṣ*) or conduct transactions (*dabbēr dāḇār*) (Isa. 58:3,13). According to Prov. 31:13, the good wife seeks wool and flax, and works *beḥēpeṣ kappeyhā*. Since *ḥēpeṣ* can mean "plea-

---

[36] W. Rudolph, *Esra und Nehemia. HAT,* XX (1949), 105.

[37] A. Schulz, *Die Bücher Samuel. EHAT,* VIII/2 (1920), 273.

sure," "will," or "business transaction," the wife works with hands that are "pleasing," "willing," or "industrious" hands; Gemser[38] translates: "with joyous hands." In Ecclesiastes (except Eccl. 5:3), *ḥēp̱eṣ* usually has the meaning "undertaking, activity, affair"; cf. Staples:[39] ". . . regularly denotes the 'business or facts' of life; and in every case it reflects the will of God."

In Eccl. 3:1, *ḥēp̱eṣ* appears in parallel with *hakkol:* "For everything there is a season (*z^emān*), and a time (*'ēṯ*) for every matter (*l^ekol-ḥēp̱eṣ*) under heaven." In vv. 2-8, *ḥēp̱eṣ* is defined more precisely by seven pairs of human activities. In 3:17, *kol-ḥēp̱eṣ,* "every matter," stands in parallel with *kol-hamma'^aśeh,* "every work." According to vv. 16-17a, these expressions refer to the actions of the righteous and the wicked, which God will judge. "Oppression of the poor (*'ōšeq rāš*)" and violation of justice (*gēzel mišpāṭ*) are nothing to get excited about, nor should one be amazed at the actions (*ḥēp̱eṣ*) of corrupt officials (5:7[8]), because "the official hierarchy looks out for itself."[40]

Even in the case of the king's own court of justice the maxim holds true (Eccl. 8:6): every matter (*ḥēp̱eṣ*) has its time and way—or better its proper moment, which determines whether the suit will be successful. For the king, *kol-'^ašer yaḥpōṣ ya'^aśeh* (8:3) means the absolute freedom to do as he wills; *ḥāp̱ēṣ* means "desire," "plan," "intend." In 12:1, too, the meaning "transaction" or "project" is probably preferable to "pleasure": when the evil days and years come, the aged man will say *'ên-lî ḇāhem ḥēp̱eṣ,* because he can no longer accomplish any "projects," any "work."

Various interpretations have been offered for the *diḇrê-ḥēp̱eṣ* (par. *diḇrê '^emeṯ*) that the Preacher sought to find (Eccl. 12:10). The usual translation is "pleasing" words; cf. Dahood:[41] "felicitous words." Staples[42] says, ". . . he was looking for solid facts upon which to base an honest thesis." Galling[43] renders the expression as "words that lead to truth." It is possible, however, that we are dealing here with "pleasing" words, i.e., words that are "convincing" or "trustworthy (*'emeṯ*)."

In Sirach, some of the *ḥēp̱eṣ* passages involve textual problems. Sir. 10:26a cautions: "Do not play the sage when you do (*la'^aḇōḏ;* B *la'^aśōṯ*) *ḥepṣ^eḵā* (*tó érgon sou*). Here *ḥēp̱eṣ* may mean "business, work." In Sir. 15:12b, however, it appears to mean "pleasure," although Codex A reads *ṣôreḵ,* "use": God has no pleasure in (use for) the wicked.[44]

According to Sir. 32:14, whoever seeks the will of God (*dôrēš 'el* par. *dôrēš tôrâ* par. *dôrēš ḥ^apāṣê 'el*) receives insight (*yiqqaḥ leqaḥ* par. *rāṣôn* par. *mûsār*). God has pleasure (*ḥēp̱eṣ*) in the phases of the moon (cf. 43:6-8). There is uncertainty about 11:23, where the LXX uses *chreía* for *ḥepṣî.* Cf. Peters:[45] *mâ ḥepṣî kî 'āśîṯî ḥepṣî,*

---

[38] B. Gemser, *Sprüch Salomos. HAT,* XVI (²1963), *in loc.*

[39] Staples, 112.

[40] K. Galling, *Die Fünf Megilloth. HAT,* XVIII (²1969), 101.

[41] M. Dahood, "The Phoenician Background of Qoheleth," *Bibl,* 47 (1966), 281.

[42] P. 112.

[43] *HAT,* XVIII, 123f.

[44] N. Peters, *Das Buch Jesua Sirach oder Ecclesiasticus. EHAT,* XXV (1913), 160; R. Smend, *Die Weisheit des Jesus Sirach* (Berlin, 1906), 141.

[45] Pp. 60f.

"What more do I need, since I have fulfilled my desire?" Smend interprets the passage differently,[46] translating *ḥepṣî* as "my work."

III. Theological Use.

1. *Sacrificial Theology and Polemic.* Like *rāṣâ/rāṣôn,* the terms *ḥāpēṣ/ḥēpeṣ* play a role in the (priestly) theology of the cult, and especially in the anticultic polemic of the prophets.

Following Mowinckel, Gunkel, Schmidt, and others, Würthwein sought to demonstrate on the basis of Am. 5:21-27 that Israel made use of oracles and augury in which, before the specific announcement of the individual oracle, the general outcome of the augury—favorable or unfavorable—was stated in general terms. In his polemic against the cult, the prophet turned the usual answer on its head by inserting *lō':* now the sacrifices and observances are no longer accepted, and the hymns of the devout are no longer heard.

Rendtorff explains the terms *rāṣâ/rāṣôn* describing a sacrifice that is "pleasing" on the basis of an "accounting" theology: a sacrifice offered correctly—that is, with proper observance of specific ritual regulations—receives the priestly declaration *'ōlâ hû'*, *ṭāme' hû'*, or the like, and is credited to the account of the one who offers the sacrifice. In the prophets' polemic against the cult, they attack the "erroneous notion of the priestly accounting theology, which holds that a ritually correct sacrifice, by virtue of a priestly credit formula, guarantees a perfect relationship with Yahweh."[47]

The priestly terminology and theology of the cult, as expressed at the beginning of the sacrificial rituals described in Lev. 1–5 (1:3f.; also 7:18; 19:5,7), appears also in Isa. 1:11ff. In an adaptation or imitation of priestly torah, Yahweh asks: "What to me is the multitude of your sacrifices? . . . I have had enough of burnt offerings of rams . . .; I do not delight (*lō' ḥāpaṣtî*) in the blood of bulls, or of lambs, or of he-goats." Declarative formulas are echoed in v. 13, where the *minḥâ* is called "vain" (*šāw'*) and the incense offering (*qᵉṭōreṯ*) an "abomination" (*tô'ēḇâ;* cf. Lev. 18:22, *tô'ēḇâ hî'*). In the prophets' polemic, the formula of pleased acceptance is turned into its opposite by means of *lō'*. The piling up of expressions for displeasure—"I cannot endure" (*lō'-'ûḵal*) (Isa. 1:13b), "my soul hates" (*śānē'*) (v. 14a), "I am weary of bearing" (*nil'â nᵉśō'*) (v. 14b)—underlines the bitter polemic against Israel's cultic practices, which Yahweh will not accept with pleasure (*ḥāpēṣ*).

In Mal. 1:10ff., *ḥēpeṣ* and *rāṣâ* appear together: Yahweh has no pleasure in the priests (*'ên-lî ḥēpeṣ bāḵem*) on account of their irreverence; he will not accept (*lō'-'erṣeh*) a *minḥâ* from their hand. In v. 13, acceptance (*rāṣâ*) and the cultic suitability of sacrificial animals occur together; referring to animals that are lame, sick, or taken by violence, Yahweh asks: "Shall I accept (*ha'erṣeh*) that from your hand?" Cf. also Mal. 2:13: "(Yahweh) no longer regards the offering or accepts it with favor at your hand" (*mē'ēn pᵉnôṯ . . . lāqaḥaṯ rāṣôn*).

---

46 P. 109.

47 Rendtorff, *ThLZ,* 81 (1956), 342.

In Ps. 51:8,18(6,16), too, *ḥāpēṣ* and *rāṣôn* serve to express criticism of the sacrificial cult: Yahweh has no delight (*lō' ḥāpēṣ*) in *zeḇaḥ*, nor is he pleased with burnt offering (*lō' rāṣâ 'ōlôṯ*) (v. 18[16]). His pleasure is in truth (*'ᵉmeṯ ḥāpēṣ*, v. 8[6]); a broken spirit is Yahweh's *zeḇaḥ* (v. 19a[17a]), a contrite heart he does not despise (*lō' bāzâ*) (v. 19b[17b]). The worshipper is confident that a contrite heart—instead of sacrifice and burnt offering—will not be rejected in God's judgment.[48] Only when Jerusalem is rebuilt (vv. 20f.[18f.]) will Yahweh once again delight (*ḥāpēṣ*) in right (legally correct—or possibly "making righteous"[49]) sacrifices.

Echoes of the sacrificial accounting theology may also be heard in Jgs. 13:23. In the face of Manoah's fear that he and his wife must die after the appearance of God's angelic messenger, his wife argues: "If it had pleased Yahweh to kill us (*ḥāpēṣ lahᵃmîṯēnû*), he would not have accepted (*lō'-lāqaḥ*) a burnt offering and a cereal offering at our hands." In other words, acceptance (*lāqaḥ*) of the offerings would imply Yahweh's pleasure, or at least mean that he did not intend to kill them.

The prophets' polemic against the cult is expressed particularly in the antithesis setting sacrifice in contrast to heart/spirit, obedience, etc. According to Hos. 6:6, Yahweh desires (*ḥāpēṣ*) fidelity to his covenant (→ חסד *ḥeseḏ*) and not (*wᵉlō'*) sacrifice, knowledge of God rather than[50] burnt offerings.

The priestly sacrificial theology with its acceptance and rejection, together with the polemic antithesis of sacrifice versus obedience, is also illustrated by the repudiation of Saul for his failure to carry out the ban. In response to Saul's objection, Samuel asks (1 S. 15:22f.): "Has Yahweh as great delight (*ḥēpeṣ*) in burnt offerings and sacrifices, as in obeying the voice of Yahweh?" Rejection (*mā'as*) of the word of Yahweh entails God's rejection of Saul as king (v. 23b). Hearkening (*šᵉmōa' haqšîḇ*) to God's voice finds acceptance (*ḥēpeṣ*), rather than sacrifice and burnt offering, which Yahweh had not demanded of Saul.

According to Rendtorff,[51] 2 S. 15:25f. also belongs to the sphere of sacrificial theology, even though there is no mention of sacrifice. The fugitive David leaves the ark behind with the explanation: "If I find favor (*māṣā' ḥēn*) in the eyes of Yahweh, he will . . . let me see both it and his habitation; but if he says, 'I have no pleasure in you' (*lo' ḥāpaṣtî bāḵ*), behold, here I am. . . ." But the mention of *ḥēn* appears also to imply for *ḥāpēṣ* an element of grace, of gracious guidance.

In Ps. 40:7-9(6-8), too, the prophetic rejection of the sacrificial cult is presupposed, especially in the contrast between sacrifice and obedience: "Sacrifice and offering thou didst not desire (*lō'-ḥāpaṣtā*), burnt offering and sin offering thou hast not required (*lō' šā'āltā*), but thou hast given me an open ear" (v. 7[6]). The obedience of the grateful worshipper is expressed particularly clearly in v. 9(8): "I delight (*ḥāpaṣtî*) to do thy will (*rᵉṣônᵉḵā*); thy law is within my heart." This displacement and,

---

[48] Cf. also Hermisson, 47.

[49] W. Beyerlin, *Die Rettung der Bedrängten in den Feindpsalmen der Einzelnen auf institutionelle Zusammenhänge untersucht. FRLANT*, 99 (1970).

[50] For a different view, see H. Kruse, "Dei 'dialektische Negation' als semitisches Idiom," *VT*, 4 (1954), 385-400.

[51] *Studien*, 259.

in a sense, spiritualization of sacrifice is carried further in Ps. 51:8(6) with *'ᵉmeṯ ḥāpaṣtā*—instead of sacrifice, God credits *'ᵉmeṯ* to mankind's account.[52]

In Isa. 66:4cβ, in the context of a prophetic or liturgical polemic, Yahweh complains that the apostate "did what was evil in my eyes, and chose (*bāḥārû*) that in which I did not delight (*lō'-ḥāpaṣtî*)." Besides pagan sacrifice,[53] the apostate delighted in "abominations" (*šiqqûṣîm*). Yahweh's *lō' ḥāpēṣ* means rejection; in the case of the apostate, *ḥāpēṣ bāḥar* means pleasure, free devotion. In Isa. 65:11f., a Deuteronomistic (?) interpolation, Yahweh's displeasure with the wicked is blamed on their forsaking Yahweh, forgetting his holy mountain, and offering worship to the deities that control destiny (v. 11).

2. *Polemic against Collective Casuistry.* In Ezk. 18:23, we are probably dealing with a cultic polemic attacking a fatalistic collectivizing legalism. Yahweh asks: "Have I any pleasure (*heḥāpōṣ 'eḥpōṣ*) in the death of the wicked, and not rather that he should turn from his way and live (*wᵉḥāyâ*)?" The promise of life to the wicked man who turns from his sins, the statement that his transgressions shall not be remembered (*lō' yizzāḵᵉrû*) against him (v. 22), fully accounts for the stylistically striking and sympathetically formulated question in the setting of an objective discourse on a point of legal casuistry.[54] The promise of life, repeated emphatically (vv. 21-23), suggests the cultic framework of a priestly temple torah. The automatic nexus of action and reward, of sin and death, does not find Yahweh's acceptance. He breaks through automatism by his free offer of repentance and return; he has pleasure in the promise of life and a new beginning.

In Ezk. 18:32, the question of 18:23 is turned into a statement and combined with a call to turn and live. In 33:11, Yahweh, using the solemn impassioned oath formula "as I live," replies that he has no pleasure in the death of the wicked, but wills salvation and therefore freely gives a new possibility of life. According to Eichrodt,[55] the promise of life includes deliverance, brought about by Yahweh's forgiveness and blessing, from the punitive state of condemnation in which the exiles feel abandoned to death. In any case, *ḥāpēṣ* expresses the prophet's polemic against and rejection of collective legal casuistry, in favor of the possibility of new life offered to individuals who repent and turn to Yahweh.

In Mal. 2:17, the faithless doubters of the Jerusalem community blasphemously turn the action-reward nexus on its head, asserting that everyone who does evil (*'ōśeh rā'*) is good in the sight of Yahweh, and that he delights in them (*ûḇāhem hû' ḥāpēṣ*). The consequences of *ra'* and *ṭôḇ* are turned into their opposites. It is claimed that Yahweh has pleasure in the evildoer, and delights no longer in the upright person who fears God. Yahweh's *ḥāpēṣ* in the upright manifests itself in blessing; the evildoer can expect disaster, extermination, and all kinds of distress. Probably this means favor

---

52 Cf. also Hermisson, 46ff.

53 Cf. G. J. Botterweck, "חזיר *ḥᵃzîr* [*chᵃzîr*]," *TDOT,* IV, 299.

54 W. Zimmerli, *Ezekiel 1. Herm* (Eng. trans. 1979), 385.

55 W. Eichrodt, *Ezekiel. OTL* (Eng. trans. 1970), 243.

toward the upright one who fears God, favor expressing in some declaration like *ṣaddîq hû'* the acceptance of walking in the fear of God, or else rejection of the evildoer.

3. *God's Pleasure and Displeasure.* In theological usage, *ḥāpēṣ* can also express God's favor or rejection. In Ps. 18:20(19), a thanksgiving hymn, a king acknowledges: "He brought me forth into a broad place; he delivered me (*y^eḥall^eṣēnî*), because he delighted in me (*ḥāpēṣ bî*)." In vv. 21-27(20-26) the king goes on to declare himself *ṣaddîq* and acknowledge God's recompense: "With the loyal thou dost show thyself loyal (*'im-ḥāsîḏ tiṯhassāḏ*)" (v. 26[25]). God's *ḥāpēṣ* is his favor toward the king, which shows itself in assistance, deliverance, and victory. The *ḥāpēṣ* of v. 20(19) is the counterpart of *hiṯhassāḏ* in v. 26(25).

According to Ps. 35:27, God delights in the *šālôm* of his persecuted servant. According to v. 28, this is a demonstration of Yahweh's righteousness (*ṣ^eḏāqâ*); all the friends who desire (*ḥ^apēṣê*) the psalmist's justification should shout for joy and be glad. In Ps. 22:9(8), the enemies of the afflicted psalmist ask mockingly that God may deliver and rescue him, since he delights in him (*ḥāpēṣ bô*). According to Ps. 41:12(11), Yahweh's graciousness and pleasure raise the psalmist up, so that his enemies do not triumph over him. The "saints in the land" enjoy Yahweh's pleasure and delight (*ḥepṣî*) (Ps. 16:3). He delights in the way (*darkô yeḥpāṣ*) of the righteous and guides his steps (Ps. 37:23), while the wicked person perishes.

Yahweh delights not in wickedness (*lō' ḥāpēṣ reša'*) (Ps. 5:5[4]); he hates (*śānē'*) all evildoers (v. 6b[5b]), destroys liars, and abhors (*tē'ēḇ*) bloodthirsty and deceitful people (v. 7[6]). The decisive rejection (*lō' ḥāpēṣ*) is effectually underlined by the parallel verbs *śānē'*, *'ibbaḏ,* and *tē'ēḇ*. Yahweh has no delight in the strength of horses or men (*lō' ḥāpēṣ* par. *lō' rāṣâ*) (Ps. 147:10), but rather in those who fear him and hope in his steadfast love (v. 11).

As an expression for omnipotence we find "he does whatever he pleases" (*kol '^ašer-ḥāpēṣ 'āśâ,* Ps. 115:3; 135:6). According to Eccl. 5:3(4), God has no pleasure in fools (*'ên ḥēpeṣ bakk^esîlîm*).[56]

If Yahweh delights (*ḥāpēṣ*) in Israel, he will lead them into the land that flows with milk and honey (Nu. 14:8). Here *ḥāpēṣ* has the sense of being favorably inclined. Yahweh's *ḥēpēṣ* gives them the confidence and strength to overcome the dangers of the land and the giants dwelling in it; cf. 13:32ff.; 14:3.

In a prophetic liturgy (Mic. 7:18), the community rejoices in Yahweh as a God who delights in steadfast love (*ḥāpēṣ heseḏ*). He pardons iniquity (*nōśē' 'āwôn*) and passes over transgression (*'ōḇēr 'al-peša'*). The people hope that he will again have compassion (*y^eraḥ^aēnû*), tread under (*yiḵbōš*) iniquities, and cast (*yašlîḵ*) all sins into the depths of the sea (v. 19). God's *ḥāpēṣ* means acceptance and acknowledgment of love; it shows itself in favor, forgiveness, and mercy. According to Jer. 9:23(24), Yahweh delights in understanding and knowledge of God.

In Jon. 1:14, before casting Jonah into the sea, the sailors pray for God's protection: "thou doest as it pleases thee." This probably meant as a kind of excuse: it seems to

---

56 For a different interpretation, see Staples.

them that Yahweh himself has decided to involve them in his vindictive intentions with respect to Jonah.[57] They are only doing Yahweh's will (*ka'ᵃšer ḥāpaṣtā 'āśîṯā*). In Job 22:3, *ḥēpeṣ kî tiṣdaq* stands in parallel with *beṣa' kî-ṯattēm dᵉrāḵeyḵā* and *sāḵan;* here *ḥēpeṣ,* like *beṣa'* and *sāḵan,* appears to mean "profit" or "gain." Eliphaz is asking what profit God is supposed to have from Job's righteousness and blameless conduct.

According to 1 S. 2:25, it pleased Yahweh or was his will to slay the sons of Eli (*ḥāpēṣ YHWH lahᵃmîṯām*). The author interprets their death theologically as a consequence of their wickedness: Yahweh had determined their premature death from the beginning (cf. also 1 S. 16:14ff.; 2 S. 24:1f.; 1 K. 22:20), thus appearing to guide the chain of events that led to the monarchy.[58] Here *ḥāpēṣ* expresses God's purpose in history, his plan and governance, which in this case was understood as manifesting itself in a kind of obduracy and predestination.[59]

Finally, in 1 K. 10:9 par. 2 Ch. 9:8 *ḥāpēṣ* stands in parallel with *'āhaḇ:* the queen of Sheba praises Solomon's God, who was pleased to set Solomon upon the throne of Israel (*ḥāpēṣ YHWH lᵉṯittᵉḵā*); because he loved (*bᵉ'ahaḇaṯ*) Israel, in order to establish it he made Solomon king to execute justice and righteousness. Thus *ḥāpēṣ,* "to be pleased," "to be inclined toward," also has the connotation of *'āhaḇ,* "love." When referring to God, *ḥāpēṣ* stands in conjunction with: *'āhaḇ* (1 K. 10:9 par. 2 Ch. 9:8), *hiṯhassāḏ* (Ps. 18:20,26[19,25]), *rānan* and *sāmaḥ* (Ps. 35:27), *nāśā' 'āwôn* par. *'āḇar 'al-peša'* (Mic. 7:18), *nāṣal/hiṣṣîl* (Ps. 22:9[8]); *lō' ḥāpēṣ* appears with *lō' rāṣâ* (Ps. 147:10).

4. *God's Will.* In Deutero-Isaiah, *ḥēpeṣ* takes on overtones of *Heilsgeschichte* and soteriology. Elliger states perceptively[60] that when *ḥpṣ* appears in Isa. 40–55 the emotional element almost always takes a back seat to the element of will. It means the will of Yahweh. In 44:28 (cf. v. 26); 46:10; 48:14, *ḥēpeṣ* stands in parallel with *'ēṣâ:* Yahweh's *'ēṣâ* stands fast, and he will accomplish (*'āśâ*) his purpose (46:10); his actions in history will carry out his plan (*'ēṣâ*) and his salvific will; he will summon Cyrus so that through him he may deliver his people and cause the temple and its city to be rebuilt (44:26,28). Yahweh himself confirms the word of his servants (*mēqîm dᵉḇar 'ᵃḇāḏāyw*) and performs the counsel of his messengers (*'ᵃṣaṯ mal'āḵāyw yašlîm*) (v. 26); Cyrus will fulfill all Yahweh's *ḥēpeṣ* (*kol-ḥepṣî yašlîm,* v. 28), that is, the rebuilding of Jerusalem and the temple (v. 26b). In addition to *'ēṣâ/ḥēpeṣ* we find the parallels *mēqîm dᵉḇar 'ᵃḇāḏāyw/'ᵃṣaṯ mal'āḵāyw yašlîm/kol-ḥepṣî yašlîm.* According to 48:14, Cyrus will perform Yahweh's purpose (*ya'ᵃśeh ḥepṣô*). Yahweh's *ḥēpeṣ* refers to a divine soteriological act, God's will to liberate Israel and restore Jerusalem.

---

57 A. van Hoonacker, *Les douze Petits Prophètes. ÉtB* (1908), 329f.

58 H. J. Stoebe, *Das erste Buch Samuelis. KAT,* VIII/1 (1973), 114.

59 On the problem of obduracy, see F. Hesse, *Das Verstockungsproblem im AT. BZAW,* 74 (1955); for a different interpretation, see M. Tsevat, "The Death of the Sons of Eli," *JBR,* 32 (1964), 355-58.

60 K. Elliger, *Deuterojesaja. BK,* XI/4, 286.

According to Isa. 53:10, Yahweh's *ḥēpeṣ* will prosper through the hand of his "bruised" and suffering servant. According to 42:1ff. and 49:1ff., this *ḥēpeṣ*, Yahweh's intention and determined plan,[61] is the deliverance of Israel and the nations. Here, too, *ḥēpeṣ* clearly refers to historical events with theological significance, deriving from Yahweh's salvific will. We may note also (42:21) that the exile and the suffering of the present were willed (*ḥāpēṣ*) by Yahweh for his righteousness' sake. Yahweh's word does not return empty without accomplishing what he purposes (*'āśâ 'eṯ-'ᵃšer ḥāpaṣtî*) and prospering in the thing for which it was sent (*hiṣlîaḥ 'ᵃšer šᵉlaḥtîw*) (55:11); it brings to fruition God's will and purpose (*ḥāpēṣ, šālaḥ*): peace, prosperity, and restoration.

The prophetical torah dealing with the admission of eunuchs and foreigners to the congregation of Yahweh and worship in the temple (Isa. 56:3-7) sets certain conditions for the eunuchs: they are to keep the Sabbath, choose the things that please God (*bāḥar ba'ᵃšer ḥāpāṣtî*), and hold fast the covenant (v. 4). The phrase *bāḥar ba'ᵃšer ḥāpāṣtî* means free choice of Yahweh's will, which becomes the will of those who choose it.[62] If this is done, they will receive from Yahweh in his temple "a monument and a name," which makes up for their having no children and gives them an "everlasting name."

Thus we see that *ḥāpēṣ* can have the meaning of "will," with salvific or historical overtones, as in the deliverance of the exiles and of Jerusalem (Isa. 42:21; 44:26,28; 48:10; 53:10), in parallel with *'ēṣâ* (44:26) and *šālaḥ*, "mission" (55:11). It is crucial that this will be realized (*'āśâ, šillēm*) (44:28; 48:14; 55:11). In the torah for eunuchs, "the things that please Yahweh" include observance of the Sabbath, the covenant, and the commandments; the eunuchs are to make this choice of their own free will (*bāḥar*).

5. *Metaphors and Names*. In Mal. 3:12, Israel is called a "land of (my?) delight" (*'ereṣ ḥēpeṣ/ḥepṣî*). The reference is probably to the land of God's pleasure, a land of wealth and magnificence because it is blessed by God (cf. Zec. 7:14). By way of contrast, the prophet calls Edom a "wicked country" (*gᵉḇûl riš'â*, Mal. 1:4).

Isa. 62:4 uses a bridal metaphor, describing Jerusalem as *ḥepṣî-ḇāh* (in contrast to *'ᵃzûḇâ*, "desolate") because Yahweh has delight in her. As a young man marries a virgin (*yiḇ'al*) or a bridegroom rejoices over his bride (*mᵉśôś*), so God rejoices over Jerusalem (*yāśîś*) (v. 5). An emotional element is given to *ḥēpeṣ/ḥāpēṣ* by the parallelism with *bā'al bᵉṯulâ* and *māśôś, śûś*. Cf. also Hephzibah, the mother of Hezekiah (2 K. 21:1).

IV. Qumran.

Usage in the Dead Sea scrolls agrees for the most part with what we have observed in the OT. The noun *ḥēpeṣ* is used for the "duties" or "tasks" of the production committee (1QS 3:17; CD 14:12 [defined in the next clause as social obligations]),

---

[61] F. Feldmann, *Das Buch Isaias. EHAT*, XIV/2 (1926), 170.

[62] *Ibid.*, 198.

as well as for the tasks of each individual, specifically on the Sabbath (CD 10:20; 11:2). During sessions of the *rabbîm, ḥēpeṣ* probably means official recognition, without which no one may speak (1QS 6:11). As in Isa. 54:12, we also find *'aḇnê-ḥēpeṣ* decorating shields (1QM 5:6), spear sockets (5:9), and sheathes for swords (5:14). Alongside cattle, silver, and gold, we find precious stones as part of the wealth of the eschatological Jerusalem.

As before mysteries (*rzym*), the worshipper stands in awe before the *ḥpṣ* of God, the wonderful and mysterious "determination" of the heavenly bodies (1QH 1:13; cf. 1QH fr. 3:7) established by the creator. God himself grants the *ḥpṣy rṣwnw*, "desires of his will," par. *'dwt ṣdqw, drky 'mtw* (CD 3:15), that mankind may fulfill them and live through them (*ḥyh bhm*).[63] God's will (*rṣwn*) is the only thing on which people should set their pleasure (1QS 9:24). It is the source of all human activity (1QH 10:5).

Botterweck

---

[63] See G. Segalla, "La volontà di Dio in Qumran," *RivBibl*, 11 (1963), 377-395.

חָפַר *ḥāpar*

Contents: I. Etymology. II. *ḥpr* I, "Dig": 1. Occurrences; 2. Theology. III. *ḥpr* II, "Be Ashamed": 1. Occurrences; 2. Theology. IV. LXX.

I. Etymology.

Most Hebrew lexica distinguish *ḥpr* I, "dig," from *ḥpr* II, "be ashamed." The semantics of the Akkadian verbs that were presumed phonologically equivalent is so disparate that the etymology of the word and its semantic history are obscure. Homophonic roots are also hypothesized for East Semitic. In both Early and Late Babylonian, as well as Assyrian, we find *ḫepēru, ḫapāru(m)* II, "dig," "scratch."[1] With its first meaning, this would correspond to *ḥpr* I. The same phonological root with the same meaning is also attested in Old South Arabic, Arabic, and Ethiopian.[2] But there has been no convincing demonstration of a semantic connection between Old Bab. *ḫapāru(m)* I, "surround," "assemble," and *ḥpr* II, as well as Arab. *ḫafira* and Ethiop. *ḫafara*, "be ashamed."[3]

ḥāpar. M. A. Klopfenstein, *Scham und Schande nach dem AT. AThANT*, 62 (1972); D. J. McCarthy, "Some Holy War Vocabulary in Joshua 2," *CBQ*, 33 (1971), 228-230; J. L. Palache, *Semantic Notes on the Hebrew Lexicon* (Eng. trans., Leiden, 1959).

[1] *CAD*, VI (1956), 170; *AHw*, I, 340.

[2] *KBL*[3], 327.

[3] *Ibid.;* cf. *AHw*, I, 321; Klopfenstein, 170f.

II. ḥrp I, "Dig." 1. *Occurrences.* The root *ḥpr* I occurs 23 times, only in the qal stem of the verb, apart from the irrelevant passage Isa. 2:20.[4] The occurrences, taken individually or in groups, exhibit several meanings. The meaning "dig" presents no philological problems; the object may be a well (Gen. 21:30; 26:15,18f.,21f.,32; Nu. 21:18) or a pit (Ps. 7:16 [Eng. v. 15]), or one digs "for" something, such as water (Ex. 7:24) or even death (Job 3:21). The object may also be implicit: a hole in the earth (Dt. 23:14[13]) or (probably) a pit (Ps. 35:7; cf. Eccl. 10:8). Something that has been hidden can also be "dug up" (Jer. 13:7). Thanks to Babylonian evidence,[5] the "pawing" of a horse is also straightforward (Job 39:21). In Job 39:29a, the meaning "spy out" for *ḥāpar* is assured by the parallel in v. 29b. Closely related is the military usage in the sense of "explore" in Dt. 1:22; Josh. 2:2f.[6]

2. *Theology.* a. In the sense of "dig," we find *ḥāpar* in early or (probably) archaizing texts. The verb *kārâ,* seemingly more common for the important work of digging wells and pits, is sometimes found in parallel (Nu. 21:18; cf. Gen. 26:25).[7] In Ps. 7:16a(15a), both occur together. Here, as in Ps. 35:7 and Eccl. 10:8, the lex talionis is at work. The image of the pit dug for others is often used for this purpose in the Psalms, but usually with more common verbs (Ps. 9:16[15]; 57:7[6]; cf. Prov. 26:27). The choice of *ḥāpar* is thus probably deliberate, lending an air of solemnity. In Jer. 13:1-11, a symbolic action on the part of Jeremiah depicted autobiographically, the recovery of the waistcloth previously buried at God's behest constitutes a central feature of the account, so that the use of this verb, which occurs nowhere else in Jeremiah, is appropriate (v. 7).

b. In Ps. 35:7b, the text just mentioned above, certain difficulties suggest that it is not appropriate to supply the object "pit" for *ḥāpar* on the basis of v. 7a, but rather to take the verb without an object in the sense of "keep a malicious eye out," "waylay," "persecute."[8] This is close in meaning to Job 3:21: those who are afflicted with suffering long in vain for death, "they dig for it (*wayyaḥpᵉruhû,* transitive!) more (doggedly) than for hid treasures." In both texts "dig" and "long for" overlap semantically.[9] In Job 39:29, God describes the sharp vision of the birds of prey, an incomprehensible wonder to the human mind. In Job 11:18b, we may have relaxed and confident "looking around." In three passages, the military sense "spy out" is assured; the scanty evidence does not permit a more precise definition. In Josh. 2:2f., the word is used only by the Canaanites when they are speaking of the Israelite spies; this is clearly a feature of the original account, since the (redactional) introduction uses other verbs (Josh. 2:1). The reverse is true in Dt. 1:22, where the author of the present context places it in the mouth of the Israelites, recounting the words of Moses,

---

4 Cf. *BHS.*

5 *AHw,* I, 340; *CAD,* VI, 170.

6 See Palache, 16, 22, 32, 76; McCarthy, 228.

7 A. Lods, *Histoire de la littérature hébraïque et juive* (Paris, 1950), 41-43.

8 M. Dahood, *Psalms I. AB,* XVI (1966), 212.

9 See below.

the speaker. Dt. 1:19-46 uses the earliest version of Nu. 13f., where the P sections use only *tûr;* in one early passage (Nu. 13:18) we find the ordinary *rā'â*. Dt. 1:22 may either have used an unaltered form of its textual source[10] or have chosen *ḥāpar* deliberately. In all later texts, the appearance of *ḥāpar* is an archaizing feature. In literary terms, it is meant to lend force to what is being said: in Dt. 1:22, for example, the burden imposed on the people and the exoneration of Moses.

III. ḥpr II, "Be Ashamed." 1. *Occurrences*. The root *ḥpr* II occurs 17 times: 13 in the qal, 4 in the hiphil. Klopfenstein[11] has recently attempted more precisely to define the meaning "be ashamed" given in the lexica; he suggests a subjective sense of shame or embarrassment in contrast to its cause, and objective "disgrace."[12] In his view, this interpretation makes the individual passages more comprehensible, exhibiting their internal structure more clearly, although Klopfenstein himself admits that the verb is subject to a strong "semantic pressure" exerted by many other verbs belonging to the same sphere, especially *bôš*, which it usually follows. Only once (Ps. 34:6[5]) do we find *ḥāpar* by itself.

2. *Theology*. Except for the image of the caravan standing disappointed and exhausted beside the dry watercourse (Job 6:20), all the occurrences are "theological."

a. The observations of life in Prov. 13:5 and 19:26 are similar: they impose no demand but make a simple statement, concluding the second member with *ḥāpar*, joined directly to the preceding verb with a simple copulative *wāw*. In Prov. 13:5, we actually have antithetical parallelism: "the righteous man hates falsehood (*w^e rāšā' yaḇ'îš w^e yaḥpîr*)." The sequence of verbs is unique; therefore the roots probably preserve their own meanings, as does the use of the hiphil: "The wicked man brings disrepute and embarrassment."[13] Since Prov. 19:26a is both syntactically and semantically complete in itself,[14] *bēn mēḇîš ûmaḥpîr* can hardly mean merely a "spoiled child" in v. 26b; its meaning is rather something like "black sheep" (cf. 10:5; 17:2).[15] The sequence *bôš–ḥāpar* is so common that the participles probably come to share much the same meaning. The second is probably a stereotyped stylistic and metrical addition. This subject matter is "theological." However "secular" the observations may have been originally, the upright person contrasted with the *rāšā'* becomes a constant theme not only in proverbial literature, but also in the prophets and Psalms.[16] Wisdom Literature deals repeatedly with the son who does not follow his parents' guidance (Prov. 1:8f.; 10:1; 20:20; 30:17; Sir. 3:1-16), as does the Law (Ex. 20:12; 21:15,17; Lev. 20:9; Dt. 5:16; 21:18-21; 27:16).

---

[10] R. de Vaux, *The Early History of Israel* (Eng. trans., Philadelphia, 1978), 524.

[11] Pp. 170-183.

[12] See also H. Seebass, "בּוֹשׁ *bôš* [*bôsh*]," *TDOT*, II, 50-60; also Klopfenstein, 182.

[13] Klopfenstein, 173.

[14] G. R. Driver, "Proverbs xix.26," *ThZ*, 11 (1955), 373f.

[15] Seebass, *TDOT*, II, 59.

[16] O. Keel (Keel-Leu), *Feinde und Gottesleugner. Studien zum Image der Widersacher in den Individualpsalmen*. *SBM*, 7 (1969), 109-131.

b. Childlessness is often the cause of *ḥāpar.* In Isa. 54:4, a promise is addressed to exiled Israel as a childless woman (vv. 1-3), who has never had a husband and finally suffers the fate of the most desolate widow (v. 4). In v. 4a, a series of four verbs, grouped into two pairs by a repeated *kî-lō'*, concludes with *kî-lō' taḥpîrî.* Apparently the reflexively transitive hiphil, like the first verb in the series, "fear not," represents the subjective side, while the two middle verbs (*bôš, klm*) stand for the objective side of the experience. In v. 4b, two nouns echo two of these verbs: *bōšeṯ* corresponds to *kî-lō' ṯēḇôšî, ḥerpâ* to *lō' ṯaḥpîrî.* Thus *ḥāpar* is strongly associated with the shame of widowhood.[17] But all this will come to an end.

On the other hand, Jer. 15:9 states clearly that a mother of seven children will lose them all (cf. v. 7, where the nation is bereft). The consequence will be *bôšâ wᵉḥāpērâ.* In Jer. 50:12b (not from Jeremiah[18]), the "mother" and "bearer" of the addressee (Babylon) will find herself in the same situation, for "the end of the nations is a wilderness dry and desert."

c. Twice *ḥāpar,* in strict (synonymous or synthetic) parallelism with *bôš,* plays a role in prophetic polemic against illegitimate cults. In Mic. 3:7, the prophet threatens the "seers" and "diviners" with disgrace and shame, and describes their outward reaction: they cover the lips. The reason is that they receive no answer from God or their idols (cf. v. 6). Together with *bôš,* then, *ḥāpar* is the consequence when one's way of life collapses: the foundation on which one has built everything has crumbled.

In Isa. 1:29 this is even more explicit, if that is possible: *ḥāpar* and *bôš* are followed by causal *min* and the "desired" (*ḥᵃmaḏtem*) and "chosen" (*bᵉḥartem*) objects of the cult, "oaks" and "gardens." Total (moral) devastation is the inescapable consequence; vv. 28 and 30f. establish a conventional framework around what the two verbs express in the categories of personal experience.

d. The metaphorical use of *ḥāpar* with nature as its subject is striking. Isa. 33:7f. describes the reaction to the unstoppable advance of an apocalyptic eschatological enemy uninhibited by any legal or moral restraints, "regarding no man." V. 9 depicts the death of the natural realm. There is a remarkable personification of Lebanon: *heḥpîr lᵉḇānôn qāmal,* "Lebanon stands confounded, withered."[19] The hiphil of *ḥpr* is used intransitively and independently, outside of its usual context.

In Isa. 24:23, *ḥāpar* and *bôš* (in that order!) take meristically as their subjects "the pale one" (the moon) and "the hot one" (the sun). At the apocalyptic irruption of Yahweh's reign, they pale before Yahweh's glory on Zion.

e. In the Psalms, *ḥāpar* usually appears in laments, with reference to enemies. In Ps. 83:18(17), which is probably preexilic (cf. "Assyria" in v. 9[8]), the imprecations against the enemy (vv. 10-18[9-17]) conclude, as in Isa. 54:4, with four different verbs set in two pairs. The third verb is *ḥāpar,* but poetic accumulation is presumably

---

[17] Klopfenstein, 77, 181f.

[18] W. Rudolph, *Jeremia. HAT,* XII (³1968), 301.

[19] O. Kaiser, *Isaiah 13–39. OTL* (Eng. trans. 1974), 337.

more important than any precise and intentional distinction. It seems that in most cases no special importance is attached to any particular nuance of the verb when it is associated with parallel verbs and expressions; they are in fact mutually interchangeable. Only Ps. 71:24 is a declarative statement, equivalent to a confession of trust. All the other occurrences are imprecations against enemies: Ps. 35:4,26; 40:15(14); 70:3(2). Only Ps. 34:6(5), *ûpᵉnêhem 'al-yeḥpārû,* "may their faces never be ashamed," represents formally a negation; semantically, however, the verse represents a positive request with a positive parallel: those who look to Yahweh, who are "radiant" for him, will endure.

f. Here we have probably touched on what is by far the dominant semantic substrate. Only in Proverbs does *ḥāpar* refer primarily to the opprobrious kind of person who is the subject of the maxim in question: he is compromised by his own actions, or, less frequently, is an example for others. Elsewhere the primary emphasis is on suffering (the consequences of one's own actions). Even the hiphil is not exclusively causative or transitive. It always has a passive subject.

What might be called the fundamental theological meaning also appears in the fact that the verb is used almost exclusively in the plural. The exceptions are only apparent. Occurrences in Proverbs do not enter into the discussion; for the rest, only the metaphors in Isa. 24:23 and 33:9 come into question. Jer. 15:9 is a symbolic usage with reference to a hostile nation. This "shame" is much more than a merely unpleasant or painful subjective "experience." In the mind of the prophet or psalmist, it refers in a radical way to the exclusion or conquest of evil, of everything hostile to God and mankind. There is no need for explicit mention of death or physical annihilation, but they are concomitant phenomena. It is not attested in this sense before the eighth century, and is restricted to eschatological and apocalyptic texts in the Prophets and prayers in the Psalms. Whether in the late period, when it is primarily attested, it ever achieved a specific semantic function distinguishing it clearly from all other related verbs is uncertain and unlikely.

Gamberoni

IV. LXX. 1. In the LXX, *ḥpr* I is usually rendered by *orýssein,* "dig" (12 times), sometimes by *anaskáptein* or *anorýssein.* We also find *ephodeúein, zētein,* and *kataskopeúein,* "explore." On several occasions a confusion between literal and metaphorical usage can be ascertained on comparison with the MT (cf. Job 3:21).

2. The usual translation of *ḥpr* II is *entrépein,* "be ashamed," "shrink from" (7 times). The use of *aischýnein* and its compounds, as well as *oneidízein,* "belittle, reproach," is remarkably rare. In comparison to the MT, the LXX emphasizes the active transitive semantic element.

Botterweck

חָפַשׂ *ḥāpaś*; חֵפֶשׂ *ḥēpeś*

Contents: I. Semitic. II. OT. III. LXX.

I. Semitic. The root is not attested in Akkadian, but the LXX translation of *hitḥappēś* as *ekrataiáōthē*, "he was determined" or "insisted," in 2 Ch. 35:22 may have taken the Hebrew word in the sense of Akk. *ḫapatu(m)*, "be or become overwhelming."[1] In Ugaritic, *ḥpš* appears once with the meaning "gather" (grain).[2] In Aramaic, Syriac, Middle Hebrew, and Modern Hebrew (often as *ḥps*[3]), the root has the basic meaning "track," "dig out." In Arabic we find *ḥafaša*, "collect" or "draw water"[4]; "trample down"; "have eye trouble or weak eyes."[5] There is also *ḥafasa*, "sink, fall."[6] These and others have given occasion for etymological speculation.[7] Ethiop. *ḥafᵉša* is used in the sense "be thick, strong," and "have much grain, rake together."[8]

The Dead Sea scrolls follow OT usage (1QH 8:29; 10:34).

II. OT. In all the certain OT occurrences, the word is to be understood in the sense of "search." The verb appears 20 times, the derived noun *ḥēpeś* once. The intensive stems predominate; their forms appear primarily in preexilic texts.

The 8 piel passages are textually unassailable. Amos has Yahweh threaten: "Though they hide themselves on the top of Carmel, from there I will search them out (*'ᵃḥappēś*[9]) and take them" (Am. 9:3). In Genesis, the piel appears twice in early narratives: Laban searches Rachel's tent for his household gods (Gen. 31:35), and Joseph's steward searches Benjamin's sack for the cup (44:12). As in these stories, the thoroughness of the search is exhibited when David is being pursued: all the hiding places are to be explored, and then Saul will go himself and search David out (1 S. 23:23[10]). As his impossible condition of peace, Ben-hadad proposes to "search" (*ḥippᵉśû*) all the houses of Israel and have his servants take whatever pleases them (1 K. 20:6); Jehu orders a thorough search (*ḥappᵉśû*) to determine that there are no servants of Yahweh among the assembled priests of Baal (2 K. 10:23).

The two other occurrences of the piel are later. The statement of Zeph. 1:12 is similar to the Amos passage cited and uses the same form: Yahweh will search Je-

---

1 *AHw*, I, 321; G. R. Driver, "Problems in the Hebrew Text of Proverbs," *Bibl*, 32 (1951), 193, n. 1.

2 *KTU*, 1.14 III, 8; IV, 52; *WUS*, no. 954.

3 *WTM*, II, 94f.

4 *GesB*, 250; cf. Lane, I/2, 601.

5 Lane, I/2, 772f.

6 R. P. A. Dozy, *Supplément aux dictionnaires arabes*, I (Leiden, ²1927; repr. 1981), 386.

7 Driver, *Bibl*, 32 (1951), 192f.

8 *TigrWb*, 104.

9 On the absence of the suffix in this form, see H. W. Wolff, *Joel and Amos*. *Herm* (Eng. trans. 1977), 335.

10 Contra A. Ehrlich, H. J. Stoebe defends the MT (*Das erste Buch Samuelis*. *KAT*, VIII/1 [1973], 425).

rusalem for the cynics who do not believe that he will intervene. In Ps. 77:7(Eng. v. 6), *wayᵉḥappēś* ("my spirit searches . . .") is read by many translators as a 1st person singular (cf. v. 4[3]); Wellhausen, followed by Gunkel,[11] emends to *wayyaḥpōz,* "is startled."

Jenni sees the piel of *ḥpś* as a typical resultative: except in Ps. 77:7(6), "a specific area mentioned as the object is thoroughly searched," while the qal expresses merely the "performance of the action."[12]

The 3 occurrences of the pual are disputed. In Prov. 28:12, Gemser[13] reads the hithpael ("make off") for the pual (*yᵉḥuppaś,* "hide themselves"); Driver, citing Arabic parallels, translates: ". . . (ordinary) men are prostrated, trampled down."[14] Others have often suggested a miswriting of different verbs such as *ḥpš* or *ḥpz.*[15] Ps. 64:7(6) will be discussed below.

The hithpael is used in 4 passages in the sense "disguise oneself." In 1 S. 28:8, Saul disguises himself from the medium; in 1 K. 20:38, Saul disguises himself from the medium; in 1 K. 20:38, the prophet disguises his face from the king; and in 1 K. 22:30 par. 2 Ch. 18:29, Ahab disguises himself so that he will not be recognized during battle. Driver[16] has defended the *hiṯhappēś* of 2 Ch. 35:22, but most scholars, following the LXX and Vulg., emend to *hiṯḥazzēq* or *ḥāšab̲*. Rudolph[17] reads *hiṯhappēš,* "because he . . . wanted to be free." Job 30:18 is also obscure; the LXX appears to have read *yiṯpōś,* which is often supplied.[18]

The qal is definitely found 3 times with the meaning "test, search" (Prov. 2:4; 20:27; Lam. 3:40). Uncertain is Ps. 64:7(6), *yaḥpᵉśû-'ôlōṯ,* which could be understood without emendation as "they contrive crimes," but is usually emended conjecturally.[19] The same verse also contains the pual participle, which would have to have the meaning "conceived" and the related noun *ḥēp̲eś* in order to be translated as "plot" or the like.

The niphal occurs once in the OT: *'êḵ neḥpᵉśû 'ēśāw,* "How Esau has been pillaged" (Ob. 6). The proposed change from the 3rd person plural to the 3rd person singular[20] (LXX *exēreunḗthē*) is unnecessary.[21]

Maass

III. LXX. The LXX renders *ḥpś* by means of *exereunán* (8 times), *ereunán* (5 times), and compounds of *kalýptein*. The translation *krataioún*[22] may be based on a

[11] *GHK,* II/2, 336.

[12] E. Jenni, *Das hebräische Pi'el* (Zurich, 1968), 130.

[13] B. Gemser, *Sprüch Salomos. HAT,* XVI (1937), 99.

[14] Driver, *Bibl,* 32 (1951), 192f.

[15] See *BHK.*

[16] G. R. Driver, "L'interprétation du texte masorétique à la lumière de la lexicographie hébraïque," *ETL,* 26 (1950), 337-353, esp. 347.

[17] *Chronikbücher. HAT,* XXI, 330.

[18] See G. Fohrer, *Das Buch Hiob. KAT,* XVI (1963), 414.

[19] *GHK,* II/2, 271.

[20] *BHK.*

[21] E. König, *Historisch-kritisches Lehrgebäude der hebräischen Sprache,* §346k; see W. Rudolph, *Obadja. KAT,* XIII/2 (1971), 304.

[22] Cf. I.1.

misreading. The noun *ḥēpeś*, "disguise,"[23] "plot,"[24] is rendered by the LXX as *exereúnēsis*, "exploration."

Botterweck

---

[23] *KBL*³, 328.
[24] H.-J. Kraus, *Psalmen. BK*, XV/1 (⁵1978), 445.

חָפְשִׁי ḥop̱šî; חֻפְשָׁה ḥup̱šâ; חָפְשִׁית ḥop̱šîṯ

Contents: I. The *ḫupše* and Heb. *ḥop̱šî*. II. Meaning. III. The Religious Position of Emancipation. IV. Absence of *ḥop̱šî* from the Vocabulary of Soteriology.

ḥop̱šî. W. F. Albright, "Canaanite ḥofšî, 'free,' in the Amarna Tablets," *JPOS*, 4 (1924), 169f.; *idem*, "Canaanite ḫapši and Hebrew ḥofsî Again," *JPOS*, 6 (1926), 106-108; U. Cassuto, *The Goddess Anath* (Eng. trans., Jerusalem, 1971), 22f.; V. Christian, "kan. ḫapši = 'Kraft, Macht,' " *OLZ*, 28 (1925), 419f.; M. Dahood, "A New Metrical Pattern in Biblical Poetry," *CBQ*, 29 (1967), 574-79, esp. 577f.; M. David, "The Manumission of Slaves under Zedekiah," *OTS*, 5 (1948), 63-79; M. Dietrich and O. Loretz, "Die soziale Struktur von Alalaḫ und Ugarit (II)," *WO*, 5/1 (1969), 57-93; M. Dietrich, O. Loretz, and J. Sanmartín, "Keilalphabetische Bürgschaftsdokumente aus Ugarit," *UF*, 6 (1974), 466f.; E. Ebeling, "Freiheit, Freilassung," *RLA*, III (1957-1971), 110f.; *idem*, "Freilassung eines Sklaven," *ibid.*, 111f.; J. J. Finkelstein, "Ammiṣaduqa's Edict and the Babylonian 'Law Codes,' " *JCS*, 15 (1961), 91-104; *idem*, "Some New *Misharum* Material and its Implications," *Festschrift B. Landsberger. AS*, 16 (1965), 233-246; J. Gray, "Feudalism in Ugarit and Early Israel," *ZAW*, 64 (1952), 49-55, esp. 52-55; P. Grelot, "*ḥofšî* (Ps. LXXXVIII 6)," *VT*, 14 (1964), 256-263; A. Guillaume, "Notes on the Psalms. II. 73-150," *JTS*, 45 (1944), 14f., esp. 15; *idem*, "Hebrew and Arabic Lexicography: A Comparative Study. IV," *Abr-Nahrain*, 4 (1963/64[1965]; repr. Leiden, 1965), 1-18, esp. 6; S. B. Gurewicz, "Some Examples of Modern Hebrew Exegesis of the OT," *ABR*, 11 (1963), 15-23, esp. 22; L. Kopf, "Das arabische Wörterbuch als Hilfsmittel für die hebräische Lexikographie," *VT*, 6 (1956), 286-302, esp. 299f. = his *Studies in Arabic and Hebrew Lexicography* (Jerusalem, 1976), 229-245; F. R. Kraus, *Ein Edikt des Königs Ammi-Ṣaduqa von Babylon. StDI*, 5 (1958); *idem*, "Ein Edikt des Königs Samsu-Iluna von Babylon," *Festschrift B. Landsberger. AS*, 16 (1965), 225-231; E. R. Lacheman, "Note on the Word ḫupšu at Nuzi," *BASOR*, 86 (1952), 6f.; N. P. Lemche, "חפשי in 1 Sam. xvi 25," *VT*, 24 (1974), 373f.; *idem*, "The Hebrew Slave: Comments on the Slave Law of Ex. xxi 2-11," *VT*, 25 (1975), 129-144; *idem*, "The Manumission of Slaves—The Fallow Year—The Sabbatical Year—The Jobel Year," *VT*, 26 (1976), 38-59; J. Lewy, "Ḫābirū and Hebrews," *HUCA*, 14 (1939), 587-623; *idem*, "A New Parallel between Ḫābirū and Hebrews," *HUCA*, 15 (1940), 47-58; *idem*, "The Biblical Institution of *D*ᵉ*rôr* in the Light of Akkadian Documents," *Eretz-Israel*, 5 (1958), 21–31; E. Lipiński, "L''esclave hébreu,' " *VT*, 26 (1976), 120-24; S. E. Loewenstamm, "Notes on the Alalakh Tablets," *IEJ*, 6 (1956), 217-225; I. Mendelsohn, "The Canaanite Term for " 'Free Proletarian,' " *BASOR*, 83 (1941), 36-39; *idem*, *Slavery in the Ancient Near East* (New York, 1949), 74-91; *idem*, "New Light on the Ḫupšu," *BASOR*, 139 (1955), 9-11; R. North, *Sociology of the Biblical Jubilee. AnBibl*, 4 (1954), xix-xxi [bibliog.]; S. M. Paul, *Studies in the Book of the Covenant in the Light of Cuneiform and Biblical Law. SVT*, 18 (1970); J. P. E. Pedersen, "Note on Hebrew ḥofšî," *JPOS*, 6 (1926), 103-105; N. M. Sarna, "Zedekiah's Emancipation of Slaves and the Sabbatical Year," *Orient and Occident. Festschrift C. H.*

I. The ḫupše and Heb. ḥopšî. Akk. *ḫupšu*[1] and Ugar. *ḫb/pṯ*[2] designate a low social stratum. According to Mendelsohn,[3] the *ḫupše* were "free proletarians" who owned small plots of ground. At Nuzi, according to Lacheman, they were semi-free. According to Dietrich and Loretz, the scribes at Alalakh considered the word to be Hurrian and preferred *namê* instead. At Alalakh the *ḫupše* were artisans, shepherds, and servants; at Ugarit and in Assyria they were also soldiers. In Assyria they did forced labor. The group at Byblos mentioned in the Rib-addi letters is hard to define. Gray[4] claims that in Canaan during the second millennium the term referred to a group of the nobility with military responsibilities and royal fiefs. This interpretation should be closely scrutinized. Gray often argues on the basis of etymology, and he cites 1 S. 17:25 without taking into account the text-critical problem of this passage.

The Heb. *ḥopšî* of Ex. 21:2-6 also seems originally to have designated a low social stratum, made up of emancipated slaves.[5] But there is no evidence for such a class in historical Israel. While Akk. *ḫupšu* and Ugar. *ḫb/pṯ* are appellatives that can be used freely, Heb. *ḥopšî* (apart from the difficult passage Ps. 88:6 [Eng. v. 5]) is invariably used as the negative of "slave," and almost always in fixed idioms referring to emancipation. Only in late texts do we find an extension of meaning and usage. This observation leads to the hypothesis that initially *ḥopšî* existed only as a linguistic relic of an earlier stage of language and society in such legal texts as Ex. 21:2-6, the only context in which it was still understood. It thus took on its typical OT meaning "emancipated slave," "freedman," and then found entrance once more into the living language: in other laws (e.g., Ex. 21:26f.), in extensions of the legal tradition of Ex. 21:2-6 (Dt. 15:12f.,18; Jer. 34:9-11,14,16), in other contexts (1 S. 17:25; Isa. 58:6; Job 3:19), and in metaphors (Job 39:5). Only when *ḥopšî* had acquired its new meaning did it give rise to new words: *ḥpš* pual, "be freed" (Lev. 19:20); *ḥupšâ*, "freedom" (Lev. 19:20); *ḥpš*, "freedom" (Sir. 7:21). Here, too, belong *bêṯ haḥopšîṯ* (2 K. 15:5; 2 Ch. 26:21 *Q*) and *bêṯ haḥopšûṯ* (2 Ch. 26:21 *K*) if we follow Qimḥi and others in interpreting the phrase as meaning "house of freedom from official duties," "(royal) retreat."

It is likely that 1 S. 17:25 is very late; it belongs to the portion of the Goliath story that is present in the MT but not in the original LXX. The way Gray and others

---

Gordon. AOAT, 22 (1973), 143-49; A. Schoors, "Literary Phrases," in *RSP,* I (1972), 1-70, esp. 27f.; H. J. Stoebe, "Die Goliathperikope 1 Sam. XVII 1–XVIII 5 und die Textform der Septuaginta," *VT,* 6 (1956), 397-413, esp. 403f.; E. Szlechter, "L'affranchissement en droit suméro-akkadien," *AHDO,* N.S. 7 (1952), 127-195; W. Thiel, *Die deuteronomistische Redaktion des Buches Jeremia* (diss., Berlin, 1970), 529-537; N. J. Tromp, *Primitive Conceptions of Death and the Nether World in the OT. BietOr,* 21 (1969), 157-59; R. de Vaux, *AncIsr,* 87f.; M. Weippert, *The Settlement of the Israelite Tribes in Palestine. SBT,* ser. 2, 21 (Eng. trans. 1971), 85-87.

1 *CAD,* VI (1956), 241f.; *AHw,* I, 357.

2 *WUS,* no. 1071; *UT,* nos. 930 and 995.

3 *BASOR,* 83 (1941); 139 (1955).

4 Cf. also Pedersen and Loewenstamm.

5 Lemche, *VT,* 25 (1975).

interpret the text arouses suspicion. The translation of *ḥop̄šî* here as "free (from paying tribute)" postulates an otherwise unattested sense, but note the extension of Akk. *andurāru šakānu,* "remit debts," "emancipate slaves," to the meaning "free from tribute" in Neo-Assyrian texts.[6] For *ḥop̄šî* in 1 S. 17:25, Stoebe assumed the normal meaning "emancipated" and finds an allusion to the Joseph story. But the word *ḥop̄šî* does not occur in the Joseph story, and our passage does not use the common expression for freeing a slave, but instead: *'ēṯ bêṯ 'āḇîw ya'ᵃśeh ḥop̄šî bᵉyiśrā'ēl.* Lemche[7] interprets *ḥop̄šî* here as a person who receives special favors from the court. Lipiński translates: "and his father's house he will make mighty in Israel." In both cases the argument is based on texts very distant in time from this late text.

In 2 K. 15:5, *bêṯ haḥop̄šîṯ* is frequently associated with Ugar. *bt ḫpṯt*[8] and interpreted as an idiom for the underworld. Ps. 88:6(5) is often cited to bolster this interpretation. But none of these texts has been really explained. It is not certain that they cast any light on each other. In addition, it is not really clear whether there is any connection between Ugar. *ḫb/pṯ* and Heb. *ḥop̄šî.* Several scholars,[9] looking for a term designating the underworld, translate *ḥop̄šî* in Ps. 88:6(5) as "my resting place," citing Ezk. 27:20. But in Ezk. 27:20 *ḥōp̄eš* does not mean "saddlecloth," referring instead to the material from which the saddlecloth (*beged*) is made. The term is probably a loanword; cf. Akk. *ḫibšu,* "a kind of hard wool."[10]

A graffito from Karnak, cited by Sayce,[11] reads: "*'[nk] b'[1] š'mr hḥpš bn . . . šr̊n̊,* "I am Baal [i]yamar, the freed, son of. . . ." Sayce considers the language to be Hebrew; *DISO*[12] is undecided. There has meanwhile come to light a Phoenician name *ḥpš,* attested in a fourth-century B.C. text from Mogador.[13] Dietrich, Loretz, and Sanmartín interpret Ugar. *b.ḫbṯh/b.yṣ 3h[m]* as "in case he is set free"/"if they flee."

In Sir. 13:11, following Barthélemy and Rickenbacher, we should probably assume that the root is *ḥpś.*

II. Meaning. According to Ex. 21:2-6, the *'eḇeḏ 'iḇrî* who ceases to be subject to his → אדון *'āḏôn* [*'ādhôn*] becomes *ḥop̄šî.* Originally the *'eḇeḏ 'iḇrî* was to be understood as a slave like those mentioned in the *wardūtu* documents of the *'apiru* at Nuzi.[14] Later, perhaps during the redaction of the Covenant Code and certainly by the time of Dt. 15, the *'eḇeḏ 'iḇrî* was understood as an "Israelite" slave; in Jer. 34 the term refers to a Judahite slave. Then *ḥop̄šî* acquired its more general meaning: "freedman." According to Lipiński, *'iḇrî* continued to designate a lower class right

---

6 *CAD,* I/2 (1964), 117a; → דרור *dᵉrôr.*

7 *VT,* 24 (1974).

8 *KTU,* 1.4 VIII, 7; 1.5 V, 15.

9 Nötscher, Dahood, Tromp, Schoors.

10 *AHw,* I, 344.

11 A. H. Sayce, "Unpublished Hebrew, Aramaic and Babylonian Inscriptions from Egypt, Jerusalem and Carchemish," *JEA,* 10 (1924), 16.

12 P. 94.

13 J.-G. Février, "Inscriptions puniques du Maroc," *Bulletin archéologique du Comité des travaux historiques et scientifiques* (Paris, 1955-58), 35.

14 Lewy, *HUCA,* 14 (1939); *idem, HUCA,* 15 (1940); Weippert; Paul.

down to the time of the exile. The word is often applied to women, although no feminine form is attested (Ex. 21:26f.; Dt. 15; Jer. 34; cf. Lev. 19:20).

Emancipation of a slave can be expressed verbally by *yāṣā'* (from the perspective of the slave) or the piel of *šlḥ* (from the perspective of the slave's owner). But with *ḥopšî* we find the two fuller expressions *yāṣā' [lᵉ]ḥopšî* and *šillaḥ [lᵉ]ḥopšî [mē'im];* these appear in 14 of the 17 occurrences of *ḥopšî*. In Dt. 15:15, → פדה *pāḏâ* is associated. In Lev. 19:20, however, *pāḏâ* is listed as an alternative to *ḥupšâ* among the various ways in which a slave relationship can be terminated. According to Jer. 34:9,15, the emancipation described in the law of Deuteronomy is the concrete form in which a → דרור *dᵉrôr* is proclaimed and validated (in this context, cf. Isa. 58:5f. with Isa. 61:1f., where a *dᵉrôr* is also proclaimed).

The meaning of *ḥopšî* is extended beyond "emancipated slave" in Isa. 58:6 ("set free from oppression or captivity") and 1 S. 17:25 ("exempted from tribute"). Nowhere is the modern concept of "freedom" attained.

III. The Religious Position of Emancipation. The legal provisions of Ex. 21:2 are less progressive than those of CH § 117, where at least in the case of resold debtor slaves[15] a maximum term of three years of service is provided. As yet, however, no extrabiblical parallels have been found for Ex. 21:5f. Even the restriction of the period of servitude to six years had a special meaning for Israel. The redaction of the Covenant Code deliberately began its collection of *mišpāṭîm* with the law in Ex. 21:2-6. Dt. 15:15 based the emancipation of slaves in the seventh year on the deliverance of Israel from Egypt. The Deuteronomistic redaction of the book of Jeremiah interpreted the *dᵉrôr* of 588 B.C. in terms of the law recorded in Dt. 15. Trito-Isaiah equated true fasting with the freeing of the oppressed (Isa. 58:6; cf. 61:1). Sir. 7:21 commended the emancipation of a slave as a good work.

The occurrences of *ḥôpšî* in Jer. 34:10f. do not appear in the LXX; they probably are among the many late interpolations found in Jer. 34. When these interpolations are removed, it is basically safe to follow Thiel in distinguishing the original account from the "Deuteronomistic" redaction. The Babylonian institution of the *mīšarum* may be compared with the *dᵉrôr* of 588.[16] It is hardly likely that the *dᵉrôr* would have been a periodic institution coinciding with the sabbatical year, for in that case there would have been no need for a → ברית *bᵉrîṯ* [*bᵉrîth*].[17] When the Deuteronomistic editors cite Dt. 15, in any case they are reinterpreting the act, whether we assume that Dt. 15:12 refers to the emancipation of each slave on an individual basis from his term of servitude, or whether (with Sarna, following a targumic tradition) we assume an emancipation of all Israelite slaves at once in the Sabbatical Year.

IV. Absence of ḥopšî from the Vocabulary of Soteriology. Slavery and emancipation took on theological significance in Israel: the whole semantic field served to interpret the exodus from Egypt, and then gave rise to a generalized soteriological

15 Szlechter.

16 Kraus; Lewy, *Eretz-Israel,* 5 (1958); Finkelstein.

17 David and Sarna take a different position.

vocabulary (cf. *yāṣā'*, *bêṯ ʿaḇāḏîm*, *pāḏâ*, *gā'al*). It appears relevant, therefore, that the word *ḥopšî* did not participate in this process. The reason why can be found as early as Dt. 6:20-25, where deliverance from Egyptian slavery serves to legitimate obedience to the law of Yahweh. The idea is developed even more directly in Lev. 25, where the word *ḥopšî* does not appear despite the thematic similarity to Ex. 21, Dt. 15, and Jer. 34. It has no place here because an Israelite who sells himself on account of his debts cannot be made a real slave. He must be treated as *śāḵîr* and *tôšāḇ* (Lev. 25:40). But the reason in turn is that all Israelites are slaves of Yahweh, by virtue of his having delivered them from slavery in Egypt (Lev. 25:45; cf. v. 55). Thus the theology of the exodus leads on the one hand to abrogation of human slavery; but on the other hand the result is not a theology of "freedom" but rather a theology of slavery to God.

Lohfink

חֵץ *ḥēṣ*

Contents: I. Etymology and Related Terms: 1. Hebrew; 2. LXX and Qumran. II. Ancient Near East: 1. Egypt; 2. Mesopotamia; 3. Asia Minor (Hittites); 4. Ugarit; 5. Ancient Greece and the Aegean. III. Construction. IV. Arrows as Weapons. V. Metaphorical Usage: 1. God's Arrow; 2. Male Potency and Offspring; 3. Lies and Slander.

I. Etymology and Related Terms.

1. *Hebrew.* The root of the Hebrew noun *ḥēṣ* is widespread in the Semitic languages: Akk. *uṣṣu* (or *ūṣu*), Ugar. *ḥẓ*, Phoen. *ḥṣ*, Imperial Aram. *ḥṣ*, Egyptian Aram. *ḥṭ*, Arab. *ḥuṭwatun*, Ethiop. *ḥṣ*. The widespread occurrence of this term for "arrow" suggests that the Semites used arrows for hunting and for war at an early date. In

---

ḥēṣ. R. D. Biggs, *ŠÀ.ZI.GA: Ancient Mesopotamian Potency Incantations. TCS*, 2 (1967); E. D. van Buren, *Symbols of the Gods in Mesopotamian Art. AnOr*, 23 (1945); C. H. Gordon, *UT* (1965); D. R. Hillers, "The Bow of Aqhat: The Meaning of a Mythological Theme," *Orient and Occident. Festschrift C. H. Gordon. AOAT*, 22 (1973), 71-80; H. A. Hoffner, Jr., "Symbols for Masculinity and Femininity: Their Use in Ancient Near Eastern Sympathetic Magic Rituals," *JBL*, 85 (1966), 326-334; S. Iwry, "New Evidence for Belomancy in Ancient Palestine and Phoenicia," *JAOS*, 81 (1961), 27-34; H. Limet, *Le travail du métal au pays de Sumer au temps de la IIIe dynastie d'Ur* (Paris, 1960); B. Meissner, *BuA;* A. Salonen, *Die Waffen der alten Mesopotamier* (1966), 109-125; J. M. Sasson, *The Military Establishments at Mari. Studia Pohl*, 3 (1969); F. H. Stubbings, "Arms and Armour," in A. Wace and F. H. Stubbings, *A Companion to Homer* (New York, 1963), 504-522, esp. 518-520; R. de Vaux, *AncIsr* (Eng. trans. 1961); M. Ventris and J. Chadwick, *Documents in Mycenaean Greek* (Cambridge, 1959), 360f.; W. Westendorf, "Bemerkungen zur 'Kammer der Wiedergeburt' im Tutanchamungrab," *ZÄS*, 94 (1967), 139-150; Y. Yadin, *The Art of Warfare in Biblical Lands in the Light of Archaeological Study* (Eng. trans., New York, 1963).

Biblical Hebrew, *ḥēṣ* is the usual term for "arrow"; besides it we find only 1 occurrence of the poetic expression *b^e^nê 'ašpâ,* "sons of the quiver" (Lam. 3:13), and *ben-qašet,* "son of the bow" (Job 41:20[Eng. v. 28]). The word *ḥēṣ* appears some 50 times in the OT, plus 4 conjectures.[1]

Hoffner

2. *LXX and Qumran.* The LXX always interprets *ḥēṣ* as a weapon, usually an "arrow" (*bélos,* 29 times; *bolís* and *schíza,* 6 times each), but sometimes as a "bow" (*tóxeuma,* 7 times; *tóxon,* 4 times). In 1 S. 17:7 we find *kontós,* "spear."

The Dead Sea scrolls use *ḥēṣ* almost exclusively in the metaphorical sense of "lying in wait"; cf. *ḥiṣṣê šaḥaṯ,* "arrows of the pit" (1QH 3:16,27).

Botterweck

II. Ancient Near East.

1. *Egypt.* The Egyptians usually used the words *'ḥ3* and *šsr* for "arrow," but on the basis of phonetic writing Gardiner suggests the existence of an even earlier term *swn/syn.*[2] Bow and arrow were widely used by Egyptian armies during the New Kingdom (16th century B.C. and after), but are also attested in earlier periods. Bows are represented on many monuments from the close of the fourth millennium (late predynastic period);[3] there are also representations in the art of the Old and Middle Kingdoms.[4]

There is evidence for symbolic use during the enthronement of the king: after his coronation, the king would shoot an arrow in each of the four directions, symbolizing victory over his enemies and his rule over all corners of the world. Four birds were released at the same time, to proclaim the king's enthronement to all four corners of the world.[5]

Westendorf showed that in Egypt the shooting of an arrow symbolized impregnation of a woman.[6] The image was understood in the same sense in Ḫatti, Mesopotamia, Ugarit, and in the OT.[7]

2. *Mesopotamia.* Since arrows were made primarily of reeds, they were referred to in Sumerian by the usual term for "reed," *ti.* In Akkadian, various terms were probably used for "arrow." The most common was *uṣṣu,* with the cognates *ḥṣ, ḥẓ,* and *ḥṭ* cited above. At various dates and in various regions, other terms sometimes supplanted *uṣṣu* or were added to it to designate a particular type of arrow: *ḫurḫutūtu* (Middle Babylonian at Nuzi), *mulmullu* (Middle Babylonian, Middle Assyrian, and

---

[1] *KBL*[3].
[2] A. H. Gardiner, *Egyptian Grammar* (London, [3]1957), Sign-list T 11.
[3] Yadin, 46f.
[4] Yadin, 46f., 62f., 81f.; pls. 118f., 146, 150f., 160ff., 200f.
[5] *RÄR,* 398.
[6] Pp. 130ff., esp. 142 and n. 11.
[7] Hoffner, 326ff.; see also below.

later), *qanû* (lit., "reed," used for "arrow" in Middle Babylonian in fringe areas of Asia Minor, Amarna, Nuzi, and Elam, as well as in Late Babylonian), and *šukūdu*.

Bows and arrows are represented in Mesopotamian art as early as the preliterary period (*ca.* 3000 B.C.) on the granite stela of Warka.[8] The earliest known representation of the compound bow is on the stela of Naram-sin at Susa (23rd century B.C.)[9] and on a fragment of limestone stela from Lagash, dating from the Akkadian period (around the 23rd century).

The arrow symbolized the deities Erra, Ninurta, and Nergal.[10] Erra was considered the god of parched earth and above all the god of pestilence. Ninurta was the god of warriors, the patron of Assyrian emperors; Ashurbanipal wrote, "Ninurta, the javelin, the great warrior, the son of Ellil, cut off the life of my enemies with his sharp arrows (*ina uṣṣišu zaqti*)."[11] Nergal is described as "[bearing] bow, arrows, and quiver."[12]

Bow and arrow stood as symbols of the warrior kings of the Neo-Assyrian period. Ashurbanipal boasts: "I held the bow, caused the arrow to fly, the ornament of my prowess."[13] In Egypt, Asia Minor, and Syria-Palestine, bow and arrow symbolized masculine sexuality in fertility rituals and incantations.[14] There is no explicit evidence in Mesopotamia for an arrow oracle like that promised the Babylonian king in Ezk. 21:26ff.(21ff.).[15] In Mesopotamian astronomical terminology, the "arrow star" was Sirius.[16]

3. *Asia Minor (Hittites).* In cuneiform Hittite, the word for "arrow" is usually represented by sumerograms; only rarely do we find syllabic orthography. It is a striking fact that archers are not mentioned in any narratives or descriptions. Only twice are archers mentioned in accounts of battles: enemy archers fought against the conqueror Suppiluliumas I.[17] On the Egyptian reliefs depicting the battle between the Egyptians and Hittites at Kadesh, the Hittite charioteers are shown without bows and arrows, in contrast to the Egyptians. The Hittites used their chariots drawn up in battle lines for attack and to bring their warriors, armed with lances, as quickly as possible into contact with any of the enemy that had not fled at the first onslaught. The Egyptians

---

8 Yadin, 46f., 118f.

9 *Ibid.*, 150.

10 Van Buren, 158f.; see also T. Solyman, *Die Entstehung und Entwicklung der Götterwaffen im alten Mesopotamien und ihre Bedeutung* (Beirut, 1968), 60, 113f.

11 Ashurbanipal, Rassam cylinder, IX, 84f.; cited from M. Streck, *Assurbanipal und die letzten assyrischen Könige bis zum Untergange Niniveh's. VAB*, 7 (1916), II, 79.

12 E. Ebeling, *Die akkadische Gebetsserie "Handerhebung." MDAW*, 20 (1953), 116, line 4; cf. E. von Weiher, *Der babylonische Gott Nergal. AOAT*, 11 (1971), 71.

13 Streck, 256, line 21.

14 Biggs, 38.

15 *BuA*, II, 65, 275; for a discussion of the technique used, see W. Zimmerli, *Ezekiel 1. Herm* (Eng. trans. 1979), 443.

16 *BuA*, II, 412f.

17 H. G. Güterbock, "The Deeds of Suppiluliuma as Told by his Son, Mursili II," *JCS*, 10 (1956), 76f.; K. K. Riemschneider, "Hethitische Fragmente historischen Inhalts aus der Zeit Ḫattušilis III," *JCS*, 16 (1962), 110-121.

improved on these tactics by arming the chariots with archers.[18] This may explain why some bows in inventory texts are referred to as "bows of Kaskaean type."[19] Nevertheless, inventories of military equipment[20] list great quantities of arrows, demonstrating that there were archers in the Hittite armies, even in the later period (*ca.* 1300-1200 B.C.).

Hunters are depicted as archers in Hittite art.[21] In magical rituals, bow and arrow symbolize both male sexuality and typically male military prowess.[22] In rituals intended to keep epidemics from Hittite armies and inflict them on the enemy,[23] the god who sends the epidemic is depicted with bow and arrow. To him the petition is addressed: "O God, shoot always upon the land of the enemy with these arrows; but if you come into the land of the Hittites, keep your quiver closed and your bow unbraced." Lions were hunted with bow and arrow.[24] A myth describes an archery contest with the warrior Gurparanzahu;[25] a palace chronicle describes similar contests in the presence of the king during the Old Kingdom.[26]

4. *Ugarit.* The Ugaritic word for "arrow" is *ḥẓ*. Occasionally *qṣ't* has been considered a poetic synonym for *ḥẓ*, but Gordon is probably correct in preferring the meaning "bow."[27] In the Ugaritic texts, arrows are mentioned in inventories of military reserves, and occasionally in military contexts within epics.[28] The fletcher is called *psl ḥẓm*, identical by Dietrich and Loretz with Hurr. *ḫdǵl*.[29] The use of arrow oracles may provide the semantic connection between *ḥẓ*, "arrow," and *ḥẓ*, "happy," in *ḥyt.ḥẓt*, "happy life."[30]

The sexual symbolism of shooting an arrow cannot be missed in *KTU*, 1.23, where it forms part of a test of El's undiminished procreative powers.[31] The bow and arrow motif is equally important in the story of Danel.[32] Danel is given a bow and arrows by the divine smith Kothar-wa-Ḫasis,[33] and he gives them in turn to his son Aqhat. The warlike goddess 'Anat desires them, and offers in return wealth and immortality.[34]

---

18 Stubbings, 521.

19 *KBo*, XVIII, 172, obv. 6, etc.

20 *KUB*, XIII, 35, obv. I, 2; III, 3, 6, 46; IV, 10; *ABoT*, 54, 6; *KBo*, XVIII, 172, obv. 6ff.; 170a, vo. 7; 160, IV, 3.

21 E. Akurgal, *The Art of the Hittites* (Eng. trans., New York, 1962), pls. 94 and 147 (black and white).

22 Hoffner, 326ff.

23 *KUB*, VII, 54, III, 19ff.; E. Laroche, *Catalogue des textes Hittites* (Paris, 1971), 425.

24 *KUB*, VIII, 1, I, 3.

25 *KUB*, XXXVI, 67, II, 18ff.

26 *KBo*, III, 34 (+) II, 33ff.

27 *UT*, no. 2258.

28 *KTU*, 1.14, III, 12.

29 M. Dietrich and O. Loretz, "Die soziale Struktur von Alalaḫ und Ugarit," *WO*, 3/3 (1966), 199.

30 *KTU*, 1.3 V, 31; 1.4 IV, 42; Iwry, 27-34.

31 Lines 37f.

32 *KTU*, 1.17.

33 V, 9-35.

34 VI, 16-33.

But Aqhat refuses: "My bow is [a weapon for] warriors; are women now to hunt [with it]?"—in other words, bow and arrows are a man's weapon, not a woman's.[35]

In Phoenician texts, the word *ḥṣ*, "arrow," occurs in three arrowhead inscriptions[36] and in the altar inscription from Kition.[37] In the latter we twice find the divine name *ršp ḥṣ*, which may be associated with *bʿl ḥẓ ršp*,[38] "Reshep, lord of the *ḥẓ*" (cf. below, V. 1). Aram. *ḥṣ*, "arrow," occurs in the eighth-century Sefire inscription; in *KAI*, 222 A.38f., the breaking of bow and arrow symbolizes the downfall of Mati'ilu's military power should he break his oath.

5. *Ancient Greece and the Aegean.* Among the Linear B tablets from Knossos was found a seal[39] that formed part of the charred remains of two wooden chests containing charred arrow shafts and points. The seal bears the Linear B logogram for "arrow," along with a syllabic writing of what was probably the Mycenean word for "arrow" (*pa-ta-ia*). The arrowheads are bronze. In the *Iliad*, the bow plays a relatively minor role and appears to be a foreign weapon (of the Lycians, Karians, and Paeonians). Only three major Greek warriors are regular archers: Philoctetes, Teucer, and Meriones of Crete. Only once in the *Iliad*[40] does Odysseus borrow a bow from Meriones. Most arrows have bronze heads; iron arrowheads are rarer.[41] It has been suggested that bows became less important during the period of the Trojan War (*ca.* 1200 B.C.). If this is true, it helps explain why in the *Iliad* only those warriors use a bow who belong to a generation before the Trojan War (e.g., Hercules). The bow and arrow as divine weapons are characteristic of Apollo, whose epithet is *hekēbólos*, "far shooting." It has been suggested that his arrows symbolize the plague, since they bring death to the camp of the enemy.[42] The compound bow of Odysseus may also have a latent sexual symbolism, since the suitors of Odysseus' wife had to be able to brace it before they could have any claim to her. Shooting with the bow has such associations among many cultures of the eastern Mediterranean in ancient times.

III. Construction. An arrow consisted of three parts, each made of a different material so that it could fulfill its specific function. The head was made of the hardest material available, to enable it to penetrate: flint, bone, or metal. The shaft had the function of transferring the energy released when the bowstring accelerated, and it was therefore long, thin, straight, stiff, and light. It usually was made of wood or reed. The tail was designed to stabilize the flight of the arrow; it was made from eagle, vulture, or kite feathers. The head was attached to the shaft by having the base of the head inserted into the shaft ("stemmed" arrowheads), or by having the shaft inserted

---

35 For interpretation of the story of Aqhat and his bow as involving sexual symbolism, see Hoffner, 326ff., and Hillers, 73f.

36 *KAI*, 20-22.

37 *KAI*, 32.

38 *KTU*, 1.82, 3.

39 Ws 1704 = Ventris and Chadwick, 361.

40 x.260.

41 iv.123.

42 E. Kirsten, "Achaoioi, 2," *KlPauly*, I, 42.

into the base of the arrowhead ("socket"). The heads might be leaf-shaped or triangular; they might be flat, ribbed, or ridged. The form was dictated by the nature of the enemy armor.[43] Arrowheads were often barbed or dipped in poison (Job 6:4). The tips of fire arrows had holes through which oil-soaked tow was threaded and then ignited (cf. Ps. 7:14[13]).

IV. Arrows as Weapons. Bow and arrow were the normal weapons of nomads (Gen. 21:20), hunters (Gen. 27:3; Isa. 7:24), robbers (Gen. 48:22; Josh. 24:12), and soldiers (Isa. 13:18; Ezk. 39:9; Hos. 1:7). Archers usually were among the footsoldiers, as were slingers (1 S. 31:3; 1 Ch. 10:3; 12:2; 2 Ch. 35:23); but they also fired from the battlements of besieged cities (2 S. 11:24; 2 Ch. 26:15),[44] from chariots (2 K. 9:24),[45] from horseback,[46] from mobile siege towers,[47] and in sea battles from ship to ship.[48] Before the invention of the catapult, bow and arrow were the most effective missile weapons used in sieges (2 K. 19:32 par. Isa. 37:33).

V. Metaphorical Usage.

1. *God's Arrow.* Bow and arrow as weapons of deities (Erra, Ninurta, Nergal, ʿAnat, Reshep, Apollo) have already been mentioned.[49] The arrows of Yahweh symbolize his attack upon the enemy. In Nu. 24:8 and Dt. 32:42, the enemies are the enemies of Israel, and the effects of the arrows are described in clear images. In Ps. 64:8(7), the arrows strike the scheming enemies of the psalmist. But Yahweh's arrows can also strike his own people, as in Dt. 32:23, a list of punishments including hunger, disease, wild beasts, and war. In laments the same image is applied to individuals: Job 6:4; Ps. 38:3(2); Lam. 3:12f. In Ps. 91:5f., "the arrow that flies by day" stands in parallel with three terms for plagues that strike by night; probably the arrow also symbolizes a disease or a demon that brings disease. In Ezk. 5:16, the arrows of Yahweh symbolize famine; v. 17 also mentions wild beasts.[50] Arrows are implements of divine punishment in Ps. 7:14(13) and Prov. 7:23.

Yahweh's arrows are often described as being bright; in theophanies, in combination with other storm imagery, they are depicted as lightning (2 S. 22:15 par. Ps. 18:15(14); Ps. 144:6 [all 3 times with *hmm,* "confusion]; Hab. 3:11; Zec. 9:14; also Ps. 77:18[17], with reference to the exodus). On occasion Yahweh uses the arrows of one nation to punish another (against Israel, Isa. 5:28; against Babylon, Jer. 50:9,14; 51:11). In Ps. 45:6(5), the king is assured that his arrows will destroy the enemy.

The use of arrows for oracles is probably connected with the idea of God's arrows;[51]

---

43 Yadin, 8f.

44 Cf. *ibid.,* 229 (Ashkelon), 422 (Gaza), 430f. (Lachish).

45 Cf. *ibid.,* 382f.

46 Cf. *ibid.,* 384f.

47 *Ibid.,* 408 (Assyrians).

48 *Ibid.,* 340f. (Medinet Habu).

49 II.2, 4, 5.

50 See above.

51 Iwry, 27-34.

it is attested in the West Semitic area and possibly (albeit not with certainty) in Mesopotamia (cf. II.2 and Ezk. 21:26ff.[21ff.]). In the double oracle given by Elisha to Joash, the king of Israel (2 K. 13:15-18), an arrow symbolizes military victory: the king shoots a "victory arrow" eastward and strikes the ground three times with arrows, a gesture intended to symbolize three victories over the Arameans; if he had struck five or six times, he would have destroyed them totally.

2. *Male Potency and Offspring.* The ancient motif of bow and arrow as a masculine symbol, with spindle and distaff as a feminine symbol,[52] can also be traced in the OT. Children, the clearest proof of virility, are likened to a quiver full of arrows (Ps. 127:4f.). The ideal wife (*'ēšeṯ-ḥayil*) puts her hands to the distaff (*kîšôr,* Prov. 31:19). But it was accounted a curse to wish that a man and his descendants should sit forever holding a spindle (2 S. 3:29).[53] The ideal man always had bow and arrow ready.[54] According to Dt. 22:5, it was strictly forbidden to attempt to change the sex of an enemy by the symbolic or magical exchange of clothing or other identifying objects.[55] The symbol of a man is here called *kᵉlî-geḇer,* "that which pertains to [or 'the weapon of'] a man." A woman is symbolized by *śimlaṯ 'iššâ,* "a woman's garments." Hittite and Ugaritic texts show clearly that such exchange of clothing or symbols, often called transvestism, frequently served to assure the desired masculine qualities of the transvestite and deny them to the enemy.

Hoffner

This interpretation of the *tô'ēḇâ* law in Dt. 22:5 as the prohibition of analogical magic has not gone undisputed; most scholars think primarily in terms of a cultic transgression: confusion of sacred objects,[56] cultic prostitution,[57] or transvestism as a sexual perversion, which is attested among the Hittites and Canaanites.[58]

Botterweck

3. *Lies and Slander.* Lies and slander in the mouth of the enemy are often compared to sharp and poisoned arrows (Ps. 57:5[4]; 64:4[3]; Prov. 25:18; 26:18; Jer. 9:7[8]). Ps. 64 depicts the slanderers as being slain with their own weapons (vv. 4,8[3,7]); in like manner the obscure verse Ps. 7:14(13) probably means that the devices of the wicked (deadly weapons, fiery arrows) return upon the user. Ps. 11:2 describes the work of the *rᵉšā'îm* as arrows shot from ambush.

Hoffner

---

52 Hoffner, 326ff.; Biggs, 38; Westendorf, 139f.; Hillers, 73f.

53 Hoffner, 329, 332; cf. also *Odyssey* xxi.350-53 with Hoffner, 329, n. 16.

54 Hoffner, 329.

55 *Ibid.*, 332ff.

56 G. von Rad, *Deuteronomy. OTL* (Eng. trans. 1966), 141; a similar interpretation is given by P. Buis and J. Leclercq, *Le Deutéronome* (Paris, 1963), 151.

57 J. L'Hour, "Les interdits *to'eba* dans le Deutéronome," *RB,* 71 (1964), 494.

58 J. N. M. Wijngaards, *Deuteronomium. BOT,* II (1971), 241f.

חָצַב *ḥāṣaḇ;* מַחְצֵב *maḥṣēḇ;* גָּזִית *gāzîṯ*

Contents: I. 1. Etymology, Occurrences; 2. Meaning. II. Secular Usage: 1. General; 2. Occupation; 3. *gāzîṯ;* 4. LXX. III. Use in Religious Contexts: 1. Preexilic Prophets; 2. Deutero-Isaiah.

I. 1. *Etymology, Occurrences.* The root *ḥṣb,* attested as early as Akkadian in the form *ḫaṣābu,* appears not only in Hebrew but also in Ugaritic, Phoenician, Aramaic, Mandaic, Yemenite, and Arabic texts.[1] It is used both as a verb (qal, pual, niphal, and hiphil) and in nouns; the Siloam inscription contains the form *ḥsbm.*[2]

2. *Meaning.* In agreement with the Akkadian parallel, we may assume "cut off" as the basic meaning (cf. Isa. 10:15). With this as the starting point, the word group developed various specialized meanings in the OT: "dig out, excavate" (Dt. 8:9; 1 K. 5:29[Eng. v. 15]), "hew out" (Dt. 6:11; Jer. 2:13), "quarry" (2 K. 12:13[12]; 1 Ch. 22:2), as well as "engrave" (Job 19:24) and "hew down" (Isa. 51:9; Hos. 6:5).

II. Secular Usage. All the passages in which the word group appears in the OT as well as in other Hebrew texts (Siloam inscription, Oxyrhynchus papyri) illustrate secular usage, with a variety of meanings. A distinction can be made only when the context is itself secular or suggests a religious reference.

1. *General.* Characteristic of secular usage is association with rocks and mining. Thus *ḥāṣaḇ* with the meaning "hew out" refers to the activity of carving various kinds of holes in the rock for wells and cisterns (Dt. 6:11; 2 Ch. 26:10; Neh. 9:25; Jer. 2:13), water supply tunnels,[3] wine presses (Isa. 5:2), and tombs (Isa. 22:16). Analogously, the meaning "break loose by digging" refers exclusively to the process of quarrying (1 K. 5:29[15]; 1 Ch. 22:15; 2 Ch. 2:1,17[2,18]) or mining (Dt. 8:9). Even when the word group is used in the sense of "carve" or "engrave" there is always a reference to stone as the material involved; this reference is made clear in 2 K. 12:13(12); 22:6; 1 Ch. 22:2; 2 Ch. 34:11 by the addition of → אבן *'eḇen* [*'ebhen*] and in Job 19:24 by the noun *ṣûr.*

ḥāṣaḇ. P. A. H. de Boer, "Notes on an Oxyrhynchus Papyrus in Hebrew," *VT,* 1 (1951), 49-57; D. Conrad, *Studien zum Altargesetz, Ex. 20:24-26* (diss., Marburg, 1968), 32-52, esp. 35f.; G. R. Driver, "Hebrew Notes," *VT,* 1 (1951), 241-250, esp. 246; R. J. Forbes, *Studies in Ancient Technology,* VII (Leiden, ²1966); W. Rudolph, *Hosea. KAT,* XIII/1 (1966), 132f., 139; S. Spiegel, "A Prophetic Attestation of the Decalogue: Hosea 6:5 with Some Observations on Psalms 15 and 24," *HThR,* 27 (1934), 105-144; I. Zolli, "Note on Hosea 6.5," *JQR,* N.S. 31 (1940/41), 79-82.

1 *KB*³, 329.
2 *KAI,* 189.
3 Siloam inscription, lines 4, 6.

2. *Occupation*. Within this word group the predominance of the participle is striking: it appears 18 times, including the Siloam inscription and the Oxyrhynchus papyri, as well as Ezr. 2:57 and Neh. 7:59, where *ḥaṣṣᵉḇāyîm* should be read.[4] This is largely because in the OT period the quarrying and shaping of stone, as well as the carving of inscriptions in stone, was the particular job of specific occupational groups, the "quarriers" and "stone-masons." Although the same word is usually used to designate both, the two occupations are distinct, as can be seen above all from 1 Ch. 22:15, which speaks of *ḥōṣᵉḇîm* alongside *ḥārāšê 'eḇen;* additional evidence is found in 1 K. 5:29(15) and 2 Ch. 2:1,17(2,18), which speak of *ḥōṣēḇ bāhār.*

Schunck

3. *gāzîṯ*. Alongside *ḥāṣaḇ* and *'aḇnê maḥṣeḇ* we find the term (*'aḇnê*) *gāzîṯ,* which appears 11 times, primarily in connection with the altar, the temple, or other elaborate buildings. It is found in the account of the building of the temple (1 K. 5:31[17]; 6:36; 7:9,11f.; 1 Ch. 22:2), in the law of the altar (Ex. 20:25), in the prophets (Isa. 9:9[10]; Ezk. 40:42; Am. 5:11), and in Lam. 3:9. The usual translation is "hewn stones" or "ashlar"; Conrad attempts to define the meaning more precisely in terms of history and archeology. From the ninth or eighth century on, *gāzîṯ* refers to the stone used as building material for elaborate buildings such as the royal palace and the temple; *'aḇnê gāzîṯ* are "hewn stones."[5] In the earlier period, which includes the altar law in Ex. 20:25, *gāzîṯ* still means only "cut stone" or simply "that which has been shaped or cut."[6] For an explanation of the law prohibiting use of *gāzîṯ,* hewn stones, for building a stone altar because they are profaned (*ḥillēl*) by a tool (*ḥereṭ*), see the survey in Conrad[7] and also this dictionary.[8]

4. *LXX*. In the LXX, *ḥṣb* is rendered by forms of *latomeín* (16 times) and occasionally by *kóptein, englýphein,* or *eklatomeín*. It is also rendered by more general verbs such as *metalleúein, orýssein,* or *poieín*. The translations of *gāzîṯ* are in part contradictory. Alongside *apelékētos,* "unhewn" (6 times), we find *xestós/xystós,* "hewn, smoothed," and *tmētós,* "cut." Sometimes *ḥṣb* is paraphrased with the verb *labeúein.*

Botterweck

III. Use in Religious Contexts.

1. *Preexilic Prophets*. The preexilic prophets use the word *ḥāṣaḇ* in two ways. First, they use it as a term for a secular image drawn from the everyday life of Israel, which they draw on to make a religious statement; besides Isa. 5:2, this usage appears especially clearly in Isa. 10:15, where the word *ḥōṣēḇ* describes Yahweh using Assyria as axe and saw to execute judgment upon his people, and in Jer. 2:13, where a hewn-out broken cistern symbolizes the foreign gods who are not Yahweh. In addition, the prophets use the verb in the sense "hew or cut (down)" to describe how Yahweh

---

4 *KBL*³, 329.

5 Conrad, 43ff.

6 *Ibid.*, 45.

7 *Ibid.*, 32ff.

8 A. S. Kapelrud, "אבן *'eḇen* [*'ebhen*]," *TDOT,* I, 49.

executes judgment through the prophets; Hos. 6:5, for example, states that Yahweh has hewn his people by the prophets.[9]

2. *Deutero-Isaiah.* Both uses of the root on the part of the preexilic prophets are continued by Deutero-Isaiah. In Isa. 51:1, using a mythological image, he likens the patriarch Abraham to a rock from which Israel was hewn;[10] in 51:9,[11] he uses mythological language to describe Yahweh's cutting the primeval Rahab in pieces.

Schunck

---

[9] For a different interpretation, see Rudolph, 132f., 139; Rudolph takes the meaning to be "incise." Following A. Klostermann, *ThLB,* 1905, 473-78, and Spiegel, 136, he thinks of Moses, functioning as a prophet, carving the Decalog on stone.

[10] P. Volz, *Jesaia II. KAT,* IX/2 (1932), 110f.; C. R. North, *The Second Isaiah* (New York, 1964), 209; N. A. van Uchelen, "Abraham als Felsen (Jes. 51 1)," *ZAW,* 80 (1968), 183-191; interpreted differently by P. A. H. de Boer, *Second-Isaiah's Message. OTS,* 11 (1956), 58-67.

[11] For discussion of the form, see I. L. Seeligmann, "Voraussetzungen der Midraschexegese," *SVT,* 1 (1953), 169, n. 4.

חָצִיר *ḥāṣîr*

Contents: I. 1. Root, Meaning; 2. Synonyms, Versions; 3. Distribution. II. 1. Grass as a Blessing; 2. "No Grass" in Curse Texts. III. 1. Image of Transitoriness; Semantic Field; 2. Human Transitoriness; 3. Transitoriness of Enemies and the Wicked.

I. 1. *Root, Meaning.* The masculine noun *ḥāṣîr,* "grass," belongs to the root *ḥṣr* I, "be green, become green," which is also attested in Punic,[1] Ethiopic (*ḥadra*), and Arabic (*ḥaḍira*).[2] The word *ḥṣr,* "grass, plants," appears also in Phoenician[3] and Old Aramaic;[4] but Kutscher thinks that Aram. *ḥṣr* is a Canaanism. The word *ḥaṣrā'* in the Aramaic Targumim is a borrowing from Heb. *ḥāṣîr.*

ḥāṣîr. W. W. Graf Baudissin, *Adonis und Esmun* (Leipzig, 1911), 204f.; J. Blau, "HEBREW *ḥâṣîr* 'reed' a ghost-word," in "Marginalia Semitica I," *Israel Oriental Studies,* 1 (Tel-Aviv, 1971), 8-11; G. W. Coats, "Self-Abasement and Insult Formulas," *JBL,* 89 (1970), 14-26; F. Crüsemann, *Studien zur Formgeschichte von Hymnus und Danklied in Israel. WMANT,* 32 (1969), 135-152; G. Dalman, *AuS,* I (1928), 334f.; E. Y. Kutscher, "Mittelhebräisch und Jüdisch-Aramäisch im neuen Köhler-Baumgartner," *Hebräische Wortforschung. Festschrift W. Baumgartner. SVT,* 16 (1967), 158-175, esp. 171; B. Meissner, *BuA,* I, 186; L. Wächter, *Der Tod im AT. ArbT,* 2/8 (1967), 97-106.

[1] *DISO,* 95.

[2] *KBL*³, 331.

[3] Baudissin.

[4] *KAI,* 222 A.28.

Alongside *ḥāṣîr,* "grass," Biblical Hebrew also has *ḥāṣîr,* "leeks" (Nu. 11:5), and *ḥāṣîr,* "reeds" (Isa. 44:4); both derive from a root *ḥṣr* II, attested only in Arabic (*ḥaṣira*).[5]

2. *Synonyms, Versions.* The word *ḥāṣîr,* "grass," shares the basic meaning "something green" with → דשא *deše'* [*deshe'*], → עשב *'ēśeḇ,* and → ירק *yereq.* All three words accordingly appear as more or less precise parallels to *ḥāṣîr,* "grass": *deše'* in Prov. 27:25; Isa. 15:6; *yereq* in Isa. 15:6; *yereq deše'* in 2 K. 19:26; Ps. 37:2; Isa. 37:27; *'ēśeḇ śāḏeh* in 2 K. 19:26; Isa. 37:27; cf. Prov. 27:25. The word *ṣîṣ* appears to be closely associated: cf. *ṣîṣ haśśāḏeh* (Ps. 103:15; Isa. 40:6) and the verb *ṣîṣ* in Ps. 90:6 alongside *ḥāṣîr,* "grass."

For *ḥāṣîr* the LXX 12 times uses *chórtos,* a general word for "cattle fodder, grass, new grass." Twice we find the general term *botánē,* "plant, pasturage." We also find *práson,* "leeks," *chlóē,* "new shoots," and *chlōrós,* a more phenomenological term for the light green of new shoots. The Vulg. mostly translates *faenum,* "hay," occasionally (esp. Jerome) *herba.*

3. *Distribution.* Unlike the common word *'ēṣeḇ* (33 occurrences), *ḥāṣîr* occurs almost exclusively in poetic texts (17 occurrences); it appears only once in a prose narrative (1 K. 18:5). It occurs in prophetic forms (Isa. 15:6; 37:27 par. 2 K. 19:26; Isa. 40:6-8; 51:12 [8 occurrences]), in the Psalms (Ps. 37:2; 90:5; 103:15; 104:14; 129:6; 147:8 [6 occurrences]), and in Wisdom Literature (Job 40:15; Prov. 27:25 [2 occurrences]). In Isa. 34:13 and 35:7, the comms. read *ḥāṣēr,* "farm," instead of *ḥāṣîr.* It is possible that Job 8:12 refers to "grass" rather than "reeds."

II. 1. *Grass as a Blessing.* Narrative, hymnic, and didactic texts refer to *ḥāṣîr* as food for the beasts of the field (*b^ehēmâ*) and domesticated animals (*bāqār*); see 1 K. 18:5; Job 40:15; Ps. 104:14; 147:8f.; Prov. 27:25. The indirect benefit to human beings is expressed in Ps. 104:14, and is implicit in 147:8f.

In both Ps. 104:14 (*maṣmîaḥ ḥāṣîr*) and 147:8 (*hammaṣmîaḥ hārîm ḥāṣîr*), the praise of the goodness of Yahweh "who causes the grass to grow" takes the form of the hymnic participle. As Crüsemann recognized, this form corresponds regularly to a specific theme: God's governance as creator and preserver of the whole created world. The "participial hymn" derives in form and content from a very ancient Babylonian hymn tradition. Even the special motif of causing vegetation to grow appears frequently in Babylonian hymns: *mudiššū urqîti,* "he who causes that which is green to grow" (and other examples from hymns to Marduk and Nergal).[6] The word *mudiššū* is cognate with Heb. *deše',* *urqîtu* with Heb. *yereq.*

2. *"No Grass" in Curse Texts.* Luxuriant grass on the fields and mountains is a sign of heavenly blessing (Ps. 65:11[Eng. v. 10]); conversely, the desiccation and withering

5 *KBL*³, 330f.

6 K. L. Tallqvist, *Akkadische Götterepitheta. StOr,* 7 (1938; repr. 1974), 84, 370, 395.

of vegetation is a sure sign of punishment or curse. In the curse section of ancient Near Eastern treaties, drought and absence of grass are among the consequences threatened if the treaty is broken: cf. *w'l ypq ḥṣr wlythzh yrq wly[thzh] 'ḥwh,* "so that no vegetation sprouts, so that no more green is seen, so that his grass is no longer [seen]" (Sefire inscription, from the middle of the 8th century B.C.);[7] the similar formulas in the treaty between Ashurnirari V and Mati'ilu of Arpad, from the same period;[8] and the threat *lō'-ya'aleh bāh kol-'ēśeḇ* (Dt. 29:22[23]) in the concluding ritual of the "covenant in Moab" (Dt. 28:69–30:20[29:1–30:20]). There may be a reminiscence of such formulas in the (exilic?) lament over Moab in Isa. 15:1-9: "the waters of Nimrim are a desolation," *kî-yāḇēš ḥāṣîr kālâ deše' yereq lō'-hāyâ* (15:6).[9] Comparable descriptions appear in Isa. 19:5-7; Jer. 12:4; 23:10.

III. 1. *Image of Transitoriness; Semantic Field.* The word *ḥāṣîr,* "grass," finds an entirely different usage in the context of biblical passages dealing with "transitoriness." The associated motifs include reference to the rapid desiccation and death of low vegetation under the influence of heat, east wind, and drought.[10]

The semantic field of such passages includes verbs like → נבל *nāḇēl,* "wither" (Ps. 37:2; Isa. 40:7f.; Job 14:2 conj.); → מלל *mll,* "wither" (Job 14:2; Ps. 37:2; 90:6; 58:8[7]?); → יבש *yāḇēš,* "dry out" (Job 8:12; Ps. 90:6; 129:6; Isa. 15:6; 40:7f.; 42:15); and → כלה *kālâ,* "perish" (Ps. 90:7; Isa. 15:6). There are occasional occurrences of *šāḏap,* "parch" (2 K. 19:26; Isa. 37:27 [1QIs^a], *hnšdp;* Ps. 129:6 conj.[11]), and the niphal of *nāṯan,* "be given over" (Isa. 51:12). The cause is the wind (*rûaḥ,* Ps. 103:16; Isa. 40:7), more specifically the east wind (*qāḏîm,* Isa. 37:27 [1QIs^a]; Ps. 129:6 conj.; cf. Ezk. 17:10; 19:12). Soonest affected is perhaps the grass "on the roofs" (*gaggôṯ,* Ps. 129:6; Isa. 37:27). The sudden death of vegetation is contrasted with its rapid sprouting and growth, expressed by such verbs as → צמח *ṣāmaḥ,* "sprout" (Ps. 104:14; 147:8; Isa. 44:4; Job 14:2 conj.), → חלף *ḥālap,* "change," in the sense of "spring forth anew" (Ps. 90:5f.; cf. hiphil in Jon. 14:7; Ps. 129:6 conj.[12]), and possibly also *ṣîṣ,* "bloom" (Ps. 90:6; 103:15).

2. *Human Transitoriness.* When the rapid withering of vegetation is compared to the transitoriness of humankind, the purpose in the first instance is to incline God to mercy and forbearance.[13] In Ps. 103, a highly individualized hymn,[14] the mention of transitoriness appears in vv. 9-18, a middle section that expatiates on Yahweh's kind forgiveness. Human transitoriness (*'enôš keḥāṣîr yāmāw,* " . . . like grass [with respect to] his days," v. 15) is set in deliberate contrast to the enduring love of Yahweh (v. 17).

---

7 See *KAI,* 222 A.28f.
8 Vo. IV, 20; *ANET*³, 533.
9 O. Kaiser, *Isaiah 13–39. OTL* (Eng. trans. 1974), 57.
10 *BuA,* I, 186; *AuS,* I, 334f.
11 *BHS.*
12 *GesB,* V.
13 Wächter, 102f.
14 Crüsemann, 302-304.

The mention of transitoriness in Ps. 90, a communal lament in which vv. 15b and 16 appear also to refer to humankind (see the reference to *ḥālap̱* above), seeks also for God's mercy (v. 13), with strong emphasis on the eternity of Yahweh (vv. 1f., 4). Similar ideas appear in Ps. 102:2(1) (cf. vv. 13f.[12f.]) and Job 14:1f. (cf. v. 3). Humankind can similarly be likened to a shadow (→ צֵל *ṣēl*) or dust (→ עפר *'āpar*) or be termed flesh (→ בשר *bāśār*).[15]

With respect to their purpose, these statements may be likened to the "self-abasement formulas" found in the language of the court and the cult, and discussed by Coats. Using rhetorical questions like "Who am I, that you . . ." or "What is man, that you . . . ," the "servant" states to his "lord" that he is not worthy of some particular treatment (usually kind).[16]

3. *Transitoriness of Enemies and the Wicked.* There is also another context in which the brevity of human life is likened to that of grass. In a series of passages (Job 8:11-13; Ps. 37:1f.; 129:5-7; Isa. 51:12; probably also Isa. 40:6-8), the simile is applied not to the individual praying to or meditating before the eternal God, but to the enemy or the wicked. A prophet, priest, or Wisdom teacher here assures whoever is oppressed by enemies or the wicked that there is no need to fear (Isa. 51:12) or fret (Ps. 37:1): even the mighty are—in the eyes of God!—as perishable and transitory as grass. The comfort intended by the comparison is obvious from the context in all the passages mentioned. In Isa. 40:6-8, however, it can be recognized only if we follow Elliger[17] instead of the usual interpretation, which sees the prophet in vv. 6b-7 attempting to evade the divine commission by referring to his own (!) mortality. Elliger sees here a connected passage, with a message of comfort given to the prophet following v. 6a (cf. v. 1). Mortal "flesh," fading "flower," and withering "grass" refer in this context neither to humankind in general nor to the devout (or the prophet) in particular, but (cf. v. 24) to the enemy who holds in his power the people to whom the prophet is to speak. However powerful he may claim to be, he is mortal, transitory "as the grass." This message is confirmed because it "stands forever" (v. 8b[18]). If v. 7 does in fact belong to the original text, at least the conclusion (*'āḵēn ḥāṣîr hā'ām*) must be considered an erroneous gloss.

Barth

15 For a discussion of Isa. 40:6-8, see III.3 below.

16 For examples of this idiom outside the Bible, in addition to those mentioned by Coats, see *ABL,* 210, vo. 8; 885, vo. 17; 965; etc.

17 *Deuterojesaja. BK,* XI/1 (1978), 22-29.

18 *Ibid.*

חָצֵר *ḥāṣēr*

Contents: I. Outside the Bible: 1. Etymology; 2. Akkadian; 3. Ugaritic; 4. Phoenician; 5. OSA; 6. Arabic; 7. Aramaic (and Greek). II. OT: 1. Settlements; 2. Courts.

I. Outside the Bible.

1. *Etymology.* On the basis of *BDB,* Orlinsky[1] and after him Malamat[2] assumed two different Protosemitic roots, the first leading to the meaning "settlement, village," the second to "enclosure, court." *KBL*[3] accepted this distinction, which can be observed primarily in Arabic. But it is probably going too far to speak of two "Protosemitic" roots. Not only are the three radicals suspiciously similar, but the semantic differences are not as great as they appear at first. More likely we are dealing with a primitive Semitic root having the meaning "surround."

2. *Akkadian.* In Old Babylonian,[3] there is a word *ḫaṣāru,* "fold, pen," attested 4 times in the Mari texts, once in the singular and 3 times in the feminine plural. The fact that in one instance[4] the *ḫaṣāru* is located in the vicinity of a city is not sufficient reason (*contra* Malamat) to assume that we are dealing with an exclusively human settlement. Furthermore, among seminomadic tribes the "enclosure" can also include the settlement of the herdsmen.[5] Late Bab. *ḫaṭ(a)ru* (*ḫaṭīru*) likewise means "fold, court," and may be an Aramaic loanword.[6]

ḥāṣēr. K. Albrecht, "Das Geschlecht der hebräischen Hauptwörter," *ZAW*, 16 (1896), 41-121; T. A. Busink, *Der Tempel von Jerusalem von Salomo bis Herodes. StFS,* 3, I (1970), 143-151; M. Dahood, "Ugaritic-Hebrew Parallel Pairs," in *RSP,* I, §II, 131,162; J. Jeremias, "Hesekieltempel und Serubbabeltempel," *ZAW*, 52 (1934), 109-112; A. Malamat, " 'Ḥāṣērîm' in the Bible and Mari," *Yediot*, 27 (1963), 180-84 [Hebrew]; *idem*, "Mari and the Bible: Patterns of Tribal Organization," *Sefer Segal. Festschrift M. H. Segal* (Jerusalem, 1964), 19-32 [Hebrew]; B. Mazar, *The Mountain of the Lord* (Garden City, 1975), 96-130; M. Noth, *The OT World* (Eng. trans., Philadelphia, 1966), "Settlements," 145-158; "Sanctuaries," 173-79ff.; F. Nötscher, *Biblische Altertumskunde. HSAT,* III (1940); H. M. Orlinsky, "*Ḥāṣēr* in the OT," *JAOS*, 59 (1939), 22-37; R. de Vaux, *AncIsr*, 271-330; E. Vogt, "Vom Tempel zum Felsendom," *Bibl*, 55 (1974), 23-64; C. Watzinger, *Denkmäler Palästinas* (Leipzig, 1933-1935); W. Zimmerli, "Ezechieltempel und Salomostadt," in *Hebräische Wortforschung. Festschrift W. Baumgartner. SVT*, 16 (1967), 398-414 = his *Studien zur alttestamentlichen Theol. und Prophetie. ThB*, 51 (1974), 148-164; → בית *bayiṯ* [*bayith*]; → היכל *hêḵāl* [*hêkhāl*].

[1] P. 24.

[2] A. Malamat, "Mari and the Bible: Some Patterns of Tribal Organization and Institutions," *JAOS*, 82 (1962), 147.

[3] *AHw,* I, 331; *CAD,* VI (1956), 130.

[4] C.-F. Jean, *Lettres diverses. ARM,* II (1959; repr. 1978), 43,7.

[5] Noth, 145.

[6] *AHw,* I, 337; see I.7.

3. *Ugaritic.* In Ugaritic we frequently find the form *ḥẓr* (the form *ḥṭr*[7] is a misreading[8]). Often *ḥẓr* occurs in parallel with *bt*; twice it appears with *hkl,* "palace."[9] Aistleitner[10] equates *bt* and *ḥẓr* completely, translating the latter as "Gehöft, Wohstätte [building, dwelling]." Gordon, Dahood, and Driver,[11] however, rightly see in *ḥẓr* (*ḥṭr*) a somewhat divergent parallel to *bt* and translate "court, courtyard," after the analogy of the parallelism between *bayiṯ,* "temple," and *ḥāṣēr* in the Psalms.[12] The other meaning, "settlements," is attested at most in 1 uncertain passage;[13] Aistleitner[14] translates "mit 1000 Höfen," Driver "1000 villages," but Gordon "1000 courts." Despite the graphic possibility, no written difference can be found; semantically, the basic meaning "enclosure, court" appears predominant, while "dwelling, settlement" is highly dubious.

4. *Phoenician.* In Phoenician, too, which like Hebrew has only the single grapheme *ṣ,* we find only the meaning "(fore)court"; and in an ancient incantation text from the seventh century B.C. we read: "The house (*bt*) into which I come . . ., the 'court' that I enter,"[15] with *bt* and *ḥṣr* in parallel, as in Ugaritic and in the OT. Another text[16] reads: *mbnt ḥṣr bt 'lm,* "the buildings of the court of the house of God." In 2 Neo-Punic texts[17] we find *ḥṣrt* (*hmqdš*), "the forecourt (of the sanctuary)."

5. *OSA.* Old South Arabic, which distinguishes the various dentals, has a noun *ḥḍr,* "dwelling" (cf. Arab. *ḥaḍara*).[18] We also find "they reached the houses (*'ḥḍr,* masc. pl.),"[19] and "from these houses (*'ḥḍrn*)."[20] But the same middle consonant appears in *mḥḍr,* "forecourt" (of a temple, with *byt* in the preceding lines). Conti Rossini[21] has: "*mḥḍr* 'vestibulum, atrium,' Pl. *mḥḍrt.*" Ryckmans discusses the proper names deriving from *ḥḍr.*[22]

6. *Arabic.* In Arabic, however, with its wealth of literature, we can distinguish two roots: (1) *ḥaẓara,* "surround, enclose," and (2) *ḥaḍara,* "betake oneself, be present,

---

7 *UT,* no. 852a.

8 See M. Dietrich, O. Loretz, and J. Sanmartín, "Untersuchungen zur Schrift- und Lautlehre des Ugaritischen (III)," *UF,* 7 (1975), 106.

9 See *WUS,* no. 960; Dahood, *RSP,* I, §II, 131, 162.

10 *WUS,* no. 960, and his *Die mythologischen und kultischen Texte aus Ras Schamra* (Budapest, ²1964).

11 *CML.*

12 See II.2.c(7).

13 *KTU,* 1.1 II, 14.

14 *WUS,* no. 960.

15 *KAI,* 27.7.

16 *KAI,* 60.2 (96 B.C.?).

17 *KAI,* 122.2 and 145.1 (1st century A.D.).

18 *CIH,* 79, 4; 82, 4.

19 A. Jamme, *Sabaean Inscriptions from Maḥram Bilqîs (Mârib)* (Baltimore, 1962), 629, 33.

20 *Ibid.,* 665, 23.

21 See *RES* 3943, 5 (Sabaean).

22 Cited in Orlinsky, 28.

dwell." The former has a derivative *ḥaẓīrat*, "enclosure, fold." Closely related is the root *ḥaṣara*, which, however, has taken on the meaning "confine, restrain, lock up."[23] In Ethiopic we still find *ḥaṣara*, "enclose with a wall."[24] The second root, *ḥaḍara*, has derivatives such as *ḥāḍirat*, "dwelling place." Although the two (or three) roots have drifted apart, here as in the other Semitic languages just discussed we are probably dealing with a basic meaning "surround, enclose." A survey of the various derivatives shows that they have occasionally changed places.

7. *Aramaic (and Greek)*. The Targumim distinguish the Hebrew etymologies of *ḥāṣēr* and translate "settlement" with *pᵉṣîḥā'* or *paṣḥā'*, but "court" with *dārᵉṯā'*. Whether the word *ḥuṭrā'*, "fold," attested 4 times in the Targumim, is cognate with Arab. *ḥaẓīrat*[25] or with *ḥōṭer*, "staff, rod,"[26] is a matter of debate. The Middle Hebrew technical term for the temple court, *'ᵃzārâ*, appears for the first time in 2 Ch. 4:9 and 6:13; in the Targumim (*'ᵃzartā'*) it appears only 5 times. In Ezekiel (Ezk. 43:14,17,20; 45:19) we still find the more general meaning "enclosure (of the altar)."[27]

The LXX also distinguished the two meanings, usually rendering "settlement" as *kṓmē* (23 times) and "court" as *aulḗ* (131 times). The LXX also uses *épaulis*, "real estate" (20 times), *skēnḗ* (6 times), *exṓteros* (3 times), *exédra*, *perípatos*, and *oikía* (once each). The passages that present textual difficulties are discussed by Orlinsky.[28]

II. OT.

1. *Settlements*. In OT Hebrew, *ḥṣr* appears only as a noun. The meaning varies on the basis of the Arabic roots.[29] In the sense of "settlement, farmstead" it is found only in the plural. According to Orlinsky,[30] it appears 47 times and is always masculine. A stereotyped formula is the phrase "cities and their (adjacent) settlements," which constitute real property and are more than mere pasturage (cf. Josh. 21:12). But they could hardly have been larger than our crossroad villages. Josh. 15:21-32, for example, mentions no less than "twenty-nine cities and their villages" along the southern edge of Judah (v. 32). The term is often applied to the settlements of seminomads, as in Gen. 25:16 ("the villages and encampments of the Ishmaelites") or Isa. 42:11 ("the villages that Kedar inhabits"). But these settlements must be distinguished from mobile encampments; the Arabic derivatives of *ḥaḍara* always refer to permanent settlements; cf. also Neh. 12:29: "The singers had built for themselves villages around Jerusalem." These villages did not have fortified walls: "the houses of the villages which have no

---

23 *Ibid.*, 23f.

24 Leslau, *Contributions*, 21.

25 Orlinsky, 25.

26 J. Levy, *Chaldäisches Wörterbuch über die Targumim und einen grossen Theil des rabbinischen Schriftthums* (Leipzig, ³1881), 252.

27 See G. R. Driver, "Ezekiel: Linguistic and Textual Problems," *Bibl*, 35 (1954), 307f.; A. Hurvitz, "The Evidence of Language in Dating the Priestly Code," *RB*, 81 (1974), 41-43.

28 Pp. 32-37.

29 See *KBL*³.

30 P. 28.

wall around them" (Lev. 25:31). They are counted as part of the open fields. But this open plan of settlement (Jer. 49:31) does not mean that the villages were totally without modest "enclosures" like folds. Here we see once more how "settlement" and "court" come together in the original basic meaning. The 5 place names incorporating *ḥāṣēr* are probably also based on the meaning "settlement."[31]

2. *Courts*. a. The Arabic roots *ḥẓr* and *ḥṣr*, "enclose," include the other meaning of *ḥāṣēr*, namely "enclosure, court." The gender[32] in this case is usually feminine (cf. also the fem. pl. *ḫaṣirātu* in the Mari texts and OSA *mḥḍrt*). In the OT, the term *ḥ^a ṣērôt* appears 20 times, apart from the oasis Hazeroth (Nu. 11:35, etc., "enclosures" [fem. pl.]). But the masculine plural also occurs 5 times—always with suffixes—, and in the singular the gender is also masculine in 10 passages (including 8 in Ezk. 40–43). Orlinsky concludes that the reference is always to the forecourt of the Jerusalem temple, understood as the dwelling place of Yahweh[33] in parallel with *bayiṯ*. The 15 occurrences of the masculine noun are limited to exilic and postexilic books and therefore constitute a late phenomenon, like the gender of *dereḵ*. Contra Albrecht,[34] who sought to restore a feminine by minor textual alterations (*p^e nîmîṯ* for *p^e nîmî* in Ezk. 40–43), Zimmerli[35] states with respect to Ezk. 40:23: "We must assume . . . [against Albrecht, *ZAW*, 16 (1896), 49] that חצר [*ḥāṣēr*] (exactly like חלון [*ḥallôn*] . . .) can be both masculine and feminine." The basic meaning "enclosure"[36] is still literally present when we have a list of the materials from which the *ḥāṣēr* is built, as in 1 K. 7:12.[37]

b. Isolated houses outside the crowded cities were probably set within a rather spacious courtyard. Elaborate palaces like that in Susa comprised an "outer court" (Est. 6:5), a "garden court" (1:5), and an "inner court" (4:11; 5:1). The harem had its own court (2:11). Palaces of square design were built around an inner court.[38]

The design and construction of Solomon's palace are described only cursorily in 1 K. 7:1-12; v. 8 speaks of "the other court" (*ḥāṣēr hā'aḥereṯ*), vv. 9 and 12 of "the great court." The "other court" is distinct from both the "great court" and the "inner court" of the temple; it surrounds the palace of Solomon. The "great court," however, "probably refers to a peripheral wall enclosing all the structure of 6:1–7:8, including the 'inner court' (for the house of Yahweh) mentioned in 6:36 and the 'other court' (for the house of Solomon) mentioned in 7:8a."[39] In the time of Hezekiah, 2 K. 20:4

---

31 *KBL*³, 332; Orlinsky, 27.
32 Orlinsky, 28-31.
33 See (7) below.
34 *ZAW*, 16 (1896), 49.
35 *Ezekiel 2*. *Herm* (1983), 339.
36 M. Noth, *Könige*. *BK*, IX/1 (1968), 140.
37 See H. Graf Reventlow, "Gattung und Überlieferung in der 'Tempelrede Jeremias' Jer 7 und 26," *ZAW*, 81 (1969), 327, n. 63.
38 See Watzinger, I, 97 for Samaria (and Assyria).
39 Noth, *BK*, IX/1, 139.

speaks of a "middle court" near the palace (assuming that *ḥāṣēr* is to be read rather than the *kethibh hā'êr.*[40] In the vicinity of the palace there was a court of the guard (*ḥ^a ṣar hammaṭṭārâ*): Neh. 3:25; Jer. 32:2, etc.

According to Ex. 8:9(Eng. v. 13) (J), the frogs died "in the houses, courtyards, and fields"; because of the feminine plural, "courtyards" is a better translation than the usual "villages." The courtyard of a private dwelling is mentioned in 2 S. 17:18, containing a well. According to Neh. 8:16, booths were set up in individual courtyards. In contrast to an enclosed courtyard, an open (market) square is called *r^e ḥôḇ*.

c. 1. Throughout the ancient Near East, sanctuaries even more than secular buildings were surrounded by one or more courts (Gk. *témenos*, Arab. *ḥaram*), in order to give the entire complex a coherent and imposing size and scale, and to hold the crowds. Religiously, the enclosed precincts possessed a numinous aura, separating the sacred from the profane (Ezk. 42:20) and placing those who entered them under the spell of the sacred.[41] In the OT, P reports that even in the desert the tent of meeting stood within a courtyard 100 cubits by 50 cubits (1 cubit = 52.5 cm.[42]) enclosed by curtains (Ex. 27:9-19; 38:9-20; 40:8,33; Lev. 6:9,19[16,26]; etc.). The details cannot be considered historical evidence, but are for the most part a retrojection of the Jerusalem temple.[43]

2. In connection with the temple of Solomon,[44] an "inner court" is mentioned, surrounded by a wall (1 K. 6:36; 7;12), in contrast to the "great court" (1 K. 7:9,12), which probably surrounded both the royal palace and the temple precincts.[45] The inner court is described as "the court before the house of Yahweh"; within it stood the altar of burnt offerings (1 K. 8:64 par. 2 Ch. 7:7). In the course of time, a second temple forecourt seems to have become distinguished from the "great court" common to the entire complex. In any case, we read of the "two courts of the house of Yahweh" in the period of Manasseh and Josiah (2 K. 21:5; 23:12). "My courts" (pl.) are also mentioned in Isa. 1:12 (although the LXX has the sg.). Baruch reads the words of Jeremiah "in the upper court (*ḥāṣēr hā'elyôn*), at the entry of the New Gate" of the temple (Jer. 36:10). Probably this was the same gate between the outer court and the somewhat elevated inner court at which Jeremiah himself addressed the people (19:14) and delivered his famous temple sermon (7:2; 26:2).[46] It is not necessary to interpret the word "court" (sg.) so narrowly as to imply that there were not two temple courts at the time of Jeremiah. When Ezekiel speaks of the temple, which was still standing, he mentions the "door of the court" (Ezk. 8:7); in 8:16 (cf. 10:3f.), however, he

[40] See the comms.; also Orlinsky, *JAOS*, 59 (1939), 22; *idem*, "The Kings-Isaiah Recensions of the Hezekiah Story," *JQR*, N.S. 30 (1939/1940), 34-36.

[41] *AncIsr*, 274-76.

[42] *BRL*², 204.

[43] See Y. Aharoni, "The Solomonic Temple, the Tabernacle and the Arad Sanctuary," in *Orient and Occident. Festschrift C. H. Gordon. AOAT*, 22 (1973), 1-8.

[44] Busink, 143-151.

[45] See II.2.b. above.

[46] See the comms.; also Reventlow, *ZAW*, 81 (1969), 327.

speaks more precisely of the "inner court of the house of Yahweh," and in 10:5 of the "outer court" (*ḥāṣēr haḥîṣōnâ*); in 9:7 we find "the courts" (pl.).

3. The description of the new temple in Ezk. 40–42 presupposes precise knowledge of the temple of Solomon,[47] and therefore provides once more for two courts. The "inner court" is mentioned in Ezk. 40:23, etc. It measures 100 cubits on a side. According to Nötscher,[48] this measurement applies only to the later "court of the priests." Two chambers in the walls beside the north and south gates serve as sacristies for the priests (40:44-46). Eight steps lower lies the "outer court" with pavement and thirty chambers (40:17-20). It serves as a place of assembly for the people (44:19). The plans no longer provide for palace buildings, and so the outer court can extend further to the south, east, and north.[49] In the temple of Solomon, the inner court was surrounded immediately by the "great court," which enclosed both temple and palace.[50] This minimal separation is described by Ezekiel as defiling the name of God (43:8). The whole temple area was to be a square 500 cubits on a side, surrounded by a wall whose purpose, we are expressly told, was to separate the holy from the profane (42:20; cf. the duties of the priests described in 22:26 and 44:23). The wall was to be surrounded in turn by a protective strip of open space 50 cubits wide (45:2, a later addition).

4. Concerning the second temple (completed in 515 B.C.[51]) we have no connected account. Like Ezekiel, Zerubbabel probably adhered as faithfully as possible to the Solomonic traditions.[52] There were undoubtedly two courts. As early as Isa. 62:9, we read: "(They) shall drink it in the courts of my sanctuary." According to Zec. 3:7, the high priest "shall rule my house and have charge of my courts." Neh. 8:16 states that the people made booths "in their courts and in the courts of the house of God." The texts in Chronicles (1 Ch. 23:28; 28:6,12; 2 Ch. 23:5) furnish evidence for their own period, not for the preexilic era. We first hear of the "court of the priests" in 2 Ch. 4:9; it belongs to the "inner court" of 1 K. 6:36. We may therefore conclude that in the period of Chronicles—as later in the Herodian temple—the inner court was reserved at least in part for the priests. The "great court" here (*ʿᵃzārâ haggᵉḏôlâ*[53]) corresponds roughly to the "great court" of 1 K. 7:9,12, or better to the "outer court" of Ezk. 10:5. In 2 Ch. 20:5 we find the term "new court," which is probably identical with the "great court" of 4:9 and was apparently renovated during the period of the Chronicler (or of King Jehoshaphat?). In 2 Ch. 24:21 we read only that the people stoned the prophet Zechariah "in the court of the house of Yahweh." According to Mt. 23:35, however, this took place "between the temple and the altar," i.e., in the

---

47 Watzinger, I, 89; Mazar, 103.

48 P. 285, n. 3; 286f.

49 Zimmerli, *SVT,* 16 (1967), 404.

50 See II.2.b above.

51 Mazar, 104f.

52 See Jeremias.

53 See I.7 above.

inner court. If so, it is correct to assume that in the time of Joash the inner court was still open to the laity. In 2 Ch. 29:16, also, which tells how the priests took everything unclean out of the *hêḵal* "into the court of the house of Yahweh," where the Levites took charge of it, we should also think of the inner court. "The courts" (pl.) are mentioned in 1 Macc. 4:38,48; 1 Macc. 9:54 speaks of tearing down "the wall of the inner court of the temple."

5. Some five hundred years after the building of Zerubbabel's temple, Herod renovated the sanctuary, adding to its courts, gates, towers, colonnades, and perimeter walls. Detailed descriptions will be found in Josephus[54] and—more reliably than in Josephus, who tends to exaggerate—in the Mishnah tractate *Middoth.*[55] From the raised temple building twelve steps led down to the inner court, the front of which measured 187 cubits from east to west and 135 cubits from north to south; this court enclosed the *hêḵal.*[56] The north and south walls of the court each had three chambers for priests.[57] The inner court (of the priests) was separated by a barrier just one cubit high from an adjacent court, the so-called court of the Israelites or court of men.[58] Further east, fifteen steps led to the "court of women," an area 135 cubits square.[59] Here and in the adjoining rooms both men and women could stay, but women were not allowed to enter the court of men. This whole inner "sacred precinct"[60] was enclosed by a high wall with several gates.[61] The "beautiful gate" to the east is mentioned in Acts 3:2. The east side of the court of women was colonnaded within.[62]

Another fourteen steps lower lay the large outer "court of the Gentiles,"[63] extending far beyond the former "outer court." It was a huge marketplace open to both Jews and Gentiles, similar to a Greek agora. By means of enormous retaining walls, some of which are still preserved, Herod nearly doubled the area of the temple complex, especially toward the south.[64] As far as can be determined today, a wall of large ashlar enclosed a square 280 meters on a side.[65] The court of the Gentiles also possessed spacious colonnades, which were much frequented.[66] A "portico of Solomon" to the east is mentioned in Acts 3:11; cf. Acts 5:12; Jn. 10:23.

6. When the archeologist's spade uncovers at least the foundations of palaces, fortresses, and temples, perimeter walls often allow us to trace outer courts; quartered

---

[54] *Ant.* xv.11.1-3, 5; *BJ* v.5.5f.
[55] See the plan in W. Baier, "Tempel," *BL,* 1723; also Vogt, 64; cf. Mazar, 113-124.
[56] *Mid.* v.1; see Nötscher, 290.
[57] *Mid.* v.3f.
[58] *BJ* v.5.6.
[59] *Ant.* xv.11.5; *Mid.* ii.5.
[60] *BJ* v.5.2.
[61] *Ant.* xv.11.5; *Mid.* i.4f.
[62] *Ant.* xv.11.3; xx.9.7.
[63] *BJ* v.5.2.
[64] *BJ* i.21.1; Watzinger, II, 34.
[65] Vogt, 28.
[66] *Ant.* xv.11.5; see Nötscher, 291f.

palaces also reveal inner courts. The famous wailing wall, for example, on the west side of the Jerusalem temple area, is not a remnant of the temple itself but of the wall built by Herod to support the temple precincts. At the north end of the west wall a remnant of the perimeter wall of the Ḥaram is still preserved.[67] Similar typically Herodian walls of ashlar have left remains by the temenoi of Hebron, Mamre,[68] and Samaria (with a square court 70 meters on a side).[69] In the Yahweh sanctuary of the citadel at Arad (10th–7th centuries B.C.), the altar of burnt offering stood within the court, in imitation of Jerusalem.[70]

7. Besides prose texts, the temple courts are spoken of 8 times in the Psalms: 4 times (Ps. 65:5[4]; 84:11[10]; 92:14[13]; 135:2) in parallelism with the house (*bayiṯ*) of God, once (100:4) with his gates, once (84:2f.[1f.]) with his dwelling place, once (116:19) with Jerusalem, and only once without parallelism (96:8). The parallelism can practically be termed synonymous, for the statements refer to the sanctuary as a whole (archaically also termed a tent: Ps. 15:1; 27:6; 61:5[4]). Zorell therefore states[71] that in poetry "courts" means "temple," and Orlinsky maintains[72] that this equivalence is the primary reason why "courts" is treated as a masculine noun in 15 passages (cf. masc. in Ps. 84:11[10] with fem. in 84:3[2]).

The fact that only the plural occurs in the Psalms may be due to the plurality of courts; but it may also, as in Ugaritic,[73] be merely a poetic plural of majesty or size (cf. "thy altars," 84:4[3]; "thy dwellings," 43:3; 46:5[4]; 84:2[1]; 132:5,7).[74] The courts thus shared in the worship and love offered to the temple[75] in Jerusalem as the place of God's cultic presence and the religious focus of Israel. God himself chose this place and thus also those who dwelt there.[76]

But apart from this somewhat imprecise poetic synecdoche, it was in fact only the courts that were open to the people, not the rooms of the temple itself. It is therefore more accurate to translate *'āḇô' bêṯeḵā* in Ps. 5:8a(7a) as "I may enter thy house,"[77] rather than "I will enter thy house."[78] V. 8b(7b) continues accurately: "I will worship toward (*'el*) thy holy temple." When 1 K. 8:31, in Solomon's prayer of dedication, speaks of someone swearing "before thine altar in this house," the word "house" refers imprecisely to the entire temple complex. The same is true in 1 K. 8:33, "make supplication to thee in this house," and more precisely "pray toward (*'el*) this place"

---

[67] See E. Mader, *Mambre* (Freiburg, 1957), 74f.

[68] Watzinger, II, 45f.; Mader, 67-81.

[69] Watzinger, I, 97; II, 48.

[70] M. Weippert, "Archäologischer Jahresbericht," *ZDPV*, 82 (1966), 287.

[71] *LexHebAram*, s.v.

[72] *JAOS*, 59 (1939), 30; cf. II.2.a above.

[73] M. Dahood, *Psalms II*. *AB*, XVII (1968), on Ps. 65:5.

[74] H.-J. Kraus, "Archäologische und topographische Probleme Jerusalems im Lichte der Psalmenexegese," *ZDPV*, 75 (1959), 129.

[75] → בית *bayiṯ* [*bayith*] III.3.

[76] *AncIsr*, 325-330, "The Theology of the Temple."

[77] F. Nötscher, *Das Buch der Psalmen*. *EB*, IV (1959), *in loc*.

[78] H.-J. Kraus, *Psalmen*. *BK*, XV, *in loc*.

(8:29,35,38,42, including foreigners); cf. Jer. 26:2, "worship in the house of Yahweh," and Isa. 56:7, "a house of prayer for all peoples."

Ps. 23:6 is poetic license: "I shall dwell in the house of Yahweh" (similarly 27:4; → ישב *yāšaḇ*). Ps. 65:5(4) macarizes those who dwell in Yahweh's courts. Despite the preceding use of "choose" and "bring near," these need not be the priests alone, but "all flesh" (v. 3[2]). Ps. 84:3(2): "My soul longs, yea, faints for the courts of Yahweh"; v. 11(10): "A day in thy courts is better than a thousand (elsewhere)"; v. 5(4): "Blessed are those who dwell in thy house." Ps. 92:14(13): "They are planted in the house of Yahweh, they flourish in the courts of our God." Ps. 96:8b: "Bring an offering, and come into his courts." Ps. 100:4: "Enter his gates with thanksgiving, and his courts with praise!" Ps. 116:18: "I will pay my vows to Yahweh in the presence of all his people, [19] in the courts of the house of Yahweh, in your midst, O Jerusalem." In Ps. 134:1, "you who stand by night in the house of Yahweh" can refer literally only to the priests and Levites; the generalizing interpolation of the LXX, "in the courts of the house of our God," derives from 135:2. There the expression "you that stand in the house of Yahweh, in the courts of the house of our God" is pure parallelism, so that we should not assume that the priests alone are meant.

To be allowed to dwell in the temple complex "before the face of God" was the highest delight of the devout, but it was also a moral obligation. The so-called entrance (or torah) liturgies (cf. Pss. 15 and 24) show that participants in the cult were confronted with the social requirements of Yahweh's law when they entered the sacred precincts. The antisacrificial words of the prophets always have in mind morally unworthy frequenters of the temple: God does not want their like to "trample his courts" (Isa. 1:12).

Hamp

חָקַק *ḥāqaq*; חָקָה *ḥāqâ*; חֹק *ḥōq*; חֻקָּה *ḥuqqâ*

Contents: I. Etymology; West Semitic. II. The Verb *ḥāqaq*/*ḥāqâ*. III. 1. Concrete Meanings; 2. "Statute" and "Ordinance"; *ḥōq* and *mišpāṭ;* 3. Use in P and H; 4. Deuteronomy and the Deuteronomistic History; 5. The Chronicler's History; 6. The Prophetic Books; 7. The Psalms. IV. LXX. V. Dead Sea Scrolls.

ḥāqaq. G. Braulik, "Bedeutungsnuancen der Ausdrücke für 'Gesetz' im deuteronomischen Sprachgebrauch," *ZDMG Sup*, 1 (1969), 343f.; *idem*, "Die Ausdrücke für 'Gesetz' im Buch Deuteronomium," *Bibl*, 51 (1970), 39-66; M. Delcor, "Contribution a l'étude de la législation des sectaires de Damas et de Qumrân," *RB*, 61 (1954), 533-553; 62 (1955), 60-75; Z. W. Falk, "Hebrew Legal Terms," *JSS*, 5 (1960), 350-54; J. Halbe, *Das Privilegrecht Jahwes: Ex. 34,10-26*.

I. Etymology; West Semitic.

The root *ḥqq* (which has the by-form *ḥqy/ḥāqâ* in Hebrew and gives rise to certain forms that appear to come from *ḥwq*) appears in Middle Hebrew and Jewish Aramaic with the meaning "hollow out," "engrave." In Mandaic it means "be in order."

In West Semitic epigraphy, occurrences are few and ambiguous. In the Hadad inscription from Zinçirli,[1] we find at the end[2] the clause *tḥq 'lyh,* which may be rendered as "You should write to him accordingly"; the context does not provide any firm grounds for interpretation. In a Phoenician funerary inscription[3] we find the word *mḥq* designating a profession; it may be translated as "sculptor" or "lawgiver." In addition, a Neo-punic inscription[4] contains the words *['r]ṣ't hmḥqt,* which may mean "the delimited properties."[5]

Arab. *ḥaqqa* means "cut a furrow" and "be genuine."[6] Kopf[7] finds a connection between a special meaning of Arab. *ḥaqqa,* "be incumbent upon," and Heb. *ḥōq,* in the sense "that which is incumbent on someone," and *m^eḥōqēq,* which he translates in Dt. 33:21 as "portion." But this juxtaposition is too dependent on accidental semantic nuances to be convincing.

The root is also attested in the South Semitic languages. In OSA there are 2 occurrences of *ḥqq* with the meaning "legally binding."[8] Ethiop. *ḥĕg* alongside *ḥĕq* means "law, precepts."[9] In Tigre,[10] the verb means "seek justice."

FRLANT, 114 (1975); R. Hentschke, *Satzung und Setzender. BWANT,* 83 [5/3] (1963); F. Horst, *Gottes Recht. GSAT. ThB,* 12 (1961); G. H. Jones, "The Decree of Yahweh (Ps. II 7)." *VT,* 15 (1965), 336-344; G. Liedke, *Gestalt und Bezeichnung der alttestamentlicher Rechtsätze. WMANT,* 39 (1971); *idem,* "חקק *ḥqq* einritzen, festsetzen," *THAT,* I, 626-633; M. Limbeck, *Die Ordnung des Heils* (Düsseldorf, 1971); N. Lohfink, *Das Hauptgebot. AnBibl,* 20 (1963); R. P. Merendino, "Die Zeugnisse, die Satzungen und die Rechte: Überlieferungsgeschichtliche Erwägungen zu Deut 6," *Bausteine biblischer Theol. Festschrift G. J. Botterweck. BBB,* 50 (1977), 185-208; S. Mowinckel, "The Hebrew Equivalent of Taxo in Ass. Mos. ix," *Congress Volume, Copenhagen 1963. SVT,* 1 (1953), 88-96; W. Nauck, "Lex insculpta (חוק תרות) in der Sektenschrift," *ZNW,* 46 (1955), 138-140; G. Östborn, *Tōrā in the OT* (Lund, 1945); J. van der Ploeg, "Studies in Hebrew Law," *CBQ,* 12 (1950), 248-259, 416-427; 13 (1951), 28-43, 164-171, 296-307; H. Graf Reventlow, *Gebot und Predigt im Dekalog* (Gütersloh, 1962); W. Richter, *Recht und Ethos. StANT,* 15 (1966); P. Victor, "A Note on חֹק in the OT," *VT,* 16 (1966), 358-361.

1 *KAI,* 214.

2 Line 34.

3 *CIS,* I, 51, 2.

4 *LidzNE,* 349.

5 For discussion of the inscriptions, see *DISO,* 95, and Hentschke, 21f.

6 A. Guillaume, "Hebrew and Arabic Lexicography: A Comparative Study. IV," *Abr-Nahrain,* 4 (1963/64[1965]; repr. Leiden, 1965), 7.

7 L. Kopf, "Arabische Etymologien und Parallelen zum Bibelwörterbuch," *VT,* 9 (1959), 255f.

8 W. W. Müller, "Altsüdarabische Beiträge zum hebräischen Lexikon," *ZAW,* 75 (1963), 309.

9 Leslau, *Contributions,* 21.

10 *TigrWb,* 77.

II. The Verb ḥāqaq/ḥāqâ.

The OT occurrences of the verb *ḥqq*/*ḥāqâ* can be assigned to three semantic groups: (1) "carve out, engrave": Shebna has a tomb carved out for himself (Isa. 22:16, *ḥqq* par. *ḥāṣaḇ*); Ezekiel engraves on a brick the plan of Jerusalem (*ḥqq*, Ezk. 4:1); Yahweh has engraved on his hands the name of Zion (*ḥqq*) to keep it ever before him (Isa. 49:16); God places Job's paths before him (*ḥāqâ*, Job 13:27); the creator draws for Job the circle of the horizon (*ḥûg*) on the face of the deep (Prov. 8:27; cf. Job 26:10). In 1 K. 6:35; Ezk. 8:10; 23:14, the participle *mᵉḥuqqeh* means "carved work" or "reliefs." (2) In 3 passages, *ḥqq* stands in parallelism with *kāṯaḇ*, "write." In Job 19:23, it applies to Job's words of complaint, which are to show for all time that he is in the right (*bassēper* means either "in an inscription"[11] or "on [a] copper [tablet]"—cf. Akk. *siparru;* note also *ḥāṣaḇ*, "carve in rock," v. 24). In Isa. 30:8, it applies to the words of Isaiah, which are to bear witness forever; here, too, *sēper* could mean "copper tablet," parallel to *lûaḥ*. In Isa. 10:1, we read: "Woe to those who decree iniquitous decrees (*haḥōqᵉqîm ḥiqᵉqê-'āwen*) and the writers who keep writing oppression." This refers either to the issuance of wicked decrees for personal gain or to legal injustice. (3) We also find the meaning "fix, determine." In Jer. 31:35, Yahweh "fixes" the moon and stars for light by night (par. *nōṯēn*, with respect to the sun). Prov. 8:15 reads: "By me (Wisdom) kings reign (*mālaḵ*), and rulers decree what is just (*yᵉḥōqᵉqû*)." In Prov. 31:5 we find *mᵉḥuqqāq*, "that which has been determined," i.e., "the law." Jgs. 5:9 probably belongs here, too: "My heart goes out to the commanders (*ḥôqᵉqê*) of Israel." In addition, the poel participle *mᵉḥōqēq* occurs 7 times; it means either "staff, scepter" (Gen. 49:10; Nu. 21:18; Ps. 60:9[Eng. v. 7] par. 108:9[8]) or "commander" (Dt. 33:21; Jgs. 5:14; Isa. 33:22). In the latter meaning, Hentschke claims to find an official title; but the occurrences are too scattered and vague to support such a conclusion.[12]

III. 1. *Concrete Meanings.* As nouns we find both *ḥōq* and the fem. form *ḥuqqâ;* they appear as terms for ordinances or legal precepts. In a few cases, however, there appears a more concrete meaning, which is probably more original. It can mean a limit or boundary, as when at creation God assigns the sea a limit (Job 38:10; Ps. 148:6; Prov. 8:29; Jer. 5:22—here the notions of "command" and "order" may also be involved). In Jer. 31:36, the expression "these *ḥuqqîm*" refers to the order of creation, described in the preceding verse.[13] In Job 28:26, God makes his *ḥōq* for the rain, that is, he guides it in its proper course or makes it fall at the proper time. In Mic. 7:11 we are dealing once more with a territorial boundary that is extended, and Isa. 5:14 says of the realm of the dead: "It has opened its mouth *bᵉlî-ḥōq*, without measure."

The noun *ḥōq* can also refer to a measured quantity, a portion, or a limited period of time. In Gen. 47:22, for example, we read that the priests in Egypt had a *ḥōq* from

---

[11] *KBL*, 665.

[12] Hentschke, 11f.; cf. Liedke, 160.

[13] See II above.

Pharaoh and lived on this *ḥōq;* the reference here is to a fixed income, probably in the form of produce. A similar meaning may be present in Ezk. 16:27: God diminished (*gāraʿ*) the *ḥōq* of Jerusalem, i.e., reduced the supply of provisions to the city (cf. Ex. 21:10), or else reduced its territory (with the meaning "a bounded area"[14]). Here, too, we should probably cite Prov. 30:8: "Give me neither poverty nor riches; feed me with *leḥem ḥuqqî,* i.e., my allotment of bread." The word can also mean a job or task, a "quota": in Ex. 5:14, the Israelites have not made their quota of bricks; cf. Prov. 31:15: the good wife provides food for her household and *ḥōq* for her maidens. In Job 14:5,13, we are dealing with the limit set on a lifetime or the lifetime itself.[15]

A *ḥōq* can also be a fixed statute: Joseph decrees a *ḥōq* in Egypt that stands "to this day," that Pharaoh is to receive a fifth of the harvest (Gen. 47:26); it became a *ḥōq* in Israel that the young girls should lament the daughter of Jephthah (Jgs. 11:39; similarly 2 Ch. 35:25); "Yahweh established the covenant for Jacob as a *ḥōq*" (Ps. 105:10); in Ps. 2:7, the *ḥōq* of Yahweh to the king appears to be the promise of sonship pronounced at the king's enthronement, probably comparable to the Egyptian royal protocol, which can also be called *ʿēḏûṯ* or *berîṯ.*[16]

A more concrete meaning for *ḥuqqâ* appears in only a few passages.[17] In Jer. 33:25, Yahweh created day and night and established the *ḥuqqôṯ* of heaven and earth, probably their "order"; Job 38:33: "Do you know the *ḥuqqôṯ* of the heavens?" In Jer. 5:24, Yahweh gives the rain in its season and keeps the *ḥuqqôṯ* of the harvest—here we could translate "appointed times."

As Liedke stresses,[18] "the *ḥōq* always involves a superior and an inferior; it is the result of an action carried out by the superior and affecting the inferior." This is reflected in the verbs that have *ḥōq* as their object: *śîm* (Prov. 8:29; Jer. 5:22), *nāṯan* (Ps. 148:6; Prov. 31:15); *ʿāśâ* (Job 14:5; 28:26), *šîṯ* (Job 14:13), etc. The superior is often Yahweh (Job 14:5,13; 23:14; 28:26; 38:10; Ps. 148:6; Prov. 8:29; 30:8; Jer. 5:22; Ezk. 16:27), but can also be Pharaoh (Gen. 47:22), Pharaoh's overseer (Ex. 5:14), or the good wife (Prov. 31:15).[19]

2. *"Statute" and "Ordinance"; ḥōq and mišpāṭ.* Most of the occurrences of *ḥōq*/*ḥuqqâ* involve the meaning "statute" or "ordinance." It is difficult to distinguish these nouns precisely from other terms for "law" and "commandment," since above all in Deuteronomy and the writings influenced by Deuteronomy words like *miṣwôṯ, ḥuqqîm*/*ḥuqqôṯ, mišpāṭîm, deḇārîm,* and *mišmereṯ* appear not to designate individual groups of laws that are formally or substantially distinct, but to be used alone or in series for the legal corpus as a whole.[20]

---

[14] Liedke, 165.

[15] According to Liedke, 167, Job 23:14 also belongs here.

[16] G. von Rad, "The Royal Ritual in Judah," in *The Problem of the Hexateuch and Other Essays* (Eng. trans., New York, 1966), 222-231.

[17] Liedke, 175f.

[18] *Ibid.*, 169.

[19] *Ibid.*, 168.

[20] Hentschke, 91.

Especially characteristic is the collocation of *ḥōq* and *mišpāṭ:* in Deuteronomy as well as in Chronicles (probably under Deuteronomic influence) *ḥuqqîm* and *mišpāṭîm,* in the Holiness Code and Ezekiel *ḥuqqôṯ* and *mišpāṭîm;* in addition, the sgs. *ḥōq* and *mišpāṭ* appear 5 times.[21] It is commonly assumed that *ḥōq* refers to the cultic ordinances and *mišpāṭ* to the civil laws.[22] Horst finds in the *ḥuqqîm* of Deuteronomy expressions of what he calls Yahweh's *Privilegrecht* ("laws defining privileges"), while the *mišpāṭîm* were civil regulations. Lohfink[23] disputes this theory and maintains that the sequence occurs in the following cases: (1) as a structural signal in Dt. 5:1; 11:32 marking the beginning and end of parenesis, and in Dt. 12:1; 26:16 marking the beginning and end of the law; and (2) in Dt. 4:45; 5:31; 6:1,20; 7:11 in apposition to *miṣwâ* or *'ēḏôṯ.*[24] Liedke[25] thinks that *mišpāṭ* refers to casuistic law, *ḥōq* to apodictic. There is no clear evidence for this last assertion (with the possible exception of Lev. 20:8, where the series of Lev. 20:9ff. is clearly called *ḥuqqôṯ*[26]), and the similarities Liedke cites[27] between *ḥōq* and apodictic law refer for the most part to occurrences of *ḥōq* that have nothing to do with law. We are left with the observation that a *ḥōq* is established by some authority.

There are a few passages containing the sg. *ḥōq ûmišpāṭ.* Josh. 24:25 refers to the covenant at Shechem, stating that Joshua "made" (*śîm*) *ḥōq* and *mišpāṭ* and wrote everything in the "book of the law of Yahweh" (v. 26). This could mean that the substance of the book of the law (*sēper tôrâ*) consisted of laws some of which could be called *ḥōq,* others *mišpāṭ.* At least this is the sense in which the Chronicler understood the passage when he alluded to it in Ezr. 7:10, and the Deuteronomistic redactor probably also took it in this way (contra Liedke,[28] who translates: "boundary and legal rights"). Ex. 15:25 tells how Moses "made a *ḥōq* and *mišpāṭ,*" but since this clause stands totally isolated in its context, we can draw no conclusions from it. Hentschke[29] translates: "cultic ordinance and law" (cf. Liedke:[30] "obligation and legal right"). In Ps. 81:5f.(4f.), *ḥōq, mišpāṭ,* and *'ēḏûṯ* all seem to refer to the festal regulations. In 1 S. 30:25, David's decision concerning division of the spoil is called *ḥōq ûmišpāṭ.* The two terms together thus designate a legally binding regulation (established by the authority of David).

These examples show that all sense of the original meaning of the terms *ḥōq* and *mišpāṭ* was soon lost, and the difference in meaning was only seldom observed.

3. *Use in P and H.* The best evidence for *ḥōq* and *ḥuqqâ* as separate technical terms

---

21 Liedke, 16f.
22 Cf. Hentschke, 73.
23 P. 157.
24 Liedke, 185.
25 *Ibid.,* 17.
26 *Ibid.,* 177f.
27 *Ibid.,* 178f.
28 *Ibid.,* 183.
29 P. 29.
30 P. 184.

for certain types of law is found in P.[31] Here *ḥōq* and *ḥuqqâ* appear "primarily in the subscriptions at the end of individual cultic regulations or minor collections of cultic ordinances, usually in the phrase *(ḥoq-) ḥuqqaṯ 'ôlām*."[32] This usage is found in Ex. 12:14,17; 27:21; 28:43; 29:9; 30:21; Lev. 7:36; 10:9; 16:31,34; 24:3; Nu. 10:8; 18:23; 19:21; 27:11; 30:17; 35:29 and in H in Lev. 17:7; 23:14,21,31,41. The phrase also appears in several superscriptions (Lev. 3:17; 16:29; Nu. 19:10: *ḥuqqaṯ 'ôlām;* Nu. 19:2; 31:21: *ḥuqqaṯ hattôrâ;* Ex. 12:43; Nu. 9:12,14: *ḥuqqaṯ happesaḥ*). As Hentschke has shown,[33] these subscriptions do not belong to the original text; they are later parenetic additions. Originally they must have referred to ritual regulations of significance for the entire cultic community. Later they came to be used also with regulations applying only to the priests.

According to Hentschke,[34] the meaning of *ḥōq/ḥuqqâ* in P can be categorized as follows:

(a) In the context of rituals and similar descriptions of cultic activities, it means roughly "(established) ceremony," e.g., Nu. 19:21, "It shall be a perpetual *ḥuqqâ* for them"; Ex. 12:43, "This is the *ḥuqqâ* of the passover." Similar usage appears in Ex. 12:14,17; 30:21; Lev. 16:29,31; 17:7; 24:3; Nu. 9:3,12,14; 10:8; 18:23; 19:10.

(b) The term *ḥōq/ḥuqqâ* can be used for both general obligations (Lev. 3:17; 10:11; 23:14,21,31,41; Nu. 15:15; 30:17 [16]) and the special ritual obligations of the priests (Ex. 28:43; 30:21; Lev. 10:9; 16:34; Nu. 18:23). The boundary between "established ceremony" and "cultic obligation" is rather vague.

(c) In some cases, *ḥuqqâ* designates the legal claim of the priests to the exclusive performance of cultic functions (Ex. 29:9) or to certain sacrificial offerings (Ex. 27:21; Lev. 7:36).

(d) The expressions *ḥōq* (Lev. 10:13f.) and *ḥoq-'ôlām* are technical terms for the sacrificial offerings assigned to the priests as their legal portion (Ex. 29:26-28; Lev. 6:11[18]; 7:34; 10:13-15; 24:9; Nu. 18:8,11,19). Here we are obviously dealing with a technical application of the particular meaning "allotted portion."[35]

(e) The phrase *ḥuqqaṯ mišpāṭ* as a subscription characterizes two minor legal corpuses, Nu. 27:8-11 (inheritance) and Nu. 35:9-29 (asylum). According to Hentschke,[36] this terminology is intended to include a *mišpāṭ* originating within the legal system in the corpus of sacral ordinances revealed by Yahweh. The best translation would be "sacral law."

---

31 Hentschke, 32-75.
32 *Ibid.*, 65.
33 *Ibid.*, 166f.
34 *Ibid.*, 72f.
35 See III.1 above.
36 P. 74.

The situation is similar in the Holiness Code. We find subscriptions referring to *ḥuqqaṯ (ḥoq-) 'ôlām* (Lev. 16:34; 17:7; 23:14,21,31,41; 24:3,9) and exhortations to keep the *ḥuqqôṯ* (Lev. 18:4f.,26; 19:19,37; 20:8,22).

4. *Deuteronomy and the Deuteronomistic History.* In Deuteronomy, *ḥōq/ḥuqqâ* appears almost exclusively in series having a parenetic function: the listeners are exhorted to keep the commandments given by Yahweh. We find a large variety of combinations: *ḥuqqîm* and *mišpāṭîm* (Dt. 4:1,5,14; 5:1; 11:32; 12:1; 26:16), *ḥuqqîm/ḥuqqôṯ, mišpāṭîm,* and *miṣwâ/miṣwôṯ* (7:11; 8:11; 11:1 [plus *mišmereṯ*]; 26:16; 30:16; *ḥuqqîm, mišpāṭîm,* and *'ēḏōṯ* (4:45; 6:20); *ḥuqqîm/ḥuqqôṯ* and *miṣwôṯ* (4:40; 5:31; 6:1f.; 10:13; 27:10; 28:15,45; 30:10 [plus *tôrâ*]), etc. The various terms have here lost their special meanings, and the combinations all refer to the law as a whole, which is also called *tôrâ* in Deuteronomy.[37]

The Deuteronomistic history exhibits the same usage as Deuteronomy. The term *ḥōq/ḥuqqâ* appears almost exclusively in parenetic speeches of the two kings David (1 K. 2:3) and Solomon (1 K. 8:58,61), but especially in words spoken by Yahweh (1 K. 3:14; 6:12; 9:4,6; 11:11) or the prophets (1 K. 11:33f.,38) bearing the mark of the Deuteronomist, and also in historical analyses and narratives in which the author or redactor himself is speaking (1 K. 3:3; 2 K. 17:8,13,15,19,34,37; 23:3). The phrase *ḥuqqaṯ haggôyîm* (2 K. 17:8) is a special case: Israel had adopted the cultic practices of other nations. Elsewhere the *ḥuqqôṯ* (with the exception of *ḥuqqôṯ dāwiḏ,* 1 K. 3:3) are given by Yahweh.

5. *The Chronicler's History.* In the Chronicler's history, legal terminology is dependent on the Deuteronomistic original.[38] Even in the sections composed by the Chronicler himself we find the typically Deuteronomistic series of terms referring to the totality of the law (1 Ch. 29:19; 2 Ch. 19:10).

In Ezra and Nehemiah, *ḥōq* is rather infrequent; apart from a document of obligation (Neh. 10:30[29]), it appears either in the Chronicler's own accounts (Ezr. 7:10f.) or in traditional prayers (Neh. 1:7; 9:13f.).[39]

6. *The Prophetic Books.* Most of the occurrences in the prophetic books are found in Ezekiel. Here the feminine form *ḥuqqâ* predominates (22 occurrences), usually in combination with the plural of *mišpāṭ,* referring to the statutes of Yahweh's covenant.[40] The form *ḥōq* appears only once (36:27) with reference to Yahweh's law; it also appears with the meaning "measure, portion" (Ezk. 16:27; 45:14) and with reference to unjust statutes (20:25). Usually Ezekiel speaks in Yahweh's name of "my *ḥuqqôṯ*" and "my *mišpāṭîm*" without any suggestion of their content. This pair of words "defines sufficiently and clearly for Ezekiel . . . the entire content of what Yahweh requires."[41] In

[37] *Ibid.,* 91ff.
[38] *Ibid.,* 95ff.
[39] *Ibid.,* 97f.
[40] *Ibid.,* 85f.
[41] *Ibid.,* 85.

Ezk. 43:11f. and 44:5, the words *ḥuqqôṯ* and *tôrôṯ* are clearly used as terms for regulations governing the cult and the temple. In 18:9, we find *ḥuqqôṯ* and *mišpāṭîm* in a context suggesting that we are dealing with "the two major domains of covenant legislation, the cult and civil law" (cf. vv. 19,21).[42] In summary, we can say that Ezekiel uses *ḥuqqâ* and *tôrâ* for cultic regulations and *mišpāṭ* for the legal norms governing life in society.

In the other prophetic books, *ḥōq* and *ḥuqqâ* occur very rarely. Isa. 24:5 speaks of transgressing the *tôrôṯ*, violating the *ḥōq*, and breaking the *b^eriṯ* as the reasons why the earth has been devastated; the relationship of the three terms to each other is not defined more precisely. Jer. 44:10,23 uses Deuteronomistic terminology: the *ḥuqqôṯ* and *'ēḏôṯ* are parts of the single *tôrâ* of God. The same is true of Am. 2:4. In Mic. 6:16 we find the expression *ḥuqqôṯ 'omrî*, comparable on the one hand to *ḥuqqôṯ dāwiḏ* (1 K. 3:3), on the other to *ḥuqqôṯ haggôyîm* (2 K. 17:8; cf. above). Zec. 1:6 refers to the words of the prophets as *ḥōq* (cf. Ps. 2:7, speaking of God's oracle to the king). In Mal. 3:7,10,22(4:4), *ḥōq* is a term for a cultic regulation. In Zeph. 2:2, *leḏeṯ ḥōq* is obscure.

7. *The Psalms*. In the Psalms, there are 30 occurrences of *ḥōq* and 3 of *ḥuqqâ;* both "are used identically as terms for specific expressions of Yahweh's will."[43] It can be stated in general that in the Psalms—as in the parenetic sections of Deuteronomy and H—"legal terms such as *ḥōq/ḥuqqâ, mišpāṭ, 'ēḏûṯ/'ēḏâ*, etc. are used for the most part as synonymous expressions, by which Yahweh's covenant will in all its variety may be extolled in fresh ways."[44]

Of the occurrences, 21 of *ḥōq* and 1 of *ḥuqqâ* appear in Ps. 119 (vv. 5, 8, 12, 16, 23, 26, 33, 48, 54, 64, 68, 71, 80, 83, 112, 117f., 124, 135, 145, 155, 171),[45] where *ḥōq* is one of the synonyms used for the word or law of God. Among the other occurrences, Ps. 2:7 refers to the divine oracle to the king, "You are my son, today I have begotten you"; and in 148:6, *ḥōq* means a limit that is not to be crossed.[46]

According to Ps. 147:19, Yahweh gave his words to Israel, *ḥuqqîm* and *mišpāṭîm*, thus exalting Israel above the nations. Ps. 99:7 speaks similarly of the revelation of the law, and says that Israel keeps his *'ēḏôṯ* and the *ḥōq* that he gave. Ps. 105:45 states that Israel was given the lands of the nations in order to keep Yahweh's *ḥuqqîm* and *tôrôṯ*.

According to Ps. 18:23(22), the psalmist kept God's *mišpāṭîm* and *ḥuqqôt* by not departing from God and remaining *tāmîm* before him; he was therefore recompensed according to his *ṣ^eḏāqâ*. Ps. 89:32(31) belongs to the tradition of Nathan's prophecy to David: even if his children violate the law (*tôrâ, mišpāṭîm, ḥuqqôṯ, miṣwôṯ*), although they may be punished, God's *ḥeseḏ* will endure. Ps. 50:16 disputes the right of the *r^ešā'îm* to take the *ḥuqqîm* and the law of Yahweh in their mouths.

---

42 *Ibid.*, 88.

43 *Ibid.*, 100.

44 *Ibid.*, 102.

45 S. Mowinckel, "Loven og de 8 termini i Sl. 119," *NTT*, 61 (1960), 95-159.

46 See III.1 above.

In Ps. 81:5(4), *ḥōq* and *mišpāṭ* are represented as a cultic ceremony ordained by God. Ps. 94:20 speaks of perversion of justice (*yōṣēr 'āmāl ʿalê-ḥōq*). Finally, Ps. 105:10 associates the giving of *ḥōq* and *berîṯ* with the promise of the land (v. 11); here *ḥōq* bears the nuance of being a divine promise.

IV. LXX. The verb *ḥāqaq*/*ḥāqâ* is usually rendered by the LXX using various compounds of *gráphein*.[47] For *ḥōqēq* and *meḥōqēq*, the LXX has a different translation in each passage. For *ḥōq* in its concrete sense we find, for example: *dósis* (Gen. 47:22), *sýntaxis* (Ex. 5:14), *hórion* (Job 38:10), *chrónos* (Job 14:5,13), *érgon* (Prov. 31:15), *tropḗ* (Job 38:33), *arithmeín* (Job 28:26), *toú mḗ dialipeín* (Isa. 5:14), *akribasmós* (Prov. 8:29), *kólpos* (= *ḥêq*) (Job 23:12), as well as *próstagma* (Gen. 47:26; Ps. 94:20; 148:6; Jer. 5:22,24; Ezk. 45:14), *nómimon* (Ezk. 16:27; Mic. 7:11), and *nómos* (Jer. 31:36 [38:37]).

As legal terms, both *ḥōq*/*ḥuqqâ* and *mišpāṭ* are translated as *nómimon, dikaíōma, próstagma,* or more rarely *nómos* or *entolḗ*.[48]

V. Dead Sea Scrolls. In the Dead Sea scrolls, the verb *ḥāqaq* is a technical term referring to God's preordaining the ages and eons of the world (1QpHab 7:13; 1QS 10:1; 1QH 1:24). This meaning shines through the noun *ḥōq* in a few passages that speak of the fixed dwelling place of the light (1QS 10:1), the regular sequence of the years (1QS 10:6), and the mighty spirits that maintain the order of the heavens (1QH 1:10). Once *ḥōq* is used for the boundaries of the earth's divisions (1QM 10:12).

Elsewhere, *ḥōq* (sg. and pl.) refers to the law, which mankind is to study (1QS 5:11; 1QM 10:10) and live by (1QS 1:7,15; 3:8; 5:7,20) in order to keep the covenant (1QS 5:22; 8:10; 10:10). But it can also mean the rules of the Qumran community, e.g., the *ḥuqqîm* for the *maśkîl* (1QS 9:12) and possibly *ḥōq hā'ēṯ* (1QS 9:14,23). The unrighteous priest is said to have been faithless toward God's *ḥuqqîm,* i.e., the law or the cultic regulations in particular (1QpHab 8:10,17). In the statement that the Kittim do not believe in God's *ḥuqqîm* (1QpHab 2:15), the meaning is probably revelation as a whole. But is also possible to speak of the "*ḥuqqîm* of darkness" by which the spirits of Belial walk (1QM 13:12). The *ḥuqqîm* of pagans were considered reprehensible; capital punishment was inflicted on those who followed them.[49] In 1QH 7:34, *ḥōq* stands in parallel synonymy with → גורל *gôrāl,* "lot."

A special case is the expression *ḥōq hārûṯ* in the Manual of Discipline (1QS 10:6,8,11). According to Nauck, this phrase refers to the ordinances of the festal calendar, "engraved" on heavenly tablets, and the associated forms of praise.

Ringgren

---

[47] See the notes in Hentschke, 7-10.

[48] For the details, see Hentschke, 105-111.

[49] Cf. Z. W. Falk, " 'Beḥuqey hagoyim' in Damascus Document IX, I," *RevQ*, 6 (1969), 569.

חָקַר *ḥāqar;* חֵקֶר *ḥēqer;* מֶחְקָר *meḥqār*

Contents: I. 1. Occurrences; 2. Etymology. II. Meaning.

I. 1. *Occurrences.* The root *ḥqr,* "explore, examine, test," exists only in Hebrew and, to a limited extent, in Aramaic (the Targumim and Mandaic). In the post-OT period, it is attested in Sirach (verb and substs. *ḥqr* and *mḥqrwtm,* "their *m.*," 44:4) and in 1QH (subst. *ḥqr*). Middle Hebrew (tannaitic) restricts the verb and the *nomen actionis ḥ^aqîrâ* almost exclusively to legal terminology: for the (cross) examination of witnesses and (much more rarely) for the examination of circumstances that have led to an oath (for the purpose of dissolving the obligation). In addition, the verb occurs very rarely in elevated diction, in prayer,[1] and in consolation.[2] Resort to Biblical Hebrew is customary in prayer, and in the brief word of consolation *ḥqr* stands alongside *lēḇāḇ* and *nāṯîḇ,* two words not normally found in Middle Hebrew. Substantives include *ḥēqer,*[3] *ḥaqrānîm,*[4] and Middle Heb. *ḥiqqûr,* "discrimination."[5] In Middle Hebrew and Aramaic, the usual root for "examine," etc., is *bdq.* In the sense "examine witnesses," it alternated originally (?) with *ḥqr;* but there is evidence of later increased terminological precision.[6] Thus *ḥqr* is one of the cases in which Biblical Hebrew and Aramaic agree against Middle Hebrew.

2. *Etymology. KBL*[3] without evidence gives "be deep" as the basic meaning;[7] this meaning was already suggested by S. P. Chajes in his 1913 Hebrew commentary on the Psalms[8] on the basis of Job 38:16, a circular argument. It would be more likely, after the example of Aram. *bdq,* to postulate a basic meaning of "divide." Since the latter means both "examine" and "divide," it would be reasonable to assume that Heb. *ḥqr,* "examine," is likewise based on a meaning "divide." This hypothesis is as good as proved by Arab. *ḥrq,* "tear apart, divide," and is further support by semantic overlaps of the same nature in Akkadian (*parāsu*) and Arabic (*baqara*).[9]

II. Meaning. The root *ḥqr* occurs 40 times in the OT: the verb is found 17 times in poetry and 10 times in prose (correcting the data in vol. II, p. 70); the noun *ḥēqer* appears 12 times and the invented form *meḥqār* once (Ps. 95:4, pl.). A certain concentration in Job (6 occurrences of the verb and 7 of the substantive) does not derive,

---

1 *Hag.* 14b.
2 *Ketub.* 8b.
3 Mekilta; cf. conclusion.
4 Sifre on Nu. 25:6; uncertain textual tradition.
5 *Aboth* vi.1.
6 Cf. Mishnah *Sanh.* vi.1.
7 Cf. J. L. Palache, *Semantic Notes on the Hebrew Lexicon* (Eng. trans., Leiden, 1959), 34.
8 P. 208.
9 See J. C. Greenfield, "Lexicographical Notes I," *HUCA,* 29 (1958), 221, n. 24.

as will be seen, primarily from the fact that the book of Job is concerned with "examining" the problem of Job.

The verb appears primarily in the qal; its meaning is illuminated to some extent by the following assignment of syntactic and semantic categories on the basis of subject and direct object. (A) Subject: a human being; object: (1) a human being (or his deeds and words). (a) Someone else: 1 S. 20:12 (Jonathan will "examine" his father Saul, i.e., "sound out" his attitude toward David); Job 32:11 (examine words, i.e., get to the root of arguments); Prov. 18:17 (the opponent in legal proceedings "fathoms" or unmasks the one who appears to be in the right); Job 28:11 (a poor man "exposes" the rich man who is wise in his own eyes). (b) The subject himself: Lam. 3:40 ("Let us test[10] and 'examine' our ways [i.e., ourselves] and return"). (2) An impersonal object: Jgs. 18:2; 2 S.10:3 par. 1 Ch. 19:3 ("spy out" [piel of *rgl*] and "examine" a land or a city); Ezk. 39:14 ("search" the land to find corpses); Job 5:27 ("this we have 'searched out' "; it is true); Job 28:3 (men "search" rock to its uttermost depth to find iron and ore); Job 29:16 (Job has "searched out" the cause of one whom he did not know and made it clear); Prov. 23:30 ("try" or taste mixed wine); Prov. 25:2 (kings are to "search out" legal cases and get to the bottom of them); also Dt. 13:15 (Eng. v. 14) (*haddāḇār,* "the matter," is implied; "you shall inquire [*dāraš*] into the matter and 'make search' and ask diligently [*šā'al*]"). (B) Subject: God; object: (1) human beings: Jer. 17:10 (Yahweh "searches" the mind and tries[11] the heart); Ps. 44:22(21) (God "searches" us and knows our hidden thoughts); Ps. 139:1,23 (God "searches" and knows or tries [*bḥn*] a person and his thoughts); Job 13:9 (when God "searches out" someone, it is impossible to deceive him like another person. (2) An impersonal object: Job 28:27 (God searches out wisdom, par. *sippēr*).

As synonyms, then, we find primarily *bāḥan, ḥāpaś, riggēl,* and *dāraš;* the outcome can be expressed by means of *yāḏa'*.

Far more than the synonyms *bḥn, nsh,* and *ṣrp,*[12] *ḥqr* stands for a purely cognitive and analytical[13] examination and testing; *nsh* and *ṣrp* emphasize more the practical aspect of testing or "trying out," and *bḥn* suggests intuitive comprehension. But borderline cases and frequent parallelism stand in the way of a uniform clear distinction. Possibly this special sense of *ḥqr* helps account for its comparatively infrequent religious use:[14] God's knowledge is not so much progressive and analytic as instantaneous and holistic; but human beings think and speak of God largely in anthropomorphic terms, and so a certain terminological inconsistency is only natural. (Knowledge gained through putting someone to the test, through leading into temptation, is something else again: here the object of knowledge, human conduct, is a successive phenomenon.)

On the other hand, when a human being is the subject, the OT person does not analyze the idea and understanding of God. The piel, which occurs only once (Eccl.

---

10 → חפש *ḥāpaś.*

11 → בחן *bḥn.*

12 → בחן *bḥn, TDOT,* II, 69-71.

13 See I.2.

14 → בחן *bḥn, TDOT,* II, 69-71.

12:9) and then in a triplet of piel forms, probably means "scan (verse)," as does the qal in Sir. 44:5.[15] This explanation of the Sirach passage, and thus also of the Ecclesiastes passage, is also supported by a marginal reading from the Genizah and by a text from Masada that reads *ḥwqry mzmwr 'l (h)qw,* where *qw* appears to mean "melody" (see Ps. 19:5[4]).

The niphal serves exclusively to express a single notion: "unfathomable, immeasurable," always in connection with a negative particle (1 K. 7:47 par. 2 Ch. 4:18: the weight of the bronze furnished by Hiram was immeasurable; Jer. 46:23: an impenetrable forest) or an unreal condition (Jer. 31:37: if the heavens can be measured [*mdd*], if the foundations of the earth can be "explored"). The force of this observation is not diminished by the argument that the occurrence of just 3 or 4 forms cannot be expected to provide information about general usage, because a similar situation exists with respect to the substantive *ḥēqer.* Of its 12 occurrences, 7 are negated, with the sense "unsearchable, immeasurable" (Job 5:9; 9:10; 34:24; 36:26; Ps. 145:3; Prov. 25:3; Isa. 40:28), 2 are the object of rhetorical questions and thus indirectly negated (Job 11:7; 38:16), 1 occurs in a corrupt text (Prov. 25:27), 1 in an uncertain text (Jgs. 5:16; cf. v. 15), and only 1 in a clear positive assertion (Job 8:8: "consider what the fathers have 'found' "). Similar remarks apply to the biblicizing Hymn Scroll, which supplies 2 instances of *lᵉ'ên ḥēqer* (1QH 3:20; 6:3), and 2 passages where it is reasonably certain that the same phrase should be supplied (8:17; 18:30), while *ḥqr* is used positively only once (1QH fr. 15:5). And finally we read in the Mekilta on Ex. 20:5: *lᵉ'ên ḥēqer wᵉ'ên mispār.* With respect to the OT negation of *ḥēqer,* it is noteworthy that 6 of the 9 certain passages refer to God or to his attributes and deeds (Job 5:9; 9:10; 11:7; 36:26; Ps. 145:3; Isa. 40:28). If this use of *ḥēqer* as a kind of *nomen actionis* is added to the usage of the qal already described, the number of religious statements using the root *ḥqr* rises from 5 to 11. All 6 verses of the second group are hymnic; their denial that it is possible to say anything about the nature of God is hymnic exaggeration and positive in the highest sense.

Tsevat

---

[15] R. Smend, *Die Weisheit des Jesus Sirach* (Berlin, 1906), 418f.; G. Rinaldi, "Alcuni termini ebraici relativi alla letteratura," *Bibl,* 40 (1959), 268f.

חָרַב *ḥārab̲* I; חָרֵב *ḥārēb̲;* חֹרֶב *ḥōreb̲;* חָרְבָּה *ḥorbâ;* חָרָבָה *ḥārāb̲â;* *חֲרָבוֹן *ḥᵃrāb̲ôn*

Contents: I. The Root. II. Dry: 1. Usage and Occurrences; 2. Theological Usage. III. Be Desolate: 1. Usage and Occurrences; 2. Theological Usage.

I. The Root. *GesB* distinguishes the verb *ḥārab̲* I, "be dry, desiccated," and *ḥārab̲* II, "be desolated," alongside a third root represented in *ḥereb̲,* "sword." According to *KBL*[2,3], no distinction should be made between the first two; we should distinguish only two roots, *ḥrb* I, with the true radicals ḪRB, and *ḥrb* II, with the radicals

ḤRB. Heb. ḥārab̲ I accordingly bears both meanings, which have led to specialized forms in other languages; cf. Akk. ḫarābu, "become a waste";[1] Ugar. ḫrb, "dry out";[2] Arab. ḫaraba, "destroy, lay waste"; and, for example, Ya'ud. ḥrb, "destroy."[3] Besides the noun ḥereb̲, Heb. ḥrb II is represented by a verb ḥārab̲ attested in 2 K. 3:23; Jer. 50:21,27, corresponding to Arab. ḥariba III, "make war on," IV, "wage war with one another."

Despite this systematic insight, the two semantic fields of ḥārab̲ I will be examined separately; the nominal derivatives, too, will be studied in two parts as necessary.

II. Dry.

1. *Usage and Occurrences*. The verb ḥārab̲ occurs in the OT with the meaning "be dry, desiccated" in the qal, with passive meaning in the pual, and with causative or resultative meaning in the hiphil. In addition, we find the nominal forms ḥārēb̲, "dry," ḥōreb̲, "dryness, drought, heat," ḥārāb̲â, "dry land," and *ḥ^a^rāb̲ôn, "dry heat."

The name ḥōrēb̲ for the mountain of God in E, Deuteronomy, and the Deuteronomistic history presents a separate problem. It may derive from this root[4] and be a substitute meaning "desert"[5] for the name Sinai, which had become suspect on account of its association with Edom. It may also, however, derive from ḥrb II,[6] in which case it would mean something like "sword-shaped." Since this problem is connected with the question of its location, we may leave it unresolved.[7]

The distinction between ḥārab̲, "dry," and → יבשׁ yāb̲ēš, "become dry," is nicely illustrated in Gen. 8:13a and 14b (P). Here ḥārab̲ designates the process, *yāb̲ēš* the result.[8] In order to avoid a contradiction, Gen. 8:13a must be translated "the waters *began* to be dried from off the earth"; cf. Isa. 19:5f.; Job 14:11; Isa. 44:27. But the distinction between ingressive ḥārab̲ and resultative-stative *yāb̲ēš* vanishes in the pual (cf. Jgs. 16:7f.) and hiphil (cf. Jer. 51:36, where *hôb̲îš* can be placed in parallelism before *heḥ^e^rîb̲;* cf. also Isa. 42:15; Hos. 13:15 conj.; Nah. 1:4 conj.;[9] also Isa. 50:2; 51:10; 2 K. 19:24 par. Isa. 37:25). The usage of the qal was not strictly ingressive, as may possibly be seen from Gen. 8:13b (J) and certainly from Ps. 106:9.

The stative meaning is inherent in the nominal derivatives. The adj. ḥārēb̲, for example, characterizes an object as being dry, without any moisture (cf. Lev. 7:10; Prov. 17:1). Of the substantives, ḥōreb̲ means "dryness," e.g., the dryness of the earth or of an object in contrast to its moistness when the dew has fallen (Jgs. 6:37,39f.); absolutely, it means "(dewless) drought" (Hag. 1:11; Jer. 50:38 MT). As a phenom-

---

1 *AHw*, I, 322; *CAD*, VI (1956), 87f.

2 *WUS*, no. 1078.

3 *DISO*, 95, 43.

4 *KBL*³, 336.

5 L. Perlitt, "Sinai und Horeb," *Beiträge zur alttestamentlichen Theol. Festschrift W. Zimmerli* (Göttingen, 1977), 302-322.

6 E. Auerbach, *Moses* (Eng. trans., Detroit, 1975), 29.

7 For earlier interpretations, see, for example, H. Holzinger, *Exodus. KHC*, II (1900), 10.

8 Cf. also E. A. Speiser, *Genesis. AB*, I (1964), 53.

9 Also K. Elliger in *BHS, in loc.*

enon of the day it means "heat," in contrast to *qeraḥ,* the cold of the night (Gen. 31:40; Jer. 36:30; Sir. 14:27). Sir. 43:3 explicitly names the sun as the cause of this heat, which can be ameliorated by the shade of clouds (Isa. 4:6; 25:4f.). In this sense it corresponds to *ḥ*ᵃ*rāb̠ōn,*[10] attested in Ps. 32:4 as *ḥarb̠ōnê qayiṣ,* "summer heat." As a bodily phenomenon, *ḥōreb̠* means "fever" (Job 30:30; possibly also [with Vulg.] in Dt. 28:22). Finally, *ḥārāb̠â*[11] refers to the dry land, in contrast to the sea, implicitly (Gen. 7:22 [J]; Ps. 78:15[12]) or explicitly (Ex. 14:21a [J]; Hag. 2:6), the waters of the Jordan (Josh. 3:17; 4:18; 2 K. 2:8), or the branches of the Nile (Ezk. 30:12).

2. *Theological Usage.* The theological use of the verb and the derived nouns springs from belief in Yahweh's dominion over nature and history, understood as a single realm in which he is at work. At the exodus, for example, he turned the sea into dry land, driving it back by a strong east wind (Ex. 14:21 [J]; cf. Ps. 106:9; Isa. 51:10). What took place then (Ps. 106:9) is a cosmic reflex of Yahweh's appearing (Nah. 1:4; cf. Hag. 2:6), possible at any time and therefore the subject of eschatological expectation; it is an aspect of his creative power (Isa. 44:27—Westermann[13] does not exclude the possibility of an allusion to the Deluge Narrative), which Deutero-Isaiah identifies characteristically with the act of deliverance at the Sea of Reeds (Isa. 51:10). This power is reflected in Yahweh's unexpected intervention in the natural order (Josh. 3:17; Jgs. 6:37ff.); it is a power shared by the prophet Elijah (2 K. 2:8). That which the king of Assyria can only boast of presumptuously (2 K. 19:24 par. Isa. 37:5), Yahweh can do in the face of his foes, drying up the branches of the Nile (Isa. 19:5f.; Ezk. 30:12) like the waters of Babylon (Jer. 50:38; 51:36), or punishing his own guilty people with a drought. The sirocco, called the wind of Yahweh, drying up the watercourses of the land, can be used as a metaphor of the imminent onslaught of the Assyrians against guilty Ephraim (Hos. 13:15). On the other hand, as the eschatological deliverer Yahweh will be for his people "a shade from the heat" (Isa. 25:4—a metaphor related secondarily in 4bα and 5aαbα to the blast of the ruthless); in the age of salvation, he will create for Jerusalem a cloud to protect from the heat of the day (Isa. 4:5f.).

III. Be Desolate.

1. *Usage and Occurrences.* In its second realm of use, too, the verb *ḥārab̠* I is intransitive in the qal. Isa. 34:10 confirms its stative meaning: *middôr lāḏôr teḥ*ᵉ*rāb̠,* "from generation to generation (Edom) shall lie waste." But in Isa. 60:12; Jer. 26:9; Ezk. 6:6; 12:20; Am. 7:9; Sir. 16:4 an ingressive translation "be laid waste, be devastated" is at least possible. The niphal, attested only in 2 participles (Ezk. 26:19; 30:7 [29:12 conj.]), serves as a passive to the qal. The causative hiphil with the meaning

---

10 Cf. *BL,* 498c.

11 Cf. *BLe,* §477z.

12 For example, H. Gunkel, *Die Psalmen. GHK,* II/2 (1929), 343 conj.; most recently discussed by M. Dahood, *Psalms II. AB,* XVII (³1979), 230.

13 *Isaiah 40–66. OTL* (Eng. trans. 1969), 157.

"lay waste, devastate" (Jgs. 16:24; 2 K. 19:17 par. Isa. 37:18; Isa. 49:17; Ezk. 19:7; Zeph. 3:6[14]) and the equivalent passive hophal, "be laid waste, be devastated" (Ezk. 26:2; 29:12) round out the usage. The objects include not only structures, buildings, cities,[15] and lands, but also populations, in whole or in part (cf. 2 K. 19:17; Isa. 60:12; Sir. 16:4).

Among the denominatives, the most important is *ḥorbâ,* "desolate place, ruins" (cf. Arab. *ḫirbat*), with 42 occurrences, 26 in the plural.[16] The following passages are only representative: Lev. 26:31; Ezr. 9:9; Ps. 9:7(6); 109:10; Isa. 5:17; 51:3; 58:12; 64:10(11); Jer. 7:34; 22:5; 44:2; 49:13; Ezk. 5:14; 25:13; 33:24; 36:10; 38:12; Dnl. 9:2; Mal. 1:4. Next come the adj. *ḥārēb̲,* "desolate, ruined" (Neh. 2:3,17; Jer. 33:10,12; Ezk. 36:35,38; Hag. 1:4,9), and the abstract noun *ḥōreb̲,* "devastation" (Isa. 61:4; Jer. 49:13; Ezk. 29:10 MT[17]). As parallel or supplementary terms, all the forms in this semantic field prefer the verb *šmm* with its derivatives *šammâ* and *šᵉmāmâ* (cf., for example, Lev. 26:31; Jer. 33:10; Ezk. 6:6; 36:35; Am. 7:9; and Jer. 25:11; 44:22; 49:13 and Lev. 26:33; Isa. 49:19; 61:4; Jer. 44:6; Ezk. 29:10). With respect to the meaning of *ḥorbâ,* it should be noted that Job 3:14 (pl.) can hardly refer to pyramids.[18] In figurative usage we find the clear metaphor of the "owl of the waste places" (*kôs ḥᵒrāb̲ôt̲,* Ps. 102:7[6]) representing the sufferer in a lament, the more obscure metaphor of the "foxes among the ruins" (*šuʿālîm boḥᵒrāb̲ôt̲,* Ezk. 13:4[19]) for the prophets of Israel, the strange mention of the *ḥorāb̲ôt̲ ʿôlām* (Ezk. 26:20), clearly located in the underworld and associated with those who dwell there,[20] and the phrase *ḥorb̲ôt̲ ʿôlām,* used in Isa. 58:12; 61:4 in the sense "ancient ruins" and in Jer. 25:9; 49:13 in the sense "everlasting ruins."[21] These figurative usages are distinct from ordinary usage, defined primarily by occurrence in threats and promises.

2. *Theological Usage.* This latter usage brings us to the specifically theological meaning of *ḥārab̲* in this semantic field. Just as, in the OT view, the God who has at his disposal the forces of nature dries up the earth, sending dryness, heat, and drought in the interests of his dominion over Israel and the nations, so too it stands in his power to punish a disobedient Israel (Lev. 26:14), Jerusalem, and Judah by laying waste their land (Jer. 7:34; 25:9ff.; 44:2,6,22), even a second time (Ezk. 33:24ff.), their sanctuaries (Am. 7:9), their cities, especially Jerusalem (Lev. 26:31ff.; Isa. 5:17; Jer. 26:9; 27:17; Ezk. 5:14; 6:6; 12:20), the king's palace (Jer. 22:5), and even the temple (Hag. 1:4,9; cf. also Jer. 26:9). The neighboring nations can be included in the same act of judgment (587: Jer. 25:9).

But because the purpose of the punishment is the prevailing of the God who, in the

---

14 Cf. also *DISO,* 95, 39ff.

15 Cf. also *KAI,* 215.4.

16 Cf. also *DISO,* 95, 43.

17 For Zeph. 2:14, see K. Elliger in *BHS, in loc.*

18 Most recently G. Fohrer, *Das Buch Hiob. KAT,* XVI (1963), 111; the contrary view is taken, for example, by M. Pope, *Job. AB,* XV (1965), 31.

19 W. Zimmerli, *Ezekiel 1. Herm* (Eng. trans. 1979), 293.

20 E. Jenni, "Das Wort ʿōlām im AT," *ZAW,* 64 (1952), 226.

21 *Ibid.,* 227.

OT view, is linked to the fate of Israel through his revelation of himself, after the catastrophe it was promised in his name that the ruins would be rebuilt, especially the ruins of Jerusalem. Isa. 44:26 shows how the fulfilled prophecy of judgment determined the self-understanding of Deutero-Isaiah, who thought he saw in Cyrus the instrument through which Yahweh would set free the exiles and rebuild Jerusalem (44:28). After the capture of Babylon by the Persian king, the Israelites held fast to the hope, now dependent solely on Yahweh, that the ruins of Jerusalem would overflow with life (49:19), so that, to the strains of a hymn of praise sung in anticipation of the comfort to come (51:3), the ruins themselves could be called upon to greet Yahweh with rejoicing at his royal entry (52:9). The theme of the rebuilding of the *'ārê ḥōreḇ* (Isa. 61:4), of the *ḥorḇôṯ 'ôlām* (Isa. 58:12; 61:4), recurs in the prophecy of Trito-Isaiah. The book of Jeremiah, probably already in consequence of theological reflection, prophesies of the new life that will fill these ruins (Jer. 33:10f.,12f.).[22] There was hope that the ruins of the "mountains of Israel," i.e., the entire land,[23] would be rebuilt, at a time when a new heart would be given and a new spirit—whether this hope was expressed by one of the prophet's contemporaries in exile[24] or by a redactor of the book of Ezekiel who can hardly be dated before the middle of the fourth century,[25] long after the problem of delayed salvation (explained concretely in Hag. 1:4,9 as being due to neglect of the temple ruins in favor of private reconstruction) was a thing of the past. How long the problem of reconstruction influenced the Jews of the postexilic period is shown by the mission of Nehemiah (Neh. 2:3,17).

The Jews of the postexilic period expected God's judgment upon the nations and an attack of the nations upon Jerusalem. These expectations are reflected in our semantic field on the one hand in the expectation of the destruction of Edom (Isa. 34:10; Jer. 49:13; Ezk. 25:13; 35:4; Mal. 1:4), a special object of hatred on account of its conduct in 587 (cf. Ob. 10f.), of commercially prosperous Tyre (Ezk. 26:20), and of Egypt (Ezk. 29:9f.), and on the other, strangely transformed, in the prophecy of the punishment of Gog from Magog upon the long desolate mountains of Israel (Ezk. 38:8).[26] Later, in Ezk. 38:10ff., it was explained on the basis of Gog's intention to destroy the restored ruins.

Ezk. 33:24,27, with its prediction of a new destruction of the people left behind in Israel, casts significant light on the tensions existing between them and the exiles, either after 586 (Zimmerli[27]) or in the fourth century (Garscha[28]).

Kaiser

---

22 S. Herrmann, *Die prophetischen Heilserwartungen im AT. BWANT,* 85 [5/5] (1965), 188, 205.

23 Zimmerli, *Ezekiel 1,* 185.

24 *Idem., Ezekiel 2. Herm* (Eng. trans. 1983), 246.

25 J. Garscha, *Studien zum Ezechielbuch. EH,* 23/23 (1974), 219, 310f.

26 G. Wanke, *Die Zionstheologie der Korachiten. BZAW,* 97 (1966), 85ff.; Zimmerli (*Ezekiel 2,* 302f.) considers the verse genuinely from Ezekiel; Garscha (237f., 310) thinks it was composed after 500 B.C.

27 *Ezekiel 2,* 200.

28 Pp. 199, 294ff.

חֶרֶב *ḥereḇ;* חָרַב *ḥāraḇ* II

Contents: I. 1. The Word; 2. Semantic Field. II. 1. Literal Usage: a. As a Weapon; b. Functions; 2. Metonymical Usage: a. As Subject; b. As Object; c. The Triad "Sword, Famine, Plague" and its Origin; 3. Metaphorical Usage.

I. 1. *The Word.* Heb. *ḥereḇ* has its reflexes in Akk. *ḫarbum,* "plow,"[1] in its Ugaritic,[2] Ya'udic, Old and Imperial Aramaic,[3] Syriac,[4] and Mandaic[5] cognates and equivalents, in Arab. *ḥarbat*^{un}, which designates a kind of javelin,[6] and in similar words of other Semitic languages.[7] As a semantic equivalent, Akk. *patrum* (Sum. *giri*$_2$), "dagger, sword,"[8] should also be mentioned.

Heb. *ḥereḇ* can designate both (1) the two-edged dagger or short sword (Jgs. 3:16,21) and (2) the single-edged scimitar or long sword, from which may derive the expression of *pî-ḥereḇ,* "the edge of the sword" (cf. Josh. 6:21, for example;[9] the expression as such does not with certainty prove the use of this weapon [cf., for example, Dt. 13:16 (Eng. v. 15); 2 K. 10:25; Jer. 21:7], which was replaced toward the end of the Late Bronze Age by a daggerlike, long thrusting sword with two edges, the *ḥereḇ pîpîyōṯ* or *pîyôṯ* [Ps. 149:6; Prov. 5:4; Isa. 41:15]).[10] From the perspective of military and religious history, the *kîḏōn* described in 1QM 5:11-14 is of special interest, because it represents a single-edged scimitar comparable to the Roman *sica,*

ḥereḇ. G. Chenet, "Ḥrb de Ras Shamra Ugarit," *Mélanges Syriens offerts à monsieur René Dussaud,* I (Paris, 1939), 49-54; *idem, Ḥrb de Ras Shamra-Ugarit et leurs rapports à l'histoire des origines israélites* (Bruges, 1939); G. R. Driver, *The Judaean Scrolls* (Oxford, 1965), 180ff.; O. Eissfeldt, "Schwerterschlagene bei Hesekiel," *Studies in OT Prophecy. Festschrift T. H. Robinson* (Edinburgh, ²1957), 73-81 = *KlSchr,* III (1966), 1-8; G. Fohrer, "Schwert," *BHHW,* III, 1750f.; H. Fredriksson, *Jahwe als Krieger* (Lund, 1945), 95ff.; H. Gressmann, *Der Ursprung der israelitisch-jüdischen Eschatologie. FRLANT,* 6 (1905), 76ff.; H. Hirsch, *Untersuchungen zur altassyrischen Religion. BAfO,* 13/14 (²1972), 6, 64f.; W. Michaelis, "μάχαιρα," *TDNT,* IV, 524-27; *idem,* "ῥομφαία," *TDNT,* VI, 993-98; P. D. Miller, Jr., *The Divine Warrior in Early Israel. HSM,* 5 (1973); A. M. Snodgrass, *Arms and Armour of the Greeks* (London, 1967); T. Solyman, *Die Entstehung und Entwicklung der Götterwaffen im alten Mesopotamien und ihre Bedeutung* (Beirut, 1968); F. Stolz, *Jahwes und Israels Kriege. AThANT,* 60 (1972); M. Weippert, "Dolch und Schwert," *BRL*², 57-63; Y. Yadin, *The Art of Warfare in Biblical Lands in the Light of Archaeological Study* (Eng. trans., New York, 1963).

1 *AHw,* I, 325.

2 *WUS,* no. 963.

3 *DISO,* 95.

4 J. Payne Smith, *A Compendious Syriac Dictionary* (1903), 156, col. 2.

5 *MdD,* 126.

6 Lane, I/2, 541.

7 *KBL*³, 335f.

8 A. Salonen, *Die Hausgeräte der alten Mesopotamier nach sumerisch-akkadischen Quellen I. AnAcScFen,* ser. B, 139 (1965), 25, 29ff., 37ff.; cf. *AHw,* II, 848.

9 Yadin, 79; this type is also discussed by Snodgrass, 97f., and Driver, 185f.

10 Yadin, 79.

from which the *sicarii* or assassins derived their name.[11] (3) The term can also be applied in general to an iron tool (Ezk. 26:9), including a chisel (Ex. 20:25). Finally, the meaning "dagger" explains the phrase *ḥarḇôṯ ṣurîm,* used for the stone knives employed for circumcision (Josh. 5:2f.).

We must also mention the verb *ḥāraḇ* II, probably to be understood as a denominative, which appears in the qal in Jer. 50:21,27 and in the niphal twice in 2 K. 3:23; in the qal it means "slay," and in the niphal "fight together."[12]

2. *Semantic Field.* We shall follow Zorell[13] in dividing the approximately 410 OT occurrences[14] into (1) literal, (2) metonymical, and (3) metaphorical usage, without necessarily drawing a line between secular and religious contexts, in accord with Israel's self-understanding and the special nature of the literature comprehended in the OT.

II. 1. *Literal Usage.*

a. *As a Weapon.* The sword or dagger (*ḥereḇ*) consists of a handle with a hilt (*niṣṣāḇ,* Jgs. 3:22), and a blade (*lahaḇ,* Jgs. 3:22; Nah. 3:3) with either a single edge (scimitar) or two edges (straight long sword; cf. *pî-ḥereḇ,* e.g., Gen. 34:26; Ex. 17:13; Nu. 21:24; Josh. 8:24; Jgs. 1:25[15] or *ḥereḇ pîpîyôṯ,* Ps. 149:6; also *pîyôṯ,* Prov. 5:4, or *šᵉtê pēyôṯ,* Jgs. 3:16). The edges were sharpened (*lāṭaš,* Ps. 7:13[12]) or whetted (*šinnēn,* Dt. 32:41; 1QH 5:13; cf. Ps. 64:4[3]) so as to produce a sharp sword (*ḥereḇ ḥaddâ,* Ps. 57:5[4]; Prov. 5:4; Isa. 49:2; Ezk. 5:1; or *ḥereḇ hahûḥaddâ,*[16] Ezk. 21:14-16[9-11]), polished by rubbing (*ḥereḇ mᵉrûṭṭâ* or *môraṭṭâ,*[17] Ezk. 21:14-16, 33[9-11,28]). The sword was kept in a sheath (*ta'ar,* 1 S. 17:51; 2 S. 20:8; Jer. 47:6; Ezk. 21:8-10,35[3-5, 30]; 1QH 5:15; also called *nāḏān,* a Persian loanword,[18] 1 Ch. 21:27). As a rule it was girded (*ḥāgar,* Jgs. 3:16; 1 S. 17:39; 25:13; 2 S. 20:8; Ps. 45:4[3]; *'āsar,* Neh. 4:12[18]), fastened (pual of *ṣāmaḏ,* 2 S. 20:8), or put (*śîm,* Ex. 32:27) over the left hip or the loins (cf. also Cant. 3:8).

According to 1QM 5:11-14, the *kîḏôn* of the Roman period consisted of a blade (*beṭen*), sometimes adorned with gold as a mark of luxury, with two lateral grooves (*sappôṯ*) running to the point (*rô'š*). The blade in turn was inserted in a hilt (*yāḏ*) made of horn (*qeren*[19]).

A sword was made (*'āśâ,* Jgs. 3:16; 1 S. 13:19) or, more precisely, forged (*kāṯaṯ,*

---

[11] Josephus *Ant.* xx.186; Acts 21:38; Driver, 183ff.; also E. Schürer, *The History of the Jewish People in the Age of Jesus Christ,* I (Eng. trans., Edinburgh, 1973), 463ff.; O. Betz, "σικάριος," *TDNT,* VII, 278-282.

[12] Cf. *KBL*³, 335.

[13] *LexHebAram,* 265f.

[14] *KBL*³, 335f.

[15] Yadin, 79.

[16] *GK,* §126w.

[17] *BLe,* §§287, 2; 357.

[18] T. Nöldeke, *GGA* (1884), 1022.

[19] Driver, 183ff.

Joel 4:10[3:10]). Stoebe[20] interprets 1 S. 13:19ff. as recalling not a deportation of Israelite smiths but a Philistine monopoly of iron goods, with the result that the average Israelite could not afford imported weapons.

At the start of a battle the sword would be taken (*lāqaḥ,* Gen. 34:25; 1 S. 17:51; Ezk. 5:1) or grasped (*'āḥaz,* Cant. 3:8) or wielded (*tāpaś,* Ezk. 38:4), then drawn (*hôṣî'*, Ezk. 21:8[3]; cf. v. 9[4]) to smite (*makkâ,* Est. 9:5; cf. Nu. 21:24, etc.), thrust (**madqērâ,* Prov. 12:18), cut (1 K. 18:28; Ezk. 23:47), or slash (Ezk. 16:40). This act could be called drawing (*šālap,* Jgs. 8:20; 9:54; 1 S. 17:51; 31:4; 1 Ch. 10:4), unsheathing (*hērîq,* Ex. 15:9; Lev. 26:33; Ezk. 12:14; 28:7; 30:11), or opening (*pātaḥ,* Ps. 37:14) the sword. A sword is accordingly described as being drawn (*šᵉlupâ,* Nu. 22:23,31; Josh. 5:13; 1 Ch. 21:16) or opened (*pᵉtûḥâ,* Ezk. 21:33[28]; cf. also Isa. 21:15). Warriors armed with swords were called *'îš šōlēp ḥereḇ* (Jgs. 8:10; 20:2,15,25; 2 S. 24:9; 2 K. 3:26; 1 Ch. 21:5), *'ᵃḥuzê ḥereḇ* (Cant. 3:8),[21] or *tōpśê ḥᵃrāḇôṯ* (Ezk. 38:4). After being used, the sword was replaced in its sheath (*hēšîḇ 'el-ta'ar,* Ezk. 21:35[30]; cf. Matt. 26:52; also Jer. 47:6; *'el nᵉḏānāh,* 1 Ch. 21:27).

b. *Functions*. Three functions of a sword can be distinguished: butcher knife (at least suggested in Isa. 34:5f.; Jer. 46:10), military weapon (e.g., 1 S. 13:19; 17:45; 21:9[8]), and sword of justice (1 K. 3:24; Isa. 66:16); but as a glance at Isa. 34:5f. shows, together with the consideration that war can be an instrument of divine punishment (Ex. 22:23[24]; Lev. 26:25,33; Isa. 1:20; 3:25; Am. 7:11,17; 9:10; etc.), the distinction is often vague, especially in the theological language of the prophets.

(1) (a). A survey of the phraseology used in the military realm provides a vivid impression of the various phases of a battle. Among the fixed idioms, combinations of a verb with *lᵉpî-ḥereḇ* clearly belong to an early linguistic stratum.[22]

First in frequency is *hikkâ lᵉpî ḥereḇ,* "slay with the edge of the sword" (Gen. 34:26; Nu. 21:24; Dt. 20:13; Josh. 8:24; 10:28,30,32,39; 11:11f.,14; Jgs. 1:8,25; 18:27; 20:37,48; 21:10; 1 S. 22:19; 2 S. 15:14; 2 K. 10:25; Job 1:15,17; Jer. 21:7); among these passages there clearly appear secondary revisions conforming to an ancient context and archaizing usage. In later usage the idiom is replaced by simple *hikkâ baḥereḇ* (Josh. 11:10; 2 S. 12:9; 2 K. 19:37; Isa. 37:38; Jer. 20:4; 26:23; 41:2). Similarly, *nāpal lᵉpî ḥereḇ,* "fall by the edge of the sword" (Josh. 8:24; Jgs. 4:16), was replaced by *nāpal baḥereḇ* (Nu. 14:3,43; 2 S. 1:12; 3:29; Isa. 3:25; 13:15; 31:8; Jer. 20:4; 39:18; Ezk. 5:12; 6:11f.; 11:10; 17:21; 24:21; 25:13; 30:5,17; 32:22-24; 33:27; 39:23; Hos. 7:16; 14:1[13:16]; Am. 7:17; Ps. 78:64; Lam. 2:21; 2 Ch. 29:9; 4QpNah. 4:4 conj.) or *nāpal lᵉḥereḇ* (Lev. 26:7f.), while nothing replaced *heḥᵉrîm lᵉpî ḥereḇ,* "put to the ban with the edge of the sword" (Dt. 13:16[15]; Josh. 6:21; 1 S. 15:8), and *ḥālaš lᵉpî ḥereḇ,* "mow down with the edge of the sword."[23]

Other available idioms included: *hārag baḥereḇ,* "slay with the sword" (Ex.

---

[20] *Das erste Buch Samuelis. KAT* VIII/1 (1973), 255f.

[21] Cf. *GK,* §50f.

[22] See also Yadin, 79.

[23] For Jgs. 4:15 see, for example, *BHK, in loc.*

22:23[24]; Nu. 31:8; Josh. 10:11; 13:22; 2 S. 12:9; 1 K. 2:32; 19:1,10,14; 2 K. 8:12; 2 Ch. 21:4; 36:17; Ezk. 23:10; 26:8,11; Am. 4:10; 9:1; cf. also Nu. 22:29; Jer. 47:6), or *nehᵉrag baḥereḇ,* "be slain with the sword" (Ezk. 26:6); *hippîl baḥereḇ,* "cause to fall by the sword" (2 K. 19:7; Isa. 37:7; Jer. 19:7; Ezk. 32:12; 2 Ch. 32:21); *hēmîṯ baḥereḇ,* "kill with the sword" (1 K. 1:51; 2:8; 2 Ch. 23:21), with the equivalent passives *mûṯ baḥereḇ,* "die by the sword" (2 K. 11:15,20; 2 Ch. 23:14,21; Jer. 11:22; 34:4; Ezk. 7:15; Am. 7:11; 9:10). Occasionally we also find *'āḇaḏ baḥereḇ,* "perish by the sword" (4QpPs 37 2:1), or *nikšal bᵉḥereḇ,* "fall by the sword" (Dnl. 11:33; cf. also Lev. 26:37).

More vivid pictures of battle are given by such expressions as: *nāṯan 'eṯ-haḥereḇ bᵉyaḏ . . .,* "put a sword in the hand of someone" (Ex. 5:21; Ezk. 30:24f.); *hippîl 'eṯ-haḥereḇ miyyaḏ . . .,* "make the sword fall from the hand of someone" (Ezk. 30:22); *qûm 'al . . . baḥereḇ,* "rise up against someone with the sword" (Am. 7:9); *nāḏaḏ mippᵉnê ḥᵃrāḇôṯ,* "flee from swords" (Isa. 21:15); *nûs mippᵉnê-ḥereḇ,* "flee from the sword" (Isa. 31:8; cf. Lev. 26:36); *rāḏap b/laḥeraḇ,* "pursue with the sword" (Jer. 29:18; Am. 1:11; CD 1:4,21; cf. Lev. 26:8). Ps. 37:15 speaks pregnantly of the heart as the target of the sword's fatal blow (*ḥarbām tāḇô' ḇᵉlibbām*), while 2 S. 23:10 reports that the bloody hand of one of David's warriors clove to his sword after a long battle.

When the battle cry sounds, which may have announced the total commitment of the fighters and their leader to Yahweh (*ḥereḇ lᵉYHWH ûlᵉgiḏ'ôn,* Jgs. 7:20), confusion can overcome the night guard; Yahweh can turn their sword against each other (*śîm 'eṯ-ḥereḇ 'îš bᵉrē'ēhû,* Jgs. 7:22; *hinnēh hāyᵉṯâ ḥereḇ 'îš bᵉrē'ēhû* (1 S. 14:20; cf. Ezk. 38:21[24]). Cursed is the one who keeps back (*māna',* Jer. 48:10) his sword from bloodshed in the battle appointed by Yahweh. The vanquished warrior falls on his sword after battle (*nāpal 'al-ḥereḇ,* 1 S. 31:4f. par. 1 Ch. 10:4f.).[25] When the attackers have taken (*lāqaḥ,* Gen. 48:22; cf. Josh. 24:12; 2 K. 6:22, and on the same subject Dt. 20:10-18, 19f.[26]) a city by sword and bow from the hand of the enemy, the *ḥalᵉlê-ḥereḇ* remain without and within the walls (Jer. 14:18; Lam. 2:21), while the female captives, called *šᵉḇuyôṯ ḥereḇ* (Gen. 31:26), are carried off. Since the *ḥalᵉlê-ḥereḇ* may, depending on the context, include those who are slain (Nu. 19:16; Dt. 21:1-9; Jer. 41:9), those slaughtered in the heat of battle (Isa. 34:1ff.; Lam. 2:21), the fallen (e.g., Isa. 22:2), or the executed (e.g., Ezk. 32:17-32; cf. v. 27), mechanical identification with the last-named group is to be avoided. As Eissfeldt points out,[27] the *ḥalᵉlê-ḥereḇ* include at least in Isa. 22:2; Jer. 14:18; Ezk. 35:8 warriors who have fallen in battle; in Lam. 4:9, it is debatable whether they should be numbered among the second group on the basis of Lam. 2:21.

In Wisdom circles, it was noted that a horse will gallop undismayed into battle without turning back (*lō'-yāšûḇ,* Job 39:22) from the sword. At the same time, there

---

[24] For Hag. 2:22, see K. Elliger, *Das Buch der zwölf Kleinen Propheten, II. ATD,* 25 (⁷1975), *in loc.*

[25] See L. Wächter, *Der Tod im AT. ArbT,* 2/8 (1967), 89ff.

[26] G. von Rad, *Studies in Deuteronomy. SBT,* 9 (Eng. trans. 1953), 45ff.

[27] Pp. 77f. (= 5).

was speculation about a fantastic monster against whom the sword does not avail (*b^elî ṯāqûm*, Job 41:4-26).[28]

Those who survived the sword (cf. *nimlaṭ mēḥereḇ*, 1 K. 19:17) were numbered among the *p^elîṭê ḥereḇ* (Jer. 44:28; Ezk. 6:8) or *ś^erîḏê ḥereḇ* (Jer. 31:2), "those who escaped the sword," and constituted the potential nucleus for the reflorescence of their people. And one day a land laid waste and depopulated by war might become *'ereṣ m^ešôḇeḇeṯ mēḥereḇ*, "a land restored from the sword," i.e., repopulated by returnees (Ezk. 38:8). The need for caution not only in war but also in peace is shown by the example of the man who did not observe the sword (*nišmar baḥereḇ*) concealed by his rival, and fell victim to a treacherous stroke (2 S. 20:10).

(b). In the notion that God alone must be relied on for aid, we come upon a bit of exilic and postexilic ideology. The nomad, as a hunter and brigand, had to "live by his sword" (Gen. 27:40);[29] Israel, however, had been delivered by Yahweh from the sword of Pharaoh (Ex. 18:4) and subsequently conquered the land without its own sword, as Ps. 44:4(3), a lament, states in the context of an historical retrospect. It must accordingly trust (*bāṭaḥ*, Ps. 44:7[6]), not in its own sword, but in Yahweh, as the confession of confidence states. Yahweh himself wielded the sword of Israel's triumph (*ḥereḇ ga'^awāṯeḵā*, Dt. 33:29; cf. 1 S. 17:47). Yahweh's failure to aid the king in battle, instead turning back his sword before the oppressor, was reason to lament (Ps. 89:44[43]); the suppliant, imitating the king's prayer, prayed to be rescued from the cruel sword of the aliens (Ps. 144:10f.).[30] In Wisdom Literature we find the analogous expectation that the righteous one at least will be redeemed from the sword in battle by Yahweh (Job 5:20; cf. also Job 27:14; Isa. 1:20; Am. 9:10). Conversely, whoever thinks he will be able to "stand" by means of his own sword will fall victim to Yahweh's punishment (Ezk. 33:26).

A critical survey of the prophetic passages cited shows that all these oracles of judgment against Israel, Jerusalem, and Judah or the nations, as well as the few promises mentioned, are at least suspected by recent scholarship to represent either contemporizing interpretation of the prophetic corpus during the exilic period or the disputes of rival postexilic factions within Judaism and their eschatological hopes.[31] (As exceptions I would cite in particular Hos. 7:16 and 14:1[13:16].)

(c). The eschatological and apocalyptic expectations of the postexilic period are thought to be represented in the following promises: a new Assyria will fall "by a

---

28 Cf. v. 18; E. Ruprecht, "Das Nilpferd im Hiobbuch: Beobachtungen zu der sogenannten zweiten Gottesrede," *VT*, 21 (1971), 223f.

29 R. de Vaux, *The Early History of Israel* (Eng. trans., Philadelphia, 1978), 169.

30 Cf. H. Gunkel, *Die Psalmen. GHK*, II/2 (⁴1926), *in loc.*

31 For a general discussion see H. W. Wolff, *Joel and Amos. Herm* (Eng. trans. 1977); O. Kaiser, *Isaiah 1–12. OTL* (Eng. trans. ²1983); *idem, Isaiah 13–39. OTL* (Eng. trans. 1974); W. Thiel, *Die deuteronomistische Redaktion von Jeremia 1–25. WMANT*, 41 (1973); G. Wanke, *Untersuchungen zur sogenannten Baruchschrift. BZAW*, 122 (1971); J. Garscha, *Studien zum Ezechielbuch. EH*, XXIII/23 (1974); H. Schulz, *Das Buch Nahum. BZAW*, 129 (1973).

sword, not of man" (Isa. 31:8; cf. also Hos. 1:7);[32] the helpers of the Messiah will rule Assyria with the sword (Mic. 5:5[6]);[33] Yahweh will break the bow, the sword, and war forever (Hos. 2:20;[34] Ps. 76:4[3][35]); swords will be beaten into plowshares (Isa. 2:4; Mic. 4:3);[36] and finally, the devout will have the praises of God on their lips and a two-edged sword in their hands to wreak vengeance on the nations (Ps. 149:6ff.).

Joel 4:10(3:10) appears as a remarkable inversion of Isa. 2:4 and Mic. 4:3; the contrary summons is issued to the nations with a view to the battles of the eschaton. Finally, we may mention the enigmatic shepherd oracles Zec. 11:17 and 13:7. To round out the picture, it should also be recalled that a dagger could represent a symbolic razor (cf. Ezk. 5:1ff.[37]).

(d). The use of a dagger or sword to inflict wounds on oneself in a state of ecstasy as part of the Ba'al cult (1 K. 18:28)[38] brings us into the realm of comparative religion. We are taken even further back by the *ḥereḇ miṯhappeḵeṯ,* "the sword turning every way," that guarded the way to the tree of life (Gen. 3:24). Gese[39] sees in it the lightning bolt of the Syro-Canaanite weather-god, in the form of a two-pronged fork or a (single or double) trident.

The two remarkably awkward scenes of the two messengers of Yahweh who encounter Balaam with drawn sword (Nu. 22:21-35; cf. v. 31)[40] and the "man" who announces himself to Joshua as the commander of Yahweh's army (Josh. 5:13-15),[41] as well as the episode of David's vision of Yahweh's messenger standing with drawn sword between heaven and earth, having just visited pestilence upon Israel and on his way to destroy Jerusalem (1 Ch. 21:16),[42] remind Miller[43] of the flaming messenger with a sharpened sword for a tongue (*ḥrb lṭšt;*[44] cf. also Rev. 1:16) sent by the Ugaritic sea-god Yamm to the assembly of the gods.

It should be noted, finally, that the apocalyptic prophecy Isa. 27:1 transfers to Yahweh the mythologem of Ba'al's victory over the sea monster Lotan:[45] on Yahweh's eschatological day of judgment, he will use his sword to punish Leviathan, presented

---

32 But see H. Barth, *Israel und das Assyrerreich* (diss., Hamburg, 1974), 57ff.

33 But see A. Weiser, *Das Buch der zwölf Kleinen Propheten, II. ATD,* XXIV (^{6}1974), *in loc.*

34 But see W. Rudolph, *Hosea. KAT,* XIII/1 (1966), *in loc.*

35 But see J. Becker, *Israel deutet seine Psalmen. SBS,* 18 (1966), 34.

36 But see H. Wildberger, *Jesaja. BK,* X/1 (1972), *in loc.*

37 But see W. Zimmerli, *Ezekiel 1. Herm* (Eng. trans. 1979), *in loc.*

38 Cf. Luc., Syr. D. 50f.; also E. Würthwein, "Die Erzählung vom Gottesurteil auf dem Karmel," *ZThK,* 59 (1962), 131-144.

39 H. Gese, "Der bewachte Lebensbaum und die Heroen," *Wort und Geschichte. Festschrift K. Elliger. AOAT,* 18 (1973), 80f. = his *Von Sinai zum Zion. BEvTh,* 64 (1974), 104f.; cf. also E. Speiser, *Genesis. AB,* 1 (1964), 24f.

40 M. Noth, *Numbers. OTL* (Eng. trans. 1968), 179.

41 *Idem, Das Buch Josua. HAT,* VII (^{2}1953), 23f.

42 See T. Willi, *Die Chronik als Auslegung. FRLANT,* 106 (1972), 174, n. 247.

43 Pp. 28ff., 128ff.

44 *KTU,* 1.2 I, 32f.

45 *KTU,* 1.5 I, 1-3.

as the incarnation of all the powers that are hostile to God. It is noteworthy that Ba'al[46] slays Yamm with two double axes.[47]

(2). As a sword of judgment, *ḥereḇ* appears in a secular context at least in 1 K. 3:24; it is used eschatologically in Isa. 66:16. If we follow Eissfeldt's interpretation of Ezk. 32:27,[48] contrasting on the one hand the heroes of former days laid to rest with their arms and the *ḥalᵉlê-ḥereḇ* on the other, we may see in these latter in Ezk. 32:17-32 those who have been executed; in this case the number of passages involving the sword of judgment increases significantly, to include Ezk. (30:11?); 31:17f.; 32:19f.; 35:8, as well as Isa. 22:2 (through its antithesis); Zeph. 2:12;[49] together with the *mᵉṭōʻᵃnê ḥereḇ* in Isa. 14:19; and the *ḥalᵉlê 'āwen* (1QM 6:3). The sinister sword in the "song of the sword" (Ezk. 21:13-22[8-17]), called *ḥereḇ ḥᵃlālîm* in 21:19(14), may then be interpreted as a "sword of judgment."[50]

Jer. 47:6f. and Zec. 13:7f. appear to allow us to equate the sword of Yahweh with his sword of judgment, which we may then recognize not only in Ezk. 30:24; 32:10f., but also in Ezk. 21:1-8 (20:45–21:3); Dt. 32:41f.; 1 Ch. 21:12; Isa. 27:1; 34:5ff.; and Jer. 12:12. To support this hypothesis, we can point out first of all that the *ḥalᵉlê 'āwen* of 1QM 6:3 are to be devoured in God's judgment by a flaming sword (*šalhôḇeṯ ḥereḇ*); cf. also 1QM 12:11f.; 15:2f.; and 19:11. In the final stage of this development, in any case, the identification of the sword of Yahweh with the sword of judgment is assured (cf. also Rev. 1:16; 2:12). For the beginning, besides Dt. 32:41f., Ps. 17:13 allows us to postulate the connection: according to Beyerlin,[51] the sword of Yahweh (*ḥarbᵉḵa*, in the language of prayer) to which the unjustly accused suppliant appeals is the sword of judgment in a cultic judicial process (cf. also Ps. 22:21[20]; 63:10f.[9f.]; Job 15:22; 19:29; 27:14; and Ps. 37:14f.).

From here we may with some justification include in our discussion Am. 9:1—presumably the earliest passage; 4:10; Lev. 26:25; CD 19:13, although we must remember that in the case of a god, as in the case of a great king, it is hardly possible to make a clean distinction between judicial execution and a punitive military expedition. That the *ḥereḇ YHWH* cannot be derived from the ancient Israelite conception of Yahweh as a warrior had already been recognized by Gressmann[52] on the basis of its late appearance in the OT, although his own derivation via the ban of Yahweh from the motif of the battle with the dragon supplemented with features borrowed from the

---

[46] *KTU*, 1.2 IV, 11ff.

[47] On the problem of identifying Lotan/Leviathan with Yamm, see the bibliog. in O. Kaiser, *Isaiah 13–39*, 221, note c; now also Miller, 24.

[48] Pp. 80f. (=7).

[49] But see K. Elliger, *Das Buch der zwölf Kleinen Propheten, II. ATD*, XXV (1951), *in loc.*

[50] See Zimmerli, *Ezekiel 1, in loc.*; also pp. 426ff. for literary criticism, and Garscha, 128ff.; also Jer. 5:35-38; 47:6f.; Zec. 13:7f.

[51] W. Beyerlin, *Die Rettung der Bedrängten in den Feindpsalmen der Einzelnen auf institutionelle Zusammenhänge untersucht. FRLANT*, 99 (1970), 107; cf. 146.

[52] Pp. 76ff.

god Resheph, a deity who still remains something of a puzzle,[53] must be considered problematic.

(a). Although there are many missing links in the chain of development, the evidence of legal documents from Old Assyrian commercial colonies is not without interest in this context. Phenomenologically, at least, it provides a certain parallel to the language and perhaps also the institution of the *ḥereḇ YHWH.* Oath formulas speak repeatedly, in what appear to be stereotyped phrases, of the "sword (*patrum*) of Ashur," which is clearly to be interpreted as an emblem of the judicial system. For example, one might swear by (or have another swear by) the sword of Ashur (*ina patrim ša Aššur tamā'um/tammu'um*), grasp or have another grasp the sword of Ashur (*patram ša Aššur ṣabātum/šaṣbutum*), or cause the sword of Ashur to go forth (*patram ša Aššur šēṣu'um*).[54] From the evidence, Hirsch concludes that in the commercial colonies various transactions were performed before the sword of Ashur, which, according to Lewy,[55] was brought from the local sanctuary to the place called the "gate of Ashur" when legal business was at hand: evidence was taken and sealed, proceedings were initiated, and documents were produced, while the parties swore by or "on" the sword of the deity and, in the case of solemn oaths, grasped the sword.[56] It may be noted that Oppenheim[57] interpreted *patram ša Aššur šēṣu'um* as referring to an oath involving an ordeal, in which the sacred dagger had to be drawn from its sheath; failure was considered evidence of perjury. His interpretation, however, appears not to have found acceptance.[58]

(b). Ezk. 23:46ff. (cf. 16:40f.) furnishes only problematical evidence for use of the sword as an instrument of sacral execution, because in this passage the swords of the *qāhāl* are not used until after stoning. The idiom *higgîr 'al-y^e^ḏê-ḥereḇ,* "give over to the power of the sword" (Ps. 63:11[10]; Jer. 18:21; Ezk. 35:5; cf. Ps. 22:21[20]; 37:11f.), probably allows us to conclude that in the judicial process, in which the institution and the notion of the sword of Yahweh were rooted, the condemned criminal was usually executed by sword. But at this point we are, at least temporarily, at the limit of our knowledge.[59]

2. *Metonymical Usage.* The boundary line between literal and metonymical usage is debatable in detail. Where we sense an abstract generalization, the ancient Israelite, at least in form of expression, clung to the specific and concrete. Only in Isa. 31:8

---

[53] As may be seen by comparing D. Conrad, "Der Gott Reschef," *ZAW,* 83 (1971), 157-183, with H. W. Helck, *Betrachtungen zur grossen Göttin und den ihr verbundenen Göttheiten* (Munich, 1971), 198ff.

[54] For the citations, see Hirsch, 6 II, 64ff.

[55] J. Lewy, "Studies in Old Assyrian Grammar and Lexicography," *Or,* 19 (1950), 23, n. 1.

[56] Hirsch, 65 II; cf. also M. San Nicoló, "Eid," *RLA,* II (1938), 310; cf. also 312.

[57] A. L. Oppenheim, "Lexikalische Untersuchungen zu den 'kappadokischen' Briefen," *AfO,* 12 (1937-39), 346.

[58] Bibliographical references kindly provided by Dr. E. von Weiher, Marburg.

[59] See also the discussion in *AncIsr,* 158ff.

can the reference to a *ḥereḇ lōʼ-ʼîš* or *lōʼ-ʼāḏām* be interpreted as evidence for a realization that the sword of Yahweh is being spoken of metonymically or symbolically, at least to the extent that we are not dealing here with deliberate linguistic mystification. Leaving aside many instances of the *ḥereḇ YHWH,* we therefore include here all the occurrences in which the sword appears as the subject of a statement that is not literally applicable, or at least strikes us as being something other than a concrete object.

In this type of usage, *ḥereḇ* means war in contrast to *šālôm,* "peace"; this is shown by the lament in Jer. 4:10 and by the sequence *ḥereḇ* "war," *šᵉḇî,* "captivity," etc. in Ezr. 9:7. As a term for an irresistible attack we find *ḥereḇ hayyônâ* (Jer. 46:16; 50:16; 25:38 conj.).[60] The phrase *ḥereḇ hammiḏbār,* "sword of the wilderness" (Lam. 5:9), refers to an enemy attack. The danger of the foe's military superiority is the meaning of Jeremiah's *ḥereḇ lᵉʼôyēḇ* (Jer. 6:25). How the meaning "war" can merge into that of a violent end is shown by the train of thought in Ezk. 11:8,10.

a. *As Subject.* If we examine the passages in which *ḥereḇ* is the grammatical subject, the idiom that speaks of the sword's "devouring" (*ʼāḵal*), which recalls the ancient expression *lᵉpî-ḥereḇ,* comes to the fore by virtue of its frequency. It refers to total annihilation in battle, usually at Yahweh's behest (Dt. 32:42; 2 S. 2:26; 11:25; 18:8; Isa. 31:8; Jer. 2:30; 12:12; 46:10,14; Hos. 11:6; Nah. 2:14[13]; 3:15; 1QM 6:3; 13:11f.; col. 16; pual in Isa. 1:20). Hos. 11:6 is the only undisputed occurrence in the prophets.[61]

The situation is similar in the case of the "coming" (*bôʼ*) of the sword (Jer. 5:12; Ezk. 30:4; 32:11; 33:3f.,6; 2 Ch. 20:9; cf. Jer. 4:10). All the occurrences refer to war that is sent by Yahweh, or is in his power to send (2 Ch. 20:9). Here we find the watchman passage Ezk. 33:1-20, a noteworthy instance of late postexilic theology of the prophets.[62]

The sword or war leaves childless the women of a nation (1 S. 15:33), Jerusalem (Lam. 1:20), or, borrowing from Lam. 1:20, Yahweh's sons and daughters (Dt. 32:25, *šikkēl;* cf. also Jer. 18:21). The sword goes through the land (*ʻāḇar,* Lev. 26:6; Ezk. 14:17), reaches its victims (*hiśśîg,* Job 41:18[26]; Jer. 42:16), and, in order to carry out Yahweh's punishment, does not depart from the house of sinful David (2 S. 12:10, *sûr*). In the last passage, we are probably dealing with an instance of exilic theology of history.[63]

b. *As Object.* Among the passages with *ḥereḇ* as object, the phrase *ḥereḇ hēḇîʼ ʻal,* "bring the sword or war upon someone," occupies first place; the subject is always

---

[60] See *GK,* §126w.

[61] On Nahum, see also J. Jeremias, *Kultprophetie und Gerichtsverkündigung in der späten Königszeit Israels. WMANT,* 35 (1970), in addition to the material cited in II.1.b(l)(b) above.

[62] Garscha, 197ff.; but see Zimmerli, *Ezekiel 2. Herm* (Eng. trans. 1983), 184.

[63] See W. Dietrich, *Prophetie und Geschichte. FRLANT,* 108 (1972), 127ff.; E. Würthwein, *Die Erzählung von der Thronfolge Davids—Theologische oder politische Geschichtsschreibung? ThSt,* 115 (1974), 24ff.

Yahweh (Lev. 26:25; Ezk. 5:17; 6:3; 11:8; 14:17; 29:8; 33:2). As a parallel we find the *šillaḥ 'aḥ^{a}rê/b^e/bēn/'al . . . 'eṯ ḥereḇ* of the book of Jeremiah (Jer. 9:15[16]; 24:10; 25:16,27; 29:17; 49:37); it is unlikely that any of the passages is pre-Deuteronomistic.[64]

It comes as no surprise that one can speak of Yahweh or *'ēl yiśrā'ēl* summoning (*qārā'*, Jer. 25:29; 1QM col. 16) a sword against the inhabitants of the earth or all nations. When Jeremiah prays to Yahweh (Jer. 18:21) to give the children of his enemies over to the power of the sword (*higgîr*), we are not dealing with the prophet's personal history, but with the history of the book that bears his name.[65]

With the meaning "consign to total annihilation" we find *nāṯan laḥereḇ* in Jer. 25:31; Mic. 6:14 (cf. also Ezr. 9:7; CD 1:4) with Yahweh or El as subject. The idiom *sāgar laḥereḇ*, "give over to the sword," means "visit war upon" in Ps. 78:62 and CD 3:11 (niphal); in CD 7:13 (hophal) it stands for total annihilation; and in CD 19:13 it means execution, so that the precise nuance of the expression is heavily dependent on its context. The synonymous phrase *nimsar laḥereḇ* (CD 19:10) likewise suggests total annihilation.

c. *The Triad "Sword, Famine, Plague" and its Origin.* The so-called triad of afflictions is limited in its occurrences to the Deuteronomistic portions of Jeremiah, the continuations of Ezekiel, and Chronicles. In its primary sequence, it envisions war as a disaster from without and its effects upon those under siege, so that we find (1) *ḥereḇ*, (2) *rā'āḇ*, "famine," and (3) *deḇer*, "plague, pestilence" (Jer. 14:12; 21:9; 24:10; 27:8,13; 29:17f.; 32:24,36; 38:2; 42:17,22; 44:13; Ezk. 6:11; 12:16; 4QpPs37 2:1). In Ezk. 14:21, the triad has been expanded by the insertion of *ḥayyâ rā'â*, "beasts of prey," after *rā'āḇ* to emphasize the danger from without. In the sequence (1) *deḇer*, (2) *ḥereḇ*, (3) *rā'āḇ* (Jer. 21:7), the author envisions a plague preceding war, then war itself with its consequences. When Jer. 34:17 alters the classic formula to (1) *ḥereḇ*, (2) *deḇer*, (3) *rā'āḇ*, the author gives primary emphasis to the more dangerous of the punishments that afflict the besieged city from within, at the expense of the usual causal sequence. Ezk. 7:15 is to be viewed from the same perspective: we find the same sequence, with an explicit contrast between affliction without (*baḥûṣ*) and within (*mibbāyiṯ*). The same formula lies behind 2 Ch. 20:9: the *š^{e}pōṭ* appended to *ḥereḇ* is, in my opinion, to be considered a gloss that has found its way into the text. The sequence (2) *deḇer*, (3) *rā'āḇ*, as comparison with 1 K. 8:37 shows, is based on the same motivation as in Jer. 34:17.

The most extreme transformation of the basic formula, with the sequence completely inverted, is found in Ezk. 5:12: (1) *deḇer*, (2) *rā'āḇ*, (3) *ḥereḇ*. This sequence, too, is quite deliberate: first, a third of the inhabitants of Jerusalem will die from pestilence and famine; then, another third will perish by the sword outside the city.

An explicit variant appears in Ezk. 28:23, where the elements are (1) *deḇer*, (2) *dām*, "blood," and (3) *ḥereḇ*. Here, too, the sequence is logical. Pestilence will ravage

64 Cf. Thiel, *in loc.*

65 A. H. J. Gunneweg, "Konfession oder Interpretation im Jeremiabuch," *ZThK*, 67 (1970), 408f., 412ff.; but cf. J. Bright, "Jeremiah's Complaints: Liturgy, or Expressions of Personal Distress?" in *Proclamation and Presence. Festschrift G. H. Davies* (London, 1970), 189-214.

besieged Tyre; when the city is taken, there will be slaughter in the streets (*dām*), while those who flee the city will perish without by the sword (cf. also Isa. 13:15).

It is at least dubious whether the sequence (1) *ḥereḇ*, (2) *šᵉḇî*, "captivity," (3) *bizzâ*, "plundering," (4) *bōšeṯ*, "shame" in Ezr. 9:7 and (1) *ḥereḇ*, (2) *lehāḇâ*, "flame" or "fire," (3) *šᵉḇî*, (4) *bizzâ* in Dnl. 11:33 should be considered variations of the triad. Likewise, the sequence (1) *ḥereḇ*, (2) *kᵉlāḇîm*, "dogs," (3) *'ôp*, "birds," (4) *bᵉhēmâ*, "beasts" in Jer. 15:3 (cf. also Dt. 28:26; 1 K. 16:4; 21:19; 2 K. 9:36), probably has a different history.[66]

A search for precursors of the classic triad turns up the short form (1) *ḥereḇ*, (2) *rā'āḇ*, likewise frequent in the book of Jeremiah (Jer. 5:12; 11:22; 14:13,15f.; 16:4; 18:21; 42:16; 44:12 [twice]; Lam. 4:9) and the pair (1) *deḇer*, (2) *ḥereḇ*, which appears as a punishment in J (Ex. 5:3). Cf. also 1 K. 8:37, where *rā'āḇ* and *deḇer* introduce a sequence of nine elements. Literarily, Jer. 5:12 probably constitutes the point of origin for the occurrences of the pair in the book of Jeremiah; in substance, however, the *Sitz im Leben* of such pairs and sequences is the lament (cf. Lam. 4:9 and Isa. 51:19).[67] Consequently it is not impossible that the lament indirectly influenced the numerous occurrences of the short and long sequences in the book of Jeremiah.

3. *Metaphorical Usage*. In comparison with the two types of usage just discussed, metaphorical usage of *ḥereḇ* proves to be very restricted. The point of departure is the metaphorical speech of Wisdom Literature, which likens the words of the "strange woman" to a two-edged sword (Prov. 5:4),[68] rash words to sword thrusts (Prov. 12:18), false witness in court to club, sword, or arrow (Prov. 25:18), and those who oppress the poor to a generation whose teeth are swords (Prov. 30:14). Similarly, a description of the enemy in a lament can identify their lips (i.e., their words) with swords (Ps. 59:8[7]) or their tongues with sharp swords (Ps. 64:4[3]). In late narrative praise, the worshipper proclaims that God has returned like a sword to its sheath the tongues of his enemies, who are likened to young lions, their teeth like swords and their tongues like sharp swords, thus averting the mortal danger that threatened (1QH 5:9-15). This brings out the point of the sword metaphor, the danger of the weapon. At the same time, we are reminded that Yahweh is and remains the lord of all war, battle, and ambush with which nations and individuals contest or embitter life.

Kaiser

---

[66] On similar lists in curses contained in ancient Near Eastern texts, see F. C. Fensham, "Common Trends in Curses of the Near Eastern Treaties and *Kudurru*-Inscriptions Compared with the Maledictions of Amos and Isaiah," *ZAW*, 75 (1963), 155-175.

[67] C. Westermann, *Isaiah 40–66*. *OTL* (Eng. trans. 1969), 245.

[68] On the identification of the "strange woman," see H. Ringgren, *Sprüch*. *ATD*, XVI (1962), 28.

חָרַד ḥāraḏ; חָרֵד ḥārēḏ; חֲרָדָה ḥ^a^rāḏâ

Contents: I. 1. Etymology; Ancient Near East; 2. Meaning and Occurrences. II. Secular Usage; Panic: 1. Bad News; 2. War. III. Religious Usage: Panic Associated with Theophanies. IV. *'ên maḥ^a^rîḏ:* Eschatological Peace or Total Security.

I. 1. *Etymology; Ancient Near East.* The root *ḥrd* appears in various Semitic languages; the distinction between *ḫ* and *ḥ* in some of these languages multiplies the potential etymological relationships. There have been repeated attempts[1] to find in the OT all the meanings attested in the ancient Near East, but without convincing success.

Closest to OT usage is Syr. *'eṯḥ^e^rēd,* "tremble" (cf. Middle Heb. *ḥrd,* "tremble," hiphil "cause to tremble, terrify"). Here belongs the designation of a god as *b'l ḥrdt,* "lord of terror," in a Neo-Punic inscription.[2] The interpretation of Ugar. *ḫrd* as "fear," "be upset" is uncertain.[3] A *ḫrd,* "vigilant, alert," occurs in *KTU,* 2.16, 13. There may be some connection with Akk. *ḫarādu* IV,[4] "wake, watch, set watch, keep awake," Arab. *ḫarida,* "be ashamed, act shamefully," and *ḥarida,* "be angry," to the extent that unusual emotional states (albeit of different sorts) are described. Akk. *ḫarādu* III, "put together," e.g. mats—*ḫurdu,* "door mat" (cf. Syr. *'eṯḥar(r)aḏ,* "be skinned"?)—might suggest in Ezk. 26:16 (the only occurrence of *ḥ^a^rāḏâ* in the pl.) a homonym meaning "mourning garments,"[5] but the argument is not compelling.[6]

The place names (which we shall not discuss) *'ên ḥ^a^rōḏ, ḥ^a^rāḏâ,* and *ḥ^a^rōḏî* are probably connected with Akk. *ḫaradum* I, "desert region[?]," Arab. *ḥārada,* "have little rain."

None of the other possible homonyms—such as Akk. *ḫurdatu,* "crossbeam," "vulva, female pudenda," Arab. *ḫarada,* "penetrate, separate oneself, set off in haste"—gives sufficient points of contact for homonymous roots with corresponding meaning in the

---

ḥāraḏ. J. Becker, *Gottesfurcht im AT. AnBibl,* 25 (1965), 10f., 66-74; J. Blau, "Etymologische Untersuchungen auf Grund des Palästinischen Arabisch," *VT,* 5 (1955), 337-344, esp. 341; H. J. van Dijk, *Ezekiel's Prophecy on Tyre (Ez. 26,1–28,19): A New Approach. BietOr,* 20 (1968), 32; G. R. Driver, "Hebrew Homonyms," *Hebräische Wortforschung. Festschrift W. Baumgartner. SVT,* 16 (1967), 54-56; J. Gray, *I & II Kings. OTL* (²1970), 495; J. Jeremias, *Theophanie: Die Geschichte einer alttestamentlichen Gattung. WMANT,* 10 (²1977), 102; N. Lohfink, "Enthielten die im AT bezeugten Klageriten eine Phase des Schweigens?" *VT,* 12 (1962), 260-277, esp. 270f.; A. Oepke, "ἔκστασις, ἐξίστημι," *TDNT,* II, 449-460, esp. 449f., 459f.; G. von Rad, *Der heilige Krieg im alten Israel* (Göttingen, ³1958), 12; F. Stolz, "המם *hmm* verwirren," *THAT,* I, 502-4; H. W. Wolff, *Hosea. Herm* (Eng. trans. 1974), 104; W. Zimmerli, *Ezekiel 2. Herm* (Eng. trans. 1983) on 26:16; 38:21.

1 See esp. Driver.

2 *KAI,* 145.5.

3 *WUS,* no. 1079.

4 *AHw,* I, 322.

5 Lohfink.

6 See II.1 below.

OT. We shall take the position that *ḥrd* and its derivatives in the OT have a single basic meaning.

2. *Meaning and Occurrences*. The meaning of *ḥrd* is frequently given as "tremble, be frightened," but the pregnant sense does not appear to be fully realized unless the element of panic is included. As a rule, *ḥrd* is used to describe crippling terror, a state of horror like that which often follows in the wake of bad news, an unpleasant surprise, or a theophany. Here the meaning of the root comes very close to that of → המם *hmm*, albeit without sharing the latter's primarily religious usage. That *ḥrd* often stands in contrast to → בטח *bāṭaḥ* [*bāṭach*] and other terms expressing a state of calm security is additional evidence that *ḥrd* is meant to suggest extreme insecurity.

There can, however, be different degrees of intensity. When panic and terror are at their height, one can speak of *ḥᵃrāḏâ gᵉḏōlâ* (Dnl. 10:7) or even *gᵉḏōlâ ʿaḏ-mᵉʾōḏ* (Gen. 27:33). It is possible that 1 S. 14:15 also belongs in this context: after we are told how a panic (*ḥᵃrāḏâ*) arose among the Philistines, which gripped the individual formations of their army (*ḥārᵉḏû*), we are finally told it became a "god-panic" (*ḥerdaṯ ʾᵉlōhîm*). It is reasonable to take this as a summary expression of an extreme (something like "colossal panic").[7] This is the more likely in that 1 S. 14:20 describes the situation as *mᵉhûmâ gᵉḏōlâ mᵉʾōḏ*. In any case, 1 S. 14:15 is meant to express the utmost intensity of panic. The pl. *ḥᵃrāḏôṯ* (Ezk. 26:16) could also be taken as a superlative. Intensity can be expressed verbally by *wayyeḥᵉraḏ mᵉʾōḏ* (1 S. 28:5) and probably also by *ḥārᵉḏû lirgāʿîm* (Ezk. 26:16; 32:10).[8]

There are 54 occurrences of *ḥrd* and its derivatives in the MT. The verb appears 23 times in the qal and 16 in the hiphil (of which Zec. 2:4 [Eng. 1:21] should be eliminated as a textual corruption, with *haḥᵃrîḏû* being conjectured in Hos. 5:8 on the basis of the LXX). Twelve occurrences are accounted for by the formula *ʾên maḥᵃrîḏ*.[9] The noun *ḥārēḏ* appears 6 times, and *ḥᵃrāḏâ* 9 times (plus the conjecture in Ezk. 38:21 on the basis of the LXX). It is noteworthy that the root never appears in the Psalms, but occurs quite frequently in 1 Samuel, Isaiah, and Ezekiel, with 8 occurrences each.

The LXX translates *ḥrd* and its derivatives primarily with *exístēmi* or *ékstasis* (24 times), together with derivatives of *phobéō* (14 times, of which 6 are *ekphóbōn* for *maḥᵃrîḏ*). In other cases the translation depends on the context. These observations confirm our conclusion that the semantic focus is on panic terror. Since this holds true generally for *ḥrd* and its derivatives, further discussion can apply universally.

II. Secular Usage: Panic.

1. *Bad News*. The use of *ḥrd* is illustrated especially well in Gen. 27:33. When Isaac realizes that he has been tricked into giving to another the blessing meant for

---

[7] D. W. Thomas, "A Consideration of Some Unusual Ways of Expressing the Superlative in Hebrew," *VT*, 3 (1953), 209-224; Becker, 71f.

[8] See Zimmerli on 26:16.

[9] See IV below.

Esau, he is completely beside himself (*wayyeḥeraḏ ḥarāḏâ geḏōlâ 'aḏ-me'ōḏ*) with terror and horror at what has happened. A somewhat less violent reaction of terror is exhibited by Boaz when he feels something at his feet in the middle of the night (Ruth 3:8). Total panic, however, breaks out at Adonijah's sacrificial feast when the news arrives that Solomon has been anointed king (1 K. 1:49): everyone rushes out, and Adonijah himself seeks asylum. The discovery that there is money in the sack of grain terrifies all Joseph's brothers (Gen. 42:28). In these cases *ḥrd* depicts the initial terrified reaction to bad news; in the last two cases, the state following the initial reaction is described by the verb → ירא *yārē'*, "be afraid" (1 K. 1:50; Gen. 42:35).

Panic terror can also anticipate the event: the priest Eli keeps watching the road because "his heart trembles" (*kî-hāyâ libbô ḥārēḏ*) for the fate of the ark, and when he receives the dreaded news he falls dead from his seat (1 S. 4:13,18). We are probably dealing with a similar situation when, at the unexpected arrival of Samuel or David, the elders of Bethlehem and the priest Ahimelech "approach trembling":[10] *ḥrd liqra'ṯ* means "approach someone trembling, in expectation of bad news" (1 S. 16:4; 21:2).

The 3 occurrences in Ezk. 26:16,18 also involve reactions to news of a disaster, the fall of Tyre, on the part of the princes of the sea and among the "isles," that is, those who dwell there. Since this is mentioned in the context of a funeral lament with mourning rites, there is justification for Lohfink's attempt to find in *lbš ḥarāḏôṯ* an otherwise unattested expression for the donning of mourning garments.[11] But metaphorical usage of *lbš* is so common—cf. the very similar Ezk. 7:27, *yilbaš šemāmâ*—that it should also be assumed here.[12]

In all these cases we are dealing with reactions that are possible under special circumstances. They are not necessary, however. Job receives the worst series of messages bearing bad news, but nothing is said of any panic on his part (cf. Job 1:13-22). Why? In Prov. 29:25 we find the maxim: *ḥerdaṯ 'āḏām yittēn môqēš ûḇôṭēaḥ beYHWH yeśuggāḇ*, "The fear of man lays a snare, but he who trusts in Yahweh is safe."

2. *War.* The root *ḥrd* finds special use in the context of war and battle, simply because unpleasant surprises and bad news are especially common here. The very alarm sounded by the → שׁופר *šôpār* creates panic (Am. 3:6; Hos. 5:8 conj.); the same is true of the sudden appearance of the enemy, especially in superior strength (1 S. 13:7; 28:5; Isa. 10:29).

Because such panic is all too common and prevents decisive action, anyone who is *ḥārēḏ*, i.e., "fearful, prone to panic," must not enter into battle (Jgs. 7:3; the choice of words may be a deliberate echo of the place named in v. 1: *'ên ḥarōḏ*). A person who is exhausted and discouraged is more vulnerable to panic. This is the basis of Ahithophel's plan in 2 S. 17:2: he plans to take David by surprise and slay him in the ensuing panic, when everyone flees.

---

10 *KBL*³.

11 See I.1 above.

12 Zimmerli, van Dijk. On use as a superlative, see I.2 above.

It is striking how rarely we find *ḥrd* in accounts of battles when the subject is panic among the enemy; here the root most often used is → המם *hmm* (but cf. also *ṣir'â*). Only in Jgs. 8:12 and 1 S. 14:15 (3 times!) do we find it so used, in each case with reference to the enemy camp, whose panic is contrasted with the confidence previously exhibited by the foes (*beṭaḥ,* Jgs. 8:11).

III. Religious Usage: Panic Associated with Theophanies. The boundary between nontheological and theological usage is fluid, for undoubtedly Yahweh is assumed to be the instigator of *ḥ^arāḏâ,* especially in battle. It is true, however, that Yahweh never appears as the subject of the verb, and only in 1 S. 14:15 is panic termed *ḥerdaṯ 'elōhîm,* "god panic"—if we are not dealing here simply with an expression of intensity.[13] This observation— at least with respect to *ḥrd*— casts some doubt on the question of whether divine terror is as well-defined a phenomenon as is often assumed.[14] In any case, *ḥrd* designates a reaction of terror in the face of a surprising event that can have a variety of causes, including an act of God.

One realm in which *ḥ^arāḏâ* is associated expressly with Yahweh's intervention is the prophetic proclamation of judgment in the context of the *yôm YHWH,* especially in the late period. In Isa. 19:16; Ezk. 30:9; 32:10, the particular reference is to judgment upon Egypt. This may occasion panic among the Egyptians themselves (Isa. 19:16), or the news of Egypt's fall may bring terror upon its allies (Ezk. 30:9; 32:10). The same is true of the princes of the sea and the "isles" at the fall of Tyre (Ezk. 26:16,18). The late interpolation Isa. 41:5, with its description of panic at the "ends of the earth," envisions similar reports. In Ezk. 38:21 conj., the panic is caused by the terrifying judgment upon Gog and his army, depicted in terms of a theophany.

It is noteworthy how rarely *ḥrd* appears in the discourses in which the prophets proclaim judgment upon their own nation. It is found only in Isa. 32:11 and Jer. 30:5, in each case preceding a turning point at which salvation is announced (Isa. 32:15ff.; Jer. 30:7ff.). The insecurity of *ḥ^arāḏâ* appears as a transition stage between a previous sense of careless security and a later stage of peace. Jer. 30:5f. depicts the panic in vivid terms: cries of terror are heard (*qôl ḥ^arāḏâ*), men appear clasping their loins like women in labor, and faces are pale.

These occurrences keep within the realm of war and battle. Other occurrences, also of early date, are found in the context of theophanies in the narrower sense. For example, the people at the foot of the mountain of God are seized with terror when thunder, lightning, cloud, and a loud trumpet blast come forth from Sinai (Ex. 19:16) or when Yahweh descends in fire upon Sinai (Ex. 19:18, where *hā'ām* should be read for *hāhār; ḥrd* takes as its subject only persons [and occasionally animals]; where we find geographical terms, as in Isa. 41:5; Ezk. 26:16; 30:9, the inhabitants are meant).

In Hos. 11:10f., too, it is the lion's roar (שׁאג *šā'ag*) of Yahweh that terrifies those in exile— with the purpose of giving them once more a secure dwelling place. In Job 37:1, too, *ḥrd* depicts the reaction to God's appearance with storm and thunder. In

[13] See I.2 above.

[14] Von Rad; more cautiously Becker, 66-74.

Dnl. 10:7, the theophany causes Daniel's companions to be gripped by panic terror (*ḥ*^*a*^*rāḏâ g*^*e*^*ḏōlâ nap*^*e*^*lâ '*^*a*^*lêhem*) and run and hide, while Daniel himself— pale with fright and incapable of moving— receives the revelation.

Here, too, belongs the usage found in Ezra and Trito-Isaiah in which *ḥ*^*a*^*rēḏîm 'al-d*^*e*^*ḇar* (or *b*^*e*^*miṣwaṯ*) of God refers to a particular group of people. Here *ḥrd* is used in a weakened sense to describe the inward distress of those who are terrified at the possible consequences of transgressing God's commandments, the very heart of the postexilic community. Ezr. 9:4 and 10:3 deal with the prohibition of mixed marriages; the *ḥ*^*a*^*rēḏîm* constitute the small circle of those who support Ezra and his measures. Isa. 66:2,5 speak similarly of those who fear the consequences of idolatry.

The much-debated passage 2 K. 4:13 is also in the final analysis to be understood from the viewpoint of reaction to a theophany. If the mere appearance of Samuel occasions panic among the elders of Bethlehem (1 S. 16:4), the extraordinary diligence of the Shunammite woman toward Elisha and Gehazi is grounded primarily in her recognition: *'îš '*^*e*^*lōhîm qāḏôš* (2 K. 4:9). In order to do justice to the holiness of the name of God, she engages in activity that can be called *ḥ*^*a*^*rāḏâ* because it recalls the confusion caused by panic.

The appearance of God (or of his messenger) can certainly occasion *ḥrd;* but it is always a human reaction, not the immediate action of God.

IV. 'ên maḥ^**a**^**rîḏ: Eschatological Peace or Total Security.** The hiphil participle found a peculiar use, attested only in the formula *w*^*e*^*'ên maḥ*^*a*^*rîḏ*. The usage is best illustrated in the two passages from the blessing and curse chapters of the Holiness Code and Deuteronomy. In Lev. 26:6, it stands in the context of a blessing, in parallel with *šālôm* and *bṭḥ,* as a description of the state of peace characterized by the absence of danger from wild beasts and the sword, when one may sleep at ease "and none shall make you afraid." In Dt. 28:26, on the contrary, the formula serves to illustrate the effects of the curse: the corpses shall be food for the birds and the beasts, with "no one to frighten them away."

In usage similar to Lev. 26:6, the formula appears also in Jer. 30:10 (= 46:27); Ezk. 34:28; 39:26; Mic. 4:4; Nah. 2:12(11); Zeph. 3:13, always with reference to the nation. In Job 11:19, a late addition, it refers to the fate of the individual. What is described is always the coming state of peace, of security from war and wild beasts, of safe dwelling in the land, of *šālôm* and *beṭaḥ*. Usage similar to Dt. 28:26 (Jer. 7:33 is a direct quotation) appears also in Isa. 17:2 (with reference to Damascus) and in Nah. 2:12(11) (Assyria). Here the beasts have taken the place of the people: they live in careless security, in terrible contrast to the insecurity of the populace.

Baumann

חָרָה *ḥārâ;* חָרוֹן *ḥārôn;* חֳרִי *ḥ°rî*

Contents: I. 1. Etymology; 2. Distribution; 3. Meaning; 4. LXX; 5. Qumran. II. Concrete Usage in the OT. III. Usage in Theological Contexts: 1. Divine Anger; 2. Human Anger; 3. Humans Angry before God.

I. 1. *Etymology.* The verbs *ḥārâ* and *ḥrr* have the basic meaning "burn." Both most probably derive from a biliteral *ḥr* in Old Hebrew. Ugar. *ḥrr* means "burn," "scorch," or "roast."[1] Akk. *erēru* and Arab. *ḥarra* also mean "burn" (although Rabin[2] takes *waḥara* to be the real Arabic cognate). The Aram. *ḥrr* of the Targumim (Ps. 2:12; 102:4 [Eng. v. 3]; Ezk. 15:4f.) has the meaning "burn" or "be blackened, charred." At Boghazköy, *re-e-ú* is attested as a Canaanite loanword = **ḥrē,* "angry."[3]

Freedman, Lundbom

2. *Distribution.* The verbal root *ḥrh* appears 93 times in the OT;[4] 82 of these occurrences are in the qal, 3 in the niphal, 2 each in the hiphil and tiphal, and 4 in the hithpael. The word is used primarily in narrative texts (33 times in the Pentateuch, 26 in the Deuteronomistic history, 4 times each in Chronicles and Nehemiah). It is surprisingly rare in the Psalms (6 occurrences) and Wisdom Literature (6 occurrences in Job, 1 each in Proverbs and Song of Solomon). It vanishes almost completely in the language of the prophets (3 occurrences in Isaiah, 2 in Jeremiah, 1 each in Hosea, Habakkuk, and Zechariah, but 4[!] in Jonah).

Botterweck

3. *Meaning.* The verb *ḥārâ* occurs mainly in the qal with *'ap̱* as the expressed or implied subject: *ḥārâ 'ap̱,* "(someone's) nose/anger burned hot." Apparently *ḥārâ* is more intense than → קצף *qṣp*, although *qāṣap̱* substitutes for *ḥārâ* in P and the Holiness Code.[5] Anger directed towards another person is expressed by *ḥārâ 'ap̱ b*[e] (except in Nu. 24:10, where *'el* is used instead). Without *'ap̱, ḥārâ* + *l*[e] means simply "(he) was angry": *wayyiḥar l*[e]*ya'*[a]*qōḇ,* "and Jacob was angry" (Gen. 31:36). The niphal appears with *b*[e] in Cant. 1:6; Isa. 41:11 and 45:24 and means "be angry (with)." The piel does not appear in Biblical Hebrew, although it may have existed later. The form *ḥryty* in 11QPs[a] Sir. 51:19 (*ḥryty npšy,* "I kindled my desire")[6] is either piel[7] or qal.

Two hiphil readings are problematic. In Neh. 3:20, *heḥ*[e]*râ* is left untranslated by

---

ḥārâ. G. Sauer, "חרה, *ḥrh* entbrennen," *THAT,* I, 633-35; W. H. Simpson, *Divine Wrath in the Eighth Century Prophets* (diss., Boston, 1968).

1 *KTU,* 1.5 II, 5; 1:23, 41, 44, 48; cf. 1:12 II, 38, 41; *UT,* no. 902.

2 C. Rabin, "Etymological Miscellanea," *Studies in the Bible. Scripta Hierosolymitana,* 8 (1961), 390f.

3 *AHw,* II, 976.

4 Cf. E. Johnson, "אנף *'ānap* ['*ānaph*]," *TDOT,* I, 355: 93 times.

5 *BDB,* 354.

6 J. A. Sanders, *The Psalms Scroll of Qumrân Cave 11 (11QPs*[a]*). DJD,* 4 (1965), 80, 82.

7 *KBL*[3], 337, under hiphil.

most modern versions, but it could mean "burned with zeal,"[8] which would reflect a meaning similar to the tiphel forms (Jer. 12:5; 22:15; see below). Job 19:11 contains a hiphil *wayyaḥar,* but this should probably be repointed as a qal.[9] Causative meaning in the sense of "provoke to anger" is expressed by the hiphil of→ כעס *kā'as* (frequent in Deuteronomy, Jeremiah, and the Deuteronomistic history). The hithpael of *ḥrh* has intensive meaning: "fly into a passion" (Ps. 37:1,7f.[4QpPs 37:8 has *tiḥar*[10]]; Prov. 24:19). Jeremiah contains two rare t-formations: *t^eṯaḥ^areh* (Jer. 12:5) and *m^eṯaḥ^areh* (22:15), which are most likely piel forms derived from a quadriliteral root *tḥrh.*[11] But the meaning in both cases is clear: "be in a heat (of a race)" or "compete." Jastrow[12] lists a *taḥ^arûṯ* in Talmudic Hebrew meaning "heat, rivalry, contention." A cognate noun *ḥārôn* means "anger" or "burning anger."[13]

Freedman, Lundbom

4. *LXX.* The LXX uses some 20 terms to represent *ḥārâ*. The reason is not clear; perhaps the root was felt to have too great an anthropopathic coloration. The most frequent terms are *thymoún* (30 times), *orgízein* (27 times), *lypeín* (5 times), *paroxýnein, ponerón phaínesthai,* and *parazēloún* (each 3 times).

5. *Qumran.* In the Dead Sea scrolls, *ḥārâ* appears 13 times; 9 occurrences are in the Damascus document (CD), with the rest distributed through the pesher literature. The noun *ḥārôn* has a similar distribution. The absence of these words in the major Qumran documents (in contrast to the frequent *'ap*) is striking. The use of the word in the Damascus document may be connected with this document's late origin, when the increasingly bitter opposition to the community evoked a harsher tone in its literature. The reference is almost always to the anger of God, which is kindled against the horde of plotters, sinners, and transgressors of the Torah (CD 1:21; 2:21; 19:26; etc.).

Botterweck

II. Concrete Usage in the OT. In the OT, anger is frequently expressed when someone has heard something—either firsthand or through a report—that makes him very displeased. It can also erupt quickly in conversation. It is a spontaneous response to a threat of some sort directed at the individual or a group to which the individual belongs. But threats to one's sense of justice, truth, or right behavior can also evoke anger. Jacob becomes angry with Rachel because she has blamed him for her barren-

---

8 *BDB*, 354.

9 See for example G. Fohrer, *Das Buch Hiob. KAT,* XVI (1963), 308.

10 H. Stegemann, "Der Pešer Psalm 37 aus Höhle 4 von Qumran (4 Qp Ps 37)," *RevQ,* 4 (1963), 247.

11 For a different view, see J. Blau, "Über die t-Form des Hif'il im Bibelhebräisch," *VT,* 7 (1957), 385-88, esp. 387f.; according to Blau, we are dealing here with a t-causative, a hitafel formed from a triliteral root.

12 M. Jastrow, *Dictionary of the Targumim* (1903; repr. Brooklyn, 1975), II, 1662.

13 → אנף *'ānap* [*'ānaph*].

ness (Gen. 30:2). An accusation by Ish-bosheth against Abner makes Abner angry (2 S. 3:8). Balak's anger is kindled against Balaam for disregarding explicit instructions and invoking a blessing on Israel rather than a curse (Nu. 24:10).

Anger is also expressed when someone has been insulted or degraded. Potiphar becomes angry after hearing a report that Joseph has insulted (*ṣḥq*) his wife (Gen. 39:17-19; cf. v. 14, where she claims an insult to the entire household: "See, he has brought among us a Hebrew to insult us"). Balaam became angry at his ass when the ass refused to move (Nu. 22:27). Saul, too, was angry when the women sang that David's exploits surpassed his own (1 S. 18:8). The Israelite troops were angry with Judah when Amaziah refused to let them join in the fight against the Edomites (2 Ch. 25:10).

In some instances, anger is expressed together with jealousy or in the heat of competition. Saul's jealousy of David led to anger towards David and Jonathan (1 S. 20:7,30). Jealousy also was behind Israel's anger at Judah when Judah took the lead in escorting King David back to Jerusalem (2 S. 19:43[42]). Sanballat and his comrades were angry when they heard that Nehemiah was rebuilding the walls of Jerusalem (Neh. 3:33[4:1]; 4:1[7]). Perhaps, too, it was sibling rivalry (*b^e^nê 'immî niḥ^a^rû-ḇî*) that made the "sons of my mother" force the bride to be a keeper of vineyards (Cant. 1:6).

News of treachery or suspicion of deceit could also arouse anger. Jacob became angry at Laban for his persistent searching for the household gods, not knowing that the real deceit lay with Rachel (Gen. 31:36; cf. v. 32). Zebul the Shechemite became angry when he heard of the plot against Abimelech (Jgs. 9:30). Eliab's anger towards David (1 S. 17:28) was prompted by his suspicion that David had ulterior motives in coming to the battle front. Elihu was angry at Job because Job justified himself instead of God; he also was angry at Job's three friends because despite their condemnation of Job they were unable to refute him (Job 32:2f.).[14] The anger of David in 2 S. 12:5 is over an injustice, although David is no doubt surprised to find out that the greedy man in Nathan's parable is none other than himself. Nehemiah is likewise angry over the injustice of the nobles in Israel forcing fellow Jews into slavery by exacting high interest (Neh. 5:6).

In the elevated speech of the patriarchs we find polite circumlocutions intended to avert another's anger. A request is prefaced with the polite formula *'al-yiḥar b^e^'ênê '^a^ḏōnî*, "let not (anger) burn in the eyes of my lord" (Gen. 31:35), or *w^e^'al-yiḥar 'app^e^ḵā b^e^'aḇdeḵā*, "let not your anger burn against your servant" (Gen. 44:18). A vestige of this remains in Ex. 32:22, where Aaron says to Moses: *'al-yiḥar 'aḇ '^a^ḏōnî*, "let not the anger of my lord burn hot."[15] When Joseph has revealed himself, he says to his brothers: *w^e^'al-yiḥar b^e^'ênêḵem*, "and do not be angry in your own eyes," i.e., at yourselves (Gen. 45:5); but in this instance we find words of genuine consolation.

III. Usage in Theological Contexts.

1. *Divine Anger.* The verb *ḥārâ* occurs most commonly in the OT with Yahweh as subject (cf. *ḥārôn*, which is used only in reference to God). Yahweh becomes angry

---

[14] For a different interpretation, see Fohrer, *KAT,* XVI, 446; cf. III.1.

[15] → חנן *ḥānan* II.2.b: *māṣā'ṯî ḥēn b^e^'êneyḵā*.

primarily because people's behavior displeases him; when his anger is kindled, it is always directed at people, whether individuals, the people of Israel, or, less commonly, the foreign nations. In Dt. 29:26(27) the phrase "against that land" means in the rhetorical language of Deuteronomy "against the people of that land." Abraham and Gideon seek to avert Yahweh's anger: *'al-nā' yiḥar la'ḏōnāy* (Gen. 18:30,32); *'al-yiḥar 'appeḵā ḇî* (Jgs. 6:39). This is more than mere politeness; both are making humble but extraordinary requests of God.

Yahweh is not recorded as becoming angry in Genesis, despite his many judgments in the primeval history. In the wilderness, however, a different situation obtains. Here we often are told of Yahweh's anger, despite the idyllic picture the later prophets paint of the wilderness period (Jer. 2:2f.; Hos. 2:16f.[14f.]). Yahweh is angry at Moses because he resists being Yahweh's mouthpiece (Ex. 4:14); this may also explain why Abraham and Gideon are cautious in presenting their arguments.

Many of the things that make humans angry make Yahweh angry also. Jealousy heads the list. Yahweh's anger with his people in the wilderness stems from their apostasy: they build a golden calf (Ex. 32:10f.; cf. v. 19; Hos. 8:5; see below). In response, Yahweh threatens to consume the people with anger. This anger is represented here as a consuming fire. He will instead make a great nation of Moses. Moses wisely rejects this idea and his intercession prevents disaster.

The consuming power of Yahweh's anger is also shown in the Covenant Code where justice is at issue. The people are told they will be judged proportionately if they wrong strangers or harm widows and orphans (Ex. 22:23[24]). The complaints of the people in the wilderness can also be answered by God's anger. The people complain in Yahweh's hearing that they lack food (Nu. 11:1,10,33). Here anger takes the form of a fire that consumes parts of the camp (v. 1) and a plague that takes the lives of numerous people (v. 33). Yahweh's anger also burns against Aaron and Miriam when they challenge Moses' right to be the sole spokesman for God (Nu. 12:9; cf. Ex. 4). Yahweh also becomes angry at Balaam for going to meet Balak (Nu. 22:22), but in light of v. 20 the reason for his anger is not at all clear. At Shittim, Israel bowed down before Ba'al of Peor, and Yahweh responds in anger with a plague that kills some twenty-four thousand (Nu. 25:3,9).

Yahweh also becomes angry when his commands are not carried out. The timidity of some in pursuing Yahweh's holy war evokes Yahweh's anger (Nu. 32:10,13; cf. Nu. 14). The punishment on this occasion is the extension of the period of wandering to forty years, so that the wicked generation would perish entirely before entering the promised land. In Deuteronomy, Yahweh becomes angry when Israel goes after other gods (*'elōhîm 'aḥērîm*, Dt. 6:14f.; 7:4; 11:16f.; 29:26f.; *'elōhê nēḵar-hā'āreṣ*, Dt. 31:16f.). Anger here results in famine (11:17) and ultimately death.

The Deuteronomistic history reflects earlier sources. Yahweh becomes angry with Israel when the Israelites seek other gods or in any way transgress the covenant (*'āḇar 'eṯ-berîṯ*, Josh. 7:1,11; 23:16; Jgs. 2:13f.,20; cf. 3:7f.; 10:6f.). This leads inevitably to defeat in battle (cf. the defeat at Ai due to Achan's sin; Josh. 7) or total subjection to the surrounding enemy (Jgs. 2:14; 3:8; 10:7). Failure to drive out all the Canaanites from the land is likewise traced to Israel's transgression of the covenant (Jgs. 2:20-23); Yahweh's lack of support is regarded as being another manifestation of Yahweh's anger.

During the monarchy, idolatry continues to be the most detestable offense against Yahweh. Now, however, the kings receive the blame (2 K. 13:3; 23:26; 2 Ch. 25:15). Even the great reform of Josiah could not prevent the anger of Yahweh from destroying the nation (2 K. 23:26).

A similar perspective appears in the historical summary of Ps. 106 (v. 40). Uzzah apparently violates a command of Yahweh not to touch the ark and in so doing is the victim of Yahweh's anger (2 S. 6:7 par. 1 Ch. 13:10), which in turn arouses the anger of David (2 S. 6:8 par. 1 Ch. 13:11). Yahweh also becomes angry when David takes a census (2 S. 24:1) and sends a plague. The background is unclear: 2 S. 24:1 states that Yahweh himself incited David against Israel, whereas 1 Ch. 21:1 says that David was incited by Satan.

The prophets use *ḥārâ* sparingly, despite their message of judgment. But their usage is consistent with that of the rest of the OT. Isaiah says that Yahweh's anger will burn against Israel for rejecting *tôrâ* (Isa. 5:24f.); the entire created order will suffer the consequences. Hosea sharply reminds Israel of Yahweh's anger over the bull cult sponsored by the government in Samaria: *zānaḥ 'eglēḵ šōm^{e}rôn ḥārâ 'appî bām* (Hos. 8:5;[16] cf. also Ex. 32:10f.). Zechariah declares Yahweh's anger at unworthy kings and their officials (Zec. 10:3).

Only twice in the OT is *ḥārâ* used to refer to Yahweh's anger towards other nations. Here his jealousy manifests itself *in behalf of* Israel. Habakkuk asks rhetorically if Yahweh's anger was against the rivers and the sea when he trampled the nations (Hab. 3:8). This mythological language probably echoes Yahweh's primordial struggle against the sea monster. In the royal psalm attributed to David (Ps. 18 = 2 S. 22), the poet recounts the cosmic manifestations of Yahweh's anger against the enemy (v. 8[7]). Finally, Job thinks Yahweh's anger is directed at him because of his lamentable plight (Job 19:11), while the epilogue speaks of anger towards Job's three friends for speaking falsely concerning Yahweh (Job 42:7; cf. II).

2. *Human Anger.* In the early period, the *rûaḥ* of God could descend upon an individual, making him angry. Samson, whose pride was injured when the answer to his riddle was discovered, went down to Ashkelon under the power of the spirit and killed thirty men, taking their garments to gather payment for his opponents (Jgs. 14:19). Saul, too, becomes angry under the influence of the *rûaḥ,* and responds to an injustice about to be done to the men of Jabesh-gilead (1 S. 11:6). As in the case of Samson, Saul's anger leads to war.

People could also reflect divine anger when the Torah was broken. Moses' anger burns hot at the sight of the golden calf (Ex. 32:19). Twice the rape of one of Israel's daughters occasioned bitter anger. David became very angry (*wayyiḥar lô m^{e}'ōḏ*) when he heard of Amnon's rape of Tamar (2 S. 13:21). Shechem's rape of Dinah (Gen. 34:7) is recalled as a similar event (cf. Gen. 38); here and elsewhere the Yahwist finds in the patriarchal history certain prototypes illuminating the history of David. But on the earlier occasion it was the sons of Jacob rather than Jacob himself who

16. J. R. Lundbom, "Double-duty Subject in Hosea VIII 5," *VT,* 25 (1975), 228-230.

became very angry (*wayyiḥar lāhem me'ōḏ*). In both cases the fathers withhold judgment while the sons mete it out to the offenders (e.g., Absalom avenges Tamar). Anger regularly leads to destructive actions, and such an action is usually carried out by the one who is angry, though occasionally by another. David thus shows unusual restraint in refraining from vengeance.

Certain Wisdom texts counsel against becoming angry, even against the wicked (Ps. 37:1,7f.; Prov. 24:19). But the exclusive use of the intensive form (hithpael) indicates that the warning is against passionate anger: *'al-tiṯḥar.* Passionate anger can only lead to evil (Ps. 37:8); besides, the wicked have no future anyway (Prov. 24:19f.).

Israel occasionally incurs the anger of their enemies, but Deutero-Isaiah asserts that Yahweh will frustrate the enemies' plans, and their anger will be of no avail. On the day of salvation they will all be shamed (*yēḇōšû*, Isa. 41:11; 45:24). Ps. 124 also asserts that, had Yahweh not been on the side of Israel, their angry enemies would surely have consumed them (vv. 2f.).

3. *Humans Angry before God.* While the OT never speaks of anyone becoming overtly angry towards God, frequently someone expresses anger in God's presence or in conversation with him. Occasionally one gets the impression that God is the real object of the anger; but if this is so, it remains hidden hidden from view. On three occasions such anger is associated with sacrifices. Cain is angry because Yahweh accepts Abel's offering but rejects his own (Gen. 4:5f.). Moses angrily tells Yahweh not to accept the offering of Korah and his rebellious priests (Nu. 16:15). And when Saul violates the requirements of the ban (→ חרם *ḥāram*), Yahweh refuses his subsequent offering and rejects Saul himself from being king (cf. Achan, III.1 above). Saul's behavior arouses Samuel's anger and he cries to Yahweh all night (1 S. 15:11).

Anger before Yahweh can also involve Yahweh's judgment, inflicted, postponed, or omitted. When Uzzah is punished for touching the ark, David verges on anger toward Yahweh (2 S. 6:7f. par. 1 Ch. 13:10f.); but he holds his peace, out of respect or fear. Jonah becomes angry during his conversation with Yahweh because Yahweh withheld punishment from Nineveh (Jon. 4:1,4); but he was also angry about the plant that perished (Jon. 4:9); and according to the biblical author the latter anger should have cancelled the former, since Jonah would understand Yahweh's mercy toward Nineveh and share his attitude.

Freedman, Lundbom

חַרְטֹם *ḥarṭōm*

Contents: I. Egyptian Background. II. Hebrew and Biblical Aramaic: 1. General; 2. Dream Interpreter; 3. Magician; 4. Daniel. III. Middle Heb. *ḥarṭôm*.

ḥarṭōm. Egyptian: H. Kees, "Der sog. oberste Vorlesepriester," *ZÄS*, 87 (1962), 119-139; A. L. Oppenheim, *The Interpretation of Dreams in the Ancient Near East, With a Translation of an Assyrian Dream-Book. TAPhS*, N.S. 46/3 (1956), esp. 238b; K. Sethe, "Miszelle," *ZÄS*, 70

I. Egyptian Background. Heb. and Biblical Aram. *harṭōm* derives from Dem. *ḥr-tb(i)* < *ḥr-tp,* "reciting priest, magician," in which the second element of Egyp. *ḫry-ḥb.(t) ḥry-tp,* "chief bearer of the ritual scrolls," i.e., chief reciter or reciting priest, has become independent. The isolation of the attributive element *ḥry-tp,* "chief," and its use in place of the entire expression appears in Egyptian as early as the magical Papyrus Harris VI, 10.[1] The chief reciting priest is not only a scholarly scribe but also the leader of the rituals. In consequence of his familiarity with sacred documents he is an expert in magic and healing; in the popular mind these arts naturally stood in the foreground, as we see from the first two tales of Papyrus Westcar[2] and the figure of Ḥor in the second Demotic narrative of Setna-Ḫa-em-wese V, 3ff.[3] As early as the Old Kingdom, the title "chief reciting priest" became an additional title of other officials, including those of lower rank.[4] The word was probably also borrowed into Hebrew as a much degraded term.

In Akkadian (Neo-Assyrian), too, the Egyptian word appears in its Demotic form as a loanword. The mention of three *ḫar-ṭi-bi* with Egyptian names[5] shows that Egyptian magicians or mantics were consulted at the Assyrian court during or before the time of Ashurbanipal. The term is closely connected with A.BA.MEŠ *mu-ṣur-a-a,* "Egyptian scribes," in a list following such priestly groups as *mašmāšu,* "incantation priests," *bārû,* "seers," A.BA[. . .]MEŠ, ". . . scribes," *kalû,* "singers," and *dāgil iṣṣūri,* "augurs." A second occurrence of the term is cited by Borger[6] in a list of booty and prisoners brought back from Egypt by Esarhaddon.[7]

II. Hebrew and Biblical Aramaic.

1. *General.* Since the Demotic term was borrowed orally into Hebrew, the change from *t* to *ṭ* presents no difficulty. The change of *b/p* to *m* is due to nasalization.[8] Volten finds Dem. *ḥry-tme* for *ḥry-tb/p* in the Instructions of Onchsheshonqy V, 13.[9]

(1934), 134; W. Spiegelberg, "Die Lesung des Titels 'Vorlesepriester, Zauberer' in den demotischen Texten," in his *Demotica I. SBAW,* Phil.-hist. Kl., 1925/6, 4-6.

Hebrew: J. M. A. Janssen, "Egyptological Remarks on *The Story of Joseph in Genesis*," *JEOL,* 14 (1955/56), 65f.; T. O. Lambdin, "Egyptian Loan Words in the OT," *JAOS,* 73 (1953), 145-155, esp. 150f.; B. H. Stricker, "Trois études de phonétique et de morphologie copte," *AcOr,* 15 (1937), 6f., 20; J. Vergote, *Joseph en Égypte. OrBibLov,* 3 (1959), 66-73.

[1] Stricker. For the hierarchical position of the *ḥry-tp,* see *RÄR,* 604, 860f.; illustrations will be found in H. Haas, *Bilderatlas zur Religionsgeschichte, 2.-4. Lieferung: Ägyptische Religion,* ed. H. Bonnet (Leipzig, 1924), no. 46, 131.

[2] S. Schott, *Altägyptische Liebeslieder* (Zurich, 1950), 176-180.

[3] F. L. Griffith, *Stories of the High Priest of Memphis* (Oxford, 1900), 182ff.

[4] Kees.

[5] C. H. W. Johns, *Assyrian Deeds and Documents* (Cambridge, ^{2}1924), 851, IV, 2.

[6] R. Borger, *Die Inschriften Asarhaddons Königs von Assyrien. BAfO,* 9 (1956), §80, I, 9, where according to *idem, AfO,* 18 (1957-58), 116b and *CAD,* VI (1956), 116b ^{lú}*ḫar-ti-i(?)-bi* should probably be read following ^{lú}MAŠ.MAŠ(?).MEŠ.

[7] Both texts are discussed by Oppenheim.

[8] Vergote.

[9] A. Volten, review of S. R. K. Glanville, *Catalogue of Demotic Papyri in the British Museum. II: The Instructions of 'Onchsheshonqy* [London, 1955], *OLZ,* 52 (1957), 127.

The term is applied to Egyptian mantics and magicians in two narrative complexes, Gen. 41 and Ex. 7f. In a third complex, Dnl. 1f.; 4f., which is patterned in many ways on the prototype of Gen. 41, it stands for Babylonian mantics. The Demotic word with the article *p3* appears in Greek transliteration in the forms *Phritobaútēs*,[10] *phritōb*, and *pherit[o]b*.[11]

2. *Dream Interpreter.* The *ḥarṭummê miṣrayim* or *ḥarṭummîm* mentioned in Gen. 41:8,24 (E) try in vain to "interpret" Pharaoh's dreams (*pāṯar,* v. 8; *ngd* hiphil, v. 24). The LXX specifies their role as dream interpreters by translating *exēgētaí*, "interpreters (of prodigies)"; cf. the translation of the Vulg.: *coniectores*, "interpreters (of dreams)." The Demotic Egyptian magician became a mantic specializing in dreams because magic also served to prevent bad dreams of their fulfilment, and perhaps also because the *ḥr-tb* dealt with dream books.

3. *Magician.* Ex. 7:11,22; 8:3f. (P) use *ḥarṭummê miṣrayim* or *ḥarṭummîm* to refer to the Egyptian magicians who attempt to emulate Moses and Aaron by performing before Pharaoh the same wonders by which Moses and Aaron legitimate themselves, an attempt that finally fails (Ex. 8:14[18]). The legendary motifs surrounding the leaders of the exodus have incorporated a fragment of a tale recounting a contest of rank between professional sages. In light of the different role represented, the LXX here translates *epaoidoí*, "singers of incantations," the Vulg. (except at 7:11) *malefici*, "witches." As a synonym for *ḥarṭummê miṣrayim*, 7:11 uses (besides *ḥᵃḵāmîm*) the Akkadian loanword *mēḵaššᵉpîm* (from *kašāpu[m]*, G and D, "bewitch"); the magico-mantic terminology pervading P is international in nature. In all these passages, the field of activity of the *ḥarṭummîm* is *lāṭîm, lᵉhāṭîm*, "the secret arts."

The miracle of Ex. 4:4 (J) and the miracle at the Sea of Reeds in Ex. 14 (*P) have parallels in the wonders performed by the chief reciting priest in the first two tales of Papyrus Westcar. The magical acts performed by Ḥor in the second tale of Setna-Ḫa-em-wese amount to a contest with the magicians of Ethiopia: one conjures up fire for Pharaoh, another produces water to put it out; one creates such a darkness that no one can see his neighbor (cf. Ex. 10:23), until another makes it light again, etc.

4. *Daniel.* Interpretation of dreams and prodigies is also the subject of Dnl. 1f.; 4f., where Daniel—like the anonymous Jewish *gzr* of 4QOrNab—plays the role of a mantic sage before the Babylonian king.[12] The term *ḥarṭōm* appears in 1:20; 2:2,10,27; 4:4,6(7,9); 5:11. The powers of the *ḥarṭummîm/n* and the other occultists mentioned in the same breath are said to consist in the interpretation of the king's dreams (2:2; 4:4[7]) and, more generally, in "showing mysteries" (*rāzâ lᵉhaḥᵃwāyâ*, 2:27; cf. 4:6[9]). Dnl. 5:12 defines more precisely Daniel's powers as chief of the *ḥarṭummîm* and related

---

[10] Josephus *Contra Apion.* i.289, 295 (B. H. Stricker, *Oudheidkundige Mededelingen*, 24 (Leiden, 1943), 30-34.

[11] J. Vergote, "Vocalisation et origine du système verbal égyptien," *ChrÉg*, 31 (1956), 41.

[12] For a discussion of Canaanite background of this figure, see H.-P. Müller, "Magisch-mantische Weisheit und die Gestalt Daniels," *UF,* 1 (1969), 79-94.

practitioners. According to 5:11, the pagan king claims that such abilities derive from "the spirit of the holy gods" and "the wisdom of the gods"; cf. 4:5f.,15 (8f.,18).

It is noteworthy that the *harṭummîm/n* are mentioned along with magicians in exhaustive didactic lists of titles, despite the difference in function: most frequently we find the *'aššāpîm/'ašᵉpîn* (from Akk. [*w*]*ašipu*[*m*]), "enchanters" (1:20; 2:2,10 [sg.!],27; 4:4[7]; 5:11); we also find the magical *mᵉkaššᵉpîm*, "sorcerers" (2:2), the nonspecific *kaśdîm/kaśdā'în*, etc., "Chaldeans" (2:2,10; 4:4[7]; 5:11), and the mantic *gāzᵉrîn*, "prognosticators" (?), i.e., "seers" (2:27; 4:4[7]; 5:11). The distinctions between the terms already appear vague. The prevalence of magicians in the immediate context explains why Theodotion renders *harṭummîm/n* uniformly as *epaoidoí*, as does the LXX in 2:2,27; the Vulg., on the contrary, mostly uses *arioli*, "soothsayers," only in 5:11 translating *princeps magorum*, "chief of the magicians."

Daniel's interpretation of dreams in chap. 4 and especially in chap. 2 legitimates him as an apocalyptic visionary, the role he plays in chaps. 7–12. It is probably true in general that mantic wisdom is one of the roots of apocalypticism.[13]

III. Middle Heb. ḥarṭôm. Middle Heb. and Jewish Aram. *ḥarṭôm/ḥarṭûmā*, "beak or mouth of an animal,"[14] is a variant of *ḥôṭām/ḥûṭmā'*, "nose"[15] (cf. Biblical Heb. denominative *ḥāṭam*, "restrain oneself"); it has no etymological connection with *ḥrṭb* > *ḥarṭōm*, "magician." Both forms appear rather to be based on Akk. *ḫuṭṭimmu*, "snout," or a corresponding Semitic form; the gemination was either replaced by a sonant[16] or was lost with lengthening of the preceding vowel. In Arabic, too, we find *ḫaṭmᵘⁿ*, "nose, beak" (cf. *ḫiṭām*, "nose rein"), and *ḫurṭūm*, "(elephant's) trunk."

Müller

---

[13] Cf. H.-P. Müller, "Mantische Weisheit und apokalyptik," *Congress Volume, Uppsala 1971*. *SVT*, 22 (1972), 268-293.

[14] *WTM*, II, 109f.

[15] *Ibid.*, 39.

[16] Cf. *VG*, I, §90; R. Růžička, *Konsonantische Dissimilation in den semitischen Sprachen*. *BAss*, 6/4 (1909), 168; and the Akkadian by-form *ḫulṭimmu*.

חָרַם ḥāram; חֵרֶם ḥērem

Contents: I. Usage, Meaning, Etymology: 1. OT Occurrences; 2. LXX Translation; 3. Contexts: a. War and Extermination; b. The Sacred; c. Punishment and the First Commandment; 4. Usage: a. *ḥērem* I; b. *ḥrm* hiphil; c. *ḥrm* hophal; 5. Idioms with *ḥērem* I; 6. Meaning; 7. Etymology. II. Ancient Parallels: 1. Mesha Stela; 2. OSA *hrg;* 3. *asakku* at Mari; 4. More Distant Parallels; 5. Wars of Extermination. III. Diachronic Survey: 1. Pre-Deuteronomistic Events and Institutions; 2. Underground Prophetic Theology during the Monarchy; 3. The Deuteronomistic Theory and its Modification; 4. Postexilic Prophecy; 5. Post-exilic Priestly Law.

ḥāram. F.-M. Abel, "L'Anathème de Jéricho et la maison de Rahab," *RB,* 57 (1950), 321-330; B. J. Alfrink, "Die Achan-Erzählung (Jos. 7)," *Miscellanea Biblica et Orientalia. Festschrift A. Miller. StAns,* 27-28 (1951), 114-129; J. Behm, " ἀνατίθημι," *TDNT,* I, 353-56; C. H. W. Brekelmans, "Le ḥerem chez les prophètes du royaume du Nord et dans le Deutéronome," *Sacra Pagina I. BETL,* 12/13 (1959), 377-383; *idem, De ḥerem in het OT* (Nijmegen, 1959); *idem,* "חֵרֶם *ḥērem* Bann," *THAT,* I, 635-39; J. Chelhod, "La notion ambiguë du sacré chez les Arabes et dans l'Islam," *RHR,* 159 (1961), 67-79; F. M. Cross, *Canaanite Myth and Hebrew Epic* (Cambridge, Mass., 1973); A. Dekkers, *Der Kriegsherem und das Naturrecht* (diss., Vienna, 1964); L. Delporte, "L'anathème de Jahvé," *RScR,* 5 (1914), 297-338; G. R. Driver, "Studies in the Vocabulary of the OT, II," *JTS,* 32 (1931), 250-57, esp. 251; *idem,* "Hebrew Homonyms," *Hebräische Wortforschung. Festschrift F. Baumgartner. SVT,* 16 (1967), 50-64; A. Fernández, "El Ḥerem biblico," *Bibl,* 5 (1924), 3-25; P. Fronzaroli, "Studi sul lessico comune semitico: IV. La religione," *AANLR,* N.S. 20 (1965), 246-269; G. Furlani, "Le guerre quali giudizi di dio presso i Babilonesi e Assiri," *Miscellanea Giovanni Galbiati, III. Fontes ambrosiani,* 27 (Milan, 1951), 39-47; A. E. Glock, *Warfare in Mari and Early Israel* (diss., Michigan, 1968); N. K. Gottwald, " 'Holy War' in Deuteronomy: Analysis and Critique," *RevExp,* 61 (1964), 296-310; M. Greenberg, "Ḥerem," *EncJud,* VIII, 344-350; J. Halbe, *Das Privilegrecht Jahwes: Ex 34,10-26. FRLANT,* 114 (1975); G. F. Hasel, *The Remnant. AUM,* 5 (1972); J. G. Heintz, "Oracles prophétiques et 'guerre sainte' selon les archives royales de Mari et l'AT," *Congress Volume, Rome 1968. SVT,* 17 (1969), 112-138; *idem,* "Le 'feu dévorant,' " *Le feu dans le Proche-Orient antique* (Leiden, 1973), 63-78, esp. 68f.; K. Hofmann, "Anathema," *RAC,* I, 427-430; H. Junker, "Der alttestamentliche Bann gegen heidnische Völker als moraltheologisches und offenbarungsgeschichtliches Problem," *TrThZ,* 56 (1947), 74-95; Y. Kaufmann, *The Religion of Israel* (Eng. trans., Chicago, 1960), 247-254; H. Kruse, "Conceptus interdicti in Lev. 27,28-29," *VD,* 28 (1950), 43-50; *idem, Ethos Victoriae in Vetere Testamento* (diss., Pontifical Biblical Institute, 1951); J. Liver, "The Wars of Mesha, King of Moab," *PEQ,* 99 (1967), 14-31; A. Malamat, "The Ban in Mari and in the Bible," *Biblical Essays 1966. OuTWP* (Stellenbosch, 1966), 40-49; H. E. del Medico, "Le rite de la guerre sainte dans l'AT," *L'Ethnographie,* N.S. 45 (1947/50), 127-170; D. Merli, "Le 'guerre di sterminio' nell'antichità orientale e biblica," *BeO,* 9 (1967), 53-68; P. D. Miller, *The Divine Warrior in Early Israel. HSM,* 5 (1973); W. E. L. Müller, *Die Vorstellung vom Rest im AT,* ed. H. D. Preuss (^{2}1973); G. von Rad, *Der heilige Krieg im alten Israel* (Göttingen, ^{3}1958); G. Schmitt, *Du sollst keinen Frieden schliessen mit den Bewohnern des Landes. BWANT,* 91[5/11] (1970); H. Schulz, *Das Todesrecht im AT. BZAW,* 114 (1969); H. Schüngel-Straumann, *Tod und Leben in der Gesetzesliteratur des Pentateuch unter besonderer Berücksichtigung der Terminologie von "töten"* (diss., Bonn, 1969); F. Schwally, *Semitische Kriegsaltertümer: I. Der heilige Krieg im alten Israel* (Leipzig, 1901); S. Segert, "Die Sprache der moabitischen Königsinschriften," *ArOr,* 29 (1961), 197-267; R. Smend, "Das Gesetz und die Völker," *Probleme biblischer Theologie. Festschrift G. von Rad* (Munich, 1971), 494-509; W. von Soden, "Die Assyrer und der Krieg," *Iraq,* 25 (1963), 131-144; F. Stolz, *Jahwes und Israels Kriege. AThANT,* 60 (1972); M. Weippert, " 'Heiliger Krieg' in Israel und Assyrien," *ZAW,* 84 (1972), 460-493; A. H. van Zyl, *The Moabites. POS,* 3 (1960).

I. Usage, Meaning, Etymology.

1. *OT Occurrences*. If Jer. 25:9 is counted, *ḥrm* hiphil occurs 48 times in the OT (34 in narrative texts, 2 in legal texts, 8 in prophetic texts; 33 occurrences are in Deuteronomy through 2 Kings). The hophal is attested 3 times (twice in legal texts, once in a narrative text, but in the context of an official decree). The noun *ḥērem* I occurs 29 times (16 in narrative texts, 9 in legal texts, 5 in prophetic texts; 18 occurrences are in Deuteronomy through 2 Kings); it appears only in the singular. It is noteworthy that both the verb and the noun are concentrated in narrative texts, more specifically in Deuteronomic and Deuteronomistic passages. By contrast, *ḥērem* II, "net," appears only in poetic contexts (4 times in Ezekiel, once in Micah, 3 times in Habakkuk, once in Ecclesiastes); 4 of its 9 occurrences are in the plural.

Ex. 22:19(Eng. v. 20) exhibits textual variants. The Samaritan Pentateuch and LXX^{A} insert *'ḥrym* before *yḥrm*. The former lacks v. 19b of the MT. Most critics assume some kind of haplography in the MT and follow LXX^{A}, but this theory does not account for the Samaritan text. A better solution is to take the earliest form of the text to be *zbḥ l'lhym yḥrm* (v. 19a of the MT). The additions of the MT and Samaritan Pentateuch exhibit two different attempts to remove any misunderstanding of *l'lhym* (only alien gods are meant!). LXX^{A} is a "contamination" of both of these attempts. The common hypothesis that *yḥrm* (itself perhaps a misreading of an original *'ḥrym*) has replaced an earlier *mwt ywmt*[1] is unlikely, because the punishments become increasingly severe in the series 22:17-19(18-20). A more likely theory is that 22:17(18) (*l' tḥyh*), vocalized as qal or pual, originally read "she shall not live," if that is not in fact the meaning of the present piel (cf. Ps. 22:30[29]).

In Josh. 6:18, the LXX *enthymēthéntes* presupposes an original *tḥmdw*. The reading of the MT is preferable, since *tḥrymw* is the first element of an enumerative verbal series. The LXX assimilates the text to Dt. 7:25 and Josh. 7:21.

The absence of a word corresponding to *bḥrm* in the LXX of Josh. 7:15 does not necessarily point to an original differing from the MT, since the LXX of Joshua generally tends to abbreviate. The entire verse 8:26 is also absent in the LXX; here we have a case of homoioteleuton (*h'y*) or deliberate textual "improvement."

In Josh. 10:28-39, the LXX harmonizes the conquest of the southern Palestinian towns not only through deletions but also through insertions. The latter include *exōléthreusan autḗn* in 10:32, without which v. 35b might have seemed illogical.

The emendation of *lmḥrtm* to *lhḥrymm* in 1 S. 30:17[2] is unnecessary.[3] The same is true of 2 K. 19:17 par. Isa. 37:18, where *hḥrybw* has been emended to *hḥrymw* since Duhm.

In Isa. 11:15, the LXX, Targum, and Syriac appear to presuppose the reading *whḥryb* for MT *whḥrym*, but this is not certain. The text is difficult. The ancient versions may have been venturing an interpretation, with the LXX possibly choosing a word similar in sound to the Hebrew original. But the MT is quite comprehensible. The parallel *hnyp ydw* refers to an action annihilating an enemy; in any case the waters

---

1 Most recently Schulz, 59.

2 First proposed by J. Wellhausen.

3 See H. J. Stoebe, *Das erste Buch Samuelis. KAT,* VIII/1 (1973), *in loc.*

of Egypt and Mesopotamia are personified as enemies. The hiphil of *ḥrm* in the meaning "utterly destroy" fits the context precisely. The MT should therefore be retained. Neither is it necessary to hypothesize a homonym.[4]

At first glance, the text-critical situation in Jer. 25:9 appears similar; the LXX and Syriac suggest an original *whḥrbtym* instead of MT *whḥrmtym*. But the MT, which is generally more extensive than the Hebrew original of the LXX in Jeremiah, twice in this passage inserts *ḥrbh*—clearly with a conscious purpose—as an interpretation of *šmh:* in v. 11 (*lḥrbh*) and in v. 9 (*wlḥrbwt*), where the original *wlḥrph* attested by the LXX has been altered. The starting point for this interpretation was probably the reading *whḥrbtym* still attested in the LXX, which was secondarily misread as *whḥrmtym* in the textual tradition leading to the MT. In the context of "disgrace" such a misreading was natural; cf. Isa. 43:28. It is therefore likely that *ḥrm* hiphil in Jer. 25:9 is not original.

There is no qal of *ḥrm*. The reading *wḥrmty* in Nu. 21:2, attested in Samaritan manuscripts, is a simplified writing adapted to Samaritan pronunciation (Macuch: *wârimti*).

In Mic. 7:2, the LXX, Vulg., Targum, Syriac, Aquila, and Symmachus find a further occurrence of *ḥērem* I; but the metaphor of hunting and pursuit in v. 2b supports *ḥērem* II. Only the LXX is consistent, presupposing a totally legal text by reading *yryby* for *y'rbw* and *yṣwrw* for *yṣwdw*. But this Hebrew original for the LXX is probably secondary with respect to the MT (assimilation to v. 3). Furthermore, if *ḥrm* is here a late gloss, as is often assumed *metri causa*, there is no evidence for *ḥērem* II before the end of the seventh century.

2. *LXX Translation*. The translation of *ḥērem* I and *ḥrm* hiphil and hophal by the LXX provides a good introduction to the semantic problems of this word group. Whenever possible in the context, the LXX chose the words *anáthēma*/*anáthema* and *anathematízō*, some 35 times. These words are used exclusively to render our word group. The starting point was probably the meaning of *anáthēma*, "votive offering placed in the temple." It must remain an open question whether the earliest non-Jewish occurrence of the Greek word group in the sense of "curse" (1st or 2nd century C.E.)[5] provides evidence for a corresponding meaning of the words even before the LXX. In any case, this group did not suffice for the LXX; apart from *aphorízein* in Lev. 27:21 and *aphórisma* in Ezk. 44:29, it made use of words meaning "destroy, slay, annihilate," especially *exoletreúein* (25 times) and in the book of Isaiah *apollýein* and *apṓleia*. These words are all used frequently in the LXX, standing above all for forms of the roots *'bd, krt, šmd, šḥt,* and *yrš*. The number of times words for destruction are used in translation slightly exceeds the number of times words for consecration or separation are used (39 versus 37). The LXX thus succeeded only about half the time in using a special group of Greek words to represent the Hebrew word group.

[4] Cf. Driver, *JTS*, 32 (1931), 251.

[5] Megara curse texts: *IG*, III App., XIV 6, 17.

3. *Contexts.*

a. *War and Extermination.* The words deriving from the root *ḥrm* I appear primarily in the context of war and extermination. War is found in Nu. 21:2f., in all occurrences from Deuteronomy through 2 Kings, in 1 Ch. 4:41; 2 Ch. 20:23; 32:14; Isa. 11:15; 34:2,5; 37:11; Jer. 50:21,26; 51:3; Dnl. 11:4; Mic. 4:13; Mal. 3:24(4:6). Josh. 11:14 almost furnishes a definition of the *heḥ*e*rîm 'ōṯam* in Josh. 11:12: *'eṯ-kol-hā'āḏām hikkû l*e*pî-ḥereḇ 'aḏ-hišmiḏām 'ōṯām lō' hiš'îrû kol-n*e*šāmâ.* The context is the Deuteronomistic summary of the military conquest of the territory west of the Jordan under Joshua.

The most frequent parallel to *ḥrm* is the hiphil of *nkh.* The two words appear together 22 times. Both verbs refer to the same act, but from different perspectives. The additional phrase *l*e*pî-ḥereb* can appear both with *nkh* (11 times[6]) and with *ḥrm* (3 times: Dt. 13:16(15); Josh. 6:21; 1 S. 15:8). Besides Josh. 11:14, total annihilation as the goal of the action in question is expressed by association with the hiphil of *šmd* in Dt. 7:24; Josh. 11:20; 2 Ch. 20:23; Dnl. 11:44). Other verbs for annihilation and killing used in combination with the hiphil of *ḥrm* include: → ירשׁ *yāraš* (Dt. 7:17), → כרת *kāraṯ* (Josh. 11:21), *'āsap* ("collect" in the sense of "destroy," 1 S. 15:6), → כלה *kālâ* (1 S. 15:18), → אבד *'āḇaḏ* [*'ābhadh*] (Dt. 7:24), → שׁחת *šāḥaṯ* (2 K. 19:11f. par. Isa. 37:11f.; 2 Ch. 20:23), → מות *mûṯ* (Josh. 11:17; 1 S. 15:3), and → חרב *ḥāraḇ* II ("annihilate," or, as a denominative from *ḥereḇ,* "sword," "slay with the sword," Jer. 50:21,27).

The fact that no surivors were left is often emphasized in the context by other formulaic expressions: Dt. 2:34; 3:3; Josh. 10:28,37,39f.; 11:12,22; 2 Ch. 20:24; Jer. 50:26; cf. 1 K. 9:21. Since the action is directed against the population of conquered cities, the formulas of a war oracle often precede (*nāṯan b*e*yāḏ,* etc., Nu. 21:2f.; Dt. 2:24,30,33,36; 3:2f.; 7:2; 20:13; Josh. 6:2,16; 8:18; 10:30,32; 2 K. 19:10 par. Isa. 37:10); first the city is taken (*lkd,* Dt. 2:34f.; 3:4; Josh. 6:20; 10:1,28,35,37,39; 11:10,12; Jer. 50:24). In many cases the fate of the cattle and plundered goods (→ בזז *bāzaz*) is more precisely specified. Often the city or booty is burned (→ שׂרף *śārap,* Dt. 7:5,25; 13:17[16]; Josh. 6:24; 7:15,25; 8:28; 11:11,13; cf. *'ēš* in Jer. 50:32 with 50:21,26).

The citations show that the hiphil of *ḥrm* belongs to the fixed framework of a generally constant narrative schema found in Deuteronomistic texts. It appears regularly in wars of conquest against enemy cities. The only weapon mentioned is the sword. In poetical contexts the weapons vary: sword (Isa. 34:5-8), bow (Jer. 51:3), hand raised to strike (Isa. 11:15).

The negative is implied when anyone survives (see above), is delivered (→ נצל *nāṣal,* 2 K. 19:11 par. Isa. 37:11; 2 Ch. 32:13-15), is released (*šillaḥ miyyāḏ,* 1 K. 20:42), is shown mercy (Dt. 7:2; Josh. 11:20; 1 S. 15:3,9,15), is saved alive (Dt. 20:11; Josh. 2:13; 6:17,25; Jgs. 21:11 [LXX^B]; 1 S. 15:8), or even is allowed to make

---

[6] Cf. Schüngel-Straumann, 69-71.

a treaty (Dt. 7:2; Josh. 11:19f.; 1 K. 20:34,42) or enter into marriage (Dt. 7:3). The taking of booty can also imply the negative (Dt. 7:25; Josh. 6f.; 1 S. 15).

Assonance establishes a special relationship with the sword (*ḥereḇ,* Dt. 13:16[15]; Josh. 6:21; 1 S. 15:8; Isa. 34:5; Jer. 50:21,26) and total destruction (*lᵉma'an hašmîḏām,* Josh. 11:20). Assonance likewise sets up the contrast with mercy toward the enemy (Dt. 7:2; 1 S. 15:8f.; Jer. 51:3), desire for booty (Dt. 7:26), and the sparing of the prostitute Rahab (Josh. 6:17). The verb can provide an etiology for ruins with the name *ḥormâ* (Nu. 21:3; Jgs. 1:17).

b. *The Sacred.* Not as extensively but still quite clearly we find *ḥrm* I in the context of the sacred, in the sense of something removed from the sphere of the profane and set apart for Yahweh. This is shown by the very expressions *heḥᵉrîm lᵉYHWH* (Lev. 27:28; Mic. 4:13; cf. the Mesha inscription) and *ḥērem lᵉYHWH* (Josh. 6:17; that the expression is merely separated by *hîʾ wᵉḵol-'ᵃšer bâ* is shown by parallel constructions such as Dt. 2:33; 3:1; cf. also *'îš-ḥermî* in 1 K. 20:42 and *'am ḥermî* in Isa. 34:5).

The occurrences of *ḥrm* in Lev. 27 and Nu. 18 appear in texts dominated by the verbal phrase *hiqdîš lᵉYHWH* and the noun *qōḏeš*. Ezk. 44:29, too, deals with offerings to the sanctuary. The *ḥērem* pronounced by Joshua over Jericho implies that the gold, silver, and vessels of bronze and iron are *qōḏeš lᵉYHWH* and are therefore to be put into the treasury of the house of Yahweh (Josh. 6:19,24). Lev. 27:28 states that every *ḥērem* is to be treated as *qōḏeš-qᵒḏāšîm*. In Josh. 6f. and Mic. 4:13, the contexts of war and sacred overlap. This is true also of Nu. 21:2f., where the *ḥērem* is undertaken in consequence of an oath (*neḏer*). According to Jgs. 21:5, the *ḥērem* is the result of a *šᵉḇû'â gᵉḏôlâ,* which is tantamount to a vow.

A few texts appear to associate *ḥrm* with sacrificial terminology: Dt. 13:16f.(15f.) (*kālîl lᵉYHWH*); Isa. 34:2 (*ḥrm* par. *ṭbḥ;* cf. 34:6, *ṭāḇaḥ* par. *zāḇaḥ*); Jer. 50:27 (*laṭṭāḇaḥ*). But it is not certain whether *kālîl* in Dt. 13:17(16) was perceived as a sacrificial term. In the Isaiah and Jeremiah passages, the common element of the comparison is probably the killing and the abundance of blood and fat, not the cultic aspect.

The precise position of *ḥrm* in the context of the sacred does not become apparent until the contrasts are noted. According to 1 S. 15:15-23, the offering as *zeḇaḥ* of animals taken as booty is the alternative, rejected by Samuel in the name of Yahweh, to the killing of them as *ḥērem*. In Isa. 43:28, we find in parallel to *wᵉ'ettᵉnâ laḥērem ya'ᵃqōḇ* the statement *wa'ᵃḥallēl śārê qōḏeš*. In the story of Achan, Joshua must "sanctify" Israel (Josh. 7:13) to be free of the *ḥērem*. The "sacred" is thus a kind of countersphere to the *ḥērem*. A cultic assembly helps avert the *ḥērem*. In Dt. 7:26; 13:15f.(14f.); 20:17f., there is a relationship between *ḥrm* and *tô'ēḇâ*. The attitude toward the *ḥērem* that is expected of Israel is expressed in Dt. 7:26 by the verbs *šqṣ* and *t'b*. In general, in the Hebrew semantic field of the sacred, the positions of the three roots *qdš, ḥrm,* and *ḥll* are distributed differently than is the case with *ḥarām* and *ḥalāl* in the corresponding semantic field in Arabic.[7]

---

[7] Cf. Chelhod.

c. *Punishment and the First Commandment.* The hophal of *ḥrm* is associated with the death sentence formula *môṯ yûmāṯ* in Ex. 22:19(20) (probably as an intensifier) and in Lev. 27:29 (which may address the same situation as Ex. 22:19). The same formula leads up to the *ḥērem* upon Jabesh-gilead in Jgs. 21:5. The fundamental crime in Ex. 22:19(20) is apostasy from Yahweh. The same transgression, described in the typical phrases of the first commandment of the Decalog, justifies the *ḥērem* upon an Israelite city in Dt. 13. In Jgs. 21, however, the point is that a city failed to obey the summons for the tribes to assemble, even though the death penalty was involved. The sin of Achan is described in Josh. 7:11,15 as transgression of the *b^erîṯ YHWH; b^erîṯ* probably means the Decalog as the list of capital offenses in Israel. The prohibition of theft might be recalled (cf. → גנב *gānaḇ* [*gānabh*] in Josh. 7:11), but it is also possible that the reference is to the first commandment, in which case Achan's conduct was viewed as apostasy from Yahweh (cf. → מעל *mā'al* in Josh. 7:1; 22:20; 1 Ch. 2:7).

The Amalekites are punished by the *ḥerem* for the sins they committed against Israel (*pāqaḏtî,* 1 S. 15:2; *'eṯ-haḥaṭṭā'îm,* 15:18). The root *ḥrm* is also associated with *ḥṭ'* in Dt. 20:18 and Isa. 43:27, and with *pqd* in Jer. 50:27. In several late prophetic passages, *ḥrm* appears in the context of statements promising punishment to the guilty. Parallel terms in Isa. 34:2,5 are *ḥēmâ, mišpāṭ, nāqām,* and *šillumîm;* in Isa. 43:28, *ḥṭ'* and *pš';* and Jer. 51:3, *'āšām, 'āwōn, n^eqāmâ,* and *šlm.* In Ezr. 10:8, *ḥērem* is the substance of a threatened punishment.

Assonance links with *ḥrm* the motifs of Yahweh's anger (Dt. 7:4; 13:18[17]; Josh. 7:1) and the word "sinners" (1 S. 15:18). The carrying out of the *ḥērem* is accompanied in Josh. 7:25 (Achan) and 1 S. 15:23f. by expressions typical of the lex talionis (cf. also 1 K. 20:42).

4. *Usage.*

a. *ḥērem I.* Brekelmans[8] sees in *ḥerem* I an original noun expressing a quality, like *qōḏeš* and *ḥōl.* He finds this character preserved in Lev. 27:21; Dt. 7:26; Josh. 6:17; 1 K. 20:42; Isa. 34:5; and Mal. 3:24(4:6). But all these passages can be understood with the word taken as a concrete noun or a noun expressing an action. The real reason for Brekelmans' theory is the analogy of *ḥērem, qōḏeš,* and *ḥōl.* But must this analogy be pressed to the point of determining grammatical class? Examination of all occurrences of *ḥērem* I shows that interpretation as a concrete noun will suffice in all cases. If so, Lev. 27:21; 1 K. 20:42; and Isa. 34:5 are epexegetic genitives, and Mal. 3:24(4:6) is an abbreviated way of saying "lest I come and smite the land and make it *ḥērem.*" It is more likely, however, that *ḥērem* is an action noun in the "prophetic" passages 1 K. 20:42; Isa. 34:5; 43:28; Zec. 14:11; Mal. 3:24(4:6), and possibly also in the late priestly passage Lev. 27:21. In all other passages it is a concrete noun.

The view that we have an action noun in the *'am ḥermî* of Isa. 34:5 is supported by the preceding verbal phrase *heḥ^erîmām* in 34:2, and in Isa. 43:28 by the parallelism

[8] *De herem,* 43-47; *THAT,* I, 636.

with *giddûpîm*. The usage in 1 K. 20:42 is to be understood analogously to that in Isa. 34:5.

What does *ḥērem* I refer to when it is a concrete noun? When we are dealing with offerings made to the sanctuary, it can refer to human beings, cattle, and other property (cf. Lev. 27:28; other passages: Nu. 18:14; Ezk. 44:29). In Lev. 27:29, in the context of punishment by *ḥērem*, the noun refers to the victim. But this may be an exceptional situation; normally in this context the statement would be expressed by means of a verb. The preceding statement may have influenced the formulation.

In the context of war, only in Josh. 6:17 does *ḥērem* (in the phrase *ḥērem l^{e}YHWH*) refer to both human beings and plunder. Elsewhere in the context of war the application to human beings is always expressed verbally. The noun is reserved for things or cattle: Dt. 7:26; 13:18(17); Josh. 6:18; 7:1,11-13,15; 22:20; 1 S. 15:21; 1 Ch. 2:7). Only as a kind of marginal possibility, then, can it refer to human beings in this context. But human beings, including Israelites, can become *ḥērem* by a kind of contamination: Dt. 7:26; Josh. 6:18; 7:12f. This usage could be summarized as follows: when human beings are exterminated in war, narrative language (essentially Deuteronomistic language) avoids labeling them with the noun *ḥērem*, although this seems to have been possible originally (cf. Josh. 6:17). To the extent that it was used as a concrete noun, *ḥērem* never lost its original cultic and sacral overtones. The verb is another matter.

b. *ḥrm hiphil*. In several passages the hiphil of *ḥrm* clearly designates a special act of consecration. Consecration for the sanctuary is involved in Lev. 27:28 (persons or things); Josh. 6:18 (objects, subject to the regulations in vv. 19 and 24); Mic. 4:13 (things). Consecration for slaughter in battle may be intended in Isa. 34:2 (cf. *nāṯan l^{e}* in the parallel). Josh. 6:19 may reflect an ancient formula of consecration belonging to this context.

At the other end of the scale we find those passages in which the hiphil of *ḥrm* is a synonym for other verbs meaning "destroy, kill," without any kind of preceding consecration. Here, for example, belong 2 K. 19:11 par. (no institution analogous to the *ḥērem* being known among the Assyrians); 2 Ch. 20:23; Isa. 11:15; Jer. 50:21 (following *ḥereḇ*),26; 51:3; Dnl. 11:44 (following the hiphil of *šmd*).

The other occurrences of the hiphil of *ḥrm* stand somewhere between these two extremes. Destruction and killing are meant, but the context does not make it entirely clear whether a preceding consecration of the enemy is also thought of. The notion of a consecration is most likely also involved in the ancient and compact texts Nu. 21:1-3 and Jgs. 1:17. In the more likely schematic accounts, which speak first of the taking of a city and then use the hiphil of *nkh* to describe the killing of the inhabitants, the hiphil of *ḥrm* always appears as the last element. Does it stand in parallelism with *nkh*? Is it a summation? In any case, the emphasis is on the element of an action that is radical and total, not on the notion of killing in consequence of a previous consecration.

When the hiphil of *ḥrm* refers to an act of consecration, objects as well as human beings can be the object of the verb (cf. above). In Nu. 21:3, where the notion of a consecration to destruction appears likely, we read: *wayyaḥ^a^rēm 'eṯhem w^e^'eṯ-'ārêhem*. Not only the population but also the cities of the Canaanites of Arad are destroyed.

In the other passages only living creatures are the object of the hiphil of *ḥrm*. Animals are mentioned expressly in Dt. 13:16(15); Josh. 6:21; 1 S. 15; several times they are probably included implicitly, and sometimes they are excluded. The focus of attention is nevertheless on the enemy population, often spoken of in summary. In Dt. 2:34; 3:6; Josh. 6:21; Jgs. 21:11 it is divided into groups (one of which is probably meant by *'îr mᵉṯîm*!). The populace is also meant in passages that speak of kings (Josh. 2:10; 11:12), lands (2 K. 19:11 par. Isa. 37:11 [but cf. 2 Ch. 32:14]), or cities (Dt. 3:6; 13:16[15]; Josh. 10:1,37; 11:12,20f.; Jgs. 1:17; Jer. 50:26). The expression "the city and everything in it" or the like is often divided between the two verbs *nkh* and *ḥrm* (Josh. 8:24,26; 10:35,37, 39). In such cases we have synonymous parallelism, in which "city" means the populace of the city. This is true also in Dt. 13:16(15) and Josh. 10:37, where the whole expression is kept together. The only possible exception is Josh. 6:17, where the verb *ḥrm* does not, however, occur. It is therefore best to translate Josh. 11:21, *'im-'ārêhem heḥᵉrîmām*, as "he destroyed them (i.e., the troops of the Anakim) together with the population of their cities." The more the hiphil of *ḥrm* becomes a synonym for verbs meaning "destroy, exterminate," the more it comes to refer only to human beings. It never takes on the meaning "destroy some*thing*."

c. *ḥrm hophal*. The occurrences of the hophal of *ḥrm* have one thing in common: they are associated with the semantic field of punishment. In Ex. 22:19(20), both crime and punishment are clear; apostasy calls for capital punishment in its most extreme form. In Lev. 27:29 the crime is not mentioned; probably the case of Ex. 22:19(20) is meant. In Ezr. 10:8, the crime consists in refusal to participate in the great action of dissolving mixed marriages—a situation that Ex. 34:16 and Dt. 7:3f. associate with apostasy. The punishment designated by *ḥrm* in this passage was once clear, but is so no longer. Presumably confiscation of property was involved. In any case, the word *ḥrm* designates only a portion of the punishment. The punishment inflicted on the guilty person himself consists in being banned (→ בדל *bdl*) from the *qᵉhal haggôlâ*. In Lev. 27:29, the hophal of *ḥrm* designates the judgment that determines the punishment or a preliminary element of the punishment, preceding the execution proper. In Ex. 22:19(20), it designates the punishment in its entirety. In Ezr. 10:8, the situation remains unclear.

5. *Idioms with ḥērem I*. Some fixed nominal idioms with *ḥērem* I are immediately comprehensible: *śᵉḏēh haḥērem* (Lev. 27:21), *ḥērem bᵉyiśrā'ēl* (Nu. 18:14; Ezk. 44:29), *ḥērem lᵉYHWH* (Josh. 6:17), *'îš-ḥermî* (1 K. 20:42; the suffix refers to Yahweh), *'am ḥermî* (Isa. 34:5; likewise). The verbal idioms are rather more obscure. It seems that *hāyâ ḥērem* (Dt. 7:26; Josh. 6:17) may replace the lacking qal of the verb. Both *hāyâ lᵉḥērem* and *śîm lᵉḥērem* refer to the contaminating extension of *ḥērem* to the entire Israelite camp. Unlike declarative *ḥērem*, this "*ḥērem* by contamination" can be reversed by appropriate measures (Josh. 6:18; 7:12). The expression *nāṯan laḥērem* (Isa. 43:28) may be equivalent to the hiphil of *ḥrm* ("consecrate to destruction").

6. *Meaning*. On the basis of the preceding discussion, and taking into account additional limitations imposed by particular contexts, we can define the following meanings. The hiphil of *ḥrm* means "consecrate something or someone as a permanent and definitive offering for the sanctuary; in war, consecrate a city and its inhabitants to destruction; carry out this destruction; totally annihilate a population in war; kill." The hophal means "be condemned to capital punishment with certain additional conditions; the execution of this punishment; confiscation (of property) (?)." The noun *ḥērem* I means "the object or person consecrated in the sense of the hiphil or condemned in the sense of the hophal or contaminated by entering into their deadly sphere; the act of consecration or of extermination and killing." The usual translation, "ban," is and always has been false and misleading. It was an appropriate rendering of the medieval Jewish *ḥērem*, corresponding to secular outlawry and ecclesiastical excommunication, but is based on a later development of the word *ḥērem* that is unattested in the OT.

Our definition is essentially quite vague; much remains obscure. Did original usage of the word group derive from an actual *ḥērem* ritual involving the magical encirclement of a city (cf. Josh. 6:3ff.) or the stretching forth of a spear (cf. Josh. 8:18)? What originally instigated a *ḥērem*—a vow (cf. Nu. 21:2) or the command of a military leader (cf. Josh. 6:17)? Was the critical element the renunciation of booty or the radical extermination? Was the destruction and razing of a city considered a part of the *ḥērem* or was it a further measure (cf. Josh. 6:24; 8:28; 11:11,13[9])? What distinguished the punishment of *ḥērem* from the other forms of capital punishment? May we draw on Josh. 7:15,25 to interpret Ex. 22:19(20)?

7. *Etymology.* Etymologically, the word group is usually traced to the common Semitic root *ḥrm*. Its reflexes in the West Semitic languages include words meaning "separate," "forbid," or "consecrate." Typical are Arab. *ḥarām*, "sacred precincts," and *ḥarim*, "harem." Akk. *(ḫ)arāmu/erēmu* on the other hand means "cover." An original meaning "separate" for this root in Akkadian is attested only by *ḫarāmu* II, found in a list, and possibly by *ḫarimtu*, "prostitute."[10] Brekelmans' monograph, for example, shows no evidence of any problem with respect to this generally accepted etymology.

The coalescence of *ḥ* and *ḫ* in Hebrew, however, suggests caution. The fact is that only in Hebrew and Moabite do we find in *ḥrm* the idea of separation combined with the idea of the destruction of what has been separated. In Arab. *ḫarrama* and *taḫarrama*, "destroy (a tribe)," the notion of destruction is associated with the root *ḫrm*, as Driver has pointed out. The usual view is that the root *ḫrm* is represented in Hebrew only by *ḥārum*, "having a divided nose" (Lev. 21:18), and *ḥērem* II, "net." Driver[11] would see in the hiphil of *ḥrm* two homonyms: "consecrate, separate," from *ḥrm*, and "destroy," from *ḫrm*. But the noun *ḥērem* I combines in its earliest occurrences the meanings "consecration" and "destruction." Even Driver, for example, is forced in

---

[9] Most recently Heintz, *Le feu*, 68f.

[10] For further discussion, see Brekelmans, *De herem;* Chelhod; Fronzaroli, 249f.

[11] *SVT*, 16 (1967), 56-59.

Isa. 34:2,5 to think in terms of homonyms in the same context. It is therefore probably best to stick with a single Hebrew verb. The question of the original root may nevertheless remain open. From the perspective of historical linguistics, one thing is clear: the noun and verb combine semantic elements that elsewhere are divided between the two roots *ḥrm* and *ḫrm*.

Heintz[12] on the other hand derives *ḥērem* II, "net," from *ḥrm*, "separate," citing the motif of the "golden net," which occurs primarily in the context of Mesopotamian victory texts, entangling the enemy. Here he finds the origin of the ancient Israelite *ḥērem:* it is the ritual of destruction in the course of a victory celebration. We still await his detailed argument.[13] In the 4 OT texts where the net motif appears together with statements celebrating victory (Ezk. 17:19f. = 12:13; 32:3; Hos. 7:12), the word *ḥērem* II is used only once for "net." There is no trace of *ḥērem* I or the verb *ḥrm* in these passages. At the very least, then, the awareness of the connection postulated by Heintz is not fully developed in the OT.

It remains unclear whether there is any etymological connection between our word group and the mountain name *ḥermōn*, the place names *ḥ°rēm* and *ḥormâ*, and the personal name *ḥārim*. In the case of *ḥormâ* some connection was perceived: cf. the etiologies in Nu. 21:1-3 and Jgs. 1:17.

II. Ancient Parallels.

1. *Mesha Stela*. The hiphil of *ḥrm*, "consecrate to destruction," appears in the Moabite Mesha inscription[14] of the ninth century:

> Chemosh spoke to me: Go, take Nebo from Israel! Then (15) I went by night and fought (*w'ltḥm*) against it [Nebo] from daybreak to noon. And (16) I took it (*w'ḥzh*) and totally destroyed it (*w'hrg kl*[*h*]): 7000 citizens and aliens, male and female (17) together with female slaves; for I had consecrated it to Ashtar-Chemosh for destruction (*ky l'štr kmš hḥrmth*). Then I took (*w'qḥ*) thence the (18) vessels of Yahweh and brought them before Chemosh.

In its verbal structure the text follows a fixed schema: oracle—departure—battle—capture of the city—slaying of the populace—*ḥērem*—taking of booty.[15] This is the same schema found in many texts of Deuteronomy and Joshua where *ḥrm* appears, although the neighbor language uses different roots in two instances (*'ḥz* for *lkd, hrg* for *nkh*). This suggests that this schema in the OT should not be viewed as a pattern originating with the Deuteronomistic narrator. The slain populace is divided into categories. The suffix referring to Nebo probably means the populace. In contrast to almost all the OT accounts of the destruction of a conquered city, the verb *ḥrm* refers here not to the actual destruction of the populace but to their preceding consecration

---

12 *SVT*, 17 (1969), 136f.

13 To be published in *CahRB*.

14 *KAI*, 181.

15 Cf. Segert, 238f.

to destruction. The sentence containing *ḥrm* is an inverted summary clause[16] interrupting the series of clauses beginning with prefix forms. It has been debated whether this was the only *ḥrm* consecration in Mesha's campaign, or whether, for instance, he also exterminated the (Israelite) population of Ataroth on the basis of such a consecration.[17] The word *ḥrm* does not appear in the passage in question, but we read: "I killed all the people from (?) (12) the city as a *ryt* (delight, satisfaction, propitiatory sacrifice?) for Chemosh and for Moab." Does *kl h'm* here mean "all the warriors" or "the whole population"? In the latter case, and if *ryt* is a sacrificial term,[18] then consecration to destruction during a war of conquest was thought of in ninth-century Moab as a sacrifice to the deity.

It is also noteworthy that, with the exception of Nebo, Mesha says something about the later fate of all the cities he conquered, telling how those he destroyed were rebuilt. Was Nebo alone left in ruins? If so, was the reason the exposed position of the city on the northern boundary of the new Moabite territory? Or was there a consecration to destruction only in the case of Nebo, making it out of the question that the city be rebuilt?

Much remains obscure, but we may conclude from this unique text that there was in Israel and Moab, and perhaps also among other neighboring peoples, a common practice of *ḥērem* in war and a common tradition for telling of it.

2. *OSA hrg*. When a city is taken, OSA *hrg* can refer to the killing of the officers and soldiers along with their wives and children on the basis of a vow made before battle.[19] The statement in → הרג *hārag* [*hāragh*] that Heb. *hrg* can mean "kill enemies to carry out the ban" is probably not true.

3. *asakku at Mari*. Following up a suggestion made by Landsberger, Malamat has worked out the relationship between the Akkadian term *asakku,* "taboo," found primarily at Mari, and the OT concept of *ḥērem*. The similarities, however, are limited. Appropriation of objects under taboo can bring guilt upon the violator of the taboo (originally subjecting him to the death penalty). This recalls the story of Achan. More specifically, a military commander could place booty under taboo. But at Mari this taboo was only temporary, so that the booty could be distributed fairly later. The major element of the biblical *ḥērem,* extermination of the populace of conquered cities, is far removed from this context. Besides the *asakku* of a god, there was also an *asakku* of the king. "In Israel *ḥerem* clearly exceeded the semantic range of *asakkum* in Mari."[20]

4. *More Distant Parallels*. In order to find more precise parallels to the OT *ḥērem,* parallels still having religious overtones, we must go beyond the geographical and

---

[16] Contra van Zyl, 141.
[17] Most recently Liver, 24f.
[18] Grimme, Ryckmans, Segert, Röllig.
[19] Ja 575, 5f.
[20] Glock, 207.

chronological boundaries of the ancient Near East, and even then we shall never find a parallel that is exact in all respects.

Aeschines[21] tells of a war of the Delphic amphictyony against the Cirrheans, members of the amphictyony who had failed to live up to their obligations. At the behest of the Pythian oracle war was declared against them, the population was sold, the city was laid waste, and the land was left totally barren. This recalls Jgs. 21.

At Rome there was a *devotio* of criminals. Criminals condemned to death were consecrated to the gods of the underworld.[22] This is reminiscent of Lev. 27:29.

Among the Celts, gold that had been consecrated (*anatetheiménos*) to the gods was inviolable.[23] Caesar records:

> To Mars, when they have determined on a decisive battle, they dedicated as a rule whatever spoil they may take. After a victory they sacrifice such living things as they have taken, and all the other effects they gather into one place. In many states heaps of such objects are to be seen piled up in hallowed spots, and it has not often happened that a person, in defiance of religious scruple, has dared to conceal such spoils in his house or to remove them from their place, and the most grievous punishment, with torture, is ordained for such an offense.[24]

There is no explicit statement that prisoners were killed, but since vi.16 says that human sacrifice was very common, it is not unlikely that prisoners were included in the spoil dedicated to the god of war.

For Germanic tribes there is explicit evidence that prisoners of war were killed as an offering to the gods. Strabo reports that this was the standing practice among the Cimbri.[25] Orosius, drawing on earlier sources, describes what took place after the battle of Arausio:

> The enemy seemed driven by some strange and unusual animus. They completely destroyed everything they had captured; clothing was cut to pieces and strewn about, gold and silver were thrown into the river, the breastplates of men were hacked to pieces, the trappings of the horses were ruined, the horses themselves were drowned in whirlpools, and men, with nooses fastened around their necks, were hanged from trees. Thus the conqueror realized no booty, while the conquered obtained no mercy.[26]

Tacitus records the actions of the Hermunduri in battle with the Chatti: "Both sides consecrated, in the event of victory, the adverse host to Mars and Mercury, a vow implying the extermination of horses, people, and all objects whatsoever."[27] There is evidence of the same practice among the Goths and Franks.

Among the Arabs, the Ghassanid prince Al-Ḥarit ibn 'Amr is said to have burned his enemies to a man while invoking the gods. The same was done under the aegis of Islam by the Wahabi Ibn Saud.[28]

---

[21] *Against Ctesiphon* 107-112.

[22] Dionysius of Halicarnassus *Roman Antiquities* ii.10.

[23] Diodorus Siculus *Library of History* v. 27.

[24] *Gallic War* vi.17.

[25] *Geography* vii.2.3.

[26] *History* v.16.5.

[27] *Annals* xiii.57.

[28] On all these parallels, see Schwally, 34-42; Junker, 77f.; Hofmann, 427; Stolz, 194f.

5. *Wars of Extermination.* Since the war *ḥērem* of Israel involved the total extermination of a population, we may ask to what extent such an action may have been carried out in the ancient Near East apart from religious consecration and taboo. At least with respect to the Assyrians it has been suggested that their military goal was the total destruction of the enemy.[29] But this theory cannot be maintained.[30] Wars were fought to stabilize the established order that had been called into question by the enemy or to destroy a neighbor's desire for independence and to incorporate into the Assyrian power structure—but not to destroy it totally.

Realistically speaking, however, wars could be conducted with extreme cruelty throughout the ancient Near East; entire cities could be destroyed, together with their populace. Two letters from Mari illustrate how matter-of-factly such slaughter could be described. Išme-dagan writes to Yasmaḫ-adad: "All the soldiers of the tribe of Ya'ilanu assembled under the command of Mar-addu to wage war. We had a battle at Tu[.]wi and I won. Mar-addu and all the members of the tribe of Ya'ilanu were killed, and all his slaves and soldiers were slain."[31] On another occasion, Yasmaḫ-adad showed mercy to a conquered city. On this occason his sovereign Šamši-adad wrote to him as follows: "You wrote to me that you took the city of Tillabnim but did not [slay] the inhabitants of the place, but rather made peace with them and allowed them to go free. What you did is highly commendable; it is worth . . . talents of gold. But formerly when you captured a city, (this conduct) was not seen."[32]

The supposedly more merciful pharaohs could also wage wars of extermination when they so desired. Of Thutmose I we read: "He hath overthrown the chief of the Nubians; the Negro is helpless, defenceless in his grasp . . ., there is not a remnant among the Curly-Haired, who come to attack him; there is not a single survivor among them."[33] From the Bible, 1 K. 9:16 may be cited by way of comparison.

There were mythological prototypes for total extermination, such as the story of the Deluge. In the Erra epic iv.26-29 we read: "Into the city to which I send you, o man, you shall not fear any god nor be afraid of any man, small and great kill together! The infant, the child: let no one escape!"[34]

Furthermore, accounts of extermination campaigns carried out by one's own army and corresponding pictorial representations had a recognized function in the political realm: they served as propaganda to arouse fear in enemies, former or potential. That this propaganda technique was used by the Assyrians against Judah is shown by 2 K. 19 par. Isa. 37.

This encounter with the deliberate display of Assyrian military ideology was probably not without its influence on the development of the Deuteronomistic *ḥērem* theory.

---

[29] Müller, 13-26.

[30] Cf. Hasel, 97f.; for the general case against the usual view of the Assyrians as an especially brutal nation, see von Soden, with bibliog.

[31] G. Dossin, *Correspondance de Šamši-Addu et de ses fils (suite). ARM,* IV (1951), 33, 5-18.

[32] *Idem, Correspondance de Šamši-Addu et de ses fils. ARM,* I (1949, repr. 1978), 10, 5-11; both texts are discussed by Glock, 177f.

[33] J. H. Breasted, *Ancient Records of Egypt,* II (Chicago, 1906), 30.

[34] Cited by Hasel, 84.

It is therefore noteworthy how often in the context of such wars we find the motif of the remnant that is saved or not saved[35]—just as in the context of most of the Deuteronomistic occurrences of *ḥrm*.

It is also worth noting that wars in the ancient Near East, even when they are better not termed "holy wars,"[36] always had a religious dimension. War was an expression of God's judgment.[37] Thus both the *ḥērem* of the Amalekites, a punitive expedition ordained by God in the early period of Israel's history, and the late prophetic oracles of salvation that speak of the divine *ḥērem* follow a widespread conceptual schema.

III. Diachronic Survey.

1. *Pre-Deuteronomistic Events and Institutions*. While the Mesha inscription certainly records a military *ḥērem* on the part of the Moabites against Israel in the ninth century, the OT does not contain a single text from which we might derive trustworthy information about an Israelite *ḥērem* for any period of Israel's history. Of the pre-Deuteronomistic material, the passages that speak of the extermination of the populace of cities named Hormah (Nu. 21:2f.; Jgs. 1:17) are suspect as being secondary etiologies. In the case of Jericho (Josh. 6f.), where a pre-Deuteronomistic narrative has been interwoven with several instances of *ḥērem* that differ from the Deuteronomistic type, the archeological evidence and literary considerations cast doubt on the historical basis.

At best a certain probability attaches to the central facts of the narrative (deriving from prophetic circles) that recounts Saul's half-hearted campaign of extermination against the Amalekites. Even here, however, the narrative interest affects fundamental points and detracts from the value of the sources. Probably the gripping account in Josh. 10f. contains several early reports of *ḥērem* wars. It is probably not accidental that the word *ḥrm* is not used of all the cities. But just as the LXX has added this term in Josh. 10:32 (Lachish), so too it is likely that the earliest form of the text available to us has been subjected to systematization; it is no longer possible to say what is a truly ancient account.

All the other Deuteronomistic accounts of *ḥērem* wars may be suspected of deriving from Deuteronomistic systematization. Jgs. 21:11 probably belongs to a text formulated at a very late date (note for example in the verse itself the P terminology of *kol-'iššâ yōḏa'aṯ miškaḇ-zāḵār*) and is therefore of dubious value as evidence. The report in 1 Ch. 4:41 (extermination of the Hamites and *me'ûnîm* [?] in the region of Gedor by the Simeonites in the time of Hezekiah) could be an historically accurate special account of the Chronicler. But does the hiphil of the verb *ḥrm* still imply here the ancient element of consecration to destruction? The account of 2 Ch. 20 is legendary in character; here, too, the hiphil of *ḥrm* simply means "destroy." This completes our survey of potential historical accounts in the OT, with negative results.

It does not follow that there were never any *ḥērem* wars. The early narratives and

---

[35] *Ibid.*, 50-134.

[36] Weippert, Stolz.

[37] Furlani.

the use of the word *ḥērem* by the prophets clearly presuppose such a practice at least on occasion in the early period of Israel's history. It is likewise not impossible that other texts describe *ḥērem* wars without using the word itself: Jgs. 18:27 or 20:48 may be examples. According to Josh. 10:35 (Deuteronomistic), Lachish had been subjected to the *ḥērem,* although vv. 31f., which actually deal with Lachish, do not use the word.

It is nevertheless unlikely—in fact, impossible—that every war in the period of the occupation in the time of the Judges was a *ḥērem* war. Nor is there any special connection between *ḥērem* and defensive war—quite the contrary. The *ḥērem* as a necessary element of a "holy war" in the sense suggested by G. von Rad stands or falls with the theory itself. Neither is a tradition of a commandment of Yahweh requiring Israel to impose a *ḥērem* on certain nations demonstrable or even likely. On the contrary, when a *ḥērem* was actually imposed, it seems to have been occasioned by a vow taken in the specific case (cf. Nu. 21:2 and the tribal oath in Jgs. 21:5), a special order of the military commander (cf. Josh. 6:17), or the words of a prophet (cf. 1 S. 15:3). Normally interest in spoliation probably prevented proclamation of a *ḥērem*. The more extensive early *ḥērem* narratives have, in fact, more to do with a taboo placed upon the booty and human violation of the taboo than with extermination of the enemy population (Josh. 6f. and 1 S. 15).

But when there finally was a *ḥērem,* the result was an orgy of destruction. The mood is perhaps best preserved in Isa. 34:1-15, a poem describing Yahweh's *ḥērem* against Edom.[38] All were killed, both human beings and cattle, and the booty was destroyed. On occasion the most valuable pieces were brought to a sanctuary (cf. Josh. 6:19,24). The treatment of the booty reveals the contagious nature of the *ḥērem* taboo (cf. the Achan narrative in Josh. 7). As evidence for the possibility of a *ḥērem* campaign against Israelites, we have the law of Dt. 13:13-19(12-18) in its pre-Deuteronomic form, as well as the historically dubious campaign against Jabesh-gilead in Jgs. 21:1-14 (and the similar campaign against Gibeah in Jgs. 20, where the word *ḥrm,* however, does not appear). Even if Dt. 13:16b(15b) (with *ḥrm*) is not pre-Deuteronomic, the phenomenon itself may be suggested in 13:16a,17*(15a,16*). In this case, *ḥērem* was thought of as a punishment.

Besides the war *ḥērem,* as Ex. 22:19(20) shows, there was a punitive *ḥērem* (on the dating of the Covenant Code and the significance of Ex. 22:19[20] for its definitive structure, see Halbe's discussion). Schmitt, citing the treatment of lèse-majesté (cf. 1 S. 22:19; 2 K. 9:26), has theorized that such punishment differed from the simple death penalty in that the children and property of the criminal were also destroyed. It was based on apostasy from the worship of Yahweh.

The special *ḥērem* consecration of persons and objects to the temple (Lev. 27:21,28; Nu. 18:14; Ezk. 44:29) is attested only in late texts; we can no longer determine whether the institution goes back to the early period of Israel's history. If so, it may have been practiced only at certain sanctuaries, and possibly did not yet benefit the priestly groups mentioned in the late texts. It was probably even then the case that

[38] Cf. *KTU,* 1.3 IV for a Ugaritic parallel.

exemption was not allowed. The practice probably developed out of the *ḥērem* consecration of booty taken in battle (cf. Mic. 4:13).

2. *Underground Prophetic Theology during the Monarchy.* With the coming of the monarchy, *ḥērem* wars probably grew even less common than before. A situation had developed in which there was abundant use for the labor forces captured during a military campaign. Previously, even if there had been no law requiring the extermination of the populace dwelling in the land claimed by the Israelite tribes, there was at least the tradition of Yahweh's promise to drive out "the inhabitants of the land" (→ גרש *gāraš* [*gārash*], → ירש *yāraš*) and the commandment prohibiting the making of any (vassal) treaty with them (Ex. 23:31b,32; 34:12,15; cf. Jgs. 2:2).[39] Where the balance of power permitted, the result was not necessarily the extermination of the Canaanites, but at least their dispossession and expulsion.

The transition to a territorial state now made it appear more desirable to allow the subject population to continue to dwell in the territory to which Israel laid claim, subject to the obligation of forced labor (cf. Jgs. 1:28,30,33,35). In more distant regions independent kingdoms were allowed to exist, subject to payment of tribute. A sense of brotherhood grew up between the heads of dynasties, regardless of the momentary balance of power: sensibilities were not easily wounded. The worship of Yahweh was expressed primarily in the full-blown sacrificial cult.

These tendencies appear to have aroused protest in prophetic circles, especially in the northern kingdom. In this context, reminiscences of the ancient *ḥērem* wars played a role, as is attested by two narratives deriving from prophetic circles. The account in 1 S. 15 accounts for the rejection of Saul on the grounds of his having spared the legendary Amalekite king Agag and used the best animals taken as booty for sacrifice instead of *ḥērem*. Samuel, the prototypical seer and king-maker, pronounces the verdict. Of interest is the phrase *rē'šîṯ haḥērem* (1 S. 15:21). The narrative is probably intended as deliberate polemic against any attempt to make *ḥērem* a sacrificial term.

The passage 1 K. 20:35-43 belongs to a narrative cycle dealing with an anonymous Israelite king, perhaps intended originally as a prototype (1 K. 20 and 22).[40] In this passage the positive picture of the king becomes negative. A prophet predicts disaster for the king because he showed mercy to his enemy, the king of Damascus, who had been defeated by Yahweh, and made a treaty with him (20:34), although this king had been consecrated to Yahweh as *ḥērem* (*'îš-ḥermî*, 20:42).

An important aspect of this underground prophetic theology should be noted: in both narratives it is external enemies (desert tribes and Arameans) who are considered *ḥērem*. This corresponds to the political situation during the monarchy. This theory differs at this point from that of the Deuteronomistic *ḥērem*, which is directed against Palestinian cities; it resembles more closely the use of *ḥērem* terminology in the oracles against the nations found in the prophetic books.

3. *The Deuteronomistic Theory and its Modification.* It is no longer possible to de-

---

39 See Schmitt and Halbe for a more extended treatment.

40 Most recently J. Gray, *I & II Kings. OTL* (Eng. trans. ²1970), 414-16.

termine whether the early recensions of the Deuteronomic law mentioned the *ḥērem*. The early stages of Dt. 7 and 13 are possible instances.

The first version of the Deuteronomistic history, probably put together during the triumphal years of Josiah,[41] makes major use of the term *ḥrm*, creating the picture of a horrible sacral war of extermination against the entire population of Palestine. The modern reader finds the picture both vivid and oppressive, usually mistaking the real intentions of the Deuteronomistic history.

The Deuteronomistic historian found *ḥērem* narratives and accounts of *ḥērem* wars in his sources for the early history of Israel (still visible in Nu. 21; Josh. 6f.,10f.; 1 S. 15). In addition, he had lists of nations that had ceased to exist. Finally, he was familiar with traditions enshrining Yahweh's promise of the land as well as the promise that Yahweh (or Israel with the help of Yahweh) would drive out or destroy (*kḥd* hiphil, Ex. 23:23) the inhabitants of the promised land (still visible in Ex. 23,34; Jgs. 2; perhaps already included in an early recension of Deuteronomy in the core of Dt. 7). There is no evidence remaining of any pre-Deuteronomistic tradition of a command to drive out the populace, but such a tradition may have existed (cf. Jgs. 1). Dt. 20:17 contains a formula recalling a commandment of Yahweh to destroy all the nations in the list of nations. Since such formulas in Deuteronomy are generally trustworthy, we must at least think in terms of the promise in Ex. 34:12,15 interpreted as a commandment (cf. Ex. 23:31b,32). Possibly the Deuteronomistic historian himself already interpreted this promise as a commandment in Dt. 7:2 (using the verb *ḥrm*). In any case, the Deuteronomistic historian frames a synthesis of the occupation according to which all the nations dwelling in the promised land were exterminated at Yahweh's command. The verb *ḥrm* becomes a catchword, losing its specific meaning and becoming a general term for radical destruction (note in Josh. 10, in the context of the Deuteronomistic redaction, the possibility of describing the same situation both with and without *ḥrm*).

Yahweh's commandment, which is presupposed (Dt. 20:17; Josh. 10:40; 11:12,15,20), renders superfluous any vow taken before a particular campaign or any special edict of a prophet or military commander. The verb now refers only to the killing of persons. In the Deuteronomistic theory of the occupation, cities, houses, wells, and animals remain unmolested. The Israelites simply take possession; there is only a change of ownership. The general principle is stated in Dt. 6:10f.; Josh. 24:13; for concrete cases, see Dt. 2:34f.; 3:4-7. In the collection of laws governing war in Dt. 20:10-18, v. 17 does not revoke v. 14b. In the case of Jericho, the tradition ran counter to the Deuteronomistic rule and was simply kept as a special case. In the case of Ai, the burning of the city could not be eliminated from the tradition; but at least a special command from Yahweh was introduced permitting booty and cattle to be taken (Josh. 8:2,27). The lists in Josh. 10f. speak of the destruction of *kol-(han)nepeš* (10:28,[30,32],35,37,39; 11:11) or—when the law in Dt. 20:16f. is cited—of the destruction of *kol-(han)n^ešāmâ* (Josh. 10:40; 11:11f.,14f.), using the language of Dt. 20:16. Josh. 11:14 states explicitly that at least to the Deuteronomist these expressions

[41] Cross, 274-289; Smend.

refer only to human beings, not to animals. The burning of Hazor, clearly also a fixed element of the tradition, is treated as exceptional (Josh. 11:13). The point of the old *ḥērem* narratives, radical renunciation of booty, has been totally eliminated.

The killing of the populace, however, is justified. The first *ḥērem* war described in the Deuteronomistic history served as a good example (cf. Nu. 21:21-31): Sihon of Heshbon is offered a peaceful agreement (*dibrê šālôm,* Dt. 2:26), which he rejects (*wᵉlô 'āḇâ,* 2:30). Only then does Israel begin the *ḥērem* war. Of course, it is made clear immediately that the rejection of peaceful compromise is itself occasioned by Yahweh: *hiqšâ YHWH 'ᵉlōhêḵā 'eṯ-rûḥô wᵉ'immēṣ 'eṯ-lᵉḇāḇô lᵉma'an tittô bᵉyāḏᵉḵā.* In Josh. 11:18-20, which summarizes the entire occupation, precisely the same is said of all the kings and cities west of the Jordan with the single exception of Gibeon. Josh. 11:19 states: *lō'-hāyᵉṯâ 'îr 'ᵃšer hišlîmâ 'el-bᵉnê yiśrā'ēl.* It would have been possible to subjugate them peacefully. But "it was Yahweh's doing to harden their hearts that they should come against Israel in battle, in order that they (the Israelites) might consecrate them to destruction without showing them mercy" (Josh. 11:20).

The war law in Dt. 20:10-18 must also be understood from this perspective: Israel's obligation to offer peaceful terms of surrender to the enemy before a war (vv. 10f.) holds not only for the cities that are "very far" (v. 15), but also for the cities that Yahweh has designated as Israel's inheritance (v. 16). The other form of war, namely *ḥrm* (vv. 16f.), is to be practiced only upon rejection of terms. That this took place, according to the Deuteronomistic history, with but a single exception, was quite another matter. But only when terms had been rejected did the ancient commandment against making any treaty come into force.

The war law Dt. 20:10-18 also limits the *ḥērem* strictly to the situation of the occupation and the inhabitants of the promised land. For later periods and other peoples, different rules apply. In principle, then, the very law that appears to demand the *ḥērem* in fact forbids it in the case of those to whom the law is actually addressed (Josiah and his contemporaries). How deliberately this restriction of the *ḥērem* is undertaken is shown by Dt. 25:17-19, where the destruction of the Amalekites is demanded—undoubtedly a proleptic legitimation of the narrative in 1 S. 15. Here, where the Deuteronomist can choose his own words, the term *ḥrm* is avoided, although it was a key word in the existing text of 1 S. 15.

In summary, then: the *ḥērem* theory of the preexilic Deuteronomistic history served to systematize various ancient traditions concerning the occupation; at the same time, however, it performed certain specific functions for the readers of the time of Josiah. It was important to undergird their sense of religious and national identity. Assyrian political hegemony and its concomitant cultural pressure had destroyed the plausibility of a religiously and politically independent Israel. Now, after the fashion of Assyrian propaganda, bloody stories of war could spread terror through Israel, too. But at the same time these stories belonged to a distant past; for its foreign policies of the present, Israel could boast of highly civilized rules of warfare, on this point too rivaling the best of the great powers.

It is important to note that the Deuteronomistic *ḥērem* theory does not appear to have been necessary to legitimize Josiah's campaigns of destruction against cultic institutions in Judah and in the former northern kingdom. The ancient commandments requiring destruction of the Canaanite cults, now enshrined in Deuteronomy, sufficed (Dt. 7:5; 12:2f.; cf. Ex. 23:24; 34:13). In any case, this purpose was served by the law in Dt. 13:13-19(12-18) (apostasy of a city from the cult of Yahweh). Even here, though, a restrictive interpretation is imposed on the ancient tradition. The law must be read in comparison with Ex. 22:19(20) and in the context of the laws in Dt. 13:2-6(1-5), 7-12(6-11); 17:2-7. Formerly, the punishment of *ḥērem* was imposed for any sacrifice to other gods. Now this punishment no longer applies to various ways of inciting to worship of other gods or to the apostasy of individuals. Only in the case of apostasy of an entire city is it prescribed.

The exilic revision of the Deuteronomistic history was faced with the task of explaining the catastrophe. An important technique used by retrospective historical interpretation was the surrender of the notion that all the inhabitants of the land had been exterminated during the occupation. Indeed, their seductive influence on Israel's faith was a major cause of the great history of apostasy. The verb *ḥrm,* which would have had to appear with a negative in the context of such statements, is avoided, presumably in order not to contradict blatantly the words of the preexilic stratum. The destruction that should have taken place but did not is viewed as Yahweh's deliberate plan, prevented by Israel's sin from being carried out. The verbs used include primarily *yrš* hiphil, *šmd* hiphil, and *krt* hiphil. Enough surviving peoples are obtained by assuming for the promised land the wide boundaries of the later Davidic kingdom.

The word *ḥrm* still plays a role in Dt. 7, which attained its final form at this time or possibly even later. In vv. 3f. (cf. also the secondary interpolation in Ex. 34:16), the ancient law against making treaties is explicated by the law against mixed marriages (*ḥrm* in 7:2 and 7:25f.). The reason for the *ḥērem* stated in Dt. 20:18 ("that they may not teach you to do according to all their abominable practices which they have done in the service of their gods, and so to sin against Yahweh your God") was undoubtedly inserted into the war law at this time. In 1 K. 9:21, we read that Solomon made a forced levy of the inhabitants of the land who had not been destroyed by the *ḥērem.* Thus the failure to carry out the *ḥērem* is used by exilic Deuteronomist to account for the catastrophe and make it intellectually assimilable. Through associative proximity, the *ḥērem* motif in Dt. 7 extends its intransigence to the prohibition of mixed marriages and the national isolation that become important in the postexilic period.

4. *Postexilic Prophecy.* The pre-Deuteronomistic usage of *ḥrm* by the prophets reappeared occasionally in the postexilic period in oracles against foreign nations (Isa. 11:15; 34:2,5; Jer. 50:21,26; 51:3; Dnl. 11:44; Mic. 4:13). What is new is that now Yahweh himself sometimes carries out the *ḥērem.* Probably through the influence of Deuteronomistic usage, the word now frequently means simply "kill, destroy." In this meaning it can appear in statements describing Yahweh's actions toward Israel (Isa. 43:28; Zec. 14:11; Mal. 3:24[4:6]).

5. *Postexilic Priestly Law.* In postexilic priestly law, we find *ḥērem* used as a term for a special form of private dedication of things and persons to the sanctuary. Such a dedication is *qōḏeš-qᵒḏāšîm* and cannot be annulled by payment (cf. Lev. 27:21,28; Nu. 18:14; Ezk. 44:29). According to Lev. 27:29, *ḥērem* survived as a form of pun-

ishment, although we are not told when it was imposed and there exists the suspicion that the verse is just a theoretical legal harmonization referring to Ex. 22:19(20), with no basis in actual practice. This view would be supported by the observation that Ezr. 10:8 threatens a *ḥērem* punishment that affects things, not persons. We are clearly dealing with confiscation of property for the sanctuary, while the delinquent himself is punished by exclusion from the *qᵉhal haggôlâ*, described by a different terminology.

This context brings us in some proximity to the talmudic *ḥērem*, which, however, is terminologically different. Isa. 43:28 may have provided a stimulus for this development (*ḥrm* in parallel with profanation and reviling; cf. the same combination of motifs in Jer. 25:9 MT, a text that has undergone late revision). See Behm for a discussion of the semantically close *anáthē/ema* of the NT and the early Church.

Lev. 27:29 was probably occasioned by the mention of persons in the preceding verse as a possible private *ḥērem* offering to Yahweh. These dedicated individuals remain alive, probably as slaves of the sanctuary. In Lev. 27:28, we find *ḥrm* hiphil, and the subject of the gift is specified: *'îš*. To distinguish this case clearly from the killing of a person, v. 29, referring to the ancient *ḥērem* punishment, was appended. The crucial point is that v. 29 uses the hophal, which shows that we are dealing with a different and distinct case. In view of the function performed by v. 29, it appears risky to reconstruct earlier forms of the "law."[42] The verse certainly has nothing to do with Jephthah's vow: he sacrificed his daughter as *'ôlâ* (Jgs. 11:30f.).

Lohfink

---

42 Most recently, Schulz, 40f.

חרם *ḥrm* II; חָרוּם *ḥārûm;* חֲרוּמַף *ḥᵃrûmap;* חֵרֶם *ḥērem* II

Contents: I. Ancient Near East: 1. Egypt; 2. Mesopotamia. II. Etymology and Distribution. III. 1. OT Occurrences; 2. Dead Sea Scrolls; 3. LXX. IV. Exegetical Conclusions: 1. *ḥārûm;* 2. *ḥērem.*

ḥrm II. D. Bidoli, *Die Sprüche der Fangnetze in den altägyptischen Sargtexten. ADAI.Ä*, 9 (1976); C. H. W. Brekelmans, "חֵרֶם *ḥērem* Bann," *THAT*, I, 635-39; G. Dalman, *AuS*, VI, 343-370; F. Daumas, "Fischer und Fischerei," *LexÄg*, II, 234-242; G. R. Driver, "Studies in the Vocabulary of the OT, II," *JTS*, 32 (1931), 250-57; *idem*, "Hebrew Homonyms," *Hebräische Wortforschung. Festschrift W. Baumgartner. SVT*, 16 (1967), 50-64; F. Dunkel, "Die Fischerei am See Genesareth und das NT," *Bibl*, 5 (1924), 375-390; K. Galling, "Fisch und Fischfang," *BRL*², 83f.; I. Gamer-Wallert, *Fische und Fischkulte im alten Ägypten. ÄgAbh*, 21 (1970); J. G. Heintz, *Le filet divin* (Jerusalem, 1965); *idem*, "Oracles prophétiques et 'guerre sainte' selon les archives royales de Mari et l'AT," *Congress Volume, Rome 1968. SVT*, 17 (1969), 112-138; P. Humbert, *Problèmes du livre d'Habacuc. Mémoires de l'Université de Neuchâtel*, 18 (1944); J. Jeremias, *Kultprophetie und Gerichtsverkündigung in der späten Königszeit Israels. WMANT*, 35 (1970); O. Keel-Leu, *The Symbolism of the Biblical World* (Eng. trans., New York, 1978); B. Meissner, *Assyrische Jagden. AO*, 13/2 (1911); P. Montet, *Les scènes de la vie privée dans les*

I. Ancient Near East.

1. *Egypt.* In Egypt, the use of nets to catch fish can be traced back to the predynastic period. The most important forms, on account of the abundant catch they supplied, were the long spindle-shaped sack net and the triangular dragnet. The top cord of these nets bore wooden floats; the bottom cord was weighted with sinkers, so that the net hung vertically in the water. It was lowered into the water between two boats, and drawn in to land by long ropes pulled by two crews on shore. There the fish were taken from the net and gathered together.

At the beginning of the Middle Kingdom, when the dead were thought to be changed into fish, the Egyptian cult of the dead considered fishermen and nets to be loci of danger for the departed. As several of the Coffin texts and the Book of the Dead 153 A(?),B show, the one who was justified before Osiris could guard himself against these dangers by knowing and speaking the names of the fishermen, the net, and its various parts.

2. *Mesopotamia.* In Mesopotamia, nets were used for fishing in the sea, although in the early period there is also evidence that they were used for freshwater fishing. Among the saltwater fishermen, those who used nets seem at times to have constituted a separate group, distinguished, for example, from those who fished for turtles. The most important word for the fishnet is the general term ^{giš}*sa* = *šētu* (also used for fowling and hunting nets); there were more than thirty additional names for various types of nets.[1] Nine each designate different forms of the two basic types, the movable net and the the casting net or dragnet. In metonymous usage, the net symbolized victory over enemies, as well as the judicial sovereignty of the deity and the king.[2] In the later period, only gods are described as retiary warriors (cf. the Vulgate stela of Eannatum[3]).

II. Etymology and Distribution. For the Hebrew root *ḥrm* II niphal, "be split," and the subst. *ḥērem*, "net," the common basic meaning is probably preserved only in Arab. *ḫarama*, "perforate," with its derivatives *'aḫram*, "having a perforated nasal septum," and *taḫrīma*, "point," "filigree."[4] Contra Driver,[5] Akk. *ḫarāmu* II, "set apart," and *ḫarimtu*, "prostitute," belong to *ḥrm* I[6] (cf. Arab. *ḥaruma*, "be forbidden," "consecrate," also attested with the meanings "take away," "exclude"[7]). The same is

---

tombeaux égyptiens de l'Ancien Empire. Publications de la Faculté des Lettres de l'Université de Strasbourg, 24 (1925); A. Salonen, *Die Fischerei im alten Mesopotamien nach sumerisch-akkadischen Quellen. AnAcScFen*, B 166 (1970); A. S. van der Woude, *Micha. PredOT* (1976); → דג *dāg* [*dāgh*]; → חרם *ḥāram* I.1,7.

[1] Salonen, 61-69.
[2] *Ibid.*, 70; Heintz, *SVT*, 17 (1969), 129ff.
[3] *ANEP*, no. 298.
[4] Wehr (^{4}1968), 212f.; *BDB*, 356f.; *GesB*, 260; *KBL*^{3}, 340.
[5] *JTS*, 32 (1931), 251; *SVT*, 16 (1967), 56.
[6] *KBL*^{3}, 340.
[7] Wehr, 171.

true of the Akkadian personal name *Ḫurrumu,* derived from *ḫarāmu* II.[8] In Middle and Modern Hebrew we find the verb *ḥāram* II, "make nets," "fish," *ḥ*ᵃ*ram,* "dock (a nose)," the subst. *ḥārām,* "fisher," and the substs. *ḥerem,* "net," "fishpond," and *ḥermā',* "net."[9] From Punic we have the word *ḥrm* for the profession of netmaker.[10]

Heintz[11] postulates a common semantic basis for *ḥrm* I and II; according to this theory, the nature of a net and the separation it expresses constitute the basis for the biblical notion of the ban.

III. 1. *OT Occurrences.* There are 11 occurrences of *ḥrm* II in the OT: the qal pass. ptcp. *ḥārûm,* "having a split nose" (Lev. 21:18), the derived name *ḥ*ᵃ*rûmap,* "Splitnose" (Neh. 3:10), and 9 occurrences of *ḥērem,* "(drag)net" (Eccl. 7:26; Ezk. 26:5,14; 32:3; 47:10; Mic. 7:2; Hab. 1:15-17).

Many emendations have been proposed for the MT. In Hab. 1:17, following 1QpHab. 6:8, it is usual to emend *ḥērem* to *ḥereḇ,* "sword,"[12] but *hērîq ḥērem,* "empty the net," makes good sense,[13] with the interpretation of the preceding verses not coming until v. 17b. In Mic. 7:2, *ḥērem* is either deleted[14] or emended to *ḥōrim,* "nobles,"[15] or *hērîmû,* "lift the hands to do evil,"[16] and linked to v. 3. In light of Aquila, Symmachus, the Syriac, the Targum, and CD 16:15, which also read *ḥērem*—albeit with the meaning "ban"—the MT should be retained. The rendering of *w*ᵉ*heḥ*ᵉ*rîm* in Isa. 11:15 as "he will split," proposed by Driver[17] and *KBL*³, is based on the erroneous association of Akk. *ḫarāmu* II with *ḥrm* II. Here we have a form of *ḥrm* I, "ban," or follow the general emendation of *ḥrm* to *ḥrb* I, "dry out."[18] The emendation of *ḥinnām* in Prov. 1:11[19] is likewise to be rejected in view of Prov. 1:17 and Ps. 35:7.[20]

2. *Dead Sea Scrolls.* In the Dead Sea scrolls, the only possible occurrence of *ḥērem* II, "net," might be in the quotation from Mic. 7:2b in CD 16:15; but there is general agreement that *ḥērem* here means "ban" or "vow."

---

[8] *AHw,* I, 323; *CAD,* VI (1956), 89f.; contra Noth, *IPN,* 226; *KBL*³, 340 (mistranscribed: *Ḫurummu*).

[9] *WTM,* II, 112.

[10] *DISO,* 96.

[11] *SVT,* 17 (1969), 136f.

[12] K. Elliger, *Das Buch der zwölf Kleinen Propheten, II. ATD,* XXV (1951), 34; Jeremias, 79; W. Rudolph, *Habakuk. KAT,* XIII/3 (1975), 209.

[13] Humbert, 42.

[14] A. Weiser, *Das Buch der zwölf Kleinen Propheten, I. ATD,* XXIV (⁵1967), 285; T. H. Robinson, *HAT,* XIV (²1954), 148.

[15] Rudolph, *Micha. KAT,* XIII/3, 121f.

[16] *KBL*³, 340; R. Vuilleumier, *Michée. CAT,* XIb (1971), 80.

[17] *JTS,* 32 (1931), 251; *SVT,* 16 (1967), 59.

[18] H. Wildberger, *Jesaja. BK,* X/1 (1972), 464.

[19] *KBL*³, 340.

[20] M. Dahood, *Psalms I. AB,* XVI (1966), 211f.; W. A. van der Weiden, *Le livre de Proverbes. BietOr,* 23 (1970), 19-22.

3. *LXX.* The LXX renders *ḥārûm* as *kolobórrin*, "mutilated," and transcribes the name *ḥ^a^rûmap̱* onomatopoetically as *Herōmaph.* For *ḥērem*, 5 times we find *sagḗnē*, "(drag?)net" (Eccl. 7:26; Ezk. 26:5,14; 47:10; Hab. 1:16), twice *amphíblēstron*, "(casting?) net" (Hab. 1:15,17), and once *ángkistron*, "fishhook" (Ezk. 32:3). In Mic. 7:2, the LXX translates very freely: *ekthlíbousin ekthlibḗ*, "they oppressed through oppression."

IV. Exegetical Conclusions.

1. *ḥārûm.* In the second law concerning priests (Lev. 21:16-23; Holiness Code), *ḥārûm* stands in a list of physical defects that exclude those who have them from priestly service. Elliger[21] interprets *ḥārum 'ô śārûa'* (v. 18) as "abnormal development of parts of the body," but the analogy of vv. 18-20 suggests specific deformities—here involving nose and ear—, so that v. 18 deals with the realms of eyesight, gait, speech, and hearing. The word *ḥārûm* designates a speech impediment caused by a perforated or twisted nasal septum, and perhaps also by a cleft palate, which lends the voice a nasal quality.

2. *ḥērem.* The noun *ḥērem* is a technical term of the fishing industry. Because of its use with *'lh* hiphil, "raise" (Ezk. 32:3); *grr,* "drag" (Hab. 1:15); and *ryq* hiphil, "empty" (Hab. 1:17), and because of the mention of drying places (*mišṭāḥ/mišṭôaḥ,* Ezk. 26:5,14; 47:10), it is usually interpreted as a "dragnet" in contrast to the *mik̠meret̠,* "casting net," which is "spread" upon the water (Isa. 19:8) and used to "gather" fish (Hab. 1:15).[22]

The relationship between hunting and fishing is shown by the parallelism of *rešet̠,* "hunting net" (Ezk. 32:3), and *m^e^ṣōḏîm,* "snares," and *'^a^sûrîm,* "fetters" (Eccl. 7:26), with *ḥērem* (cf. also Jer. 16:16), and by the use of *ṣûḏ,* "hunt," in the context of fishing (Mic. 7:2).

The occurrences of *ḥērem* are all metaphorical, and appear only in the prophets.

a. The "divine net" in the hand of Yahweh or used by others at his behest is a symbol of power and sovereignty. In Ezk. 32:3 it illustrates Yahweh's superiority to Pharaoh, who is depicted (v. 2) as a young lion and a crocodile (→ תנין *tannîn*). Yahweh himself—"with a host of many peoples," a secondary addition—undertakes to punish and destroy Pharaoh by throwing his "hunting net" (*rešet̠*) over the lion and hauling the crocodile out of the water with his *ḥērem.* The corpse Yahweh will cast upon the ground and on the open field, so that all the beasts of the earth can gorge themselves. This act of Yahweh's judgment will be so mighty that it will affect not only the whole earth, but the very cosmos as well. (For Marduk's net as a possible analog, cf. EnEl IV, 95.)

According to Hab. 1:14-17, the power of the Babylonians has become so great (with Yahweh's approval) that they can catch the men of other nations at will like fish,

---

[21] *Leviticus. HAT,* IV (1966), 291f.

[22] *AuS,* VI (1939), 361; Galling, 84; → דג *dāg* [*dāgh*], 136.

with *ḥakkâ*, "hook," *mikmereṯ*, "casting net," and *ḥērem*, without resistance. The high value placed on such equipment is illustrated by the divinization of the nets (v. 16), to which the Babylonians sacrifice.[23]

b. When a person or his actions are compared to a *ḥērem*, the danger emanating from such a person is expressed. According to Mic. 7:2, the corruption of Judah is so great that each person is the enemy of his neighbor. As a hunter lies in wait for his prey, and as a fisher goes after the fish with his net, so each goes after his brother (cf. van der Woude, who interprets *ḥērem* as the "destruction" [*ḥērem* I] that all pursue).

Eccl. 7:26 uses similar terminology to describe the danger of the seductive woman, comparing her to *m^e^ṣōḏîm*, "snares." Her heart is like *ḥ^a^rāmîm*, "dragnets," because she is always out to befool and capture men; her hands are like *'^a^sûrîm*, "fetters," so that the victim cannot break loose.

c. The *mišṭaḥ ḥ^a^rāmîm* of Ezk. 26:5,14, in the prophecy of judgment against Tyre, uses "a place of spreading nets to dry" as an image for the total destruction of this flourishing commercial center; the island, now uninhabitable, will mean nothing except to fishermen, who will spread their nets on its rocks to dry.

In Ezk. 47:10, the *mišṭôaḥ laḥ^a^rāmîm* is used in a positive rather than negative sense: the Dead Sea will be full of fish, from En-gedi to En-eglaim the drying places for the fishermen's nets will proclaim the immeasurable wealth of fish provided by what had once been a dead sea, now brought to life by the water flowing from the temple spring.

Giesen

---

[23] For additional instances of the "divine net" and ancient Near Eastern parallels, see Heintz, *SVT*, 17 (1969), 129-138; Keel-Leu, 89-93, 235.

חרף *ḥrp* I

Contents: I. Philological History. II. *ḥrp* I: 1. Occurrences; 2. *ḥōrep* and the Etymology of *ḥrp* I; 3. Verb; 4. Names; 5. Parallel Terms and Antonyms; 6. Versions.

ḥrp I. J. Barth, *Wurzeluntersuchungen zum hebräischen und aramäischen Lexicon* (1902); G. R. Driver, "Studies in the Vocabulary of the OT. IV," *JTS*, 33 (1932), 38-47; I. Eitan, "The Bearing of Ethiopic on Biblical Exegesis and Lexicography," *JPOS*, 3 (1923), 136-143; G. Gerleman, *Studies in the Septuagint. I. The Book of Job. LUÅ*, N.S., Avd. 1, 43/2 (1946); S. Krauss, *Talmudische Archäologie*, II (1911; repr. Hildesheim, 1966); B. Landsberger, "Schwierige akkadische Wörter. 2. 'Früh' und 'spät,' " *AfO*, 3 (1926), 164-172; Leslau, *Contributions;* J. D. Michaelis, *Supplementa ad Lexica Hebraica*, VI (Göttingen, 1792), 933-940; F. Rundgren, "Arabisches *xarīf*- 'Herbst' und *xarūf*- 'Lamm,' " *OrSuec*, 18 (1969), 137-141; A. Schultens, *Liber Jobi* (Leiden, 1737); M. Wagner, *Die lexikalischen und grammatikalischen Aramaismen im alttestamentlichen Hebräisch. BZAW*, 96 (1966).

I. Philological History. There are two roots *ḥrp* in Biblical Hebrew. From one derives the substantive *ḥōrep,* usually translated "fall" or "winter";[1] from the other derives *ḥerpâ,* which means "disgrace, shame." Despite the significant difference in meaning, many scholars have attempted to derive the two substantives and their associated verbs from a single root. Gesenius[2] takes *ḥrp* to mean "*carpsit,*" "pluck," and thus arrives at the meaning "*carpsit conviciis . . . probris affecit*" ("pick at with abuse . . . abuse"). For the Jewish Aram. *ḥ^a^rap,* on the basis of a (hypothetical) basic meaning "be small, insignificant," Levy[3] arrives at the meaning "direct sharp words against someone, abuse, revile," as well as the meaning "be early, be young," from which comes *ḥ^a^rîpûṯā',* "youth" (Job 29:4). And Dalman[4] notes for an Aramaic root *ḥrp* the meanings "sharpen, bring to a point" and "revile" (pael) and "be early" (aphel).

Most scholars, however, find at least two roots *ḥrp.* Even in this case, however, many start with a root *ḥrp,* "pluck," derived from Arab. *ḫarafa* (cf. Akk. *ḫrp* II, "pull off"[5]). In this etymology there are two basic approaches. In the first, a meaning "pick at (with words)," "abuse (verbally)" is found in the root, and another *ḥrp* is derived (a) denominatively from *ḥōrep̱* (without any etymology of its own)[6] or (b) from a sense "overflow," "be juicy, fresh," which leads in turn to *ḥōrep,* "autumn," as well as "sap of life," "dew of youth."[7] In the second, more common approach, *ḥrp* I is derived from Arabic in the sense of "pluck, pick," leading to *ḥōrep̱* as the "time of picking," i.e., "autumn" (with its denominative verb in Isa. 18:6), together with *ḥrp* II from Jewish Aramaic, Syriac, and Arabic derivatives of a root *ḥrp* II from Jewish Aramaic, Syriac, and Arabic derivatives of a root *ḥrp* (Arab. *ḥrf*), "be pointed or sharp," from which we have "abuse," "revile."[8]

In Ps. 57:4(Eng. v. 3), Driver and *KBL*[2,3] find a third root *ḥrp.*[9] The niphal ptcp. *neḥ^e^repeṯ* in Lev. 19:20[10] is sometimes associated with *ḥrp* II, "abuse": "abused by the man" (among others, Luther and the Luther Bible until the 1964 revision) or "set free by the man" (Fürst;[11] similarly Levy[12] for the qal pass. ptcp. *ḥ^a^rûpâ,* "lit. given over to disgrace; i.e., belonging to a man"). It is also associated with *ḥrp* I (*ḥōrep̱*)

---

1 P. Fronzaroli, "Studi sul lessico comune semitico: III. I fenomeni naturali," *AANLR,* N.S. 20 (1965), 142, 148.

2 F. Gesenius, *Thesaurus philologicus criticus linguae hebraeae et chaldaeae Veteris Testamenti* (Leipzig, 1829-1858), 522ff.

3 J. Levy, *Chaldäisches Wörterbuch über die Targumim und einen grossen Theil des rabbinischen Schriftthums* (Leipzig, ³1881), I, 283; cf. *WTM,* II, 113f.

4 G. Dalman, *Aramäisch-neuhebräisches Handwörterbuch zu Targum, Talmud und Midrash* (Frankfort, ²1922), 161b.

5 *AHw,* I, 323.

6 C. F. A. Siegfried, *Hebräisches Wörterbuch zum AT* (Leipzig, 1893), 225.

7 J. Fürst, *Hebräisches und chaldäisches Handwörterbuch über das AT* (Leipzig, 1861), 442f.

8 *GesB,* 261; E. König, *Hebräisches und aramäisches Wörterbuch zum AT* (Leipzig, ⁴·⁵1931), 126; *KBL*², 335f.; *KBL*³, 341.

9 → חרף *ḥrp* II, II.1.

10 See II.3 below.

11 *Handwörterbuch,* 442.

12 *WTM,* II, 114.

(König:[13] "as though plucked, i.e., betrothed"; *KBL*[1]: "intended [for another man]"[14]). Still others derive it from a different root.[15]

De facto, the occurrences involve two roots: *ḥrp* I, associated with Akk. *ḫarāpu(m)*, "be early,"[16] and *ḥrp* II, associated with Arab. *ḥarafa*.[17]

II. ḥrp I.

1. *Occurrences*. The occurrences associated with *ḥrp* I include the verb in Isa. 18:6 (qal) and Lev. 19:20 (niphal), and the subst. *ḥōrep* in Gen. 8:22; Job 29:4; Ps. 74:17; Prov. 20:4; Jer. 36:22; Am. 3:15; Zec. 14:8. The assignment of the names *ḥārip* (Neh. 7:24; 10:20[19]) and *ḥārēp* (1 Ch. 2:51) to this root is not certain; they are more likely derived from *ḥrp* II (like the gentilic name *ḥ^a rîpî*/*ḥ^a rûpî* in 1 Ch. 12:6[5]).

2. *ḥōrep and the Etymology of ḥrp I*. The subst. *ḥōrep* designates the winter—for Palestine, the rainy season.[18] Accordingly, *ḥōrep* stands alongside *qayiṣ*, "summer" (Gen. 8:22; Ps. 74:17; Zec. 14:8; cf. Am. 3:15). The two together designate an entire year (Ps. 74:17; Zec. 14:8). The Israelite king Jeroboam II, and perhaps also members of the upper class, had both a "winter house" and a "summer house" (Am. 3:15). A winter house of Zedekiah, king of Judah, was equipped with a brazier because of the cold season (Jer. 36:22).

As Jer. 36:22 shows, the period designated by *ḥōrep* includes the ninth month (Chislev, November-December). This is the period when it rains (Ezr. 10:13; cf. 1 [Eth.] En. 2:3) and when people shiver on account of the rain (Ezr. 10:9).

Nowhere do we read that *ḥōrep* includes the time of harvest, which concludes with the Feast of Booths, the feast of "ingathering" (*ḥag hā'āsip*, "at the end of the year" [Ex. 23:16]) from threshing floor and winepress (Dt. 16:13), in the seventh month (September-October). 1 (Eth.) En. 82:19 expressly includes the harvesting of the fruits of the land and the produce of the field, together with the vintage, in the season characterized by "great heat and drought," i.e., the summer, which the "astronomical book" of 1 (Eth.) En. 72–82 assigns to the fourth through sixth months, the period between the summer solstice and the autumnal equinox (82:18; 72:15-20).

The period of heat and therefore of ingathering belongs to the summer (*qayiṣ*; cf. also Prov. 6:8; 10:5; Jer. 8:20) rather than the winter (*ḥōrep*), characterized by cold (cf. Gen. 8:22 and, for example, *B. Meṣ*. 107b).

That *ḥōrep* has nothing to do with the time of harvest is emphasized by the fact that the rabbinic division of the year into six periods of two months each (*zera'*, "seedtime"; *ḥōrep*, "winter"; *qîr*, "cold"; *qāṣîr*, "cutting"; *qayiṣ*, "fruit harvest"; *ḥōm*, "heat") assigns *ḥōrep* to the second position: "half of Chislev (the ninth

---

13 *Wörterbuch*, 126.

14 Citing Landsberger, 170.

15 *GesB*, 261 ("uncertain stem"); *KBL*[3], 342 (*ḥrp* IV).

16 Landsberger; *AHw*, I, 323; *CAD*, VI (1956), 90.

17 → חרף *ḥrp* II.

18 See *AuS*, I/1 (1928), 34ff.

month), Marcheshvan (the tenth), half of Shebat (the eleventh)," in other words, December through January.[19]

Thus the common derivation of *ḥōrep* from Arab. *ḫarafa*, "pluck,"[20] and its interpretation as "harvest time," "autumn," is untenable.[21] The meaning "autumn" for OSA *ḫrp* and Arab. *ḫarīf* is secondary.[22] The subst. *ḥōrep* derives in fact from a root *ḥrp*, "be early." The root has this meaning in Akkadian, where the verb *ḫarāpu(m)* is used with the sun, rain, high water, etc., and the adj. *ḫarpu(m)* is used with rain, high water, sowing, harvest, the morning, etc.[23] In Ugaritic (if *ḫprt* is a metathesized form of *ḫrpt*, with the meaning "yearlings") we find the same etymology.[24] This meaning of the root *ḥrp*, apart from the niphal in Lev. 19:20 and the associated qal passive participle in the Talmud, reappears in Jewish Aramaic: *ḥ^a^rap* aphel, "do something early";[25] *ḥ^a^rāpā'*, "premature" (of the early rain and of lambs born in the month of Adar, in contrast to "late" ['^a^pîlôṯ] lambs born in Nisan);[26] *ḥ^a^rîpûṯā'*, "youth, early manhood" (Job 29:4[27]), with its probable derivative *ḥurpā'*, simply "lamb" (also in Syriac and Mandaic; cf. Arab. *ḫarūf*, "lamb"); cf. Akk. *ḫurāpu*, "spring lamb."[28] Here belong also OSA *ḫrp* and Ethiop. *ḫarīf*, "year,"[29] where the semantic development from "spring" to "year" is clearly similar to that of *ḥōḏeš* from "new moon" to "month."

Thus *ḥōrep* means the early season of the year (that is, of the agricultural year, which begins in the fall), or "spring." Climatologically, this is "winter" in Palestine.

This meaning is also present in Prov. 20:4.[30] This is the basis on which we must determine the meaning of *ḥōrep* in Job 29:4. Job recalls his former good fortune (vv. 2ff.): "As I was *bîmê ḥorpî*, when God still 'guarded'[31] my tent." Here *ḥōrep* does not mean "autumn," as the period of a person's mature vigor (the view of most interpreters since Schultens), but "spring," that is, youth and early adulthood (with Symmachus, *en hēmérais neótētós mou*, and Vulg., *in diebus adulescentiae meae*).[32] Fohrer[33] thinks here not of "youth" but of "earlier days," the days of prosperity. It is not necessary to postulate a hapax legomenon.[34]

---

19 *B. Meṣ.* 106b; Tosefta *Ta'an.*, i.7, ccxv.15; cf. Krauss, II, 149.

20 Schultens, 801f.; Gesenius, *Thesaurus; GesB; KBL*²; cf. also Eitan, 142.

21 Cf. Landsberger, 170f.

22 Cf. also Lane, I/2, 725ff.

23 *AHw*, I, 323, 326; *CAD*, VI, 90, 105f.; cf. also *ḫarpu*, "autumn."

24 *KTU*, 1.4 VI, 48; *UT*, no. 992.

25 *Sanh.* 70b; *WTM*, II, 114a.

26 *Roš Haš.* 8a, etc.

27 See below.

28 *AHw*, I, 357f.

29 Leslau, *Contributions*, 22.

30 Cf. *AuS*, I/1 (1928), 36, 164.

31 *BHK*.

32 Barth, 23f.; N. Peters, *Das Buch Job. EHAT*, 21 (1928), 314; G. Hölscher, *Das Buch Hiob. HAT*, XVII (²1952), 70 (citing the derivatives of *ḥōrep* in Levy, *Chaldäisches Wörterbuch*, I, 284); *KBL*³; etc.

33 G. Fohrer, *Das Buch Hiob. KAT*, XVI (1963), 402, 405.

34 *KBL*².

3. *Verb*. In Isa. 18:6, the qal of *ḥrp* is a denominative verb from *ḥōrep*, meaning "spend the winter" (like the qal of *qyṣ* in the same verse from *qayiṣ*, "summer"; cf. Gk. *cheimṓn/cheimázō*, Lat. *hiems/hiemare*).

The niphal of *ḥrp* appears in a legal dictum in Lev. 19:20: "If a man lies carnally with a woman who is a slave, *neḥ^erepeṯ l^e'îš*, and not yet ransomed or given her freedom, there shall be a *biqqōreṯ*.[35] They shall not be put to death, because she was not free." In this case we are dealing with a woman (slave) with whom a man (neither her master nor her spouse) has had intercourse. She is described as "*neḥ^erepeṯ* to a man." It is unlikely that *neḥ^erepeṯ* means "already selected for marriage,"[36] so that the marriage has not yet taken place and the death penalty is not required: v. 20b justifies the absence of the death penalty not on the grounds that there was no marriage, but on the grounds that the woman was not free. Furthermore, if the woman, who is (still) a slave, does not have the legal status of a wife, there would be no occasion for capital punishment and no motivation for the express stipulation that the slave and the man are not to be put to death.

The case in fact resembles that in Dt. 22:23f.,25-27, which treats as a crime intercourse of a man with a virgin who is *m^e'ōrāśâ l^e'îš*, "espoused," i.e. "betrothed," to a man. Through the act of *'rś* the woman is "espoused" to her spouse (the term "engaged" is commonly but imprecisely used). Legally she is already his wife, even if she is still living in her father's house and has not yet been "taken" in marriage (cf. Dt. 20:7aα). It is this act of espousal that is referred to by *neḥ^erepeṯ* in Lev. 19:20.[37] Instead of the niphal participle, the Talmud later uses the qal pass. ptcp. *ḥ^arûpâ*,[38] equated in *Qidd.* 6a with *'rsh* (= Biblical Heb. *'rśh*) with the qualification that the latter was employed generally, the former specifically in Judea.[39]

Intercourse with an espoused girl or woman was punishable by death for both parties (cf. Dt. 22:23f. and the special case in vv. 25-27). The fact that this punishment is not invoked in the case described in Lev. 19:20 (cf. v. 20bα) is due to the woman's being (still) a slave, neither (as is stressed) ransomed nor given her freedom. The legal rights of the slave's owner take precedence over those of the spouse of the "espoused" woman. Semasiologically, *neḥ^erepeṯ* means neither "rejected," "abandoned," nor "plucked,"[40] but rather "given *early* (to a man),"[41] or better, "given an early status," a notion referring to her "premarital"[42] status.[43]

---

35 K. Elliger, *Leviticus. HAT,* IV (1966), 243, 260: "rebuke"; more likely: "liability for damages" (*KBL*³, 145).

36 M. Noth, *Leviticus. OTL* (Eng. trans. ²1977), 142.

37 See also II.6 below.

38 *Šabb.* 72a, etc.

39 The *ḫarūpu* cited under *ḥrp* IV by *KBL*³, 342 (E. Ebeling, *Die babylonische Fabel und ihre Bedeutung für die Literaturgeschichte. MAOG* 2/3 [1927], 44, line 39) does not mean "fiancé," but rather "carob"; cf. *BWL,* 216, 39; *AHw,* I, 329; *CAD,* VI, 120.

40 See I above.

41 Landsberger, 170.

42 P. Koschaker, "Eheschliessung und Kauf nach alten Rechten," *ArOr,* 18 (1950), 228.

43 Cf. M. David, review of E. Jacob, *Die altassyrischen Gesetze* [*ZVR Sond,* 41 (1925)], in *OLZ,* 30 (1927), 1072f.

4. *Names.* Assignment of the personal names *ḥārîp* (Neh. 7:24; 10:20[19]) and *ḥārēp* (1 Ch. 2:51)[44] to *ḥrp* I is supported by the observation that in the list of those returning from exile recorded in Neh. 7 par. Ezr. 2, the name *yôrâ* appears in Ezr. 2:18 for the name *ḥārîp* in Neh. 7:24. The former is obviously associated with *yôreh,* "early rain," which suggests that for the Israelites the name *ḥārîp* meant "early." If so, the name would be explained as something like "the early one," early born, in contrast to the Akkadian name *Uppulti,* "(late fruit =) the late one," "late born" (from *apālu,* "be late").[45] But see → חרף *ḥrp* II.

5. *Parallel Terms and Antonyms.* Corresponding to the Akkadian antonyms *ḫa-rāpu*/*apālu,* "be early/be late,"[46] the Hebrew of the OT has as an antonym to *ḥrp* I the root *'pl,* found in the adj. *'āpîl,* "late" (Ex. 9:32 [late addition to J], applied to a late harvest).

Additional parallels and antonyms are not derived etymologically but from the concrete meaning of the noun formed from *ḥrp* I. For the period of *ḥōrep* the OT uses the word *s^e^tāw* (Cant. 2:11), standing explicitly in parallel with "rain." The word is borrowed from Old Aramaic (inscription of Barrākib, king of Sam'al, dating from the second half of the eighth century B.C.);[47] it appears also in Jewish Aramaic and Syriac. It is related to Akk. *šatû,* "drink,"[48] and Arab. *šitā',* "rainy period," "winter."[49] As an antonym to *ḥōrep,* "winter," we find *qayiṣ,* "summer" (Gen. 8:22; Ps. 74:17; Zec. 14:8; cf. Am. 3:15); corresponding to the denominative qal *ḥrp,* "spend the winter," we find the qal of *qyṣ,* "spend the summer" (Isa. 18:6).

6. *Versions.* In Isa. 18:6, the verb *ḥrp* I was misunderstood by the LXX (*hḗxei*); the Targum (*y'bdwn stw'*) and Vulg. (*hiemabunt*) understood it correctly. In Lev. 19:20, the LXX renders the meaning correctly (*diapephylagménē*); this verb stands for *šmr* (14 times) and *nṣr* (Dt. 32:10). Targum Yerušalmi I translates exactly (*mt'rs',* "espoused") and Targum Onqelos appropriately (*'ḥyd',* "dedicated"), while Targum Neofiti 1 with *mš'bdh,* "subjected to service," has in mind the status of the slave with respect to her owner. The Vulg. (*nubilis*) thinks of her marriageability.

The original meaning of the subst. *ḥōrep* is reflected in the LXX in the rendering *éar,* "spring," in Gen. 8:22; Ps. 74:17; Zec. 14:8; the meaning "winter" appears in the adj. *cheimerinós* in Jer. 36:22. In Am. 3:15, the *oíkos therinós,* "summer house," has as its counterpart the *oíkos perípteros,* a house surrounded by colonnades for protection against the sun, but also against rain.

In Job 29:4, the LXX translates *bîmê ḥorpî* as *epibríthōn hodoús* (B) /*hodoís* (AS^2). It is unlikely that this rendering represents a different consonantal text and that the

---

44 For a Hebrew seal, see *LidzEph,* I (1900), 274.

45 Cf. Landsberger, 168; for the form in compound names see *AN,* 131, 155.

46 Landsberger.

47 *KAI,* 216.18f.

48 *AHw,* II, 1202.

49 Cf. Wagner, no. 207.

Greek translator has before him *b^e^mōaḥ rōp̱eh* (*bmḥ rph* for *bymy ḥrpi*).[50] There is no obvious semantic development from "becoming weak in the marrow, drooping" to the postulated meaning "when I sank down owing to corpulence" > "when I walked heavily on the roads." It is more likely that the LXX—unable to understand the MT—derived its formulation from Job's description in vv. 7ff.: "when I (weighing heavily =) weightily (= commanding and receiving honor) (walked) upon the roads."[51] Jerome followed this lead with *florens in viis,* while the Targum, Symmachus, and Vulg. correctly render the MT.[52] In Prov. 20:4, *oneidizómenos,* "abused," is based (wrongly) on *ḥrp* II.

The Targum uses *s(y)tw'* 5 times to translate *ḥōrep̱* (Gen. 8:22; Ps. 74:17; Jer. 36:22; Am. 3:15; Zec. 14:8).[53] In Job 29:4 it uses *ḥ^a^rîpûṯa',* "springtime," "youth,"[54] and in Prov. 20:4—misunderstanding like the LXX—*mtḥsd,* "abused."

The Vulg. uses for *ḥōrep̱ ver,* "spring" (Ps. 74:17), *hiems,* "winter" (Gen. 8:22; Zec. 14:8) or the adj. *hiemalis* (Jer. 36:22; Am. 3:15); in Job 29:4, *adulescentia* renders the meaning correctly. In Prov. 20:4, with *propter frigus,* the Vulg. also has in mind "winter," but changes the meaning by substituting a cause ("on account of the cold") for a statement of time ("in the winter").

Kutsch

---

[50] Gerleman, 21.
[51] Cf. Gerleman.
[52] See II.2 above.
[53] See II.5 above.
[54] See II.2 above.

חרף *ḥrp* II

Contents: I. 1. The Root *ḥrp* II; 2. Statistics; 3. Semantic Field. II. 1. Verb; 2. Noun; 3. Theological Statements; 4. Names. III. 1. LXX, Targum, Vulg.; 2. Sirach, Qumran.

I. 1. *The Root ḥrp II.* The root represented by *ḥrp* II appears outside of Biblical Hebrew in Middle Hebrew, in Jewish and Christian Palestinian Aramaic, in Syriac, in Mandaic, and in Arabic, where it sometimes has the meaning "be sharp" or the like. The details are as follows: The verb has the meaning (1) "be sharp" in Syriac (with the pael "sharpen" and ethpael "be sharpened") and Mandaic; (2) "stimulate, incite" in Christian Palestinian Aramaic (aphel) and Syriac (pael, aphel); and (3) "abuse, mock, belittle" in Biblical Hebrew, Middle Hebrew, and Jewish Aramaic. (According

---

ḥrp II. G. R. Driver, "Studies in the Vocabulary of the OT. IV," *JTS,* 33 (1932), 38-47; J. Schneider, "ὄνειδος," *TDNT,* V, 238-242; R. Smend, *Die Weisheit des Jesus Sirach* (Berlin, 1906); Y. Yadin, *The Ben Sira Scroll from Masada* (Jerusalem, 1965).

to von Soden, it is questionable whether a stative verb like "be sharp" can belong together with the transitive "abuse.")

The nouns mean (1) "sharpness," with the corresponding adj. "sharp," in Jewish Aramaic, in Syriac, and (adj. only) in Christian Palestinian Aramaic and Mandaic. (Middle Heb. *ḥārôp,* "graving tool," presupposes this meaning; Arab. *ḥarf* means "edge.") In Syriac, two nouns and an adjective developed the meaning "speed(y)," which also lies behind Jewish Aram. *ḥ*ᵃ*rîpûṯā'*, "swift current," as well as "sharp(ness) (of intellect)" in Jewish Aramaic and Syriac. Here probably belong personal names and one geographical name from Biblical Hebrew, and personal names from Jewish Aramaic.[1] In Christian Palestinian Aramaic we find a noun with the meaning "incitement." (2) On the other hand, Heb. *ḥerpâ,* Jewish Aram. *ḥerp*ᵉ*ṯā'*, *ḥêrûpā'* mean "abuse, slander, insult."

The variety of meanings exhibit a semantic development. The meaning "sharp" develops into "speedy" (cf. Biblical Heb. *ḥdd:* hophal [Ezk. 21:14-16(Eng. vv. 9-11)] "be sharpened"; qal [Hab. 1:8] "be speedy" par. *qll* qal). "Make sharp" develops into "incite," "abuse." This shows clearly that—as is generally assumed today—we are dealing with a single root in these cases. That this root has nothing to do with *ḥrp* I[2] can be seen from the absence of any convincing semantic connection, and from the fact that in Arabic the two roots differ in their initial consonant (*ḫarūf,* "lamb"/*ḥarāfa,* "sharpness").[3]

The basic meaning of the root *ḥrp* II, "be sharp," piel "make sharp, sharpen," may appear in proper names in Biblical Hebrew,[4] but cannot be seen in the verb or noun (*ḥerpâ*). The meaning "incite," attested in Christian Palestinian Aramaic and Syriac, does appear in Sir. 43:16: "His (Yahweh's) word impels the south wind" (hiphil of *ḥrp* in M,[5] piel in B[6]).

2. *Statistics.* The verb *ḥrp* II appears 39 times in the OT: 4 times in the qal, 34 times (plus Ps. 57:4[3]) in the piel. It is especially frequent in the context of 1 S. 17 (5 occurrences, plus 2 S. 21:21; 23:9 [gloss]; also 11QPs^a 28:14) and 2 K. 19 par. Isa. 37 (4 occurrences each). It occurs 11 times in the Psalter (plus Ps. 57:4[3]), as well as in Jgs. 5:18 (the earliest occurrence); 8:15; 1 Ch. 20:7; 2 Ch. 32:17; Neh. 6:13; Job 27:6; Prov. 14:31; 17:5; 27:11; Isa. 65:7; Zeph. 2:8,10. The noun *ḥerpâ* appears 73 times, most frequently in Jeremiah, Ezekiel, and Lamentations (12, 7, and 3 times, respectively) and in the Psalter (20 times). The 31 additional occurrences range from 1 S. 11:2 to Nehemiah and Daniel (4 occurrences each).

3. *Semantic Field.* Together with and parallel to *ḥrp* II we find → גדף *gāḏap* [*gādhaph*] piel, "revile" (2 K. 19:6 [with v. 4],22 par. Isa. 37:6 [with v. 4],23; Ps.

---

1 See II.4 below.

2 → חרף *ḥrp* I.1.

3 See F. Rundgren, "Arabisches *xarîf-* 'Herbst' und *xarūf-* 'Lamm,' " *OrSuec,* 18 (1969), 137-141.

4 See II.4 below.

5 Yadin, 32.

6 Smend, 46.

44:17[16]; [1QpHab. 10:13]); *hll* III polel, "deride" (Ps. 102:9[8]); *l'g,* "mock" (Prov. 17:5; *n'ṣ* piel, "blaspheme" (Ps. 74:10,18); *'mr 'l,* "speak against someone" (2 Ch. 32:17); *k's* hiphil, "provoke" (Isa. 65:3, with v. 7). The semantic field also includes *bûz* and → בזה *bāzâ* [*bāzāh*], "despise" (Prov. 1:7; Nu. 15:31; etc.); *ḥsd* I piel, "bring shame upon" (Prov. 25:10; Sir. 14:2); *klm* hiphil, "reproach" (Ruth 2:15; 1 S. 20:34; etc.); *mûq* hiphil, "scoff" (Ps. 73:8[7]); *nqb* qal (Lev. 24:11,16a,16b) in the sense "blaspheme"; *qll* piel, "curse" (Lev. 24:11, etc.; rendered by some of the Targumim with the piel of *ḥrp*); *š'ṭ,* "despise" (Ezk. 16:57; 28:24, 26); and *bôš* hiphil in the sense "bring shame" (Prov. 10:5; etc.). The opposite is expressed by the piel of *kbd,* "treat as important," "honor" (Prov. 14:31).

Corresponding to the noun *ḥerpâ* we find *bûz, bûzâ,* "contempt" (Ps. 119:22; Neh. 3:36[4:4]); *bōšeṯ,* "shame" (Isa. 30:5); *giddûpîm* and *giddûpâ,* reviling" (Zeph. 2:8; Ezk. 5:15); *dērā'ôn,* "contempt" (Dnl. 12:2); *ḥeseḏ* I, "defamation" (Sir. 41:22), "reproach" (Lev. 20:17; Prov. 14:34); *la'ag,* "derision" (Ps. 44:14[13]); *qeles/qallāsâ,* "derision" (Jer. 20:8; Ezk. 22:4); *nega'-wᵉqalôn,* "wounds and dishonor" (Prov. 6:33); and above all *kᵉlimmâ* and *kᵉlimmûṯ,* "dishonor" (Jer. 51:51; "originally physical in contrast to verbal [*ḥerpâ*] abuse";[8] Jer. 23:40). In expressions like "make/become a reproach," *ḥerpâ* appears with *'ālâ* and *qᵉlālâ,* "curse" (Jer. 42:18); *za'ᵃwâ,* "horror" (Jer. 24:9); *šammâ/mᵉšammâ,* "waste" (Jer. 25:18; Ezk. 5:15); *šᵉrēqâ,* "whistling" (to ward off demons) (Jer. 29:18); *māšāl,* "byword," and *šᵉnînâ,* "taunt" (Jer. 24:9). The etymology of this last from *šnn,* "sharpen" (a sword: Dt. 32:41; a tongue: Ps. 64:4[3]), illustrates the connection of *ḥrp* piel and *ḥerpâ* with *ḥrp,* "be sharp." Cf. also *šᵉ'āṭ,* "malice" (Ezk. 25:6). On the use of *ḥerpâ* in parallel with *'erwâ,* "shame" (Isa. 47:3), see II.2 below.

II. 1. *Verb.* In Biblical Hebrew, *ḥrp* II means "abuse (verbally)," "blaspheme," "scoff": "How long, O God, is the foe to scoff (*ḥrp* piel)? Is the enemy to revile (*n'ṣ* piel) thy name forever?" (Ps. 74:10). The immediate context lends various nuances. The one who scoffs at another seeks to denigrate the latter in significance, worth, and ability; he makes clear that he scorns and despises the other.

The leaders of the city of Succoth refuse Gideon and his party the provisions they request, and underline their scorn by asking whether Gideon already has in his hand the Midianite "kings" he has been pursuing (Jgs. 8:15; cf. v. 6). The victorious enemies taunt the beaten Davidides (Ps. 89:52[51]). The enemies of Nehemiah would "taunt" him if he had taken refuge in the temple in the face of attack (Neh. 6:13). Such "taunting" in the sense of contempt is the opposite of *kbd* piel, "treat as important," "honor": one who oppresses a poor person or mocks (*l'g*) him insults his maker (Prov. 14:31a; 17:5a), but one who is kind to the needy honors him (14:31b).

Frequently the taunts are accompanied by emphasis on one's own greatness and abilities. For example, Sennacherib, king of Assyria, "mocks" Yahweh, "the living God" (2 K. 19:4,16,22f. par. Isa. 37:4,16,23f.; 2 Ch. 32:17), by denying that he has

---

7 *GesB*, *KBL*² s.v.

8 *KBL*², 440b.

the power to intervene on behalf of Jerusalem; at the same time he boasts of himself and his victories (2 K. 18:30,32b-35; 19:10-13 par. Isa. 36:15,18-20; 37:10-13; 2 Ch. 32:11-19). Likewise according to 1 S. 17 the Philistine Goliath "defies" the "ranks of Israel" (v. 10) by challenging them to send forth a representative to engage in single combat to decide the issue; he considers himself invincible, assuming that no Israelite would have a chance against him, even if one were prepared to accept the challenge (vv. 11,24). The Philistine "disdains" (*bzh*) the youth David who comes to meet him (v. 42) and "curses" him (*qll* piel, v. 43). The Philistine mocks not only Israel (vv. 10,25) but "the armies of the living God" (vv. 26,36; cf. 11QPs^{a} 28:14), and thus ultimately Yahweh himself. With his victory over the Philistine, David takes the "reproach" from Israel (cf. v. 26a). For *ḥrp* in such contexts see also 2 S. 21:21 par. 1 Ch. 20:7; 2 S. 23:9.[9]

The boasting that goes hand in hand with "scoffing" finds terminological expression in the use of *gdl* (hiphil) *'l*, "claim to be greater or better than someone," in parallel with *ḥrp*: both enemy and friend boast their superiority to the psalmist in Ps. 55:13(12); Moab and Ammon boast before the people of God (Zeph. 2:8,10), whose downfall is announced by Yahweh because of their own "pride" (*gā'ôn*, v. 10).

If the subject of the taunts is mightier, they incite him to action: he will take vengeance on those who would humiliate him; he will punish them. So Gideon deals with the inhabitants of Succoth (Jgs. 8:15f.); so Yahweh takes vengeance on the Israelites for the blasphemy of their illegitimate cults (Isa. 65:6f.; cf. *k's* [hiphil] *'al-pānîm*, "provoke me to my face," in v. 3). The military and political catastrophe of Israel in 587 B.C. caused the nations to ask maliciously, "Where is their God?" (Ps. 79:10); but a faith grounded in hope encourages the humiliated Israelites to pray to Yahweh that he will avenge their disgrace sevenfold (v. 12; cf. also Ps. 74:10,18,22). This same question can also be addressed to an individual as a taunt by his enemies (Ps. 74:10; cf. v. 4) when he is suffering from an otherwise undefined affliction (cf. also Ps. 102:9[8]). On the other hand, the psalmist can be supported by God's steadfast love, by the coming of God's promised salvation, so that he can "answer" those who taunt him (Ps. 119:41f. [qal]), just as a father can "answer" reproaches if his son is wise and thus makes his heart glad (Prov. 27:11 [qal]).

In two passages, Jgs. 5:18 and Job 27:6, the element of "slander" or the like is very much secondary to the meaning "despise." In Jgs. 5:18, the expression *ḥērēp nāpšô lāmûṯ* means literally: "He (the tribe of Zebulun) despised his life to (*l^{e}*, 'in the direction of'[10]) death." In other words, the members of the tribe preferred to sacrifice their own lives rather than lose the battle. One could also translate: "They sacrificed themselves." Job 27:6 also yields perfectly good sense: "I hold fast my righteousness, and will not let it go; my heart (= conscience) does not (despise =) regret any of my days (*lō'-yeḥ^{e}rap l^{e}ḇāḇî miyyāmāy*)." This is true whether one follows the MT reading the qal (cf. Ps. 69:10[9]; 119:42; Prov. 27:11) or, following Budde, replaces it with the piel.[11]

---

[9] See F. Willesen, "The Philistine Corps of the Scimitar from Gath," *JSS*, 3 (1958), 327-335.

[10] See *GK*, § 114m.

[11] K. Budde, *Das Buch Hiob*. *GHK*, II/1 (^{2}1913), 156.

In Ps. 57:4(3)—"He (Yahweh) will send from heaven and save me, *ḥērēp šō'ªpî*"—it is probably best to follow most interpreters in reading the participle as a construct plural.[12] The subject is probably not Yahweh (LXX; cf. II.3 below) but the *šō'ªpîm,* whether the singular is retained[13] or replaced by the pl. *ḥērᵉpû.* "They taunt who trample upon me" is an asyndetic clause motivating the petition in v. 4aα(3aα); cf. Gen. 17:14 and *GK,* §158a, as well as the "reproach of the daughters of Edom . . . who despise [ptcp.] you" (Ezk. 16:57). It is therefore unnecessary to postulate another root *ḥrp* with the meaning "frustrate, disappoint,"[14] whose semantic derivation from Arab. *ḥarifa,* "be feeble-minded" > "drivel" (cf. Syr. *ḥraf,* "mix"; Tigré "babble"), is unconvincing, or an emendation such as *yaḥpᵉrû,* "let them be confounded."[15]

2. *Noun.* The meaning of the noun *ḥerpâ* varies with the sense of the context. It means "slander" or "the act of slandering" (Neh. 5:9; Job 16:10; Isa. 51:7; Dnl. 11:18; Mic. 6:16[16]) in the sense of "speech against someone" (cf. 2 Ch. 32:17), the reproach that one "takes up" (*nś'*, Ps. 15:3) or "hears" (Jer. 51:51; Lam. 3:61; Zeph. 2:8). It can also mean (one's own) reproachful behavior (Hos. 12:15[14], of Israel's conduct toward God, par. *dāmîm,* "bloodguilt") together with its consequences (Jer. 31:19: *nāśā'tî ḥerpaṯ nᵉ'ûrāy*). Above all, *ḥerpâ* designates the disgrace that one party can "put" on another (1 S. 11:2; Ps. 78:66; Jer. 23:40), the reproach that rests on an individual (Gen. 30:23; 1 S. 25:39; Ps. 69:8[7]; Prov. 6:33; Jer. 15:15; Lam. 3:30), a group (Isa. 4:1), or a nation (1 S. 17:26; Isa. 25:8; Jer. 31:19; Lam. 5:1; Ezk. 36:30; Zeph. 3:18). We also find the idiom "become" (1) *ḥerpâ* or (2) *lᵉḥerpâ,* or "be made" (*ntn, śym*) (3) *ḥerpâ* or (4) *lᵉḥerpâ* applied to (a) an object, (b) an individual, (c) a city, (d) a nation, or the like (1.b: the psalmist, Ps. 31:12[11]; 109:25; a descendant of David, Ps. 89:42[41]; 1.c: Jerusalem, Ezk. 5:15; 1.d: Israelites or Judeans, Ps. 79:4; Neh. 2:17; 2.a: the word of Yahweh for the inhabitants of Jerusalem, Jer. 6:10 [they scorn it] or for Jeremiah, Jer. 20:8 [he is reproached]; 2.c: Bozrah, Jer. 49:13; 2.d: the Judeans, Jer. 42:18; 44:8,12; 3.b: the psalmist, Ps. 39:9[8]; 3.c: Jerusalem, Ezk. 22:4; 3.d: the Israelites, Ps. 44:14[13]; 4.c: Jerusalem, Ezk. 5:14; 4.d: the king and inhabitants of Jerusalem after 597 B.C., Jer. 24:9; 29:18; the Israelites, Joel 2:17; cf. v. 19). In these passages, *ḥerpâ*—like the terms *'ālâ, za'ªwâ* (*Q*), *māšāl, qᵉlālâ, šammâ, šᵉnînâ,* and *šᵉrēqâ* used in parallel or in similar constructions (see I.3 above)—becomes as it were a term for those on whom "reproach" rests, who find themselves scorned.

In Isa. 47:3, where *ḥerpâ* appears in parallel with *'erwâ,* both words probably refer to the female pudenda (cf. Jer. 13:26).

Various situations are considered by the OT to be a "reproach": thinking of David

---

[12] On *napšî* at the beginning of v. 5(4), see *BHS.*

[13] *GK,* § 145l.

[14] Driver, *KBL*[2,3].

[15] H.-J. Kraus, *Die Psalmen. BK,* XV/1 (⁴1972), 411, following H. Gunkel, *Die Psalmen. GHK,* II/2 (⁴1926), 245 (with additional suggestions).

[16] See *BHK, BHS.*

as a runaway slave (1 S. 25:39 [cf. vv. 10f.]), celibacy (Isa. 4:1), widowhood (Isa. 54:4), childlessness (Gen. 30:23; cf. Luke 1:25), and quite generally any suffering or humiliation (Ps. 22:7[6]; 31:12[11]; 39:9[8]). Self-humiliation before Yahweh can also be a "reproach" to the psalmist (Ps. 69:11[10]). Adultery (Prov. 6:33) and wickedness (Prov. 18:3) are a "disgrace" to those who commit them. It is a disgrace for a family to give a woman in marriage to an uncircumcised male (Gen. 34:14). Slavery in Egypt was a "reproach" to the people of Israel (Josh. 5:9;[17] possibly uncircumcision[18]), as was maiming members of the populace (1 S. 11:2). Other examples include Goliath's contempt (1 S. 17:26; see II.1 above), famine (Ezk. 36:30; cf. the Targum on Joel 2:19), political humiliation (Isa. 25:8; 30:5; Babylon in 47:3), the result of attack by the apocalyptic army in Joel 2:19,[19] scattering in defeat (Ps. 44:14[13]), the capture and destruction of Jerusalem and the temple (Ps. 79:4; Jer. 51:51), loss of the *naḥ^{a}lâ* (Lam. 5:1f.), and the defenseless situation of those left behind after 587 (Neh. 1:3)—the rebuilding of the walls puts an end to this "disgrace" (2:17).

3. *Theological Statements*. Human abuse can be inflicted on God as well as on other human beings. Foreign enemies mock Yahweh with their arrogance (2 K. 19:4, etc.), by destroying his sanctuary (Ps. 74:10,18,22), by asking "Where is their God?" (Joel 2:17); but even his own people insult him (Ps. 69:10[9]), especially by participation in alien cults (Isa. 65:7).

Yahweh is never the subject of *ḥrp* (qal and piel) as a reprehensible action (on Sir. 43:16, see I.1 above). But as part of Yahweh's judgment he can "disgrace" the guilty (Ephraim, Hos. 12:15[14]; the Judeans, Ps. 44:14[13]; Jer. 24:9; 29:18; [42:18]; Jerusalem, [Ezk. 5:14f.]; 22:4; Bozrah, Jer. 49:13; his enemies, Ps. 78:66; cf. the confession of faith in Dnl. 9:16). The people plead with Yahweh to remember the disgrace inflicted on his anointed (Ps. 89:51[50]), to behold the disgrace of the people (Lam. 5:1), to turn back the taunts of their enemies on their own heads (Neh. 3:36[4:4]); the psalmist prays to be delivered from *ḥerpâ* (Ps. 119:22,39) and from the "scorn of the fool" (39:9[8]). For a new future, Yahweh proclaims the deliverance of Israel from the reproach of the nations (Ezk. 36:15; cf. Zeph. 3:18; also Joel 2:19) and the removal of "the reproach of his people from all the earth" (Isa. 25:8). And according to Dnl. 12:2f., "some shall awake to everlasting life, and some 'to shame' (gloss?) and everlasting contempt."

4. *Names*. The personal names *ḥārîp̄* (Neh. 7:24; 10:20[19]) and *ḥārēp̄* (1 Ch. 2:51),[20] derived from *ḥrp,* (originally) "be sharp," mean "sharp, fresh,"[21] or more likely "sharp-witted" (*ḥārîp̄* in this sense appears in the Targum on Job 11:12; Targum Yerušalmi I on Nu. 13:3; *Hor.* 14a). In Gen. 25:15, Targum Yerušalmi I substitutes *ḥ^{a}rîpā'* for the name of Ishmael's son *ḥ^{a}ḏaḏ,* identifying it with *ḥdd,* "be

---

17 O. Eissfeldt, *Hexateuchsynopse* (Darmstadt, ^{2}1922; repr. 1973), 32.
18 *KBL*^{3}, 342.
19 H. W. Wolff, *Joel and Amos. Herm* (Eng. trans. 1977), 62.
20 *LidzEph,* I (1900), 274.
21 *IPN*, 228.

sharp, quick," and interpreting the name *ḥarîpā'* as deriving from *ḥrp* II. The additional evidence and more likely meaning make this etymology preferable to derivation from *ḥrp* I.

The name of Solomon's Egyptian scribe *'elîḥōrep* (1 K. 4:3) has not been satisfactorily explained.[22] The element *ḥōrep* does not convey any appropriate meaning, and derivation from an Egyptian name (**'r-ḥp* = **'elîḥap,* "Apis is my god"[23]) is uncertain.

The gentilic name *ḥarûpî* (*Q*)/ *ḥarîpî* (*K*) (1 Ch. 12:6) suggests an unidentified place named *ḥārû/îp;* this name, likewise derived from *ḥrp* II, probably reflects a geographical term meaning "crag" or the like; cf. the use of the noun *šēn* with the same meaning (1 S. 14:4f.; Job 39:28) and Middle Heb. *šenûnîṯ*[24] from *šnn,* "be sharp."

III. 1. *LXX, Targum, Vulg.* The versions usually render *ḥrp* qal and piel and *ḥerpâ* appropriately. The LXX uses *oneidízein,* "insult," for the verb (34 times; Jgs. 5:18, etc.), *óneidos,* "insult, disgrace" (24 times; Gen. 34:14, etc.), and *oneidismós,* "act of insulting" (44 times; 1 S. 25:39, etc.), for the noun. The Targumim render the verb with *ḥsd,* "suffer disgrace," pael "insult, disgrace" (30 times; Jgs. 8:15, etc.; also Ps. 57:4[3]), the noun with *ḥsd* (1 and 2 Samuel) and *qln,* "shame, disgrace" (10 times plus Isa. 47:3 and Lam. 3:30). The Vulg. renders the verb with *exprobrare,* "cast aspersions" (26 times; Jgs. 8:15, etc.), the noun with *opprobrium* (65 times; Gen. 30:23, etc.). That the translators of the LXX were also familiar with the meaning "be sharp" for *ḥrp* is shown by the use of *paroxýnein,* "make sharp," "incite," "make bitter," for the verb (Prov. 14:31; 17:5) and the adj. *oxýs,* "sharp," for the substantive (Job 16:10).

2. *Sirach, Qumran.* In Sirach and the Dead Sea scrolls, apart from Sir. 43:16 (see I.1 above), the verb and noun are used as they are in the OT. The verb has the meaning "insult": Sir. 34:31 Bm (a friend, LXX *exouthenoún*); 41:22 M (after an act of charity, LXX *oneidízein*); 1QpHab. 10:13 (with *gdp;* the deceived insult the elect of God); 11QPs^a 28:14 (see the discussion of 1 S. 17 in II.1 above); it can also mean "act disgracefully" (Sir. 42:14, a daughter; cf. Hos. 12:15[14], discussed in II.2 above, LXX *kataischýnein*). The noun means "disgrace": in Sirach as a consequence (5:14 A, par. *bōšeṯ,* LXX *katágnōsis;* 6:1 A, with *qālôn,* LXX *óneidos;* 34:2 B, not in the LXX; 41:6 M, LXX *óneidos;* 42:14 Bm, LXX *oneidismós*), and as a qualifier for words (34:2c) or a quarrel (6:9 A, LXX *oneidismós* [twice]). In the Dead Sea scrolls, the noun appears in the idiom "become/make (*le*)*ḥerpâ*" (1QS 4:12, par. *za'awâ;* 1QH 2:9, par. *qeles;* 2:34, par. *bûz;* 4QpHos^a 2:13, par. *qālôn;* cf. 1Q34 3:1.3, where the context is unclear).

Kutsch

---

[22] M. Noth, *Könige. BK,* IX/1 (1968), 56.

[23] *KBL*³, 54a.

[24] *WTM,* IV, 586b.

חָרַץ ḥāraṣ; חָרוּץ ḥārûṣ; חָרִיץ ḥārîṣ

Contents: I. 1. Etymology; 2. Meaning; 3. LXX; 4. Qumran. II. Concrete Usage in the OT: 1. Sharp Cutting Instruments; 2. The Sharp Individual; 3. Decisive Speech. III. Usage in Theological Contexts: 1. *ḥārûṣ* as a Divine Punitive Instrument; 2. Decisive Speech and Action in Holy War; 3. Divinely Decreed Ends.

I. 1. *Etymology.* In Hebrew, the root *ḥrṣ* has the basic meaning "cut," as can be seen from Lev. 22:22, where the qal pass. ptcp. *ḥārûṣ* denotes "cut (naturally mutilated?) animals." The verb *ḥāraṣ* has a range of meanings closely comparable to those of its Akkadian cognate *ḫarāṣu,* which means (1) "cut down, cut off"; (2) "set, determine" (cf. *parāsu*); (3) "cut in (deeply), dig a furrow"; (4) "make clear, clarify"; (5) "become ready, treat, consider"; and (6) "deduct, correspond."[1] In Ugaritic, the noun *ḥrṣ*[2] may mean "threshing sled"[3] or "wrinkle, furrow."[4] The meaning of a related verb in *KTU,* 1.19 I, 10 is obscure. The text *KTU,* 1.17 VI, 37 is especially unclear; several alternative translations have been proposed.[5] Of special interest are occurrences of *ḥrṣ,* perhaps also with the meaning "threshing sled," together with *ṣmd(m)* (biblical *ṣemeḏ*) in several texts.[6] The noun *ṣmd* can mean "stick, war club" or "yoke of oxen," or possibly a land measure related to the area a yoke of oxen can plow or thresh in some limited amount of time.[7] In *KTU,* 4.145, 8, it appears in a list of military supplies, and it is similarly associated with horse-drawn chariotry in *KTU,* 4.363, 9. The meaning "graven" has been proposed for the Phoen. adj. *ḥrṣ,*[8] but all its occurrences seem to admit of the meaning "golden," so we must suspend judgment. On *KAI,* 145.10, see the discussion below; *KAI,* 81.2 is obscure. In the Targumim, Midrashic literature, and the Talmud, *ḥᵃraṣ* means "dig a cavity, cut a trench" and "decree, designate."[9] The noun *ḥᵃrîṣ* means "moat, canal, incision," as it does also in 3Q15 8[10] (cf. *ḥārûṣ* in Dnl. 9:25) and in Old Aramaic.[11]

2. *Meaning.* a. In the OT, the usual verb meaning "cut" is → כרת; *ḥāraṣ* is also displaced by *ḥāraš,* which denotes the cutting done by an engraver or sculptor. Like its Arabic cognate *ḥaraṯa, ḥāraš* can also mean "plow." The verb *ḥāraṣ* and its sub-

---

1 *AHw,* I, 323f.; *CAD,* VI (1956), 92-95.

2 *WUS,* no. 971.

3 *KTU,* 1.19 I, 8.

4 *KTU,* 1.17 VI, 37.

5 Cf. *UT,* no. 900, and Supplement, 543; J. A. Sasson, in *RSP,* I, III, 56a.b; *ANET*³, 151.

6 *KTU,* 4.145, 8; 4.169, 4, 7f.; 4.384, 11; 4.377, 5, 6.

7 *UT,* nos. 900; 2168.

8 *KAI,* 10.4, 5, 12; 11; 38.1; 60.3, 5.

9 M. Jastrow, *A Dictionary of the Targumim, the Talmud Babli and Yerushalmi, and the Midrashic Literature* (1903; repr. Brooklyn, 1975), I, 505.

10 M. Baillet, J. T. Milik, and R. de Vaux, *Les 'petites grottes' de Qumrân. DJD,* 3 (1962), 244.

11 *KAI,* 202.A 10; cf. Akk. *ḫarīṣu, AHw,* I, 326.

stantives occur a total of 28 times in the OT, including 1 instance of a proper name (2 K. 21:19). This and comparable Ugaritic names[12] may reflect the Egyptian idiom *dm rn* discussed below. There are 7 occurrences in the qal.

Apart from Lev. 22:22, the idea of cutting or sharpening appears only in the idiom *ḥāraṣ lāšôn l^e*, "cut or sharpen the tongue." This refers to a forceful way of speaking, but it is not clear whether it means decisive speaking or speaking that is sharp, i.e., meant to inflict injury upon one at whom words are directed (as we speak of a "cutting remark" or "sharp words"). Several considerations suggest the former: (1) talmudic usage (possibly influenced by the late first-millennium practice of engraving decrees; but the sense "engrave" is not clearly attested); (2) Akkadian usage; and (3) the Egyptian idiom *dm rn,* "pronounce (lit., 'cut'; cf. *dm.t,* 'knife') someone's name," normally in a context involving joy or favor.[13] Sharpness of mouth or tongue is mentioned in Ps. 52:4(Eng. v. 2); 140:4(3); Isa. 49:2; Jer. 9:7(8). In fact, the secondary meaning "decide, determine" is more common in the OT. In the niphal we find only the ptcp. *neḥ^{e}rāṣâ/neḥ^{e}reṣeṯ* (5 occurrences), meaning "decisive" or "determined."

b. Originally, *ḥārûṣ* may have been an adjective meaning "sharp"; but in the OT it appears only as a substantive (Isa. 41:15 is a gloss[14]), referring primarily to a sharp threshing sled or a sharp individual. (The noun *ḥārûṣ* meaning "gold" is a different root; → זהב *zāhāḇ* [*zāhābh*].) The noun *ḥārûṣ* is the indigenous Hebrew word for "threshing sled." The synonymous *môrāg* may be a loanword from Sumerian;[15] it occurs only 3 times in the OT: 2 S. 24:22 (par. 1 Ch. 21:23) and Isa. 41:15. In 2 S. 24:22 par., *môrāg* is used by a foreigner, Araunah the Hittite Jebusite, who is speaking to David. In Isa. 41:15, *môrāg* has intruded as a late gloss.

The *môrāg* is a sled made of wood (2 S. 24:22). It is slightly upturned in front; underneath are sharp stones or pieces of iron to rip up the stalks of grain. The sled is pulled by a yoke of oxen, while someone stands on it to supply weight.[16] The *ḥārûṣ* was a similar instrument. Job gives us an impression of the underside of the *ḥārûṣ* when he describes Leviathan the sea monster: "His underparts are like sharp potsherds; he spreads himself like a threshing sled on the mire" (Job 41:22[30]). Although modern sleds in the Near East make use of basalt or other hard stones (cf. Driver), the ancient Hebrew *ḥārûṣ* appears to have contained sharp pieces of iron, at least occasionally. Am. 1:3 refers to *ḥ^{a}ruṣôṯ habbarzel* (the qualifier suggesting that other materials were sometimes used), and the Targumim render *ḥārûṣ* in Isa. 28:27 by *môrîgê barz^{e}lā'* (cf. *neḥ^{e}rāṣâ* in Isa. 28:22). The underside was thus comparable to a mouth filled with sharp teeth (cf. Isa. 41:15 and *KTU,* 1.19 I, 8: *kḥrṣ 'bn ph,* "as a threshing sled with stones is its mouth"[17]).

---

12 *PNU,* 136.

13 *WbÄS,* V, 449-459.

14 J. Reider, "Etymological Studies in Biblical Hebrew," *VT,* 2 (1952), 116f.; cf. B. Duhm, *Das Buch Jesaia. HKAT* (^{5}1968, ^{4}1922 = *GHK,* III/1), 306.

15 Reider.

16 S. R. Driver, *The Books of Joel and Amos. CBSC* (1915), 227f.; *AuS,* III (1933), 78-85.

17 *WUS,* no. 971.

In the book of Proverbs, ḥārûṣ generally refers to the sharp individual (Prov. 12:27; 21:5; and *passim*). Here ḥārûṣ is usually rendered "diligent" or the like,[18] but it may in fact mean something more like "alert, discerning, thoughtful." Since ḥārûṣ is often contrasted with → רמיה *r^emiyyâ* (Prov. 10:4; 12:24,27), it may signify an ambitious person. In Prov. 21:5 ḥārûṣ may designate an abstract quality and not an individual. In Joel 4:14 (3:14) (2 occurrences), it is a noun[19] meaning "decision" in the phrase *'ēmeq h^eḥārûṣ*, "valley of decision." In Dnl. 9:25, ḥārûṣ is a noun meaning "cut place," i.e., a "moat" or "street."[20]

c. The noun ḥārîṣ means either "something cut" or "a sharp (cutting) instrument." The phrase *ḥ^ariṣê heḥālāḇ*, "pieces of cheese," in 1 S. 17:18 refers to several small whole cheeses or slices of cheese. In 2 S. 12:31 (par. 1 Ch. 20:3), *ḥ^arîṣê habbarzel* are "iron picks."

Freedman, Lundbom

3. *LXX*. The LXX uses five different words to translate the verb, with a certain preference for *syntémnein* (4 times) and *grýzein* (3 times). In rendering ḥārûṣ it exhibits complete uncertainty (eleven different words) in the passages where "gold" is meant (*chrysós/chrysíon*).

4. *Qumran*. In the Dead Sea scrolls, ḥāraṣ occurs 7 times, almost exclusively in eschatological contexts, where it refers to the "appointed" time (1QS 4:20,25; 1QM 15:6), the "determined" end (1QH 3:36). But the concrete meaning is still preserved in 1QM 5:9, which refers to the grooves on a lance head. In 3Q15 5,8, ḥārîṣ means "Solomon's canal."[21]

Botterweck

II. Concrete Usage in the OT.

1. *Sharp Cutting Instruments*. The pick (ḥārîṣ) was a common laboring tool and the threshing sled (ḥārûṣ) a farm tool. We find the pick used in construction work in 2 S. 12:31 (par. 1 Ch. 20:3), where David has the Ammonites put to forced labor. The threshing sled is properly the possession of a farmer, used during harvest to thresh grain. But we also find it used in wartime as an instrument of torture.[22] Amos bitterly criticizes the Arameans (i.e., Hazael?) for viciously threshing the people of Gilead with these sleds (Am. 1:3).

2. *The Sharp Individual*. The OT contains five proverbs exalting the person who is ḥārûṣ. One who is ḥārûṣ has complete control over his own life, along with some degree of control over the lives of others. The ḥārûṣ attains power and will rule, while

---

18 *BDB*, RSV, *KBL*³.
19 *BLe*, §472x.
20 See I.1 above.
21 See Baillet, Milik, and de Vaux, *DJD*, 3 (1962), 244.
22 W. R. Harper, *Amos and Hosea*. *ICC* (1905; repr. 1953), 17f.

the slothful (*r*ᵉ*miyyâ*) will be put to forced labor (Prov. 12:24). He also accumulates great wealth, whereas the slothful person (*'āṣēl*) is reduced to poverty (Prov. 10:4; cf. also 12:27, where *hôn-'āḏām* is obscure; 13:4). Cf. the modern proverb "The early bird catches the worm"; a similar idea appears in Prov. 12:27: "A slothful man will not catch his prey, but the diligent man (*ḥārûṣ*) will get precious wealth." But to be *ḥārûṣ* does not always imply acting quickly. It refers rather to the carefully calculated move that succeeds. The *ḥārûṣ* is not like the hasty or precipitate person (*'āṣ*), whose haste brings poverty (Prov. 21:5).

3. *Decisive Speech.* In Hebrew psychology, the act of speaking can be compared to a cutting operation. Not only can the tongue be sharp,[23] but words uttered by the tongue are also likened to fragments, which, once cut, have a kind of finality. They cannot be recalled. King Ahab considers the judgment of the disguised prophet final, since the prophet himself has cited the (presumably fictitious) order he received and failed to carry out. Therefore the king claims he has no voice in the matter when he tells the prophet: "You yourself have decided it" (1 K. 20:40).

III. Usage in Theological Contexts. With the exception of Lev. 22:22, all usages of the verb and substantives that are in any way theological occur in contexts of judgment and war. Lev. 22:22 prohibits the use of mutilated animals as an offering to Yahweh.

1. *ḥārûṣ as a Divine Punitive Instrument.* The threshing sled appears twice in the Isaiah tradition as a metaphor of divine punishment. Yahweh does not use it against Israel, however, for it does too much damage. Israel to him is like dill and cumin and must be beaten with a rod or stick (Isa. 28:27). But Yahweh will use the *ḥārûṣ/môrāg* at the restoration of Israel, when Israel itself will be Yahweh's threshing sled, which he will use to cut up the mountains and hills—and perhaps the foreign enemy as well (Isa. 41:15).

2. *Decisive Speech and Action in Holy War.* In holy war—as in any war—decisiveness or its absence determines the outcome. During the Philistine wars, the sound of marching in the tops of the balsam trees is to be the signal for engaging the enemy, and Yahweh tells David to "act decisively" (*'āz teḥ*ᵉ*rāṣ*), i.e., attack, when he hears the signal (2 S. 5:24). This idiom also occurs in the Neo-Punic Great Mactar lintel:[24] *'qṣb ḥb'rt šḥrṣ drkn,* "He cut off the tribes (*ḥbrt*) who attacked our roads (*drkn*)."[25]

Equally important in holy war is the enemy's inability to speak out sharply or decisively in opposition to Israel. At the exodus, Yahweh assures his people that "not even a dog shall cut his tongue" (*lō' yeḥ*ᵉ*raṣ-keleḇ l*ᵉ*šōnô*) against them; a fortiori, no person will speak either (Ex. 11:7). During the conquest likewise there was no opposition to Joshua and his army when they fought the Canaanites near Makkedah (Josh. 10:21). Joel refers alternately to a "valley of decision" (*'ēmeq heḥārûṣ,* Joel

---

23 See I.2.a above.

24 *KAI,* 145.10.

25 C. R. Krahmalkov, "Two Neo-Punic Poems in Rhymed Verse," *RSF,* 3 (1975), 196.

4:14[3:14]) and a "valley of Jehoshaphat." This is probably where an earlier war—unknown to us—was decided; but Joel has the site in mind because Yahweh will there win a future victory against the Gentiles.

3. *Divinely Decreed Ends*. Certain things are "pre-cut" by Yahweh, i.e., they are determined well in advance of the time when they are to take place. According to Job 14:5 (cf. Dnl. 9:27), the number of a person's days has been determined by God, who thereby sets up a boundary the individual cannot pass. The number of a nation's days is likewise decreed by Yahweh. Isaiah tells the people that Jerusalem's destruction has been determined beforehand (Isa. 28:22), as has the destruction of Assyria (10:22f.). Daniel echoes Isaiah, saying that although the desolation of Jerusalem by Antiochus was similarly decreed (Dnl. 9:26; 11:36), so is the end of the one who carries out this desolation (9:27). Cf. the discussion of the Dead Sea scrolls in I.4 above.

Freedman, Lundbom

חָרַשׁ *ḥāraš* I; חָרָשׁ *ḥārāš;* חֲרָשִׁים *ḥ^a^rāšîm*

Contents: 1. Cut, Plow, Engrave; 2. Plow = Prepare; 3. Craftsmen; Magicians; 4. LXX.

1. *Cut, Plow, Engrave*. The root *ḥrš* is assigned several meanings by *KBL*[2,3]: (1) plow, (2) engrave, (3) prepare, (4) (ptcp.) craftsman. The series appears to reflect a logical semantic development based on the common meaning "cut (into)."[1] But there is no evidence for the general meaning "cut" in the ancient Semitic languages. The specific meaning "plow"[2] (Akk. *erēšu,* "plow";[3] Canaanite *a/iḫrišu*[4]) is already found in Ugar. *ḥrṯ,* which is clearly distinct from *ḥrš,* "craftsman."[5] Arab. *ḥaraṯa,* "plow," is likewise distinct from *ḥarīs,* "careful." Müller[6] and Delcor,[7] following Loewenstamm, are therefore correct in postulating separate roots.

The meaning "engrave" could constitute a bridge between "plow" and "fashion," but it appears only in Jer. 17:1, and there only in a metaphorical sense: the sin of

---

ḥāraš I. G. R. Driver, "Hebrew Poetic Diction," *Congress Volume, Copenhagen 1953. SVT,* 1 (1953), 26-39, esp. 27; S. E. Loewenstamm, "The Hebrew root חרש in the light of Ugaritic texts," *JJS,* 10 (1959), 63-65; H.-P. Müller, "Magisch-mantische Weisheit und die Gestalt Daniels," *UF,* 1 (1969), 79-94; M. Wagner, *Die lexikalischen und grammatikalischen Aramaismen im alttestamentlichen Hebräisch.* BZAW, 96 (1966), 59: no. 110.

1 Cf. also *GesB, BDB,* and *LexHebAram*², *s.v.*

2 Cf. *KBL*³.

3 *CAD,* IV, 285ff.; *AHw,* I, 238f.

4 EA 226, 1.

5 *WUS,* nos. 976, 980.

6 See below.

7 M. Delcor, "חרש *ḥrš* schweigen," *THAT,* I, 639.

Judah is "engraved" (par. "written") on the tablet of the heart. Loewenstamm connects this sg. *ḥrš* totally with Ugar. *ḥrṯ* and postulates for this pair alone the basic Proto-Semitic meaning "cut." Thus the *ḥrš* in Jer. 17:1 is a by-form of the semantically identical *ḥārûṯ,* "engraved (writing)," in Ex. 32:16 (E), as well as Sir. 45:11; 1QS 10:6,8,11; cf. 1QM 12:3; 1QH 1:24,[8] which is entirely separate from "plow" in the OT and represents more than just an Aramaic form. "Arab. *ḫarata,* 'dig,' alongside *ḥaraṯa,* 'plow,' and Pun. *ḥrt,* 'engrave, write' . . . casts doubt on the theory that the form is an aramaism."[9] Sznycer[10] discusses the meaning "artisan, specialized worker" for Pun. *ḥrš.* The Targumim never translate *ḥrš* as *ḥrt,* but usually as *rd';* the Syriac, too, uses periphrastic expressions like "guide the plow" (*paddānā'*). The verb *ḥrt* occurs only twice in the Targumim; as expected, it means "scratch, engrave" (Lev. 19:28 [marks of mourning] and Jer. 17:1, our passage). Loewenstamm emphasizes the close relationship between "plow" and "incise" in Ugaritic, citing the sentence: "He plows his breast like a garden."[11] Finally, there may be a distant connection with the similar root → חרץ *ḥāraṣ;* cf. also *ḥereṭ,* "stylus," in Isa. 8:1; 1QM 12:3; but *ḥereṯ* in 1QH 1:24.[12]

Hamp

The meaning "plow" occurs primarily in the concrete sense. According to the law of the king in 1 S. 8:11ff., the Israelites will have to plow and harvest and do other work for the king (v. 12). Elijah found Elisha plowing when he called him to be his successor (1 K. 19:19). The oxen were plowing when the enemy attacked (Job 1:14). The sluggard does not plow and therefore cannot expect a harvest (Prov. 20:4). The law prohibits plowing with an ass and ox together (Dt. 22:10).

But plowing is also used in various contexts as a metaphor or illustration. The prophetic threat in Mic. 3:12, cited in Jer. 26:18, is still reasonably concrete: Zion shall be plowed and Jerusalem turned into a heap of ruins. In Isa. 28:24, *pāṯaḥ* ("open, break up the ground") and *śdd* ("harrow") refer to two different kinds of *ḥrš,* which, together with sowing, constitute the skilled labor of the farmer: God will so deal with his people. Am. 6:12 asks whether one plows the sea with oxen,[13] expressing an absurdity (par. "Do horses run upon rocks?"; on Am. 9:13, see 2 below). As a punishment, Hosea threatens Judah with plowing, i.e., hard labor (Hos. 10:11; on 10:13, see 2 below). In Ps. 129:3, the statement "The plowers plowed upon my back" refers to enemy oppression. Finally, Samson says, "If you had not plowed with my heifer," referring to how his wife was exploited to guess his riddle (Jgs. 14:18).

Ringgren

---

8 On the meaning of *ḥrš* in the Dead Sea scrolls, see S. H. Levey, "The Rule of the Community III, 2," *RevQ,* 5 (1964/65), 239-243.

9 Wagner, 59.

10 M. Sznycer, "Une inscription punique trouvée a Monte Sirai (Sardaigne)," *Sem,* 15 (1965), 35-43, esp. 38ff.

11 *KTU,* 1.5 VI, 20f.; cf. *WUS,* no. 980, and *KTU,* 1.6 I, 4.

12 See *KBL*³.

13 Conj. *BHK* and *BHS.*

2. *Plow = Prepare.* For the semantic development of the root *ḥrš* I, *KBL*³ gives as the third meaning "process, prepare." The word "process" is undoubtedly meant to lead to the fourth meaning, "technician." Loewenstamm[14] more reasonably associates it with "plow," citing Rashi's explanation that "plowing" is preparation for sowing. The meaning "prepare" appears only in metaphorical and ethical usage: to prepare (i.e., plan) good deeds, evil deeds, schemes (1 S. 23:9; Prov. 3:29; 6:14,18; 12:20; 14:22; Sir. 7:12; 8:2). The fundamental point of contact with "plow" is suggested by Hos. 10:13 ("You have plowed iniquity, reaped injustice, and eaten the fruit of lies") and Job 4:8 ("Those who plow iniquity and sow trouble reap the same"). Dalman[15] describes how closely related sowing is to plowing in the Near East, since the seed grain is plowed into the ground. Messianic fertility is illustrated by a harvest lasting until fall plowing (Am. 9:13). In the metaphors cited, *GesB* leaves open the question of derivation from "plow" or from "process." In Ezk. 21:36(Eng. v. 31) we find the expression *ḥārāšê mašḥîṯ,* "smiths of destruction," if the vocalization is correct. The Hebrew could hear both meanings in *ḥrš* simultaneously.

Hamp

3. *Craftsmen; Magicians.* a. The OT speaks of *ḥārāšîm,* "craftsmen," 31 times. The kind of *ḥārāš* can be further specified by the addition of *'ēṣ* or *'eḇen:* 2 S. 5:11; 1 Ch. 22:15 (both); Ex. 28:11 (*'eḇen*); 2 K. 12:12(11); Isa. 44:13 (*'ēṣ*); cf. 1 Ch. 14:1 (*qîr* instead of *'eḇen*); Dt. 27:15; Isa. 41:7; 45:16 (*ṣîr,* "idol"). The *ḥārāšîm* are mentioned together with *bōnîm* (2 K. 22:6; 2 Ch. 34:11), *ḥōṣᵉḇîm,* "masons" (Ezr. 3:7; 2 Ch. 24:12), *ḥōšēḇ* and *rōqēm* (Ex. 35:35; 38:23), *masgēr,* "smith" (2 K. 24:14,16; Jer. 24:1; 29:2, all referring to the deportation under Jehoiachin), and with *ṣōrēp* (Isa. 41:7; Jer. 10:9). Albright has a different interpretation,[16] deriving *ḥrš* from Arab. *ḥaris,* "watchman," and taking *ḥārāš wᵉhammasgēr* as "guardian of the prison." The *ḥārāšîm* can thus be workers of stone, wood, or metal (weaponsmiths, 1 S. 13:19; Isa. 54:16).

The *ḥārāšîm* are mentioned above all in connection with the building or ornamentation of the temple (or tent of meeting, Ex. 35:35; 38:23): 2 S. 5:11 par. 1 Ch. 14:1; 2 K. 22:6; 1 Ch. 29:5; 2 Ch. 24:12; 34:11; Ezr. 3:7, and as makers of idols: Isa. 40:19; 41:7; 44:13; 45:16; Jer. 10:3; Hos. 13:2. The theological point is that idols are *ma'ᵃśê yᵉḏê ḥārāš,* the work of human hands (Dt. 27:15), or as Hos. 8:6 says, *ḥārāš 'āśāhû wᵉlō' 'ᵉlōhîm hû':* they are not gods.

Ringgren

b. *KBL*³ lists an *ḥrš* III, "practice magic." In fact we appear once more to have a different root. The only likely OT occurrence is *ḥᵃrāšîm,* "charms," in Isa. 3:3.[17] Elsewhere a variety of words is available for magic (*lḥš, nḥš, kšp, 'nn*). This meaning

---

[14] P. 65.

[15] *AuS,* II (1932), 179-185.

[16] W. F. Albright, review of J. A. Montgomery, *The Books of Kings* [*ICC* (1951)], *JBL,* 71 (1952), 253.

[17] See the comms., most recently H. Wildberger, *Jesaja. BK,* X/1 (1972), *in loc.*

of *ḥrš* is reasonably well attested in Ugaritic (twice) as well as in Jewish Aramaic, Syriac, Samaritan, and Ethiopic, but not in Akkadian and Arabic.[18]

On the basis of the identical spelling, H.-P. Müller proposes an intimate connection between artistic craftsmanship and magic. "The root *ḤRŠ III* . . . illustrates a way of thinking in which technical craftsmanship is pointless without accompanying magic."[19] Heb. *ḥārāš*, "craftsman," he derives from this root. "To *ḤRŠ III* probably also belong the verb forms in Gen. 4:22; 1 K. 7:14, "work iron," and Prov. 3:29; 6:14 (with the obj. *ra'[ā]*), "work black magic (?)."

Undoubtedly such thought and activity were widespread in the ancient Near East, including Israel. But it must not be overemphasized, and in the case of the OT it must be remembered that Yahwism strictly forbade occult practices (Ex. 22:17[18] [Covenant Code]; Lev. 19:26; 20:27; Dt. 18:9-14; 1 S. 28:3),[20] albeit without being able to eradicate them completely, as the groups mentioned in Isa. 3:3 illustrate (similarly Jer. 27:9). In the person of the sage,[21] and in part also of the prophet and the oracle priest (as Müller and others show in detail), superstition could be disarmed and incorporated into Yahwism. This is shown particularly in P, where the artistic craftsmanship employed in fabricating the tent of meeting and the priestly vestments is ascribed to a charisma imparted by God (Ex. 28:3; 31:3,6; 35:26; 36:1f.). Hiram of Tyre was also "full of wisdom" (1 K. 7:14). The principle of theocentric causality even ascribes the practical lore of the farmer to special instruction on the part of God (Isa. 28:23-29).

All of this is quite in line with OT religion. But it is unlikely that the term *ḥārāš* applied to such persons included the notion of "magician." The 2 occurrences of *ḥrš*, "practice magic," in Ugaritic and the evidence of the late Semitic languages do not provide sufficient basis for such a conclusion. In the early use of the noun "craftsman" and the adj. "skilled" outside the Bible in Ugaritic[22] and Phoenician[23] there is no recognizable connection with magic. More likely, as is so often true in the Semitic languages, we are dealing with a different root. The derivation from Neo-Bab. *harāšu*, "bind, tie on,"[24] is uncertain.

Hamp

4. *LXX*. The LXX renders *ḥrš* I by *arətrián* (12 times), *tektaínein/téktōn* (11 times), *therízein*, and *litourgikós* (twice each); *aischýnein* (Prov. 20:4), *aloētós* (Am. 9:13), and *hamartōlós* (Ps. 128:3) probably come from misreadings.

The LXX clearly places the *ḥārāš* in the technological realm: *téktōn* (19 times; Vattioni discusses this equivalence[25]), *technítēs* (5 times), *chalkeús* (3 times), *oikodómos* (twice), and *architéktōn* (once).

Fabry

חָרַשׁ *ḥārāš* II → דמה II/דמם *dāmâ [dāmāh]/dmm*

---

[18] See the lexica, esp. *KBL*³.

[19] P. 80.

[20] Cf. P. van Imschoot, "Magie," *BL*², 1074f.; "Traum," *ibid.*, 1781.

[21] → חכם *ḥāḵam* [*chākham*].

[22] *WUS*, no. 976; *UT*, no. 903.

[23] *DISO*, 97.

[24] *AHw*, I, 324.

[25] F. Vattioni, "Il mestiere di Gesù," *Studi Sociali*, 2 (1962), 107-129.

חָשַׂךְ *ḥāśak*

Contents: I. Meaning; Occurrences. II. With Human Subject. III. With God as Subject.

I. Meaning; Occurrences. The root *ḥśk* appears in the OT only as a verb; it means "hold back, spare." This meaning is confirmed by the comparable use of *ḥśk*/*ḥsk* in Middle Hebrew and of *ḥ^a sak* in Aramaic, with no significant shift of meaning. The South Semitic cognates, Arab. *ḥašaka,* "knock in, fill in," OSA *ḥškt,* "wife, consort," and *mḥškt,* "ambassador," exhibit a more distant semantic connection. The latter appear to refer to persons who are "prohibited, inviolable," and thus members of a harem.[1] A cognate verb *ḥšk* appears in Ugaritic.[2] The identification of this verb, however, is disputed by Whitaker,[3] who discounts any occurrences of a verb *ḥšk* in Ugaritic, finding instead forms of *ḥš,* "hurry," followed by the prep. *k.* The uncertainty in Ugaritic, however, in no way affects the clarity with which the meaning is attested in OT usage.

The verb *ḥāśak* occurs 28 times, 2 of which are almost certainly due to errors in the textual tradition. In Ezk. 30:18, *ûḇiṯhapn^e ḥēs ḥāśak hayyôm,* the verb is certainly a mispointing for *ḥāšak,* "become dark."[4] In Ezr. 9:13, *ḥāśaktā l^e maṭṭâ mē'^a wōnēnû,* "you have held back from our sins," is awkward, and should probably be corrected to *ḥāšaḇtā,* "you reckoned less than our sins (against us)."[5] Of the remaining 26 occurrences, 13 appear in the Wisdom books of Job and Proverbs.

II. With Human Subject. In 19 occurrences of *ḥāśak,* a human being is the subject of the action, with the meaning "hold back, restrain." The object of this restraining activity is either a human being in the fulness of his personality or some physical faculty such as speech or movement. This gives rise to an extended or metaphorical meaning of desisting from certain types of activity, so that the verb acquires a moral connotation with respect to refraining from doing or saying certain things.

The more concrete meaning, "hold back, restrain," is well illustrated by 2 S. 18:16, where the soldiers of Joab are called off by a trumpet from pursuing the supporters of Absalom. The verb *ḥāśak* designates the act of "calling off" or "holding back" the pursuing troops. Isa. 14:6 describes the opposite situation: a victorious commander refuses to hold back his soldiers from pursuing a defeated enemy. In this satirical poem on the downfall of a tyrannical emperor, identified in v. 4 as the king of Babylon,

---

ḥāśak. G. R. Driver, "Problems in 'Proverbs,'" *ZAW,* 50 (1932), 141-48; *idem,* "Problems in the Hebrew Text of Proverbs," *Bibl,* 32 (1951), 173-197; F. V. Winnett, "A Monotheistic Himyarite Inscription," *BASOR,* 83 (1941), 22-25.

1 Winnett, 24.

2 *KTU,* 1.3 III, 18; IV, 11; 1.1 II, 21; III, 10; cf. *CML,* 138; *WUS,* no. 983; G. Rinaldi, "Ebr. *ḥśk,*" *BiOr,* 8 (1966), 126.

3 Whitaker, 266.

4 Cf. LXX, Vulg., Targum, Syriac.

5 Cf. *KBL*³.

the scope of his power is shown by his pursuit of his enemies, "without desisting" (*mᵉraddēp̄ bᵉlî ḥāśāk̲*).[6]

OT usage frequently extends metaphorically this direct meaning of "hold back" by a signal or word of command. Hence *ḥāśak̲* appears in injunctions urging others to perform or refrain from certain types of action. In Prov. 13:24, the wise father is urged not to hold back the rod with which he beats his son to teach him discipline. A similar appeal to the human will is found in Isa. 54:2, where the survivors of the Babylonian exile, who are to repopulate Jerusalem and the land of Judah, are urged not to refrain from pitching their tents in order to reclaim their homeland. This particular image is part of an exhortation addressed to the exiles, preparing them to return to Judah to reestablish Israel as a nation. Similarly in Isa. 58:1 God urges the prophet not to restrain his voice in proclaiming to his people the severity of their sins. Job tells his friends (Job 16:5) that if their respective positions were reversed—if they and not he were in pain—he, too, would find it easy to emulate them in alleviating (*ḥśk*) pain with comforting words. He insists, however, that his speaking in no way lessens (v. 6, *ḥśk*, "holds back") his pain.

The notion of restraining one's speech occurs in Job 7:11: "I will not restrain my mouth," because life is so brief and Job's sufferings so bitter. We may compare Prov. 10:19, where the one who restrains his lips is counted prudent. This theme of economy of speech is popular with the Wisdom teachers and appears in various contexts. The underlying notion is that the talkative person readily falls into any of a number of sins by revealing thoughts and feelings that are best concealed. Speech, like emotions, must be controlled; failure to do so quickly arouses hostility and resentment. This idea appears again in Prov. 17:27, where the one who "holds back" (*ḥāśak̲*) his words shows himself to have knowledge. By controlling his feelings and not putting them into words, the wise person avoids the enmity and bitterness that words spoken hastily or in anger would provoke. The underlying reason for enjoining such caution and self-control in speech is the need to keep in check emotions that too much speaking would betray.

The notion of restraining certain parts of the body is used metaphorically for desisting from particular types of action. This usage is exemplified in Jer. 14:10, where Israel is accused of turning aside from Yahweh. Here it is simply said that they have not restrained their feet from wandering away from him. By resorting to other forms and traditions of worship than those approved by Yahweh and by indulging in actions contravening the morality he has disclosed, Israel has failed to display the obedience Yahweh demands. Another situation in which refusal to hold something back takes on extended metaphorical meaning appears in Job 30:10, where Job complains that his friends and neighbors have not withheld spitting (*rqq*) from him, thus displaying their contemptuous disregard for him and his sufferings. Several passages speak of withholding property or possessions. Prov. 11:24 draws a paradoxical contrast between the generous person, whose liberality makes him richer, and the miser, who refrains from giving to others. His refusal to give what he should (*ḥōśēk̲ miyyōšer*) only makes him

---

6 *BHS*.

poorer. This may mean that one who refuses to give becomes spiritually impoverished; more likely a direct economic penalty is envisaged. Refusal to be generous and give gifts results in a failure to make friends and to build up relationships of trust with others. This paradoxical idea finds eloquent expression in Prov. 21:26: "All day long he covets greedily" (*hiṯʾawwâ ṯaʾ"wâ;* LXX *asebḗs* suggests the reading *ḥaṭṭāʾ* for *ṯaʾ"wâ,*[7] but the more neutral MT is probably correct as it stands), "but the righteous gives and does not hold back." The Wisdom teacher notes the paradoxical and contrasting results that follow from the two different types of behavior. Whoever shows by his attitude that he is out to make a profit and get what he can is disliked and distrusted; he receives no gifts and is not trusted in business. In contrast, one who gives generously makes friends and establishes relationships that ultimately redound to his advantage.

In 2 K. 5:20, we find a much more subtle expression of the Israelite conception of honor and privilege as they relate to the giving and receiving of gifts. The Aramean leper Naaman is described as seeking out the prophet Elisha in order to be healed of his disease; he brings an enormous gift of silver, gold, and lavish garments (2 K. 5:5). After showing Naaman how to be healed, Elisha refuses to accept any of the gift, thereby "sparing Naaman" (*ḥāśaḵ . . . naʾ"mān,* v. 20). Since the spiritual wealth of Elisha is regarded as greater than the material wealth of the Aramean commander, it is the privilege of the truly great to give to the less privileged. Elisha's servant Gehazi, however, covets at least a part of the proposed gift, and is punished for his greed by being afflicted with Naaman's leprosy.

The great religious and ethical importance attaching to willingness to give of one's material possessions is illustrated by two stories of the Hebrew patriarchs. In the Joseph saga, Joseph's success and his favor in the house of Pharaoh's officer Potiphar are shown by Potiphar's allowing Joseph full use of all his possessions. He withholds nothing in his house from Joseph's use (Gen. 39:9 [E], *wᵉlōʾ-ḥāśaḵ . . . mᵉʾûmâ*). Only his wife is excluded from this generosity, because of the special ties created by marriage.

An even more striking illustration of the total commitment and trust expressed by refusal to withhold anything, even one's most precious possession, is Abraham's readiness to give his son Isaac to God. Abraham's willingness to give to God is the central point of the narrative of Gen. 22:1-19 (E). Twice it is affirmed that Abraham's obedience to God is wholehearted because he is prepared not to withhold (*ḥāśaḵ,* vv. 12,16) Isaac, his only son, from God. This willingness displays Abraham's regard for God, for which he is richly blessed (vv. 16-18).

In Prov. 24:11, in a context with marked Egyptian affinities, the verb *ḥāśaḵ* occurs in an admonition whose precise meaning is obscure in a number of details. The second hemistich reads *ûmāṯîm lahereḡ ʾim-taḥśōḵ,* which may be rendered "hold back [asseverative use of *ʾim*[8]] those who are stumbling to the slaughter." If the text is pointed to read *ûmuṭṭîm lahereḡ ʾal-tēḥāśēḵ* (hophal ptcp. of *nṯh*[9]), it may be rendered "do

---

[7] Cf. *BHK*³.
[8] *GK,* §149.
[9] Cf. *BHK*³.

not hold yourself back from those who are being taken to slaughter," i.e., execution. The admonition would then enjoin help for those who are wrongly sentenced to death. Driver[10] would see here an extended sense of *ḥśk* in line with Syr. *ḥsk,* "preserved, kept safe." The NEB, following this suggestion, translates, "and save those being hurried away to their death."[11] This rendering does not specify the kind of misfortune described as *hereg,* "slaughter, execution." Most probably the reference is to capital punishment, very probably based on a miscarriage of justice. Setting aside Driver's suggestion, we would bear in mind the possibility that the admonition urges compassion on those under sentence of death, without any reflection on the justice of the sentence.

III. With God as Subject. In the other uses of the verb *ḥśk* in the OT, God is the subject, either directly or indirectly (when the verb is passive). In Job 21:30, for example, the wicked man is spared or held back in the day of calamity, a sign of the great mercy of God, who does not punish people as they deserve. Job 33:18 affirms a similar idea: as an expression of his mercy, God keeps people back from the pit; in other words, he spares them from the death they deserve on account of their misdeeds. In Ps. 78:50, God's refusal to act thus for the rebellious Egyptians is stated quite simply: he does not hold back their lives from death, but allows them to succumb to the plague he inflicts upon Egypt. The same general idea of God's holding back trouble and calamity for mankind is expressed more poetically in Job 38:23, where Job is shown the heavenly storehouses in which God keeps the snow and hail, holding them back for use in time of trouble and war.

In three other instances God appears as the subject of *ḥāśak* with reference to his power to control human actions. This striking usage has its counterpart in the belief that God can harden (→ קָשָׁה *qāšâ*) people's hearts, inciting them to rebel and disobey his will. In Gen. 20:6 (E), God reveals in a dream to Abimelech, king of Gerar, that Sarah, who had been introduced to him as Abraham's sister, was in fact Abraham's wife. Since he had taken her to be his wife, the fact that he had not had intercourse with her is revealed as an overruling act of God, who had kept Abimelech from touching Sarah to prevent him from committing an unwitting sin.

A similar understanding of God's power to control human actions is found in 1 S. 25:39. Nabal has incurred David's anger and hostility by insulting him and refusing to give him or his men any material assistance. David therefore threatens and plans to kill him, until Nabal's wife Abigail intervenes to dissuade David from such an act of murder. Within a short time Nabal dies suddenly, which is interpreted as a divine punishment. David can therefore thank God for having saved him for incurring blood guilt through an act of murder (*w^e' eṯ-'aḇdô ḥāśaḵ mērā'â*). God has overruled David's plans to prevent him from sinning.

Most likely the same idea is expressed in Ps. 19:14 (Eng. v. 13), where the meaning, however, is somewhat uncertain. The psalmist prays to God to keep him back from

---

[10] *Bibl,* 32 (1951), 188f.

[11] W. McKane, *Proverbs. OTL* (1970), 400-402.

zēḏîm. The simplest interpretation is to regard this as a reference to "arrogant actions." But *zēḏ* refers more usually to arrogant and insolent persons, which may be the meaning here. The LXX translates the noun as *allotríōn*, apparently misreading it as *zārîm*. It is quite possible to take the psalmist's plea as a request to be spared the unpleasantness of being confronted with and ruled by arrogant people. In view, however, of the markedly inward and spiritual tenor of Ps. 19B, it is more likely that we should interpret the request as an indication that the psalmist is so conscious of his weakness and proneness to sin that he asks God to control his thoughts and actions, to prevent him from committing such actions.

Clements

חָשַׁב *ḥāšab*; חֹשֵׁב *ḥōšēḇ*; חֶשְׁבּוֹן *ḥešbôn*; *חִשָּׁבוֹן *ḥiššāḇôn*; מַחֲשֶׁבֶת *maḥᵃšeḇeṯ*

Contents: I. 1. Occurrences; 2. Semantics. II. General Usage: 1. Fixed Idioms with Qal and Niphal; 2. Piel; 3. Negation; 4. Nouns; 5. Literary Use; 6. Linguistic Strata. III. Theological Usage: 1. Anthropological Statements; 2. Theological Confrontations; 3. Planning; 4. "Crediting"; 5. Names; 6. Gen. 15:6; 7. Ps. 32:2; 8. Eccl. 7:23ff.

I. 1. *Occurrences*. a. The root *ḥšb* appears in OT Hebrew in various forms. First is the verb in qal, piel, and hithpael, with the nominalized qal act. ptcp. *ḥōšēḇ* designating the profession of "fabric worker, embroiderer" (Ex. 25–31; 35–40 [P]) or "technician" (2 Ch. 26:15). The subst. *maḥᵃšeḇeṯ*, a feminine verbal noun with the prefix *ma-*, sometimes appearing as *maḥᵃšāḇâ*, is a term for an action or its result, a

---

ḥāšab. H. Z. Dimitrovsky, "Notes Concerning the Term 'חשבון,' " *Tarbiz*, 39 (1969/70), 317 [Hebrew]; G. R. Driver, "Technical terms in the Pentateuch," *WO*, 2 (1954-59), 254-263; M. D. Goldman, "Lexical Notes on Exegesis: 'Thinking' in Hebrew," *ABR*, 1 (1951), 135-37; F. Hahn, "Genesis 156 im NT," *Probleme biblischer Theologie. Festschrift G. von Rad* (Munich, 1971), 90-107; H. W. Heidland, *Die Anrechnung des Glaubens zur Gerechtigkeit. BWANT*, 71[4/18] (1936); *idem*, "λογίζομαι," *TDNT*, IV, 284-292; E. Jenni, *Das hebräische Pi'el* (Zurich, 1968), 226-28; K. Koch, "Tempeleinlassliturgien und Dekaloge," *Studien zur Theologie der alttestamentlichen Überlieferungen. Festschrift G. von Rad* (Neukirchen-Vluyn, 1961), 45-60; N. Lohfink, *Die Landverheissung als Eid. SBS*, 28 (1967); F. Nötscher, *Zur theologischen Terminologie der Qumran-Texte. BBB*, 10 (1956), 52f.; G. von Rad, "Faith Reckoned as Righteousness," in his *The Problem of the Hexateuch and Other Essays* (Eng. trans., New York, 1966), 125-130; R. Rendtorff, *Die Gesetze in der Priesterschrift. FRLANT*, N.S. 44 [62] (²1963); *idem*, "Priesterliche Kulttheologie und prophetische Kultpolemik," *ThLZ*, 81 (1956), 339-342; G. Rinaldi, "Ebr. *ḥšb*, sir. *ḥšab*, arab. *ḥasaba* 'contare' e *ḥasiba* 'pensare, ritenere,' etiop. *ḥassāb* 'computo,' " *BeO*, 5 (1963), 141f., 169; W. Schottroff, "חשב *ḥšb* denken," *THAT*, I, 641-46; D. Sperber, "On the Term חשבון," *Tarbiz*, 39 (1969/70), 96f. [Hebrew], VI [English]; *idem*, "Calculo—Logistes—Ḥasban," *Classical Quarterly*, 19 (1969), 374-78; E. Würthwein, "Amos 5, 21-27," *ThLZ*, 72 (1947), 143-152 = his *Wort und Existenz* (Göttingen, 1970), 55-67; *idem*, "Kultpolemik oder Kultbescheid?" *Tradition und Situation. Festschrift A. Weiser* (Göttingen, 1963), 115-131 = his *Wort und Existenz*, 144-160; → צדק *ṣdq*.

"plan," hence "invention," "piece of work" (with the technical term *ḥōšēḇ).* Two nouns appear only in later strata (Ecclesiastes, Chronicles, Sirach): *ḥešbôn,* an abstract formation meaning "accounting, investigation,"[1] and **ḥiššāḇôn* (pl. only), "invention, construction" (2 Ch. 26:15, referring to catapults and similar weapons).[2] For *ḥešeḇ,* "girdle," see Rinaldi,[3] *KBL*[3,4], and Schottroff[5] (from *ḥbš* by metathesis); a different etymology is proposed by Driver[6] (from *ḥšb,* "bring together"[7]). The root is also used to form masculine personal names: *ḥᵃšuḇâ, haššûḇ, ḥᵃšaḇyāh(û), ḥᵃšaḇnâ,* and *ḥᵃšaḇnᵉyâ.*[8] There is no demonstrable relationship with either of the roots *'sp,* "collect," or *ḥpś,* "seek."[9] The hypothesis of a homonymous root, possibly attested in Arabic, for the hithpael passages Nu. 23:9; 1QS 3:1,4 ("form an alliance, join together with"[10]) is superfluous.[11]

b. Outside of Hebrew, the root appears in Ugaritic (*ḥṯbn,* a noun meaning "account"[12]) and Phoenician-Punic (qal ptcp. *ḥšb*[13] and piel ptcp. *mḥšbm,*[14] a term for an official, "quaestor," or the like). The qal participle also appears in the expression *ḥšb n'm,* "benevolent."[15]

The root appears in Biblical Aramaic as a verb with the meaning "account (as)" (Dnl. 4:32 [Eng. v. 35], peal). As a noun, "account," it appears in Egyptian Aramaic (*ḥšbn,* const. sg.[16]), Jewish Aramaic (*ḥušbānā',* "accounting"[17]), Palmyrene (in the formula *lḥšbn,* "on account of,"[18] and the itpael inf. "be accounted"[19]), Nabatean (*kl' nḥšb byny lbynyk,* probably a hebraism, "be accounted as nothing," in the context of an agreement canceling debts[20]), and the Hatra inscriptions (*ḥšbn' dbyt b'šmn,* a title:

---

1 See I.2 below; on the place name *ḥešbôn,* "Heshbon," see *KBL*³, 346f.

2 See II.4 below.

3 Pp. 142, 169.

4 P. 346.

5 P. 642.

6 Pp. 255ff.

7 See I.2.a below.

8 See III.5 below.

9 Rinaldi, 141.

10 Goldman, 136f.

11 Rinaldi, 141; also Driver, 258f.

12 H. Donner, review of C. Virolleaud, *Le Palais royal d'Ugarit,* II [Paris, 1957], *BiOr,* 17 (1960), 181; M. Dahood, "Hebrew-Ugaritic Lexicography, II," *Bibl,* 45 (1964), 409; *Ugaritic-Hebrew Philology. BietOr,* 17 (1965), 58f.; *WUS,* no. 990.

13 *CIS,* I, 74, 4.

14 *DISO,* 97.

15 *KAI,* 160.5; 161.2.

16 *AP,* 81, 1.

17 *KBL*³.

18 *CIS,* II, 3913 II, 75, 115.

19 *DISO,* 97f.

20 J. Starcky, "Un contrat Nabatéen sur papyrus," *RB,* 61 (1954), 161-181; J. J. Rabinowitz, "A Clue to the Nabatean Contract from the Dead Sea Region," *BASOR,* 139 (1955), 11-14.

"chief accountant of the B. temple"[21]). In Syriac and Mandaic we also find the verb with the meaning "credit (to), plan,"[22] and the noun with the meaning "account."[23]

In South Semitic, the root appears in the Arabic verb *ḥasaba,* "count, account," and its derivatives, especially *ḥusbān,* "account,"[24] and in Ethiop. *haṣ(a)ba,* "think, account."[25]

The only possible Akkadian cognate suggested to date is *epēšu,* "make, do." But any relationships with *epēšu* and its derivatives,[26] which have a very broad semantic range,[27] can hardly be defined.[28]

In Egyptian, from the Pyramid texts on we find the loanword *ḥśb,* with the meaning "account, calculate."[29]

2. *Semantics.* a. The Hebrew verb *ḥšb* exhibits two basic semantic elements. The first is the element of calculation, with its modifications "account, compute, charge, settle (accounts)," thus "count, value, calculate." The second is the element of planning: "think out, conceive, invent." Both elements appear in the derived nouns, and can also be recognized in part in non-Hebrew cognates. According to Rinaldi,[30] they are the deposit of a semantic development from "think, account" to an "attività esternà," something like "frame plans."

Whether we can go on to hypothesize a basic meaning "weave" for *ḥšb* is dubious. Starting with *ḥōšēb̲,* "embroiderer," one who embroiders patterns on linen (in contrast to *'ōrēg,* "linen weaver," and *rōqēm,* "tapestry weaver"),[31] and *ḥešeb̲,* "girdle" (Egyp. *ḥśb,* "wrapper"; *ḥśb.t,* "pulled in"), Driver, like Goldman, comes to the following conclusion:[32]

> Primarily חשב means 'drew, put together'; and this, the literal sense, appears in התחשב 'was banded together' (Num. xxiii 9). In a secondary sense חשב is used of putting together figures, *i.e.* calculating or reckoning, and plans, *i.e.* scheming, so that it comes to mean also 'reckoned' and 'planned' just as נסך 'wove' means 'planned, schemed' (Is. xxxi 1). If this reasoning is correct, the meaning of חֵשֶׁב 'band' must be referred to the primary

---

21 *DISO,* 97f.; A. Caquot, "Nouvelles inscriptions araméens de Hatra (III)," *Syr,* 32 (1955), 54, no. 49, 3.

22 *MdD,* 154a; F. Rosenthal, ed., *Aramaic Handbook. PLO,* N.S. 10 (1972), II/2, 72; cf. also I/1, 7; I/2, 3 (cf. *KAI,* 215); I/2, 61.

23 O. Eissfeldt, *Neue keilalphabetische Texte aus Ras-Schamra. SDAW,* 1965/6, 34, line 2; *MdD,* 138b.

24 Wehr, 175.

25 *TigrWb,* 73a.

26 Cf. *GesB, KBL* [1,2].

27 Cf. *AHw, CAD.*

28 Rinaldi, 141; see I.2.b below.

29 *WbÄS,* III, 166f.; W. Vycichl, "Grundlagen der ägyptisch-semitischen Wortvergleichung," *Festschrift H. Junker. MDAI,* 16 (1958), 375.

30 Pp. 141f.

31 Cf. D. Barthélemy and J. T. Milik, *Qumran Cave I. DJD,* 1 (1955), 18-38, pls. IV-VII.

32 Pp. 258f.

sense of the root, as denoting binding or drawing tight, while that of חֹשֵׁב 'embroiderer' will come from the secondary sense importing a specialized skill in designing patterns.

*KBL*³ also gives "weave" as the primary meaning.[33] It is difficult to explain, however, why both *ḥēšeḇ* and *ḥōšēḇ* in its technical meaning belong to the same late stratum P. Nu. 23:9 (reflexive, "reckon oneself among") does not provide evidence of such an original meaning. But the semantic development outlined above is not inherently impossible.

If the verb exhibits a semantic development parallel to that of the noun derivatives ("embroiderer," "account," "plan"),[34] it is important to take note of the two semantic focuses "calculate" and "plan." In this context one may speak of "thought"[35] or "thinking,"[36] although we are dealing in general with an act of ratiocination[37] that is not made epistemologically distinct by use of *ḥšb*.

b. The semantic focus "calculate," especially common in the piel forms, substantive, and economic contexts (also outside of Hebrew), can be understood as the center of a semantic field that comprises primarily the verbs of counting (→ ספר *spr* and → מנה *mnh*), as well as the rare *kss*, "count off" (*miḵsâ*, "number, total"; Ex. 12:4; Lev. 27:23).

But *ḥšb* goes beyond the meaning of reckoning with numbers and quantities, referring rather to values and factors in general: weighing, evaluating, calculating, rational assignment of place and rank, the technical accounting of a merchant. This special sense of *ḥšb* is underlined by the occasional parallel use of verbs like → חפץ *ḥpṣ* or → רצה *rṣh*, "be pleased with," → בזה *bzh*, "despise," → מאס *m's*, "reject," and → נשׂא *nś'* or → כסה *ksh* piel, "forgive (*'āwôn*, 'sin')."

The second semantic element, "plan," often appearing with undefined object as in the use of the cognate acc. *maḥ*ᵃ*šeḇeṯ*, seems likewise to be dominated by this internal nucleus of calculated accounting. In contrast to → יעץ *y'ṣ*, "advise, determine, intend," and → זמם *zmm*, "devise, think," as well as the nouns *'ēṣâ—maḥ*ᵃ*šeḇeṯ—m*ᵉ*zimmâ (zimmâ)*, or in comparison with other terms in the semantic field of "planning," such as → דמה *dmh* piel, "liken, devise," → זכר *zkr*, "remember," → הגה *hgh*, "murmur, consider," and → ידע *yd'*, "know," the element of rational calculation shines through; when directed toward persons, it conveys the often noted "negative intention behind such 'plans,' "[38] an intention not so evident in technical contexts.[39]

The notion of rational, scientific calculation is inherent in *ḥšḇ*. Along with *kss*, it

---

33 P. 346.

34 Rinaldi, 141f.

35 Heidland, von Rad.

36 Schottroff.

37 Jenni, 226.

38 Schottroff, 644.

39 But see III.1 below.

is the only known Hebrew verb that refers to arithmetical calculation beyond mere counting, an observation supported by the late derivatives *ḥešbôn* and *ḥiššāḇôn*. From this perspective—to return to the question of Akkadian equivalents—it appears to be the case that Heb. *ḥšb* corresponds to the following Akkadian verbs: *kapādu*, "devise, plan, intend"; *ḫasāsu*, "think, remember, plan"; *manû*, "count, account, pay,"[40] and probably also *epēšu*, "do, make," which is etymologically closest to Heb. *ḥšb*, and exhibits a partial analogy in its specialized use in mathematical texts (*nipišu*, "[mathematical] calculation").[41]

c. The same semantic structure is reflected in the translations of the LXX. In three quarters of all the *ḥšb* passages, the verb is represented by *logízesthai* and its compounds—reserved almost exclusively for *ḥšb*—used as a technical term for "mercantile accounting": "calculate the value, account, calculate with reference to person and amount," more rarely "consider to be," not in the sense of classical Greek philosophy. The noun *logismós*, "account(ing)," is used similarly, albeit in only about a half of all the occurrences of derivatives of *ḥšb*. Here, too, the classical meaning "arithmetic" is possible only in the latest *ḥšb* passages.

The LXX exhibits great variety in its treatment of the other *ḥšb* passages. This applies above all to the passages that express the element of constructive planning (aside from special preferences, such as *poieín* in Est. 8:3, *dokeín* in Gen. 38:15, *hēgeísthai* in Job, and *mnēsikakeín* in Zechariah), which obviously cannot be expressed by *logízesthai* (cf. *architektoneín*, Ex. 35:32; *mēchanḗ*, *mēchaneúesthai*, 2 Ch. 26:15), or where the translators attach more importance to the emotional or subjective nature of the statement (e.g., *bouleúein* throughout Genesis; *dianoeísthai* in Gen. 6:5, etc.; *diánoia* in Isa. 55:9; etc.). This distribution of emphasis agrees by and large with the semantic range of *ḥšb*. Heidland claims [42] that the Hebrew term influenced the Greek above all by bringing out the "subjective, emotional, or even voluntary nature" of the "thinking" referred to, emphasizing emotion and choice in personal and emotional value judgments in a manner foreign to the thinking of the Greeks. This claim cannot be supported, however, because the meaning of *ḥšb* cannot be qualified as being fundamentally "emotional" or "voluntaristic," although it has to do with "planning, thinking, accounting."

II. General Usage.

1. *Fixed Idioms with Qal and Niphal.* The usage of *ḥšb* may be characterized as follows:

a. The active verbal forms and the verbal noun occur only with personal subject.

---

[40] See III.5.

[41] See W. von Soden, "Leistung und Grenze sumerischer und babylonischer Wissenschaft," *Die Welt als Geschichte*, 2 (1936), 509-557, esp. 531 = *Libelli*, 142 (1965), 75-123, esp. 97; citations will be found in *CAD*, XI/1 (1981), 248f.

[42] *TDNT*, IV, 284-292.

Apparent exceptions like Job 41:19,24 (27,32) (Leviathan); Ps. 52:4(2) (tongue); Prov. 16:9 (heart) are easily explained as metaphors (possibly also Jon. 1:4, "the ship threatened to break up"[43]). The activity designated is thus typically and exclusively human. This probably accounts for the absence of causative forms: with *ḥšb* it is impossible to conceive of an external cause or a dependent secondary subject.

b. The natural and almost instinctive element of such reckoning and planning makes itself felt in a substantial number of passages in which *ḥšb* is associated in a stereotyped phrase with *maḥ*^{a}*šeḇeṯ*, expressing in general terms the repeated and repeatable activity (pl.: 2 S. 14:14; Jer. 11:19; 18:18; 29:11; 49:20; 50:45; Dnl. 11:24f.; cf. Zec. 8:17; sg.: 2 Ch. 26:15; Est. 8:3; 9:25; Jer. 18:11; 49:30; Ezk. 38:10).

c. The personal and subjective element is emphasized in various passages by the addition of *b*^{e}*lēḇ*, "in the heart," stressing in these passages that the reckoning and planning is to be interpreted subjectively as an internal thought process (Ps. 140:3[2]; Isa. 10:7; 32:6 [*Q*, LXX]; Zec. 7:10; 8:17; also Gen. 6:5; 1 Ch. 29:18; Prov. 16:9; 19:21; Jer. 4:14; Ezk. 38:10).

d. The activity is nonevaluative when *ḥšb* refers to a material object. Isa. 13:17 says of the Medes that they "have no regard for silver and do not delight (*ḥpṣ*) in gold," i.e., do not reckon monetary value. According to 1 K. 10:21 par. 2 Ch. 9:20, in the days of Solomon silver "was not considered as anything" (*lō' neḥšāḇ*); it had lost its value. The notion of weighing and counting is also recognizable in Isa. 40:15,17, where we read: "Behold, the nations are like a drop from a bucket, and are accounted as the dust on the scales," and in the bitter statement of Job 6:26f.: "To reprove words—do you count on that? . . . You would even cast lots over the fatherless, and bargain over your friend" (cf. also Lam. 4:2; Dnl. 4:32[35]).

Besides taking account of quantities and values (which includes the passages using the piel, the niphal in 2 K. 22:7, and some usages outside Hebrew[44]), it is invention (Ex. 31:4; 35:32; 2 Ch. 2:13[14]; Am. 6:5) and categorization that appear in neutral formulations, for example: "Beeroth also is reckoned to Benjamin" (2 S. 4:2); "it is reckoned as Canaanite" (Josh. 13:3); "that also is known as a land of Rephaim" (Dt. 2:20; cf. Dt. 2:11; Lev. 25:31; Isa. 29:17; 32:15).

e. The negative overtones previously mentioned[45] appear when the verb has a personal object. More is involved than just "taking someone to be such-and-such," without further consequences, when Judah thinks the woman sitting by the wayside is a prostitute (Gen. 38:15), when Eli takes Hannah to be drunk (1 S. 1:13), or when Job's maidservants count him as a stranger (*zār,* Job 19:15), as we can see from Gen. 31:15: "Are we (Rachel and Leah) not regarded by him (Laban) as foreigners, for he has

---

43 Jenni, 228; for a different interpretation, see D. N. Freedman, "Jonah 1 4b," *JBL,* 77 (1958), 161f.

44 I.1.b; II.1.b.

45 See the discussion of Job 6:26 above.

sold (*mkr*) us. . . ." What is expressed is a personal devaluation, a categorization defining a personal and general assessment (*l*[e]). The depreciative comparison is often expressed by a noun with the particle *k*[e], "like": clay, earthenware, a speck of dust, nothing, zero, dross (conj.), cattle, sheep to be slaughtered, foreigners, an enemy, etc., but a double accusative is also found ("we esteemed him stricken," Isa. 53:4). It seems that this negative element was not sensed as merely the result of a given set of circumstances; it was obviously experienced and looked upon as an injury, an evil, similar to a curse in its effect. The negative connotation can also be seen in expressions of purpose (e.g., 1 S. 18:25; Neh. 6:2,6; Est. 9:24f.).

In many cases, the verb for reckoning and planning, calculating and classifying, has a negative object, most often *rāʿâ* (Gen. 50:20; Ps. 35:4; 41:8[7]; 140:3[2]; Prov. 16:30; Ezk. 38:10; Zec. 7:10; 8:17; cf. Ezk. 11:2; Mic. 2:1;[46] Ps. 36:5[4]; 1QIs[a] 32:6; Ps. 52:4[2]; Isa. 53:3f. Positive expressions are almost totally lacking.[47] Mal. 3:16 MT (*ḥōš*[e]*ḇê š*[e]*mô*, "those who value his name") is not without its textual problems, but could possibly be interpreted within this general framework (to reckon with the presence of Yahweh = to fear Yahweh). Prov. 17:28, "A silent fool is deemed intelligent," comments ironically on the deceptiveness of such esteem (cf. Neh. 13:13).

Our general observations are supported, finally, by the appearance of enemies as the subject of *ḥšb* in about a quarter of its occurrences. The frequent use of the preposition *ʿal*, "against," indicates the meaning.

f. The construction with an impersonal accusative object (sometimes double) and a dative of the person involved, introduced by *l*[e], appears to be a fixed idiom meaning "reckon something (as something) to someone's account," pass. "be reckoned (as something) to someone's account." An example that is also theologically significant[48] is Shimei's prostrate plea to David in 2 S.19:20(19): "Let not my Lord reckon to me (*ʾal-yaḥ*[a]*šōḇ-lî*) my guilt (*ʿāwōn*), or remember (*zkr*) how your servant did wrong (*ʿwh* hiphil) on the day my lord the king left Jerusalem; let not the king bear it in mind (*śûm ʾel-libbô*)." Variants and analogies include Gen. 15:6; 50:20; Job 35:2; Ps. 32:2; Ezr. 9:13 (mss.). The association with *ʿāwōn* might suggest a connection with the law of debts, or at least its terminology (opposite of *ṣ*[e]*ḏāqâ*). Among occurrences of the passive, we may single out Lev. 17:4: "As blood guilt (*dām*) it shall be imputed to that man" (cf. Lev. 7:18; Nu. 18:27; Prov. 27:14, "[His hypocritical blessing] will be reckoned to him as cursing"[49]).

2. *Piel*. The piel of *ḥšb* shifts the semantic emphasis to the result of the thought process.[50] Attention is directed to planning that issues in action ("A man's mind plans his way," Prov. 16:9), effective strategy ("He shall devise plans against strongholds," Dnl. 11:24), purposeful undertakings ("What do you plot against Yahweh?" Nah. 1:9;

---

46 See J. T. Willis, "On the Text of Micah 2,1aα-β," *Bibl*, 48 (1967), 534-541.

47 The theologically relevant passages are discussed in III below.

48 III.6.

49 Cf. I.1.b.

50 Resultative; Jenni, 226ff.

"They devise evil [*rā'*] against me," Hos. 7:15), absorbed calculation leading to the final outcome ("to understand this," Ps. 73:16; "the days of old," Ps. 77:6[5]; "thy ways," Ps. 119:59; "the son of man," Ps.144:3—probably in the sense of "discover, find out" [par. *yd'*]: "What is the son of man? You found out"), the concrete result of calculated planning.[51]

From here it is but a step to the technical use of the piel in a mathematical or commercial sense: "And they did not ask an accounting from the men into whose hand they delivered the money to pay out to the workmen" (2 K. 12:16[15]); cf. Lev. 25:27,50,52; 27:18,23 (instructions for settling accounts), as well as the Aramaic passages with the same meaning[52] and the substantives.[53]

The hithpael in Nu. 23:9 is unique: "Lo, a people dwelling alone, and not reckoning itself among the nations" (cf. *mnh,* "count," and *mispār,* "number," in v. 10 of the MT). Here, too, the notion of ranking hovers in the background. We are dealing with graspable quantities that can be counted and compared; this fact makes it possible to single out this one people from all the nations.

3. *Negation.* Negated usage is important because it directs attention to the frustration and disappointment of expectations that *ḥšb* normally raises. It is an extraordinary situation when people like the Medes have no regard for money (silver, Isa. 13:17), when silver is reckoned as nothing in the days of Solomon (1 K. 10:21 par.), when no accounting is required for expenditures for labor (2 K. 12:16[15] piel = the money is not accounted for; 2 K. 22:7 niphal). The failure to take any notice of the Servant of God (Isa. 53:3; cf. v. 4) and the lack of regard for human life (Isa. 33:8) reveal a lamentable state of desolation. According to Nu. 23:9, Israel's assessment of itself is quite extraordinary and in fact paradoxical. The element of calculation inherent in the verb appears particularly where the negation ("not to account") takes on a mathematical sense ("account as nothing"), as in the condensed formulation of 1 K. 10:21: *'ên kesep̠ lō' neḥšāb̠ . . . limᵉ'ûmâ* (cf. 2 Ch. 9:20), "there was no silver—it was reckoned as nothing." Isa. 40:17 is similar: "They are accounted by him as less than nothing (*mē'epes*) and emptiness (*tōhû*)," as is Dnl. 4:32(35): "All the inhabitants of the earth are accounted as nothing (Aram. *kᵉlâ*)." Cf. also the expression *kl' nḥšb* in the Nabatean contract mentioned in I.1.b. The same idea lies behind 2 S. 19:20(19); Ps. 32:2; and Lev. 7:18, which deal with the question of whether something (guilt, sacrifice) is to be accounted and put down as a quantity in being. The yes/no alternative points to an act of decision.

4. *Nouns.* The nouns *maḥᵃšab̠â* and *maḥᵃšeb̠eṯ,* usually in the plural and without the definite article, are also used in combination with *ḥšb*. They are strongly dependent on the meaning of the verb. Since this meaning is not restricted by the presence of an object, there is an emphasis on "creative calculation," i.e., "purposes, plans," with

---

51 On Eccl. 7:23ff., see III.8 below.

52 I.1.b.

53 II.1.d.

more stress on the technical element in late passages, as we see in the context of Ex. 31:4; 35:32ff.; 2 Ch. 2:13(14); 26:15 (cf. the use of the verb in Am. 6:5).[54]

The noun *ḥešbôn* I is not found in Hebrew until late. Ecclesiastes and Sirach use it in the sense of "calculated result," "practical outcome," "the sum achieved by 'adding one thing to another' " (Eccl. 7:27), "total"—a resultative sense already visible in the usage of the piel ("investigation," Sir. 27:5f.; 42:3). The reference in 1QH 1:29 is to sacred song; it is possible that *ḥešbôn* here means artistic rhythmic performance, as in Am. 6:5.[55]

The situation is similar in the case of the pl. *ḥiššᵉḇōnôṯ* (no sg.), which appears twice. It is not a technical term, as the differing contexts that determine its meaning show. In 2 Ch. 26:15—an attempted description using *ḥšb* 3 times: *ḥiššᵉḇōnōṯ maḥᵃšeḇeṯ ḥôšēḇ*, "engines, the invention of a skillful person," i.e., "a technological miracle"—the reference is to catapults and ballistae shooting arrows in defense of Jerusalem, for which there was no technical term.[56] In Eccl. 7:29, in the context of the *ḥešbôn* maxim developed in 7:23ff., it refers to a fundamental anthropological observation: "They seek out many devices" (i.e., ideas and strategies for self-realization).[57]

5. *Literary Use*. a. Forms of the root *ḥšb* are used with conscious repetition (i.e., more than once and apart from etymological figures) in the following texts or textual strata and complexes: JE, Gen. 50:20; P, Ex. 25–39; Lev. 25,27; Nu. 18:27,30; Dt. 2:11,20; only sporadically in the Deuteronomistic corpus and the Chronicler's history (2 S. 14:13f.; 2 Ch. 26:15; Neh. 6:2,6); more frequently in the prophetic writings, Isa. 29:16f.; Isa. 40:15ff.; 53:3f.; 55:7ff.; Jer. 18:8ff.; 29:11; Mic. 2:1,3; Nah. 1:9,11; in Job 19:11,15; 41:19,21(27,29); Ps. 33:10f.; 35:4,20; 40:6,18(5,17); 140:3,5(2,4); Lam. 3:60f.; Dnl. 11:24f.; and finally Eccl. 7:25ff. In most passages the repetition can be ascribed to deliberate usage; in a few it derives from the contextual material (lists, instructions, etc.).

b. The root appears most often in Wisdom aphorisms (Prov. 6:18; 12:5; 15:22,26; 16:3,9,30; 17:28; 19:21; 20:18; 21:5; 24:8; 27:14; Isa. 2:22?) and Wisdom poetry (Job 5:12; 6:26; 13:24; 18:3; 19:11,15; 21:27; 33:10; 35:2; 41:19,21,24[27,29,32]; Eccl. 7:23ff.; cf. Sir. 9:15; 27:5f.; 42:3). It also appears with great frequency in the preaching of the prophets (Hos. 7:15; 8:12; [Am. 6:5]; Mic. 2:1,3; 4:12; Isa. [2:22]; 5:28; 10:7; [13:17]; 29:16f.; [32:15; 33:8]; Nah. 1:9,11; Jer. 4:14; 6:19; 11:19; 18:8,11f.,18; 23:27; 26:3; 29:11; 36:3; 48:2; 49:20,30; 50:45; 51:29; Ezk. 11:2; 38:10; Isa. 40:15,17; 53:3f.; 55:7ff.; 59:7; 65:2; 66:18; Zec. 7:10; 8:17; Mal. 3:16; cf. Dnl. 4:32[35]; 11:24f.). There is no discernible affinity for any specific literary genre. Although they are not bound to a specific genre, words deriving from this root

---

54 Rinaldi, 142.

55 *Ibid.*

56 See P. Welten, *Geschichte und Geschichtsdarstellung in den Chronikbüchern. WMANT,* 42 (1973), 111ff.

57 III.8.

appear frequently in connection with enemies in the Psalms (Ps. 10:2; 21:12[11]; 33:10; 35:4,20; 36:5[4]; 41:8[7]; 44:23[22]; 52:4[2]; 56:6[5]; 88:5[4]; 140:3,5[2,4]; also 32:2; 33:11; 40:6,18[5,17]; 73:16; 77:6[5]; 92:6[5]; 94:11; 119:59; 144:3). The root is used technically (piel and niphal ptcp.) in priestly instruction (Ex. 31,35; Lev. 25,27; Nu. 18), and also occurs in passing remarks (e.g., Josh. 13:3; 2 S. 4:2; 1 K. 10:21 par. 2 Ch. 9:20; 2 K. 22:7). But it appears as well in various key positions, in part redactional (Gen. 6:5; 15:6; 50:20; Nu. 23:9; 1 S. 18:25; 2 S. 14:13f.; 19:20[19]; 2 Ch. 26:15; Eccl. 7:23-29; Jer. 18:8ff.).

6. *Linguistic Strata*. The question whether *ḥšb* belongs to specific linguistic strata or groups can be answered only in part. Its casual use in narrative and descriptive texts, in brief notices, in passages from the Psalms, in prophetic oracles, in priestly instruction appears to indicate that in the OT period *ḥšb* and *maḥᵃšeḇeṯ*—as well as *ḥešbôn*, to judge from extrabiblical evidence (Ugaritic, Aramaic, Sirach)—were everyday colloquial words. Passages like Gen. 31:15 and 2 S. 19:20(19) confirm this conclusion. The root *ḥšb* was the common term for the process of reckoning and planning, as well as matters having to do with commerce (money, debt), government records (persons and places), and the technical planning of certain enterprises (siege technology, inventions). It is therefore hardly surprising that Wisdom teachers above all made extensive use of the root—they must at least have been concerned with training and education in the fields just mentioned. That they then also took a theoretical interest in the nature and performance of these *ḥšb* actions is attested by the passages from Proverbs (e.g., Prov. 15:22; 20:18), and especially by the discussion of *ḥešbôn* in Eccl. 7:23ff. But this term for calculation and planning was also needed by prophets and priests for theological statements, as well as for anthropological and technological statements. Only in late texts (P, Ecclesiastes) and then only in part (ptcp., piel) does it appear to have taken on specialized meaning (cf. 2 Ch. 26:15).

III. Theological Usage.

1. *Anthropological Statements*. The act of calculating or planning designated by *ḥšb* is dealt with by the OT fundamentally from an anthropological perspective. In Prov. 15:22 ("Without counsel [*sôḏ*] plans go wrong, but with many advisers they succeed") and 20:18 ("Plans are established by counsel [*'ēṣâ*], and [only] by wise guidance wage war") we are still dealing with the consequences of faulty political planning, i.e., with the necessary conditions for the successful planning and execution of an enterprise, and in 21:5 ("The plans of the diligent lead surely to abundance, but every one who is hasty comes only to want") with commercial calculation and its effectiveness, but *ḥšb* quickly becomes the mark of how human nature expresses itself. Thus the first part of Prov. 16:9 makes the fundamental observation that the human will (*lēḇ 'āḏām*) plans or calculates (piel) the course of each individual life; Prov. 19:21 goes on to state that such plans are many. Both statements already suggest that these plans are subject to a fundamental appraisal. Whether they will endure is not just a matter of careful preparation and skillful execution. They have their own inherent qualifications,

which can also be brought to light: "The plans of the righteous are just; the counsels of the wicked are treacherous" (Prov. 12:5).

The negative overtones of passages where one human being reckons with another have already been mentioned.[58] The statements about enemies in the Psalms follow this lead. In the Psalms that speak of the enemies of the king or of the community (Ps. 21:12[11]; 33:10; 44:23[22]; 56:6[5]) the concrete political background is visible—not so in the case of the enemies of the individual. It may be asked whether the use of *ḥšb* here suggests an economic setting (cf. Gen. 31:15). The general and formulaic phraseology precludes analysis in terms of specific situations. The image of the political enemy appears to have influenced these passages. But their clear purpose is merely to express the destructiveness and danger of such people—against a background of fear when one is faced with being "totaled" (cf. 2 S. 24 par.).

The appraisal is more radical in passages dominated by the theology of creation, which voice a fundamentally negative judgment on all human planning. Cf. Gen. 6:5f. (J): "Yahweh saw that the wickedness of man was great in the earth, and that every imagination of the thoughts of his heart (*kōl-yēṣer maḥšᵉḇōṯ libbô*) was only evil continually, and Yahweh was sorry . . ." and Gen. 8:21: "The imagination of man's heart is evil from his youth," at the beginning and the end of the Deluge pericope. The plural suggests an uninterrupted chain of human schemes producing the most varied results—understood here as a fundamental human phenomenon and appraised theologically as marking the beginning of a movement to create an independent world in opposition to God.

Eccl. 7:29 reads like a commentary on Gen. 6:5 and 8:21: "Behold, this alone I found, that God made man upright (*yāšār*), but they have sought out many devices (*ḥiššᵉḇōnôṯ rabbîm*)," in the sense of calculated technological activity that is nevertheless contrary to God's purpose for mankind, superfluous, and purposeless.[59] Ps. 94:11 likewise—again in the context of creation (vv. 9ff.)—states that Yahweh looks upon the plans of humans as → הבל *heḇel* [*hebhel*], "a breath" (cf. Ecclesiastes), something insubstantial and ephemeral, worthless.

2. *Theological Confrontations*. Especially illuminating are the passages where *ḥšb* with a human subject is contrasted to *ḥšb* with God as subject. Thus Gen. 50:20 states climactically the quintessence of the Joseph story: "You planned (*ḥšb*) evil against me, but God planned (*ḥšb*) it for good." The verb *ḥšb* is used twice, once with the accusative plus *'al* (in the sense of free creative planning and calculating with and against a person), once with the accusative plus *lᵉ* (in the sense of appraisal and evaluation of an existing situation, with overtones of fiscal accounting for a person). In other words, a cruelly calculated plan became when carried out a factor in a higher and more comprehensive plan whose purpose was good. So taken, Gen. 50:20 is merely an application, albeit unusual, of the experience enshrined in Prov. 16:3,9; 19:21, which

---

[58] II.1.e.

[59] See III.8.

have as their theme the confrontation of two sets of plans. The most pregnant formulation is Prov. 16:9: "A man's mind plans his way, but Yahweh directs his steps."[60]

The same confrontation determines the structure of Mic. 2:1-5. In 2:3 ("Therefore thus says Yahweh: Behold, against this family I am devising evil") Yahweh reacts with a kind of recompense to the actions castigated in v. 1 ("Woe to those who devise wickedness . . . upon their beds"). It is the logic of offsetting accounts; contrary to Gen. 50:20, Yahweh appears as punitive judge.

Ps. 33:10f. extols Yahweh as creator and lord of the world, bringing his policies to fruition, who "brings the counsel of the nations to nought; he frustrates the plans of the peoples." His plan "stands for ever, the thoughts of his heart to all generations" (cf. Job 5:12).

Isa. 55:7ff. seeks reconciliation through appeal to forsake unrighteous plans and return to Yahweh's mercy and forgiveness. But this means acknowledgment of higher plans and preparations that are not identical with human goals: "For my plans are not your plans, neither are your ways my ways, says Yahweh. For as the heavens are higher than the earth, so are my ways higher than your ways and my plans than your plans" (vv. 8f.). Conversion and submission—culticly realized in the presence of God (vv. 6f.)—are the correct attitude, since God's plans have come to term (vv. 10f.).

In several passages fixed idioms are manifestly applied to the relationship between mankind and God: Hos. 8:12; Job 13:24; 19:11 (cited in 33:10); Nah. 1:9 (piel),11. The first two exhibit reciprocal usage. Yahweh's laws are accounted like those of a stranger (*k^emô-zār*) (for the idiom cf. Gen. 31:15; Job 19:15); Yahweh himself allegedly counts Job "as his adversaries" (Job 19:11 MT), rates him "as an enemy" (13:24; cf. Gen. 38:15; 1 S. 1:13; Job 18:3; Ps. 44:23[22]). Nah. 1:9,11 are singular statements describing a *ḥšb* that does not cease even in the face of Yahweh ("What do you plot [piel] before [*'el*] Yahweh," 1:9) and becomes Yahweh's declared enemy ("one plots evil against Yahweh," 1:11).[61]

3. *Planning*. If *ḥšb* and its derivatives are used for human planning and calculating, it is conceivable that they could be applied in this function to the person of the deity as well. We do in fact find statements that speak of Yahweh's plan in history and the world. This concept appears to have become a theologoumenon above all in the Jeremiah tradition, especially in such secondary passages as Jer. 18:8,11; 26:3; 36:3; 49:20,30; 50:45. Usually the reference is to concrete plans and purposes with respect to Babylon (51:29), Edom (49:20), and even the city of Jerusalem (Lam. 2:8). The concept is then extended to abstract planning and general purpose: Isa. 55:8f. ("high plans"); Jer. 29:11 ("plans for welfare and not for evil"); Mic. 4:12. In hymnic texts, God's plans become the subject of praise (Ps. 33:11) and worship (Ps. 92:6[5]: "How great are thy works, O Yahweh! Thy plans are very deep!"; Ps. 40:6[5]; 144:3). Ps. 40:18(17) is textually uncertain (cf. Ps. 70:6[5], which reads *ḥušâ-llî,* "hasten to me"). If the MT is correct (*$yaḥ^a$šōḇ lî*), we have here evidence for Yahweh's concern for the

---

[60] On Gen. 15:6, see III.6 below.

[61] On the enemies in the Psalms, see III.1; on Ps. 32:2, see III.7.

individual ("the Lord plans on my behalf")—a theological statement in its own right alongside 40:6(5).[62]

4. *"Crediting."* In the corpus of priestly traditions, *ḥšb* appears to have developed a third use as a technical term, in addition to the use of the participle ("embroiderer") in Ex. 25ff. and the piel ("settle accounts") in Lev. 25 and 27. This third usage appears in the niphal passages Lev. 7:18; 17:4; Nu. 18:27,30.

Ever since von Rad's study of "Faith Reckoned as Righteousness" and Rendtorff's analysis of the declaratory formulas in the laws of P, it has been assumed that the expression belongs to the "conventional phrases of the cultus" and refers to a "declaratory act" in which the priest accepts or rejects the sacrifice.[63] "To acknowledge that a sacrifice has been properly performed, however, is of course nothing more nor less than to 'reckon' it to the worshipper."[64] This priestly declaration is accordingly an expression and manifestation of a cultic "credit theology" that is also presupposed by decisions concerning what is clean and other cultic qualifications (entrance liturgies).[65] It is possible, however, to express some doubts.

a. The small number of occurrences (4, leaving aside Gen. 15:6 and Ps. 106:31 for the moment) is itself suspicious. Furthermore, Nu. 18:27,30 (which states that the tithe of the tithe of all offerings, which belongs to the Levites, is reckoned as the portion they themselves owe the priests: it "shall be reckoned to the Levites as produce of the threshing floor, and as produce of the wine press") is a general rather than a technical usage (niphal of *ḥšb* with *l*^{e} *k*^{e}, as in Isa. 40:17; Prov. 27:14 or Isa. 5:28; 29:16; and Job 41:21[29]). Thus Lev. 17:4 with its uniquely harsh condemnation of secular animal slaughter ("bloodguilt [*dām*] shall be imputed to that man; he has shed blood") and the explanatory interpolation in Lev. 7:18 about eating sacrificial flesh on the third day after the sacrifice ("neither shall it be credited to him; it is *piggûl*") remain the only evidence for such a priestly "credit theology." Closer examination shows that even these passages do not support the hypothesis.

b. In the context of Lev. 7:11-21, v. 18aγ is clearly parenthetical. If there is any technical priestly terminology here, it is clearly in the crucial statement of v. 18aβ: "he who offers it shall not be accepted" (niphal of *rṣh;* cf. Rendtorff and Würthwein). What follows are explanatory clauses stating that on account of this breach of regulations the whole sacrifice is rendered unacceptable and cannot be credited.

Examination of the basic text Lev. 19:5-8 shows that 19:7 refers only to the *rṣh* declaration and *piggûl* qualification; the *ḥšb* clause should be considered a secondary interpretative addition, expressing in cold economic terms the invalidity of such a sacrifice. The same is true of Lev. 17:4. Here, too, the *ḥšb* clause of this "verdict" together with its justification belong to a later stage of interpretation.[66]

---

[62] See III.5 below; on 1QM 14:14, see Rinaldi, 142.
[63] Von Rad, 126.
[64] *Ibid.*, 127.
[65] See Koch, 45ff.; Schottroff, 644f.
[66] K. Elliger, *Leviticus. HAT,* IV (1966), 222ff.

c. It is far from clear that these niphal passages have any theological relevance. The context in each case deals with acknowledgment and acceptance of sacrificial offerings, but nowhere is there any special emphasis on the *ḥšb* statement. On the contrary, it appears—in harmony with usage elsewhere—to refer parenthetically to a specific regulation applying to the priests (Lev. 7:18; Nu. 18:30) or the persons concerned (Lev. 17:4; Nu. 18:27), indicating that the matter is regulated in a particular way. Of course, theological implications are not precluded. But the passive formulation itself shows that no specifically theological statements can be made beyond the general determination of validity or evaluation (cf. Lev. 25:31).

As the passages cited show, the *ḥšb* idioms and the ideas associated with them found a place in priestly theory and practice, where they met with an organized mode of thought (reckoning, planning) that was highly valued. In 2 passages, *ḥšb* entered into the language used to rule on the validity of sacrifice, where it added the precision of "accounting" terminology (Lev. 7:18; 17:4). But these isolated passages do not support the hypothesis of a "credit theology."[67]

5. *Names*. The following names are derived from *ḥšb: ḥ^a^šuḇâ, ḥ^a^šaḇyâ, ḥ^a^šaḇyāhû, ḥ^a^šaḇnâ, ḥ^a^šaḇn^e^yâ*, and *ḥaššûḇ*.[68] All are masculine. Some 20 bearers of such names can be distinguished in the OT. The great majority are known to be Levites (about two-thirds being explicitly so identified). About half belong to the time of Nehemiah, appearing exclusively in Chronicles, Nehemiah, and Ezra. The names thus appear to be traditional Levite names. Their basic structure is the perfect of *ḥšb* plus a theophorous element, which constitutes the subject even in the passive forms (the presence of the nasal being unexplained), so that the name may be interpreted as a confessional statement: "Yah(weh) planned" or "planned by Yah(weh)." The suggestion that these "thanksgiving names" imply that "upright conduct was rewarded with the gift of a child"[69] is only one possibility among many, and not the most probable (Gen. 15:6; but cf. Ps. 106:31). There is a possible connection with Ps. 40:6(5) ("be concerned about"[70]), and especially the reference to Yahweh's wondrously kind disposition, experienced in the gift of a child—in other words, *ḥšb* is used in the sense of beneficent planning, probably in the context of creation theology as in Ps. 33:11; 92:6(5); 144:3; 1QM 14:14. The unexplained Akkadian thanksgiving names derived from the verb *manû*, "count," may offer an analogy.[71]

6. *Gen. 15:6*. Unquestionably *ḥšb* attained its greatest theological significance and influence in the context of Gen. 15:6:[72] "He (Abram) believed Yahweh, and he reckoned it to him as righteousness." The verse has been assigned to various literary

---

67 On Gen. 15:6, see III.6.

68 On *ḥešbôn*, see *KBL*³; on the formation of these names, see *IPN*, 20f., 33, 38, 188f., 244.

69 *IPN*, 188.

70 See III.3 above; cf. Rinaldi, 142.

71 *AN*, 192f.; cf. I.2.b.

72 Heidland, Hahn.

strata: E,[73] J,[74] JE^R,[75] etc. There is more agreement concerning its function. It refers back to 15:1-5, summarizes from a distance, interprets, and states the conclusion. It is a "solemn statement" and "almost has the quality of a general theological tenet."[76]

This conclusion is in agreement with the syntactic structure. The narrative consecutive imperfect (*wayyaḥšeḇehā*) still dominates, but it is introduced by a perfect with *we* (*wehe'emîn*), which—whether categorized as temporal ("and when . . .") or frequentative ("and repeatedly . . .")—is in turn subordinate to the consecutive imperfect.[77] The verbal suffix appended to *ḥšb* transforms the perfect clause into an object clause ("and the fact that Abram believed Yahweh"), thus establishing the dependency of the introductory clause on the main clause. Here *we* does not function as a tense marker; it serves instead to interrupt the narrative and establish distance; at the same time, in the manner of clauses linked by means of *we* (often with the effect of surprise[78]), it marks the transition to a conclusion introduced by a confirming perfect.

Gen. 15:6 makes use of three semantic elements: the phrase *he'emîn be*, "trust in, believe in"; the term *ṣedāqâ*, "righteousness" (i.e., being in proper order); and the phrase *ḥšb* with accusative suffix plus *le* and an accusative object, "account something to someone as something." Various interpretations base themselves on the origin of these three elements and the way they are combined.

Von Rad looked for the origin of the latter two elements (i.e., v. 6b) in "the conventional phrases of the cultus." On the basis of the *ḥšb* niphal passages, he arrives at a "process which results in a cultic judgment" occupying an important place in the cultus, a "declaratory act" performed by the priest in the name of Yahweh, using "declaratory formulae"[79] to state the cultic acceptance of the sacrifice. Considering the term *ṣedāqâ* and its use in the cult, he arrived at a "quite different aspect of the Yahwistic cultus": the "temple-gate liturgies."

In the central statement of these liturgies (in the form of some such declaratory formula as "He is righteous; he shall have his life" [Ezk. 18:9]) he thought to find once again a "cultic reckoning," although as he admits the verb *ḥšb* does not occur in these texts. In these two areas of the cult—sacrifice and entrance liturgy—he identified the traditio-historical roots of Gen. 15:6b, although he describes the passage itself as "polemical and revolutionary," breaking the cultic dependence on an act of sacrifice and transferring the "reckoning" to the "sphere of a free and wholly personal relationship between God and Abraham"—in other words, spiritualizing it.

Lohfink[80] criticizes von Rad's explanation on three points: (1) the traditio-historical setting is not clearly defined, i.e., the context of Gen. 15:6a and 15:1-5 is not taken into account; (2) the passage does not in fact represent a spiritualization of cultic acts

---

73 Since Wellhausen.

74 Cf. Lohfink.

75 Identified as the Deuteronomist by R. Smend, "Zur Geschichte von האמין," *Hebräische Wortforschung. Festschrift W. Baumgartner. SVT*, 16 (1967), 284-290.

76 G. von Rad, *Genesis. OTL* (Eng. trans. ^{2}1973), 185; cf. Lohfink, 32, n. 2.

77 W. Schneider, *Grammatik des biblischen Hebräisch* (Munich, 1974), §48.

78 *GK*, §154.

79 See Rendtorff.

80 Lohfink, 58ff.

but rather an interpretation of the promise to Abraham on the basis of cultic experiences and ideas; and (3) the term *ṣ*ᵉ*ḏāqâ,* "righteousness," does not occur in the context of "cultic reckoning," at least when sacrifice is offered (cf. Lev. 7:18; 17:4). Lohfink, following Kaiser[81] and others, thinks that the "oracle of salvation" was the realm of experience "that was drawn upon to interpret the ancient Abraham tradition," and that the interpretative elements of Gen. 15:6 all fit within this framework: confidence in the acceptance of the divine oracle, "perhaps in the form of a hymn of praise"; "correctness" (*ṣ*ᵉ*ḏāqâ,* Akk. *kittu*) in the oracular ritual; and the crediting or reckoning, consisting (as in the case of von Rad) in a "declaration of correctness made by the priest" ("cultic use of *ḥšb*").

Both discussions are imprecise at one crucial point: the meaning of the *ḥšb* phrase. Von Rad observes that *ḥšb* occurs only in the first of his cultic contexts (sacrifice), and focuses precisely on its use there as an interpretative element, reflecting cultic acts: "The difference between the declaratory formulae and the occurrences of the cultic term חשב is simply that the latter are found in directions to the priests, instructing them in the kind of tests they are to apply. The former prescribe the exact form of words on the declaration to be made to the worshipper."[82] But he is unable to explain the relationship of these very late and secondary[83] instructions dealing with peripheral cultic themes to Gen. 15:6. The entrance liturgy is the setting for *ṣ*ᵉ*ḏāqâ* and the oracle of salvation may well be the setting for *he'*ᵉ*mîn,* but neither is the setting for *ḥšb.* We can only conclude that in the use of *ḥšb* in Gen. 15:6 we are dealing with a situation independent of the P passages but parallel to them and to Gen. 50:20 and Ps. 32:2 as well, where *ḥšb* has been employed ad hoc to interpret a cultic and theological circumstance.

The specific contribution of this element to the total statement made by Gen. 15:6 may be described in two ways:

a. The summary nature of the passage is underlined. The act(s) of accepting faith is finally reckoned as a deciding factor in the relationship with Yahweh. The expression, probably shaped by notions associated with the law of debts (cf. 2 S. 19:20[19]),[84] calls the outcome of the events depicted a settlement of accounts in a theological sense, deliberately echoing commercial language—as the context shows. The interpretation of the promise to Abraham found in Gen. 15:1-6 uses such expressions and ideas throughout. Note the promise of great reward (v. 1), the question of how it is to be paid (v. 2), the negotiations about property and inheritance (3 occurences of *yrš* in vv. 3f.), and the demonstration of numbers (v. 5). All of this leads up to *ḥšb.* The reckoning of belief as *ṣ*ᵉ*ḏāqâ* documents the conclusion of the transaction. (On the

---

[81] O. Kaiser, "Traditionsgeschichtliche Untersuchung von Genesis 15," *ZAW,* 70 (1958), 107-126.

[82] Von Rad, 129.

[83] III.4.

[84] H. H. Schmid, *Gerechtigkeit als Weltordnung. BHTh,* 40 (1968), 108, n. 139.

commercial style of the pericope [cf. also Gen. 31:25ff. and esp. 18:20ff.] as an interpretative element, see the discussion by von Rad.[85])

b. Since the verb in its origin exhibits a personal and rational semantic structure in its usual subject, its use in Gen. 15:6 evokes a sense of what has been termed "inwardness, subjectivity, spiritualization," a transfer "to the sphere of a free and wholly personal relationship." The term that appears primarily in Wisdom Literature is here used uniquely to designate an extraordinary occurrence. Together with the (cultic?) notion of *ṣᵉḏāqâ* it serves to define Yahweh's momentary reaction theologically as an act of conscious judgment.

7. *Ps. 32:2.* Ps. 32:2 is structurally parallel to the macarism in v. 1, paraphrasing and explicating the cultic formulas appearing there; these in turn refer to the ceremony of absolution described in v. 5. The explication makes use of the phrase *ḥšb lᵉ:* "Blessed is the man to whom Yahweh imputes no iniquity, and in whose spirit there is no deceit." As in Gen. 15:6, the interpretative use of *ḥšb* conveys the idea that the act of absolution—active in v. 5, passive in v. 1—has personal consequences for both Yahweh and the person (*'āḏām*) concerned. Yahweh waives his inherent rights and refuses to impute iniquity (i.e., he declares it null and void); the person renounces his deceit. The point is therefore a theological subjectivization, involving the attitude of both Yahweh and his human counterpart. Once again, *ḥšb* is suggested by the context and its basic ideas of thinking and planning (cf. the close association of *ḥšb* and *'śh rᵉmiyyâ* in Ps. 52:4[2]), and from it the authorship of the Wisdom Psalms took root here.[86] Once again, *ḥšb* is used to give cultic acts a personalistic theological interpretation; their effect is traced to the inward mind of God (par. *rûaḥ*).

8. *Eccl. 7:23ff.* The nouns *ḥešbôn* and *ḥiššᵉḇōnôṯ* play an especially important role in Eccl. 7:23(26)-29, an aphoristic passage devoted to an anthropological theme. For the method of conducting his inquiries (*tûr*)—from the seeking to the finding of wisdom and knowledge—Ecclesiastes borrows the term *ḥešbôn,* "reckoning," with its fiscal overtones and with its double meaning: in the constructive sense of "plan"—as in 9:10, in the series listing the marks of life not found in Sheol, between "work" and "knowledge, wisdom"—and in the mathematical sense of "result, total, formula," as in 7:25,27, where it refers to the humanly unattainable goal of his intellectual labors. In this context it is impossible to arrive at a calculable result, a sum or a formula; the findings are negative (cf. the results of investigating relationships between the sexes in 7:26 and 7:28—quantified!).

The *ḥšb* terms serve several purposes for the Preacher: (a) They underline the failure of the wise person to arrive at a tangible result in his anthropological investigations, despite his adding one thing to another, i.e., proceeding methodically (Prov. 7:27),

---

[85] *Theol. des ATs,* I⁶, 390ff., 407f.; II (⁵1968), 404; Heidland takes a different line.

[86] For an attempt at a general interpretation, see K. Seybold, *Das Gebet des Kranken im AT. BWANT,* 99[5/19] (1973), 159ff.

although this would normally be expected (9:10). (b) Drawing on Gen. 6:5,[87] they relate these very efforts self-critically and pessimistically to the OT doctrine of creation. (c) In this passage they constitute a theological verdict, formulating a generalized anthropological insight on the basis of the corrupted relationship between man and woman: the human (*'āḏām*) striving after "many arts"[88]—inventions, devices, technologies, methods of self-realization—twists a world that was created upright. The subjection of his own work to this verdict typifies the thought of the Preacher.

On the Dead Sea scrolls, see Nötscher; on the NT, see Heidland and Hahn.

Seybold

---

[87] See III.1 above.
[88] M. Claudius.

חָשָׂה *ḥāśâ* → דמה II / דמם *dāmâ [dāmāh] II / dmm*

חָשַׁךְ *ḥāšaḵ*; חֹשֶׁךְ *ḥōšeḵ*; חֲשֵׁכָה *ḥašēḵâ*; חָשֹׁךְ *ḥāšōḵ*; מַחְשָׁךְ *maḥšāḵ*

Contents: I. Etymology, Distribution, Semantic Field. II. Ancient Near East: 1. Egypt; 2. Mesopotamia; 3. Ugarit. III. Literal Meaning: 1. Darkness and Creation; 2. Darkness in Israel's History; 3. Other Literal Uses. IV. Metaphorical Usage: 1. Darkness as Evil; 2. Darkness as Ignorance; 3. Darkness as Disaster; 4. Darkness as Death; 5. Darkness in Curses; 6. Darkness as Punishment. V. LXX. VI. Dead Sea Scrolls.

I. Etymology, Distribution, Semantic Field. The Hebrew root *ḥšk* has cognates in Phoenician and Punic, biblical and extrabiblical Aramaic, and later Semitic languages. The root does not appear in Ugaritic or Akkadian texts. In the MT the verb occurs only in the qal ("be/become dark") and hiphil ("make dark, darken"). The noun *ḥōšeḵ* means "darkness, gloom, blackness." Derivatives include *ḥašēḵâ*, "darkness," *maḥšāḵ*, "dark/secret place," and the adj. *ḥāšōḵ*, "dark, obscure."

The root occurs 112 times in the Hebrew of the MT, once in Aramaic (Dnl. 2:22). The verb occurs 17 times (11 in the qal, 6 in the hiphil). The subst. *ḥōšeḵ* occurs 79 times, *ḥašēḵâ* 8 times, *maḥšāḵ* 7 times, and the adj. *ḥāšōḵ* only once (Prov. 22:29).

ḥāšaḵ. S. Aalen, *Die Begriffe "Licht" und "Finsternis" im AT, im Spätjudentum und im Rabbinismus*. SNVAO (1951); H. Conzelmann, "σκότος B., C.," *TDNT*, VII, 426-433; E. Hornung, "Licht und Finsternis in der Vorstellungswelt Altägyptens," *StudGen*, 18 (1965), 73-83; *idem, Nacht und Finsternis im Weltbild der alten Ägypter* (1956); F. Nötscher, *Zur theologischen Terminologie der Qumran-Texte. BBB*, 10 (1956), 73-83; H. Ringgren, "Light and Darkness in Ancient Egyptian Religion," *Liber Amicorum. Festschrift C. J. Bleeker* (Leiden, 1969), 140-150; W. H. Schmidt, *Die Schöpfungsgeschichte der Priesterschrift. WMANT*, 17 (³1973); W. von Soden, "Licht und Finsternis in der sumerischen und babylonisch-assyrischen Religion," *StudGen*, 13 (1960), 647-653; D. W. Thomas, "צַלְמָוֶת in the OT," *JSS*, 7 (1962), 191-200; N. J. Tromp, *Primitive Conceptions of Death and the Nether World in the OT. BietOr*, 21 (1969); J. Zandee, *Death as an Enemy according to Ancient Egyptian Conceptions. Numen*, 5 (1960).

The semantic field of *ḥšk* includes the following: *'ᵃpēlâ*, "darkness"; *kēhâ, kāhâ* (→ כהה), "dim"; *laylâ* (→ ליל), "night"; *nešep,* "twilight"; *'ēpâ,* "obscurity"; *'ᵃlāṭâ*, "darkness"; *'ānān* (→ ענן), "cloud"; *'ārāḇ* (→ ערב), "be/become dark"; *'ᵃrāpel*, "darkness"; *ṣēl* (→ צלל), "shade, shadow"; *ṣālal,* "be/become dark"; *ṣalmāweṯ* (→ צלמות), "darkness"; *qaḏrûṯ,* "darkening." Antonymns include: *'ôr* (→ אור), "light"; *yôm* (→ יום), "day"; *nāgâ, nōgâ* (→ נגה), "shine, shining"; *nēr, nîr,* "lamp"; *ṣohᵒrayim,* "noon"; *šemeš* (→ שמש), "sun"; cf. also *hālal,* "shine," and *zāhar,* "be bright."

The root is relatively infrequent in the Pentateuch (11 occurrences), but appears more frequently in the Prophets (34 occurrences, 20 of which are in Isaiah). In the Writings, more than three quarters of the 62 occurrences are in Job (26) and Psalms (21).

II. Ancient Near East.

1. *Egypt.* The concepts of light and darkness (Egyp. *kkw*[1]) occupy an important place in the religion of Egypt.[2] According to the creation myth of Hermopolis, two of the eight primeval deities, Kuk (*kkw*) and Kauket (*kwk.t*), represent darkness. All eight originally emerged from chaos and darkness in the primeval ocean (Nun). These eight gods created light. Sometimes the roles of Kuk and Kauket are divided: Kuk brings light and sunrise, Kauket brings night.

The great hymn to the sun of Akhenaten[3] calls night the time of darkness, when thieves and beasts of prey go about undetected. Enshrouded in darkness, the earth is still. At dawn, however, the darkness is driven back and a seemingly dead world recovers its normal rhythm and vitality.

This daily alternation of darkness and light is understood as a daily renewal of the creative struggle of light against darkness, with each sunrise a reenactment of the primeval victory of light. Apophis, dragon of darkness, is defeated by Re and his company.[4]

The Egyptian netherworld is described as a place of darkness. Akhenaten's death is described in terms of sundown and darkness, and Amon's rise to power after him in terms of light.[5] One of the Coffin texts[6] refers to the deceased as entering the dark realm of Nun confident in the help of Hu and Sia.

Light and darkness also become metaphors for health and suffering. The sun-god gives light and life both to the living and to the dead in the netherworld, through which the sun boat makes its nightly journey toward the dawn.

According to Hornung,[7] darkness was considered an outward sign of disaster, and

---

1 *WbÄS,* V, 142ff.
2 Ringgren; Hornung; Zandee, 88-94.
3 *ANET*³, 369-71.
4 Ringgren, 144f.
5 *Ibid.*, 147f.
6 *CT,* II, spell 80.
7 E. Hornung, "Dunkelheit," *LexÄg,* I, 1153f.

from the Amarna period on served as a metaphor for affliction and separation from the gods.

Mitchel

2. *Mesopotamia.* Akkadian has several terms for darkness, essentially synonymous in their metaphorical meaning: (1) *ekletu(m)*[8] and (2) *uklu(m),* from the verb *eklu(m),* "be/become dark," both appearing only in Babylonian; (3) *eṭutu* (Late Babylonian and Assyrian), from a verb *eṭû,* likewise meaning "be/become dark"; and (4) *da'ummatu(m)* (only Babylonian), from *da'āmu(m)* I, "be dusky." In Sumerian, the word for darkness is *kukkú*; it is represented by a double writing of the sign GI_6, which by itself means "black" and "night." For other terms, often obscure, see the lexicons' discussion of entries in lexical lists; for *ganzir,* "entrance to the netherworld, darkness," see *CAD,* V (1956), 43b.

In Babylonian and Assyrian, darkness is always seen as negative and threatening to humans; only in Sumerian do we find the association "dark = cool" in a positive description of a temple chamber.[9] In omen interpretations hunger and darkness are closely connected; "he will walk in constant darkness" stands in contrast to "he will be rich." Darkness surrounds the sick person or afflicts his body; he prays that a god "may pluck out his darkness."

The face is often said to darken in threatening situations. Curses contain the wish that the person cursed "wander in perpetual darkness" or that "bright day become for him deep darkness." The bright light of day is contrasted to the darkness of death. Special note should be taken of the historical omens associated with King Sargon of Akkad, where we read: "The sacrificial liver of Sargon, who entered into darkness, and for whom then light shone forth," and: " . . . who wandered through darkness and then saw light."[10] In his journey to Utnapishtim, Gilgamesh conquered an obstacle never before conquered by a human being: he traveled for twelve double hours through the absolute darkness within the mountains until he "emerged before the dawn."[11]

Incantation texts contain numerous statements indicating that darkness is the preferred realm of demons. They "sit in the darkness" and "fly like birds of night in the place of darkness." Demons are compared to dense clouds or dust storms; even in bright daylight they bring darkness, especially for any sick person they attack. Demons travel quick as lightning in the darkness; they are said to be halted in the tomb.

We gain the impression that demons are intimately associated with the realm of darkness proper, the netherworld, which is often called the "house of darkness." There the spirits of the dead (*eṭemmu*) dwell in darkness and see no light. On the other hand, in Sumerian hymns to the sun-god Utu or his son Gibil we find the statement that he brings light to the netherworld, the place of darkness; he is also called the torch of Arallu, the netherworld. These statements probably derive from the idea that, after

---

[8] Entered as *ikletu* in *CAD,* VII (1960), 60f.

[9] Å. W. Sjöberg, *The Collection of the Sumerian Temple Hymns. TCS,* 3 (1969), 57.

[10] V. Scheil, "Nouveaux présages tirés du Foie," *RA,* 27 (1928), 151; W. G. Shileico, "Ein Omentext Sargons von Akkad und sein Nachklang bei römischen Dichtern," *AfO,* 5 (1928), 216.

[11] Gilg. IX.

setting in the evening, the sun-god passes through the netherworld; this idea is probably also connected with the epithets "lord of the spirits of the dead" and "lord of the dead and the living."

Illumination of darkness in the context of establishing order and justice on the earth is also ascribed to a series of other gods such as Nusku, Nabu, Ninurta, and Adad. In particular the moon-god Sin is extolled as illuminator of the darkness. Was the relatively weak light of the moon-god of such great importance to the Babylonians because it kept the darkness of night from turning into the darkness of the netherworld, and thus becoming the unimpeded domain of demons, which are often termed unresting *eṭemmū* (spirits of the dead)? In any event, light is the enemy of demons, and Šamaš is said to keep them at a distance. This would also explain the peril perceived in the night of the new moon and especially in eclipses of the sun or moon, during which everyone was exposed to arbitrary attack on the part of demons, which could not be influenced by magic in advance. This would account for the intense concern with eclipses, totally absent in the OT, which would be directly related to the religious world of Sumerian and Babylonian cosmology.

Lutzmann

3. *Ugarit.* There is no certain mention of darkness in the Ugaritic texts. In *KTU*, 1.4 VII, 54f., the messenger of the gods *Gpn-w'ugr* is called *bn ǵlmt* and *bn ẓlmt.* If these are not proper names, they might be translated "son of seclusion" (cf. Heb. *'ālam*) and "son of darkness" (cf. Heb. *ṣalmāweṯ*), referring to the double deity as the offspring of the god of the netherworld.[12]

Ringgren

III. Literal Meaning.

1. *Darkness and Creation*. a. Any theological discussion of the concept of darkness must begin with Gen. 1 (P), where v. 2 presumes darkness to be one of the constitutive elements of chaos: " . . . and darkness was upon the face of *t^ehôm*." Although the prior existence of darkness is assumed, so that it is not a part of God's creation (in apparent contrast to Isa. 45:7, "I form light and create darkness," although here the context clearly argues against a dualistic view that would see darkness as an alien power in the universe), it is more than the absence of light (although passages such as Am. 5:18,20 describe it as the absence of light). It possesses a quality of its own that unmitigated makes it inimical to life. Therefore something must be done with it before the earth can be habitable.

According to Gen. 1:3f., God created light and "separated (→ בדל *bdl* hiphil) the light from the darkness." The separation is conceived in spatial terms, at least in Job 26:10 and 38:19f. In the former verse, Job (or Bildad?) says that God "described a circle upon the face of the waters at the boundary between light and darkness." This circle must be the horizon (cf. Prov. 8:27, → חוג *ḥûg* [*chûgh*]). In the latter passage,

[12] J. C. de Moor, *The Seasonal Pattern in the Ugaritic Myth of Ba'alu. AOAT,* 16 (1971), 172.

Yahweh personifies light and darkness, asking Job whether he knows the abode of each, whence they return after completing their work. Thus the first day of creation not only separated light from darkness but also assigned each its own dwelling place.

But the concept is obviously temporal as well. At daybreak darkness returns to its abode while light comes forth from its home; at night the process is reversed. At creation, therefore, darkness was not abolished but subordinated. It was not called into being or seen as "good," but the act of separation gave it a place in the ordering of the cosmos.

Gen. 1:5 goes on to say that God "called the darkness night." This naming is more than an act of identification; by naming darkness, God characterized it, expressed its nature and even indicated his control over it. Only by naming darkness does God endow it with complete existence (cf. again Isa. 45:7), as comparison with EnEl I, 1f. shows. Having made light and darkness separate entities, on the fourth day of creation he put them under the "rule" of the heavenly bodies, which were "to separate the light from the darkness" (Gen. 1:18). The function of darkness in the cosmos finds further expression in such texts as Ps. 104:20, where it is the function of light and darkness to mark time for the daily routine of man and beast.

b. The association of darkness with creation naturally has a bearing on its nature. But beyond that, darkness is spoken of as "falling" (*napal,* Gen. 15:12) upon Abram and as "silencing" (*ṣmt,* Job 23:17); one may be "thrust" (*hdp,* Job 18:18) or "perish" (*dmm,* 1 S. 2:9) in it. Darkness "covers" (*kāsâ,* Is. 60:2) things and thus can serve as a place of escape (Ps. 139:11); therefore the wicked work in darkness (Job 24:16).

People are spoken of as "walking" (*hālak,* Ps. 82:5; Eccl. 2:14; Isa. 9:1[Eng. v. 2]; 50:10), "sitting" (*yāšab,* Ps. 107:10; 143:3; Isa. 42:7; Mic. 7:8), and "groping" (*mšš,* Job 12:25) in darkness. Darkness is often caused by "clouds" (2 S. 22:12 par. Ps. 18:12[11]; Isa. 5:30), and so the two words are frequently associated in the OT. It can also be caused by a swarm of locusts (Ex. 10:15) or by the extinguishing of a lamp (Job 18:6; 29:3). Though darkness can be dispelled by a human being (Job 28:3), the sun (Ps. 112:4), or simply "light" (Isa. 58:10), it is primarily and finally under the control of God (2 S. 22:29 par. Ps. 18:29[28]; Job 19:8; Isa. 42:16; Jer. 13:16).[13] Darkness is inferior when compared to light (Eccl. 2:13).

c. The OT is emphatic that darkness is under God's control; this has been so from the very first, when God stripped it of its arbitrariness by including it in his work of creation.[14] As mentioned above, he separated it, named it, and placed it under the rule of the heavenly bodies (Gen. 1:4f.,18). Am. 5:8 ("he darkens the day into night") also presupposes God's direct control over the alternation of day and night. An illustration of God's power over darkness is provided by the ninth of the Egyptian plagues (Ex. 10:21f.): at God's command, Moses stretched out his hand toward heaven, and "there was thick darkness (*ḥōšek-'ªpēlâ*) in all the land of Egypt three days." This was all the more astonishing because Pharaoh, the son and representative of the sun-

---

[13] For further discussion, see below.

[14] H. W. Huppenbauer, "Finsternis," *BHHW,* I, 482.

god, was considered the illuminator of his land.[15] Before the God of Israel, Pharaoh and Re were powerless. Ps. 105:28 recalls this episode along with other events fundamental to the creation of the nation of Israel.

Even in the wilderness, God demonstrated his power over darkness by using it to protect his people (Ex. 14:20; cf. Josh. 24:7). According to Deutero-Isaiah, the same phenomenon would be repeated in Israel's second exodus, from Babylon: "I will turn the darkness (*maḥšāḵ*) before them into light" (Isa. 42:16). Ps. 18:29(28) par. says: "My God lightens (*ngh*) my darkness"; and elsewhere in the Psalms the same confession is repeated: "Thou makest darkness, and it is night" (Ps. 104:20). In fact, in the presence of Yahweh darkness loses its essence: "Even the darkness is not dark to thee, the night is as bright as the day" (Ps. 139:12). Job, too, confesses God's control over darkness: "He uncovers the deeps (*ʿamuqôṯ*) out of darkness, and brings deep darkness to light" (Job 12:22); "He has set darkness upon my paths" (Job 19:8; cf. 26:10).

Three prophetic texts are important in this connection. Isa. 45:7 (see above) asserts the universality of God's creative and controlling power; not even darkness lies outside his dominion. Offering a last chance for repentance, Jeremiah says to Judah: "Give glory to Yahweh your God before he brings darkness . . . and while you look for light he turns it into gloom and makes it deep darkness" (Jer. 13:16).

The sole occurrence of the term for darkness in Biblical Aramaic (*ḥašôḵā'*) states that God has all wisdom and reveals everything that is hidden: "He knows what is in the darkness, and the light dwells with him" (Dnl. 2:22). What is dark to mankind is known to God; in truth darkness does not exist for him, because he controls it.

2. *Darkness in Israel's History.* Darkness in the literal sense plays an important role in several crucial events in the national history of Israel. The first is Yahweh's covenant with Abraham, recorded in Gen. 15. The age-old ritual was accompanied by great darkness (*ḥašēḵâ gᵉḏōlâ,* v. 12). This prototype was followed in the later covenants between Yahweh and his people described in Ex. 20 and Dt. 5. The darkness apparently represented the "terror of Yahweh," prefiguring the symbolic darkness into which the covenant breaker would be cast.

Darkness also played a key role in the plagues preceding the deliverance of the Israelites from Egyptian servitude. The Egyptians considered darkness the realm of evil, a fact that made the last three plagues especially effective. The eighth plague was a swarm of locusts that "covered the face of the whole land, so that the land was darkened" (*watteḥšak,* Ex. 10:15). The plague of locusts in Joel 2:2 with its accompanying darkness clearly recalls this passage. The ninth plague was even more severe: it was a darkness "to be felt" (*wᵉyāmēš ḥōšeḵ,* Ex. 10:21), a "thick darkness" (*ḥōšeḵ-'apēlâ*) lasting three days (Ex. 10:22). This darkness struck directly against the great sun-god of Egypt. It also furnishes the background for a proper understanding of Ezekiel's lament over Pharaoh (Ezk. 32:1-16), an incantation designed to send Egypt and all it represents to the netherworld. Ezk. 32:8 states expressly: "All the bright lights of heaven will I make dark over you, and put darkness upon your land." Thus

---

[15] *ANET*[3], 431.

darkness and other portents become harbingers of judgment. The same elements appear together in Joel 3:4(2:31), describing the day of Yahweh.

Just before Israel's miraculous crossing of the Sea of Reeds, God again used darkness in Israel's behalf, this time to protect the people from the pursuing Egyptians (Ex. 14:20; cf. Josh. 24:7).

Just as darkness was part of the covenant ceremony between God and Abraham, it also played an important role in the Sinai theophany associated with the giving of the law. Dt. 4:11 summarizes what took place: "And you came near and stood at the foot of the mountain, while the mountain burned with fire to the heart of heaven, wrapped in darkness (*ḥōšek*), cloud, and gloom" (cf. Dt. 5:23). Ex. 20:21 uses the word *ʿarāpel*. Collocation of terms for "darkness" is characteristic of theophanies.[16]

Darkness is mentioned again on one occasion during the conquest. Rahab, speaking of the Israelite spies, says to the king of Jericho: "When the gate was to be closed, at dark (*baḥōšek*), the men went out" (Josh. 2:5). Although the expression is used here only in its literal sense, it is worth noting that once again darkness protected the Israelites before a crucial battle.

3. *Other Literal Uses*. The derived noun *maḥšāk* is best translated "dark place." It usually refers to a place that is literally dark. In Ps. 74:20, for example, we read that "the dark places of the land (*maḥašakkê-'ereṣ*) are full of the habitations of violence," probably as hiding places for the violent (or their victims?). Ps. 143:3 says, "The enemy . . . has made me sit in darkness (*maḥašakkîm*) like those long dead," an expression probably quoted directly in Lam. 3:6. The term may refer to actual imprisonment or symbolically to the realm of the dead as a place of darkness.

That *ḥōšek*, too, could be thought of as a dark place may be deduced from the parallelism in Isa. 45:3: "I will give you the treasures of darkness (*ḥōšek*) and the hoards in secret places (*mistārîm*)," i.e., treasures hidden in dark places (cf. Job 3:21; Prov. 2:4). When the psalmist exclaims, "Let only darkness cover me" (Ps. 139:11), he must also have been thinking of darkness as a place of escape or concealment.

b. Darkness is the sphere of the wicked. Prov. 2:13 speaks of the wicked who forsake the paths of uprightness "to walk in the ways of darkness (*darkê-ḥōšek*)." It is obviously quite natural for evil to seek the concealment of darkness. Job 24:13-17 elaborates on this theme with specific examples: murderers kill in the dark, thieves steal at night, adulterers disguise themselves at twilight, and people break into houses in the dark (*ḥōšek*), "for deep darkness (*ṣalmāweṯ*) is morning to all of them; for they are friends with the terrors of deep darkness (*ṣalmāweṯ*)." Another example appears in Isa. 29:15, where the prophet describes the conspirators planning a revolt against Assyria: "Woe to those who hide deep from Yahweh their counsel, whose deeds are in the dark (*maḥšāk*)." Ezk. 8:12 reports the prophet's vision in which he saw the elders of Israel practicing their abominations "in the dark" (*baḥōšek*). In Job 34:22,

[16] See below.

Elihu says of such deeds: "There is no gloom (ḥōšeḵ) or deep darkness (ṣalmāweṯ) where evildoers may hide themselves"—all must appear before God's judgment.

c. Interestingly enough, darkness describes not only the sphere of the wicked but also the abode of God, especially when he reveals himself in a theophany. The locus classicus is 2 S. 22:8-16 par. Ps. 18:8-16(7-15). After a description of God's appearance in smoke, fire, and lightning, v. 12(11) states: "He made darkness (ḥōšeḵ) around him his canopy, thick clouds, a gathering of water." Despite minor textual problems, it is clear that the darkness of the clouds is the tent in which God shrouds his majesty. This darkness conceals God from human sight. As was mentioned above, when the law was given at Sinai the majesty of Yahweh was veiled in darkness (several synonyms) and clouds (Dt. 4:11; 5:23; cf. Ex. 20:18,21). At the dedication of the temple, Solomon reminded the people that Yahweh had said he would dwell in darkness (ʿᵃrāpel) (1 K. 8:12 par. 2 Ch. 6:1). Both Eliphaz (Job 22:13f.) and Ps. 97:2 describe God as being wrapped in thick clouds and darkness.

IV. Metaphorical Usage.

1. *Darkness as Evil.* In the prophets, darkness is sometimes used as a symbol of evil. But here light and darkness are more than images or symbols; one has the sense that there is an inherent relationship between light and darkness on the one hand, good and evil on the other.[17] An illustration appears in Isa. 5:20: "Woe to those who call evil good and good evil, who put darkness for light and light for darkness, who put bitter for sweet and sweet for bitter!" These are people who confuse ethical distinctions.

The image can also suggest false worship, as in Isa. 45:18f.: "I am Yahweh, and there is no other. I did not speak in secret, in a land of darkness (bimᵉqôm ʾereṣ ḥōšeḵ); I did not say to the offspring of Jacob, 'Seek me in chaos (ṯōhû) [or: in vain].' " The point seems to be that Yahweh's revelation did not take place in secret; it is open and accessible. It is unnecessary to take refuge in magic or, as v. 20 suggests, worship wooden idols. Above all the verse probably refers to Yahweh's open appearance, in contrast to working in secret. Ezk. 8:12 combines the notion of deeds done in secret with the idea of idolatrous evil: "Have you seen what the elders of the house of Israel are doing in the dark, every man in his room of pictures?"

2. *Darkness as Ignorance.* Especially in Wisdom Literature, darkness appears as a symbol of ignorance, in contrast to enlightened wisdom. Dahood even suggests a semantic relationship between darkness and ignorance in the verb ʿālam, "conceal; be dark, be ignorant"[18] (e.g., Job 22:15, "the path of ignorance"; Job 42:3, "he who obscures counsel"; Eccl. 3:11, "darkness/ignorance"; Jer. 18:15, "bypaths of darkness/ignorance"). In any case, such a semantic relationship is likely in Job 37:19, where Elihu says, "Teach us what we shall say to him; we cannot draw up our case

---

[17] F. Delitzsch, *The Prophecies of Isaiah. KD,* VII (1877; repr. 1954), I, 177.
[18] See M. Dahood, *Psalms I. AB,* XVI (1966), 162; *Psalms II. AB,* XVII (1968), 30f., 270.

because of darkness (*ḥōšeḵ*)." Pope translates: "We cannot argue from ignorance."[19] In Job 38:2, Yahweh says, "Who is this that darkens (*maḥšîḵ*) counsel by words without knowledge?" The question implies that Job has spoken out of ignorance and has thus obscured what was otherwise plain. In Job 12:24f., Job himself says of God: "He takes away understanding from the chiefs of the people of the earth, and makes them wander in a pathless waste; they grope in the dark without light; and he makes them stagger like a drunken man." The difficulty of finding the right way in the dark becomes an image for the situation of the ignorant. Ps. 82:5 speaks similarly of the wicked: "They have neither knowledge nor understanding (*lōʾ yāḏeʿû wᵉlōʾ yāḇînû*), they walk about (hithpael of *hlk*) in darkness (*ḥᵃšēḵâ*)." Here the context gives ignorance a clearly ethical sense. Eccl. 2:13f. contrasts wisdom and light with folly and darkness: the former surpass the latter, "the wise man has his eyes in his head, but the fool walks in darkness." Isa. 60:2, "Darkness (*ḥōšeḵ*) shall cover the earth, and thick darkness (*ʿᵃrāpel*) the peoples," may refer to lack of knowledge of God; in any case, it stands in contrast to the appearance of the light and glory (*kāḇôḏ*) of Yahweh.

In several passages in the prophets and in Wisdom Literature, darkness is associated with blindness or captivity. Blindness may be brought on by old age, as in Eccl. 12:3 ("those that look through the windows [i.e., the eyes] are dimmed [*ḥāšᵉḵû*]"), or by traumatic events, as in Lam. 5:17 ("for these things [the fall of Jerusalem] our eyes have grown dim [*ḥāšᵉḵû*]"). The plight of the blind is described graphically: "they meet with darkness by day and grope at noonday as in the night" (Job 5:14); "they grope in the dark without light" (Job 12:25; cf. Gen. 19:11; Dt. 28:29; 2 K. 6:18; Isa. 59:10). Ps. 69:24(23) contains a curse on the psalmist's enemies: "Let their eyes be darkened (*teḥšaḵnâ*), so that they cannot see." There are several extrabiblical parallels to such curses, e.g., in the oath taken by Hittite soldiers[20] and in Baʿal's oath.[21]

By contrast, Isa. 29:18 promises restoration of sight to the blind: "In that day . . . out of their gloom and darkness (*mēʾōpel ûmēḥōšeḵ*) the eyes of the blind shall see." We read similarly in Deutero-Isaiah: "I will lead the blind in a way that they know not, in paths that they have not known I will guide them. I will turn the darkness (*maḥšāḵ*) before them into light, the rough places into level ground" (Isa. 42:16). This passage deals with the return of the exiles from Babylon, brought about by the appearance of Yahweh.

The gloom of a prison makes darkness an apt metaphor for imprisonment or captivity. Initial examples include three passages from the Servant Songs in Deutero-Isaiah. The first is Isa. 42:6f.: "I have given you as a covenant to the people, a light to the nations, to open the eyes that are blind, to bring out the prisoners from the dungeon, from the prison those who sit in darkness." The blind and the prisoners here represent peoples who lack the right knowledge of God. Separation from God, who is light, means darkness.[22] The second is Isa. 49:9: "Say to the prisoners, 'Come

---

[19] M. H. Pope, *Job. AB,* XV (1965), 240.

[20] *ANET*³, 353f.

[21] *KTU,* 1.14 IV, 5.

[22] For a different interpretation, see K. Elliger, *Deuterojesaja. BK,* XI/1 (1970), 235f.; Elliger finds reference to the freeing of prisoners.

forth,' to those who are in darkness, 'Appear.' " Freedom and light go together. The third passage, Isa. 50:10, is not entirely clear: "Who among you fears Yahweh, let him obey the voice of his servant; who walks in darkness (*ḥ^a^šēkîm*) . . . , let him trust in the name of Yahweh and rely upon his God." Whether these words are meant as a description of the Servant, as rhetorical questions with the answer "no one," or as directives to those whom the Servant will free,[23] the connection between darkness and captivity is plain.

The same image probably lies behind Mic. 7:8: "When I sit in darkness, Yahweh will be a light to me"; in any case, the verse alludes to the distress in which Zion finds itself. Ps. 107:10,14 speaks plainly of those who "sat in darkness and in gloom (*ḥōšek w^e^ṣalmāwet*), prisoners in affliction and in irons," who, however, have been freed by Yahweh. In a taunt song against Babylon, Deutero-Isaiah promises the tyrant the same fate he has inflicted on Israel: "Sit in silence, and go into darkness" (Isa. 47:5); here there are probably also overtones of darkness as disaster and punishment.

Here, too, belongs the symbolic use of darkness with reference to the Babylonian capture of Jerusalem. Lam. 4:7f. states that the princes of Jerusalem, who had been "purer than snow, whiter than milk," have become "blacker than soot" (*ḥāšak miššeḥôr*). This is consonant with Jeremiah's warning: "Give glory to Yahweh your God before he brings darkness (*yaḥšîk*), before your feet stumble on the twilight mountains (*hārê nāšep*), and while you look for light he turns it into gloom (*ṣalmāwet*) and makes it deep darkness (*"ărāpel*)" (Jer. 13:16). Thus darkness becomes a symbol of captivity, where prisoners are incarcerated. The term is used in this sense in Ps. 107:10,14;[24] Isa. 9:1(2); 42:7; 49:9; Mic. 7:8.

3. *Darkness as Disaster.* The OT often links both imprisonment and disaster in general with Sheol, the realm of the dead, as a place of darkness. In specific cases it is often impossible to decide the exact meaning of a metaphorical expression.

The book of Job often uses darkness as an image for the fate of the wicked. Eliphaz employs it several times: "They meet with darkness by day and grope at noonday as in the night" (Job 5:14); "He does not believe that he will return out of darkness" (15:22; the preceding verses describe the terror of the wicked); "He knows that a day of darkness is ready at his hand" (15:23); because of Job's sin he is suddenly overwhelmed with terror, "your light is darkened, so that you cannot see" (22:11). Bildad says: "The light of the wicked is put out, and the flame of his fire does not shine. The light grows dark (*ḥāšak*) in his tent, and his lamp is put out" (18:5f.). A burning lamp often symbolizes intact fortune, while a light going out suggests disaster. Bildad may also be alluding to the feeling of horror when a family dies out (cf. 18:18). This may also be the point of 20:26, where Zophar says, "Utter darkness is laid up for him."[25]

But darkness can also represent the lot of the upright. Thus Job can say, "He has walled up my way, so that I cannot pass, and he has set darkness upon my paths" (Job 19:8), or, "By his light I walked through darkness" (29:3). Here we should also

---

[23] See the comms.

[24] See above.

[25] Text emended, following *BHK*³.

mention the difficult passage Job 23:17: "I perish [or: I am struck dumb; *ṣmt* niphal] through darkness, and thick darkness covers my face." This translation omits the negative *lō'*; otherwise the passage would read: "I was not struck dumb before the darkness," which also yields acceptable sense.[26] In Ps. 18:29(28) (par. 2 S. 22:29), the psalmist speaks of God's help in distress: "You are my lamp, O Yahweh, and my God lightens my darkness (*ḥoškî*)." Eccl. 5:16(17) describes the common lot of mankind: "All his days he spends in darkness." Darkness is here an image of joyless life. Eccl. 12:1f. speaks of the burdens brought on by old age: ". . . before the sun and the light and the moon and the stars are darkened (*ḥāšaḵ*), and the clouds return after the rain."

In the prophets, too, light signifies prosperity and darkness adversity. This explains Isa. 58:10: "Then shall your light rise in the darkness (*ḥōšeḵ*) and your gloom (*'ᵃpēlâ*) be as the noonday." The darkness represents chaos, and the break of day Yahweh's victory over the dark forces of chaos.[27] A similar contrast appears in Isa. 59:9: "We look for light, and behold, darkness (*ḥōšeḵ*), and for brightness, but we walk in gloom (*'ᵃpēlâ*)" (cf. Isa. 9:1[2]; 50:10; 60:2). According to Muilenburg,[28] this contrast is characteristic of Israel's reflection about beginning and end.

God himself sometimes brings adversity. In Jer. 13:16,[29] it is likened to a mountain traveler being overtaken by darkness. Lam. 3:2 expresses the same thought: "He has driven and brought me into darkness but not into light (*ḥōšeḵ wᵉlō'-'ôr*)." But God also delivers: "When I sit in darkness, Yahweh will be a light to me" (Mic. 7:8).

4. *Darkness as Death.* The ultimate calamity to befall mankind is death. The abode of the dead, *šᵉ'ōl*, is a realm of darkness and gloom. "Darkness" thus becomes a poetic name for Sheol. The context argues for such a meaning, for example, in 1 S. 2:9: "He will guard the feet of his faithful ones; but the wicked will perish in darkness (*baḥōšeḵ yiddāmmû*)." Other passages that may refer to Sheol include: Job 15:30, "He will not escape from darkness"; Job 17:13, "If I look for Sheol as my house, if I spread my couch in darkness"; Job 18:18, "He (the wicked) is thrust from light into darkness, and driven out of the world (*tēḇēl*)"; Job 22:11, "Your light [LXX] is darkened, so that you cannot see, and a flood of water covers you"; Ps. 35:6, an imprecation, "Let their way be darkness and slipperiness (*ḥᵃlaqlaqqôṯ*)"; Ps. 88:13(12), "Are thy wonders known in the darkness, or thy saving help in the land of forgetfulness?" (v. 11[10] speaks of the dead and the *rᵉpā'îm;* v. 12[11] calls the realm of the dead the grave and *'ᵃḇaddôn*); Ps. 88:19(18), "My companions are in darkness (*maḥšāḵ*)"; Ps. 143:3, "The enemy . . . has made me sit in darkness like those long dead" (cf. the similar statement in Lam. 3:6, "He has made me dwell in darkness like the dead of long ago"); Eccl. 6:4, with reference to a stillborn child, "For it comes into vanity and goes into darkness (*ḥōšeḵ*), and in darkness (*ḥōšeḵ*) its name is covered" (unnamed, it never achieves full reality and has no guarantee of life beyond the

---

26 See the comms.

27 E. Jacob, *TheolOT* (Eng. trans., New York, 1958), 265.

28 "Isaiah 40–66: Introd. and Exegesis," *IB,* V, 690.

29 See above.

grave[30]); Eccl. 11:8, "For if a man lives many years. . . , let him remember that the days of darkness (*ḥōšeḵ*) will be many"; Nah. 1:8, "He (Yahweh) will pursue his enemies into darkness."

Other passages, too, associate darkness with death, but without directly identifying it with Sheol. Such passages include: Job 3:4ff., where Job curses the day of his birth: "Let that day be darkness (*ḥōšeḵ*)! May God above not seek it, nor light shine upon it. Let gloom (*ḥōšeḵ*) and deep darkness (*ṣalmāweṯ*) claim it. Let clouds dwell upon it; let the blackness of the day terrify it. That night—let thick darkness seize it. . . . Let the stars of its dawn be dark (*yeḥšᵉḵû*)"; Job 10:20-22: "Let me alone, that I may find a little comfort before I go whence I shall not return, to the land of gloom (*ḥōšeḵ*) and deep darkness (*ṣalmāweṯ*), the land as gloomy as black night (*'ereṣ 'êpāṯâ kᵉmô 'ōpel ṣalmāweṯ*), the land of chaos, where light is as darkness (*wattôpa' kᵉmô-'ōpel*)";[31] Job 15:22f.: "He (the wicked) does not believe that he will return out of darkness. . . . He knows that a day of darkness is ready at his hand";[32] Job 17:12 (text obscure): "They make night into day; 'The light,' they say, 'is near to the darkness' (*'ôr qārôḇ mipnê-ḥōšeḵ*)"; Job 18:6: "The light (of the wicked) is dark (*ḥāšaḵ*) in his tent, and his lamp above him is put out"; Job 20:26, again of the wicked: "Utter darkness is laid up for his treasures"; Job 23:17: "I was not silenced in the face of darkness";[33] Ps. 88:7(6): "Thou hast put me in the depths of the Pit, in the regions dark (*maḥᵃšakkîm*) and deep"; Prov. 20:20: "If one curses his father or his mother, his lamp will be put out in utter darkness"; cf. Isa. 45:19.[34]

5. *Darkness in Curses*. Since darkness often symbolizes disaster and death, the expression is often used in curses. The passages in question have already been cited: Job 3:4ff. (Job's cursing the day of his birth); Ps. 35:6; Ps. 69:24(23) (curses against enemies); Isa. 47:5 (against Babylon); Prov. 20:20 (against parents).

6. *Darkness as Punishment.* As was noted above, darkness often appears as the fate of sinners. In such cases the calamity suggested can be considered judgment or punishment. This is especially true in the prophets. Isaiah, for example, describes the fate of his people in terms of darkness: "If one look to the land, behold, darkness (*ḥōšeḵ*) and distress; and the light is darkened (*ḥāšaḵ*) by its clouds" (Isa. 5:30). Isa. 8:22 describes the situation of the land after the Assyrian conquest in similar terms: "They will look to the earth, but behold, distress and darkness (*ḥᵃšēḵâ*), the gloom (*mᵉ'ûp*) of anguish; and they will be thrust into thick darkness (*'ᵃpēlâ*)." If this verse goes with 9:1(2), it depicts the situation on which the light suddenly shines. In Isa. 47:5 it is Babylon, the enemy of Israel, that is punished: "Go into darkness, O daughter of the Chaldeans." Jeremiah uses expressions like "bring darkness" and "turn light

---

30 See W. Zimmerli, *Prediger. ATD*, XVI/1 (1962), 198.

31 Here the various words for darkness are amassed in order to depict the deep darkness of the realm of the dead; see the comms.

32 See above.

33 See above.

34 See IV.1 above.

into gloom" when he threatens Jerusalem with punishment (Jer. 13:16).[35] Micah castigates the prophets of Israel on account of social injustice: "Therefore it shall be night to you, without vision, and darkness to you, without divination. The sun shall go down upon the prophets, and the day shall be black over them" (Mic. 3:6). Here darkness symbolizes the failure of the prophets' powers and the end of their work, as well as general disaster (and possibly death). Nahum speaks of Yahweh's vengeance upon Nineveh: "He will make a full end of his adversaries, and will pursue his enemies into darkness" (Nah. 1:8).

God's anger also expresses itself in the natural world. The judgment of Yahweh is accordingly often pictured as a return to chaos. One of the primary characteristics of the day of Yahweh is darkness, perhaps even primordial darkness. Am. 5:18-20 shows that the day of Yahweh was generally considered a day of light and happiness, when the enemies of Israel would be judged. Quite the contrary, says Amos: "It is darkness and not light; . . . gloom (*'āpēl*) with no brightness in it."

A century later, Zephaniah echoes the same warning: "A day of wrath is that day, a day of distress and anguish, a day of ruin and devastation, a day of darkness (*ḥōšeḵ*) and gloom (*'ᵃpēlâ*), a day of clouds (*'ānān*) and thick darkness (*'ᵃrāpel*)" (Zeph. 1:15). The sequence of synonyms summarizes everything that is symbolized by the word *ḥōšeḵ*. The imagery was developed within the theophany tradition; here it is applied to Yahweh's appearance as judge. Similar expressions reappear in Joel 2:1f., where we once more find the terms *ḥōšeḵ, 'ᵃpēlâ, 'ānān,* and *'ᵃrāpel*. Three of these are used in Dt. 4:11 with reference to the appearance of God on Sinai. Both passages are probably dependent on the ancient theophany tradition. There may also be an allusion to the plague of locusts in Ex. 10:15. Joel 2:10 continues: "The earth quakes before them, the heavens tremble. The sun and the moon are darkened, and the stars withdraw their shining." Features that may derive from a concrete description of a swarm of locusts take on an almost mythological character, becoming harbingers of the eschatological day of Yahweh. The theme is developed further in 3:3f.(2:30f.): "I will give portents in the heavens and on the earth, blood and fire and columns of smoke. The sun shall be turned to darkness, and the moon to blood, before the great and terrible day of Yahweh comes."

Isa. 13 applies the notion of the day of Yahweh to Babylon. Here we read once more: "The stars of the heavens and their constellations will not give their light; the sun will be dark at its rising and the moon will not shed its light" (v. 10). Thus at the end the earth returns to its primordial condition, as it was before light was created.

Ezekiel, too, without explicitly mentioning the day of Yahweh, speaks of darkness as a punishment upon the enemies of Israel. In a prophecy threatening Egypt, he says: "At Tehaphnehes the day shall be dark, when I break there the dominion of Egypt . . . she shall be covered by a cloud . . ." (Ezk. 30:18). Here features of the ninth plague are combined with those of the day of Yahweh. And again: "When I blot you out, I will cover the heavens, and make their stars dark; I will cover the sun with a

[35] See above.

cloud, and the moon shall not give its light. All the bright lights of heaven will I make dark (*hiqdartî*) over you, and put darkness (*ḥōšeḵ*) upon your land" (32:7f.).

Ringgren

V. LXX. In the vast majority of cases, the LXX translates Heb. *ḥōšeḵ* and *maḥšāḵ* with *skótos* or *skoteinós* (9 times). Once (Job 17:13) a rarer synonym *gnóphos* is used to render *ḥōšeḵ*, and once (Ps. 74:20[LXX 73:20]) *maḥ^a^šakkê* is translated by *eskotisménoi*. In 3 passages *ḥōšeḵ* is not translated (1 S. 2:9; Isa. 5:30b; Ezk. 8:12). Once (Dt. 5:23) the LXX follows a text attested only in a few Hebrew manuscripts, and once (Job 37:19) it appears to follow a different tradition entirely. Five times the LXX gives its own interpretation of the term for darkness: Job 34:22, *tópos;* Job 38:2, *krýptōn;* Ps. 88:19(18)(LXX 87:19), *talaipōría;* Ps. 107:14(LXX 106:14), *skótos;* Prov. 22:29 (translating *ḥāšōḵ*), *nōthrós*. The verb *ḥāšaḵ* is translated by *skotízō*, **syskotázō*, or *skotáō*. Once the LXX presupposes a different textual tradition (Ex. 10:15, *phtheírō*).

Geraty

VI. Dead Sea Scrolls. The contrast between light (→ אור *'ôr*) and darkness (*ḥōšeḵ*) is of fundamental importance for the dualistic theology of the Qumran community. God created an "angel (spirit) of light" and an "angel (spirit) of darkness" (or "injustice," → עול *'āwlâ* or *'āwel*) (1QS 3:18f.,25), and everyone walks under the dominion of one or the other (1QS 3:19ff.). The generations of the unjust spring forth from the fountain of darkness (*m^e^qôr ḥōšeḵ*, 1QS 3:19). Those outside the community are "sons of darkness" (1QS 1:10; cf. 1QM 1:1,7,10,16; 3:6,9; 13:16; 14:17), and the members of the community should "hate" them (1QS 1:10). They do "works of darkness" (1QS 2:7; cf. 1QM 15:9) or "walk in the ways of darkness" (1QS 3:21; 4:11) or follow the "laws" (*ḥuqqîm*) of darkness (1QM 13:12). Their ultimate fate is "the fire of darkness" (*'ēš maḥ^a^šakkîm*, 1QS 4:13), also called "the darkness of fire" (*'^a^pēlaṯ 'ēš*). Here we obviously have a confusion of two different places of punishment, one characterized by darkness, the other by fire.

The War scroll envisions an eschatological battle between the sons of light and the sons of darkness (1QM 1:1 and *passim*). It will last until the end of the "times of darkness" (*mô'^a^ḏê ḥōšeḵ*, 1QM 1:8), and when it ends the sons of darkness will be destroyed (1QM 1:16; 13:16).

In the Thanksgiving scroll there are notably few occurrences of *ḥōšeḵ;* the primary emphasis is on the victory of the light. God "caused a light (*mā'ôr*) to shine out of the darkness" (1QH 9:26) and freed the human race from "the dwelling place of darkness" (1QH 12:26). Darkness and gloom (*qaḏrûṯ, mšḥwr, ṣalmāweṯ*) are used in 1QH 5:31-33 as images for the distress of the psalmist. Here we also find *ḥōšeḵ* in its literal sense: according to 1QH 12:6, "the beginning of the dominion of darkness" marks one of the times for communal prayer.

We also find *ḥōšeḵ* in some fragmentary texts. In the so-called Book of Mysteries, we read: "Injustice will vanish before justice, as darkness vanishes (*gālâ*, 'go into exile') before the light" (1Q27 5f.). In an astrological text (4Q186 1f.,7f.) we find the statement *w^e^šālōš b^e^ḇōr haḥōšeḵ*, "and three (parts) in the pit of darkness." Here the "pit of darkness" is obviously the opposite of the *bêṯ hā'ôr*, "house of light." The exact meaning is obscure, but the text clearly concerns the relationship of human beings to the twin principles of good and evil.[36] In 4Q184 1,6, "darkness" appears to be associated with a "prostitute" (*zônâ*) who dwells in darkness (*ḥōšeḵ 'ᵃpēlâ*) and has some connection with the netherworld; probably, however, something else is meant, perhaps Rome or its Jewish collaborators.

An Aramaic text recording the visions of Amran[37] contains references to the contrast between *nᵉhôrā'*, "light," and *ḥᵃšôḵā'*, "darkness," as well as to the "sons of light."

Ringgren, Mitchel

---

[36] See M. Delcor, "Recherches sur un horoscope en langue hébraïque provenant de Qumran," *RevQ*, 5 (1966), 531.

[37] J. T. Milik, "4Q visions de 'Amram et une citation d'Origène," *RB*, 79 (1972), 77-97.

חֹשֶׁן *ḥōšen*

Contents: I. Occurrences; Etymology. II. Cultural Development and Theological Significance: 1. Oracle Pouch; 2. Breastpiece; 3. Symbolism.

I. Occurrences; Etymology. The noun *ḥōšen*—apart from Sir. 45:10f.—occurs 25 times in P. It is found in texts that discuss the fashioning of the priestly vestments (Ex. 25:7; 28:4,15-30; 35:9,27; 39:8-21) or the investiture of Aaron (Ex. 29:5; Lev. 8:8), and refers to the pectoral ornament of the high priest. A formal extrabiblical parallel is the breastpiece of the Egyptian high priest of Memphis.[1] In a Middle Bronze tomb at Byblos has been found the pectoral ornament of a king: an approximately rectangular plate of gold, encrusted with jewels and suspended from a golden chain (cf. Ezk. 28:13).[2]

The etymology of *ḥōšen* is obscure. The suggested derivations have not been uninfluenced by the currently accepted interpretations of the biblical passages. Arab. *ḥasuna*, "be beautiful," suggests especially the elaborate decoration of the *ḥōšen*. The

---

ḥōšen. H. Bonnet, *RÄR*, 125f.; K. Elliger, "Ephod und Choschen: Ein Beitrag zur Entwicklungsgeschichte des hohepriesterlichen Ornats," *VT*, 8 (1958), 19-35 = *Erlanger Forschungen*, ser. A, 10. *Festschrift F. Baumgärtel* (1959), 9-23; I. Friedrich, *Ephod und Choschen im Lichte des Alten Orients. Wiener Beiträge zur Theologie*, 20 (1968); J. Gabriel, *Untersuchungen über das alttestamentliche Hohepriestertum mit besonderer Berücksichtigung des hohepriesterlichen Ornates* (Vienna, 1933); J. S. Harris, "The Stones of the High Priest's Breastplate," *ALUOS*, 5 (1966), 40-62; J. Maier, "Urim und Tummim: Recht und Bund in der Spannung zwischen Königtum und Priestertum im alten Israel," *Kairos*, N.S. 11 (1969), 22-38; O. Nussbaum, *Das Brustkreuz des Bischofs* (Mainz, 1964), 7ff.; E. Sellin, "Noch einmal der alttestamentliche Efod," *JPOS*, 17 (1937), 236-251; H. Thiersch, *Ependytes und Ephod* (Stuttgart, 1936).

[1] See illustrations in K. Koch, "Hoherpriester," *BHHW*, II, 739.

[2] Cf. P. Montet, *Byblos et l'Égypte* (Paris, 1929), pl. 94.

derivation from *ḥsn,* "hide, keep, preserve," as in Aram. *'assānā'*, "provisions," is an attempt to establish the meaning "container, pouch."

II. Cultural Development and Theological Significance.

1. *Oracle Pouch.* The development of the *ḥōšen* can be traced in the two literary strata that can be distinguished in Ex. 28.[3] Ex. 28:15f.,22,30 show that the *ḥōšen,* together with the *'ēpôḏ baḏ* (a kind of leather apron), was a separate item in the priestly vestments.[4] It had the form of a square pouch about 23 centimenters (9 inches) on a side, made of a piece of cloth folded and sewed along two edges; the opening was at the top. It was worn over the breast, held by two cords fastened at the neck. The name *ḥōšen (ham)mišpāṭ* in vv. 15 and 30 indicates the original purpose of this pouch: it held the oracle stones Urim and Thummim (→ גורל *gôrāl;* the *ḥōšen* may even be implicit when the ephod is mentioned in 1 S. 14:3; 21:10[Eng. v. 9]; 23:9; 30:7). In the case of the high priest as chief steward of the oracle (Exod. 28:15, par. 39:8), the *ḥōšen* was made of the same precious cloth as the ephod, a blend of four fabrics. Lev. 8:8 reflects roughly the same stage of tradition.

2. *Breastpiece.* In the second stratum (Ex. 28:17-21,23-28 par. 39:10-14,16-21), the *ḥōšen* has become a stiffened breastpiece encrusted with precious stones. At the same time it was incorporated into the ephod. The jewels were arranged in four rows of three stones each, "set in gold that was spirally interwoven with the fabric, so that they could not fall out."[5] The significance of the names given the individual jewels by the MT is totally obscure; the first interpretation was ventured by the LXX. The names of the twelve tribes were engraved on the stones, but there is no discernible connection between the names of the tribes and the names of the stones. A similar collection of precious stones appears in Ezk. 28:13 (cf. Rev. 21:19f.). According to Ex. 25:7 and 35:9, the jewels were an offering of the community. The decoration may have been copied from the ornamentation of the royal breastpiece.

The increased weight of the breastpiece led to a different way of attaching it. Four rings were sewn to it, two to the upper corners and two to the lower. From the upper rings, two golden cords led up to the shoulder-pieces of the ephod, where they were attached to rosettes. Through the lower rings, which were fastened to the rear of the *ḥōšen,* a blue lace was passed; attached to two additional rings on the lower portion of the shoulder-pieces of the ephod, it bound the two vestments tightly together, preventing the *ḥōšen* from shifting.

3. *Symbolism.* Each of the two traditions concludes with a symbolic interpretation of the *ḥōšen.* Ex. 28:30 has Aaron "bear the judgment of the people of Israel before Yahweh continually" as he wears the *ḥōšen* containing the Urim and Thummim. This interpretation shows "how the significance of the *ḥōšen* was reinterpreted at an early

[3] Cf. also Elliger.
[4] See → גורל *gôrāl* III.2.
[5] Josephus *Ant.* iii.7.5.

date, probably in the preexilic period. The Urim and Thummim are no longer brought forth to determine God's 'decision' when a disjunctive question is asked in a dubious situation; they remain upon Aaron's heart."[6] The directive that Aaron is "continually" to bear Israel's judgment before Yahweh may derive from the tendency to link jurisprudence totally to the judicial power of the high priest.[7]

Ex. 28:29 connects its interpretation with the precious stones. By the *ḥōšen*, the high priest is continually to bring the twelve tribes of Israel into remembrance before Yahweh. This central element of the high priest's regalia thus functions as a visible symbol of the intercessory role of its bearer. This reinterpretation takes from the empty *ḥōšen* the last trace of its original mantic significance. Sir. 45:10f., with its rapturous glorification of Aaron's priestly dignity, unites these two traditions once more.

The Greek translations *peristḗtion, podḗrēs, logeíon/lógion,* and *docheíon/dóchion* (Symmachus) reflect various interpretations, in part contradictory.

Dommershausen

---

[6] Elliger, 30.
[7] Maier, 31.

חָשַׁק *ḥāšaq;* חֵשֶׁק *ḥēšeq;* חִשֻּׁק *ḥiššuq;* חָשׁוּק *ḥāšûq*

Contents: I. 1. Etymology; Meaning; 2. Use in Original Sense. II. Metaphorical Meaning: 1. Secular; 2. Theological.

I. 1. *Etymology; Meaning.* The root *ḥšq* with the prep. b^e[1] or l^e plus the infinitive construct occurs 8 times in the OT and once in Sirach in the qal; once in Sirach in the niphal; once in the OT in the piel; and twice in the OT in the pual. On the basis of other Semitic idioms such as Akk. *ešēqu,* "be united,"[2] and possibly also Tuareg *aseġ,* "unite," we may postulate for the Hebrew root the basic meaning "adhere to, be united."[3] The relationship to Arab. *'ašiqa/'asiqa,* "love passionately," proposed by *KBL*[3] [4] has more to do with the metaphorical meaning.

2. *Use in Original Sense.* The original meaning occurs in the OT only in the tech-

---

ḥāšaq. H. J. Franken, *The Mystical Communion with JHWH in the Book of Psalms* (Leiden, 1954), 36; I. Husik, "Joseph Albo, the Last of the Medieval Jewish Philosophers," *PAAJR,* 1 (1930), 70f.; G. Quell, " ἀγαπάω," *TDNT,* I, 21-35.

[1] *Synt.* §106a.
[2] *AHw,* I, 249; O. Rössler, "Der semitische Charakter der lybischen Sprache," *ZA,* 50 (1952), 131.
[3] Franken.
[4] See also A. Guillaume, "Hebrew and Arabic Lexicography," *Abr-Nahrain,* 1 (1959/60 [1961]; repr. Leiden, 1965), 25.

nical terminology of P's account of the construction of the tabernacle: piel (Ex. 38:28), "join," and pual (Ex. 27:17; 38:17), "be joined." The word *ḥāšûq* (Ex. 27:10f.; 38:10-12,17,19) refers to a connecting pole or beam;[5] this explains *ḥiššuq*, "spoke (of a wheel)," as a rod connecting the felly of a wheel with the hub (1 K. 7:33).

II. Metaphorical Meaning.

1. *Secular.* The association of the root *ḥšq* with the subject → נפשׁ *nepeš* allows it to be applied to individual human bonds: between a man and a woman (Gen. 34:8, LXX *prosairéomai*), between a wise man and wisdom (Sir. 51:19, *diamáchomai*, "be zealous for"). The context equates the meaning with *dāḇaq b*[e6] (Gen. 34:3) and *lō' hāpaḵ pānîm min* (Sir. 51:19). Unlike *dāḇaq*,[7] *ḥāšaq* always has a positive sense, never a hostile sense like "stick to in pursuit." Dt. 21:11 (LXX *enthyméō*) takes account of such human bonds, permitting marriage (*lāqaḥ l*[e]*'iššâ*) with a foreign captive to whom one is attracted in this way. Sir. 40:19 praises a woman of loving devotion (niphal; *ámōnos*, "irreproachable").

The segholate noun *ḥēšeq* deriving from this root means inward devotion to or pleasure in a project, for example Solomon's pleasure in his public works (1 K. 9:19, LXX *pragmateía*) in parallel with 1 K. 9:1 (*ḥāpēṣ la'*[a]*śôṯ*); 2 Ch. 7:11 (*kol-habbā' 'al-lēḇ š*[e]*lōmōh la'*[a]*śôṯ*). Finally, the word designates the prophet's longing for twilight (*nešep hišqî*, Isa. 21:4; the LXX has a variant reading).

The root is not used to refer to friendship between men.[8]

2. *Theological.* The OT quite naturally applies this term for devotion to the relationship between God and mankind. Ps. 91:14 characteristically places its description of mankind's devotion to Yahweh in Yahweh's own mouth (*bî ḥāšaq*, LXX *ep' emé ēlpisen*) and equating this attitude with *yiqrā'ēnî, yāḏa' š*[e]*mî*. The psalmist thus depicts this devotion not as an emotional bond but as a firm and deliberate attestation of trust.

This mode of expression is strongly reminiscent of Deuteronomistic style. It is therefore not surprising to find that the root *ḥšq* occurs in Deuteronomy, albeit not very frequently. Dt. 10:15 connects the bond between Yahweh and the patriarchs of Israel with his love for them (*l*[e]*'ah*[a]*ḇâ 'ōṯām*)[9] and his choosing of their descendants (*wayyiḇḥar b*[e]*zar'ām*); the LXX is therefore correct in translating *proeílato*. The same situation is also found in Dt. 7:7f., where the parallelism of *'ah*[a]*ḇâ* and *bāḥar* is extended by *šomrô 'eṯ-hašš*[e]*ḇu'â* (v. 8). Thus the bond of love between Yahweh and his own people does not spring from any qualities inherent in the latter, but from his own past decision, incomprehensible to mankind.[10]

---

[5] M. Noth, *Exodus. OTL* (Eng. trans. 1962), 217; E. Jenni, *Das hebräische Pi'el* (Zurich, 1968), 163.

[6] → דבק *dāḇaq* [*dābhaq*] II.1(a).

[7] *Ibid.*, II.1(b).

[8] → אהב *'āhaḇ* [*'āhabh*] II.3.

[9] *Ibid.*, IV.2.

[10] Husik.

Theological usage, like secular usage, does not suggest a sudden surge of emotion; it presupposes not just an unconditional erotic attraction but also a reasoned and unconditional decision. Just as Shechem longed for Dinah so much that he asked his father to request her in marriage (Gen. 34:3,8), just as the warrior determines to take a foreign slave as his wife (Dt. 21:11),[11] just as Solomon pursues his building projects (1 K. 9:19), so the psalmist knows Yahweh's name and calls to him in his distress, whereupon Yahweh grants him an oracle expressing his favor. In the same way, Yahweh knows his people and feels bound to the promises he has given. This adherence presupposes an already established bond between God and mankind, which remains unbroken. In this sense the textually problematical passage Isa. 38:17 can be interpreted as expressing the worshipper's confidence that Yahweh will preserve (LXX *heílou* [impv.]) his life and not surrender it to destruction. The root *ḥšq* thus refers neither to a mystical union between God and mankind nor to an emotional certainty, but rather to a conscious attitude of devotion on the part of an individual and fidelity on the part of God, maintained even under stress.

Wallis

[11] See above.

חָתַם *ḥāṯam*; חוֹתָם *ḥôṯām*

Contents: I. Etymology; Occurrences. II. Archeological Evidence. III. Context. IV. Secondary Meanings of the Verb. V. The Verb in Prophetic and Apocalyptic Tradition. VI. Metaphorical Usage of the Noun.

I. Etymology; Occurrences. The root *ḥtm* is found in West and South Semitic. The verb may mean either "affix a seal" or "seal shut." The noun everywhere has the

ḥāṯam. D. Diringer, *Le iscrizioni antico-ebraïci palestinesi* (Florence, 1934); L. Fischer, "Die Urkunden in Jer. 32,11-14 nach den Ausgrabungen und dem Talmud," *ZAW,* 30 (1910), 136-142; K. Galling, "Beschriftete Bildsiegel des ersten Jahrtausends v. Chr. vornehmlich aus Syrien und Palästina," *ZDPV,* 64 (1941), 121-202; A. H. J. Gunneweg, *Mündliche und schriftliche Tradition der vorexilischen Prophetenbücher als Problem der neueren Prophetenforschung. FRLANT,* N.S. 55[73] (1959); D. Jones, "The Traditio of the Oracles of Isaiah on Jerusalem," *ZAW,* 67 (1955), 226-246; T. O. Lambdin, "Egyptian Loan Words in the OT," *JAOS,* 73 (1953), 145-155; S. Moscati, "I sigilli nell'AT: Studio esegetico-filologico," *Bibl,* 30 (1949), 314-338; *idem, L'epigrafia ebraica antica 1935-1950. BietOr,* 15 (1951); H. H. von der Osten, *Altorientalische Siegelsteine der Sammlung Hans Silvius von Aulock* (Uppsala, 1957) (bibliog., pp. 180-84); S. Schott, "Wörter für Rollsiegel und Ring," *WZKM,* 54 (1957), 177-185; F. Vattioni, "I sigilli ebraici," *Bibl,* 50 (1969), 357-388; P. Welten, *Die Königs-Stempel. ADPV* (1969).

meaning "seal" and "seal ring." The root does not appear in East Semitic, where we find instead the noun *kunukku* and the verb *kanāku*.[1]

The absence of the root in East Semitic raises the question whether the root itself is Semitic or represents a loanword in West and South Semitic. The latter conclusion is supported by the fact that the Hebrew noun form *qāṭal,* on which the noun *ḥôṯam* must be based, is extremely rare. It is therefore commonly assumed that the Semites borrowed the noun from Egyptian and that the Semitic verb is denominative; in Egyptian, the noun *ḫtm,* "seal," is found as early as the Old Kingdom.[2] In the Old Kingdom the noun referred only to a cylinder seal; later it could also mean a seal ring.[3] It probably derived from the verb meaning "affix a seal," found from the early period on.[4] The meaning "seal shut" for the verb is probably secondary both in Egyptian and in the Semitic languages.[5]

The Hebrew noun occurs 15 times in the OT (once in the byform *ḥōṯemeṯ*). Of these 15 occurrences, however, almost half appear in the phrase *pittûḥê ḥôṯām,* "seal engraving" (Ex. 28 and 39, describing the priestly vestments). Seals found in Palestine use *ḥtm* 27 times. The corresponding Aramaic verb is found in Dnl. 6:18(Eng. v. 17). The piel and hiphil have the secondary meaning "seal shut." It is also worth noting that the verb appears most commonly in later documents, more than half its occurrences being in Nehemiah, Esther, Job, and Daniel.

Besides *ḥôṯām,* OT Hebrew has another noun *ṭabba'aṯ,* also deriving from Egyptian (*ḏb'.t,* "seal [ring]").[6] In Egyptian, this word occurs most often in ritual texts, *ḫtm* in magical texts.[7] The word has taken on an extended meaning in Hebrew, designating the rings used to carry the ark of the covenant or forming part of the priestly regalia, etc. (Ex. 25–29), or ornamental rings in general (Ex. 35:22; Nu. 31:50; Isa. 3:21). Only in the book of Esther does it refer clearly to seal rings (Est. 3:10,12; 8:2,8,10)—and probably also Gen. 41:42.[8]

II. Archeological Evidence. Four main types of seals have been found in excavations in Palestine.

(1) Scarabs. These include both genuine Egyptian scarabs and indigenous imitations. They are quite plentiful, probably numbering several thousand (about 1000 at

---

[1] For a survey, see Moscati, *Bibl,* 30 (1949), 326f.
[2] See, for example, *VG,* I, 342, n. 1; most recent lexicons and grammars; Moscati, *Bibl,* 30 (1949), 329f.; Lambdin, 151.
[3] Schott, 181f.
[4] *Ibid.,* 183.
[5] Moscati, *Bibl,* 30 (1949), 330; *GesB* differs.
[6] Moscati, *Bibl,* 30 (1949), 331-34; Lambdin, 151; Schott, 178-181.
[7] Schott, 183.
[8] Moscati, *Bibl,* 30 (1949), 324.

Tell el-ʿAjjûl near Gaza, some 550 at Lachish, about 400 at Gezer, etc.).[9] Their hieroglyphic inscriptions show that most of them date from the Middle or Late Bronze Age. In the early period they were usually made of steatite (soapstone); later harder stones were used, as well as gemstones, faience, bone, etc.[10]

(2) Cylinder Seals. These include genuine Mesopotamian seals and indigenous imitations. They are less common: about 200 were known in 1949;[11] later 20 were discovered at Hazor and a very few others elsewhere.[12] Some date from the Chalcolithic period; most date from the Middle and Late Bronze Age, and quite a few can be assigned to the preexilic period of Israel's history. They are made of stones like steatite and hematite, as well as faience, glass, and similar plastic materials. Their decoration consists of formalized human and animal figures. They do not contain inscriptions.

Scarabs and cylinder seals did not bear the name of their owner and probably served as both amulets and seals. They generally had a hole bored through them so that they could be worn on a cord around the neck.[13]

(3) Israelite Name Seals. More than 200 of these seals (often called private seals) have been discovered. In addition there are about 100 impressions of such seals on pottery.[14] In outward form they often resemble Egyptian scarabs, being made out of harder types of stone[15] and often having a hole through them; they were rarely made into rings.[16] They exhibit a reasonably regular form: about half of them have illustrations (human or animal forms, stylized figures, usually borrowed from foreign seals); nearly all have a proper name preceded by a *lamedh* of possession, often followed by a patronymic or an appellative such as "servant of N." or "servant of the king," or on occasion "son of the king." A very few bear feminine names with the qualification "wife of N." or "daughter of N." Almost all of these date from the late period of the monarchy. There are a few from the postexilic period, mostly pictorial, though often bearing an Aramaic inscription.[17]

---

[9] F. Petrie, *Ancient Gaza,* I-IV (London, 1931-34); O. Tufnell, *Lachish,* III (London, 1953), 368-373; IV (London, 1958), 113-126; R. A. S. Macalister, *The Excavation of Gezer* (London, 1912), II, 314-330; also A. Rowe, *A Catalogue of Egyptian Scarabs, Scaraboids, Seals, and Amulets in the Palestine Archaeological Museum* (Cairo, 1936).

[10] K. Galling, "Amulett," *BRL*², 10f.; S. Morenz, "Skarabäus," *BHHW,* III, 1812f.

[11] B. Parker, "Cylinder Seals from Palestine," *Iraq,* 11 (1949), 1-43; cf. J. Nougayrol, *Cylindres-sceaux et empreintes de cylindres trouvés en Palestine* (Paris, 1939), v-vi.

[12] Y. Yadin, *Hazor,* III-IV (plates) (Jerusalem, 1961), cccxix-cccxxii; G. E. Wright, "Selected Seals from the Excavations at Balâṭah (Shechem)," *BASOR,* 167 (1962), 5-13; etc.

[13] For further details, see Galling, *BRL*², 10f.; P. Welten, "Siegel und Stempel," *BRL*², 299.

[14] Diringer, 119-127, 159-261; Galling, *ZDPV,* 64 (1941), 172-198; Moscati, *L'epigrafia,* 47-65, 72-82; Vattioni, 376-385. It is impossible to determine the ratio of actual seals to seal impressions, since several excavation reports do not make a distinction; see Vattioni, 359.

[15] Cf. Job 41:7(Eng. v. 15) LXX; Ex. 28:11,21,36; 39:6,14,30.

[16] For further details, see Welten, *BRL*², 299-307; and G. Sauer, "Siegel," *BHHW,* III, 1786-1790.

[17] See, for example, F. M. Cross, "Judean Stamps," *Eretz-Israel,* 9 (1969), 20-27.

(4) Royal Seals. These seals are known only from their impressions on jar handles. They are heavily represented: more than 800 in all, of which more than 300 come from Lachish alone, and some 150 from Ramat Raḥel.[18] They all bear a symbol showing two or four wings together with the caption *lmlk,* "belonging to the king," and one of four Judean city names. The jars were probably intended for delivering oil and wine from the crown properties of Judah to Judean garrisons, during the reigns of Hezekiah and Josiah.[19]

III. Context. The archeological evidence suggests that seals with Hebrew inscriptions were far from common in ancient Israel. The situation almost certainly differed from that in Mesopotamia, where, according to Herodotus, each man had his seal. In the OT—especially in late and imaginative texts—those who possess seals are primarily kings and officials. Seals appear to have symbolized royal and official dignity. The OT passages that speak concretely of affixing a seal always depict it as a legal act, usually performed by a king or queen: Jezebel seals the letters containing charges against Naboth with the seal of the king (1 K. 21:8). The letters of Haman that were to destroy the Jews are likewise sealed with the king's seal (Est. 3:12); later Esther and Mordecai are permitted to countermand Haman's orders through letters that likewise bear the royal seal, "for an edict written in the name of the king and sealed with the king's ring cannot be revoked" (Est. 8:7ff.). Similarly, when Daniel had been cast into the den of lions a stone was laid upon the mouth of the den, "and the king sealed it with his own signet (*'izqâ*) and with the signet of his lords" (Dnl. 6:18[17]). Here, too, affixing a seal is an official act. At the covenant renewal presided over by Ezra, the first to set his seal on the document was Nehemiah the governor; a series of officials follow suit (Neh. 10:1-28[9:38–10:27]). Those with lower social rank did not take part in the ceremonial sealing, but joined "their noble brethren" (10:29f.[28f.]). The whole ceremony is depicted as an official act.[20] This same valuation of affixing a seal is evident in one of the patriarchal narratives: when Judah can give his daughter-in-law Tamar his seal and cord (Gen. 38:18,25), it is because he is not just a random passerby; he makes his appearance as the head of a tribe (as in Test. Judah 15:3, a late Jewish retelling of the story, in which Judah is presented as designated king and the seal has been transformed into a royal diadem).

When Jeremiah buys the field at Anathoth (Jer. 32), the point is precisely that he conducts the transaction as officially as possible. This is why there are so many legal details in the account, and the sealing of the documents is mentioned several times (vv. 10f.,14,44). We are clearly dealing with a private transaction that—even without participation of appropriate officials—is made legally binding through correct procedure.

Fischer and Jones[21] discuss the purely technical details of how leather or papyrus documents were sealed in their treatment of the special "double" document in Jer. 32:

---

18 Details in Welten.

19 Welten; a different interpretation in Cross, *Eretz-Israel,* 9 (1969), 20-22, etc.

20 On the problems of textual and literary criticism raised by this chapter, see, for example, W. Rudolph, *Esra und Nehemia. HAT,* XX (1949), 172-76.

21 Pp. 227f.

the document was tied with a cord secured by a small lump of clay (cf. Job 38:14), on which an impression of the seal was left.[22]

The OT view of sealing as being primarily an official legal action is in remarkable agreement with the observation that comparatively many of the Hebrew name seals discovered in Palestine belonged to royal officials: *lgdlyhw (')šr 'l hby(t);*[23] four persons called *'bd hmlk;*[24] and four persons called *bn hmlk.*[25] Finally, six persons are referred to as "servants" or "officials" (*'bd, n'r*) of *'brm* or *yrb'm, 'zyw, ywkn,* and *'ḥz.*[26] These names could refer to the corresponding kings of Israel and Judah.[27] At best, then, 15 seals belonged to royal officials (16 if the Jotham on the seal from Elath is not the king but a high official[28]).

That officials were naturally assumed to have seals is clear from a letter found on an ostracon at Arad: Nahum, an official (probably military), is ordered to get a jug of oil; the letter continues: "Send it to me quickly and seal it with your seal (*ḥtm 'th bḥtmk*).[29] The royal seals mentioned above also attest to the official character of the act of affixing a seal, as do (if they are interpreted correctly) the so-called "satrap seals," a dozen seal impressions from the Persian period with the inscription *pḥw',* "satrap, governor."[30]

IV. Secondary Meanings of the Verb. The less precise meaning of the verb *ḥāṯam,* "seal shut," occurs in various contexts. In the symbolic language of the Song of Solomon, we read that the unattainable beloved is like "a fountain sealed" (Cant. 4:12). The wicked are said to shut themselves up during the day for fear of the light (Job 24:16; piel, "seal for themselves"). In medico-legal terminology, venereal disease can affect the male organ so that it is "stopped from discharge" (*ḥtm* hiphil), making the person unclean (Lev. 15:3). There are also two passages in Job that use the verb in describing Yahweh as lord of the forces of nature: during the storms of winter he keeps people from going outside ("seals shut for them," Job 37:7, emended on the basis of 9:7[31]), and he has the power to darken the stars ("seal shut for them," 9:7).

There are several interesting passages where Yahweh is still the active subject but the verb has the meaning "store up, preserve." In his fourth speech, Job expresses his desire to hide in Sheol until God's wrath is past, but his desire is not granted: Yahweh

---

22 Cf. *ANEP,* no. 265.

23 Moscati, *L'epigrafia,* 61f.

24 Diringer, 229-231; Moscati, *L'epigrafia,* 52.

25 Diringer, 127, 232f.; Vattioni, 381, 385. "Son of the king" may be an official title; see Welten, *BRL*², 304.

26 Diringer, 224-28, 221-24, 126; Moscati, *L'epigrafia,* 59.

27 Welten, *BRL*², 303f.

28 N. Avigad, "The Jotham Seal from Elath," *BASOR,* 163 (1961), 21.

29 Y. Aharoni, "The Use of Hieratic Numerals in Hebrew Ostraca and the Shekel Weights," *BASOR,* 184 (1966), 14-16.

30 *Idem, Excavations at Ramat Raḥel,* vol. 1: *Seasons 1959 and 1960* (Rome, 1962), 5-10, 29-34; vol. 2: *Seasons 1961 and 1962* (Rome, 1964), 19-22, 43-45; a different interpretation in Cross, *Eretz-Israel,* 9 (1969), 24-26.

31 G. Fohrer, *Das Buch Hiob. KAT,* XVI (1963), 481.

preserves Job's sins sealed up in a bag, so that the punishment can last forever (Job 14:13-17).[32] The idea has close parallels in Dt. 32:34f. and Hos. 13:12.[33] Dt. 32:34 likewise uses the verb *ḥtm*, but states that the wickedness of Yahweh's enemies is sealed up in his treasuries until his day of vengeance. As we have seen above, sealing was considered a legally binding action; both passages thus express the notion that Yahweh's storing up of sin is an act of divine justice and hence irrevocable.

Characteristically, the idea reappears with modifications in apocalyptic literature. The "sealing of sin" in Dnl. 9:24 (*K*) does not look forward to a punishment in the distant future, but means that the sin is forgiven. In this passage the angel Gabriel comes to Daniel and announces to him that the seventy years spoken of by Jeremiah must be understood as seventy weeks of years. At the end of this period, sin will be "sealed" and iniquity atoned for.[34] Then will come the time of glory with "everlasting righteousness" and "sealing of vision and prophet."[35]

V. The Verb in Prophetic and Apocalyptic Tradition. The verb *ḥtm* occurs in 2 passages from Isaiah that appear similar in meaning at first glance but are shown by closer inspection to be antithetical. Isaiah gives command to "bind up the testimony (*teʿûḏâ*; → עוד *ʿwd*)" and "seal the teaching (→ תורה *tôrâ*)" (Isa. 8:16-20).[36] It remains unresolved whether these expressions refer to the oral preaching of Isaiah or to a written message (as the parallel in Jer. 36 might suggest).[37] The appended *belimmuḏāy*, "among my disciples," does not settle the question; the whole verse can be taken literally (the binding and sealing of a scroll) or figuratively (the transmission of a message to Isaiah's disciples). The literal interpretation is supported by the observation that the terminology used to describe what is happening derives from the legal realm, i.e., the binding and sealing are viewed as a legal act similar to the drawing up of a will. This action on the part of the prophet will not succeed unless it is carried out to the letter. Isaiah's purpose is the same as in 8:1-4, where witnesses are summoned: it must be possible at a later date to determine whether the message really agrees with what has come to pass.[38]

In the other passage, the prophet's message is compared to "the words of a book that is sealed" (Isa. 29:11f.). The short prose passage is probably to be explained as a postexilic extension of the oracle in vv. 9f., and can be understood only in the light of these verses.[39] The subject matter is the hardness of heart introduced in Isa. 6:9f.: the prophet is convinced that the inhabitants of Judah are not only unwilling to hear his message, but—according to the will of God—unable to hear and understand. In

---

32 For the structure of the passage, see *ibid.*, 257-260.

33 Fohrer.

34 The text is usually emended from *lḥtm* to *lhtm* on the basis of the *qere;* see O. Plöger, *Das Buch Daniel. KAT,* XVIII (1965), 134.

35 See below.

36 On the form of the verb, see H. Wildberger, *Jesaja. BK,* X/1 (1972), 342f., and Jones, 232.

37 Gunneweg, 32-34, 45f.

38 See Jones, 235f., and O. Kaiser, *Isaiah 1–12. OTL* (Eng. trans. 1972), 120; a somewhat different interpretation is offered by Gunneweg, 45-49.

39 O. Kaiser, *Isaiah 13–39. OTL* (Eng. trans. 1974), 269-271.

contrast to the first passage, the content is here entirely negative; Isaiah's message will not succeed.[40]

The notion that the prophetic message might be sealed so that later the prophet might be proved to have truly predicted what was to come took on great importance in late Jewish apocalyptic. Now, however, great weight is placed on the notion that what takes place in the last times follows the divine plan that had been revealed in earlier times. Dnl. 9:24 states that at the end of the ages "vision and prophet" will be sealed. This could mean simply that prophetic vision and preaching are superfluous when all is consummated. More likely, however, it means that the revelation received earlier by the prophets is confirmed by being fulfilled at the eschaton. In this sense the ministry of the prophets is past, it is "closed" and no longer has any purpose.[41] The two passages in Dnl. 12 where Daniel is commanded to shut up the words and seal the book until the time of the end (vv. 4,9) are to be interpreted in the technical apocalyptic sense. The entire fiction that Daniel received the message some five hundred years before the end is preserved by the notion that all was kept hidden until the period just before the end.[42]

VI. Metaphorical Usage of the Noun. It has already been emphasized[43] that seals may be considered tokens of royal and official dignity. Therefore a seal or seal ring can also be used to symbolize a person one values. The loving bride says to her beloved, "Set me as a seal upon your heart, as a seal upon your arm" (Cant. 8:6). The image includes both the seal worn on a cord about the neck and the seal ring worn on one's finger (or are we to imagine an armlet with a seal,[44] despite the absence of archeological evidence?). The image also occurs in Egyptian love songs.[45]

The same image can express the special relationship between God and the king. At his enthronement, the king takes on the function of "attesting" and instantiating the dominion of God.[46] In Jer. 22:24, Jehoiachin is described as the signet ring on Yahweh's right hand—which will still be "torn off." It is probably this passage from which Haggai borrowed his image when he describes Yahweh's choosing of Zerubbabel with the words: "I will make you like a signet ring" (Hag. 2:24). Just as Jehoiachin was "torn off" as a signet ring at the beginning of the exile, at the end of the exile Zerubbabel is chosen anew and placed as a signet ring on Yahweh's finger.[47]

The text of Ezk. 28:12 is obscure.[48] It is possible that in the original text the king of Tyre was likened to a seal.[49]

Otzen

---

40 R. Kilian, "Der Verstockungsauftrag Jesajas," in *Bausteine biblischer Theologie. Festschrift G. J. Botterweck. BBB,* 50 (1977), 209-225.

41 N. Porteous, *Daniel. OTL* (1965), 140.

42 *Ibid.,* 171.

43 See III above.

44 Moscati, *Bibl,* 30 (1949), 319.

45 E. Würthwein, *Das fünf Megilloth. HAT,* XVIII (^{2}1969), 68.

46 A. Weiser, *Das Buch Jeremia 1–25:14. ATD,* XX (^{6}1969), 194.

47 F. Horst, *Die zwölf Kleinen Propheten. HAT,* XIV (^{3}1964), 209.

48 W. Zimmerli, *Ezekiel 2. Herm* (1983).

49 Cf. LXX.

חתן *ḥtn*; חָתָן *ḥāṯān*; חֹתֵן *ḥōṯēn*

Contents: I. 1. Ancient Near East; 2. Etymology. II. 1. Meanings and Occurrences; 2. Distribution; 3. Related Terms; 4. Versions. III. Ex. 4:24-26.

I. 1. *Ancient Near East.* The root *ḥtn* has to do with a relationship of affinity, in contrast to consanguinity. This relationship is brought into being by marriage between one spouse (or by extension the spouse's family) and the blood relatives (cognates) of the other spouse. It occurs primarily in West Semitic languages and also in Akkadian, although it may represent a West Semitic loanword there.[1] We will start with the nouns that designate persons, then go on to abstract nouns and verbs, most of which are probably denominative.

In each case the most important noun is a form corresponding to Biblical Heb. *ḥāṯān*. Everywhere it refers primarily to a son-in-law: Ugar. *ḫatnu;*[2] Middle Heb.

ḥtn. F. Delitzsch, *Prolegomena eines neuen hebräisch-aramäischen Wörterbuchs zum AT* (Leipzig, 1886); A. Goetze, "Short or long *a*? (Notes on Some Akkadian Words)," *Or,* 16 (1947), 239-250; J. Hoftijzer and G. van der Kooij, *Aramaic Texts from Deir 'Alla. DMOA,* 19 (1976); A. Jamme, *Sabaean Inscriptions from Maḥram Bilqîs (Mârib)* (Baltimore, 1962); J. D. Michaelis, *Supplementa ad lexica hebraica,* II (Göttingen, 1785), 988f.; T. C. Mitchell, "The Meaning of the Noun *ḥtn* in the OT," *VT,* 19 (1969), 93-112; W. W. Müller, "Altsüdarabische Beiträge zum hebräischen Lexikon," *ZAW,* 75 (1963), 304-316; T. Nöldeke, *Mandäische Grammatik* (1875; repr. Darmstadt, 1964); J. Wellhausen, *Reste arabischen Heidentums* (^{2}1897); A. J. Wensinck, "Khitān," in his *Handwörterbuch des Islam* (Leiden, 1941), 314-17; H. von Wissmann, *Zur Geschichte und Landeskunde von Alt-Südarabien. SAW,* Phil.-hist. Kl., 246 (1964).

On III (besides the comms.): W. Beltz, "Religionsgeschichtliche Marginalie zu Ex 4 24-26," *ZAW,* 87 (1975), 209-211; Y. Blau, "The *Ḥatan Damim* (Ex. IV:24-26)," *Tarbiz,* 26 (1956/57), 1-3 [Hebrew], I [English]; B. S. Childs, *Myth and Reality in the OT. SBT,* 27 (1960); J. Coppens, "La prétendue agression nocturne de Jahvé contre Moïse, Séphorah et leur fils," *ETL,* 18 (1941), 68-73; W. Dumbrell, "Exodus 4:24-26: A Textual Re-Examination," *HThR,* 65 (1972), 285-290; G. Fohrer, *Überlieferung und Geschichte des Exodus. BZAW,* 91 (1964), 45ff. (bibliog.); J. de Groot, "The Story of the Bloody Husband (Exodus IV 24-26)," *OTS,* 2 (1943), 10-17; J. Hehn, "Der 'Blutbräutigam' Ex 4 24-26," *ZAW,* 50 (1932), 1-8; H. Junker, "Der Blutbräutigam: Eine textkritische und exegetische Studie zu Ex 4 24-26," *Alttestamentliche Studien Friedrich Nötscher. BBB,* 1 (1950), 120-28; H. Kosmala, "The 'Bloody Husband,' " *VT,* 12 (1962), 14-28; P. Middlekoop, "The Significance of the Story of the 'Bloody Husband' (Ex 4:24-26)," *Southeast Asia Journal of Theology,* 8 (1966/67), 34-38; J. Morgenstern, "The 'Bloody Husband' (?) (Exod. 4:24-26) Once Again," *HUCA,* 34 (1963), 35-70; G. Richter, "Zwei alttestamentliche Studien. I. Der Blutbräutigam," *ZAW,* 39 (1921), 123-28; L. F. Rivera, "El 'esposo sangriento' (Ex 4,24-26)," *Rev Bíbl,* 25 (1963), 129-136; H. Schmid, "Mose, der Blutbräutigam: Erwägungen zu Ex 4,24-26," *Jud,* 22 (1966), 113-18; S. Talmon, "The Bloody Husband," *Eretz-Israel,* 3 (1954), 93-96 [Hebrew], IV [English]; G. Vermès, *Scripture and Tradition in Judaism. StPb,* 4 (1961), 178-192 ("Circumcision and Exodus IV 24-26").

1 Goetze, 247.

2 *UT* 77, 25 = *KTU,* 1.24, 25; *PRU,* III, 233.

ḥāṯān; Jewish Aram.,[3] Syr., Christian Palestinian Aram., Sam. *ḥaṯna'*, usually representing Heb. *ḥāṯān*; Nabatean *ḥtn;*[4] Mand. *hatna;*[5] Arab. *ḫatan;* Akk. *ḫatanu(m), ḫatnu;*[6] OSA *ḫtn*[7] (not "relative"[8] but "son-in-law,"[9] possibly also "brother-in-law").

Besides "son-in-law," the meaning "brother-in-law" is found in Syriac ("sister's husband"), Mandaic (fem. *hatnan,* "sister-in-law"[10]), and Akkadian.[11] The meaning "bridegroom" (the nonconsanguineous male married to a woman) is found in Old Aramaic,[12] Jewish Aramaic, Syriac, Christian Palestinian Aramaic (primarily representing Heb. *ḥāṯān* in these last three), Mandaic, Arabic, and possibly once in Akkadian, if in Gilg. VI, 7 (Ishtar to Gilgamesh: "You shall be my spouse") a Late Babylonian variant[13] has *ḫatanu* instead of *ḫā'iru,* "spouse."[14] Lane[15] also records for Arab. *ḫatan* the meanings "father-in-law" and "husband of an aunt (paternal or maternal)." The meaning "father-in-law" is also given for Mand. *hatna.*[16] In a Hittite letter, Akk. *ḫadanu* refers to an affine relationship of the second degree, designating the son-in-law of a woman in relationship to the woman's brother.[17]

In Ugaritic, *ḫtn* appears as a personal name;[18] at Mari (early 2nd millennium) it is an element of West Semitic personal names.[19]

Various abstract nouns have the meaning "affinity": Jewish Aram. *ḥîttûnā'*, Syr. *m*ᵉ*ḥattnūṯā, ḥuttānā* (also "marriage"); or "marriage," "wedding": Middle Heb. *ḥîttûn,* Syr. *ḥaṯnūṯā* (Cant. 3:11[20]). In Akkadian, too, if we are not dealing with a Canaanite loanword, *ḫatnūtu* means "wedding" (in the idiom *ḫatnūtam epēšu,* "celebrate a marriage," "marry," in a letter from Tell Ta'annak[21]). An occurrence of *ḥtn* in Imperial Aramaic[22] is uncertain both in reading and meaning ("marriage"?).[23] Also obscure

---

3 Also Bab. *Yebam.* 52a; *CIJ,* I, 290, 1.
4 *CIS,* II, 209, 7; see Mitchell, 110f.
5 *MdD,* 128b.
6 *CAD,* VI (1956), 148; *AHw,* I, 335b.
7 *RÉS* 4878, 2.
8 Müller, 309.
9 Von Wissmann, 398.
10 *MdD,* 128b.
11 E.g., G. Boyer, *Textes juridiques et administratifs. ARM,* VIII (1958), 68, 6, referring to several men.
12 Deir 'allā, combination II, 7; Hoftijzer-van der Kooij, 173ff.
13 *KAR,* 115, 8.
14 *CAD,* VI, 148b; but *AHw,* I, 335b suggests a possible error.
15 I, 704.
16 *MdD,* 128b, and Nöldeke, 107, 2; neither includes a citation.
17 *KUB,* XXIII, 85, 8; *CAD,* VI, 148b.
18 *UT* 1099, 20, 23, 27 = *KTU,* 4.269, 20, 23, 27.
19 *APNM,* 101 and 205f.
20 See II.1.d below.
21 W. F. Albright, "A Prince of Taanach in the Fifteenth Century B.C.," *BASOR,* 94 (1944), 23, including n. 73; *CAD,* VI, 150a; *AHw,* I, 336a.
22 *RÉS,* 1785, G.
23 Cf. *DISO,* 98.

are the etymology and meaning of OSA *mḫtn:* "ceremonial place,"[24] "cultic site?"[25] "house of circumcision."[26]

Except for Arabic, all verbal forms of *ḥtn* are denominative; they are mostly reflexive with the meaning "become related by marriage": Middle Hebrew (hithpael), Jewish Aramaic (ithpael), and Syriac (ethpael). Middle Hebrew, like Biblical Hebrew, uses the qal participle with the meaning "father-in-law." Up to this point, the usage of the verb is dependent on Biblical Hebrew. In addition, Late Rabbinic Hebrew has a pual ptcp. *m*e*ḥuttān*, "related by marriage," applied to both fathers-in-law, the father of the husband and the father of the wife.[27] Syr. *ḥtn* paal stands in Gen. 38:8 for *gambreúesthai*, "marry": here it does not represent Heb. *ḥtn* but rather the piel of *ybm*, "marry a (dead) brother's wife" (→ יבם *ybm*). In Ugaritic, *ḥtn* means "marry,"[28] in OSA, "join (two families) through marriage."[29] In Mandaic, the paal of *htn* means "join (a man and a woman) in marriage."[30]

Arabic exhibits a unique and important development: in stem III, the verb *ḫatana*, denominative from *ḫatan*, has the meaning "become related by marriage."[31] In stems I and VIII (pass.), the verb also means "circumcise," hence the derived nouns *ḫatn*, *ḫitān*, "circumcision."[32]

2. *Etymology.* There are two possibilities to be considered for the semasiological development of *ḥāṯān*, etc.

a. Besides the noun *ḫatanu(m)*, Akkadian has a verb *ḫatānu* with the meaning "protect."[33] Delitzsch[34] had already suggested that the two are related.[35] Therefore *KBL*³ explains Heb. *ḥāṯān* as follows: "One who through marriage (as son-in-law or brother-in-law) is related to someone else and his family, and enjoys their protection."[36] This explanation assumes that the *ḥāṯān* ("son-in-law"; the meaning "brother-in-law" does not occur in Hebrew[37]) joins the household of his father-in-law and thus receives his protection.[38] Such an occurrence was possible, for example, in the case of an *errēbu* marriage,[39] but it was certainly not the rule. Normally the wife becomes part of her husband's family. Since it is hardly appropriate to derive the basic meaning of

---

24 Jamme, 55f.
25 Müller, 309.
26 *LexSyr*, 264b; cf. Arab. *ḫatana*, "circumcise."
27 *WTM*, II, 129b.
28 *KTU*, 1.24, 32; also *UT*, no. 1025; but Mitchell, 110, n. 1, reads "marriage."
29 Ja 651, 14; Jamme, 155f.
30 *MdD*, 155.
31 Lane, I, 703.
32 See I.2.b below.
33 *CAD*, VI, 148f.; *AHw*, I, 335f.
34 Pp. 90f.
35 See also Goetze, 247.
36 P. 350b.
37 See II.1.a below.
38 Delitzsch, 91.
39 E. Ebeling, "Ehe," *RLA*, II (1938), 283; F. Horst, "Ehe im AT," *RGG*³, II, 316.

a word from a secondary usage, we may conclude that *ḥāṯān*, "son-in-law," does not derive from Akk. *ḫatānu*, "protect."

b. The fact that Arab. *ḫatana* can (also) mean "circumcise" has led scholars to posit for Heb. *ḥtn* an association involving circumcision, the bridegroom, and marriage in general.[40] Levy[41] even postulates for Heb. *ḥāṯān* the basic meaning "the child on whom circumcision is performed," from which in turn the meanings "bridegroom" and "son-in-law" are derived. The only OT text exhibiting a connection between *ḥāṯān* and circumcision is Ex. 4:26b; but this very passage shows that reference of the root *ḥtn* to circumcision is here unique.[42]

II. 1. *Meanings and Occurrences.* a. In OT Hebrew, the noun *ḥāṯān* is the basic word. It means primarily a (young) man in relationship to his father-in-law, then also in relationship to the young woman to whom he is espoused before their marriage, his "bride"; thus *ḥāṯān* means "son-in-law" or "bridegroom." Thus the OT speaks of Lot's sons-in-law (Gen. 19:12 [or delete *ḥāṯān û*[43]],14), calls Samson the son-in-law of an anonymous Timnite (Jgs. 15:6), calls the Levite from the hill country of Ephraim the son-in-law of a man from Bethlehem (Jgs. 19:5), speaks of David as the son-in-law of King Saul (1 S. 18:18; 24:12[Eng. v. 11]), calls Tobiah, the opponent of Nehemiah, the son-in-law of Shecaniah (Neh. 6:18), and refers to one of the sons of Jehoiada the high priest as the son-in-law of Sanballat the Horonite (Neh. 13:28).

Whenever *ḥāṯān* means "bridegroom" in the OT, it never refers to a specific individual. Instead, the "bridegroom"—like the "bride" (*kallâ*) who is usually associated with him—almost always appears as the typical representative of a person who is especially happy. A bridegroom's rejoicing over his bride is like God's rejoicing over Jerusalem in the day of salvation (Isa. 62:5); the author of the short hymn of praise in Isa. 61:10 likens his rejoicing in God to that of a bridegroom and bride adorning themselves for their wedding. As the typical expression of happiness, the joyous voice of bridegroom and bride will be silenced when the threatened disaster comes to pass (Jer. 7:34; 16:9; 25:10), just as it will be heard again when God's favor is restored (Jer. 33:11). The rising sun is compared to a bridegroom leaving his chamber (Ps. 19:6[5]). And even the bride and bridegroom are summoned from their chambers to participate in the penitential liturgy (Joel 2:16). The meaning "bridegroom" is usually also posited in the phrase *ḥ^{a}ṯan dāmîm* (Ex. 4:25f.), which is accordingly translated "bridegroom of blood."[44]

Finally, the noun *ḥāṯān* can be used in a general sense for someone related through marriage. The marriage of Jehoram, king of Judah, to Athaliah, the sister of Ahab, king of Israel (she was the "daughter of Omri" [2 K. 8:26], not the "daughter of

---

[40] Wellhausen, 175, etc.
[41] *WTM*, II, 129b.
[42] See III below.
[43] *KBL*^{3}, 350b.
[44] See III below.

Ahab" [v. 18][45]) means that his son Ahaziah was *ḥ^a^tan bêṯ-'aḥ'āḇ,* an "affine of the house of Ahab" (2 K. 8:27).[46]

b. The verb *ḥtn* is a denominative from the subst. *ḥāṯān.*[47] The qal is represented only by the participle.[48] The hithpael means "enter into a relationship of affinity." The Israelites would enter into such a relationship with the previous inhabitants of the land (of Canaan) if they gave their daughters to (the sons of) the Canaanites and took for themselves or their sons daughters of the Canaanites—a course of action desired by the Shechemites (Gen. 34:9) but forbidden the Israelites in Dt. 7:3 and threatened with punishment in Josh. 23:12.

Ezra is forced to learn that the Israelites, including the priests and Levites, have entered into a relationship with "abominable people" by intermarrying with women of foreign ancestry (Ezr. 9, esp. v. 14). And Jehoshaphat, king of Judah, had made a marriage alliance with the Israelite king Ahab (2 Ch. 18:1) by allowing his son Jehoram to marry Athaliah, Ahab's sister.[49] A special case arises when through marriage a man becomes the son-in-law of the bride's father, as in the case of David and Saul (1 S. 18:21-23,26f.), as well as Solomon and Pharaoh (1 K. 3:1).

c. The qal ptcp. *ḥōṯēn,* "one who has a son-in-law," "father-in-law,"[50] refers to the father of a bride or wife. Examples include the father-in-law of the Levite from the hill country of Ephraim (Jgs. 19:4,7,9); the father-in-law of Moses, who has different names in different traditions: Jethro (Ex. 3:1; 4:18 [*yeṯer*]; 18:1f.,5-8,12ab,14f.,17, 24,27), priest of Midian (3:1; 18:1), or Hobab, son of Reuel the Midianite (Nu. 20:29) or Kenite (Jgs. 1:16[LXX]; 4:11), also Reuel, priest of Midian (Ex. 2:21; cf. vv. 16,18). The corresponding feminine form *ḥōṯeneṯ* refers to the mother of a bride or wife as mother-in-law: "Cursed be he who lies with his mother-in-law (*ḥōṯeneṯ*, Dt. 27:23)"; cf. Lev. 20:14: "If a man takes a wife and her mother also, it is wickedness (*zimmâ*)."

d. From the denominative verb *ḥtn* is derived the subst. *ḥ^a^ṯunnâ,*[51] which occurs in the OT only in Cant. 3:11: "Go forth, O daughters of Zion, and behold King Solomon, with the crown with which his mother crowned him on the day of his *ḥ^a^ṯunnâ*, on the day of the gladness of his heart." Usually *ḥ^a^ṯunnâ* is translated "wedding";[52] more precisely—as the association of *ḥ^a^ṯunnâ* with *ḥāṯān* in the sense of "bridegroom" shows and the parallelism with "day of the gladness of his heart"

---

45 J. Begrich, "Atalja, die Tochter Omris," *ZAW,* 53 (1935), 78f.; cf. W. Rudolph, *Chronikbücher. HAT,* XXI (1955), 264.

46 Cf. the discussion of 2 Ch. 18:1 in the next section.

47 *GesB*, 269a; *KBL*³, 350b.

48 See the next section.

49 See the discussion of 2 K. 8:27 in II.1.a above.

50 *KBL*³, 350b.

51 On the form, see *BLe,* § 467r ′ ′ ′.

52 *KBL*³, 351a; also "marriage."

suggests—what is here expressed is the significance of this day from Solomon's perspective: it is the day on which he becomes a bridegroom.

2. *Distribution.* The noun *ḥōṯān* occurs 20 times in the OT. The occurrences with the meaning "son-in-law" (9 times) and "related by marriage" (once) are found in the "historical books"; those with the meaning "bridegroom" appear in the prophetic books (7 times) and the Psalter (once). The other 2 occurrences are in Ex. 4:25f. The hithpael of *ḥtn* occurs 11 times, *ḥōṯēn,* "father-in-law," 21 times, and *ḥōṯenet̲,* "mother-in-law," and *ḥᵃṯunnâ,* "marriage," "bridegrooming," once each.

3. *Related Terms.* When the root *ḥtn* does not refer to relationship through marriage in general—*ḥāṯān,* "related by marriage" (2 K. 8:27); *ḥtn* hithpael, "enter into an affine relationship" (Gen. 34:9; Dt. 7:3; Josh. 23:12; 2 Ch. 18:1; Ezr. 9:14)—it has to do with the relationship of a man to his wife's family. He is *ḥāṯān,* "son-in-law," to his *ḥōṯēn,* "father-in-law," and *ḥōṯenet̲,* "mother-in-law"; he is *ḥāṯān,* "bridegroom," to his *kallâ,* "bride"; he "becomes the son-in-law" (*ḥtn* hithpael) of a man (1 S. 18:21-23,26f.; 1 K. 3:1).

On the other hand, *kallâ* refers to a girl or woman not only in her relationship as "bride" to her "bridegroom" (Isa. 49:18; 61:10; 62:5; Jer. 7:34; 16:9; 25:10; 33:11; Joel 2:16; cf. Cant. 4:8-12; 5:1; also 2 S. 17:3 conj.:[53] "as a bride turns to her husband" [on *šûḇ,* "turn to," see, for example, Ps. 9:18(17); 119:79; Isa. 19:22]), but also as daughter-in-law to her husband's father (Gen. 11:31; 38:11,16,24; Lev. 18:15; 20:12; 1 S. 4:19; 1 Ch. 2:4; Ezk. 22:11; Hos. 4:13f.) or mother (Ruth 1:6-8,22; 2:20,22; 4:15; Mic. 7:6).

Biblical Hebrew has separate words for the wife's in-laws: *ḥām,* "husband's father" (Gen. 38:13,25; 1 S. 4:19,21); *ḥāmôṯ,* "husband's mother" (Ruth 1:14; 2:11,18f.,23; 3:1,6,16f.; Mic. 7:6).

Just as *ḥᵃṯunnâ* refers to the relationship of a bridegroom to his bride from the groom's perspective, "bridegrooming" (Cant. 3:11), so *kᵉlûlôṯ* refers to the "bride time" (Jer. 2:2).

The terminological differentiation between the parents of the husband and the parents of the wife is eliminated in Middle Hebrew: *ḥām* and *ḥāmôṯ* refer to the father-in-law and mother-in-law of both the husband and the wife,[54] just as in late Rabbinic Hebrew the pual ptcp. *mᵉḥuttān* refers to both fathers-in-law.[55]

On the special case of a brother-in-law, the brother of a man who has died without offspring, who is required to take the widow (*yᵉḇāmâ*) in levirate marriage (*ybm* piel), → יבם *ybm.*

4. *Versions.* The Targumim and Syriac keep the root *ḥtn.*[56] The LXX and Vulg. make a distinction in translating *ḥāṯān.* When it means "son-in-law," they use *gam-*

[53] See *BHK, BHS,* and the comms.
[54] *WTM,* II, 68b.
[55] *Ibid.,* II, 129b.
[56] See I.1 above.

brós/*gener* (Gen. 19:12,14a,14b [LXX only]; Jgs. 15:6; 19:5; 1 S. 18:18 [vv. 17-19 are absent in LXX^B]; 22:14; Neh. 6:18; 13:28 [not LXX]; [cf. 1 Macc. 16:12]), as well as in 2 K. 8:27 (Origen, Lucian), where the meaning is "related through marriage." When it means "bridegroom," they use *nymphíos*/*sponsus* (Ps. 19:6[5]; Isa. 61:10; 62:5; Jer. 7:34; 16:9; 25:10; 33:11; Joel 2:16). Sometimes there is uncertainty: in Jgs. 15:6 and 19:5, LXX^B uses *nymphíos* for *ḥāṯān*, "son-in-law," as does the entire LXX tradition in Neh. 13:28. Ex. 4:25f. is discussed below.

The LXX distinguishes the fathers-in-law, translating *ḥōṯēn*, "husband's father-in-law," as *gambrós* (20 times; in Ex. 18:14, *ḥōṯēn* is not translated), and *ḥām*, "wife's father-in-law," as *pentherós* (Gen. 38:13,25; 1 S. 4:19,21); for *ḥōṯeneṯ* (and 12 times for *ḥāmôṯ*) it uses *pentherá* (Dt. 27:23 [A; B instead curses intercourse with the *nýmphē*, "bride"]). The Vulg. distinguishes for *ḥōṯēn* between *socer* (Jgs. 19:4,7,9, and 4 times for *ḥām*), corresponding to *socrus* for *ḥōṯeneṯ*, and *cognatus* (Ex. 3:1; 4:18; 18:1,5-8,12a,14,27; Nu. 10:29; Jgs. 1:16; 4:11). For *ḥ^a^ṯunnâ* we find the unusual *nýmpheusis*/*desponatio*.

The hithpael of *ḥtn* is rendered by the LXX without distinction as *gambreúein* (Dt. 7:3; Ezr. 9:14 [B]) or *epigambreúein* (Gen. 34:9; 1 S. 18:21 [except B],22f.,26f.; 2 Ch. 18:1; Ezr. 9:14 [A]; [cf. 1 Macc. 10:54,56]), as well as *epigamían poieín* (Josh. 23:12). In 1 S. 18:21-23,27, the Vulg. appropriately uses *gener esse* (or *gener fieri*, v. 26); elsewhere it uses various expressions for entering into an affine relationship: *affinitate coniungi* (1 K. 3:1; 2 Ch. 18:1), *connubia iungere* (Gen. 34:9) or *miscere* (Josh. 23:12), *matrimonia iungere* (Ezr. 9:14), *coniugia sociare* (Dt. 7:3).

III. Ex. 4:24-26. The phrase *ḥ^a^ṯan dāmîm* poses a special problem. It occurs in only a single passage, Ex. 4:25f., and is usually translated "bridegroom of blood." The complete passage (vv. 24-26) reads as follows:

> At a lodging place on the way Yahweh met him and sought to kill him.
> (25) Then Zipporah took a flint and cut off her son's foreskin, and touched Moses' feet with it, and said, "Surely you are a *ḥ^a^ṯan-ddāmîm* to me!"
> (26) So he let him alone. Then it was that she said, "You are a *ḥ^a^ṯan dāmîm*," because of the circumcision.

Among the versions, the LXX and Targumim (except for the Samaritan), not understanding the Hebrew text, have instead of *ḥ^a^ṯan dāmîm* "blood of circumcision." Symmachus and Theodotion (and Aquila?), with *nymphíos haimátōn*, follow the MT, as does the Samaritan Targum, with *ḥmwy mdmym*, "my father-in-law (for Heb. *ḥōṯēn*) by blood." The Syriac paraphrases: "By bond of blood you are my bridegroom."

The question of what *ḥ^a^ṯan dāmîm* means involves other difficulties deriving from the text. It is as inappropriate here as in Gen. 32:25; 38:7; 2 S. 24:1 to inquire after a reason for Yahweh's hostility.[57] That the object of the attack was not the child[58] but Moses himself (as the Syriac already saw) is clear from the observation that there is

57 E.g., Wellhausen, 175: Moses was uncircumcised.
58 E.g., Morgenstern, 44, 66f.

no mention of the son until v. 25aα,[59] as well as the original connection of v. 24 to v. 20a, which initially spoke only of a single son of Moses and Zipporah (cf. 2:22), not two sons (MT, following 18:3). In addition, Zipporah touches the foreskin of her son not to the "feet" (i.e., the genitals) of her son[60]—which would bleed automatically because of the circumcision—but to those of Moses. That Yahweh leaves him alone (v. 26a)—not because of the circumcision[61] but because the blood was applied to Moses—shows that this blood ritual (like that in Ex. 12:22f.) was considered apotropaic.

The observation that the blood for this ritual was obtained through circumcision leads us to the purpose of the brief narrative. The point is not to justify the circumcision of young children instead of adults,[62] but to explain the phrase *ḥ^a^ṯan dāmîm*,[63] as the concluding clause of v. 26b underlines. Ex. 4:25f. is the only text we have from Northwest Semitic that connects the root *ḥtn* with circumcision. It is commonly assumed that circumcision played a role here with the use of *ḥāṯān*, etc., but this assumption is improbable. If so, the phrase *ḥ^a^ṯan dāmîm*, deriving from another linguistic background (Midianite bedouin?—cf. Gen. 25:2), would need to be explained for Israelites. If we assume a semantic connection with Arab. *ḫatana*, "circumcise," *ḥ^a^ṯan dāmîm* can be interpreted as "blood-circumcised (person),"[64] at least in v. 26. In v. 25, however, the "to me" suggests a reinterpretation for Israelites: "You are a blood-relative (by marriage) to me." The translation "bridegroom of blood" is inappropriate for Moses, who is already long married; the assumption of a connection between circumcision and marriage[65] is superfluous.

Kutsch

---

[59] Fohrer, 47.
[60] For a different interpretation, see Kosmala, 24; Fohrer, 47.
[61] M. Noth, *Exodus*. *OTL* (Eng. trans. 1962), 49f.
[62] Wellhausen, 175; Childs, 60; Fohrer, 47f.
[63] Schmid, 115.
[64] Kosmala, 27; Fohrer, 47.
[65] E.g., Junker, 123; Noth, 35f.

חָתַת *ḥāṯaṯ*; חַת *ḥaṯ*; חִתָּה *ḥittâ*; חִתִּית *ḥittîṯ*; חֲתַת *ḥ^a^ṯaṯ* I and II; חַתְחַתִּים *ḥaṯḥattîm*; מְחִתָּה *m^e^ḥittâ*

Contents: I. Semitic. II. OT.

I. Semitic. Akk. *ḫatû(m)* II means "strike down" (the land of the enemy by disease); philologically, we would expect the Hebrew equivalent to be *ḥṭ'*, but the etymological relationship is obvious. Closer to Heb. *ḥtt* is Akk. *ḫātu(m), ḫattu(m)* I, "terror, panic."[1]

In Ugaritic we find *ḫt* I, "broken," in the Keret epic.[2] The close connection with a root ending with *aleph* is evidenced by Arab. *ḥata'a* VIII, "be broken"; Arab. *ḫatta* means "wear down or away," "destroy," "break"; *ḫattun* means "death," "destruction"; *ḫatatun* is disease affecting trees.[3] As Arabic parallels *GesB* cites *ḫatatun,* "lack of vigor," *ḫatit,* "slight, contemptible," *ḫatta* IV with *min,* "be ashamed," all with *ḫ*.[4]

Aram. *ḥ^aṯaṯ,* "break," is a hebraism.[5] Syriac also borrows the Hebrew word. Whether Syr. *ḥaṯhet,* "lead astray," *ḥaṭîṭâ,* "precise," and their associated substantives are associated with the Hebrew word is dubious.[6] In Middle Hebrew such analogical forms as *ḥty, ḥt',* and *ḥth* are common. Derived substantives include *ḥittûy,* "breaking," *ḥittûṯ, ḥittîṯ,* "terror."[7] There are three nominal hapax legomena in the OT (*ḥittâ, ḥ^aṯaṯ,* and *ḥaṯḥattîm*) that are common in Modern Hebrew, as well as *ḥaṯ* and *m^eḥittâ*.[8] In Ethiopic we find *ḫatāt,* "be torn to pieces."[9]

In the Dead Sea scrolls, the word occurs in the War scroll, the Thanksgiving scroll, and the Isaiah commentary. In the first, it appears in the biblicizing exhortation "do not be afraid and do not be terrified" (1QM 15:8 [restored]), twice in the Thanksgiving scroll in the sense of "lose courage" (1QH 2:35; 7:8), and in 4QpIs[a] in the expression *wḥtw wnms 1[b..]* (on Isa. 10:24f.), translated by Allegro: "And they will be dismayed, and will melt the he[art of . . .]."[10]

II. OT.

1. The prophetic books contain 37 of the 56 occurrences, the Pentateuch only 2 (Dt. 1:21; 31:8). Apart from the derived substantives, the root does not occur in Psalms and Proverbs. The basic meaning of the passive stems is "be terrified," that of the active stems, "terrify." Jenni goes into more detail: "be filled with terror (not simply 'be afraid')," and piel, "terrify (fill with terror)."[11] Joüon lists the various translations and notes that the meaning of the root is in fact rather vague. Depending on the context, the root can stand for fear, confusion, or weakness.[12]

---

1 *AHw,* I, 336.

2 *WUS,* no. 1101.

3 Lane, I/2, 508f.; R. Dozy, *Supplément aux dictionnaires arabes,* I (Leiden, [2]1927; repr. 1981), 246f.; Wehr, 155.

4 P. 269.

5 G. Dalman, *Aramäisch-neuhebräisches Handwörterbuch zu Targum, Talmud und Midrasch* (Frankfort, [2]1922), 155.

6 *LexSyr,* 263f.

7 *WTM,* II, 125f.

8 See below.

9 *TigrWb,* 81.

10 J. M. Allegro, "Further Messianic References in Qumran Literature," *JBL,* 75 (1956), 174-187; Document III, Fragment C, 179.

11 E. Jenni, *Das hebräische Pi'el* (Zurich, 1968), 67f.

12 P. Joüon, "Notes de lexicographie hébraique. III. Racine חתת," *MUSJ,* 5 (1911/12), 425-432.

Two usages stand out in the OT. On the one hand, the word is used to depict the terror evoked when Yahweh comes to punish. On the other, the root has a firm place in the Deuteronomistic exhortation "Fear not." In the OT it appears in company with *'āzar,* "gird," → בּוֹשׁ *bôš* [*bôsh*], *b't,* → זעק *zā'aq, hêlîl* (→ ילל *yll*), → ירא *yārē',* → כרת *krt,* → לכד *lāḵaḏ,* → ערץ *'āraṣ,* → פקד *pāqaḏ,* → רעע *r"*, and → שׁדד *šdd.* It is noteworthy that the root is not paired with → פחד *pḥd.* When the cause of the terror is mentioned, it is linked with the verb by means of *min* or *mippᵉnê.*

2. Isa. 8:9 uses the plural qal imperative 3 times in poetic language: when God comes, the peoples are to gird themselves and be "dismayed."[13] The verse has been the subject of several special investigations;[14] its provenance is disputed. Wildberger[15] considers it Isaianic, calling *ḥtt* a "favorite expression" on the part of Isaiah and finding in the "ironic imperatives" an exact parallel to Isa. 6:9b. In fact the word occurs 10 times in Isaiah I (21 times in Jeremiah), although the genuineness of most of the Isaiah passages is disputed. There can hardly be any doubts about Isa. 20:5: the inhabitants of Judah will be "dismayed" (par. *bôš*) when Yahweh takes Egypt and Ethiopia captive through the agency of the king of Assyria. But even the officers of Assyria will desert their standards in panic (Isa. 31:9). Isa. 37:27 (par. 2 K. 19:26) announces to the Assyrians that they will be dismayed and confounded (*bôš*) (perfect tense). Jeremiah, too, takes aim at both the Israelites and their enemies: the wise men (Jer. 8:9, *ḥtt* together with the hiphil of *bôš* and the niphal of *lkd*), Moab (48:1 [sg.],20,39 [*ḥat*], alongside the pual of *šdd,* the hiphil of *bôš,* the niphal of *lkd, hêlîl,* and *zā'aq*), Babylon (50:2 [twice], alongside the niphal of *lkd* and the hiphil of *bôš*), and its diviners (50:36).

Jer. 14:4, *hā'ᵃḏāmâ ḥattâ,* "the ground is dismayed," is usually emended, although it can be supported, especially on the basis of Arabic parallels; Rudolph reads *heḥārâ* and cites other proposals.[16] Ob. 9 tells the mighty men of Teman that they will be dismayed (*wᵉḥattû*) because the inhabitants of Mt. Esau will be slaughtered (niphal of *krt*). These passages can all be interpreted as looking forward to God's eschatological judgment. Whoever takes them in this sense while denying the existence of a preexilic eschatology must date them in the exilic or postexilic period.[17] Job 32:15 has nothing to do with eschatology; Elihu takes Job's friends to task for being discomfited (*ḥattû*) and having no word to say.

3. The niphal is the stem most frequently found in the OT. All attempts to make a clear semantic distinction between the qal and niphal remain problematical. There is a preponderance of noneschatological occurrences of the niphal, but it occurs also in clearly eschatological contexts.

---

13 On the problems of the text, esp. the first word *rō'û,* see H. Wildberger, *Jesaja. BK,* X/1 (1972), 329.

14 K. Budde, H. Schmidt, M. Saebø.

15 *BK,* X/1, 331.

16 *Jeremia. HAT,* XII (³1968), 98.

17 G. Fohrer, "Die Struktur der alttestamentlichen Eschatologie," *ThLZ,* 85 (1960), 416.

The niphal, too, occurs most frequently in Jeremiah; its appearances will be tallied here. The account of Jeremiah's call associates the niphal and hiphil in a punning sense: "Do not be dismayed (*'al-tēḥaṯ*) by them, lest I dismay you before them" (Jer. 1:17). For the hiphil form, the LXX uses *ptoēthḗs*. That the repetition of the verb is an intentional poetic device is shown by the prayer in Jer. 17:14-18 ("Heal me, O Yahweh, and I shall be healed . . ."); in v. 18a, both *bôš* and the niphal of *ḥtt* are repeated: " . . . let them be dismayed, but let me not be dismayed." Here we have antithetical parallelism. In other places (like v. 14a), the second verb form indicates the result of the action described by the first.[18] Also contrastive (although not from Jeremiah) is the warning against idolatry in 10:2: " . . . do not be dismayed at the signs of the heavens because (*kî*) the nations are dismayed at them" (both with *min*). In 23:4, we read that under the righteous branch of David and his good shepherds the people will fear (*yārē'*) no more, nor be dismayed (*w^e lō'-yēḥattû*), nor be afflicted (*pāqaḏ*). Like the whole pericope (23:1-4), this verse is in prose; the messianic prophecy immediately following (vv. 5f.) is in rhythmic form. The intransitive niphal is also used in Jer. 30:10, stylistically related to Deutero-Isaiah: "Then fear not (*yārē'*), O Jacob my servant, . . . nor be dismayed (*w^e' al-tēḥaṯ*), O Israel. . . ."[19] The verse reappears word for word in 46:27, and is probably a redactional addition in the MT.

The parallelism with *yārē'* found in all these Jeremiah passages reappears in 1 S. 17:11, as well as in all the passages in Deuteronomy, Joshua, and Chronicles, although they lack the eschatological element. The exhortation not to fear or be dismayed obviously found stereotyped expression in the encouraging exhortations of the Deuteronomistic school. Moses addresses all the people (Dt. 1:21) and Joshua (Dt. 31:8): "Do not fear or be dismayed"; 1:21 uses the negated imperative with *'al* and the short aorist, 31:8 uses *lō'* and the long aorist. In the parallel text Josh. 1:9,[20] *'al-tēḥāṯ* is preceded by *'al-ta'^a rōṣ*. The Deuteronomistic expression reappears with minor variations in Josh. 8:1 (sg.) and 10:25 (pl.); Chronicles also incorporates it in David's exhortation to Solomon (1 Ch. 22:13; 28:20), Jahaziel's exhortation to Judah (2 Ch. 20:15,17 [pl.]), and Hezekiah's exhortation to the inhabitants of Jerusalem (2 Ch. 32:7). Ezekiel is exhorted not to be afraid of or dismayed at the "rebellious house" (Ezk. 2:6; 3:9); in the former passage *yārē'* is construed with *min*, in the latter with the accusative, while *tēḥāṯ* uses *mipp^e nê(hem)*, as in Jer. 1:17 and Mal. 2:5.

The two verbs also appear juxtaposed in early prose. In the story of David and Goliath, the Israelites' fear of the Philistines is described in the words *wayyēḥattû wayyir^e' û m^e' ōḏ* (1 S. 17:11). Only in Mal. 2:5 is the pair of synonyms used for the fear of God: Yahweh's covenant with Levi consisted in giving him life and peace, and causing him to fear God and be in awe (*niḥaṯ*)[21] of his name.[22]

In a different sense, the verb is associated with Yahweh twice in Proto-Isaiah: the

---

18 M. Held, "The Action-Result (Factitive-Passive) Sequence of Identical Verbs in Biblical Hebrew and Ugaritic," *JBL*, 84 (1965), 272-282.

19 On the background of chaps. 30 and 31, see Rudolph, *HAT*, XII, 188-207.

20 Niphal or qal according to M. Noth, *Das Buch Josua. HAT*, VII (²1953), 22.

21 On the vocalization, see *GK*, §67u.

22 S. Plath, *Furcht Gottes. ArbT*, 2/2 (1962), 39, 45.

Assyrians will be terror-stricken at the voice of Yahweh (Isa. 30:31); just as a lion is not terrified (*yēḥaṯ*) by the shouting of the shepherds, so Yahweh will not be daunted from punishing Assyria (31:4). In Isa. 7:8, *yēḥaṯ* predicts the destruction of Ephraim as a people.

There are 2 occurrences of the verb side by side in Deutero-Isaiah (Isa. 51:6f.): although heaven and earth will pass away, Yahweh's deliverance will never waver (*lō' tēḥaṯ*), and (again par. *yārē'*) those who know righteousness are not to be dismayed (*'al-tēḥattû*) at the revilings of those who do not. In 51:6, *tēḥaṯ* was obviously read differently in the ancient versions; the LXX has *eklípē* (for *teḥdal?*). The Song of Hannah ends (1 S. 2:10) with a vision of Yahweh's universal judgment and the exaltation of the Messiah: "Yahweh—his adversaries will be dismayed" (there is no need for the proposed emendation of the 3rd person pl. niphal impf. *yēḥattû* to the 3rd person sg. impf. *yāḥēṯ*[23]). Job 39:22 describes the fearlessness of a warhorse (*wᵉlō' yēḥāṯ*). Job 21 describes the unadulterated happiness of the wicked. V. 13b appears inappropriate: "In a moment they go down in dismay to Sheol"; but *reg̲a'* can be interpreted to mean "peace,"[24] and *yēḥattû* can be read as *yēḥāṯû* (qal impf. of *nḥt*), following most of the ancient versions.[25]

4. The piel appears intransitively in Jer. 51:56. This construction is considered possible,[26] but both the LXX and Syriac read a variant text here; the text is suspect and probably incorrect. Job 7:14 is an apodosis beginning with the consecutive perf. piel *wᵉḥittattanî:* "Thou dost scare me with dreams and terrify me with visions." The consecutive perfect here is a frequentative relating to previous experiences, following conditional clauses with *kî*.[27]

5. There are 5 occurrences of the hiphil in Isaiah, Jeremiah, Habakkuk, and Job. Its causative function is hard to distinguish from that of the piel. In the messianic prophecy of Isa. 9:3(Eng. v. 4), the imagery appears to be interrupted by the hiphil of *ḥtt,* "terrify": ". . . the rod of his oppressor *haḥittōṯā*"; as in 1 S. 2:4, the smooth translation "thou hast broken" has been adopted. Jer. 49:37 uses the rare uncontracted form *wᵉhaḥtattî*.[28] The hiphil form in Jer. 1:17 was discussed above.

Hab. 2:17 threatens that the beasts will terrify the wicked on account of their violence and deadly destruction (*yᵉḥîṯan*[29]). The Qumran commentary reads *yḥth* or *wḥth,* the LXX *ptoḗsei;* the text is usually emended to *yᵉḥitteḵā*.[30] But the MT form can also be explained as a quantitative metathesis between consonant and vowel, often observed in later Hebrew, or as a form derived by analogy to the hollow verbs.[31] Job

---

23 H. J. Stoebe, *Das erste Buch Samuelis. KAT,* VIII/1 (1973), 102.

24 *GesB*, 746.

25 G. Fohrer, *Das Buch Hiob. KAT,* XVI (1963), 337f.

26 *GK,* §52k.

27 *Ibid.*, §112hh.

28 *Ibid.*, §67aa; Rudolph, *HAT,* XII, 272, eliminates the *h.*

29 On the connecting vowel *a,* see *GK,* §60d.

30 *BHS.*

31 *GK,* §20n.

asserts that he did not stand in fear (*'e'erôṣ*) of the multitude or allow the contempt of families to terrify (*y^eḥittēnî*) him (31:34).

This complete list of OT occurrences could be added to by emendations. In Jer. 21:13, *yāḥēṯ* (hiphil of *ḥtt*) is often read for *yēḥaṯ* (from *nḥt*), following the LXX; in Prov. 17:10, *tāḥēṯ* (hiphil of *ḥtt*) is similarly read for *tēḥṯ* (from *nḥt*), again with the LXX.[32] But the Masoretic derivation from *nḥt* has been strongly defended in both cases.[33]

6. The adj. *ḥaṯ* appears in 1 S. 2:4 and Jer. 46:5; it has also been explained as a qal participle. In the Song of Hannah it refers to the bows of the mighty (cf. Isa. 9:3[4]). The plural should not be emended to the singular;[34] it appears regularly following the genitive of the construct phrase.[35] Jer. 46:5 describes the flight of the vanquished Egyptians; *ḥattîm* is best taken here as meaning "dismayed" (Rudolph: "shocked"). In Gen. 9:2 (P), the word occurs again in conjunction with the root *yārē':* "The fear of you and the dread of you shall be upon every beast. . . ."[36] Job 41:25(33) calls the crocodile a creature *liḇlî-ḥāṯ;* here Fohrer, following Hölscher, reads the noun *ḥ^aṯaṯ,*[37] while earlier the emendation *l^eḇa'al ḥayyôṯ* was proposed.[38] In Modern Hebrew, *liḇlî-ḥaṯ* is commonly used in the sense "undismayed."

Another derivative (also used in Modern Hebrew) is *ḥittâ,* which appears only once in the OT, in Gen. 35:5 (E): when Jacob sets out for Bethel, a "terror from God" (*ḥittaṯ '^elōhîm*) falls upon the neighboring cities, preventing them from pursuing Jacob's family on account of their crime against Shechem.

The noun *ḥittîṯ,* "terror," appears only in two places in Ezekiel: 32:23-32 (7 times) and 26:17. In the description of Egypt's descent into the netherworld, there is a list of those slain and fallen by the sword who once spread terror (*nāṯ^enû ḥittîṯ[ām],* 32:23f., 26; of Tyre in 26:17; with *nittan* in 32:25; with *nāṯattî* in 32:32). In 32:27 we find the construct phrase *ḥittîṯ gibbôrîm,* in 32:30 the questionable *b^eḥittîṯām migg^eḇûrāṯām.*[39]

The noun *ḥ^aṯaṯ* appears only in Job 6:21, where fear is spoken of as a consequence of seeing calamity: "You see my calamity, and are afraid."

A pl. *ḥaṯḥattîm* (Modern Heb. "dangers") is found in Eccl. 12:5; Hertzberg translates "terrors."[40]

The later sections of Proverbs use the noun *m^eḥittâ* (also found in Modern Hebrew) in the sense of "ruin." It provides the link between Prov. 10:14 and 15: "The babbling

---

[32] O. Rössler, "Die Präfixkonjugation Qal der Verba Iae Nûn im althebräischen und das Problem der sogenannten Tempora," *ZAW,* 74 (1962), 127.

[33] Rudolph, *HAT,* XII, 138; B. Gemser, *Sprüch Salomos. HAT,* XVI (²1963), 73.

[34] *BHK.*

[35] *GK,* §146a; Stoebe, *KAT,* VIII/1, 102.

[36] The formula is discussed by C. Westermann, *Genesis 1-11* (Eng. trans., Minneapolis, 1984), 462f.

[37] *KAT,* XVI, 527.

[38] *BHK.*

[39] W. Zimmerli, *Ezekiel 2. Herm* (Eng trans. 1983), 169.

[40] H. Hertzberg, *Der Prediger. KAT,* XVII/4 (1963), *in loc.*

of a fool brings ruin near" (cf. 13:3; 18:7), and "The poverty of the poor is their ruin." Lack of people means ruin for a prince (14:28). Both the doing of justice (Prov. 21:15) and Yahweh himself (10:29) are *m^eḥittâ* to evildoers. Jeremiah prays that Yahweh will not be *m^eḥittâ* to him, but a refuge in the day of trouble (Jer. 17:17), and Deutero-Isaiah promises safety from fear and terror (Isa. 54:14). Moab will become a terror (or horror) to all its neighbors (Jer. 48:39). The only passage from the Psalms to use the root is Ps. 89:41(40): "Thou hast breached all his walls; thou hast made his strongholds a *m^eḥittâ*"; here the context suggests the meaning "destruction."

Finally, there is a proper name derived from *ḥtt: ḥ^aṯaṯ* (1 Ch. 4:13), which may contain an echo of the *paḥaḏ yiṣḥāq* (Gen. 31:42,53).

Maass

טַבּוּר *ṭabbûr* → הַר *har,* III, 437f.

טָבַח *ṭāḇaḥ;* טַבָּח *ṭabbāḥ;* טֶבַח *ṭeḇaḥ;* טִבְחָה *ṭiḇḥâ;* מַטְבֵּחַ *maṭbēaḥ*

Contents: I. Etymology and Semantics: 1. Ancient Near East; 2. OT Statistics; 3. *ṭabbāḥ;* 4. Secular Usage; 5. Versions. II. Ethical and Theological Usage: 1. Humans as Subject; 2. God as Subject.

I. Etymology and Semantics.

1. *Ancient Near East.* The root *ṭbḥ* is well represented in all the Semitic languages; its reflexes are semantically homogeneous.[1] Akk. *ṭabāḫu* and OSA *ṭbḫ* mean "slaughter." In Ugaritic, only verbal forms of *ṭbḫ* are known to occur.[2] The specialized meaning "cook" is found in the (damaged) passage "They cooked a kid in milk"[3] (→ גדי *g^eḏî* [*g^edhî*], → חלב *ḥālāḇ* [*chālābh*]); elsewhere it is not always possible to make a clear distinction between "slaughter" and "cook," e.g., "Slaughter/cook a lamb that I may eat it."[4] The basic meaning "slaughter" refers primarily to the preparation of festal banquets, but also to the slaughter of sacrificial animals (funerary sacrifice to Ba'al[5] or sacrifice to El[6]). Of frequent occurrence is the root *dbḥ,* "sacrifice";[7] less frequent is *šḫṭ,* "slaughter."

In Aramaic, Syriac, Mandaic, and Punic the root also can mean either "slaughter"

ṭāḇaḥ. J. Behm, "θύω," *TDNT,* III, 180-190; G. Dalman, *AuS,* VI (1939), 70-103; S. Grill, "Der Schlachttag Jahwes," *BZ,* N.S. 2 (1958), 278-283; O. Michel, "σφάζω," *TDNT,* VII, 925-938.

1 Cf. *KBL*³.

2 Citations in *UT,* no. 1029; *WUS,* no. 1111.

3 *KTU,* 1.23, 14.

4 *KTU,* 1.16 VI, 17; see Michel, 930, n. 27.

5 *KTU,* 1.6 I, 18-28.

6 *KTU,* 1.1 IV, 30.

7 → זבח *zāḇaḥ* [*zābhach*].

or "cook," as in Hebrew. In Arabic, however, *ṭabaḫa* means only "cook," while *ḏabaḥa* (or *saḥaṭa*) is used for "slaughter" or "sacrifice."

2. *OT Statistics*. The verb occurs 11 times, always in the qal. There are 2 occurrences of the noun *ṭabbāḥ*, "(male) cook" (1 S. 9:23f.), 1 of the fem. pl. *ṭabbāḥôṯ*, "(female) cooks" (1 S. 8:13), 31 occurrences of the masc. pl. *ṭabbāḥîm*, "bodyguards," 13 of *ṭeḇaḥ*, "slaughter," including Ezk. 21:20b conj., 3 of the synonymous *ṭiḇḥâ*, and 1 of *maṭbēaḥ*, "place of slaughter" (Isa. 14:21; cf. *mizbēaḥ*, "altar"). There are 3 occurrences of the cognate acc. *ṭbḥ ṭeḇaḥ*, "slaughter a slaughter (= an animal)" (Gen. 43:16 [J]; Prov. 9:2; Ezk. 21:15 [Eng. v. 10]). The similar *ṭbḥ ṭiḇḥâ* is also found (1 S. 25:11). Finally, there is the personal name Tebah (Gen. 22:24) and the toponym Tebah (2 S. 8:8 conj. = Tibhat of 1 Ch. 18:8).

3. *ṭabbāḥ*. There is no discernible development in usage and meaning except in the case of *ṭabāḥîm*, "bodyguards" of the king, a meaning that appears only in the OT. By etymology, they were (at least originally) involved with slaughtering and cooking (cf. the "chief butler" and "chief baker" in Gen. 40:2). They may also have functioned as executioners.[8] The title *śar haṭṭabbāḥîm* is given the Egyptian Potiphar 6 times (Gen. 37:36; 39:1; 40:3f.; 41:10,12). The passages are usually assigned to the Elohist; the use of the technical term cannot be dated. The Babylonian commander Nebuzaradan is likewise titled *raḇ-ṭabbāḥîm* (7 times in 2 K. 25:8-20, 17 times in Jer. 39:9–52:30). As late as Dnl. 2:14, Arioch is still called "captain of the bodyguard" (Aram. *raḇ-ṭabbāḥayyā'*). The somewhat narrower meaning "cook"—probably identical with "slaughterer" in earlier days—appears in 1 S. 8:13 and 9:23f.[9] Slaughtering was the job of men (Gen. 18:7; Jgs. 6:19; 1 S. 25:11).[10]

4. *Secular Usage*. Only in the OT do we find the limitation of *ṭbḥ* to the ordinary nonreligious slaughter of domestic animals to provide for a banquet (Gen. 43:16; Ex. 21:37[22:1] [Covenant Code]; Dt. 28:31; Prov. 9:2; cf. Mt. 22:4; Lk. 15:23). It is therefore comparatively infrequent, and remains distinct from the root → זבח *zbḥ*, undoubtedly related in Proto-Semitic, which occasionally refers to secular slaughter (1 S. 28:24; Ezk. 34:3[11]), but in the vast majority of occurrences means cultic slaughter for sacrifice.

The same is true of the much more common root → שׁחט *šāḥaṭ*, which focuses on the actual process of slaughtering and is usually—although not exclusively—used for cultic slaughtering. It became a technical term in P.[12]

Especially before Josiah's centralization of the cult in 621 B.C., secular slaughtering was probably joined with quasi-sacrificial ritual; in any case, consumption of blood had always been prohibited in Israel, and animals were always slaughtered by having their

---

[8] H. Gunkel, *GHK*, I/1 (^{3}1910), 410.

[9] See above.

[10] Cf. *AuS*, VI, 74, 102.

[11] Cf. *KBL*^{3}, *s.v.*

[12] N. H. Snaith, "The Verbs *zābaḥ* and *šāḥaṭ*," *VT*, 25 (1975), 244.

throats slit. For example, sheepshearing was a harvest festival celebrated with banqueting and wine by the owners of the flocks (2 S. 13:23); the festivities probably included religious sacrifices.[13] But in 1 S. 25:11, Nabal lists only the provisions of "bread, water, and the meat that I have killed for my shearers"—nothing more than normal slaughtering for food.

Following the usage of the OT, the rabbis also distinguish secular slaughtering without any ritual element (*ṭbḥ,* on the basis of Ex. 21:37[22:1]) and ritual slaughtering in a context either cultic or secular (*šḥṭ*); the professional slaughter is called *ṭabbāḥ.*[14]

5. *Versions.* a. To render *ṭbḥ,* the LXX uses both *spházein* and *thýein,* both of which can mean "slaughter" for either cultic or secular purposes, "which is from the very first very close to ancient concepts."[15] The verb *thýein,* with the fundamental meaning "sacrifice," is regularly used for *zbḥ* (only 4 times for the root *ṭbḥ*[16]). The usual translation of *šḥṭ* and *ṭbḥ* is *spházein,* in each case with appropriate derivatives.

The desire for variation and specification appears especially in the 4 instances of the cognate acc. *ṭbḥ ṭeḇaḥ* or *ṭiḇḥâ.* Gen. 43:16 reads *spháxon thýmata,* but *thýmata* hardly suggests sacrificial animals, especially in the context of a hastily prepared meal for Joseph's brothers in Egypt. Prov. 9:2 uses the same expression to describe the meal provided by personified Wisdom. In 1 S. 25:11 *thýmata há téthyka* is even used for Nabal's preserved meat;[17] Ezk. 21:15(10), on the other hand, uses *spháxēs sphágia.*

In Jer. 11:19, the LXX may be seeking to state explicitly that the prophet is like an innocent lamb led to its slaughter (*agómenon toú thýesthai*); in Jer. 25:34(LXX 32:34) and 51:40(LXX 28:40, and so probably translated by the same hand as chap. 11), the same word *liṭbôaḥ* is rendered *eis sphagḗn.*

The slaughter of human beings is expressed only by *spházein* or *sphagḗ* (Ps. 37:14[LXX 36:14]; Isa. 14:21; 34:2; 65:12; Jer. 25:34[LXX 32:34]; 48:15[31:15]; [50:27(27:27)]). The "lamb for the slaughter" is also rendered by the common formula *epí/eis sphagḗn* (Prov. 7:22; Isa. 53:7; Jer. 12:3); *próbata sphagḗs* is used in Zec. 11:4,7 for *ṣō'n hah^{a}rēḡâ* (cf. Ps. 44:23[22, LXX 43:23]). The LXX rendering in Lam. 2:21 is totally unique: "Thou hast slain them, cooked (*emageíreusas*) them, not spared them." The translator was obviously familiar with the meaning "cook" and used it literally, probably having in mind the slaughtering and dismemberment of a sacrifice.

In the Vulg., too, *immolare* (Dt. 28:31; Prov. 9:2) and *victima* (Gen. 43:16; Prov. 9:2; Jer. 11:19; 12:3; 51:40; Ezk. 21:15[10]) need not refer to cultic slaughtering.[18] Both the LXX and Vulg. show through their choice of words that they, like the classic authors, could use cultic terminology in a secular sense.

---

13 A. Wendel, *Das Opfer in der altisraelitischen Religion* (Leipzig, 1927) (cited in Michel, 930, n. 27).

14 M. Jastrow, *A Dictionary of the Targumim, the Talmud Babli and Yerushalmi, and the Midrashic Literature* (1903; repr. Brooklyn, 1975), 516, 1546f.; Michel, 933.

15 Behm, 181.

16 See below.

17 See above.

18 H. Georges, ed., *Ausführliches Lateinisch-Deutsches Handwörterbuch* (Basel, [9]1951), *s.v.*

b. The Targumim and Syriac usually render verbal *ṭbḥ* by means of the common verb *nks* (with the subst. *nikseṯā'*),[19] which means "slaughter" in general, without being limited—like OT *ṭbḥ*—to secular slaughtering; for "sacrifice" they have the common term *dbḥ*. From the pael of *ṭbḥ* there is derived the ptcp. *meṭabbeḥayyā'* (Targum Yerušalmi on Lev. 1:5; Ezk. 40:43). The Targumim and Syriac also have the noun *ṭabbāḥā'*, "slaughterer" (Lev. 1:5,11),[20] as well as "cook" (1 S. 8:13; 9:23f.), and *ṭeḇāḥā'*, "slaughter" (Prov. 7:22). Especially when human beings are involved (Isa. 14:21; 34:2; 65:12; Jer. 25:34; 48:15; 50:27; 51:40; Ezk. 21:15,33[10,28]), *qaṭlā'* often appears as a noun. This typically Aramaic root[21] often represents other Hebrew equivalents. For "bodyguards" we find the pl. *qāṭôlayyā'*, corresponding to Syr. *daḥšê'*, "*satellites, lictores.*"[22]

II. Ethical and Theological Usage.

1. *Humans as Subject.* The victims of slaughter—real or metaphorical—can also be human beings. The root *ṭbḥ,* as well as *šḥṭ,* is more expressive of bloody massacre than more general expressions such as the hiphil of → מות *mûṯ* and → נכה *nkh* or → הרג *hāraḡ* [*hāragh*]. The wicked slaughter the upright (Ps. 37:14). The young men of Moab go down to slaughter (Jer. 48:15). In poetic texts the "slaughter" of human beings is often associated with the simile "like a lamb" or "like sheep for slaughter."[23] The simile suggests unsuspecting innocence (Jer. 11:19) or the gentle submissiveness of the Servant of Yahweh (Isa. 53:7). The last passage is cited in the NT as a messianic prophecy (Acts 8:32); the Targum, however, as it often does, reverses the meaning of the bitter passage: "The mighty of the nations he will hand over like a lamb to the slaughter."[24] Here the comparison expresses the ruthless ease of the killing, like Akk. *kīma immeri iṭbuḫšu;*[25] cf. Jer. 12:3; Prov. 7:22: ". . . as an ox goes to the slaughter"; Ps. 44:23(22): "we are accounted as sheep for the slaughter" (*keṣō'n ṭiḇḥâ;* v. 12[11], *keṣō'n ma'aḵāl*). Ps. 44:23(22) is cited in the NT (Rom. 8:36) and in rabbinic texts as an example of martyrdom.[26]

2. *God as Subject.* In descriptions of judgment, God himself can function as subject of *ṭbḥ,* directly or indirectly, either slaying the enemies of his people or appearing as an executioner in the midst of his own people. The shepherds are slaughtered and dispersed (Jer. 25:34); the apostate must bow down to the slaughter (Isa. 65:12). Similar statements appear in the "song of the sword" (Ezk. 21:15,20,33[10,15,28])

---

[19] *WTM, s.v.*

[20] *WTM, s.v.;* Jastrow, *Dictionary of the Targumim, s.v.; LexSyr, s.v.*

[21] M. Wagner, *Die lexikalischen und grammatikalischen Aramaismen im alttestamentlichen Hebräisch. BZAW,* 96 (1966), 100f.

[22] *LexSyr, s.v.*

[23] See I.5 above; cf. Michel, 936.

[24] H. Hegermann, *Jesaja 53 in Hexapla, Targum und Peschitta. BFChTh,* 2/56 (1954).

[25] F. Delitzsch, *Assyrisches Handwörterbuch* (1896; repr. 1968), 299.

[26] Michel, 937f.

and Zec. 11:4,7, with the phrase *ṣō'n hah^{a}rēḡâ;* Jer. 12:3: "Pull them out like sheep for the slaughter (*k^{e}ṣō'n l^{e}ṭiḇḥâ*), and set them apart for the day of slaughter."

The apocalyptic and eschatological extension of such statements is the notion of Yahweh's "day of slaughter," which appears during the exilic period, especially in Jeremiah;[27] here the prophetic "day of Yahweh" is described in more detail as a "day of wrath" (Prov. 11:4; Isa. 13:13; Lam. 1:12; 2:1,21f.; Ezk. 7:19; Zeph. 1:15,18; 2:3) and "day of vengeance" (Isa. 34:8; 63:4; Jer. 46:10). The term *zeḇaḥ* appears often in these pronouncements of judgment, but now it refers only analogically and sarcastically to a "sacrifice" to which the birds and wild beasts are invited (Ezk. 39:17-20). The basic meaning "slaughter" is everywhere apparent here (cf. *yôm hereḡ/h^{a}rēḡâ,* Isa. 30:25; Jer. 12:3; *yôm zeḇaḥ,* Zeph. 1:8). Note the parallelism in Isa. 34:6: Yahweh has a sacrifice (*zeḇaḥ*) in Bozrah, a great slaughter (*ṭeḇaḥ gāḏôl*); he has given all the nations over for slaughter (34:2). According to Jer. 46:10, the sword of Yahweh will be drunk with blood when he holds a sacrifice (*zeḇaḥ*) in the north country.[28] In Jer. 50:27, the Babylonians are compared to bulls: "Slay all her bulls, let them go down to the slaughter." According to Jer. 51:39f., Yahweh holds a figurative revel (*mišteh*) and brings the Babylonians down "like lambs to the slaughter" (*k^{e}kārîm liṭḇôaḥ*). Even Israel was slain by Yahweh on the day of his wrath and slaughtered without mercy (Lam. 2:21[29]). But even here this harsh understanding of God is accepted without criticism or objection.

Hamp

---

[27] Grill.
[28] Grill, 279.
[29] For the LXX, see I.5.a above.

טָהַר *ṭāhar;* טָהוֹר *ṭāhôr;* טֹהַר *ṭōhar;* טָהֳרָה *ṭoh^{o}râ*

Contents: I. Ancient Near East: 1. Egypt; 2. Mesopotamia. II. Etymology; Semantic Field; OT Occurrences. III. OT Usage: 1. Pure Gold, etc.; 2. Cultic Purity; 3. Figurative Meaning. IV. LXX. V. Dead Sea Scrolls.

ṭāhar. H. Cazelles, "Impur et sacré à Ugarit," *Al-Baḥîth. Festschrift J. Henninger. Studi Instituti Anthropos,* 28 (Bonn, 1976), 37-47; J. Döller, *Die Reinheits- und Speisegesetze des ATs in religionsgeschichtlicher Beleuchtung. ATA,* 7/2-3 (Münster, 1917); W. H. Gispen, "The Distinction between Clean and Unclean," *OTS,* 5 (1948), 190-96; F. Hauck and R. Meyer, "καθαρός," *TDNT,* III, 413-431; H. J. Hermisson, *Sprache und Ritus im altisraelitischen Kult. WMANT,* 19 (1965), 84-99; H. W. Huppenbauer, "טהר und טהרה in der Sektenregel von Qumran," *ThZ,* 13 (1957), 350f.; W. Kornfeld, "Reine und unreine Tiere im AT," *Kairos,* 7 (1965), 134-147; F. Maass, "טהר *ṭhr* rein sein," *THAT,* I, 646-652; W. Paschen, *Rein und Unrein: Untersuchung zur biblischen Wortgeschichte. StANT,* 24 (1970).

I. Ancient Near East.

1. *Egypt.* Egyp. *w'b*[1] means both "purify" and "be or become pure"; it is also used as an adjective, "pure." In its transitive sense, the verb is sometimes used concretely, "wash," "make clean" (e.g., clothing), sometimes figuratively, "purify" (e.g., the king, priests, a temple, or an altar), i.e., make free from impurity or evil. In the sense "be pure" it is used of persons, parts of the body, clothing, buildings, sacrifices, etc., as well as the cloudless sky. Especially common is the phrase *w'b 'wy,* "with pure hands," describing priests in the presence of a god or attendants in the presence of the king. In the context of ritual purity it is often used in the formulas *w'b w'b,* "pure, pure (is) . . .," and *(ỉw w'b,* "it is pure," when sacrifice is offered, during purification ceremonies, or upon entering a temple. The one who offers the sacrifice says *(ỉw.y w'b.kwy,* "I am pure." As an adjective, *w'b* exhibits a semantic shift from "pure" = "clean" to "pure" = "consecrated, sacred," and to "pure" = "unused." It is applied to persons, objects of all kinds, buildings, localities, etc.[2]

Purity plays a highly important role in worship and in the cult of the dead.[3] It is an absolute precondition for any cultic act. The temple, the cultic vessels, and above all the one who performs the act must be pure. The word *w'b* even becomes the ordinary term for "priest." "Whoever enters the temple, let him be pure";[4] but also: "Everyone who enters this tomb, after he has purified himself as he purifies himself for the temple of the great god. . . ."[5]

Purification is accomplished by means of water (washing the body or clothing) or soda, but it also includes avoidance of everything repugnant to the deity (abstinence, dietary prohibitions, intercourse with impure persons).

The purification of the king at his coronation is depicted in many scenes that show Horus and Thoth purifying the king with libation flasks. From the flasks instead of water pour the hieroglyphs "life" and "happiness."[6] The purification of the king thus not only removes his impurity but endues him with new life. There may be an echo here of the purification of the sun-god in the heavenly ocean before his rising.[7] In like manner the purification of the dead not only effects ritual purity but also brings life.[8]

A ritual for purification of the pharaoh has been discussed by Schott.[9] This ritual also involves removal of everything evil and abominable. It is also stated that the

---

1 *WbÄS,* I, 280-82.
2 For citations, see *WbÄS.*
3 *RÄR,* 631-33.
4 *Urk.,* IV, 831.
5 *Ibid.,* I, 174.
6 A. H. Gardiner, "The Baptism of Pharaoh," *JEA,* 36 (1950), 3-12.
7 A. M. Blackman, *RT,* N.S. 39, 44ff.; cf. *RÄR,* 634.
8 *RÄR,* 635.
9 S. Schott, *Die Reinigung Pharaos in einem memphitischen Tempel. NAWG,* Phil.-hist. Kl., 1957/3.

purity of the king resembles the purity of the gods of the four corners of the earth, so that it fills the whole world.[10]

2. *Mesopotamia*. The Akkadian word for "pure" is *ebbu*[11] or *ellu;*[12] the two are largely synonymous, but each has certain special nuances. The former (equivalent to Sum. *dadag*) means "gleaming" (metals, gold, precious stones, wood), "clean" (clothing), "sacred" or "pure" (objects, materials, or animals for cultic use; also rituals and divine beings), and "trustworthy." The latter (equivalent to Sum. *ku, sikil*) can also mean "gleaming" (precious stones, light, a face; cf. expressions like "pure as the heavens," "as the sun," "as milk"[13]); it can also mean "pure" (= "unmixed" ?; gold, naphtha, oil, etc.), but it never refers to physical cleanness. It is often applied to objects, materials, or animals used in the cult; it indicates the ritual purity of a person, and it has a meaning that comes close to the concept "holy,"[14] as applied to gods, kings, priests, their acts, dwelling places, etc. Incantations, for example, may be called "pure" or "holy." Finally, it can also mean "free."

The verb *ebēbu*[15] and *elēlu*[16] are likewise largely synonymous and often appear together. In the D stem, with the meaning "purify," they are often associated with verbs meaning "wash." Water often serves as a means of purification; for example: "Sanctify, purify (*ullulu, ubbubu*) this man with holy (*ellu*) water from Apsu"[17]—showing that the water of purification is mythologically equivalent to Apsu; "I washed my hands, I purified (*ubbubu*) my body in the pure (*ellu*) water of the spring."[18] Gilgamesh washes his hair and cleanses (*ubbubu*) his weapons.[19] Shalmanezer cleanses his weapons in the sea.[20] Even the gods cleanse themselves in the pure water of the *bīt rimki* (washhouse).[21] The tamarisk and other plants are also used for purification ("May the tamarisk free [*pašāru*] me;[22] note here the "freeing" from impurity and sin). Also of interest is the association with *kuppuru:* "You shall purify (*tukappar*) the king with holy (*ebbu*) rites of purification (*takpirāte*)."[23]

---

[10] Cf. K. I. A. Engnell, *The Call of Isaiah. UUÅ*, 1949/4, 36f.; the purity of the king is also discussed by E. Otto, *Gott und Mensch nach den ägyptischen Tempelinschriften der griechisch-römischen Zeit. AHAW*, Phil.-Hist. Kl., 1964/1, 67f.

[11] *AHw*, I, 180; *CAD*, IV (1958), 1-4.

[12] *AHw*, I, 204f.; *CAD*, IV, 102-106.

[13] *CAD*, IV, 81.

[14] A. O. Haldar, *Associations of Cult Prophets among the Ancient Semites* (Uppsala, 1945), 202-206.

[15] *AHw*, I, 180f.; *CAD*, IV, 4-8.

[16] *AHw*, I, 197f.; *CAD*, IV, 80-83.

[17] CT 17, 5 III, 1f.

[18] Maqlû VII, 119.

[19] Gilg. VI, I.1, probably used in the literal sense.

[20] *KAH* 2, 113 I,10.

[21] V R 51, no. 3, 38f.

[22] Maqlû I, 23.

[23] H. Zimmern, *Beiträge zur Kenntnis der babylonischen Religion. Assyriologische Bibliothek*, 12 (Leipzig, 1901), no. 26 II, 2.

Temples, princes, and the people are purified.[24] The king is "purified"[25] for his throne. Lepers are purified so that they can reenter their house.[26] Sacrifices are to be "kept pure" so that no error (*ḫiṭītu*) is committed.[27]

The verb *ullulu* also means "consecrate": Nabonidus consecrated and gave his daughter to the moon-god.[28]

II. Etymology; Semantic Field; OT Occurrences. The root *ṭhr* appears in Biblical and later Hebrew as well as Jewish Aramaic; it is also found in Arabic (*ṭahara, ṭahura,* "be pure," "be upright"), OSA (*ṭhr*, "purity";[29] cf. Soq. *ṭahir,* "pure"), and in Ethiopic (*ṭahara,* "be pure"; similarly Tigré[30]). In Ugaritic, *ṭhr* (var. *ẓhr*) is used of precious stones, probably with the meaning "gleaming."[31] Syriac uses *zᵉḵā* or *dᵉḵā* (→ זכה *zāḵâ* [*zākhāh*]).

Certain Hebrew passages suggest "gleaming" as a fundamental meaning. Ex. 24:10, for example, says that Moses, Aaron, and the elders of Israel saw the God of Israel, with a sapphire pavement under his feet gleaming like the clear heaven (*kᵉʿeṣem haš-šāmayim lāṭōhar*). Ps. 89:45(Eng. v. 44) says of the king *hišbattā miṭṭᵉhorô,* possibly to be amended to *miṭhārô,* meaning that he was robbed of his royal splendor; cf. Iran. *xvarᵉnah* and Akk. *melammu* as terms for the divine splendor of the king.[32] The same is true of Mal. 3:3, where the piel of *ṭhr* and *ṣrp* are used with reference to the refining of silver, and Job 37:21, where the wind clears (piel of *ṭhr*) the skies.

This basic meaning is supported in part by a survey of the semantic field. Synonyms include → ברר *brr,* "be pure, be clear"; → זכה *zāḵâ* [*zākhāh*], "be pure," "be upright"; and occasionally → לבן *lbn,* "be white." In association with *ṭhr* we also find verbs meaning "purify" such as *zqq* and *ṣrp,* as well as the root → נקה *nāqâ,* which represents the same idea transferred to the ethical realm. The use of → כפר *kipper* in combination with *ṭhr* is discussed below.[33] There are also points of contact with → קדש *qdš,* "holy." The antonym is provided by → טמא *ṭāmēʾ* and its various snyonyms.

The verb *ṭāhar* occurs 29 times in the qal, 40 times in the piel, and 20 times in the hithpael. There are 2 possible occurrences of the pual: 1 S. 20:26 conj. in place of the second *ṭāhôr,* and (less certainly) Ezk. 22:24, where *humṭārâ* might be read for

---

24 *KAV* 218 A, II, 22; *CAD*, IV, 7.

25 *CAD*, IV, 83.

26 *Ibid.*, IV, 7.

27 A. T. Clay, *Miscellaneous Inscriptions in the Yale Babylonian Collection. YOSBT,* 1, 45 II, 24; *CAD*, IV, 82.

28 *YOSBT,* 1, 45 II, 10.

29 ContiRossini, 159.

30 *TigrWb*, 606; possibly also borrowed from Hebrew: T. Nöldeke, *Neue Beiträge zur semitischen Sprachwissenschaft* (Strasbourg, 1910), 36; E. Ullendorf, *Ethiopia and the Bible*. Schweich lectures, 1967 (London, 1968), 123.

31 Cazelles.

32 G. Widengren, *Die Religionen Irans. RdM,* 14 (1965), 58f.; E. Cassin, *La splendeur divine. Civilisation et sociétés*, 8 (The Hague, 1968).

33 Cf. Paschen, 37-42.

*m*ᵉ*ṭōhārâ*. Derivatives include *ṭāhôr,* "pure," *ṭōhar,* "purity, purification," *toh*ᵒ*râ*, "purity, purification," and possibly *miṭhār.*[34]

III. OT Usage. Most occurrences of *ṭhr* in the OT refer to cultic purity. There are also some figurative occurrences: some with the meaning of "moral purity" and others where *ṭāhôr* seems to mean "pure, unadulterated." These latter will be considered first.

1. *Pure Gold, etc*. Some cultic utensils are to be made of *zāhāḇ ṭāhôr.* In the regulations governing the making of the tabernacle (Ex. 25; 30:3) and the account of its construction (Ex. 37), the term "pure gold" alternates with simple *zāhāḇ,* "gold." The ark is to be overlaid with "pure gold" (25:11; 37:2); the *kapporeṯ* is to be fashioned of "pure gold" (25:17; 37:6), as is the table (25:24, *'āśâ;* 37:11, *ṣph* piel, "overlaid"). Cultic vessels are also to be made of "pure gold" (25:29; 37:16). Several passages speak of "pure gold" as the material of the lampstand (25:31,39; 37:17,22,24). Finally, the snuffers and trays are of "pure gold" (25:38; 37:23), and the incense altar is overlaid with it (30:3; 37:26). There are other references to "pure gold" in the context of the priestly vestments and their fashioning (Ex. 28, 39): two chains for the ephod (28:14), two chains for the breastpiece (28:22; 39:15,17), bells on the skirts of the outer robe (28:33, *zāhāḇ;* 39:25, *zāhāḇ ṭāhôr*), and a plate with the inscription *qōḏeš l*ᵉ*YHWH* (28:36; 39:30, with the addition of *nēzer-haqqōḏeš*).

It is uncertain whether there is any real difference between the most common expression *zāhāḇ* and the more precise *zāhāḇ ṭāhôr.* The Chronicler occasionally uses other terms. We read in 1 Ch. 28:15f. that the lampstands and the table for the showbread were made of *zāhāḇ,* while according to 28:17 the forks, basins, and cups were made of *zāhāḇ ṭāhôr;* 1 K. 7:50 uses *zāhāḇ sāgûr.* According to 1 Ch. 28:18, the altar of incense was made of *zāhāḇ m*ᵉ*suqqāq*. According to 2 Ch. 3:4, the inside of the vestibule of Solomon's temple was covered with *zāhāḇ ṭāhôr,* while *zāhāḇ ṭôḇ* was used for the nave and most holy place (3:5,8; v. 7 mentions only *zāhāḇ*). According to 2 Ch. 9:17, finally, the king's ivory throne was overlaid with "pure gold" (1 K. 10:18 has *zāhāḇ mûpāz*).

These synonyms suggest that the phrase refers to pure, unalloyed gold. Since, however, almost all the passages deal with cultic objects, it is undeniable that there may be overtones of "cultic purity." Job 28:19 uses *keṯem ṭāhôr,* "pure gold," metaphorically for the value of wisdom. Similar is Ps. 12:7(6): the promises of Yahweh are *ṭāhôr,* comparable to purified (*ṣārûp, m*ᵉ*zuqqāq*) silver.

2. *Cultic Purity.* a. Most frequently, *ṭāhôr* is a cultic term, with → טמא *ṭāmē'* as its antonym. It is the function of the priests to distinguish (*hiḇdîl* [→ בדל *bdl*]) between the unclean and the clean (Lev. 10:10; cf. 20:25; Ezk. 44:23). Ezk. 22:26 asserts that the priests have not been doing their job. The law governing clean and unclean animals is intended to distinguish *ṭāmē'* from *ṭāhôr,* those that may be eaten from those that

34 See above.

may not be eaten (Lev. 11:47). The law of leprosy shows how to tell when one is clean and when one is unclean (Lev. 14:57). The general principle that something unclean does not produce something clean finds figurative application in Job 14:4: the unclean human race cannot bring forth a single individual who is clean in the eyes of God.

b. Only those who are clean may take part in the cult. All who are clean may eat the flesh of the *šᵉlāmîm* sacrifice; whoever eats of it while unclean shall be cut off from the community (Lev. 7:19f.). According to Deuteronomy, on the other hand, the flesh of animals that are not slaughtered for sacrifice may be eaten by clean and unclean alike (Dt. 12:15,22; cf. also 15:22). When David absents himself from Saul's table on the day of the new moon, Saul thinks it is because he is unclean (1 S. 20:26).

Everyone who is clean must keep the Passover (Nu. 9:13); those who are not clean or have not sanctified themselves are forbidden to eat the Passover lamb (2 Ch. 30:17f.; Ezr. 6:20). Some cultic acts can be performed only by an *'îš ṭāhôr* (Nu. 19:9,18f.).

A priest who is clean may eat of the wave offering (Nu. 18:11; Lev. 10:14 adds: "in a clean place"[35]) and of the firstfruits (Nu. 18:13). Lev. 22:4 states that a priest may eat of the holy things (*qoḏāšîm*) of the Israelites only when he is clean.[36]

A special purification ceremony associated with the consecration of the Levites is described in Nu. 8:5-22. They are sprinkled with the water of expiation (*mê ḥaṭṭā'ṯ*); they shave themselves[37] and wash their clothes (v. 7); propitiatory sacrifice is offered (*kipper,* vv. 12,21). Finally the Levites are brought before Yahweh. Thus they are separated (*hiḇdîl*) from the people, and now belong to Yahweh (*wᵉhāyû lî,* v. 14). Then they can perform the sacred rites.

According to Neh. 12:30, the priests and Levites purified themselves before purifying the people, the gates, and the wall.

c. Cultic ceremonies are to be performed at a clean place (*māqôm ṭāhôr*). The remains of the bull sacrificed as a sin offering are burned in a clean place outside the camp (Lev. 4:12); the ashes are conveyed to a clean place outside the camp (Lev. 6:4[11]); a man who is clean is to deposit the ashes of the heifer in a clean place outside the camp (Nu. 19:9). The breast that is waved and the thigh that is offered are eaten by the priests in any clean place (Lev. 10:14; cf. LXX *hagíō*); compare the cereal offering, which is to be eaten beside the altar, in a *holy* place (Lev. 10:12f.), as well as the goat of the sin offering (Lev. 10:16ff.).

d. There are clean and unclean animals (Lev. 11:47; 20:25, *ṭāhôr—ṭāmē';* cf. Gen. 7:2,8 [J], clean versus not clean); they are listed in Lev. 11. The clean animals may be eaten, the unclean may not be eaten (Lev. 11:47; Dt. 14:11,20). Noah offered sacrifice of every clean animal and bird (Gen. 8:20[J]). For further discussion → טמא *ṭāmē'*.

---

[35] See below.

[36] K. Elliger, *Leviticus. HAT,* IV (1966), 292.

[37] → גלח *gillaḥ* [*gillach*].

e. Certain cultic objects are referred to expressly as "clean" or "pure." These include the table for the showbread (Lev. 24:6; 2 Ch. 13:11—possibly an abbreviated way of saying "table of pure gold," cf. Ex. 25:23f.; 37:10f.;[38] the things set on the table include pure incense, *l^eḇōnâ zakkâ*) and the lampstand (Ex. 31:8; 39:37; Lev. 24:4—also a possible abbreviation; cf. Ex. 25:31; 37:17[39]). According to Ex. 30:35, the incense is to be both *ṭāhôr* and *qōḏeš;* its constituents include *l^eḇōnâ zakkâ* (v. 34; Ex. 37:29 speaks only of *q^eṭōreṯ hassammîm ṭāhôr*). According to Isa. 66:20, cereal offerings are presented in clean vessels. Mal. 1:11 speaks of "pure offerings" throughout the world, in contrast to the unacceptable sacrifices offered by the priests of Israel; but here there are echoes of the notion of proper intention.

f. Another group of passages refers to the cleansing of cultic objects so that they may be used in the cult. Noteworthy here is the association with *qiddēš*, "sanctify," and *kipper,* "propitiate," as well as the mention of what the objects are to be purified of. According to Lev. 16:19, the altar is to be sprinkled on the Day of Atonement with blood "to cleanse (*ṭhr* piel) it and hallow (*qdš* piel) it from the uncleannesses (*ṭum'ōṯ*) of the people of Israel." According to v. 16, the ceremony pertains to *ṭum'ōṯ, p^ešā'îm,* and *ḥaṭṭō'ṯ*. The cultic terminology of uncleanness is here linked with the idea of sin. Ezk. 43:26 states that for seven days the altar shall be atoned for (*kpr* piel), purified (*ṭhr* piel), and consecrated (*millē' yāḏ*!); in the preceding verses we also find the verb *ḥiṭṭē'*, "cleanse from sin." According to 2 Ch. 29, during the reformation of Hezekiah the priests sanctified themselves (*hiṯqaddēš*) in order to cleanse (*ṭhr*) the temple (v. 15). They cleansed the inside of the temple and removed all the uncleanness (*ṭum'â*, v. 16); they sanctified (*qdš*) the temple for eight days (v. 17) and then reported to Hezekiah: "We have cleansed (*ṭhr,* v. 18; cf. *hēḵîn, hiqdîš*, v. 19) all the house of Yahweh." Such terminology is not used in the parallel, 2 K. 18:4. The reformation of Josiah is described as follows in 2 Ch. 34: Josiah began to purge (*ṭhr,* v. 3) Judah and Jerusalem of high places, Asherim, and idols; the cleansing included the burning of the bones of the idolatrous priests (v. 5). The whole is summarized in v. 8 in the words "he purged the land and the temple." The parallel text in 2 K. 23 uses instead the verb *ṭimmē'*, "defile" (vv. 8,10,13), i.e., make unclean through contact with the bones of the dead.

According to Neh. 12:30, the priests and Levites purify themselves (*ṭhr* hithpael) and then purify (piel) the people, the gates, and the wall of Jerusalem. Neh. 13:9 states that Nehemiah cleansed the chambers in the temple court and brought thither the cultic vessels. The function of the Levites is described summarily in 1 Ch. 23:28 as "cleansing all that is holy" (*ṭoh^oraṯ l^eḵol-qōḏeš*); cf. Neh. 12:45: priests and Levites are obligated to perform the service of purification as well as the service of their God.

g. A large number of the occurrences of *ṭāhôr* and the verb *ṭhr* (qal, piel, and hithpael) appear in the ritual laws dealing with uncleanness and purification from uncleanness.

---

[38] See above.

[39] See above.

The law of leprosy contains several examples of the declaratory formula *ṭāhôr hû'* (Lev. 13:13,17,39-41; also 11:37, with reference to seed that a carcass falls upon). The piel is used for the priest's declaration of cleanness (Lev. 13:17,23,28,34f.,37); the qal appears in 13:6,34; 14:8f.,20; the hithpael participle designates the person to be cleansed (Lev. 14:4,7f.,11,14,17-19). The cleansing includes sprinkling with water (Lev. 14:7); the final cleansing involves a *kipper* act (Lev. 14:10-20).

A concrete example is provided by the story of Naaman in 2 K. 5: he is advised to bathe in the Jordan in order to become clean (vv. 10,13); although he does not understand the meaning of the order (v. 12), he is cleansed (v. 14).

Other references to purification refer to genital discharge (Lev. 12:7f., qal; *kipper* appears in the same passage). Uncleanness is removed by bathing ("bathe in water . . . and be clean," Lev. 17:15; 22:7; Nu. 19:19 [also *ḥiṭṭē'*]; Nu. 31:24; washing clothes, Lev. 11:32; 13:58; 17:15; Nu. 31:23). In Nu. 19:12 we find "cleanse oneself (*hiṯḥaṭṭē'*) and become clean."

Ezk. 39 speaks of cleansing the land defiled by the corpses of Gog (vv. 12,14,16).

3. *Figurative Meaning*. Just as the boundary line between uncleanness and sin is fluid,[40] cleanness or purity is closely related to what is ethically and religiously good. Eccl. 9:2 lists a contrasting series: righteous/wicked (*ṣaddîq/rāšā'*), good/evil (*ṭôḇ/ra'*, if we may assume that one element has been dropped), clean/unclean (*ṭāhôr/ṭāmē'*); all are treated the same, claims the author. Of course it is possible that the reference here is to cultic purity, but the context suggests ethical judgment. The same is true of Job 14:4, already cited above: the (ethically) unclean human race cannot produce an individual who is (ethically) clean in the eyes of God. Three variations on the same theme occur elsewhere in the book of Job: "Can mortal man be righteous (*ṣāḏaq*) before God? Can a man be pure (*ṭāhar*) before his Maker?" (4:17); "What is man, that he can be clean (*zāḵâ*)? Or he that is born of a woman, that he can be righteous (*ṣāḏaq*)?" (15:14); "How then can man be righteous (*ṣāḏaq*) before God? How can he who is born of woman be clean (*zāḵâ*)?" (25:4). Here we see that *ṭāhar*, *zāḵâ*, and *ṣāḏaq* are closely related in meaning.

The boundary between literal and figurative meaning is also fluid in Zec. 3:5. The high priest Joshua has his filthy (*ṣō'îm*) garments removed and is given a "clean" turban, which also signifies that his iniquity (*'āwôn*) has been taken away (v. 4). "Filthy" here clearly symbolizes sin or iniquity; the clean garments are "not filthy" in the literal sense, but also symbolize ethical purity. A similar association appears in Prov. 30:12: "There are those who are pure in their own eyes, but are not cleansed of their filth (*ṣō'â*)." The context shows that the reference is to ethical qualities.

In Job 17:9, *ṭ^ehor-yāḏayim*, "clean of hands," stands in parallel with *ṣaddîq;* in the preceding verse, *nāqî* and *yāšār* are synonymous. Prov. 22:11 praises the one who loves purity of heart and speaks graciously (*ḥēn*); the precise meaning is not clear, but Prov. 15:26 states that pleasant (*nō'am*) words are pure, while wicked thoughts are an abomination. According to Ps. 12:7(6), the promises (*'imrâ*, pl.) of Yahweh are pure,

---

40 → טמא *ṭāmē'*.

like silver that is refined and purified (*ṣārûp, mᵉzuqqāq*). Since the preceding verses speak of the false speech of the wicked, the meaning "true" or "trustworthy" suggests itself. Ps. 19:8-11(7-10) contains a series of predicates describing the word (law, commandment, etc.) of Yahweh; these include *ṭāhôr* (describing the "fear" of Yahweh, perhaps read mistakenly for *'imrâ,* "promise") and *bar* (→ ברר *bārar*); synonyms include *ne'ᵉmān, yāšār, 'ᵉmeṯ,* and *ṣāḏaq*. The purpose of the psalm appears primarily to be the praise of God's word as being true and trustworthy; there may also be echoes of the clarity of God's commands. According to Hab. 1:13, Yahweh is too pure to behold *ra'* and *'āmāl;* nevertheless, laments the prophet, he lets the faithless hold sway.

Sometimes the subject is purification from idolatry, for example Gen. 35:2, "Put away the foreign gods . . . and purify yourselves"; Josh. 22:17, where the congregation is not yet cleansed from the *'āwôn* of Ba'al-Peor; Jer. 13:27, "I have seen your abominations (*šiqqûṣ*). . . . How long will it be before you are made clean?"; Ezk. 36:25, "I will sprinkle clean water upon you, and you shall be clean from all your uncleannesses, and from all your idols I will cleanse you" (cf. Ezk. 37:23 with *šiqqûṣ, gillûl,* and *peša'*); cf. also Neh. 13:30: "Thus I cleansed them from everything foreign (*nēḵār*)."

"Cleanse" can also refer to forgiveness of sins in general. In Jer. 33:8, "cleanse from *'āwôn*" stands in parallel with *sālaḥ;* cf. Ezk. 36:33, where we find only "cleanse from *'āwôn.*" Ezk. 24:13 speaks of the impossibility of cleansing from filthiness caused by "lewdness," i.e., idolatry. Lev. 16:30 links cleansing from sins (*ḥaṭṭō'ṯ*) with the notion of atonement (*kipper*). Prov. 20:9 speaks of the impossibility of purifying oneself from sin (or keeping oneself pure) and having a clean (*zikkâ*) heart. In Ps. 51:4(2), the psalmist prays that God will cleanse him from his sin (*ḥaṭṭa'ṯ*); the parallel clause, "wash me from my *'āwôn,*" alludes to purification ceremonies. V. 9(7) associates the purification with washing and with hyssop as a means of purification (cf. Lev. 14:46f. in the case of leprosy and Nu. 19:18 in the case of cultic uncleanness). The result is given in v. 12(10): a clean heart. Mal. 3:3 promises that the sons of Levi will be purified like the refining of silver and gold (*ṣrp, zqq* piel); as a result they will present offerings in righteousness (*ṣᵉḏāqâ*).

IV. LXX. The LXX usually uses *katharós* and *katharízein* to translate *ṭhr* and its derivatives. Sometimes other words are picked: *hagnós,* Ps. 12:7(6, LXX 11:7); 19:10(9, LXX 18:10); *hósios,* Prov. 22:11; *díkaios,* Prov. 30:12; *dókimos,* 2 Ch. 9:17; *hágios,* Lev. 10:14 (assimilation to v. 13?); *hagnízein,* 2 Ch. 29:16,18; 30:18; *hagnismós,* Nu. 8:7; *aphagnízein,* Nu. 8:6,21. In Ezk. 22:24, *bréchein* presupposes a reading *mumṭār.*

V. Dead Sea Scrolls. The statements concerning purification in the Dead Sea scrolls can be divided into two groups. On the one hand, the Manual of Discipline and sometimes the Damascus Document speak of "the purity of the many" (*ṭohᵒraṯ hārabbîm,* 1QS 6:16,25; 7:3,16,19) or "the purity of the holy men" (*ṭohᵒraṯ 'anšê haqqōḏeš,* 1QS 5:13; 8:17), or simply *ṭohᵒrâ* (1QS 6:22; 7:25; 8:24; CD 9:21,23) as something that outsiders are forbidden to touch. It is not clear whether these passages refer to the ritual washing, the common meals, or something else.[41] In any case, the exclusivity of the Qumran community in its separation from all outsiders is clearly expressed.

On the other hand, the Hodayoth contain several occurrences of the verb *ṭhr,* mostly in the piel, with reference to cleansing from sin and iniquity (*'āwôn,* 1QH 1:32; *peša',* 3:21; 7:30; 11:10; *'ašmâ,* 4:37; 6:8). One passage (15:16) compares cleansing to the refining (*zqq*) of silver; another (6:8) uses *zqq* without mentioning silver. According to 3:21, the result of this cleansing is incorporation into the community. Finally, 16:12 states that the cleansing takes place through the holy spirit of God. The Temple scroll (published in 1977) contains many additional occurrences.

Ringgren

[41] Paschen, 94ff.

טוֹב *ṭôḇ;* טוּב *ṭûḇ;* יטב *yṭb*

Contents: I. 1. Etymology; 2. Usage Outside the Bible. II. 1. OT Occurrences; 2. Utilitarian Meaning in Secular Usage; 3. *ṭôḇ l^e^* Expressing Benefit; 4. *ṭôḇ lēḇ;* 5. *ṭôḇ* in Ethical and Theological Usage; 6. Names. III. Dead Sea Scrolls. IV. LXX.

ṭôḇ. W. F. Albright, "The Refrain 'and God saw ki ṭôb' in Genesis," *Festschrift A. Robert. Travaux de l'Institut Câtholique de Paris,* 4 (1957), 22-26; *idem,* "The Son of Tabeel (Isaiah 7:6)," *BASOR,* 140 (1955), 34f.; *idem,* "Contributions to Biblical Archaeology and Philology. 1. Chaos and the Origin of Light in Genesis I," *JBL,* 43 (1924), 363-69; J. Barr, "Theophany and Anthropomorphism in the OT," *Congress Volume, Oxford 1959. SVT,* 7 (1960), 31-38; J. B. Bauer, "Der priesterliche Schöpfungshymnus in Gen. 1," *ThZ,* 20 (1964), 1-9; J. Becker, *Das Heil Gottes. StUNT,* 3 (1964); E. Beyreuther, "Good, Beautiful, Kind," *NIDNTT,* II, 98-107; H. H. Blieffert, *Weltanschauung und Gottesglaube. im Buche Kohelet* (diss., Rostock, 1938); T. Boman, *Hebrew Thought Compared with Greek* (Eng. trans. 1960; repr. New York, 1970); *idem, Das hebräische Denken im Vergleich mit dem griechischen* (Göttingen, [5]1968) [his revised edition is not available in English]; J. Bottéro, "L'Ecclésiaste et le problème du Mal," *Nouvelle Clio,* 7-10 (1955-57), 133-159; D. Boyarin, "Studies in the Aramaic Legal Papyri," *JANES,* 31 (1971), 57-62; M. Buber, *Good and Evil* (Eng. trans., New York, 1952); G. W. Buchanan, "The OT Meaning of the Knowledge of Good and Evil," *JBL,* 75 (1956), 114-120; W. M. Clark, "A Legal Background to the Yahwist's Use of 'Good and Evil' in Genesis 2–3," *JBL,* 88 (1969), 266-278; J. Coppens, *La connaissance du bien et du mal et le péché du paradis. ALBO,* ser. 2, 3 (1948); J.-S. Croatto, "ṬÔBÂ como 'amistad (de Alianze)' en el AT," *AION,* N.S. 18 (1968), 385-89; M. Dahood, *Proverbs and Northwest Semitic Philology. SPIB,* 113 (1963); *idem,* "Ugaritic and the OT," *ETL,* 44 (1968), 35-54; O. Eissfeldt, *Der Maschal im AT. BZAW,* 24 (1913); I. Eitan, "A Contribution to Isaiah Exegesis," *HUCA,* 12/13 (1937-38), 55-88; K. H. Fahlgren, *Ṣ^e^dākā* (Uppsala, 1932), repr. in part in *Um das Prinzip der Vergeltung in Religion und Recht des AT,* ed. K. Koch. *WdF,* 125 (1972), 87-129; R. Fey, *Amos und Jesaja. WMANT,* 12 (1963); J. Fischer, "טוב וָרָע in der Erzählung von Paradies und Sündenfall," *BZ,* 22 (1934), 323-331; M. Fox, "Ṭôḇ as Covenant Terminology," *BASOR,* 209 (1973), 41f.; R. Gordis,

I. 1. *Etymology.* The root *ṭb* belongs to the small group of originally biliteral substantives; like most roots in this group, it is of Proto-Semitic origin.[1] Analogy to the triliteral roots at an early date[2] gave rise to a triliteral perfective by-form *yṭb*[3] with supplementary function[4] alongside the biliteral perfective form *ṭb*. Gray[5] theorizes that

---

"The Knowledge of Good and Evil in the OT and the Qumran Scrolls," *JBL*, 76 (1957), 123-138; L. H. Gray, *Introduction to Semitic Comparative Linguistics* (1934; repr. Amsterdam, 1971); W. Grundmann, "ἀγαθός," *TDNT*, I, 10-18; *idem*, "καλός," *TDNT*, III, 536-550; D. R. Hillers, "A Note on Some Treaty Terminology in the OT," *BASOR*, 176 (1964), 46f.; L. Jacquet, "Abîme de malice et abîme de bonté: Psaume 36," *BVC*, 81 (1968), 36-47; A. Jirku, "Der 'Mann von Ṭob' (II. Sam 10 6. 8)," *ZAW*, 62 (1949/50), 319; I. Johag, "*Ṭôḇ*—Terminus technicus in Vertrags- und Bündnisformularen des Alten Orients und des ATs," *Bausteine biblischer Theologie. Festschrift G. J. Botterweck. BBB*, 50 (1977), 3-23; K. Koch, " 'denn seine Güte währet ewiglich,' " *EvTh*, 21 (1961), 537-544; H. Kruse, "Die 'dialektische Negation' als semitisches Idiom," *VT*, 4 (1954), 385-400; A. Kuschke, "Die Menschenwege und der Weg Gottes im AT," *StTh*, 5 (1952), 106-118; A. G. Lamadrid, "Pax et bonum (. . . *šālôm*, *ṭôb* et *bĕrît* . . .)," *Antonianum*, 44 (1969), 161-181; *idem*, "Pax et bonum, 'Shālôm' y 'ṭôb' en relación con 'bĕrît,' " *EstBíb*, 28 (1969), 61-77; L. J. Liebreich, "Psalms 34 and 145 in the Light of their Key Words," *HUCA*, 27 (1956), 181-192; I. Löw, "טובתיו Neh. 6 19," *ZAW*, 33 (1913), 154f.; H. D. A. Major, "The Tree of the Knowledge of Good and Evil (Gen. ii.9, 17)," *ExpT*, 20 (1908-1909), 427f.; M. Mannati, "Ṭûb-Y. en Ps. XXVII 13: *La bonté de Y.*, ou *Les biens de Y.*?" *VT*, 19 (1969), 488-493; G. Mensching, *Gut und Böse im Glauben der Völker* (Stuttgart, ²1950); A. R. Millard, "For He is Good," *TynB*, 17 (1966), 115-17; W. L. Moran, "A Note on the Treaty Terminology of the Sefîre Stelas," *JNES*, 22 (1963), 173-76; *idem*, "The Ancient Near Eastern Background of the Love of God in Deuteronomy," *CBQ*, 25 (1963), 77-87; W. W. Müller, "Altsüdarabische Beiträge zum hebräischen Lexikon," *ZAW*, 75 (1963), 304-316; F. Nötscher, *Zur theologischen Terminologie der Qumran-Texte. BBB*, 10 (1956); *idem*, *Gotteswege und Menschenwege in der Bibel und in Qumran. BBB*, 15 (1958); G. S. Ogden, *The Tôb-Spruch in Qoheleth* (diss., Princeton, 1975); B. Reicke, "The Knowledge Hidden in the Tree of Paradise," *JSS*, 1 (1956), 193-201; F. Rosenthal, "Yôm Ṭôḇ," *HUCA*, 18 (1943/44), 157-176; H. H. Schmid, *Wesen und Geschichte der Weisheit. BZAW*, 101 (1966); W. H. Schmidt, *Die Schöpfungsgeschichte der Priesterschrift. WMANT*, 17 (³1973); F. L. R. Stachowiak, *Chrestotes. Studia Friburgensia*, N.S. 17 (1957); *idem*, "Goodness," *EncBTh*, I, 321-28; W. Staerk, "L'arbre de vie et l'arbre de la science du bien et du mal," *RHPR*, 8 (1928), 67; J. J. Stamm, *AN*; H. S. Stern, "The Knowledge of Good and Evil," *VT*, 8 (1958), 405-418; H. J. Stoebe, "Gut und Böse in der Jahwistischen Quelle des Pentateuch," *ZAW*, 65 (1953), 188-204; *idem*, "טוב *ṭōb* gut," *THAT*, I, 652-664; R. von Ungern-Sternberg, *Redeweisen der Bibel. BSt*, 54 (1968); R. de Vaux, review of J. Coppens, *La connaissance*, *RB*, 56 (1949), 300-308; E. Vogt, " 'Regen in Fülle' (Psalm 68, 10-11)," *Bibl*, 46 (1965), 359-361; *idem*, "*Filius Ṭāb'ēl* (Is 7,6)," *Bibl*, 37 (1956), 263f.; K. Weiss, "χρηστός," *TDNT*, IX, 483-492; C. Westermann, *Creation* (Eng. trans., Philadelphia, 1974); H. Wildberger, "Israel und sein Land," *EvTh*, 16 (1956), 404-422; H. W. Wolff, *Joel and Amos. Herm* (Eng. trans. 1977); W. Zimmerli, "Concerning the Structure of OT Wisdom," in *Studies in Ancient Israelite Wisdom*, ed. J. L. Crenshaw (New York, 1974), 175-207.

[1] Cf. J. Barth, *Die Nominalbildung in den semitischen Sprachen* (Leipzig, ²1894), §1a, b; *BLe*, §270, n. 5. V. Christian, *Untersuchungen zur Laut- und Formenlehre des Hebräischen. SSAW*, 228/2 (1953), 111, sees in Heb. *ṭôḇ* an analog to the Akkadian permansive participle, used as both verb and noun.

[2] Cf. Barth, §1c.

[3] Cf. *LexLingAram*, 75.

[4] Cf. Barth, §1c, d; *BLe*, §§378, 392j.

[5] §103; cf. *VG*, §71a, c.

the vocalization is based on a Proto-Semitic secondary infix *-ai-/-au-* that was assimilated to stressed *ā*. This changed to *ô* in Canaanite (and in part back to *ā* at a later time) and was sometimes lowered to *û*.[6]

In Ugaritic we find the noun *ṭbn*, "harmony,"[7] and *ṭbt;* the meaning "goodness" for the latter is strongly contested on account of the fragmentary nature of the text.[8] We also find the adj. *ṭb*, pl. *ṭbm*, "good, pleasant, sweet."[9] No corresponding verb appears in Ugaritic. Elsewhere in Northwest Semitic the following forms occur, with a variety of semantic nuances: noun, Old Aram. *ṭbt*, Syr. *ṭ'b* or *ṭwb';* verb, Old Aram. *ṭyb/ṭ'b* and *yṭb*, Syr. *ṭ'b;* adjective, Old Aram., Syr., Nab., Palmyr. *ṭb*, Biblical Aram. *ṭ'b*, Hatra, Targ., Pun. *ṭb';* and adverb, Targ. *ṭb*, Palmyr. *ṭbyt*.

In East Semitic, of special importance is the Akkadian noun *ṭābtu*, "good deed, favor," alongside *ṭābūtu* or *ṭūbtu*, "friendship, good will." We also find the adj. *ṭābu*, "good," with *ṭābiš*, "good," *ṭūbu*, "that which is good." As in other languages—similar to Egyp. *nfr*—the verb *ṭiābum/ṭābu* appears here with the meaning "become/make good, beautiful."

Of disputed etymology is the word *ṭwb* that appears in Aramaic and North Arabic with the meaning "rumor, report," frequently with the negative qualification "slander." Here we are dealing with an independent homonym, a monosyllabic form that could easily develop. It belongs with *ṭbb/ẓbb*, a by-form of *dbb*.[10]

2. *Usage Outside the Bible*. Examination of the root *ṭb* at its very earliest stage of usage reveals a variety of applications that did not develop out of a single conceptual meaning to which they could be traced etymologically. The meanings coexist synchronically (polysemy), and must be classified according to the particular situation and application at hand. No real semantic innovation for *ṭb* appears at any time. We are always dealing with semantic extensions and specializations of the term in specific areas.

a. The basic meaning of *ṭb* and its derivatives refers in general to the qualities that make an object desirable. Here the emphasis is an originally pure utilitarianism, both qualitative and quantitative. When used in this way, *ṭb* can become a fixed element in the definition of an object, e.g., Ugar. *tql ksp ṭb*, "a shekel of fine silver"[11] (cf. Gen. 2:12; Josh. 7:21; 1 S. 25:8; 2 K. 3:19,25; 2 Ch. 3:5,8; Est. 8:17; Eccl. 7:14; Isa. 5:9;

---

[6] *BLe*, §2i, 14j; Gray, §45f, 93, 96f; for a different approach, see Christian, 109; G. J. Botterweck, *Der Triliteralismus im Semitischen erläutert an den Wurzeln GL KL ḲL*. *BBB*, 3 (1952), 48.

[7] *KTU*, 1.19, 46.

[8] *KTU*, 1.82, vo. 34; cf. *WUS*, no. 1110.

[9] *KTU*, 1.43, 12, 15; 1.3 I, 20; 4.213 *passim*.

[10] *KBL*[3], 352; J. Barr, *Comparative Philology and the Text of the OT* (Oxford, 1968), 16f.; R. Gordis, "The Text and Meaning of Hosea XIV 3," *VT*, 5 (1955), 88-90 = his *The Word and the Book* (New York, 1976), 347-49; Löw, 154f.; M. Wagner, *Die lexikalischen und grammatikalischen Aramaismen im alttestamentlichen Hebräisch*. *BZAW*, 96 (1966), 59; E. Zolli, "טוב II," *Bibl*, 34 (1953), 121-23.

[11] *KTU*, 1.43, 12, 15.

etc.) or *yn ṭb*[12] alongside *yn d l ṭb,*[13] in the sense of variously flavored wines such as honeyed wine or spiced wine[14] (cf. Ps. 34:9[Eng. v. 8]; 133:1f.; Cant. 1:2f.; 7:10[9]; Isa. 5:20; Virolleaud[15] takes the meaning instead to be "wine that is good" and "wine that is not good"). The element of sweetness appears in Arab. *ṭiyāb,* which is used by metonymy for a kind of date, as well as in Akk. *ṭābu,* "sweetmeat."

Oil had a wide range of uses in the ancient Near East: it was an essential addition to food, it provided a source of illumination, it was used for medicinal purposes, and it was used for anointing when sacrifice was offered.[16] This fact explains the numerous references to great quantities of *šmn ṭb,* "fine oil," as a gift or commodity (the reference is to crushed oil, purified of all foreign elements[17]). In Arabic usage, *šmn ṭb* refers only to spiced oil for secular use, not the oil used for cultic anointing[18] (cf. 2 K. 20:13; but in Jer. 6:20 *qāneh haṭṭôḇ* appears together with "frankincense from Sheba" in a sacral context, synonymous with *tyb*).

As a designation of the purest quality, *ṭb* is also used with *eru,* "copper,"[19] *eqla,* "field," etc.

The Akkadian fem. noun *ṭābtu* (sumerogram MUN), "salt," is not connected with the root *ṭb,* "good." Here we are dealing with an "etymological homonym," which is the product of phonetic convergence and was finally associated by metonymy with *ṭb,* "good," and fem. *ṭābtu,* "goodness," because salt was looked upon as an indispensable product. We are clearly dealing with a semantic transference based on homonymy.

A true example of synecdoche, by contrast, is Neo-Bab. *tyb,* "fragrance,"[20] and Min. *tyb,* which designates a substance producing this fragrance, probably a resin used with other aromatics when incense was offered.[21]

b. In all the Semitic languages, *ṭb* is used in the context of everyday life to designate the practical utility of an object, an action, or a situation, with reference to its being "useful" or "advantageous." The particular purpose in each case lends the word its specific meaning.

In Assyrian, this usage appears only in the use of the D stem of the verb to mean

---

[12] *KTU,* 4.213, 1, 4, 6, 9, 11, 14, 16, 20, 22.

[13] *KTU,* 4.213, 2, 5, 7, 10, 12f., 15, 17, 19, 23; cf. line 3: *ḥlq.*

[14] Cf. *AuS,* IV (1935), 375; M. Dahood, *Ugaritic-Hebrew Philology. BietOr,* 17 (1965), 59, no. 1028; O. Eissfeldt, "The Alphabetical Cuneiform Texts from Ras Shamra Published in 'Le Palais Royal d'Ugarit,' vol. II, 1957," *JSS,* 5 (1960) = *KlSchr,* II (1953), 389; *UT,* no. 1028; *WUS,* no. 1110; J. Aistleitner, "Lexikalisches zu den ugaritischen Texten," *AcOrASH,* 11 (1960), 29-34.

[15] *PRU,* II, 84.

[16] S. H. Langdon, *Die neubabylonischen Königsinschriften. VAB,* 4 (1912), 62, 52.

[17] Cf. *AuS,* IV, 247, 256; EA 14 I, 32; II 50; III 34-45; 17, 44; etc.

[18] H. Gunkel, "Psalm 133," *Beiträge zur alttestamentlichen Wissenschaft. Festschrift K. Budde. BZAW,* 34 (1920), 73f.

[19] EA 40, 13.

[20] Langdon, 256, 5.

[21] *CIH,* 308, 4 (meaning disputed); 681; 686; *RÉS* 2771, 4f.; 2778, 12; 2839, "pleasant odor of God"; etc. Cf. W. W. Müller, *Die Wurzeln med. und tertiae Y/W im Altsüdarabischen* (diss., Tübingen, 1962), 72.

"prepare, make ready."[22] Ugar. *ṭb/ṭbn ql*[23] probably suggests less the "pleasantness" than the "power" of a voice.[23] Delitzsch[24] interprets *muṭi-ib-tum,*[25] a synonym for *da-al-tum*[26] and applied to a door as a poetic epithet, in the sense "making glad (the one returning home)." Akk. *kī ūmu iṭṭību* means for the sailor "good (i.e., favorable) weather."[27] Aram. *m'n ṭb* is a "seaworthy ship."[28] It is important for a speaker to find the right words, i.e., to have the gift of eloquence and use it in appropriate situations: "May your lips be friendly (*šaptāka lū ṭābā*) when you wish them to be. . . ."[29]

c. The relationship between human beings and the gods is also defined in part in terms of "right" words and deeds,[30] i.e., those that serve to fulfill the will of the gods and are therefore rewarded by the gods: "The great gods look with joy upon my good (*damqāte*) works, and at their exalted command I sit *ṭābiš* upon the throne of my father. . . ."[31] The word *ṭābiš*, "in good fashion, well," can also be interpreted as "with favorable auspices." In the annals of Ashurbanipal,[32] the pleasure of the gods is coupled with the rainfall of Adad, i.e., with the fertility of the land and its associated prosperity. In response to human beings the gods speak favorable and propitious words, not least in oracles.[33] Every important undertaking is dependent on the favorable interpretation of such oracles in order to determine the days best suited to the project (*ūmī ṭābūti;*[34] *ina arḫi ṭābi*, "in a favorable month"[35]).

In the Babylonian hymns, the king frequently prays to the gods for *šīru ṭābu;*[36] this prayer may express the desire for physical health, but it may also indicate the desire for a favorable omen. Juxtaposition with a prayer for "protection of the soul"[37] or "joy of heart"[38] supports the meaning "health of body," but the texts often associate this prayer with a prayer for an oracle (cf. esp. the highly poetic prayer of Nebuchadnezzar to the goddess Ninkarrak[39]).

In Neo-Babylonian letters from the king to his inferiors, the stereotyped salutation

---

22 Prism of Tiglath-pileser I, IV, 70; cf. II, 10.

23 *KTU*, 1.3 I, 20; 1.19, 45f. For a different view, see C. Virolleaud, *La déesse 'Anat* (Paris, 1938), *in loc.* Cf. I Danel 46.

24 F. Delitzsch, *Assyrisches Handwörterbuch* (1896; repr. Leipzig, 1968), 300.

25 *AHw*, II, 691b.

26 *AHw*, I, 154.

27 EA 7, 59.

28 Ahikar, 109.

29 CT 29.

30 Langdon, Neb. 86 I, 15-23.

31 M. Streck, *Assurbanipal und die letzten assyrischen Könige bis zum Untergang Niniveh's. VAB*, 7 (1916), L⁴, II, 10f.

32 *Ibid.*, Rm I, 44ff.

33 *Ibid.*, 344-46; K 1285, 11, 13, 26.

34 H. Hunger, *Babylonische und assyrische Kolophone. AOAT*, 2 (1968), 179a.

35 Streck, 640.

36 Langdon, 130, 53; Streck, L², 21; S², 42; S³, 71; Col. n, 12; etc.

37 Langdon, 78, 46.

38 Streck, Cyl. L², 20f.; cf. Langdon, 112, 56.

39 Langdon, 76, 38–78, 52.

was a wish for the recipient's welfare: *libbaka lū ṭābka,* "may your heart be happy," i.e., "may you prosper." Well-being in the sense of peace and contentment in the land is to extend to subjects, especially recently subjugated peoples, thanks to the generous and upright government of their (new) ruler. Thus despite variations in wording one could speak of a "pacification formula."[40]

d. According to Assyrian and Babylonian texts, the king's gracious will is manifested in his *šāru ṭābu,* his "good breath."[41] This places him on a plane with gods such as Marduk, the *il šāri ṭābi,*[42] "whose good breath we breathe when in terrible distress."[43] The *šāru ṭābu* of the king makes itself known in a positive response for anyone who calls on him for support (usually military), as well as in material aid. Cf. the related passages in the Amarna letters: *šāru balāṭi-ia,*[44] *ša-ri-ia.*[45] Here we may be dealing with a personalized synecdoche representing the king. The *šāru* designates a totally positive element. Its refusal means punishment, denial of material aid, displeasure on the part of the ruler, depriving the person concerned of "peace of heart," his personal security,[46] making him helpless in the face of his enemies.[47]

e. From the Old Assyrian period until at least the sixth century B.C., in suzerainty treaties as well as in "official" letters and communications between individual rulers, the making, keeping, and breaking of political alliances are often discussed. Besides Akk. *aḫḫūtu/i,* "brotherhood," a central role is played in these contexts by the active verb (present *iṭāb/iṭib/iṭibbu;* permansive *ṭāb*) and the noun *ṭābūtu* (*ṭūbtu/ṭūbu,* and the collective pl. *ṭub[b]āti*), "benevolence, friendship."[48] The loyalty of the parties manifests itself in various ways. The phrase *ṭūbtu u sulummû* is a term for peace resulting from a treaty. Used with *itti* ("with, under") and *bīri* ("between"), *ṭābūtu/i* designates those relationships between two states that are defined by formal treaty. A common variant is juxtaposition of covenant friendship (*ṭābūtu/i*) and brotherhood (*aḫḫūtu/i*).[49] These terms can stand side by side or be used as synonyms for each other. The relationship is especially close when the subst. *aḫḫūtu* appears with the attributive adj. *ṭābtu.*[50] These terms suggest less a lord/vassal relationship than ties between equal or almost equal sovereigns defined by mutual treaty obligations in the realm of commerce[51] or matrimonial politics.[52]

---

40 *Ibid.,* 172, 35-37; cf. 102, 11-16; M. Schorr, *Urkunden des altbabylonischen Zivil- und Prozessrechts. VAB,* 5 (1913; repr. 1971), 110, 17; *KAI,* 222 B.6.
41 EA 297, 18.
42 EnEl, VII, 20.
43 EnEl, VII, 23.
44 EA 141, 2.
45 EA 281, 3.
46 EA 297, 17f.
47 EA 137, 67-80.
48 → ברית *bᵉrîṯ* [*bᵉrîth*], III.2, 258f.
49 EA 4, 15, 17; 17, 51; 11 vo., 22; etc.
50 EA 1, 64.
51 EA 11 vo., 22f.; 16, 32.
52 EA 4, 15-18; cf. 1, 64.

As early as the Amarna letters we find as parallel terms for making a treaty the expressions *šalmu* (for *salīma*[53]) *epēšu*, *ṭābūta epēšu*, and *kitta(m) epēšu*.[54] The contrary, "break a treaty" or "offend against a treaty," has a prominent place especially in the annals of Ashurbanipal. The terms *adû* and *ṭābtu* appear here with the same verbs, but are not (*pace* Lamadrid and Moran) synonymous and interchangeable.

The term *adû* has in the two parties who together conclude a treaty two reference points on the same plane; *ṭābtu* starts explicitly from the perspective of the sovereign and describes the obligations of the vassal. In this latter case the parties are anything but equal; in expressions using *ṭābtu* we are always dealing with vassal treaties, as is also shown by the statement in certain texts that the traitor has refused homage and tribute.[55] The onesidedness of this relationship is further underscored by the fact that treaties with the Assyrian king involve the gods of Assyria themselves, and are confirmed by oath in their presence, but not in the presence of the gods of the other party (unlike the Sefire treaty), so that the treaty can be broken only by the vassal.[56]

f. The use of *ṭôḇ* in the administration of justice is particularly well attested in Aramaic.[57] Of particular importance in the realm of word formation is the distinction between the passive and active uses of the verb, which are in part characteristic of specific types of cases.

In all linguistic usage, *ṭb* in combination with *lbb* is to be considered a term belonging to the law of personal property. In civil and forensic law it applies to commerce and the transfer of ownership through purchase or inheritance (not through gift). It is a fixed technical term for "satisfaction"; in the concluding clauses of a contract or protocol it documents the fulfilment of obligations and makes the associated renunciation of further claims legally binding.

The connection between the notion of satisfaction and that of fulfilment of obligations is made clear in quitclaims and conveyances by the active form *hwṭbt lbby b* . . . , "you have satisfied my heart with. . . ."[58] This expression combines two aspects that the passive form expresses by means of two terms: (1) *yhbt ly dmwy/ym't ly,* "you have given me its price"/"you have sworn me an oath"; (2) *wṭyb lbby bgw,* "and my heart is satisfied thereby." From this perspective the passive form is the direct result of the active. Fulfilment of the required conditions and "satisfaction of heart" are identical.

g. As an attribute applied to persons, Ugar. *ṭb* (pl. *ṭbm*) may appear with the meaning "happy."[59]

---

53 Cf. *AHw,* III, 1149b.

54 EA 136, 8-13, 27-32; 138, 53; cf. Lamadrid, *EstBíb,* 28 (1969), 61-77.

55 Streck, Rm VII, 89f.; B 7, 95; Rm IX, 9, 117-19; cf. also Rm VIII, 66, *lā ḫāsis ṭābti* in its context; etc.

56 For details, see Johag.

57 See Y. Muffs, *Studies in the Aramaic Legal Papyri from Elephantine. StDI,* 8 (1969).

58 *Ibid.*, 46f., 70f.; *AP,* 6, 12; 20, 8.

59 Cf. F. B. Knutson, in *RSP* II, 158; *KTU,* 1.108, 4f. reads *ẓbm*.

The Aramaic *māšāl* sayings from Elephantine exhibit an ethical component. They use concrete terms by metonymy as images for abstract concepts.[60] A large number of these proverbs are general maxims pertaining to daily life in society; they bear on ethical conduct and furnish concrete guidelines: "Good eyes (*'ynyn ṭbn*) should not be darkened and good ears (*'dnyn ṭbn*) should not be stopped, and a good mouth (*pm ṭb*) will love the truth and speak it."[61]

h. In Palmyrene and Nabatean graffiti, some as late as the Christian era, *ṭb* appears in combination with various forms of the root → זכר *zāḵar* [*zākhar*]; these are memorial and dedication inscriptions. The expression often appears in parallel with → שׁלם *šlm*[62] and *bryk*[63] with a personal name. Schottroff[64] distinguishes between secular and sacral usage in Palmyrene and Nabatean, and points out[65] the OT correspondences in Neh. 5:19 and 13:31 (with k^e, "according to"). The devout worshipper is confident that God will remember him and vouchsafe his lasting blessing on account of his actions. The act of remembering assures salvation (*hyyn*); thus *ṭb* takes on a religious sense: *dkrn ṭb*, "devout remembrance."[66] On memorial tablets, the exclamatory formula *dkyr l/bṭb*, "be it remembered for/as good,"[67] requests "good remembrance" not only for the person of the departed, but also for his "good name" (*šm ṭb*) or for the "beauty" and "excellence" of a woman: "So excellent and beautiful was she that no one was like her in excellence."[68] Some texts[69] invoke a curse on anyone who ignores this request; whoever obeys it will receive the same "good remembrance" as the departed.[70]

II. 1. *OT Occurrences*. Forms of *ṭôḇ* are found in all the OT books except Obadiah, Habakkuk, and Haggai: 738 occurrences are Hebrew and 3 are Aramaic (Ezr. 5:17; Dnl. 2:32; 6:24); it also occurs 13 times in names. Besides the perfective root *ṭwb* there are 123 occurrences of the imperfective by-form *yṭb* (44 in the qal, 73 in the hiphil [there are only 3 occurrences of the hiphil of *ṭwb*], 6 in the form of the superlative subst. *mêṭāḇ*). In many passages it is difficult to determine whether the form *ṭôḇ* represents the adjective (masc. sg.) or the verb (qal stative, ptcp., or inf.); Lisowsky and Mandelkern differ in 70 cases.[71] The adj. *ṭôḇ/â* is frequently nominalized. We also find an abstract noun *ṭûḇ* (32 occurrences) formed from *ṭôḇ* after the analogy of *quṭl* abstracts. When we investigate diachronic and geographical distribution, we find

---

60 Ahikar, 86,109,151f.,159; cf. 115,123,163-65.

61 Ahikar, 86.

62 *CIS*, II, 228; *RÉS* 1106, 1-4; 1116 A^2 (?); 1136 A, C^2; etc.

63 *KAI*, 224.1f., etc.

64 W. Schottroff, *"Gedenken" im Alten Orient und im AT. WMANT*, 15 (^{2}1967).

65 *Ibid.*, 219.

66 *Ibid.*, 80.

67 *KAI*, 238.8f.; 244.2f., 5; 246.3; 251.3; 256.3 with l^e; *RÉS* 1137 A; 1171, 1; 1192, 11; 1383; 1389; etc. with b^e.

68 *KAI*, 226.3; 276.9, 11.

69 *Ibid.*, 245.1-3.

70 *Ibid.*, 240.2f.

71 See *KBL*^{3}, 354-56.

that the root is used throughout the whole of Israel from the early period down to the latest period of the OT canon, albeit partially restricted to certain areas of life.

The following is a survey of OT occurrences. *ṭôḇ* (verb or adj.; note the caveat above) occurs in J 31 times; E, 14; P, 15; Dt. 1–11 and 27–34, 24; Dt. 12–26, 6; Josh., 8; Jgs., 14; Ruth, 3; 1 S., 39; 2 S., 26; 1 K., 24; 2 K., 12; 1 Ch., 8; 2 Ch., 23; Ezr., 7; Neh., 12; Est., 23; Job, 12; Ps., 69; Prov., 62; Eccl., 52; Cant., 4; Isa., 9; Deutero-Isa., 3; Trito-Isa., 2; Jer., 37; Lam., 7; Ezk., 9; Dnl., 4; Hos., 5; Joel, 1; Am., 4; Jon., 2; Mic., 4; Nah., 2; Zec., 4; Mal., 1. Occurrences of *ṭôḇ* hiphil are 1 K., 1; 2 K., 1; 2 Ch., 1. *ṭûḇ* is found in J 2 times; E, 2; P, 1; Dt., 2; 2 K., 1; Ezr., 1; Neh., 4; Job, 2; Ps., 7; Prov., 1; Isa., 1; Trito-Isa., 2; Jer., 3; Hos., 2; Zec., 1. *yṭb* qal occurs in J 3 times; E, 2; P, 2; Dt. 1–11 and 27–34, 6; Dt. 12–26, 3; Josh., 2; Jgs., 3; Ruth, 2; 1 S., 2; 2 S., 2; 1 K., 2; 2 K., 1; Neh., 2; Est., 5; Ps., 1; Eccl., 1; Jer., 4; Nah., 1. *yṭb* hiphil is found in J 9 times; E, 1; P, 2; Dt. 1–11 and 27–34, 6; Dt. 12–26, 4; Josh., 1; Jgs., 2; Ruth, 1; 1 S., 4; 1 K., 1; 2 K., 2; Job, 1; Ps., 6; Prov., 5; Eccl., 1; Isa., 2; Deutero-Isa., 1; Jer., 14; Ezk., 2; Hos., 1; Jon., 3; Mic., 2; Nah., 1; Zeph., 1. *mêṭāḇ* occurs in P 4 times and in 1 S. twice.

The root is especially frequent in the southern kingdom from the eighth to the sixth centuries and after the exile. It is very common in the Deuteronomistic history; in a special portion of the Psalms, where it takes on a refined, although not totally abstract, meaning; in Wisdom Literature, where it usually has no religious overtones; and in Jeremiah.

The by-form *yṭb* is most common in the hiphil, with a causative meaning; it describes active intervention rather than durative possession of a characteristic or the result of an action in the past. But the hiphil of *yṭb* is not totally distinct in usage from the qal or from the qal of *ṭôḇ*.

2. *Utilitarian Meaning in Secular Usage*. The most common meaning of *ṭôḇ* in the OT is utilitarian. From the perspective of the suitability of an object or person, the focus is on the functional aspect, as being in proper order or suited for the job. We are thus dealing with "goodness for something," with a very concrete and tangible meaning in the background.

The approval formula of the Creation Narrative is a parade example: *wayyar' 'ᵉlōhîm kî ṭôḇ* (Gen. 1:1,4,10,12,18,21,25,31). Essential to the interpretation of *ṭôḇ* is its use with → ראה *rā'â,* which means "see" in the sense of "regard," "examine," or even "think proper," so as to arrive at the conclusion: "Truly, it is good." In this way the functionality of the work is emphasized, the fact that the world God has created is "in good order." Mesopotamian parallels indicate that the expression "see that something is good" or "see how good something is" was used by craftsmen on completion of their work.[72] The utilitarian interpretation is underscored by indicating the functions served by the works of creation. They are good for the purpose for which they were fashioned, without any suggestion of objective evaluation.[73]

---

[72] Schmidt, 62.

[73] Westermann, 61.

The adj. *ṭôḇ* takes on an active sense when applied to counsel (2 S. 17:14) that serves to accomplish a project, as well as to favorable interpretation of a dream (Gen. 40:16). The hiphil of *yṭb* is also used for conduct appropriate to a situation (Gen. 4:7; Jon. 4:4,9). In OT secular usage, the same form can have the active meaning "prepare for use" (Ex. 30:7) or more specifically "reach a decision" (1 S. 20:13) or "adorn one's head" (2 K. 9:30); the result of an action is used to express its cause. The hiphil of *yṭb* also serves to express the special excellence of some action (1 S. 16:17; Ps. 33:3; Isa. 23:16; Jer. 1:12; Ezk. 33:32) when the finite form of *yṭb* is constructed with the infinitive of a second verb or with a substantive. Jer. 2:33 describes cunning and shrewd behavior (cf. Mic. 7:3 with the oxymoron *'al-hāra' . . . lᵉhêṭîḇ*); the same idiom can characterize special love and kindness (Ruth 3:10). As an infinitive absolute with a finite verb or participle it provides elative or superlative meaning. The action is intensified to the ultimate degree: "seek diligently" (Dt. 13:15[14]; 17:4; 19:18); "grind to dust" (idols; Dt. 9:21; 2 K. 11:18; etc.).

In the context of agriculture, there is emphasis on the element of fertility. Plump ears of grain of the highest quality are *šibbᵒlîm ṭôḇôṯ* (cf. Gen. 41:5,22,24,26). Cows (Gen. 41:26; 1 S. 8:16) or asses (1 S. 8:16) called *ṭôḇ* are well-nourished, well-built, strong beasts of burden or fat stock.

In secular usage, the noun *ṭûḇ* or *ṭôḇâ* designates not so much a quality as the cause or source of that quality. Both words are general terms for the produce of the land (Ezr. 9:12; Neh. 9:25; Jer. 2:7). In Jer. 17:6, *ṭôḇ* has by metonymy the specialized meaning "rain," i.e., the good that occasions the fertility of the soil (cf. v. 8, where *ḥōm* is the opposite of *ṭôḇ*). In the farewell discourse of Moses (Dt. 28:12), rain is spoken of as a good from the "rich treasury" (*'ôṣārô haṭṭôḇ*) of God, a blessing on human labor, in parallel with abundant prosperity "in the fruit of your body, and in the fruit of your cattle, and in the fruit of your ground" (v. 11; cf. Neh. 9:36; Ps. 65:12[11]; 68:10f.[9f.]; Isa. 4:2; 30:23f.; Jer. 31:12-14; Hos. 2:23f.[21f.]).[74]

In Solomon's prayer of dedication (1 K. 8), there is a clear connection between the lack of rain and the sins of the people (vv. 35f.). Prayer for the forgiveness of sins is linked with prayer for rain (cf. Jer. 3:3; 5:25). Both Jer. 31:12 and Ps. 85:13(12) associate rain (*ṭôḇ*) and fertility with the coming age of salvation.

Of particular importance is the phrase *'ereṣ ṭôḇâ* (Ex. 3:8; Nu. 14:7; Dt. 1:25,35; 3:25; 4:21f.; 6:18; 8:7,10; 9:6; 11:17; Josh. 23:16; Jgs. 18:9; 1 Ch. 28:8; Hos. 10:1) or *hā'ᵃdāmâ haṭṭôḇâ* (Josh. 23:13,15; 1 K. 14:15). As the land promised to the Israelites, it is viewed from a twofold perspective. First, *ṭôḇ(â)* comprehends here all the positive material elements that make the land desirable to the Israelites during the exodus from Egypt and the period of wandering in the desert. Second, in the context of the blessings the land is to receive from Yahweh, *ṭôḇ* appears as a term of promise in a series of terms describing the promise of the land. The element of promise in the description of the land as God's gracious gift and Israel's heritage finds particular expression in the "confessional" statement *ṭôḇâ hā'āreṣ 'ᵃšer-YHWH 'ᵉlōhênû nōṯēn*

---

[74] See M. Dahood, "Hebrew-Ugaritic Lexicography, II," *Bibl,* 45 (1964), 393-412, esp. 411.

lānû (Dt. 1:25; 4:21; 8:10; etc.), in which Plöger[75] claims (probably correctly) to find a cultic responsory.

When applied to persons, *ṭôḇ* emphasizes a special ability, excellence, or positive quality: a newborn child is called *ṭôḇ* if it is strong and handsome (Ex. 2:2); marriageable girls are *ṭōḇōṯ* (Gen. 6:2; cf. Egyp. *nfr.t*[76]). The construct phrase *ṭôḇaṯ-śeḵel* refers to the ability to think in practical terms, to show a particular skill (1 S. 25:3; 2 Ch. 30:22). In the case of an *'îš-ṭôḇ*, the quality of an action is transferred to the person who performs it (2 S. 18:27; 1 K. 2:32): "a worthy man brings good news" (1 K. 1:42). Here is clear evidence of the esteem a reliable messenger enjoyed; in Egypt, the instruction of a messenger was even a formal subject of study.[77]

Contrary to the opinion of numerous exegetes, the messenger in Isa. 52:7 is not in the narrower sense to be taken as a messianic bearer of tidings of salvation; the context (vv. 1-12) makes it clear that the author is not thinking of a distant future but of Israel's deliverance from exile. It is not universally true that the piel of *bśr* has positive meaning, but it tends in this direction. In v. 7b, *ṭôḇ* is to be construed as a noun in synthetic parallelism with *šālôm* and *yešûʿâ*, which are connected with *mašmîaʿ*. All three terms look beyond present deliverance to the proclamation of God's reign.

It is especially required of the king that he be good and upright (2 K. 10:3, *ṭôḇ* par. *yšr*); this refers not to his political abilities as a ruler, but to his keeping of the covenant (cf. 1 S. 15:26-28), an allusion to the king's position in religious history and in the political history of Israel. This applies equally to the princes and judges of the people, over whom the prophet Micah delivers a devastating judgment: in terms of social justice, "the best of them is like a brier, the most upright of them a thorn hedge" (Mic. 7:4).

In Semitic thought and usage, a person is valued less for his appearance than for his abilities. For the Greeks, the abstract intellectual notion of beauty is paramount; for the Semites, it is sensuous beauty that matters. That which is beautiful is pleasing and serviceable. Aesthetic beauty in the ancient Near Eastern sense is never characterized in the OT by the use of *ṭôḇ* alone, which always appears in this sense in combination with a substantive, usually in a construct phrase with *mar'eh* (Gen. 24:16; 26:7; 2 S. 11:2; Est. 2:2f.,7; Dnl. 1:4), *tō'ar* (1 K. 1:6), or *rō'î* (1 S. 16:12), i.e., always in combination with the root *r'h* or *t'r*, "see," or more accurately "observe," so that this "beauty" is not objective, but resides in the subjective viewpoint of the observer. There is always an emphasis on being materially "desirable" or "useful."[78] The "beauty" of the promised land finds expression primarily in its fertility. Persons demonstrate their excellence through special characteristics: Saul surpasses the rest of his people in stature (1 S. 9:2, *ṭôḇ* par. *bāḥûr*), David in his vivacity, musical skill, and bravery (1 S. 16:12,18).

---

[75] J. G. Plöger, *Literarkritische, formgeschichtliche und stilkritische Untersuchungen zum Deuteronomium. BBB*, 26 (1967), 51, 88.

[76] *WbÄS*, II, 258.

[77] See B. Gemser, *Sprüch Salomos. HAT*, XVI (^{2}1963), 59; A. Erman, *The Ancient Egyptians: A Sourcebook of Their Writings* (Eng. trans., New York, ^{2}1966), 58, 68.

[78] Boman, 84f.

3. *ṭôḇ lᵉ Expressing Benefit.* In impersonal nominal constructions with the particles *lᵉ*, *bᵉ*, and *'el,* together with a pronominal suffix, *ṭôḇ* expresses the benefit someone gains through another person, a thing, or an action. The playing of the lyre is intended to have a beneficial effect on Saul's sick soul, so that the "evil spirit" will leave him (1 S. 16:16,23). In combination with *dbr,* the meaning is to speak favorably of someone, for instance on account of the value of his previous actions (1 S. 19:4; cf. 20:12; 27:1; 2 S. 18:3). In the midst of the perils of the wilderness, it appears better to the Israelites to return to Egypt than to go forward (Nu. 11:18; 14:3), because there they had enough to eat. Similarly a freed slave might stay with his master if he fared well there (Dt. 15:16; 23:17[16]). In all these cases, the emphasis is on securing the necessary or accustomed conditions of life, either in strictly economic terms or with political overtones having to do with peace and prosperity (Jgs. 9:2; cf. 2 Ch. 10:7). All the passages involve subjective personal advantage.[79]

When construed personally as a statement concerning Yahweh's good deeds toward someone (*ṭôḇ YHWH lᵉ*), *ṭôḇ* takes on historico-theological significance, deriving from the contrast between the upright and the wicked and conveying the notion of hope in the midst of misfortune (Ps. 73:1; 145:9; Lam. 3:25f.; but cf. Ps. 39:3[2]). Yahweh is good to the *yᵉšārîm* and *ṣaddîqîm*. In addition, *ṭôḇ* is found in synonymy or parallelism with *ṣᵉḏāqâ* (→ צדק *ṣāḏaq*) as a term for the faithfulness of Yahweh.

4. *ṭôḇ lēḇ*. The phrase *ṭôḇ lēḇ* appears as the vehicle of emotions in the sense "being of good cheer." It is especially common in secular usage in the context of festivals and banquets (Jgs. 16:25; 1 S. 25:36, with the addition "he was very drunk"; 2 S. 13:28; Est. 1:10; cf. Jgs. 19:6,9; Ruth 3:7; Prov. 15:15). Here *ṭôḇ lēḇ* refers to a state in which one is incapable of perception, decision, or action, without any negative connotations. The expression alludes not only to the outward consequences of indulgence, but also in part to an inward attitude; this is especially clear in Eccl. 9:7, where the summons to eat with enjoyment and drink wine with a merry heart is grounded on the notion that such conduct is pleasing to God.

Another nuance appears in the meaning "be of good cheer" or (ingressively) "take heart" (1 K. 21:7; Est. 5:9; Eccl. 7:3; cf. Prov. 15:13; 17:22, where the hiphil of *yṭb* expresses the possibility of becoming cheerful). The inward feelings are expressed by the facial mien: "A glad heart makes a cheerful countenance, but by sorrow of heart the spirit is broken" (Prov. 15:13; cf. 17:22; Eccl. 7:3).

The people of Israel are threatened with disaster because in their abundance they forgot to serve Yahweh with joyfulness and gladness of heart (*bᵉṭûḇ lēḇāḇ,* Dt. 28:47). This (postexilic) verse implies the charge of breaking the covenant. Not to serve Yahweh with gladness of heart means to turn away from him, to reject his law, to turn to other gods (v. 45). In the postexilic period, *lēḇ* in combination with *ṭûḇ* takes on the meaning of "felicity" in the positive theological sense (Isa. 65:14).

---

79 On the use of the expression in the language of treaties, see Johag.

5. *ṭôḇ in Ethical and Theological Usage*. a. Alongside → ישׁר *yāšar*, → חפץ *ḥāpēṣ*, and → רצה/רצון *rāṣâ/rāṣôn*, the semantically passive phrase *ṭôḇ* b^{e}*'ênê* (42 occurrences; with *lipnê* or *'al* in late texts), "be/seem good in the eyes of someone," or its active equivalent *yṭb* qal (16 occurrences[80]), "prove good," frequently in combination with the action verb *'āśâ*, is often translated "please" without consideration of its various nuances. This usage is found primarily in the context of everyday life; it points to something that appears beneficial to someone for the purposes of his own life, by a kind of "visual estimate."[81] In this totally subjective estimate an independent expression of will is heard: "Do what you please" (Gen. 20:15; 1 Ch. 21:23; Est. 1:19; 3:9,11; 5:4,8,14; 7:3; 8:5,8; 9:13; cf. Jer. 40:4 [*ṭôḇ* par. *yšr*]; 1 S. 14:36,40; 2 S. 19:19[18]; 24:22; 2 K. 10:5; Zec. 11:12). In such cases we may be dealing with a formula of approbation or approval, with reference, say, to good news (Gen. 45:16), sagacious words (Gen. 34:18; 41:37; Lev. 10:20; Josh. 22:30,33; 2 S. 18:4; Est. 1:21), or a decision (Dt. 1:23; 2 S. 3:19). Someone's general conduct can be found good if it is in accord with the "proper estimate" (1 S. 18:5; 29:6,9; 2 S. 3:36; cf. 22:26), since the eye discloses the inward disposition (cf. Sir. 31:13; *'Aboth* ii.9; v.19).

From another perspective, the expression *ṭôḇ* b^{e}*'ênê* can indicate conscious submission to someone else's authority on the basis of formal status (Gen. 16:6; Josh. 9:25; 1 S. 24:5[4]; Jer. 26:14). In Jgs. 10:15, the Israelites submit to the will and judgment of Yahweh in consequence of their sins against the covenant (cf. 1 S. 11:10; 2 S. 15:26; 19:28[27]). Just as the relationship between a king and his subjects is defined by what the king commands (cf. Dnl. 6:24[23]; Ezr. 5:17; Neh. 2:5-7), so the worshipper submits in prayer to the objective will of God. Obedience to the covenant is met with the promise that all will go well (*yîṭaḇ lāḵ*). But Israel can only choose to accept or reject the laws of the covenant, which Yahweh created and is therefore "just" and "good" (Dt. 6:18; 12:28; 2 K. 10:30; 2 Ch. 14:1[2] [ṭôḇ par. *yšr*]; cf. 1 S. 3:18; Mic. 6:8).

The use of the phrase *ṭôḇ* b^{e}*'ênê* or *ṭôḇ lipnê* as legal terminology associated with the covenant can be seen clearly in the contrast between the one who is pleasing to God and the sinner, who must come to judgment (Eccl. 2:26; 7:26; cf. Lev. 10:19; Mal. 2:17). God demands absolute obedience of human beings even when they lack the necessary knowledge on which to act, as in the case of Balaam, who was compelled to bless Israel contrary to his own will and original plan (Nu. 24:1). In 2 K. 20:3 (par. Isa. 38:3; cf. 2 Ch. 31:20), "doing what is good in God's sight" involves walking before Yahweh in faithfulness and with a whole heart. Yahweh will hear the prayer of one whose conduct is good (2 K. 20:3-5; cf. 1 S. 3:18; 2 S. 10:12 par. 1 Ch. 19:13). Also dependent on the pleasure of Yahweh is the successful completion of a project involving the entire nation (1 Ch. 13:2).

If → ישׁר *yāšar* takes the place of *ṭôḇ*, the "objective criterion of critical evaluation"[82] is being applied—usually by God, rarely by a human being (Ex. 15:26; Dt.

---

80 For Aramaic, see *AP*, 27, 19, 21f.
81 Ungern-Sternberg, 62.
82 *Ibid.*, 64.

6:18; 12:25; 13:19[18]; 21:9; 1 S. 18:20,26; 2 S. 17:4; etc.). In this case the "proper estimate" of an action lies outside human judgment.

On the other hand, → חפץ *ḥāpēṣ*, "delight," embodies an affective judgment (which can also be negative). It is therefore used primarily of human beings and their desires,[83] just like → רצה/רצון *rāṣâ/rāṣôn*, "be pleased" (Gen. 33:10; Dt. 33:24; 2 Ch. 10:7), usually with an element of arbitrariness (Prov. 14:35; 16:13,15; 19:12; Dnl. 8:4; etc.).

b. With 79 occurrences, the juxtaposition of *ṭôḇ* with its antonym *ra'* (→ רעע *rā'a'*) is quite frequent, especially in Jeremiah (15 times). The antithesis appears almost as a formula in several expressions. In the first instance it has no ethical or theological overtones, meaning simply "pleasant" and "unpleasant" to the taste and other senses (Gen. 3:6; 2 S. 19:36[35]), then "salutary"/"harmful" with various nuances, and finally "good"/"evil" in the ethical sense.[84] In combination with *yd'* or *da'aṯ* (→ ידע *yāḏa'*) (Gen. 2:9,17; 3:5,22; Dt. 1:39) the expression refers to "functional knowledge" of what is helpful or hurtful for mankind.[85] In Gen. 3:6, *l^ehaśkîl* demonstrates an intellectual interpretation of the expression (cf. 2 S. 14:17,20; Ps. 36:4[3]; Eccl. 4:13). The ability to make the ethical distinction between what is "good" and what is "evil" will give mankind autonomous mastery over life. To eat of the "forbidden tree" is to impugn the authority of God, to seek to be like God; for he "knows the opposites of being, . . . he has direct intercourse with them [*yd':* be in direct contact with]. . . . He who is above all opposites has intercourse with the opposites of good and evil that are of His own making."[86] Here the expression takes on preeminent theological meaning as characterizing the gulf between creature and creator.

The ability to distinguish between *ṭôḇ* and *ra'* is not found in young children, who are not yet responsible for their actions and are therefore innocent (Dt. 1:39; Isa. 7:15f.; cf. Nu. 14:31). An ethical element also appears in the antithesis "spurn"/"choose" (Ps. 36:5[4]; Jon. 4:11). In 1 K. 3:7-12, Solomon's prayer for the ability to discern between good and evil is identical with the desire to be able to judge justly (vv. 11f.; cf. 2 S. 14:17). According to Jer. 4:22, stupidity is the inability to do good rather than evil, i.e., to fulfill the requirements of the covenant. The people described are "stupid children," who have no accurate estimate of important matters. An aged man may also claim inability to distinguish between *ṭôḇ* and *ra'* (2 S. 19:36[35]). Like Gen. 3:5, Isa. 7:15 sees a connection between food and the knowledge of good and evil: "to nourish judgment."[87]

"Discerning good and evil" (2 S. 14:17: *šāma' haṭṭôḇ w^ehārā';* 1 K. 3:9: *bîn bên-ṭôḇ l^erā'*) appears as a synonym for "distinguishing right from wrong," and thus also has a place in legal terminology. It is characteristic of a good king to hear both truth

---

83 See G. Gerleman, "חפץ *ḥpṣ* Gefallen haben," *THAT,* I, 624f.

84 Fischer, 323-25.

85 C. Westermann, *Genesis 1–11* (Eng. trans., Minneapolis, 1984), 241.

86 Buber, 20f.

87 H. W. Wolff, *Frieden ohne Ende. BSt,* 35 (1962), 45.

(*ṭôḇ*) and falsehood (*ra'*) and to distinguish correctly between them through the wisdom of God that is within him.

Also ethical in meaning is the expression *šillam rā'â taḥaṯ ṭôḇâ* (Gen. 44:4; 1 S. 25:21; Ps. 35:12; 38:21[20]; 109:5; Prov. 17:13; cf. 1 S. 24:18f.[17f.]; Jer. 18:20) or *l^e^rā'â w^e^lō' l^e^ṭôḇâ* with the directional particle *l^e^* (Jer. 21:10; 39:16; 44:27; Am. 9:4; etc.). The complaint "someone has requited me evil for good" derives from a forensic context; it is an indictment or a pleading of innocence (Ps. 35:12; 38:21[20]; 109:5; etc.). In individual laments the innocent accused brings his case before God to counter the wicked lies of false witnesses. To requite good with evil is a great injustice, which will be punished with constant misfortune (Prov. 17:13). But a reward will be given to anyone who repays good even to his enemy or lets him go away safe (cf. 1 S. 24:18-20[17-19]). In several passages we find the contrast between fortune and misfortune in material terms but with theological and ethical overtones (1 K. 22:8,18 par. 2 Ch. 18:7,17; Jer. 21:10; 39:16; 44:27; Am. 9:4). Yahweh is described as watching over Israel for evil and not for good, punishing Israel for transgressing the covenant and eradicating the Israelites from the land he had given them (Jer. 44:27).

In some instances the phrases *ṭôḇ wārā'* or *'im-ṭôḇ w^e^'im-rā'* (with *min-'aḏ* in prepositional constructions) are viewed as a polar merism expressing totality: positively "everything," neutrally "something," negatively "nothing";[88] this interpretation holds for Nu. 24:13; Prov. 15:3; Isa. 41:23; Jer. 10:5. But most of the passages in question deserve a more nuanced examination. As a declarative phrase, the expression expresses the dependence of a decision on the judgment of someone having authority, e.g. when a priest declares a sacrificial animal to be clean or unclean (Lev. 27:12). In combination with → דבר *dāḇar* [*dābhār*] the idiom belongs in a forensic context (Gen. 31:24,29; 2 S. 13:22).

Of course Laban is not to say "nothing" to Jacob, as the merism theory might suggest; he is simply not to charge him with any crime. Absalom similarly takes no legal action against Amnon. Judgment is not a matter of human decision, only its execution (cf. Gen. 24:50; Lev. 5:4; Lam. 3:38; Zeph. 1:12). The Israelites who want to flee to Egypt look for Yahweh's judgment (Jer. 42:6; cf. Eccl. 12:14). In this context the idiom does not reflect the desire for an oracle, favorable or unfavorable; it is a technical term for a specific yes-or-no judgment.

Of special import is the exhortation of the prophet Amos: "Seek good, and not evil, that you may live; and so Yahweh, the God of hosts, will be with you" (Am. 5:14, alluding to the oracle in 5:4). The conditional assurance of salvation *l^e^ma'an tiḥyû* (v. 14) *'ûlay yeḥ^e^nan* (v. 15) is the direct consequence of *diršû-ṭôḇ w^e^'al-rā'*, which is identical with *diršûnî wiḥ^e^yû* (v. 4) and *diršû 'eṯ-YHWH wiḥ^e^yû* (v. 6), so that Yahweh and *ṭôḇ* appear synonymous. The "good" with which Amos is concerned has nothing to do with the cult (v. 5), but rather with return to the eternally valid law of Yahweh,

---

88 A. M. Honeyman, "*Merismus* in Biblical Hebrew," *JBL*, 71 (1952), 11-18; P. P. Boccaccio, "I termini contrari come espressioni della totalità in ebraico," *Bibl*, 33 (1952), 173-190; Buchanan, 114-120; Hillers, 46f.; H. A. Brongers, "Merismus, Synekdoche und Hendiadys in der bibel-hebräischen Sprache," כה *1940-1965*. *OTS*, 14 (1965), 100-114; Clark, 266-278; Fox, 41f.

with the establishment of justice and with rejection of falsehood, evil, and indifferent cultic ceremonial (v. 15; cf. Ps. 34:11,14f.[10,13f.]; 36:4[3]; 37:3; Prov. 11:27; Mic. 3:2; etc.). Establishment of justice in the gate is for Amos the "fundamental requirement of obedience."[89] It is the purpose of his theological statements and his social criticism (cf. also Neh. 9:13; Ps. 119:39,112; Prov. 20:23; 24:23,25). The identification of *ṭôḇ* with → משפט *mišpāṭ* is based on the requirements of social solidarity; *ṭôḇ* in the active sense means "social fidelity" (cf. 2 Ch. 24:16; Ps. 14:1,3; Prov. 3:27; Mic. 3:2). "In Israel, evil is always evil because it offends against the idea of community; similarly, the good is good only by virtue of being in accord with the principle of community."[90]

c. Conduct in accordance with the law of Yahweh's covenant can be termed *dereḵ haṭṭôḇâ*, "the right way of life," "the way of salvation." It involves corresponding social and ethical demands (Jer. 7:5), as a rule norms governing the life of the community. Jeremiah links walking in the fear of God with the right to dwell in the promised land. Trito-Isaiah, on the other hand, points out the special mercy of God: he does not desert his people even when they walk in a way that is not good (Isa. 65:2). This notion bears the mark of Israel's experience of deliverance from the exile.

The direct opposite of *dereḵ haṭṭôḇâ* is *dereḵ lō'-ṭôḇ* (Ps. 36:5[4]; Prov. 16:29; Isa. 65:2); the first is a nominal phrase, the second verbal. This "not good" way is further characterized as being "wicked" (*rš'*, Ezk. 3:18f.); more often the more general term *ra'* is used (1 K. 13:33; 2 K. 17:13; 2 Ch. 7:14; Ps. 119:101; Prov. 2:12; 8:13; Jer. 18:11; 23:22; 25:5; Ezk. 13:22; 33:11; etc.). As *'ōraḥ mišpāṭ* (Isa. 40:14; Prov. 2:8; 17:23; etc.), the *dereḵ haṭṭôḇâ* or *dereḵ ṭôḇîm* or *dereḵ hayyᵉšārîm* also includes the element of secular prosperity, of "living securely" (1 S. 24:20[19]; 1 K. 8:36 par. 2 Ch. 6:27f.; Prov. 2:7f.; 12:15; 15:19).[91]

d. The term *ṭôḇ* plays an important role in covenantal and legal terminology.[92] The hiphil of *yṭb* serves to express God's act of salvation as an offer and guarantee of later intervention (Gen. 32:10,13[9,12]; Ex. 1:20; Dt. 8:16; 28:63; Josh. 24:20; Jgs. 17:13; Ps. 51:20[18]; Jer. 18:10; Ezk. 36:11; etc.). In combination with the noun *dāḇār* or the piel of the verb *dbr,* which is especially frequent in the historical books and Jeremiah, before the establishment of the monarchy and urbanization we find expressed the legal authority of the head of the clan or family, and later that of priestly, royal, or prophetic functionaries; the combination comes very close to the meaning of *ṭôḇ bᵉ'ênê* (cf. Dt. 1:14; 5:28; 18:17; Josh. 22:33; 1 S. 9:10).

When inquiry is made through an oracle or prophet, the response *dbr ṭôḇ* means "yes," i.e., a positive outcome (2 Ch. 10:7), *dbr ra'* a negative (1 K. 22:8,18 par. 2 Ch. 18:7,17). To do what all Israel thinks good to do (2 S. 3:19) or (synonymously)

---

89 Fey, 36.
90 Fahlgren, 106.
91 Nötscher, *Gotteswege und Menschenwege,* 50.
92 Johag.

to speak good words (1 K. 12:7) is the necessary condition for a covenant between David or Rehoboam and the northern tribes; a specific set of obligations is implied (cf. 1 S. 3:12f.,21). "Good words" (*d^eḇārîm ṭôḇîm*) or "good things" (*ṭôḇâ/ṭôḇôṯ*) appears in some passages together with → חסד *ḥeseḏ*, → שלום *šālôm*, or *'aḥwâ* (Zec. 11:14)—frequently in pairs—as a synonym for the "covenant" (→ ברית *b^erîṯ* [*b^erîth*]) itself or a designation of its substance.

The phrase *šālôm w^eṭôḇ* (cf. Gen. 26:29; Dt. 23:7; Ezr. 9:12; Isa. 52:7; Jer. 8:15; etc.) designates in the first instance material prosperity, security, and harmony.[93] In Gen. 26:29 it is a technical term for the covenant between Abraham and Abimelech (cf. Gen. 21:22-34; 31:44-53; Ps. 34:15[14]). Conditions are set down that must be fulfilled by whoever desires life and wishes to enjoy "goods" (*ṭôḇ/ṭôḇâ*). From the accommodation of differing interests, the meaning of *ṭôḇ* is extended into the ethical realm (often with the qal of *yṭb* used factitively or the hiphil used statively with active meaning).

For Jeremiah, Ezekiel, and Micah, the touchstone that distinguishes true from false prophets is *šālôm* (Jer. 6:14; 8:11; Ezk. 13:10,16; Mic. 3:5); for Micaiah ben Imlah it is *ṭôḇ* (1 K. 22:8,13,18 par. 2 Ch. 18:7,12,17). Both *šālôm* and *ṭôḇ* stand as antonyms to *rā'â*.

In 2 S. 7:28, *ṭôḇâ* refers to the covenant of Yahweh with the house of David (cf. v. 29; 1 S. 25:30; 2 Ch. 24:16; Akk. *dabābu ṭābūta* = Heb. *dabbēr ṭôḇ*). Some kind of formal treaty is probably also involved in 2 K. 25:28 (par. Jer. 52:32). Ezr. 9:12 discusses the negative attitude of the Torah toward mixed marriages, the prohibition of which is presented as part of Yahweh's covenant, as is also apparent from the context of Ezr. 9, "the biblical document *par excellence* of the covenant."[94]

In Jer. 12:6, *y^eḏabb^erû ṭôḇôṯ* is used in antithesis to *bāg^eḏû* (v. 6a), "deal treacherously." Here we are dealing with the informal offer of friendly relations, not an established treaty, so that there is no need to guarantee observance of the conditions.[95]

Above all, *haddāḇār haṭṭôḇ* represents covenant terminology in connection with the promise of the land and the fulfilment of that promise (Josh. 21:43-45; 23:14-16). Yahweh kept his part of the agreement: "Not one of all the good promises which Yahweh had made to the house of Israel had failed; all came to pass" (Josh. 21:45; cf. 1 K. 8:56). The polarity of *haddāḇār haṭṭôḇ* and *haddāḇār hārā'* leaves open not only the gift of the land, but also the possibility of judgment and the destruction of Israel, if the people do not in turn fulfill their covenant obligations (Josh. 23:15f.; cf. Neh. 5:9; *lō'-ṭôḇ haddāḇār* means to act wickedly; 1 S. 26:16; 1 K. 14:13; Jer. 29:32; Hos. 8:1-3; 14:3[2]; Mic. 1:12). As a term for God's benevolence, *dibbēr ṭôḇ* is used in parallel with *dibbēr šālôm* (Nu. 10:29; 1 S. 25:30; cf. Ps. 85:9[8]).

A new theological element appears in the Deuteronomistic redaction of Jeremiah: announcement of salvation without prior performance on the part of the people (Jer.

---

93 Lamadrid, *EstBíb*, 28 (1969), 63.

94 Moran, *CBQ*, 25 (1963), 82; cf. Hillers, 47.

95 Fox, 42.

32:42; cf. 24:5-7; 29:10; etc.). Association with *lēḇ* in Ps. 45:2(1), a prophetical song in praise of the king, suggests that *dāḇār ṭôḇ* refers to a message of joy or salvation.[96]

In 2 S. 15:3, the plural of *dāḇār ṭôḇ* is used to indicate that someone is legally in the right. The statement *ṭôḇ haddāḇār* is an expression of approval (1 K. 2:18,38,42; 18:24). In informal contexts, *dāḇār ṭôḇ* can also mean a "friendly word" (Prov. 12:25); *dibbēr ṭôḇâ* means "speak on someone's behalf" (Jer. 18:20) or find the right word in season (Prov. 15:23). The expression can also refer to appropriate behavior (Ex. 18:17 [negated]; Est. 7:9).

e. Typical of Wisdom Literature, especially Proverbs and Ecclesiastes, is the *ṭôḇ min* formula. Here we find antithetical couplets in *māšāl* form; their original setting was ethical instruction for family and clan, with the aim of practical mastery of life measured in terms of ability and resistance (cf. Prov. 12:9; 15:16f.; 18:22; 21:9,19; 25:7; 27:5,10;[97] Eccl. 4:6,9; 5:4[5]; 7:10; etc.). They reply to the anthropocentric question *mâ ṭôḇ/yiṯrôn lā'āḏām* (Eccl. 1:3; 2:3,22; 3:9; 5:15b[16b]; 6:8,12; 10:10f.; etc.).

Ecclesiastes, Proverbs, and Job use the neutral term *'āḏām*,[98] which ignores the element of covenant relationship with Yahweh.

In prose we find similar rhetorical questions or statements of alternatives that admit only a single answer: Ex. 14:12; Jgs. 8:2; 11:25; 18:19; 1 S. 1:8; 15:28; 1 K. 19:4; 2 K. 5:12; Am. 6:2; Jon. 4:3,8; Nah. 3:8. The question remains open in Gen. 29:19; Jgs. 15:2; 1 S. 9:2; 21:2[1]; Isa. 56:5.

In terms of intent, there is a distinction between comparative ("better than") and adversative ("what is good is . . . and not . . .") forms.[99] The first applies only to cases involving human norms, determining what is good or evil, advantageous or disadvantageous, on the basis of human preferences; the ethical claim is not ethical but pragmatic (cf. 2 K. 10:3). In this context we may speak of a scale of values within Wisdom Literature. The situation is different when the statement is based on the antithesis obedience/disobedience, thus invading the theological realm, where nothing is relative; here we face unconditional obligations (1 S. 15:22; Ps. 69:32[31]; cf. Prov. 17:1).

The *ṭôḇ min* form exhibits variations. The antithetical statements may be distributed over two hemistichs, or they may be embedded in a single hemistich, coupled with a second that provides their motivation; they may also themselves serve to justify a previous statement.[100] All share the purpose of pointing the way to human happiness. Thus alongside *ṭôḇ* we find such terms as *ḥyh/ḥayyîm* (→ חיה *ḥāyâ* [*chāyāh*]), *'ōšer* (→ עשׁר *'āšar*), *kāḇôḏ* (→ כבד *kāḇaḏ*), *yāmîm* (→ יום *yôm*), *'ōreḵ*, etc.

---

96 For a different view, see H.-J. Kraus, *Psalmen. BK*, XV/1 (⁵1978), *in loc.;* but see also R.-J. Tournay, "Les affinités du Ps. xlv avec le Cantique des Cantiques et leur interprétation messianique," *Congress Volume, Bonn 1962. SVT*, 9 (1963), 168-212.

97 Aramaic: Ahikar, 57; Egyptian: Ptah-hotep, 13 (Erman, 59f.).

98 Zimmerli, 179.

99 Schmid, n. 69; for a different view, see Kruse, 391f., 397.

100 Zimmerli, 192.

Here belong the Wisdom sayings that in a congratulatory style[101] call something *ṭôḇ*, especially when emphasized by the exclamation *mâ ṭôḇ*, sometimes strengthened by a deictic *hinnēh* or affirmative *kî* (Ps. 127:3ff.; 133:1; Sir. 25:4f.). Such sayings reflect a life rooted in *ṣᵉḏāqâ* and *mišpāṭ* (Ps. 112:5; Isa. 3:10; Lam. 3:25), as well as harmonious communal life (Gen. 2:18; 2 K. 2:19).

One of the major themes of the *ṭôḇ min* sayings is the evaluation of poverty and riches (Ps. 37:16; Prov. 15:16; 16:8,19; 19:1,22; 28:6; etc.). The antithesis "upright/wicked" often appears as equivalent to "poor/rich." Wealth as such is not condemned, but only the unjustly acquired possessions of the wicked (but cf. Ps. 49). The striving for the worldly good of joy and contentment is much discussed in Ecclesiastes (Eccl. 2:24; 3:22; 5:17[18]; 8:15; cf. 3:12), where *ṭôḇ* can stand for the "naive enjoyment of life."[102] The meaning of earthly life is found in enjoyment of human goods; in light of the discrepancy between righteousness and prosperity, wickedness and misfortune, attention is focused on the reward and punishment nexus (Eccl. 2:1; 3:13; 4:8; 5:17[18]; 6:3,6; 8:12f.,15). But it is clear that despite the secular tone Ecclesiastes views worldly goods as gifts of God's grace. Ecclesiastes deals in its pessimistic passages with the irresponsibility of human wickedness, calling the dead and the unborn happier than the living—not only because the latter must behold the works of the wicked, but also because they can themselves become involved (Eccl. 4:3; cf. 7:2f.; Prov. 17:20).

The possession of life and good fortune above all material goods and power is assured by wisdom (*ḥoḵmâ;* → חכם *ḥāḵam* [*chākham*]) and knowledge (*da'aṯ;* → ידע *yāḏa'*) in the full range of their meanings (Prov. 3:14; 8:10f.,19; 16:16; 19:8; Eccl. 4:13; 7:5,11; 9:16,18; etc.). Together with the fear of God and trust in God, they represent the highest good. In them the force of the covenant relationship is expressed, and they occur frequently in confessional statements (Ps. 63:4[3]; 84:11[10]; 118:8f.; 119:72; cf. Prov. 16:20 with *'ašrê;* in Ps. 111:10, Dahood takes *ṭôḇ* as an objective genitive depending on *śēḵel*, interpreting it in a personal sense as "the good man" related through chiasmus to *yir'aṯ YHWH* in the first colon of the verse).

f. As "the good" par excellence, the noun *ṭûḇ* or *ṭôḇâ* (as well as the neuter use of the adj. *ṭôḇ*) has two senses in religious contexts, related as cause and effect, as an abstract concept and its (collective) concrete manifestation.[103] As an abstraction, *ṭûḇ/ṭôḇ(â)*, that which is good in itself, refers to Yahweh; it is personified and identified with him, no longer meaning "the good" but rather "the good one" (Ps. 16:2; 119:122; cf. 104:28; Prov. 13:21; as a negative counterpart, Ps. 36:2[1]). In this sense *ṭûḇ* in Ex. 33:19 should be taken as a theophanic term parallel to the → פנים *pānîm*, *kāḇôḏ* (→ כבד *kāḇaḏ*), or *nō'am* (→ נעם *nā'am*) of Yahweh. The notion of Yahweh as the source of human well-being and prosperity is developed most extensively in the thanksgiving and historical psalms, as well as Jeremiah (Jer. 15:11; 17:6; 33:11; 44:17; etc.).

The brief hymn in imperative form *hôḏû lᵉYHWH kî-ṭôḇ kî lᵉ'ôlām ḥasdô* (1 Ch.

---

101 Kraus, *BK*, XV/2, on Ps. 112:5.

102 F. Ellermeier, *Untersuchungen zum Buche Qohelet*, I (Herzberg am Harz, 1967), 87.

103 Mannati.

16:34; Ps. 106:1; 107:1; 118:1,29; etc.; cf. Ps. 52:11[9]; 54:8[6], with *kî-ṭôḇ* as an abbreviated formula) is the central confessional statement of the OT, based on Israel's concept of an historical and personal God. Its *Sitz im Leben* is the communal thanksgiving as an expansion of the Song of Moses and the Song of Miriam (Ex. 15; cf. Ps. 68:5ff.[4ff.]). Yahweh's concrete acts of salvation are encompassed by the term *ṭôḇ;* despite its historical references, the formula thus achieves generality (cf. Isa. 63:7). The imperative summons to praise and the mention of those addressed is followed by a *kî* clause recounting the praise; *kî* is therefore affirmative and proclitic, not causative. The hymnic form, the mention of instrumental accompaniment and sacrifice, as well as mention of the *bêṯ YHWH,* point in the direction of the temple liturgy. The benefit of God's presence, which the upright experience even before entering the temple (Ps. 23:6; 65:5[4]; 73:28; 84:11[10]; cf. 100:5), finds expression in the thanksgiving hymns of the community and in individual laments and thanksgivings (Ps. 54:8[6]; 86:5; 119:122; etc.). The notion of God's goodness, manifested in concrete acts, runs parallel to his righteousness as the supreme norm by which actions are judges, as one of the fundamental themes of the OT (in the late period of Israel's history, the formula is used to praise God at the end of a battle [1 Macc. 4:24]).

In Jeremiah, *ṭôḇ* frequently appears in the context of *Heilsgeschichte,* referring to the future well-being of both nation and individual (Jer. 8:15; 14:11,19; 17:6; etc.). It takes on special importance as the substance of the new covenant, the *b^erîṯ ʿôlām* (Jer. 32:40-42; cf. 33:9,11,14). The *ṭûḇ YHWH* is his response to active human *ṭôḇ* (cf. Job 21:13; 36:11; Ps. 23:6; Jer. 8:15). Thus Fox[104] sees *ûpāḥ^adû ʾel-YHWH w^eʾel-ṭûḇô* (Hos. 3:5) in combination with the verbs *šûḇ* and *biqqēš* as expressing a covenantal quality, synonymous with *yārēʾ YHWH* (Ps. 31:20[19]; 34:3,9-15[2,8-14]; 68:10f.[9f.]; Nah. 1:7).

Human beings experience God's goodness in the form of good things, which, however, as gifts of God's grace, are not absolutely at human disposal (Job 2:10). The reference is to material goods that make for a happy life (Ps. 34:9,13[8,12]), without regard to moral qualities (for example, a good harvest, prosperity, power, the blessing of children; cf. Dt. 26:11; 28:11; 30:9; Job 2:10; 9:25; etc.). Gifts already received are for the devout a guarantee of further demonstrations of *ṭôḇ,* not only for the devout themselves but also for their descendants (Ps. 25:13; Prov. 13:22).

The consequence of God's active doing of good (*ʿāśâ ṭôḇ[â]*) is passive human well-being (*yṭb* qal and hiphil). Both are conditional upon obedience or repentance (Gen. 32:10,13[9,12]), and are therefore often introduced by conditional *waw* or *l^emaʿan.* The well-being that results from faithful adherence to the covenant takes the form, for example, of long life and possession of the promised land (Dt. 4:40; 5:16,29; cf. Ex. 18:9; Nu. 10:32; etc.), signs of a specific quality of life (cf. esp. 1 Ch. 29:28). From the human perspective, *ʿāśâ ṭôḇ* in the Psalms and Wisdom Literature takes on the meaning "righteousness," "fear of God"; *ʿāśâ lōʾ ṭôḇ* as a reference to "wicked" actions (Job 24:21; Ps. 14:1,3; 53:2,4[1,3]; Eccl. 7:20; etc.) can become a general

[104] P. 41.

term for "sin."[105] The antithesis is the positive expression *'āśâ ṭôḇ:* total realization of goodness and uprightness in human life (Ps. 14:1,3; 37:3; 53:4[3]).

6. *Names*. We find *ṭôḇ* or *ṭûḇ* as part of a name in the OT in *'ᵃḥiṭûḇ* (1 S. 22:9) and *'ᵃḇîṭûḇ* (1 Ch. 8:11). There are corresponding Old Babylonian names *abu-ṭābu* and *aḫu-ṭābu*, which suggest that the *ṭwb* element is an adjectival component of an attributive name.[106] There may possibly be a lowering of an original *ô* to *û*, frequently observed in Phoenician. From a later period comes the name *ṭôḇîyāh(û)* or *ṭāḇ'ēl* (Neh. 6:19; Isa. 7:6), with *ṭôḇ* as its first element combined with a theophorous *yāhû* or *'ēl;* here we are dealing with a name expressing confidence.[107]

A toponym *ṭôḇ* is found in Jgs. 11:3,5; 2 S. 10:6, 8. It is frequently identified with modern eṭ-Ṭaiyibeh, northeast of the Jordan. According to Abel,[108] *ṭôḇ* corresponds to the *twby* found in the Palestine list of Thutmose III[109] and the *du-bu* of the Amarna tablets.[110] Noth[111] in particular has disagreed. If *ṭôḇ* in the phrase *'îš ṭôḇ* is interpreted geographically, "a man from *ṭôḇ*," the expression corresponds to Akk. "*amēlu* of the city N," which designates a ruler of low rank.[112]

III. Dead Sea Scrolls. In the texts from Cave 1 (plus CD), *ṭôḇ* appears 33 times:[113] twice as a verb, 15 times as a noun, and 16 times as an adjective. The meaning is usually ethical or moral. There are 15 additional occurrences from 4Q, 11Q, and Murabba'āt.

The Hodayoth in particular extol God's goodness as "the only source of grace under the law,"[114] in parallel with such terms as *ḥeseḏ*, *raḥam*, *sᵉlîḥâ*, and *ṣᵉḏāqâ*. God's "goodness" and "righteousness" are interchangeable (1QH 7:30; 11:9,31; 1QS 11:14). Like faithfulness to the covenant and to the law, *ṭwb* is required for the way of salvation (1QS 1:2; cf. 1:5; 4:3; 10:12,18; 1QH 14:17; 15:18; cf. 14:26; 16:18; 17:24). Goodness is an expression of the aid that God gives his covenant people against the enemy (1QM 18:8); it is the highest good and a source of delight for the righteous (1QH 10:16; 11:6; 12:21; 18:14).

Essential to the definition of "good" and "evil" is the conflict with dualism under the headings of truth vs. falsehood, light vs. darkness, good vs. evil. Here mankind

---

105 W. Zimmerli, *Ezekiel I. Herm* (Eng. trans. 1979), p. 385.

106 For a different view, see H. Ringgren, → אב *'āḇ* [*'ābh*], *TDOT*, I, 16.

107 *IPN*, 147; H. Bauer, "Die hebräischen Eigennamen als sprachliche Erkenntnisquelle," *ZAW*, 48 (1930), 73-80, esp. 75; Stamm; Vogt, *Bibl*, 37 (1956), 263; Albright, *BASOR*, 140 (1955); A. Alt, "Menschen ohne Namen," *ArOr*, 18 (1950), 9-24, esp. 22f.

108 F.-M. Abel, *Géographie de la Palestine*, II (Paris, ³1967), 10.

109 No. 22.

110 EA 205, 3.

111 M. Noth, "Die Nachbarn der israelitischen Stämme im Ostjordanlande," *ZDPV*, 68 (1949), 1-50 = his *Aufsätze zur biblischen Landes- und Altertumskunde* (Neukirchen-Vluyn, 1971), I, 438, n. 6.

112 EA 141, 4; 162, 2; 174, 4; etc.

113 K. G. Kuhn, *Konkordanz zu den Qumrantexten* (Göttingen, 1960).

114 Becker, 161.

is both subject and object.[115] Called to rule over the world, they have been assigned the task of choosing between good and evil, and deciding in favor of the good (1QS 3:17f.; 4:26). The division that splits the human world extends to the "spirits of truth and wickedness" in the human heart (1QS 4:26; cf. 4:3; 1QH 14:12). It is the duty of the individual within the community to practice "good humility" (*'nwt ṭwb*, par. *'hbt ḥsd* and *mḥšbt ṣdq*, 1QS 2:24), and to repay evil with good in recognition of God as the only righteous judge (1QS 10:18). In the priestly blessing he is therefore armed with the gifts of wisdom and understanding (1QS 2:3; cf. Nu. 6:24-26).

IV. LXX. The LXX uses many nuances in its attempt to reproduce the semantic richness of *ṭôḇ*. In order of frequency, the commonest word groups are: *agathós*, *kalós*, *chrēstós*, *eú* (in combination with *gígnesthai*, *eínai*, *poieín*, and *chrásthai*), *kreíttōn*, *aréskein*, *orthós*, *sphódra*, *dokeín*, and *cháris*. Most frequent (416 occurrences) are forms of *agathós*, the majority in Wisdom Literature. It is typical of Greek and Hellenistic thought that when *ṭôḇ* refers to God it is translated by the neuter *agathón*.

The noun *agathōsýnē* (15 occurrences), unlike *chrēstótēs*, refers not only to the goodness of God but also to material goods and human actions. The verb *agathopoieín* (together with *agathoún* and *agathýnein*) translates *hêṭîḇ*, expressing "realization of the good through action."[116]

The translation *kalós* or *kalṓs* can mean "useful," but more frequently means "ethically good."[117] In most cases, *kalós* and *agathós* are used synonymously (cf. Nu. 24:1; Dt. 6:18; 12:28; 2 Ch. 14:1; Prov. 3:4; Isa. 1:17; Am. 5:14f.; etc.).[118] The use of *kalós* in Gen. 1 to translate *ṭôḇ* is indicative of the Greek notion of beauty. Unlike *ṭôḇ*, *kalós* is here "perceived in objective terms; a specific function is fulfilled."[119]

Also of interest is the use of *chrēstós* not only for the excellence or value of an object (Jer. 24:2f.,5; Dnl. 2:32) but also and more often to characterize persons. As a title of honor and as an epithet applied to rulers, *chrēstós* is well suited to describe persons who make "beneficent use"[120] of their power and influence (cf. Ps. 112:5[LXX 111:5]; Jer. 52:32). Primarily, however, it is used for the wealth of Yahweh's goodness. What is noteworthy in this usage, especially in the Psalms and in prophetic texts, is the use of additional terms to illuminate or specify the meaning, especially *éleos*, corresponding to Heb. *ḥsd*.[121] The noun *chrēstótēs* is used almost exclusively in praise of Yahweh, primarily in the Psalms.

The adj. *eú*, in combination with *gígnesthai*, *eínai*, *poieín*, and *chrásthai*, refers to good deeds done by both God and humans, as well as to well-being in general. In the stereotyped formula *hína eú soi génētai* it appears primarily in the parenetic sections of Deuteronomy (cf. Dt. 4:40; 6:18; 10:13; 12:25,28; etc.).

Höver-Johag

---

115 Nötscher, *Terminologie*, 79.
116 Grundmann, *TDNT*, I, 17.
117 Grundmann, *TDNT*, III, 545.
118 Beyreuther, 103.
119 Schmidt, 151.
120 Weiss, 485.
121 *Ibid.*

טוּחַ *ṭûaḥ*; טָחָה *ṭāḥāh;* טִיחַ *ṭîaḥ;* טֻחוֹת *ṭuḥôṯ*

Contents: I. 1. Etymology, Occurrences; 2. Meaning. II. Secular Usage. III. Use in Cultic and Religious Texts: 1. Legal Texts; 2. Prophetic Texts; 3. Job and Psalms (*ṭuḥôṯ*).

I. 1. *Etymology, Occurrences.* The root *ṭwḥ,* which probably had a by-form *ṭḥḥ* (cf. Isa. 44:18), is found outside of Hebrew in Ugaritic, Middle Hebrew, Jewish Aramaic, Punic, Arabic, and Ethiopic. It is used as a verb in the qal and niphal, and as a noun in the derivatives *ṭîaḥ* (Ezk. 13:12) and (probably) *ṭuḥôṯ* (Ps. 51:8[Eng. v. 6]; Job 38:36).

2. *Meaning.* All the passages suggest the fundamental meaning "plaster" for this group of words (Lev. 14:42; Ezk. 13:10). The verb then took on such specialized meanings as "paint over (with whitewash)" (Ezk. 22:28) and "overlay" (1 Ch. 29:4), as well as "be covered" or "be stuck together" (Isa. 44:18), while the noun *ṭîaḥ* acquired the meaning "coating," "whitewash" (Ezk. 13:12). The noun *ṭuḥôṯ,* "darkness," "obscurity," reflects the concrete result of being plastered or covered over.[1]

II. Secular Usage. The verb is typically used with nouns meaning plaster, mud, or whitewash (7 of 11 occurrences). This usage is also reflected in the postexilic period by a separate noun *ṭîaḥ* from *ṭwḥ* with the meaning "plaster," "whitewash."[2] Thus *ṭwḥ* means primarily the purely secular process of plastering the wall of a house (Lev. 14:42f.,48) or covering a wall with mud or whitewash (Ezk. 13:10-12,14f.). By analogy, it comes to mean the process of overlaying interior walls with gold or silver (1 Ch. 29:4).

Similarly, *ṭwḥ* or *ṭḥḥ* used with reference to human eyes means their being covered over or stuck together, i.e., blind (Isa. 44:18, where *ṭaḥû* from *ṭḥḥ* should be read,[3] or *ṭāḥ* from *ṭwḥ,* which would follow the consonantal text and obviate the hypothesis of a by-form *ṭḥḥ*).

III. Use in Cultic and Religious Texts.

1. *Legal Texts.* Within the laws dealing with clean and unclean things, the section pertaining to "diseased" houses uses *ṭwḥ* for the replastering of walls with fresh plaster

---

ṭûaḥ. S. Mowinckel, "טחות und שׂכוי: Eine Studie zur Astrologie des ATs," *AcOr,* 8 (1929), 1-44.

[1] H. Gunkel, *Die Psalmen. GHK,* II/2 (⁴1926), 227, and H.-J. Kraus, *Psalmen. BK,* XV/1 (⁴1972), 382, following the LXX, which translates *tà ádēla* in Ps. 51:8(LXX 50:8). A different translation and derivation, based solely on Job 38:36 and irreconcilable with Ps. 51:8, will be found in G. Hölscher, *Das Buch Hiob. HAT,* XVII (²1957), 95-97, and G. Fohrer, *Das Buch Hiob. KAT,* XVI (1963), 508-9.

[2] See W. Zimmerli, *Ezekiel I. Herm* (Eng. trans. 1979), 296.

[3] Following B. Duhm, *Jesaja. GHK,* III/1 (⁴1922), 336.

after the affected stones and the old plaster have been removed (Lev. 14:42f.,48). The application of fresh plaster indicates that the house is clean, although this cleanness can itself turn unclean (Lev. 14:43f.).[4]

2. *Prophetic Texts.* Among the prophets, only Ezekiel and Deutero-Isaiah use derivatives of *ṭwḥ.* Like the law governing "diseased" houses, Ezekiel is concerned in the first instance with coating a wall—although in this case the coating is whitewash, which, unlike plaster, does not bond the stones it covers but merely improves their appearance. Ezekiel uses this image of a thin, deceptive coat of whitewash to illustrate his attack on the false prophets: their words and actions are like the work of a person who whitewashes a wall to give it an appearance of solidity and thus imbues those who live in the house with a false sense of security (Ezk. 13:10,14; 22:28 [Ezk. 13:11f.,15 are additions made by later redactors[5]]). Here *ṭwḥ* symbolizes false promises of deliverance.

The verb is also used symbolically in Isa. 44:18, a later interpolation in Deutero-Isaiah:[6] the covered eyes (i.e., blindness) of those who make and worship idols stands for their lack of knowledge and understanding.

3. *Job and Psalms (ṭuḥôṯ).* The meaning and translation of *ṭuḥôṯ* is a difficult problem and is still disputed.[7] If the most probable meaning, "darkness, obscurity," is correct,[8] both Ps. 51:8(6) and Job 38:36 associate darkness or obscurity with the truth and wisdom imparted by Yahweh in secret. Thus *ṭuḥôṯ* stands for the darkness provided by Yahweh, a notion typical of Wisdom Literature; it is of a piece with the hidden secrecy of wisdom in 1 Cor. 2:7.

Schunck

---

4 See K. Elliger, *Leviticus. HAT,* IV (1966), 176f.

5 See G. Fohrer, *Ezechiel. HAT,* XIII (1955), 71-73; Zimmerli, *Ezekiel I,* 296.

6 C. Westermann, *Isaiah 40–66. OTL* (Eng. trans. 1969), 151.

7 See Gunkel, *GHK,* II/2, 227; Fohrer, *KAT,* XVI, 508-9.

8 See I.2.

טוֹטָפֹת *ṭôṭāpōṯ*

Contents: I. Ornament. II. Symbolism.

ṭôṭāpōṯ. M. Caloz, "Exode, XIII, 3-16 et son rapport au Deutéronome," *RB,* 75 (1968), 5-62; H. Grimme, "Hebr. טֹטָפֹת und טֹת, zwei Lehnwörter aus dem Ägyptischen," *OLZ,* 41 (1938), 148-152; C. A. Keller, *Das Wort OTH als "Offenbarungszeichen Gottes"* (Basel, 1946), esp. 65f.; G. Klein, "Die Totaphot nach Bibel und Tradition," *JPTh,* 7 (1881), 666-689; E. König, *Das Deuteronomium. KAT,* 3 (1917); R. Růžička, *Konsonantische Dissimilation in*

I. Ornament. Apart from the Egyptian uraeus[1] and horns,[2] there is considerable iconographic evidence for forehead ornaments ("between the eyes," Ex. 13:9,16; Dt. 6:8; 11:18).[3] There is also literary evidence for related ideas: "Upon my belly, upon my back, I bear the word of the king my lord";[4] "Behold, I have told you the best that is within me, let it stand as a firm rule before your eyes."[5] But there is no extrabiblical evidence for *ṭôṭāpōṯ* itself. That the word refers to an apotropaic amulet is purely hypothetical.[6] What may be the same root in Arabic and Mandaic has no obvious connection with the OT.[7] A material or historical connection between *ṭôṭāpōṯ* and phylacteries (Mt. 23:5; cf. the Targum on 2 S. 1:10 and Middle Hebrew) is not to be assumed.[8]

II. Symbolism. The uniformly defective Masoretic spelling *ṭ(w)ṭpt* (Ex. 13:16; Dt. 6:8; 11:18), the use of a corresponding singular in Ex. 13:9, and the Greek (*asáleuton*),[9] Syriac, and Vulg. suggest the possible assimilation of a segholate singular ending to the preceding *'ôṯ*. The noun *ṭôṭāpōṯ* is always qualified by the phrase *bên 'êneyḵā* or *'ênêḵem;* it is preceded by *'ôṯ 'al-yāḏᵉḵā* or *yaḏᵉḵem*. In Ex. 13:16, *lᵉṭôṭāpōṯ* is used as a second predicate noun alongside *lᵉ'ôṯ* dependent on *wᵉhāyâ*, while in Dt. 6:8; 11:18 it alone depends on *wᵉhāyû* and *lᵉ'ôṯ* is the indirect object of the verb *ûqᵉšartām*/*ûqᵉšartem*. The scanty evidence, itself formulaic and contextually homogeneous, does not support the existence, form, or function of a material object[10] on the basis of cultural or religious origins.

There remains the question of the word's function and meaning in its literary context. In its earliest occurrence, Ex. 13:16, which dates from the early Deuteronomic or pre-Deuteronomic period,[11] *ṭôṭāpōṯ* is determined semantically by *'ôṯ,* as we would

---

den semitischen Sprachen. BAss, 6/4 (1909), 129; E. A. Speiser, "ṬWṬPT," *JQR,* 48 (1957), 208-217; *idem,* "*Pālil* and Congeners: A Sampling of Apotropaic Symbols," *Festschrift B. Landsberger. AS,* 16 (1965), 389-394; B. Stade, "Beiträge zur Pentateuchkritik. 1) Das Kainszeichen," *ZAW,* 14 (1894), 250-318, esp. 308-318; J. Swetnam, "Why Was Jeremiah's New Covenant New?" *Studies on Prophecy. SVT,* 26 (1974), 111-15; M. Weinfeld, *Deuteronomy and the Deuteronomic School* (Oxford, 1972), 299-303.

1 See Grimme.

2 See *ANEP,* index under "horn."

3 E.g., *ANEP,* nos. 37, 74-75, F., 464; *AOB,* nos. 283f.; cf. various symbols at eye level of the persons depicted, esp. on cylinder seals: e.g., *ANEP,* nos. 687, 690, 698, 700f., etc.

4 EA 147; *ANET*³, 484.

5 The Instruction of King Merikare, 143f., *ANET*³, 418.

6 Speiser, *AS,* 16 (1965), 389-393.

7 Cf. *KBL*³, 357.

8 L. I. Rabinowitz, "Tefillin," *EncJud,* XV, 898-904.

9 O. Betz, "στίγμα," *TDNT,* VII, 659, n. 20.

10 Cf. Speiser, *AS,* 16 (1965), esp. 392f.

11 Caloz; Weinfeld, 179-190, 301; cf. N. Lohfink, *Das Hauptgebot. AnBibl,* 20 (1963), 121-24; C. Brekelmans, "Die sogenannten deuteronomischen Elemente in Gen.-Num.: Ein Beitrag zur Vorgeschichte des Deuteronomiums," *Volume de Congès, Genève 1965. SVT,* 15 (1966), 90-96; *idem,* "Éléments deutéronomiques dans le Pentateuque," *Aux grands carrefours de la révélation et de l'exégèse de l'AT. Recherches bibliques,* 8 (1967), 77-91.

expect from the syntax and from the sequence of a very common word[12] followed by what is almost a hapax legomenon. The later redactor of Ex. 13:3-10 therefore replaced it with the clearer *zikkārôn.*[13]

Literarily, the occasion or subject matter in Ex. 13:11-16 is specifically the law of the first-born; but the rhetorical situation (the child's question in Ex. 13:14; cf. v. 8) involves the exodus and the law in their entirety (cf. v. 9, the only occurrence in the Pentateuch of *tôraṯ YHWH*), as is stated explicitly in Dt. 6:8; 11:18 (6:7; 11:19). Comparison (esp. of Dt. 11:18a) with figurative language in Prov. 1–9 (Prov. 1:9; 3:21f.; 4:4,9; 6:21f.; cf. Isa. 49:18) shows that the context and style, especially the figurative use of *qāšar* (Prov. 3:3; 6:21; 7:3), are typical of Wisdom Literature; but the combination of *qāšar 'al* with *le* and the sequence *qāšar—hāyâ le* are unique. A sage thus expands on a pregnant phrase (Ex. 13:16) in order to clarify it. He does nothing with the word *ṭôṭāpōṯ,* even leaving it with the neutral verb *hāyâ le* (as in Ex. 13:16; cf. v. 9), presumably because it suggested nothing specific and there was no alternative in common usage for this barely comprehensible word, so that he did not dare to express himself in clear, concrete terms (cf. the more graphic treatment of the mezuzoth in Dt. 6:9; 11:20; see also Isa. 57:8 as an illustration of the religious background). Instead, he made do with vague parenetic references, since the word *ṭôṭāpōṯ* was a fixed element of the traditional form.

This may have been only a *pis aller,* but it made a degree of sense: it appears that with the passage of time it became increasingly easy to find religious meaning, historical or symbolic, in extant materials, which could be interpreted on the basis of specific ideas. Religious or cultic symbols could even be woven together on the basis of a conscious plan (see, for example, the treatment of the priestly vestments in Ex. 28 and 39, and of the tassels in Nu. 15:37-41). Such symbols enhanced the value and importance of what they symbolized. The "signet on the hand," for example (Jer. 22:24; cf. Cant. 8:6; Hag. 2:23), can signify a special intimacy. Similarly the *ṭôṭāpōṯ* "between the eyes" had a very personal meaning, reminding the individual of deliverance and the law, just as stelae, inscribed (Dt. 27:1-8; Josh. 8:30-35) or uninscribed (Ex. 24:3-8; Josh. 4:4-7; 24:26f.), served as reminders for the nation.

A later age found in the *ṭôṭāpōṯ* the tefillin or phylacteries to be worn on the forehead; this identification is probably due to the tendency to bring Scripture and religious observance into total agreement.[14]

Gamberoni

[12] Cf. W. Schottroff, "זכר *zkr* gedenken," *THAT,* I, 509.

[13] → זכר *zāḵar* [*zākhar*].

[14] Cf. Speiser, *AS,* 16 (1965), 391-93; F. J. Helfmeyer, "אות *'ôṯ* [*'ôth*]," *TDOT,* I, 180.

טִיט *ṭîṭ*

Contents: I. Etymology, Meaning. II. 1. OT Usage; 2. Figurative Usage.

I. Etymology, Meaning. Haupt[1] proposed to find in *ṭîṭ* a word connected with Aram. *ṭînā'*. The original form would then have been *ṭint,* giving rise to the later form *ṭîṭ* through partial assimilation of the fem. ending *t.* But in Arabic we find the forms *maṭiṭat* and *ṭinnun* with the meaning "mud," and in Akkadian the forms *ṭēṭu, ṭeṭṭu,* and *ṭîṭu* with the meaning "mud, clay, muck." Since *ṭîṭ* has this same meaning in Hebrew, it is reasonable to conclude that the word came to Canaan from Mesopotamia, especially because it was clearly in constant use in Assyria and Babylonia. The term does not seem to have reached Ugarit. From Hebrew it has been incorporated into Modern Hebrew.

II. 1. *OT Usage*. The word *ṭîṭ* was a common term for muck and mire in the streets and alleys of the ancient world, similar to the dust of the earth (2 S. 22:43 par. Ps. 18:43[Eng. v. 42]; Mic. 7:10). It can also be used for the silt stirred up by the raging sea (Isa. 57:20). In Ps. 69:15(14), too, *ṭîṭ* is associated with the depths of the sea; here we read of sinking in *ṭîṭ.* The word is likewise associated with the depths in Job 41:22(30). The passage describes the monster Leviathan in a series of images illustrating how dangerous the beast is. The image is not totally clear, and translations vary. There may be confusion between the imagery and the thing represented. Weiser translates: "He has sharp potsherds beneath, he pushes a threshing sledge in the mire."[2]

The word is also used for the mud on the bottom of wells and cisterns. Jer. 38:6 speaks of the prophet Jeremiah sinking in such mire. As in Akkadian, the word also means potter's clay (Isa. 41:25; Nah. 3:14).

2. *Figurative Usage*. The word *ṭîṭ* is used figuratively in Isa. 41:25, a prophetic oracle. The one who comes from the north, from the rising of the sun, will trample all rulers as a potter treads his clay with his feet. The word is used in a similar way in 2 S. 22:43 and Ps. 18:43(42).

The image of a dark, mucky pit is used to depict the deep despair from which Yahweh has rescued his worshippers: "He drew me up from the desolate pit, out of the miry bog" (Ps. 40:3[2]). The worshipper could cry out, "Rescue me from sinking in the mire" (Ps. 69:15[14]), in a context that is clearly figurative. The worshipper in his need brings his prayer before God, to be rescued "from the desolate pit."

Kapelrud

ṭîṭ. J. Barth, *Wurzeluntersuchungen zum hebräischen und aramäischen Lexicon* (Leipzig, 1902), 25; G. Dalman, *AuS*, II (1932); J. L. Kelso, *The Ceramic Vocabulary of the OT. BASORSup*, 5/6 (1948); A. W. Schwarzenbach, *Die geographische Terminologie im Hebräischen des ATs* (Leiden, 1954).

[1] P. Haupt, "The Book of Nahum," *JBL*, 26 (1907), 1-53, esp. 32.

[2] A. Weiser, *Das Buch Hiob. ATD*, XIII (^{6}1974), 253.

טַל *ṭal*

Contents: I. Etymology. II. Meteorology. III. Wisdom Literature. IV. Blessings and Curses. V. Figurative Usage. VI. Mythological Ideas in the Ugaritic Texts and the OT.

I. Etymology. The word *ṭal* is found in the West and South Semitic languages, in all of which it has the meaning "dew" or "light rain." The root is *ṭll;* denominative verbs meaning "be moist," "moisten," "cause dew to fall," etc.[1] occur in most of the languages but not in Hebrew. There is clearly no original connection with the homonymous Aramaic root,[2] which is related to Heb. *ṣll,* "overshadow" (basic meaning "be dark"[3]).

II. Meteorology. It is only the dew that provides a certain amount of moisture for plants during the long, dry Palestinian summer.[4] The summer dew is thus as necessary for life as the winter rain;[5] in the OT, a time of famine can be called simply a time "without dew or rain" (1 K. 17:1). The pairing of dew and rain occurs several times (Dt. 32:2; 2 S. 1:21; Job 38:28). Dew is therefore of great importance, and several passages in the OT[6] show that the Israelites made observations concerning the dew as a meteorological phenomenon. The dew "falls" (*yāraḏ* or *nāpal;* Nu. 11:9; 2 S. 17:12; Ps. 133:3). It comes from the heavens (Gen. 27:28,39; Dt. 33:13; cf. Dt. 33:28; Prov. 3:20; and Sir. 43:22, according to which the heavens or the clouds "drop" [*'rp*] dew, and the parallel Ugaritic idiom *ṭl šmm*[7]). It falls during the night (Nu. 11:9; Jgs. 6:36-40; Cant. 5:2; cf. Dnl. 4:12,20,22,30[Eng. vv. 15,23,25,33]; 5:21, where the repeated statement "let him be wet with the dew of heaven" indicates that Nebuchad-

---

ṭal. D. Ashbel, "On the Importance of Dew in Palestine," *JPOS,* 16 (1936), 316-321; A. Bentzen, *Messias, Moses redivivus, Menschensohn. AThANT,* 17 (1948); G. Dalman, *AuS,* I (1928); P. Humbert, "La rosée tombe en Israël: A propos d'Esaïe 26, 19," *ThZ,* 13 (1957), 487-493; J. C. de Moor, *The Seasonal Pattern in the Ugaritic Myth of Ba'lu. AOAT,* 16 (1971); P. Reymond, *L'eau, sa vie, et sa signification dans l'AT. SVT,* 6 (1958); R. B. Y. Scott, "Meteorological Phenomena and Terminology in the OT," *ZAW,* 64 (1952), 11-25; F. Vattioni, "La rugiada nell'AT," *RivBibl,* 6 (1958), 147-165; G. Widengren, *Psalm 110 och det sakrala kungadömet i Israel. UUÅ,* 1941/7:1 [available in German in *Zur neueren Psalmenforschung* (1976), 185-216].

1 Cf. the lexica.

2 Contra *KBL*², 352f. and *KBL*³, 358f.; but see *GesB,* 276; *BDB,* 378; and Baumgartner, *KBL*², 1079, which find two distinct roots; cf. also Dnl. 4:9 and Neh. 3:15, the latter aramaizing Hebrew.

3 Basic meaning "be dark"; see B. Halper, "The Participial Formations of the Geminate Verbs," *ZAW,* 30 (1910), 216.

4 For meteorological and statistical information about dew, see *AuS,* I, 89-96, 310-14, 514-19; Ashbel, 316-321; M. Gilead and N. Rosenan, "Ten Years of Dew Observations in Israel," *IEJ,* 4 (1954), 120-23; Scott, 21f.; Reymond, 25-27; Vattioni, 147f.

5 → מטר *māṭār.*

6 Cf. Humbert, 487f.

7 *KTU,* 1.3 II, 39f.

nezzar is to spend the night in the open like the animals[8]) and vanishes quickly in the morning (Ex. 16:13f.; Hos. 6:4; 13:3). The dew "lies" on the ground (Ex. 16:13f.) and appears in large concentrations on uneven surfaces, as the sign given to Gideon presupposes (Jgs. 6:36-40). The expression "like a cloud of dew in the heat of harvest" in Isa. 18:4 may be based on the observation that dew increases in quantity as summer progresses.[9] A similar observation appears in Sir. 18:16 (not found in the Hebrew fragments): "Can the dew not bring to an end the burning heat?" (cf. Sir. 43:22, where the Hebrew text is obscure).

The OT considers hoarfrost (*kᵉpôr*) to be frozen dew (*kᵉpōr šāmayim,* Job 38:29[10]); it is also mentioned in Ex. 16:14; Ps. 147:16; Sir. 3:15; 43:19.

III. Wisdom Literature. Behind nearly all the mentions of dew in the OT (some 30 in all) stands the conviction that the dew is a gift of Yahweh,[11] just as in the religion of Ugarit it is a gift of Ba'al.[12] Yahweh is the giver of fertility, and without dew there is no fertility. The dew is thus an expression of Yahweh's blessing, belonging as it were to the order of creation. This can be seen above all in Wisdom texts. Characteristic of the doctrine of creation in Wisdom Literature is the listing of examples of Yahweh's creative power. Such lists often include dew alongside other natural phenomena.

The words spoken by God in the book of Job make use of rhetorical questions to depict the creation, ordering, and preservation of the created world, including the question "Has the rain a father, or who has begotten the drops of dew?"—with the implied answer "None but Yahweh" (Job 38:28; Fohrer[13] is probably wrong in seeing this verse as a gloss on v. 29, which asks a similar question concerning the hoarfrost). Likewise typical of Wisdom is the shorter statement in Prov. 3:19f.: by wisdom Yahweh founded the earth and the heavens; by his knowledge the deeps are opened and the clouds drop down the dew (cf. Job 28:25f.; Prov. 8:28; Jer. 10:12f.;[14] also Ps. 147:16 [*kᵉpôr*]).

This notion of creation is extended in later Wisdom Literature, with some shift of emphasis: Yahweh is at work in all periods of history, ordering and preserving his creation. The great hymn in praise of the created order in Sirach mentions a series of natural phenomena including the dew, which brings refreshment in the burning heat (Sir. 43:22;[15] cf. also 43:19). The basic idea of this passage (that natural phenomena are a revelation of Yahweh's *kāḇôḏ*[16]) reappears in different form in the LXX additions to Dnl. 3: here the natural phenomena share in the praise of Yahweh. The dew is mentioned several times in this connection (LXX Dnl. 3:64,68).[17]

---

8 Cf. Reymond, 26f.

9 See *AuS,* I, 93, 311; but cf. O. Kaiser, *Isaiah 13–39. OTL* (Eng. trans. 1974), 95.

10 Cf. Reymond, 28; Scott, 17.

11 Cf. Humbert, 488-490.

12 Cf. Reymond, 41-48; also *KTU,* 1.19 I, 38-46.

13 G. Fohrer, *Das Buch Hiob. KAT,* XVI (1963), 492.

14 B. Gemser, *Sprüch Salomos. HAT,* XVI (1937), 30.

15 On the difficulty of the Hebrew text, see Vattioni, 165f.

16 See J. Marböck, *Weisheit im Wandel. BBB,* 37 (1971), 145-151.

17 Cf. C. Kuhl, *Die drei Männer im Feuer. BZAW,* 55 (1930), 114f., 118.

It is thus to be expected that a natural phenomenon like the dew should be mentioned in theological contexts, especially in the creation texts of Wisdom Literature. It is in the Wisdom doctrine of creation above all that a truly theological view of nature is developed.[18] This doctrine plays a certain role in later apocalyptic cosmological speculations. In such a context, for instance, Enoch receives instruction concerning the chambers containing the various natural phenomena, including those for dew (1 [Eth.] En. 34:1f.; 36:1; 60:20; 75:5).

IV. Blessings and Curses. The dew is thus linked indissolubly with the order of creation, with fertility and God's blessings. It is therefore natural for the promise of dew to be included in blessing formulas, and conversely for absence of dew to be threatened in curse and punishment formulas. Such formulas probably originated in cultic ritual, but they can also appear apart from this setting. A typical contrast between blessing and curse is found in Gen. 27. Through cunning, Jacob receives his father's blessing: "May God give you of the dew of heaven, and of the fatness of the earth, and plenty of grain and wine" (Gen. 27:28). Esau receives a "negative" blessing resembling a curse: "Far away from the fatness of the earth shall your dwelling be, and away from the dew of heaven on high" (Gen. 27:39; cf. in Ugaritic the juxtaposition of *ṭl šmm* and *šmn 'arṣ*[19]). Although in Gen. 27 the two formulas are embedded in one of the stereotyped narratives of the farewell discourse of a dying father, and are furthermore intended in their final recension to illuminate the relationship between Israel and Edom, they can be considered sayings that originally circulated independently, referring to the relationship between pastoral tribes and hunters in Palestine and east of the Jordan.[20]

Curses can also be pronounced against inanimate objects. There is a lament over Saul and Jonathan that has been interpolated into the Deuteronomistic history (2 S. 1:17-27).[21] Verse 21 states that the mountains of Gilboa, where the warriors fell, shall never again receive dew or rain, but remain barren. The idea is either that the place is to remain in eternal mourning or that it is to suffer punishment for having received innocent blood.[22]

The word *ṭal* appears in another punishment described in the Deuteronomistic history, this time upon Israel, which thinks that Ba'al, not Yahweh, is the giver of fertility; the punishment will be deprivation of "dew and rain" for many years (1 K. 17:1). The passage provides a deep insight into this religious crisis; in the Ugaritic Aqhat epic almost the identical words are used to state that Ba'al will withhold fertility for seven

---

[18] See G. von Rad, *OT Theology*, I (Eng. trans., New York, 1962), 463; cf. W. Eichrodt, *TheolOT*, II. *OTL* (Eng. trans. 1967), 489-495.

[19] *KTU*, 1.3 II, 39; *CML*, 85; Vattioni, 151f.

[20] M. Noth, *A History of Pentateuchal Traditions* (Eng. trans. 1972; repr. Chico, Calif., 1981), 110f.; cf. V. Maag, "Jakob—Esau—Edom," *ThZ*, 13 (1957), 418-429.

[21] More details on the position of the poem in the historical narrative in R. A. Carlson, *David the Chosen King* (Eng. trans., Stockholm, 1964), 47-49; J. H. Grønbaek, *Die Geschichte vom Aufstieg Davids. Acta theologica danica*, 10 (Ger. trans., Copenhagen, 1971), 221f.

[22] Cf. Vattioni, 155f.; H. L. Ginsberg in *ANET*³, 153, n. 34.

or eight years, "without dew, without rain" (*bl ṭl bl rbb*).[23] Because the dew is a divine gift, its absence is subject to religious interpretation, both at Ugarit and in Israel.

Rather more specialized blessing formulas are found in the tribal sayings of Gen. 49 and Dt. 33, which go back to the premonarchic period, at least in their original form. Their most likely *Sitz im Leben* was the amphictyonic cult.[24] Some of them promise fertility or success in battle. A prime example is the long passage devoted to Joseph in Dt. 33:13-17, in which his land is to be blessed "with the choicest gifts of heaven, of dew, and of the deep that couches beneath" (v. 13). The syntax is somewhat labored, and most scholars, following the Targum, Peshitta, and Gen. 49:25, substitute *mē'āl*, "above," for *miṭṭāl;* this emendation also improves the parallelism.[25] But the juxtaposition of *ṭal* and *tᵉhôm* in Job 38:28-30; Prov. 3:20 can be cited in support of the text. The theophany that provides the framework for the tribal sayings (Dt. 33:2-5,26-29) betrays the cultic background of both the individual sayings and the composition as a whole.[26] Here, too, we find a blessing (v. 28) that promises all Israel dew, grain, and wine.

Elements of these ancient blessings reappear quite naturally in the eschatologizing words of the prophets. Zec. 8:9-15 speaks of the happy time to come when the temple will be rebuilt and Israel will no longer be a curse, but a blessing.[27] In concrete terms, this means the return of fertility (the fruit of the vine, the increase of the ground, and the dew of the heavens). Like the blessing of Jacob in Gen. 27, this promise of blessing has a negative equivalent; Hag. 1:2-11 (a passage related to the verses from Zechariah through the shared theme of rebuilding the temple[28]) ascribes the failure of the land's fertility to the failure of the people to restore the temple and describes the consequences: the heavens have withheld the dew and the earth its produce; drought has hit the grain and wine and oil (vv. 10f.). In the Aramaic Balaam prophecy from Tell Deir 'allā, *ṭl* and *šr* (rain?) appear together in an obscure context.[29]

In apocalyptic literature, the prophetic notion of nature's extraordinary abundance in the last days is taken even higher: all the normal natural phenomena—dew included—will vanish, leaving only the radiance of the glory of the Most High (4 Esd. 7:39-44).

V. Figurative Usage. In the figurative language of the OT, dew appears in two different usages: it can stand for the meteorological phenomenon, or serve as a met-

[23] *KTU*, 1.19 I, 44; cf. *CML*, 58f.; Ginsberg in *ANET*³, 153.

[24] See A. H. J. Gunneweg, "Über den Sitz im Leben der sog. Stammessprüche (Gen. 49 Dtn. 33 Jdc. 5)," *ZAW*, 76 (1964), 245-255, esp. 254; cf. J. Scharbert, "ברך *brk*," *TDOT*, II, 306f.

[25] Cf. Vattioni, 154.

[26] Cf. A. Weiser, "Zur Frage nach den Beziehungen der Psalmen zur Kult: Die Darstellung der Theophanie in den Psalmen und im Festkult," in *Festschrift A. Bertholet* (Tübingen, 1950), 518; Gunneweg, *ZAW*, 76 (1964), 254.

[27] Scharbert, *TDOT*, II, 299.

[28] See K. Elliger, *Das Buch der zwölf Kleinen Propheten, II. ATD*, XXV (⁴1963), 140.

[29] Combination II, 35f.; see J. Hoftijzer and G. van der Kooij, *Aramaic Texts from Deir 'Allā. DMOA*, 19 (1976), 175, 181, 251f.

aphor to express Yahweh's blessing. In the former case, the image is mostly used negatively; in the latter, of course, it is always used positively. The attack of an overwhelming army can be likened to the dew that falls everywhere and covers everything (2 S. 17:12, with reference to Absalom's plan to attack David; cf. a similar usage in 1QM 12:9). Hosea makes frequent use of the dew in his imagery, sometimes in a negative sense. Observing how quickly dew vanishes in the morning, he describes the covenant love of Israel, which is "like a morning cloud, like the dew that goes early away" (Hos. 6:4; cf. Sir. 3:15: your sins will vanish as the frost [frozen dew] vanishes before the heat of the day). The same imagery is used as a threat in Hos. 13:3: the nation will be "like the morning mist or like the dew that goes early away."

Elsewhere dew can symbolize a favorable state or event. If the people will return to him, Yahweh will "be as the dew to Israel; he shall blossom as the lily" (Hos. 14:6[5]). Yahweh is the life-giving and life-preserving power for the Israel of the future.[30] Mic. 5:6(7), if it is not postexilic, refers to the exile of the northern kingdom; it speaks of "the remnant of Jacob that shall be in the midst of many peoples like the dew from Yahweh," i.e., it will mediate the blessing that is granted to the nations.[31] The image in Isa. 18:4 is obscure: Yahweh waits quietly "like a cloud of dew at harvest time (or: in the heat of harvest)," until he destroys the enemy.[32]

Finally, dew can symbolize various human relationships. A king's favor can be compared to dew upon the grass (Prov. 19:12). The righteous Job likens his situation to that of a tree whose roots spread out to the waters and whose branches are wet with dew (Job 29:19). In the Song of Moses (Dt. 32:2),[33] the "didactic invocation," which is based on Wisdom tradition, likens Moses' words to the rain and dew on grass and herb. In Ps. 133:3, a somewhat exaggerated metaphor extols unity amongst the brethren as being comparable to the beneficial effects of oil upon the head or dew upon Mt. Hermon.[34]

VI. Mythological Ideas in the Ugaritic Texts and the OT. In two or three OT passages, mythological ideas appear in connection with the dew. The meaning of these texts (Job 38:28; Ps. 110:3; Isa. 26:19) is not entirely clear. Comparison with analogous ideas in the religion of Ugarit, however, strongly suggests allusion to ancient myths.

Some of the Ugaritic passages have been cited in sections III and IV above. These passages demonstrate above all that the dew is understood as the gift of Ba'al. But several female figures also appear to be associated with the dew:

a. After her great battle with the enemies of Ba'al, 'Anat draws water and washes "with the dew of the heavens, with the oil of the earth, with the rain of the cloud-

---

30 A. Weiser, *Das Buch der zwölf Kleinen Propheten, I. ATD*, XXIV (^{3}1959), 103.

31 *Ibid.*, 275.

32 See Reymond, 30f.

33 See G. von Rad, *Deuteronomy. OTL* (Eng. trans. 1966), 196.

34 See H.-J. Kraus, *Psalmen. BK*, XV (^{4}1972), 889-891.

rider—dew, which the heavens pour; rain, which the stars pour."[35] It is possible that we are dealing here with a magical ritual intended to produce rain and dew.[36]

b. Of Danel's daughter Puġat we read: "You bear water upon your shoulders, you pour dew upon the barley, you know the path of the stars."[37] It is possible to interpret this statement as meaning that Puġat recites the rain and dew ritual of 'Anat.[38]

c. At most, however, these two rituals show that magical means were used in the Ugaritic cult to cause rain and dew, and that the dew also played some role in the myths of the gods. More important is the fact that among the daughters (or wives?) of Ba'al we find the name Ṭallai, "Bedewed."[39] She is almost always mentioned in stereotyped expressions that speak of her and her two sisters in conjunction with Ba'al: "Pidrai, daughter of the honey-dew . . . Ṭallai, daughter of the mist . . . 'Arṣai, daughter of full bloom" (the meanings of the epithets have been the subject of much discussion).[40] The three figures appear together in several texts;[41] only in one does Ṭallai appear alone:[42] "Ṭallai made his (Ba'al's) head beautiful between his eyes," which probably means she ornamented his hair with drops of dew; cf. Cant. 5:2. Although much remains obscure, it is clear that the dew appears in the Ugaritic pantheon as one of Ba'al's daughters, although she does not play a major role.[43]

This may cast some light on three OT passages:

a. Job 38:28 might be a veiled polemic against the notion that someone other than Yahweh—namely Ba'al—begot the dew.

b. Isa. 26:19 speaks of the resurrection of the dead, and adds: *kî ṭal 'ôrōṯ ṭalleḵā*, "for thy dew is a dew of lights."[44] The passage is undoubtedly quite late, and 26:19 may only be trying to say that Yahweh "in his world of light disposes of a miraculous and miracle-working dew, which is able to bring to life the shades in the underworld."[45]

---

[35] *KTU*, 1.3 II, 38-41; cf. IV, 42-44.

[36] Esp. clear in *KTU*, 1.3 IV; *CML*, 89; see de Moor, 98-100, 104f.; cf. A. S. Kapelrud, *The Violent Goddess* (Oslo, 1969), 100-103.

[37] *KTU*, 1.19 II, 5-7; cf. 10f. and IV, 28ff.

[38] De Moor, 100.

[39] Cf. M. H. Pope, "Ṭlj," *WbMyth*, I, 312.

[40] Here following de Moor, 81-84, where many other proposed interpretations are cited.

[41] *KTU*, 1.3 I, 23-25; III, 5-7; (IV, 49-51); 1.4 I, 17-19; IV, 55-57; 1.5 V, 10f. (first two only).

[42] *KTU*, 1.101, 5 (see J. C. de Moor, "Studies in the New Alphabetic Texts from Ras Shamra I," *UF*, 1 [1969], 180f.).

[43] See de Moor, *Seasonal Pattern*, 81-84, 188, 317 (*s.v.* dew).

[44] Recent studies of the many problems surrounding this verse include: Humbert, 490-93; M.-L. Henry, *Glaubenkrise und Glaubensbewährung in den Dichtungen der Jesajaapokalypse*. *BWANT*, 5/6 (1967), 106-108; Kaiser, 215-220; F. J. Helfmeyer, "'Deine Toten—meine Leichen': Heilszusage und Annahme in Jes 26, 19," in *Bausteine biblischer Theologie. Festschrift G. J. Botterweck*. *BBB*, 50 (1977), 245-258, esp. 255ff.

[45] Kaiser, 218; cf. Reymond, 215f.

But a closer connection with mythological ideas is also possible: de Moor connects *ṭal 'ôrōṯ* with the epithet of Ba'al's first daughter, Pidrai, *bt 'r,* and translates, "daughter of the honey-dew," a special kind of dew that is clearly also used by 'Anat in her fertility rites. Perhaps, then, the puzzling *ṭal 'ôrōṯ* has a specialized meaning here: Yahweh's dew, which can bring about the resurrection of the dead, is of a special kind, i.e., it is identical with the age-old life-giving honey-dew.[46]

c. The text of Ps. 110:3[47] is undoubtedly corrupt and requires emendation. Here we shall discuss the reference to dew. The passage in question can be read: *mēreḥem šaḥar lēḵ keṭal yeliḏtîḵā,* "go forth from the womb of the dawn, I have given birth to you like the dew."[48] This statement is addressed to the king of Judah, probably at his enthronement and speaks of his birth—understood from the perspective of cultic ideology—in mythological language. The question is how the king, the dew, and the dawn are related. Widengren makes a radical proposal: the royal ceremony reflected in Ps. 110 dates from the Canaanite period of Jerusalem. Citing the Ugaritic text SS, he interprets v. 3 as follows: in *KTU,* 1.23,[49] El begets the two deities Šaḥar and Šalem; the former (fem. according to Widengren[50]) can be identified with the dawn, the latter with sunset and also with El Elyon of Jerusalem. Thus the Jerusalem king was thought of as the child of these two divine figures and himself identified with the dew (Widengren translates: "From the womb of the dawn, *as* dew I have begotten you"[51]). Bentzen has a different interpretation of the prepositional phrase: "On holy mountains I have begotten him, from the womb, *before* the morning star and the dew."[52] It is probably best to take *keṭal* as nothing more than a simile, so that in its original ("Canaanite") form the passage means that the Jerusalem king is the child of El and Šaḥar, just as the dew is the daughter of Ba'al (and the dawn Šaḥar?). In the royal cult of Israel and in Ps. 110, these mythological notions are quite veiled (although Isa. 14:12 can be very direct in saying much the same thing about the Babylonian king).

---

[46] De Moor, *Seasonal Pattern,* 82-84; 104f.; also Widengren, 11f. (= 195f.); H. Riesenfeld, *The Resurrection in Ezekiel XXXVII and in the Dura-Europos Paintings. UUÅ,* 1948/11, 10-13; Vattioni, 157-160. For a different approach, see G. Schwarz, "'. . . Tau der Lichter. . .'? Eine Emendation," *ZAW,* 88 (1976), 280f.; Schwarz proposes the reasonable emendation *ṭal 'ōḇōt,* "dew of the spirits of the dead." On the later Jewish notion of the "dew of resurrection," see Riesenfeld, 10, and St.-B., IV, 1177.

[47] For earlier studies, see Kraus, *BK,* XV, 752; more recent discussions include: J. Coppens, "Les apports du Psaume CX (Vulg. CIX) à l'idéologie royale israélite," *The Sacral Kingship. SNumen,* 4 (1959), 337-343; R.-J. Tournay, "Le Psaume CX," *RB,* 67 (1960), 10-18; G. Cooke, "The Israelite King as Son of God," *ZAW,* 73 (1961), 200-224, esp. 218-224.

[48] See above all Widengren, 9-11 (= 193-96); Bentzen, 14f.; the comms.; and the studies by Coppens, Tournay, and Cooke mentioned above.

[49] Lines 51-53; *CML,* 112f.

[50] Pp. 10f.; cf. Coppens, 338, n. 10.

[51] See his *Sakrales Königtum im AT und im Judentum* (Stuttgart, 1955), 44-47; cf. *Psalm 110,* 9-12 (= 193-97).

[52] Bentzen, 15; cf. his *Fortolkning til de gammeltestamentlige salmer* (Copenhagen, 1939), 557-560.

The names of two Judahite queens, Abital and Hamutal (cf. the masc. name *yhwṭl*[53]), may contain the element *ṭal*, "dew."[54] Usually, however, they are taken as aramaizing forms (*ṭl* = *ṣl*, "shadow").[55]

Otzen

---

[53] *AP*, nos. 22, 57; 23, 4.

[54] See the lexica.

[55] See H. Bauer, "Die hebräischen Eigennamen als sprachliche Erkenntnisquelle," *ZAW*, 48 (1930), 76, 80; A. Vincent, *La Religion des Judéo-Araméens d'Éléphantine* (Paris, 1937), 402f.; *IPN*, 39; further discussion in Vattioni, 148-150.

טָמֵא *ṭāmē'*; טֻמְאָה *ṭum'â*

Contents: I. Etymology, Semantic Field, Occurrences. II. Ritual Uncleanness in the OT: 1. General; 2. Unclean Animals; 3. The Dead; 4. Leprosy; 5. Other Forms of Human Uncleanness; 6. Cultic Unfitness. III. Metaphorical Usage: Idolatry and Sin. IV. LXX. V. Dead Sea Scrolls.

I. Etymology, Semantic Field, Occurrences. The root that appears in *ṭāmē'*, "be unclean," appears with the same meaning in Jewish Aramaic, Syriac, and Middle Hebrew. It is not attested in classical Arabic, but later Arabic has a verb *ṭamā*, "be choked with mud," and a noun *ṭammay*, "mud of the Nile." Paschen proposes "wet dirt" as the basic meaning.[1]

The verb (qal, piel, and hithpael) occurs 155 times in the OT, the noun *ṭum'â*, "uncleanness," 136 times. The semantic field includes → שׁקץ *šqṣ* (verb; substs. *šeqeṣ* and *šiqqûṣ*), with the meaning "abominate," "abomination"; → נדה *niddâ*, which refers to sexual uncleanness; → תועבה *tô'ēḇâ*, "abomination"; and *piggûl*, "sacrificial flesh not fit to eat." Uncleanness often appears in the same context as *gillulîm*, "idols," and the various words for "sin" and "guilt."[2]

ṭāmē'. J. Döller, *Die Reinheits- und Speisegesetze des ATs in religionsgeschichtlicher Beleuchtung. ATA*, 7/2-3 (1917); W. H. Gispen, "The Distinction between Clean and Unclean," *OTS*, 5 (1948), 190-96; F. Hauck, "καθαρός," *TDNT*, III, 414-17, 427-29; K. Koch, "Haggais unreines Volk," *ZAW*, 79 (1967), 52-66; W. Kornfeld, "Reine und unreine Tiere im AT," *Kairos*, 7 (1965), 134-147; F. Maass, "טמא *ṭm'* unrein sein," *THAT*, I, 664-67; M. Noth, *The Laws in the Pentateuch and Other Studies* (Eng. trans., Philadelphia, 1966), 49-60; W. Paschen, *Rein und Unrein: Untersuchung zur biblischen Wortgeschichte. StANT*, 24 (1970); G. von Rad, *OT Theology*, I (Eng. trans., New York, 1962), 272-79; L. E. Toombs, "Clean and Unclean," *IDB*, I, 641-48; K. Wigand, "Die altisraelitische Vorstellung von unreinen Tieren," *ARW*, 17 (1914), 413-436; R. K. Yerkes, "The Unclean Animals of Leviticus 11 and Deuteronomy 14," *JQR*, N.S. 14 (1923/24), 1-29; W. Zimmerli, *OT Theology in Outline* (Eng. trans., Atlanta, 1978), 97, 130f.; J. K. Zink, "Uncleanness and Sin: A Study of Job XIV 4 and Psalm LI 7," *VT*, 17 (1967), 354-361.

[1] P. 27.

[2] See below.

II. Ritual Uncleanness in the OT.

1. *General.* In the OT, one of the duties of a priest is to distinguish (*bdl* hiphil; e.g., Lev. 10:10; Ezk. 22:26; 44:23) the unclean from the clean, the sacred from the profane. What matters is ritual uncleanness, which cannot be reconciled with the holiness of Yahweh.

Things that are unclean include certain animals and groups of animals, serious diseases, sexual discharges and aberrations, death, and (metaphorically) certain activities, especially all those associated with the alien cult.

The OT does not explain why certain things lead to uncleanness and others do not. But animals that were "sacred" to Israel's neighbors or played a role in the alien cult are unclean in Israel. The combination of sexual uncleanness with polemic against all forms of alien cult suggests that the laws concerning sexual uncleanness might be based on a refusal to divinize any aspect of sexuality.

Ritual uncleanness is often linked with the sphere of death. The distinction between clean and unclean animals applies only to those used for sacrifice, offering of the first-born, or food, for all of which only "clean" animals are permitted. A leper was kept apart like a corpse. The sexual discharge of a male and the menstruation of a female are life that is never realized and therefore have an aspect of death about them. Sexual intercourse, ejaculation, and parturition all contribute to the emergence of life, but they are also felt to be unclean and require purification.

Instances of outward uncleanness require purification through water, but sometimes a ceremony of expiation is also needed because the uncleanness can be understood as sin and guilt.

André

The religio-historical similarity between uncleanness and taboo has often been pointed out. In fact there are many contexts, especially those involving sex or death, in which the Israelite laws governing uncleanness are probably connected with ancient taboos; in other cases, uncleanness is more likely rooted in the rejection of alien cultic practices.

In an earlier day, under the influence of evolutionary thought, the history of religions viewed holiness and uncleanness as differentiated aspects of what had once been a single notion of taboo: the "good" divine taboo became holiness, the "evil" demonic taboo, which could be destructive, became uncleanness. Within the context of historical Israel and the OT, this interpretation is without any support. In the OT, holiness and uncleanness are absolutely antithetical (e.g., Isa. 6:3f.; 35:8; 52:1,11).[3] The only evidence for a connection between uncleanness and holiness is a passage from the Mishnah[4] stating that the scriptures "make the hands unclean" (*m*^{e}*ṭamm*^{e}*'în 'eṯ-hayyāḏayim*). But this expression probably means only that the scriptures are so holy that the hands must seem unclean in comparison.[5]

Akk. *ikkibu* (Sum. *emgeb*) has often been called an expression of taboo.[6] The

---

[3] Cf. H. Ringgren, *Israelite Religion* (Eng. trans., Philadelphia, 1966), 141f.; R. Dussaud, *Les origines cananéennes du sacrifice israélite* (Paris, [2]1941), 30ff.

[4] *Yad.* 3:2f.

[5] H. Ringgren, *The Prophetical Conception of Holiness. UUÅ*, 1948/12, 16.

[6] *CAD*, VII (1960), 55-57; *AHw*, I, 368f.

primary meaning of the word is "something forbidden": an object, place, or action barred by divine prohibition. Hemerologies mention certain animals that must not be eaten or taken because they are *ikkibu;* often the God who issues the prohibition is named and a punishment is threatened. To cross a river is an *ikkibu* of Ea, which connotes both "forbidden by Ea" and "sin against Ea." The verb *akālu,* "eat," often is used for transgression of the prohibition, not necessarily in its literal sense. In later texts, *ikkibu* is used imprecisely as a synonym for "sin" or "punishment."[7] In certain cases it also suggests that something is reserved to a god or to the king. The *CAD* uses the translation "sacred, reserved," but the meaning could also be "protected by divine prohibition." Much the same applies to the (near) synonym *asakku,*[8] except that it refers to what is sacrosanct to a god or to the king, whereas *ikkibu* usually refers to something terrible that causes human pain or disease.[9]

Both *ikkibu* and *asakku* therefore mean something other than a mechanical taboo; they presuppose a divine prohibition. In certain cases, however, they come close to the meaning "sacred, sacrosanct (to someone)." They are therefore hardly comparable to the Israelite term *ṭāmē'*.

The OT occasionally treats uncleanness and sin as more or less identical. Both are damaging to the community as a whole, and can be viewed "as expressions of the hostile reality that permeates life, attempting again and again to penetrate the sphere of what is divine and good. There is, so to speak, a sphere of evil and death that continually threatens man's life: it is called uncleanness, sin, chaos."[10]

Ringgren

2. *Unclean Animals*. Except for Hos. 9:4 and Ezk. 4:14, unclean animals are mentioned only in the laws, above all in Lev. 11 (34 occurrences; cf. Dt. 14). The detailed list in Lev. 11:4-8 (cf. Dt. 14:7f.) names as unclean animals the camel, the rock badger, the hare, and the (wild) swine. They are defined as being quadrupeds that chew the cud or part the hoof, but not both. According to Lev. 11:3, the only clean quadrupeds are those that both chew the cud and part the hoof. Lev. 11:24-26 states that all quadrupeds that do not part the hoof as well as those that do not chew the cud are unclean. The same is true of all quadrupeds with paws (11:27f.) and certain small creeping animals, not defined more precisely (11:29-31). Dt. 14:10 calls all marine animals without fins and scales *ṭāmē'*, while Lev. 11:9-12 terms the same animals *šeqeṣ*. Likewise according to Dt. 14:19 all flying insects are *ṭāmē'*, while being described as *šeqeṣ* in Lev. 11:20,23. The *ṭāmē'-ṭāhôr* passage in Dt. 14:4-20 is prefaced by the general statement "You shall not eat any *tô'ēḇâ*" (v. 3), whereas the corresponding section in Lev. 11 ends with the prohibition against eating *šeqeṣ* (v. 43).[11]

An unclean animal renders unclean everything and everyone that comes in contact

---

7 *CAD,* VII, 57.

8 *AHw,* I, 79; *CAD,* I/2 (1964), 326f.

9 B. Landsberger, "Lexikalisches Archiv. 2. *asakku* II = 'tabu'," *ZA,* N.S. 41 (1933), 218f.; cf. also F. Thureau-Dangin, "Asakku," *RA,* 38 (1941), 41-43; → חרם *ḥrm* I, II.3.

10 Ringgren, *Israelite Religion,* 142.

11 Cf. G. J. Botterweck, "חזיר *ḥ^azîr* [*ch^azîr*]," *TDOT,* IV, 297ff.; K. Elliger, *Leviticus. HAT,* IV (1966), *in loc.*

with it. It must not be eaten (Lev. 11:47; Jgs. 13:4-7). Anyone who picks it up or touches (*nāga'*) it is unclean until evening (*ṭāmē' 'aḏ-hā'ereḇ*). Anything upon which any of them falls when they are dead is unclean until evening (Lev. 11:32). An earthen vessel, an oven, or a stove that is made unclean in this way must be destroyed (vv. 33, 35). Any food prepared with water from an unclean vessel and any beverage in an unclean vessel are unclean (v. 34). If the body of a dead animal falls on dry seed, the seed is not unclean (*ṭāhôr hû'*) unless it has previously been wet by water (v. 38).

Clean quadrupeds that die or are torn render unclean until evening anyone who eats, picks up, or touches them (Lev. 11:39f.; 22:8; cf. Ezk. 4:14). According to Dt. 14:21, such animals should be given to an alien (*gēr*) or sold to a foreigner (*noḵrî*), since they are not governed by the holiness laws. But according to Lev. 17:15, both the native (*'ezrāḥ*) and the sojourner are unclean until evening if they eat of it. The instructions about clean and unclean animals in Lev. 11 end with a prohibition against defiling oneself with any swarming thing that crawls upon the earth, concluding with and underlined by the holiness formula: "I am Yahweh your God; therefore keep yourselves holy (*hiṯqaddeš*) and be holy, for I am holy" (v. 44), "for I am Yahweh who brought you up out of the land of Egypt . . ." (v. 45).

If someone discovers afterwards that he has come into contact with an unclean animal (Lev. 5:1-13) and has therefore not been able to carry out the required purification, he has brought guilt upon himself (*ṭāmē' w^e'āšēm*, v. 2); he is to confess his error (*ḥaṭṭā'ṯ*) and offer a guilt offering. The priest is to make atonement (*kipper*) for him for his error.

Animals for sacrifice must be clean; when they are sacrificed to Yahweh, they become holy (*qōḏeš*, Lev. 27:9). Unclean animals must not be sacrificed; they are to be redeemed or sold (Lev. 27:11-13,27; Nu. 18:15). The flesh of a sacrificial animal that has come in contact with anything unclean must be burned (Lev. 7:19; cf. Hag. 2:14).

Water for impurity (*mê niddâ*, Nu. 19) contains the ashes of a heifer sacrificed as a sin offering (v. 9). The priest (v. 7) in whose presence the animal is sacrificed, the man who burns it (v. 8), and the clean (*ṭāhôr*) man who gathers the ashes (v. 10) are all unclean until evening, as is everyone who touches the water (v. 21). Clearly the uncleanness that the ashes are meant to remove is associated with them proleptically.

According to Hos. 9:4, the exiles who eat of the sacrifice (*zeḇaḥ*) become unclean. This means either that no sacrifice is possible in an alien land without the temple, as is suggested by the addition of "it shall not come into the house of Yahweh," or that the uncleanness is brought about through eating the holy sacrifice, which should instead be offered to Yahweh (cf. "for their hunger only," i.e., it is used for secular purposes).[12]

Flesh that is not sacrificial may be eaten by anyone, clean or unclean (Dt. 12:15,22; 15:22).

3. *The Dead.* Anyone who comes in contact with a corpse, regardless of the cause of death, with human remains, or with a grave is unclean for seven days (Nu. 19:11-22;

---

12 Cf. H. W. Wolff, *Hosea. Herm* (Eng. trans. 1974), 155; W. Rudolph, *Hosea. KAT,* XIII/1 (1966), 176.

16 occurrences). Two versions of the law appear: 11-13 and 14-22. In both cases purification with water takes place on the third day and on the seventh day. The results of omitting this purification differ somewhat in the two versions: the first states (v. 13) that whoever does not cleanse himself (lit. "free himself from sin," *hiṯḥaṭṭē'*) defiles the tabernacle (*miškān*) of Yahweh and shall be cut off (*nikraṯ*) from Israel; the second (v. 20) speaks of the sanctuary (*miqdāš*) of Yahweh and being cut off from the assembly (*mittôk haqqāhāl*). Purification involves cleansing with "water for impurity" (vv. 12f.,17-20), after which the person affected must wash his clothes and bathe himself. All the vessels in the vicinity of the corpse (vv. 15,18) are also unclean and must be sprinkled with the water. Whoever comes into contact with someone who has become unclean in this way becomes unclean in turn until evening (v. 22; cf. Lev. 22:4).

Anyone who is unclean must stay outside the camp in whose midst Yahweh dwells, lest it be defiled (Nu. 5:2f.). Corpses in the courts of the temple defile the house of Yahweh (Ezk. 9:7).

During the period of his separation, a Nazirite must not even go near a dead body (Nu. 6:6-12) because he is holy to Yahweh (*qāḏōš lᵉYHWH*). If someone dies in his presence, he must be purified: he must shave his head on the seventh day, and have the priest offer a sin offering and a burnt offering and make atonement for him on the eighth day. The high priest must not go near a dead body (not even that of a blood relative), because he is holy (Lev. 21:11). If this does happen, he is unclean for fourteen days. His purification concludes with a sin offering. According to Lev. 21:9, a priest is defiled by his daughter's unchastity.

Anyone who is unclean through contact with a dead body shall keep the Passover as provided by the law, but in the second month rather than in the first (Nu. 9:4-14). Someone who has been crucified must be buried before nightfall, because he is accursed of God. The corpse defiles the land given by Yahweh for an inheritance (Dt. 21:23). That uncleanness (especially when death is involved) is contagious, unlike holiness, can also be seen from Hag. 2:13f. The prophet considers his own people, himself included, to be unclean because the temple has not been rebuilt, so that complete purification is impossible.[13]

4. *Leprosy.* A person or object afflicted with or suspected of leprosy[14] is unclean. The occurrences are found in Lev. 13 (24 times), Lev. 14 (8 times), and Nu. 5:3. The term → טהר *ṭhr* appears 19 times in Lev. 13 and 24 times in Lev. 24. In addition, *ṭhr* appears 4 times in 2 K. 5:10-14.

The regulations deal with "leprosy" affecting human beings (Lev. 13:2-46; 14:2-32), garments (13:47-59), and houses (14:34-53,57). A person suspected of leprosy must be brought to the priest, who decides whether or not it is a case of true leprosy (Lev. 13). If it is, the priest declares the person unclean (*ṭimmē'*, v. 3). The leper must go about with torn clothes, let his hair hang loose, and cover his beard; he must warn others by crying *ṭāmē' ṭāmē'*. He must dwell apart (*bāḏāḏ*) outside the camp (13:45f.), because the camp, in whose midst Yahweh dwells, must not be defiled (Nu. 5:3).

---

13 On *hā'ām-hazzeh,* see Koch, contra Rothstein, *et al.*

14 → צרעת *ṣāra'aṯ.*

A person with the symptoms of leprosy (a white spot on the skin, raw flesh in a swelling, a boil, a burn scar, an itch, or baldness) must be kept in isolation for seven days. After being examined by the priest, he is kept in isolation an additional seven days. If the priest then finds that he is not leprous, he is to declare him clean (*tihar hakkōhēn*). The sick person must then wash his garments.

The color white plays an important role in the diagnosis. If a white spot on the skin fades, raw flesh becomes white, or white or reddish-white swellings or burns fade or fail to spread, the person is clean. But if the hair of the affected area turns white, the person is to be declared unclean. Strangely, someone who has turned white all over because the leprosy has covered his whole body is clean (Lev. 13:12f.)! Cf. 2 K. 5:27, where the servant of Elisha turns white as snow with leprosy as a punishment (*m^{e}ṣōrā' kaššāleg*).

A leprous garment is to be kept in isolation for seven days (Lev. 13:47-58). If the spot spreads, the garment is infected with malignant leprosy (*ṣāra'aṯ mam'ereṯ,* vv. 51f.) and must be burned. If the garment remains unchanged, it is washed and kept in isolation another seven days. If the priest determines that the spot is worse, the garment must be burned. If it has faded, it is torn out of the garment. If it disappears through washing, the garment is to be washed again; then it is clean. The section 13:47-58 does not use the formulas *ṭimmē' hakkōhēn* and *ṭihar hakkōhēn,* but it concludes: "This is the law for a leprous disease . . . , to decide whether it is clean or unclean (*l^{e}ṭah^{a}rô 'ô l^{e}ṭamm^e'ô*)."

A house having yellowish or reddish spots on its walls deeper than the surface has a leprous disease; it must be shut up for seven days (Lev. 14:34-53). If the spot has then spread, the affected stones must be taken out and thrown away in an unclean place outside the city. If the disease breaks out again after the wall has been replastered, the house must be torn down. If the leprosy is gone, the priest is to pronounce the house clean. Nothing that was in the house but was removed before the priest's inspection is unclean (v. 36). Anyone who enters the house while it is shut up is unclean (vv. 46f.).

The purification of a leper who has been healed takes place in two stages (Lev. 14:2-32). The priest meets the person to be purified (hithpael ptcp. of *ṭhr*) outside the camp and sprinkles him with the blood of a bird that has been killed. A living bird that has been dipped in the same blood is released. After he has washed his clothes, shaved off his hair, and bathed, the cured leper is clean (v. 8) and may enter the camp; but he must repeat the procedure seven days later. The second part of the purification takes place before Yahweh at the door of the tent of meeting (vv. 11,23). It is carried out by the priest, and comprises a cereal offering, a guilt offering, and a burnt offering. The blood of the guilt offering is applied to the right earlobe of the one to be purified, to the thumb of his right hand, and to the great toe of his right foot. The same places are then touched with oil. The priest sprinkles some of the same oil seven times before Yahweh and pours the rest on the head of the person to be purified. Vv. 18-20 and 29 state explicitly that this portion of the purification makes atonement (*kipper 'ālāyw hakkōhēn*). The purification of a house that has been affected with leprosy also culminates in a ceremony of atonement involving the sprinkling of blood (14:49-53). According to 2 K. 5:10-14, Elisha orders the Aramaean Naaman to wash seven times in the Jordan to be cleansed of his leprosy. After washing, Naaman is clean, that is, his flesh "returns" (*šûḇ*) and is like the flesh of a little child. Elisha had said that only Yahweh can cure leprosy (v. 7); Naaman's cure convinces him and he becomes a worshipper of Yahweh (v. 15).

5. *Other Forms of Human Uncleanness*. Ritual uncleanness (other than leprosy) can occur in five forms: a discharge or an emission of semen in the case of a man, menstruation or parturition in the case of a woman, and sexual intercourse. The relevant passages are found primarily in Lev. 15, where *ṭāmē'* occurs 36 times and *ṭāhar* 6 times.

A discharge (*zûḇ*) (Lev. 15:3-15) makes the man himself unclean (v. 3), anything on which he sits or lies (vv. 4,9), and anyone who comes in contact with such an object (vv. 5f.,10) or with the man (v. 7). If the man spits on someone (v. 8) or touches a person or a vessel without having rinsed his hands in water (vv. 11f.), they are unclean. Anyone who comes into direct or indirect contact with him is unclean until evening (*ṭāmē' 'aḏ-hā'ereb*). When the man has been cleansed of his emission, i.e., when it ceases, a two-stage purification ceremony is performed seven days later (cf. leprosy): first he washes his clothes and bathes in running water (v. 13); then follows atonement (*kipper 'ālāyw hakkōhēn*) before Yahweh at the door of the tent of meeting, with sin offering and burnt offering (vv. 14f.).

The law concerning emission of semen (*šiḵbaṯ-zera'*, Lev. 15:16-18,32) applies to the man himself (v. 16), anything with which the semen comes in contact (v. 17), and the woman with whom he has had intercourse (v. 18). The stereotyped formula *ṭāmē' 'aḏ-hā'ereḇ* applies to both, as well as to garments; but the regulations governing purification involve the bathing of the man and the washing of the garments, with no mention of an atonement ceremony.

In the case of a woman, the same regulations govern both normal menstruation (*niddâ*, Lev. 15:19-24,33; 18:19) and prolonged or irregular menstruation (15:25-27). The woman herself is unclean for seven days, but every person or object that comes in direct or indirect contact with her is unclean until evening. If, however, any of her blood is left on the man during sexual intercourse, he is also unclean for seven days (v. 24; cf. Ezk. 22:10). The regulations governing purification (15:28-30), which involves bathing and an atonement ceremony, are identical with those that apply to a man with an emission.

When a woman gives birth to a son (Lev. 12) she is unclean for seven days, but fourteen days in the case of a daughter. During her days of purification (*yᵉmê ṭohᵒrâ*), 33 for a son, 66 for a daughter, she must remain at home, not touching anything sacred or entering the sanctuary. The regulations governing purification say nothing about washing or bathing; the woman is clean when she has offered a guilt offering and a burnt offering and the priest makes atonement for her before Yahweh at the door of the tent of meeting.

In the case of sexual intercourse with an emission of semen (Lev. 15:18; cf. above), both parties are unclean until evening. The man is unclean for seven days if he gets any of the woman's blood on him (Lev. 15:24; cf. above). The man is also unclean if he has intercourse with another man's wife (Lev. 18:20) or an animal (18:23). For the two latter events, Lev. 20:10,15 prescribes the death penalty, as does v. 18 for intercourse with a woman during menstruation.

David saw Uriah's wife Bathsheba bathing on the roof (2 S. 11:2-4) and had intercourse with her "after she had purified herself from her uncleanness" (*qdš* hithpael); this suggests that the bath was part of her purification. Although an atonement ceremony is not mentioned, the text frees David from the suspicion of having defiled himself with an unclean woman. He did, however, defile himself through intercourse with another man's wife, but the text does not mention this uncleanness!

If a wife is unfaithful to her husband (Nu. 5:11-31) or he is jealous of her, he is to take her to the priest and offer a jealousy offering (*minḥaṯ qinā'ōṯ, minḥaṯ zikkārôn mazkereṯ 'āwōn*) for her. The question is whether or not she has defiled herself (*ṭm'* niphal, vv. 13f.,20,27,29; piel, 19). The priest brings her before Yahweh, makes her swear an oath against herself, and makes her drink the water of bitterness that brings the curse. If her body swells and her thighs fall in (v. 27), she is guilty and must bear her iniquity (v. 31). If she is innocent, the water will not harm her; she is clean (*ṭhr,* v. 28) and may conceive children.

A divorced woman who remarries and then is divorced or becomes a widow may not be taken back by her first husband, for she has defiled herself (hothpael) through her second marriage (Dt. 24:4). To take her back would be an abomination (*tô'ēḇâ*) before Yahweh and a sin (*ḥēṭ'*).

6. *Cultic Unfitness*. A person who is unclean is excluded from the cult. No one who is unclean may enter the temple (2 Ch. 23:19). Transgression of the laws governing cleanness brings death, because it defiles the dwelling place of Yahweh (Lev. 15:31). The penal regulations for transgression of these laws lead into a general parenesis directed especially against defilement through animals (Lev. 20:25f.); the passage has been intruded into a chapter comprising penal regulations for sins of unchastity that carry the death penalty.[15] Lev. 7:20f. states clearly that whoever has been defiled through contact with an unclean animal and nevertheless eats of the *šelāmîm* sacrifice is to be put to death. A priest who eats of the sacrifice before purifying himself of such uncleanness is to be put to death away from the presence of Yahweh, because he has brought guilt upon himself by bringing what is unclean in contact with what is holy (Lev. 22:3-9). Someone who is unclean must not remove any of the sacred tithe (Dt. 26:14).

III. Metaphorical Usage: Idolatry and Sin. Metaphorically *ṭāmē'* is used of unclean conditions and actions. Often apostasy from Yahweh is involved, including pagan practices and the cult of other gods, sometimes in the form of unchastity. Frequently the uncleanness is explicitly called sin, guilt, and wickedness.

The collection of laws in Lev. 18:6-23 contains regulations prohibiting sexual transgressions, with an intrusive prohibition against sacrificing children to Molech (v. 21). A man is unclean if he has intercourse with a woman during her period (v. 19),

---

15 Cf. Elliger, *HAT,* IV, *in loc.*

with the wife of another man (v. 20), or with an animal (v. 23; see above). The summary in vv. 24-30 (where *ṭāmē'* appears 6 times) refers to all the sexual contacts mentioned in the collection as unclean. With such practices the nations have defiled themselves (v. 24, niphal), so that the land became defiled (vv. 25,27, qal). These *tô'ēḇôṯ* brought guilt (*'āwôn*), so that the land vomited out (*qy'*) its inhabitants through the visitation (*pqd*) of Yahweh. An Israelite who defiles himself through any of these *ḥuqqôt hattô'ēḇôṯ* (v. 30) is to be cut off from among his people. These sexual aberrations, then, are condemned as unclean pagan practices and are considered sinful.

Lev. 19:2-37 is a collection of miscellaneous holiness laws, roughly half of which conclude with *'ᵃnî YHWH 'ᵉlōhêḵem*. In v. 31, *ṭāmē'* is used of defilement through consultation of departed spirits (*'ōḇōṯ*) and "wizards" (*yiddᵉ'ōnîm*). All forms of spiritualism and divination are punishable by death (Lev. 20:6,27; cf. Zec. 13:2-6). Divination is alien to the nature of Yahweh.

Ezekiel often associates uncleanness with idols (*gillûlîm*): Ezk. 14:11; 20:7,18,31; 22:3f.; 23:7,13-17, 30,38; 36:18,25; 37:23. As an example of the Israelites' obstinacy, Ezk. 20 speaks of their refusal to forsake (*šlk* hiphil) the idols of Egypt before the exodus (v. 8). Through these idols, they are defiled themselves (v. 7). This disobedience is repeated in the desert (vv. 18-21) and continues in Ezekiel's day (vv. 30-32). Vv. 23-26 blame the exile on the apostasy of the desert generation, which caused Yahweh himself to defile the people through their offerings and child sacrifice (*ṭāmē'* hiphil), so that he might punish them later. When the long-postponed punishment (vv. 9,14,17,22) has been carried out through the exile, Israel will worship Yahweh instead of the idols on Mt. Zion (v. 40), and abhor the evil things through which it has defiled itself (v. 43) and profaned the holy name of Yahweh (v. 39).

Ezk. 23 also states that Israel has defiled itself through idols since it was in Egypt. Apostasy from Yahweh is pictured as the harlotry of two women with their lovers (cf. Hos. 5:3; 6:10). Oholah (= Samaria) defiled herself with the idols of Assyria (Ezk. 23:7), and Oholibah (= Jerusalem) with Assyria (v. 13), Babylon (v. 17), and the nations (v. 30). Because they also took part in the cult of Yahweh, they defiled and profaned his temple (vv. 38f.). These abominations are summarized in v. 49 as sin (*ḥēṭ'*). The Israelites have taken their idols into their hearts (*he'ᵉlû gillûlêhem 'al-libbām*) and "set the stumbling block of their iniquity before their faces" (Ezk. 14:3f.,7), and have defiled themselves through their transgressions (*peša'*, v. 11). Those who act thus will be cut off from the people, as the law requires (*krt* hiphil, v. 8). The list of Jerusalem's sins (Ezk. 22:3-12) that have defiled her name includes among its abominations (*tô'ēḇôṯ*) uncleanness through idolatry (vv. 3f.), sexual intercourse with a woman during her period (time of uncleanness, v. 10), and intercourse with a daughter-in-law (v. 11; cf. Ezk. 33:26). This uncleanness will be punished by dispersal (v. 15). In Ezk. 36, conversely, purification is associated with deliverance. The iniquities and abominations (v. 31) of which Israel is to be cleansed by being sprinkled with water include unclean conduct and idolatry (vv. 17f.,25,29; cf. Ezk. 37:23). By cleansing Israel, Yahweh vindicates the holiness of his profaned name. In similar fashion, Ps. 106:34-39 states that Israel has become unclean through its idolatry, which has polluted (*ḥānēp*) the land and made the people of Yahweh abhorred (*t'b* piel, v. 40).

Uncleanness is sometimes equated explicitly with sin, transgression, and iniquity

(Lev. 16:16,19; 18:25; 22:9; Eccl. 9:2; Isa. 6:5; 64:5[Eng. v. 6]; Lam. 1:8f.; 4:15; Ezk. 14:11; 18:6,11,15; 37:23; 39:24; Zec. 13:1f.). The uncleanness of Isaiah and the people stands in sharp contrast with the holiness of Yahweh. When the prophet's lips are purified, his sin is forgiven (*kpr* pual, Isa. 6:7) so that he can proclaim the word of the Holy One. The purification of the prophet also symbolizes Yahweh's purification of his people (6:3-13).

A priest who is unclean and eats of the sacrificial gifts has sinned through contact with what is holy and must be put to death (Lev. 22:2-9). On the Day of Atonement, the sanctuary and altar are to be cleansed from all uncleannesses (*ṭum'ōṯ*), transgressions (*pᵉšā'îm*), and sins (*ḥaṭṭō'ṯ*) (Lev. 16:16,19). The purification involves sprinkling with the blood of the goat of the sin offering or daubing and sprinkling with the blood of the goat and of the bull that is also offered as a sin offering (cf. the ceremony of purification in the case of leprosy).

Lam. 4:15 calls the priests in their bloodstained garments unclean; their sin and iniquity (*ḥaṭṭā'ṯ, 'āwôn*) consists in having shed the blood of the righteous (v. 13; cf. Ezk. 24:11,13). The combination of unclean persons, polluted garments, and iniquities is also found in Isa. 64:5(6), where Israel confesses its guilt (*'āwôn*) before Yahweh. "Defiling (*ṭimmē'*) a neighbor's wife" is mentioned 3 times in lists of sins (Ezk. 18:6,11,15), together with "eating with its blood" (text emended[16]), "lifting up one's eyes to idols (*gillûlîm*)," "approaching a woman in her time of impurity (*niddâ*)," etc. All of these are called sin, iniquity, and transgression, and are punishable by death. Their opposite is *mišpāṭ* and *ṣᵉḏāqâ*, which bring life. According to Ezk. 37:23, Yahweh will save the dispersed of Israel from all their backslidings (reading *mᵉšûḇôṯ*[17]) through which they have defiled themselves by sinning in idolatry, detestable things (*šiqqûṣîm*), and transgressions (cf. Ezk. 39:23f., where the dispersion of Israel is depicted as a consequence of uncleanness and transgression [*peša'*]).

The land of Israel's inheritance must not be defiled, because it is the dwelling place of Yahweh (Nu. 35:34). The land is polluted (*ḥnp* hiphil, v. 33) by blood (= murder) and expiation can only be made by blood (v. 33b). To defile the land means to profane the holy God. Jeremiah accuses Israel of having defiled the land immediately after the occupation through idolatry, making Yahweh's heritage an abomination (Jer. 2:7); the people deny the accusation (v. 23), but their guilt is a stain (*ktm* niphal) before Yahweh (v. 22). When Israel defiled the sanctuary with *šiqqûṣîm* and *tô'ēḇôṯ* (Ezk. 5:11; cf. 2 Ch. 29:16), their conduct was worse than that of the nations (Ezk. 5:6), for they rejected the *mišpāṭîm* and *ḥuqqôṯ* of Yahweh. In the time of Zedekiah, the priests and leaders of the people defiled with the *tô'ēḇôṯ* of the nations the temple that Yahweh had hallowed (*qdš* hiphil, 2 Ch. 36:14), thus incurring the punishment of exile. Ezk. 43:7f. speaks of profanation (*ḥll*) of the temple through the burial of kings and the alien cult, also defiling the holy name of Yahweh. With references to holiness, therefore, "profane" and "defile" are almost synonymous. An Israelite or sojourner who offers any of his children to Molech defiles the sanctuary and profanes (*ḥll* piel) the

---

16 See *BHK*³.

17 See *BHK*³.

holy name of Yahweh, and is to be stoned to death (Lev. 20:2f.). Sacrifice to Molech in the valley of Hinnom and *šiqqûṣîm* in the temple defile the name of Yahweh, because they are contrary to his will (Jer. 7:30f.; 32:34f.).

According to 2 K. 23, Josiah defiled the sanctuaries of the pagan cult in his reformation. On the high places (2 K. 23:8,13) and at Topheth (v. 10), the altars, masseboth, and asherahs were broken down, and the sites were filled with human bones. The altar at Bethel was defiled (v. 16) by having the bones from the tombs burned upon it. In 2 Ch. 34:3,5,8, the verb *ṭhr* is used to refer to these actions. The Jeremiah passages thus stress defilement through contact with human remains, whereas Chronicles stresses purification from pagan practices.

Non-Israelites are rarely the subject of *ṭāmē'*. The sexual aberrations that are forbidden Israel (Lev. 18:6-23) had been practiced by the nations, who had thus defiled themselves and the land and been vomited out (*qy'*, vv. 24f.) of the land. Ezr. 9:10-15 refers to the passage when it warns the returning Israelites not to intermarry with non-Israelites. Some of the latter, however, appear to have separated themselves from their uncleanness and joined the worshippers of Yahweh (Ezr. 6:21). Although Ps. 79:1 speaks of the ruins of Jerusalem, the defilement of the holy temple does not necessarily refer to the destruction of the sanctuary. More likely is the profanation of Yahweh's holiness by the appearance of unclean non-Israelites in the temple (cf. Dt. 23:1-5[22:30–23:4]; Lam. 1:10). This same idea that the uncleanness of idolators is irreconcilable with holiness appears in Isa. 35:8-10, which states that the unclean shall not go on the holy way to Zion, but only the redeemed people. No one who is uncircumcised or unclean may enter the holy city of Jerusalem (Isa. 52:1). Anyone on the road who is carrying an idol of silver or gold must see that it is unclean and cast it aside (Isa. 30:22).

As a narrative tale, Gen. 34 differs from the other texts that speak of defilement through unchastity. The rape of Dinah by the uncircumcised Shechem (34:5,13,27) causes her brothers to take vengeance on Shechem and his family, who defiled (v. 27, *ṭm'*) her.

If Mic. 2:10 is meant to summarize the preceding section, the use of *ṭum'â* is peculiar: nowhere else is oppression termed uncleanness. Sellin therefore suggests the emendation *mᵉ'aṭ mᵉ'ûmâ taḥbᵉlû ḥᵃḇōl*, "For the sake of a tiny amount you take an inhuman pledge," which fits the context better.[18]

Residence in an alien land makes it difficult or impossible to observe the purity laws. In contrast to the land where Yahweh's sanctuary is found, an alien territory can be considered unclean (Josh. 22:19; Isa. 52:11; Am. 7:17). Among the Gentiles it is impossible to follow the dietary laws (Ezk. 4:13f.; Hos. 9:3).

For Job, the distance between God and mankind is as great as the distance between clean and unclean (Job 14:4).

IV. LXX. The usual LXX equivalents are *miaínein* (qal, niphal, piel, adj., *ṭum'â*), *akatharsía* (qal, piel, adj., *ṭum'â*), *akáthartos* (qal, niphal, adj., *ṭum'â*), and *akáthartos*

[18] For another interpretation, see W. Rudolph, *Micha. KAT,* XIII/3 (1975), 56ff.

gínesthai (qal, Lev. 14:36). For the qal, we also find *ekmiaínesthai* (Lev. 18:20,23,25; 19:31), and for the piel *míansis* (Lev. 13:44). In addition, for the piel we find *bebēloún*, for profaning the holy name of God (Ezk. 43:7f.); *exaírein*, with reference to the silver and gold of idols (Isa. 30:22); for the adjective: *apokathēménē*, an unclean woman (Lev. 15:33); *hrýpos*, "Can a *katharós* come from a *hrýpos*?" (Job 14:4); *tum'â: hamartía*, in the context of making atonement for the uncleanness of leprosy (Lev. 14:19).

V. Dead Sea Scrolls. When the Dead Sea scrolls speak of separating the clean from the unclean, the sacred from the profane (CD 6:17; 12:20), the emphasis is on the difference between the full members of the community and those who are willing to repent. Sometimes several terms for uncleanness occur together: *niddaṯ ṭum'â* (1QpHab 8:13), *darḵê niddâ ba'ᵃḇōḏaṯ ṭum'â* (1QS 4:10), *'ᵃḇōḏat niddaṯ ṭum'āṯām* (1QM 13:5).

In the purity catechesis 1QS 5:13-20 (cf. CD 10:10-13; 11:18–12:2; 12:8-20), the members of the community (*'anšê hayyaḥad*) are forbidden to admit those desiring to repent to the bath of purification on the grounds that all who transgress God's word are unclean (1QS 5:13f.). Such people one must keep apart (*bdl* hiphil, 5:10). No one touched (*mᵉnuggā'*) by any human uncleanness may enter the assembly of God or have a position in the community (1QSa 2:3-5). No one who is uncircumcised, unclean, or violent may go on the way of holiness (1QH 6:20f.). As long as they reject the ordinances of God, they may not cleanse themselves with the water of purification (*mê niddâ*), sea water or river water, or any kind of wash water (*mê raḥaṣ*, 1QS 3:4-6). Their works are filth (*ma'ᵃśêhem lᵉniddâ*) and their possessions are unclean (1QS 5:19f.; CD 6:15). The water of a tiny pool, insufficient to cover someone, is defiled when someone unclean touches it (CD 10:13). The same is true of trees, sand and stones, tools, nails, and pegs (CD 12:15-18). Anyone who blasphemes by saying that the ordinances of God's covenant are not firmly fixed defiles his holy spirit (*rûaḥ qoḏšᵉhem*), the spirit of truth (CD 5:11; 7:3; cf. 1QS 4:2-8). To the spirit of wickedness (*rûaḥ 'awlâ*) belong ways of filth in the service of uncleanness (1QS 4:10).

The sanctuary can be profaned in various ways. In 1QpHab 12:6-9 (on Hab. 2:17), we find *middᵉmê qiryâ* for *middᵉmê 'āḏām*, interpreted with reference to the wicked priest, who has done abominable deeds (*ma'ᵃśê tô'ᵃḇôṯ*) and defiled the sanctuary of God. When sacrifice is offered it must not be brought by someone who is unclean, which would defile the altar; the sacrifice of the wicked is an abomination (*tô'ēḇâ*, CD 11:18-21). No one may enter a house of prayer (*bêṯ hištaḥᵃwôṯ*) in a state of uncleanness requiring cleansing; when the trumpets of the community sound, he must do so before or afterwards (CD 11:21-23). Intercourse with a woman who is menstruating defiles the sanctuary (CD 5:6). According to CD 12:1f., a man must not have intercourse with a woman in Jerusalem, so as not to defile the city of the sanctuary with their uncleanness (*niddâ*). Whether or not this is a universal prohibition depends on the gap in the final word in 11:23. Lohse suggests [*hšb*]*t*, limiting the prohibition to the Sabbath. A pesher on Isa. 24:17f. (CD 4:14ff.; cf. 1QM 13:5) speaks of three snares of Belial: unchastity, riches, and pollution of the sanctuary. Whoever escapes one will be caught by another. The association of riches with the filth of uncleanness appears also in 1QpHab 8:12f., where the wicked priest is said to have acted faithlessly against the commandments for the sake of riches.

A peculiar interpretation appears in CD 20:23, where "defile the sanctuary" stands in contrast to "rely on God" and "return to God." The interpretation of the parallel verbs *š'n* niphal, "rely on God," *ṭm'* piel, "defile" or "declare to be defiled" (with the sanctuary as object), and *šûḇ*, "return to God," is uncertain.[19]

Anyone who has an infirmity or is touched by uncleanness (*m^e^nuggā' b^e^ṭum'aṯ b^e^śārô*) must not go forth to war (1QM 7:4), since war is a holy enterprise. The priests must not pollute themselves (*gā'al* hithpael) with the unclean blood of the slain, for they are holy (1QM 9:9).

André

---

19 Cf. the translations and comms. by J. Maier, A. Dupont-Sommer, E. Lohse, L. Moraldi, etc.

טָמַן *ṭāman*; מַטְמוֹן *maṭmôn*

Contents: I. 1. Etymology; 2. OT Occurrences. II. OT Usage. III. *maṭmôn*.

I. 1. *Etymology.* The Hebrew root *ṭmn* is a dissimilated form of *ṭmr,* as the occurrences of *ṭmr* in other Semitic languages suggest. It appears in Akk. *ṭ/tamāru*, "bury"; OSA *ṭmrm*,[1] "something kept secure"; Arab. *ṭamara*, "bury"; and probably also Meḥri *ṭamōr,* "hide, conceal," which differs too much in meaning from Arab. *ṭamara* to be considered a loanword. In Aramaic, *ṭmr* is widely attested: Jewish Aramaic "hide, preserve," Christian Palestinian "hide," Syriac "bury, hide," and Mand. "preserve." Ethiop. *ṭafara*, "cover, arch over," and *ṭafar,* "roof, vault (of the heavens)," also have meanings that can be associated with the root *ṭmr.*

The Arabic noun *maṭmūra*, "subterranean cellar for storing grain," does not require a verb *ṭmr* with the meaning "store, preserve";[2] it can be derived easily from the basic meaning of the root *ṭmr,* "hide." This also settles the question of associating *ṭmn* with Arab. *iṭma'anna*, "bend, come to rest," and *ṭammana*, "calm," which (as their vastly different meaning shows) can hardly have any connection with Heb. *ṭmn*.[3]

It is hardly possible[4] to see in *ṭmn* the original consonants and take the forms of *ṭmr* as exhibiting dissimilation (*n* to *r*). The opposite dissimilation proposed here from *ṭmr*

---

1 *RÉS*, 3910, 7.

2 S. Fränkel, *Die Aramäischen Fremdwörter im Arabischen* (Leiden, 1886), 137.

3 Contra T. Nöldeke, *Zur Grammatik des classischen Arabisch* (1897; repr. Darmstadt, 1963; *DKAW,* Phil.-hist. Kl., 45/2), 8.

4 R. Růšička, *Konsonantische Dissimilation in den semitischen Sprachen*. *BAss*, 4/4 (1909), 100.

to Heb. *ṭmn* may be explained as a case of phonetic assimilation to the verb *ṣāpan*, which also means "hide."[5]

2. *OT Occurrences*. The qal of *ṭmn* occurs 28 times in the OT (3 in the Pentateuch, 3 in Joshua, 7 in Jeremiah, 7 in the Psalms, 6 in Job, and 2 in Proverbs); the niphal in Isa. 2:10 (the entire verse is lacking in 1QIs^{a}) has the expected reflexive meaning "hide oneself."

The hiphil, which occurs twice in 2 K. 7:8, has been challenged,[6] but is in fact a "direct causative"[7] with the meaning "they hid for themselves a secret treasure." The existence of the hiphil is confirmed by the marginal reading (Ms. B) of Sir. 41:15, where the hiphil of *ṭmn* takes the place of the hiphil of *ṣpn*.

II. OT Usage. In the OT, *ṭāman* appears with the meaning "hide by burying." In Gen. 35:4, Jacob buries all the foreign gods under the *'ēlâ* at Shechem.[8] In Ex. 2:12, when Moses covers the body of the Egyptian with sand, his purpose is not to bury the corpse but to hide it. The same is true in Job 3:16, where Job wishes he were like a *nēpel ṭāmûn;* again, the miscarriage is not so much buried as hidden in shame. Only in Job 40:13, where Job is commanded, if he would be like God, to bury (*ṭomnēm*) the proud and the wicked in the dust, to enclose them in the *ṭāmûn*, do we find the meaning "burial" and the notion of the underworld as a place of enclosure.

In Jer. 13:4-7, also, *ṭāman* is used in the sense "hide by burying" in the account of Jeremiah's symbolic act (whether it is interpreted realistically, allegorically, or as a vision): Jeremiah is to hide a linen waistcloth in a cleft of the rock by the Euphrates. According to Jer. 43:9f., Jeremiah buries (*ṭāman*) stones in the pavement at Tahpanhes as a hidden foundation for the throne of Nebuchadnezzar.

In Josh. 7:21f., in the story of Achan, a beautiful mantle and silver are buried, just as in 2 K. 7:8 (hiphil), in the story of the Aramean war, the lepers bury silver, gold, and clothing. The hidden (*ṭāmûn*) treasures of the sand to be received by Issachar (and Zebulun?) according to Dt. 33:19 are probably purple snails, sponges, and glass.[9] Besides earth or sand, stalks of flax can also be used as a cover; cf. Josh. 2:6, which tells how Rahab hides the spies under such stalks.

In the language of the Psalms, *ṭāman* can mean the stealthy rigging of a net (*rešeṯ*, Ps. 9:16[Eng. v. 15]; 31:5[4]; 35:7f.) or laying of a snare (*paḥ*, Ps. 140:6[5]; 142:4b[3b]; *paḥîm*, Jer. 18:22b; 1QH 2:29; *môqᵉšîm*, Ps. 64:6[5]; *ḥeḇel*, Job 18:10). These images from the hunt describe the situation of the psalmist: his enemies lie in wait for him, but their own foot can be caught in the net that they have hidden (Ps. 9:16[15]; cf.

---

[5] Oral communication from W. W. Müller, Marburg.

[6] Cf. *GesB;* also *BDB* and *LexHebAram;* according to J. Barth, "Vergleichende Studien. III," *ZDMG*, 43 (1889), 180, a qal i-imperfect.

[7] E. König, *Hebräisches und aramäisches Wörterbuch zum AT* (Leipzig, [6,7]1937), 136; cf. *idem*, *Historisch-kritisches Lehrgebäude der hebräischen Sprache*, III (Leipzig, 1897), §191d-f.

[8] Cf. O. Keel, "Das Vergraben der 'fremden Götter' in Genesis XXXV 4b," *VT*, 23 (1973), 305-336.

[9] C. Steuernagel, *GHK*, I/3/1 (1923), 179; for a different interpretation (associated with caravan trade) see H.-J. Zobel, *Stammesspruch und Geschichte*. *BZAW*, 95 (1965), 39.

also 35:8). In this context, *ṭāman* emphasizes the secrecy and hence the maliciousness of the snare. Perhaps Job 20:26 also belongs here: Zophar's second reply describes how the wicked cannot escape judgment, saying that *kol-ḥōšeḵ ṭāmûn,* "all darkness is hidden (for him)," so that darkness becomes a snare for him.

The term is also used metaphorically in Isa. 2:10 (variant of 2:19), a command to hide in the dust on the day of Yahweh before the terror of Yahweh and the glory of his majesty (cf. Rev. 6:15).

In an ironic description of the awful indolence of the sluggard who can only do half of anything (normally even the laziest person will eat with enthusiasm), Prov. 19:24 (variant of 26:15) states that the sluggard buries (*ṭāman*) his hand in the dish but does not bring it back to his mouth. Sir. 41:14f. points out that buried wisdom is useless, and that someone who hides his folly is better than someone who hides his wisdom.

When Job tries to prove his innocence, he can point out in Job 31:33 that he never concealed his transgressions before(!) mankind by hiding (*ṭāman*) his iniquity in his bosom. CD 5:4 states that the book of the Torah was hidden from the days of Eleazar and Joshua to the day of Zadok.

The LXX almost invariably uses forms of *krýptein* to translate *ṭāman,* the Vulg. forms of *abscondere,* the Targumim for the most part forms of *ṭmr* alongside *kmn* and *ṭmn',* and the Syriac, as would be expected, forms of *ṭmr.*

III. *maṭmôn.* The noun *maṭmôn* occurs only once in the singular (Gen. 43:23), 4 times in the plural (Job 3:21; Prov. 2:4; Isa. 45:3; Jer. 41:8; also Sir. 42:9). The meaning ranges from "storage pit" to "buried treasure." According to Jer. 41:8, ten of the Samaritan pilgrims promise Ishmael, the murderer of Gedaliah, stores (cf. Arab. *maṭmūra*) of wheat, barley, oil, and honey from their storage pits in the field if he will spare them.

In Isa. 45:3, in the context of the Cyrus oracle, Yahweh promises his anointed treasures of darkness (*'ôṣᵉrôṯ ḥōšeḵ*) and hoards in secret places (*maṭmunê mistārîm*), that he may know Yahweh. According to Prov. 2:4, the only way to achieve knowledge of God is to search out wisdom like hidden treasures (*kammaṭmônîm*). Job, however, knows that those who are miserable and bitter seek for death "as the greedy dig for buried treasures" (Job 3:21).[10] Gen. 43:23 uses the singular as a general term for treasure, in this case referring to the money paid for the grain, which Joseph has replaced in the sacks. According to Sir. 42:9, a daughter is a treasure that keeps her father awake (LXX) because worry about her prevents him from sleeping.

The association of *maṭmôn* with *māmôn/mamōnás,* still suggested by *KBL*², cannot be maintained.[11]

Kellermann

---

10 G. Fohrer, *Das Buch Hiob. KAT,* XVI (1963), 125.

11 Cf. H. P. Rüger, "Μαμωνας," *ZNW,* 64 (1973), 127-131.

טָעַם ṭā'am; טַעַם ṭa'am; טְעֵם ṭe'ēm; מַטְעַמִּים maṭ'ammîm

Contents: I. Etymology, Meaning. II. OT Usage. III. Usage in Theological Contexts.

I. Etymology, Meaning. The root *ṭ'm* is attested not only in the West Semitic languages (Hebrew, Modern Hebrew, Biblical Aramaic, other dialects of Aramaic)[1] but also in East Semitic (Akk. *ṭêmu*[2]) and South Semitic (Arab. *ṭa'm, ṭa'ima;*[3] Ethiop. *ṭe'ma, ṭa'ma*[4]).

The basic meaning of the verb is "taste" (both solid and liquid foods), i.e., "perceive with the sense of taste," and hence also "enjoy, eat" (Hebrew, Aramaic, Arabic, Ethiopic) and by extension "perceive" (Hebrew). The derived nouns refer usually to "tasty food" or the "taste (of food)," with extensions of meaning through "discernment, understanding, judgment" to "command, decree, report" (cf. Akk. *ṭêmu* as well as Heb. *ṭa'am* and Biblical Aram. *ṭe'ēm*).

II. OT Usage. In the OT, we find the verb *ṭ'm* 10 times in the qal; the derived noun *ṭa'am* occurs 13 times, *maṭ'ammîm* 8 times. In the Aramaic of the OT, we find the verb 3 times in the pael and the derived noun *ṭe'ēm* 28 times, as well as 2 occurrences of *ṭa'am*.

The original meaning of the verb, "taste, perceive with the sense of taste," which is located in the gums (Job 12:11; 34:3) and atrophies with increasing age (2 S. 19:36[Eng. v. 35]), is clearly attested in Hebrew. Since what is involved is the perception and distinction of the specific taste of various foods and drinks, the verb with accusative object—like *'āḵal* and *šāṯâ* or *lāḥam*—can also mean the objective process of tasting, the ingestion of nourishment with the intent of tasting it, so that *ṭ'm* can best be translated "enjoy" or "eat" (1 S. 14:24; 2 S. 3:35; 19:36; Jon. 3:7), or, in conjunction with *me'aṭ,* "take a taste of" (1 S. 14:29, 43). In Biblical Aramaic, the verb in the pael with an accusative object is used in parallel with *'āḵal* with the meaning "feed" (Dnl. 4:22,29[25,32]; 5:21; cf. 4:30[33]).

In addition, the accent of *ṭ'm* can lie on the careful tasting and test of a food, controlled by the gums, so that the verb with an accusative object, like the parallel term *bāḥan* (→ בחן *bḥn*), can mean "test by tasting" (Job 12:11; 34:3 conj. *lô 'ōḵel*). In the OT, *ṭ'm* followed by a *kî* clause as a way of expressing perception appears only in the figurative sense of "take note that" (Prov. 31:18; Ps. 34:9[8] par. *rā'â*).

The derived noun *maṭ'ammîm* means "tasty food" (Gen. 27:4,9,14,17,31) or "delicacies" (Prov. 23:3,6), but the noun *ṭa'am* exhibits a broad spectrum of meanings. First, it can be used in the original sense of "taste" (of food or drink); with reference

---

1 *BDB; KBL*[3]; *LexLingAram.*

2 W. Muss-Arnolt, *A Concise Dictionary of the Assyrian Language* (Berlin, 1905), 355f.; *BDB*, 380f.

3 Lane, 1853f.

4 *TigrWb*, 619; *LexLingAeth*, 1241ff.

to wine, it can be qualified as unchanged (Jer. 48:11, applied figuratively to Moab), or it can be further defined by comparison (*k^e^-*) to other foods (Ex. 16:31; Nu. 11:8). It can also be used in the positive sense of "tastiness" (Job 6:6).

When used figuratively the noun can also mean subjective taste or the perception of taste on the part of individuals, and thus the gift of discrimination, so that *ṭa'am* can be used for the "good judgment" of the devout believer (Ps. 119:66) or of elders (Job 12:20), the "discretion" of a wise (1 S. 25:33) or beautiful (Prov. 11:22) woman. The phrase *hēšîḇ ṭa'am* therefore means "answer discreetly" (Prov. 26:16), and *šinnâ ṭa'am* means "feign madness" (1 S. 21:14[13]; Ps. 34:1[superscription]; lit., "disarrange the sense of judgment"; cf. Akk. *ṭēma šanû;*[5] also Sir. 25:18, *b^e^lō' ṭa'am,* "involuntarily"). In addition, *ṭa'am* can be used as an aramaism in the sense of the result of critical examination, hence "judgment, decree" (Jon. 3:7).

The common noun *ṭ^e^'ēm* in Biblical Aramaic also exhibits the original meaning "taste" (of food or drink) in the phrase *biṭ'ēm ḥamrā'*, "under the influence of wine" (Dnl. 5:2; lit., "[influenced] by the taste of wine"[6]). Elsewhere, however, it appears only in its later meanings. In the figurative sense of careful perception it appears in the idiom *śîm ṭ^e^'ēm 'al,* "direct attention to someone," i.e., "pay heed to someone" (Dnl. 3:12; 6:14; cf. *śîm bāl l^e^-*, Dnl. 6:15); and, like Heb. *hēšîḇ ṭa'am,* it appears with the same meaning in the phrase *h^a^ṯîḇ ṭ^e^'ēm,* "answer someone wisely" (Dnl. 2:14).

In the most cases, however, the noun in Biblical Aramaic has the meaning "instruction, decree, command" (Ezr. 6:14; 7:23; the vocalization *ṭa'am,* found only here, is obviously patterned on the Hebrew noun to underline the fact that it is a "divine" command[7]), above all in the phrase *śîm ṭ^e^'ēm,* "give command" (Ezr. 4:19,21; 5:3, 9,13,17; 6:1,3,8,11f.; 7:13,21; Dnl. 3:10,29; 4:3[6]; 6:27[26]), but also in the construct phrase *b^e^'ēl-ṭ^e^'ēm,* "commander" (Ezr. 4:8f.,17; possibly the designation of an official, the "chancellor"; cf. Akk. *bêl ṭêmi*[8]). Finally, *ṭ^e^'ēm* can have the further nuance of "report" (Ezr. 5:5), which also appears in the idiom *y^e^haḇ ṭ^e^'ēm,* "give account" (Dnl. 6:3[2]; cf. also Akk. *turru ṭêmu,* "report").

III. Usage in Theological Contexts. In theological contexts, *ṭ'm* is used in its original meaning where it is forbidden by required fasting, whether occasioned by an oath taken before a war of Yahweh (1 S. 14:24,29,43) or by an edict ordaining public penance (Jon. 3:7). The root also has theological overtones occasioned by wisdom influence, in the figurative sense of careful discrimination and discretion, characteristic primarily of those who are old and wise, and desirable in a beautiful woman. Human discretion and judgment are thus thought of as a divine gift, which Yahweh can bestow to carry out his purpose (1 S. 25:33), but which he can also take away from the wise (Job 12:20). Or it can refer to the knowledge that belongs specifically to the devout, to the sense of Yahweh's saving goodness (*ṭûḇ*) that is given to the believer in distress

---

5 *BWL,* 325.

6 See *KBL*²; cf. *BDB*, *LexLingAram.*

7 Cf. *BLe,* §§228f.

8 *KBL*², 1079.

(Ps. 34:9[8]), or to the good judgment concerning Yahweh's statutes and commandments that is the prayer of those devoted to the Torah, which can be learned only through Yahweh's help (Ps. 119:66). Finally the noun *ṭa'am* in Biblical Aramaic, which is both analogous to and distinct from the human command *ṭ*ᵉ*'ēm,* designates the command given by the God of heaven through the prophetic word (Ezr. 6:14; 7:23).

Schüpphaus

טַף *ṭap*

Contents: I. Etymology. II. Meaning: 1. General; 2. Household; 3. Dependents; 4. Children. III. Theological Usage: 1. Totality; 2. Election of the Lowly.

I. Etymology. The etymology and Semitic background of *ṭap* are disputed. The word is often associated[1] with Ethiop. *ṭaff,* "infant." Others cite Arab. *ṭanifa,* "be uneasy, be suspicious,"[2] *nṭp*/*ṭpp,* "drip," or *ṭpp* II (= Arab. *ṭaffa*), "collect, amass."[3]

Also uncertain is the association of *ṭap* with the verb *ṭpp,* found only in Isa. 3:16, which is usually translated (on the assumption that it is related to *ṭap* = "infant") "walk like a small child, trip,"[4] but sometimes[5] "go quickly" or "dance, leap, jump."

II. Meaning.

1. *General.* Overemphasis on the possible connection with Ethiop. *ṭaff* has favored the still current assumption that *ṭap* refers exclusively to infants or young children. This restricted range of meanings[6] does not do justice to the 42 OT occurrences of *ṭap.* The interpretation "those belonging to a wandering tribe who are unable to keep up,"[7] based on cultural history, is also too narrow (although appropriate in a few passages where the *ṭap* remain behind during military campaigns: Nu. 32:16f.,24,26; Dt. 3:19; Josh. 1:14; cf. Gen. 50:8) and too dependent on the uncertain etymological association with *ṭpp* or *ṭnp.* Deuteronomy at least (cf. Dt. 25:18) has another term (*neḥ*ᵉ*šālîm*) for those who lag behind.

ṭap. L. Koehler, "Ṭapp = Nicht oder wenig Marschfähige," *ThZ,* 6 (1950), 387f.; J. A. L. Lee, "'ΑΠΟΣΚΕΥΗ *in the Septuagint,*" *JTS,* N.S. 23 (1972), 430-37; P. Weigandt, "Zur sogenannten 'Oikosformel,' " *NovT,* 6 (1963), 49-74, esp. 53-63 and 71-74.

1 *LexLingAeth,* 1251.

2 *KBL*².

3 J. Fürst, *Hebräisches und Chaldäisches Handwörterbuch über das AT,* I (Leipzig, ³1876).

4 Cf. *KBL*³ and even F. Gesenius, *Thesaurus philologicus criticus linguae hebraeae et chaldaeae Veteris Testamenti* (Leipzig, ²1835-1858).

5 *LexHebAram,* with Arabic parallels.

6 Accepted, for example, by H. W. Wolff, *Anthropology of the OT* (Eng. trans., Philadelphia, 1974), 120.

7 Köhler in *KBL*² and *KBL*³.

Apart from Dt. 20:14, the collective noun *ṭap* appears only in narrative texts of the OT. It appears frequently in series with other nouns, especially *nāšîm* (24 out of 42 passages), *'ᵃnāšîm, mᵉṯîm,* and *gᵉḇārîm,* as well as various terms (always clearly distinguished from *ṭap*) for domestic animals, cattle, or possessions. The word does not always refer to the same concrete group, but there is probably no semantic development observable in the OT. The basic meaning is probably something like "hangers-on," i.e., those who are "dependent," the "remainder" (cf. Jer. 48:16 LXX [41:16 MT] *tá loipá,* which is not, as is commonly suggested, a mistake for *tá nḗpia*), "not so important" (often with pejorative connotations, as in Ex. 10:10,24; Dt. 1:39). Both linguistically and semantically, then, *ṭap* has a "complementary" function: only the context shows what *ṭap* refers to, when the groups mentioned before or after *ṭap* have been subtracted.

2. *Household.* In its most general sense—usually in isolation—*ṭap* probably means something like "hangers-on, family, household," including women, children, the aged, slaves, etc. (Gen. 43:8; 47:12 [see below],24; 50:8,21; Ex. 10:10,24 [with pejorative overtones]; 12:37; Nu. 31:17f. [see below]; 32:16f.,24; Jgs. 18:21 [see below]; 2 S. 15:22; Ezr. 8:21).

In 2 Ch. 20:13 and 31:18, this usage is defined more precisely by an explanatory gloss:[8] "their *ṭap,* i.e., their wives and their sons (and their daughters)." It may remain an open question whether the gloss "their wives and sons" in 20:13 is a correct gloss and "their wives and sons and daughters" in 31:18 incorrect (because it contradicts 31:16);[9] the meaning of *ṭap* is not affected. In any case, these two passages show that the general meaning of *ṭap* was largely unfamiliar at an early date and needed further explanation.

The translation of the unique phrase *lᵉpî haṭṭāp* in Gen. 47:12 as "according to the size of the household" explains the passage completely. The translation "down to the youngest"[10] is forced. The derivation from a root *ṭpp* II, "drip,"[11] suggested by Driver[12] and accepted, for instance, by *KBL*³ (as *ṭap* II), which yields the meaning "within a drop," i.e., "in full measure," contradicts the close association of Gen. 47:12 with 45:11 and 50:21 in both style and content (cf. also the analogous function of the formulas "you and your house"—e.g., in Gen. 45:11—and "you and your *ṭap,*" Gen. 50:21, translated as *oikía* by the LXX).

The distinctions made by Nu. 31:17f., against the background of this general meaning of *ṭap,* do not support the conclusion that *ṭap* itself means "just the male children" in v. 17 and "only the female children" in v. 18.[13]

The conjecture of *'eṯ-hannāšîm wᵉeṯ-haṭṭap* instead of *'eṯ-haṭṭap* in Jgs. 18:21[14]

---

[8] W. Rudolph, *Chronikbücher. HAT,* XXI (³1968), *in loc.*

[9] *Ibid.*

[10] E. A. Speiser, *Genesis. AB,* I (³1979), *in loc.,* among others.

[11] See I above.

[12] G. R. Driver, "Two Problems in the OT Examined in the Light of Assyriology," *Syr,* 33 (1956), 70-78, esp. 73.

[13] Weigandt, 54, following *KBL*².

[14] K. Budde, *Das Buch der Richter. KHC,* VII (1897), *in loc.,* and *BHK*³.

is inappropriate and superfluous if the general meaning of *ṭap̱* is taken into account. This interpretation is confirmed by LXX^A and Theodotion (*tḗn panoikían*).[15]

3. *Dependents.* A more restricted meaning—something like "dependents, those unfit for military service" (i.e., children, the elderly, slaves, etc.)—is exhibited by *ṭap̱* in the following passages, where it stands in contrast to the males/warriors mentioned explicitly or implicitly and to the women spoken of either directly before or after: Gen. 45:19; 46:5; Nu. 16:27; 32:26; Dt. 2:34; 3:6,19; 29:10; 31:12; Josh. 1:14; 8:35; Jgs. 21:10; Est. 8:11; Jer. 40:7; 41:16; 43:6 (cf. 1QSa 1:4 and possibly 1:8 emended). This usage is especially common in descriptions of booty (cf. → בזז *bzz*) taken or to be taken: Gen. 34:29; Nu. 14:3 (cf. 14:31 and Dt. 1:39); 31:9; Dt. 20:14.

Comparison of Nu. 32:26, where *ṭap̱* is distinguished from *nāšîm*, with 32:16f.,24, where *ṭap̱* appears by itself (cf. Gen. 50:8), speaks quite clearly for distinguishing a general meaning of *ṭap̱,* including women, and a restricted meaning excluding women. Women can be included in *ṭap̱,* but whether they are in a particular instance must be determined from the context rather than from the meaning of the word alone.

In Deuteronomy and Jeremiah we find a uniform usage that amounts to a cliche: all the passages in these books exhibit the narrower meaning of *ṭap̱.* Note especially the formulas *m^{e}ṯîm w^{e}hannāšîm w^{e}haṭṭāp̱* (Dt. 2:34; 3:6) and *'^{a}nāšîm w^{e}hannāšîm w^{e}haṭṭap̱* (Dt. 31:12; Jer. 40:7; cf. also Jer. 41:16 and 43:6).

The occurrence of *zāqēn* in Dt. 29:9(Eng. v. 10); Est. 3:13; Ezk. 9:6 appears to contradict the statement that *ṭap̱* could also include the elderly. In Dt. 29:9(10), however, *ziqnêḵem* means "elders," i.e., officials. In Est. 3:13, two pairs of complementary terms (*minna'ar w^e'aḏ-zāqēn* and *ṭap̱ w^{e}nāšîm*) are conjoined with some overlap. In Ezk. 9:6 we either find the same situation (*zāqēn bāḥûr ûḇ^{e}ṯulâ* and *w^{e}ṭap̱ w^{e}nāšîm*) or *zāqēn* refers to the idolatrous elders of Ezk. 8:11, who are the first to be slain.

4. *Children.* The context of Nu. 14:31 and Dt. 1:39 (*w^{e}ṭapp^{e}ḵem* par. *ûḇ^{e}nêḵem '^{a}šer lō'-yāḏ^e'û hayyôm ṭôḇ wārā'*)—and possibly also Dt. 29:10(11); 31:12; Josh. 8:35—suggests the meaning "children" in these passages, which is often taken to be the basic meaning of *ṭap̱* (cf. also 1QpHab. 6:11).

III. Theological Usage. No specifically theological usage of *ṭap̱* is found, but two aspects are of interest.

1. *Totality.* The noun often appears in contexts that emphasize inclusive totality: cf. the formulaic language of Deuteronomy and Jeremiah[16] and the descriptions of booty,[17] and also Est. 3:13; 8:11. In this usage, *ṭap̱* indicates the completeness of God's judgment or total annihilation (Nu. 16:27; 31:17; Ezk. 9:6; for the same idea but

---

15 See Lee for a general discussion of the LXX equivalents for *ṭap̱.*

16 See II.3 above.

17 See above.

without ṭap, cf. Josh. 6:21; 1 S. 15:3; 22:19). In a similar fashion, 2 Ch. 20:13 emphasizes by mentioning the ṭap that "all Judah stood before Yahweh" (the unity and totality of Israel being a major theme of the Chronicler's theology) and that worship no longer involves just the adult males. Finally, in the Deuteronomic and Deuteronomistic passages Dt. 29:10(11); 31:12; Josh. 8:35, ṭap corroborates the fact that the making of the covenant and the reading of the Torah involve the entire people—even the coming generations, "those who are not here with us this day" (Dt. 29:14[15]).

2. *Election of the Lowly.* The use of ṭap in Deuteronomy has overtones of the biblical (and specifically Deuteronomic) theme of "election of the lowly." The promise of the land will not be fulfilled for the rebellious generation of the desert, but specifically for the ṭap, the little ones, the weak and unimportant, who can easily fall prey to enemies and "have no knowledge of good or evil" (Dt.1:39; cf. Nu.14:31). It is therefore also fitting that the ṭap—together with the *gērîm*,[18] likewise a group needing protection—should take part in the cultic assembly (Dt. 29:10[11]; 31:12; Josh. 8:35).[19]

Locher

[18] D. Kellermann, "גּוּר *gûr*," *TDOT,* II, 445.
[19] See III.1 above.

טָרַף *ṭārap;* טֶרֶף *ṭerep;* טְרֵפָה *ṭ^erēpâ;* טָרָף *ṭārāp*

Contents: I. Root: 1. Etymology; 2. Occurrences; 3. Meaning. II. General Usage: 1. Literal Meaning; 2. Secular and Sacral Ordinances; 3. Human Nourishment. III. Theological Usage: 1. Figurative Applications to Historical Entities with Pejorative Meaning; 2. Figurative Applications to Historical Entities with Positive Meaning; 3. Usage with Yahweh as Subject.

I. Root.

1. *Etymology.* The root *ṭrp* has not been found in Ugaritic or Akkadian; it is attested only in Hebrew, Middle Hebrew, Jewish Aramaic, and Coptic, with the meaning "tear (to pieces), tear away, steal." Undoubtedly the Syriac equivalent with the meaning "slay" and the Arabic word for "graze bare" are related to this Semitic root.

2. *Occurrences.* Forms of *ṭrp* occur 56 times in the OT, together with 2 occurrences (Gen. 8:11 [J] and Ezk. 17:9), which must be derived from a noun *ṭārāp,* with the meaning "freshly plucked" (off a plant). It is not necessary to postulate a different root for this meaning; the extension of meaning is well within the semantic range of *ṭrp.* It is noteworthy that in the OT the verbal forms are in the minority; the nouns *ṭ*ᵉ*rēpâ* and *ṭerep,* with a variety of meanings, predominate. Of the verbal stems we

find the qal with the meaning "tear, steal," the niphal and pual as the equivalent passives, and a single occurrence of the hiphil (Prov. 30:8) as the causative of the qal, with the weakened meaning "cause to enjoy."[1] Instances of this root appear in only 16 of the books of the OT; it is noteworthy that there is not a single occurrence in the narrative sections (*ṭrp* does not appear at all in the Deuteronomistic history or in the Chronicler's history). Neither does it appear in the Five Scrolls, Deutero-Isaiah, Daniel, Joel, Obadiah, Jonah, Habakkuk, Zephaniah, Haggai, or Zechariah. Since the only occurrence in Deuteronomy is found in the Blessing of Moses (Dt. 33:20) and the passage in Numbers (23:24 [E]) belongs to one of the sayings of Balaam—in other words, both occurrences must be assigned to earlier material that has been incorporated into the books—it is actually true to say that *ṭrp* is not found in extensive portions of the Pentateuch. The 4 occurrences in Exodus (all in Ex. 22) are in the Covenant Code; in Genesis, the story of Joseph (chaps. 37 and 44) includes 4 of the 8 occurrences (including a single instance of *ṭārāp̱,* as noted above). The root occurs once in Jeremiah, Micah, and Malachi, and twice in Proverbs, Isaiah, Hosea, and Amos (the form in Am. 1:11 is disputed). Most of the occurrences are found in Nahum (5), Ezekiel (11, including 1 instance of *ṭārāp̱*), the Psalms (8), and Job (6). The 3 occurrences in Leviticus are in the law governing the priesthood. The various forms of *ṭrp* clearly appear in highly specialized and limited literary contexts, which depend on the semantic range of the root. Because it is used in tribal sayings (Gen. 49:9,27; Dt. 33:20), the Balaam cycle, and eighth-century prophetic texts, we must conclude that the root was in use at a very early date; it was not retrojected into the early period on the basis of late prophetic and Wisdom texts.

3. *Meaning*. The basic meaning is "tear (to pieces)," especially with large beasts of prey as the subject; in the OT, it is above all the lion (lionness, cub: *'aryeh, 'ᵃrî* [→ ארי *'ᵃrî*], *lāḇî, kᵉpîr, layiš, šaḥal*) and wolf (→ זאב *zᵉ'ēḇ* [*zᵉ'ēbh*]) that are associated with the term. Occasionally the panther or leopard (*nāmēr,* Jer. 5:6) is mentioned, or an unspecified wild beast (*ḥayyâ rā'â,* Gen. 37:33). A beast of prey must get food by "tearing to pieces" if it is not to starve; this natural quest for nourishment, however, involves an element of violence, which can be exploited in figurative usage. It is easy to see how *ṭrp* in its various forms can take on the meaning "(de)spoil, prey, booty."

In some cases it is possible to take the noun *ṭerep̱,* apart from the modalities of the quest for food, in the neutral or even positive sense of "food" (Ps. 111:5; Prov. 31:15; Mal. 3:10). The association with the basic meaning is still clear. In this sense, Job 24:5 states that the zebras (*pᵉrā'îm*)[2] seek *ṭerep̱,* i.e., food. Even here, the tearing off of the grass that grows on the steppes may furnish a connection with the basic meaning. The same notion of tearing a leaf or twig from a plant has led to the meaning "fresh, freshly plucked" (Gen. 8:11 [J]; Ezk. 17:9). This extension of meaning led in turn to a separate Masoretic substantive form, *ṭārāp̱.* The other substantive derived

---

1 *KBL.*

2 "Wild asses" according to P. Humbert; see *KBL.*

from *ṭārap, ṭᵉrēpâ,* always means "something torn," usually a domestic or sacrificial animal attacked by a beast of prey.

The OT often uses *ṭārap* metaphorically with historical entities as subject or object. People, nations, kings, and social classes can act like beasts of prey; and individuals, groups, or entire populations can be the target of such actions. Finally, it is possible to apply the functional characteristics of *ṭārap* to God's active intervention: in judgment and in salvation he will be like a lion towards his people.

II. General Usage.

1. *Literal Meaning*. The many early passages in which *ṭārap* is used figuratively[3] demonstrate indirectly what is also proven by the less frequent instances of the literal meaning: "tearing" or "spoliation" goes naturally with beasts of prey. The point is made by one of the rhetorical questions in Amos (Am. 3:4): "Does a lion roar in the forest, when he has no prey?" A lion's behavior is common knowledge; no judgment is passed. A lion would perish without prey (Job 4:11; cf. 24:5). It is part of the order of creation, according to which it is Yahweh himself who provides *ṭerep* (hunts) for the lioness (Job 38:39). The young lions roar for prey and seek their food (*'oḵlām,* Ps. 104:21) from God. Human beings as well as animals can fall victim to beasts of prey. A passage in the story of Joseph uses this possibility as a motif. Joseph's brothers attempt to make their father Jacob think that Joseph has not returned because a wild beast has torn and devoured him (Gen. 37:33: *ṭārōp ṭōrap yôsēp,* with *'āḵal* in parallelism; cf. 44:28; the qal infinitive absolute precedes the pual perfect as an intensifier).

2. *Secular and Sacral Ordinances*. Occurrences like those just described can involve questions of property law, leading in the ancient Near East and in the OT to specific regulations governing compensation. If the person to whom domestic animals have been entrusted can show the owner the torn carcass or parts of it (according to Am. 3:12, two legs or a piece of an ear are sufficient evidence [*'ēḏ*]), there is no obligation to make restitution (Ex. 22:12[Eng. v. 13]: *'im-ṭārōp yiṭṭārēp*). The Yahwist, too, in the story of Jacob and Laban (Gen. 31:39) is aware of this law contained in the Covenant Code. Jacob did not, however, take advantage of the law, although he had the opportunity and right to do so. In both instances, *ṭᵉrēpâ* is a legal term. The passage from the Joseph story mentioned in the preceding section also shows that bloody garments were considered evidence that someone had been killed by a wild beast (Gen. 37:33).

The noun *ṭᵉrēpâ* also plays a role in the ordinances of sacral law. Ezekiel claims not to have eaten flesh torn by beasts from his youth to the time Yahweh requires him to eat unclean food (Ezk. 4:14).[4] He has accepted the obligation of observing certain priestly laws governing purity, such as are still mentioned in Leviticus. Unfortunately

---

3 See below.

4 See W. Zimmerli, *Ezekiel 1. Herm* (Eng. trans. 1979), 170f.

it is impossible to date the ordinances in Leviticus precisely, so that Ezk. 4:14 may be the earliest evidence for such "laws of the priesthood." Lev. 17:15 (Holiness Code) gives the impression of being earlier, however. It does not forbid absolutely the eating of an animal that has died or been torn, but declares that anyone—native or sojourner—who eats such flesh is unclean until evening. He must bathe and wash his garments (cf. Lev. 11:40a). This ordinance must be observed by all.

In its present context, Lev. 22:8 (Holiness Code) states that priests must not eat *n*e*ḇēlâ ûṭ*e*rēpâ*, which would render them unclean; but in this context the verse is secondary.[5] Ex. 22:30(31) is also thought not to be a part of the Covenant Code; it is out of place in both form and content, presupposing an ideal of purity and holiness that is not developed until Leviticus.[6] Lev. 7:24, likewise secondary, forbids Israelites to eat the fat of an animal that dies or is torn by beasts, although they are free to use it for other purposes (v. 24 interrupts the continuity of vv. 23 and 25[7]). Therefore the ordinance in Ezk. 44:31, in Ezekiel's description of the ideal temple, which forbids the priests to eat anything that has died or is torn, is probably also not authentic, since it is clearly borrowed from Lev. 22:8.[8]

On the basis of the evidence cited, we may conclude that, according to the sacral law of the preexilic period, the eating of *ṭ*e*rēpâ* was not forbidden; it did, however, render the eater unclean and necessitated certain acts of purification. In the exilic and postexilic period, the priests and eventually the laity were forbidden to eat *ṭ*e*rēpâ*.

3. *Human Nourishment.* The sense of "human nourishment" that developed from the basic meaning of *ṭerep* took on positive overtones in the OT. Prov. 31:15 is a familiar passage praising the virtuous woman who provides *ṭerep* for her entire *bayiṯ*. According to Ps. 111:5, one of Yahweh's wonderful works is his provision of *ṭerep* for those who fear him. In Mal. 3:10, the term *ṭerep* is even used for the tithes of the people that are stored in the second (postexilic) temple, "provisioning" the house of God. Proper observance of the regulations governing the tithes will lead to economic prosperity throughout the land. The needful food that the wise one requests from God is also called *ṭerep* (Prov. 30:8): *haṭrîpēnî leḥem ḥuqqî*, "let me 'tear' the bread that I need."

III. Theological Usage.

1. *Figurative Applications to Historical Entities with Pejorative Meaning*. a. The harsh policies of conquest and oppression practiced by the Assyrians in the eighth century B.C. are likened to the behavior of a beast of prey, especially a lion. The earliest passage is Isa. 5:29, in an oracle of doom addressed to the entire nation. The lion's actions are described in detail: he roars, then growls and seizes his prey (*yō'ḥēz ṭerep*), carrying it off so that none can rescue (*w*e*'ên maṣṣîl*). The context (vv. 26-28)

5 Cf. M. Noth, *Leviticus. OTL* (Eng. trans. 1965), 160.
6 Cf. *idem, Exodus. OTL* (Eng. trans. 1962), 188.
7 See Noth, *Leviticus, in loc.*
8 Cf. W. Zimmerli, *Ezekiel 2. Herm* (Eng. trans. 1983), 463, 468.

speaks of various military actions, such as might also be seen in v. 29,[9] either described figuratively in a simile introduced by the particle *k*ᵉ- or (on the assumption that *lāḇî'* refers to a military unit) mentioned explicitly. Probably the image and the reality are intertwined.

A little more than a century later, Nahum uses the image of a lion for Assyria and Nineveh in his prophecy of disaster. The city of Nineveh is a lion's cave, in which dwells a pride of lions (lionesses and whelps); they have filled (*wayᵉmallē'*) the cave with *ṭerep* and *ṭᵉrēpâ*. This is undoubtedly a reference to the booty collected during various military campaigns. For both the action and its result, Nahum uses the verb *ṭārap* and the nouns *ṭerep* and *ṭᵉrēpâ*, which describe the violence and brutality of the events (Nah. 2:13[12]). The image is carried over in 3:1, although the central term of the comparison, the lion, is not mentioned. The lament over Nineveh calls the Assyrian city *'îr dāmîm,* which *lō' yāmîš ṭārep,* "does not cease from plunder" (or "plundering," since *ṭerep* has strong verbal overtones; the imperfect tense, implying incomplete action, is used as a frequentative). But Assyria-Nineveh will perish through the actions of Yahweh, through which the sword will devour the young lions (*ûkᵉpîrayiḵ tō'ḵal ḥāreḇ*) and the prey will be cut off from the earth (*wᵉhiḵrattî mē'ereṣ ṭarpēḵ*) (Nah. 2:14[13]). Once again there is an immediate juxtaposition of image and reality: the prophet speaks explicitly of the chariots, which will be burned and destroyed.

The prophecy of disaster in Isa. 31:4 goes even further: Yahweh himself is likened to an angry, growling lion, or a young lion with its prey (*ka'ᵃšer yehgeh hā'aryeh wᵉhakkᵉpîr 'al-ṭarpô*), which cannot be restrained from its gruesome work of destruction. Assyria will be destroyed in the same way as it brought destruction on others.

In the great poetic oracle of Amos against the nations, the guilt of Edom is exemplified by the statement that "his anger tore perpetually (*wayyiṭrōp lā'aḏ*)" (Am. 1:11). Here again the image is used without explicit mention of a beast of prey.[10] In Jer. 5:6, on the other hand, lion, wolf, and leopard are mentioned, together with their characteristic actions (*nāḵâ* hiphil, *šāḏaḏ, šāqaḏ*). They lie in wait for Jerusalem, and everyone who goes out will be torn in pieces (*kol-hayyōṣē' mēhēnnâ yiṭṭārēp*). This prophecy of disaster looks for destruction through the agency of an historical entity, which is not named explicitly.

b. In a sermon addressed to the various classes (Ezk. 22:23-31), Ezekiel castigates the social conduct of various groups among his people: the princes, the priests, the officials, the prophets, and the rural gentry (*'am hā'āreṣ*). Specifically, the princes (Ezk. 22:25, reading *'ᵃšer nᵉśî'eyhā* with the LXX instead of *qešer nᵉḇî'eyhā*) are

---

[9] Cf. B. Mazar, "The Military Élite of King David," *VT,* 13 (1963), 312; H. Wildberger, *Jesaja. BK,* X/1 (1972), 225.

[10] For the argument against Amos' authorship, see H. W. Wolff, *Joel and Amos. Herm* (Eng. trans. 1977), 160; for a more nuanced discussion, see W. Rudolph, *Amos. KAT,* XIII/2, 120, 134f.; both comms. rightly reject the emendation of *wayyiṭrōp* to *wayyiṭṭōr* (from *nāṭar*) on the basis of the Syriac and Vulg., which was popular at one time; see also S. Wagner, "Überlegungen zur Frage nach den Beziehungen des Propheten Amos zum Südreich," *ThLZ,* 96 (1971), 663ff.

described as roaring lions, tearing the prey (*ṭōrēp̱ ṭārep̱*). The parallels in the context clearly suggest social oppression and exploitation (*nep̱eš 'āḵālû ḥōsen wîqār yiqqāḥû* . . .). The *śāreyhā*, the officials of the land (probably judges), are depicted as wolves tearing the prey (*kiz'ēḇîm ṭōr*ᵉ*pê ṭārep̱*); their activity is likewise characterized as "shedding blood, destroying lives," for the sake of dishonest gain (22:27; cf. Zeph. 3:3f.).[11] In this passage, *ṭārap* and *ṭerep̱* are terms for social injustice.

Ezk. 19:3,6, in a lament for the "princes of Israel," appear to refer to the last representatives of the Davidic monarchy.[12] It is not quite clear whether the comparison of the monarchy and these representatives to a lioness and her young lions has these negative overtones. In the first instance, only the natural behavior of lions is described: the lioness brings up her whelps, and they learn to catch prey (*wayyilmaḏ liṭrāp-ṭerep̱*). But the next clause, *'āḏām 'āḵāl*, is striking. If it is meant to refer to the general nature of royal conduct, a certain antimonarchical element is implied. The lament looks back on the destruction of the Judahite monarchy, described in part by means of the metaphor of a lion hunt (Ezk. 19:2-9).

c. In the individual laments or prayers of those who are unjustly persecuted, the personal enemy is sometimes depicted as a tearing lion. The supplicant turns to Yahweh for help, lest the pursuer (*rōḏēp̱*, Ps. 7:2[1][13]) rend like (*k*ᵉ-) a lion and there be none to rescue (*w*ᵉ*'ēn maṣṣîl*). It has been suggested that in *nap̱šî* as the object of *pen-yiṭrōp̱* we find the original meaning of *nep̱eš* = "throat" (v. 3[2]).

The same idea appears in Ps. 17:12: personal persecutions are like (*dāmâ*) a lion eager to tear (*yiḵsôp̱ liṭrôp̱*). The parallel expressions suggest not only physical violence (vv. 9,11) but also slander or false accusation (v. 10b).

Ps. 22, an individual lament, speaks of a ravening (*ṭōrēp̱*, v. 14[13]) and roaring lion (vv. 14,22[13, 21]), as well as bulls (v. 13[12]), dogs (v. 17[16]), and wild oxen (v. 22[21]), albeit without using *ṭārap* in connection with these other animals. Thus the tearing of prey by a wild beast (usually a lion) can be used as a metaphor to describe the various ways in which one person can be threatened by another.

If Yahweh has come to the supplicant's aid, the hymn of thanksgiving often mentions his former peril, as in Ps. 124:6: "Blessed be Yahweh, who has not given us as prey (*ṭerep̱*) to their teeth!" The action is that of a beast of prey, but the subject is stated to be other people (*'āḏām*) (vv. 2f.,6). In his protestations of innocence, Job states with pride that in earlier days when he was highly esteemed he espoused the cause of the poor and downtrodden, tearing the prey from the fangs of the unrighteous (Job 29:17, where *ṭerep̱* stands for property unlawfully seized by the "fangs" of the unrighteous). Once again the question of social justice is in the background (cf. the context). In another passage (16:9), Job describes his own persecution by an enemy, whose wrath has torn him: this adversary is God himself. All the disasters that have fallen upon Job are a consequence of devastation wrought by God, who tears like a beast of prey in his wrath (*'appô ṭārap̱*). Bildad's charge that Job is tearing himself

---

[11] Zimmerli, *Ezekiel 1*, 469.

[12] See the discussion in *ibid.*, 395f.

[13] Probably to be read as a singular; see H.-J. Kraus, *Psalmen. BK*, XV/1 (^{4}1972), 53.

in his anger (*ṭōrēp̱ napšô be'appô,* 18:4) sounds like a direct response to Job's audacious charge against God.[14]

2. *Figurative Applications to Historical Entities with Positive Meaning.* The metaphor of the tearing lion can also be applied to Israel, individual tribes, or the "remnant of Jacob." In these cases, however, it is understood positively as an image of strength and power, of irresistibility and victory. The points of comparison are the same as in pejorative usage. In the second oracle of Balaam (Nu. 23:24 [E]), Israel is glorified in the simile (with the particle *ke*-) of a lion that rises up and does not lie down until it has devoured its *ṭerep̱* and drunk the blood of the slain. In the tribal sayings of Gen. 49, Judah is singled out for special praise: it is from prey that he rises for further action (*miṭṭerep̱ . . . 'ālîṯā*). He is depicted as a lion (*gûr 'aryēh yehûḏâ,* v. 9), strong, powerful, successful, irresistible. The image of a tearing wolf similarly depicts Benjamin (*binyāmîn ze'ēḇ yiṭrāp̱,* v. 27) as mighty and victorious in battle; both morning and evening he has prey to devour. The saying about Gad in Dt. 33:20 is much later. The image of a lion again depicts his success; the verb *ṭārap̱* is used in the sense of "dismember." The sayings can be interpreted historically.[15]

This imagery is still used in the postexilic period to describe Israel's ascendancy over the nations. The "remnant of Jacob" in the midst of many peoples is like (*ke*-) a lion that treads down and tears to pieces unimpeded (*'ašer 'im 'āḇar werāmas weṭārap̱ we'ên maṣṣîl,* Mic. 5:7[8]). In all these descriptions, the imagery is meant to express the special blessing possessed by Israel, its might and special position among the nations.

3. *Usage with Yahweh as Subject.* In a few passages, *ṭārap̱* is used as a metaphor for Yahweh's actions in judgment and salvation. The clearest instance is Hosea's oracle of disaster addressed to "Ephraim" (Hos. 5:14 and context). Here it is Yahweh himself who attacks Israel with violence, not some other power like the Assyrians. The Syro-Ephraimite War is lost, "for," says the threat, with Yahweh speaking in the 1st person, "I will be like a lion to Ephraim, and like a young lion to the house of Judah. I, even I, will rend and go away, I will carry off, and none shall rescue." The prayer of repentance in Hos. 6:1 refers to this image by calling for return to the one who has torn, since he alone can heal. The image of a lion depicts Yahweh in his destructive power.[16]

The oracle concerning Assyria in Isa. 31:4 draws on the same set of ideas. This time, however, Yahweh takes the part of Jerusalem and Judah against those who afflict the people of God. We may also recall Job's audacious description of the violence he sees inflicted on him by God, in which Yahweh in his wrath acts like a tearing beast of prey (Job 16:9).

---

14 Cf. A. Weiser, *Das Buch Hiob. ATD,* XIII (⁶1974), *in loc.;* G. Fohrer, *Das Buch Hiob. KAT,* XVI (1963), 296f., deletes the passage as an explanatory gloss, probably mistakenly.

15 See H.-J. Zobel, *Stammesspruch und Geschichte. BZAW,* 95 (1965); K.-D. Schunck, *Benjamin. BZAW,* 86 (1963).

16 Cf. H. W. Wolff, *Hosea. Herm* (Eng. trans. 1974), 117.

That this imagery also found its way into cultic and liturgical documents is shown by Ps. 50:22, in the context of a prophetic judgment liturgy that is probably postexilic.[17] A warning is addressed to those who would forget God, citing a 1st-person divine oracle: *pen-'eṭrōp̱ we'ên maṣṣîl,* "lest I rend, and there be none to deliver." The terrible acts that Yahweh is capable of inflicting on the wicked and negligent are depicted appropriately by this harsh term *ṭārap̱.* Yahweh is not explicitly called a lion, but the verb inevitably brings to mind a beast of prey. The occurrence in Ps. 76:5(4), in a hymn to the might of the God of Zion, is unfortunately in a corrupt passage.[18] It is barely possible to extract the following sense from the MT: "Terrible art thou [emendation based on the Syriac and Targum], mightier than one who makes [or: has] mountains of spoil." Of course, this reading itself presupposes an interpretation of *'addîr mēharerê-ṭārep̱.*

Wagner

---

[17] *Kraus, BK,* XV/1, *in loc.;* see also G. Fohrer, *IntrodOT* (Eng. trans., Nashville, 1968).

[18] See the apparatus in *BHK*³ and *BHS* for the attempts at reconstruction, which have a long history; see also the discussion in the comms.

יאל *y'l*

Contents: I. Etymology and Grammar. II. Meaning and Use. III. Denominative.

I. Etymology and Grammar. The verb *y'l* has been the subject of much etymological speculation, as though this could penetrate to the heart of the word. Like many other words, it has been associated with the root *'wl,* of which Buhl says: "This root is the basis of a great number of words, whose meanings are so diverse that it must represent the coalescence of a variety of originally independent roots." The derivation from *'wl,* proposed by Haupt,[1] is based on an analogy suggested by de Lagarde, who pointed out the similarity to Arab. *'āwwal;* Haupt related the root to *wa'ala.* Pedersen[2] preferred to focus on the use of the verb instead of a dubious etymology. He called *y'l* a verb that, by virtue of its meaning, has the character of an auxiliary, such as "begin," "stop," "do again," etc. The syntax of these verbs often involves a main verb in the infinitive construct, with or without *le-,* for example, *hô'altî ledabbēr,* "I have taken upon myself to speak" (Gen. 18:27). But the syntax can also involve a main verb in the same form as the auxiliary without any connective

---

y'l. P. Haupt, "The Etymology of Mohel, Circumciser," *AJSL,* 22 (1905/1906), 249-256; P. A. de Lagarde, *Übersicht über die im aramäischen, arabischen und hebräischen übliche Bildung der Nomina* (Göttingen, 1889).

[1] P. 255.

[2] J. P. E. Pedersen, *Hebraeisk grammatik* (Copenhagen, ²1933; repr. 1950), 234.

particle, for example, *hô'alnû wannēšeḇ,* "would that we had been content to dwell beyond the Jordan" (Josh. 7:7). The two examples show that the translation must vary with the context.

II. Meaning and Use. The meaning varies with the situation. If one takes the basic meaning of the Arabic as the point of departure, it may be possible to postulate a meaning "be first," as Köhler does, but this meaning is hardly appropriate in actual contexts. The most frequent use suggests that the verb refers to a beginning that is not easy, a beginning made difficult by a sense of modesty, politeness, or some other obstacle. But this meaning can be extended to "undertake" or "decide to do" something. The phrase *hô'altî l^eḏabbēr* (Gen. 18:27,31) cited above can also be translated: "Only with difficulty have I decided to speak."

The occurrences of the verb are therefore open to a variety of translations. In Ex. 2:21, we read: *wayyô'el mōšeh lāšeḇeṯ 'eṯ-hā'îš,* which Noth translates: "Moses found himself ready to stay with the man."[3] The RSV reads: "And Moses was content to dwell with the man"; the NEB: "So it came about that Moses agreed to live with the man." One might say simply: "Moses decided to stay with the man." The difficult beginning is clear in Jgs. 1:27,35, but there is no beginning involved in Josh. 17:12: "The Canaanites persisted in dwelling in that land." The two imperatives in Jgs. 19:6, *hô'el-nā' w^elîn,* are usually translated: "Do me the favor of spending the night." In Dt. 1:5, the author may also be suggesting a difficult beginning: "Moses began to explain." Jgs. 17:11 may involve an element of consent, but the most likely translation is: "He decided." It is possible that 1 S. 12:22 exhibits a similar meaning: "It has pleased Yahweh to make you a people for himself"; but it is also possible to translate: "Yahweh had already begun to make you a people for himself." The same problem seems to be present also in 1 Ch. 17:27; here, too, the first translation is usually preferred: "Now therefore may it please thee to bless the house of thy servant, that it may continue for ever."

The notion of "being pleased" is found also in 2 S. 7:29; 2 K. 5:23; 6:3; Job 6:9,28; Hos. 5:11; this is doubtless the situation in many instances. But the "pleasure" often appears to be more forced that joyous, involving an element of concession, although this is not always the case.

III. Denominative. There is a second verb *y'l,* deriving from → אויל *'^ewîl* [*'^evîl*], "fool"; it is used in the niphal with the meaning "be a fool, act foolishly" (Nu. 12:11; Jer. 5:4) or "prove oneself a fool" (Isa. 19:13; Jer. 50:36; Sir. 37:19). This verb is restricted in both use and meaning.

Kapelrud

---

[3] M. Noth, *Exodus. OTL* (Eng. trans. 1962), 28.

יְאֹר *y^{e}'ōr*

Contents: I. Occurrences and Etymology. II. Egyptian Background. III. Yahweh and the Nile. IV. Mythology. V. The Nile in Sirach.

I. Occurrences and Etymology. The noun *y^{e}'ōr*/*y^{e}'ôr* (plene 6 times) occurs 45 times in the OT in the singular as a term for the Nile;[1] there are 3 additional passages in Sirach (Sir. 39:22; 47:14; also 24:27 conj.[2]). The plural occurs 16 times, designating the delta branches or channels of the Nile. In Dnl. 12:5-7 *y^{e}'ōr* refers to the Tigris, in Job 28:10 to a water tunnel.

The noun derives from Egyp. *ỉtrw* (written *ỉrw* from the eighteenth dynasty on).[3] When it was borrowed by Hebrew, it was probably pronounced *ya'ru(w);* in the Amarna period the *a* became *o,* leading to the Hebrew pronunciation *yōr.*[4]

The OT also uses the word *šîḥôr,* "Pool of Horus," for the Nile (Josh. 13:3; 1 Ch. 13:5; Isa. 23:3; Jer. 2:18).

Despite its foreign etymology, *y^{e}'ōr* does not seem to have been taken as a proper name; it is usually used with the article (always in Genesis, Exodus, and Daniel). Only in Job 28:10; Isa. 19:7; Ezk. 30:12 is it used absolutely. In Isa. 7:18; Am. 8:8; 9:5 *miṣrāyim* is added, and in 2 K. 19:24; Isa. 19:6; 37:25 *māṣôr,* as though the term needs further definition.

The same conclusion is suggested by the LXX, which uses *potamós* not only for *nāhār* but also for *y^{e}'ōr* (50 times, as against 4 for *diṓryx*). This interpretation also allows Daniel to use *y^{e}'ōr* for the Tigris. In a few cases, *nāhār* is also used for the Nile (Isa. 19:5; Jer. 46:7f.; Ezk. 32:2); in addition, *n^{e}hārîm* in Isa. 18:2,7 probably refers to the Blue Nile and the White Nile. It is also noteworthy that the LXX uses *Gēṓn* in Jer. 2:18 (for *šîḥôr*) and Sir. 24:27, identifying the Nile with the second of the rivers of Paradise.[5]

Eising

---

y^{e}'ôr. D. Bonneau, *La crue du Nil, divinité égyptienne* (Paris, 1964); A. de Buck, "On the Meaning of the Name *Ḥ'pj,*" *Orientalia Neerlandica,* 1948, 1-22; J. A. Fitzmyer, *The Genesis Apocryphon of Qumran Cave I. BietOr,* 18A (^{2}1971), 108-110,152f.; A. Hermann, "Der Nil und die Christen," *JAC,* 2 (1959), 30-69; T. O. Lambdin, "Egyptian Loan Words in the OT," *JAOS,* 73 (1953), 145-155; S. Morenz, *Die Geschichte von Joseph dem Zimmermann. TU,* 56 (1951), 29-34; *idem, Egyptian Religion* (Eng. trans., Ithaca, N. Y., 1973); C. H. A. Palanque, *Le Nil à l'époque pharaonique, son rôle et son culte en Égypte. Bibliothèque de l'école des hautes études,* 144 (1903); K. H. Rengstorf, "ποταμός," *TDNT,* VI, 595-607; P. Reymond, *L'eau, sa vie, et sa signification dans l'AT. SVT,* 6 (1958); A. Schwarzenbach, *Die geographische Terminologie im Hebräischen des ATs* (Leiden, 1954), 64f.; B. H. Stricker, *De overstroming van de Nijl. MEOL,* 11 (1956); W. Vycichl, "Ägyptische Ortsnamen in der Bibel," *ZÄS,* 76 (1940), 79-93.

[1] Cf. also the conjecture in Isa. 33:21b by H. Gunkel, "Jesaia 33, eine prophetische Liturgie," *ZAW,* 42 (1924), 179.

[2] Cf. N. Peters, *EHAT,* XXV (1913), 204.

[3] *WbÄS,* I, 146.

[4] Vycichl, 82.

[5] → גִּיחוֹן *gîḥôn.*

II. Egyptian Background. The use of the Egyptian name for the Nile in the OT raises the question whether we may also find Egyptian ideas concerning the Nile.[6] With respect to religious ideas and cultic practices, the answer is negative.

The Egyptians worshipped the Nile—or rather its annual inundation—as a god, with the name Ḥapi (*ḥ'py*).[7] The Nile was commonly associated with the primal sea Nun,[8] and both were termed "father of the gods." The Nile was thought to rise from the depths of the earth as two springs; these were originally located in the vicinity of Silsile,[9] later in the vicinity of the first cataract, at Elephantine.[10]

The Nile was considered primordial, and could be addressed accordingly as "the only one who has called himself into being." At Elephantine, the chief god Khnum was protector of the sources of the Nile and thus also giver of the inundation. Other deities also appear in the same role, e.g., Amon-Re, Aten, Sobk, and Isis (often as Isis-Sothis). Osiris is well attested as lord of the Nile's inundation; indeed, he is often identified with the water of the Nile. The identification of the Nile with Osiris gave rise to the late belief that death in the Nile effects deification. There is also a pair of Nile deities, interpreted as the Nile-gods of Upper and Lower Egypt. In addition, the late temples contain illustrations depicting long processions of Nile-gods presenting to the chief god of the temple the offerings of the nomes they represent. These deities have characteristic fat bodies and pendulous breasts.

Special feasts were observed to celebrate the Nile, which was extolled as "the great Nile, bringing life to the whole land through its foodstuffs." Several hymns to the Nile have been preserved.[11] Kings and princes can boast that they are "the Nile to their people."[12]

Bergman

III. Yahweh and the Nile. In Genesis and Exodus the Nile is not deified; in the Joseph narrative it amounts to little more than a large river. In Pharaoh's dream, the fat cows and the thin cows come out of the Nile (Gen. 41:1-3,17ff.), which might suggest that the land depends on it for fertility or famine. But it should be noted that the full ears and withered ears are not explicitly associated with the Nile. The emergence of the cows from the Nile could also be due to their being pastured near the river. In any case, there is considerable evidence that the Israelites were familiar with the Nile and its surroundings. The volume of the Nile and its rising made a deep impression. A city surrounded by such a wide river enjoys special protection (Nah. 3:8). It provides drinking water (Ex. 7:18f.) and brings fertility to the land. Fishing and farming depend on it, including the growing of flax, on which weavers and rope makers depend for their livelihood (Isa. 19:5-9). Vessels of papyrus are used for traffic on the Nile (Isa. 18:2). But when the river dries up, its canals become foul (Isa. 19:6f.)

---

6 Cf. *RÄR*, 525ff.; Palanque, Bonneau.

7 *WbÄS*, III, 42; de Buck.

8 *WbÄS*, Bel. II, 215, 9f.

9 The Nile stela found there (nineteenth dynasty): P. Barguet, *BIFAO*, 50 (1952), 49-63.

10 Cf. Herodotus ii.28.

11 *ANET*³, 372f.

12 H. Grapow, *Die bildlichen Ausdrücke des Ägyptischen* (Leipzig, 1924), 62.

and swarms of flies can appear, which can symbolize the Egyptian army (Isa. 7:18). Modern biology can connect the third of the Egyptian plagues, the plague of gnats, with the Nile; but Ex. 8:12(Eng. v. 16) and Wis. 19:10 think that the gnats were brought forth from the sand by God's power.

The plague narratives of Exodus frequently connect the Nile with acts of God. God turns its water into blood and causes frogs to infest the land. Ex. 4:9 already assigns Moses a sign making use of water from the Nile, which will turn into blood when Moses pours it on the ground. In the first plague, this takes place when Moses stretches out his staff over the river (Ex. 7:18,20). Initially y^{e}*'ōr* is used here in the singular (Ex. 4:9; 7:15,17f.,20f.,25,28; 8:5,7[9,11]; 17:5); in 7:19, however, the plural and three additional terms for bodies of water express the universality of the punishment. But it is also possible that "the Niles" refers to the several branches of the river at its mouth; cf. Ex. 8:1(5) in the case of the plague of frogs, as well as Ps. 78:44. Despite the similarity of these events to natural phenomena like the fertile mud that clouds the water and the frogs that are always present in the Nile, Exodus is concerned to point out that everything is at God's behest.

Am. 8:8 and 9:5 refer in the first instance to an earthquake brought about by God, but it is likened to the rising and falling of the Nile. We may therefore conclude that these movements of the Nile also depend on God's power. God can even cause the mighty Nile to dry up (Isa. 19:5-9), so that it becomes foul and all who depend on it must suffer.

IV. Mythology. In these passages, God uses the Nile to demonstrate his power; there are other passages in the prophets that appear to associate mythological conceptions with the Nile.

In Ezk. 29:3-5, y^{e}*'ōr* occurs 6 times; the king of Egypt boasts that the Niles (i.e., the branches of the Nile[13]) belong to him, that he has even made them. In Egyptian texts, Amon-Re is the lord and creator of the Nile; Pharaoh thus proclaims himself lord of the Nile and therefore divine, placing himself in conflict with the true God of Israel. The latter responds to Pharaoh's boast, addressing him three times, speaking of "your Nile" and calling him "the great crocodile that lies between the arms of the Nile" (29:3). That Yahweh is the true lord of the Nile and of the Nile-god Pharaoh he demonstrates by catching the crocodile, drawing it up with all the fish out of the stream, and casting it forth into the wilderness (29:4f.).

This passage should be compared with the lament over Pharaoh in Ezk. 32; here the word y^{e}*'ōr* does not appear, but its waters and those of the sea are called *mayim* and n^{e}*hārôṯ*. As in chap. 29, however, the crocodile is captured in a net and cast forth upon the dry land (32:3-6). The destruction of Pharaoh and all the foes of Israel described here (vv. 13f.) is coupled with a promise to the now subject nations; when it is fulfilled, "then they will know that I am Yahweh" (v. 15). An important element here is the accusation against the crocodile: "You have bubbled with your nostrils, clouded the waters with your feet, and muddied their rivers" (v. 2).[14] What seems at

[13] Cf. W. Zimmerli, *Ezekiel 2. Herm* (Eng. trans. 1983), 110.
[14] *Ibid.*, 154.

first glance to be the natural behavior of a crocodile in the Nile may be an echo of "the mythological background of political hegemony,"[15] because the rising of the Nile and the fertile mud that clouds it appear to be understood as the work of the crocodile. We may think of the crocodile-god Sobk, the lord and giver of the Nile at Fayyum, where he had a temple at Crocodilopolis; here the inundation of the Nile was also celebrated.[16] It is of course strange that the crocodile-god was worshipped in Egypt while at the same time the crocodile was an object of fear, against which magical spells were employed.[17]

Job 40:25f.(41:1f.) provides additional evidence of a mythological background. In order to demonstrate his power in contrast to human impotence, God asks Job: "Can you draw out the crocodile with a fishhook, or . . . put a rope in his nose?" "Crocodile" here translates → לִוְיָתָן *liwyāṯān,* which Yahweh will kill along with the "dragon in the sea" (Isa. 27:1). This triumph of Yahweh is also extolled in Ps. 74:14: "Thou didst crush the heads of Leviathan, thou didst give him as food, as fodder for the jackals."[18] All this is in agreement with our *y*^e^*'ōr* passages Ezk. 29:4f. and 32:3-5. Job 3:8 also alludes to a mythological dawn of time, and Ps. 104:26 says that God created Leviathan "for the sport of it."

The mythological Rahab (→ רהב *rhb*) also belongs in this context. In passages like Ps. 87:4(3) and Isa. 30:7, Rahab is only a poetic term for Egypt, but all other passages involve more. Ps. 89:10f.(9f.) speaks of a raging of the sea that is stilled by God and of a crushed Rahab; the verses occur in a context describing God's creation of the world and his dominion over it. Isa. 51:9 also mentions the primal age explicitly. The sea and Rahab are also mentioned together in Isa. 51:9; Ps. 89:10f.(9f.); Job 26:12f. All these passages, as well as Job 9:13,[19] share a common subject: God's victory in battle over the primeval waters.

The fact that God shows his power by drying up the sea or the great waters is in harmony with his ability to dry up the Nile (Isa. 19:6f.). The drying up of the Nile as a sign of power is also mentioned in 2 K. 19:24 par. Isa. 37:25; Zec. 10:11. It is Sennacherib who boasts that he "dried up all the streams of Egypt," thus claiming divine power. He has not stopped to consider that what he claims to have done was planned by God "from the days of old" (2 K. 19:25 par. Isa. 37:26). In the face of Sennacherib's arrogance, God asserts his superiority by "putting a ring through his nose" and "placing a bit in his mouth" (2 K. 19:28 par. Isa. 37:29). This is similar to what befalls the crocodile in Job 40:25(41:1) and Ezk. 29:4, but it could also describe the fate of other kings taken captive by the king of Assyria.[20]

Jer. 46:7-9 compares the pharaoh Necho and his army to the Nile. The rising of the Nile represents the mighty army of Egypt; Pharaoh boasts that his power is like the

---

15 *Ibid.*, 159.

16 *RÄR*, 394, 755f.

17 *RÄR*, 392-94.

18 H. Gunkel, *Einleitung in die Psalmen. HAT,* II/2 (1933), 321; R. Kittel, *Die Psalmen. KAT,* XIII (5,6 1929), 249.

19 Cf. F. Horst, *Hiob. BK*, XVI (1968), 147f.

20 *VAB*, 7, 80; 9, 107; *AOB*, no. 144.

inundation of the land, destroying the cities and their inhabitants (v. 8). Here, too, God triumphs over such arrogance; his "day of vengeance" is coming (v. 10), although this time not represented by the drying up of the Nile.

According to Zec. 10:10-12, God will smite the waves of the sea on behalf of his people and cause the Nile to dry up. The statement that Assyria will also be laid low is probably unconnected with the fate of the crocodile in Ezk. 29:3.

In both Isa. 33:21 and Nah. 3:8, a wide river brings security and blessing to a city. Since "broad rivers and streams" are promised Jerusalem in Isa. 33:21, the much debated passage probably refers to an act of God involving the water of salvation and fertility, assuming that the name of Yahweh or the mention of him in *'addîr* is retained.[21] Whether one finds here a statement that God will be a mighty protection "in place of" broad rivers depends on the interpretation of *māqôm;* König[22] proposes that in the eschaton God himself will personally take over the protection of his people. In the case of the sun's light, an eschatological promise assumes that God himself, rather than sun and moon, will be the everlasting sun of Zion (Isa. 60:19f.). But to use our passage by itself to suggest this "in place of" also for the river and its life-giving water is risky, even though it is not uncommon to find a spring and streams of water in association with Zion as an eschatological motif (Ps. 36:9f.[8f.]; 46:5[4]; 65:10[9]; Ezk. 47:1-12; Joel 4:18[3:18]).[23] In Jer. 17:13, Yahweh is even called "the fountain of living water" (cf. also Isa. 8:6; 11:9; 12:3).

V. The Nile in Sirach. The 3 passages in Sirach are based on the notion of the Nile as a symbol of fertility and the wellspring of God's salvation. In Sir. 39:22, "His (God's) blessing overflows like the Nile" refers to the fertility of the land, vouchsafed by God, since the antithesis in v. 23 states that Yahweh's wrath creates a salt desert. Sir. 24:27 says of the book of God's covenant, "It overflows with instruction like the Nile,"[24] an image for the overflowing riches of the law.

Sir. 47:14 states that Solomon "overflows with knowledge like the Nile." The author uses the simile of the Nile to say how rich and abounding in wisdom this idealized king is.

Eising

---

21 In favor, for example: B. Duhm, *Jesaja. GHK,* III/1 (^{5}1968), 246; O. Procksch, *Jesaja I. KAT,* IX/1 (1930), 421; change to *yihyeh,* for example: J. Ziegler, *Das Buch Isaias. EB,* III (1958), 108; O. Kaiser, *Isaiah 13–39. OTL* (Eng. trans. 1974), *in loc.*

22 E. König, *Das Buch Jesaja* (Gütersloh, 1926), 289.

23 Cf. H.-J. Kraus, *Psalmen. BK,* XV (^{4}1972), 343f.; W. Zimmerli, *Ezekiel 2,* 510.

24 Cf. N. Peters, *EHAT,* XXV, 205.

יבל *ybl;* יבול *y^e^bûl*

Contents: I. Etymology. II. Ancient Near East: 1. Akkadian; 2. Ugaritic; 3. Aramaic; 4. Phoenician and Punic. III. The Verb *ybl.* IV. The Noun *y^e^ḇûl.*

I. Etymology. West Semitic *ybl* (found in Hebrew, Aramaic, Ugaritic, and Phoenician/Punic) corresponds to *wbl* in the other Semitic languages.[1]

In Old Babylonian and Old Akkadian, the first radical *w* is represented by the sign PI, which stands for *wa, wi, wu,* and occasionally *b* (cf. *bābilu*). In Middle Babylonian, Middle Assyrian, and later, the *w* is either not represented at all orthographically or is represented by signs that normally stand for *m* followed by a vowel.[2] A secondary root *tabālu* also came into existence in Akkadian, expressing movement away from a given point of reference: "carry away, take away."

Other verbs with a weak first radical have given rise to secondary roots beginning with *t* in Akkadian: *awû* (**hwy?*) and *taw/mû,* "speak, swear"; *abākū* and *tabāku,* "turn upside down, pour out";[3] *wukkūlu* (D stem of *wkl*) and *takālu,* "(en)trust";[4] *warû* and *tarû,* "bring, lead."[5] Like other roots beginning with *w, wbl/ybl* exhibits some forms (primarily imperatives of the G stem and certain verbal nouns) that do not have the initial syllable of *w* followed by a vowel, as though we were dealing with an originally biliteral root *bl.*[6]

The Akkadian noun *biltu,* "burden, talent, yield, tribute," derives from the shorter root *bl,* as may *bu/ibbulu,* "inundation, flood," and *bibiltu,* "decimation, destruction." Since an emphatic *l* is sometimes represented orthographically in hieroglyphic Egyptian by *n* or *r,* Egyp. *bnbn,* "flow (as a river)," and *bnn,* "overflow, beget," could be considered related. All the verbs associated with this root share the notion of linear motion, with the emphasis sometimes on appearance (*y^e^ḇûl,* "produce, yield," Egyp. *bnn,* "beget"), sometimes on disappearance (Akk. *bu/ibbulu,* "inundation, flood," *bibiltu,* "destruction," Heb. *mabbûl,* "flood."

II. Ancient Near East.

1. *Akkadian.* The Akkadian verb *wabālu* has several meanings: "present (offerings), surrender (animals) for use, prepare (a tablet or letter), transport (goods), carry (a load), wash away (by water), accompany or guide (persons)."

---

ybl. R. Dussaud, *Les origines cananéennes du sacrifice israélite* (Paris, ^{2}1941); H. A. Hoffner, *Alimenta Hethaeorum: Food Production in Hittite Asia Minor. AOS,* 55 (1974); M. J. Lagrange, *Études sur les religions sémitiques. ÉtB* (^{2}1905); S. Moscati, *An Introduction to the Comparative Grammar of the Semitic Languages. PLO,* N.S. 6 (^{2}1969).

1 Moscati, no. 8, 64f.
2 Cf. *GaG,* §21.
3 Cf. *CAD,* I/1 (1964), 8f., *abāku* B.
4 Cf. von Soden, *Ergänzungsheft zum GAG. AnOr,* 47 (1969), §103d.
5 Cf. *GaG,* §§102m, 103d.
6 Moscati, no. 16, 119; *GaG,* §103; *UT,* §9.48.

The related nouns are: *babbilu/bābilu,* "bearer, tenant"; *bu/ibbulu; bibiltu;*[7] *bibil libbi,* "desire"; *biblu,* "dowry, yield, flood"; *bibil pāni,* "reconciliation"; *biltu;*[8] *mubabbilu,* "bearer"; *šē/ubultu/šūbiltu,* "shipment, transport"; *šutabultu,* "mixture"; *tabālu,* "carry away."

2. *Ugaritic.* In Ugaritic texts, the verb *ybl,* "bring, expedite," is used in the simple stem, in contrast to Biblical Hebrew, where it occurs only in the hiphil or hophal. It is found with the following objects: tribute (*'rgmn, mnḥ*), gift or payment (*trḫ,* "bride-price"; *ksp,* "pay"; *ks,* "gift"; *qš,* "present"; *3lqṣm* [a kind of stone]; *qšt,* "bow"), message (*rgm, bšrt*). The verb has the meaning "furnish with" in conjunction with straps (*qblbl*). The noun *ybl* (vocalized **yabul,* the passive of the simple stem) is found in the phrase *ybl 'rṣ* (cf. Heb. *y^e^bûl hā'āreṣ*), "produce of the earth, that which the earth brings forth."[9]

3. *Aramaic.* In Ya'udic and Imperial Aramaic, *ybl* occurs with the meaning "bring, transport."[10] According to *DISO,* the verb occurs only in the qal or simple stem, whereas *KAI*[11] postulates the D stem for Ya'udic. A noun *ybl,* "income, revenue," is found in the fragmentary context of Panammuwa 21.[12]

4. *Phoenician and Punic.* In the Amarna tablets,[13] the Canaanite substrate has occasioned *ūbil* (for *yōbil?*), the active participle of the G stem, instead of the expected *bābil.* In the Marseilles sacrificial tariff (Punic),[14] *ybl* refers to a sacrificial animal, probably a sheep or ram. The vocalization *yābil* and the meaning are confirmed by Akk. *yābilu,* "sheep, ram,"[15] a Neo-Assyrian loanword from West Semitic → יובל *yôḇēl.* According to Dussaud,[16] *ybl* designates a castrated animal, *'yl* an uncastrated animal.

III. The Verb ybl. In the OT, the verb *hôḇîl* and its pass. *hûḇal* are used for the escorting of important persons, often in ceremonial contexts. In Ps. 45:15f.(Eng. vv. 14f.), for example, the foreign princess (*baṯ-meleḵ*), who has been selected to be the bride of the Judahite king, is led to him with her escort of virgins (*b^e^ṯûlôṯ*). Ps. 60:11(9) and 108:11(10) describe the retinue God provides for the victorious Judahite king in the conquered enemy city (*'îr māṣôr*); the attendance of Yahweh provides not only glory but security (cf. the following verses in each Psalm). According to Isa.

---

7 See above.

8 See above.

9 *UT,* no. 1064; *WUS,* no. 1129; cf. IV below.

10 *DISO,* 103.

11 II, 229.

12 Lagrange, 497, and G. A. Cooke, *A Text-Book of North Semitic Inscriptions* (Oxford, 1903), 180; cf. *KAI,* 215.21, which does not recognize such a noun.

13 EA 287, 55.

14 *CIS,* I, 165; *KAI,* 69.7.

15 *AHw,* I, 411; *CAD,* VII (1960), 321.

16 Pp. 139f.

55:12, the accompanying presence of Yahweh furnishes security (*b^e šālôm*), happiness, and rejoicing (*yipṣ^e ḥû . . . rinnâ*) when the exiled Jews depart from Babylon and return to their homeland. The mountains, the hills, and the trees of the field will sing and clap their hands. A corpse is also escorted ceremoniously to the grave (Job 10:19; 21:32).

A second major semantic component of the verb is the offering of gifts or tribute to a superior in order to obtain his favor. Tribute (*šāy,* Ps. 68:30[29]; 76:12[11]; Isa. 18:7 or *minḥâ,* Hos. 10:6; Zeph. 3:10[17]) is brought to kings throughout the OT and offered to them (Hos. 10:6; *minḥâ* is also used as the object of the hiphil of → בוא *bô'* [Gen. 4:3; 43:26; Lev. 2:8; 1 S. 10:27; 1 K. 10:25; etc.], the hiphil of *qrb* [Lev. 2:14; 9:17; Jgs. 3:18; etc.], and *šālaḥ* [Jgs. 3:15, etc.]). But just as in the political sphere the inferior king (the vassal) brings tribute to the superior king (cf. Ugar. *dybl lšpš mlk rb*) so Ps. 68:30(29) expects that kings will bring their tribute to Yahweh: *l^e ḵā yôḇîlû m^e lāḵîm šāy.* Israel is Yahweh's people and the Israelites are his subjects. As such, they bring him their gifts and offerings as a kind of tribute. Therefore the verb *hôḇîl* is also used for the bringing of a sacrificial animal to the temple for slaughter (Isa. 53:7, *kaśśeh laṭṭeḇaḥ;* Jer. 11:19, *k^e ḵeḇeś . . . liṭbôaḥ*). In Job 21:30, we appear to have the same use of *yôḇîlû* as in the Akkadian idiom *pānī wabālu,* "forgive, spare, show favor";[18] cf. *ḥillâ pānîm*[19] and Akk. *bibil pānī,* "reconciliation."

IV. The Noun y^e ḇûl. The noun *y^e ḇûl,* formally a passive participle, confirms the use of the qal in the early period of the language. Although it is possible that the hiphil and hophal replaced the original use of the qal in early Hebrew, it is more likely that *y^e ḇûl* was borrowed from a Canaanite dialect in which the qal of *ybl* was the normal form of the verb. This was the case in Ugaritic and Punic;[20] in Ugaritic we even find the phrase *ybl 'rṣ.* As a passive, *y^e ḇûl* refers to the produce of the land (*y^e ḇûl hā'āreṣ/hā'^a ḏāmâ*) or of the vine (*y^e ḇûl bagg^e pānîm,* Hab. 3:17). Since practically all plants are dependent on the soil, the semantic range of *y^e ḇûl* is very broad and deliberately vague, although (in contrast to *p^e rî*) it never refers explicitly to the fruit of trees.

The Vulg. translates *y^e ḇûl* as *fructus* (Ps. 78:46[Vulg. 77:46]; 85:13[12, Vulg. 84:13]) *germen* (Lev. 26:4,20; Dt. 11:16; 32:22; Ezk. 34:27; Hab. 3:17; Hag. 1:10; Zec. 8:12), *in herbis cuncta* (Jgs. 6:4), and *proventus* (Ps. 78:46). The LXX usually translates it as *karpós* (Dt. 11:17; Jgs. 6:4; Ps. 78:46[LXX 77:46]; 85:13[12, LXX 84:13]), less frequently as *gennḗmata* (Lev. 26:4; Dt. 32:22; Hab. 3:17), *ischýs* (Ezk. 34:27), *ekphória* (Hag. 1:10), or *spóros* (Lev. 26:20). From the versions we would conclude that this word was not found originally in Job 20:28.

In terms of the immediate sense of the word, it is not Yahweh who gives *y^e ḇûl;* it is the land (*hā'āreṣ* or *hā'^a dāmâ*) that gives (*nāṯan,* Lev. 26:4, 20; Dt. 11:17; Ps.

---

[17] Cf. II.2 above, Ugar. *'rgmn* and *mnḥ.*

[18] *CAD,* I/1, 18; A. Goetze, "Fifty Old-Babylonian Letters from Ḥarmal," *Sumer,* 14 (1958), 28ff.

[19] → חלה *ḥālâ* [*chālāh*].

[20] See above.

67:7[6]; 85:13[12]; Ezk. 34:27; Zec. 8:12; cf. with *p^e rî* [Lev. 25:19; 26:4,20; Ps. 1:3; Ezk. 34:27; Zec. 8:12; etc.]) or withholds its produce, through human agency. Of course Yahweh is always presupposed as the ultimate causality. The *y^e ḇûl* of the land depends on Yahweh's favor towards his people. If he is angry, the earth withholds its *y^e ḇûl* (Hag. 1:10), or the fire of Yahweh's wrath (*'ēš . . . b^e' appî*) devours the earth and its *y^e ḇûl* (Dt. 32:22). A similar fate overtakes the enemies of Yahweh. He inflicts his wrath upon Egypt by giving its *y^e ḇûl* to the caterpillar (*ḥāsîl*, Ps. 78:46).

The noun is not used metaphorically for human actions, like *p^e rî* and its Greek translation *karpós*.[21]

The OT has many synonyms for *y^e ḇûl: dāgān, šeḇer, karmel, '^a ḇûr, qāṣîr, p^e rî, t^e ḇû'â, bar.* It cannot be determined with certainty that *y^e ḇûl* was the preferred term for agricultural produce in any of the major source documents of the OT. In the Hexateuch, it is used by both D (Dt. 11:17; 32:22; Jgs. 6:4) and P (Lev. 26:4,20; cf. Ezk. 34:27). It is also used by Habakkuk (Hab. 3:17) and the postexilic prophets (Hag. 1:10; Zec. 8:12). Even though there is no undisputed occurrence of the term in the early biblical sources, the Ugaritic evidence suggests that it was used in Hebrew at an early date.

Hoffner

---

[21] Cf. F. Hauck, "καρπός," *TDNT,* III, 614f.

יבם *ybm;* יָבָם *yāḇām;* יְבָמָה *y^e ḇāmâ*

Contents: I. 1. Meanings and Occurrences; 2. Statistics; 3. The Root in Other Semitic Languages; 4. Etymology; 5. Versions. II. The Institution of Levirate Marriage: 1. Israel; 2. Ancient Near East.

---

ybm. S. Belkin, "Levirate and Agnate Marriage in Rabbinic and Cognate Literature," *JQR,* N.S. 60 (1969/1970), 275-329; M. Burrows, "Levirate Marriage in Israel," *JBL,* 59 (1940), 23-33; *idem,* "The Marriage of Boaz and Ruth," *JBL,* 59 (1940), 445-454; *idem,* "The Ancient Oriental Background of Hebrew Levirate Marriage," *BASOR,* 77 (1940), 2-15; E. Chiera, *Mixed Texts. Publications of the Baghdad School,* 5 (1934); G. R. Driver and H. C. Miles, *The Assyrian Laws* (Oxford, 1935), 240ff.; H. Gese, M. Höfner, and W. Rudolph, *Die Religionen Altsyriens, Altarabiens und der Mandäer. RdM,* 10/2 (1970), 1-232; S. D. F. Goitein, "Zur heutigen Praxis der Leviratsehe bei orientalischen Juden," *JPOS,* 13 (1933), 159-166; C. H. Gordon, *Ugaritic Literature. SPIB,* 98 (1949); J. Gray, *The Legacy of Canaan. SVT,* 5 (²1965); F. Horst, "Leviratsehe," *RGG³*, IV, 338f.; P. Koschaker, "Zum Levirat nach hethitischem Recht," *RHA,* 2 (1933), 77-89; D. A. Leggett, *The Levirate and Goel Institutions in the OT* (Cherry Hill, N.J., 1974) (with bibliog.); J. M. Mittelmann, *Der altisraelitische Levirat* (Leipzig, 1934); J. Morgenstern, "The Book of the Covenant, Part II," *HUCA,* 7 (1930), 19-258, esp. 159ff.; A. F. Puukko, "Die leviratsehe in den altorientalischen Gesetzen," *ArOr,* 17/2 (1949), 296-99; L. I. Rabinowitz, "Levirate Marriage and Ḥaliẓah," *EncJud,* XI, 122-131; K. H.

I. 1. *Meanings and Occurrences.* The root *ybm* refers to a special kind of relationship by marriage,[1] i.e., the relationship between members of two families that has come into being through the marriage of persons belonging to these families. The crux of the relationship is defined by the directives in Dt. 25:5-10. Here *ybm* relates the brother (*yāḇām*) of a man who has died without a son to the latter's widow, who is termed *yᵉḇāmâ** (or *yāḇemeṯ**) in relationship to "her" *yāḇām*. It is implicit in the term that the *yāḇām* is obligated to take "his" *yᵉḇāmâ* in levirate marriage (piel of *ybm*). In the narrative in Gen. 38, Judah asks his second son Onan to consummate a levirate marriage with his brother's widow (*wᵉyabbēm 'ōṯāh*) and "raise up" offspring for his brother (v. 8). Almost everywhere in the OT and in later Jewish literature, the root *ybm* has this specialized meaning, referring to the obligation of a *yāḇām* to his *yᵉḇāmâ*. An exception is found in Ruth 1:15,[2] where a *yᵉḇāmâ* is associated with a woman, Ruth, referring to the widow of the deceased brother of her likewise deceased husband, and in Bab. *Šeb.* 102a par. *Lev. r.* 20, 163b, where Moses is referred to as the *yāḇām* of Elizabeth, the wife of his (still living!) brother Aaron.

2. *Statistics.* The noun *yāḇām* occurs twice in the OT (Dt. 25:5,7); the fem. equivalent *yᵉḇāmâ** (or *yāḇemeṯ**) occurs 5 times (Dt. 25:7a,b,9; Ruth 1:15a,b). The piel of *ybm* (a denominative verb from *yāḇām*[3]) occurs 3 times (Gen. 38:8; Dt. 25:5,7). The suggestion of a Hebrew verb *ybm*, meaning "create," in Ps. 68:18 (Eng. v. 17)[4] is not as convincing as the usual emendation *b' msyny* (for MT *bm syny*), "(Yahweh) 'came from' Sinai (to the sanctuary)."

3. *The Root in Other Semitic Languages.* Both nouns, *yāḇām* and *yᵉḇāmâ*, are found also in Middle Hebrew, Jewish Aramaic, and Syriac, as is the verb (in the piel or pael). Middle Hebrew has two additional nouns, *yibbûm*, "levirate marriage,"[5] and *yᵉḇāmûṯ*, "consummation of levirate marriage." It also uses the hithpael and nithpael of the verb *ybm*, with the *yᵉḇāmâ* rather than the *yāḇām* as subject: "be taken in levirate marriage."[6] Syriac also has *yaḇmûṯā'*, "levirate."

Rengstorf, *Jebamot. Die Mischna*, III/1 (Giessen, 1929); H. H. Rowley, "The Marriage of Ruth," *HThR*, 40 (1947), 77-99 = his *The Servant of the Lord* (Oxford, ^{2}1965), 169-194 (with bibliog.); W. Rudolph, *Das Buch Ruth. KAT*, XVII/1 (1962), 60ff.; J. Scheftelowitz, "Die Leviratsehe," *ARW*, 18 (1915), 250-56; T. Thompson and D. Thompson, "Some Legal Problems in the Book of Ruth," *VT*, 18 (1968), 79-99; M. Tsevat, "Marriage and Monarchical Legitimacy in Ugarit and Israel," *JSS*, 3 (1958), 237-243; B. N. Wambacq, "Le mariage de Ruth," *Mélanges Eugène Tisserant*, I. *Studi e Testi*, 231 (Rome, 1964), 449-459.

[1] Cf. → חתן *ḥtn*.

[2] As in *Yebam.* ii.3; iii.3; xv.4a; cf. Rengstorf, 17.

[3] Rengstorf, 3*, n. 1; *KBL*^{3}, 367a.

[4] M. Dahood, "Hebrew-Ugaritic Lexicography III," *Bibl*, 46 (1965), 313f., on the basis of Ugaritic (see I.3).

[5] Rengstorf, 3*, n. 1.

[6] Cf. Rengstorf on *Yebam.* i.2b and 4b.

According to *KBL*³,[7] Arabic has a verb *wabama*, "beget," but such a verb does not appear in the standard lexica.[8]

The meaning of *ybm* and *ybmt* in Ugaritic is disputed. On the basis of Heb. *yāḇām*, *ybm*[9] has been translated "brother-in-law,"[10] but the fragmentary texts give no further information about the person so designated. More important is the discussion of the epithet *ybmt l3mm* applied to 'Anat, which frequently stands in parallel with *btlt 'nt*, "virgin 'Anat."[11] Initially, the translation "sister-in-law" was preferred on the basis of Heb. *yᵉḇāmâ;*[12] more recently, the meaning "progenitress" has found increasing acceptance. It was first proposed by Albright on the basis of *yāmām**, "progenitor,"[13] then in connection with the root *wbm* (cf. Arab. *wabama* [?]).[14] If *l3m* means "people"[15] (cf. Heb. *le'ōm*) or "prince,"[16] we have four possible translations: "sister-in-law of peoples,"[17] "sister-in-law of princes,"[18] "progenitress of peoples,"[19] or "progenitress of princes."[20] "Sister-in-law" could be meant only in a general and atypical sense, especially if *l3mm* is considered a singular referring to "Prince" Ba'al, so that *ybmt l3mm* is translated "sister of Ba'al."[21] If *ybmt*, however, means "progenitress," then *ybm* must be interpreted similarly if it is not to be separated from *ybmt*, and translated "progenitor." In at least one passage, however,[22] this interpretation is problematic: "progenitor for (?) the gods (or: for El)." In yet another passage,[23] *l3mm* appears without *ybmt* in parallel with *btlt;* Gese[24] considers it a special name for 'Anat, "while *ybmt* characterizes her status as an independent woman." This leaves open the question of what *ybmt* means in combination with *l3mm*. In view of these problems, it is not surprising that Aistleitner terms the root *ybm* "obscure."[25]

---

7 P. 367a.

8 Lane; *Lisān al-'arab;* M. al-Murtaḍā al-Zabīdī, *Tāğ al-'arūs* (1888; repr. 1965); G. W. F. Freytag, *Lexicon arabico-latinum* (Halle, 1830-37); A. al-Bustānī, *Fākihat al-Bustan* (Beirut, 1927-1930; repr. 1930); *Muḥīṭ al-Muḥīṭ;* R. P. A. Dozy, *Supplément aux dictionnaires arabes* (²1927; repr. Leiden, 1981).

9 *KTU*, 1.6 I, 31; 1.16 II, 32.

10 Gordon, 43, 79; *CML*, 166b.

11 *KTU*, 1.4 II, 15; 1.10 III, 3; 1.3 II, 33; also 1.17 VI, 25 and in line 19 as 'Anat's epithet for herself; cf. also *KTU*, 1.3 III, 12.

12 Gordon, 29, 50, 18, 90; also 19; *CML*, 166b ("relative by marriage").

13 W. F. Albright, "Recent Progress in North-Canaanite Research," *BASOR*, 70 (1938), 19, n. 6.

14 In a letter to M. Burrows; cf. Burrows, 6f.; cf. *UT*, no. 1065.

15 *UT*, no. 1346; *WUS*, no. 1433.

16 *CML*, 158b.

17 Gordon.

18 *CML*.

19 Albright.

20 *UT*, no. 1065.

21 Gray, 43, n. 8.

22 *KTU*, 1.6 I, 31.

23 *KTU*, 1.13, 20.

24 Gese, 157.

25 *WUS*, no. 1130.

4. *Etymology.* What does this evidence suggest for the etymology of Heb. *yāḇām?* If the terms *ybm* and *ybmt* designate in-laws in Ugaritic, "brother-in-law" and "sister-in-law," then this would be the primary meaning. The interpretation of *yāḇām* as designating the brother of a man who has died without a son, having the obligation of entering into levirate marriage (piel of *ybm*), would then represent a special development within Hebrew and other languages depending on Hebrew for this meaning. The original (broader) meaning would still be visible in Ruth 1:15 and Bab. *Šeb.* 102a. But it is in this broader meaning that *yāḇām* cannot be associated with Arab. *wabama,* "beget," assuming that there is such a root. A brother-in-law has nothing inherent to do with the begetting of children. But if Ugar. *ybmt* means "progenitress," then it can hardly have anything to do with Heb. *yāḇām* and related words. The begetting of children is the purpose of every marriage, not just levirate marriage; the special feature of such a marriage, the fact that the first son is reckoned as the son of the deceased husband, is not brought out by the term "beget." There is thus no evidence for an etymological connection of Heb. *yāḇām* with Ugaritic or Arabic.

5. *Versions.* Among the versions, the Targumim and Syriac use nouns and verbs derived from the root *ybm.*[26] In targumic expansions of the MT we also find nouns like *yaḇmā'* in Nu. 27:4; Dt. 25:9 (both Pseudo-Jonathan); Ruth 1:13; *yeḇimtā'* in Dt. 25:4 (Pseudo-Jonathan; cf. Bab. *Yebam.* 4a); *ybm* pael in Ruth 4:5.

Lacking a corresponding technical term, the LXX translates *yāḇām* literally as *adelphós toú andrós* (Dt. 25:5bα,7bα, even where it erroneously read the noun (*yeḇāmî*) instead of the verb (*yabbemî*)(Dt. 25:7bβ). For the fem. *yeḇāmâ* it similarly uses *gynḗ toú adelphoú* in Dt. 25:7a,9, repeating only *gynḗ* in v. 7bα. In Ruth 1:15, where *yeḇāmâ* has the more general meaning "sister-in-law,"[27] it uses the word *sýnnymphos,* "co-bride," found only here. For the verb, it uses *synoikeín* (Dt. 25:5b; see above for v. 7bβ) or, more appositely, *gambreúein* (Gen. 38:8; in Dt. 7:3; 2 Esd. 9:14 Cod. B for *ḥtn* hithpael).

For *yāḇām,* the Vulg. does not use *levir* (which is attested, though rare, from the 3rd century on) but *frater viri* (Dt. 25:7bα) or *frater eius* (v. 5bα); for *yeḇāmâ* it uses *uxor fratris* (Dt. 25:7a) or simply *mulier* (vv. 7bα,9), and in Ruth 1:15a *cognata,* represented in v. 15b by *ea.* For the verb, it uses *sociare* (Gen. 38:8) or *in coniugium sumere* (Dt. 25:7bβ), while in v. 5b it paraphrases *weyibbemâ* with *et suscitabit semen fratris sui* (cf. v. 7bα).

II. The Institution of Levirate Marriage.

1. *Israel.* The institution of levirate marriage in the strict sense is presupposed in Israel and Judaism when a man dies without a son (LXX in Dt. 25:5: without offspring); the brother takes the widow, his sister-in-law, to wife, and the first-born son of this marriage is accounted the son of the deceased. With few exceptions,[28] only in

---

26 See I.3 above.
27 See I.1 above.
28 See I.1 above.

this situation are brother-in-law and sister-in-law called *yāḇām* and *yᵉḇāmâ,* with the relationship itself (from the perspective of the male) being called *yibbēm*. It is disputed whether the relevant OT texts in Gen. 38; Dt. 25:5-10; Ruth 4 reflect various stages (five according to Morgenstern) in the development of the institution, itself possibly Canaanite in origin,[29] or whether the narratives in Gen. 38 and Ruth 4 and the legislation in Dt. 25:5-10 presuppose the same idea of a widow's remarriage within the family of her deceased husband.[30] That the piel of *ybm* refers to a permanent marriage, not just the begetting of a son for the deceased brother, can be seen from Dt. 25:6 ("first-born") and from Gen. 38:14b (the widow becomes the *'iššâ* of her brother-in-law), in what is probably the earliest passage (J).

According to Gen. 38, the brothers of the deceased are obligated to enter into levirate marriage with his widow. The obligation passes in order of birth (vv. 7f.,11)—here for narrative reasons, but probably in agreement with actual practice.[31] The theory that the father of the deceased also has this obligation[32] is contrary to the narrative: Judah sees that he should have given his grown son Shelah to Tamar (v. 26a); the sons she has borne him belong to him, not to the deceased Er.[33] Voluntary levirate marriage on the part of a distant relative is not presupposed in Ruth 4; it is therefore highly unlikely in Gen. 38, although not totally out of the question.[34] Dt. 25:5-10 also speaks of a levirate obligation only on the part of the brothers of the deceased. V. 5a states explicitly that they "dwell together," either in their father's house or without dividing their inheritance. This is also assumed in Gen. 38:8, where the father urges his son Onan to fulfill his levirate obligation, while refusing to give his third son to his daughter-in-law; both sons are therefore still under his authority. Dt. 25:7-10 provides the *yāḇām* the right to refuse levirate marriage, even though the refusal involves public defamation on the part of the *yᵉḇāmâ,* who pulls (*ḥlṣ*) a sandal off his foot and spits in his face (v. 9). Whether the narrator of Gen. 38 was aware of this possibility remains unknown; in any case the plot of his story precludes it: Onan cannot escape his levirate obligation, but can only prevent the begetting of a son that would not belong to him.

Many legal and historical problems are raised by Ruth 4. There is no question of levirate marriage, either in word (the root *ybm* does not occur, nor is there any reason for it to) or in fact: the marriage in question is not that of a brother but of a distant relative of Elimelech (to whom the first "redeemer" is more closely related than Boaz), and not to his widow Naomi, but to her (likewise widowed) daughter-in-law. The point of the narrative in Ruth 4 is that Boaz marries Ruth; but the legal institution involved is not levirate marriage but *gᵉ'ullâ,* "redemption," the right or obligation of close relatives to buy (or buy back) real property that an Israelite is forced to sell (cf. Lev. 25:25ff.; Jer. 32:6ff.; → גאל *gā'al*). According to Ruth 4:5,10, the "redeemer" (*gō'ēl*), a distant (!) relative—the practice of the period or (more likely?) a special feature of

[29] Burrows, 30.

[30] Thompson.

[31] Cf. later *Yebam.* iv.5f.

[32] Among others, Morgenstern, 180; for the ancient Near East, see II.2 below.

[33] Rengstorf, 16*f.; Rudolph, 63.

[34] Rudolph, 62f.

this particular narrative—must "buy" Ruth as well as the property. Only the stated purpose, restoring the name of the dead (Elimelech? Mahlon?) (vv. 5,10), recalls Dt. 25:5-10; neither is it stated that the son to be born belongs to the "deceased."

The purpose of levirate marriage is to "raise up" offspring (Gen. 38:8; cf. v. 9), a "name" (Dt. 25:7; cf. vv. 6,9), for a man who has died without a son, to preserve his "lineage" in the clan or "in Israel" (Dt. 25:7; cf. v. 6). Protection and economic security for the widow[35] are not mentioned in Gen. 38 or Dt. 25:5-10 (for Ruth 4, see the paragraph above), but are achieved by levirate marriage; the widow, however, is prevented from marrying anyone outside the family of her deceased husband (Dt. 25:5aβ). There would be no need to fear the loss of family property in such a situation, since the woman herself does not represent such property[36] and as a widow has no right of inheritance.[37]

Lev. 18:16 and 20:21 deal only with illegal intercourse between a man and his sister-in-law. Later Judaism devoted much discussion to problems of family law growing out of levirate marriage, as well as the possibility of refusal (*ḥaliṣa*). Cf. also Mk. 12:18-27 par.

2. *Ancient Near East.* In the ancient Near East, something comparable to levirate marriage in Israel with respect to the parties and purposes involved is discussed to varying degrees in the Hittite and Middle Assyrian laws (not in the Code of Hammurabi), and in one text each from Nuzi and Ugarit.

According to Hittite law,[38] a widow is taken in marriage by a relative of her deceased husband in the sequence brother–father; if the latter dies, she may be taken in marriage by a brother of the father or a brother (in this case probably already married) of the deceased, or by a brother's son. The absence of a son or offspring is not specified, but may be presupposed[39] when the widow is given economic security through inheritance of her husband's property.[40]

According to Driver-Miles, §33 (fragmentary), if a widow living in her father's house has sons, she remains with them. If she has no sons, her father-in-law gives her as wife to another of his sons.[41] If there is no brother of her deceased husband available, her father can give her as wife to her father-in-law. If there is no surviving brother-in-law or father-in-law, the woman is a "widow" and legally free. According to §43, if a son for whom his father has "anointed" a girl to be his bride[42] or given nuptial gifts to her father dies or runs away, the son's father may give the girl as wife to another of his sons, provided the latter is at least ten years old. If the only son is less than ten years old, the bride's father can either agree to the marriage or return the

---

35 Thompson, Leggett.

36 Contra Puukko, 298f.

37 Thompson disagrees.

38 *HG,* II, §79*; cf. Leggett, 21f.

39 Cf. Koschaker, 80.

40 *HG,* II, §II, 78*.

41 Cf. also Driver-Miles, §30.

42 Cf. also E. Kutsch, *Salbung als Rechtsakt im AT und im alten Orient. BZAW,* 87 (1963), 29ff.

nuptial gifts; if there is no other son, the nuptial gifts are returned. According to §31, on the other hand, if a man's wife dies and he does not wish to take back the nuptial gifts, he can, with the consent of his father-in-law, marry a sister of his deceased wife.

There is a parallel to Driver-Miles, §43 at Nuzi: according to one text,[43] a man who has purchased a wife for his son can give her to another of his sons if the first dies. At Ugarit, there is a text[44] presupposing that the widow of a king, presumably sonless,[45] will be married by his brother. At Nuzi—in contrast to Israel—the existence of children is presupposed.[46]

This survey shows clear differences from the Israelite institution reflected in the root *ybm*. Among both the Hittites and the Assyrians, the obligation to marry a man's widow extends beyond his brothers; in Driver-Miles, however, it is limited to a woman, married (§33) or espoused (§43), living in her father's house. There are substantial differences in §31. Since by Hittite law a widow inherits her husband's property,[47] the regulation of her remarriage appears intended to keep this property in the (deceased) husband's family if possible. The Assyrian laws, on the contrary, protect the rights of the husband and his family, which exist by virtue of gifts given to the bride's father (§§30f., 43); for this purpose they expand the possibilities for exercising these rights before the final recourse, the reclaiming (§§30f.) or return (§43) of the gifts. The motif of guaranteeing the "name," the hereditary lineage of a man who has died sonless, through levirate marriage does not appear elsewhere in the ancient Near East, except possibly at Ugarit.

Kutsch

---

43 Chiera, no. 441.
44 RS 16.144 (*PRU*, III, 76).
45 Tsevat, 239.
46 Leggett, 24.
47 *HG*, II, §78*.

יָבֵשׁ *yāḇēš;* יַבָּשָׁה *yabbāšâ;* יַבֶּשֶׁת *yabbešeṯ*

Contents: I. Occurrences and Meaning: 1. Root; 2. Verb; 3. Derivatives; 4. Toponym. II. Usage: 1. General; Negative; 2. Sayings Concerning Judgment and Salvation; 3. "Dry Land" at the Exodus; 4. Dry Land and Sea.

I. Occurrences and Meaning.

1. *Root.* The root *ybš,* which is found also in other Semitic languages,[1] is found in Hebrew primarily as a verb; it also appears as a *qaṭil* adjective and in the derived

---

1 Cf. *KBL*³, *s.v.*

nouns *yabbāšâ* and *yabbešeṯ*. Since the verb, adjective, and nouns appear in similar semantic contexts and in similar types of texts, not rarely in combination, it is both appropriate and necessary to treat them together.

All the forms have something to do with "(being or becoming) dry" (cf. → חרב *ḥāraḇ* I, which also appears in combination with *yāḇēš:* Isa. 42:15; 44:27; Jer. 51:36; Nah. 1:4), usually in the literal sense, more rarely (but more significantly) in a metaphorical sense. Phenomena of daily life may be involved, such as dry bread or dried grapes. In texts of more theological importance, apart from the group of texts that describes the route of Israel through the sea when they were delivered out of Egypt[2] as a path on dry land in the midst of the sea,[3] dryness is viewed as something negative, something to be avoided.[4] It is something that is or should be overcome, especially when metaphorical usage is involved.[5]

It is also a negative counterpart to positive concepts (cf. its frequent contrast with *laḥ*), and in combination with such positive terms it can mean something like "everything, everywhere."[6] It is especially common to speak of "dryness" in pejorative descriptions, as in announcements of judgment.[7]

It may be seen already that within the OT *ybš* and its derivatives, despite their occasional association with the exodus that is also reflected in statements about Yahweh's power over the dry land and the sea, have no special theological significance and certainly no positive overtones; what they express never has any connection with a beneficial act of God or with human prosperity.

2. *Verb*. According to the usual count, the verb occurs 38 times in the qal; in this stem it usually means "be dry" or more rarely "become dry" (Gen. 8:7,14; Josh. 9:5,12; 1 K. 13:4; 17:7; Job 8:12; 12:15; 14:11; 18:16; Ps. 22:16[Eng. v. 15]; 90:6; 102:5,12[4,11]; 129:6; Isa. 15:6; 19:5,7; 27:11; 40:7f.,24; Jer. 12:4; 23:10; 50:38; Lam. 4:8; Ezk. 17:9f. [3 times]; 19:12; 37:11; Hos. 9:16; Joel 1:12,20; Am. 1:2; 4:7; Jon. 4:7; Zec. 11:17). Isa. 50:2 should be added to these passages, where *tîḇaš* should be read, following the LXX and 1QIs^a. In Gen. 8:7 and Isa. 27:11, the form *y^{e}ḇōš(eṯ)* should be interpreted as the qal infinitive construct, rather than being derived from the noun *yabbešeṯ*.[8]

The piel appears only in Job 15:30 and Prov. 17:22 (both times metaphorically) in the sense of "make dry" (as in Akkadian) or "dry" (transitive). In Nah. 1:4 the hiphil should probably be read.[9] According to Jenni, the piel is used for statements about universal human experience (cf. Prov. 17:22: "A downcast spirit dries up the bones"), where the subject is emphasized and the resulting condition is considered in isolation.

---

2 → יצא *yāṣā'* and → עלה *'ālâ*.
3 → ים *yām*.
4 See II.3.
5 See II.1.
6 See II.4.
7 II.2.
8 *GK*, §70a 1, n. 2.
9 Cf. *BLe*, §382, and E. Jenni, *Das hebräische Pi'el* (Zurich, 1968), 104.

There are 12 occurrences of the hiphil (Josh. 2:10; 4:23 [twice]; 5:1; Ps. 74:15; Isa. 42:15 [twice]; 44:27; Jer. 51:36; Ezk. 17:24; 19:12) with the meaning "cause to dry out" (with the accusative), plus Zec. 10:11 with the intransitive meaning "dry out" (internally transitive).[10] Nah. 1:4[11] should be added to this list. The hiphil is used for "processes involving special circumstances; the emphasis is on the process itself, which is brought into relationship with other processes."[12] When the piel or hiphil is used, Yahweh is always the subject, directly or indirectly; even the east wind in Ezk. 19:12 is under his control and comes from him.[13]

The LXX uses *apoxēraínein* for the qal and piel, *xēraínein* for the qal, piel, and hiphil; it also uses *xērós gígnesthai* for the qal (Ezk. 37:11) and *exaírein* for the hiphil (Jer. 51:36[LXX 28:36]). We also find *kataxēraínein* and *maraínein*.

3. *Derivatives*. There are 9 occurrences of the adj. *yāḇēš*. Besides the meaning "dry," it is frequently used metaphorically (often in contrast to *laḥ*) in the sense of "decaying" or something similarly negative and undesirable (Nu. 6:3; 11:6; Job 13:25; Isa. 56:3; Ezk. 17:24; 21:3(20:47); 37:2,4; Nah. 1:10). To these occurrences should be added Sir. 6:2; 14:10 (metaphorical usage; also cf. Sir. 14:9 conj.) and 1QH 3:30; 8:19 (LXX: *xērós, katáxēros*).

The noun *yabbāšâ* occurs 14 times. It can mean "dry ground" (Isa. 44:3), "dry land" (Ex. 14:16,22,29; 15:19; Josh. 4:22; Neh. 9:11 [possibly "dryshod"?]), or simply "land" in contrast to "sea" (→ ים *yām*) (Gen. 1:9f.; Ex. 4:9; Jon. 1:9,13; 2:11; Ps. 66:6). This last meaning is also found in 1QH 3:31; 8:4; in 1QH 17:4 the meaning is unclear. In Palmyrene, also, the hendiadys *bym' wbybš'* means something like "everywhere."[14] The LXX uses *ánydros, xērós*, and sometimes simply *gḗ*.

Finally, the noun *yabbešeṯ* occurs twice (Ex. 4:9 [in combination with *yabbāšâ*]; Ps. 95:5). Here the LXX reads *xērós* and *gḗ*. For discussion of Gen. 8:7 and Isa. 27:11, see I.2 above.

In the Dead Sea scrolls, besides 1QH 3:30f. (the fire of Belial destroys both the green and the dry, as well as the land; cf. Ezk. 21:3[20:47][15]), 1QH 8 is of special importance: the community is compared to a sacred colony living beside brooks and springs in the midst of a dry land, for which it praises Yahweh. In 1QH 8:4,19f., the noun, adjective, and verb appear together. The meaning of 8:19f., however, is obscure. On 8:4, cf. Isa. 44:3.

4. *Toponym*. The village Jabesh (in) Gilead is mentioned in Jgs. 21:8f.; 1 S. 11; 31:11,13 and *passim;* 1 Ch. 10:11f. It has not been definitely identified, despite the

---

[10] Cf. Jenni, 46, 104.

[11] On the close relationship of this hiphil to similar forms of *bôš*, as well as the deliberate play on the meanings "dry up" and "perish," see H. Seebass, "בוש *bôš* [*bôsh*]," *TDOT*, II, 57, 59f.; also M. Dahood, "Hebrew-Ugaritic Lexicography III," *Bibl*, 46 (1965), 314f.

[12] Jenni, 104.

[13] Contra Jenni, 104.

[14] *DISO*, 103.

[15] The subject is discussed in F. Lang, "πῦρ," *TDNT*, VI, 939.

common references to Wâdī (el-)Yâbis and (possibly) the Yabiši of the Amarna letters.[16] Whether "Jabesh" in 2 K. 15:10,13f. is a personal name or a toponym (of a different village) is a matter of debate.

II. Usage.

1. *General; Negative.* Used in a general sense and without particular theological relevance, *ybš* or one of its derivatives first appears in Nu. 6:3 (the Nazirites must eat neither fresh [*laḥ*] nor dried [LXX: *staphís*] grapes) and Josh. 9:5,12 (the Gibeonites take hard, dry bread along as part of their stratagem). Both these occurrences involve the adjective. In the passages mentioned below, the verb in the qal is used unless otherwise mentioned.

Human death is like the drying up of a river (Job 14:11).[17]

During their desert wanderings, the people complain that their throats are dry (Nu. 11:6 [J]; adj.); v. 5a describes the contrasting positive in detail.

As these occurrences already suggest, *ybš* and its derivatives are frequently found in contexts where "dryness" (literal or figurative) is looked on as something negative to be overcome, to be changed into something positive.

Thus the psalmist in Ps. 22:16(15) laments: "My palate [conj. *ḥikkî*] is dried up like a potsherd," possibly describing a fever that grips him (cf. v. 15[14]). This motif reappears in similar descriptions of distress in individual and community laments: Ps. 90:6; 102:12(11) (cf. Isa. 15:6). Ps. 90:6 compares human beings to the grass, which soon "withers"; this is a common motif in other passages (Ps. 129:6; Isa. 40:7f.; Ezk. 17:10; 19:12), where it is the hot wind that causes the sudden change (cf. Ezk. 19:12; hiphil).

In Ezk. 37:11, the people likewise lament, "Our bones are dried up," lamenting their distress in exile; the whole vision of Ezekiel, which describes the situation of the exilic community, grows out of this motif. V. 11b characteristically interprets "dried up" as meaning "without hope." Ezk. 37:2,4 (adj.) describe the bones emphatically as being "very dry"; but they can and must hear the word of Yahweh spoken to them through the mouth of Ezekiel. Here again the interpretation of v. 11 given above may be cited: Ezk. 37:1ff. repeatedly states the prophet's part in "reviving" the people!

Finally, Job complains to Yahweh that he is like dry (adj.) chaff before him (Job 13:25; cf. Nah. 1:10),[18] so that Yahweh's power as judge is totally disproportionate to Job's impotence and meaninglessness.

2. *Sayings Concerning Judgment and Salvation.* Since it is Yahweh who holds sway

[16] EA 256, 28; but cf. J. A. Knudtzen, ed., *Die El-Amarna-Tafeln. VAB*, 2 ([2]1964), 1320, n. See M. Noth, "Jabes-Gilead: Ein Beitrag zur Methode der alttestamentlicher Topographie," *ZDPV*, 69 (1953), 28-41 = his *Aufsätze zur biblischen Landes- und Altertumskunde* (Neukirchen-Vluyn, 1971), I, 476-488; K. Elliger, "Jabes," *BHHW*, II, 790f. Noth and Elliger identify the site with Tell el-Maqlûb. Cf. also J. J. Simons, *The Geographical and Topographical Texts of the OT. StFS*, 2 (1959), §671.

[17] Cf. F. Horst, *Hiob. BK*, XVI/1 (1968), *in loc.*

[18] *AuS*, III (1933), 137.

over the sea and the dry land, the waters dry up when he withholds them (Job 12:15) and the waters of the Deluge dry up (Gen. 8:7 [P]; cf. the dating of this event in v. 14 [P]). Yahweh causes streams to dry up (Ps. 74:15; hiphil) and Jonah's castor bean plant withers when Yahweh sends a worm to attack it (Jon. 4:7).

Yahweh's causing something to dry up or causing something green to wither as a sign or consequence of his judgment is therefore an especially common motif in proclamations or descriptions of this divine judgment (cf. → חרב *ḥāraḇ* I), characterizing it as imminent. The passages discussed in II.1 therefore have some relationship with those to be discussed here in II.2, which may indicate that the use of *ybš* and its derivatives in these two semantic clusters is the earliest.

That God's judgment brings or consists in dryness is also stated by not a few important ancient Near Eastern texts from outside Israel. Before punishing them with the flood, Enlil sends a drought to decimate raging (rebelling?) humanity.[19]

Never in the OT is a drought associated with the (or a) "death" of Yahweh, as such a drought is associated in a Ugaritic text with the death of Ba'al.[20] Similar passages appear in the Ugaritic epics of Aqhat[21] and Keret.[22] There it was also the god Mot who was the god of drought.

According to the OT, the brook Cherith dries up because Yahweh withholds the rain, which is to be understood as a punishment (1 K. 17:7; cf. Am. 4:7). At Yahweh's rebuke the fish dry up, since they are without water (Isa. 50:2 conj.[23]). The hand that the king stretches forth against the prophet dries up (1 K. 13:4). It is also Yahweh who dries up the green tree (Ezk. 17:24; hiphil). Misfortune comes upon the city of Nineveh, since it is consumed like dry (adj.) stubble in Yahweh's judgment (Nah. 1:10; cf. Job 13:25); misfortune likewise befalls the worthless shepherd, whose arm will wither (Zec. 11:17). The lament over Moab speaks of the grass that is withered (Isa. 15:6). The Nile, too, dries up and all the adjacent farmland with it (Isa. 19:5,7), when Yahweh so desires and decrees. Yahweh's fire will consume every green tree and every dry (adj.) tree (Ezk. 21:3[20:47]). The judgment upon Babylon that leads to the freeing of the exiles will have as one of its consequences the drying up of the canals there (Jer. 50:38; cf. 51:36 [hiphil]). Drying up or withering as an element of judgment is also found in Ezk. 17:9; Hos. 9:16; Joel 1:12,20. The exiled community, having experienced God's judgment themselves, lament that the daughter of Zion and her youths have become as dry as wood (Lam. 4:8); Isa. 27:11 shows that the dry branches of trees were broken off for firewood. And those who hate Zion are like grass that withers (when it is pulled up? Ps. 129:6).

In Nah. 1:4, the fact that Yahweh dries up (hiphil) the rivers is an element and consequence of his coming as judge; it is part of the theophany of judgment. The

---

19 Atraḫasis, II, 1, 15. On dryness as a divine punishment, cf. also the entries under "Dürre" in *WbMyth*, I, 574; also H. Gese in Gese, M. Höfner, and K. Rudolph, *Die Religionen Altsyriens, Altarabiens und der Mandäer. RdM*, 10/2 (1970), 79, 85, 89f., 136, 184.

20 *KTU*, 1.3 V, 17ff.

21 *KTU*, 1.19 I, 30.

22 *KTU*, 1.16 III, 12ff.

23 See above, I.2.

same idea is also present in Am. 1:2, where *yāḇēš* should not be emended to *yᵉḇōš* (on the basis of Isa. 19:8; 33:9). Parallelism with → אבל *'āḇal* [*'ābhal*] is also found in Jer. 12:4; 23:10, both of which are probably later additions.[24] Since Amos also speaks of drought as an act of Yahweh's judgment in Am. 4:7,[25] there is no reason on that account to deny Amos' authorship of 1:2.[26] The passage speaks of Yahweh's coming and its results (cf. Nah. 1:4). His coming in a storm (or earthquake?) is not beneficial but destructive. It will move from south to north, i.e., it will be directed against the northern kingdom. Here, as elsewhere in Amos, judgment is proclaimed against northern Israel; Carmel[27] is singled out as a particular symbol of fertility, because it, too, will fall victim to the destruction of this theophany (somewhat altered in form because only its effects are described) of Yahweh come to judgment.[28]

Wisdom texts also speak of "drying up" or "withering" as a punishment and judgment within the reward/punishment schema.[29] The wicked and godless are compared to plants without water, which quickly wither (Job 8:12f.; 18:16; cf. 15:30 [piel] and Prov. 17:22 [piel]; also Sir. 6:2; 14:10 as a general maxim).

It is a generally recognized observation, frequently mentioned in the context of Yahweh's judgment, that grass withers quickly in the hot wind (cf. Ps. 90:6; 102:12[11]; 129:6; also Ezk. 17:10; 19:12; cf. the discussion in II.1 above). For this very reason, because everything earthly withers away in the face of Yahweh's judgment, the theme of Deutero-Isaiah's preaching is the antithetical endurance and effectiveness of Yahweh's word (Isa. 40:7f.; cf. 40:24). In Isa. 42:15 (hiphil), too, Yahweh's act of judgment is only the negative background to his work of salvation for Israel; he who dries up the "depths" (Isa. 44:27 [hiphil]) can also bring salvation for Israel (v. 28), since he pours streams on the "dry ground" (Isa. 44:3 [noun]). Here, too, Deutero-Isaiah borrows from the usual message of judgment preached by his prophetic predecessors, but gives it a characteristic positive twist, having it surpassed by assurances of salvation promised after the judgment to a people that have passed through the judgment (Isa. 40:2).

Even Ezekiel could promise that all the trees would know that Yahweh has dried up the green (*laḥ*) tree (Ezk. 17:24 [hiphil]), but makes the dry tree flourish. According to Isa. 56:3 (adjective), therefore, no eunuch may say that he is a dry tree; he may become a member of the community.

3. *"Dry Land" at the Exodus.* P's exaggerated account of the exodus event, describ-

---

[24] See I. Meyer, *Jeremia und die falschen Propheten. OBO*, 13 (1977), 117f.

[25] Cf. W. Rudolph, *Amos. KAT,* XIII/2 (1971), *in loc.*, contra H. W. Wolff, *Joel and Amos. Herm* (Eng. trans. 1977), *in loc.*

[26] For a discussion of this passage and the metaphor involved, see M. Weiss, "Methodologisches über die Behandlung der Metapher dargelegt an Am. 1,2," *ThZ,* 23 (1967), 1-15; S. Wagner, "Überlegungen zur Frage nach den Beziehungen des Propheten Amos zum Südreich," *ThLZ,* 96 (1971), 659-661; K. Koch, "Die Rolle der hymnischen Abschnitte in der Komposition des Amos-Buches," *ZAW,* 86 (1974), 530-34.

[27] → כרמל *karmel.*

[28] For the mention of Zion (→ ציון *ṣiyyôn*), cf. also Ps. 50:2; for "roaring," cf. Am. 3:8 (→ שאג *šā'ag*).

[29] Cf. H. D. Preuss, "בוא *bô'*," *TDOT,* II, 25f., with bibliog.

ing Israel's deliverance at the Sea of Reeds in terms that include *ybš* and its derivatives, is undoubtedly not the earliest statement of this act of deliverance on the part of Yahweh; but it is theologically the most important, although it merely builds upon what J (and E?) already said about this event. Ex. 14:16,22,29 (cf. the addition in 15:19; all nouns) describe the revelation of Yahweh's glory during the passage through the sea, culminating in the statement that the waters were divided and Israel passed through the midst of the sea[30] on "dry ground."

This motif reappears in Ps. 66:6 and Neh. 9:11 (both nouns); it is also echoed in Zec. 10:11 (hiphil). According to Josh. 2:10, the Canaanites had also heard of this event. In Josh. 4:22f. (verb in the hiphil plus noun), the answer to the catechetic question about the meaning of the stones in the Jordan also refers to what happened at the Sea of Reeds. According to Josh. 5:1 (hiphil), the kings of the Amorites and the Canaanites had heard of the passage of Israel through the Jordan,[31] during which Yahweh "dried up" the water of the river, a clear parallel to what happened at the Sea of Reeds. It is also P that speaks of the "drying up" of the waters in the context of the Deluge narrative (Gen. 8:7; cf. v. 14), illustrating its particular interest in this word cluster.

Ex. 4:9 (J; noun *yabbešet*) names as a sign[32] of Moses' call his potential power to change into blood water that he pours out onto dry ground.

4. *Dry Land and Sea.* "Dry land" (always the noun) is also contrasted to "sea" (*yām*) in Gen. 1:9f. (P), which state that God "made" the sea and the dry land (Ps. 95:5 and Jon. 1:9; therefore both are subject to him) by "separating" the dry land from the sea.[33]

Jonah's initially theoretical statement in Jon. 1:9 has immediate practical consequences in v. 13: no one can reach "land" from the sea against the will of Yahweh, to whom both are subject. Only at his command, therefore, can the fish vomit Jonah out on "dry land" (2:11[10]). This juxtaposition of "dry land" and "sea" shows further that Yahweh rules over "everything," as is expressed by the antithetical hendiadys, like "heaven and earth," and is present and at work "everywhere."[34]

Preuss

---

30 → ים *yām*.

31 → ירדן *yardēn*.

32 F. J. Helfmeyer, "אות *'ôṯ* [*'ôth*]," *TDOT,* I, 184.

33 See C. Westermann, *Genesis 1–11* (Eng. trans., Minneapolis, 1984), 120-22; also → בדל *bdl*. Cf. also Hag. 2:6 and L. Schmidt, *"De Deo." BZAW,* 143 (1976), 83.

34 Cf. *DISO*, 103; also I.3 above.

יָגָה yāḡâ; יָגוֹן yāḡôn; תּוּגָה tûḡâ

Contents: I. Occurrences and Meaning. II. General Usage. III. Theological Usage: 1. yāḡâ
and its Derivatives in Laments; 2. Prophetic Lament; 3. Announcement of Salvation; 4. Prediction of Disaster; 5. Summary.

I. Occurrences and Meaning. In the OT yāḡâ and its derivatives occur 26
times; the verb appears 8 times, a noun 18 times. Two noun forms derive from the
root: yāḡôn (14 occurrences) and tûḡâ (4 occurrences). The verb appears in the
niphal (passive) and hiphil (active); the piel is used once (like the hiphil). To date
there is no evidence for any forms of yāḡâ in ancient Semitic languages (Ugaritic,
Akkadian) or in Biblical Aramaic.

It is possible that a noun y'gn (ygn) in a Neo-Punic inscription from the beginning
of the first century B.C. (found at Leptis in 1955) should be assigned to the root ygy.[1]
But it is also possible that the 'ayin is not a mater lectionis but a misplaced radical of
the verb yg'. In this context the meaning of the latter root would also be appropriate.

Depending on the stem involved, yāḡâ has the meaning "grieve" or "be grieved."
The nouns can always be translated "sorrow." It is also possible, depending on the
particular context and the parallel terms, to use other synonyms like "pain" or "suffering." For the Neo-Punic noun, the meaning "travail" has been suggested.

This "sorrow" is not an isolated pain of body or mind, but a fundamental way of
reacting to such varied experiences as pain, suffering, or affliction. "Sorrow" is the
opposite of joy and gladness.

The semantic field presupposes a subjective element for both the active infliction of
pain and the passive suffering of pain. What happens in yāḡâ always involves a
personal subject or object. The root is often used in laments or in accounts of laments
after alleviation of their cause (5 times each in Psalms and Lamentations, 9 times in
the prophets, and once in Job). As might be expected, wisdom aphorisms contain
reflections on this human experience (3 occurrences in Proverbs). The other 3 occurrences are found in the Joseph saga (twice) and Esther (once).

II. General Usage. In the Joseph saga, Jacob laments that his sons would bring
his gray hairs with yāḡôn into Sheol if they were to take from him his youngest son
Benjamin after the loss of Joseph. The anticipated potential loss of the youngest son
gives rise to sorrow. Sorrow is a process. The actualization of sorrow leads eventually
to a wretched and joyless death (Gen. 42:38; 44:31). Pain and suffering and their
consequences can be conceptualized and can be proleptically experienced and defined.
They can be properly so identified before their onset.

The 3 passages in Proverbs all use tûḡâ ("sorrow"). All occur in a collection
(10:1–2:16) made up of two earlier collections (an observation of no further relevance). The core of this collection comprises wisdom aphorisms dating from the

---

yāḡâ. J. Scharbert, Der Schmerz im AT. BBB, 8 (1955).

[1] KAI, 119.6; II, 124f.

preexilic period. Prov. 10:1; 14:13; 17:21 are bipartite aphorisms expressing universal insights gained through experience. Prov. 10:1 agrees in content with 17:21: a foolish child is a *tûgâ* ("sorrow") to his parents, while a wise (*ḥāḵām*) son makes his father glad. The noun *tûgâ* refers therefore not to an isolated pain, but to the basic nature of a life dominated by the present reality of an unfortunate situation.

Prov. 14:13 is not entirely clear: "Even in laughter the heart can be sad, and the end of joy is sorrow" (reading *'aḥ*ᵃ*rîṯ haśśimḥâ* instead of the suffixed form *'aḥ*ᵃ*rîṯâ śimḥâ*). Ringgren[2] finds here and in v. 10 an acute psychological observation: "One's inmost feelings are unknown to others." Secret sorrow is veiled by an outward display of joy.[3] But *'aḥ*ᵃ*rîṯ* can also be translated "border," so that the aphorism could mean that grief "borders" on joy— pleasure and pain lie side by side in the human heart.

That one can inflict sorrow on others through words is stated in Job 19:2 (cf. the context). Job accuses the others of breaking him in pieces with words and "tormenting" (*tôg*ᵉ*yûn*) him with reproaches and unjustified reproofs. "Public opinion" as represented by Job's friends, with its tendency to judge and condemn, tears the nonconformist apart with anguish.

In Mordecai's establishment of Purim, an historical explanation is given along with the date and nature of the festival (Est. 9:22). The feast is to recall the days when the Jews found relief from all the pogroms, and the month "that had been turned for them from *yāgôn* into *śimḥâ,* from mourning into a holiday." Here *yāgôn* refers to the emotional experience of an entire people. Sorrow is the result of outward and inward oppression and persecution. The term *yāgôn* is used as a sociological expression of a people's existential state.[4]

III. Theological Usage.

1. *yāgâ and its Derivatives in Laments.* That the root *yāgâ* in its various verbal and substantival forms has its particular locus in lament can be seen from its frequent usage in literary contexts depicting lamentation. The first group to claim our attention are the individual laments.

In Ps. 13:3(Eng. v. 2), for example, the absence of God creates *yāgôn* in the → לבב *lēḇāḇ* and *'ēṣôṯ* (probably *'aṣṣeḇeṯ,* although there is much to support the MT[5]) in the *nepeš*. God has turned away, causing pain and sorrow. These dominate the life of the worshipper to his very core, making it unbearable. The same situation is described in Ps. 31:11(10), the lament of one who is persecuted unjustly. In addition to laments and petitions, the psalm includes an expression of confidence and a thanksgiving after the prayer has been heard. The worshipper sees his life spent in sorrow and sighing (*yāgôn* and *'*ᵃ*nāḥâ*). Both these passages could be preexilic.

Ps. 107:39 and 116:3, however, are postexilic. Ps. 116:3 belongs to an individual thanksgiving, in which a description of need and a lament precede the thanksgiving proper. The expressions used do not give a clear picture of the specific need or suf-

---

2 H. Ringgren, *Sprüch. ATD,* XVI/1 (³1980), *in loc.*

3 *Ibid.*

4 Cf. H. Bardtke, *KAT,* XVII/5 (1963), 389-393; Ringgren, *ATD,* XVI/1, *in loc.*

5 See also H.-J. Kraus, *Psalmen. BK,* XV/1 (⁵1978), *in loc.*

fering. "Snares of death" and "pangs of Sheol" are mentioned in parallelism with *yāḡôn* and *ṣārâ* (→ צרר *ṣrr*). The thanksgiving festival liturgy in Ps. 107 contains in vv. 33-43 a hymnic expansion expressing general theologoumena concerning Yahweh's power. This section exhibits features typical of Wisdom. Yahweh's social intervention on behalf of the "needy" (→ אביון *'eḇyôn* [*'ebhyôn*]) takes place against the background of his oppression of the rich and powerful (*n*e*ḏîḇîm;* → נדב *ndb*). That the latter must submit to *rā'â* and *yāḡôn* is due solely to Yahweh (Kraus[6] would like to transpose vv. 39 and 40, which would undoubtedly improve the logic of vv. 38-41; it is also possible to interpret v. 39 as anticipating v. 40).

Ps. 107:39, part of a thanksgiving festival liturgy, is associated only indirectly with a lament; the association is once again direct in the case of Ps. 119:28 (in the context of vv. 25-32). The despair of the psalmist is expressed in general terms: *dāl*e*pâ napšî mittûḡâ* ("I am sleepless with sorrow"; cf. v. 25: *dāḇ*e*qâ l*e*'āpār napšî*), followed immediately by a prayer for revival or strengthening through God's word (*kiḏ*e*ḇār*e*ḵā*). Sorrow may encompass the psalmist on account of his lack of devotion. He senses that his life is not in agreement with God's Torah. Nothing more precise can be made out.

A typical lament situation lies behind the quotation in Jer. 45:3, where Jeremiah cites Baruch's lament before addressing words of comfort to him: "Woe is me! for Yahweh has added sorrow (*yāḡôn*) to my pain (*maḵ'ōḇî*). I am weary with my groaning (*b*e*'anḥāṯî*), and I find no rest (*m*e*nûḥâ*)." This statement gives such a routine impression that it might be considered a stereotyped expression. In the present context, it refers to the interweaving of Baruch's personal fortunes with the disastrous fate of the people. Jeremiah must proclaim judgment to the people.

There is no dispute that the 5 occurrences in Lamentations derive from OT lament genres. But all attempts to define the genre of the individual poems more precisely run into difficulties. In addition to the dirge, both individual and collective lament are found. One poem contains elements from all the various lament genres.[7] As to date, there is relative unanimity that the poems of Lamentations were occasioned by the fall of Jerusalem and the destruction of the temple, and were probably composed not long afterwards.[8]

Lam. 1 is a dirge with Zion as its subject (so that Kraus suggests the designation "lament for the destroyed sanctuary"). V. 4 describes the lamentable situation after the historical catastrophe—the desolation of the city and the suffering of the population. In particular, the maidens (*b*e*ṯûlôṯ*), who had been carefree and at ease during the rejoicing and dancing of the festivals, are now described as being afflicted with sorrow (*nûḡôṯ,* niphal ptcp.). In this form of *yāḡâ* is expressed all the pain and sorrow that the populace, and especially the young women, could suffer in an ancient Near Eastern city taken in battle. Lam. 1:5 designates the reason for the suffering in strictly theological terms. It is not enemies and oppressors who have "made her suffer

---

[6] *BK,* XV/2 (⁵1978), *in loc.*

[7] See the discussion in the comms., for example H.-J. Kraus, *Klagelieder (Threni). BK,* XX (³1968); O. Plöger, *Die fünf Megilloth. HAT,* XVIII (²1969); A. Weiser, *Klagelieder. ATD,* XVI/2 (²1958).

[8] On the individual problems of chaps. 1 and 3, see the comms.

(*hôgâ,* hiphil perfect with suffix)," but Yahweh himself, quite actively (as the lament goes on to state in detail) on account of the transgressions committed by the city. The worshippers do not turn away from Yahweh, who has occasioned their suffering, but confess the rightness of his act of judgment. Even in v. 12, when the lament turns into a graphic description of pain and anguish, nothing is said to qualify the statement that Yahweh in his fierce anger has inflicted this sorrow (*hôgâ;* the LXX reads Heb. *hôgānî*).

Lam. 3 is complex in its structure. Elements of an individual lament appear to predominate. Since the *yāgâ* passages appear within a section of the individual lament that expresses the motif of confidence, the formal problems of the chapter as a whole can be ignored here. The confidence motif makes use of traditional statements affirming Yahweh's true nature, confessing his everlasting goodness and mercy.[9] Lam. 3:31 reaffirms that Yahweh does not cast off for ever (*l^e^'ôlām*), but rather that when he has caused grief he will have compassion according to his abundant mercy (v. 32: *kî 'im-hôgâ w^e^riḥam k^e^rōḇ ḥ^a^sāḏāw* [*Q ḥ^a^sāḏāyw;* pl.]), that he does not willingly afflict and grieve people (v. 33: *wayyaggeh,* probably mispointed; the piel imperfect should be *way^e^yaggeh;* the hiphil impf. *wayyô-geh* has also been suggested). In this passage the attempt to overcome the religious crisis following the catastrophe of 587 B.C. in a kind of theodicy achieves a kind of high point. In a timely application of certain aspects of Israel's faith, Yahweh's true nature and earlier acts are affirmed: he shows love and acts with mercy. A deserved judgment has come to pass, but it will be limited in duration. Yahweh's causing *yāgâ* is not his *opus proprium.* This passage has marked affinities with Deutero-Isaiah.

2. *Prophetic Lament.* Jeremiah is noted for his "confessions," in which he provides information about his inward experience as a prophet, and above all about the suffering involved in his office. Jer. 20:18 is part of a curse on the day of his birth: "Why did I come forth from the womb to see (only) *'āmāl* and *yāgôn*?" What has preceded explicates the substance of *yāgôn* and *'āmāl* (→ עמל *'ml*): insecurity, persecution, calumny, and mockery, as well as the failure of his message. These are what Jeremiah feels are his fate as a prophet called by Yahweh. He feels betrayed by his God (20:7ff.). In contrast to the other writing prophets of the OT, Jeremiah reveals much of how the disaster that befalls his people affects him inwardly: *yāgôn 'ālay libbî dawwāy,* "My grief is beyond healing, my heart is sick" (8:18). The message of Yahweh's judgment that he must deliver makes him sick himself and makes his whole life a life of suffering. He suffers with his people.

3. *Announcement of Salvation.* In Deutero-Isaiah, *yāgôn* plays a role in the message of salvation. Isa. 51:11 states that sorrow and sighing have fled away (*nāsû yāgôn wa'^a^nāḥâ*) from those whom Yahweh shall redeem, who will come to Zion. Those who once tormented (*môgayiḵ,* hiphil ptcp.) Jerusalem must now take the cup of wrath and judgment and drink from it (51:23), just as Jerusalem had to drink from it

---

[9] See Plöger, *HAT,* XVIII, *in loc.* Kraus, *BK,* XX, discusses the author's didactic-parenetic style.

(v. 22). The *môgîm* are understood to be the historical entity of the Neo-Babylonians with their program of military conquest, subjection, and deportation. Isa. 35:10 corresponds so closely to 51:11 that it can only be taken as a quotation from Deutero-Isaiah.

The transformation of mourning into joy and sorrow into gladness forms part of the complex of ideas behind the message of salvation in Jer. 31:13; vv. 10-12 of the larger context also contain the notions of redemption through Yahweh and the joyous return of the diaspora to Zion. This is so reminiscent of Isa. 51:11 (35:10) that, despite all attempts to ascribe these verses to Jeremiah, they are probably to be dated in the exilic or postexilic period. That is where these messages of salvation have their *Sitz im Leben,* their locus in history.[10]

4. *Prediction of Disaster.* To Ezekiel's allegory of the two unfaithful sisters Oholah and Oholibah has been added the pericope of the cup of wrath, in which *yāgôn* is also used (Ezk. 23:31-34). Oholibah (Jerusalem) must drink from the cup like Oholah (Samaria); she will be filled with *šikkārôn* and *yāgôn* (v. 33). Zimmerli[11] calls this pair of words a zeugma meaning "drunkenness that causes sorrow." The context shows that *yāgôn* refers to terrible devastation, the military destruction of the city and its subsequent desolation. It is still a matter of debate whether this passage goes back to Ezekiel himself or is a product of his school. Zimmerli emphasizes that there is no reason to doubt Ezekiel's authorship.

The phrase *nûgê mimmô'ēḏ* in Zeph. 3:18 ("tormented away from the festival"; niphal ptcp., pl. const.) is unfortunately incomprehensible. The entire verse is corrupt, and in particular the phrase in question is usually reconstructed on the basis of the LXX and appended to v. 17: *k^{e}yôm mô'ēḏ,* "as on the day of assembly."[12] The present context is a collection of messages of salvation.

5. *Summary.* In theological usage of *yāgâ* and its derivatives, an individual person or a group is always affected. People inflict *yāgôn* on others. The theological point is that individuals or groups may see in this an act of God's judgment, accept it as such, and take comfort in the assurance that the God who can cause sorrow also knows how to transform pain into joy. Trust in God's true nature, in his unmerited mercy, is accompanied by a willing acknowledgment that he is righteous when he brings disaster.

The *yāgâ/yāgôn/tûgâ* situations affecting individuals, brought about by interpersonal conflict, are also brought before God in laments and related to God in prayers for protection, justice, and relief. Here, too, the motivating force is confidence in God's ability and willingness to help, rooted in turn in the affirmations and traditions of ancient Israel. According to the witness of the OT, God himself is the subject of *yāgâ,* bringing judgment and disaster upon his people; but this power can also be used to bring deliverance to Israel and disaster to the enemies of God's people. Never, though, is God himself the object of a *yāgâ* event.

Wagner

---

[10] The problem is discussed by S. Herrmann, *Die prophetischen Heilserwartungen im AT. BWANT,* 85 [5/5] (1965), 215ff.

[11] W. Zimmerli, *Ezekiel 1. Herm* (Eng. trans. 1979), *in loc.*

[12] See the text and apparatus in *BHK*[3] and *BHS.*

יָגַע *yāga‘*; יְגִיעַ *ye gîa‘*; יְגִיעָה *ye gî‘â*; יָגָע *yāgā‘*; יָגֵעַ *yāgēa‘*; יָגִיעַ *yāgîa‘*

Contents: I. Ancient Near East: 1. East Semitic; 2. West Semitic. II. 1. Etymology; 2. Statistics; 3. Distribution; 4. LXX; 5. Meanings. III. Semantic Domains: 1. Profane/Secular; 2. Religious and Theological.

I. Ancient Near East.

1. *East Semitic*. The Akkadian verb *egû(m)* with the meaning "tire"[1] or "be careless, neglectful (of duty)"[2] is attested from Old Babylonian to Neo-Babylonian and Neo-Assyrian.

In Old Babylonian laws we frequently find the expression, "If the boatman [or: watchman, shepherd, tradesman, etc.] was careless,"[3] referring to an economic or social offense. Hammurabi assures the people: "I was never careless."[4] Old Babylonian letters contain instructions not to be careless with silver[5] or a building.[6] In addition, one should not "tire" when on watch.[7]

Religious texts often speak of neglect of or on the part of a deity. A prayer may state, "I did not neglect to offer your sacrifices,"[8] or confess, "I have been neglectful, I have sinned. . . ,"[9] or pray, "Be gracious to your servant, who has been neglectful."[10] The idea of sin and transgression is expressed directly by *egû(m)*. In the vassal treaty of Esarhaddon we read in the context of an oath: "Whoever . . . sins (*ša e-gu-u i-ḫa-ṭu-u*) against the oaths of this tablet. . . ."[11] One can also sin against Esagil.[12] King Nabonidus, however, insists, "I did not tire (*lā ēgî*), did not forget my duty, was not

---

yāga‘. G. Fohrer, "Twofold Aspects of Hebrew Words," *Words and Meanings. Festschrift D. W. Thomas* (Cambridge, 1968), 95-103; H. L. Ginsberg, "Lexicographical Notes," *ZAW*, 51 (1933), 308f.; E. Jenni, *Das hebräische Pi‘el* (Zurich, 1968), 71f., 99; F. Perles, "A Miscellany of Lexical and Textual Notes on the Bible, *JQR*, N.S. 2 (1911/12), 130ff.; S. Segert, "Zur Habakkuk-Rolle aus dem Funde vom Toten Meer III," *ArOr*, 22 (1954), 452f.

1 *AHw*, I, 191.

2 *CAD*, IV (1958), 48f.

3 Eshnunna, §§5, 25; 6, 34; cf. *ANET*³, 161; CH §§105, 47; 125, 75; 236, 32; 237, 46; 267, 82; cf. *ANET*³, 170f., 176f.

4 CH Epilogue, 40, 15; cf. *CAD*, IV, 49; *ANET*³, 177.

5 H. F. Lutz, *Early Babylonian Letters from Larsa. YOSBT*, 2 (1917), 11, 12; 134, 17; *MDP*, 18, 240, 14.

6 G. R. Driver, *Letters of the First Babylonian Dynasty. OECT*, 3 (1924), 62, 17.

7 O. Schroeder, *Altbabylonische Briefe. VAS*, 16 (1917), 107, 6.

8 *KAR*, 128, vo. 19.

9 J. V. Scheil, *Une saison de fouilles à Sippar* (Cairo, 1902), 2, 10.

10 D. W. Myhrman, *Babylonian Hymns and Prayers. PBS*, 1/1 (1911), 2, ii, 36.

11 D. J. Wiseman, *The Vassal-Treaties of Esarhaddon. Iraq*, 20 (1958), 57, line 397; cf. *AHw*, I, 191.

12 *BWL*, 56p.

careless (*lā addû*)"[13] when it was necessary to carry out the words of his deity. The tutelary deities "at your right hand and at your left shall not neglect to watch over you,"[14] i.e., they shall not grow weary with watching. None of the astral gods shall "commit an error."[15]

The noun *egû* means a "loose woman"[16] or a "sinner,"[17] and thus a "sinful person."[18] The derived noun *egîtu,* "carelessness, careless sin,"[19] appears in the sentence: "He made the wind bear away my offenses."[20] Such a "careless sin," however, can also provoke a curse[21] or—if committed against a particular deity—lead to the destruction of the temple tower.[22] The noun *egûtu,* "carelessness,"[23] is used in the context of "forgiving the carelessness of the soothsayer,"[24] and the noun *mēgūtu(m),* "carelessness,"[25] appears in casuistic laws.[26]

2. *West Semitic.* In West Semitic, words formed on the root *yg'* are especially common in Arabic. The Arabic root *wǧ'* is attested in the verbal forms *waǧi'a,* "have pain, suffer," *'awǧa'a,* "cause pain," *tawaǧǧa'a,* "express pain or suffering," and the noun *waǧa',* "pain, sickness."[27]

Morphologically related is OSA *'gw,* "exert oneself,"[28] and the Ethiopic verb *wag'a,* "worry," found in Tigré.[29] In Neo-Punic the morphologically related noun *ygn,* "labor,"[30] is attested once.

There is no known instance of the root *yg'* in Ugaritic. One of its semantic elements appears to be found in the disputed verb *dlp,* "be exhausted."[31]

In Middle Hebrew the verbal forms of the root *yg'* (qal, piel, hiphil, hithpael) are

---

13 W. Röllig, "Erwägungen zu neuen Stelen König Nabonids," *ZA,* N.S. 22 [56] (1964), 223, line 18; cf. C. J. Gadd, "The Harran Inscriptions of Nabonidus," *AnSt,* 8 (1958), 64, line 18.

14 A. Ungnad, *Babylonian Letters of the Ḫammurapi Period. PBS,* 7 (1915), 106, 14.

15 EnEl, V, 7; cf. A. Heidel, *The Babylonian Genesis* (Chicago, ²1963), 44; *ANET*³, 67; *CAD,* IV, 49.

16 Antagal, F, 127f.

17 *BWL,* 56; Ludlul bēl nēmeqi, III, p.

18 *CAD,* IV, 47.

19 *AHw,* I, 190; *CAD,* IV, 46.

20 *BWL,* 50, line 60, Ludlul bēl nēmeqi, III, 60.

21 Šurpu, III, 142.

22 L. Legrain, *Royal Inscriptions and Fragments from Nippur and Babylon. PBS,* 15 (1926), 69, 6.

23 *AHw,* I, 191; *CAD,* IV, 51.

24 E. Klauber, *Politisch-religiöse Texte aus der Sargonidenzeit* (Leipzig, 1913), 128, 5.

25 *AHw,* II, 640.

26 Cf. M. Civil, "New Sumerian Law Fragments," *Festschrift B. Landsberger. AS,* 16 (1965), 6.

27 Lane, VIII, 3049.

28 *RÉS,* 3854, 2; cf. W. W. Müller, "Altsüdarabische Beiträge zum hebräischen Lexicon," *ZAW,* 75 (1963), 309.

29 *TigrWb,* 448b.

30 *DISO,* 103; *KAI,* 119.6 (→ יגה *yāgâ*).

31 *KTU,* 1.2 IV, 17, 26; *UT,* no. 666; cf. *WUS,* no. 749: "oppress" or "convulse"; J. Obermann, "How Baal Destroyed a Rival: A Mythological Incantation Scene," *JAOS,* 67 (1947), 201: "quiver"; E. A. Speiser, "The Semantic Range of *dalāpu,*" *JCS,* 5 (1951), 64-66.

attested as well as the nominal forms *yāgā'*, "work, effort," and *y*^{e}*gî'â*, "labor, toil."[32]

II. 1. *Etymology.* The root *yg'* is of common Semitic origin. Points of contact and some degree of overlapping, especially in the Akkadian and Hebrew use of the verbal forms, suggest the cautious hypothesis of a common basic Semitic meaning "be/become weary," on the basis of which it is possible to explain the distinctive usages and semantic fields in the individual Semitic languages.

In Hebrew usage of the verb and various derivatives, the primary emphasis is on the basic meaning "be/become weary." Extended semantic fields arise from the effort exerted while being or becoming weary, so that one "toils" or "labors." By metonymy, the result of such labor is its "yield" and hence its "return." Extended by synecdoche, finally, it means "property" and "wealth." In view of this development, it is unnecessary to postulate two relatively independent semantic fields, "be/become weary" and "toil," which rarely touch or overlap in Hebrew.

2. *Statistics.* The various verbal and nominal forms, including adjective derivatives, of the Hebrew root *yg'* appear 48 times in the OT. The verb is used 26 times: 20 times in the qal, 4 in the hiphil (Isa. 43:23f.; Mal. 2:17a,b), and twice in the piel (Josh. 7:3; Eccl. 10:15). The masc. verbal noun *y*^{e}*gîa'*, an aramaizing[33] *qaṭîl* form,[34] is attested 16 times. The fem. *qaṭîl* form *y*^{e}*gî'â*[35] is attested only once (Eccl. 12:12), written defectively as *y*^{e}*gia'*.[36] The hapax legomenon *yāgā'* (Job 20:18) is a masculine verbal noun formed as a *qaṭal*, often eliminated by the conj. *y*^{e}*gî'ô*.[37] But it is probably better to follow Fohrer[38] and Gerleman[39] in retaining the MT, possibly reading the form *y*^{e}*gā'ô*, "his gain,"[40] from which the suffix may have been lost by haplography. The adj. *yāgēa'*, a *qaṭil* formation,[41] appears 3 times (Dt. 25:18; 2 S. 17:2; Eccl. 1:8). Gunkel's emendation of MT *gōwēa'* to *yāgēa'* in Ps. 88:16(Eng. v. 15)[42] on the basis of the LXX[43] represents a misguided weakening of the statement.[44] The hapax legomenon *yāgîa'* (Job 3:17) is a *qaṭil* formation.[45]

---

32 *WTM*, II, 218f.

33 Cf. R. Meyer, *Hebräische Grammatik* (Berlin, ^{3}1969), II, §28.

34 Cf. J. Barth, *Die Nominalbildungen in den semitischen Sprachen* (Leipzig, ^{2}1894), 84; *BLe*, §471.

35 *KBL*^{3}; cf. *y*^{e}*gîa'* in the lexica: E. König, *Hebräisches und aramäisches Wörterbuch zum AT* (Leipzig, ^{6,7}1937), 141, and *LexHebAram*, 292.

36 Cf. *WTM*, II, 219 for the plene orthography in Middle Hebrew.

37 Budde, Graetz, Beer, Dhorme, and others; cf. *BHK* with a reference to יגיע in V$^{Ken\ 145}$.

38 G. Fohrer, *Das Buch Hiob. KAT*, XVI (1963), 325.

39 *BHS*.

40 Cf. *BHS*.

41 Barth, 12, 165; Meyer, II, §25.

42 H. Gunkel, *Psalmen. GHK*, II/2 (^{5}1968), 383f.; cf. *BHS; KBL*^{3}, 369.

43 Syriac and Jerome.

44 Cf. H.-J. Kraus, *Psalmen. BK*, XV (^{4}1972), 607; M. Dahood, *Psalms III. AB*, XVIIA (1970), 302.

45 Cf. *BLe*, §470n.

In the Hebrew text of Sirach, we find 1 occurrence each of the verb in the qal (Sir. 11:11), the noun *ye gîa'* (14:15), and the adj. *yāgîa'* (37:12).[46] In the Dead Sea scrolls, the root *yg'* is attested in the qal form *yg'w* (1QpHab. 10:7, quoting Hab. 2:13). This is presumably an imperfect written defectively, but it is also possible to vocalize it as a perfect.[47] The defective hiphil inf. *lwgy'* (1QpHab. 10:11) should probably be read as *l^e hôgîa'*.[48] The reading *'yg['\]* is uncertain.[49]

3. *Distribution*. The 48 occurrences of the root *yg'* appear in 17 OT books. The Pentateuch contains 3 forms (2 in Deuteronomy, 1 in Genesis), the Prophets 24 (14 in Isaiah 40–66, 4 in Jeremiah, 1 in Ezekiel, 5 in the Minor Prophets), Wisdom Literature 10 (6 in Job, 3 in Ecclesiastes, 1 in Proverbs), the poetic books 6 (5 in Psalms, 1 in Lamentations), and the historical books 5 (2 each in Joshua and 2 Samuel, 1 in Nehemiah). This wide distribution shows that the derivatives of *yg'* are not limited to a particular genre.

4. *LXX*. The LXX renders the Hebrew verbal forms 15 times as *kopián*,[50] twice as *paroxýnein* (Mal. 2:17a,b), and once each as *anágein* (Josh. 7:3), *apothnḗskein* (Job 9:29), *énkopos poieín* (Isa. 43:23), *proistánai* (Isa. 43:24), *manthánein* (Isa. 47:12), *mochtheín* (Isa. 62:8), *ekleípein* (Hab. 2:13), *parekteínein* (Prov. 23:4), and *kopoún* (Eccl. 10:15). The noun *ye gîa'* is rendered 8 times as *pónos* and twice each as *érgon* (Job 10:3; 39:11),[51] *kópos* (Gen. 31:42; Neh. 5:13), *kopián* (Job 39:16; Isa. 45:14), and *móchthos* (Isa. 55:2; Ezk. 23:29). The noun *ye gî'â* is rendered as *kópōsis* and the noun *yāgā'* as *kopián*. The adj. *yāgēa'* is rendered twice as *kopián* and once as *énkopos* (Eccl. 1:8). For the adj. *yāgîa'* we find *katákopos*. This multiplicity of Greek terms does not exhibit any systematic approach to translation, but reflects an abundance of semantic nuances.

5. *Meanings*. The basic verbal meaning of the root *yg'* may properly be defined as "be/become weary" in the objective sense of bodily fatigue, i.e., "be/become weak, weary, exhausted," rather than in the subjective psychological sense of "be/become weary of something." The prep. *b^e-*, "through," with such objects as moaning (Ps. 6:7[6]; Jer. 45:3), crying out (Ps. 69:4[3]; Isa. 43:22), and wandering (Isa. 57:10), indicates the source of the physical exertion that brings weariness. The state of "weariness" appears to precede the process of "becoming weary."[52]

The piel has the atemporal meaning "make weary" in Eccl. 10:15. In Josh. 7:3,[53]

---

[46] Cf. I. Lévi, *The Hebrew Text of the Book of Ecclesiasticus* (1904; repr. Leiden, 1969), 41, with the conj. *yāgēa'*.

[47] K. Elliger, *Studien zum Habakuk-Kommentar vom Toten Meer. BHTh*, 15 (1953), 56; Segert, 452f.

[48] Cf. E. Lohse, *Die Texte aus Qumran* (Munich, [2]1971), 240.

[49] K. G. Kuhn, *Konkordanz zu den Qumrantexten* (Göttingen, 1960), 82; for a different view, see E. L. Sukenik, *'Ôṣar ham-m^e gillôt hag-g^e nûzôt* (Jerusalem, 1954), 58.

[50] Cf. F. Hauck, "κόπος," *TDNT*, III, 827-830.

[51] Cf. G. Bertram, "ἔργον," *TDNT*, II, 635ff.

[52] Jenni, 72.

[53] Jenni, 99.

with future reference, it means "make weary"[54] or "tire,"[55] although others suggest the extended sense "toil."[56] The hiphil has the causative sense "cause someone to be weary,"[57] i.e., "weary someone."[58] The prep. *b^e-* with such objects as incense (Isa. 43:23), words (Mal. 2:17a), or sins (Isa. 43:24) designates the means by which someone is made weary.

Extended meanings appear as the natural consequence of toil in the state of being weary and the process of wearying. The qal can be used alone after *'ašer* in the sense of "labor" (Isa. 47:15).[59] Here again the prep. *b^e-* indicates the object *for* which (land, Josh. 24:13; wine, Isa. 62:8; fire, Hab. 2:13; nought, Jer. 51:58) or *with* which (sorceries, Isa. 47:12) one labors. It is also possible to be weary of Yahweh (Isa. 43:22).

The Masoretic pointing in 2 S. 5:8 reads *yigga‘*, a qal imperfect of the root *ng‘*,[60] its meaning in this context is obscure. Ginsberg[61] repoints the MT so as to read *w^eyigga‘*, a piel form of the root *yg‘*, and suggests the meaning "torture" on the basis of Arabic. This suggestion has found no support,[62] in part because *ṣinnôr* is understood to mean "spear"[63] rather than "water shaft."[64] It is probably necessary to stay with some form of *ng‘*,[65] although it is impossible to decide whether in this context the meaning "reach"[66] or "climb up"[67] better represents what is being said.

The passive state "weary" is expressed by the adj. *yāgēa‘* (Dt. 25:18; 2 S. 17:2). The adj. *y^egē‘îm* in the obscure passage Eccl. 1:8a appears to designate an active process. Its meaning is dependent in part on the word *d^eḇārîm*,[68] which here does not have the meaning "things"[69] but rather "words,"[70] as it does in 13 other passages

54 E. König, 140.
55 *GesB*, 283.
56 *BDB*, 388; *KBL*³, 369.
57 Jenni, 72.
58 *KBL*³, 369.
59 J. L. McKenzie, *Second Isaiah. AB*, XX (1968), 90.
60 Cf. *KBL*², 593.
61 Ginsberg, *ZAW*, 51 (1933), 308.
62 Cf. J. Mauchline, *1 and 2 Samuel. NCB* (1971), 217f.
63 Following E. L. Sukenik, "The Account of David's Capture of Jerusalem," *JPOS*, 8 (1928), 12-16.
64 Cf. J. J. Simons, *Jerusalem in the OT* (Leiden, 1952), 168-174, with bibliog.
65 *KBL*³, 369, without accepting Ewald's suggestion of a hiphil form *w^eyagga‘*, "plunge into," or following S. R. Driver, *Notes on the Hebrew Text of the Books of Samuel* (Oxford, ²1913), 259, emending the MT to *wayya‘al;* cf. *BHK*.
66 Simons, 169-173; H. W. Hertzberg, *I & II Samuel. OTL* (Eng. trans. 1964), 268f.
67 F. W. Birch, L.-H. Vincent, and G. Bressan, "L'espugnazione di Sion in 2 Sam 5:6 // 1 Cron 11:4-6 e il problema del 'Ṣinnôr,' " *Bibl*, 25 (1944), 377-381, and others.
68 → דבר *dāḇar* [*dābhar*].
69 Also R. Gordis, *Koheleth: The Man and His World* (New York, ³1968), 146; H. Lamparter, *Das Buch der Weisheit. BAT*, 16 (²1959), *in loc*.
70 H. W. Hertzberg, *KAT*, XVII/4 (1963), 72; K. Galling, *Die fünf Megilloth. HAT*, XVIII (²1969), 85f.; R. B. Y. Scott, *Proverbs–Ecclesiastes. AB*, XVIII (1965), 210; F. Ellermeier, *Untersuchungen zum Buche Qohelet*, I (Herzberg am Harz, 1967), 202f.; and others.

in Ecclesiastes. Therefore the emendation suggested by Ehrlich[71] and adopted by Zimmermann,[72] reading the piel ptcp. *m*ᵉ*yagg*ᵉ*‘îm* instead of the adjective, is neither desirable nor necessary. The statement in Eccl. 1:8a can be translated literally: "All words are wearying."[73] The active aspect of *yāgēa‘* thus indicates that it is not the words that are weary; they "weary" those who speak and hear them.

The noun *y*ᵉ*gî‘â*[74] in Eccl. 12:12, in the construct with *bāśār,*[75] means "weariness of body." Here the reference is to the "weariness of body" that comes from the exertion of intensive studying. For this reason the meanings "exertion"[76] and "labor"[77] are inappropriate to the sense of the passage.

The adj. *yāgîa‘* appears in Job 3:17 in the construct with *kōaḥ*,[78] with the combination suggesting the concept "those whose strength is wearied or exhausted,"[79] or, in short, "the weary."[80]

The noun *yāgā‘*[81] is used metonymically in Job 20:18, where it means "profit" as the result of laborious and wearying toil.

The noun *y*ᵉ*gîa‘* reveals various shades and extensions of meaning, revealing a semantic development of cause and effect. It can, for example, refer to the wearying activity itself, i.e., "work" or "labor" (Job 39:11,16; Ps. 78:46; Isa. 55:2), as well as the result of what has been achieved by the wearying activity, i.e., the product in the form of "yield" or "profit" (Dt. 28:33; Ps. 109:11; Jer. 3:24). It can also be used by synecdoche for the "property" so acquired (Neh. 5:13; Hos. 12:9[8]; cf. Sir. 14:15) and quite generally for "wealth" (Isa. 45:14; Jer. 20:5; Ezk. 23:29). The genitive phrase *y*ᵉ*gîa‘ kappayim* (often with pronominal suffix) means literally "the labor of one's hands" (Gen. 31:42; Ps. 128:2; Hag. 1:11). With reference to human beings, it refers by metonymy to what has been attained through the wearying work of one's hands, i.e., "profit"[82] or "yield."[83] With reference to God, it refers to what he has brought about or created (Job 10:3).

Roughly synonymous terms with the nuance of "gain" include *'ōn,* "wealth,"[84] *saḥar,* "profit" (Isa. 45:14), *kesep,* "money" (Isa. 55:2);[85] what is gained can include cattle, sons, and daughters (Jer. 3:24), as well as "wealth" (*ḥōsen*) and "treasure" (*y*ᵉ*qār*) of all kinds (Jer. 20:5).

---

71 A. B. Ehrlich, *Randglossen zur hebräischen Bibel,* VII (1914; repr. Hildesheim, 1968), 56.
72 F. Zimmermann, "The Aramaic Provenance of Qohelet," *JQR,* N.S. 36 (1945/46), 41.
73 König, 140.
74 For discussion of the form and orthography see II.2 above.
75 → בשׂר *bāśār.*
76 König, 141.
77 *GesB,* 283.
78 → כח *kōaḥ.*
79 *GesB,* 283; cf. A. Dillmann, *Hiob. KEHAT,* II/4 (^{3}1869), 31: "tired out."
80 Cf. A. S. van der Woude, "כֹּחַ *kōᵃḥ* Kraft," *THAT,* I, 823.
81 For a discussion of the form and a conjectural emendation, see II.2 above.
82 Ehrlich, I (1908; repr. Hildesheim, 1968), 158f.
83 Fohrer, *BK,* XVI, 99, 101.
84 *KBL*^{3}, 22.
85 Cf. J. Barr, *Comparative Philology and the Text of the OT* (Oxford, 1968), 153.

The verb *yg'* appears 5 times in parallelism with synonymous *y'p*[86] (Isa. 40:28,30f.; Hab. 2:13 = Jer. 51:58) and once each in parallelism with the hiphil of *'bd*[87] (Isa. 43:23) and the noun *'āmāl*[88] (Eccl. 10:15). In Dt. 25:18 the adj. *yāgēa'* appears with the adj. *'āyēp.*[89] Similar in meaning to *y^egîa'* is *yiṯrōn*, "profit, advantage."[90]

III. Semantic Domains.

1. *Profane/Secular.* Physical or bodily weariness can be occasioned by flight (2 S. 17:2), battle (2 S. 23:10), ritual weeping (Ps. 6:7[6]; Jer. 45:3) and crying (Ps. 69:4[3]; cf. Isa. 43:22), words (Eccl. 1:8;[91] 10:15; Mal. 2:17), study (Eccl. 12:12[92]), and the offering of sacrifice (Isa. 43:23) or other cultic acts (Job 9:29). A sober sense of realism finds expression in the appreciation of human achievement in agriculture. One does not leave the hard-won "fruits of one's labor" to the wild ox (Job 39:11). Although human beings are not, like the ostrich, indifferent to the fruits of their labor (Job 39:16; cf. Isa. 65:23), they must always remember the proverb: "Do not exhaust yourself to acquire wealth" (Prov. 23:4).[93] Life in its true fulness cannot be bought through labor (Isa. 55:2); it is God's free gift (Isa. 55:1-5).

Deep resignation and pessimism about life are reflected in Job's saying about the "weary" who find rest only in the grave (Job 3:17).

2. *Religious and Theological.* The notion that God has no "profit" (Job 10:3) in the destruction of human beings derives from the intimate relationship between Creator and creature. One wisdom passage promises that those who walk in God's ways will enjoy the fruit of the "labor of (their) hands" (Ps. 128:2). The patriarchal tradition contains a recollection of this statement: God came to Jacob's aid when the "labor of (his) hands," which had taken years, was in danger (Gen. 31:42).[94] A sudden change from violence and injustice to divine protection and security is also implicit in the description of the salvation to come.

The judgmental prediction that the "peoples labor only for naught (fire)" (Hab. 2:13 = Jer. 51:58)[95] demonstrates the vanity of political coercion that seeks renown and security through the exploitation of forced labor on the part of subjects. Ephraim

---

86 → יעף *yā'ap.*

87 → עבד *'āḇaḏ.*

88 → עמל *'āmal.*

89 → יעף *yā'ap.*

90 Cf. M. Wagner, *Die lexikalischen und grammatikalischen Aramaismen im alttestamentlichen Hebräisch. BZAW,* 96 (1966), 63, no. 123.

91 See II.5 above.

92 See II.2, 5 above.

93 For a critical comparison with Amenemope, IX, 9-15, see W. McKane, *Proverbs. OTL* (1970), 382.

94 Cf. E. A. Speiser, *Genesis. AB,* I (1964), 247, with reference to Akk. *mānaḫātu,* "earnings."

95 See II.3 above. B. Duhm's emendation *wayyîg^e'û* (*Das Buch Habakuk* [Tübingen, 1906], 58), adopted by W. Nowack, *GHK,* III/4.2 (1903), 274, and E. Sellin, *Das Zwolfprophetenbuch. KAT,* XII/2 (^{2,3}1929-1930), 354, has been made highly unlikely by 1QpHab; cf. Segert, 453.

makes a daring claim in response: "With all my labor no guilt that is sin can be found in me" (Hos. 12:9[8]).[96] The senselessness of all the labor Israel has expended on idolatry is sharply attacked: "You are wearied with all your wandering" (Isa. 57:10). No matter how great the effort, all the divination and occult science[97] at which Babylon "has labored from (its) youth" (Isa. 47:12[98]), with their modern heritage of astrology and occultism, contribute nothing to spiritual or religious well-being and security or to deliverance from danger (Isa. 47:15).

In contrast to the inadequacy of pagan gods, Yahweh proves to be the God who gave Israel a land that "cost no labor" (Josh. 24:13). Israel received from its God a land that was already arable and cultivated. The crime of the Amalekites consisted in their cutting off the weak who were lagging behind when Israel was "faint and weary" from the hardships of the desert (Dt. 25:18). The whole people (military levy) need not "toil" up to the city of Ai (Josh. 7:3), because Yahweh drives out the people of Canaan for Israel (cf. 24:11,18). God is with his people as long as they abide within the covenant. But if they become disobedient and rebellious, then the curse will be fulfilled that others shall enjoy the fruit of Israel's labor: "A nation which you have not known shall eat up the fruit of your ground and of all your labors" (Dt. 28:33; cf. Ps. 78:46; 109:11; Jer. 20:5; Ezk. 23:9; Hag. 1:11). The wisdom teachers already knew that the wicked cannot enjoy the fruit of their toil (Job 20:18). Finally, we hear the lament that Israel is weary under the alien yoke of exile (Lam. 5:5) and finds no rest.

Several of the most significant theological statements using our root appear in Isa. 44–66. Yahweh is the creator God and Lord of history, who "does not faint (→ יעף *y'p*) or grow weary (*yg'*)" (Isa. 40:28). He is a source of inexhaustible strength, who helps the faint and weary (v. 30). He is also the Lord of those who hope in him (v. 31) and call upon him (Ps. 6:7[6]; 69:4[3]): "He gives power to the faint, and to him who has no might he increases strength. Even youths shall faint and be weary, and young men shall fall exhausted; but they who wait for the Lord shall renew their strength, they shall mount up with wings like eagles, they shall run and not be weary, they shall walk and not faint" (Isa. 40:29-31). Yahweh gives the faint and weary physical vitality and spiritual support.

Isa. 43:22-25 levels a terrible accusation against Israel. The sins of the people have turned the Lord into a servant; they have wearied him through their misdeeds: "No, you have caused me to serve through your sins, you have wearied me with your iniquities" (v. 24). The astonishing change from "Lord" to "servant"[99] is caused by Israel's claim to have served God faithfully with many sacrifices. But God did not desire of his people any onerous cultic ceremonies (v. 23b). The weariness brought about by God's service (v. 24b; the LXX avoids the anthropomorphism by deliberate

---

[96] Cf. W. Rudolph, *Hosea. KAT,* XIII/1 (1966), 222f.; H. W. Wolff, *Hosea. Herm* (Eng. trans. 1974), *in loc.,* with reference to the emendations suggested by the LXX.

[97] G. E. Wright, *The OT against its Environment. SBT,* 2 (1950), 77-93.

[98] To be retained, following the MT and 1QIs^a, contra Duhm and Ewald.

[99] The latter is an allusion to the Servant Songs; cf. C. Westermann, *Isaiah 40–66. OTL* (Eng. trans. 1966), 130f.

variation,[100] as does the Targum: "You have made it strong before me with your transgressions") reveals the whole tragedy of the people's sinful conduct. The notion of the divine servant seems to have some connection with the exhausting labor of the Servant of God: "I have labored in vain, I have spent my strength for nothing and vanity" (Isa. 49:4; cf. 53:10-12). The labor of the Servant of God is in vain.

The description of the salvation to come is guaranteed by Yahweh's oath, which looks forward to the time when the faithful will enjoy the fruit of the field and the grape of the vine: "I will not again give your grain to be food for your enemies, and foreigners shall not drink your wine for which you have labored" (Isa. 62:8). Yahweh is the herald of peace, who determines the fate of his people. Among the major themes of the apocalyptic poem describing the "new heaven and new earth" (65:8-25) are the statements that the elect shall enjoy "the work of their hands" (v. 22) and "shall not labor in vain" (v. 23). This future realization of true abundance (Isa. 55:1-5) includes life within God's protection.

Hasel

---

[100] Cf. J. Ziegler, *Untersuchungen zur Septuaginta des Buches Isaias. ATA*, 12/3 (1934), 154.

יָד *yāḏ*; זְרוֹעַ *zᵉrôaʿ*; יָמִין *yāmîn*; כַּף *kap*; אֶצְבַּע *ʾeṣbaʿ*

Contents: I. Ancient Near East: 1. Egypt; 2. Mesopotamia. II. 1. *yāḏ:* Philology; 2. *yāḏ:* Cognates, Denominatives, Homographs; 3. *yāḏ:* Meaning; 4. Other Biblical Terms; 5. Biblical Aramaic; 6. LXX. III. Usage: 1. Holding; 2. Personal Responsibility; 3. Possession and Control; 4. *bᵉyāḏ;* 5. Gestures. IV. Iconography. V. Theological Aspects: 1. Power; 2. Divine Power; 3. Hostile Divine Power; 4. Divine Impotence; 5. Transmission of Power; 6. Divine Gestures; 7. Idols.

---

yāḏ. H. Altenmüller, "Hand," *LexÄg*, II, 938-943; H. Braun, *Qumran und das NT* (Tübingen, 1966), I, 89f.; L. H. Brockington, "The Hand of Man and the Hand of God," *Baptist Quarterly*, 10 (1947), 191-97; M. A. Canney, *Givers of Life and their Significance in Mythology* (London, 1923), 88-103; M. Dahood, "Congruity of Metaphors," *Hebräische Wortforschung. Festschrift W. Baumgartner. SVT*, 16 (1967), 40-49, esp. 44-46; D. Daube, *The NT and Rabbinic Judaism* (London, 1956), 224-246; M. Delcor, "Two Special Meanings of the Word יד in Biblical Hebrew," *JSS*, 12 (1967), 230-240 = his *Religion d'Israël et Proche Orient ancien* (Leiden, 1976), 139ff.; *idem*, "מלא *mlʾ* voll sein, füllen," *THAT*, I, 897-900, esp. 898f.; R. C. Dentan, "Hand," *IDB*, II, 520f.; É. P. Dhorme, *L'emploi métaphorique des noms de parties du corps en hébreu et en akkadien* (1923; repr. Paris, 1963), 137-154; R. du Mesnil du Buisson, *Les peintures de la synagogue de Doura-Europos. SPIB*, 86 (1939); E. Edel, "Zur Etymologie und hieroglyphischen Schreibung der Präpositionen *mn* und *mdj*," *Or*, N.S. 36 (1967), 74f.; A. Fitzgerald, "Hebrew *yd* = 'Love' and 'Beloved,' " *CBQ*, 29 (1967), 368-374; J. A. Fitzmyer, "Some Observations on the *Genesis Apocryphon*," *CBQ*, 22 (1960), 284; D. Flusser, "Healing through the Laying-on of Hands in a Dead Sea Scroll," *IEJ*, 7 (1957), 107f.; P. Fronzaroli, "Studi sul lessico comune semitico," *AANLR*, 19 (1964), 259, 273, 279; K. Galling, "Erwägungen zum Stelenheiligtum von Hazor," *ZDPV*, 75 (1959), 1-13; B. de Geradon, "Le coeur, la bouche, les

I. Ancient Near East.

1. *Egypt.* a. The usual Egyptian word for "hand"[1] is *ḏr.t,*[2] probably a paraphrastic expression meaning "grasper." The original words for "hand" common to the Semitic languages apparently became taboo at an early date in colloquial language,[3] so that the correspondence to *yd* is preserved only in hieroglyph for *d;*[4] *kp* (cf. Heb. *kap̱*) is used only for the severed hands of the enemy.[5]

Individual words for right hand (*wnmy*)[6] and left hand (*snmḥy*)[7] appear in the New Kingdom.The noun *ḏr.t* has a wide range of use; it can mean, for instance, both the trunk of an elephant and the paw of a cat.[8] All kinds of implements are considered "hands," and in an extended sense ʿAnat and ʿAstarte are "the hands of the chariot."[9] Often no distinction is made between "hand" and "arm." In sacrificial formulas both words appear in parallel.[10] The word for "fist" is *ḫfʿ*,[11] with a determinative of a clenched hand, whereas *ḏr.t* has the determinative of an outstretched hand—like the hieroglyph for *d.* But this distinction is not always maintained: either a "hand" (*ḏr.t*) or a "fist" (*ḫfʿ*) can hold a scepter, seize the enemy, or have power over human life.

---

mains: Essai sur un schème biblique," *BVC,* 1/4 (1953), 7-24; H. Holma, *Die Namen der Körperteile im Assyrisch-Babylonischen. AnAcScFen,* ser. B, 7/1 (1911), 110-128; J. Holman, "Analysis of the Text of Ps 139," *BZ,* N.S. 14 (1970), 37-71, esp. 53f.; P. Humbert, "Étendre la main," *VT,* 12 (1962), 383-395; A. R. Johnson, *The Vitality of the Individual in the Thought of Ancient Israel* (Cardiff, ²1964), 50-60; O. Keel[-Leu], *The Symbolism of the Biblical World* (Eng. trans., New York, 1978), esp. IV.3, VI.1; *idem, Wirkmächtige Siegeszeichen im AT. OBO,* 5 (1974); P. Lacau, *Les noms des parties du corps en Égyptien et en Sémitique* (Paris, 1970), 136f.; E. Lohse, "χείϱ," *TDNT,* IX, 424-437; U. Luck, *Hand und Hand Gottes: Eine Beitrag zur Grundlage und Geschichte des biblischen Gottesverständnisses* (1959); T. Nöldeke, *Beiträge zur semitischen Sprachwissenschaft* (Strasbourg, 1904), 124-136; *idem, Neue Beiträge zur semitischen Sprachwissenschaft* (Strasbourg, 1910), 113-16; R. North, "*Yâd* in the Shemitta-Law," *VT,* 4 (1954), 196-99; J. L. Palache, *Semantic Notes on the Hebrew Lexicon* (Eng. trans., Leiden, 1959), 38; R. Péter, "L'imposition des mains dans l'AT," *VT,* 27 (1977), 48-55; G. Révész, *Die menschliche Hand* (New York, 1944); H. Riesenfeld, *The Resurrection in Ezekiel XXXVII and in the Dura-Europos Paintings. UUÅ,* 1948/11, 32-34, 36f.; G. Rinaldi, "*jād,*" *BeO,* 6 (1964), 246; G. Robinson, "The Meaning of יָד in Isaiah 56$_5$," *ZAW,* 88 (1976), 282-84; K. Rupprecht, "Quisquilien zu der Wendung מלא (את) יד פלוני und zum Terminus מלאים," *Sefer Rendṭorff. Festschrift R. Rendtorff. BDBAT,* 1 (1975), 73-93; H. Schlier, "βϱαχίων," *TDNT,* I, 639f.; H. W. Wolff, *Anthropology of the OT* (Eng. trans., Philadelphia, 1975), 67f.; A. S. van der Woude, "יד *jāḏ* Hand," *THAT,* I, 667-674.

[1] Cf. *WbÄS,* VI, 73, *s.v. "Hand."*

[2] *WbÄS,* V, 580ff.; cf. also the variant *ḏ3.t, ibid.,* 516.

[3] Altenmüller, 938, including n. 5.

[4] *WbÄS,* V, 414.

[5] *WbÄS,* V, 118; attested from the New Kingdom on; possibly a loanword.

[6] *WbÄS,* I, 322.

[7] *WbÄS,* IV, 140.

[8] *WbÄS,* V, 584, 9f.

[9] W. R. Dawson and T. E. Peet, "The So-called Poem of the King's Chariot," *JEA,* 19 (1933), 169, 173.

[10] E.g., *WbÄS,* Bel. V, 101, on 581, 3 and 582, 1.

[11] *WbÄS,* III, 272; cf. the verb *ḫfʿ*, "grasp, seize."

b. Hands are not often represented empty. All kinds of implements and insignia in the hands of human beings and gods manifest their power and authority, their vigor and their readiness to act: lash and scepter in the hands of the pharaoh and Osiris; ankh and scepter in the hands of the gods (usually a papyrus scepter in the hands of goddesses); staff of office, writing implements, etc. in the hands of various officials. The power to act can be emphasized textually by an epithet like "having many hands" (said of Amon).[12] The same notion finds ingenious visual expression in the Amarna representations of the sun disk: its many rays terminate in hands that give the royal family "life" and "sovereignty" or receive offerings from them. The accompanying texts speak of both the "rays"[13] and the "hand"[14] bearing "life and sovereignty."

c. The dominant role of the hand—as a symbol of action—among the parts of the body is attested by these Amarna pictures, which otherwise eschew all anthropomorphism. The same notion finds expression in another area in the way the severed hands of slain enemies are treated in the New Kingdom: they are displayed as victory trophies or placed in a great heap before the deity, which is probably a foreign custom.[15]

At creation, the divine act par excellence, the "hand of the deity" (*ḏr.t nṯr*) plays an important role in some versions. On the basis of the cosmogony of Heliopolis, which draws on the concept of the masturbating primal god Atum,[16] from the First Intermediate period on the "hand of Atum" appears as an independent goddess, later equated with Hathor-Nebhet-Hetepet and Iusas.[17] Mut and Isis also appear in the role of "hand of the deity." From the Middle Kingdom on, the same term is also used as a title for the divine consorts.[18]

The worshipper "with beautiful hands" (holding sistra) will please the god.[19] "To lay one's hand on what is beautiful," i.e., to touch the sistrum, stands symbolically for both imposition of hands and embrace.

d. The way one holds one's hands (and arms) is the clearest of gestures: in greeting or prayer, rejoicing or lamentation. Special gestures emphasize protection and defense. In representations of a protective attitude the hands and arms not uncommonly are depicted with wings to strengthen the effect, as in the case of Isis protecting her mate. The outstretched hands of the *ka* glyph indicate readiness to accept offerings. A hand at the mouth can indicate the status of a child (Harpocrates); in late antiquity it was

[12] Papyrus Boulaq, 17, 6f.

[13] M. Sandman, *Texts from the Time of Akhenaten. Bibliotheca aegyptiaca,* 8 (Brussels, 1938), 69, 10.

[14] *Ibid.,* 75, 10.

[15] Altenmüller, 940, including nn. 44-46.

[16] Already found in *Pyr.,* 1248, but with *ḥf*ʿ (masc.) instead of *ḏr.t* (fem.).

[17] See J. Vandier, "Iousáas et (Hathor)-Nébet-Hétépet," *RÉg,* 16 (1964), 55-146; 17 (1965), 89-176; 18 (1966), 67-142.

[18] J. Leclant, "Gotteshand," *LexÄg,* II, 813-15.

[19] Cf. H. Brunner, "Das Besänftigungslied im Sinuhe (B 169-179)," *ZÄS,* 80 (1955), 7f.

interpreted as a sign for the requirement of silence in the mysteries.[20] Amulets and some objects for cultic use are often made in the form of hands (incense bowls, unguent spoons, etc.).

e. In cultic scenes the hands often play an important role as bearers and receivers of various offerings and instruments, and as the primary vehicles of the gestural language used in the cultic drama. The accompanying texts often speak of "life, health, sovereignty" in the hands of the pharaoh or the deity. The hand of the pharaoh or the deity can also be an object of fear, when the hand is conceived of as punishing. A memorial stone of the Ramesside period from Thebes says of the goddess Meritseger: "She showed mercy to me after letting me see her hand." But being in the hand of a deity is primarily an expression of enjoying that deity's protection. In the Instruction of Amenemope we read: "Do not scorn a man who is in the hand of god"[21] and "How happy is he who reaches the west if he is safe in the hand of the god."[22] Of Amon-Re, the god of destiny, it is said: "The years are in his hand,"[23] and an early Ramesside wisdom text asks the rhetorical question: "Are not both yesterday and tomorrow in the hands of the god?"[24] At Hierakonpolis "the two hands of Horus" are important cultic objects; according to a myth Isis severed them from her son's arms, probably because of attempted violence. Cultic officials are to appear before the deity "with pure hands," "with open hand (generosity)," "with friendly hand," and "with knowing hand." In the ritual of Amon[25] the officiating king states: "I am Horus in my purity; my hands are the hands of Horus, my arms the arms of Thoth." "Hand" and "heart" occasionally stand for the combination of purpose and act.[26] A Middle Kingdom text praises a man, using the phrases "with friendly hand" and "with friendly heart" in parallel.[27]

Bergman

2. *Mesopotamia*. Akkadian uses the word *idu* (which goes back to the Proto-Semitic noun *yad*) only in the sense "arm, side, strength."[28] Of the words for "hand," by far the most common is *qātu*, used in a variety of ways (including such meanings as "achievement; disposition; portion; surety").[29] Cultic acts often require "cleansing (verbs: *mesû, ullulu, ubbubu*) the hands." "Lifting up" (verb: *našû;* cf. the noun phrase *nīš qāti* and the Sumerian loanword *šu'illakku*[30]) probably accompanies every prayer.[31] "Grasping (*ṣabātu*) the hand" is also used as an image for divine aid, and "the hands

[20] For additional gestures see Altenmüller, 938f.

[21] XXIV, 11.

[22] XXIV, 19f.

[23] Papyrus Berlin 3049, XII, 2.

[24] Cited by S. Morenz, *Egyptian Religion* (Eng. trans., Ithaca, N. Y., 1973), 75f.

[25] I, 6.

[26] *WbÄS*, V, 582, 15.

[27] K. Sethe, *Ägyptische Lesestücke* (Leipzig, ²1928), 75, 20.

[28] *CAD*, VII (1960), 10ff.; *AHw*, I, 365.

[29] *AHw*, II, 908ff.

[30] *AHw*, II, 797; III, 1262b.

[31] See W. Mayer, *Untersuchungen zur Formensprache der babylonischen "Gebetsbeschwörungen." Studia Pohl*, ser. maior, 5 (1976), 8, 25f.

of the god created humankind." Diseases, however, are often referred to as "the hand of Ishtar (or Ninurta, etc.)," and the hands of demons often bring disaster. In other passages *qātu* refers to a god's power or sphere of influence; here belong such names as *Āmur-qāssa*, "I recognized her power."

Another common word for "hand" is *rittu*.[32] With reference to deities, it appears particularly in expressions meaning "hold in the hand" (a goddess *tamḫat rittušša*), including the cosmic sense: *itmuḫ Marduk rittuššu . . . markas* (the bond) *ša[mê u erṣeti]*.[33] Ea is prayed to smite the toothache worm "with his strong hand" (*ina dannati rittī-šu*). In the case of demons, a *rittu* is usually an animal's claw.

The noun *upnu* is much more common than its Hebrew equivalent *hōpen;* both mean "hollow of the hand." In prayer "my hands are opened" (*petâ upnā-ya*),[34] "the king opened his hands,"[35] etc. But a worshipper can also lament: "My hands are full (*malâ upnā-ya*) of suffering, curse, sins, etc."[36] A very rare word for "both hands" is *atulimānu/talīmānu;*[37] the worshipper "raises both hands." The final word for "hand," *kappu* II,[38] corresponding to Heb. *kap,* does not appear in religious texts.[39]

Von Soden

II. 1. *yāḏ: Philology.* The most common word for "hand" in the OT is *yāḏ*. It occurs more than 1600 times. A statistical survey appears in *THAT,*[40] but it is doubtful whether this survey does more than indicate that the use of the word is fairly evenly distributed, the longer books having more examples. No useful conclusion can be drawn from the observation that the greatest number of occurrences is found in 1 Samuel, Jeremiah, and Ezekiel (in that order), since these are all substantial books.

The fact that this word is used primarily for one particular part of the human body, and that a very important one, makes it reasonable to infer that the word is ancient; the occurrence of cognates in the main Semitic languages confirms as probable the view that it is a basic Semitic word.[41] Examples of cognates are Akk. *idu,* Ugar. *yd* (also *d*, with *bd* for *byd* as in Phoenician and Punic),[42] Amarna *badiu* as a gloss to *ina qātišu,*[43] Phoen. and Pun. *yd,* Syr. *'īḏ,* Jewish Aram. *yd,* Ethiop. *'ed,* OSA *yd* and *'d,* Arab. *yad;* cf. Egyp. *d.*

---

[32] *AHw,* II, 990.

[33] *KB,* VI/2, 114, 8.

[34] Mayer, 1.c, 470, 12.

[35] *KB,* VI/2, 138, 1.

[36] Šurpu V, 123f.

[37] *AHw,* I, 88b; *CAD,* I/2 (1968), 521f.

[38] *Ahw,* I, 444b; in *CAD,* VIII (1971), 187, this word is identified with *kappu* I, "wing."

[39] See V.1 below.

[40] Van der Woude, 667f.

[41] W. Gesenius-G. Bergsträsser, *Hebräische Grammatik,* 29th ed., II (Leipzig, 1926; repr. 1962), 184; Fronzaroli, 259, 273, 279.

[42] *UT,* no. 633.

[43] F. M. T. de Liagre Böhl, *Die Sprache der Amarnabriefe* (Leipzig, 1909), §37m, EA 245, 35; *WUS,* no. 1138.

No verbal root has been put forward satisfactorily as basic to the word, so that the original may have been a biliteral form.[44]

An alternative is to view the basic word as simply *d* = "hand."[45] Rabin argues for three types of form: (1) *yāḏ*, as in Hebrew, Arabic, Aramaic, Ugaritic, and Phoenician, comparable also to Akk. *idu*, Syr. *'īḏā*, etc.; (2) *'d*, exemplified by Ethiop. *'d*, *'ad* in some Arabic dialects, and *'id* in some colloquial dialects of Arabic; and (3) *d*, arguable from Ugar. *bd*, attested also in EA *ba-di-u*, which contains *di* as the element meaning "hand," and Isa. 16:6; Jer. 48:30, where, according to Rabin, *lô'-ḵēn baddāw* means "non-truth is in his hands," i.e., "he has a wrong opinion of himself." For this meaning he compares the saying of R. Jannai:[46] *'ên b^eyāḏēnû*, interpreted correctly by Obadiah of Bertinoro as meaning "we do not know why." The Hebrew proper name *bēḏyâ* (Ezr. 10:35; LXX^L *Badaia*) means "in the hand of God"; cf. Samaria ostracon 58 *bdwy* and Ugar. *bd'il*. Rabin argues further for *day*, "sufficiency," as derivative, being the old dual of *d*, "hand" = "power, ability" and hence "sufficiency," noting also Isa. 45:9 *ûpā'āl^eḵā 'ên-yāḏayim lô*, "your work has no hands," i.e., "your work is no good," and Jer. 49:9 = Ob. 5 as meaning "they steal as much as they can (*dayyām*). He also notes that the Egyptian letter *d* pictures a hand and cites the existence of reduplicated forms (Akk. *idd*, colloquial Arab. *yadd*, *'idd*) as further examples of an original simple form.

2. *yāḏ: Cognates, Denominatives, Homographs*. That *yāḏ* is not derived from a verb *yāḏâ*, "throw," appears clear. But various denominatives deriving from *yāḏ* have been suggested, primarily by Palache.[47] He connects with this noun: (1) *yāḏâ*, "throw," a not unnatural supposition based on the action of the hand; (2) Arab. *wadā*, Aram. *'d'*, "hand over, pay," again a natural connection; (3) Heb. *yāḏâ* hiphil, "pay, render thanks," comparing such constructions as *šillēm tôḏôṯ*, *nāṯān tôḏôṯ*; (4) Arab. *'adā(y)*, *'addā*, "hand over, pay";[48] (5) Arab. *'āda*, "be strong," where the initial guttural would seem to be a counterindication; (6) *yāḏâ* in Isa. 11:8, in the expression *gāmûl yāḏô hāḏâ*, understood as "offer, present his hand." This text is often considered corrupt; the suggested emendation *y^eḏahdeh*, "dance"[49] or "play pebbles,"[50] eliminates the "hand" concept in either case. The verb *hāḏâ* is also compared to Aram. *haddî* and Arab. *hadā*, "lead."

It must be acknowledged that verbal derivatives based on actions of the hand are not improbable. Of those proposed, "throwing" and "handing over" are most natural; if *yāḏâ* hiphil, "give thanks," is connected with *yāḏ*, the link might most naturally be seen in the hand gestures appropriate to such an expression of respect or homage.[51]

---

44 Cf. *VG*, I, 333, §115dβ.

45 C. Rabin, "Hebrew *D* = 'Hand,' " *JJS*, 6 (1955), 111-15; erroneously cited as Rabinowitz, *JSS*, by *KBL*³, 369.

46 *'Aboth* iv.15.

47 P. 38.

48 Cf. (2) above.

49 NEB.

50 J. Reider, "Etymological Studies in Biblical Hebrew," *VT*, 2 (1952), 115.

51 Cf.III.5.j below.

Quite different questions are raised by the suggestion of a distinct root, a homograph of *yāḏ*, with the meaning "love" and "beloved."[52] As Delcor clearly shows, this area of discussion impinges directly on the question of the sense of several passages where the meaning "phallus" is at least possible. This theory would suggest that such usage is due not to some extension of the normal meaning of *yāḏ* or its use as a euphemism for some other word for the male organ, but to the existence of a homograph of *yāḏ* that admits either confusion or wordplay. Basically the question is whether the root *ydd*, assumed for Hebrew as the root of → ידיד *yāḏîḏ*, *yᵉḏîḏôṯ*, *yᵉḏîḏâ*, etc., also produces a noun *yāḏ* comparable to Arab. *wadd*, Ugar. *yd*, "love." *KBL*³ admits this for Ps. 16:4, reading *miyyaddām* for *miyyāḏām*.[53] Fitzgerald goes on to suggest tentatively such a meaning in a number of other passages: Lam. 3:3, where *hāpaḵ yāḏ* is understood in the sense of "reversing love" (but cf. below on *hāpaḵ yāḏ* as a charioteer's action); Eccl. 7:26, where the parallelism of *lēḇ* and *yāḏ* suggests the translation "bonds are her love." In Isa. 11:11, Fitzgerald suggests *yaddô*, "his love": "he will love them all the more the second time." Other passages considered are Ps. 78:42; 80:18 (Eng. v. 17); 88:6(5); 95:7. In Isa. 66:14 and Jer. 15:17, *yāḏ* stands in contrasting parallelism with *za'am*, "wrath."[54] Isa. 57:8 is a problematic passage where a sexual meaning for *yāḏ* has often been suggested; this passage will be discussed below. In addition, Fitzgerald suggests the meaning "loved ones" in Job 20:10 and Lam. 4:6, and draws attention to the proper names *yiddô* (1 Ch. 27:21; Ezr. 10:43 *K*) and *yaddai* (Ezr. 10:43 *Q*).

The arguments of Delcor take account of the use of *yd'il* in Ugaritic.[55] The word appears alongside *mṭ* and *ḥṭ*, "staff, scepter," also "penis." Thus *yd* can be regarded as a euphemism, as in Hebrew. Delcor argues, however, that a root *yd* is sufficiently documented in South Arabic, Arabic, Syriac, Ugaritic, Hebrew, and Akkadian. Cf. also *WUS*, which distinguishes *yd* I, "hand,"[56] from *yd* II, "penis,"[57] leaving open the question whether they are connected or whether *yd* II is linked to *yd* III, "love."[58]

The philological arguments are inevitably inconclusive, but the existence of a root *ydd*, "love," is clear. Two aspects of the discussion need further investigation, and some relevant points will be addressed below. First, there is the question in any given passage—such as those discussed by Fitzgerald—whether the meaning "love" is necessarily more appropriate than the metaphorical sense associated with *yāḏ*, "hand." As will be seen, the use of this word in the sense of "power" not only in Hebrew but also in other Semitic languages allows a perfectly satisfactory interpretation of Isa. 11:11, the passages from Psalms, Isa. 66:14, and Jer. 15:17. Eccl. 7:26 may be understood

---

52 Fitzgerald; Delcor, *JSS*, 12 (1967), 230-240.

53 See C. Schedl, "Die 'Heiligen' und die 'Herrlichen' in Psalm 16 1-4," *ZAW*, 76 (1964), 174; on the basis of Ugar. *yd*, "love," Schedl translates *middām* as "ihnen zuliebe," "for their sake."

54 → זעם *zā'am*.

55 *KTU*, 1.23, 33-35.

56 No. 1138.

57 No. 1139.

58 No. 1140.

literally with *yāḏ* in the sense of "arm."[59] Lam. 3:3 involves metaphorical usage. The meaning "love" is not absolutely excluded, but does not appear essential in any instance.

Second, granted the existence of *ydd,* "love," there is the more difficult question whether it is to be treated as being entirely separate from the word *yāḏ,* "hand." The possibility that the extension of meaning from "hand" to "power" includes "sexual power" may be considered. The possible use of "hand" for "phallus" allows such a development. The questions raised by the use of *yāḏ* for "monument"[60] also suggest sexual overtones. The evidence can only be weighed; some considerations based on cognate languages and the use of terms for the human body in other languages may contribute to the discussion.

3. *yāḏ: Meaning.*

a. The normal meaning of *yāḏ* is "hand," but the hand is not distinguished sharply from the wrist and arm. Gen. 24:22, for example, speaks of bracelets placed upon the *yāḏ,* understood to include both hand and forearm. A separate word for "arm," → זרוע *zᵉrōa',* allows a distinction to be made; and the Amarna letters show a distinction between the glossing of *ina qātišu,* "in his hand," by *badiu,*[61] and of *qātu* by *zuruḥ.*[62] But the same overlap of meaning is found in Akk. *idu,* and Akk. *aḫu* also denotes both arm and hand.[63] In Zec. 13:6, *bên yāḏeyḵā* means "between the arms," i.e., "the chest"; similarly in 2 K. 9:24 *bên zᵉrō'āyw* means "between the shoulders." In Jer. 38:12, *'aṣṣîlôṯ yāḏeyḵā* refers to the "armpits," and in Ezk. 13:18 *'aṣṣîlê yāḏay* refers to the "wrists." A similar usage in Sir. 9:9; 41:19 refers to the "elbow." In Ezk. 41:8, *'aṣṣîlâ* is an architectural term.

Parts of the hand are specified more precisely by such terms as *bōhen yāḏ,* "thumb" (e.g., Exod. 29:20), and *'eṣbᵉ'ôṯ yāḏ,* "fingers" (e.g., 2 S. 21:20). The term *kap yāḏ* is also found (e.g., Dnl. 10:10), but must be considered in relation to the meanings of *kap* and the extent of overlap between these two main terms for "hand."[64]

b. (1) Like Akk. *idu,* Heb. *yāḏ* is used for the side of the body or the side in general, e.g., *yaḏ dereḵ* (1 Sam. 4:13 *Q*), *lᵉyaḏ-ma'gāl* (Ps. 140:6[5]), *lᵉyaḏ-šᵉ'ārîm* (Prov. 8:3). Closely similar is the virtually prepositional expression *'al-yᵉḏêhem,* "beside them" (Job 1:14); cf. *ṣillᵉmḵā 'al-yāḏ yᵉmîneḵā* (Ps. 121:5). Some phrases associated with this usage, however, may in fact involve a metaphorical element of "strength." For example, 1 Ch. 23:28 uses the expression *ma'ᵃmāḏām lᵉyaḏ-bᵉnê 'ahᵃrōn* for the Levites' support of the Aaronite priests.

An extension of this usage refers to direction (*miyyaḏ kittîm,* Nu. 24:24) or an extent

---

[59] See below.
[60] See below.
[61] See above.
[62] EA 287, 27; 288, 34.
[63] Holma, 110ff.
[64] See II.4 below.

of space defined by both arms (*raḥᵃḇaṯ-yāḏayim*, e.g., Gen. 34:21); *rᵉḥaḇ yāḏāyim* (Ps. 104:25) means "broad." A related development uses *yāḏ* to mean "border," as in Nu. 34:3 and Josh. 15:46, and to denote the bank of a river (like Akk. *aḫu*), as in Ex. 2:5.

(2) Also derivative is the meaning "portion" (Jer. 6:3) in the sense of a parcel of pasture land that falls under someone's hand or control;[65] a portion or share of seed (Gen. 47:24); portions of the people (Neh. 11:1); metaphorically a share in the king (2 S. 19:44[43]). In Neh. 10:32(31), *kol-yāḏ* appears to mean "debts of every kind," although *yāḏ* here may indicate "control," as possibly in the similar expression in Dt. 15:2. Possibly related is the meaning "military division" (2 K. 11:7), although this may be seen as linked to the meaning "power" and hence "military might."[66] When *yāḏ* means "hand," the dual *yāḏayim* is used, but for the derived meanings the pl. *yāḏôṯ*.

(3) Other meanings of *yāḏ* refer to handlike objects; cf. the analogous use of *kap* in the sense of "socket."[67] Thus *yāḏ* may refer to "armrests" (1 K. 10:19), the "axle (boss?)" of a wheel (1 K. 7:32f.), or a "peg" (Ex. 26:17). The same may possibly be true for the use of *yāḏ* to denote some kind of monument or stela, which according to 2 S. 18:18 may be identified as a *maṣṣēḇâ:* "He set up for himself the *maṣṣēḇâ* which is in the King's Valley . . . and it is called Absalom's monument to this day." The same meaning, though presumably in a metaphorical sense, is found in Isa. 56:5, where there is to be established for the eunuchs in the temple precincts *yāḏ wāšēm;* as in the Absalom narrative, this is connected with remembrance, being described as better than sons and daughters, "a perpetual *šēm*."[68] Such a monument is probably also referred to in 1 S. 15:12 and 1 Ch. 18:3, where the hiphil of *nāṣaḇ* suggests the actual setting up of a monument, apparently a victory stela. But 2 S. 8:3, which corresponds to 1 Ch. 18:3, reads *lᵉhāšîḇ yāḏô binᵉhar-(pᵉrāṯ Q)*, which could mean "to recover his victory stela from the river Euphrates" but more naturally would mean "to restore his control at (as far as) the river Euphrates." Ezk. 21:24(19) uses *yāḏ* in the sense of a "pointer," a signpost at a road junction (the MT is not entirely in order, but the meaning is clear); such a pointer could presumably resemble a hand, although no archaeological evidence confirms the existence of such an object.

(4) The relationship between *yāḏ*, "hand," and *yāḏ*, "monument," is not immediately apparent. Delcor[69] provides a careful discussion of the evidence, showing that, although there is no philological evidence in cognate languages, there is clear archaeological evidence. He discusses the raised stones of Gezer (though accepting the

---

65 Cf. Robinson; for *yāḏ*, "portion, property," see below.

66 See below.

67 See below.

68 Robinson takes *yāḏ* here to mean "possession" [see above; cf. Gen. 35:4] in parallel with *šēm*, "heritage."

69 *JSS*, 12 (1967), 230-34.

dubious conclusions of Albright as to their funerary character[70]) and the stelae of Hazor. A closer parallel is provided by the Punic stelae on which a hand is engraved, interpreted as the hand of the deity raised in blessing. There is an additional parallel from Hazor, a stela showing in relief two hands surmounted by the lunar disk; there are comparable Palmyrene monuments with two praying hands. From this it would appear that *yāḏ*, "monument," may derive either from representation of the hand of the deity in blessing or protection, or from the hand(s) of the votary in prayer.[71] Delcor also notes the appearance of the toponym *yaḏ hammeleḵ* in the Shishak inscription.[72] But the possible phallic connection with *maṣṣēḇôṯ*, associated in shrines with the female symbol of the *'ᵃšērâ*, allows the alternative that the use of *yāḏ* in this context is linked to the sexual use of the term.[73]

(5) As we have seen, this sexual use may derive from another verbal root, *ydd*, "love." But there are other possibilities. Just as "cover the feet" is a euphemism for "urinate" (e.g., *lᵉhāsēḵ 'eṯ-raglāyw*, 1 S. 24:4[3]) and "the hair of the feet" for genital hair (*śa'ar hāraglāyim*, Isa. 7:20; similarly Isa. 6:2 uses *regel* as a surrogate for the genital region), so *yāḏ* may be a surrogate for some other term for "phallus." A similar surrogate is *bāśār* (Lev. 6:3[10]; 15:2; Ezk. 23:20) or *bᵉśar 'orlâ* (Gen. 17:11), *bᵉśar 'erwâ* (Ex. 28:42). In Ezk. 8:17 *zᵉmôrâ* is sometimes thought to have this meaning, although it seems unlikely. In 1 S. 21:6(5) *kᵉlî* has likewise been so interpreted;[74] also, rather less probably, *qōṭen* in 1 K. 12:10. To these may be added *'ammâ*, "forearm, cubit"; *'eḇer*, "wing"; and *'eṣba'*, "finger," used in Rabbinical Hebrew for "penis," the third perhaps already at Qumran.[75] In Lev. 12:7; Prov. 5:18 and the Mishnah, *māqôr*, "fountain," is used for the female genitalia; it is used for the male organ in 1QM 7:6 and Rabbi Eliezer xxii.[76] This meaning of *yāḏ* could then be linked to the phrase *yāḏ miḥûṣ lammaḥᵃneh* in Dt. 23:13(12), meaning "latrine," and more specifically the phrase *mᵉqôm hayyāḏ* in 1QM 7:6f., presumably with allusion to the Deuteronomy passages.[77] It is not clear, however, that *yāḏ* here does not simply mean "side." The meaning "penis" for *yāḏ* occurs in 1QS 7:13.[78] Isa. 57:8 has *yāḏ ḥāzîṯ*, where the context strongly suggests an alien religious object; Isa. 57:10 has *ḥayyaṯ yēḏēḵ*, which may also be taken as a reference to virility, although others prefer a different meaning (e.g., NEB "you earned a livelihood," which is rather pedestrian).

---

70 Cf. now P. H. Vaughan, *The Meaning of bāmâ in the OT. SOTS Mon*, 3 (1974).

71 See IV below.

72 Cf. B. Mazar, "The Campaign of Pharaoh Shishak to Palestine," *Volume du Congrès, Strasbourg 1956. SVT*, 4 (1957), 57-66.

73 Cf. Delcor's cautious discussion, pp. 236f., with references to the literature.

74 But see H. J. Stoebe, *Das erste Buch Samuelis. KAT*, VIII/1 (1973), 396.

75 See Delcor, *JSS*, 12 (1967), 237, for references.

76 See Y. Yadin, *The Scroll of the War of the Sons of Light against the Sons of Darkness* (Eng. trans., Jerusalem, 1957), 291; cf. also 1QH 1:22 and Y. Yadin, "A Note on DSD IV:20," *JBL*, 74 (1955), 40-43.

77 See also Y. Yadin, *Jerusalem Revealed* (Eng. trans., New Haven, 1974), 90, on the same expression in the Temple scroll (11QT 46:13).

78 See A. R. C. Leaney, *The Rule of Qumran and its Meanings. NTL* (1966), 207.

A more complex metaphor is perhaps found in Cant. 5:4f. A door and its opening as an image for love is also found in Egyptian poetry;[79] while it is perfectly possible to understand the wording literally—and this may be part of the intention—it is not improbable that sexual imagery is also intended, with a reference both to the *yāḏ* of the man and the *yāḏayim* of the woman "dripping with myrrh."[80]

The second possible alternative explanation appears already in Isa. 57:10, where the meaning "power, vitality" lies near to hand. The wider metaphorical use of *yāḏ*, "power," is discussed below; here the question is whether it is proper to assume that one aspect of this power may be sexual. It may be natural to see the primary metaphorical sense developing from the hand as an instrument in powerful action, in connection with warfare and weapons; but the related idea of power as virility should not be considered totally separate from this sense. The meaning "penis" for *yāḏ* may therefore be considered a possible extension of *yāḏ*, "power." Further parallels may be seen in the wide range of illustrative material from various cultures somewhat haphazardly gathered by Canney[81] and in *ERE*.[82]

4. *Other Biblical Terms.*

a. The second most frequent word for "hand" in Biblical Hebrew is *kap,* which occurs nearly 200 times;[83] the distribution does not appear to have any particular significance. Heb. *kap* is parallel to Ugar. *kp,*[84] Arab. *kaff,* Ethiop. *kaf,* Egyp. *kp,* and Akk. *kappu*. Copt. *ḫop* is also cited by *KBL*³, but it is more appropriately associated with Heb. *ḥōp̄en*.[85] Fronzaroli[86] compares the verbal *kpup,* "bend, be crooked." A by-form of *kap, 'eḵep,* has been proposed to explain Job 33:7; if this is correct, the hand would be undertaking hostile action (par. *'ēmâ,* as in Job 13:21[87]).

The two main words for "hand," *yāḏ* and *kap,* have given their names to letters of the alphabet (*yôḏ* [*yodh*] and *kap* [*kaph*], Gk. *iota* and *kappa*). This would seem clearly to suggest that there are two different representations of the form of the hand, although in both instances a sketch of the hand with its fingers appears to be basic. It is not in fact possible on the basis of the representations to determine precisely what aspects of the shape of the hand are really in mind. In 1 K. 18:44, *k*ᵉ*ḵap-'îš* is used to describe a small object.

The noun *kap* tends to denote the open hand, ready to receive something. Thus it is used for the hand of Pharaoh holding his cup (Gen. 40:11); this passage appears to indicate a difference between *yāḏ* and *kap,* since it says that Pharaoh's cup (*kôs*)

---

79 See G. Gerleman, *Ruth–Das Hohelied. BK,* XVIII (1965), 167ff.

80 See also the discussion of *kap* below.

81 Pp. 62f.

82 J. A. MacCulloch, "Hand," *ERE,* VI, 495. See also Lacau, 81, who connects Egyp. *mt,* "phallus," with Heb. *mēṯ, m*ᵉ*ṯîm,* "men."

83 For statistics, see W. Schottroff, "ידע *jd'* erkennen," *THAT,* I, 689.

84 *UT,* no. 1286; *WUS,* no. 1364.

85 See II.4.b below.

86 P. 259.

87 Cf. *KBL*³, 46.

is in the hand (*bᵉyāḏ*) of the butler, who places (*nāṯan*) it in the hand (*'al-kap*) of Pharaoh. But such a distinction is too precise, since Gen. 40:13, repeating the sense, says, "You will place (*nāṯan*) the cup in his hand (*bᵉyāḏô*)." The theme of "the cup in the hand of God" always uses *yāḏ* (e.g., Isa. 51:17).

Whereas a *yāḏ*, "hand," can hold a wide range of objects, the usage of *kap̱* is much more restricted. It denotes especially the hollow hand into which oil (e.g., Lev. 14:15) or meal (Nu. 5:18) may be poured; it is used for the open hands of the priest (Ex. 29:24) and hands that hold pieces of silver (2 S. 18:12). But the *kap̱* can likewise hold a staff (Ex. 4:4, although 4:2 uses *yāḏ*), darts (2 S. 18:14), a sword (Ezk. 21:16[11]), or a reed (Ezk. 29:7).

Prov. 31:19 speaks of implements for spinning held in the hand (*yāḏ, kap̱*); Isa. 62:3 speaks of a crown (*'ᵃṭereṯ*) in the hand (*yāḏ*) and a *ṣānîp̱* in the hand (*kap̱*) of God. These two parallels make it clear that the distinction between the terms is by no means precise; they might suggest the break-up of a stereotyped phrase.[88] Melamed cites the phrase *yāḏ yāmîn* as one that is frequently broken into its component parts in parallel units, e.g., in Isa. 48:13. The phrase *kap̱ yāḏ*, "palm of the hand," the hand as holding, may have been divided similarly into its two parts, with the result that the two words, now appearing in parallel clauses, might each acquire the fuller sense. Such a break-up might thus lead to the use of *kap̱* alone as "the hand holding an object," as distinct from its more proper sense, "hollow palm."

Our discussion makes it clear enough that *kap̱* is unlikely to denote the closed hand or fist.[89] When a more precise description is given, *kap̱* may denote the palm of the hand as a flat surface (e.g., Isa. 49:16, where "Jerusalem" is engraved upon God's hands; Dnl. 10:10, which speaks of "my knees and the palms of my hands" [*kappôṯ yāḏāy*]). The palm is referred to in 2 K. 18:21 (par. Isa. 36:6), where *ûḇā' bᵉḵappô* refers to the penetration of the hand by a reed (contrast Ezk. 29:7 where *tāpaś bᵉḵap̱* refers to taking hold of a reed). In Prov. 6:3, however, *bô' bᵉḵap̱* means "get into the power or control of." The text of Job 36:32 is problematic. The MT reads *'al-kappayim kissâ*, "he conceals light within his hands" (cf. Isa. 49:2: *bᵉṣēl yāḏô*); but a reading *kēp̱îm*, "thunderbolts," has been proposed.[90]

The noun *kap̱* also appears to denote the hand severed from the body (as in Egyptian, where *kp* is used for hands cut from dead enemies and presented to the deity by the king[91]). Thus we read of the discovery of Jezebel's *kappôṯ hayyāḏāyim* (2 K. 9:35), the cutting off (*qṣṣ*) of a woman's hand (*kap̱*) as punishment (Dt. 25:12), and the severed hands of Dagon (*kappôṯ yāḏāyw*, 1 S. 5:4). The text of Jgs. 8:6,15 (*hᵃḵap̱ zeḇaḥ . . . 'attâ bᵉyāḏeḵā*) has been subject to debate. If correct, it would appear to mean: "Is the severed hand of (dead) Zebah . . . in your hand?" In both cases, however, *hᵃḵap̱* might be an error for *ha'ap̱*. The repetition of the same slip seems

---

[88] See E. Z. Melamed, "Break-Up of Stereotype Phrases as an Artistic Device in Biblical Poetry," *Studies in the Bible*. *ScrHier*, 8 (1961), 143f.

[89] Contra W. Ewing and E. R. Rowlands, "Hand," *HDB*, 363, and a number of renderings of *kap̱* in the NEB.

[90] Cf. NEB.

[91] Lacau, 136f.

unlikely, however, and perhaps we have here (see also below) a reference to the cutting off of hands as a token of victory.

When used in connection with the foot or leg (*regel*), *kap* denotes the foot or the sole of the foot. In Ezk. 1:7, there is a clear distinction between *regel,* "leg," and *kap regel,* "foot." The word is used for the soles of the feet in 2 K. 19:24 (*kap-pᵉʿāmay*). It can be used for the feet of birds, animals, and humans (Gen. 8:9; Lev. 11:27; Josh. 3:13). It can also be used for "handlike" objects. The pl. *kappôṯ* frequently refers to bowls or saucers for religious use (e.g., 1 K. 7:50, and repeatedly in Nu. 7). Parallel to this is the use of the corresponding term in cognate languages for scales for weighing (cf. Akk. *kappu,*[92] Ugar. *kp mzm*). Attention has also been drawn to bowls "with hands carved on their backs" and to bowls with a hollow tube opening into them, perhaps for libations. It is likely that bowls of this kind were understood as representing the hollow hand, which itself could perform functions in religious rites.[93]

Similar is the use of *kap* to denote "the hollow socket of the thigh" (Gen. 32:26,33[25,32]) and the hollow of a sling (1 S. 25:29; cf. Arab. *kiffat* for the pan of a catapult).

Less certain is the meaning of *kappôṯ hammanʿûl* in Cant. 5:5. Does it denote the hollowing containing a door bolt[94] or the handles of the bolt?[95] "Knob" is one meaning for *yāḏ*.[96] The issue is confused by the use of sexual imagery here, as we have already seen, although it seems likely that the phrase was a familiar one referring to part of the door furniture. The metaphorical use of *kap* is discussed below.

b. Heb. *ḥōpen* (6 occurrences) also denotes an open hand, a hollow hand, or a handful. Cognates include Akk. *ḫapnu, upnu,* "hands outstretched to heaven";[97] Arab. *ḥafnat, ḥufnat;* Ethiop. *ḥefn;* Egyp. *ḫfʿ;* cf. Gk. *kóphinos,* "basket"; Copt. *ḫop.*[98] The word is always used in the dual, denoting the two hands held together forming a hollow. Eccl. 4:6 contrasts one *kap* full to two *ḥōpen,* bringing out the meaning of both words. Fronzaroli[99] defines *ḥupn* as the fist or what the fist can contain, a handful.

c. The noun *šōʿal* also denotes a hollow hand or handful. In later Hebrew it also indicates the depths (of the sea?). In 1 K. 20:10; Ezk. 13:19 the plural is used in the ordinary sense for handfuls of dust and barley respectively; in Isa. 40:12, *mî-māḏaḏ*

---

92 Holma, 117f.

93 See above. Cf. also J. L. Kelso, *The Ceramic Vocabulary of the OT. BASORSup,* 5/6 (1948), §42; G. E. Wright, *Biblical Archaeology* (Philadelphia, ²1962), 142 and fig. 96; J. L. Kelso, "Solomon's Temple Resurrected," *BA,* 4 (1941), 30.

94 *KBL*¹.

95 *KBL*³; *BDB,* 497, which specifies: "the [bent] handles of the bolt."

96 See above.

97 Holma, 118f.

98 See II.4.a above.

99 P. 260.

b^ešo'^olô mayim refers to the single hollow hand, although the conjectural reading *b^ešo'^olîm yām* is often preferred.

d. The noun *'egrōp̄* (only in Ex. 21:18; Isa. 58:4) is variously understood. The LXX (*gygmḗ*) and Vulg. (*pugnus*) suggest "fist," but "spade, shovel" has been proposed on the basis of derivation from *grp* (cf. Jgs. 5:21). "Shovel away" has been proposed as the meaning of this root on the basis of Arab. *grf.* The use of *'eḇen* in parallelism (Ex. 21:18) does not solve the problem, although one might expect two objects: a wooden object and some other implement. Cf. also *b^e'eḇen yāḏ* (Nu. 35:17), *biḵ^elî 'ēṣ-yāḏ* (Nu. 35:18), but simply *b^eyāḏô* in Nu. 35:21; the construction is not entirely clear.

e. Several other terms will be mentioned briefly. The first, → זרוע *z^erôa'*, has the meaning "arm," which overlaps with that of *yāḏ yāmîn* and *ś^emō'l* for right and left hand respectively. The former in particular is often used in the same metaphorical sense as *yāḏ*, "power."[100] The second, *'ammâ*, "forearm, cubit," appears most often as a unit of measure. The third, *'eṣba'*, "finger, toe,"[101] is often used closely with *yāḏ* or *kap;* it has its own particular theological use.[102] The magical use of Akk. *ubānu* is comparable;[103] cf. Heb. *bōhen, b^ehôn*, e.g., in Jgs. 1:6. Special significance evidently attaches to the placing of sacrificial blood on the right thumbs and big toes of the priests (Ex. 29:20; Lev. 8:23f. includes the lobes of their right ears as well). Cf. also Lev. 14:14,25 and the use of oil in rituals (Lev. 14:17,28) connected with cleansing from *ṣāra'aṯ*.

5. *Biblical Aramaic*. Aram. *yāḏ* is used both for the hand itself (Dnl. 5:5, with reference to the fingers [*'eṣb^e'ān*] of a person's hand) and metaphorically for "power, control" (Dnl. 6:28, "the power [*yāḏ*] of the lion," although the "paw" of the lion could also be meant; cf. Ezr. 5:8). "Put in the power of" is expressed by *y^ehaḇ b^eyaḏ* in Dnl. 2:38 (cf. Heb. *nāṯan b^eyaḏ*); "deliver from the power of" is *šêzîḇ min-yaḏ* (Dnl. 3:15). Human life (breath) is in the control of God (*nišm^eṯāḵ bîḏēh*, Dnl. 5:23). In Dnl. 2:34,45, *dî-lā' bîḏayin* (cf. Heb. *'epes yāḏ*) denotes a nonhuman agency.

As in Hebrew, *š^elaḥ yaḏ* (Ezr. 6:12) means "undertake." In Ezr. 7:14,25 occur two expressions for Ezra's law: *dāṯ '^elāhāḵ dî ḇîḏāḵ* and *ḥoḵmaṯ '^elāhāḵ dî-ḇîḏāḵ*. The parallel use of *siprā'* in the Elephantine papyri[104] suggests the sense "the law(book) in your hand, your possession," although a possible meaning is "under your authority, control."

In Dnl. 4:32(35), the idiom *y^emaḥē' ḇîḏēh* means "no one may strike him (God) on the hand," i.e., stop him from doing as he pleases; "the hand of God" is used metaphorically for what lies within his power.

---

100 See below.
101 See above.
102 See below.
103 Holma, 123f.
104 *AP*, 10, 12.

Biblical Aram. *pas yᵉḏā'* (Dnl. 5:5,24) means "the flat back of the hand" or "the whole hand below the wrist," but not "the palm of the hand" (cf. Phoen. *pst,* "tablet"); in later Hebrew *pas* means "piece" or "flat of the hand or foot"; cf. Aram. *passa'*, "spade," and possibly *kᵉṯōneṯ passîm* (Gen. 37:3, etc.), "garment of pieces." Biblical Aram. *'ammâ* (Dnl. 3:1; Ezr. 6:3) is used only in the sense of "cubit."

In 1QapGen 20:4f., *yāḏ* and *kap* are used in parallel in the description of Sarah's beauty.[105] In 1QapGen 21:15, *lyd ym'* is used for the shore of the sea.

6. *LXX*. The normal word for "hand" in Greek, and the usual equivalent for *yāḏ,* is *cheír.*[106] It denotes both the human hand and the divine hand, with its protecting and healing functions.[107] In a transferred sense it means "side" (cf. Hebrew), "power," "work," and "handful" or "troop." Not only does *cheír* render *yāḏ* but also *kap* (e.g., Jgs. 6:13), *ḥōpen* (e.g., Ezk. 10:2 LXX^{A}), *šō'al* (Isa. 40:12), *tāw* (Job 31:35), and *yāmîn* (Gen. 48:14). In Nu. 14:17, *kōaḥ* is rendered *cheír* by LXX^{A} but *ischýs* by LXX^{B}. A wide range of other terms is used also, particularly for the special extended meanings of *yāḏ;* detailed discussion of these is not necessary here.

III. Usage.

1. *Holding*. The use of *yāḏ* simply to denote a part of the human body is clearest in the many expressions that describe the hand as holding something. The range of objects held is wide. As has been noted,[108] *kap* finds similar and at times identical usage. Objects held may be weapons (e.g., *ḥereḇ* [Nu. 22:23]; more generally *kēlîm* [2 K. 11:8]; *ḥᵃnîṯ* [1 Ch. 11:23]; *kîḏôn* [Josh. 8:18]), everyday household articles (e.g., *kôs* [Gen. 40:11]; *kaddîm* [Jgs. 7:19]; *kᵉlî* [Jer. 18:4] in the sense of a potter's vessel; *kesep* [Dt. 14:25]); sacrificial offerings (*'ēš* [Gen. 22:6]; *minḥâ* [Nu. 5:25]; *šôr* [1 S. 14:34]; *'eglaṯ bāqār* [1 S. 16:2]), for which *kap* is also commonly used. In the last two instances we may note that the sense "hold in the hand" is extended to cover the broader meaning "have in one's possession." A similar extension is implied in the expression *mᵉ'ûmâ min-haḥērem* (Dt. 13:18). The range is so great that there is no need to cite more than these few examples. We may also observe that the same usage holds whether the object is concrete or metaphorical; Yahweh may hold a *kôs* in his hand (e.g., Isa. 51:17), and a weapon such as a *qešeṯ* may be referred to metaphorically (as in Job 29:20). Most often the object, whether real or metaphorical, is described as being *bᵉyāḏ,* but in Ezr. 8:33 silver is weighed into (*'al*) the hands. "Hold" is expressed by *ḥāzaq* (thus *hanna'ar hammaḥᵃzîq bᵉyāḏô* [Jgs. 16:26]) or *'āḥaz* (Ps. 73:23). But these verbs have in fact an extended or metaphorical sense suggesting guidance (cf. more clearly Isa. 51:18, par. *mᵉnahēl,* and Jer. 31:32 in a covenant

---

105 See also J. T. Milik, "Le Testament de Lévi en Araméen: Fragment de la grotte 4 de Qumrân," *RB*, 62 (1955), 400, citing a phrase from the Testament of Levi in Aramaic: *w'ṣb't kpy wydy.*

106 On *cheír* in Classical Greek, see Lohse.

107 On the latter see below.

108 See II.4 above.

context) or encouragement (e.g., Ezk. 13:22 [piel]). In Ps. 37:24, *sāmaḵ* is used of the hand of God that holds or protects.

In a number of cases the boundary between literal usage (holding an object in the hand) and the extended senses of being under someone's control (e.g., Ps. 95:4) or of the hand as a substitute for the person (e.g., Mal. 1:10[109]) is very difficult to define. In Zec. 4:12, it is not clear whether *b^eyaḏ* with reference to *šibb^alê hazzēṯîm* expresses "holding" or, as is more probable, "beside" or "through."

The idiomatic expression *maqqēl yāḏ* (Ezk. 39:9) clearly indicates a weapon held in the hand.

2. *Personal Responsibility.* As we have seen, it is sometimes not easy to say whether *yāḏ* is used literally in the sense of "hand" or less precisely in the sense of a person who controls (or whose hand controls) some object.[110] In some of these instances the literal sense may dominate. In Ex. 32:4, for example, *wayyiqqaḥ miyyāḏām* implies that what was taken was being held in the hand of the persons concerned, though the sense is naturally given as "he took (it) from them." In Prov. 6:17, *yāḏayim šōp^eḵôṯ dām-nāqî* can evidently be understood literally, since the hands hold the instruments by which murder is committed; but there is a clear implication that the persons are guilty of murder. To "require at someone's hand" means "impute responsibility," as in 1 S. 20:16. Alert servants (Ps. 123:2) watch for the hand gesture (*'el-yaḏ '^aḏônêhem*) indicating what is to be done, but the expression is understood more precisely to indicate regard for their master's authority.

The extended meaning appears more clearly in *'^aśēh l^eḵā '^ašer timṣā' yāḏeḵā* (1 S. 10:7), which implies the appropriate military action but also has a wider sense. There is an easy development from this to the next example, where a quality belonging to a person is ascribed to his hands. In Ezk. 7:27, *wîḏê 'am-hā'āreṣ tibbāhalnâ* expresses distress; it is evident that this is an extended meaning in which the hand really stands for the person. Compare the similar expression in Ps. 6:3f.(2f.), where *'^aṣāmîm* and *nepeš* are used with *bāhal*. What the hands hold or do may express metaphorically the state of the person. Thus *'āwen b^eyāḏ^eḵā* (Job 11:14) indicates the evil power of the person; *ṭ^ohor-yāḏayim* (Job 17:9) and *bōr yāḏay* (Ps. 18:21[20]) express the person's state of purity in terms of the hands that may be defiled through contact with what is impure. In Ps. 18:21(20), the parallel to *bōr yāḏay* is *ṣeḏeq,* making clear the wider implications of the expression. The wicked have *zimmâ* in their hands (Ps. 26:10). Blood on one's hands (e.g., Gen. 4:11), responsibility for blood (Gen. 9:5), and more general responsibility (Gen. 31:39) all have to do with the hands of the person responsible. The quality of the person *'ên b^eyāḏî rā'â wāpeša'* (1 S. 24:12[11]) is comparable, as is *y^eḏêḵem dāmîm mālē'û* (Isa. 1:15), to which 1QIs^a adds *'ṣb'wtykm b''wn*.

The problem of defilement through contact with what is unclean is often expressed in terms of hands; its removal is expressed in terms of acts of cleansing.[111] Thus

109 See III.2.
110 See Johnson.
111 → טמא *ṭāmē';* cf. Lohse, 426.

purificatory washing (*rāḥaṣ*) may involve the hands and feet (Ex. 30:19; 40:31). A person who is unclean by reason of some bodily discharge (*zāḇ*) transmits this uncleanness to another person unless he has rinsed his hands (*w^e^yāḏāyw lô'-šāṭap bammāyim* [Lev. 15:11]).

Touching with the hand (*yāḏ nāg^e^'â bî* [Dnl. 10:10]) may be understood in the sense of protection; but the analogy of Isa. 6:7, where Isaiah's mouth is touched (*nāga' 'al*) with an ember from the altar, suggests that purification may also be meant.

The hand may be protective, as in *tānûaḥ yaḏ-YHWH bâhār hazzeh* (Isa. 25:10). Cf. also *yāḏ . . . hāy^e^ṯâ 'eṯ* in Jer. 26:24. But the similar verb *nāḥaṯ* is used in a hostile sense in Ps. 38:3(2), where *wattinḥaṯ 'ālay yāḏeḵā* is in parallel with *ḥiṣṣeyḵā niḥ^a^ṯû ḇî,* with a wordplay on *nûaḥ* and *nāḥaṯ.* Eccl. 7:18 uses the same verb in the sense "hold firmly" (*'al-tannaḥ 'eṯ-yāḏeḵā,* par. *'āḥaz*). A comparable extended sense of the verb with *yāḏ* is found in Eccl. 11:6: "not withholding the hand," i.e., not being idle. It is evident that the range of meanings of *nûaḥ* with *yāḏ* varies according to context. A different protective idea is expressed in Jer. 33:13, where *'al-y^e^ḏê môneh*[112] describes the safety of the flock under the shepherd's care, interpreted as a metaphor for divine care.

The same usage appears also with *kap.* In people's hands are *ḥāmās,* "violence" (e.g., Jon. 3:8), as well as *'āwel* (Ps. 7:4[3]) and *ra'* (Mic. 7:3). In Isa. 59:3, *kap* parallels *'eṣba'* with reference to the defilement through bloodshed and *'āwen* (cf. Isa. 1:15 and 1QSIs[a]). Similarly *kap* can be used in expressions of innocence and purification (e.g., Ps. 24:4; 26:6). In Ps. 78:72, *wayyir'ēm k^e^ṯōm l^e^ḇāḇô ûḇiṯ^e^ḇûnôṯ kappāyw yanḥēm* is used figuratively with reference to divine action.

3. *Possession and Control.* Expressions denoting possession and control also use *yāḏ;* the latter sense provides the basis for much wider metaphorical use. At the literal level, even stolen property may be in the possession (*b^e^yāḏô* [Ex. 22:3]) of a person. Particular territories may be in the possession of a king and may therefore be taken out of his possession or control (*miyyāḏô* [Dt. 3:8]). Something that is *taḥaṯ yāḏ* is in the possession or under the control of a particular person (e.g., 1 S. 21:4[3]).

Possibly related is the use of the verb *mālē'* with reference to institution and dedication. The common expression *millē' yāḏ* (e.g., Ex. 28:41) is used of priestly institution; Jgs. 17:12 suggests that this may be connected with an agreement to make a suitable payment (cf. v. 10, which speaks of regular payment of ten [shekels] of silver, garments, and sustenance). The expression *millē' yāḏ* then implies actual placing of something in the hands of the person being instituted, in either full or token payment. The MT of Ezk. 43:26 would appear to extend this usage to dedication of the altar; here it is the third term in the description, alongside *kipper* and *ṭihar.* Some versions, however, connect this phrase with consecration of the priests.[113]

The same construction is used in 1 Ch. 29:5; 2 Ch. 29:31 for generous contribu-

---

112 On the use of *pāqaḏ* in Ps. 31:6(5), see below.

113 Cf. W. Zimmerli, *Ezekiel 2. Herm* (Eng. trans. 1983), 430.

tions, possibly in connection with the use just mentioned. A different use is present in the cases where a contrast is drawn between what is spoken with the mouth and what is fulfilled (*millē'*) with the hands, e.g. in Jer. 44:25. Also different is the use of *millē'* with reference to the drawing of a bow (*millē' yāḏô baqqešeṯ*; 2 K. 9:24).[114]

A different metaphorical extension may be seen in Eccl. 7:26 where the hands of a woman are described as fetters. An alternative interpretation takes *yāḏ* here as meaning "love."[115]

4. *b^eyāḏ*. A specialized related use appears in the prepositional form *b^eyāḏ*, used frequently to designate the agent through whom a particular action is performed. This may involve simply the carrying out of a commission, as in *b^eyaḏ rē'ēhû* (Gen. 38:20), or it may involve a particular agent, as in *b^eyaḏ gō'ēl haddām* (Josh. 20:9). God may save through the agency of a specially chosen person (*môšîa' b^eyaḏî* [Jgs. 6:36]).

The dividing line between such expressions and those referring to an actual hand is not always clear; Jgs. 3:15, for example, describes the sending of tribute (*minḥâ*) *b^eyāḏ*—in the hand of or through the agency of Ehud. In reference to God (e.g., *b^eyaḏ-YHWH* [Ex. 16:3]) the rendering "by the power of" is better. The use of *b^eyaḏ* with reference to prophetic activity is found in Hag. 1:1,3; 2:1,10 (where some mss. read *'el*) and Mal. 1:1. In Zec. 7:7,12 and Hos. 12:11(10), it is used of the prophets as a body.

It is likewise difficult to distinguish clearly between *b^eyaḏ* in the sense of agency and its use in the sense "under the control of." In 2 Ch. 26:11 both *b^eyaḏ* and *'al yaḏ* are used, although it is by no means clear that there is any distinction between them. Neither is it entirely clear whether the expressions mean "through the agency of" or "under the control or direction of."

In Job 8:4 the expression *b^eyaḏ-piš'ām* is likewise ambiguous. Job's sons may be delivered "into the power of their sins," or we may understand the phrase to mean "on account of" their sins,[116] or judgment brought about "through the agency of" sin.

5. *Gestures*. A wide range of expressions seems to describe gestures made with the hand or movements of the hand. In some instances the meaning is quite clear, but in others even the context leaves doubt as to the precise nature of the gesture. Definition of the hand movements involved depends on interpretation of the iconographic evidence.[117]

a. A number of phrases denote gestures associated with bargaining and pledging. In Prov. 11:21; 16:5, *yāḏ l^eyāḏ* appears to refer to some kind of solemn assurance, a pledge that what is related is true and reliable.[118] The verb *tāqa'*, "strike," exhibits the same meaning. Thus in Job 17:3 *mî hû' l^eyāḏî* (for which a reading *yiṯqa'* has also

[114] Cf. the use of *z^erôa'* in F. J. Helfmeyer, *TDOT*, IV, 131-140.

[115] Cf. II.3 above.

[116] Svi Rin, "Ugaritic-OT Affinities," *BZ*, N.S. 7 (1963), 32f., comparing Ugar. *bd 'iṯt*, "because of a woman," with Jer. 41:9, *b^eyaḏ-g^eḏalyāhû*.

[117] See IV below and Révész, 92-114.

[118] Cf. W. McKane, *Proverbs*. *OTL* (1970), 437, who relates the phrase to bargaining.

been proposed) in parallel with *śîmâ-nā 'orḇēnî,* "provide a surety," evidently means "warrant," "be answerable for." The same root is also used in the qal with *kap.* In Prov. 22:26, however, the meaning "pledge" is clear from the parallel in 6:1; 17:18. In Ps. 47:2(1), the parallel with *rûa'* makes the meaning "acclamation" likely; the same is probably true of Nah. 3:19. Other gestures of joy expressed with the verbs *māḥā'* and *nāḵâ* are discussed below. The striking of hands evidently constitutes some kind of guarantee or agreement.

Closely related are *tᵉśûmeṯ yāḏ* (Lev. 5:21), which denotes the giving of a pledge, and *nāṯan yāḏ* (Ezk. 17:18; cf. 2 K. 10:15), in parallel with *bᵉrîṯ,* denoting an agreement or covenant.[119] In Gen. 38:28, *nāṯan yāḏ* seems to have a different meaning, simply "put forth the hand" (cf. *šālaḥ* below). In Jer. 50:15 and Lam. 5:6, the sense appears to be "surrender"; in Ex. 7:4, the phrase has a hostile meaning. In 1 Ch. 29:24 (with *taḥaṯ*) and 2 Ch. 30:8 (with *lᵉ*) it means "swear allegiance," a sense related to the meaning "agreement" noted above.

Another expression that seems to indicate some kind of agreement is *šîṯ yāḏ,* which is used in Ex. 23:1 in connection with the wicked and false witness, and in Job 9:33 in connection with the referee who places his hand on two parties in litigation. But the phrase is also used in Gen. 46:4 to mean "shut someone's eyes (in death)," perhaps in some way like the gesture of placing one's hand to one's mouth for silence.[120] In Gen. 48:17 the words seem at first sight simply to mean "lay one's hand on," but the blessing context suggests that it carries the meaning of conveying blessing through the hand gesture. It is therefore perhaps comparable to the later use of *śāmaḵ* in connection with the ordination of priests.[121]

b. The oath of allegiance suggested by two instances of *nāṯan yāḏ*[122] appears more clearly in a range of other expressions, especially in the use of *śîm* in this sense in combination with *taḥaṯ yārēḵ* in Gen. 24:2,9; 47:29. This may be compared with the phrase *tᵉśśûmeṯ yāḏ* noted above. Other meanings of *śîm* in combination with *yāḏ* and *kap* are discussed below.

The raising of the hands as a gesture denoting or accompanying an oath is expressed in Gen. 14:22 with the hiphil of *rûm* (cf. also Dnl. 12:7, which specifies the raising of both the right and the left hand). Elsewhere this expression has quite different senses.[123] The phrase *nāśā' yāḏ* is commonly used for swearing an oath (e.g., Ex. 6:8); it is also used for pronouncing a blessing (Lev. 9:22; Ps. 134:2, par. *bērēḵ YHWH*). The same sense may be present in Ps. 10:12, although here the raising of the hand, parallel with *qûm* and *'al-tiškaḥ,* is more likely to refer to battle, suggesting a show of power against the enemy. In Ps. 106:26, a hostile sense may be implicit in the oath; such a sense is clearer in 2 S. 18:28; 20:21; and in Isa. 49:22, in parallel with *'ārîm nissî,* as a gesture against the nations or possibly—in spite of the implied

---

119 W. Zimmerli, *Ezekiel 1. Herm* (Eng. trans. 1979), 365f.

120 See below.

121 See below.

122 See above.

123 See below.

warfare and hostility—as a summons to the nations to assemble to carry the sons and daughters of Israel. The phrase *nāśā' yāḏ* also appears in Ps. 28:2 as a gesture of appeal to the deity.[124]

c. A wide range of meanings attaches to the very common expression *šālaḥ yāḏ*.[125] It may denote simply extension of the hand to perform an appropriate action (e.g., Gen. 3:22, the picking of fruit; Gen. 8:9, Noah's taking the dove into his hand on its return). It is also used of a supernatural hand extended holding a scroll (*yāḏ šᵉlûḥâ* [Ezk. 2:9]). It is frequently used in a hostile sense, as in Gen. 37:22, closely parallel to *nāṭâ*. Related is the sense of extending power and control (Dnl. 11:42). As in Ps. 125:3, a hand may be extended for evil purposes; this is perhaps the sense of *šālaḥ yāḏ 'al* in 1 Ch. 13:10 with reference to Uzzah's touching the ark, with the prep. *'al* expressing a hostile act. Instead of *wayyišlaḥ 'uzzâ 'el-'ᵃrôn hā'ᵉlōhîm wayyōḥez bô* (2 S. 6:6), 1 Ch. 13:9 has the simpler *wayyišlaḥ 'uzzā' 'eṯ-yāḏô*, which has a hostile sense in 13:10.

The phrase *šālaḥ yāḏ* can be used in the legal sense of "touch" (Ex. 22:7[8]). Possessions are denoted by the expression *mišlaḥ yāḏ* (e.g., Dt. 12:7), apparently used in a related metaphorical sense in Isa. 11:14. Prov. 31:19f. uses *šālaḥ yāḏ* in the piel twice, the first time in the neutral sense "take hold of," parallel to *kappeyhā tāmᵉḵû*, the second time as a gesture of kindliness to the poor, parallel to *kappāh pārᵉśâ le'ānî*. In Cant. 5:4,[126] *dôḏî šālaḥ yāḏô min-haḥôr* can be interpreted as meaning "put his hand through the opening," allowing for both the imagery of love and the possibility of a double meaning; but it could also mean "removed his hand from." In either case the sexual reference is perceptible. A further expression *šālaḥ miyyaḏ* (1 K. 20:42) means "release."

A hostile sense is often expressed by *nāṭâ yāḏ* (e.g., Isa. 5:25) and the related phrase *hayyāḏ hannᵉṭûyâ* (e.g., Isa. 14:26), although the more common word is *zᵉrōa'*.[127] In Prov. 1:24, *nāṭâ yāḏ* is a gesture of appeal. Wildberger[128] considers this basically a protective gesture, often transposed to express hostility; but there does not appear to be any passage in which the protective sense is clear.

The opposite of "extending the hand" is "drawing it back," expressed by the hiphil of *šûḇ* (e.g., Gen. 38:29); Jer. 6:9 illustrates the use of this expression in the practical sense of what the vintager does when cutting the grapes. But in Am. 1:8 and elsewhere the expression also has a hostile sense; this appears in Lam. 2:8; 3:3 as well. A person's hand may be drawn back from evil (Ezk. 18:8), and God may draw back his hand so as not to destroy (Ezk. 20:22). In Isa. 1:25, the expression appears to denote such a withdrawal of hostility or an act of restoration. Ps. 74:11 expresses this more vividly by speaking of God's keeping his *yāḏ* and *yāmîn* within the fold of his garment

---

124 See j(4) above.

125 Humbert; Keel, *Wirkmächtige Siegeszeichen im AT*, 153-58, on *šālaḥ* and *nāṭâ*.

126 Cf. II.3, 4 above.

127 Helfmeyer, 135ff.

128 H. Wildberger, *Jesaja. BK*, X/1 (1972), 217, on Isa. 11:9.

(*miqqereḇ ḥêqᵉḵā* [*Q*]). In Ex. 4:6f., the same sense is expressed first by the hiphil of *bô'*, then by the hiphil of *šûḇ*.

d. The use of *śîm* with *yāḏ* and *kap* is associated with gestures of silence.[129] It also expresses protection (*kap* [Ps. 139:5]) and hostility (*kap* [Job 40:32]). The metaphorical *śîm nepeš bᵉḵap* (Jgs. 12:3; 1 S. 19:5; 28:21) also means "take a risk"; it is used in Job 13:14 in parallel with *'eśśā' bᵉśārî bᵉṣinnāy.* The meaning of the same phrase in Ps. 119:109 in parallel with *wᵉṯôrāṯᵉḵā lō' šāḵaḥtî* is very unclear.

e. The verb *māṣā'* used with *yāḏ* (e.g., *māṣᵉ'â yāḏî* [Isa. 10:10]) means "reach" or "seize," with Assyria the subject (as also in Isa. 10:14). In Ps. 21:9(8), *yāḏ* is used in parallel with *yāmîn* (both with *māṣā'*, the former with *lᵉ* and the latter with the accusative) in the sense of "reach." In Job 31:25, it means "acquire wealth"; in Eccl. 9:10 (in a quite general sense), it means "what the hand finds to do," as also in 1 S. 10:7 (where military action is clearly implied[130]).

f. Jer. 38:23 (cf. also 34:3) has *tāpaś* in the sense of "grasp" or "seize," and hence "take captive."

g. The use of *rāpâ* with *yāḏ*, whether verbally as in *herep yāḏeḵā* (2 S. 24:16), "let your hand relax," or adjectivally, as in *yāḏayim rāpôṯ* (e.g., Isa. 35:3), expresses weakness, slackness, or relaxation of tension. In Jer. 38:4 and Ezr. 4:4, the piel of *rāpâ* is used for "cause to be weak," i.e., "discourage." Expressions of this kind appear often with words of fear or encouragement. The image of hands that hang loose in contrast to strong and powerful hands (*ḥāzaq* qal and piel, used with *yāḏ* in Jgs. 9:24, for example;[131] cf. the common use of *yāḏ ḥᵃzāqâ*[132]). In 2 Ch. 15:7, *ḥāzaq* appears in parallel with *'al-rāpâ*. Dt. 32:36 has *'āzᵉlaṯ yāḏ* in the similar sense of "power disappearing," with reference to Israel's loss of strength. Eccl. 10:18 employs *šiplûṯ yāḏayim* in the same way for "slackness, lack of activity."

h. When used with the hand as its object, *qāṣar*[133] expresses essentially the opposite of *šālaḥ*. It is used of the divine hand kept close to the body instead of being stretched forth in action.[134]

i. In 1 K. 22:34, for example, *hāpaḵ yāḏ* is used of the driver's action in turning a chariot around.

---

[129] See j(2) below.
[130] See III.2 above.
[131] See also j(3) below.
[132] See V below.
[133] → קצר *qāṣar* II.
[134] See below.

j. There are many expressions that clearly denote hand gestures but whose meaning is not precisely clear in every case.

(1) Job 31:27 has *wattiššaq yāḏî lᵉpî* in a context suggesting worship of the sun and moon; this may be assumed to refer to a gesture of worship, although its precise significance is unknown.

(2) In Prov. 30:32, *yāḏ lᵉpeh* appears to indicate a gesture of silence when someone is involved in presumptuous actions; the relation of this to Job 31:27 is not clear. Job 21:5 (*yāḏ*) and 29:9 (*kap*) express silence with *śîm* plus the same phrase.

(3) Zec. 14:13 has *wᵉheḥᵉzîqû 'îš yaḏ rē'ēhû wᵉ'ālᵉṯâ yāḏô 'al-yaḏ rē'ēhû*. The context suggests panic created by divine intervention, and v. 14a speaks of conflict between Judah and Jerusalem. Since the first clause indicates encouragement, freeing from fear[135] suggests that the second might have similar meaning. In this case both phrases would indicate the response of the people to a catastrophic situation, and the second would presumably be related to the theme of "surety" conveyed by *yāḏ lᵉyāḏ*.[136] Alternatively,[137] the first clause might suggest encouragement and the second hostility between associates at the very moment they seek to strengthen each other. The verb *'ālâ* with *'al* does indeed naturally suggest hostility; the two clauses are often rendered in this sense, with the hiphil of *ḥāzaq* understood to have the inimical meaning "seize hold of." If v. 14a is intrusive,[138] introducing an alien note of civil war into a passage concerned with God and the nations, then either sense would be possible: the hostile meaning would refer to panic created among the nations, while the encouraging sense would indicate the reaction in Judah to the divine action. The precise meaning remains doubtful, since *'ālâ 'al* could also mean "in support of."

(4) In Neh. 8:6, *bᵉmō'al yāḏayim*, also from *'ālâ*, is possibly related; the most natural assumption is that it refers to the raising of the hands when *'āmēn* is solemnly pronounced. The fact that there is no suggestion of hostility may support the encouraging sense in Zec. 14:13.

(5) The verb *māḥā'* is used with both *yāḏ* and *kap*. In Ezk. 25:6, *māḥā' yāḏ* parallels *rāqa' regel*, and these in turn are paralleled by *śāmaḥ*. We may therefore see here an act of rejoicing; this appears also to be the sense in Isa. 55:12 (*kap*) and Ps. 98:8 (*yāḏ*), in parallel with *rānan*. The phrase *tāqa' kap* (Ps. 47:2[1], par. *rûa'*) expresses acclamation; so too presumably in Nah. 3:19. Other verbs meaning "strike," however, express anger or hostility: *sāpaq kappayim* (Nu. 24:10), anger; also Lam. 2:15; Job 27:23 (*śāpaq*), both with *šāraq* in parallel, whistling here being regarded as hostile. This construction has also been conjectured for Isa. 2:6, *bîlᵉḏê noḵrîm*

---

135 See III.5.g above.

136 See III.5.a above.

137 NEB.

138 P. D. Hanson, *The Dawn of Apocalyptic* (Philadelphia, 1975), 371.

yaśpîqû; but the sense of *śpq* II, "abound," is more appropriate, for the meaning "make a bargain" does not occur with *sāpaq* I (*śāpaq*).

The verb *nāḵâ,* likewise with *kap,* expresses distress (Ezk. 6:11, hiphil with *b*e*-ḵap,* par. *rāqa' b*e*regel* and continued with *'āmar-'āḥ;* also Ezk. 21:19[14], where *w*e*haḵ kap 'el-kap* suggests distress at the pronouncement of doom). In Ezk. 22:13, Yahweh strikes (*nāḵâ;* hiphil) with his hand (*kap*) in anger; in 21:22(17) the same expression found in 21:19(14) is associated with Yahweh, "who causes his anger to rest" (*nûaḥ;* hiphil); this may mean either "causes it to abate" or, more likely, "causes it to settle" on the object of divine wrath (cf. Zec. 2:13[9]).

(6) In Zeph. 2:15, *yānîa' yāḏô* represents a presumably hostile gesture, since it parallels *šāraq*. But the hiphil of this verb in Dnl. 10:10 refers to Daniel's resting on his knees and the palms of his hands (*kappôṯ yāḏî*); the form may be an error for *'ûr.*

(7) The hiphil of *nûp* also appears to indicate a hostile gesture. The common rendering "wave" has been shown by Milgrom[139] to be unsatisfactory; the verb means "lift." This is clear in Isa. 10:32; 11:15; Zec. 2:13(9); Job 31:21. In Isa. 13:2 it could denote a threat or a signal; the latter fits the context better, with *ś*e*'û-nēs* and *hārîmû qôl*. All three expressions would then refer to summoning the warriors. But the use of the same expression in 2 K. 5:11 points to a different sense; Naaman may have expected Elisha to drive his disease away by means of a hostile gesture, but more likely the prophet's raising his hand was thought to involve some magic power.[140]

(8) We have already mentioned the hiphil of *rûm,*[141] but there is also a more literal sense of "raising" a hand or foot (Gen. 41:44) to perform an action; cf. Moses' "lifting" and "lowering" (*nûaḥ*; hiphil) of his hand (Ex. 17:11) during the battle with the Amalekites. In 1 K. 11:26f.; Mic. 5:8, the gesture is hostile and may be analogous to the action of Moses. Related is the common use of *yāḏ rāmâ* in the sense of "triumphant" (Ex. 14:8; Nu. 33:3; Dt. 32:27; possibly also Isa. 26:11). In Nu. 15:30 the expression could well have the negative sense "deliberately, defiantly." In Dt. 12:6,17, *t*e*rûmaṯ yaḏ*e*ḵem* denotes what has been offered or held up before the deity.

(9) When used with *yāḏ 'al rô'š* (2 S. 13:19), *śîm* evidently denotes a gesture of distress or shame (cf. Jer. 2:37).

(10) The expression *yāḏāyw 'al-ḥ*a*lāṣāyw kayyôlēḏâ* (Jer. 30:6) denotes a gesture of distress.

(11) The phrase *nō'ēr kappāyw* (Isa. 33:15) denotes a gesture refusing a bribe.

---

139 J. Milgrom, "The Alleged Wave-Offering in Israel and in the Ancient Near East," *IEJ*, 22 (1972), 33-38 = his *Studies in Cultic Theology and Terminology. StJLA,* 36 (1983), 133-38.

140 See, for example, Révész, 114-121.

141 See III.5.b above.

(12) The expression *yāṣaq mayim ʿal-yāḏayim* (2 K. 3:11) may indicate a gesture of respect or an act of service.

(13) A number of gestures are particularly associated with various kinds of worship, most clearly in the use of the qal or piel of *pāraś*. In Isa. 25:11, this verb is used of a swimmer spreading his hands (*yāḏ*); the clear opening stich and comparison are followed by an obscure reference to *ʿim ʾorᵉḇôṯ yāḏāyw,* perhaps to be interpreted as "skill" (cf. Arab. *ʾirbatun*).[142] Lam. 1:10 uses the verb with *yāḏ* to mean "stretch out the hands to plunder." More often, however, it is used in connection with an appeal to the deity: Ps. 143:6; Lam. 1:17, both with *yāḏ* (the latter has *bᵉyaḏ*); more frequently with *kap,* as in Isa. 1:15. Isa. 65:2 uses the same idiom for God's appeal to his people. In Prov. 31:20,[143] the qal of *pāraś* with *kap* stands in parallel to the piel of *šālaḥ* with *yāḏ*, referring to outstretched hands as a gesture of kindness. With this may be compared the single occurrence of the piel of *šāṭaḥ* with *kap* in Ps. 88:10(9), parallel to *qārāʾ*.

(14) The verb *nāśāʾ* is used with *yāḏ* and *kap* in the sense of "appeal" (Lam. 2:19; Ps. 63:5[4]; 119:48 [*ʾel-miṣwôṯeyḵā*]; 141:2—all with *kap;* Ps. 28:2; 63:5[4] with *yāḏ*). The verb is also used with *nepeš* in a similar sense in Ps. 86:4. When *nāśāʾ* is used absolutely without an object, we may ask whether it is correct to assume in every case[144] that *qôl* is to be supplied ("lift up the voice"); there might instead be a reference to a hand gesture or some other use of hand or voice by synecdoche for the whole person as *nepeš* is used.

(15) In Dt. 15:8,11, *pāṯaḥ* is used with *yāḏ* to express generosity; in Ps. 104:28; 145:16, God opens his hands (*yāḏ*) in blessing, in both instances in the context of supplying food for created beings. Dt. 15:7 expresses the opposite by means of *qāpaṣ yāḏ,* parallel to *ʾimmēṣ lēḇāḇ*.

(16) The procedure by which Elijah restores a child to life is described in 2 K. 4:34; the verb used is *śîm:* Elijah places *kappāyw ʿal kappāyw,* and similarly with *peh* and *ʿênayim*. It is evident that here, too a strong element of magic is present, expressing the conveying of life from one person to another and presumably suggesting the revivification of each part of the body by contact with its corresponding part.

(17) Blessing and curse are transmitted through certain gestures of the hands.[145] The laying of hands on a person is associated with blessing (*šālaḥ* and *šîṯ* in Gen. 48:14), as is the raising of hands (*nāśāʾ* in Lev. 9:22).

The wide variety of gestures discussed in this survey suggests both the difficulty of determining the precise nature of each particular one and also the likelihood that in

---

142 O. Kaiser, *Isaiah 13–39. OTL* (Eng. trans. 1974), 204.

143 See above.

144 See, for example, *KBL*², 636.

145 See H.-D. Wendland, "Handauflegung. II. Biblisch," *RGG*³, III, 53f.

actual life situations the meaning of a gesture would be made clear by its context and also perhaps by words or other circumstances accompanying the gesture. This is evident from the number of instances in which the same expression is used to convey very different meanings. In any case, information concerning the context is needed to determine the meaning of the hands and their gestures. In some instances, it must also be noted—although it is not possible to be absolutely clear as to which—there is likely to be some degree of magical association. This point will be clarified in the next section, where we shall briefly discuss the iconographic evidence.[146]

We may also note that in a number of instances the same expressions are used to describe both divine and human actions; gestures are quite naturally attributed to the deity.

IV. Iconography.

1. Representation of hands and arms in the ancient Near East provides a variety of illustrations of the gestures described above. It is evident that a sharp distinction between hand and arm is not always possible in such portrayals, as indeed the word *yāḏ* may be used for both. Thus the references to illustrations in *ANEP*[147] given under → זרוע *z^e^rôa'* all provide evidence for deities holding weapons in their hands (either the right hand or both hands). In most instances the right arm is raised above the head. Basically these illustrations portray the deity as a warrior. Keel makes a very precise distinction between portrayal of a figure holding a weapon (whether the *kîḏôn* of Josh. 8:18ff. or the *maṭṭeh* of Moses) and that of a figure with raised hands (cf. Moses in Ex. 17:8ff.).

The variety of terminology used for raising hands and the different meanings that may be attached to most usages[148] point to the need for caution in interpreting iconographic evidence wherever the precise function of the gesture is not made absolutely clear by other elements in the picture. In many instances the hands are raised as a token of power, or blessing, or worship; in other instances the precise significance of the gesture is as difficult to ascertain as in many of the texts.[149]

2. Something different is involved in portrayal of the hand to represent the deity by synecdoche in a number of pictures from the synagogue at Dura-Europos.[150] The open right hand of God or of the angel of God emerges from the clouds or from heaven in the following pictures: the sacrifice of Abraham (No. 1; cf. the same representation of the divine hand with the words *'al tišlaḥ* in the mosaic of the synagogue

---

146 Cf. Révész, 114-121.

147 Nos. 476, 479, 486, 490, 501, etc.

148 See above.

149 See, for example, *ANEP,* 239.

150 The instances are fully listed by du Mesnil du Buisson; those in the Ezekiel series are discussed by Riesenfeld, 33f.

at Beth Alpha[151]), the crossing of the sea (No. 4), Moses at the burning bush (No. 5), Elijah reviving the widow's son (No. 27), and 5 times in Ezekiel's vision of the bones (No. 20). In this last, the hand of God points in 4 instances to people who are rising from the ground. Riesenfeld cites some examples of the later use of this motif in connection with resurrection, and finds analogies also in the appearance of the hand on ancient tombstones as a symbol of life. Du Mesnil du Buisson[152] argues that the portrayal of the hand in effect merely separates the scenes in the Ezekiel picture and marks the moments at which God speaks. These pictures are much later than the biblical period, and represent in some measure the development of means for portraying the presence of the deity without actually depicting him. But they also represent the use of the hand to represent the person and as a vehicle of power.

3. The Ezekiel pictures from Dura-Europos also provide examples, natural enough in the context, of the portrayal of *disjecta membra,* including hands, on the ground. It is clear that they are designed to suggest the dead and dislocated bodies that are about to be brought together and restored to life.

Portrayals of heads and hands in battle scenes have been held to symbolize victory.[153] Gordon suggests that such amputated members were used for statistical purposes; one might be tempted to compare the counting of foreskins in 1 S. 18:24-27. But it would seem more probable to consider them—and the actual amputations carried out during or after battle (cf. Jgs. 8:6, if the MT is correct; Jgs. 1:6f. for a comparable amputation of thumbs and big toes)—as indicating the removal of the enemy's power, symbolized by his hand, head, or penis. Gordon[154] points to parallels in the Ras Shamra texts,[155] where "Anath's success in the chase is coupled with her victory in war, expressed in terms of her human victims' heads and hands flying in mid-air like balls and grasshoppers respectively."[156] The offering of the hand (and also of the penis) of a dead enemy to the deity is discussed by Lacau.[157] This material, too, exemplifies the problems of interpreting iconographic material, even where textual evidence may reasonably be adduced as parallel.[158]

V. Theological Aspects.

1. *Power.* The metaphorical use of the hand or arm[159] has already been adumbrated in much of the material adduced in II above, especially in II.3, where the idea of

---

151 Cf. E. R. Goodenough, *Jewish Symbols in the Greco-Roman Period,* I (New York, 1953), 246-48; E. L. Sukenik, *The Ancient Synagogue of Beth Alpha* (Eng. trans., Jerusalem, 1932), pl. xix.

152 E.g., 99.

153 E.g., C. H. Gordon, *Introduction to OT Times* (Ventnor, N. J., 1953), 140; *idem, The World of the OT* (New York, 1958), 153f.

154 C. H. Gordon, "Near East Seals in Princeton and Philadelphia," *Or,* N.S. 22 (1953), 244.

155 *KTU,* 1.3 II, 2f.

156 Lines 9f.

157 Pp. 136f.

158 For later material, see H. Jursch, "Hand Gottes," *RGG*[3], III, 52.

159 Helfmeyer, 131ff.

power is associated with it. This metaphorical use is not limited to the OT, but must be viewed within the wider context of other languages of the ancient Near East. Indeed the very naturalness of the metaphor makes it easy to see why it may be distributed so widely. Dhorme[160] has compared Akkadian and Hebrew usage of the upper limbs of the body, including the hand.

The use of *yāḏ* in the sense of "power" or "control" covers a wide range. Quite general terminology appears in Gen. 31:29, *yeš-l*e*'ēl yāḏî,* and in Dt. 28:32 (the opposite), *'ên l*e*'ēl yāḏeḵā*. Gen. 49:24 speaks of military power in the parallel between *qešeṯ* and *z*e*rō'ê yāḏāyw.* In Josh. 8:20, *w*e*lō'-hāyâ ḇāhem yāḏayim* expresses impotence; cf. also Dt. 32:36. A ruler has control (*yāḏ*) over the affairs of his kingdom (e.g., Gen. 41:35); in Ps. 89:26(25), such royal power is expressed by *yāḏ* and *yāmîn*. The relationship between the royal power here over *yām* and *n*e*hārôṯ* and the wording of 2 S. 8:3[161] is complex; perhaps the latter should be understood as a literal and historical form of the psalm verse, confined by the *qere* to the Euphrates. Soldiers are "under the hand," i.e., the control, of their officers (e.g., Nu. 31:49). The phrase *taḥaṯ yāḏô* may mean "within his ability" (Ezk. 46:5) or "under his control" (e.g., Jgs. 3:30). The noun *yāḏ* is also used in the sense of "support," as in 1 S. 22:17, where the priests of Nob are described as supporting David: *kî gam-yāḏām 'im-dāwiḏ*. A wide range of such expressions is used for "control" in various areas of life.

Metaphorical usage is found also in such expressions as *kol-yāḏ 'āmēl* (possibly to be read *'āmāl*) *t*e*ḇô'ennû* (Job 20:22) with the meaning "force of misfortune." Prov. 18:21 speaks of the power (*yāḏ*) of the tongue over life and death.

The expressions *b*e*'epes yāḏ* (Dnl. 8:25) and *lō' ḇ*e*yāḏ* (Job 34:20) appear to mean "without military power" or possibly "without any human agency." In the latter case, a distinction is made between *yāḏ* in the sense of ordinary human powers and the power wielded by God, which is often expressed by *yāḏ*. In Ex. 9:3, *yāḏ* can be seen as hostile and destructive when the hand of God is described as *hôyâ b*e*miqn*e*ḵā;* this hostile sense is also found elsewhere (e.g., Dt. 2:15).

2. *Divine Power.* Divine power is expressed in a variety of ways through reference to the hand of God; the more general idea of the powerful hand is associated with various divine actions. Divine power is expressed as *'ōṣem yāḏ*e*ḵā* in Job 30:21 (*kōaḥ y*e*ḏêhem* is used in 30:2 for human power; cf. Isa. 10:13, where *kōaḥ* parallels *ḥoḵmāṯî*). In some instances divine power can be mediated through human hands, being conveyed from the deity to the recipient through an agent.[162] In Ps. 89:14(13), divine power is expressed by *yāḏ, z*e*rōa'*, and *yāmîn* in parallel phrases (cf. also v. 22[21]).

Ex. 8:15(19) uses *'eṣba' '*e*lōhîm* generally for the cause of the disasters that have come upon Egypt. The same term is used in Ps. 8:4(3) for the divine creative power with reference to the heavens. In Ex. 31:18; Dt. 9:10, it is used for God's writing of the law, as a way of authenticating the law's divine origin.

---

160 Pp. 137-154.

161 See *yāḏ,* "stela," above.

162 See Wendland.

Creative power is also expressed by the use of *yāḏ:* God's hands *nāṭû šāmayim* (Isa. 45:12), his hand *yāsᵉḏâ 'ereṣ* (Isa. 48:13). In Ps. 95:4, *bᵉyāḏô meḥqᵉrê-'āreṣ* could refer to possession, although the more natural interpretation is control linked with the theme of creation in the following verse. The verb *'āśâ* with *yāḏ* is used for creation (Isa. 66:2) and more generally for any divine action associated with creation (Isa. 41:20). In Ex. 15:17, *kûn* expresses this creative power, in parallel with *pā'al* and associated with the establishment of a sanctuary (cf. Ps. 89:22[21], with reference to the strengthening of the king).

The hand of God provides protection (1 K. 18:46; Ezr. 8:22 with *'al;* 1 Ch. 4:10 with *'im*). Ps. 37:24 uses *sāmaḵ* with *yāḏ* for such protection. Ex. 33:22f. tells how God covers Moses in the rock cleft with his hand (*kap*) and removes (*sûr;* hiphil) it after passing by. In Isa. 49:2 (cf. 51:16), *bᵉṣēl yāḏô* refers to hiding. Two expressions denoting "security" occur in Ps. 31: *bᵉyāḏᵉḵā 'apqîḏ rûḥî* (v. 6[5]) and *bᵉyāḏᵉḵā 'ittōṯāy* (v. 16[15]), both with reference to the divine protecting hand. In Ps. 139:5, *wattāšeṯ 'ālay kappeḵâ* also expresses protection. Ps. 80:18(17) describes the *yāḏ* of God as being upon the *'îš yᵉmîneḵā* (par. *'immaṣtā*); the sense is that of protection or strengthening. In Ps. 91:12, protection is provided by angelic beings who *'al-kappayin yiśśā'ûnᵉḵā*. Israel is described as *ṣō'n yāḏô* (Ps. 95:7 MT; often emended, but the meaning "protection" appears quite appropriate). Job 12:10 has *bᵉyāḏô nepeš kol-ḥāy,* a phrase that in another context could well mean "in his protection," but here moves toward the sense "under his control, at his disposition." When Ps. 88:6(5) speaks of being cut off (*gāzar*) from the hand of God, the reference is to the realm of death, Sheol, where the power and protection of God are not present. The verb *gāzar* is used in this technical sense of being separated in a number of passages: from God (Ps. 31:23[22]), from the land of the living (Isa. 53:8), from the cult (2 Ch. 26:21).

The powerful activity of God is often expressed by the use of *yāḏ* in association with forms of the root *ḥzq*. In Ex. 13:3 and elsewhere we find *bᵉḥōzeq yāḏ,* but the most common expression is *bᵉyāḏ ḥᵃzāqâ* (Ex. 3:19, etc.), often in parallel with *zᵉrōa' nᵉṭûyâ* (e.g., Ps. 136:12).[163] We also find *yāḏ nᵉṭûyâ* (e.g., Isa. 9:11[12]). The outstretched hand may be hostile to Israel's enemies, viewed equally as enemies of God (Egypt in Ex. 15:12), or to Israel (e.g., Isa. 9:11[12]). A more literal use of the expression appears in Nu. 20:20, where *bᵉ'am kāḇēḏ ûḇᵉyāḏ ḥᵃzāqâ* means "with substantial military force."

It might be asked whether *yāḏ* is being used here in the sense of "military division," so that such language with reference to the deity is best understood as originating in warfare concepts. Certainly when Ex. 14:31 and Dt. 7:19 speak of "seeing" the mighty hand of God, there is an appeal to ideas expressed more tangibly, for example, in Jgs. 5:4,20, where Yahweh marches to the battle and the stars are engaged in the conflict. This supports the view that *YHWH ṣᵉḇā'ôṯ* has a military connotation; cf. also Ps. 44:3(2), which describes *'attâ yāḏᵉḵā* as achieving the conquest. The theme is elaborated in battle narratives such as Josh. 5:13-15, where the captain of the divine

---

163 → זרוע *zᵉrōa'*.

army appears to Joshua, and also in the eventual stylizing of these battle narratives (as in 1 S. 7 and the writings of the Chronicler) so that the whole of the military action is attributed to God.

The root *ḥzq* is also used in connection with prophetic inspiration. Ezk. 3:14 gives a vivid account of how the *rûaḥ* takes hold of Ezekiel and *yaḏ-YHWH 'ālay ḥāzāqâ*. This corresponds to a number of passages (e.g., Ezk. 1:3) in which the hand of God is simply upon the prophet (*watt^{e}hî 'ālāyw;* cf. also Jer. 15:17, *mipp^{e}nê yāḏ^{e}ḵā*). With this we may compare the description of Elisha's inspiritation in 2 K. 3:15. More problematic is Isa. 8:11, where *kōh 'āmar YHWH 'ēlay* is followed by *b^{e}ḥezqaṯ hayyāḏ*. In the light of usage in Ezekiel, this may be seen as expressing the moment of prophetic inspiration, on the assumption that *yāḏ* refers to the hand of God. It is also possible to understand the expression in the protective sense, i.e., "when God took me by the hand" (cf. *ḥāzaq* with *yāmîn* in Isa. 45:1), a sense continued in the following phrase, whether we follow Isa. 8:11 MT *w^{e}yiss^{e}rēnî,* "he disciplined me," or emend to *way-^{e}sîrēnî,* "he removed me." But this seems less probable, and the parallel in Isa. 45:1 is itself better understood to refer to commissioning. The impression created by the Ezekiel and Isaiah passages is that of the overwhelming nature of prophetic inspiration and its irresistible demand (cf. also Jer. 20:7). Wildberger[164] argues that the prophet hesitates to express his experience in words, not speaking explicitly of the hand of God and not stating that it is he himself who has been "seized." There does not appear to be an adequate basis for this argument. More relevant is Wildberger's point that Isaiah is using an established formula and that such a formulaic phrase would imply quite clearly that the prophet himself is seized by the hand of God.

Divine power finds expression particularly in the two themes of deliverance from alien control and deliverance into the control of aliens. A wide range of expressions is used for both.

The most common verb for expressing deliverance from hostile forces, in both an actual (often military) sense and metaphorically, is *nāṣal*. Jacob, for example, prays to be delivered from the hand of his brother (Gen. 32:12[11]); God proposes to deliver Israel from the power of Egypt (Ex. 3:8). It is said of God (e.g., Dt. 32:39): *'ên miyyāḏî maṣṣîl*. The same verb is used of human deliverance in Nu. 35:25, with reference to protection of a homicide from the *gō'ēl haddām*. Prov. 6:5 is probably textually corrupt (read perhaps *ṣayyāḏ* for *yāḏ*); if correct, it would refer to deliverance from hostile power. The hiphil of *nāṣal* is used a number of times with *mikkap* (e.g., 2 K. 20:6 [of God]; 2 Ch. 32:11; cf. also 2 S. 14:16, where David is the deliverer, as well as 2 S. 10:10[9] in parallel with *ml.t* [piel] *mikkap*). The hiphil is used in Mic. 4:10 of divine deliverance, in parallel with *gā'al mikkap* (cf. also the use of the hiphil in Hab. 2:9, of those who seek to save their wicked gains from attack). Jer. 15:21 has *pāḏâ mikkap* for divine deliverance, parallel to *hiṣṣîl miyyāḏ*. In the parallel texts Ps. 18:1 (superscription) and 2 S. 22:1, the former has *yāḏ* where the latter has *kap*.

The hiphil of *yš'* occurs frequently, in Ps. 106:10 in parallel with *gā'al*. In Ex.

---

164 H. Wildberger, *BK*, X/1, 336f.

14:30, it appears in a summary of the deliverance from Egypt. In the context of divine deliverance, 1 S. 4:3 has *mikkap;* Jgs. 6:14 (Gideon) and 2 K. 16:7 (the kings of Assyria) use the same construction for human deliverers. In 1 S. 25:26, we find *wᵉhôšēaʿ yāḏᵉḵā lāḵ,* apparently in the sense of "(not permitting) that your own hand should deliver you,"[165] in contrast to deliverance through divine power.

Ps. 107:2 uses *gā'al* for divine deliverance, as do Ps. 106:10 in parallel with *yšʿ* and Jer. 31:11 in parallel with *pdh.* Dt. 7:8 uses *pāḏâ miyyāḏ* for deliverance from Pharaoh, Ps. 49:16(15); Hos. 13:14 from the power of Sheol, Job 5:20 from the power of the sword, and Job 6:23 from the ruthless. Neh. 1:10 has a fuller expression for God's deliverance: *bᵉḵōḥᵃḵā haggāḏôl ûbᵉyāḏᵉḵā haḥᵃzāqâ.* Ps. 71:4 alone uses the piel of *plt* for divine deliverance from the power (*yāḏ*) of the wicked, paralleled by *mikkap* with two other terms for evil people. We find *šāpaṭ* for divine deliverance from human enemies in 1 S. 24:16(15); 2 S. 18:19,31.

Related to these are certain other expressions. Thus 2 K. 13:5 speaks of God's providing a *môšîaʿ* for Israel, *wayyēṣᵉ'û mittaḥaṯ yaḏ-'ᵃrām,* where the idea of divine deliverance is expressed obliquely through reference to the agent. Ps. 140:5(4) uses *šāmar* virtually in the sense of "deliver," although the idea of "keep safe" is clearly present, with reference to the hand of the wicked (par. *nāṣar*); Ps. 141:9 exhibits the same usage in a metaphor of preservation from the snares of the wicked.

The expression *pōrēq 'ên miyyāḏām* (Lam. 5:8) corresponds precisely to *'ên miyyāḏî maṣṣîl* (Dt. 32:39). The niphal of *mlṭ* is used neutrally of escape from the power of enemies (e.g., 1 S. 27:1; negatively, e.g., Jer. 32:4). The piel in parallel with *pāḏâ* in Job 6:23 refers to an appeal to others to deliver from the power of an adversary.

An implicit reference to divine deliverance appears in 2 Ch. 30:6: *happᵉlêṭâ hanniš'ereṯ lāḵem mikkap malḵê 'aššûr.*

Am. 9:2 describes God's hand as taking (*lāqaḥ*) the fugitives of his justice from Sheol; the sense suggests a parallel to passages where *lāqaḥ* appears to be used in a technical sense of divine transport to another realm.

3. *Hostile Divine Power.* God also gives people into the power of their enemies; in addition, his own power can be hostile.

The theological significance of a range of phrases used for the deliverance of people to judgment rests, of course, in what these statements say about God's control of events. The hostile hand of the enemy who comes to control those put under him in judgment can be seen as the agent through which God acts. The most common expression for this is *nāṯan bᵉyāḏ* (e.g., Josh. 2:24; also with *kap* in Jgs. 6:13; Jer. 12:7; cf. also Aram. *yᵉhaḇ,* Dnl. 2:38). In 1 K. 5:17(3), *nāṯan tāḥaṯ kappôṯ raglāyw* refers to God's subduing of David's enemies. The expression is also used commonly with reference to the subjection of Israel in judgment to alien powers, as well as to the *gō'ēl haddām* (Dt. 19:12). We also find the simple meaning "put under the control or rule of" with no hostile sense (e.g., Jgs. 9:29). In Job 9:24, the niphal of *nāṯan*

---

165 For a possible forensic sense here, see J. F. A. Sawyer, "What Was a *mošiaʿ*," *VT,* 15 (1965), 484.

denotes control of the land by the wicked; the context makes it clear that Job attributes this to God (cf. v. 23).

The same meaning obtains with the use of *māḵar* (e.g., Jgs. 2:14, par. *nāṯan*); the verb occurs twice in this sense in Judges (the text of 1 S. 23:7 being probably corrupt), and otherwise only in Ezk. 30:12; Joel 4:8(3:8).

The verb *sāgar* has the same meaning in the piel (e.g., 1 S. 17:46) and the hiphil (e.g., Ps. 31:9[8] with reference to God; 1 S. 30:15 with reference to David's deliverance into the power of someone else; Josh. 20:5 with reference to deliverance of the *gō'ēl haddām*). Job 16:11 uses the hiphil of *sāgar* with *'el,* in parallel with *wᵉ'al-yᵉḏê rᵉšā'îm yirṭēnî.* Cf. also the corresponding Aramaic term in 1QapGen 22:7.

Other words, rarely used, include *'āzaḇ* (Neh. 9:28; 2 Ch. 12:5) and the piel of *śkr* (Isa. 19:4).

The same idea of divine judgment is expressed by *nāpal bᵉyāḏ* (e.g., 2 S. 24:14), "fall into the power of God." Ruth 1:13 implies a hostile action of God in the expression *yāṣ'ā ḇî yaḏ-YHWH,* and Job 13:21 with *kap* (God's hand, which Job wishes to see removed).

Hostility (against Behemoth) is expressed in Job 40:32 by *śîm kap 'al.* In Ezk. 21:29(24), a judgment oracle on Judah, "falling into the power of the enemy" is expressed by *bakkap tittāpēśû.*

In all these expressions for the power of God, whether they refer to God's hand as showing power or express the deliverance of Israel into the power of enemies as instruments of divine judgment, it is evident that the same phrases may be used equally of both divine and human action. There is no distinctive terminology here for the action of God.

4. *Divine Impotence*. The opposite of a display of divine power, particularly as expressed through the outstretched hand of God, is indicated by the use of *qāṣar* (Nu. 11:23; Isa. 50:2; 59:1), which is also used of human impotence (2 K. 19:26 par. Isa. 37:27).

5. *Transmission of Power.* The phrase *sāmaḵ yāḏ* is used about 20 times in the OT; often it clearly conveys the idea of transmitting something from a person to another person or a sacrificial animal. Am. 5:19 uses it neutrally of a person leaning his hand on a wall, and Ps. 37:24 uses it of God's hand that holds and protects. Its specialized meaning appears in Nu. 27:18, for example, where it is used of the commissioning or ordaining of Joshua as Moses' successor, and in Ex. 29:10 with respect to a sacrificial animal. In Lev. 16:21, the significance of the action is described: Aaron places (*sāmaḵ*) both his hands on the head of the goat and confesses Israel's sins over it (*'ālāyw*); he places (*nāṯan*) the sins upon the head of the goat, which carries them away (*nāśā'*). Lev. 24:14 describes the same action; everyone who has heard a blasphemer is required to place his hand on the head of the person when he has been brought before the camp; the whole congregation then stones him. In each of these cases where more precise information is given it would appear that there is some transmission involved in the act of placing hands on the animal or person; the same may also be said of the commissioning of Levites or of Joshua. It is therefore appro-

priate to see here a transmission of power. (Péter distinguishes imposition of *a hand*, which expresses identity between the person and the sacrificial animal, and imposition of *hands*, which expresses transmission.) The same terminology is used later for rabbinic ordination, and is explained (e.g., in *Nu. r.* on 27:20) as the pouring of personality "as from one vessel into another."[166]

There is no evidence in the OT for the use of this terminology in acts of healing, although the LXX renders *wᵉhēnîp yāḏô 'el-hammāqôm* in 2 K. 5:11[167] as *kaí epithḗsei tḗn cheíra autoú epí tón tópon*. This is clearly an interpretative translation; it is noteworthy that *epithḗsei* is a natural equivalent for *sāmaḵ*. Apart from NT usage, the closest parallel is now found in 1QapGen 20:22,29: *w'smwk ydy 'lwhy wyḥh,* which provides evidence for the extension of *sāmaḵ* to acts of healing and for revealing the background of NT usage.[168]

6. *Divine Gestures*. In our discussion of the various usages of *yāḏ* and *kap,* it has become clear that many of these expressions are used equally of actions performed by the deity or by human beings. Thus Yahweh holds a *kôs* in his hand (e.g., Isa. 51:17). The hand of God may rest on someone in hostile fashion (*nûaḥ,* Ps. 38:3[2]). His hands have skill in shepherding his people (Ps. 78:72). He expresses his power with his hand (Ex. 13:9). He raises (*nāśā'*) his hand, a gesture probably to be understood as expressing hostility to the wicked (Ps. 10:12; NEB "set thy hand to the task" misses the sense, although the phrase could be understood to refer to protection); in Ps. 37:24, *sômēḵ yāḏô* denotes a divine protective gesture. In Isa. 49:22, *nāśā' yāḏ* is used to express hostility or a summons. God may keep his hand in or it may be short (*qāṣar,* Nu. 11:23; Isa. 50:2; 59:1); he may draw back his hand (*šûḇ*; hiphil) so as not to destroy (Ezk. 20:22). In an angry gesture (Ezk. 22:13) he strikes (*nāḵâ*) with his hand (*kap*—the open hand, not the clenched fist as NEB renders). In Ezk. 21:22, he strikes hand on hand (*nāḵâ kap*) "causing his anger to rest" (*nûaḥ;* hiphil), i.e., abate, or more probably to settle on the object of his wrath. He stretches out (*pāraś*) his hands in appeal to his people (Isa. 65:2); he opens (*pāṯaḥ*) his hands in blessing (Ps. 104:28; 145:16) and raises (*nāśā'*) his hands to swear an oath (e.g., Ex. 6:8).

This brief summary of hand gestures (discussed more fully above) makes it clear that here, too, there are many instances of the same expressions used for both the deity and human beings. The fact that in a few cases a particular phrase appears only with reference to human beings would be a dubious basis for saying that it could not be used of the deity or that it was deliberately avoided. Thus *nāśā' yāḏ,* "swear an oath," is used of both; *rûm* (hiphil) *yāḏ* is used only of human persons (Gen. 14:22). It would be fallacious reasoning to assume that the latter could not also be used of the deity.

This general observation makes it desirable to view with caution the detailed ar-

---

166 See Daube, 224-246, with a full discussion and references.

167 See above.

168 See J. A. Fitzmyer, *The Genesis Apocryphon of Qumran Cave I. BietOr,* 18A (^{2}1971), 140; also *idem, CBQ,* 22 (1960), 284; Braun, 89f.; Flusser, *IEJ,* 7 (1957), 107f.

guments adduced by Humbert[169] to suggest a distinction between *šālaḥ yāḏ* and *nāṭâ yāḏ*, the former being primarily a human gesture, the latter a gesture "properly and exclusively divine."[170]

Analysis of usage points to a wide range of contexts for *šālaḥ yāḏ*, most of which refer to human gestures; but there are 5 passages where it is used of the deity: Ex. 3:20; 9:15; 24:11 (all J); Ps. 138:7; Ezk. 8:3. Humbert's argument that they are exceptional is undermined by his comment on Ps. 138:7, to the effect that it involves a deliberate martial anthropomorphism. Can one really distinguish between a deliberate anthropomorphism and the very common and indeed quite natural attribution to the deity of actions exactly comparable to human actions? Humbert's case is further weakened by his refusal to include 3 references to *šālaḥ yāḏ* associated with divine beings other than the deity. Thus in 2 S. 24:16 the subject is *mal'aḵ YHWH;* Ezk. 2:9 refers to *yāḏ šᵉlûḥâ*, clearly implying either the deity or an angelic being, more likely the former since the context involves hearing what is evidently God's voice; Ezk. 10:7 uses the expression of a *kᵉrûḇ*. Humbert's argument that these expressions refer to creatures and do not involve the deity himself totally misunderstands the relationship in the OT between God and the angelic beings that act on his behalf. This is especially clear in passages where the narrative moves imperceptibly from one to the other (see, e.g., Jgs. 6:11f.,14,22f.).[171]

These observations on Humbert's comments concerning *šālaḥ yāḏ* make one suspicious of his confident statements about *nāṭâ yāḏ*. His examination of the usage shows that it is used of God or of God's agents, with the possible sole exception of Job 15:25. The agents in question are Moses (e.g., Ex. 9:22), Aaron (e.g., Ex. 7:19), Joshua (Josh. 8:18,26), and *ḥoḵmâ* (Prov. 1:24). In claiming that the expression belongs to description of the deity alone, Humbert gets round the Job 15:25 passage by claiming it is an example of hubris, a case where a human person improperly undertakes a gesture belonging to the deity alone.

The total number of occurrences of *nāṭâ yāḏ* is 41; even if Humbert is right in saying that Job 15:25 is not a real exception, one may doubt whether it is a statistically viable conclusion that the expression was so restricted. In light of the extensive overlap of divine and human gestures, this conclusion could be no more than tentative. It must be added that, while it is quite proper to see Aaron and Moses and Joshua as agents of the deity, and therefore to regard their actions as tantamount to actions of the deity, the argument is not entirely convincing when Humbert dismisses as not attributable to the deity those instances of *šālaḥ* where the agent is an angelic being. In Josh. 8:18, God commands Joshua to extend his hand; but it is no more proper to say that it is really God who acts and not Joshua than it would be to claim in Ex. 17:8-13 that it is God who raises his hands and not Moses, though it is evident in both instances that the narrator would see the deity as the operative power.

It is also open to question whether Humbert is right in describing the gesture as

---

169 *VT*, 12 (1962), 383-395.

170 *Ibid.*, 392.

171 See also J. Barr, "Theophany and Anthropomorphism in the OT," *Congress Volume, Oxford 1959. SVT*, 7 (1960), 31-38.

"point the hand." This would reasonably suggest a hostile gesture toward or against particular places or people. But the usage of the verb is not so limited. In Isa. 45:12, it is said of God *yāḏay nāṭû šāmayim* (also Ps. 104:2, without *yāḏ*); here and elsewhere it is clear that the meaning is "stretch" or "spread." In Prov. 1:24, Wisdom is said to stretch out her hands, but no one pays attention; clearly the gesture is one of appeal. Again we observe how the same gesture may express more than one meaning, or, possibly, the same expression may describe more than one gesture.

7. *Idols*. Various expressions denote what people produce with their hands. The phrase *y^e^gîa' kappayim* (e.g., Gen. 31:42) is used in this sense; in Job 10:3 it is used of Job as the product of the divine hands. Similarly we find *p^e^rî* with both *kap̱* (e.g., Prov. 31:16) and *yāḏ* (Prov. 31:31), and *g^e^mûl* with *yāḏ* (e.g., Jgs. 9:16), used in Prov. 12:14 for the reward that follows from good deeds. Gen. 5:29 expresses the labor of human hands by *'iṣṣ^e^ḇôn yāḏênû*, parallel to *ma'^a^śēnû*. The latter is the most common word for this idea, and is widely used to denote anything human beings can make. Thus Cant. 7:2 refers to the work of the craftsman's (*'ommān*) hands. Dt. 2:7, for example, speaks of divine blessing on all the work of human hands, and such expressions are commonly found in a range of contexts.

More specifically, however, the expressions refer to idolatrous objects, as for example in Jer. 1:16, where *ma'^a^śê y^e^ḏêhem* parallels *'^e^lōhîm '^a^ḥērîm*. Such an example is entirely clear, and the expression is particularly characteristic of Deuteronomy and Jeremiah; cf. also Ps. 115:4; 135:15; Hos. 14:4(3). In some passages it is difficult to be certain whether the phrase means "deeds" or "idolatrous objects." Dt. 31:29 is probably to be taken in the latter sense, but the more general meaning is also possible (so NEB; RSV translates literally and therefore ambiguously). The ambiguity is a natural outcome of emphasizing that idols are mere objects made by human beings; both senses occur frequently in the Deuteronomic and Jeremianic writings. This is brought out fully in such a passage as Isa. 17:8, where first altars and then *'^a^šērîm* and *ḥammānîm* are described as *ma'^a^śēh yāḏāyw* and *'^a^šer 'āśû 'eṣb^e^'ôṯāyw*, respectively. People should turn instead to their maker (*'ōśēhû*), the Holy One of Israel (v. 7). The same phraseology in Dt. 27:15 refers explicitly to the maker of an image.

The phrase *ma^a^'śēh yāḏāyw* is equally used for God's works. In Isa. 5:12, it parallels *pō'al YHWH;* cf. also Ps. 92:5(4). God's created order is also so described (Ps. 102:26[25]). In particular, human beings are the work of God's hands (Ps. 138:8; Job 14:15; 34:19); the term is also applied to Assyria in Isa. 19:25, and more generally to the people of God in Isa. 60:21; 64:7(6). In Ps. 111:7, the works of God's hands are *'^e^meṯ* and *mišpāṭ*.

Ackroyd

ידה *ydh;* תּוֹדָה *tôḏâ*

Contents: I. Etymology and Occurrences. II. Meaning: 1. Hebrew; 2. Egyptian; 3. Akkadian. III. Usage: 1. Confession as Praise; 2. Penitential Confession.

I. Etymology and Occurrences. Apart from Hebrew, the root *ydh* (*yd'*, *wdy*) appears only in Aramaic (Biblical: Dnl. 2:23; 6:11) and Arabic.[1] The fundamental meaning is "confess." It appears in the OT as a verb (about 100 occurrences), a noun (*tôḏâ,* about 30 occurrences), and in the form of the personal name *hôḏawyāh*(*û*) (1 Ch. 3:24; 5:24; 9:7; Ezr. 2:40).[2]

---

ydh. D. Bach, *Tôdâh dans l'AT* (diss., Strasbourg, 1972); *idem,* "Rite et parole dans l'AT: Nouveaux éléments apportés par l'étude de Tôdâh," *VT,* 28 (1978), 10-19; K. Baltzer, *The Covenant Formulary in OT, Jewish, and Early Christian Writings* (Eng. trans., Philadelphia, 1971); A. Barucq, *L'expression de la louange divine et de la prière dans la Bible et en Égypte. Bibl. d'étude,* 33 (1962), esp. 323-335; W. Beyerlin, "Die *tôdā* der Heilsvergegenwärtigung in den Klageliedern des Einzelnen," *ZAW,* 79 (1967), 208-224; H. J. Boecker, *Redeformen des Rechtslebens im AT. WMANT,* 14 (²1970); P. A. H. de Boer, *De voorbede in het OT. OTS,* 3 (1943); H. Brunner, "Gebet," *LexÄg,* II, 452-59; H. Cazelles, "L'Anaphore et l'AT," *Eucharisties d'Orient et d'Occident. Lex orandi,* 46 (Paris, 1970), 11-21; F. Crüsemann, *Studien zur Formgeschichte von Hymnus und Danklied in Israel. WMANT,* 32 (1969); A. Erman, *The Ancient Egyptians: A Sourcebook of their Writings* (Eng. trans., New York, ²1966); M. Gilbert, "La prière de Daniel, Dn 9,4-19," *RThL,* 3 (1972), 284-310; A. E. Goodman, "חסד and תודה in the Linguistic Tradition of the Psalter," *Words and Meanings. Festschrift D. W. Thomas* (Cambridge, 1968), 105-115; H. Grimme, "Der Begriff von hebräischen הודה und תודה," *ZAW,* 58 (1940/41), 234-240; H. Gunkel and J. Begrich, *Einl. in die Psalmen. GHK,* sup. vol. (²1966); K. Heinen, *Das Gebet im AT* (Rome, 1971); H.-J. Hermisson, *Sprache und Ritus im altisraelitischen Kult. WMANT,* 19 (1965); F. Horst, "Die Doxologien im Amosbuch," *ZAW,* 6 (1929), 45-54 = his *Gottes Recht. GSAT. ThB,* 12 (1961), 155-166; B. W. Jones, "The Prayer in Daniel IX," *VT,* 18 (1968), 488-493; D. Kellermann, *Die Priesterschrift von Numeri 1*1 *bis 10*10 *literarkritisch und traditionsgeschichtlich untersucht. BZAW,* 120 (1970); U. Kellermann, *Nehemia: Quellen, Überlieferung und Geschichte. BZAW,* 102 (1967); K. Koch, " 'denn seine Güte währet ewiglich,' " *EvTh,* 21 (1961), 537-544; A. Lacocque, "The Liturgical Prayer in Daniel 9," *HUCA,* 47 (1976), 119-142; F. Mand, "Die eigenständigkeit der Danklieder des Psalters als Bekenntnislieder," *ZAW,* 70 (1958), 185-199; W. Mayer, *Untersuchungen zur Formensprache der babylonischen "Gebetsbeschwörungen." Studia Pohl,* ser. maior, 5 (1976), 307ff.; O. Michel, "Gebet II (Fürbitte) (A. Nichtchristlich I, Alter Orient)," *RAC,* IX (1972 [1976]), 1-11; *idem,* "ὁμολογέω," *TDNT,* V, 199-220; O. Plöger, "Reden und Gebete im deuteronomistischen und chronistischen Geschichtswerk," *Festschrift G. Dehn* (Neukirchen-Vluyn, 1957), 35-49; R. Rendtorff, *Studien zur Geschichte des Opfers im alten Israel. WMANT,* 24 (1967); E. von Severus, "Gebet (III. Jüdisch)," *RAC,* VIII (1972), 1162-69; A. Stuiber, "Eulogia," *RAC,* VI (1966), 900-928, esp. 900-906; C. Westermann, *Praise and Lament in the Psalms* (Eng. trans., Atlanta, 1981); *idem,* "ידה *jdh* hi. preisen," *THAT,* I, 674-682; D. Wohlenberg, *Kultmusik in Israel* (diss., Hamburg, 1967).

1 *KBL*³, 372.
2 *IPN,* 194f.

II. Meaning.

1. *Hebrew.* The verb *ydh* occurs in the hiphil and hithpael, and conveys two ranges of meaning. The first is "praise, sing a hymn"; the second is "confess." Thanksgiving is a form of praise.[3] There is no semantic distinction in the use of the two stems. It is true that the hiphil usually expresses praise, the hithpael confession. But the antithetical parallelism with the piel of *ksh* in Prov. 28:13 and the synonymous parallelism based on the negated hiphil of *yd'* and piel of *ksh* in Ps. 32:5 demand the meaning "confess," especially since *peša'* is the object in both cases. By contrast, the use of the hithpael of *ydh* in 2 Ch. 30:22 points to the first meaning. Here we find the object *l*ᵉ*YHWH,* which is not used elsewhere with the hithpael, but with the hiphil (e.g., Ezr. 3:11; Ps. 33:2; 105:1; Isa. 12:4). Furthermore, in 2 Ch. 30:22 *miṯwaddîm* parallels *m*ᵉ*zabb*ᵉ*ḥîm ziḇḥê š*ᵉ*lāmîm.*[4] But the offering of praise (*tôḏâ*[5]) is a qualified *zeḇḥê š*ᵉ*lāmîm.*[6] The hithpael is found only in prose. When the hiphil appears in prose, it is being used in a technical sense. Association with the piel of → הלל *hll* (1 Ch. 23:30; 25:3; 2 Ch. 5:13; 31:2; Neh. 12:24,46), with the statement "for his steadfast love endures for ever" (1 Ch. 16:41; 2 Ch. 7:3,6), or with both (Ezr. 3:11) characterizes hymnody. In his prayer at the dedication of the temple (1 K. 8:23-53; 2 Ch. 6:14-42), Solomon prays that God may hear his people when they turn (*šûḇ*) to him, pray (*pll*) and make supplication (*ḥnn*) in the temple, and praise (*ydh;* hiphil) his name. Here a penitential liturgy including a communal lament is presupposed. Communal laments on the occasion of a defeat or drought are found in Ps. 79 and Jer. 14:2-9, respectively. At least Ps. 79 ends, as its genre would lead us to expect,[7] with a vow of praise in v. 13; we may therefore assume that this is what the hiphil of *ydh* in 1 K. 8:33,35; 2 Ch. 6:24, 26 refers to. This assumption is supported by Neh. 11:17: *y*ᵉ*hôḏeh latt*ᵉ*pillâ,* "he begins the praise in the communal lament."[8] Ps. 106, with its combination of hymnic introit and confession of sins, may also be noted here. The use of the hiphil is therefore peculiar to poetry, while prose uses the hithpael. This is true despite the hiphil in 1 Ch. 29:13, where it has found its way into a prose prayer as a technical term synonymous with the piel of *brk* (cf. 1 Ch. 29:10,20).

The noun *tôḏâ* derived from the hiphil of the verb[9] corresponds to the verb in its meanings: (1) praise or thanksgiving, offering of praise or thanksgiving, the choir (that sings the hymn of praise); (2) confession. The noun *huyy*ᵉ*ḏôṯ,* found only in Neh. 12:8, is synonymous with the plural of *tôḏâ,* "choir."

Bach, who connects the two meanings of *tôḏâ* with the offering of sacrifice, proposes the translation "sacrifice of confession."[10]

G. Mayer

---

[3] Westermann, *Praise and Lament in the Psalms,* 25.
[4] Cf. Rendtorff, 153.
[5] See III.1.c below.
[6] Hermisson, 33.
[7] See III.1.a below.
[8] Gunkel-Begrich, 119.
[9] *BLe,* §495.
[10] Bach, *VT,* 28 (1978), 19.

2. *Egyptian*. Egyptian has no words that clearly mean "(offer) thanksgiving" or "prayer of thanksgiving," etc. Several words and phrases for "praise"[11] probably involve thanksgiving and may therefore be considered as possible tokens of thanksgiving. It is difficult, however, to define the precise nuances of these various words, since the gestures and attitudes suggested by the determinatives convey insufficient information. In a double procession comprising twenty-four persons, for example, *nhm*[12] is used to describe the action of a single individual participant;[13] one may reasonably ask whether his attitude is really more thankful than that of the others. A parallel text[14] uses the two other expressions that the *WbÄs* translates as "thank": *ḥsy-R'*[15] and *dw3-nṯr.*[16] The formation of these two expressions is interesting. According to the *WbÄS*, "give thanks for something" is thus expressed by saying "praise Re (or god) for something." It is important to note that these expressions can have both human beings and gods as subject, and that thanks can be given for persons, pharaohs, cities, etc. In a dedication inscription from Denderah,[17] Hathor thanks the pharaoh, her beloved son, as well as the city for the temple and its precincts; i.e., she "praises Re" for the pharaoh and the city.

In his study of the more personal elements of praise in Egypt, Barucq[18] notes that explicit thanksgiving is rarely attested. The best evidence appears in the well-known group of stelae from the Ramesside period devoted to "personal religion" and school texts from the same period.[19] Particularly noteworthy is the unique vow of praise in the stela of Neb-Re: "I will set up this memorial to your name and set your worship on it in writing if you save for me the scribe Nekhtamon." The erection of the stela and the narrative of the deity's benefaction are concrete tokens of thanksgiving.

Indirectly, of course, all kinds of theophorous personal names and divine epithets proclaiming the mercies of various deities and their healing or saving intervention can serve as evidence of thanksgiving. Barucq[20] points out that the phrases *m nfrw.k* and *m ḥśwt.k* that occur frequently in the private inscriptions at Amarna can be interpreted as expressions of thankfulness to the king on the part of these individuals.

Praise of the gods, which finds its natural locus in a general disposition, is a dominant element in hymns and prayers;[21] confession of sin, however, is extremely rare in the material available to us, and is found primarily in the group of texts mentioned above. The so-called negative confessions,[22] which would be better termed

---

11 *WbÄS*, VI, 100, *s.v.* "Lobpreis" (8 references), and 119, *s.v.* "preisen" (22 references).
12 The meaning is "thank" according to *WbÄS*, II, 286.
13 *Urk.*, VIII, no. 55k, 13.
14 *Ibid.*, 56k, 22f.
15 *WbÄS*, III, 155; all citations late.
16 *WbÄS*, V, 428.
17 A. Mariette, *Dendérah*, I (Paris, 1870), 54a.
18 P. 327.
19 See Barucq's collection of penitential prayers, 569, and the translations in Erman, 282ff.
20 P. 334.
21 Barucq, Brunner; J. Assmann, "Aretalogien," *LexÄg*, I, 425-434.
22 Book of the Dead, chap. 125.

declarations of innocence,[23] provide a wide-ranging catalog of sins expressed in negative form. But they bear the title "Separation of NN from all the evil he has done," and the Instruction of Amenemope states explicitly: "Do not say, I have no sin,"[24] which clearly bears witness to a sense of sin on the part of the Egyptians.[25]

Bergman

3. *Akkadian.* Linguistically, there is no analog in Akkadian to *hôḏâ, tôḏâ,* and *hiṯwaddâ.* In statements, *dalālu* (II), "praise" (verb), and *dalīlu* I (also *dilīlu*), "praise" (noun), are largely used like *hôḏâ* and *tôḏâ.*[26] Most commonly—and almost always in the concluding doxologies of prayers—we find *dalīlī-ka/ki/kunu ludlul,* "I will praise you." But *dalālu* can also have as its objects such terms as *qurdu,* "warlikeness," *tanittu,* "glory," or *narbû,* "great deeds"; the last is found most often with *šūpû,* "glorify." A deity as object appears most often in names like *Šin-ludlul;* more common, however, are short forms like *Adallal.* W. Mayer discusses in detail expressions like *dalīlī-ka ludlul,*[27] with many references to the OT. A "vow of praise" is thanksgiving to the deity; neither Akkadian nor Hebrew has a word for "thank." The fact that gods and human beings stand in constant interrelationship finds eloquent expression in vows of praise, some of which appear already in Sumerian letters addressed to gods, penitential prayers, and incantations;[28] there is an intimate connection between life and praise. Other verbs of praising include:[29] *šurruḫu* and *nu''udu,* "glorify," *šit(am)muru,* "honor," *kitarrubu,* "hail repeatedly," and *šurbû,* "magnify, praise." There are further phrases compounded with "say" and "make." The wealth of expressions and their frequent use not only in fixed formulas show the importance attached to praising the deity.

Confession of sin is a different matter. Akkadian lacks a word equivalent to Heb. *hiṯwaddâ; ḫīṭa petû,* "disclose sin," appears only rarely in the Amarna letters.[30] Confession of sin nevertheless has a firm place in Babylonian prayers,[31] because sin was looked on as one of the major causes of suffering, from which the supplicant seeks deliverance. Normally the reference to sin appears in relative clauses or nominal constructions within a lament that bemoans suffering and prays for deliverance, e.g.: "on account of the sin that I know or do not know, wherein I was negligent, sinned, offended, went badly astray."[32] But we also find confession in main clauses, e.g.: "I was negligent, sinned, offended, went badly astray; these all are my sins and my misdeeds. I was unknowingly neglectful, transgressed your commandment, swore

---

23 Cf. C. Maystre, *Les déclarations d'innocence* (Cairo, 1937).
24 XIX, 19.
25 S. Morenz, *Egyptian Religion* (Eng. trans., Ithaca, N. Y., 1973), 130ff.
26 *AHw,* I, 153f.; *CAD,* III (1959), 46f., 50f.
27 Pp. 307ff.
28 *Ibid.,* 315ff.
29 *Ibid.,* 319ff.
30 *AHw,* II, 860b: 20.
31 Cf. Mayer, 1.c, 111ff.
32 E. Ebeling, *Die Akkadische Gebetsserie "Handerhebung." MDAW,* 20 (1953), 8, 10f.

falsely by you, did not obey your ordinances."[33] In addition to general confession, we find special confession in which individual sins are named, e.g.: "I spoke and then changed it, I demanded trust and did not give it; I did what was improper, what was harmful was in my mouth; I told what had never been said."[34] Guides for self-examination before confession contain catalogs of sins comparable to those of the Christian tradition. The second and third tablets of the Šurpu incantation series, dating probably from the end of the second millennium B.C., speak of some three hundred possible ways to fall into separation from the deity (called *māmītu*, "curse") through misconduct or unwitting sin.[35] There are also a few confessions of sin on the part of kings; these name individual sins, albeit in conjunction with a list of good works. Thus Ashurnasirpal I (*ca.* 1050 B.C.), being in poor health, says: "I was not mindful of your lordship, I did not pray continually; the people of Assyria were not well informed, they did not always turn to your divinity."[36] Religious attitudes and convictions are often older than the concepts and terms that refer to them, and can continue to develop without conceptual form.

Von Soden

III. Usage.

1. *Confession as Praise.* a. Characteristic and instructive with respect to the use of the verb is J's interpretation of the names Reuben, Simeon, Levi, and Judah in Gen. 29:31-35.[37] What Leah lacks in comparison with her sister Rachel is the love of her husband (vv. 32-34). Her distress is that she is neglected (v. 31). When Yahweh looks upon her affliction (v. 32), when he hears her (v. 33), her prayer to Yahweh is presupposed. The birth of her fourth son, the fulfillment of this prayer, leads to praise: "This time I will praise the Lord" (v. 35). In other words, as early as the eighth century B.C., and probably even earlier, the elements of description of need, prayer, fulfillment, and thanksgiving through praise are conjoined. The statement *'ôḏeh 'eṯ-YHWH* is a vow of praise but also a brief form of a hymn of praise, a kind of prototype arising from the occasion.

A vow of praise, usually expressed through a voluntative 1st person singular hiphil, concludes individual laments (Ps. 7:18[Eng. v. 17]; 28:7; 35:18; 42:6,12[5,11]; 43:4f.; 52:11[9]; 54:8[6]; 57:10; 71:22; 86:12; 109:30; 119:7). The supplicant can also use an infinitive construct to describe the vow of praise. The voluntative may be retained, as in Ps. 119:62: "I will rise to praise," or the vow may appear as a petition: "Bring me out of prison, that I may praise" (Ps. 142:8[7]). A wish in the 3rd person plural (*yôḏû*) can also take the place of the vow of praise. The situation is similar in the case

---

33 W. G. Lambert, "Three Literary Prayers of the Babylonians," *AfO*, 19 (1959-1960), 51, lines 67ff.

34 E. Reiner, "Lipšur Litanies," *JNES*, 15 (1956), 142, 53f.; W. G. Lambert, "Dingir.šà.Dib.Ba. Incantations," *JNES*, 33 (1974), 280, 124/6.

35 E. Reiner, *Šurpu. BAfO*, 11 (1958).

36 W. von Soden, "Zwei Königsgebete an Ištar aus Assyrien," *AfO*, 25 (1974-77), 39 and 43, lines 23f.

37 M. Noth, *A History of Pentateuchal Traditions* (Eng. trans. 1972; repr. Chico, Calif., 1981), 25, 29.

of communal laments. The vow of praise may be expressed through the voluntative of the 1st person plural (Ps. 79:13) or it may be replaced by a petition using the infinitive construct: "Help us . . . to praise" (Ps. 106:47). In Ps. 44:9(8), where *nôḏeh* follows statements of confidence, the vow is in a sense anticipated.

The occasions leading to a vow of praise can be stated only in general terms, since the imagery of the laments is standardized: the life of the supplicant is threatened. Description of constantly recurring situations dominates, involving above all the experience of persecution (Ps. 71:10; 86:14). The innocent supplicant is being persecuted. His enemies lay a net and dig a pit for him without cause (Ps. 35:7; cf. 57:7[6]); they oppress him for no reason (Ps. 7:5[4]). The enemies of the devout overwhelm them with their wickedness (Ps. 52:3-6[1-4]). Cunning and violence are joined (Ps. 140:2-5[1-4]). The description of Ps. 109:3f. is moving: "With words of hate they beset me; they attack me without cause. For my love they accuse me, although my prayer was for them."[38] Forced exile also separates from the life-giving presence of God, which is experienced in the cult (Pss. 42f.). Imprisonment resembles death, where there is no praise of God (Ps. 142:5,8[4,7]).

The basic situation that evokes a vow of praise in a communal lament is the same as in an individual lament: a threat to life. Now, however, it is transferred to the group. It is actual or predictable (cf. 2 Ch. 20:4ff.) national catastrophe. Dispersion among the nations resulting from defeat (Ps. 44:10-12[9-11]; 106:47) parallels the destruction of Jerusalem and the desecration of the temple (Ps. 79). Despite many attempts to assign Ps. 79 to a specific historical event, it remains uncertain whether it refers to the capture of Jerusalem by Nebuchadnezzar in 587/586 B.C. or to an event of the Maccabean period. For later generations, the fall of Jerusalem and the Babylonian captivity became the archetypes of radical collective disaster.

Praise is actually expressed in the *tôḏâ* (Neh. 12:27; Ps. 26:7; 42:5[4]; 69:31[30]; 95:2; 100:1,4; 147:7; Isa. 51:3; Jer. 30:19; Jon. 2:10[9]). It is a joyful song in which exultation over God's mercy makes itself heard (Ps. 42:5[4]); it is among the messages of rejoicing that will be heard concerning the "new salvation,"[39] the renewed favor of God after the destruction of the Judahite state (Isa. 51:3; Jer. 30:19). In the individual thanksgiving song, which we should conceive of as fulfilling the vow of praise, the verb *ydh* has a fixed place. The introduction often consists of *'ôḏeh* plus object (Ps. 9:2[1]; 108:4[3]; 118:21; 138:1f.; Isa. 12:1; 25:1). If this place is already occupied by another expression of praise, *'ôḏeh* comes at the end (Ps. 18:50[49] par. 2 S. 22:50; Ps. 30:13[12]; 118:19,28). The oath here moves from singular thanksgiving to continual praise.[40] In the vow of praise, it is possible for the voluntative of the 1st person to be replaced by the optative of the 3rd person masculine plural (Ps. 107:8,15,21,31). In hymns the formula occurs only twice. Once it serves as an introduction (Ps. 111:1), and in the psalm of creation the worshipper proclaims his praise toward the end (Ps. 139:14).

Usually hymns are introduced by the impv. *hôḏû*, "praise" (2 Ch. 20:21; Ps. 30:5[4]; 97:12; 136:1-3; Isa. 12:4; Jer. 33:11). The same is true of the historical psalms (1 Ch.

---

38 Trans. following H.-J. Kraus, *Psalmen. BK*, XV/2 (⁵1978), 744.

39 A. Weiser, *Psalms. OTL* (Eng. trans. 1962), 349.

40 Crüsemann, 236.

16:8; Ps. 105:1; 106:1) and liturgies (Ps. 107:1; 118:1), if these forms are in fact not simply variants of the hymn. An introduction using a different verb may also be continued by *hôḏû* (Ps. 100:4). Repetition at the end can turn the introduction into a framework (1 Ch. 16:34; Ps. 118:29; 136:26). Exceptionally, the summons to praise can come at the conclusion (Ps. 97:12). It can be replaced by the optative of the 3rd person masculine plural (Ps. 67:4,6[3,5]; 89:6; 99:3; 145:10) or the 3rd person feminine singular (Ps. 76:11[10]). Forms using the infinitive construct also appear (Ps. 92:2[1]; 122:4). Crüsemann[41] admits neither *yôḏû* nor *tôḏekkā* (Ps. 76:11[10]) as variants of the vow of praise or of the imperative summons to praise; instead he puts these forms under the heading of "optative praise," an independent hymnic form whose variability he is quite ready to recognize.

It is helpful to list the occasions with which *ydh* is associated in thanksgiving songs.[42] In view of the fate that awaited those conquered in battle—depending, of course, on their social rank (cf. 2 K. 25)—victory was perceived as newly bestowed life, demonstrating the harmony between Yahweh and his believers (Ps. 18:36-39,50[35-38,49] par.; Isa. 25:1-5); similarly, healing of a disease felt to be mortal causes the worshipper to rejoice and exult (Ps. 30:3,13[2,12]). The blessing of children, which guarantees a woman's position and gains the love of her husband (Gen. 29:35), also belongs here.

The praise is developed by means of a clause beginning with *kî*. When *'ôḏeh* introduces the *tôḏâ*, the *kî* clause recounts the divine benefaction the worshipper has experienced. Additional clauses may continue the narrative. The perfective verbal clause is the rule. Only in Ps. 108:5(4) do we find a noun clause. The narrative is couched in direct address: "Thou hast maintained my right and my cause" (Ps. 9:5[4][43]; cf. Ps. 108:4[3]; 118:21; 138:2; Isa. 12:1; 25:1). No narrative is associated with the vow of praise that concludes the *tôḏâ*, for the future praise of God remains open. Only where the concluding vow is represented by the hymnic form of optative praise do we find in two instances a summary narrative in the 3rd person (Ps. 107:9,16), to be understood as recapitulating the detailed narrative that has gone before.

Despite its great similarity, the situation is not so clear in the vow of praise found in individual laments. In Ps. 7:18(17); 28:7; 35:18; 42:6,12(5,11); 43:4f.; 71:22; 119:7, there is no *kî* clause; the vow is open-ended. Elsewhere it takes on a variety of forms. In a perfective verbal clause the worshipper may anticipate the divine benefaction out of assurance that he will be heard. He addresses God in the 2nd person, as in the introduction to the *tôḏâ*. Other forms of direct address include the noun clause in Ps. 57:11(10) (cf. 108:4[3]) and Ps. 86:13, a verse combining noun and verb clauses: "Thy steadfast love is greater than I; thou hast delivered my soul from the depths of Sheol." Ps. 54:8(6) is in the 3rd person; once again, *kî ṭôḇ* is explicated by "for he has delivered me from every trouble." Here, however, the suffix *-nî* confirms

---

[41] *Ibid.*, 184-191.

[42] The terminology is discussed by C. Westermann, *Gewendete Klage*. *BSt*, 8 (1955); and *idem*, "Die Rolle der Klage in der Theologie des ATs," *Forschung am AT. ThB*, 55 (1974), 250-268 [= "The Role of the Lament in the Theology of the OT," *Int*, 28 (1974), 20-38].

[43] Kraus, *BK*, XV/1, *in loc*.

the specific reference to the worshipper. In Ps. 109:31, the *kî* clause changes to the 3rd person, with the verb in the imperfect. The *kî* clauses that follow the imperative summons to praise (*hôḏû*) are all in the 3rd person. In contrast to the thanksgiving song, there is no narrative but rather some variation of a statement concerning Yahweh and his → חסד *ḥeseḏ* (Ps. 100:4; 107:1; 136:1-3; Jer. 33:11; etc.) or his favor (*rāṣôn*[44] [Ps. 30:6(5)]). When optative praise (*yôḏû*) replaces the imperative (*hôḏû*), the *kî* clause takes the form of an imperfective verbal clause. Whether Yahweh is described as just and merciful (Ps. 67:5[4]) or his greatness is described in a rhetorical question, there is no reference to any specific crucial deed. The statement is intended to describe his nature. After *'ôḏeh,* however, even in a hymn, the direct address and mention of the particular deed are retained (Ps. 139:14).

We see, then, that *'ôḏeh,* regardless of its place and function in the various literary types, always implies a transaction between Yahweh and the human world, which is recounted in a *kî* clause, whereas the *kî* clause following a summons to praise constitutes a statement about Yahweh. This significant difference leads Westermann to speak of declarative praise in the former case, descriptive praise in the latter. On the basis of this difference in content, he terms the thanksgiving song a declarative praise psalm and the hymn a descriptive praise psalm.[45]

The particle *kî* both designates content and motivates praise. This double function leads to some uncertainty in translation, as comparison of recent comms. will attest. In Ps. 9:5(4), Gunkel[46] renders *kî* as "for," Weiser[47] as "that"; Kraus[48] does not translate it at all. In Ps. 30:6(5), Gunkel has "for"; Weiser leaves the word untranslated, and Kraus renders it as "indeed." In Isa. 12:1, Kaiser[49] translates it as "for," Wildberger[50] as "truly." Since "for" overemphasizes the motivating function, the use of a deictic particle is most appropriate: of the translations given, "truly" and "indeed" best represent the double function. Both point to content without excluding motivation. Crüsemann,[51] too, has elected to translate *kî* as "indeed," albeit only when it follows an imperative summons to praise, since he sees in the *kî* clause not only the content of the praise but also the carrying out of the summons. Elsewhere he retains the motivating "for."

b. As the wealth of parallel verbs and other expressions shows, praise involves intense emotion. It includes joy (1 Ch. 16:10; Ps. 9:3[2]; 67:5[4]; 105:3; etc.), singing and playing[52] (Ps. 7:18[17]; 18:50[49]; 30:5,13[4,12]; 108:4[3]; etc.), exultation[53]

---

44 → רצה *rāṣâ.*
45 *Praise and Lament in the Psalms,* 31.
46 H. Gunkel, *Die Psalmen. GHK,* II/2 (1926).
47 *In loc.*
48 *BK,* XV/1.
49 O. Kaiser, *Isaiah 1–12. OTL* (Eng. trans. ²1983).
50 H. Wildberger, *Jesaja. BK,* X/1 (1972).
51 Pp. 32-35.
52 → זמר *zmr.*
53 → עלץ *'ālaṣ.*

(Ps. 9:3[2]; *'lz*, Ps. 28:7), rejoicing[54] (Ps. 33:1; 67:5[4]; 71:23; 100:2; Isa. 12:6), glorifying[55] (Ps. 35:18; 109:30; etc.). There are many verbs that mean "rejoice": → רוע *rw'*, Ps. 100:1; → גיל *gyl*, Ps. 43:4; *ṣhl*, Isa. 12:6. Worshippers seldom rest content with a single expression. In the ecstasy of joyous excitement they pile verb upon verb (Ps. 9:3[2]; 67:5[4]; Isa. 12:6). The voice of someone who summons others to praise is like a voice of mirth (*śāśôn*[56]) and gladness, the voice of the bridegroom and the bride (Jer. 33:11).

Praise cannot be a private matter involving only those who praise and are praised. The impv. *hôḏâ* is addressed to all and sundry. There is a summons to tell others, or the worshipper suggests such a summons by announcing his intention to speak (Ps. 9:2[1]; 79:13). He describes those who will hear as the "godly" (Ps. 52:11[9]), the company of the upright, a congregation[57] of indefinite size (Ps. 111:1). It comprises many (Ps. 109:30), appears as a great congregation and a mighty throng (Ps. 35:18). Ultimately it includes the entire world. The peoples (*gôyim*, Ps. 18:50[49] par.; *'ammîm*, 1 Ch. 16:8; Ps. 57:10[9]; 105:1; 108:4[3]; Isa. 12:4) and nations (*le'ummîm*, Ps. 57:10[9]; 108:4[3]) are to experience the praise.

The object may be connected with the verb by means of *'ṯ* or *le*, or it may remain unstated. It is almost always God. Only 4 times is a human person the object of *ydh:* Gen. 49:8; Job 40:14; Ps. 45:18(17); 49:19f.(18f.). In the first two passages, the authors had the royal power as a reflection of divine sovereignty before their eyes; the last two passages make it clear, indeed insist, that praise can never refer to human persons, who would in this case take the place of God. The praise of human persons vanishes with its object, who can be praised only ironically. The absolute use of *ydh* to express praise of God (Neh. 11:17; 12:24; 2 Ch. 31:2) follows naturally.

Praise is addressed to God or speaks of him. Its object may therefore be in the 2nd or 3rd person singular; they appear about equally. It must be noted, of course, that the imperative requires the 3rd person. When the object is in the 2nd person, it is expressed by means of the appropriate personal suffix attached to the verb (25 times), *lekā* (1 Ch. 29:13; Ps. 6:6[5]; 79:13; 119:62), or an hypostasis expressed with the 2nd person suffix. Among these we find God's "name"[58] (11 times), including his "holy name" (1 Ch. 16:35; Ps. 106:47), which post-Deuteronomic literature uses as an alternative form of "Yahweh,"[59] and the striking "wonders"[60] (Ps. 89:6[5]). The tetragrammaton never appears.

The situation is entirely different in the case of the 3rd person. Here the tetragrammaton clearly predominates (32 times), whereas the hypostatized name appears only as "the name of Yahweh" (Ps. 122:4) and as "his holy name"[61] (*zēḵer qoḏšô*, Ps.

---

54 → רנן *rānan*.
55 → הלל *hll* II.
56 → שׂישׂ *śîś*.
57 → עדה *'ēḏâ*.
58 → שׁם *šēm*.
59 O. Grether, *Name und Wort Gottes in AT. BZAW*, 64 (1934), 35ff.
60 → פלא *pele'*.
61 Cf. W. Schottroff, *"Gedenken" im Alten Orient und im AT. WMANT*, 15 (²1967), 297ff.

30:5[4]; 97:12). The same role as the tetragrammaton is played by the terms *'ᵉlōhîm* (Neh. 12:46; Ps. 136:2), *'ēl haššāmāyim* (Ps. 136:26), and *'āḏōn* (Ps. 136:3). The 3rd person suffix with the verb is used only rarely (Ps. 28:7; 42:6,12[5,11]; 43:5), as is *lô* (Ps. 100:4).

The three determinative elements of praise—joy, involvement of others, and exclusive reference to God—lead to a fourth fundamental factor: the association of praise with life. Only the living can praise God (Isa. 38:19). Those who have become dust are no longer able to do so (Ps. 30:10[9]). The shades of the dead (Ps. 88:11[10]) and the shadowy realm of Sheol (Isa. 38:18), which is separated from God, know nothing of *ydh;* to ask of it is purely rhetorical.

c. To praise the name of Yahweh, people go up to Jerusalem, to the temple (Ps. 118:19). This is required by an ordinance of Israel (Ps. 122:1-4). The setting of praise is worship, its site the temple. Within the temple precincts, praise takes place in a variety of places.

The altar and *tôḏâ* go together. The faithful go about the altar with a *tôḏâ* (Ps. 26:7). They desire to praise (*'ôḏᵉḵā,* Ps. 43:4) at the altar. Before the *hêḵāl*—used by synecdoche for the temple structure—they prostrate themselves in worship (Ps. 138:2), i.e., in the courtyard where the altar of burnt offering stands.[62] This agrees with Jon. 2:10(9), where fulfillment of the vow of sacrifice includes *tôḏâ*. Ps. 54:8(6) speaks of a vow of sacrifice and praise (*'ezbᵉḥâ, 'ôḏeh*). The optative praise (*yôḏû*) that takes the place of a vow of praise in Ps. 107:21f. also includes a summons to sacrifice (*yizbᵉḥû*), referred to here as *zibḥê ṯôḏâ*.

The passages cited show that there is a connection between the individual song of thanksgiving and sacrifice; both go back to a vow (*nēḏer*)[63] made in distress, and both are performed together.[64] The association finds expression in shared terminology. Instead of *zeḇaḥ tôḏâ* (Ps. 116:17) we may find simply *tôḏâ* (2 Ch. 29:31; 33:16; Ps. 56:13[12]; Jer. 17:26; 33:11), a usage attested very early (Am. 4:5). More details about the freewill thank offering are found in P (Lev. 7:11ff.). The *zeḇaḥ tôḏâ* is a peace offering (*zeḇaḥ šᵉlāmîm*[65]) that also includes cereal offerings. There are two versions of what is involved in this supplementary offering, of which the priest receives his portion. The main difference between the two is that the former, through assimilation to the *minḥâ,* requires unleavened bread (v. 12), while the latter permits leavened bread (v. 13). Read in the light of Am. 4:5, v. 13 cannot originate as a mitigation; there are instead alternative ways of carrying out the offering, of which the latter represents the earlier practice. The offering of unleavened bread is a postexilic usage.[66] The requirement that none of the flesh of the sacrifice be left until morning (v. 15) is also inculcated by the Holiness Code (Lev. 22:29f.). Cattle, sheep, and goats can serve

---

62 T. A. Busink, *Der Temple von Jerusalem von Salomo bis Herodes. StFS,* 3, I (1970), 322.

63 → נדר *nāḏar.*

64 Rendtorff, 136f.

65 → שׁלם *šālam.*

66 K. Elliger, *Leviticus. HAT,* IV (1966), 99.

as sacrificial animals for the peace offering.[67] The same is probably true of the *tôḏâ*. Ps. 69:31f.(30f.) at least indicates that a *tôḏâ* usually involved the sacrifice of an ox (*šôr*) or bull (*par*).

It is natural to ask into the locus of such an individual element in the context of worship, especially when one considers the resources required. A congregation must be present, as well as priestly and levitical specialists. Only two passages, both in Chronicles, speak of specific occasions on which thanksgiving offerings were offered. At the "dedication" of the temple inaugurating the restoration of the cult after the cleansing of the temple (715/14–697/96[68]), Hezekiah calls on the people to offer *zᵉḇaḥîm wᵉṯôḏôṯ*, i.e., thank offerings defined as animal sacrifices (2 Ch. 29:31). Freewill burnt offerings are also mentioned in this context. All this takes place after the fixed sequence of official sacrifices (Nu. 29; 2 Ch. 29:21; Ezr. 6:17; 8:35) is concluded. It appears, therefore, that in the postexilic period the festal liturgy provided an open slot for freewill offerings (cf. Nu. 29:39), here devoted to thanksgiving offerings. It is true that 2 Ch. 33:15f. speaks only of a cleansing of the temple; but the "peace offerings as thanksgiving offerings" offered by Manasseh (697/96–642/41[69]) in thanksgiving for Yahweh's deliverance from the hand of the Assyrian emperor Ashurbanipal should certainly be considered analogous to the sacrifices at the festival concluding the cleansing of the temple. When the Deuteronomistic editor of the book of Jeremiah speaks of *tôḏâ* being offered, accompanied by hymns (Jer. 33:11), he is assimilating the private thank offering to the regular morning and evening sacrifices as well as to the prescribed festival sacrifices; these are accompanied by hymnody sung by the temple singers (1 Ch. 23:30f.; 2 Ch. 7:6), as can be seen from the association of the peace offering meal with the singing of the Levites (2 Ch. 30:22), a description that probably reflects the editor's own period.

The Chronicler, in order to emphasize the importance of the levitical office, assigns the hymnody of the Levites a totally independent status within the cult (1 Ch. 16:4,7,37,41). It is the music and singing in the temple that evoke the divine presence (2 Ch. 5:12f.). Now no longer associated with sacrifice and the priesthood, levitical hymnody moves outside the temple precincts, becoming a part of any cultic celebration, as when Zerubbabel and Jeshua lay the cornerstone of the temple (Ezr. 3:11) or when the city wall of Jerusalem is dedicated (Neh. 12:27). When war is described in liturgical terms, it takes the place of the battle cry (2 Ch. 20:21).[70] This would probably not have been possible if hymnody had not actually had a place in war understood as a cultic act. The extent to which cultic elements influence the description of war can also be seen in 1 Macc. 4:24; 13:51, where the formula for levitical hymnody is used for the victory song after battle.

Without thanksgiving song there can be no thanksgiving offering. On the other hand, we hear of thanksgiving songs being sung without an associated sacrifice. A

---

[67] Rendtorff, 161f.

[68] S. Herrmann, *A History of Israel in OT Times* (Eng. trans., Philadelphia, 1975), 257.

[69] *Ibid.*

[70] Cf. G. von Rad, *Der heilige Krieg im alten Israel* (Göttingen, ⁴1965), 80f.

tôḏâ can in fact take the place of sacrifice (Ps. 69:31f.[30f.]).[71] The *tôḏôṯ* localized elsewhere are necessarily not connected with sacrifice. There is a *tôḏâ* at the gate, of which we can learn much from Ps. 100, explicitly called *mizmôr l^eṯôḏâ* by its superscription. A group is called upon to enter (*bōʾû*) with *tôḏâ*, later referred to as *t^ehillâ*. At the end, this call is summarized by the impv. *hôḏû* (v. 4). The plural imperatives together with the associated terms *tôḏâ* and *t^ehillâ* show that we are dealing here with a hymn sung during entrance into the temple precincts. The features of an entrance and plural summons also appear in Ps. 95:2,6. Pilgrims (Ps. 122) sang such hymns, as the worshipper of Ps. 42:5(4) sadly recalls.

The Psalms furnish scanty information about how the praise was actually performed. It was sung to instrumental accompaniment. If the "I" and "we" or the "you" of the imperative are not merely literary fictions,[72] the singing could be either solo (individual thanksgiving song, individual hymn) or collective (communal thanksgiving song, hymn). Antiphonal singing is likely in the case of several hymns (e.g., Ps. 136). Various instruments could be used for accompaniment, apparently not associated with particular genres: zither (*kinnôr*), harp (*nēḇel*), ten-stringed bow harp (*ʿāśôr*). Whether singers accompanied themselves or were accompanied by an orchestra or instrumental soloists remains an open question. The playing of two instruments simultaneously by the same "I" (Ps. 57:9f.[8f.]; 71:22; 92:2,4[1,3]) argues against self-accompaniment. Perhaps there were various styles of performance.

The Chronicler's history provides more evidence. The singing of praise is entrusted to the Levites (1 Ch. 16:4f.,7,42; 23:30; 25:6; 2 Ch. 5:12; 7:6; 31:2), who are singers and musicians (2 Ch. 7:6), playing the instruments mentioned above and also cymbals (*m^eṣiltayim*) (1 Ch. 16:5; 2 Ch. 5:12; Neh. 12:27). A musician would master a particular instrument (1 Ch. 16:5; 25:3). Certain individuals functioned as leaders: Mattaniah (Neh. 11:17; 12:8,24f.), Jeduthun (1 Ch. 25:3), Asaph (Neh. 12:46). The first two are also mentioned as soloists: Mattaniah as a singer (Neh. 11:17), Jeduthun as a zither player (1 Ch. 25:3). Even if the division of the Levites into twenty-four classes serving in turn (1 Ch. 25) is a fiction on the part of the Chronicler, we do read of choirs and orchestras being assembled out of their total number (2 Ch. 20:21; Neh. 12:31,38,40). When they appear in temple worship, they stand in the courtyard east of the altar (2 Ch. 5:12). Their times of service include at least the times of sacrifice. During performance of the music it is important that the singing be in unison with the instrumental music (2 Ch. 5:13). Sometimes their number is augmented by priests sounding trumpets (2 Ch. 5:12; Neh. 12:35). Subordination of the temple musicians to the Levites is postexilic, although it is ascribed to David (2 Ch. 7:6; Ezr. 3:10). It is probably historically accurate that there were temple musicians ever since the Jerusalem temple existed.

The information derived from the Psalms can easily be correlated with what we learn from Chronicles. The instruments are the instruments of the temple orchestra. Both solo and choral performance are possible. The open questions are whether the "I" of the psalmist is identical with the "I" of the performer and how the "congre-

71 Hermisson, 38.

72 Wohlenberg, 576, 583.

gation" participated. There is much to be said for the theory that in the temple performers were recruited from the ranks of the professional musicians.[73] This would suggest a development analogous to that of the sacrificial system, in which the individuals present their offerings but the priests are responsible for the technical details of the sacrifice.

2. *Penitential Confession*. a. According to P, confession of sins constitutes a part of the sacrificial ritual in certain cases (Lev. 5:1-6; Nu. 5:5-10). The sequence of acts to be performed begins with a consecutive perfect (*wᵉhiṯwaddâ* [Lev. 5:5], *wᵉhiṯwaddû* [Nu. 5:7]). The action of an individual that is to be confessed is called a sin, and is attached to a verb by means of a relative clause (*'ᵃšer ḥāṭā' 'ālêhā* [Lev. 5:5]) or as an object (*'eṯ-ḥaṭṭā'ṯām* [Nu. 5:7]).

(1) Lev. 5:1-6. Confession is followed by the sacrifice of a sin offering (*ḥaṭṭā'ṯ*), which may be a sheep or a goat, for restitution (*'āšām*).[74] Then, as in the case of any sin offering,[75] the priest gives the chance to make atonement for the sin. The passage deals with the procedure in a series of four cases, two of which derive from the legal sphere and have to do with failure to testify and rash swearing of oaths (vv. 1, 4), while the two others have to do with failure to carry out the cleansing rituals prescribed by Lev. 11–15, arising from subsequent knowledge (vv. 2f.). The sacrifice provides a way to mitigate the consequences of sins committed unknowingly or rashly.[76]

(2) Nu. 5:5-10. As in the previous text, following the introduction the ritual begins with a confession of sin. This passage omits the expected continuation, expressed in consecutive perfects, in which the priest makes atonement through a sacrifice. The sequence of actions concludes with restitution, and we find instead a conditional clause that mentions the rest of the ritual in passing. The procedure is undoubtedly meant to end with an act of atonement, but the passage is dominated by the case in which there is no one to whom restitution can be made. On the one hand, the crime is described as a breach of faith with Yahweh; on the other, restitution is owed primarily to a private individual who has suffered injury. Lev. 5:20-26(6:1-7) governs such cases. To deny possession of property that has been given as security, lent, taken by violence, or lost represents a breach of faith with Yahweh. The true owner has a right to damages in the amount of six fifths of the property's value (by rabbinic reckoning five fourths, since the fifth is calculated on the basis of the entire quantity). But because the offense is termed a *ma'al bᵉYHWH,* Yahweh is also owed damages, a ram without blemish, which belongs to the priest who makes atonement. Only then can the mitigation of consequences take place. The action described in the conditional clause in Nu. 5:5ff. is here the central ritual. In Nu. 5:5-10, therefore, we have a special provision ("codicil") relating to Lev. 5:20-26 and applying to the case when there is no one authorized

[73] *Ibid.,* 582.
[74] Elliger, *HAT,* IV, 76.
[75] Rendtorff, 230.
[76] Cf. Elliger, *HAT,* IV, 73f.

to receive restitution. Payment is to be made to the officiating priest. With respect to Lev. 5:20-26, the confession of sin is also a new element. Possibly it is also presupposed in the Leviticus passage.[77] But if one considers that in the "amendment," as in Lev. 5:1-6, there is no longer any real legal recourse, it is only here that the confession is fully necessary.

(3) Lev. 16:21f. The ritual of the Day of Atonement also includes a confession. Its content is the sins of the Israelites. The use of the multiple terms *'āwōn, peša'*, and *ḥaṭṭā'ṯ,* all in the plural, is intended to provide the most inclusive and general formulation possible. The confession is spoken by a single individual (*hiṯwaddâ*). The high priest represents the people. In the present version of the text, the triple action of confession, sacrifice, and atonement, familiar from Lev. 5:1-6 and Lev. 5:20-26(6:1-7) plus Nu. 5:5-8, is repeated in v. 24. The integration of the scapegoat into the atonement ritual gives concrete form to the verbal ritual, but at the same time also "demythologizes" what was originally a magical process for the transfer of sins.

(4) Lev. 26:40. In Lev. 26:14-38, the concluding chapter of the Holiness Code proclaims the punishment for Israel's faithlessness in a style recalling prophetic speech, through which we can hear echoes of the events of 587 B.C. Progressing stage by stage, the punishment culminates in the destruction of the people. The following passage (vv. 39-45) robs this final threat of its radical nature by interpreting it as a pedagogical device on the part of God. Deportation is the consequence of sin that has been accumulating for generations, but it also provides the chance to remove this sin. Restitution is preceded by a collective confession of sin (*weʰhiṯwaddû 'eṯ-'ᵃwōnām weʾ eṯ-'ᵃwōn 'ᵃḇōṯām*), described more precisely as treachery and blind disobedience (*mā'al* and *hālaḵ beqerî*).[78] That the place as well as the manner of this confession is not arbitrary is shown by comparison with 1 K. 8:46-50 par. 2 Ch. 6:36-39, a comparison justified by the fully formulated confession there (v. 47 par. v. 37). This text is itself a reworking of 1 K. 8:33f. par. 2 Ch. 6:24f., made necessary by the deportation of 587 B.C. For the deportees, turning toward the land, toward Jerusalem, toward the temple has replaced the temple itself as the place of prayer. For the rest, the form has scarcely been altered. If one also includes the list of prayers God is called upon to hear in the prayer of dedication, it is likely the second version also points to a penitential liturgy in the midst of which stood a confession of sin. Such a penitential liturgy—obviously not involving any sacrifice—was probably also the locus of the confession in Lev. 26:40.

When it comes to the form and content of the confession, the passages just discussed leave us in the lurch. The text associated with Lev. 16:21 has been preserved in rabbinic literature. The high priest confesses (*miṯwaddeh*): "Ah, YHWH, before thee thy people, the house of Israel, has transgressed (*'awû*), offended (*pāšeʾ'û*), sinned (*ḥāṭeʾû*). Make atonement, we pray (*kapper-nā'*), for the sins, offenses, and misdeeds with which thy

[77] D. Kellermann, 66.

[78] Elliger, *HAT,* IV, 378.

people, the house of Israel, has transgressed, offended, and sinned before thee."[79] Now one might assume that the wording is the result of scribal composition based on Lev. 16:21, especially since the sequence of verbs is not absolutely certain. Rabbi Jose (*ca.* 130-160 C.E.) knows a tradition that runs: "Thy people, the house of Israel, has sinned (*ḥāṭeʾû*), transgressed (*ʿāwû*), offended (*pāšeʿû*) before thee."[80] But the special tradition itself derives from rabbinic combination, as is clear from a discussion elsewhere.[81] The version that begins with *ḥṭʾ* is based on the observation that in the other tripartite confessions (1 K. 8:47; Ps. 106:6; Dnl. 9:5) this verb also comes first.

Similar confessions in a cultic context, likewise introduced explicitly by *ydh,* are found also in nonrabbinic strands of Jewish tradition. In the covenant formulary of the Manual of Discipline from Qumran,[82] praise of God on the part of priests and Levites and a listing of *ʿwwnt, pšʿy ʾšmtm,* and *ḥṭʾtm* by the Levites are followed by two confessions in the 1st person plural. The first is tripartite with the verbs in the same order as in the list. As in Mishnah *Yoma,* therefore, *ʿwh* comes first and *ḥṭʾ* last. The text of the second is damaged, but can be reconstructed with the help of CD 20:29. The "wickedness" (*ršʿ*) of both the present and previous generations is explained as "disobedience" (*hlk qry*) to God's ordinances. This expression is also used by Lev. 26:40 to describe the sin of Israel, again with the inclusion of earlier generations.

These postbiblical confessions exhibit two characteristic features. (1) They are brief and limited to stating the fact of transgression; at most a brief explanation is added. (2) Their verbs repeat the terminology of the liturgical introduction. Their brevity is understandable if one assumes that the persons using them also spoke for themselves. It is hard to imagine a private individual reciting a complex composition within the cult. The same is true for groups assembled more or less by accident and therefore varying in membership. The short formula may therefore be taken as the basic form of the confession. This agrees with the biblical evidence. Individuals or groups confess their sin using a sequence of one or more verbs in the 1st person singular or plural (*ḥāṭāʾṯî* [Ex. 9:27; 10:16; Nu. 22:34; 1 S. 15:30; 2 S. 12:13; 19:21(20); 2 K. 18:14]; *ḥāṭāʾṯî . . . heʿewêṯî* [2 S. 24:17; cf. 1 Ch. 21:17]; *ḥaṭāʾnû* [Jgs. 10:15; 1 S. 7:6]; *ḥāṭāʾnû wehe ʿewînû rāšāʿnû* [1 K. 8:47 par. 2 Ch. 6:37]). A brief reference to the act judged to be a sin appears in Jgs. 10:10; 1 S. 15:24; and 2 S. 24:10 par. 1 Ch. 21:8.[83] The use of verbs identical with the roots appearing in the terms found in the liturgical instructions shows that the latter imply the form of the confession. They do not need to include a detailed formulary, since they make allusion in each case to the appropriate fixed formula of confession.[84] It is true, however, that various genres made use of confession as a motif informing in part an entire literary unit.[85]

79 Mishnah *Yoma* vi.2.
80 Tosefta *Kippurim* iii.12 (ed. S. Lieberman [New York, 1962], 245).
81 Tosefta *Kippurim* ii.1 (*ibid.*, 233).
82 1QS 1:16ff.
83 On Josh. 7:20, see III.2.b below.
84 Boecker, 111f.
85 See III.2.c below.

b. When Achan makes the confession recorded in Josh. 7:20, he is obeying the command stated in v. 19. Now while the command consists of the three impvs. *śîm-nā' kāḇôḏ, tēn tôḏâ, hagged-nā'*, the response consists of only two members: an admission of sin (*ḥāṭā'ṯî*) and a reference to the act (*wᵉḵāzō'ṯ wᵉḵāzō'ṯ 'āśîṯî* [v. 20]; the detailed account is a later elaboration). Since the two first imperatives have Yahweh as indirect object (*lᵉYHWH, lô*), the first part of the confession, addressed to Yahweh (*lᵉYHWH*), must refer to both, especially since the second part with its repetition of the verb *'śh* clearly takes up the third imperative, so that *ḥāṭā'ṯî lᵉYHWH* is both confession and doxology.[86] The command and the confession belong to a procedure of sacral law ordained by oracle (vv. 10-15) in response to Joshua's inquiry (vv. 7-9). The basis is that the people have sinned (*ḥṭ'*) by taking some of the devoted things (*ḥērem*) (7:11), and have thus broken faith (*m'l*) (7:1). The guilty party, whose responsibility is shared by the people, is determined by lot in assembly before the sanctuary. When the misappropriated property is produced, the old status consonant with the *bᵉrîṯ* (vv. 11,15) is restored. This actually concludes the judicial process. The punishment of the guilty party follows (v. 15: burning, because *ḥērem* is involved; v. 25: stoning for theft). The *tôḏâ* finds its place between determination of the guilty party and restitution.

A procedure of sacral law is also involved in Ezr. 10. The similarities to Josh. 7 are evident. The facts of the case—here mixed marriages—are defined as breach of faith (*m'l* [Ezr. 10:2,10]). The guilty parties are to be identified in the assembly before the sanctuary (10:7-9). The process concludes with restitution (10:18-44). In contrast to Josh. 7, the call to confession (*tᵉnû ṯôḏâ* [v. 11]) comes before determination of the guilty party; this is probably not due to a fundamentally different sequence but to the impossibility of identifying the guilty on the spot, so that the actual investigation must be assigned to a commission (10:16f.). The invitation to doxology is also missing. The text of the confession itself is not recorded. This was later felt to be a serious omission, and the gap was filled with a long prayer (Neh. 9).[87]

If we disregard the rationalization manifested in Ezr. 10 by omission of the doxology and substitution of detailed committee work for determination of the guilty by lot, not only has the form of sacral legal proceedings remained constant over a period of more than four hundred years,[88] but so has the form of the invitation to confession, expressed by the imperative of *ntn* with *tôḏâ* as direct object and Yahweh as indirect object.

c. Among the prayers in the Chronicler's history and the book of Daniel, confessions are found in Ezr. 9:6-15 (v. 6; cf. v. 15); Neh. 1:5-11 (vv. 6f.); 9:6-37 (v. 33); and Dnl. 9:4-19 (v. 5; cf. v. 15). The genre involved is a collective prayer of repentance, related to the communal lament. The hithpael of *ydh* is used to introduce the prayer (Neh. 9:2f.; in Neh. 1:6 the introduction has been incorporated as a relative clause into the request that the prayer be heard; only then does the 1st person sg. shift to the 1st person pl.), conclude it (Ezr. 10:1), or frame it (Dnl. 9:4,20). Except in Neh.

---

86 Grimme, 234ff.; Horst, 50 (162).

87 See III.2.c below.

88 M. Noth dates the "collector" of the etiological stories in Josh. 1–12 around 900; *Das Buch Josua. HAT,* VII (³1971), 13.

9:12, *ydh* stands in parallel with the hithpael of *pll*. The worshippers express grief and humility. They fast (Neh. 1:4; 9:1; Dnl. 9:3), wear mourning (Neh. 9:1; Dnl. 9:3), tear their clothing and pull hair from their heads (Ezr. 9:3f.), and put earth upon their heads (Neh. 9:1; Dnl. 9:3), or are described in general terms as mourning (Neh. 1:4). Proskynesis is mentioned in Ezr. 10:1 (*miṯnappēl;* cf. Ezr. 9:5) and Neh. 9:3 (*mištaḥ^awîm*). Alongside absolute use (Ezr. 10:1; Neh. 9:3; Dnl. 9:4) we find the object *ḥaṭṭā'ṯ* (Neh. 1:6; Dnl. 9:20) or *ḥaṭṭā'ṯ* par. *'āwōn* (Neh. 9:2). The terminology of the confessions corresponds only in part to this object. The confession in Ezr. 9:6—which also exhibits other peculiarities—contains the nouns *'āwōn* and *'ašmâ;* Neh. 9:33 has the hiphil of *rš'*. Neh. 1:6f. does have *ḥṭ'*, but expands on it in v. 7 by means of the rare verb *ḥbl,* "do evil." Dnl. 9:5 is also expanded (and generalized), this time with *'wh* and *rš'* hiphil (v. 15 only *rš'* qal).

In addition, confession is found in penitential liturgies (Ps. 106:6), laments (Ps. 41:5-11[4-10]; 51; Jer. 3:21-25; 14:7-9, 19-22), and thanksgiving songs (Job 33:27), which is not surprising in view of the close connection between lament and thanksgiving. There is therefore a special form of lament characterized by confession of sin. These observations allow us to conclude that the passages listed use the hithpael of *ydh* as a technical term for the recitation of a particular kind of prayer, namely, a prayer of repentance or a lament including a confession of sin.

The forms found (consecutive impf. [Neh. 9:2; Dnl. 9:4; inf. constr. with k^e [Ezr. 10:1]; ptcp. [Neh. 1:6; 9:3; Dnl. 9:20]) are typical of narrative style. They place the prayers within the setting of the narrative and also relate them to the narrator's intentions, revealed by the placement of the prayers. The hero—whether an individual or the people—always prays at a moment of crisis, i.e., when the people are in danger. The turning point is brought about immediately by the prayer of confession. Following the prayer in Ezr. 9:6-15, the people purify themselves and are ready to do penance (Ezr. 10:1-6). Nehemiah's prayer (Neh. 1:5-11) exhibits its effect in the king's agreement to his mission (Neh. 2). After the people have confessed their guilt in Neh. 9:5-37, they renew their obligation to the commandments (Neh. 10). As a consequence, the new city wall can be solemnly dedicated (Neh. 12:27ff.). The prayer of repentance in the mouth of Daniel (Dnl. 9:4ff.) leads in vv. 21ff. to God's intervention: Gabriel brings the interpretation of the seventy years spoken of in Jer. 25:11; 29:10 that must be fulfilled upon the ruins of Jerusalem (Dnl. 9:2).[89] In Ezr. 9/10; Neh. 9/10; Dnl. 9 there may be echoes of a covenant renewal formulary;[90] for the Chronicler, however, the prayers are primarily expository material.[91] The same is true in the book of Daniel. They arise from the fundamental conviction that prayer and confession can end the distress that has come about as a consequence of sin, giving both the individual and the people a future.[92] This is the attitude to life of Wisdom Literature, summarized pregnantly in Prov. 28:13 (cf. Ps. 32): "Those who conceal their transgressions will not prosper, but those who confess (*môḏeh*) and forsake them will obtain mercy."

G. Mayer

---

89 See O. Plöger, *Das Buch Daniel. KAT,* XVIII (1965), 136f.

90 Baltzer, 43-49.

91 Plöger, *Festschrift G. Dehn,* 44.

92 *Ibid.,* 48.

יָדִיד yāḏîḏ

Contents: I. Etymology; 2. Occurrences; 3. Meaning. II. 1. Secular Usage; 2. Religious Usage. III. Religio-Historical Conclusions.

I. 1. *Etymology.* The noun *yāḏîḏ* found in the Hebrew OT is also attested in Ugaritic,[1] Amorite,[2] and possibly Phoenician.[3] There can be no doubt that it is a *qaṭîl* form based on the root *ydd,* despite the absence of this root in Hebrew, since the verb appears in other Semitic languages (Ugar. *ydd,* Arab. *wadda,* OSA *waddada,* Akk. *namaddu*)[4] and besides our noun other derivatives of this root occur in OT Hebrew as well as some other Semitic languages. These include the abstract nouns *y^eḏîḏûṯ* (Jer. 12:7) and *y^eḏîḏōṯ* (Ps. 45:1[Eng. superscription], possibly to be read *y^eḏîḏûṯ* with *BHS*), as well as several personal names: *y^eḏîḏâ,* the name of Josiah's mother,[5] *y^eḏîḏyâ,* Solomon's surname, and the masc. name *mêḏāḏ,* also attested elsewhere (LXX *Mōdad;* cf. also the Ugaritic name *mdd-b'l*[6] and the *mwdd* of two Aramaic inscriptions[7]). Other personal names formed on the root *ydd* are attested in Ugaritic: *ydd, yddn, bn yddn.*[8]

It is dubious at best whether Hebrew, like Arabic and Ugaritic, has a noun *yaḏ* II derived from *ydd* II, as postulated by Schedl[9] for Ps. 16:4 (emending MT *middām* to *miyyāḏām,* "for the sake of their love," "for their sake"). There has been little acceptance of Fitzgerald's[10] proposal to find this noun *yd(d)* in Eccl. 7:26; Isa. 11:11; Lam. 3:3; and possibly also Ps. 88:6(5); 95:7; Isa. 57:8; 66:14; Jer. 15:17; cf. Wildberger on Isa. 11:11: "*yd* hardly ever means 'love.' "[11]

2. *Occurrences.* The noun *yāḏîḏ* appears 8 times in the OT. The earliest occurrence is in the tribal saying concerning Benjamin in the Blessing of Moses (Dt. 33:12),

---

yāḏîḏ. P. A. H. de Boer, "2 Samuel 12:25," *Studia Biblica et Semitica. Festschrift T. C. Vriezen* (Wageningen, 1966), 25-29; O. Eissfeldt, "Renaming in the OT," *Words and Meanings. Festschrift D. W. Thomas* (Cambridge, 1968), 69-79; A. Fitzgerald, "Hebrew *yd* = 'Love' and 'Beloved,' " *CBQ,* 29 (1967), 368-374; M. Noth, *IPN;* J. J. Stamm, "Hebräische Frauennamen," *Hebräische Wortforschung. Festschrift W. Baumgartner. SVT* 16 (1967), 301-339 = his *Beiträge zur hebräischen und altorientalischen Namenkunde* (1980), 97-135; see also the bibliogs. under → אהב *'āhaḇ* [*'āhabh*] and → דוד *dôḏ* [*dôdh*].

[1] *WUS,* no. 140.
[2] *APNM,* 209.
[3] Cf. *KBL*[3].
[4] Cf. *KBL*[3].
[5] Stamm, 325.
[6] *PNU,* 399.
[7] *KAI,* II, 221, with bibliog.
[8] *PNU,* 390f.
[9] C. Schedl, "Die 'Heiligen' und die 'Herrlichen' in Psalm 16 1-4," *ZAW,* 76 (1964), 174.
[10] *CBQ,* 29 (1967), 368-374.
[11] Cf. H. Wildberger, *Jesaja. BK,* X/1 (1972), 463.

which very likely dates from even before the Israelite state.[12] We next find *yāḏîḏ* twice in Isaiah's Song of the Vineyard (Isa. 5:1) and once in Jeremiah (Jer. 11:15). The other occurrences are in exilic or postexilic Psalms of various genres: Ps. 60:7(5) (communal lament) par. 108:7(6) (liturgy); 84:2(1) (hymn); 127:2 (wisdom song). There is also *y^eḏîḏûṯ* in Jer. 12:7 and *y^eḏîḏōṯ* in Ps. 45:1 (superscription; preexilic). If we include the names listed above (Jedidah [2 K. 22:1]; Jedidiah [2 S. 12:25]; Medad [Nu. 11:26f.; assigned by Eissfeldt to E, treated by Noth[13] as an addition to a J passage]), we find that our noun occurs, albeit infrequently, in a relatively wide variety of genres dating from different periods.

3. *Meaning*. In Ugaritic the verb *ydd* means "love (sexually)." El says to Tlš, a woman who serves the gods: "Love the gods of the field, labor and give birth."[14] The fem. noun *mddt,* "beloved," undoubtedly has the same meaning; Keret uses it to refer to his own wife.[15] The corresponding Arabic and Ethiopic verbs *wadda* and *waddada* have the same meaning. The translation of the noun *yāḏîḏ* as "beloved" is therefore a given. It is worth noting, however, that in other contexts in Ugaritic this word has lost completely or at least to a great extent its sexual reference. The phrase *ydd 3l,* for example, is a fixed epithet for the god Mot; the expression *bn 3l mt,* "the son of El, Mot," finds its parallel in *ydd 3l gzr,* "the beloved of El, the powerful one."[16] The same is true in the case of the title *mdd 3l,* "beloved of El," solemnly bestowed by El upon the god Yam.[17] The Ugaritic personal names, which are masculine, are more likely to mean "favorite (of the god N)" than "beloved (of the god N)." In any case, there are never any sexual overtones.

These observations suggest that it is also appropriate to assume that Heb. *yāḏîḏ* means "favorite" or "friend." Noth makes the same suggestion, explaining the female name "Jedidah" as a secular name: "Parents often call a child 'darling' or 'favorite.' "[18] Finally, it may be noted that the LXX always renders our word as *agapētós* or the like, thus placing it in the semantic field of → אהב *'āhaḇ* [*'āhabh*].

II. 1. *Secular Usage*. It would seem desirable to start with the assumption that the noun *yāḏîḏ* belonged by nature to the secular sphere, and expressed a relationship between individuals or groups based on positive feelings of attraction. The fem. name "Jedidah" could well be an illustration. When a child is called "beloved," the "darling" of its parents, the name expresses the loving and benevolent relationship of the parents toward the child. In support of such a secular interpretation, reference has been made[19] to linguistic and semantic parallels in other Semitic languages, with

[12] H.-J. Zobel, *Stammesspruch und Geschichte. BZAW,* 95 (1965), 53-59, 108-112.
[13] M. Noth, *Numbers. OTL* (Eng. trans. 1968), 83.
[14] *KTU,* 1.12 I, 24f.
[15] *KTU,* 1.14 II, 50; IV, 28.
[16] *KTU,* 1.5 II, 9; 1.6 VI, 30f.; etc.
[17] *KTU,* 1.4 II, 34; VI, 12; 1.1 IV, 20; etc.
[18] *IPN,* 223; also Stamm, 325.
[19] Most recently Stamm, 325.

reference to both girls and boys. At the same time, however, we find references to a deity in the case of the Ugaritic names *ydd-3l* and *mdd-b'l,* an observation that calls into question the secular interpretation of the name Jedidah and strongly suggests a theophoric interpretation of the OT name Medad as a hypocoristic form of *medad-'el.* This interpretation is reinforced by the parallel theophoric name "Eldad," "El has loved."[20]

Further evidence for a secular interpretation of *yāḏîḏ* may possibly be found in Ps. 45:1 (superscription), which calls the Psalm a *šîr yᵉḏîḏōṯ.* There can be no doubt that this is a royal song, more precisely a song for the marriage of a king, possibly the marriage of Ahab and Jezebel.[21] But this very fact complicates interpretation of the superscription, for the usual rendering "love song" does not fit the content of the Psalm. Wildberger[22] therefore suggests the translation: "song of the (female) friends," viz., of the bride. But even this interpretation clashes with v. 11(10), where the royal bride is addressed as "my daughter." Since this song owes its inclusion in the Psalter to its having been reinterpreted as referring to the relationship between Yahweh and his people, the superscription in v. 1 should probably be considered redactional and interpreted from this new perspective. This means that the term "love song" must refer to the love of Yahweh for Israel.

The other passages where *yāḏîḏ* can be interpreted in a secular sense are likewise ambiguous. The prophet sings the Song of the Vineyard for his *yāḏîḏ,* stating that this *yāḏîḏ* had a vineyard (Isa. 5:1). As the song goes on to show, Yahweh is the *yāḏîḏ* of Isaiah, and as such is also the possessor of the vineyard "Israel." Although *yāḏîḏ* has a clear parallel in → דוד *dôḏ* [*dôdh*], nothing in the song calls Yahweh anything like the beloved of Israel.[23] Therefore the translation "friend" appears most appropriate. This would still mean that Yahweh is the object of Isaiah's friendship and affection, which is surprising in that elsewhere in the OT subject and object in this relationship are reversed.[24] This would support the other interpretation, which sees in *yāḏîḏ* and *dôḏ* references to the bridegroom. Although in the course of the song the bridegroom is identified with Yahweh, this theory sees no religious reference in the term *yāḏîḏ* itself. It is used totally in a secular sense, indicating feelings and demonstrations of friendship and affection.

There is still Ps. 84:2(1): "How lovely (*yeḏîḏôt*) are your dwellings, Yahweh Sabaoth!" This verse is generally held to reflect the love of the singer for the Jerusalem sanctuary. But it is also possible to interpret Yahweh as the subject of the loving and the temple as a visible sign of Yahweh's affection. In any case, this passage is the only instance in which our term is applied to an inanimate object, a late usage.

2. *Religious Usage.* The observation that in the OT *yāḏîḏ* refers almost exclusively to something loved by Yahweh is of some importance. There are various objects of

---

20 *IPN,* 183.

21 O. Eissfeldt, *The OT: An Introd.* (Eng. trans., New York, 1965), 99.

22 H. Wildberger, *BK,* X/1, 167.

23 Contra J. Sanmartín-Ascaso, "דוד *dôḏ* [*dôdh*]," *TDOT,* III, 150.

24 See below, II.2.

Yahweh's love: the tribe of Benjamin (Dt. 33:12), the people of Israel (Ps. 60:7[5] par. 108:7[6]; Jer. 11:15; 12:7 [?]), and an individual (Ps. 127:2; also Jedidiah in 2 S. 12:25). Yahweh can be mentioned explicitly in the 3rd person, as in the Blessing of Moses or the naming of Solomon, or the reference can be indirect through a 3rd person or 2nd person singular suffix, as in Ps. 60:7(5) and 127:2. Only in Jeremiah do we find the 1st person singular suffix: "my beloved," "beloved of my soul."

It is very risky to venture a conclusion on the basis of these few scattered occurrences dating from many different periods. A few comments are nevertheless in order. The most informative passage is the Benjamin saying in the Blessing of Moses (Dt. 33:12).[25] The phrase "beloved of Yahweh" is explained by the following statements: "he dwells in safety"; " 'Elyon' encompasses him all the day long, and he makes his dwelling between his cliffs." The expression "beloved of Yahweh" suggests security and protection. One is reminded of the play on "Benjamin"/"Son of Happiness" (Gen. 35:18).[26]

The substance of 2 S. 12:25 is very similar. Solomon, the second son of David and Bathsheba, is given the name "Beloved of Yahweh" by Yahweh through the prophet Nathan.[27] Since 2 S. 12:24f. concludes the story of David's adultery with Bathsheba, the point of the solemn naming is probably that Yahweh will preserve the life of the second child of this marriage and will in fact take it under his special protection.[28] Similar incidents are found in the royal literature of Egypt, but it is uncertain whether there was any direct influence.[29]

This helps explain how the expression "beloved of Yahweh" comes to be applied in Jeremiah to the people of God: it expresses Yahweh's favor towards his people, demonstrated repeatedly since the exodus, and also the uniqueness of Israel in comparison to other nations. Since Jer. 11:15 and 12:7 appear in the context of an accusation and a lament on the part of Yahweh, it is clear that there are overtones of obligation in the term "beloved of Yahweh"; for if the people of God had responded to Yahweh's love, God would not have had to drive his people from their homes or deliver them over to their enemies. It is interesting that Ps. 60:7(5) is also in a communal lament. The supplicants refer to themselves as "thy beloved," and in parallel (v. 6[4]) as "those who fear thee" (*yᵉrēʾêḵā*). It would therefore be possible, on the basis of the parallelism, to interpret our *yāḏîḏêḵā* as "those who love thee, Yahweh." It must be noted, however, that this passage would be the only example of this reversal of subject and object.[30]

Finally, the conviction that Yahweh gives everything his favorite child needs takes the form of a wisdom aphorism (Ps. 127:2)[31] This is the last evidence for the notion

---

[25] Most recently C. J. Labuschagne, "The Tribes in the Blessing of Moses," *Language and Meaning. OTS,* 19 (1974), 97-112.

[26] Eissfeldt, *Festschrift D. W. Thomas,* 73.

[27] For a different view, see G. Fohrer, "Ζιών," *TDNT,* VII, 302.

[28] Eissfeldt, *Festschrift D. W. Thomas,* 70, 78f.

[29] Cf. J. Bergman, "אהב *ʾāhaḇ* [*ʾāhabh*]," *TDOT,* I, 100.

[30] But see the discussion of Isa. 5:1 in II.1 above.

[31] Cf. however V. Hamp, "Der Herr gibt es den Seinen im Schlaf," *Wort, Lied und Gottesspruch. Festschrift J. Ziegler. FzB,* 1-2 (1972), II, 71-79.

of affection inherent in our term, the protection afforded quite personally to the people and the individual adherent of the God of Israel.

III. Religio-Historical Conclusions. The fact that the name *yāḏîḏ* and other derivatives of the root *ydd* II appear very infrequently in the OT, coupled with the fact that the common notion of God's love for his people and the individual is expressed not by *ydd* but by → אהב *'āhaḇ* [*'āhabh*], suggests that the *yāḏîḏ* notion was felt to be somewhat alien and was therefore avoided. This could mean that the notion originated in Israel's Canaanite environment and was borrowed at an early date. Within the OT, this theory is supported by the observation that the two earliest occurrences date from the period before the Israelite state and the early monarchy and that the Benjamin saying with its use of Elyon for Yahweh probably points back to El Elyon. Furthermore, the titles *ydd 3l* and *mdd b'l* appear in Ugaritic texts. And since El Elyon seems to have been the specific form of the El deity worshipped at Jerusalem, and the naming of Solomon likewise took place at Jerusalem, the *yaḏîḏ* notion within Yahwism could go back to Jerusalem cultic terminology. In view of the paucity of the literary sources, however, we must always remember that such theories are hypothetical.

Zobel

יָדַע *yāḏaʿ*; דַּעַת *daʿaṯ*; דֵּעַ *dēaʿ*; דֵּעָה *dēʿâ*; מוֹדָע *môḏāʿ*; מֹדַעַת *mōḏaʿaṯ*; מַדָּע *maddāʿ*; מַנְדָּע *mandāʿ*

Contents: I. 1. Etymology; 2. Contaminations and Conjectures; 3. Occurrences; 4. LXX. II. Ancient Near East: 1. Egyptian; 2. Akkadian; 3. Ugaritic; 4. Names. III. 1. Secular Usage; 2. Religious Usage; 3. Revelation; 4. Derivatives; 5. Dead Sea Scrolls.

---

yāḏaʿ. P. R. Ackroyd, "Meaning and Exegesis," *Words and Meanings. Festschrift D. W. Thomas* (Cambridge, 1968), 1-14; J. Barr, *Comparative Philology and the Text of the OT* (Oxford, 1968), 19ff., 325, 328; F. Baumann, "ידע und seine Derivate," *ZAW*, 28 (1908), 22-41, 110-143; *idem*, " 'Wissen um Gott' bei Hosea als Urform der Theologie?" *EvTh*, 15 (1955), 416-425; G. Bertram, "φρήν," *TDNT*, IX, 220-235, esp. 224-230; G. J. Botterweck, *"Gott erkennen" im Sprachgebrauch des ATs. BBB*, 2 (1951); *idem*, "Vom Wesen der alttestamentlichen Gotteserkenntnis," *Wissenschaft und Weisheit*, 14 (Düsseldorf, 1951), 48-55; G. W. Buchanan, "The OT Meaning of the Knowledge of Good and Evil," *JBL*, 75 (1956), 114-120; R. Bultmann, "γινώσκω," *TDNT*, I, 689-719; J. de Caevel, "La connaissance religieuse dans les hymnes d'action de grâces de Qumrân," *ETL*, 38 (1962), 435-460; D. J. A. Clines, "The Tree of Knowledge and the Law of Jahweh," *VT*, 24 (1974), 8-14; M. Dahood, "Canaanite Words in Qoheleth 10,20," *Bibl*, 46 (1965), 210-12; *idem*, "Hebrew-Ugaritic Lexicography II," *Bibl*, 45 (1964), 403; *idem*, "Hebrew-Ugaritic Lexicography III," *Bibl*, 46 (1965), 316f.; *idem*, "Hebrew-Ugaritic Lexicography XII," *Bibl*, 55 (1974), 381-393, esp. 388f.; *idem*, "Qoheleth and Recent Discoveries," *Bibl*, 39 (1958), 302-318, esp. 312; *idem*, "Northwest Semitic Philology and Job," *The Bible in Current Catholic Thought. St. Mary's Theology Studies*, 1. *Gruenthaner Memorial Volume* (New York, 1962), 5-74, esp. 72; *idem*, *Proverbs and Northwest Semitic Philology.*

I. 1. *Etymology.* The root *yd‘*, "know," is found throughout the range of the Semitic languages, with the possible exception of Arabic: Akk. *idû/edû*,[1] Ugar. *yd‘*,[2] Ethiop. *ayde‘a*, OSA *yd‘*,[3] as well as the modern South Arabic dialects,[4] Phoen. and Aram. *yd‘*,[5] Christian Palestinian, Syr., and Mand.[6] *y^eda‘*. According to Nöldeke,[7] Arabic retains only vestiges of *yd‘*, which was replaced by *‘arafa* and *‘alima*. Neo-Egyp. *yd‘*, "clever,"[8] is a borrowed West Semitic participle.[9] According to Rössler,[10] Egyp. *rḫ*, "know," is the regular phonological equivalent of Hamito-Semitic *yd‘*.

SPIB, 113 (1963), 18, 20f., 31; *idem*, "Ugaritic studies and the Bible," *Greg*, 43 (1962), 55-79, esp. 63f.; W. D. Davies, " 'Knowledge' in the Dead Sea Scrolls and Matthew 11:25-30," in his *Christian Origins and Judaism* (Philadelphia, 1962), 119-144; R. C. Dentan, *The Knowledge of God in Ancient Israel* (New York, 1968); G. R. Driver, "Hebrew Notes on Prophets and Proverbs," *JTS*, 41 (1940), 162-175, esp. 162; *idem*, "Hebrew Notes," *JBL*, 68 (1949), 57-59; *idem*, "Linguistic and Textual Problems: Isaiah I–XXXIX," *JTS*, 38 (1937), 36-50, esp. 49; J. H. Eaton, "Some Misunderstood Hebrew Words for God's Self-Revelation: ידע 'Know,' " *BT*, 25 (1974), 333; I. Eitan, *A Contribution to Biblical Lexicography* (New York, 1924), 48ff.; J. A. Emerton, "A Consideration of Some Alleged Meanings of ידע in Hebrew," *JSS*, 15 (1970), 145-180; *idem*, "Notes on Jeremiah 12 9 and on some suggestions of J. D. Michaelis about the Hebrew Words *naḥā*, *‘æbrā*, and *jadă‘*," *ZAW*, 81 (1969), 182-191, esp. 189f.; *idem*, review of *KBL*³, II, *VT*, 25 (1975), 810-16, esp. 811f.; H. M. Féret, *Connaissance biblique de Dieu* (Paris, 1955); J. Fischer, "טוֹב וָרָע in der Erzählung von Paradies und Sündenfall," *BZ*, 22 (1934), 323-331; A. Fitzgerald, "Hebrew *yd‘* = 'Love' and 'Beloved,' " *CBQ*, 29 (1967), 368-374; F. Gaboriau, "La connaissance de Dieu dans l'AT," *Angelicum*, 45 (1968), 145-183; *idem*, "Enquête sur la signification de connaître: Étude d'une racine," *Angelicum*, 45 (1968), 3-43; *idem*, *La signification de "connaître" dans l'AT* (Rome, 1968); *idem*, *Le thème biblique de la connaissance* (Paris, 1969); J. Goldingay, " 'That You May Know that Yahweh is God': A Study of the Relationship between Theology and Historical Truth in the OT," *TynB*, 23 (1972), 58-93; M. D. Goldman, "Lexicographical Notes on Exegesis, 4: The Root *wd‘* and the Verb 'To Know' in Hebrew," *ABR*, 3 (1953), 45-51, esp. 46f.; R. Gordis, "The Knowledge of Good and Evil in the OT and the Qumran Scrolls, *JBL*, 76 (1957), 123-138; O. Haggenmüller, "Erinnern und Vergessen Gottes und der Menschen," *BiLe*, 3 (1962), 1-15, 75-89, 193-201; J. Haenel, *Das Erkennen Gottes bei den Schriftpropheten*. *BWANT*, 29[2/4] (1923); H. H. Hirschberg, "Some Additional Arabic Etymologies in OT Lexicography," *VT*, 11 (1961), 373-385, esp. 379; H. B. Huffmon, "The Covenant Lawsuit in the Prophets," *JBL*, 78 (1959), 285-295; *idem*, "The Treaty Background of Hebrew *yāḏa‘*," *BASOR*, 181 (1966), 31-37; *idem* and S. B. Parker, "A Further Note on the Treaty Background of Hebrew *yāḏa‘*," *BASOR*, 184 (1966),

(continued on p. 450)

1 *AHw*, I, 187f.; *CAD*, VII (1960), 20-34.

2 *WUS*, no. 1148; *UT*, no. 1080.

3 ContiRossini, 162.

4 Leslau, *Contributions*, 24.

5 *DISO*, 104f.

6 *MdD*, 188f.

7 T. Nöldeke, review of F. Delitzsch, *Prolegomena eines neuen hebräisch-aramäischen Wörterbuchs zum AT*, *ZDMG*, 40 (1886), 725; *idem*, *Neue Beiträge zur semitischen Sprachwissenschaft* (1910), 202f.

8 Papyrus Anastasi, I, 17, 8.

9 *WbÄS*, I, 153.

10 O. Rössler, "Das ältere ägyptische Umschreibungssystem für Fremdnamen und seine sprachwissenschaftlichen Lehren," in *Neue Afrikanische Studien*, ed. J. Lukas. *Festschrift A. Klingenheben*. *Hamburger Beiträge zur Africa-Kunde*, 5 (1966), 218-229, esp. 228.

Besides Akk. *idû/edû* with its initial consonant *y* we also find the variant root *wadû*. According to von Soden,[11] this form with initial *w* is a back formation from the D stem.[12] The Ethiopic causative *ayde‘a* also has an initial *y*, although, as in Heb. *yd‘*,[13] the analogical influence of verbs with initial *w* must be taken into account.

Etymological attempts to derive *yd‘* from *yāḏ*[14] or Arab. *wd‘*, "lay down, become quiet,"[15] or "be quiet" > (inchoative) "become quiet" > "become aware of," "know,"[16] etc. are purely hypothetical.[17]

2. *Contaminations and Conjectures*. The etymology of the common Semitic root *yd‘* is uncertain, and it is difficult to derive from the numerous passages containing this root a meaning that is independent of the context. Several scholars, especially Thomas and Dahood, following earlier lexicographers, have attempted to identify other roots behind *yd‘*. Their conclusions have often met with skepticism or rejection on account of their hypothetical and frequently arbitrary character.[18]

a. *yāḏa‘* < Arab. *wada‘a*, "be quiet, humiliated": Jgs. 8:16; 16:9; 1 S. 6:3; Am. 3:3; Hos. 6:3; 9:7; Isa. 8:19; 9:8(Eng. v. 9); 45:4; 53:3,11; Jer. 2:16; 14:18; 15:12; 24:1; 31:8,19; Ezk. 19:7; Zec. 14:7; Dnl. 12:4; Ezr. 4:13; Ps. 14:4; 35:15; 53:5(4);

36-38; J. P. Hyatt, "A Note on *yiwwāda‘* in Ps. 74:5," *AJSL*, 58 (1941), 99f.; J. A. Illundain, *El conocimiento de Dios en el AT* (diss., Louvain, 1972); R. Knierim, "Offenbarung im AT," *Probleme biblischer Theologie. Festschrift G. von Rad* (Munich, 1971), 206-235; H. Kosmala, "Die 'Erekenntnis der Wahrheit,' " in his *Hebräer, Essener, Christen. StPB*, 1 (1959), 153-173; R. Kümpel, *Die Berufung Israels: Ein Beitrag zur Theologie des Hosea* (diss., Bonn, 1973), 110f., 233-35; N. Lohfink, "Die priesterliche Abwertung der Tradition von der Offenbarung des Jahwenamens an Mose," *Bibl*, 49 (1968), 1-8, esp. 2f.; J. L. McKenzie, "Knowledge of God in Hosea," *JBL*, 74 (1955), 22-27; J. Miklík, "Der Fall des Menschen," *Bibl*, 20 (1939), 387-396; W. Moran, review of A. Goetze, *The Laws of Eshnunna* [*AASOR*, 31 (1956)], *Bibl*, 38 (1957), 218; S. Mowinckel, *Die Erkenntnis Gottes bei den alttestamentlichen Propheten. NTTSup* (1941); T. Nöldeke, *Neue Beiträge zur semitischen Sprachwissenschaft* (Strasbourg, 1910), 194f.; F. Nötscher, *Zur theologischen Terminologie der Qumran-Texte. BBB*, 10 (1956), 15-79; G. Pidoux, "Encore les deux arbres de Genèse 3!," *ZAW*, 66 (1954), 37-43; B. Reicke, "The Knowledge Hidden in the Tree of Paradise," *JSS*, 1 (1956), 193-201; *idem*, "The Knowledge of the Suffering Servant," *Das ferne und nahe Wort. Festschrift L. Rost. BZAW*, 105 (1967), 186-192; J. Reider, "Egyptological Studies: ידע or ירע and רעע," *JBL*, 66 (1947), 315-17; W. Reiss, " 'Gott nicht Kennen' im AT," *ZAW*, 58 (1940/41), 70-98; H. H. Schmid, *Wesen und Geschichte der Weisheit. BZAW*, 101 (1966), 199-201; W. Schottroff, "ידע *yd‘* erkennen," *THAT*, I, 682-701; W. von Soden, *AHw*, I, 187f.; II, 666f., 682; III, 1259; J. A. Soggin, "Observazioni filologico-linguistiche al secondo capitolo della Genesi: 1) l'expression עֵץ הַדַּעַת טוֹב וָרָע v. 9. 17," *Bibl*, 44

(continued on p. 451)

[11] *GaG*, §103e.

[12] *GaG*, §106q.

[13] Cf. W. Gesenius-G. Bergsträsser, *Hebräische Grammatik*, 29th ed., II (Leipzig, 1926; repr. 1962), 124-131.

[14] Hänel, 225, n. 2.

[15] G. M. Redslob, "Zur hebräischen Wortforschung," *ZDMG*, 25 (1871), 506-508.

[16] Botterweck, *"Gott erkennen,"* 11.

[17] Cf. Gaboriau, *Angelicum*, 45 (1968), 6-17; D. W. Thomas, "The Root ידע in Hebrew," *JTS*, 35 (1934), 298-301.

[18] Barr, Emerton, Liebreich, Reider.

74:5; 119:152; 138:6; Job 9:5; 20:20,26; 21:19; 37:7,15; 38:33; Eccl. 10:20; Prov. 5:6; 9:13; 10:9,21; 12:16; 13:20; cf. Sir. 7:20.[19] This suggestion is very old, going back to Reiske (1779), Michaelis, and Kennicott.[20]

b. *yāḏa'* < Arab. *wada'a* with the special meaning "leave alone, neglect": Ex. 3:7; Prov. 14:7.[21]

c. *yāḏa'* < Arab. *wada'a* with the figurative meaning "punish": Gen. 18:21; Jgs. 8:16 (Peshitta); 16:9; Hos. 6:3 (Quinta: *paideúein*); 9:7; Isa. 53:3; Jer. 31:19; Ezk. 19:7; Dnl. 12:4; Job 20:20; Prov. 10:9; Sir. 7:20.[22] Cf. the reconstructed semantic development of *yāḏa'*, "know" > "bring to knowledge" > "punish," first suggested by Pococke for Jgs. 8:16 and Hos. 9:7.[23]

d. *yāḏa'* < Arab. *wada'a* III, "say farewell, leave, send away": Ex. 3:7; 1 S. 21:3(2); 22:6; Prov. 14:7.[24]

e. *yāḏa'* < Arab. *wadi'a,* "care for": Ex. 2:25; Ps. 31:8(7).[25]

f. *yāḏa'* < Arab. *wadi'a* III, with the special meaning "be reconciled": Am. 3:3.[26]

(1963), 521-23; *idem,* "Philological-linguistic Notes on the Second Chapter of Genesis," *OT and Oriental Studies. BietOr,* 29 (1975), 169-178, esp. 169ff.; H. S. Stern, "The Knowledge of Good and Evil," *VT,* 8 (1958), 405-418; H. J. Stoebe, "Gut und Böse in der Jahwistischen Quelle des Pentateuch," *ZAW,* 65 (1953), 188-204, esp. 195ff.; D. W. Thomas, "A Note on נוֹדַע in 1 Samuel XXII.6," *JTS,* N.S. 21 (1970), 401f. (for other articles on *yāḏa'* by Thomas see "Bibliog. of the Writings of David Winton Thomas," comp. A. Phillips, in *Words and Meanings. Festschrift D. W. Thomas* [New York, 1968], 217-228); R. de Vaux, review of J. Coppens, *La connaissance du bien et du mal et le péché du paradis* [*ALBO,* ser. 2, 3 (1948)], *RB,* 56 (1949), 300-308; S. Wagner, "ידע in den Lobliedern von Qumran," *Bibel und Qumran. Festschrift H. Bardtke* (Berlin, 1968), 232-252; H. W. Wolff, " 'Wissen um Gott' bei Hosea als Urform von Theologie," *EvTh,* 12 (1952/53), 533-554 = *GSAT. ThB,* 22 (²1973), 182-205; *idem,* "Erkenntnis Gottes im AT," *EvTh,* 15 (1955), 426-431; W. Zimmerli, "Knowledge of God According to the Book of Ezekiel," in his *I Am Yahweh* (Eng. trans. 1982), 29-98; *idem,* "Die Quellen der alttestamentlichen Gotteserkenntnis," *Theologie und Wirklichkeit. Festschrift W. Trillhaas* (Göttingen, 1974), 226-240; *idem,* "Das Wort des göttlichen Selbsterweises (Erweiswort), eine prophetische Gattung," *Festschrift A. Robert. Travaux de l'institut catholique de Paris,* 4 (1957), 154-164 = his *Gottes Offenbarung. ThB,* 19 (²1969), 120-132.

19 Goldman; Thomas; Barr; Robinson, 268; B. Gemser, *Sprüche Salomos. HAT,* XVI (²1963), 111ff.; Hyatt; Liebreich.

20 B. Kennicott, *Remarks on Selected Passages in the OT* (1787), 222.

21 D. W. Thomas, "Additional Notes on the Root ידע in Hebrew," *JTS,* N.S. 15 (1964), 54-57.

22 Schindler, Ben Yehuda, Liebreich, Yalon, Thomas, Barr.

23 E. Pococke, *A Comm. on the Prophecy of Hosea* (Oxford, 1685), 455.

24 D. W. Thomas, *JTS,* N.S. 15 (1964), 54-57; 21 (1970), 401f.

25 *Idem,* "A Note on וַיֵּדַע אֱלֹהִים in Exod. II. 25," *JTS,* 49 (1948), 143f.

26 Barr, 19f., 328.

g. *yāḏa'* < Arab. *da'ā,* "seek, ask after"; Hos. 6:3; Prov. 10:32; 24:14; 29:7.[27]

h. *yāḏa'* < Arab. *da'ā* III, "tear down, destroy": Ps. 74:5; Ezk. 19:7.[28]

i. *yāḏa'* < Arab. *da'a,* "call": Ps. 91:14; Job 6:3; 23:3; Prov. 3:5.[29]

j. *yāḏa'* < Arab. *waḏa'a,* "flow, sweat" (cf. Akk. *zu'tu, zutu,* Ugar. *d't,* Heb. *zē'ā*): Isa. 53:11; Prov. 10:9,32;[30] 14:7,33; Sir. 12:1.[31]

k. *yōḏēa'* < Ugar. *d't,* "friend": Eccl. 10:20; Prov. 8:12; 22:12.[32]

l. *yāḏa'* < Ugar. *yd't,* "obedience": 1 S. 2:12.[33]

m. *maddā'* < Ugar. *mnd',* "messenger": Eccl. 10:20.[34]

Finally, textual emendation has often been resorted to in the case of many allegedly obscure *yd'*-passages: (n) *yā'aḏ* instead of *yāḏa':* 1 S. 21:3(2)[35] or the reverse: Jer. 24:1.[36] (o) *yāra'* instead of *yāḏa'* with subsequent dittography giving *rā'a':* Jgs. 8:16; Isa. 53:3; Ezk. 19:7; Ps. 138:6; Job 21:19; Prov. 10:9;[37] Job 35:15.[38] (p) *yāza'* instead of *yāḏa':* Isa. 53:11;[39] Prov. 10:9,32; 14:7,33.[40] (q) *ḏā'â,* "request, wish," instead of *yāḏa':* Ezk. 19:7; Ps. 74:5; Prov. 10:32; 15:14; 24:14; 29:7.[41] (r) *gāḏa'* instead of *yāḏa':* Gen. 18:21; Jgs. 8:16; Isa. 53:3; Jer. 31:19; Ezk. 19:7; 38:24; Prov. 10:9.[42] (s) *'ārâ* instead of *yāḏa':* Prov. 10:32.[43] (t) *rā'â* instead of *yāḏa':* Ex. 2:25.[44]

---

27 *KBL*³, 219; Barr, 24; D. W. Thomas, "Textual and Philological Notes on Some Passages in the Book of Proverbs," *Wisdom in Israel and in the Ancient Near East. Festschrift H. H. Rowley. SVT,* 3 (1955), 284f.

28 Barr, 25, 325; Driver, *JBL,* 68 (1949), 57-59.

29 E. Zolli, "Contributo alla semántica de *yd',*" *Sef,* 16 (1956), 23-31.

30 Cf. J. J. Reiske, *Coniectvrae in Iobvm et Proverbia Salomonis* (Leipzig, 1779), Arab. *ḏā'a,* "effundere, expirare."

31 Following an old suggestion by Nöldeke, *Neue Beiträge zur semitischen Sprachwissenschaft,* 194f.; now Dahood, *Proverbs and Northwest Semitic Philology,* 21; *Bibl,* 46 (1965), 316f.

32 Dahood, *Bibl,* 46 (1965), 316f.; cf. *KAI,* II, 125. On Prov. 22:12, cf. however D. W. Thomas, "A Note on דַּעַת in Proverbs XXII. 12," *JTS,* N.S. 14 (1963), 93f.: "lawsuit."

33 S. E. Löwenstamm, "Ugaritic Gleanings," *Lešonénû,* 30 (1965), 66, 85-91 [Hebrew].

34 Dahood, *Bibl,* 39 (1958), 312.

35 *BDB.*

36 G. R. Driver, "Hebrew Notes on the 'Wisdom of Jesus Ben Sirach,' " *JBL,* 53 (1934), 288.

37 Reider.

38 Emerton, *JSS,* 15 (1970), 154f.

39 Dahood, *Proverbs and Northwest Semitic Philology,* 21, contra Barr, 22f.

40 Dahood, *ibid.,* 18, 20, 31f.; cf. already Nöldeke, *Neue Beiträge zur semitischen Sprachwissenschaft,* 194f.

41 Barr, 24f., 325; on Proverbs, cf. also Thomas, *SVT,* 3 (1955), 284; *KBL*³, 219.

42 Fürst, contra D. W. Thomas, "Julius Fürst and the Hebrew Root ידע," *JTS,* 42 (1941), 64f.

43 M. Scott.

44 Dillmann, Kautzsch, Bertholet.

3. *Occurrences.* According to Lisowsky, the root *yd'* and its derivatives occur 1058 times in the Hebrew OT, 51 times in the Aramaic sections. The verb *yāḏa'* does not appear in Obadiah, Haggai, Lamentations, or Ezra; in the other books it appears 948 times (947 by Schottroff's count): 822 qal, 71 hiphil, 42 niphal (41 Schottroff), 6 pual, 3 hophal, 2 hithpael, 1 piel, 1 poel. It is especially common in Ezekiel (99 times), Psalms (93 times), Jeremiah (77 times), Isaiah (75 times), and Job (70 times). It occurs 174 times in the Pentateuch (only 9 times in Leviticus and 17 in Numbers) and 181 times in the Deuteronomistic history, but only 38 times in the Chronicler's history. Proverbs and Ecclesiastes, with 35 occurrences each, use the word frequently, but it appears only twice in Song of Songs. This last observation may indicate that *yāḏa'* later leveled a certain semantic component of the early period.

The noun *da'aṯ* occurs 90 times (11 times as subject, 37 as object): 40 times in Proverbs, 11 in Job, 8 in Ecclesiastes; substantially less frequently in Isaiah (9 times), Hosea (4 times), and Malachi (once).

The derivative *dēa'* is restricted to the Elihu speeches in Job (5 times). There are 6 occurrences of *dē'â* (twice in Isaiah, once each in Jeremiah, Psalms, Job, and 1 Samuel; conjectured in Prov. 24:14); *maddā'* (6 occurrences), *mōḏa'aṯ* (1 occurrence), and *môḏā'* (2 occurrences) are late derivatives (Daniel, 2 Chronicles, Ruth, Ecclesiastes, Proverbs, Sirach).

The Aramaic verb *y^eḏa'* occurs 47 times (36 in Daniel, 11 in Ezra), of which 22 are peal and 25 haphel. The nominal derivative *manda'* occurs 4 times in Daniel. Sirach uses the verb 29 times, the noun *da'aṯ* 9 times, *madda'* twice, *dea'* and *dē'â* once each.

4. *LXX.* The LXX uses 22 verbs, 3 nouns, and 8 adjectives to render *yāḏa'*.[45] We find *gignṓskein* (490 times), with its compounds *apogignṓskein* (once), *diagignṓskein* (twice), and *epigignṓskein* (52 times), and *eidénai* (185 times) with its compound *syneidénai* (once), *epístasthai* (42 times), *ideín* (16 times), and *gnōrízein* (3 times). The verbs *aisthánesthai, akoúein,* and *manthánein* each occur twice.

The niphal is rendered similarly: 3 times with *gígnesthai;* here and in the pual we find *gnōstós* 5 times. For the piel we find *ideín,* etc., and for the poel *diamartyreín.* The hiphil is rendered primarily by *gnōrízein* (30 times), by *gignṓskein,* etc., 3 times. The element of revelation is heard in *angéllein,* etc. (10 times), *dēloún* (4 times), and *deiknýein,* etc. (5 times). Through its comparatively rare use of *didáskein* (only 6 occurrences), the LXX limits the pedagogical element found in the hiphil of *yd'*. In Sirach, with the same terminology, we also find 1 occurrence of *noeín.*

The subst. *da'aṯ* has 21 equivalents:[46] *gnṓsis* (29 times) and *epígnōsis* (5 times), *aísthēsis* (19 times), *sýnesis* (6 times) and *epistḗmē* (5 times), *boulḗ/boúlēma* (3 times), *sophía* (twice), and *noús, paideía,* and *phrónēsis* once each. In rendering the other derivatives, the LXX remains within the semantic realm just outlined.

Aram. *y^eḏa'* is rendered variously in the Greek translations of the Bible. For the peal we find *gignṓskein, eideín, gnōstós,* and *epigignṓskein.* The aphel is rendered by

---

[45] See E. C. Dos Santos, *An Expanded Hebrew Index for the Hatch-Redpath Concordance to the Septuagint* (Jerusalem, n.d.), 77.

[46] *Ibid.,* 44.

dēloún, sēmaínein, ap/anangéllein, and *hypodeiknýein,* while Theodotion almost invariably uses *gnōrízein.* Aram. *mandaʿ* is rendered by *psychḗ,* while Theodotion uses *phrḗn.*

Botterweck

II. Ancient Near East.

1. *Egyptian.*

a. *rḫ, ʿrk, ʿm.* The most important Egyptian word for "know" is *rḫ.*[47] Another word is *ʿrḳ.*[48] The regular antonym is *ḫmy,* "be ignorant."[49] For "come to know," besides *rḫ* and *ʿm*[50] we find words for "see" (*ptr, m33*) and "hear" (*śḏm*). Later for "have knowledge" we also find *śy3;*[51] cf. Sia, the personification of knowledge and understanding, alongside Hu, the embodiment of the word.[52] The important phrase *m ḫm-f* (etc.), "without the knowledge of (someone),"[53] appears in negated statements to express the omniscience and sovereignty of a god or pharaoh. For "knowing," in addition to *rḫ* and *rḫ-św,*[54] we find a variety of words.[55] The fact that several of them are compounded with *ỉb,* "heart" (*3ḫ-ỉb, wb3-ỉb, wḥʿ-ỉb,* etc.) shows that the heart was considered the seat of knowledge and understanding.[56] For other terms such as *ś33/ś3.e* and *ś3r/ś3r.t* → חכם *ḥāḵam* [*chākham*].[57]

b. *Expert, Craftsperson, Magician, Ritualist.* Egyp. *rḫ* can refer to all kinds of knowledge. The phrase *rḫ ḫt* refers to a specialist, whether a scholar, a craftsperson, a magician, or a ritualist. More precise expressions like *rḫ ʿwy,* "with skillful arms," and *rḫ ḏbʿw,* "with skillful fingers," are applied to the king as ritual officiant. In this context the king is "one who knows the powerful words."[58] In the autobiographical inscriptions, those who speak often boast of their wisdom, knowledge, and expertise.[59] The ideal is "to know better than the learned, to be truly expert. . . ." In the high value this literature places on knowledge it has points of contact with Wisdom Literature. These instructions are meant to bring the ignorant to knowledge.[60]

---

47 *WbÄS,* II, 442ff.
48 *WbÄS,* I, 212.
49 *WbÄS,* III, 278ff.
50 *WbÄS,* I, 184.
51 *WbÄS,* IV, 30.
52 See Bonnet, "Sia," *RÄR,* 715.
53 *WbÄS,* III, 280.
54 *WbÄS,* II, 445.
55 See *WbÄS,* VI, 88 and 84 *s.v.* "kundig" and "klug."
56 See A. Piankoff, *Le "coeur" dans les textes égytiennes* (Paris, 1930), 47ff.
57 M. Krause, *TDOT,* IV, 368-370.
58 E. Chassinat, *Le temple de Denderah,* I (Cairo, 1934), 135; cf. II (1934), 144.
59 See J. M. A. Janssen, *De traditioneele egyptische Autobiografie voor het Nieuwe Rijk* (Leiden, 1946).
60 Ptahhotep, 47; Amenemope, XXVII, 10.

c. *Knowing the Forms and Names of God.* To know people is important. The Eloquent Peasant declares proudly that he knows all the people of the nome.[61] A favorite title is *rḫ (n) nśw,* "familiar of the king,"[62] also found in the feminine. It is even more important to know God. Texts often speak of the mutual knowledge of king and god. Akhenaten declares of the god Aten: "There is none other who knows you but thy son."[63] Those who are devout should know the divine forms and the names. Often, however, it is stressed that one cannot know the true form and the true name of the deity. "God is too great to be worshipped, too powerful to be known," we read in the great Leiden Hymn to Amon.[64] God's plans cannot be known: "If you cannot know the plans of god, you cannot know the coming day."[65] The instructions frequently emphasize the limitations of human knowledge, even when they stress the ideal of the true sage.

d. *Knowledge of the Dead.* Special knowledge plays an important role in mortuary literature. The dead person declares: "I know the names of the nomes, the cities, and the sea."[66] The dead person must know all kinds of sayings, as well as the names of the gods and demons. Some sections of the Book of the Dead bear that title: "Sayings for knowing the souls of the sacred places." By virtue of these sayings the dead person becomes master of all kinds of mysteries. The dead person boasts of divine omniscience: "There is nothing that I do not know in the heavens, on earth, and in the water; there is nothing that I do not know in Hapi; there is nothing of which Thoth does not know that I do not know."[67] He surpasses even Thoth, the sage par excellence.[68]

e. *"Know" Sexually.* Like *yāḏa‘*, *rḫ* can also mean "know" in the sexual sense;[69] in this case it often has a phallus as a determinative. In the late period, the same determinative is sometimes used in jest for *rḫ* in the sense of "know." There is a good text to illustrate this sexual usage of *rḫ* in a hymn to Min from Edfu,[70] which substitutes *rḫ* for the *nk,* "have intercourse with," of the early version.[71]

Bergman

2. *Akkadian.*

a. *idû and Its Stems.* The root *idû, edû (wadû),* "know," is very common in Akkadian

---

61 Line 16.
62 *WbÄS,* II, 446, 14.
63 Amarna, VI, 27, 12.
64 IV, 19.
65 Wisdom of Amenemope, XXII, 5-8.
66 *CT,* V, 364.
67 *CT,* V, 305f.
68 Cf. P. Boylan, *Thoth, the Hermes of Egypt* (Oxford, 1922), 98-106.
69 *WbÄS,* II, 446, 8.
70 E. Chassinat, *Le temple d'Edfou,* II (Cairo, 1938), 390f.
71 Cf. H. Gauthier, *Les fêtes de dieu Min* (Cairo, 1931), 239f.

from the Old Babylonian period on.[72] The forms of *wadû* are obviously back formations based on the D stem;[73] the G stem "know" forms an adj. *edû*, "well-known, famous," and an irregular ptcp. *mudû* (< *muda'u*),[74] "wise, knowledgeable, well-informed," found also in the meaning "familiar."[75] We also find the nouns *mūdûtu*, "knowledge" (Old Babylonian), "wisdom" (Neo-Babylonian), **idūtu*, "knowledge," and *mūdânūtu*, negated in the meaning "ignorance" (Neo-Assyrian). The D stem *(w)uddû* means "inform, reveal"; the Š stem *šūdû*, "announce, make known," is similar. From the latter are formed the nouns *mušēdû*, "reporter," and *šūdûtu*, "announcement" (both only Late Babylonian). The Št stem *šutēdû* means "acquire knowledge." The few occurrences of the N stem have passive meaning.

b. *Secular Knowing*. As in Hebrew, the semantic field of "knowledge" and "wisdom" is highly developed. The terminology usually builds on concrete perception: in parallel with "know" we find *amāru*, "see, recognize"; *aḫāzu*, "grasp, learn"; *ḫāṭu*, "see, grasp, learn"; *lamādu*, "experience, know (both intellectually and sexually)"; *ṣabāru*, "grasp, understand"; *šamū*, "hear, perceive." Equally concrete is the expression *pīt uzni*, "wise" (lit., "having open ears").

The verb *idû/edû* denotes in the first instance secular "acquaintance" (with persons, their age, where they are staying, circumstances, facts, the right time, etc.), "expertise" (in craftsmanship, military strategy, geography), then "knowledge" of a specific sort (when to harvest, what roads and canals are blocked, a disaster), and finally specialized "expertise" (in astronomy, liturgy, warfare, irrigation, treatment of diseases.

People are characterized socially by what they know (*idû*). Highlanders and murderers do not "know" good manners,[76] and the wicked "do not know" how to keep an oath.[77] Sages (*eršu*), however, know moderation;[78] they can understand how the deities are disposed toward them, but even they are ignorant of how the gods punish.[79] For the most part, however, the old human self-estimate holds: people are "dull" (*sukkuku*), for they know nothing.[80]

Akkadian epistolary literature understands *idû* primarily in the sense of "be informed" (about the plans of others, the commands of the king, imminent dangers, military positions); cf. the stereotyped informatory formula: *šarru bēlī ú-da*, "Know my lord the king that. . . ."[81]

---

72 Cf. *AHw*, I, 187f.; II, 666f., 682; III, 1259; *CAD*, IV (1959), 34f.; VII, 20-34; X/1 (1978), 263; X/2 (1978), 263-68.

73 *GAG*, §106q.

74 Cf. *GAG*, §56d and P. C. A. Jensen, "Akkadisch *mudū*," *ZA*, N.S. 1 [35] (1924), 124-132.

75 Cf. R. Yaron, *The Laws of Eshnunna* (Jerusalem, 1969), 43, 100, 216.

76 *TCL*, 3, 93.

77 *ABL*, 1237, 16.

78 Review of R. C. Thompson and R. W. Hutchinson, "The Site of the Palace of Ashurnasirpal at Nineveh" [*Annals of Archaeology and Anthropology*, 18 (1931), 79-112], *AfO*, 7 (1931-32), 281, vo. 7.

79 D. W. Myhrman, *Babylonian Hymns and Prayers*. *PBS*, 1/1 (1911), 14, 24.

80 IVR 10, vo. 29ff.

81 *ABL*, 482, 9.

Declarations of loyality and solidarity use the same form to address the king, as do letters of accreditation from (foreign) diplomats[82] and priests.[83]

c. *Family Law.* In family law and the law of inheritance, the expression "someone who does not know his father" appears as a term for a (semi)orphan and his obscure family background.[84] In the mouth of Ashurbanipal, *ul i-di aba u umme,* "I know neither father nor mother,"[85] refers to the king's divine descent. In the law of oaths *idu* appears in several variations: "(I swear that) I know nothing of it";[86] "May your gods and Šamaš be my witnesses that I. . . ."[87] The standard oath formula is: "May god be my witness."[88]

d. *Magic and Religion.* In the realm of magic, gods "known and unknown" (*idû u la idû*) are invoked. Felt to be especially dangerous were the machinations of demons one might encounter unsuspectingly[89] or curses of which one is unaware.[90] One has no power over a person whose name and location are unknown.[91] One may pray to the gods for help against demons because they are unknown and their effect is therefore unpredictable.[92] There were also prayers against unknown diseases,[93] and people sought to protect themselves against unwitting sins.[94]

Unless the name of the deity is known, there can be no communication between a human being and a god. Generally people have only slight knowledge of the gods: their dwelling places and plans are unknown, so that people are prevented from gaining insight into their own future.[95] But this ignorance extends to the divine plane: the gods do not know the plans of Tiamat,[96] and therefore cannot prevent the deluge. On the other hand, Šamaš is said to know the plans of other deities, and Ea is "versed" in all things.[97] Ea, Šamaš, and the Anunnaki are therefore given the epithet *mūdê kalāma,* "knowing everything" (cf. also the mother of Gilgamesh[98]). Knowledge and wisdom are attributes of the gods. Marduk, "who knows all wisdom" (*mudû gimri usnu*),[99]

---

82 Cf. EA 149, 47.
83 Cf. *ABL,* 65, 11; also the summary formulation in *ABL,* 85, vo. 10; 768, 4; etc.
84 *BE,* XIV, 8, 6.
85 *OECT,* 6 (1927), pl. 11.
86 *ABL,* 896, 12; cf. 287, vo. 9.
87 EA 161, 33; cf. also *ABL,* 390, vo. 7; *MDP,* 24, 393, 16.
88 *TCL,* 14, 32, 15.
89 IVR 55, no. 2, 4.
90 Šurpu, II, 82.
91 Maqlû, II, 209.
92 Cf. Maqlû, VI, 123.
93 *KAR,* 73, vo. 20.
94 E. Reiner, "*Lipšur* Litanies," *JNES,* 15 (1956), 136, 83.
95 IVR 10, vo. 29ff.
96 EnEl III, 128.
97 Gilg. XI, 176.
98 Gilg. I, V.15.
99 EnEl II, 116.

knows the hearts of the Igigi,[100] and therefore is given the epithet *ᵈŠA.ZU* (= *mudê libbi ilî*);[101] cf. the instructive parallelism here: soothe the hearts of the gods, preserve righteousness, accomplish justice, etc.

Hammurabi similarly receives the title *mudē igigallim,* "absorbed in wisdom";[102] Ashurbanipal is *eršu, mudû, ḫasīsu, pit uzni,* and possessor of *nēmequ,* "wisdom";[103] Esarhaddon is described as *lē'ū, itpēšu, ḫassu,* and *mudú;*[104] and finally Šamaš-šum-ukin claims the title *enqu, mudú,* and *ḫasis kal šipri,* "one who understands all works."[105] Gilgamesh is called "the mighty one, renowned and experienced."[106]

The *mudū šarri,*[107] "friend of the king" (cf. Egyp. *rḫ [n] nśw*) enjoys special privileges and may rank with those who belong to a warrior caste (*mariannu šarri*). Goetze[108] claims to see in the *mudū šarri* a fugitive who has found asylum at the king's court.

e. *Revelation.* The forms *uddû* and *šūdū* function as terms for revelation. The gods reveal themselves in the cosmos by "showing" the heavens their course[109] and "assigning" the moon to ornament the night.[110] Marduk "makes known" to the gods their various domains (*mu'addî qirbēti ana ilî*).[111] The domains of Sin and Šamaš can be found (*utaddû*) throughout the entire cosmos.[112] The gods can "make known" their will through signs and oracles,[113] above all by designating priests, kings, and governors; cf. Enlil's title "designator of governors" and Nabû's title "designator of the kingship."[114] The basis of all religious observance is laid by the deity's revelation of its name, which can then be "named" (*zakāru*). Even though there is no extant Akkadian discourse on "revelation," we see everywhere how important the fact of revelation was felt to be. By means of oracles and omens, people attempted to discover the will of the gods and learn what human fate holds in store; it was considered a sign of impending disaster when a desired omen was "not revealed" (*ul utaddû*).[115]

---

100 S. Langdon, *Die neubabylonischen Königsinschriften. VAB,* 4 (1912), 214, I, 17.

101 EnEl VII, 35.

102 CH, III, 17.

103 E. A. W. Budge and L. W. King, *The Annals of the Kings of Assyria* (London, 1902), 1197, IV, 5.

104 R. Borger, *Die Inschriften Asarhaddons, Königs von Assyrien. BAfO,* 9 (1956), §45, II, 19.

105 F. X. Steinmeltzer, "Die Bestallungsurkunde des Königs Šamaš-šum-ukîn von Babylon," *AnOr,* 12 (1935), 303, I, 9.

106 Gilg. I, II.26.

107 *RS* 15.137, 12; 16.239, 18.

108 A. Goetze, *The Laws of Eshnunna. AASOR,* 31 (1951-52 [1956]), 111, n. 13.

109 EnEl V, 6.

110 EnEl V, 13.

111 EnEl VII, 84.

112 *TCL* 6, 51, vo. 5f.

113 A.T. Clay, *Miscellaneous Inscriptions in the Yale Babylonian Collection. YOSBT,* 1 (1915), 45, I, 7.

114 *BWL,* 114, 54.

115 *PBS,* 1/2 (1911), 116, 41f.

3. *Ugaritic*.

a. *Occurrences*. To date *ydʻ* is attested 48 times in Ugaritic,[116] as a verb and as the nouns *dʻt* and *mndʻ*. The derivation and meaning of the latter noun are disputed. Dietrich and Loretz[117] translate it as "possibly, in case"; Driver[118] derives it from *ydʻ*: "assuredly" > "it is something known." Virolleaud[119] takes the same approach. Whitaker's assignment of *mdʻ*[120] to our root has been cast in doubt by Loretz's objection.[121] Here *mdʻ* probably means "why," while in the two economic texts[122] it refers to a person who stands in a position of confidence, one who is "well known" to the king; cf. *mûdu* in the Akkadian syllabic texts from Ugarit in the sense "companion; one who knows or associates with a person."[123]

b. *Message or Warning*. For the verb, the meaning "know" is undisputed.[124] In secular usage—almost entirely Ugaritic epistolary literature—the object of the knowledge is a message (*rgm*)[125] or warning[126] brought by a messenger;[127] in this context, *ydʻ* means "ponder, take to heart."

Letters are written to inform the recipient of specific news:[128] a mother, for example, learns (*ydʻ*) of her son's successful audience with the Great King.[129] In official correspondence, *ydʻ* refers to official cognizance—of a raid, for example: "Our town is destroyed; be this known to you!"[130]

c. *Personal Knowledge*. In Ugaritic, *ydʻ* also touches the personal realm; it is used, for example, for Keret's wise understanding of his daughter Ṯitmanet, whom he wishes to preserve from hardship.[131] And El knows (*ydʻ*) the true nature of fierce ʻAnat, who has killed Aqhat[132] and even plans to kill El.[133]

---

116 Whitaker, 303f.
117 M. Dietrich and O. Loretz, "Zur ugaritischen Lexikographie (I)," *BiOr*, 23 (1966), 131.
118 *CML*, 162.
119 In *PRU* on *KTU*, 2.34, 10f.; 2.45, 31: "messenger."
120 *KTU*, 1.107, 39.
121 M. Dietrich, O. Loretz, and J. Sanmartín, "Einzelbemerkungen zu RS 24.251 = Ug. 5,S.574-578 Nr. 8," *UF*, 7 (1975), 128.
122 *KTU*, 4.387, 12; 4.609, 4.
123 *PRU*, III, 234; cf. also M. Dahood, *Ugaritic-Hebrew Philology. BietOr*, 17 (1965), 61.
124 *WUS*, no. 1148; *UT*, no. 1080.
125 *KTU*, 2.8, 6; possibly also 2.3, 24.
126 *KTU*, 2.17, 8.
127 É. Lipiński, "*Skn* et *sgn* dans le sémitique occidental du nord," *UF*, 5 (1973), 199.
128 *KTU*, 2.34, 30; 2.9, 3.
129 *KTU*, 2.16, 7.
130 *KTU*, 2.61, 13; cf. M. Dietrich, O. Loretz, and J. Sanmartín, "Brief über die Auswirkungen einer Razzia (RS 19.11 = *PRU*, V, 114)," *UF*, 7 (1975), 532.
131 *KTU*, 1.16 I, 33; cf. H. Sauren and G. Kestemont, "Keret, roi de Ḫubur," *UF*, 3 (1971), 211.
132 *KTU*, 1.18 I, 16.
133 *KTU*, 1.3 V, 27; cf. A. S. Kapelrud, *The Violent Goddess* (Oslo, 1969), 65.

d. *Sexual Knowledge.* Ugar. *ydʻ* can also mean "know" in the sexual sense, as is clear from its use in synthetic parallelism with *hry,* "conceive, become pregnant."[134] Baʻal "surrounded" ʻAnat (*ʻzrt*) and "knew" her (*ydʻ*); she "became pregnant" (*hry*) and "gave birth" (*wld*).[135] Textually disputed is the passage[136] in which, in the context of an incubation rite, Kaṯirat is termed *ydʻt.*[137]

e. *Magic and Mythology.* There is a fixed formula *ydʻ hlk kbkbm,* "know the course of the stars,"[138] which may refer to special magical wisdom.[139]

In Ugaritic mythology, the gods are often subjects of a knowledge not defined in greater detail.[140] A charm against snake venom invokes the god who "knows" the bite, i.e., knows how to diagnose it, and "understands" (*ypq*) how to draw the poison.[141] After the death of Baʻal, the search for a competent successor is the primary problem confronting the assembly of the gods.[142] The summons of the goddess Aṯirat, *nmlk ydʻ ylḥn,* eludes precise interpretation, since *ylḥn* is obscure.

Although it is a common mythologoumenon that the gods understand what is hidden and know the future, *ydʻ* almost never occurs in these contexts (cf. Ugar. *ḥdy, ph,* "see"). The root *ydʻ* is not used to express visionary knowledge and mantic or magical revelation. This can also be seen clearly in *KTU,* 1.6 III, 8. El learns in a dream that the heavens drop oil and the valleys flow with honey. Only then can ʻAnat conclude (*ydʻ*) that Baʻal, who was dead, is alive once more (*k ḥy ʼl3yn bʻl*) and that the infirmity of the cosmos has come to an end.

The inability of the cosmos and human world to picture (*ydʻ* par. *byn*) the enormous divine palace of Baʻal[143] on Mt. Zaphon[144] appears to be a frequent theme.[145] Baʻal alone understands (*byn*) the nature of lightning and thunder, the message of trees and stones, of heaven and earth, of sea and stars; he sees the total context of which human beings know nothing (*l tdʻ nšm*). These abilities of Baʻal constitute the explication of *ydʻ ylḥn,* which is expected of the highest god.[146]

4. *Names.* In almost all Semitic languages, the root *ydʻ* appears as an element of

---

134 *KTU,* 1.13, 31.

135 Cf. H. Cazelles, "L'hymne ugaritique a Anat," *Syr,* 33 (1956), 52, 55f.

136 *KTU,* 1.17 II, 41.

137 Cf. A. Caquot, M. Sznycer, and A. Herdner, *Textes Ougaritiques, I: Mythes et légendes. LAPO,* 7 (1974), 426.

138 *KTU,* 1.19 II, 2, 7; IV, 38.

139 Cf. H. P. Müller, "Magisch-mantische Weisheit und die Gestalt Daniels," *UF,* 1 (1969), 94.

140 *KTU,* 1.3 I, 25; 1.10 I, 3.

141 *KTU,* 1.107, 35; cf. Loretz, *UF,* 7(1975), 128.

142 *KTU,* 1.6 I, 48.

143 Aistleitner.

144 Cf. L. R. Fisher, *RSP,* I, II, 221.

145 *KTU,* 1.1 III, 15, 26, 27; IV, 15, 18; cf. also 1.7, 32.

146 Cf. H. Donner, "Ugaritismen in der Psalmenforschung," *ZAW,* 79 (1967), 328-330; A. R. Ceresko, "The A:B::B:A Word Pattern in Hebrew and Northwest Semitic with Special Reference to the Book of Job," *UF,* 7 (1975), 74.

proper names. Most common are names of thanks, comprising *yd'* plus a theophorous element such as *'el, yahû, b'l, šm, nabû,* Ea, etc.

a. *Ancient Near East.* At Ugarit, for example, we find the name *b'l-d' (ba'lī-yada'*[147]), "Ba'al knew," and the short forms *ad', ad'y, yd',* and *md'.*[148]

In Akkadian, names with *edû/idû,* with or without a theophorous element, were obviously very popular. We find clausal lament names: *ar-ni-ú-ul-i-dam,* "I do not know my sins";[149] *dbēl-ḫi-ṭu-ul-i-di,* "Ba'al, I do not know my transgressions" (cf. *dea-ḫi-i-ṭi-ul-i-di*[150]), and the religious confidence names *ili(AN)-i-da-an-ni, ili(AN)-ú-dan-ni,* "My god knows me," i.e., "My god cares for me,"[151] *dnabû-idanni,* "Nabû knows me."[152] The clausal names often include an additional element: *da-šur-ki-ti-i-di,* "Ashur knows my righteousness,"[153] *ilí-ki-nam-i-di,* "My god knows the righteous one," *dša-maš-ki-nam-i-di,* "Šamaš knows that I am righteous."[154] The name *fman-nu-i-da-at/as-su-i-di,* "Who knows his power?" is obviously a name of praise in the form of a question.[155] In the case of *a-ba-am-la-i-di, a-ba-ul-i-di,* "I do not know the father," and *ul-i-di-ul-a-mur,* "Neither do I know the father nor have I seen him," we are probably dealing with the names of foundlings.[156] The Amorite names on the pattern *ya-da-AN* or *ya-daḫ-AN* are discussed by Huffmon.[157]

b. *OT.* These names based on *yāḏa'* are also common in the OT: *'aḇyāḏā'* and *'aḇîḏā'* (Gen. 25:4; 1 Ch. 1:33), *'elyāḏā'* (2 S. 5:16), *be'elyāḏā'* (1 Ch. 14:7), *yô/yehôyāḏā'* (2 S. 8:18), *yeḏa'yâ* (1 Ch. 9:10), *yeḏî'a'ēl* (1 Ch. 7:6), *šemîḏā'* (Nu. 26:32; cf. Samaria ostracon 29[158]), and *de'û'ēl* (Nu. 1:14[159]); various short forms also occur: *yāḏā'* (1 Ch. 2:28), *yaddûa'* (Neh. 10:22[21]), and *yiddô* (1 Ch. 27:21).

III. 1. *Secular Knowledge.*

a. *Visual and Auditory Perception.* External knowledge or recognition (*yāḏa'*) is often paralleled by visual sensory perception: *rā'â,* Nu. 24:16f.; Dt. 11:2; 1 S. 26:12; Neh. 4:5(11); Job 11:11; Ps. 138:6;[160] Eccl. 6:5; Isa. 29:15; 41:20; 44:9,18; 58:3; 61:9; Jer. 2:23; 5:1; 12:3; cf. also the attention-getting formula *da' ûre'ēh:* 1 S. 12:17;

---

147 *PNU,* 39.
148 *PNU,* 142f.
149 H. H. Figulla, *Altbabylonische Verträge. VAS,* 13 (1914), 103, 13.
150 *AN,* 164.
151 *IPN,* 181.
152 *AN,* 198; Tallqvist, *APN,* 150b.
153 *APN,* 41a; a large number of similar formations in C. Saporetti, *Onomastica Medio-Assira, II. Studia Pohl,* 6 (1971), II: *Studi, vocabulari ed elenchi,* 124.
154 *AN,* 239f.
155 *AN,* 238.
156 *AN,* 321, with additional examples; cf. also *APN,* 90f.
157 *APNM,* 38, 209.
158 J. C. L. Gibson, *Textbook of Syrian Semitic Inscriptions,* I (Oxford, ^{2}1973), 9.
159 *KBL*^{3}, 375.
160 Reider, 317.

14:38; 23:22; 24:12(11); 25:17; 2 S. 24:13; 1 K. 20:7,22; 2 K. 5:7; Jer. 2:19. This *rā'â* often precedes the *yāḏa'* and makes it possible (Gen. 18:21; Ex. 2:25; Dt. 4:35; 1 S. 6:9; 18:28; Ps. 31:8[7]; Isa. 5:19); we also find *ḥāzâ* (Nu. 24:16; Dnl. 5:23), *šûr,* "behold" (Nu. 24:16f.), hithpael of *š'h,* "gaze at" (Gen. 24:21), hiphil of *nkr* (Dt. 33:9; Isa. 61:9), and *šāzap* (Job 28:7).

An auditory process can also precede *yāḏa': šāma',* Ex. 3:7; Dt. 9:2; Neh. 6:16; Ps. 78:3; Isa. 33:13; 40:28; 48:7f.; Jer. 5:15. Both elements are constitutive of the epistemic process *rā'â—šāma'—yāḏa'* in Ex. 3:7; Lev. 5:1; Nu. 24:16f.; Dt. 29:3(4); 33:9; Isa. 32:3f.; 48:6. In such parallelisms, *yāḏa'* can function as the superior term, summarizing the sensory perception and processing it intellectually (e.g., Ex. 3:7). The great semantic range of *yāḏa'* from purely apperceptive knowledge to "be careful of, pay attention to" is clear from its use in parallel with *śîm,* "take to heart" (Isa. 41:20,22), *śāḵal,* "consider" (Isa. 41:20; 44:18), → בקשׁ *biqqēš* [*biqqēsh*], "seek" (Jer. 5:1), *bāḥan,* "test with care" (Jer. 12:3), and *qāšaḇ,* "pay attention" (Isa. 32:3).

The complexity of many epistemic processes is expressed by an accumulation of various verbs belonging to the semantic field of "knowing," without distinguishable emphasis on the various nuances of the individual meanings.[161] "Seeing, knowing, considering, and understanding" (Isa. 41:20: *rā'â, śîm, śāḵal, yāḏa'*) do not always point to a deliberate distinction between sensory and intellectual apperception; more generally the totality of human knowledge is addressed. Cf. also the combination of *yāḏa'* with *šāma'* and *bîn* (Isa. 40:21); *bîn, rā'â,* and *śāḵal* (Isa. 44:18); *rā'â* and *bîn* (Isa. 6:9); *rā'â, šāma', qāšaḇ,* and *bîn* (Isa. 32:3f.); *šāma', ḥāzâ, rā'â,* and *šûr* (Nu. 24:16f.); and finally Aram. *ḥ*^{a}*zâ* and *š*^{e}*ma'* (Dnl. 5:23).

b. *Subject.* The subject who knows must have the physical ability to apprehend. Eyes are needed (Dt. 29:3[4]), which must be able to see (*rā'â,* Isa. 44:18) and not be blind (*šā'â* or *š",* Isa. 32:3f.). They must be opened (*pāqaḥ,* Gen. 3:7; *š*^{e}*ṯum,* Nu. 24:13,15) and uncovered (→ גלה *gālâ* [*gālāh*], Nu. 24:16). Ears are needed (Dt. 29:3), which must be opened (*pāṯaḥ,* Isa. 48:8) and attentive (*qāšaḇ,* Isa. 32:3f.). A heart is needed (Dt. 29:3), which must be discerning (*śāḵal,* Isa. 44:18), not fat (*šāman,* Isa. 6:9f.) or rash (*nimhar,* Isa. 32:3f.). One must not sleep (*yāšēn,* Gen. 19:33,35; 1 S. 26:12), be drunk (*šaḵar,* Dt. 29:5[6]; cf. Gen. 19:33,35), or be blinded (*ṭaḥ,* Isa. 44:18). In his pain and suffering, Job does not see what is going on around him (Job 14:21).

c. *Heart.* In the epistemic realm, the heart (→ לב *lēḇ*) has many functions as an organ of perception and knowledge. Starting with outward perception, the *lēḇ* supports understanding and decision on the basis of what is perceived (cf. Ex. 7:23; 9:21; etc.).[162] As the seat of memory, the heart makes it possible to incorporate particular apperceptions into a larger realm of experience (cf. Dt. 4:9; Isa. 33:18; 65:17; etc.),[163]

---

161 K. Elliger, *Deuterojesaja II. BK,* XI/1 (1978), 168f.

162 For other citations see F. H. von Meyenfeldt, *Het Hart (LEB, LEBAB) in het OT* (Leiden, 1950), 142.

163 *Ibid.,* 143.

providing the basis for judgment and responsible action with respect to what is perceived (cf. Josh. 14:7).

In the heart, the various objects of perception become concentrated to form insight into the true nature of the world, on the basis of which people may consciously frame their lives (Dt. 8:5; Prov. 2:2; 8:5; 19:8; etc.). Here the foundations are laid for repentance and covenant loyalty.[164] Confronted with a multitude of heterogeneous perceptions, for example when dwelling among the Gentiles (Dt. 30:1), people should reflect and focus on true values (Dt. 4:39; Isa. 32:4; etc.).

d. *"Seeking" Knowledge.* It takes effort to gain specific knowledge. It must be "sought" (*biqqēš*, Eccl. 7:25; 8:17; Jer. 5:1; *dāraš*, Ps. 9:11[10]; *šā'al*, Jgs. 18:5 [with reference to an oracle]) or laboriously "searched out" (*tûr*, Eccl. 7:25) and "investigated" (piel of *šûṭ*, Jer. 5:1) until it is found (*māṣā'*, Job 23:10; 28:13; Prov. 8:9; Eccl. 8:17; Jer. 5:1). Thus knowledge is the result of systematic searching (*ḥāqar*, Ps. 139:1,23), trying (*bāḥan*, Job 23:10; Ps. 139:23; Jer. 6:27; 12:3), effort (*'āmal*, Eccl. 8:17), testing (piel of *nissâ*, Jgs. 3:4; with God as subj., Dt. 8:2; 13:4[3]; 2 Ch. 32:31), and judgment (*bāḥar mišpāṭ*, Job 34:4). All these passages show that *yd'* exhibits a wealth of implications that cannot be defined explicitly in either the sensate or noetic realm.

The object of knowledge and perception must be fundamentally perceptible, i.e., it must be within the grasp of the knowers: before them (*neged*, Ps. 51:5[3]; 69:20[19]), before their eyes (*'ēṯ*, Isa. 59:12), immediately with them (*'im*, with the connotation of a claim to possession, Job 15:9; Ps. 50:11), or near them (*qārab*, Isa. 5:19); only Yahweh can know from afar (Ps. 138:6; 139:2). It must not be hidden (*lō'-nikḥad min*, Ps. 69:6; Hos. 5:3), but must come (*bô'*, Isa. 5:19). The normal process of perception cannot deal with things that are great (*g^eḏōlôṯ*, Jer. 33:3), hidden (*sēṯer*, Isa. 29:15; Jer. 40:15; Dnl. 2:22; *b^eṣurôṯ*, Jer. 33:3; *n^eṣurôṯ*, Isa. 48:6), dark (*ḥōšeḵ*, Ps. 88:13[12]; Isa. 29:15; Dnl. 2:22), deep (*'^amîq*, Dnl. 2:22), or new (*ḥ^aḏāšôṯ*, Isa. 48:6).

Certain conditions are necessary for perception and knowledge to take place: the object must be near (*qārôḇ*, Isa. 33:13) or in the midst (*tôḵ*, Neh. 4:5[11]); otherwise one may approach it (*rûṣ*, Gen. 24:17,21; *nāgaš*, 1 S. 14:38) or rely on a witness (*'ēḏ*, Lev. 5:1; negatively, Isa. 44:9). In the underworld there is no possibility of knowledge (Ps. 88:13[12]).

Finally, several objects in tradition are made known through telling (*sāpar*, Ps. 78:3) or revelation (*gālâ*, 1 S. 3:7; hiphil of *yāḏa'* or *rā'â*, Ex. 6:3; Jer. 11:18; *nāgad*, Isa. 40:12).

e. *Historical Knowledge and Skill.* Ex. 1:8 speaks of a "new king over Egypt, who did not know Joseph" in the sense of historical knowledge. Cf. the Anakim in Dt. 9:2, whom Israel itself "knows." Cf. also *yd'* in the sense of acquaintance with someone living (Gen. 29:5; Dt. 22:2; Job 19:13; 29:16; 42:11; Ezk. 28:19). For the phrase "a nation which you do not know," see Dt. 28:33,36; Ruth 2:11; 2 S. 22:44; Isa. 55:5;

---

164 See also below.

Jer. 9:15(16); Zec. 7:14; cf. Ezk. 28:19. For the expression "a land which you do not know," see Jer. 15:14; 16:13; 17:4; 22:28; Ezk. 32:9.

For personal knowledge of what someone is like, see 2 K. 9:11: "You know the fellow and his talk." According to 2 S. 3:25, David "knows" Abner through unfortunate experience. Cf. also 1 S. 10:11; 1 K. 5:17(3); 18:37; Prov. 12:10; Cant. 6:12.

We find *yd'* with a noun or infinitive object also in the sense of skill or technical knowledge: *'îš yōḏēa' ṣayiḏ,* "a skillful hunter" (Gen. 25:27); the *'anšê 'ᵒnîyyôṯ* are *yōḏ'ê hayyām,* "sailors" (1 K. 9:27 par. 2 Ch. 8:18); cf. the one who is "skilled in what is written (*sēper*)" in Isa. 29:12 and the skillful lyre players in 1 S. 16:16,18, who know how to play the funeral lament (*nehî,* Am. 5:16). Cf. also *yd'* with *l* plus the infinitive: hewers of wood (1 K. 5:20[6]), architects (2 Ch. 2:6), craftspeople who work in gold, silver, bronze, and iron, as well as materials like crimson and purple cloth (2 Ch. 2:7). Finally, *yd'* can also refer to skill in speaking (Jer. 1:6), doing good (Jer. 4:22), and doing evil (Eccl. 4:17), etc.

f. *Emotional and Sexual Knowledge.* In addition to technical skill, *yd'* can also mean practical, emotional, and volitional "acquaintance" and "concern"; cf. *yd'* par. *pqd* (Job 5:24; 35:15); *yd'* par. *šmr* (Job 39:1; Jer. 8:7); *yd'* par. *mṣ' ḥēn* (Ex. 33:12,17); etc. Potiphar, for example, "had no concern" (*yāḏa'*) about anything in his house when Joseph was there (Gen. 39:6,8). Prov. 27:23 admonishes: "Know well (*yāḏōa' tēḏa'*) the condition of your flocks, and give attention (*šîṯ libbᵉḵā*) to your herds." Job "regards" (*yd'*) not himself and "loathes" (*m's*) his existence (Job 9:21; cf. also 35:15).

In the sense of "acquaintance" or "love," *yd'* then comes to mean sexual intercourse of a man with a woman (Gen. 4:1,17,25; 38:26; Jgs. 19:25; 1 S. 1:19; 1 K. 1:4) or a woman with a man (Gen. 19:8; Jgs. 11:39; cf. *yd' miškaḇ zāḵār* [Nu. 31:17f.,35; Jgs. 21:11f.]); for homosexual intercourse, see Gen. 19:5; Jgs. 19:22. The sexual reference has been explained as deriving from the unveiling of a woman on her wedding night[165] or first intercourse,[166] but these explanations are not convincing. More likely we are dealing with a euphemism for sexual relations.[167]

g. *(Tree of the) Knowledge of Good and Evil.* The knowledge of good and evil (*yd' bên-ṭôḇ wārā'*), i.e., the ability to distinguish between them, is beyond the capacities of immature children, because they cannot yet judge the consequences of what is involved (Dt. 1:39; 1 K. 3:7; Isa. 7:15f.; Jer. 4:22). Such knowledge is available to adults (1QSa 1:10f.), while the old man Barzillai questions it in himself (2 S. 19:36[35]). Solomon's prayer for "an understanding heart (*lēḇ šōmēa'*) to govern (*lišpōṭ*) the people and to discern between good and evil (*lᵉhāḇîn bên-ṭôḇ lᵉrā'*)" (1 K. 3:9) probably refers to the ability to judge and distinguish between justice and injustice (cf. 3:11).

The knowledge of the forbidden "tree of the knowledge of good and evil" (Gen. 2:9,17) and the godlike (*hāyâ kē'lōhîm,* Gen. 3:5; *hāyâ kᵉ'aḥaḏ mimmennû,* 3:22)

---

165 A. Socin.

166 K. Schwally, K. Budde.

167 Gaboriau, *Angelicum,* 45 (1968), 37-40; Schottroff, 691; cf. *AHw,* I, 188, and B. Landsberger, "Das 'gute Wort,' " *MAOG,* 4 (1928-29), 321.

knowledge that comes from eating its fruit have been interpreted variously, because of the wide semantic range of *ṭôḇ/rā‘*: those who interpret *ṭôḇ/rā‘* as "good/bad," "beneficial/harmful" in a functional or utilitarian sense, will also interpret *yd‘* in a value-free sense.[168] Budde,[169] on the other hand, interprets *yd‘ ṭôḇ wārā‘* as the ability to make ethical decisions. Buber[170] linked the ethical and functional aspects of "knowing good and evil": the ability to make a moral distinction between good and evil is intended to secure for us the power to live autonomously. By seeking to be like God, we impugn the authority of God; God "knows the opposites of being, . . . he has direct intercourse [*yd‘*] with them . . . he is above all opposites."[171] Similar interpretations have also been suggested by others.[172]

Many interpret *yd‘* as sexual knowledge and experience, knowledge of what it means to beget and bear children; this sexual knowledge of joy and suffering, life and death, had been forbidden because it makes human beings like God.[173] Many associate the serpent as a symbol of the Canaanite fertility cult with the "knowledge of good and evil."[174]

Besides these explanations, the interpretation of *ṭôḇ wārā‘* as expressing polar totality, "everything," is of interest.[175] According to von Rad, "knowledge of good and evil" means "omniscience in the broadest sense of the word"; according to Pidoux, the fruit of the tree of the knowledge of good and evil would convey "a power that would be godlike . . . the power that is one of the characteristics of the deity."[176]

h. *Wisdom*. In the OT, *ḥoḵmâ* (wisdom) refers to more than the wisdom of Israel; this can be seen in its frequent association with other closely related concepts.[177] In Proverbs, for example, *da‘aṯ* (40 occurrences) and *ḥoḵmâ* (39 occurrences), which can be used interchangeably,[178] take up substantial space. In "almost playful coordination"[179] we find *m^e^zimmâ*, "discretion" (Prov. 1:4; 2:10f.; 5:2; 8:12), *t^e^ḇûnâ*, "under-

---

[168] Cf. J. Wellhausen, *Die Composition des Hexateuchs und der historischen Bücher des ATs* (Berlin, [3]1899).

[169] K. Budde, *Die biblische Urgeschichte* (Giessen, 1883), 65-72.

[170] M. Buber, *Images of Good and Evil* (Eng. trans., New York, 1952), 13-26.

[171] *Ibid.*, 20.

[172] Stoebe, de Vaux; cf. also W. M. Clark, "A Legal Background to the Yahwist's Use of the 'Good and Evil' in Genesis 2–3," *JBL*, 88 (1969), 266-278.

[173] H. Schmidt, *Die Erzählung von Paradies und Sündenfall* (Tübingen, 1931), 13-31; I. Engnell, " 'Knowledge' and 'Life' in the Creation Story," *Wisdom in Israel and in the Ancient Near East. Festschrift H. H. Rowley. SVT*, 3 (1955), 103-119; L. F. Hartmann, "Sin in Paradise," *CBQ*, 20 (1958), 26-40; etc.

[174] Coppens, Hidding, Loretz, Soggin, etc.

[175] A. M. Honeyman, "*Merismus* in Biblical Hebrew," *JBL*, 71 (1952), 11-18; P. P. Boccaccio, "I termini contrari come espressioni della totalità in ebraico," *Bibl*, 33 (1952), 173-190; D. R. Hillers, "An Alphabetic Cuneiform Tablet from Taanach (TT 433)," *BASOR*, 173 (1964), 46f.; etc.

[176] P. 41.

[177] G. von Rad, *Wisdom in Israel* (Eng. trans., Nashville, 1972), 75.

[178] J. Becker, *Gottesfurcht im AT. AnBibl*, 25 (1965), 214.

[179] Von Rad, *Wisdom in Israel*, 53.

standing" (2:6,10f.; 17:27; 24:3f.), *'ᵒrmâ*, "prudence" (1:4; 8:12), and *bînâ* (9:10), frequently in parallelism with *ḥoḵmâ* (1:7; 2:6,10; 8:12; 9:10; 14:6; 24:3f.; 30:3).

Two different understandings of *da'aṯ* can be traced back to an earlier (Prov. 10–29) and a later (Prov. 1–9) corpus of proverbs. In the earlier view, *da'aṯ* refers to the secular realm, especially interpersonal relationships. This is illustrated by the frequent antithetical parallelism of sage and fool: *da'aṯ* is what characterizes the wise (*ḥᵃḵāmîm*, Prov. 10:14; 15:2,7), the righteous (*ṣaddîqîm*, 11:9; 29:7), the prudent (*'ārûm*, 13:16; cf. 14:8), and those with understanding (*nāḇôn*, 14:6; 15:14; 18:15); nothing is said about its source.

Those who are wise lay up (*ṣāpan*, Prov. 10:14) or conceal (*kāsâ*, 12:23) their *da'aṯ*. While scoffers seek *ḥoḵmâ* in vain, *da'aṯ* is easy for those of understanding (14:6); while the simple acquire folly, the prudent are crowned (*krt* [?] with *da'aṯ* (14:18).[180] Heart and ear seek (*biqqēš*, 15:14; 18:15) *da'aṯ*, the tongue and lips of the wise dispense (*taṭṭîp*, 15:2) and spread (*zārâ*, 15:2,7) *da'aṯ*. Those who love "discipline" (*mûsār*) or "instruction" love *da'aṯ* (12:1; cf. 19:27; 23:12). When those of understanding are reproved, they gain *da'aṯ* (19:25; cf. 12:1); when they are instructed, they receive *da'aṯ* (21:11; cf. Dnl. 1:4). They exhibit *da'aṯ* and *tᵉḇûnâ* by being restrained in speech and cool in spirit (Prov. 17:27). We find a sense of processes obeying their own inner laws.

The later section of the book of Proverbs appears to be the product of more theological reflections. Here Yahweh gives *ḥoḵmâ;* from his mouth come *da'aṯ* and *tᵉḇûnâ* (Prov. 2:6). He is an aid to the upright (2:7); those who receive and accept this aid gain *ḥoḵmâ* and *da'aṯ* (2:10). Through the *ḥoḵmâ* and *da'aṯ* of Yahweh the earth and the heavens were founded and developed (3:19f.).

Knowledge is not given to human beings by nature;[181] Yahweh himself and the "divine authority of wisdom"[182] cooperate to produce *da'at.* The corresponding statement from the human perspective is that the fear of Yahweh is the beginning of wisdom (*yir'aṯ YHWH rē'šîṯ dā'aṯ,* Prov. 1:7). The relationship between *yir'aṯ YHWH* and *da'aṯ* is clear from the parallels: *da'aṯ* par. *ḥoḵmâ, yir'aṯ YHWH* par. *rē'šîṯ da'aṯ* (Prov. 1:7); *yir'aṯ YHWH* par. *da'aṯ* (1:29); *da'aṯ 'ᵉlōhîm* par. *ḥoḵmâ, tᵉḇûnâ, bînâ,* and *da'aṯ* (2:5f.); *da'aṯ qᵉḏōšîm* par. *bînâ* and the *tᵉḥillâ* of *ḥoḵmâ* (9:10). The concepts cannot be sharply distinguished, but they should probably be understood as different aspects of a fundamental religious attitude referring ultimately to the same reality (cf. esp. 2:5; 9:10).[183]

It is characteristic of Proverbs to use fear of Yahweh and knowledge of God synonymously (*da'aṯ, da'aṯ 'ᵉlōhîm,* and *da'aṯ qᵉḏōšîm* being ultimately identical[184]), esp. in Prov. 2:5 (cf. 1:29; 9:10). As the gift of wisdom, *da'aṯ* par. *yir'aṯ YHWH* conveys the meaning of (true) religion, if *yir'aṯ YHWH* is understood as reverential awe, finding expression in uprightness and devotion, and *da'aṯ* means acquaintance with God and

---

180 Cf. W. A. van der Weiden, *Le livre des Proverbs. BietOr,* 23 (1970), 110: "acquérir, acheter."

181 Von Rad, *Wisdom in Israel,* 55.

182 B. Lang, *Frau Weisheit: Deutung einer biblischen Gestalt* (Düsseldorf, 1975), 171.

183 Cf. Becker, *Gottesfurcht im AT,* 220.

184 *Ibid.*, 217f.

walking in his ways (cf. Isa. 11:2). Not only does Yahweh give wisdom; from him come knowledge and understanding (Prov. 2:6). He is a shield and protection (Prov. 2:7f.) for those who trust in him (3:5).

While for the most part Proverbs speaks positively of knowledge, Ecclesiastes exhibits a pessimistic attitude toward *da'aṯ*. Although *ḥoḵmâ* and *da'aṯ* (7 occurrences) reinforce each other,[185] they ultimately convey no benefit (Eccl. 1:16-18). Similarly, *ḥoḵmâ* and *da'aṯ*, which are given by God's free will (2:26), are only of relative advantage in comparison to folly and riches (2:21; 7:11f.), for in the realm of the dead there is neither *ḥoḵmâ* nor *da'aṯ* (9:10).

In Sirach, *yāḏa'* occurs 29 times and *da'aṯ* 9 times, but the text of Sir. 7:3,20; 9:10; 46:6,10; 51:15 is uncertain. In any case, Sirach prefers *ḥkm* and *byn* and their derivatives. In Sirach, *śkl, yd', ḥšb* and their derivatives refer almost without exception to human knowledge and wisdom.[186] Wisdom and knowledge are characteristic of the physician (Sir. 38:3), the sage, and the scribe (37:22f.). Perhaps the author is drawing on the Greek idea of the *lógos* when he states that the "word" is the place where wisdom is revealed (*yd'*, pass.; 4:24; cf. 5:10).

Most of the occurrences of *yāḏa'* are in the context of "wisdom concerning secular matters,"[187] which formulates the results of experience in every conceivable situation. According to Sir. 40:29, the knowledgeable (*yôḏēa'*) and well-educated (*ysr*) are characterized by caution in their dealings with others and a refusal to jump to conclusions. They take counsel only with those who keep the Torah (37:12) and are incorruptible (37:8); they are marked by their reserve (35:8).

In the variety of his counsels, the author is especially concerned for people's well-being. To intensify his admonitions he occasionally uses the impv. *da'*, "know." He warns against envy (Sir. 34:13) and the violent (9:13), and clearly echoing the law of love (Dt. 6:5; Lev. 19:18) he exhorts his readers to love their neighbors as themselves (Sir. 34:15). He warns against hedonism (11:19), gullibility (8:18; cf. 12:11), and premature judgment (9:11; cf. 34:24), basing his cautions on the human inability to predict the course of events.

Sirach often looks to sacred history to illustrate God's wisdom in history and his pedagogical governance of human affairs. He made the water in the desert drinkable (Sir. 38:5; cf. Ex. 15:23f.), hardened the heart of Pharaoh (Sir. 16:15; cf. Ex. 7:3), caused David to fell mighty Goliath (Sir. 47:5; cf. 1 S. 17:40ff.), and made Enoch (Sir. 44:16; Gen. 5:24) an example of repentance (LXX), of conversion of the nations (Latin), of *da'aṯ* (Hebrew, possibly a reference to Enoch's role in revelation).

Sirach also uses the recognition formula, in Sir. 36:17(22) as an element supporting a prayer,[188] in 36:5 in a double form: ". . . that they [the Gentiles] may know, as we have known, that there is no God except thee."

For Sirach, God possesses all knowledge (Sir. 1:1); he discerns all cognition (42:18).

---

185 A. Lauha, *Kohelet. BK*, XIX (1978), 47.

186 J. Marböck, *Weisheit im Wandel. BBB*, 37 (1971), 14f.

187 *Ibid.*, 126f.

188 See the Northwest Semitic parallels in T. Penar, *Northwest Semitic Philology and the Hebrew Fragments of Ben Sira. BietOr*, 28 (1975), 60.

God can also perceive the secret sins (16:17,21); from him nothing is hidden (17:15-20),[189] for the entire created order is his work.

2. *Religious Usage.*

a. *God's Knowledge.* We find *yd'* in Am. 3:2 as an expression for the special relationship between Yahweh and Israel or election to service: "You only have I chosen from all the families of the earth." Despite the Deuteronomistic language, Am. 3:2 does not use the election term *bḥr* (cf. Dt. 7:7; 14:2), but rather the ambivalent term *yd'* for the special association of Yahweh with Israel or with individual leaders.[190] According to Gen. 18:19; Ex. 33:12,17; Dt. 34:10; 2 S. 7:20 par. 1 Ch. 17:18; Jer. 1:5, Yahweh entered into a special relationship of selection and election with Abraham, Moses, Jeremiah, and David. Yahweh chose Abraham, to "charge his children . . . to keep the way of Yahweh by doing righteousness and justice" (Gen. 18:18f.). In Ex. 33:12,17, Yahweh says to Moses, "I know you by name (*yd' b^ešēm*), and you have found favor (*mṣ' ḥēn*)"; *yd' bešēm* par. *mṣ' ḥēn* characterize the special election (and call); cf. also Dt. 34:10. Cf. the verbs *lqḥ* par. *bḥr* par. *yd'* for the gracious election of David in 2 S. 7:20 par. 1 Ch. 17:18. In Jer. 1:5, the appointment of Jeremiah to prophetic office is characterized by *yd'* par. *qdš* hiphil; long before his birth (*yṣ'* par. *yṣr*), Jeremiah had been chosen as a prophet (*yd'* par. *qdš* hiphil par. *nāḇî' n^eṯattîḵā*).

Huffmon[191] seeks to connect *yāḏa'* with Hitt. *šek/šak,* Akk. *idû,* Ugar. *yd'* in Near Eastern treaties and interpret OT *yd'* as a term for mutual recognition.[192]

On rare occasions we find *yd'* as a term for Yahweh's "care" or "protection." In Nah. 1:7f., for example, in the context of a hymn, we read: "Yahweh is good, a stronghold in the day of trouble; he knows those who take refuge in him." Yahweh answers trust with care and benevolence; see, for example, Ps. 1:6; 31:8(7); 37:18; 144:3.

In the Song of Hannah (1 S. 2:1-10) we find this theologoumenon: "A God of knowledge (*'ēl dē'ôṯ* [pl. intensitatis? or 'perceptions'?]) is Yahweh, a God who weighs actions (*w^e'ēl tôḵēn* [emended] *'^alîlôṯ*)" (v. 3). Yahweh is a God who knows (*yd'*), who tests and judges (*tkn*); *yd'* means "know well," "test," "weigh," "judge"; cf. Ps. 94:11, "Yahweh knows the thoughts of man"; Job 23:10; Prov. 24:12. In a declaration of innocence, the worshipper says: "If we had . . . spread forth our hands to a strange god, would not God discover (*ḥqr*) this? For he knows (*yd'*) the secrets of the heart" (Ps. 44:21f.[20f.]; cf. Job 31:6; Ps. 40:10[9]; Jer. 12:3), and in a confession of sin: "Let not thy anger burn hot, Yahweh; thou knowest thy people, that they are set on evil" (Ex. 32:22; cf. Ps. 69:6[5]). In a statement of confidence, the worshipper prays:

---

[189] Cf. Marböck, 136.

[190] See, for example, Botterweck, *"Gott erkennen,"* 18-22; T. Vriezen, *Die Erwählung Israels nach dem AT. AThANT,* 24 (1953), 36f.; H. Wildberger, *Jahwes Eigentumsvolk. AThANT,* 37 (1960), 108.

[191] *BASOR,* 181 (1966), 37.

[192] Cf. also Huffmon-Parker; McKenzie.

"Search (*ḥqr*) me . . . and know (*yd'*) my heart, try (*bḥn*) me, know (*yd'*) my thoughts, and see (*r'h*) if there be any wicked way in me" (Ps. 139:23f.; cf. vv. 1f.,4). In Yahweh's knowing, testing, and judging, the devout see the occasion of divine intervention (Ps. 69:20[19]; Jer. 15:15; 18:23; cf. Neh. 9:10). On the pair *yd'* par. *nsh* piel, cf. Dt. 13:4(3): "For Yahweh your God is testing (*nsh;* piel) you, to know whether you love Yahweh . . ."; cf. also Dt. 8:2; Jgs. 3:4; and 2 Ch. 32:31: "God left him [Hezekiah] to himself, in order to try him (*lᵉnassôṯô*) and to know (*lāḏaʿaṯ*) all that was in his heart." In some passages, Yahweh answers in a dream: "I know that you [Abraham] have done this in the integrity of your heart" (Gen. 20:6; cf. also 2 K. 19:27 par. Isa. 37:28; 48:4; Jer. 48:30; Ezk. 11:5; Am. 5:12).

b. *Knowledge of God.* "To know Yahweh" refers to a practical, religio-ethical relationship. Yahweh will deliver (*plṭ;* piel) and protect (*śgb;* piel) those who know (*yd'*) his name and cleave (*ḥšq*) to him (Ps. 91:14). Cf. the parallelism *lō' yd'* par. *qr' bᵉšēm* (Ps. 79:6; Jer. 10:25). All who are upright of heart (*yišrê-lēḇ*) know him (Ps. 36:11[10]). Only those who are prepared to refrain (*rph;* hiphil) from idolatry and sin know God. Cf. *yd'* par. *drš,* "seek" (Ps. 9:11[10]), *yd'* par. *yr'* (1 K. 8:43; 2 Ch. 6:33; Ps. 119:79; Prov. 1:7; 2:5; 3:6; Isa. 11:2). Those who "know" (*yd'*) Yahweh in all their ways (Prov. 3:6), i.e., "trust" (*bᵉṭaḥ*) in him with all their heart (v. 5a), "fear" (*yᵉrā'*) him, and turn away from evil (*sûr mērā'*) (v. 7) will find their paths made straight. Cf. *yd'* par. *'bd* (1 Ch. 28:9), *yd'* par. *'mn* hiphil (Isa. 43:10), *yd'* par. *drš* (Ps. 9:11[10]).

c. *Ignorance of God.* "Not to know Yahweh" appears in combination with parallel verbs as a way of expressing apostasy and religio-ethical decline. Those who do not know Yahweh "sin" (*ḥāṭā'*) against him (1 S. 2:25), they are "ungodly" (*'awwāl*) (Job 18:21), they "swear, lie, kill, steal, and commit adultery" (Hos. 4:1f.), they are treacherous adulterers (Jer. 9:1[2]), they "deceive" (v. 2[3]) and "slander" (v. 3[4]). Whole series of sins stand in parallel with *lō' yd'*. The expression *lō' yd'* stands for the "rebellion" (*pš'*) of those who "forsake" (*'zb*) Yahweh (Isa. 1:4; Hos. 4:10), "forget" (*škḥ*) him (Hos. 4:6), "despise" (*n'ṣ;* piel) him (Isa. 1:4), or "disregard" (*bûz*) him (1 S. 2:12,30); cf. "play the harlot" (*znh,* Hos. 2:7[5]), "prophesy by Ba'al" (Jer. 2:8).

As an expression of religious inexperience due to the absence of previous revelation or encounter, Samuel did not yet "know" (*yd'*) or recognize the voice of Yahweh; "a revelation of Yahweh had not yet come to him (*ṭerem yiggāleh 'ēlāyw*)" (1 S. 3:7). Only after his dream vision at Bethel did Jacob "know" that Yahweh was in the place, so that he was afraid (Gen. 28:16). Cf. also Jgs. 13:6. The new settlers in conquered Samaria do not "know" the cult of the local deity and need to be instructed.[193]

The Gentiles do not "know" Yahweh; they are unwilling to "hear his voice" (Ex. 5:2) or "call upon his name" (Ps. 79:6; Jer. 10:25) and worship him. They have no relationship to him.

---

[193] Cf. Baumann, *ZAW,* 28 (1908), 39-41, 110-141; Botterweck, *"Gott erkennen,"* 42-98; Denton, 34-41; Schottroff, 694f.

The expression "not know other gods" refers to the absence of any relationship between Israel and the gods of foreign nations. They have never revealed themselves to Israel in word or deed; Israel has nothing to do with them (Dt. 11:28; 13:3,7, 14[2,6,13]; 28:64; 29:25[26]; 32:17; cf. also Jer. 7:9; 19:4; 44:3; Dnl. 11:38).

3. *Revelation.*

a. *Terminology.* Hebrew expresses the notion of revelation by means of the roots *glh,* "uncover"; *ngd* hiphil, "report"; *yd'* hiphil, "make known," niphal, "make oneself known"; *r'h* niphal, "be seen, appear." There are also *dbr* piel, *'mr, šm',* etc. There is theological significance in the varying terminology of Ex. 6:3: "I appeared (*wā'ērā'*) to Abraham, to Isaac, and to Jacob as *'ēl šadday,* but by my name Yahweh I did not make myself known to them (*lō' nôḏā'tî lāhem*)." P assigns the "appearance of Yahweh" to a preliminary stage of the patriarchal religion; with Moses there begins something new: Yahweh makes himself known in person, as *'ᵃnî YHWH.* Moses is to begin his speech with *'ᵃnî YHWH* (v. 6) and emphasize its conclusion with *'ᵃnî YHWH* (v. 8).[194]

b. *History, Salvation Oracle (?), Torah (?).* Revelation (*yd';* hiphil or niphal) is involved when Yahweh makes his name known in historical demonstrations of power (Ps. 76:2[1]; Isa. 64:1f.[2f.]; Jer. 16:21; Ezk. 39:7). Cf. Yahweh's revelation of himself in such hymnic statements as Ps. 9:17(16); 48:4(3); 77:15,20 (14,19); 79:10; 88:13 (12); 103:7. The revelation often conveys specific information from Yahweh: he reveals the new king to Samuel (1 S. 16:3) and the duration of the Davidic dynasty to Nathan (2 S. 7:21 par. 1 Ch. 17:19). Cf. also the announcement of the commandments in Ex. 25:22; Ezk. 20:11; also Gen. 41:39; Neh. 9:14; Jer. 11:18.

In Ps. 25:4, the worshipper, oppressed by his enemies, prays, "Make known to me (*hôḏî'ēnî*), Yahweh, thy ways, thy paths teach me (*lammᵉḏēnî*)." In Ps. 39:5(4), he prays to know (*yd';* hiphil) his end, that he may know (*yd'*) how mortal he is. According to 51:8(6), insight into sinfulness is not the result of human thought but a gift of divine communication (*yd';* hiphil). Cf. the prayer of the community to Yahweh in 90:12: "Teach us (*yd';* hiphil) to number our days that we may get a heart of wisdom (*lᵉḇāḇ ḥoḵmâ*)" and v. 16: "Let thy work be manifest (*r'h;* hiphil) to thy servants." The oppressed psalmist in 143:8 prays: "Let me hear (*šm';* hiphil) . . . thy steadfast love. . . . Teach (*yd';* hiphil) me the way I should go." Cf. also the expressions of confidence in Ps. 16:11; 25:14.

It is possible that this communication or instruction (*yd';* hiphil) should be thought of as involving a salvation oracle or Torah instruction.[195] In the case of Torah instruc-

---

[194] Cf. R. Rendtorff, "The Concept of Revelation in Ancient Israel," in *Revelation as History,* ed. W. Pannenberg (Eng. trans., New York, 1968), 30.

[195] H. Gunkel and J. Begrich, *Einl. in die Psalmen. GHK,* sup. vol. (⁹1975), 224; Begrich, "Das priesterliche Heilsorakel," *ZAW,* 52 (1934), 81-92 = *GSAT. ThB,* 21 (1964), 217-231; H.-J. Kraus, *Psalmen. BK,* XV/1-3 (⁵1978).

tion, one might recall with Robert[196] and Deissler[197] that "way" and "path" are often used as synonyms for "law."

c. *yd' kî 'ᵃnî YHWH.* Corresponding to the use of *yd'* niphal, "make oneself known," and *yd'* hiphil, "make known," as terms of the divine self-revelation, we find the recognition statement *yd' kî 'ᵃnî YHWH,* usually preceding a statement about God's action. In the prophetic oracle of divine self-demonstration,[198] *yd' kî 'ᵃnî YHWH* constitutes the end and purpose of the oracle, while the divine message *ntn bᵉyāḏ* as a probative sign is subordinate to the self-introduction of Yahweh that is to be demonstrated.[199] These recognition statements surely belong neither to the realm of priestly *da'aṯ* nor to the realm of wisdom *da'aṯ.* The recognition statement has its roots in crucial symbolic events, in the traditions of the exodus or the wars of Yahweh, and in apodictic legislation (Ex. 6:2ff.; Ezk. 20:5ff.; cf. Ex. 29:46; Lev. 22:32f.; Nu. 15:41).

The question of how revelation and history are related points ultimately to whether an event could be recognized as an act of Yahweh only "when preceded immediately by a declarative word of Yahweh."[200] According to Rendtorff, "A third party is not necessary, . . . a mediator between the event and the one who experiences it. . . . The event itself can and must effect recognition and knowledge of Yahweh in the one who sees it and understands it in its context as an act of Yahweh."[201] According to Zimmerli, however, "history is only ancillary to Yahweh's self-demonstration, for the 'I am Yahweh' addressed to the listener is the real focus."[202] History "does not conceal within itself a hidden meaning that we could approach through the power of human interpretation. But God, by appointing someone to proclaim the name of Yahweh over this event, can cause history to address people personally."[203] In the case of a revelatory event, Rendtorff focuses more on the significance of the act, whereas Zimmerli emphasizes the significance of the word.

The expression *yd' kî 'ᵃnî YHWH,* "and you will/shall know that I am Yahweh," which has its setting in prophetic speech, is more or less fixed and formulaic; it is almost always preceded by a statement about an act of Yahweh. Often the recognition statement constitutes the climax; occasionally there follows a more detailed motivation or a summary conclusion. Of the 947 occurrences of *yd'* as a verb, the short form *yd' kî 'ᵃnî YHWH* with minor variations occurs 71 times in Ezekiel alone.[204]

---

196 A. Robert, "Le sens du mot Loi dans le Ps. CXIX (Vulg. CXVIII)," *RB,* 46 (1937), 182-206.

197 A. Deissler, *Psalm 119 (118) und seine Theologie. MThS,* 1/11 (1955), 71.

198 Zimmerli, *ThB,* 19 (1963), 120-132.

199 *Ibid.,* 124.

200 R. Rendtorff, "Geschichte und Wort im AT," *EvTh,* 22 (1962), 621-649; repr. in *GSAT. ThB,* 57 (1975), 60-88.

201 Rendtorff, *Revelation as History,* 47.

202 W. Zimmerli, " 'Offenbarung im AT,' " *EvTh,* 22 (1962), 30.

203 *Ibid.,* 28f.

204 See the concordances of Mandelkern and Lisowsky, as well as Botterweck, *"Gott erkennen,"* 14-17, and Zimmerli, *I Am Yahweh.*

The expression can be further defined by an adverbial phrase consisting of b^e plus the infinitive: ". . . know that I am Yahweh, when their slain lay among their idols . . ." (Ezk. 6:13; 12:15; 15:7; 20:42,44; 25:17; 28:22; 30:8; 33:29; 34:27; 35:12; 36:23; 37:13). Also common is a statement of purpose with *l^ema'an*, e.g., Ezk. 16:62f.: ". . . and you shall know that I am Yahweh, that you may remember and be confounded, and never open your mouth again." Outside of Ezekiel, a statement of purpose also appears in Ex. 7:5,17; 8:18(22); 14:4,18; 31:13; 1 K. 20:13,28; Ps. 46:11(10); Jer. 24:7. In addition to the interpolation "your God" into the recognition statement, we also find *'^elōhîm* with the emphatic article, as in Dt. 4:35,39; 7:9; 1 K. 8:60; 2 Ch. 33:13; etc.; cf. also 1 K. 18:37; 2 K. 19:19; Isa. 37:20; Sir. 36:5; Ps. 83:19(18): ". . . know that thou alone . . . art the Most High over all the earth." Occasionally the objective clause *kî '^anî YHWH* is expanded by means of a relative clause: ". . . know that I am Yahweh, who sanctify Israel when my sanctuary is in the midst of them for evermore" (Ezk. 37:28; cf. Isa. 43:10; 45:3; 49:23,26; 52:6). Only in Ezekiel do we find the expression ". . . know that I, Yahweh, do . . ." (Ezk. 5:13; 14:23; 17:21,24; 22:22; 36:36; 37:14). Often the object clause with *yd'* states Yahweh's action, e.g., "that Yahweh sent me" (Nu. 16:28; Zec. 2:13,15(9,11); 4:9; 6:15.[205] Elsewhere in the object clause it is Yahweh's word that is known: 2 K. 10:10; Isa. 9:8(9); Jer. 32:8; 44:28f.; Zec. 11:11. We also find Yahweh's name (Jer. 16:21), his hand (Josh. 4:24; 1 S. 6:3); his judgments (Ps. 119:75), and his mercy (Jon. 4:2).

d. *Signs, Wonders, the Exodus*. The recognition statement in the context of crucial symbolic events is especially clear in the traditions of the exodus and the plagues. In the plague of flies (Ex. 8:18[22] [J]), the symbolic nature of the divine act is obvious when at Yahweh's behest Moses says to Pharaoh: "On that day I will set apart the land of Goshen . . . so that no swarms of flies shall be there; that you may know that I am Yahweh in the midst of the land. . . . This sign (*'ôṯ*) shall take place tomorrow" (8:18,19b[22,23b]). The threat to slay the first-born states: ". . . not a dog shall growl; that you may know that Yahweh makes a distinction between the Egyptians and Israel" (Ex. 11:7). Yahweh's actions effectively compel recognition, acknowledgment, confession, and gratitude. According to Ex. 8:6(10), the end of the plague is to be a demonstration to Pharaoh, so that he may know "that there is no one like Yahweh our God." The cessation of the hail causes Pharaoh to know "that the earth is Yahweh's" (Ex. 9:29); similarly, the pollution of the Nile (Ex. 7:17 [J]) is to be for Pharaoh and the Egyptians a sign of divine self-demonstration and a source of painful surprise and knowledge.

Signs (*'ôṯ*), wonders (*môpēṯ*), trials (*massōṯ*), and terrors (*môrā'îm*) (Dt. 4:34f.) evoke recognition and knowledge; their strangeness and their unexpected appearance in the midst of everyday life are a cause of spontaneous recognition. The most frequent function of an *'ôṯ* is to evoke the knowledge "that I am Yahweh." This formula of recognition[206] or majesty[207] appears first in the Yahwist, and is intended to promote

---

[205] Additional citations in Botterweck, *"Gott erkennen,"* 16.
[206] Rendtorff.
[207] Elliger.

the sovereignty of the one God Yahweh in the cosmopolitan kingdom of David and Solomon (Ex. 8:18[22]ff.; 10:2f.).[208] From this starting point the functional schema then penetrates later literature. Such signs (*'ôṯōṯ*) include—besides the Egyptian plagues—victory over enemies (1 K. 20:13), the Sabbath (Ex. 31:13; Ezk. 20:12), and the elimination of idolators (Ezk. 14:8). Occasionally the monotheistic purpose of the recognition formula is made even more pointed: all the *massōṯ, 'ôṯōṯ, môp̄eṯîm,* and *môrā'îm* of the exodus are to lead to the knowledge that there is no God but Yahweh (Dt. 4:34f.); in the contest on Mt. Carmel, the sacrificial fire is to demonstrate that Yahweh is God rather than the baals (1 K. 18:37).

In Ex. 6:2-12 (P), a revelation discourse, Israel is to "know that I am Yahweh your God, who has brought you out from under the burdens of the Egyptians" (v. 7). By the realization of the promises to the patriarchs, but above all by the deliverance (*yṣ'* hiphil, *nṣl* hiphil, *g'l*) from Egypt, the Israelites are to recognize and know that Yahweh is among them and makes himself known in power. Even "the Egyptians shall know that I am Yahweh, when I stretch forth my hand upon Egypt and bring out the people of Israel from among them" (7:5). For the Egyptians this knowledge is a painful and helpless surprise. By the miracle at the sea, "the Egyptians shall know that I am Yahweh, when I have gotten glory (*behikkāḇeḏî*)" (14:18; cf. the similar statement in 14:4).

In the manna tradition of Ex. 16, the murmuring Israelites are assured: "At evening you shall know (*yd'*) that it was Yahweh who brought you out of the land of Egypt, and in the morning you shall see (*r'h*) the glory of Yahweh, because he has heard your murmurings" (vv. 6f.; cf. also v. 12). According to Ex. 29:45f., Yahweh "will dwell among the people of Israel and will be their God. And they shall know that I am Yahweh their God, who brought them forth . . . that I might dwell among them. I am Yahweh their God." Here the recognition statement is expanded by the Egypt motif. By observing the Sabbath as a sign between God and the people, "you may know that I am Yahweh, who sanctify you" (Ex. 31:13), i.e., separate you from the nations.

In the supplement dealing with the Feast of Booths (Lev. 23:39-43), the instructions to Moses concerning dwelling in booths are given historical motivation: "That your generations may know that I made the people of Israel dwell in booths when I brought them out of the land of Egypt; I am Yahweh your God" (v. 43); here Israel is to be reminded of the beginnings of its national existence in the Mosaic period. According to Nu. 14:34 (secondary), the present generation will not enter the promised land because of their lack of trust in God's guidance; only their children shall share in the gift of the land after forty years of penance (God's judgment).

The recognition statements in P are based on God's acts in the exodus and deliverance from Egypt (Ex. 6:7; 7:5), in the miracle at the sea (14:4,8), and in the feeding with quails and manna (16:6f.,12). The tent of meeting (Ex. 29:45f.), observance of the Sabbath (Ex. 31:13), and dwelling in booths during the Feast of Booths (Lev. 23:43) are signs reminding the community of its beginnings.

---

208 For a criticism of the early dating, see H. H. Schmid, *Der sogenannte Jahwist* (Zurich, 1976).

e. *Parenesis in Deuteronomy and the Deuteronomistic History.* In Deuteronomy and in the Deuteronomic history in its various recensions the recognition statement has undergone parenetic transformation. In the sermonic passage Dt. 7:1-11, a hymnically expanded recognition statement (v. 9) constitutes the conclusion to a parenetic series of commandments and prohibitions: "Know therefore that Yahweh your God is God, the faithful God who keeps covenant and steadfast love with those who love him and keep his commandments." Cf. in the parenesis Dt. 11:2-32 the assurance, "Your eyes have seen all the great work of Yahweh which he did" (v. 7). In Dt. 4:32-40, Israel is called on to ask "whether such a great thing as this has ever happened or was ever heard of" (v. 32); then in broad strokes are listed the signs and wonders that "Yahweh your God did for you in Egypt before your eyes" (v. 34b). The purpose of these signs and deeds experienced by the Israelites is given in a recognition statement (v. 35): "To you it was shown, that you might know that Yahweh is God: there is no other besides him." Cf. also Dt. 4:39: "Know therefore (*w^eyāḏa'tā*) this day, and lay it to your heart (*wa^hašēḇōṯā*), that Yahweh is God." To "know Yahweh" means to "lay it to one's heart," to hear and obey the divine commandments.

Despite the signs and wonders before Pharaoh, Yahweh has to this day not given his people "a heart to understand (*lēḇ lā^eḏa'aṯ*), or eyes to see (*'ênayim lir'ôṯ*), or ears to hear (*'oznayim lišmōa'*)" (Dt. 29:3-5[4-6]).

The expression "know that Yahweh is God" appears in the Deuteronomistic history to emphasize the uniqueness of Yahweh or his name. Solomon, for instance, prays that Yahweh will maintain the cause of Israel "that all the peoples of the earth may know (*l^ema'an da'aṯ kol-'ammê*) that Yahweh is God; there is no other" (1 K. 8:60). Hezekiah, too, when faced with the threat from Sennacherib, prays to Yahweh for deliverance, "that all the kingdoms of the earth may know that thou, Yahweh, art God alone" (2 K. 19:19 par. Isa. 37:20; cf. 2 Chr. 6:33). Cf. also Solomon's prayer for the foreigner: "Hear thou in heaven . . . that all the peoples of the earth may know (*l^ema'an yēḏ^e'ûn*) thy name and fear (*l^eyir'â*) thee . . . and that they may know (*w^e-lāḏa'aṯ*) that this house . . . is called by thy name" (1 K. 8:43 par. 2 Ch. 6:33). The deeds of Yahweh and Yahweh's response to prayer in the temple bring the foreigner to fear of God, knowledge and confession of Yahweh, who can be called upon by name.

f. *Prophetic Demonstration.* The recognition statement *yāḏa' kî 'anî YHWH* is especially common in prophetic utterances, often constituting their climax; it is usually preceded by a statement about God's acts. Zimmerli[209] sees in the two prophetic utterances in 1 K. 20:13,18 a form of the divine statement two to three centuries earlier than that found in Ezekiel, on the grounds of the "almost classic economy of their diction," "their theology of optimistic North Israelite nationalism," and the ideology of the holy war that they reflect. At the center of each oracle stands a prediction that God will intervene in Ahab's battle with Ben-hadad: "Behold, I will

[209] Zimmerli, *I Am Yahweh.*

give it into your hand this day (*hin^enî nōṯ^enô b^eyāḏ^eḵā hayyôm*); and you shall know (*w^eyāḏaʿtā*) that I am Yahweh" (v. 13).

By intervening against the Arameans and delivering them into the hand of Judah, Yahweh seeks to demonstrate to his people as well as to the Gentiles that it is he who says, "I am Yahweh" (1 K. 20:28). In 1957, Zimmerli[210] proposed the term "prophetic utterance of divine self-demonstration," in brief "demonstration utterance," for the messenger saying expanded by the inclusion of a recognition statement. In this originally tripartite "demonstration utterance," the recognition of the divine self-demonstration (*yāḏaʿtā kî ʾ^anî YHWH*) constituted the climax and goal of the prophetical utterance, while the oracle promising that God would give the enemy into Judah's power (*nāṯattî b^eyāḏ^eḵā*) plays a subordinate role as a sign of the self-introduction of Yahweh that is to be demonstrated.[211]

The phrase *ntn b^eyāḏ*,[212] often termed a "formula of surrender or conveyance,"[213] appears in the context of military conflict with reference to Yahweh's deliverance of the enemy or the land into the power of Israel or other nations. According to von Rad,[214] "it is evident that the phrase [*ntn b^eyāḏ*] is rooted in the holy war"; the oracle with its promise "lays the foundation for that unshakable assurance of victory. . . ."[215] The oracle promising that God will deliver the enemy in the hands of Israel is the sign confirming Yahweh's self-introduction.

In Ezekiel's oracles against the nations we find "the purest formal examples of the demonstration utterance, which is then made use of in astonishingly novel contexts."[216] Because the Ammonites have mocked the Jerusalem sanctuary and the people of Israel, Yahweh will give them over to the "people of the East": "then you will know that I am Yahweh" (Ezk. 25:5b). Yahweh will stretch forth his hand against Ammon, cut it off and make it perish, that it may know (*w^eyāḏaʿtā*) God's self-demonstration (25:7). For the Philistines, God's self-demonstration will come in his vengeance (25:17), and for Tyre in the destruction, plundering, and slaughter of its mainland settlements (26:6). Cf. Ezk. 29:6,9,16; 35:3f.,5-9,10-13, with 14f. as a conclusion. For a combination of recognition statement with judgment oracle, see Jer. 16:21: "Therefore, behold, I will make them know (*môḏîʿām*), this once I will make them know (*ʾôḏîʿēm*) my power and my might, and they shall know (*ydʿ*) that my name is Yahweh." Cf. also Mal. 2:4.

In Deutero-Isaiah, the statement of recognition points in the direction of the priestly

---

210 Zimmerli, *Festschrift A. Robert.*

211 *Ibid.*, 124.

212 → יד *yāḏ*.

213 W. Richter, *Traditionsgeschichtliche Untersuchungen zum Richterbuch. BBB*, 18 (²1966), 21ff.; J. G. Plöger, *Literarkritische, formgeschichtliche und stilkritische Untersuchungen zum Deuteronomium. BBB*, 26 (1967), 61ff.; etc.; but cf. the reservations expressed by F. Stolz, *Yahwes und Israels Kriege. AThANT*, 60 (1972), 21f.; C. J. Lambuschagne, "נתן *ntn* geben," *THAT*, II, 117-141, esp. 135, 137; etc.

214 G. von Rad, *Der heilige Krieg im alten Israel* (Göttingen, ⁵1969), 6-9.

215 *Ibid.*, 9.

216 Zimmerli, *Festschrift A. Robert*, 130.

salvation oracle.[217] According to Begrich,[218] the prophet speaks in the style of the priestly oracle in order to present to his hearers as a vivid reality the comforting image of God familiar to all from the words of the oracle. Begrich and Zimmerli are probably right in holding that, in contrast to 1 K. 20 and Ezekiel, where the recognition statement appears in the context of prophetic forms of speech, in Deutero-Isaiah it has its locus in the priestly oracle of answered prayer.

Within the context of a great oracle addressed to Cyrus (Isa. 45:1-7), Yahweh promises to give him hidden treasures and secret hordes, "that you may know that I am Yahweh, who called you by your name, the God of Israel" (45:3; cf. 45:6). The statements of recognition are preceded by Yahweh's acts.

The promise of Yahweh to the exiles climaxes in a recognition statement: "Then you shall know that I am Yahweh; those who trust in me shall not be put to shame" (Isa. 49:23). In Yahweh's victory over the enemy, "all flesh shall know that I am Yahweh your Savior, and your Redeemer, the Mighty One of Jacob" (49:26; cf. 60:16; cf. also Joel 2:27; 4:17[3:17]). Features of Deuteronomic parenesis appear in Isa. 41:20: "That people may see (*r'h*) and know (*yd'*) and take (*śîm*) to heart and understand (*śkl*) together that the hand of Yahweh has done this . . ."; cf. also 43:10; 41:23, 26 (forensic). Cf. also Ps. 20:7(6); 41:12(11); 56:10(9); 135:5; 140:13(12). After the Reubenites state that their copy of the altar of Yahweh is intended solely as a witness between Israel and Reuben and that they have no intention of turning aside from Yahweh, Phinehas says: "Now we know that Yahweh is in the midst of us, because you have not committed this treachery against Yahweh" (Josh. 22:31; cf. Jgs. 17:13; 2 S. 5:12 par. 1 Ch. 14:2; 2 K. 5:15; Neh. 6:16).

g. *da'aṯ 'ᵉlōhîm in Prophetic Criticism*. In the prophets, especially Hosea and Jeremiah, the "knowledge of God" (*da'aṯ 'ᵉlōhîm*) appears primarily in oracles of judgment: Jer. 2:8; 4:22; 9:2,5(3,6); Hos. 4:1,(6); 5:4; 8:2; cf. Hos. 2:10(8) and the salvation oracles Jer. 31:34; Hos. 2:22(20); cf. Isa. 11:2,9; 33:6; also Isa. 28:9; Jer. 22:16; Dnl. 11:32; Hos. 6:3; 13:4; Mal. 2:7.

In prophetic criticism attacking absence or rejection of *da'aṯ 'ᵉlōhîm*, we find *škḥ* as a parallel: "Since you have forgotten (*škḥ*) the *tôrâ* of your God, I also will forget your children" (Hos. 4:6). The absence or neglect of *da'aṯ 'ᵉlōhîm* stands in parallel with apostasy (*bdg*, 5:7; 6:7), rebellion (*srr*, 7:14; 9:15; *mārâ*, 14:1[13:16]), adultery (1:2; 2:4,7[2,5]; 3:2; 4:12; 5:4; 6:10; 8:9f.; 9:1), iniquity (*kḥš*, 10:13; 12:1[11:12]), deceit (*mirmâ*, 12:1[11:12]), faithlessness (*'āḇar bᵉrîṯ*, 6:7; 8:1; *ḥālaq lēḇ*, 10:2). In invective we find *da'aṯ 'ᵉlōhîm*, *'ᵉmeṯ* and *ḥeseḏ* (4:1: 6:6), *tôrâ* (4:6; Mal. 2:7), and *ṣeḏeq* (Isa. 53:11; 58:2) in parallel.

The special meaning of *da'aṯ* is clear from Hos. 6:6: "I desire *ḥeseḏ* and not [or: more than] sacrifice (*zeḇaḥ*), *da'aṯ* rather than [more than] burnt offerings (*'ōlôṯ*)."

---

[217] Begrich, *ZAW*, 52 (1934), 61-92; *idem*, *Studien zu Deuterojesaja*. *BWANT*, 77[4/25] (1938), 6-19; Zimmerli, "Erkenntnis Gottes," *ThB*, 19 (²1969), 69-71, 81f., 97; Schottroff, 698; for a different view, see C. Westermann, *Isaiah 40–66*. *OTL* (Eng. trans. 1969), 78-80; Elliger, *BK*, XI/1, *passim*.

[218] *ZAW*, 52 (1934), 91 [= 217].

Absence of *da‘aṯ* (*lō’ yāḏa‘* or *mibbᵉlî da‘aṯ*) and disaster often constitute the causal nexus for the present or future situation: "Therefore my people go into exile for want of *da‘aṯ*" (Isa. 5:13; cf. Jer. 2:8; 4:22; 9:2,5[3,6]; Hos. 4:1,6; 13:4; etc.). A vivid picture of life without faithfulness and knowledge of God is painted by Hos. 4:2: "There is swearing, lying, killing, stealing, adultery, violence, and murder follows murder."

h. *The Day of Salvation.* In the promised day of salvation, Yahweh will give his people righteousness (*ṣeḏeq*), justice (*mišpaṭ*), steadfast love (*ḥeseḏ*), mercy (*raḥᵃmîm*), faithfulness (*'ᵉmunâ*), and knowledge of Yahweh (Hos. 2:21f.[19f.]). In that day knowledge (*da‘aṯ*) will be given to all; "the earth shall be full of the knowledge of Yahweh" (Isa. 11:9). This situation of peace is a gift from Yahweh, who gives this *da‘aṯ* (Jer. 24:7; Hos. 2:22[20]). The Messiah, too, bears this sign; upon him rests the spirit of *da‘aṯ* (Isa. 11:2) and the fear of God (cf. Isa. 33:6 and the juxtaposition of *yir'aṯ YHWH* and *da‘aṯ* in Proverbs, e.g., Prov. 1:7,29; 2:5.

In these announcements of the messianic kingdom (Isa. 11:2,9; 33:6; 53:11; Jer. 9:23[24]; 24:7; 31:34; Hos. 2:22[20]; etc.) against the background of proclamations of disaster the prophetic understanding of *da‘aṯ* stands out clearly: it is an active concern for Yahweh that is required of all, a type of religio-ethical conduct; the presence or absence of *da‘aṯ* is crucial for the salvation of society as a whole, so that there is a shared responsibility with respect to this *da‘aṯ* that remains in force until the day of salvation: "They shall all know me . . . ; for I will forgive their iniquity, and I will remember their sin no more" (Jer. 31:34). It is the forgiveness of sins that makes "knowledge of God" possible (cf. Isa. 53:11) and leads to intimate communion with God.[219] According to Jer. 24:7, it is Yahweh's purpose to give the exiled community a new heart, "to know that I am Yahweh; and they shall be my people and I shall be their God, for they shall return to me with their whole heart"; cf. Jer. 31:31-34.

i. *Origin of da‘aṯ 'ᵉlōhîm.* In addressing the question of origin, Baumann,[220] Fohrer,[221] and Eichrodt[222] suggest the context of marriage and a relationship of marital fidelity. This marriagelike relationship between Yahweh and Israel is supported by Hos. 2:21f.(19f.), "I will betroth (*'rś*) you to me in righteousness and in justice, in steadfast love and in mercy . . . and you shall know (*yd‘*) Yahweh," or Hos. 5:4 (*rûaḥ zᵉnûnîm* par. *'eṯ-YHWH lō yd‘;* cf. also 6:6,10; 8:2,9f. According to Baumann,[223] in Hosea *da‘aṯ 'ᵉlōhîm* and *da‘aṯ YHWH* refer to a "relationship with God," "communication with God," "respect, love, and trust shown toward God."

---

219 Cf. S. Herrmann, *Die prophetischen Heilserwartungen im AT. BWANT,* 85 [5/5] (1965), 179-185, esp. 183.

220 *ZAW,* 28 (1908), 31; *EvTh,* 15 (1955), 416-425.

221 G. Fohrer, *Studien zur alttestamentlichen Prophetie, 1949-1965. BZAW,* 99 (1967), 228 (n. 16), 275.

222 W. Eichrodt, " 'The Holy One in Your Midst': The Theology of Hosea," *Int,* 15 (1961), 259-273, esp. 264.

223 *ZAW,* 28 (1908), 124f.

Others[224] connect *yd'* and *da'aṯ 'ᵉlōhîm* with the terminology of Near Eastern treaties, proposing that "know" is a technical term for mutual legal recognition of sovereign and vassal, e.g., Suppiluliumas and Ḫuqqan.[225] It is said of both Suppiluliumas and Ashurbanipal that the gods "know" them, i.e., recognize them as legitimate rulers.[226] Huffmon[227] claims to find this legal meaning in the OT (Gen. 18:19; Ex. 33:12 [cf. 33:17] *yd' bᵉšēm;* 2 S. 7:20; Isa. 45:3f.; Jer. 1:5). Other texts deal with the relationship or covenant between Yahweh and Israel (Dt. 9:24; 34:10; Jer. 12:3; Hos. 13:4f.; Am. 3:2). Finally, Huffmon claims that *yd'* also stands for recognition of the sovereign on the part of the vassal (Hos. 8:2; 2:22[20]; 5:4; cf. 4:1). Goetze,[228] however, rejects the similarity to Hittite terminology postulated by Huffmon, thus leaving the theory without foundation.

McKenzie takes as his point of departure the variation in form between *da'aṯ 'ᵉlōhîm* and *yd' 'eṯ-YHWH.* "To know Yahweh" involves not just theoretical knowledge but acceptance of the divine will for one's own life (cf. Hos. 2:22[20]; 5:4; 6:3). The phrase *da'aṯ 'ᵉlōhîm* means knowledge and practice of traditional Hebrew morality.[229] "To know Yahweh" includes everything we understand by "religion" in the broadest sense of the word.

Wolff[230] has offered a new explanation of *da'aṯ 'ᵉlōhîm:* it is rooted in the ministry of the priests and means "the priestly task of preserving and handing on a specific body of knowledge concerning God, which can be learned but also forgotten."[231] In Hosea, Wolff sees "the transition from the free forms of the ancient Israelite creed to a Deuteronomic theology constituting a school."[232] "Knowledge of the acts of God in the exodus, in the events of the desert, and in the gift of the land," as well as "the establishment of the covenant and Torah," constitute the basic form of "theology."[233]

It is true that Wolff sees the subject matter of *da'aṯ 'ᵉlōhîm* as being not God himself but "the acts of God in the early period of Israel and the ancient sacral law"[234]; but he also states that "this knowledge never appears in isolation, but always in contact with its object."[235] "It is therefore clearly qualified by its object as a personal relationship growing out of a living encounter with God."[236]

---

224 Huffmon, Parker, and others.

225 Huffmon, *BASOR,* 181 (1966), 31.

226 *Ibid.,* 32f.

227 Pp. 34-37.

228 A. Goetze, "Hittite *šek-/šak-* '(Legally) Recognize' in the Treaties," *JCS,* 22 (1968-69), 7f.

229 Cf. the argument in J. L. McKenzie, "The Appellative Use of El and Elohim," *CBQ,* 10 (1948), 170-181.

230 *ThB,* 22 (²1973), 182-205.

231 *Ibid.,* 192.

232 *Ibid.,* 205.

233 *Ibid.*

234 *EvTh,* 15 (1955), 428.

235 *Ibid.,* 427.

236 Kümpel, 234.

Begrich[237] has discerned a change of terminology in priestly *da'aṯ* and *tôrâ* (cf. Hos. 4:6; Mal. 2:7). In the P laws, the priestly *tôrâ* is addressed to the laity in person, instructing them in cultic questions. Priestly *da'aṯ* as professional lore comprises for internal use specific information about performance of the cult.[238] According to Begrich,[239] it was only the restoration accomplished by Ezra that made the *da'aṯ* of priestly professional lore common knowledge and brought this concept of *tôrâ* into general usage.

Finally, the hiphil of *yd'* is used of those who proclaim the revelation: Moses (Ex. 18:16,20), Samuel (1 S. 10:8); priests (Ezk. 44:23). In addition, all those who are redeemed (Isa. 12:4) and the devout (Ps. 105:1; 145:12) are to make this known to the nations.

5. *Derivatives.*

a. *dēa'*. The noun *dēa'* is a nominalized qal infinitive construct[240] with the abstract meaning "knowledge." It is restricted to the speeches of Elihu in the book of Job. Elihu makes a clear distinction between this word and *da'aṯ,* using the latter only in a negative sense. He also sees *dēa'* as the knowledge of a youth in contrast to the *ḥoḵmâ* of the old, which, in Elihu's opinion, has not stood the test (Job 32:6,10,17). This *dēa'* he claims to have fetched from afar (36:3); indeed, it ultimately belongs to God alone (37:16). In Sir. 16:25 it is the knowledge of the scribes (par. *rûaḥ*).

The fem. form *dē'â* means "knowledge" and appears 6 times. It, too, refers in the first instance to the omniscience of Yahweh, who is described in the Song of Hannah (1 S. 2:3) as *'ēl dē'ôṯ;*[241] cf. *'l d'wt* in 1QS 3:15; 1QH 1:26: God knows even the most secret human sins. Elihu also uses this plural to indicate the source and fulness of his knowledge (Job 36:4). The wicked (*r^ešā'îm*) in their "boundless hybris"[242] dispute this *dē'â* on the part of God (Ps. 73:11). In a judgment oracle Isaiah attacks the drunken priests and prophets who "err in vision and stumble in giving judgment," but claim nonetheless as spokesmen for God's will and as interpreters of oracles and visions to share in the knowledge of God. They reject Isaiah, who wishes to teach them knowledge (*dē'â*) and interpretation like a teacher of children (Isa. 28:7,9).

For the messianic age of salvation, Yahweh promises shepherds with insight and knowledge, who will teach the people to do God's will (Jer. 3:15; Deuteronomistic or post-Deuteronomistic redactor). In the context of messianic expectation (Isa. 11:9), *dē'â 'eṯ-YHWH* is the comprehensive gift given by Yahweh to his people for their salvation; according to v. 9b, it is the precondition for cosmic peace. According to v. 2b, the Messiah is endowed with the spirit of knowledge (*rûaḥ da'aṯ*) and of the fear

---

237 J. Begrich, "Die priesterliche Tora," *BZAW*, 66 (1936), 63-88 = *GSAT. ThB*, 21 (1964), 232-260, esp. 251-58.

238 Cf. R. Rendtorff, *Die Gesetze in der Priesterschrift. FRLANT,* N.S. 42[62] (1954), 77.

239 *ThB*, 21 (1964), 258.

240 *GK*, §69m.

241 *GK*, §124e.

242 Kraus, *BK*, XV/2, 669.

of Yahweh (*yir'aṯ YHWH*). The future perspective of *dē'â* (Prov. 24:14) and *ḥokmâ* is also brought out by proverbial wisdom. In Sir. 51:16, *dē'â* has the sense of "practical knowledge" as a consequence of habitual *ḥoḵmâ*.

b. *maddā'*. The 6 occurrences of the noun *maddā'* are all from the late postexilic period. Schottroff[243] points to the Aramaic equivalent *mandā'*, "understanding," which may occur as an adjective (!) form at Elephantine (*kmnd'*, "as is well known"), although this is disputed. The Chronicler connects *maddā'* with *ḥoḵmâ* (2 Ch. 1:10-12), seeing in both the ideal characteristics of King Solomon. In the parallel account 1 K. 3:9,11f., however, *bîn* and *nāḇôn* take the place of *maddā'*. Dnl. 1:4,17 (cf. also Aram. *mandā'* in Dnl. 5:12) sees in *maddā'* a characteristic that candidates for high official office must exhibit: comprehensive knowledge and intellectual flexibility. According to Sir. 3:13, one must not despise one's father simply because his intellectual flexibility decreases with advancing age. In intercourse with others one should conduct oneself judiciously, with *maddā'*, adapt with intellectual flexibility, and not act superior (Sir. 13:8).

The meaning of *maddā'* is disputed in the exhortation: "Even on your bed (*miškāḇ*), do not curse the king, nor in your *maddā'* curse the rich" (Eccl. 10:20). The majority of commentators suggest the meaning "bedchamber" for *maddā'* on the basis of the parallelism, either taking the verbal root *yd'* in the sexual sense[244] or postulating a misreading of *mṣ'*.[245] Also uncertain are derivations from Akk. *md'*, "friend," or Ugar. *mnd'*, "messenger,"[246] or the interpretation "quiet."[247] Still others retain the original meaning of *maddā':* one should not curse anyone even in thought.[248]

c. *mandā'*. Like Heb. *maddā'* (cf. Dnl. 1:4,17), the Aramaic nominal derivative *mandā'* (4 occurrences in Daniel) refers to Daniel's intellectual gift, which together with *rûaḥ* and *śkl* enables him to interpret dreams (Dnl. 5:12). When Nebuchadnezzar was restored after having changed into a kind of beast, his understanding and ability to engage in rational thought (*maddā'*) returned, making him fully human once more (Dnl. 4:31,33). Finally, *mandā'*, like *ḥoḵmᵉṯā'*, is a gift from God (Dnl. 2:21).

d. *môḏā'* and *mōḏa'aṯ*. The usual interpretation of *môḏā'* and *mōḏa'aṯ* as "relative"[249] is based on Prov. 7:4, which calls for a particularly intimate relationship with *ḥoḵmâ* and *bînâ*, which should be taken as sister and *môḏā'*. Grammatically, how-

---

243 P. 684.

244 *KBL*^{2,3}; R. Braun, *Kohelet und die frühhellenistische Popularphilosophie*. *BZAW*, 130 (1973), 126.

245 F. Perles, "A Miscellany of Lexical and Textual Notes on the Bible," *JQR*, N.S. 2 (1911/12), 130ff.; Lauha, *BK*, XIX, 196f.

246 Dahood, *Bibl*, 46 (1965), 210ff.

247 D. W. Thomas, "A Note on בְּמַדָּעֲךָ in Eccles. X. 20," *JTS*, 50 (1949), 177.

248 McNeile, G. A. Barton (*ICC* [1908]); Gordis, Hertzberg, Loretz; C. F. Whitley, *Koheleth: His Language and Thought*. *BZAW*, 148 (1979), 90f.

249 *KBL*³, 521.

ever,[250] and on the basis of Ruth 2:1 (*Q*); 3:2 (Boaz described as *môḏā'* or *mōḏa'aṯ* [fem. in form]), the most one can think of is a distant relationship (cf. the distinction from *qārôḇ* in Ruth 3:12), or more likely, a close acquaintance.

5. *Dead Sea Scrolls*. In the published scrolls from Qumran and Murabba'āt, *yd'* appears 140 times, *da'aṯ* 50 times, *dē'â* 16 times, and *maddā'* 4 times. For *yd'*, the majority of the occurrences are in the hymnic literature (1QH; 1Q22; 1Q34; 1Q36; 4QDibHam; 11QPs^{a}; etc. [92 occurrences]), while the regulatory literature exhibits only 30 occurrences. The nouns are more evenly distributed: *da'aṯ* occurs 24 times in the Hymns (plus 4QŠir Šab, etc.) and 22 times in the Rule; *dē'â* occurs 7 times in the Hymns, 8 times in the Rule; *maddā'* occurs 3 times in 1QS.

At Qumran, *yd'* can mean special knowledge in the realm of anthropology, cosmology, and especially soteriology. Since *sôḏ* and *rāz* often appear as objects, *yd'* frequently stands for the secret esoteric knowledge of the sect. According to Kuhn,[251] we have here a nascent Gnosticism introduced into the Jewish religion of the law and late Jewish apocalypticism.[252]

A special meaning is conveyed by *yd'* in the Hymns.[253] God gives human beings a share in knowledge (1QH 4:27; 7:27; 10:4; 11:4,16); apart from his will no knowledge is possible (1:8; 20:9). Right ethos is dependent on *yd'*, for whoever is graced with the *rûaḥ da'aṯ* scorns the way of the wicked (1QH 14:25f.) and resists those who do evil (14:12ff.). It is within a community that one experiences *yd'*;[254] it is a good that must be used for the benefit of the community (1QS 1:11f.). In the formulaic acceptance of the soteriological confession,[255] *yd'* stands for acknowledgment that God has acted to bring salvation to his elect.

Botterweck

---

[250] *GesB*, 400.

[251] K. G. Kuhn, "Die in Palästina gefundenen Handschriften und das NT," *ZThK*, 47 (1950), 203-205.

[252] Cf. also K. G. Kuhn, "Die Sektenschrift und die iranische Religion," *ZThK*, 49 (1952), 306f., and the criticism by F. Nötscher, *Zur theologischen Terminologie der Qumran-Texte. BBB*, 10 (1956), 38ff.

[253] De Caevel, Wagner, etc.

[254] Wagner, 250.

[255] Cf. H. W. Kuhn, *Enderwartung und gegenwärtiges Heil. StUNT*, 4 (1966), 26ff., 139-181, esp. 165.

יְהוּדָה y^e*hûḏâ*

Contents: I. 1. Occurrences; 2. Etymology; 3. Meaning. II. Territory. III. 1. Tribe; 2. Patriarch. IV. History. V. Theology.

I. 1. *Occurrences.* The proper name y^e*hûḏâ* is found primarily in the OT. Lisowsky-Rost lists 814 occurrences of the Hebrew noun, Mandelkern only 805; both add 7 occurrences of the Aramaic form y^e*hûḏ*. In the Dead Sea scrolls the name occurs 23 times. Finally, there are 76 occurrences of the Hebrew gentilic y^e*hûḏî,* 6 of the fem. form y^e*hûḏîṯ,* and 10 of the Aram. y^e*hûḏāy.* The extrabiblical occurrences, primarily in Assyro-Babylonian inscriptions, refer to the same entity as the OT occurrences, and therefore have nothing significant to contribute to our discussion.

2. *Etymology.* With respect to the etymology of the word "Judah," *KBL*[3] says laconically and accurately: "etymology uncertain."

---

y^e*hûḏâ.* Y. Aharoni, *The Land of the Bible* (Eng. trans., Philadelphia, [2]1979); *idem,* "The Northern Boundary of Judah [Jos. 15, 10f]," *PEQ,* 90 (1958), 27-31; W. F. Albright, "The Names 'Israel' and 'Judah'. . . ," *JBL,* 46 (1927), 151-185; A. Alt, "Bemerkungen zu einigen judäischen Ortslisten des ATs," *BBLAK,* 68 (1951), 193-210 = *KlSchr,* II (1953), 289-305; *idem,* "Festungen und Levitenorte im Lande Juda," *KlSchr,* II (1953), 306-315; *idem,* "The God of the Fathers," in his *Essays on OT History and Religion* (Eng. trans., Garden City, 1966), 1-78; *idem,* "Judas Gaue unter Josia," *PJ,* 21 (1925), 100-116 = *KlSchr,* II (1953), 276-288; *idem,* "The Monarchy in the Kingdoms of Israel and Judah," *Essays,* 239-259; K. T. Andersen, "Die Chronologie der Könige von Israel und Juda," *StTh,* 23 (1969), 69-112; E. Auerbach, "Der Wechsel des Jahres-anfangs in Juda im Lichte der neugefundenen Babylonischen Chronik," *VT,* 9 (1959), 113-121; K. Baltzer, "Das Ende des Staates Juda und die Messias-frage," *Studien zur Theologie der alttestamentlichen Überlieferungen. Festschrift G. von Rad* (Neukirchen-Vluyn, 1961), 33-43; J. Bright, *A History of Israel* (Philadelphia, 1959; [3]1981); A. Caquot, "La parole sur Juda dans le testament lyrique de Jacob (*Genèse* 49, 8-12)," *Sem,* 26 (1976), 5-32; F. M. Cross, "A Reconstruction of the Judean Restoration," *JBL,* 94 (1975), 4-18; *idem* and G. E. Wright, "The Boundary and Province Lists of the Kingdom of Judah," *JBL,* 75 (1956), 202-226; O. Eissfeldt, " 'Juda' in 2. Könige 14,28 und "Judäa' in Apostelgeschichte 2,9," *WZ Halle-Wittenberg,* 12 (1963), 229-238 = *KlSchr,* IV (1968), 99-120; *idem,* " 'Juda' und 'Judäa' als Bezeichnung nordsyrischer Bereiche," *FuF,* 38 (1964), 20-25 = *KlSchr,* IV (1968), 121-131; J. H. Grønbaek, "Benjamin und Juda: Erwägungen zu 1 Kön. xii 21-24," *VT,* 15 (1965), 421-436; *idem,* "Juda und Amalek: Überlieferungsgeschichtliche Erwägungen zu Exodus 17, 8-16," *StTh,* 18 (1964), 26-45; H. H. Grosheide, "Juda als onderdeel van het Perzische rijk," *GThT,* 54 (1954), 65-76; M. Haran, "The Rise and Decline of the Empire of Jeroboam ben Joash," *VT,* 17 (1967), 266-297; J. Hempel, "Juda 1," *BHHW,* II, 898-900; S. Herrmann, "Autonome Entwicklungen in den Königreichen Israel und Juda," *Congress Volume, Rome 1968. SVT,* 17 (1968), 139-158; *idem, A History of Israel in OT Times* (Eng. trans., Philadelphia, 1975); S. H. Horn, "The Babylonian Chronicle and the Ancient Calendar of the Kingdom of Judah," *AUSS,* 5 (1967), 12-27; F. Huber, *Jahwe, Juda und die anderen Völker beim Propheten Jesaja. BZAW,* 137 (1976); Ihromi, "Die Königinmutter und der 'amm ha'arez im Reich Juda," *VT,* 24 (1974), 421-29; E. Janssen, *Juda in der Exilszeit. FRLANT,* 69 (1956); A. Jepsen, "Ein neuer Fixpunkt für die Chronologie der israelitischen Könige?" *VT,* 20 (1970), 359-361; *idem,* "Noch einmal zur israelitisch-jüdischen Chronologie," *VT,* 18 (1968), 31-46; *idem* and R. Hanhart,

In OT tradition, the name is connected with the verb → ידה (*ydh*), "praise." Gen. 29:35 (J) has Leah say: "This time I will praise Yahweh"; and the tribal saying about Judah in the Blessing of Jacob (Gen. 49:8) begins with the play on words: "Judah, your brothers shall praise you." In both cases we are dealing with popular etymology with no claims to any scientific validity, being based on associational wordplay.[1]

As far as a scientific etymology of the name "Judah" goes, there is most general agreement on the negative statement that "Judah" is not a theophorous name. This theory was once proposed by Procksch,[2] who claimed that "Judah" contained the name "Yahweh." Hempel[3] suggests that "Judah" is a shortened form of "Yehud-'el," "praised be El," although he appends a question mark to this etymology. A similar suggestion was made by Meyer,[4] who proposed that the short form "Yehuda" developed from the longer "Yehuda-'el," "El is majestic," deriving from → הוד *hôḏ* [*hôdh*], "majesty." Nyberg[5] takes the opposite approach, explaining our name as deriving from a divine name *yhwd*, and citing "the group of *yhwd*-worshippers" and other names he interprets in the same way: Abihud, Ahihud, and Ammihud. Lewy[6] explains the biblical "Judah" and the form "Iaudi" found in inscriptions as being compounds of the short form of the OT divine name "Iau" (*yhw*) with the Hurrite possessive suffix *-di*/*-da*. Finally, Albright[7] and most recently Millard consider our name an originally theophorous form that was later shortened, consisting of the jussive hophal of *hôḏâ* and the name of Yahweh, with the meaning "Yahweh let be praised." This etymology is accepted by

---

Untersuchungen zur israelitisch-jüdischen Chronologie. *BZAW*, 88 (1964); Z. Kallai-Kleinmann, "The Town Lists of Judah, Simeon, Benjamin, and Dan," *VT*, 8 (1958), 134-160; U. Kellermann, "Die Listen in Nehemia 11 eine Dokumentation aus den letzten Jahren des Reiches Juda?" *ZDPV*, 82 (1966), 209-227; A. Kuschke, "Kleine Beiträge zur Siedlungsgeschichte der Stämme Asser und Juda," *HThR*, 64 (1971), 291-313; E. Kutsch, "Das Jahr der Katastrophe: 587 v.Chr.: Kritische Erwägungen zu neueren chronologischen Versuchen," *Bibl*, 55 (1974), 520-545; *idem*, "Zur Chronologie der letzten judäischen Könige (Josia bis Zedekia)," *ZAW*, 71 (1959), 270-74; J. Lewy, "Influences Ḫurrites sur Israël," *RÉS*, 1938, 49-75; *idem*, "The Old West Semitic Sun-God Ḥammu," *HUCA*, 18 (1943/44), 429-488; E. Lipiński, "L'Étymologie de 'Juda,'" *VT*, 23 (1973), 380f.; N. Lohfink, "Die Einheit von Israel und Juda," *Una Sancta*, 26 (1971), 154-164; G. C. Macholz, "Zur Geschichte der Justizorganisation in Juda," *ZAW*, 84 (1972), 314-340; A. Malamat, "Jeremiah and the Last Two Kings of Judah," *PEQ*, 83 (1951), 81-87; *idem*, "The Last Kings of Judah and the Fall of Jerusalem: An Historical-Chronological Study," *IEJ*, 18 (1968), 137-156; *idem*, "The Last Wars of the Kingdom of Judah," *JNES*, 9 (1950), 218-227; *idem*, "The Twilight of Judah: In the Egyptian-Babylonian Maelstrom," *Congress Volume, Edinburgh 1974*. *SVT*, 28 (1975), 123-145; B. Mazar, "David's Reign in Hebron and the Conquest of Jerusalem," *In the Time of Harvest. Festschrift A. H. Silver* (New York, 1963), 235-244; A. R. Millard, "The Meaning of the Name Judah," *ZAW*, 86 (1974), 216-18; H.-P. Müller, "Phönizien und Juda in exilisch-nachexilischer Zeit," *WO*, 6 (1971), 189-204; J. M.
(continued on p. 484)

1 See most recently J. Barr, "Etymology and the OT," *Language and Meaning*. *OTS*, 19 (1974), 1-28.

2 O. Procksch, *Genesis*. *KAT*, I (^{2,3}1924), 178.

3 P. 898.

4 E. Meyer, *Die Israeliten und ihre Nachbarstämme* (Halle, 1906), 441.

5 H. S. Nyberg, *Studien zum Hoseabuche*. *UUÅ*, 1935/6, 77.

6 J. Lewy, "Influences Ḫurrites sur Israël," *RÉS*, 1938, 54f.; *ḤUCA*, 18 (1943/44), 479.

7 *JBL*, 46 (1927), 151-185.

Zorell.[8] Albright cites also the earlier explanations by Haupt ("Yehuda" is a "feminine collective" of *yᵉhôḏeh* with the meaning "he acknowledges allegiance to the religion [of Yahweh]") and Jastrow (the name is a compound of "Yahu" and *yûḏâ* or *da'â*).

A change in the etymological approach was marked by Alt's observation[9] that "Judah" is not a personal name but a "place-name like Jogbeha." Alt was followed by others, including Waterman[10] and Noth,[11] to the extent that they also saw in the name a geographical term or regional name like "Ephraim" or "Naphtali." This theory is largely accepted today.[12]

On this basis, Lipiński, citing Yeivin,[13] has suggested deriving the name "Judah" from Arab. *wahda,* "ravine," "gorge," interpreting the proper noun as a *qaṭul* form meaning "the washed-out or excavated land," with reference to the geomorphology of the land of Judah. The noun *wahda* does not occur in the OT, however, so that this etymology must remain hypothetical.

Myers, "Edom and Judah in the Sixth-Fifth Centuries B.C.," *Near Eastern Studies in Honor of William Foxwell Albright* (Baltimore, 1971), 377-392; M. Noth, *IPN; idem, Das System der Zwölf Stämme Israels. BWANT,* 52 [4/1] (1930); *idem,* "Eine Siedlungsgeographische Liste in 1. Ch. 2 und 4," *ZDPV,* 55 (1932), 97-124; *idem,* "Die Ansiedlung des Stammes Juda auf dem Boden Palästinas," *PJ,* 30 (1934), 31-47 = his *Aufsätze zur biblischen Landes- und Altertumskunde* (Neukirchen-Vluyn, 1971), I, 183-196; *idem,* "Zur historischen Geographie Südjudäas," *JPOS,* 15 (1935), 35-50 = *Aufsätze,* I, 197-209; *idem, The OT World* (Eng. trans., Philadelphia, 1966); V. Pavlovský and E. Vogt, "Die Jahre der Könige von Juda und Israel," *Bibl,* 45 (1964), 321-347; J. Potin, "David roi de Juda à Hébron," *BTS,* 80 (1966), 4f.; G. von Rad, "Ἰσραήλ," *TDNT,* III, 356-59; B. Reicke, "Juda 2-4," *BHHW,* II, 900f.; L. Rost, *Israel bei den Propheten. BWANT,* 78[4/19] (1937); C. Schedl, "Textkritische Bemerkungen zu den Synchronismen der Könige von Israel und Juda," *VT,* 12 (1962), 88-119; K.-D. Schunck, "Juda und Jerusalem in vor- und frühisraelitischer Zeit," *Schalom. Festschrift A. Jepsen* (1971), 50-57; R. Smend, "Gehörte Juda zum vorstaatlichen Israel?" Fourth World Congress of Jewish Studies, *Papers,* I (Tel-Aviv, 1967), 57-62; L. A. Snijders, "Het 'volk des lands' in Juda," *GThT,* 58 (1958), 241-256; J. A. Soggin, "Der judäische 'am-ha'areṣ und das Königtum in Juda," *VT,* 13 (1963), 187-195; *idem, Das Königtum in Israel. BZAW,* 104 (1967); *idem,* "Zur Entwicklung des alttestamentlichen Königtums," *ThZ,* 15 (1960), 401-418; E. L. Sukenik, "Paralipomena Palaestinensia," *JPOS,* 14 (1934), 178-184; S. Talmon, "The Judean Am Ha'aretz in Historical Perspective," Fourth World Congress of Jewish Studies, *Papers,* I (Tel-Aviv, 1967), 71-76; E. R. Thiele, "A Comparison of the Chronological Data of Israel and Judah," *VT,* 4 (1954), 185-195; *idem,* "The Chronology of the Kings of Judah and Israel," *JNES,* 3 (1944), 137-186; T. C. G. Thornton, "Charismatic Kingship in Israel and Judah," *JTS,* N.S. 14 (1963), 1-11; R. de Vaux, *The Early History of Israel* (Eng. trans., Philadelphia, 1978); H. C. M. Vogt, *Studie zur nachexilischen Gemeinde in Esra-Nehemia* (Werl, 1966); L. Waterman, "Jacob the Forgotten Supplanter," *AJSL,* 55 (1938), 25-43; P. Welten, *Die Königs-Stempel. ADPV* (1969); W. R. Wifall, "The Chronology of the Divided Monarchy of Israel," *ZAW,* 80 (1968), 319-337; G. E. Wright, "The Provinces of Solomon," *Festschrift E. L. Sukenik. Eretz-Israel,* 8 (1967), 58-68; Y. Yadin, "The Fourfold

(continued on p. 485)

[8] *LexHebAram,* 298a.

[9] *Essays,* 1-78, 6, n. 6.

[10] Pp. 29-31.

[11] M. Noth, *Das Buch Josua. HAT,* VII (^{3}1971), 125; *The OT World,* 55f.

[12] De Vaux, 546; Herrmann, *History,* 109f., n. 56; R. Bach, "Juda," *RGG*^{3}, III, 963; W. Thiel, "Verwandschaftsgruppe und Stamm in der halbnomadischen Frühgeschichte Israels," *Altorientalische Forschungen,* 4 (1976), 151-165, esp. 157.

[13] S. Yeivin, "Yᵉhūdā," *EMiqr,* III (1958), 487-508.

3. *Meaning*. If we start with the sequence of occurrences within the OT, "Judah" is the name of the fourth son of Jacob by his wife Leah, after Reuben, Simeon, and Levi. Such an individual appears both in the ancient tribal story of Gen. 38 and in the Joseph novella, where (in the earlier J version) he functions as spokesman for the group of brothers (Gen. 37:26; 43:3,8; 44:14,16,18; 46:28). But even in the various strata of the Judah saying in the Blessing of Jacob (Gen. 49:8,9,10-12) the personal name is transparent, revealing behind it the tribe of the same name, which appears as such in the Blessing of Moses (Dt. 33:7) and other ancient traditions (e.g., Jgs. 1:2-7; note the pl. verb forms in vv. 4-7). At the latest when David is advanced to kingship over the "house of Judah" (2 S. 2:4), we note that Judah comprises several tribes or groups; but this advancement takes place at Hebron, which belongs to Caleb, not Judah. It is natural that "Judah" should be the political designation of the kingdom of the same name.

At the same time, however, we learn in the Samson narrative (Jgs. 15:9), for example, where the Philistines come up and camp "in (b^e) Judah," or in a statement in Josh. 20:7 that Hebron lies in the "hill country of Judah," that "Judah" is a geographical term designating the land or the mountains within it. In 1 S. 23:3, also, according to Noth,[14] "Judah" is clearly used as a geographical term.

Still another meaning is found in Jer. 40:15; 42:15,19; 43:5; 44:12,14,28, where the group that flees to Egypt after the murder of Gedaliah is called the "remnant of Judah"; the inhabitants of the military colony at Elephantine also refer to themselves as "Judeans" or "Jews."[15] Last but not least, in the exilic and postexilic writings "Judah" is the term used for the Golah,[16] which became an independent Persian province under Nehemiah (cf. Neh. 5:14 and the Elephantine papyri),[17] and—under the name "Judea"—formed part of various Hellenistic kingdoms (1 Macc. 3:34).

The theory that the "Judah" of 2 K. 14:28 (and also Acts 2:9) refers to *y'dy*, a small state in northwest Syria attested in Assyrian texts and the Zenjirli inscriptions, has been forcefully defended by Eissfeldt.[18]

The Dead Sea scrolls reflect initially the usage of the OT: "Judah" can refer to the land (CD 4:3; 6:5) and its cities (1QM 12:13; 19:5; 1QpHab. 12:9), the people (CD 7:12; also 4:11: "house of Judah") and their leaders (CD 8:3; 19:15), and finally also the tribe of Judah (4 QPB 1). But this last passage with its messianic interpretation of Gen. 49:10 makes it clear that the notion of Judah is privately shifting so as to refer to the Qumran community. Judah consists of those who—although there may be evil

---

Division of Judah," *BASOR*, 163 (1961), 6-12; H.-J. Zobel, "Beiträge zur Geschichte Gross-Judas in früh- und vordavidischer Zeit," *Congress Volume, Edinburgh 1974. SVT*, 28 (1975), 253-277; *idem*, "Das Selbstverständis Israels nach dem AT," *ZAW*, 85 (1973), 281-294; *idem*, *Stammesspruch und Geschichte. BZAW*, 95 (1965); *idem*, "Ursprung und Verwurzelung des Erwählungsglaubens Israels," *ThLZ*, 93 (1968), 1-12.

14 Noth, *The OT World*, 55.

15 *AP*, 21, 2, 4, 11; 22, 1; 30, 22.

16 Rost, 114.

17 *AP*, 30, 1: "Bagohi, governor of Judah."

18 *KlSchr*, IV, 99-131, citing Gordon, Driver, and Mauchline.

in Judah (4QT 27) and wicked people in Judah (CD 20:27)—fulfill the law and are faithful to the Teacher of Righteousness (1QpHab 8:1; 12:4), of those who, together with the Sons of Levi and Benjamin, fight against the Sons of Darkness (1QM 1:2).

As noted above,[19] there is a tendency today to consider the geographical use of the name "Judah" to be primary. This change is reflected dramatically in the editions of *KBL*. In the second edition (1958), the article "Judah" is divided into three sections: (1) masculine personal name; (2) name of a tribe; (3) the empire or state of Judah. In the third edition (1978), we find: (1) name of a territory, the tribe of Judah, originally *hr yhwdh;* (2) Judah the son of Jacob (eponym); (3) empire and state of Judah; (4) province of Judah; (5) masculine personal name. In other words, the tribe that settled in the hill country of Judah took the name of the region or was named by other groups on the basis of its territory. In a further transposition, then, the tribe was personified in the patriarch Judah, who now appeared as the fourth son of Jacob and Leah. This personification of the tribe in its eponymous ancestor is clearest in Gen. 49 and 38.

In the postexilic period, there was a tendency to name children after personalities of Israelite history. "Judah" is one of the first names we find, as early as the fifth century B.C.: it is the name of a Levite (Ezr. 10:23), a Benjaminite (Neh. 11:9), and two priests (Neh. 12:34,36). Following Hölscher, Noth maintains that these names emphasize pure genealogical descent.[20]

Even though the meanings shade into each other, so that statistical data can only be approximate, the following survey is interesting because it draws attention to the absolute importance of the name "Judah." Some 40 times it refers to an individual, about 290 times it refers to the tribe or people, and about 480 times it refers to the land or political entity. The latter, therefore, is of primary importance in the OT.

II. Territory. Genitive phrases in which Judah is combined with *'aḏmaṯ* (Isa. 19:17), with *'ereṣ* (Dt. 34:2; 1 S. 22:5; 30:16; 2 K. 23:24; 25:22; plus 18 additional instances) or the pl. *'arṣôṯ* (2 Ch. 11:23), with *har* (Josh. 11:21; 20:7; 21:11; 2 Ch. 27:4) or the pl. *hārê* (2 Ch. 21:11), with *miḏbār* (Jgs. 1:16; Ps. 63:1[Eng. superscription]), or with *negeḇ* (1 S. 27:10; 2 S. 24:7) refer clearly to the territory or regions of Judah, describing them as farmland, mountains, steppe, and desert. Similar descriptions of the geographical extent of Judah are also found elsewhere in the OT. In Jer. 17:26, the Shephelah, the hill country, and the Negeb are listed (also Jer. 32:44; 33:13); Yadin,[21] drawing also on Dt. 1:7; Josh. 11:16; 12:8,15; 2 Ch. 26:10, points out that in these passages the territory of Judah is divided into four regions: desert, hill country, Shephelah, and Negeb; these clearly correspond to the natural features of the land of Judah.

With respect to the extent of the area covered by the geographical term "Judah," the formula containing "Shephelah" and the description of Judah's borders in Josh. 15:1-12 both consider the Mediterranean to be the western boundary. This theory does

---

19 I.2.

20 Cf. *IPN*, 60.

21 P. 11, n. 30.

not agree with the actual state of affairs: the Shephelah contained a string of powerful Canaanite cities that Judah had not conquered (Jgs. 1:19); during the twelfth century B.C. these belonged to the sphere of the Philistine pentapolis. Even in the early Davidic period the fact that the Philistines were Judah's neighbors to the west was accepted without question (1 S. 23:1ff.; 27:8-12; etc.);[22] the Blessing of Noah (Gen. 9:25-27), which probably dates from the Davidic period, locates the Philistines (Japheth) alongside the Israelites—or better alongside the groups belonging to greater Judah (Shem)—as sharing equally in the possession of Canaan.

Everywhere in the OT, the Dead Sea is considered Judah's eastern boundary; for, as the designations "Midbar of Ziph" (1 S. 23:14; 26:2), "Midbar of Maon" (1 S. 23:24f.), and "Midbar of En-gedi" (1 S. 24:2[1]) show, the *miḏbār* of Judah (cf. Jgs. 1:16; Ps. 63:1[superscription]) is the stretch of land constituting the eastern slope of the hill country of Judah down to the Dead Sea.[23]

The southern boundary is defined by the "Negeb." Even though geographically vague, the term is geopolitically clear; nowhere in the OT is the name "Judah" connected with the desert bordering the Negeb in the south (cf. for example the "Midbar of Beer-sheba" in Gen. 21:14).

Only to the north is there no natural geographical boundary of the territory of Judah. The political structure linked with the regional structure in the Jeremiah passages cited above speaks of the "cities of Judah," the "region of Jerusalem," and the "land of Benjamin." This makes it clear that although Jerusalem and Benjamin belonged to the kingdom of Judah, for Jeremiah at least they had nothing to do with the term "Judah." We may conclude that in the time of Jeremiah the "region of Jerusalem" marked the northern boundary of Judah as a geographical entity. That Jerusalem did not belong to Judah but represented an independent political entity follows from the capture of Jerusalem by David (2 S. 5:6-12). He took it with the aid of "his people," i.e., his mercenaries, and consequently viewed the city as the independent and exclusive property of the crown, so that the politically accurate term continues to be "Judah and Jerusalem." Thus the southern boundary of the former city-state of Jerusalem constituted the northern boundary of Judah as a geographical entity.

This statement is indisputably true for the duration of the kingdom of Judah, i.e., from David to 586 B.C. For the pre-Davidic and early Davidic period, there is no clear information about whether Jerusalem belonged to the territory of Judah. Recently Schunck has argued vigorously on the basis of Jgs. 1:3-8 for a destruction of Jerusalem by Judahite clans around 1270 B.C., but without any subsequent settlement of the city. Of course this would mean that Jerusalem and its region had belonged to the territory of Judah, or at least that Judah's claim to the city could be supported on this basis. But this is never the case. On the contrary, the "theoretical tribal geography of the premonarchic period" clearly assigns Jerusalem to the "sphere of influence of the tribe

---

[22] Cf. also O. Eissfeldt, "Israelitisch-philistäische Grenzverschiebungen von David bis auf die Assyrerzeit," *ZDPV*, 66 (1943), 115-128 = *KlSchr*, II (1963), 453-463.

[23] Cf. Noth, *Aufsätze*, I, 198.

of Benjamin" (Josh. 15:8; 18:16;[24] cf. also Dt. 33:12[25]), even though the Benjaminites, as Jgs. 1:21 clearly states, were unable to take the city. The acceptance of the Judahites' claim to Jerusalem in Josh. 15:63 says nothing to the contrary, since this passage is secondary with respect to Jgs. 1:21. As Noth rightly emphasizes,[26] it runs counter to both the system of boundary descriptions (Josh. 15:8; 18:16) and the views of the redactor (Josh. 18:28), who did not count Jerusalem as part of Judah. This makes it likely that Jerusalem was not conquered in the premonarchic period by Benjamin, not to mention Judah, so that the territory of Jerusalem could not have belonged to the territory of Judah.[27]

Finally, the territory of Judah was further bounded by the string of Canaanite city-states extending west on the heights of Jerusalem.[28]

This gross geographical demarcation of the territory of Judah is confirmed and refined by additional information. First we shall mention briefly the cities that are expressly said by the OT to belong to (l^e) or lie within (b^e) Judah. The former applies to Socoh (Kh. 'Abbâd,[29] 1 S. 17:1), the latter to Kirjath-jearim (Dēr el-Azhar[30]) (Jgs. 18:12; but cf. 1 Ch. 13:6: l^e), Beer-sheba (Bîr es-Seba') (1 K. 19:3), and Beth-shemesh (er-Rumeileh[31]) (2 K. 14:11). When Ezr. 1:2f. qualifies "Jerusalem" by adding *'ašer bîhûḏâ*, "which is in Judah," it calls attention to the political change the end of the Davidic dynasty brought to Jerusalem. Now this city belonged to Judah—here probably the province of Judah, which did not extend far geographically, especially to the south.[32]

Finally, there are two other statements of some importance. The fact that Socoh and Beer-sheba belonged to Judah shows that Judah did indeed extend geographically far to the south; the description of Hebron in Josh. 20:7 as a city "in the hill country of Judah" (cf. Josh. 11:21, which mentions Debir and Anab along with Hebron as cities in the hill country of Judah) makes it clear that the territory of Judah stretched from Jerusalem in the north to the Negeb in the south. This is also presupposed by 1 S. 30:14, which speaks of the Negeb of the Cherethites, the Negeb of Caleb, and the Negeb "which belongs to Judah." The "Negeb of Judah" is also mentioned in 2 S. 24:7. This expression sounds like the term "Negeb of Arad" in Jgs. 1:16. Perhaps 1 S. 27:10 should be included; it lists the Negeb of Judah together with the Negeb of the Jerahmeelites and the Negeb of the Kenites; but because v. 12 speaks of the people, it is more likely that "Judah" refers to the Judahites.[33]

---

[24] *Idem*, "Jerusalem und die israelitische Tradition," *OTS*, 8 (1950), 28-46 = *GSAT*, I. *ThB*, 6 (³1966), 172-187, esp. 172f.

[25] Zobel, *Stammesspruch und Geschichte*, 35.

[26] Noth, *HAT*, VII, 100.

[27] Cf. A. Alt, "Jerusalems Aufstieg," *KlSchr*, III (1959), 248, and the discussion of the size of the city-state, *ibid.*, 251f.

[28] Noth, *The History of Israel* (Eng. trans., New York, ²1960), 32, 54.

[29] Noth, *HAT*, VII, 94.

[30] *Ibid.*, 110.

[31] *Ibid.*, 89.

[32] Herrmann, *History*, 315f.

[33] Zobel, *SVT*, 28 (1975), 265f.

The second comment is more important, and has to do with the toponyms "Bethlehem" and "Baalath." In the case of both names, the geographical qualification "Judah" is added directly, without either *l*ᵉ or *b*ᵉ (Bethlehem-Judah: Jgs. 17:7-9; 19:1f., 18; 1 S. 17:12; Ruth 1:1f.; Baalath-Judah: 2 S. 6:2 conj.). There is thus clearly a difference between those cities that were associated directly with Judah and the other cities that did not belong to Judah from the start but only during the course of history. That in these two names "Judah" is to be interpreted as a geographical term and in the same sense is clear, not least from the fact that the clan residing in Bethlehem was called Ephrathah or Ephrath (cf. Ruth 1:2; 1 S. 17:12).

This terminology then suggests that the geographical term "Judah" can be used in a narrower and a wider sense. The most likely theory is that the word "Judah" was a geographical term referring initially to the hill country bearing that name, then extending to all the Israelite groups settled in the southern part of Palestine.

III. 1. *Tribe*. There is a consensus today that the group of Israelites settling in the hill country of Judah was consolidated as a tribe in consequence of the settlement process and took the name Judah.[34] This is evident from the fact that the territory settled by the tribe of Judah is not coextensive with the hill country of Judah: Hebron, which is located in the hill country of Judah, is considered a city of Caleb. This also shows that the clans or tribes of the Calebites, Kenizzites, Kenites, and Jerahmeelites bordering Judah on the south had already occupied their territories and thus set certain limits to the southward expansion of Judah.

The name of the tribe was probably always Judah. At least this is its name in the texts Gen. 49:8-12 and Dt. 33:7, which are historically reliable and clearly date from the period when the tribes were vital political units. The other Israelite tribes, too, bore names consisting solely of a personal name. We may also consider the term *bᵉnê yᵉhûḏâ* relatively early. It appears 53 times in the OT, but can be used not only for the tribe (e.g., Nu. 10:14; Josh. 15:12f.,63; 18:11,14; Jgs. 1:16) but also for the people of the kingdom of Judah (in Jeremiah, esp. Jer. 7:30; 32:30,32; etc.) and even the Jews (Dnl. 1:6), and finally quite literally for the sons and descendants of the patriarch Judah (1 Ch. 2:3f.; 4:1; etc.). The expression *maṭṭēh bᵉnê yᵉhûḏâ* (Josh. 15:1,20f.; 21:9; etc.) is undoubtedly a late combination, since the simple *maṭṭēh yᵉhûḏâ* on which it is based (some 10 occurrences) appears exclusively in P or other late passages (Ex. 31:2; 35:30; 38:22; Nu. 1:27; 7:12; 13:6; 34:19; Josh. 7:1,18; 21:4). Finally, we find the term *šēḇeṭ yᵉhûḏâ* in Josh. 7:16; 1 K. 12:20; 2 K. 17:18; Ps. 78:68). Here, too, we seem to be dealing with a title appearing first in the period of the monarchy, perhaps even not until the division of the kingdom of even later. The subdivision of the *šēḇeṭ* into "families" (*mišpāḥâ*) is presupposed in Nu. 26:22 (P); Josh. 7:17 (emended), and Jgs. 17:7.

---

34 Most recently Noth, *The History of Israel*, 52f.; de Vaux, 547; Herrmann, *History*, 110f., n. 56.

2. *Patriarch.* Even in what we have taken to be the earliest texts in which "Judah" designates a tribe, a process of abstraction can already be observed. The tribal sayings personify the tribe, representing it as an individual, capable of pronouncing a blessing (as in the Blessing of Moses, Dt. 33:7) and having brothers and a father (as in the Blessing of Jacob, Gen. 49:8), or described as a ruler whose entrance into Shiloh is awaited (Gen. 49:10-12).[35] In similar fashion, the phrase *b^enê y^ehûḏâ* can be understood quite literally as referring to the sons and descendants of the patriarch Judah, as is in fact the case in Gen. 46:12; Nu. 26:19f.; etc. Because this abstracting personification is already attested in the earliest passages, it may be considered a natural and original process. The development of the tribe of Judah is therefore linked with the development of its eponymous patriarch Judah.

Judah appears as this individual in Gen. 38, a narrative that reflects the primitive circumstances of tribal development. Judah, married to the Canaanite Shua, begets Er, Onan, and Shelah, of whom Er and Onan die. Er's widow Tamar, mistaken for a prostitute by Judah (who is likewise widowed), becomes pregnant by him and gives birth to the twins Perez and Zerah. In Nu. 26:19-22, then, the Shelanites, Perezites, and Zerahites appear as the actual sons of Judah as well as being Judahite families; for some reason only the Perezites are further divided into Hezronites and Hamulites. In Ruth 4:12, Perez is associated with Bethlehem-Ephrathah, and Ruth 4:18-22 contains the genealogy of Perez through Hezron, Ram, Amminadab, Nahshon, Salmon, Boaz, and Obed to Jesse and David. Finally, we may cite the lists in 1 Ch. 2:3-55 and 4:1-23, where Kenaz (4:13), Caleb (2:42; 4:15), Jerahmeel (2:25), and Cain (2:55) are included among the Judahite families and—at least in 4:24-43—the genealogy of Simeon is appended directly to that of Judah before Reuben, expressing an association between Simeon and Judah that is not unexampled in the OT (cf. Josh. 19:1; Jgs. 1:3). Thus even these genealogies still make a distinction between the original Judah and an extended Judah, between a Judah with its center in Bethlehem-Ephrathah and the Judah that includes Kenaz, Caleb, Jerahmeel, and Cain, and possibly also Simeon. It is noteworthy that this genealogical differentiation is still reflected in Josiah's administrative division of the kingdom.[36]

It is more important for the OT genealogy, however, that the patriarch Judah is a member of the family of Jacob. As the fourth son of Jacob with Leah, Judah was incorporated into the twelve tribe system after Reuben, Simeon, and Levi (Gen. 29:35 [J]; 35:23 [P]). Although this schema underwent many changes, including the removal of Levi and consolidation of Ephraim and Manasseh to form Joseph, the place of Judah remained untouched except for being advanced from fourth to third place. This is important as showing that there was an attempt in the OT to harmonize the actual distribution of power perhaps in the period of David and Solomon with the ranking implicit in the genealogy. The J version of the Joseph story makes Judah rather than the first-born Reuben the spokesman for the brothers. The Chronicler explains laboriously that, although Judah was the strongest of the brothers, the birthright of Reuben

---

[35] Zobel, *Stammesspruch und Geschichte*, 10-14.

[36] Alt, *KlSchr*, II, 285ff.

went to Joseph rather than to Judah; but Joseph was not himself entered in the family genealogy, because the Nagid came forth out of Judah (1 Ch. 5:1f.). Finally, the sequence of tribal sayings in the Blessing of Jacob should be noted: after negative words about Reuben, as well as Simeon and Levi, the first positive saying is devoted to Judah. Furthermore, this saying with its eight lines is among the longest sayings in the Blessing of Jacob. We may interpret this as meaning that Judah is the actual recipient of Jacob's blessing. With all appropriate caution, we may conclude from the texts cited that by the time of David and Solomon this genealogical system with Judah in fourth place was already so fixed in its basic structure that it was no longer possible to revise the ranking of the sons within the system so as to correspond to reality.

IV. History. One of the most difficult problems with respect to the history of Judah is constructing an account of its early history in the pre-Davidic period; the sources are scanty and far from unambiguous. Opinions differ as to whether Judah entered its territory from the east across the lower Jordan[37] or from the south.[38] The scholars who favor the east point to the inclusion of Judah in the "Leah group," for which—or at least for Simeon and Levi—Gen. 34 suggests an early settlement in the central area west of the Jordan, followed—at least for Simeon—by forced migration to the extreme south. This settlement in and around Shechem could have been preceded by a penetration into the settled territory from the east. Because Simeon and Judah dwell together and because according to Jgs. 1 both tribes occupied their territory together, Judah, already associated with Simeon, could also have entered from the east. Others such as Aharoni and Schunck attempt to substantiate this purely hypothetical settlement of Judah in central Palestine by citing the statement about a conflict at Bezek between Judah and Adoni-bezek (Jgs. 1:4ff.): if this site is identical with Kh. Ibzîq, then the events (themselves quite obscure) narrated here took place in the central territory west of the Jordan.

It is nevertheless debatable whether the settlement of the Leah group or even part of it in the region of Shechem really requires entrance from the east, or whether advance into this region from the south is not conceivable. This theory might gain support from the subsequent history of Simeon, which, after the conflicts at Shechem, retreated whence it had come.

The primary evidence for the southern hypothesis is the story of the spies (Nu. 13f.), based on a Calebite occupation tradition. Like Caleb, the argument runs, the other tribes dwelling in the southern region west of the Jordan (such as Kenaz, Cain, and Jerahmeel, together with Judah and Simeon, and possibly even Levi) advanced from the region around Kadesh directly into their later territory. Persuasive as this theory is, the question here remains whether this Calebite tradition can simply be extended to Judah and Simeon. Our study of the geographical data suggested that Hebron and the southern part of the hill country of Judah were already occupied when

---

[37] Most recently Noth, *The History of Israel,* 74; Bright, 136f.; Aharoni, *The Land of the Bible,* 215-220; Schunck.

[38] Most recently J. Scharbert, "Juda," *LThK*², V, 1150; de Vaux, 540-546; Herrmann, *History,* 91, 103.

Judah entered its territory. This suggests a split in the process of occupation between Judah and Simeon on the one hand and Caleb together with the remaining tribes on the other. But does this cast doubt on the southern hypothesis? Hardly—precisely because the geopolitical situation favors advance from the south rather than from the east.[39] One must also note that Judah obviously settled in the vicinity of Caleb, Kenaz, Cain, and Jerahmeel and even (as we shall see) merged with them precisely because there had obviously been contacts between them before the occupation.

With respect to the date of settlement, the lack of clear evidence likewise compels us to resort to conjecture. Noth includes the Judahite occupation in the general Israelite occupation of Canaan, suggesting the end of the thirteenth century B.C.[40] or possibly the second half of the fourteenth century B.C.[41] But those who think the inclusion of Judah in the Leah group represents an historical datum separate the occupation of Canaan by this group from the occupation by the Rachel group both geographically and temporally, considering it an earlier independent event. This might account for the remarkable fact that Gen. 35:21f.; 34; and 38 contain special traditions relating solely to members of this Leah group, which were incorporated into the patriarchal narrative because they reflect a similar historical period, or at least reflect events from the time before the occupation of Canaan by the house of Joseph (cf. Gen. 34). The settlement of Judah may consequently be dated in the fourteenth century B.C.

The actual occupation of the high country between Jerusalem and Hebron by Judah was obviously followed almost at once by the steady, peaceful advance of Judah into the foothills to the west (the Shephelah), with the acquiescence of the Canaanites. This process constitutes the historical background of Gen. 38 and explains the inclusion of city names from this area in the genealogy of Judah.[42] Thus the entire territory delimited by the desert to the south and east and by the Canaanite cities to the north and west came to be settled.

The next discernible political event of any importance was the merger of the Judahites and Simeonites, the Calebites, Kenizzites, Kenites, and Jerahmeelites to form the league of greater Judah, probably because of constant pressure from such elements as the Amalekites, and possibly also the Edomites and other groups, pushing north out of the desert around Kadesh.[43] This league was probably referred to as the "house of Judah," a term found a total of 41 times, beginning with 2 S. 2:4. It referred originally to the monarchy of David at Hebron (cf. the later accurate term "house of Judah and Jerusalem" in Isa. 22:21; Zec. 8:15), but then came to be used mostly in contrast to "house of Israel" (2 S. 12:8; 1 K. 12:21; and 12 other occurrences), "house of Joseph" (Zec. 10:6), or simply "Ephraim" (Hos. 5:12). The narrative in 2 S. 2:1-4, with its inclusion of Hebron among the cities of Judah and its use of "elders of Judah" and "house of Judah" in v. 4, makes it clear that the entity called the "house of Judah"

---

[39] Herrmann, *History,* 91.
[40] Noth, *Aufsätze* I, 189.
[41] Noth, *The History of Israel,* 80f.
[42] See de Vaux, 540-42.
[43] See Zobel, *SVT,* 28 (1975), 253-277.

was already in existence before David became king.[44] Furthermore, the term *bayiṯ* suggests something like a league or covenant uniting the various groups that made up the "house of Judah."[45]

The territory of greater Judah was organized regionally, generally on the basis of cities. Only the Kenites and Jerahmeelites appear to have constituted an exception in that they maintained their old tribal organization for some time (1 S. 30:29). These regions were represented by elders who met in the common capital of Hebron to govern the fortunes of their larger commonwealth.

This league probably came into being in the course of the twelfth century B.C. It achieved its political goal, in that it helped its six members by and large to preserve the wealthy territory of which they had taken possession. Despite repeated attempts, the Amalekites never really succeeded in gaining a foothold in greater Judah. Neither do there seem to have been serious conflicts with the Philistines, who had settled on the western edge of the territory; our sources give the impression of a reasonably well-defined boundary between the adjacent groups.[46] This does not mean, however, that greater Judah was outside the wider sphere of influence of the Philistines. But in contrast to the hill country of Ephraim, we never hear of a Philistine occupation of the hill country of Judah; and the elders of Judah clearly had enough of a free hand at least internally that they could anoint David to be king over them.

But before we turn to this event, we must examine the question of whether Judah belonged to the kingdom of Saul.[47] The primary evidence that it did is Saul's pursuit of David in the land of Judah described in 1 S. 23f. and 26f. and the story of Saul's successful battle with the Amalekites (1 S. 15), which Noth,[48] however, rightly describes as a special tradition without any discernible connection, literary or historical, with the other stories about Saul. Those who maintain the contrary rely primarily on the statement in 2 S. 2:9 that Ishbaal was king over Israel but not king over Judah. This argument has been countered by the assertion that Judah had split off from the former kingdom of Saul in the course of David's rebellion and become independent.[49] This argument, however, is not persuasive. The Philistines also ruled de facto over the other portions of Saul's heritage west of the Jordan, so that the entire statement of 2 S. 2 is nothing more than a postulate, and Judah could well have been included. And we may follow Herrmann in seeing the extension of Saul's pursuit of David to Judahite territory as an "exceptional" measure, so that nothing compels us "to conclude that Saul was also king over Judah."[50] The fact that there is no mention of major

---

[44] For a different view, see de Vaux, 549; and H. J. Stoebe, *Das erste Buch Samuelis. KAT,* VIII/1 (1973), 518.

[45] H. A. Hoffner, "בַּיִת *bayiṯ* [*bayith*]," *TDOT,* II, 114.

[46] See Zobel, *SVT,* 28 (1975), 271ff.

[47] Most recently K.-D. Schunck, *Benjamin. BZAW,* 86 (1963), 124-26; Smend; Aharoni, *The Land of the Bible*, 289-291; Bright, 189, 193f.; de Vaux, 548f.; also Scharbert, 1150.

[48] *The History of Israel*, 175.

[49] *Ibid.*, 182; Aharoni, 289-291.

[50] Herrmann, *History,* 140.

or minor judges from Judah[51] and the absence of Judah from the Song of Deborah may also be cited in evaluating the independent development of Judah well into the early period of the monarchy.

With the kingship of David over Judah we are finally standing on historically firm ground. David had won the favor of the elders of greater Judah through gifts of spoil taken in battle (1 S. 30:26-31); at Hebron they now anoint him king over the house of Judah (2 S. 2:1-4). Even when the monarchic principle is incorporated into the democratic organization of greater Judah, we find the elders as the locus of the political power that decides the fate of their commonwealth. Those referred to in 1 S. 30:26 as "elders of Judah" (*ziqnê y^ehûḏâ*) are called "men of Judah" (*'anšê y^ehûḏâ*) in 2 S. 2:4. That both expressions refer in fact to the same entity is shown by the three other passages in the OT where we find the phrase "elders of Judah." According to 2 S. 19:12(11), after the death of Absalom the elders of Judah are to bring the king back, and in v. 15(14) the "men of Judah" (*'îš-y^ehûḏâ*) send word to David to return. In this narrative vv. 17(16) and 42-44(41-43) also speak of the "men of Judah" (*'îš*). There is a similar situation in 2 K. 23:1 (par. 2 Ch. 34:29): the "elders of Judah and Jerusalem" spoken of here are called in v. 2 "all the men [sg.] of Judah and all the inhabitants of Jerusalem." Finally, Ezk. 8:1 speaks of the elders of Judah, i.e., the elders of the exiled Judahites. The concept "elders of Judah" can also be represented by the expression "men [sg.] of Judah." In the rarer plural this phrase also means the same thing. In 2 S. 2:4, we are told that the "men of Judah" (pl.: *'anšê y^ehûḏâ*) anointed David king over the house of Judah, and then the king states in v. 7 that the "house of Judah" has anointed him king over them. In other words, the entities "men [pl.] of Judah" and "house of Judah" are identical, just as the term "house of Judah" always takes a plural verb (2 S. 2:7,10; Jer. 3:18; 36:3; Ezk. 8:17; 25:3; cf. Neh. 4:10; Jer. 11:10). Like the "elders" in 1 S. 30:26, the "men" represent the "house." In other words, the "men" (sg. or pl.) or "elders" represent the political power of the house of Judah. This is also the situation in 1 K. 1:9, where Adonijah invites all his brothers and "all the men [pl.] of Judah" to have them recognize his claim to the throne. In addition to this meaning, the phrase "men of Judah and Benjamin" in Ezr. 10:9 means all the marriageable men. In 1 S. 17:52, the "men of Judah" are introduced secondarily alongside the "men of Israel" as taking part in the pursuit of the Philistines when they are put to flight by David's victory over Goliath. Here "men" means the warriors of the militia.

This broad spectrum of meanings also holds for the sg. *'îš y^ehûḏâ*, "men of Judah," found 31 times. We have already pointed out that "men" and "elders" here have the same meaning. It is appropriate to add that our phrase also appears in Jgs. 15:10; 2 S. 19:15,17,42-44(14,16,41-43); 2 K. 23:2 in the sense of "the men who carry out the business of government." The legal community is addressed in Isa. 5:3,7. Frequently the militia is intended (Jgs. 15:11; 1 S. 11:8; 15:4; 2 S. 20:2,4; 24:9; 2 Ch. 13:15; 20:27; 34:30). This expression also serves to designate the people of Judah as a

[51] K.-D. Schunck, "Die Richter Israels und ihr Amt," *Volume de Congrès, Genève 1965. SVT,* 15 (1966), 252-262, esp. 257.

political entity comprising Judahites and Jerusalemites (Jer. 4:3f.; 11:2,9; 17:25; 18:11; 32:32; 35:13; 36:31; also Dnl. 9:7). Finally, Jer. 44:26f. refers to the Judahites who emigrated to Egypt. In all these passages, as we can see, the term has a political meaning. It refers to those Judahites who as full citizens are subject to militia duty, who administer justice in the gate, who as elders take responsibility for government; it can be extended to mean the citizens of the state of Judah in general.

Finally, all the expressions so far discussed can be included under the category "people of the land" (*'am hā'āreṣ*) when this term refers to the body of full citizens of Judah, property owners, assembled for political purposes (cf. Gen. 23:7,12f.; 2 K. 11:14,18-20; 21:24 [twice]; 23:30; 25:19 [twice]; possibly also 2 K. 15:5; 16:15; 23:35; 24:14; 25:3). Würthwein[52] already pointed out that at least the term "men of Judah" is identical with the expression "people of the land" and has the same meaning. Finally, it may be noted that at least in 2 K. 14:21 (par. 2 Ch. 26:1) the term "people of Judah" (*'am* y^e*hûḏâ*), found also in five other passages, is identical with the "people of the land." The point at issue is the choice of Azariah by "all the people of Judah" to replace the murdered Amaziah as king of Judah, a duty otherwise performed by the "people of the land." In 2 S. 19:41(40), we read that "all the people of Judah" and "half the people of Israel" went with David; since vv. 42-44(41-43) go on to speak of "all the men [sg.] of Judah and Israel," it is the soldiers who appear to be involved. And the Jeremiah passages (Jer. 25:1f.; 26:18) use "people of Judah" for those to whom the word of Yahweh is addressed, meaning simply the Judahites. In Ezr. 4:4, finally, our expression refers to the Judahites preparing to rebuild the temple.

There is no Israelite parallel to the Judahite term *'am hā'āreṣ;* the group referred to is therefore exclusively Judahite. This is further evidence that Judah and Israel are two disparate political entities, which underwent separate and distinct development until the time of David. It may be noted here merely for the sake of completeness that the kingship developed along charismatic lines in Israel and along dynastic lines in Judah because of the difference in origin.[53]

For the subsequent history of Judah, it is worth noting that the title "king of Judah," used 150 times in the OT, appears for the first time in 1 K. 12:23, where the man of God Shemaiah uses it of Rehoboam. Even the pl. "kings of Judah" appears only once, in 1 S. 27:6, before 1 K. 14:29 speaks of the "Book of the Chronicles of the Kings of Judah"; the Samuel passage explains why Ziklag belongs to the "kings of Judah"—an apparently late addition, dating in its literary form at least from after the division of the kingdom.[54]

The literary evidence is of some importance in view of the fact that Saul is called "king of Israel" by David (1 S. 24:15[14]; 26:20) as well as by the Philistine Achish (1 S. 29:3), so that it is highly possible that he bore this title. Even though only an isolated statement is involved, it is of interest that David is also called "king of Israel" by Michal in 2 S. 6:20. The expressions "David was king over the house of Judah"

[52] E. Würthwein, *Der 'amm ha'arez im AT* (Stuttgart, 1936), 15.

[53] Cf. Alt, *Essays,* 239-259; most recently, Herrmann, *SVT,* 17 (1968), 139-158; *History,* 152.

[54] Cf. Stoebe, *KAT,* VIII/1, 478f.

(2 S. 2:4,7), "Ishbaal was king over all Israel" (2 S. 2:9), and "David ruled over all Israel and Judah" (2 S. 5:5) are value-free statements of political fact; the title "king of Israel," however, probably always implies a special dignity, having overtones of the sacral status enjoyed by the king of Israel as Yahweh's anointed, at least in the case of Saul, and inherent in the name "Israel" from the very beginning. It is therefore likely that David, and probably Solomon as well, like Saul before them, bore the title "king of Israel." With the division of the kingdom this title devolved upon Jeroboam, the king of the northern kingdom, so that Rehoboam received the analogous title "king of Judah." He was the first to be called king of Judah, and Jehoiachin was the last (2 K. 25:27). In this case Judah included both the land bearing that name and the territory of Jerusalem;[55] in other words, it was the name of the whole political entity, just as it was to be again in the time of Nehemiah, whose intent it was finally to eliminate the distinction between city and countryside in Judah by requiring the resettlement of families from the rural areas to Jerusalem (Neh. 7:4f.; 11:1f.).

The terminological rivalry that ultimately created a contrast like that explicit in Isa. 5:7[56] between the two names "Israel" and "Judah" with their unequal shares in historical tradition came to an end with the end of the political independence of the northern kingdom in 722 B.C. As Rost has shown, in the period that followed, Judah unhesitatingly adopted the name "Israel" along with the Israelite tradition behind the name. As a result of this process, which may have extended into the reign of Josiah,[57] "Judah" became once more an exclusively secular political term, which it remained thenceforth. The reign of Josiah represented a last political golden age for the southern kingdom; he was able to extend the northern boundary of Judah far into the former territory of the northern kingdom and at the same time effect the internal stabilization of Judah through cultic reform. Even so, however, the name "Judah" occurs only once, for example, in Dt. 1–29, buried in the list of tribes standing on Mt. Gerizim (Dt. 27:12), while the name "Israel" is found 46 times there.

On the whole, the most difficult problem related to the history of the monarchy is that of chronology. Since it also involves the northern kingdom and goes beyond the limits of this article, we will not discuss it here.[58] For the same reason, we pass over the history of Judah in the exilic and postexilic period, referring the reader to the current literature.

V. Theology. We are fully in the dark as to the beginnings of Yahweh worship among the groups that came together to form Judah. Down to the time of David, Judah and the Judahite tribes and clans had a history separate from that of the central Palestinian tribes; it is therefore likely that they also found their way to Yahwism independently. The manner in which this took place must remain hypothetical. We can think of the Kenites, who were associated with Judah and probably had Yahweh

---

[55] Rost, 3.

[56] Cf. H. Wildberger, *Jesaja. BK*, X/1 (1972), 172.

[57] Herrmann, *History*, 268.

[58] See most recently *ibid.*, 188f., and the literature cited in nn. 2-8.

as their God before the Judahites.[59] But we can also think of the Levites, who belonged to the Leah group, as the agents of Yahwism, especially since the exodus tradition assigns Moses to the tribe of Levi (Ex. 2:1-10) and the Levites claim to have been entrusted with the priestly office at or near Kadesh (Dt. 33:8-11). And if we decide that Judah entered Canaan from the south, we can think of the oasis of Kadesh quite apart from the Levites, assigning it the function of imparting Yahwism to the Judahites and affiliated groups during their temporary stay there, especially since it has long been known that a number of Kadesh traditions are included in the total corpus of desert and Sinai traditions, to which they have taken a back seat, so that we must recognize an independent role played by Kadesh vis-à-vis Sinai. It is impossible to decide with any assurance among the different possibilities, various combinations of which are also conceivable.

But one observation is germane at this point: in the early period, the intensity and importance of Yahwism were clearly less in Judah than in Israel. The exodus and Sinai traditions, which are fundamental to the faith of Israel, were the exclusive property of the northern kingdom; they are intimately associated with the name "Israel." The same is true of the notions of covenant and election. Even the early Israelite cultic symbols of the ark and the golden bull, associated by tradition totally with the events at Sinai, may be considered typically Israelite. That Judah had nothing even remotely similar to offer can be seen from David's efforts to gain his new capital the status of a cultic metropolis by recalling the Israelite ark and bringing it to Jerusalem. Obviously there was nothing more appropriate at his disposal, nor do our sources say anything about typically Judahite cultic symbols.

For the period of Judahite religious history before the introduction of Yahwism, as for the other proto-Israelites, we can assume the religion of El.[60] For Jerusalem (then a Jebusite city), Gen. 14:18-20 names El Elyon; for Calebite Hebron or the nearby sanctuary of Mamre, Gen. 13:18; 17:1; 18:1ff. name El Shaddai; for the sanctuary of Beer-sheba, Gen. 21:33 names El 'Olam; and for the oasis of Beer-lahai-roi, somewhere in the Negeb, Gen. 16:11-14 names El Roi (cf. Gen. 24:62). Thus OT tradition links the patriarchs Abraham and Isaac with sites in the territory that was later to be greater Judah. It is noteworthy that nothing is said of any sanctuary peculiar to the tribe of Judah itself; it is clear that we should think of Judah as taking part from the beginning in the cult of other sanctuaries, possibly even that of Hebron/Mamre. Even in the religious realm we thus discern the nascent outlines of a kind of Judahite state, corresponding to a markedly nationalistic sense of identity in Judah and contrasting in roughly the same period with a more religious sense of identity in Israel.[61] The dynastic kingship of Judah is rooted in the same intellectual milieu. It had a purely political origin; only after the fact was it legitimized religiously by the prophecy of

---

[59] See H. Heyde, *Kain, der erste Jahwe-Verehrer. ArbT,* 1/23 (1965).

[60] See O. Eissfeldt, "El und Jahwe," *JSS,* 1 (1956), 25-37 = *KlSchr,* III (1966), 386-397; *idem,* "Der kanaanäische El as Geber der den israelitischen Erzvätern geltenden Nachkommenschaft- und Landbesitzverheissungen," in *Festschrift C. Brockelmann. WZ Halle-Eittenberg,* 17 (1968), 45-53 = *KlSchr,* V, 50-62.

[61] Cf. Zobel, *ZAW,* 85 (1973), 281-294.

Nathan (2 S. 7). It thus differed from the charismatic kingship of Israel, which was inaugurated by divine election and then constituted by popular acclamation.

We must also consider the incorporation into Yahwism of Canaanite religious notions, initiated by the inclusion of the priest Zadok[62] (probably a pre-Israelite Jebusite) in David's cabinet and institutionalized by Solomon's building of the Jerusalem temple. Faith in a creator-God,[63] linked with El in the Ugaritic texts, is explicitly connected by the OT itself (Gen. 14:19) with El Elyon of Jerusalem, thus becoming a Jerusalemite theologoumenon. This makes it probable that the notion of God as creator entered into Yahwism through Jerusalem or Judah; the earliest witness to this belief is Gen. 2:4bff., from the hand of the Yahwist, who was certainly from Judah, as was the exilic prophet Deutero-Isaiah, who brought new life to this notion after it had lain dormant for centuries. Jerusalem can probably also be looked on as the access point for other credal statements of Israel that are rooted in the religious milieu of Canaan.

Apart from the Abraham and Isaac traditions, which, as we have seen, were indigenous to greater Judah, the traditions of David and Zion may be singled out as being typically Judahite. Although we encounter these traditions in the preexilic period in Isaiah and Jeremiah,[64] it was Judah's loss of independence in 586 B.C. and the exile that lent them enhanced significance. The exile confronted the David tradition above all with the question of whether the divine promise addressed to David through Nathan remained in force. Deutero-Isaiah deals with the question by democratizing the promise and treating the people as the true recipients of God's eternal grace shown to David (Isa. 55:3-5).[65] The other possibility of securing the unbroken vitality of Nathan's promise for the faith of Israel in the exilic and postexilic period is to interpret it eschatologically: it is not yet fulfilled and is therefore still in force. Its awaited fulfillment can involve the "restoration of the Davidic dual monarchy,"[66] as in Jeremiah (Jer. 23:5f.; 30:9; 33:15f.); Ezekiel (Ezk. 37:24; cf. 34:23f.) expects reunification of Judah and Joseph to form a new Israel under the rule of the coming David.[67] Trito-Isaiah (Isa. 65:9) possibly and Zechariah (Zech. 2:16[12]), like Micah (Mic. 5:1ff.[2ff.]) before them, expect salvation limited to Judah. The name "Judah" in the religious sense is clearly linked with this expectation.

Other messianic hopes also work their way into this context, in that they look for a coming ruler from the house of David (cf. Ps. 89; Isa. 8:23–9:6[9:1-7]; 11:1-5; Hos. 3:5; Am. 9:11f.) and thus hope, even if not always explicitly, that a new age will dawn for Jerusalem and Judah. In any case, in the early postexilic period the hopes centering on the governor Zerubbabel or on Zerubbabel and the high priest Joshua (Hag. 2:20-23; Zec. 4:14) point to the existence of such expectations with immediate consequences

---

[62] Cf. H. H. Rowley, *Worship in Ancient Israel* (Philadelphia, 1967), 72-75.

[63] → אל *'ēl*.

[64] Cf. G. von Rad, *OT Theology*, I (Eng. trans., New York, 1962), 40ff., 73ff.

[65] O. Eissfeldt, "Die Gnadenverheissungen an David in Jes 55,1-5," *KlSchr*, IV (1968), 44-52 [= "The Promise of Grace to David in Isaiah 55:1-5," in *Israel's Prophetic Heritage. Festschrift J. Muilenburg* (New York, 1962), 196-207].

[66] Rost, 3.

[67] See W. Zimmerli, *Ezekiel II. Herm* (Eng. trans. 1983), 563ff.

for Judah; Nehemiah himself was accused of wanting to be acclaimed "king in Judah" (Neh. 6:7). This messianic hope, already exhibiting a variety of forms in the OT, underwent further development in Judaism; its fixed elements are always the origin of the Messiah from the lineage of David and his work on behalf of Judah and Jerusalem (cf., e.g., 2 Esd. 12:31-34; Pss. Sol. 17f.; T. Sim. 7; and the texts from Qumran).

The second of the two traditions, the Zion tradition, is, as von Rad has cogently emphasized, an independent tradition of divine election. It represents the latest of these traditions.[68] Since it is dominated by a "consciousness of unrestricted safety and security with Jahweh,"[69] it differs from the typically Israelite election tradition, the exodus tradition; while the latter is characterized by marked dynamism, the former exhibits a static steadfastness[70] that may also be considered part of the ancient Judahite ideology. In any case, it is thanks to this tradition that "Judah" became the name of the Golah and, in the postexilic period, the "official term for the cultic community gathered about the Jerusalem temple, as well as for the Persian province that had been independent of Samaria since the time of Nehemiah,"[71] and that finally the religion of Yahweh could survive as "Judaism" (cf. Zec. 8:23).[72]

Subject to the qualifications outlined here, to the effect that despite the wealth of theological statements associated with the name "Israel" there are some theologoumena in the OT linked with the name "Judah," von Rad's categorical statement is true: "Judah is the name of a tribe, and it remains . . . throughout the whole range of OT literature . . . the secular name for a tribe."[73]

Zobel

---

68 Von Rad, *OT Theology,* I, 46f.
69 *Ibid.*
70 See also Zobel, *ThLZ,* 93 (1968), 1-12.
71 Rost, 3; Bach, 964, gives the archaeological evidence for the name *yhd.*
72 Hempel, 899; cf. Scharbert, 1151.
73 Von Rad, *TDNT,* III, 356f.

יהוה YHWH

Contents: I. The Word. II. Evidence for Vocalization and Extrabiblical Use: 1. Biblical; 2. Extrabiblical; 3. Greek; 4. Second Millennium Sources; 5. Summary. III. Amorite. 1. Evidence; 2. Phonology of the Tetragrammaton. IV. Meaning: 1. General; 2. Biblical Evidence; 3. Other Theories. V. The Figure of Yahweh.

I. The Word. The Tetragrammaton *YHWH* is the personal name of the God of Moses. The correct pronunciation of the name was lost from Jewish tradition some time during the Middle Ages; late in the period of the Second Temple the name had come to be regarded as unspeakably holy and therefore unsuitable for use in public reading, although it continued to be used privately. Early in the modern period, scholars began to try to recover the pronunciation. The form *yahweh* is now accepted almost universally.[1] The structure and etymology of the name have been much discussed. While no consensus exists, the name is generally thought to be a verbal form derived from the root *hwy,* later *hyh,*[2] "be at hand, exist (phenomenally), come to pass." Whether the verb was originally a qal or a hiphil formation is not entirely clear. The weight of the evidence is on the side of the latter.

The problems associated with the Tetragrammaton are manifold and all somewhat technical. Biblical orthography and onomastics must be surveyed, together with extrabiblical evidence for the vocalization and use of the name; phonological and typological arguments must also be reviewed before the biblical narrative itself can be discussed.

Freedman

YHWH. F. M. Cross, *Canaanite Myth and Hebrew Epic* (Cambridge, Mass., 1973); G. R. Driver, "The Original Form of the Name 'Yahweh': Evidence and Conclusions," *ZAW,* 46 (1928), 7-25; Z. S. Harris, *Development of the Canaanite Dialects. AOS,* 16 (1939); J. P. Hyatt, "The Origin of Mosaic Yahwism," *The Teacher's Yoke. Festschrift H. Trantham* (Waco, 1946), 85-93; E. Jenni, "יהוה *Jhwh* Jahwe," *THAT,* I, 701-707; J. Kinyongo, *Origine et signification du nom divín Yahvé àla lumière de récents travaux et de traditions sémitico-bibliques. BBB,* 35 (1970); J. L'Hour, "Yahweh Elohim," *RB,* 81 (1974), 524-556; *D. J. McCarthy, "Exod. 3:14: History, Philology and Theology," *CBQ,* 40 (1978), 311-322; S. Mowinckel, "The Name of the God of Moses," *HUCA,* 32 (1961), 121-133; A. E. Murtonen, *A Philological and Literary Treatise on the OT Divine Names* אל*,* אלוה*,* אלוהים *and* יהוה (Helsinki, 1952); S. Norin, "Jô-Namen und J^e^hô-Namen," *VT,* 29 (1979), 87-97; *G. H. Parke-Taylor, *Yahweh: The Divine Name in the Bible* (Waterloo, Ont., 1975); B. Porten, *Archives from Elephantine* (Berkeley, 1968); W. H. Schmidt, "Der Jahwename und Ex. 3,14," *Textgemäss. Festschrift E. Würthwein* (Göttingen, 1979), 123-138; M. W. Stolper, "A Note on Yahwistic Personal Names in the Murašû Texts," *BASOR,* 222 (1976), 25-28; R. de Vaux, *The Early History of Israel* (Eng. trans., Philadelphia, 1978); *idem,* "The Revelation of the Divine Name YHWH," *Proclamation and Presence. Festschrift G. H. Davies* (London, 1970), 48-75, esp. 67-69; *L. Viganò, *Nomi e titoli di YHWH alla luce del semitico del Nord-Ovest. BietOr,* 31 (1976); *B. N. Wambacq, "*'Eh^e^yeh, 'ašer 'eh^e^yeh,*" *Bibl,* 59 (1978), 317-338. [*Appeared after completion of article]

[1] The history of modern interpretations is discussed by Kinyongo, 51-53.

[2] → היה *hāyâ* [*hāyāh*].

II. Evidence for Vocalization and Extrabiblical Use.

1. *Biblical.*

a. *Orthography.* In the MT, *YHWH* is an example of a *qere perpetuum:* the consonants are supplied with the vowels of the spoken form *'ᵃḏōnāy,*[3] or, if *'ᵃḏōnāy* preceded, with the vowels of *'ᵉlōhîm,* without indication of the appropriate consonants in the margin. The impossible form *yᵉhōwāh* (Eng. "Jehovah") came into being when Renaissance Christians either failed to recognize or chose to ignore the Masoretic convention. The Masoretes did not, however, supply the precise vowel points required for their pronunciation, which would have yielded the form *yᵃhōwāh;* this form would have violated the very taboo they sought to observe if the first syllable had contained an *a* vowel. They therefore wrote *yᵉhōwāh* with the most colorless vowel in their system. The writing *yᵉhōwih* for *'ᵉlōhîm* similarly does not violate the taboo. These writings thus contain indirect evidence that the first syllable of the Tetragrammaton did not contain *ᵉ* or a similar vowel.[4]

This reading of the divine name is probably much older than the MT. In some (though by no means all) of the Dead Sea scrolls, the use of the archaic script to write the name may indicate a special pronunciation. In 4Q139, two dots before the name *YHWH* may serve the same function.[5] Material from Jewish sources will be found in Reisel and Rosh-Pinnah.[6] According to Driver,[7] the Tetragrammaton was abbreviated to *y* in early biblical texts, but his argument is not convincing.

b. *Onomastic Evidence.* Personal names compounded with the name *YHWH* are common in the OT.[8] In initial position, the element has two forms: *yô-* and *yᵉhô-*. In the received text, these alternate rather freely, e.g., *yônāṯān* and *yᵉhônāṯān, yôyāḵîn* and *yᵉhôyāḵîn;* the short form is more common in early monarchic and postexilic texts, the longer in late monarchic texts.[9] The longer form is obviously original. In regular Hebrew phonology, an *h* can be elided only at a formative boundary (*maqṭîl* < *mahaqṭîl, babbayiṯ* < *bahabbayiṯ*), but it is hardly surprising to find such elision within a word in the case of a personal name.[10] At the end of a name, the Tetragrammaton also has two forms: *-yāhû* and *-yāh,* e.g., *malkiyyāhû* and *malkiyyāh/yâ, ma'ᵃśēyāhû* and *ma'ᵃśēyāh/yâ.* Here, too, priority must be assigned to the longer form, which suggests that both derive from **yahw* with vocalization of the *w* to *u.*[11] In the

---

3 → אדון *'āḏôn* [*'ādhôn*].

4 *UT,* no. 1084; for another explanation, see R. Kittel, "Yahweh," *Schaff-Herzog,* XII, 470f.

5 J. Strugnell, 164 and n. 27, in J. P. Siegel, "The Employment of Palaeo-Hebrew Characters for the Divine Names at Qumran in the Light of Tannaitic Sources," *HUCA,* 42 (1971), 159-172.

6 M. Reisel *The Mysterious Name of Yahweh* (Assen, 1967); E. Rosh-Pinnah, "The Sefer Yetzirah and the Original Tetragrammaton," *JQR,* N.S. 57 (1967), 212-226.

7 G. R. Driver, "Abbreviations in the Massoretic Text," *Textus,* 1 (1960), 111-131.

8 See *IPN* and Kinyongo, 47f.

9 Driver, *ZAW,* 46 (1928), 22.

10 Harris, 52-56.

11 *BLe,* §25c', d'.

longer form, the *u* has been preserved through lengthening; in the shorter, the *u* was not lengthened and was therefore lost.

We will not discuss here the short form *yāh,* which appears in poetry as early as the tenth century (e.g., Ps. 68:5,19[Eng. vv. 4,18]) and in the liturgical formula *halᵉlû-yāh.* It strangely appears also in Ex. 15:2. In Ex. 17:16, *kēs yāh* should probably be read as a verbal form of the root *ksy (kāsâ).* Cross[12] maintains that at least in later sources the form *yāh* has nothing to do with the divine name but is a vocative particle like Ugar. *y* and Arab. *yā*. According to other scholars, the short form represents the original form of the divine name; according to Driver,[13] divine names are never shortened in other Semitic languages, and it is therefore unlikely that so sacred a name as "Yahweh" could be abbreviated. Examples to the contrary are rare, but they are found, e.g., *ḥîrōm* < *'ᵃḥîrōm,* possibly *'eldāḏ* < *'el-hᵃḏad,* "Hadad is God," and *mêḏāḏ* < *mê-hᵃḏaḏ,* "water of Hadad (?)."

2. *Extrabiblical.*

a. *The Name Itself.* The extremely early date of the meager extrabiblical evidence makes it an appropriate starting point for our study. With one noteworthy exception, the occurrences of the name "Yahweh" are limited to blessing and cursing formulas and allusions to such formulas in cultic references and titles. These texts are cited here in chronological order. Instances where the divine name is restored are omitted, e.g., the Fort Shalmaneser inscription[14] and the two ostraca from Megiddo and Samaria with *lyh.*[15]

(1) The earliest extrabiblical evidence is the Mesha inscription,[16] where we read: *w'qḥ mšm '[t k]ly yhwh wśḥb hm lpny kmš,* "and I took the vessels [cf. Isa. 52:11] of Yahweh and dragged them before Chemosh." The appearance of the Tetragrammaton is unquestionable.

(2) An eighth-century seal in the Harvard Semitic Museum collection bears the inscription *lmqnyw 'bd.yhwh,* "belonging to Miqneyaw, the servant of *yhwh.*" The name seems to be levitical (cf. 1 Ch. 15:18,21); the owner of the seal was probably a priest serving the sanctuary.[17]

---

[12] F. M. Cross, "The Cave Inscriptions from Khirbet Beit Lei," *Near Eastern Archaeology in the Twentieth Century. Festschrift N. Glueck* (Garden City, 1970), 306, n. 17.

[13] *ZAW,* 46 (1928), 23.

[14] A. R. Millard, "Alphabetical Inscriptions on Ivories from Nimrud," *Iraq,* 24 (1962), 41-51.

[15] De Vaux, *The Early History of Israel,* 340, nn. 83f.

[16] *KAI,* 181.17f.

[17] Cross, *Canaanite Myth and Hebrew Epic,* 61.

(3) A funerary inscription from Khirbet el-Qôm, southwest of Lachish, dating from around 750 B.C.,[18] contains the words *brk 'wryhw lyhwh,* "blessed be Uriyahu by Yahweh."[19]

(4) An inscription in four fragments found at Kuntillat 'Ajrud near the Sinai peninsula includes the letters *hyṭb yhwh* and the divine name "Ba'al" in Phoenician script.[20]

(5) The Lachish letters from the last days of the monarchy contain several formulas employing the Tetragrammaton. The largest number of occurrences are in greetings: *yšm' yhwh 't 'dny š[m]'t šlm 't kym 't kym,* "May Yahweh make my lord hear good news soon";[21] *yr' yhwh 't 'dny 't h't hzh šlm,* "May Yahweh make my lord see this season in good health."[22] The common OT oath formula *ḥy yhwh,* "As Yahweh lives,"[23] also occurs at Lachish, once with the biblical spelling[24] and once with the eccentric spelling *ḥyhwh,*[25] probably scriptio continua or possibly haplography.[26] The name also occurs in the context *ybrk yhwh 't '[??]y,*[27] an unexplained passage, and possibly also in a badly damaged portion of a text.[28]

(6) The Arad ostraca discovered by Aharoni have been published only in part. One of the letters[29] contains two references to Yahweh, the first in the introductory greeting: *'l 'dny 'lyšb yhwh yš'l lšlmk* (lines 1-3), "To my lord Elyashib; may Yahweh seek your peace" (lit., "ask after," probably equivalent to "grant"; cf. 1 S. 1:28 and a similar formula in Aramaic[30]), the second in lines 7-10: *wldbr 'šr ṣwtny šlm byt yhwh h' yšb,* "And as for the matter concerning which you commanded me—it has been settled. In the house of Yahweh he remains." The writer may have been stationed at the Jerusalem temple. The reference to staying in the temple is odd; cf. Ps. 23:6, where *bêṯ-YHWH* may mean Yahweh's territory or land, which is also possible here.[31]

---

[18] W. G. Dever, "Iron Age Epigraphic Material from the Area of Khirbet el-Kôm," *HUCA,* 40-41 (1969-1970), 139-204.

[19] A. Lemaire, "Les Inscriptions de Khirbet El-Qôm et l'Ashérah de YHWH," *RB,* 84 (1977), 595-608.

[20] Z. Meshel, "Kuntilat 'Ajrud—An Israelite Site on the Sinai Border," *Qadmoniot,* 9 (1976), 122.

[21] *KAI,* 192.1-3; variants in *KAI,* 193.2f.; 194.1f.; 195.1-3; 197.1f.

[22] *KAI,* 196.1f.

[23] → חיה *ḥāyâ* [*chāyāh*].

[24] *KAI,* 196.12.

[25] *KAI,* 193.9.

[26] Harris, 31, 57; M. Greenberg, "The Hebrew Oath Particle *Ḥay/Ḥē,*" *JBL,* 76 (1957), 34-39.

[27] *KAI,* 192.5f., unexplained.

[28] *KAI,* 194.7f.

[29] Y. Aharoni, "Hebrew Ostraca from Tell Arad," *IEJ,* 16 (1966), 1-7.

[30] *AP,* 30, 1f.

[31] → ישב *yāšaḇ.*

(7) The most difficult of the preexilic uses of the Tetragrammaton occurs in some wall inscriptions from Khirbet Beit Lei, a few miles from Lachish.[32] Inscription A, as given by Cross, reads: *[']ny yhwh 'lhykh 'rṣh 'ry yhdh wg'lty yršlm,* "I am Yahweh, your God, I will accept the cities of Judah and I will redeem Jerusalem." Cross regards the text as poetic and speculates that it might be a prophecy from the time of the fall of Jerusalem. Cross reads text B as follows: *nqh yh 'l ḥnn nqh yh yhwh,* "Absolve [us], O merciful God; absolve [us], O Yahweh." Text C reads: *hwš' yhwh,* "Deliver [us], Yahweh." Although Cross and Naveh differ in their readings, they agree on the occurrence of the Tetragrammaton and also think that the texts are not merely formulaic.

(8) The remaining occurrences are limited to Aramaic texts from Egypt. Two spellings of the divine name occur: *yhw* (almost always in papyri) and *yhh* (once in a papyrus,[33] otherwise on ostraca). The spelling *yh,* attested once,[34] is probably the result of the fading of original *yhw.*

The name occurs 8 times on ostraca in the formula *ḥy yhh.* That the expression is common can be seen from a letter to a woman: "I am sending you vegetables tomorrow. Meet the boat tomorrow on Sabbath lest they get lost/spoiled. By the life of *yhh,* if not, I shall take your life. Do not rely upon Meshullemeth or upon Shemaiah. Now, send me barley in return. . . . Now, by the life of *yhh,* if not, you will be responsible for the bill."[35] The form *yhh ṣb't* occurs on ostraca in greeting formulas.[36] Particularly interesting is the greeting, "I send you peace and life. I bless you by *yhh* and *ḥn[m???],*" an apparently syncretistic formula linking Yahweh with the local Egyptian god Khnum.[37] References to swearing by *byhw 'lh' byb byrt',* "by the god *yhw* in the fortress of Elephantine," and the like occur in the same papyri.[38]

A number of the references to *yhw* involve the cult of the temple at Elephantine, usually called *'gwr'* (Akk. *ekurru,* from Sum. *é-kur*), but once *byt* and once *byt mdbh'*.[39] One Aramaic text refers apparently to harassment of the Judahite garrison for their religious observance.[40] The temple of *yhw* was probably destroyed around 410 B.C., when this text was written. In a later text, written around 408, the members of the garrison request permission to rebuild the temple.[41] Yet another text may contain a reference to the rebuilding.[42] Two people in one text are called *khny' zy yhw 'lh',*

---

[32] J. Naveh, "Old Hebrew Inscriptions in a Burial Cave," *IEJ,* 13 (1963), 74-96; cf. Cross, *Festschrift N. Glueck,* 299-306.

[33] *AP,* 13, 14.

[34] *BMAP,* 3; see Porten, 106, n. 5.

[35] Clermont-Ganneau text 152; cf. Porten, 126.

[36] Porten, 106, n. 6; 109.

[37] *Ibid.,* 159, 275.

[38] *AP,* 6, 4, see Porten, 237-240; *AP,* 45, see Porten, 153.

[39] Porten, 109.

[40] *AP,* 27.

[41] *AP,* 30, cf. 31; F. Rosenthal, *An Aramaic Handbook. PLO,* N.S. 10 (1967), I/1, 10f.

[42] *AP,* 33; Porten, 110-15, 284-296.

"priests of the god *yhw.*" The term "servitor (*lḥn*) of *yhw*" probably refers to some religiously sanctioned position.[43]

Especially noteworthy is the collection list, which is headed: *znh šmht ḥyl' yhwdy' zy yhb ksp lyhw 'lh' lgbr l[g]br ksp [š 2],* "This is [a list of the] names of [the people of] the Judahite garrison who gave money for the god *yhw,* each in the sum of [two shekels]."[44] The end of the text seems to contradict this superscription by recording that more than a third of the money went to *yhw,* a similar amount to 'Anath-Bethel, and the rest to Ešem-Bethel. This appears to reflect a partially syncretized cult, although other interpretations are possible.[45]

(9) Thus some 19 occurrences of the Tetragrammaton in the form *yhwh* bear witness to the reliability of the MT in this respect; more may be expected, notably from the Arad archives.

The vocalization of the form *yhwh* has sometimes been taken as *yahwō* on the basis of forms like *nbh,* "Nebo," and *'th,* Biblical Heb. *'ôṯô.*[46] It has been demonstrated, however, that the South Canaanite dialects (Hebrew, Moabite) were consistent in their use of final matres lectionis: *y* stood for *ī, w* for *ū,* and *h* for *ē, ā,* or *ō.*[47] The reading *ō* is therefore not supported by the evidence.

The Elephantine forms *yhw* and *yhh* are more than twice as numerous as the form *yhwh,* although the diversity of spelling is confusing. The ostracon form *yhh* is probably more advanced linguistically (*ū* > *ō*) than the papyrus form (*û*). One could interpret this as indicating that the sound shift was in process at the time, but it is simple to assume that it was already complete and that the form *yhw* was a slight archaism.

We may therefore summarize: (a) the consonants of the name are *yhw;* (b) the name ended in a long non-high vowel, which was not *ī* or *ū;* (c) a shorter form of the name appears around the time of the exile, which may be derived from the prefixed (*yᵉhô-yô-*) or suffixed (*-yāhû, -yāh*) forms used in compounds; (d) after the final vowel was lost, *w* changed to *ū* (later > *ō*).

There is a problematic occurrence on a fifth-century incense altar from Lachish,[48] where *yh* may be a divine name, but the reading is dubious.[49] Jar handles from the

---

[43] *AP,* 38, 1; see Porten, 35, 74, 106, n. 5, 109, 214.

[44] *AP,* 22.

[45] Porten, 160-179.

[46] Mesha, *KAI,* 181.14; Lachish III, *KAI,* 193.12; cf. de Vaux, *The Early History of Israel,* I, 340f.; Kinyongo, 49-51; most recently L. Delekat, "Yáhō-Yahwǽ und die alttestamentlichen Gottesnamenkorrekturen," *Tradition und Glaube. Festschrift K. G. Kuhn* (Göttingen, 1971), 23-75. On the forms, see F. M. Cross and D. N. Freedman, *Early Hebrew Orthography. AOS,* 36 (1952; repr. 1981), and *KAI, in loc.*

[47] Cross-Freedman; see M. P. O'Connor, "Writing Systems, Native Speaker Analyses, and the Earliest Stages of Northwest Semitic Orthography," in *The Word of the Lord Shall Go Forth. Festschrift D. N. Freedman. ASOR, Special Volume,* 1 (Winona Lake, Ind., 1983), 439-465.

[48] O. Tufnell, *Lachish,* III (London, 1953), 358f.; see Porten, 292, n. 27.

[49] Defended by Y. Aharoni, "Trial Excavation in the 'Solar Shrine' at Lachish; Preliminary Report," *IEJ,* 18 (1968), 163; rejected by F. M. Cross, "Two Notes on Palestinian Inscriptions of the Persian Age" (with Postscript), *BASOR,* 193 (1969), 21-24.

fifth or fourth century stamped *yhw* or *yh*[50] probably do not contain the divine name,[51] but a shortened or debased form of the ordinary stamp *yhwd*.

b. *Onomastic Evidence*. Personal names provide much more material than the documentation for the independent form. A large portion of the evidence cannot be considered here, however, because the dates of many of the texts, especially the West Semitic seals and bullae, are uncertain. We shall summarize here the more clearly datable West Semitic materials and then the Akkadian data.

(1) West Semitic Sources. The various forms of the divine name in personal sentence names are not uniformly attested. Early occurrences are also limited. The only tenth-century names that might be relevant are the two on the edge of the Gezer calendar,[52] written *'by* and *pny;* the restoration of an *h* at the end of the former is far from certain, as is the completeness of the latter.[53] The ninth century also offers but two names, both clearly legible: *šm'yhw* and *'zryhw.*[54] The Harvard Semitic Museum seal mentioned earlier yields the name *mqnyw.*[55] A seal of the eighth or seventh century contains the name *yhwmlk.*[56] A seal from Ramat Raḥel (eighth century) reads *ywbnh.*[57]

Names terminating with the divine name are well attested for the seventh and sixth centuries. The Judahite form is generally *-yhw,* as the following examples witness: *'wryhw,*[58] *'ḥyhw,*[59] *'šyhw,*[60] *bqyhw,*[61] *brkywh,*[62] *grmyhw,*[63] *hwdyhw,*[64] *hwš'yhw,*[65] *hṣlyhw,*[66]

---

[50] E.g., Y. Aharoni, *et al., Excavations at Ramat Raḥel,* vol. 2: *Seasons 1961 and 1962* (Rome, 1964), 20f.

[51] See, for example, Driver, *ZAW,* 46 (1928), 22.

[52] *KAI,* 182.

[53] *KAI,* II, 181f.

[54] D. Diringer, *Le iscrizioni antico-ebraïci Palestinesi* (Florence, 1934), 199f.; J. C. L. Gibson, *Textbook of Syrian Semitic Inscriptions,* I (Oxford, ²1973), 61.

[55] Cross, *Canaanite Myth and Hebrew Epic,* 61.

[56] G. R. Driver, "Brief Notes. (I) A New Israelite Seal," *PEQ,* 77 (1945), 5.

[57] Y. Aharoni, "Hebrew Jar-Stamps from Ramat Raḥel," *Eretz-Israel,* 6 (1960), 56-60 [Hebrew], 28* [English].

[58] Arad, *ca.* 625: Y. Aharoni, "Three Hebrew Ostraca from Arad," *Eretz-Israel,* 9 (1969), 17 [Hebrew], 134 [English]; Khirbet el-Qôm, *ca.* 750: Lemaire, *RB,* 84 (1977), 599.

[59] Lachish: *KAI,* 193.17; Ophel ostracon: *KAI,* 190; both seventh century.

[60] Letter from Arad: Y. Aharoni, "The Use of Hieratic Numerals in Hebrew Ostraca and the Shekel Weights," *BASOR,* 184 (1966), 14; seal from Arad: *idem,* "Seals of Royal Functionaries from Arad," *Eretz-Israel,* 8 (1967), 101-103 [Hebrew], 71* [English]; seventh-sixth centuries.

[61] Ophel ostracon: *KAI,* 190.

[62] Seal from Arad: Aharoni, *Eretz-Israel,* 8 (1967), 101-103.

[63] Arad: Aharoni, *Eretz-Israel,* 9 (1969), 17; Lachish I, 1.

[64] Lachish: *KAI,* 193.17.

[65] Yabneh Yam (*ca.* 625): *KAI,* 200.7; F. M. Cross, "Epigraphic Notes on Hebrew Documents of the Eighth-Sixth Centuries B.C.: II. The Murabba'ât Papyrus and the Letter Found Near Yabneh-Yam," *BASOR,* 165 (1962), 35; Lachish: *KAI,* 193.1.

[66] Lachish I, 1.

ḥyhw (< *'ḥyhw*),[67] *ṭbyhw*,[68] *y'znyhw*,[69] *yd'yhw*,[70] *yḥ[z]qyhw*,[71] *yrmyhw*,[72] *knyhw*,[73] *mbṭḥyhw*,[74] *mlkyhw*,[75] *mtnyhw*,[76] *nḥmyhw*,[77] *nryhw*,[78] *ntnyhw*,[79] *sbryhw*,[80] *smkyhw*,[81] *'nnyhw*, *'śyhw*, *ṣpnyhw*, and *šbnyhw*,[82] *šlmyhw*,[83] *šm'yhw*,[84] *šmryhw*.[85]

The (northern) Israelite form in the eighth century was *-yw;* traces may be found in the LXX, which presumably antedates the Judahite normalization: *Ēleioú* instead of *Ēlía(s);* cf. 1 K. 17:2, where the MT reads *'elāyw*, the LXX *prós Ēleioù*.[86] The following examples may be cited: *'byw*,[87] *gdyw*,[88] *dlyw*,[89] *yd'yw*,[90] *mrnyw*,[91] *'bdyw*,[92] *qlyw*,[93] *šmryw*.[94] Some names with the northern form have also been found at Kuntillat 'Ajrud: *'mryw*, *hlyw*, *'bdyw*, and *sm'yw*.[95]

The Israelite initial form was the same; it is attested in the eighth-century name

---

67 Tell Qasile, Text 1 (eighth century): B. Maisler (Mazar), "Two Hebrew Ostraca from Tell Qasîle," *JNES*, 10 (1951), 265f.; cf. S. Moscati, *L'epigrafia ebraica antica 1935-1950*. *BietOr*, 15 (1951), 113.

68 Lachish: *KAI*, 193.19.

69 Lachish I, 2f.

70 Arad: Aharoni, *Eretz-Israel*, 9 (1969), 17.

71 Ophel ostracon: *KAI*, 190.

72 Lachish I, 4; ostracon from Arad (*ca.* 600); Aharoni, *Eretz-Israel*, 9 (1969), 11; Lachish solar shrine (last period of the monarchy): Aharoni, *IEJ*, 18 (1968), 166-69.

73 Lachish: *KAI*, 193.15.

74 Lachish I, 4.

75 Arad: Aharoni, *Eretz-Israel*, 9 (1969), 11; Neḥemyahu ostracon from Arad, *ca.* 701: *ibid.*, 15.

76 Lachish I, 5.

77 Arad: Aharoni, *Eretz-Israel*, 9 (1969), 17; Neḥamyahu: ibid., 15.

78 Arad: *ibid.*, 17; Lachish solar shrine: *idem*, *IEJ*, 18 (1968), 166-69; Lachish I, 5.

79 Khirbet el-Qôm (*ca.* 750): Lemaire, *RB*, 84 (1977), 596f.

80 Arad: Aharoni, *Eretz-Israel*, 9 (1969), 17.

81 Lachish: *KAI*, 194.6; 198.2; Lachish XI, 5.

82 Lachish solar shrine: Aharoni, *IEJ*, 18 (1968), 166-69.

83 Seal from Arad: *idem*, *Eretz-Israel*, 8 (1967), 101-103.

84 Arad: *idem*, *Eretz-Israel*, 9 (1969), 17; Murabba'āt 17B (1700-50): P. Benoit, J. T. Milik, and R. de Vaux, *Les gróttes de Murabb'ât*. *DJD*, II (1961), 93-100; cf. Cross, *BASOR*, 165 (1962), 42; Lachish: *KAI*, 194.6; 199.4.

85 Ostracon from Arad: Aharoni, *IEJ*, 16 (1966), 5f.

86 D. Diringer and S. P. Brock, "Words and Meanings in Early Hebrew Inscriptions," *Words and Meanings. Festschrift D. W. Thomas* (Cambridge, 1968), 39-45.

87 Sam. 52, 2 (*ca.* 735): G. A. Reisner, C. S. Fischer, and D. G. Lyon, *Harvard Excavations at Samaria, 1908-1910*, I. *HSS*, 1 (1924), 227-246; for dating, see Cross, *BASOR*, 165 (1962), 35.

88 Sam. 4, 2; 5, 2; 6 = *KAI*, 185.2f.; etc. (15 occurrences in all).

89 Hazor text 8: Y. Yadin, *et al.*, *Hazor*, II (Jerusalem, 1960), 75.

90 Sam. 1 = *KAI*, 183.8; Sam. 42, 2; 48, 1.

91 Sam. 42, 3; 45, 2f.; 47, 2f.

92 Sam. 50, 2.

93 Samaria sherd C1012 (*ca.* 722); cf. Cross, *BASOR*, 165 (1962), 35, n. 7.

94 Sam. 1 = *KAI*, 183.1f.; Sam. 13, 2; 14, 2; 21, 1f.

95 See the preliminary report, Z. Meshel, *Kuntillet 'Ajrud, a Religious Centre from the Time of the Judaean Monarchy on the Border of Sinai. Exhibition Catalog of the Israel Museum*, 175 (Jerusalem, 1978); cf. Norin.

ywyšb.[96] In the seventh and early sixth centuries, the Judahite form varied between the dominant *yhw-* and the less common *yw-*, as seen in *yhw'z,*[97] *yhw'l* and *yhwkl,*[98] and *yw'zr.*[99]

The Elephantine forms varied widely. Initially, *yhw-* predominates, as in *yhw'wr, yhwḥnn, yhwṭl, yhwntn,* and *yhwšm'*, but other forms are known.[100] The form *yhh-* occurs in *yhh'wr* and *yhhdd,*[101] *yw-* in *ywntn,*[102] and *yh-* in *yhntn* and *yh'šn.*[103] The standard final form was *-yh,*[104] although *-yw* also occurs.[105]

We may also mention in passing that the form *yhw* is well attested in both initial and final position in material from the late biblical period, alongside *yw-*, *-yw,* and *-yh,* probably as an archaism. Of the 30 names in the index to Lidzbarski's *Handbuch,* 14 are formed with *-yhw.*[106] On Hasmonean coins, Jonathan is called *yhwḥnn* and Antigonus *mttyh,* while Alexander Jannaeus' name appears in both a short and a long form: *yhwntn* on a royal coin series and *ywntn* on a priestly coin series.[107]

(2) Assyrian Sources. The names of at least three Palestinian rulers with *yhwh*-names are attested in the Assyrian royal annals. One initial form of the Tetragrammaton appears in the transcription of Ahaz' name as *ia-ú-ḫa-zi,* reflecting Heb. **yahū-ḥazⁱ*. Azariah is referred to as *az-ri-ia-a-ú,* Heb. **'azrⁱ-yahū*. Hezekiah's name appears in two different forms: *ḫa-za-qi-ia-ú/ḫa-za-qi-a-ú* (Heb. **ḥāzaqⁱ-yahū*) and *ḫa-za-qi-ia* (Heb. **ḥāzaqⁱyāh*).[108] There is a king of Hamath named *ia-ú-bi-i'-di.*[109] The meaning of this name is unclear; *ywrm* as the name of a prince of Hamath in 2 S. 8:10 may be analogous.[110] There are still other names from East Semitic sources that may contain the Tetragrammaton.[111] The names with Yahweh as their final element exhibit the same form as the royal names; those with the divine name at the beginning are unclear. The important firm of Murašû and Sons at Nippur (fifth century) had dealings with many members of the Judahite diaspora, and names formed with the Tetragrammaton are

---

[96] Sam. 36, 3; cf. also 35, 3; 57, 1.

[97] Arad: Aharoni, *Eretz-Israel,* 9 (1969), 17.

[98] Lachish solar shrine: *idem, IEJ,* 18 (1968), 166-69.

[99] Murabba'āt 17B: *DJD,* 2, 93-100.

[100] See *AP* and *BMAP,* indexes.

[101] *AP,* 1, 2; 11, 13; for the reading of the latter, see Porten, 106, n. 5; 136, n. 83; for a defense of Cowley's reading, see M. D. Coogan, "Patterns in Jewish Personal Names in the Babylonian Diaspora," *JSJ,* 4 (1973), 186, n. 2.

[102] *AP,* 81, 14, 29.

[103] *AP,* 2, 21; *BMAP,* 5, 4, 7, 9; 6, 2; 10, 21?

[104] See *AP* and *BMAP,* indexes.

[105] *AP,* 5, 15; 6, 18; 10, 22; 11,16.

[106] Additional material in *LidzEph.*

[107] Examples in G. A. Cooke, *A Text-Book of North-Semitic Inscriptions* (Oxford, 1903), no. 149C, a-d.

[108] *APN, s.v.;* the variant *ḫa-za-qi-a-a-ú* is not entirely clear.

[109] *Ibid.*, 92b; for discussion, see E. Lipiński, "An Israelite King of Hamat?" *VT,* 21 (1971), 371-73, and Kinyongo, 24-26.

[110] Driver, *ZAW,* 46 (1928), 9, n. 9.

[111] *Ibid.*, 10f.

common in their records.[112] Six different names in the archives have initial *ia-a-ḫu-*, as in *ia-a-ḫ-u-natan* (with a corresponding Aramaic docket *yhwntn*), reflecting Heb. **yahū-nāṯan*. Two dozen names have the final element *-ia-a-wa*$_6$ (e.g., *abi-ia-a-wa*$_6$), corresponding to Heb. *-yaw*.

3. *Greek*. In the early centuries of this era, the Tetragrammaton became more common epigraphically than it had been in the first millennium B.C. The context is so different, however, that it would take us far afield to do it justice.[113] The name now appears as *iaō*, the name of an all-powerful deity appealed to by magicians together with Adonai and Abraxas. The name enjoyed high esteem: "When this name is but spoken, the earth moves from its foundation."[114]

One amulet from this period reads: "Iaō Adōnai Sabaōth, give luck, friendship, good fortune, and a healthy sex life to the bearer of this amulet."[115] The name is also common in magical spells such as *iaō sabaōth adōnai akrammachammerei*.[116] It also occurs in the form *iabezebuth*.[117] The other forms are more difficult to interpret, since vowel sequences are often a regular part of magical spells; many obviously reflect a form like *iaō*, e.g., *iaōou, iauo iau, ieou, ieaō*.[118]

Patristic and classical authors present a similar picture. The dominant form is a shortened one, e.g., *iaō*,[119] *iaou*,[120] Lat. *yaho*,[121] Gk. *ieuō*,[122] or *iō*.[123] An interesting hybrid form is Irenaeus' *yaōth*, presumably modeled on *sabaōth*.[124] Despite the fact that the name was often mutilated almost beyond recognition, the full form does appear to occur: *iasse*[125] and perhaps *iaē*.[126] Theodoret calls this form Samaritan, citing *aia* as the Judahite form.[127] The occurrence of this form in papyri as well makes the common explanation that it is a reflex of *'ehyeh* doubtful but not impossible, since

---

112 See Coogan, *JSJ*, 4 (1973), 183-191; "More Yahwistic Names in the Murashu Documents," *JSJ*, 7 (1976), 199f.

113 See esp. R. Ganschinietz, "Iao," *PW*, IX/1 (1914), 698-721; also D. Wortmann, "Neue magische Texte," *Bonner Jahrbücher*, 168 (1968), 56-111; K. Preisendanz, *Papyri Graecae magicae*, II (Leipzig, 1931); *idem*, "Zur Überlieferung der griechischen Zauberpapyri," *Miscellanea Critica*, ed. J. Irmscher, *et al.* (1951), I, 203-217.

114 Wortmann, *Bonner Jahrbücher*, 168 (1968), 56-111, esp. 59.

115 *Ibid.*, 106.

116 Preisendanz, *Papyri Graecae magicae*, 10.

117 Ganschinietz, 706, 4.

118 *Ibid.*, 700, 44, 50; 702, 43, 45.

119 Macrobius, Diodorus Siculus: *Ibid.*, 708, 8; 707, 5.

120 Clement of Alexandria: *Ibid.*, 700, 29; but cf. Kinyongo, 51.

121 Jerome: Ganschinietz, 699, 28.

122 Porphyry: *Ibid.*, 702, 33.

123 Jerome, *Onomastica sacra: Ibid.*, 702, 17.

124 *Ibid.*, 701, 55.

125 Epiphanius, Theodoret: *Ibid.*, 707, 63; cf. Kinyongo, 57.

126 Origen: Ganschinietz, 704, 65; for another interpretation, see de Vaux, *The Early History of Israel*, 341, n. 89.

127 Ganschinietz, 705, 12.

the latter was recognized in rabbinic tradition as a divine name.[128] The classical material is also discussed by Eerdmans and Thierry.[129]

4. *Second Millennium Sources.*

a. *Egyptian.* Of the Egyptian evidence, a list of toponyms from the temple of Amon at Soleb (Amenhotep III, 1402-1363) is the earliest; here we find an entry *t3 š3św yhw[3],* "the land of Shasu-*yhw.*" Similar references occur in a block from Soleb (Amenhotep III) and twice in lists from Medinet Habu (Rameses III, 1198-1166).[130] The name might reflect the Tetragrammaton. Albright vocalized it as *y(a)hw(e?),* and Cross has recently suggested *ya-h-wí.*[131] It must be emphasized that the vocalization of foreign words in Egyptian is problematic.

b. *Ugaritic.* In a damaged passage of a Ugaritic text[132] we read: *šm bny yw . . . wp'r šm ym,* "My son's name is *yw,* he shall be called *ym.*" The presence of the word *yw* is indisputable; it is probably a name. Many scholars have connected it with the Tetragrammaton.[133] The connection is unlikely for several reasons. The form *yw* could not be derived from *yhw* in the second millennium unless the latter had become opaque, which is unlikely. However the Ugaritic text is read, the verbal play on the similarity between *yw* and *ym* (the sea-god Yam) must be taken into account. The association of a verb form with the name *yammu* would be odd even in a folk etymology; in poetry it seems better to look for an explanation in simple *w/m* alternation. The same alternation lies behind the Greek form *ieuō* for *yammu* in Eusebius.[134] Earlier Canaanite hypotheses are discussed by Kinyongo.[135]

c. *Cuneiform Evidence.* None exists. The form *aḫi-yami* on a Late Bronze tablet from Tell Ta'anak is based on the divine name *yam,* not *yhw.*[136] The forms *iaūm, iau,*

---

[128] Siegel, 167.

[129] B. D. Eerdmans, "The Name Jahu," *OTS,* 5 (1948), 1-29; G. J. Thierry, "The Pronunciation of the Tetragrammaton," *OTS,* 5 (1948), 30-42.

[130] See R. Giveon, *Les bédouins Shosou des documents Égyptiens. DMOA,* 18 (1971), 27; reviewed in M. Weippert, "Semitische Nomaden des zweiten Jahrtausends: Über die *Š3'św* der ägyptischen Quellen," *Bibl,* 55 (1974), 265-280, 427-433; see also S. Herrmann, "Der alttestamentliche Gottesname," *EvTh,* 26 (1966), 281-293.

[131] W. F. Albright, *Yahweh and the Gods of Canaan* (1968; repr. Winona Lake, 1978), 149; Cross, *Canaanite Myth and Hebrew Epic,* 61f., following W. Helck.

[132] *KTU,* 1.1 IV, 14f.

[133] Originally by Virolleaud, later by Gordon (*UT,* no. 1084). For another reconstruction of the text and discussion, see J. C. de Moor, *The Seasonal Pattern in the Ugaritic Myth of Ba'lu. AOAT,* 16 (1971), 116, 118f.; cf. de Vaux, *The Early History of Israel,* 341f., and Kinyongo, 34-36.

[134] *Praep. ev.* i. 19, 21.

[135] Pp. 32f., 44f.

[136] F. Hrozný in E. Sellin, ed., *Tell Ta'annek. DKAW,* Phil.-hist. Kl., 50/4 (1904), II, 5-17, 121; de Vaux, *The Early History of Israel,* 341f.

and *ia* are not to be taken as Akkadian transcriptions of *yhw*: the first is the 1st person possessive pronoun; the second and third are hypocoristic endings.

Freedman–O'Connor

d. *Nabatean*. Cazelles[137] has drawn attention to the Nabatean divine name *'hyw*, of which there are some 15 occurrences, including a personal name *'bd 'hyw*.[138] He suggests that Moses discovered this name as the name of the local deity of Horeb (Ex. 3:1f.) and associated it with the verb *hāyâ*. The problem with this hypothesis is the extremely long period separating the time of Moses and the inscriptions.

Ringgren

5. *Summary*. The consonants of the Tetragrammaton are firmly established as *yhw*. Also established are the vowel of the first syllable, *a*, and the fact that the first syllable was closed. The vowel of the second syllable is problematic. West Semitic orthography confirms that it was non-high. Since there is good reason to accept the Masoretic rule that all final vowels are long, we are left with four possibilities: *āē*, *ē*, *ō*, and *ā*. Of these only the first two are supported by Greek evidence; the Greek forms with *ō* are probably connected with the short form *yahō*.

III. Amorite.

1. *Evidence*. The Mari archives, still only partially published, constitute the principal source for the sentence names that form the basis for our knowledge of Amorite, a Northwest Semitic dialect attested from the Ur III period down to the Amarna period.[139] The evidence of these names is problematic. There are several relevant groups. The first contains a verbal element *ya-wi*, e.g., *ya-wi-^{d}IM*, *ya-wi-AN*, *ya-wi-i-la*, *ya-wi-^{d}d[a-gan]*, *ya-wi-ya*, *ya-wi-um*, *ya-wi-e*.[140] The first four are made up of a divine name and a form of the verb *hwy*, and can be normalized as *yahwī-hadd*, *yahwī-il(a)* (twice), and *yahwī-dagan*. The fifth and sixth names comprise the verb plus a hypocoristic ending. The last name, normalized as *yahwē*, is important because it bears witness to the optional shift of *ī* to *ē* in Amorite. Compare *yi-i-ti-ba'-al* = *yi'itī-ba'al*, "Ba'al will come,"[141] with *ya-al-e-^{d}da-gan* = *yal'e-dagan*.[142]

The second group contains the verbal element *ya-aḫ-wi*, e.g., *ya-aḫ-wi-na-si*, *ya-aḫ-*

---

137 H. Cazelles, "Dieu et l'Etre," *Études Augustiniennes* (Paris, 1978), 27-44, esp. 31, 43.

138 J. Cantineau, *Le Nabatéen* (Paris, 1930), 57; cf. J. Euting, *Nabatäische Inschriften aus Arabien* (Berlin, 1885); B. Moritz, *Der Sinaikult in heidnischer Zeit. AKGW*, Phil.-hist. Kl., N.S. 16/2(1917).

139 On Ur III, see G. Buccellati, *The Amorites of the Ur III Period* (Naples, 1966), 125-231; on Amarna, see C. R. Krahmalkov, "Northwest Semitic Glosses in Amarna Letter No. 64: 22-23," *JNES*, 30 (1971), 140-43.

140 *APNM*, 160; names with *la-wi-* may be related, *APNM*, 79ff., 225; Cross, *Canaanite Myth and Hebrew Epic*, 62.

141 *APNM*, 208.

142 *APNM*, 224.

wi-AN.[143] These names have been associated with the Tetragrammaton but should probably be derived from the root *ḥwy,* "live," i.e., *yaḥwī-naśi* and *yaḥwī-il(a).*[144]

The verbal element in *ya-u-ì-lí* is unique; it probably reflects a short form of *hwy*[145] and should be normalized as *yahū-ilī.* Some difficult Ur III forms are discussed by Buccellati.[146]

Thus Amorite contains a verb form remarkably similar to the reconstruction of the Tetragrammaton, but there is no reason to "identify" the two. The Amorite form is an imperfect from the root *hwy,* which probably means "exist, be at hand," as in Hebrew and Aramaic. Morphologically, the form can be either the simple or the causative stem.[147] The attempt to demonstrate the existence of an Amorite god *yahwe*[148] must be considered unsuccessful.[149]

2. *Phonology of the Tetragrammaton.* Although Amorite and Hebrew are distinct languages, their verbal systems have much in common. There is no reason to doubt that at a certain stage of development Hebrew had a form *yahwī* (without the shift *w* > *y*) or *yahwē.* Since the Hebrew verbal system dictates the ending *ē,* we can conclude that the pronunciation of the Tetragrammaton in the biblical period was *yahwēh.* The other forms can be explained on the basis of various phonological processes. This development is connected with the shift of the Tetragrammaton from a verb to a proper noun, which lightens the grammatical burden of the word.

The various forms can be explained as follows. Wherever possible, closed syllables tend to change to open syllables. The final vowel, which could not be dropped in a verbal form, was no longer necessary after the semantic shift. It was therefore shortened and eventually dropped, like all short concluding vowels. The result is **yahw,* an impossible form. The *w* was vocalized and could be lengthened, resulting in the form *yahū.*[150] If it was not lengthened, the final had to be dropped, leaving the form **yah,* which became *yāh* through regular lengthening of the vowel.

From the form *yahū* two other short forms were derived. (a) If the rule that syncopates intervocalic *h* at formative boundaries is extended to *yahū,* the result is *yaū.* Since such vowel sequences are unstable in Hebrew, this easily becomes *yaw.* (b) The final vowel *ū* can become *ō,* giving *yahō.* This shift probably occurred first in names and was later extended to the divine name elsewhere. It could also result by analogy to the archaic ending *-ō* in such words as *yᵉrîḥô* and *šilōh.* These two forms give rise to two others: (c) *yahō* > *yᵉhō* through regular reduction of the unaccented vowel, and (d) *yaw* > *yô* by contraction.

143 *APNM,* 191f.

144 *APNM,* 71f.

145 *APNM,* 160.

146 P. 136.

147 Similar conclusions by Kinyongo, 66-69; Cross (*Canaanite Myth and Hebrew Epic,* 63-65) favors the causative.

148 A. Finet, "Iawi-Ilâ, roi de Talḫayûm," *Syr,* 41 (1964), 118-122.

149 W. von Soden, "Jahwe 'Er ist, Er erweist sich,' " *WO,* 3 (1964-66), 179-181; *APNM,* 70-72; de Vaux, *The Early History of Israel,* 342f.

150 *BLe,* §25c'd'; cf. Cross, *Canaanite Myth and Hebrew Epic,* 61.

Finally, the form *'ehyeh* in Ex. 3:14 deserves attention. As we have seen, it occurs also in patristic and classical sources (cf. also Hos. 1:9, where instead of the expected "I am not your God" we find "I am not your *'ehyeh*"[151]). This word is commonly understood as a 1st person singular imperfect. There is some evidence, however, that this may be a popular interpretation and that the form may in fact be identical with *yahweh* with the shift *y* > *'*. This shift is known in Amorite, as the names *a-bu-um-ya-qar* and *a-bi-e-qar* show,[152] although its status is obscure because 1st person verbs are rare in the available texts. In fact, it has been suggested[153] that the Amorite name *e-wi-ma-lik* from Alalakh should be normalized as *'ehwī-malik*, "the (divine) king is at hand." Thus the form *'ehyeh* might be equivalent to *yahweh.* If, however, *yahweh* is a hiphil form, then *'hyh* might represent a parallel aphel formation. The form could also be a 1st person imperfect hiphil or even a noun formation with a prosthetic aleph.

Freedman–O'Connor

IV. Meaning.

1. *General.* The consensus of modern scholarship supports the biblical text in associating the name Yahweh with the root → היה *hāyâ* [*hāyah*], "become." The parallel Amorite form furnishes the final link in the chain of evidence. As we pointed out above, the Amorite evidence poses the problem of what stem is involved, since in Amorite the verb could be either the simple stem or the causative. In Hebrew, however, *yahweh* must be a causative, since the dissimilation of *yaqṭal* to *yiqṭal* did not apply in Amorite, while it was obligatory in Hebrew. The name *yahweh* must therefore be a hiphil. Although the causative of *hwy* is otherwise unknown in Northwest Semitic (with the exception of Syriac, which is of little relevance here[154]), it seems to be attested in the name of the God of Israel.[155]

All reconstructions that recognize a verbal form in *YHWH* associate it with a sentence name or with a sentence from a cultic litany.[156] This conclusion is usually based on typological arguments deriving from other sentence names: since causative forms

---

151 De Vaux, *The Early History of Israel*, 356f.

152 G. Dossin, *Correspondance du Ismaḫ-Addu. ARM,* V (1952), 4, 5; *APNM,* 214; cf. also H. L. Ginsberg, "Gleanings in First Isaiah," *Mordecai M. Kaplan: Jubilee Volume* (New York, 1953), 257; W. R. Arnold, "The Divine Name in Exodus iii.14," *JBL,* 24 (1905), 107-165.

153 C. R. Krahmalkov, *Studies in Amorite Grammar* (diss., Harvard, 1965); cf. Cross, *Canaanite Myth and Hebrew Epic,* 68, n. 92.

154 On the form *yhwh* in the Sefire inscription, II A,4, see J. A. Fitzmyer, *The Aramaic Inscriptions of Sefîre. BietOr,* 19 (1967), 87.

155 Cf. P. Haupt, "Der Name Jahwe," *OLZ,* 12 (1909), 211-14; W. F. Albright, "Contributions to Biblical Archaeology and Philology: The Name *Yahweh,*" *JBL,* 43 (1924), 370-78; *idem,* review of B. N. Wambacq, *L'épithète divine Jahué Sᵉba'ôt* [Paris, 1947], *JBL,* 67 (1948), 373-381; *idem, Yahweh and the Gods of Canaan,* 168-172; Cross, *Canaanite Myth and Hebrew Epic,* 60-75; D. N. Freedman, "The Name of the God of Moses," *JBL,* 79 (1960), 151-56; Kinyongo, 69-82; on the meaning, J. P. Hyatt, "Was Yahweh Originally a Creator Deity?" *JBL,* 86 (1967), 369-377.

156 Albright.

of other verbs meaning "be" occur in sentence names, we may assume that an analogous causative form underlies the Hebrew divine name.

Most Semitic verbs for "be" derive from the root *kwn,* although this root does not always mean "be." Akk. *kānu* means "be firmly in place." In Ugaritic the root appears in the El epithet "Bull El his father, King El who created (*yknn*) him."[157] Both simple and causative forms occur in names from Ugarit[158] and Mari.[159] In Aramaic the root is rare,[160] and is not productive of proper nouns. In Phoenician and Punic texts, only the simple stem appears to be attested; in names the causative appears as well.[161] In Hebrew, the names exhibit chiefly hiphil and polel forms. The most interesting of the former is *y^e^hôyāḵîn,* with the curious variant *y^e^ḵōnyâ.* The root *hwy* generally does not form names. Akk. *bašû,* "be, exist," occurs in names, especially in the causative Š form, e.g., *sin-aḫa-šubšī,* "Sin, call a brother into being."[162] Thus the typological evidence shows that both simple and causative stems were used in the formation of names.

2. *Biblical Evidence.* It is impossible here to do justice to the complexity of the biblical material regarding Yahweh; recent research has nevertheless provided several firm points of reference.

a. *Ancient Poetry.* Analysis of the oldest poems in the Bible has been greatly refined in recent years, and a probable sequence dating can be established.[163] The typology of the divine name in ancient poetry allows us to distinguish three periods. The twelfth century was the period of militant Mosaic Yahwism; in this period the name Yahweh predominates (Ex. 15; Ps. 29; Jgs. 5). In the eleventh century, the syncretistic fusion of Yahweh, a southern god, with El, a major Levantine deity, was under way; this fusion is reflected in the poetry by the use of the name "El," but also in the revival of the patriarchal terms for El, especially El Shaddai, El Elyon, and El 'Olam (Gen. 49, the poetic sections of Nu. 23f., Dt. 33). Syncretistic tendencies progress during the period of the early monarchy (tenth and ninth centuries), represented by 1 S. 2; 2 S. 1; 22 (par. Ps. 18); 2 S. 23; Dt. 32; Ps. 78; 68; 72.

In this corpus of material, the name "Yahweh" is generally dominant. Since we may assume that the name was introduced into Israelite tradition no earlier than 1200 B.C., we have a clear terminus post quem. The single exception is all the more striking in that the only poem without the name "Yahweh," Gen. 49 (except for v. 18, which belongs to the liturgical setting and is secondary), is attributed to a pre-Mosaic figure.

---

157 *KTU,* 1.3 V, 35f.; 1.4 IV, 47f.

158 *PNU, s.v.*

159 *APNM, s.v.*

160 *DISO, s.v.*

161 F. L. Benz, *Personal Names in the Phoenician and Punic Inscriptions. Studia Pohl,* 8 (1972), 332.

162 *APN,* 198.

163 Albright, *Yahweh and the Gods of Canaan;* D. N. Freedman, "Divine Names and Titles in Early Hebrew Poetry," *Magnalia Dei. Festschrift G. E. Wright* (Garden City, 1976), 55-107 (= his *Pottery, Poetry, and Prophecy* [Winona Lake, 1980], 77-130).

The Elohistic Pss. 78 and 68 and the oracles of Balaam all focus on other divine names, but "Yahweh" occurs a few times. Thus it is possible that Gen. 49 is in fact of non-Yahwistic origin.

The contribution of this corpus to our investigation is crucial. In all these archaic poems, "Yahweh" clearly appears both grammatically and syntactically as a personal name. Its original verbal form and force have left no trace.[164]

b. *Later Material*. In later texts, however, there are instances where we may assume that the name has verbal force, but these must be viewed as revivals of archaic usage. The following formulas result from this revival: (1) *yahweh šālôm*, "he creates peace," the name of Gideon's altar in Jgs. 6:24; (2) *yahweh ṣᵉḇā'ôṯ*, "he creates armies," the first part of the legend on the ark in 1 S. 4:4; the second part of the legend, *yōšēḇ hakkᵉruḇîm*, "the one enthroned on cherubs," is either the subject or in apposition to the divine name El (cf. 2 S. 6:2; 1 Ch. 13:6);[165] (3) *yahweh qannā'*, "he creates zeal" (Ex. 34:14); the sentence following means "he is a [not: the] zealous God; (4) *yahweh nissî*, "he creates my refuge," the name of Moses' altar (Ex. 17:15; according to the LXX, *kataphygḗ*; cf. *mᵉnûsî* in 2 S. 22:3; Ps. 59:17[Eng. v. 16]); Jer. 16:19.

In his unpublished *History of the Religion of Israel*, Albright reconstructs several other such formulas: (1) *yhwh yir'eh* for *yahweh yir'â*, "he creates fear" (Gen. 22:14); (2) *'ēl 'ᵉlōhê yiśrā'ēl* for *'ēl yahweh yiśrā'ēl*, "El creates Israel" (Gen. 33:20); (3) *'ēl 'ᵉlōhê hārûḥôṯ* for *'ēl yahweh rûḥôṯ*, "El creates the winds."

The shape of these sentences is unusual, but similar oddities are found in names. From these formulas we may conclude that expressions made of *yahweh* plus an object are sentences describing the god El, reintroduced during the eleventh-century period of El/Yahweh synthesis. The name "Yahweh" itself is a typical hypocoristicon; the original form must have been *yahweh 'ēl*, "El creates." It could not have been a title of El, but only of a deity attached to the court of the chief god.

The divine name in Ex. 3:12,14[166] appears in the form *'ehyeh*.[167] Whether the form is a phonological or morphological variant of *yahweh* or a related verbal form in the 1st person we cannot say. There is some basis, as we have seen, for the first explanation. The expression *'ehyeh 'ᵃšer 'ehyeh* is, at least according to Masoretic analysis, an idem per idem construction, employed "where the means, or the desire, to be more

---

164 For examples of isolated verbs as divine names in the Mari archives, see H. B. Huffmon, "Yahweh and Mari," *Near Eastern Studies in Honor of William Foxwell Albright* (Baltimore, 1971), 283-89; there are two pre-Islamic Arabic examples: *yaġūṯ*, "he helps," and *ya'ūq*, "he protects"; cf. de Vaux, *The Early History of Israel*, 346.

165 See J. de Fraine, "La royauté de Yahvé dans les textes concernant l'arche," *Volume de Congrès, Genève 1965. SVT*, 15 (1966), 134-149; J. P. Ross, "Jahweh Ṣᵉḇā'ôṯ in Samuel and Psalms," *VT*, 17 (1967), 76-92; cf. M. Liverani, "La preistoria dell'epiteto 'Yahweh ṣĕbā'ōt,' " *AION*, N.S. 18 (1967), 331-34.

166 Kinyongo, 127-132; H. Schmid, "Jhwh, der Gott der Hebräer," *Jud*, 25 (1969), 257-266.

167 On the verse in general, see J. Lindblom, "Noch einmal die Deutung des Jahwe-Namens in Ex. 3,14," *ASTI*, 3 (1964), 4-15; Kinyongo, 91-116; B. Albrektson, "On the Syntax of אהיה אשר אהיה in Exodus 3:14," *Words and Meanings. Festschrift D. W. Thomas* (London, 1968), 15-28; cf. de Vaux, *The Early History of Israel*, 343-357.

explicit does not exist."[168] The use of this construction is illuminated by the unusual grammar of Ex. 3:2f., where the verb *b'r* is apparently used in two different senses: "be on fire" (v. 2) and "be consumed by fire" (v. 3).[169] A similar phrase occurs in Ex. 33:19, in a description of Yahweh as a merciful and gracious God: "I favor whomever I favor and I have mercy on whomever I have mercy." The stress here is on action; there is no suggestion of willfulness or arbitrariness. The statement in Ex. 3:14, "I create whatever I create," i.e., "I am the creator par excellence," could be meant as a counterpart to these expressions. If so, we should translate it: "I create whatever I create," and regard showing favor and having mercy as theological glosses on the unusual verb form in the divine name.

Freedman

3. *Other Theories*. Lack of space forces us to deal briefly with the endless array of explanations proposed for the Tetragrammaton. We pass over entirely eccentric theories such as derivation from Proto-Indoeuropean *dja-*, found in the names "Zeus" and "Jupiter."[170]

a. *Other Verbal Etymologies*. A number of Semitic verbal roots, most attested largely or exclusively in Arabic, have been pressed into service as etymons for *yahweh*. As Driver has wisely said, "such arabizing interpretations are a priori doubtful, and the traditional Hebrew explanation is in itself as reasonable as anything else hitherto proposed."[171] The three most important etymologies are: (1) Arab. *hawā*, "fall";[172] (2) Arab. *hawā*, "blow," linked with Yahweh as a supposed storm-god[173]; and (3) Arab. *hawā*, "love, be passionate."[174] A fourth etymology has the virtue of being associated with the ancient period: a supposed Ugar. *hwy*, "speak."[175] But the verbal root is not attested in the Ugaritic texts, and the noun *hwt* is best considered an Akkadian loanword (*awātu*, "word").

b. *The Short Form Theory*. The theory that the form *yhwh* is not primary has had a number of advocates, above all Driver and Mowinckel.[176] Driver espouses the untenable view that all the short forms of the name were pronounced identically as *yā*, and that the form *yāhū* arose through a misreading of orthographic *yhw*.[177] The evi-

---

[168] S. R. Driver, *The Book of Exodus*. *CBSC* (1911; repr. 1953), 363; cf. Ex. 16:23 and see Albrektson, 26f.; de Vaux, *Festschrift G. H. Davies*, 67-69.

[169] See D. N. Freedman, "The Burning Bush," *Bibl*, 50 (1969), 245f., with a different explanation.

[170] De Vaux, *The Early History of Israel*, 344; Kinyongo, 27-31, 37f., 42-46; the theory has been revived by D. Broadribb, "La Nomo Javeo," *Biblia Revuo*, 6 (1970), 162f.

[171] G. R. Driver, "Jehovah," *Encyclopaedia Britannica* ([14]1929), XII, 996.

[172] De Vaux, *The Early History of Israel*, 345.

[173] T. J. Meek, *Hebrew Origins* (New York, [2]1960), 99-101.

[174] S. D. Goitein, "*YHWH* the Passionate: The Monotheistic Meaning and Origin of the Name *YHWH*," *VT*, 6 (1956), 1-9; cf. de Vaux, *The Early History of Israel*, 345f.

[175] R. A. Bowman, "Yahweh the Speaker," *JNES*, 3 (1944), 1-8; Murtonen, 90, considers the name a noun with a *y-* prefix meaning "commander."

[176] For earlier forms of the suggestion, see Kinyongo, 53-56.

[177] Driver, *ZAW*, 46 (1928), 20-25.

dence he cites for writing *yā* as *ywh* all involves non-Semitic names. The problems of transcribing foreign words are irrelevant for Hebrew orthography as practiced by Hebrew speakers. The theory of orthographic confusion in a common word is unacceptable, since silent reading was virtually unknown until the early Middle Ages. Driver believes that *yā* probably originated as an ejaculation.[178] The form *yahweh* arose when the primitive cry or name was elongated to *ya(h)wa(h);* then the similarity to the verb form was noticed and the etymology of Ex. 3 created. Driver considers this etymology very ancient; the long form originated around the time of the exodus but was regarded as too holy for ordinary use, so that the form *yā(h)* survived in names.

Mowinckel[179] finds the origin of the name in a supposed form **yā huwa,* "O He!" comprising the vocative particle *yā,* found in both Ugaritic and Arabic, and Arab. *huwa,* "he." Although the 3rd person pronoun is used as a divine epithet in the OT (notably in Deutero-Isaiah, e.g., Isa. 43:10; also Ps. 102:28[27]; and in ancient poetry, Dt. 32:4,6,39; Ps. 78:38; 68:36[35]), and although the analogies cited are very interesting, the explanation is phonologically untenable. Old Canaanite and Amorite attest the shift of *w* to ' in the personal pronoun in the Old Babylonian period. The ' of the biblical form *hû'* is not a vowel letter but a true consonant that cannot be ignored. Mowinckel's reference to the Arabic pronoun is therefore out of place; Proto-Canaanite **yā huwa* would have become *yā hū'a* by the Middle Bronze age, but there is no trace of an ' in *yahweh.*

V. The Figure of Yahweh. The God of Israel is the central figure of the OT; the ways in which he is portrayed are the subject of this entire dictionary. Here we can treat only a few aspects from the earliest poetry.[180]

The origins of Yahwism are obscure, but for more than a century scholars have found that the biblical traditions hint at Midianite or Kenite provenance.[181] The narrative in Ex. 18 is usually taken as prime evidence that Jethro, Moses' Midianite father-in-law, initiated Moses into the cult of Yahweh. It therefore seems reasonable

---

178 Cf. Kinyongo, 59-61; a similar position is taken by Eerdmans.

179 Similar positions are taken by E. C. B. Maclaurin, "YHWH: The Origin of the Tetragrammaton," *VT,* 12 (1962), 439-463; H. Kosmala, "The Name of God (YHWH and HU)," *ASTI,* 2 (1963), 103-106 (= his *Studies, Essays, and Reviews* [Leiden, 1978], I, 1-4); cf. Kinyongo, 61-64; de Vaux, *The Early History of Israel,* 344.

180 Other aspects are considered in G. E. Mendenhall, *The Tenth Generation* (Baltimore, 1973). A catalogue of literary studies would be endless. A survey of the most common Yahweh formulas is given in Murtonen, 67-90, but his conclusion about the name itself is untenable. On monotheism in the Early Iron age, see W. L. Lambert, "The Reign of Nebuchadnezzar I: A Turning Point in the History of Ancient Mesopotamian Religion," *The Seed of Wisdom. Festschrift T. J. Meek* (Toronto, 1964), 3-13.

181 The classic statement of this thesis remains H. H. Rowley, *From Joseph to Joshua* (London, 1950), 149-163; A. H. J. Gunneweg, "Mose in Midian," *ZThK,* 61 (1964), 1-9 (= his *Sola Scriptura* [Göttingen, 1983], 36-44); R. de Vaux, "Sur l'origine Kénite ou Madianite du Yahvisme," *Eretz-Israel,* 9 (1969), 28-32; see also Kinyongo, 7-19, 39-41. For a different perspective, see A. Cody, "Exodus 18,12: Jethro Accepts a Covenant with the Israelites," *Bibl,* 49 (1968), 153-166; and de Vaux, *The Early History of Israel,* 330-38.

to suppose that the mention of "the god of your father" in Ex. 3:6 means the god of Moses' spiritual father and actual father-in-law, Jethro, priest of Midian. This cultic borrowing may be reflected in Nu. 25, if the Ba'al of Beth-peor can be identified with (Midianite) Yahweh; the narrative would then refer to a new encounter between the two cults after a period of separate development.[182]

There are many objections to this reconstruction, but no other is cogent. The best alternative is the suggestion of Hyatt[183] that the father referred to in Ex. 3:6 is Moses' physical father; but the special Yahwistic character of Moses' mother's name, Jochebed, is dubious.[184]

The epithets of Yahweh in ancient poetry form a diverse collection.[185] Some derive from Syrian traditions, e.g. *rōkēḇ šāmayim,* "sky mounter" (Dt. 33:26); *rōkēḇ bāʿᵃrāḇôṯ,* "cloud mounter" (Ps. 68:5[4]); and *rōkēḇ bišᵉmê šᵉmê-qeḏem,* "mounter of the ancient and remote skies" (Ps. 68:34[33]), all reflecting the Ugaritic Ba'al epithet *rkb 'rpt.*[186] Others are well-known titles of El: *'ēl 'ôlām, 'ēl 'elyôn, 'ēl šaddai.*[187] Others, although less common, are not found outside the OT: → צור *ṣûr,* "rock"; *zᵉmîrôṯ,* "fortress." Many others are completely transparent: *ṣaddîq,*[188] "the just one"; *yāšār,*[189] "the honest one"; *'ēl dēʿôṯ,* "the God of knowledge"; *'el hakkāḇôḏ,* "the God of glory"; *'ēl rᵒʾî,* "the God of my vision"; *mēmîṯ ûmᵉḥayyeh,* "killer-quickener"; *mᵉlammēḏ,* "teacher"; *māginnî,*[190] "my suzerain."

Other titles derive from the prose tradition. J's version of the revelation of the name to Moses naturally emphasizes the qualities or attributes of the deity, since in J's view the name itself had long been known. In Ex. 34:6f., the list of attributes begins with *'ēl raḥûm wᵉḥannûn,* "God compassionate and gracious" (cf. 33:19, discussed earlier). The succeeding terms *'ereḵ 'appayim,* "very patient," *raḇ-ḥeseḏ we'ᵉmeṯ,* "very merciful and faithful," *nōśē' 'āwōn wāp̄ešaʿ wᵉḥaṭṭā'â,* "who forgives iniquity and rebellion and sin," bring out this central aspect of Yahweh's character, his readiness to forgive. In tension and contrast are the expressions *wᵉnaqqēh lō' yᵉnaqqeh,* "but he never acquits [the guilty]," and *pōqēḏ ʿᵃwōn 'āḇôṯ,* "visiting the iniquity of parents upon children." Retributive justice is balanced against forgiving love. The Mosaic representation of the covenant deity hangs between these attributes. The people of Yahweh was established by divine grace and survives only through his continuing mercy. But it must obey its suzerain and live according to his just commandments. Disobedience and rebellion cannot be condoned, nor can the guilty go unpunished.

---

182 Mendenhall, *The Tenth Generation,* 105-121; cf. also the Kenite-Rechabite connection in 1 Ch. 2:55.

183 Hyatt, *Festschrift H. Trantham,* 85-93.

184 De Vaux, *The Early History of Israel,* 339, n. 75.

185 For a full discussion, see Freedman, *Festschrift G. E. Wright,* 55-107. The Syro-Palestinian background is surveyed by Cross, *Canaanite Myth and Hebrew Epic,* 44-111, and P. D. Miller, *The Divine Warrior in Early Israel. HSM,* 5 (1973).

186 See S. P. Brock, "Νεφεληγερέτα = *rkb 'rpt,*" *VT,* 18 (1968), 395-97.

187 F. M. Cross, "אל *'ēl,*" *TDOT,* I, 253-261.

188 → צדק *ṣāḏaq.*

189 → ישר *yāšar.*

190 → מגן *māḡēn.*

The paradox of divine justice and mercy is that they go hand in hand and cannot be separated. Israel, the holy nation, is established and preserved by divine grace and compassion, but is defined as a people by the covenant demands and the principles of justice. Without justice Israel cannot be the people of Yahweh; without mercy it cannot be at all.

It is difficult to summarize the character of Yahweh in early poetry.[191] The centrality of the divine warrior has recently been emphasized;[192] the importance of the deity who fights actively and directly for his people cannot be gainsaid (cf. Ex. 15, where the mythological background has been partly suppressed).[193] But this figure must not be collapsed with the image of the omnipotent nature deity who sponsors the defense of his own people by offering them his troops, the stars and other meteorological phenomena (Jgs. 5:20; 2 S. 22:14; Josh. 10:12f.). In Ps. 29 and other theophanic traditions of Dt. 33:2-5,26-29; Ps. 68:18(17); Hab. 3:3-15, this latter figure appears to be independent of the active warrior. In fact, the prose traditions of the divine warrior appear to be more explicit than the poetic ones.[194] Furthermore, in the old poetry Yahweh is also a God who inspires and controls mantic utterances (Nu. 23f.). Later Yahweh is seen as presiding over a just society (Dt. 32), in particular a monarchy (1 S. 2; 2 S. 23). The poetry reflects throughout the various historical situations of Israel in the early period: an era of intensive religious expansion, depicted under the image of divine warfare, is succeeded by a period of relative stability, which eventually is assimilated to monarchy, the dominant social pattern of the ancient Near East.

The nature of Mosaic monotheism is often misconstrued as insisting that Yahweh is the only god in existence. This notion is foreign to the earliest OT materials. There are other gods, who fall into two categories: those who work for Yahweh (and appear later as angels) and those who oppose him. All these figures derive from pre-Mosaic Yahwistic mythology. Mention of these groups is most common in old poetry.

Yahweh's subordinates are the members of the *sôḏ-qᵉḏōšîm*, "the council of the holy ones" (Ps. 89:8[7];[195] cf. also the ideologically "later" passages Ps. 35:10; 71:19; 89:9[8]; 1 K. 8:23 par. 2 Ch. 6:14; also Dt. 10:17; Ps. 136:2). They surround him as he moves (Dt. 33:2f.; Zec. 14:5). His superiority is obvious: "Who is like you, Yahweh, among the gods? Who is like you, awesome one, among the holy ones?" (Ex. 15:11; cf. Ps. 89:6-8[5-7]).

The motif of the divine council,[196] although usually associated in the OT with Yahweh, is the result of Yahweh's fusion with El. The council of El, well known from

---

[191] See esp. de Vaux, *The Early History of Israel,* 383f.; D. N. Freedman, "God Compassionate and Gracious," *Western Watch,* 6 (1955), 7-24.

[192] Cf. Miller.

[193] De Vaux, *The Early History of Israel,* 383f.; F. M. Cross and D. N. Freedman, "The Song of Miriam," *JNES,* 14 (1955), 237-250; Cross, *Canaanite Myth and Hebrew Epic,* 112-144; D. N. Freedman, "Strophe and Meter in Exodus 15," *A Light Unto My Path. Festschrift J. M. Myers* (Philadelphia, 1974), 163-203 (= *Pottery, Poetry, and Prophecy,* 187-228).

[194] Miller, 128-135.

[195] *Ibid.,* 66-69.

[196] → סוד *sôḏ.*

Ugaritic texts, appears in its original form only once in the OT, namely in Dt. 32:8f., where the primordial apportioning of the inheritance of El's sons is described: "When Elyon assigned the nations their inheritance, when he divided up humankind, he set up the peoples' territories according to the number of El's sons;[197] Yahweh's portion was his people, Jacob was his hereditary share."

Most of these and similar passages allude to an undifferentiated mass of gods around Yahweh. Hab. 3:15, however, in the context of an archaizing poem, names Yahweh's two bodyguards: *deḇer,* the plague god, walks before him, and *rešep,* the pestilence god, follows him. Demythologized minor deities appear in later Israelite literature as hypostatized virtues: *ṭôḇ* and *ḥeseḏ,* "goodness" and "loyalty," accompany the psalmist (Ps. 23:6); in Ps. 85:11f.(10f.), an allegory of virtue is acted out by three minor deities: *'ᵉmeṯ, ṣeḏeq,* and *ḥeseḏ,* "truth," "justice," and "loyalty." The "sons of god" in Gen. 6:1f. and the cherubs and bulls associated with cultic installations may also be minor deities. However, rather than a pair of mother-goddesses, *šāḏayim* and *reḥem,* "breasts" and "womb," in Gen. 49:25 probably describe a single goddess, demythologized even in that archaic context.

The original home of Yahweh was in the south, in or among the mysterious mountains Sinai (Dt. 33:2), Seir (Dt. 33:2; Jgs. 5:4), Paran (Dt. 33:2; Hab. 3:3), and Teman (Hab. 3:3), probably in the vicinity of Edom, Midian, and Cushan. Although many scholars prefer the traditional association with the Sinai peninsula, the area is probably to be sought in the region east and south of Aqabah, in the northern part of the Arabian Shield. This home is reflected preeminently in Yahweh's title *zeh sînay,* "the one of Sinai" (Jgs. 5:5; Ps. 68:9[8]). He reached his later home Zion after a long trek north;[198] Ps. 48:3(2) explicitly identifies Zion with Zaphon in the far north, the home of Ugaritic Ba'al. The northern mountains also appear as "the mountains of the ancient one, the hills of the eternal one" (Dt. 33:15).

Yahweh's opponents include the mythical monsters Leviathan,[199] Rahab,[200] Tehom,[201] and the serpent.[202] Also among them may be the "new gods" (*'ᵉlōhîm ḥᵃḏāšîm* of Jgs. 5:8 and Dt. 32:17, but the exact sense of the phrase is elusive.

The figure of Yahweh has some general similarity to the figures of Chemosh of Moab, Milcom/Molech of the Ammonites, and Qaus of Edom, to the extent we are acquainted with them. None of the four appears in the Ugaritic epic texts, but Chemosh and Milcom seem to have been known at Ugarit.[203] The development of the four cults in the Early Iron age may well have been parallel, and Solomon indeed worshipped Yahweh, Molech, and Chemosh (1 K. 11:7) as well as Astarte of the Sidonians (cf. also 2 Ch. 2:4[5]). The name of the Levite Qushayahu (or better Qaus-yahu) (1 Ch.

---

197 With the LXX and a Qumran text published in P. W. Skehan, "A Fragment of the 'Song of Moses' (Deut. 32) from Qumran," *BASOR,* 136 (1954), 12.

198 See D. N. Freedman, "A Letter to the Readers," *BA,* 40 (1977), 46-48.

199 → לויתן *liwyāṯān.*

200 → רהב *rhb.*

201 → תהום *tᵉhôm.*

202 → נחש *nāḥāš;* Ps. 68:23(22); cf. P. D. Miller, "Two Critical Notes on Psalm 68 and Deuteronomy 33," *HTR,* 57 (1964), 240-43.

203 *KTU,* 1.100, 36; 1.107, 16; 1.123, 5; and *UT,* no. 1484.

15:17) may stem from an identification of Qaus and Yahweh, but the evidence is slender.[204] The name *y^e^hôšû'â* may also be syncretistic, since *šû'â* appears elsewhere as a divine name.

The syncretistic identification of Yahweh with other deities was a fairly constant phenomenon throughout the first millennium, as is well known from the prophets. The use of the title *'^e^lōhê haššāmayim*. "God of heaven," in the Persian period may reflect a partial but marginal syncretism with Ahura Mazda.[205] The Elephantine deities Ešembethel and 'Anath-bethel were linked with Yahweh, though whether as hypostases of certain of his features or as subordinate but independent deities we cannot say.[206] Later syncretism, like the identification of (Yahweh) Sabaoth with the deity Sabazios, falls outside our scope.

The name "Yahweh" is relatively rare in Wisdom Literature (in Ecclesiastes it is absent entirely); it occurs only once in the poetry of Job (Job 12:9; cf. Isa. 41:20), but appears in the prose framework in Job 38:1 and 40:1. This rarity reflects a common tendency in ancient Near Eastern wisdom to prefer general terms for the deity.[207] Certain Qumran texts also avoid the name except in biblical quotations. The substitution of *'l* for *YHWH* in quotations cannot be taken as evidence of polemic intent because of the text-critical problems involved.[208] Fitzmyer claims that the Palestinian Jews of the first century C.E. called Yahweh *mārē'* (Aramaic) and *'āḏôn* (Hebrew).[209] The standard LXX rendering of the name is *kýrios;* Origen, Aquila, Symmachus, and Theodotion prefer to use ΠΙΠΙ, which resembles יהוה visually.[210] The proper epilogue to these developments is the magical material discussed above.

Freedman–O'Connor

---

[204] N. Glueck, "The Topography and History of Ezion-Geber and Elath," *BASOR*, 72 (1938), 11, n. 36.

[205] D. K. Andrews, "Yahweh the God of the Heavens," *The Seed of Wisdom. Festschrift T. J. Meek* (Toronto, 1964), 45-57.

[206] Porten, 151-186.

[207] R. Gordis, *Poets, Prophets, and Sages* (Bloomington, 1971), 159-168.

[208] *Ibid.*, 168, 193; Siegel.

[209] J. A. Fitzmyer, "Some Reflections on the Semitic Background of the *Kyrios*-title in the NT," a paper delivered at the thirty-seventh meeting of the Catholic Biblical Association, Chicago, Aug. 20, 1974; cf. *CBQ*, 36 (1974), 562.

[210] Cf. W. G. Waddell, "The Tetragrammaton in the LXX," *JTS*, 45 (1944), 158-161.